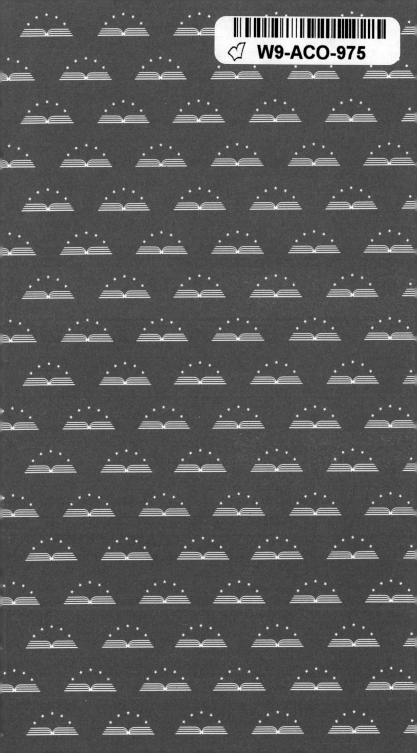

WILLIAM JAMES

WILLIAM JAMES

WRITINGS 1902–1910

The Varieties of Religious Experience
Pragmatism
A Pluralistic Universe
The Meaning of Truth
Some Problems of Philosophy
Essays

THE LIBRARY OF AMERICA

The paper used in this publication meets the minimum
requirements of the American National Standard for
Information Sciences—Permanence of Paper for
Printed Library Materials, ANSI Z39.48—1984.

Distributed to the trade in the United States and
Canada by the Viking Press.

Library of Congress Catalog Card Number: 87 3301
For cataloging information, see end of *Notes* section.
ISBN 0-940450-38-0

Third Printing
The Library of America—38

Manufactured in the United States of America

BRUCE KUKLICK
WROTE THE NOTES AND SELECTED
THE CONTENTS FOR THIS VOLUME

*Grateful acknowledgment is made to the
National Endowment for the Humanities, the Ford Foundation,
and the Andrew W. Mellon Foundation for their
generous financial support of this series.*

*The publishers express their appreciation
to the Houghton Library at Harvard University for the use
of William James materials.*

Contents

THE
VARIETIES OF RELIGIOUS EXPERIENCE

A STUDY IN HUMAN NATURE

BEING
THE GIFFORD LECTURES ON
NATURAL RELIGION DELIVERED AT
EDINBURGH IN 1901–1902

TO

E. P. G.

IN FILIAL GRATITUDE AND LOVE

Preface

THIS BOOK would never have been written had I not been honored with an appointment as Gifford Lecturer on Natural Religion at the University of Edinburgh. In casting about me for subjects of the two courses of ten lectures each for which I thus became responsible, it seemed to me that the first course might well be a descriptive one on 'Man's Religious Appetites,' and the second a metaphysical one on 'Their Satisfaction through Philosophy.' But the unexpected growth of the psychological matter as I came to write it out has resulted in the second subject being postponed entirely, and the description of man's religious constitution now fills the twenty lectures. In Lecture XX I have suggested rather than stated my own philosophic conclusions, and the reader who desires immediately to know them should turn to pages 456–463, and to the 'Postscript' of the book. I hope to be able at some later day to express them in more explicit form.

In my belief that a large acquaintance with particulars often makes us wiser than the possession of abstract formulas, however deep, I have loaded the lectures with concrete examples, and I have chosen these among the extremer expressions of the religious temperament. To some readers I may consequently seem, before they get beyond the middle of the book, to offer a caricature of the subject. Such convulsions of piety, they will say, are not sane. If, however, they will have the patience to read to the end, I believe that this unfavorable impression will disappear; for I there combine the religious impulses with other principles of common sense which serve as correctives of exaggeration, and allow the individual reader to draw as moderate conclusions as he will.

My thanks for help in writing these lectures are due to Edwin D. Starbuck, of Stanford University, who made over to me his large collection of manuscript material; to Henry W. Rankin, of East Northfield, a friend unseen but proved, to whom I owe precious information; to Theodore Flournoy, of Geneva, to Canning Schiller, of Oxford, and to my colleague Benjamin Rand, for documents; to my colleague Dickinson

S. Miller, and to my friends, Thomas Wren Ward, of New York, and Wincenty Lutoslawski, late of Cracow, for important suggestions and advice. Finally, to conversations with the lamented Thomas Davidson and to the use of his books, at Glenmore, above Keene Valley, I owe more obligations than I can well express.

HARVARD UNIVERSITY,
    March, 1902.

Contents

LECTURE X

LECTURES XI, XII, AND XIII

LECTURE XIX

LECTURE XX

LECTURE I

RELIGION AND NEUROLOGY

IT IS WITH no small amount of trepidation that I take my
place behind this desk, and face this learned audience. To
us Americans, the experience of receiving instruction from the
living voice, as well as from the books, of European scholars,
is very familiar. At my own University of Harvard, not a winter passes without its harvest, large or small, of lectures from
Scottish, English, French, or German representatives of the
science or literature of their respective countries whom we
have either induced to cross the ocean to address us, or captured on the wing as they were visiting our land. It seems the
natural thing for us to listen whilst the Europeans talk. The
contrary habit, of talking whilst the Europeans listen, we have
not yet acquired; and in him who first makes the adventure it
begets a certain sense of apology being due for so presump-
tuous an act. Particularly must this be the case of a soil as
sacred to the American imagination as that of Edinburgh.
The glories of the philosophic chair of this university were
deeply impressed on my imagination in boyhood. Professor
Fraser's Essays in Philosophy, then just published, was the
first philosophic book I ever looked into, and I well remember the awestruck feeling I received from the account of Sir
William Hamilton's class-room therein contained. Hamilton's
own lectures were the first philosophic writings I ever forced
myself to study, and after that I was immersed in Dugald
Stewart and Thomas Brown. Such juvenile emotions of reverence never get outgrown; and I confess that to find my humble self promoted from my native wilderness to be actually
for the time an official here, and transmuted into a colleague
of these illustrious names, carries with it a sense of dreamland
quite as much as of reality.

But since I have received the honor of this appointment I
have felt that it would never do to decline. The academic career also has its heroic obligations, so I stand here without
further deprecatory words. Let me say only this, that now
that the current, here and at Aberdeen, has begun to run from

west to east, I hope it may continue to do so. As the years go by, I hope that many of my countrymen may be asked to lecture in the Scottish universities, changing places with Scotsmen lecturing in the United States; I hope that our people may become in all these higher matters even as one people; and that the peculiar philosophic temperament, as well as the peculiar political temperament, that goes with our English speech may more and more pervade and influence the world.

As regards the manner in which I shall have to administer this lectureship, I am neither a theologian, nor a scholar learned in the history of religions, nor an anthropologist. Psychology is the only branch of learning in which I am particularly versed. To the psychologist the religious propensities of man must be at least as interesting as any other of the facts pertaining to his mental constitution. It would seem, therefore, that, as a psychologist, the natural thing for me would be to invite you to a descriptive survey of those religious propensities.

If the inquiry be psychological, not religious institutions, but rather religious feelings and religious impulses must be its subject, and I must confine myself to those more developed subjective phenomena recorded in literature produced by articulate and fully self-conscious men, in works of piety and autobiography. Interesting as the origins and early stages of a subject always are, yet when one seeks earnestly for its full significance, one must always look to its more completely evolved and perfect forms. It follows from this that the documents that will most concern us will be those of the men who were most accomplished in the religious life and best able to give an intelligible account of their ideas and motives. These men, of course, are either comparatively modern writers, or else such earlier ones as have become religious classics. The *documents humains* which we shall find most instructive need not then be sought for in the haunts of special erudition—they lie along the beaten highway; and this circumstance, which flows so naturally from the character of our problem, suits admirably also your lecturer's lack of special theological learning. I may take my citations, my sentences and paragraphs of personal confession, from books that most of you at some time will have had already in your hands, and yet this will be no detriment to the value of my conclusions. It is true that some more adventurous reader and investigator, lecturing here in future, may unearth from the shelves of libraries documents that will make a more delectable and curious entertainment to listen to than mine. Yet I doubt whether he will necessarily, by his control of so much more out-of-the-way material, get much closer to the essence of the matter in hand.

The question, What are the religious propensities? and the question, What is their philosophic significance? are two entirely different orders of question from the logical point of view; and, as a failure to recognize this fact distinctly may breed confusion, I wish to insist upon the point a little before we enter into the documents and materials to which I have referred.

In recent books on logic, distinction is made between two orders of inquiry concerning anything. First, what is the nature of it? how did it come about? what is its constitution, origin, and history? And second, What is its importance, meaning, or significance, now that it is once here? The answer to the one question is given in an *existential judgment* or proposition. The answer to the other is a *proposition of value*, what the Germans call a *Werthurtheil*, or what we may, if we like, denominate a *spiritual judgment*. Neither judgment can be deduced immediately from the other. They proceed from diverse intellectual preoccupations, and the mind combines them only by making them first separately, and then adding them together.

In the matter of religions it is particularly easy to distinguish the two orders of question. Every religious phenomenon has its history and its derivation from natural antecedents. What is nowadays called the higher criticism of the Bible is only a study of the Bible from this existential point of view, neglected too much by the earlier church. Under just what biographic conditions did the sacred writers bring forth their various contributions to the holy volume? And what had they exactly in their several individual minds, when they delivered their utterances? These are manifestly questions of historical fact, and one does not see how the answer to them can decide offhand the still further question: of what use should such a volume, with its manner of coming into existence so defined, be to us as a guide to life and a revelation? To answer this other question we must have already in our mind some sort of a general theory as to what the peculiarities in a thing should be which give it value for purposes of revelation; and this theory itself would be what I just called a spiritual judgment. Combining it with our existential judgment, we might indeed deduce another spiritual judgment as to the Bible's worth. Thus if our theory of revelation-value were to affirm that any book, to possess it, must have been composed automatically or not by the free caprice of the writer, or that it must exhibit no scientific and historic errors and express no local or personal passions, the Bible would probably fare ill at our hands. But if, on the other hand, our theory should allow that a book may well be a revelation in spite of errors and passions and deliberate human composition, if only it be a true record of the inner experiences of great-souled persons wrestling with the crises of their fate, then the verdict would be much more favorable. You see that the existential facts by themselves are insufficient for determining the value; and the best adepts of the higher criticism accordingly never confound the existential with the spiritual problem. With the same conclusions of fact before them, some take one view, and some another, of the Bible's value as a revelation, according as their spiritual judgment as to the foundation of values differs.

I make these general remarks about the two sorts of judgment, because there are many religious persons—some of you now present, possibly, are among them—who do not yet make a working use of the distinction, and who may therefore feel at first a little startled at the purely existential point of view from which in the following lectures the phenomena of religious experience must be considered. When I handle them biologically and psychologically as if they were mere curious facts of individual history, some of you may think it a degradation of so sublime a subject, and may even suspect me, until my purpose gets more fully expressed, of deliberately seeking to discredit the religious side of life.

Such a result is of course absolutely alien to my intention; and since such a prejudice on your part would seriously obstruct the due effect of much of what I have to relate, I will devote a few more words to the point.

There can be no doubt that as a matter of fact a religious life, exclusively pursued, does tend to make the person exceptional and eccentric. I speak not now of your ordinary religious believer, who follows the conventional observances of his country, whether it be Buddhist, Christian, or Mohammedan. His religion has been made for him by others, communicated to him by tradition, determined to fixed forms by imitation, and retained by habit. It would profit us little to study this second-hand religious life. We must make search rather for the original experiences which were the pattern-setters to all this mass of suggested feeling and imitated conduct. These experiences we can only find in individuals for whom religion exists not as a dull habit, but as an acute fever rather. But such individuals are 'geniuses' in the religious line; and like many other geniuses who have brought forth fruits effective enough for commemoration in the pages of biography, such religious geniuses have often shown symptoms of nervous instability. Even more perhaps than other kinds of genius, religious leaders have been subject to abnormal psychical visitations. Invariably they have been creatures of exalted emotional sensibility. Often they have led a discordant inner life, and had melancholy during a part of their career. They have known no measure, been liable to obsessions and fixed ideas; and frequently they have fallen into trances, heard voices, seen visions, and presented all sorts of peculiarities which are ordinarily classed as pathological. Often, moreover, these pathological features in their career have helped to give them their religious authority and influence.

If you ask for a concrete example, there can be no better one than is furnished by the person of George Fox. The Quaker religion which he founded is something which it is impossible to overpraise. In a day of shams, it was a religion of veracity rooted in spiritual inwardness, and a return to something more like the original gospel truth than men had ever known in England. So far as our Christian sects to-day are evolving into liberality, they are simply reverting in essence to the position which Fox and the early Quakers so long ago assumed. No one can pretend for a moment that in point of spiritual sagacity and capacity, Fox's mind was unsound. Every one who confronted him personally, from Oliver Cromwell down to county magistrates and jailers, seems to have acknowledged his superior power. Yet from the point of view of his nervous constitution, Fox was a psychopath or *détraqué* of the deepest dye. His Journal abounds in entries of this sort:—

"As I was walking with several friends, I lifted up my head, and saw three steeple-house spires, and they struck at my life. I asked them what place that was? They said, Lichfield. Immediately the word of the Lord came to me, that I must go thither. Being come to the house we were going to, I wished the friends to walk into the house, saying nothing to them of whither I was to go. As soon as they were gone I stept away, and went by my eye over hedge and ditch till I came within a mile of Lichfield; where, in a great field, shepherds were keeping their sheep. Then was I commanded by the Lord to pull off my shoes. I stood still, for it was winter: but the word of the Lord was like a fire in me. So I put off my shoes, and left them with the shepherds; and the poor shepherds trembled, and were astonished. Then I walked on about a mile, and as soon as I was got within the city, the word of the Lord came to me again, saying: Cry, 'Wo to the bloody city of Lichfield!' So I went up and down the streets, crying with a loud voice, Wo to the bloody city of Lichfield! It being market day, I went into the market-place, and to and fro in the several parts of it, and made stands, crying as before, Wo to the bloody city of Lichfield! And no one laid hands on me. As I went thus crying through the streets, there seemed to me to be a channel of blood running down the streets, and the market-place appeared like a pool of blood. When I had declared what was upon me, and felt myself clear, I went out of the town in peace; and returning to the shepherds gave them some money, and took my shoes of them again.

But the fire of the Lord was so on my feet, and all over me, that I did not matter to put on my shoes again, and was at a stand whether I should or no, till I felt freedom from the Lord so to do: then, after I had washed my feet, I put on my shoes again. After this a deep consideration came upon me, for what reason I should be sent to cry against that city, and call it The bloody city! For though the parliament had the minister one while, and the king another, and much blood had been shed in the town during the wars between them, yet there was no more than had befallen many other places. But afterwards I came to understand, that in the Emperor Diocletian's time a thousand Christians were martyr'd in Lichfield. So I was to go, without my shoes, through the channel of their blood, and into the pool of their blood in the market-place, that I might raise up the memorial of the blood of those martyrs, which had been shed above a thousand years before, and lay cold in their streets. So the sense of this blood was upon me, and I obeyed the word of the Lord."

Bent as we are on studying religion's existential conditions, we cannot possibly ignore these pathological aspects of the subject. We must describe and name them just as if they occurred in non-religious men. It is true that we instinctively recoil from seeing an object to which our emotions and affections are committed handled by the intellect as any other object is handled. The first thing the intellect does with an object is to class it along with something else. But any object that is infinitely important to us and awakens our devotion feels to us also as if it must be *sui generis* and unique. Probably a crab would be filled with a sense of personal outrage if it could hear us class it without ado or apology as a crustacean, and thus dispose of it. "I am no such thing," it would say; "I am MYSELF, MYSELF alone."

The next thing the intellect does is to lay bare the causes in which the thing originates. Spinoza says: "I will analyze the actions and appetites of men as if it were a question of lines, of planes, and of solids." And elsewhere he remarks that he will consider our passions and their properties with the same eye with which he looks on all other natural things, since the consequences of our affections flow from their nature with the same necessity as it results from the nature of a triangle that its three angles should be equal to two right angles. Similarly M. Taine, in the introduction to his history of English literature, has written: "Whether facts be moral or physical, it makes no matter. They always have their causes. There are causes for ambition, courage, veracity, just as there are for digestion, muscular movement, animal heat. Vice and virtue are products like vitriol and sugar." When we read such proclamations of the intellect bent on showing the existential conditions of absolutely everything, we feel—quite apart from our legitimate impatience at the somewhat ridiculous swagger of the program, in view of what the authors are actually able to perform—menaced and negated in the springs of our innermost life. Such cold-blooded assimilations threaten, we think, to undo our soul's vital secrets, as if the same breath which should succeed in explaining their origin would simultaneously explain away their significance, and make them appear of no more preciousness, either, than the useful groceries of which M. Taine speaks.

Perhaps the commonest expression of this assumption that spiritual value is undone if lowly origin be asserted is seen in those comments which unsentimental people so often pass on their more sentimental acquaintances. Alfred believes in immortality so strongly because his temperament is so emotional. Fanny's extraordinary conscientiousness is merely a matter of over-instigated nerves. William's melancholy about the universe is due to bad digestion—probably his liver is torpid. Eliza's delight in her church is a symptom of her hysterical constitution. Peter would be less troubled about his soul if he would take more exercise in the open air, etc. A more fully developed example of the same kind of reasoning is the fashion, quite common nowadays among certain writers, of criticising the religious emotions by showing a connection between them and the sexual life. Conversion is a crisis of puberty and adolescence. The macerations of saints, and the devotion of missionaries, are only instances of the parental instinct of self-sacrifice gone astray. For the hysterical nun, starving for natural life, Christ is but an imaginary substitute for a more earthly object of affection. And the like.[1]

We are surely all familiar in a general way with this method of discrediting states of mind for which we have an antipathy. We all use it to some degree in criticising persons whose states of mind we regard as overstrained. But when other people criticise our own more exalted soul-flights by calling them

[1] As with many ideas that float in the air of one's time, this notion shrinks from dogmatic general statement and expresses itself only partially and by innuendo. It seems to me that few conceptions are less instructive than this re-interpretation of religion as perverted sexuality. It reminds one, so crudely is it often employed, of the famous Catholic taunt, that the Reformation may be best understood by remembering that its *fons et origo* was Luther's wish to marry a nun:—the effects are infinitely wider than the alleged causes, and for the most part opposite in nature. It is true that in the vast collection of religious phenomena, some are undisguisedly amatory—e. g., sex-deities and obscene rites in polytheism, and ecstatic feelings of union with the Saviour in a few Christian mystics. But then why not equally call religion an aberration of the digestive function, and prove one's point by the worship of Bacchus and Ceres, or by the ecstatic feelings of some other saints about the Eucharist? Religious language clothes itself in such poor symbols as our life affords, and the whole organism gives overtones of comment whenever the mind is strongly stirred to expression. Language drawn from eating and drinking is probably as common in religious literature as is language drawn from the sexual life. We 'hunger and thirst' after righteousness; we 'find the Lord a sweet savor;' we 'taste and see that he is good.' 'Spiritual milk for American babes, drawn from the breasts of both testaments,' is a sub-title of the once famous New England Primer, and Christian devotional literature indeed quite floats in milk, thought of from the point of view, not of the mother, but of the greedy babe.

Saint François de Sales, for instance, thus describes the 'orison of quietude': "In this state the soul is like a little child still at the breast, whose mother, to caress him whilst he is still in her arms, makes her milk distill into his mouth without his even moving his lips. So it is here. . . . Our Lord desires that our will should be satisfied with sucking the milk which His Majesty pours into our mouth, and that we should relish the sweetness without even knowing that it cometh from the Lord." And again: "Consider the little infants, united and joined to the breasts of their nursing mothers, you will see that from time to time they press themselves closer by little starts to which the pleasure of sucking prompts them. Even so, during its orison, the heart united to its God oftentimes makes attempts at closer union by movements during which it presses closer upon the divine sweetness." Chemin de la Perfection, ch. xxxi.; Amour de Dieu, vii. ch. i.

In fact, one might almost as well interpret religion as a perversion of the respiratory function. The Bible is full of the language of respiratory oppres-

'nothing but' expressions of our organic disposition, we feel outraged and hurt, for we know that, whatever be our organism's peculiarities, our mental states have their substantive value as revelations of the living truth; and we wish that all this medical materialism could be made to hold its tongue.

Medical materialism seems indeed a good appellation for the too simple-minded system of thought which we are con-

---

sion: "Hide not thine ear at my breathing; my groaning is not hid from thee; my heart panteth, my strength faileth me; my bones are hot with my roaring all the night long; as the hart panteth after the water-brooks, so my soul panteth after thee, O my God." *God's Breath in Man* is the title of the chief work of our best known American mystic (Thomas Lake Harris); and in certain non-Christian countries the foundation of all religious discipline consists in regulation of the inspiration and expiration.

These arguments are as good as much of the reasoning one hears in favor of the sexual theory. But the champions of the latter will then say that their chief argument has no analogue elsewhere. The two main phenomena of religion, namely, melancholy and conversion, they will say, are essentially phenomena of adolescence, and therefore synchronous with the development of sexual life. To which the retort again is easy. Even were the asserted synchrony unrestrictedly true as a fact (which it is not), it is not only the sexual life, but the entire higher mental life which awakens during adolescence. One might then as well set up the thesis that the interest in mechanics, physics, chemistry, logic, philosophy, and sociology, which springs up during adolescent years along with that in poetry and religion, is also a perversion of the sexual instinct:—but that would be too absurd. Moreover, if the argument from synchrony is to decide, what is to be done with the fact that the religious age *par excellence* would seem to be old age, when the uproar of the sexual life is past?

The plain truth is that to interpret religion one must in the end look at the immediate content of the religious consciousness. The moment one does this, one sees how wholly disconnected it is in the main from the content of the sexual consciousness. Everything about the two things differs, objects, moods, faculties concerned, and acts impelled to. Any *general* assimilation is simply impossible: what we find most often is complete hostility and contrast. If now the defenders of the sex-theory say that this makes no difference to their thesis; that without the chemical contributions which the sex-organs make to the blood, the brain would not be nourished so as to carry on religious activities, this final proposition may be true or not true; but at any rate it has become profoundly uninstructive: we can deduce no consequences from it which help us to interpret religion's meaning or value. In this sense the religious life depends just as much upon the spleen, the pancreas, and the kidneys as on the sexual apparatus, and the whole theory has lost its point in evaporating into a vague general assertion of the dependence, *somehow*, of the mind upon the body.

sidering. Medical materialism finishes up Saint Paul by calling his vision on the road to Damascus a discharging lesion of the occipital cortex, he being an epileptic. It snuffs out Saint Teresa as an hysteric, Saint Francis of Assisi as an hereditary degenerate. George Fox's discontent with the shams of his age, and his pining for spiritual veracity, it treats as a symptom of a disordered colon. Carlyle's organ-tones of misery it accounts for by a gastro-duodenal catarrh. All such mental over-tensions, it says, are, when you come to the bottom of the matter, mere affairs of diathesis (auto-intoxications most probably), due to the perverted action of various glands which physiology will yet discover.

And medical materialism then thinks that the spiritual authority of all such personages is successfully undermined.[1]

Let us ourselves look at the matter in the largest possible way. Modern psychology, finding definite psycho-physical connections to hold good, assumes as a convenient hypothesis that the dependence of mental states upon bodily conditions must be thorough-going and complete. If we adopt the assumption, then of course what medical materialism insists on must be true in a general way, if not in every detail: Saint Paul certainly had once an epileptoid, if not an epileptic seizure; George Fox was an hereditary degenerate; Carlyle was undoubtedly auto-intoxicated by some organ or other, no matter which,—and the rest. But now, I ask you, how can such an existential account of facts of mental history decide in one way or another upon their spiritual significance? According to the general postulate of psychology just referred to, there is not a single one of our states of mind, high or low, healthy or morbid, that has not some organic process as its condition. Scientific theories are organically conditioned just as much as religious emotions are; and if we only knew the facts intimately enough, we should doubtless see 'the liver' determining the dicta of the sturdy atheist as decisively as it does those of the Methodist under conviction anxious about his soul. When it alters in one way the blood that percolates it, we get the methodist, when in another way, we get

[1] For a first-rate example of medical-materialist reasoning, see an article on 'les Variétés du Type dévot,' by Dr. Binet-Sanglé, in the Revue de l'Hypnotisme, xiv. 161.

the atheist form of mind. So of all our raptures and our dry-nesses, our longings and pantings, our questions and beliefs. They are equally organically founded, be they of religious or of non-religious content.

To plead the organic causation of a religious state of mind, then, in refutation of its claim to possess superior spiritual value, is quite illogical and arbitrary, unless one have already worked out in advance some psycho-physical theory connecting spiritual values in general with determinate sorts of physiological change. Otherwise none of our thoughts and feelings, not even our scientific doctrines, not even our *dis*-beliefs, could retain any value as revelations of the truth, for every one of them without exception flows from the state of their possessor's body at the time.

It is needless to say that medical materialism draws in point of fact no such sweeping skeptical conclusion. It is sure, just as every simple man is sure, that some states of mind are inwardly superior to others, and reveal to us more truth, and in this it simply makes use of an ordinary spiritual judgment. It has no physiological theory of the production of these its favorite states, by which it may accredit them; and its attempt to discredit the states which it dislikes, by vaguely associating them with nerves and liver, and connecting them with names connoting bodily affliction, is altogether illogical and inconsistent.

Let us play fair in this whole matter, and be quite candid with ourselves and with the facts. When we think certain states of mind superior to others, is it ever because of what we know concerning their organic antecedents? No! it is always for two entirely different reasons. It is either because we take an immediate delight in them; or else it is because we believe them to bring us good consequential fruits for life. When we speak disparagingly of 'feverish fancies,' surely the fever-process as such is not the ground of our disesteem—for aught we know to the contrary, 103° or 104° Fahrenheit might be a much more favorable temperature for truths to germinate and sprout in, than the more ordinary blood-heat of 97 or 98 degrees. It is either the disagreeableness itself of the fancies, or their inability to bear the criticisms of the convalescent hour. When we praise the thoughts which health brings, health's peculiar chemical metabolisms have nothing to do with determining our judgment. We know in fact almost nothing about these metabolisms. It is the character of inner happiness in the thoughts which stamps them as good, or else their consistency with our other opinions and their serviceability for our needs, which make them pass for true in our esteem.

Now the more intrinsic and the more remote of these criteria do not always hang together. Inner happiness and serviceability do not always agree. What immediately feels most 'good' is not always most 'true,' when measured by the verdict of the rest of experience. The difference between Philip drunk and Philip sober is the classic instance in corroboration. If merely 'feeling good' could decide, drunkenness would be the supremely valid human experience. But its revelations, however acutely satisfying at the moment, are inserted into an environment which refuses to bear them out for any length of time. The consequence of this discrepancy of the two criteria is the uncertainty which still prevails over so many of our spiritual judgments. There are moments of sentimental and mystical experience—we shall hereafter hear much of them—that carry an enormous sense of inner authority and illumination with them when they come. But they come seldom, and they do not come to every one; and the rest of life makes either no connection with them, or tends to contradict them more than it confirms them. Some persons follow more the voice of the moment in these cases, some prefer to be guided by the average results. Hence the sad discordancy of so many of the spiritual judgments of human beings; a discordancy which will be brought home to us acutely enough before these lectures end.

It is, however, a discordancy that can never be resolved by any merely medical test. A good example of the impossibility of holding strictly to the medical tests is seen in the theory of the pathological causation of genius promulgated by recent authors. "Genius," said Dr. Moreau, "is but one of the many branches of the neuropathic tree." "Genius," says Dr. Lombroso, "is a symptom of hereditary degeneration of the epileptoid variety, and is allied to moral insanity." "Whenever a man's life," writes Mr. Nisbet, "is at once sufficiently illustrious and recorded with sufficient fullness to be a subject of profitable study, he inevitably falls into the morbid category. . . . And it is worthy of remark that, as a rule, the greater the genius, the greater the unsoundness."[1]

Now do these authors, after having succeeded in establishing to their own satisfaction that the works of genius are fruits of disease, consistently proceed thereupon to impugn the *value* of the fruits? Do they deduce a new spiritual judgment from their new doctrine of existential conditions? Do they frankly forbid us to admire the productions of genius from now onwards? and say outright that no neuropath can ever be a revealer of new truth?

No! their immediate spiritual instincts are too strong for them here, and hold their own against inferences which, in mere love of logical consistency, medical materialism ought to be only too glad to draw. One disciple of the school, indeed, has striven to impugn the value of works of genius in a wholesale way (such works of contemporary art, namely, as he himself is unable to enjoy, and they are many) by using medical arguments.[2] But for the most part the masterpieces are left unchallenged; and the medical line of attack either confines itself to such secular productions as every one admits to be intrinsically eccentric, or else addresses itself exclusively to religious manifestations. And then it is because the religious manifestations have been already condemned because the critic dislikes them on internal or spiritual grounds.

In the natural sciences and industrial arts it never occurs to any one to try to refute opinions by showing up their author's neurotic constitution. Opinions here are invariably tested by logic and by experiment, no matter what may be their author's neurological type. It should be no otherwise with religious opinions. Their value can only be ascertained by spiritual judgments directly passed upon them, judgments based on our own immediate feeling primarily; and secondarily on what we can ascertain of their experiential relations to our moral needs and to the rest of what we hold as true.

[1] J. F. NISBET: The Insanity of Genius, 3d ed., London, 1893, pp. xvi, xxiv.
[2] MAX NORDAU, in his bulky book entitled *Degeneration*.

Immediate luminousness, in short, *philosophical reasonableness*, and *moral helpfulness* are the only available criteria. Saint Teresa might have had the nervous system of the placidest cow, and it would not now save her theology, if the trial of the theology by these other tests should show it to be contemptible. And conversely if her theology can stand these other tests, it will make no difference how hysterical or nervously off her balance Saint Teresa may have been when she was with us here below.

You see that at bottom we are thrown back upon the general principles by which the empirical philosophy has always contended that we must be guided in our search for truth. Dogmatic philosophies have sought for tests for truth which might dispense us from appealing to the future. Some direct mark, by noting which we can be protected immediately and absolutely, now and forever, against all mistake—such has been the darling dream of philosophic dogmatists. It is clear that the *origin* of the truth would be an admirable criterion of this sort, if only the various origins could be discriminated from one another from this point of view, and the history of dogmatic opinion shows that origin has always been a favorite test. Origin in immediate intuition; origin in pontifical authority; origin in supernatural revelation, as by vision, hearing, or unaccountable impression; origin in direct possession by a higher spirit, expressing itself in prophecy and warning; origin in automatic utterance generally,—these origins have been stock warrants for the truth of one opinion after another which we find represented in religious history. The medical materialists are therefore only so many belated dogmatists, neatly turning the tables on their predecessors by using the criterion of origin in a destructive instead of an accreditive way.

They are effective with their talk of pathological origin only so long as supernatural origin is pleaded by the other side, and nothing but the argument from origin is under discussion. But the argument from origin has seldom been used alone, for it is too obviously insufficient. Dr. Maudsley is perhaps the cleverest of the rebutters of supernatural religion on grounds of origin. Yet he finds himself forced to write:—

"What right have we to believe Nature under any obligation to do her work by means of complete minds only? She may find an incomplete mind a more suitable instrument for a particular purpose. It is the work that is done, and the quality in the worker by which it was done, that is alone of moment; and it may be no great matter from a cosmical standpoint, if in other qualities of character he was singularly defective—if indeed he were hypocrite, adulterer, eccentric, or lunatic. . . . Home we come again, then, to the old and last resort of certitude,—namely the common assent of mankind, or of the competent by instruction and training among mankind."[1]

In other words, not its origin, but *the way in which it works on the whole*, is Dr. Maudsley's final test of a belief. This is our own empiricist criterion; and this criterion the stoutest insisters on supernatural origin have also been forced to use in the end. Among the visions and messages some have always been too patently silly, among the trances and convulsive seizures some have been too fruitless for conduct and character, to pass themselves off as significant, still less as divine. In the history of Christian mysticism the problem how to discriminate between such messages and experiences as were really divine miracles, and such others as the demon in his malice was able to counterfeit, thus making the religious person twofold more the child of hell he was before, has always been a difficult one to solve, needing all the sagacity and experience of the best directors of conscience. In the end it had to come to our empiricist criterion: By their fruits ye shall know them, not by their roots. Jonathan Edwards's Treatise on Religious Affections is an elaborate working out of this thesis. The *roots* of a man's virtue are inaccessible to us. No appearances whatever are infallible proofs of grace. Our practice is the only sure evidence, even to ourselves, that we are genuinely Christians.

"In forming a judgment of ourselves now," Edwards writes, "we should certainly adopt that evidence which our supreme Judge will chiefly make use of when we come to

[1] H. MAUDSLEY: Natural Causes and Supernatural Seemings, 1886, pp. 257, 256.

stand before him at the last day. . . . There is not one
grace of the Spirit of God, of the existence of which, in any
professor of religion, Christian practice is not the most decisive evidence. . . . The degree in which our experience
is productive of practice shows the degree in which our
experience is spiritual and divine."

Catholic writers are equally emphatic. The good dispositions which a vision, or voice, or other apparent heavenly favor leave behind them are the only marks by which we may
be sure they are not possible deceptions of the tempter. Says
Saint Teresa: —

"Like imperfect sleep which, instead of giving more
strength to the head, doth but leave it the more exhausted,
the result of mere operations of the imagination is but to
weaken the soul. Instead of nourishment and energy she
reaps only lassitude and disgust: whereas a genuine heavenly vision yields to her a harvest of ineffable spiritual
riches, and an admirable renewal of bodily strength. I alleged these reasons to those who so often accused my visions of being the work of the enemy of mankind and the
sport of my imagination. . . . I showed them the jewels
which the divine hand had left with me: —they were my
actual dispositions. All those who knew me saw that I was
changed; my confessor bore witness to the fact; this improvement, palpable in all respects, far from being hidden,
was brilliantly evident to all men. As for myself, it was impossible to believe that if the demon were its author, he
could have used, in order to lose me and lead me to hell,
an expedient so contrary to his own interests as that of up-
rooting my vices, and filling me with masculine courage
and other virtues instead, for I saw clearly that a single one
of these visions was enough to enrich me with all that
wealth."[1]

I fear I may have made a longer excursus than was necessary, and that fewer words would have dispelled the uneasiness which may have arisen among some of you as I announced my pathological programme. At any rate you must

[1] Autobiography, ch. xxviii.

all be ready now to judge the religious life by its results exclusively, and I shall assume that the bugaboo of morbid origin will scandalize your piety no more.

Still, you may ask me, if its results are to be the ground of our final spiritual estimate of a religious phenomenon, why threaten us at all with so much existential study of its conditions? Why not simply leave pathological questions out?

To this I reply in two ways: First, I say, irrepressible curiosity imperiously leads one on; and I say, secondly, that it always leads to a better understanding of a thing's significance to consider its exaggerations and perversions, its equivalents and substitutes and nearest relatives elsewhere. Not that we may thereby swamp the thing in the wholesale condemnation which we pass on its inferior congeners, but rather that we may by contrast ascertain the more precisely in what its merits consist, by learning at the same time to what particular dangers of corruption it may also be exposed.

Insane conditions have this advantage, that they isolate special factors of the mental life, and enable us to inspect them unmasked by their more usual surroundings. They play the part in mental anatomy which the scalpel and the microscope play in the anatomy of the body. To understand a thing rightly we need to see it both out of its environment and in it, and to have acquaintance with the whole range of its variations. The study of hallucinations has in this way been for psychologists the key to their comprehension of normal sensation, that of illusions has been the key to the right comprehension of perception. Morbid impulses and imperative conceptions, 'fixed ideas,' so called, have thrown a flood of light on the psychology of the normal will; and obsessions and delusions have performed the same service for that of the normal faculty of belief.

Similarly, the nature of genius has been illuminated by the attempts, of which I already made mention, to class it with psychopathical phenomena. Borderland insanity, crankiness, insane temperament, loss of mental balance, psychopathic degeneration (to use a few of the many synonyms by which it has been called), has certain peculiarities and liabilities which, when combined with a superior quality of intellect in an individual, make it more probable that he will make his mark and affect his age, than if his temperament were less neurotic. There is of course no special affinity between crankiness as such and superior intellect,[1] for most psychopaths have feeble intellects, and superior intellects more commonly have normal nervous systems. But the psychopathic temperament, whatever be the intellect with which it finds itself paired, often brings with it ardor and excitability of character. The cranky person has extraordinary emotional susceptibility. He is liable to fixed ideas and obsessions. His conceptions tend to pass immediately into belief and action; and when he gets a new idea, he has no rest till he proclaims it, or in some way 'works it off.' "What shall I think of it?" a common person says to himself about a vexed question; but in a 'cranky' mind "What must I do about it?" is the form the question tends to take. In the autobiography of that high-souled woman, Mrs. Annie Besant, I read the following passage: "Plenty of people wish well to any good cause, but very few care to exert themselves to help it, and still fewer will risk anything in its support. 'Some one ought to do it, but why should I?' is the ever reëchoed phrase of weak-kneed amiability. 'Some one ought to do it, so why not I?' is the cry of some earnest servant of man, eagerly forward springing to face some perilous duty. Between these two sentences lie whole centuries of moral evolution." True enough! and between these two sentences lie also the different destinies of the ordinary sluggard and the psychopathic man. Thus, when a superior intellect and a psychopathic temperament coalesce—as in the endless permutations and combinations of human faculty, they are bound to coalesce often enough—in the same individual, we have the best possible condition for the kind of effective genius that gets into the biographical dictionaries. Such men do not remain mere critics and understanders with their intellect. Their ideas possess them, they inflict them, for better or worse, upon their companions or their age. It is they who get counted when Messrs Lombroso, Nisbet, and others invoke statistics to defend their paradox.

To pass now to religious phenomena, take the melancholy

[1] Superior intellect, as Professor Bain has admirably shown, seems to consist in nothing so much as in a large development of the faculty of association by similarity.

which, as we shall see, constitutes an essential moment in every complete religious evolution. Take the happiness which achieved religious belief confers. Take the trance-like states of insight into truth which all religious mystics report.[1] These are each and all of them special cases of kinds of human experience of much wider scope. Religious melancholy, whatever peculiarities it may have *quâ* religious, is at any rate melancholy. Religious happiness is happiness. Religious trance is trance. And the moment we renounce the absurd notion that a thing is exploded away as soon as it is classed with others, or its origin is shown; the moment we agree to stand by experimental results and inner quality, in judging of values,—who does not see that we are likely to ascertain the distinctive significance of religious melancholy and happiness, or of religious trances, far better by comparing them as conscientiously as we can with other varieties of melancholy, happiness, and trance, than by refusing to consider their place in any more general series, and treating them as if they were outside of nature's order altogether?

I hope that the course of these lectures will confirm us in this supposition. As regards the psychopathic origin of so many religious phenomena, that would not be in the least surprising or disconcerting, even were such phenomena certified from on high to be the most precious of human experiences. No one organism can possibly yield to its owner the whole body of truth. Few of us are not in some way infirm, or even diseased; and our very infirmities help us unexpectedly. In the psychopathic temperament we have the emotionality which is the *sine quâ non* of moral perception; we have the intensity and tendency to emphasis which are the essence of practical moral vigor; and we have the love of metaphysics and mysticism which carry one's interests beyond the surface of the sensible world. What, then, is more natural than that this temperament should introduce one to regions of religious truth, to corners of the universe, which your robust Philistine type of nervous system, forever offering its biceps to be felt, thumping its breast, and thanking Heaven that it has n't a

---

[1] I may refer to a criticism of the insanity theory of genius in the Psychological Review, ii. 287 (1895).

single morbid fibre in its composition, would be sure to hide forever from its self-satisfied possessors?

If there were such a thing as inspiration from a higher realm, it might well be that the neurotic temperament would furnish the chief condition of the requisite receptivity. And having said thus much, I think that I may let the matter of religion and neuroticism drop.

The mass of collateral phenomena, morbid or healthy, with which the various religious phenomena must be compared in order to understand them better, forms what in the slang of pedagogics is termed 'the apperceiving mass' by which we comprehend them. The only novelty that I can imagine this course of lectures to possess lies in the breadth of the apperceiving mass. I may succeed in discussing religious experiences in a wider context than has been usual in university courses.

LECTURE II

CIRCUMSCRIPTION OF THE TOPIC

MOST BOOKS on the philosophy of religion try to begin with a precise definition of what its essence consists of. Some of these would-be definitions may possibly come before us in later portions of this course, and I shall not be pedantic enough to enumerate any of them to you now. Meanwhile the very fact that they are so many and so different from one another is enough to prove that the word 'religion' cannot stand for any single principle or essence, but is rather a collective name. The theorizing mind tends always to the oversimplification of its materials. This is the root of all that absolutism and one-sided dogmatism by which both philosophy and religion have been infested. Let us not fall immediately into a one-sided view of our subject, but let us rather admit freely at the outset that we may very likely find no one essence, but many characters which may alternately be equally important in religion. If we should inquire for the essence of 'government,' for example, one man might tell us it was authority, another submission, another police, another an army, another an assembly, another a system of laws; yet all the while it would be true that no concrete government can exist without all these things, one of which is more important at one moment and others at another. The man who knows governments most completely is he who troubles himself least about a definition which shall give their essence. Enjoying an intimate acquaintance with all their particularities in turn, he would naturally regard an abstract conception in which these were unified as a thing more misleading than enlightening. And why may not religion be a conception equally complex?[1]

Consider also the 'religious sentiment' which we see

[1] I can do no better here than refer my readers to the extended and admirable remarks on the futility of all these definitions of religion, in an article by Professor Leuba, published in the Monist for January, 1901, after my own text was written.

referred to in so many books, as if it were a single sort of mental entity.

In the psychologies and in the philosophies of religion, we find the authors attempting to specify just what entity it is. One man allies it to the feeling of dependence; one makes it a derivative from fear; others connect it with the sexual life; others still identify it with the feeling of the infinite; and so on. Such different ways of conceiving it ought of themselves to arouse doubt as to whether it possibly can be one specific thing; and the moment we are willing to treat the term 'religious sentiment' as a collective name for the many sentiments which religious objects may arouse in alternation, we see that it probably contains nothing whatever of a psychologically specific nature. There is religious fear, religious love, religious awe, religious joy, and so forth. But religious love is only man's natural emotion of love directed to a religious object; religious fear is only the ordinary fear of commerce, so to speak, the common quaking of the human breast, in so far as the notion of divine retribution may arouse it; religious awe is the same organic thrill which we feel in a forest at twilight, or in a mountain gorge; only this time it comes over us at the thought of our supernatural relations; and similarly of all the various sentiments which may be called into play in the lives of religious persons. As concrete states of mind, made up of a feeling *plus* a specific sort of object, religious emotions of course are psychic entities distinguishable from other concrete emotions; but there is no ground for assuming a simple abstract 'religious emotion' to exist as a distinct elementary mental affection by itself, present in every religious experience without exception.

As there thus seems to be no one elementary religious emotion, but only a common storehouse of emotions upon which religious objects may draw, so there might conceivably also prove to be no one specific and essential kind of religious object, and no one specific and essential kind of religious act.

The field of religion being as wide as this, it is manifestly impossible that I should pretend to cover it. My lectures must be limited to a fraction of the subject. And, although it would indeed be foolish to set up an abstract definition of religion's essence, and then proceed to defend that definition against all comers, yet this need not prevent me from taking my own narrow view of what religion shall consist in *for the purpose of these lectures*, or, out of the many meanings of the word, from choosing the one meaning in which I wish to interest you particularly, and proclaiming arbitrarily that when I say 'religion' I mean *that*. This, in fact, is what I must do, and I will now preliminarily seek to mark out the field I choose.

One way to mark it out easily is to say what aspects of the subject we leave out. At the outset we are struck by one great partition which divides the religious field. On the one side of it lies institutional, on the other personal religion. As M. P. Sabatier says, one branch of religion keeps the divinity, another keeps man most in view. Worship and sacrifice, procedures for working on the dispositions of the deity, theology and ceremony and ecclesiastical organization, are the essentials of religion in the institutional branch. Were we to limit our view to it, we should have to define religion as an external art, the art of winning the favor of the gods. In the more personal branch of religion it is on the contrary the inner dispositions of man himself which form the centre of interest, his conscience, his deserts, his helplessness, his incompleteness. And although the favor of the God, as forfeited or gained, is still an essential feature of the story, and theology plays a vital part therein, yet the acts to which this sort of religion prompts are personal not ritual acts, the individual transacts the business by himself alone, and the ecclesiastical organization, with its priests and sacraments and other go-betweens, sinks to an altogether secondary place. The relation goes direct from heart to heart, from soul to soul, between man and his maker.

Now in these lectures I propose to ignore the institutional branch entirely, to say nothing of the ecclesiastical organization, to consider as little as possible the systematic theology and the ideas about the gods themselves, and to confine myself as far as I can to personal religion pure and simple. To some of you personal religion, thus nakedly considered, will no doubt seem too incomplete a thing to wear the general name. "It is a part of religion," you will say, "but only its unorganized rudiment; if we are to name it by itself, we had better call it man's conscience or morality than his religion. The name 'religion' should be reserved for the fully organized system of feeling, thought, and institution, for the Church, in short, of which this personal religion, so called, is but a fractional element."

But if you say this, it will only show the more plainly how much the question of definition tends to become a dispute about names. Rather than prolong such a dispute, I am willing to accept almost any name for the personal religion of which I propose to treat. Call it conscience or morality, if you yourselves prefer, and not religion—under either name it will be equally worthy of our study. As for myself, I think it will prove to contain some elements which morality pure and simple does not contain, and these elements I shall soon seek to point out; so I will myself continue to apply the word 'religion' to it; and in the last lecture of all, I will bring in the theologies and the ecclesiasticisms, and say something of its relation to them.

In one sense at least the personal religion will prove itself more fundamental than either theology or ecclesiasticism. Churches, when once established, live at second-hand upon tradition; but the *founders* of every church owed their power originally to the fact of their direct personal communion with the divine. Not only the superhuman founders, the Christ, the Buddha, Mahomet, but all the originators of Christian sects have been in this case;—so personal religion should still seem the primordial thing, even to those who continue to esteem it incomplete.

There are, it is true, other things in religion chronologically more primordial than personal devoutness in the moral sense. Fetishism and magic seem to have preceded inward piety historically—at least our records of inward piety do not reach back so far. And if fetishism and magic be regarded as stages of religion, one may say that personal religion in the inward sense and the genuinely spiritual ecclesiasticisms which it founds are phenomena of secondary or even tertiary order. But, quite apart from the fact that many anthropologists—for instance, Jevons and Frazer—expressly oppose 'religion' and 'magic' to each other, it is certain that the whole system of thought which leads to magic, fetishism, and the lower superstitions may just as well be called primitive science as called primitive religion. The question thus becomes a verbal one again; and our knowledge of all these early stages of thought and feeling is in any case so conjectural and imperfect that farther discussion would not be worth while.

Religion, therefore, as I now ask you arbitrarily to take it, shall mean for us *the feelings, acts, and experiences of individual men in their solitude, so far as they apprehend themselves to stand in relation to whatever they may consider the divine.* Since the relation may be either moral, physical, or ritual, it is evident that out of religion in the sense in which we take it, theologies, philosophies, and ecclesiastical organizations may secondarily grow. In these lectures, however, as I have already said, the immediate personal experiences will amply fill our time, and we shall hardly consider theology or ecclesiasticism at all.

We escape much controversial matter by this arbitrary definition of our field. But, still, a chance of controversy comes up over the word 'divine,' if we take it in the definition in too narrow a sense. There are systems of thought which the world usually calls religious, and yet which do not positively assume a God. Buddhism is in this case. Popularly, of course, the Buddha himself stands in place of a God; but in strictness the Buddhistic system is atheistic. Modern transcendental idealism, Emersonianism, for instance, also seems to let God evaporate into abstract Ideality. Not a deity *in concreto*, not a superhuman person, but the immanent divinity in things, the essentially spiritual structure of the universe, is the object of the transcendentalist cult. In that address to the graduating class at Divinity College in 1838 which made Emerson famous, the frank expression of this worship of mere abstract laws was what made the scandal of the performance.

"These laws," said the speaker, "execute themselves. They are out of time, out of space, and not subject to circumstance: Thus, in the soul of man there is a justice whose retributions are instant and entire. He who does a good deed is instantly ennobled. He who does a mean deed is by the action itself contracted. He who puts off impurity thereby puts on purity. If a man is at heart just, then in so far is he God; the safety of God, the immortality of God, the majesty of God, do enter into that man with justice. If a man dissemble, deceive, he deceives himself, and goes out of acquaintance with his own being. Character is always known. Thefts never enrich; alms never impoverish; murder will speak out of stone walls. The least admixture of a lie—for example, the taint of vanity, any attempt to make a good impression, a favorable appearance—will instantly vitiate the effect. But speak the truth, and all things alive or brute are vouchers, and the very roots of the grass underground there do seem to stir and move to bear you witness. For all things proceed out of the same spirit, which is differently named love, justice, temperance, in its different applications, just as the ocean receives different names on the several shores which it washes. In so far as he roves from these ends, a man bereaves himself of power, of auxiliaries. His being shrinks . . . he becomes less and less, a mote, a point, until absolute badness is absolute death. The perception of this law awakens in the mind a sentiment which we call the religious sentiment, and which makes our highest happiness. Wonderful is its power to charm and to command. It is a mountain air. It is the embalmer of the world. It makes the sky and the hills sublime, and the silent song of the stars is it. It is the beatitude of man. It makes him illimitable. When he says 'I ought'; when love warms him; when he chooses, warned from on high, the good and great deed; then, deep melodies wander through his soul from supreme wisdom. Then he can worship, and be enlarged by his worship; for he can never go behind this sentiment. All the expressions of this sentiment are sacred and permanent in proportion to their purity. [They] affect us more than all other compositions. The sentences of the olden time, which ejaculate this piety, are still fresh and fragrant. And the unique impression of Jesus upon mankind, whose name is not so much written as ploughed into the history of this world, is proof of the subtle virtue of this infusion."[1]

Such is the Emersonian religion. The universe has a divine

[1] Miscellanies, 1868, p. 120 (abridged).

soul of order, which soul is moral, being also the soul within the soul of man. But whether this soul of the universe be a mere quality like the eye's brilliancy or the skin's softness, or whether it be a self-conscious life like the eye's seeing or the skin's feeling, is a decision that never unmistakably appears in Emerson's pages. It quivers on the boundary of these things, sometimes leaning one way, sometimes the other, to suit the literary rather than the philosophic need. Whatever it is, though, it is active. As much as if it were a God, we can trust it to protect all ideal interests and keep the world's balance straight. The sentences in which Emerson, to the very end, gave utterance to this faith are as fine as anything in literature: "If you love and serve men, you cannot by any hiding or stratagem escape the remuneration. Secret retributions are always restoring the level, when disturbed, of the divine justice. It is impossible to tilt the beam. All the tyrants and proprietors and monopolists of the world in vain set their shoulders to heave the bar. Settles forevermore the ponderous equator to its line, and man and mote, and star and sun, must range to it, or be pulverized by the recoil."[1]

Now it would be too absurd to say that the inner experiences that underlie such expressions of faith as this and impel the writer to their utterance are quite unworthy to be called religious experiences. The sort of appeal that Emersonian optimism, on the one hand, and Buddhistic pessimism, on the other, make to the individual and the sort of response which he makes to them in his life are in fact indistinguishable from, and in many respects identical with, the best Christian appeal and response. We must therefore, from the experiential point of view, call these godless or quasi-godless creeds 'religions'; and accordingly when in our definition of religion we speak of the individual's relation to 'what he considers the divine,' we must interpret the term 'divine' very broadly, as denoting any object that is god*like*, whether it be a concrete deity or not.

But the term 'godlike,' if thus treated as a floating general quality, becomes exceedingly vague, for many gods have flourished in religious history, and their attributes have been

[1] Lectures and Biographical Sketches, 1868, p. 186.

discrepant enough. What then is that essentially godlike quality—be it embodied in a concrete deity or not—our relation
to which determines our character as religious men? It will
repay us to seek some answer to this question before we proceed farther.

For one thing, gods are conceived to be first things in the
way of being and power. They overarch and envelop, and
from them there is no escape. What relates to them is the first
and last word in the way of truth. Whatever then were most
primal and enveloping and deeply true might at this rate be
treated as godlike, and a man's religion might thus be identified with his attitude, whatever it might be, towards what he
felt to be the primal truth.

Such a definition as this would in a way be defensible. Religion, whatever it is, is a man's total reaction upon life, so
why not say that any total reaction upon life is a religion?
Total reactions are different from casual reactions, and total
attitudes are different from usual or professional attitudes. To
get at them you must go behind the foreground of existence
and reach down to that curious sense of the whole residual
cosmos as an everlasting presence, intimate or alien, terrible
or amusing, lovable or odious, which in some degree every
one possesses. This sense of the world's presence, appealing
as it does to our peculiar individual temperament, makes us
either strenuous or careless, devout or blasphemous, gloomy
or exultant, about life at large; and our reaction, involuntary
and inarticulate and often half unconscious as it is, is the completest of all our answers to the question, "What is the character of this universe in which we dwell?" It expresses our
individual sense of it in the most definite way. Why then not
call these reactions our religion, no matter what specific character they may have? Non-religious as some of these reactions
may be, in one sense of the word 'religious,' they yet belong
to *the general sphere of the religious life*, and so should generically be classed as religious reactions. "He believes in No-
God, and he worships him," said a colleague of mine of a
student who was manifesting a fine atheistic ardor; and the
more fervent opponents of Christian doctrine have often
enough shown a temper which, psychologically considered, is
indistinguishable from religious zeal.

But so very broad a use of the word 'religion' would be inconvenient, however defensible it might remain on logical grounds. There are trifling, sneering attitudes even towards the whole of life; and in some men these attitudes are final and systematic. It would strain the ordinary use of language too much to call such attitudes religious, even though, from the point of view of an unbiased critical philosophy, they might conceivably be perfectly reasonable ways of looking upon life. Voltaire, for example, writes thus to a friend, at the age of seventy-three: "As for myself," he says, "weak as I am, I carry on the war to the last moment, I get a hundred pike-thrusts, I return two hundred, and I laugh. I see near my door Geneva on fire with quarrels over nothing, and I laugh again; and, thank God, I can look upon the world as a farce even when it becomes as tragic as it sometimes does. All comes out even at the end of the day, and all comes out still more even when all the days are over."

Much as we may admire such a robust old gamecock spirit in a valetudinarian, to call it a religious spirit would be odd. Yet it is for the moment Voltaire's reaction on the whole of life. *Je m'en fiche* is the vulgar French equivalent for our English ejaculation 'Who cares?' And the happy term *je m'en fichisme* recently has been invented to designate the systematic determination not to take anything in life too solemnly. 'All is vanity' is the relieving word in all difficult crises for this mode of thought, which that exquisite literary genius Renan took pleasure, in his later days of sweet decay, in putting into coquettishly sacrilegious forms which remain to us as excellent expressions of the 'all is vanity' state of mind. Take the following passage, for example,—we must hold to duty, even against the evidence, Renan says,—but he then goes on:—

"There are many chances that the world may be nothing but a fairy pantomime of which no God has care. We must therefore arrange ourselves so that on neither hypothesis we shall be completely wrong. We must listen to the superior voices, but in such a way that if the second hypothesis were true we should not have been too completely duped. If in effect the world be not a serious thing, it is the dogmatic people who will be the shallow ones, and the worldly minded whom the theologians now call frivolous will be those who are really wise.

"*In utrumque paratus*, then. Be ready for anything—that perhaps is wisdom. Give ourselves up, according to the hour, to confidence, to skepticism, to optimism, to irony, and we may be sure that at certain moments at least we shall be with the truth. . . . Good-humor is a philosophic state of mind; it seems to say to Nature that we take her no more seriously than she takes us. I maintain that one should always talk of philosophy with a smile. We owe it to the Eternal to be virtuous; but we have the right to add to this tribute our irony as a sort of personal reprisal. In this way we return to the right quarter jest for jest; we play the trick that has been played on us. Saint Augustine's phrase: *Lord, if we are deceived, it is by thee!* remains a fine one, well suited to our modern feeling. Only we wish the Eternal to know that if we accept the fraud, we accept it knowingly and willingly. We are resigned in advance to losing the interest on our investments of virtue, but we wish not to appear ridiculous by having counted on them too securely."[1]

Surely all the usual associations of the word 'religion' would have to be stripped away if such a systematic *parti pris* of irony were also to be denoted by the name. For common men 'religion,' whatever more special meanings it may have, signifies always a *serious* state of mind. If any one phrase could gather its universal message, that phrase would be, 'All is *not* vanity in this Universe, whatever the appearances may suggest.' If it can stop anything, religion as commonly apprehended can stop just such chaffing talk as Renan's. It favors gravity, not pertness; it says 'hush' to all vain chatter and smart wit.

But if hostile to light irony, religion is equally hostile to heavy grumbling and complaint. The world appears tragic enough in some religions, but the tragedy is realized as purging, and a way of deliverance is held to exist. We shall see enough of the religious melancholy in a future lecture; but melancholy, according to our ordinary use of language,

[1] Feuilles détachées, pp. 394–398 (abridged).

forfeits all title to be called religious when, in Marcus Aurelius's racy words, the sufferer simply lies kicking and screaming after the fashion of a sacrificed pig. The mood of a Schopenhauer or a Nietzsche,—and in a less degree one may sometimes say the same of our own sad Carlyle,—though often an ennobling sadness, is almost as often only peevishness running away with the bit between its teeth. The sallies of the two German authors remind one, half the time, of the sick shriekings of two dying rats. They lack the purgatorial note which religious sadness gives forth.

There must be something solemn, serious, and tender about any attitude which we denominate religious. If glad, it must not grin or snicker; if sad, it must not scream or curse. It is precisely as being *solemn* experiences that I wish to interest you in religious experiences. So I propose—arbitrarily again, if you please—to narrow our definition once more by saying that the word 'divine,' as employed therein, shall mean for us not merely the primal and enveloping and real, for that meaning if taken without restriction might well prove too broad. The divine shall mean for us only such a primal reality as the individual feels impelled to respond to solemnly and gravely, and neither by a curse nor a jest.

But solemnity, and gravity, and all such emotional attributes, admit of various shades; and, do what we will with our defining, the truth must at last be confronted that we are dealing with a field of experience where there is not a single conception that can be sharply drawn. The pretension, under such conditions, to be rigorously 'scientific' or 'exact' in our terms would only stamp us as lacking in understanding of our task. Things are more or less divine, states of mind are more or less religious, reactions are more or less total, but the boundaries are always misty, and it is everywhere a question of amount and degree. Nevertheless, at their extreme of development, there can never be any question as to what experiences are religious. The divinity of the object and the solemnity of the reaction are too well marked for doubt. Hesitation as to whether a state of mind is 'religious,' or 'irreligious,' or 'moral,' or 'philosophical,' is only likely to arise when the state of mind is weakly characterized, but in that case it will be hardly worthy of our study at all. With states that can only by courtesy be called religious we need have nothing to do, our only profitable business being with what nobody can possibly feel tempted to call anything else. I said in my former lecture that we learn most about a thing when we view it under a microscope, as it were, or in its most exaggerated form. This is as true of religious phenomena as of any other kind of fact. The only cases likely to be profitable enough to repay our attention will therefore be cases where the religious spirit is unmistakable and extreme. Its fainter manifestations we may tranquilly pass by. Here, for example, is the total reaction upon life of Frederick Locker Lampson, whose autobiography, entitled 'Confidences,' proves him to have been a most amiable man.

"I am so far resigned to my lot that I feel small pain at the thought of having to part from what has been called the pleasant habit of existence, the sweet fable of life. I would not care to live my wasted life over again, and so to prolong my span. Strange to say, I have but little wish to be younger. I submit with a chill at my heart. I humbly submit because it is the Divine Will, and my appointed destiny. I dread the increase of infirmities that will make me a burden to those around me, those dear to me. No! let me slip away as quietly and comfortably as I can. Let the end come, if peace come with it.

"I do not know that there is a great deal to be said for this world, or our sojourn here upon it; but it has pleased God so to place us, and it must please me also. I ask you, what is human life? Is not it a maimed happiness—care and weariness, weariness and care, with the baseless expectation, the strange cozenage of a brighter to-morrow? At best it is but a froward child, that must be played with and humored, to keep it quiet till it falls asleep, and then the care is over."[1]

This is a complex, a tender, a submissive, and a graceful state of mind. For myself, I should have no objection to calling it on the whole a religious state of mind, although I dare say that to many of you it may seem too listless and half-

[1] Op. cit., pp. 314, 313.

hearted to merit so good a name. But what matters it in the end whether we call such a state of mind religious or not? It is too insignificant for our instruction in any case; and its very possessor wrote it down in terms which he would not have used unless he had been thinking of more energetically religious moods in others, with which he found himself unable to compete. It is with these more energetic states that our sole business lies, and we can perfectly well afford to let the minor notes and the uncertain border go.

It was the extremer cases that I had in mind a little while ago when I said that personal religion, even without theology or ritual, would prove to embody some elements that morality pure and simple does not contain. You may remember that I promised shortly to point out what those elements were. In a general way I can now say what I had in mind.

"I accept the universe" is reported to have been a favorite utterance of our New England transcendentalist, Margaret Fuller; and when some one repeated this phrase to Thomas Carlyle, his sardonic comment is said to have been: "Gad! she'd better!" At bottom the whole concern of both morality and religion is with the manner of our acceptance of the universe. Do we accept it only in part and grudgingly, or heartily and altogether? Shall our protests against certain things in it be radical and unforgiving, or shall we think that, even with evil, there are ways of living that must lead to good? If we accept the whole, shall we do so as if stunned into submission,—as Carlyle would have us—"Gad! we'd better!"— or shall we do with enthusiastic assent? Morality pure and simple accepts the law of the whole which it finds reigning, so far as to acknowledge and obey it, but it may obey it with the heaviest and coldest heart, and never cease to feel it as a yoke. But for religion, in its strong and fully developed manifestations, the service of the highest never is felt as a yoke. Dull submission is left far behind, and a mood of welcome, which may fill any place on the scale between cheerful serenity and enthusiastic gladness, has taken its place.

It makes a tremendous emotional and practical difference to one whether one accept the universe in the drab discolored way of stoic resignation to necessity, or with the passionate happiness of Christian saints. The difference is as great as that between passivity and activity, as that between the defensive and the aggressive mood. Gradual as are the steps by which an individual may grow from one state into the other, many as are the intermediate stages which different individuals represent, yet when you place the typical extremes beside each other for comparison, you feel that two discontinuous psychological universes confront you, and that in passing from one to the other a 'critical point' has been overcome.

If we compare stoic with Christian ejaculations we see much more than a difference of doctrine; rather is it a difference of emotional mood that parts them. When Marcus Aurelius reflects on the eternal reason that has ordered things, there is a frosty chill about his words which you rarely find in a Jewish, and never in a Christian piece of religious writing. The universe is 'accepted' by all these writers; but how devoid of passion or exultation the spirit of the Roman Emperor is! Compare his fine sentence: "If gods care not for me or my children, here is a reason for it," with Job's cry: "Though he slay me, yet will I trust in him!" and you immediately see the difference I mean. The *anima mundi*, to whose disposal of his own personal destiny the Stoic consents, is there to be respected and submitted to, but the Christian God is there to be loved; and the difference of emotional atmosphere is like that between an arctic climate and the tropics, though the outcome in the way of accepting actual conditions uncomplainingly may seem in abstract terms to be much the same.

"It is a man's duty," says Marcus Aurelius, "to comfort himself and wait for the natural dissolution, and not to be vexed, but to find refreshment solely in these thoughts— first that nothing will happen to me which is not conformable to the nature of the universe; and secondly that I need do nothing contrary to the God and deity within me; for there is no man who can compel me to transgress.[1] He is an abscess on the universe who withdraws and separates himself from the reason of our common nature, through

[1] Book V., ch. x. (abridged).

being displeased with the things which happen. For the same nature produces these, and has produced thee too. And so accept everything which happens, even if it seem disagreeable, because it leads to this, the health of the universe and to the prosperity and felicity of Zeus. For he would not have brought on any man what he has brought, if it were not useful for the whole. The integrity of the whole is mutilated if thou cuttest off anything. And thou dost cut off, as far as it is in thy power, when thou art dissatisfied, and in a manner triest to put anything out of the way."[1]

Compare now this mood with that of the old Christian author of the Theologia Germanica: —

"Where men are enlightened with the true light, they renounce all desire and choice, and commit and commend themselves and all things to the eternal Goodness, so that every enlightened man could say: 'I would fain be to the Eternal Goodness what his own hand is to a man.' Such men are in a state of freedom, because they have lost the fear of pain or hell, and the hope of reward or heaven, and are living in pure submission to the eternal Goodness, in the perfect freedom of fervent love. When a man truly perceiveth and considereth himself, who and what he is, and findeth himself utterly vile and wicked and unworthy, he falleth into such a deep abasement that it seemeth to him reasonable that all creatures in heaven and earth should rise up against him. And therefore he will not and dare not desire any consolation and release; but he is willing to be unconsoled and unreleased; and he doth not grieve over his sufferings, for they are right in his eyes, and he hath nothing to say against them. This is what is meant by true repentance for sin; and he who in this present time entereth into this hell, none may console him. Now God hath not forsaken a man in this hell, but He is laying his hand upon him, that the man may not desire nor regard anything but the eternal Good only. And then, when the man neither careth for nor desireth anything but the eternal Good

[1] Book V., ch. ix. (abridged).

alone, and seeketh not himself nor his own things, but the honour of God only, he is made a partaker of all manner of joy, bliss, peace, rest, and consolation, and so the man is henceforth in the kingdom of heaven. This hell and this heaven are two good safe ways for a man, and happy is he who truly findeth them."[1]

How much more active and positive the impulse of the Christian writer to accept his place in the universe is! Marcus Aurelius agrees *to* the scheme—the German theologian agrees *with* it. He literally *abounds* in agreement, he runs out to embrace the divine decrees.

Occasionally, it is true, the Stoic rises to something like a Christian warmth of sentiment, as in the often quoted passage of Marcus Aurelius:—

"Everything harmonizes with me which is harmonious to thee, O Universe. Nothing for me is too early nor too late, which is in due time for thee. Everything is fruit to me which thy seasons bring, O Nature: from thee are all things, in thee are all things, to thee all things return. The poet says, Dear City of Cecrops; and wilt thou not say, Dear City of Zeus?"[2]

But compare even as devout a passage as this with a genuine Christian outpouring, and it seems a little cold. Turn, for instance, to the Imitation of Christ:—

"Lord, thou knowest what is best; let this or that be according as thou wilt. Give what thou wilt, so much as thou wilt, when thou wilt. Do with me as thou knowest best, and as shall be most to thine honour. Place me where thou wilt, and freely work thy will with me in all things. . . . When could it be evil when thou wert near? I had rather be poor for thy sake than rich without thee. I choose rather to be a pilgrim upon the earth with thee, than without thee

[1] Chaps. x., xi. (abridged): Winkworth's translation.
[2] Book IV., § 23.

to possess heaven. Where thou art, there is heaven; and where thou art not, behold there death and hell."[1]

It is a good rule in physiology, when we are studying the meaning of an organ, to ask after its most peculiar and characteristic sort of performance, and to seek its office in that one of its functions which no other organ can possibly exert. Surely the same maxim holds good in our present quest. The essence of religious experiences, the thing by which we finally must judge them, must be that element or quality in them which we can meet nowhere else. And such a quality will be of course most prominent and easy to notice in those religious experiences which are most one-sided, exaggerated, and intense.

Now when we compare these intenser experiences with the experiences of tamer minds, so cool and reasonable that we are tempted to call them philosophical rather than religious, we find a character that is perfectly distinct. That character, it seems to me, should be regarded as the practically important *differentia* of religion for our purpose; and just what it is can easily be brought out by comparing the mind of an abstractly conceived Christian with that of a moralist similarly conceived.

A life is manly, stoical, moral, or philosophical, we say, in proportion as it is less swayed by paltry personal considerations and more by objective ends that call for energy, even though that energy bring personal loss and pain. This is the good side of war, in so far as it calls for 'volunteers'. And for morality life is a war, and the service of the highest is a sort of cosmic patriotism which also calls for volunteers. Even a sick man, unable to be militant outwardly, can carry on the moral warfare. He can willfully turn his attention away from his own future, whether in this world or the next. He can train himself to indifference to his present drawbacks and immerse himself in whatever objective interests still remain accessible. He can follow public news, and sympathize with

---

[1] Benham's translation: Book III., chaps. xv., lix. Compare Mary Moody Emerson: "Let me be a blot on this fair world, the obscurest, the loneliest sufferer, with one proviso,—that I know it is His agency. I will love Him though He shed frost and darkness on every way of mine." R. W. EMERSON: Lectures and Biographical Sketches, p. 188.

other people's affairs. He can cultivate cheerful manners, and be silent about his miseries. He can contemplate whatever ideal aspects of existence his philosophy is able to present to him, and practice whatever duties, such as patience, resignation, trust, his ethical system requires. Such a man lives on his loftiest, largest plane. He is a high-hearted freeman and no pining slave. And yet he lacks something which the Christian *par excellence*, the mystic and ascetic saint, for example, has in abundant measure, and which makes of him a human being of an altogether different denomination.

The Christian also spurns the pinched and mumping sick-room attitude, and the lives of saints are full of a kind of callousness to diseased conditions of body which probably no other human records show. But whereas the merely moralistic spurning takes an effort of volition, the Christian spurning is the result of the excitement of a higher kind of emotion, in the presence of which no exertion of volition is required. The moralist must hold his breath and keep his muscles tense; and so long as this athletic attitude is possible all goes well—morality suffices. But the athletic attitude tends ever to break down, and it inevitably does break down even in the most stalwart when the organism begins to decay, or when morbid fears invade the mind. To suggest personal will and effort to one all sicklied o'er with the sense of irremediable impotence is to suggest the most impossible of things. What he craves is to be consoled in his very powerlessness, to feel that the spirit of the universe recognizes and secures him, all decaying and failing as he is. Well, we are all such helpless failures in the last resort. The sanest and best of us are of one clay with lunatics and prison inmates, and death finally runs the robustest of us down. And whenever we feel this, such a sense of the vanity and provisionality of our voluntary career comes over us that all our morality appears but as a plaster hiding a sore it can never cure, and all our well-doing as the hollowest substitute for that well-*being* that our lives ought to be grounded in, but, alas! are not.

And here religion comes to our rescue and takes our fate into her hands. There is a state of mind, known to religious men, but to no others, in which the will to assert ourselves and hold our own has been displaced by a willingness to close our mouths and be as nothing in the floods and waterspouts of God. In this state of mind, what we most dreaded has become the habitation of our safety, and the hour of our moral death has turned into our spiritual birthday. The time for tension in our soul is over, and that of happy relaxation, of calm deep breathing, of an eternal present, with no discordant future to be anxious about, has arrived. Fear is not held in abeyance as it is by mere morality, it is positively expunged and washed away.

We shall see abundant examples of this happy state of mind in later lectures of this course. We shall see how infinitely passionate a thing religion at its highest flights can be. Like love, like wrath, like hope, ambition, jealousy, like every other instinctive eagerness and impulse, it adds to life an enchantment which is not rationally or logically deducible from anything else. This enchantment, coming as a gift when it does come,—a gift of our organism, the physiologists will tell us, a gift of God's grace, the theologians say,—is either there or not there for us, and there are persons who can no more become possessed by it than they can fall in love with a given woman by mere word of command. Religious feeling is thus an absolute addition to the Subject's range of life. It gives him a new sphere of power. When the outward battle is lost, and the outer world disowns him, it redeems and vivifies an interior world which otherwise would be an empty waste.

If religion is to mean anything definite for us, it seems to me that we ought to take it as meaning this added dimension of emotion, this enthusiastic temper of espousal, in regions where morality strictly so called can at best but bow its head and acquiesce. It ought to mean nothing short of this new reach of freedom for us, with the struggle over, the keynote of the universe sounding in our ears, and everlasting possession spread before our eyes.[1]

This sort of happiness in the absolute and everlasting is what we find nowhere but in religion. It is parted off from all

[1]Once more, there are plenty of men, constitutionally sombre men, in whose religious life this rapturousness is lacking. They are religious in the wider sense; yet in this acutest of all senses they are not so, and it is religion in the acutest sense that I wish, without disputing about words, to study first, so as to get at its typical *differentia*.

mere animal happiness, all mere enjoyment of the present, by that element of solemnity of which I have already made so much account. Solemnity is a hard thing to define abstractly, but certain of its marks are patent enough. A solemn state of mind is never crude or simple—it seems to contain a certain measure of its own opposite in solution. A solemn joy preserves a sort of bitter in its sweetness; a solemn sorrow is one to which we intimately consent. But there are writers who, realizing that happiness of a supreme sort is the prerogative of religion, forget this complication, and call all happiness, as such, religious. Mr. Havelock Ellis, for example, identifies religion with the entire field of the soul's liberation from oppressive moods.

> "The simplest functions of physiological life," he writes, "may be its ministers. Every one who is at all acquainted with the Persian mystics knows how wine may be regarded as an instrument of religion. Indeed, in all countries and in all ages, some form of physical enlargement—singing, dancing, drinking, sexual excitement—has been intimately associated with worship. Even the momentary expansion of the soul in laughter is, to however slight an extent, a religious exercise. . . . Whenever an impulse from the world strikes against the organism, and the resultant is not discomfort or pain, not even the muscular contraction of strenuous manhood, but a joyous expansion or aspiration of the whole soul—there is religion. It is the infinite for which we hunger, and we ride gladly on every little wave that promises to bear us towards it."[1]

But such a straight identification of religion with any and every form of happiness leaves the essential peculiarity of religious happiness out. The more commonplace happinesses which we get are 'reliefs,' occasioned by our momentary escapes from evils either experienced or threatened. But in its most characteristic embodiments, religious happiness is no mere feeling of escape. It cares no longer to escape. It consents to the evil outwardly as a form of sacrifice—inwardly it knows it to be permanently overcome. If you ask *how* religion

[1] The New Spirit, p. 232.

thus falls on the thorns and faces death, and in the very act annuls annihilation, I cannot explain the matter, for it is religion's secret, and to understand it you must yourself have been a religious man of the extremer type. In our future examples, even of the simplest and healthiest-minded type of religious consciousness, we shall find this complex sacrificial constitution, in which a higher happiness holds a lower unhappiness in check. In the Louvre there is a picture, by Guido Reni, of St. Michael with his foot on Satan's neck. The richness of the picture is in large part due to the fiend's figure being there. The richness of its allegorical meaning also is due to his being there—that is, the world is all the richer for having a devil in it, *so long as we keep our foot upon his neck.* In the religious consciousness, that is just the position in which the fiend, the negative or tragic principle, is found; and for that very reason the religious consciousness is so rich from the emotional point of view.[1] We shall see how in certain men and women it takes on a monstrously ascetic form. There are saints who have literally fed on the negative principle, on humiliation and privation, and the thought of suffering and death,—their souls growing in happiness just in proportion as their outward state grew more intolerable. No other emotion than religious emotion can bring a man to this peculiar pass. And it is for that reason that when we ask our question about the value of religion for human life, I think we ought to look for the answer among these violenter examples rather than among those of a more moderate hue.

Having the phenomenon of our study in its acutest possible form to start with, we can shade down as much as we please later. And if in these cases, repulsive as they are to our ordinary worldly way of judging, we find ourselves compelled to acknowledge religion's value and treat it with respect, it will have proved in some way its value for life at large. By subtracting and toning down extravagances we may thereupon proceed to trace the boundaries of its legitimate sway.

To be sure, it makes our task difficult to have to deal so much with eccentricities and extremes. "How *can* religion on the whole be the most important of all human functions,"

[1] I owe this allegorical illustration to my lamented colleague and friend, Charles Carroll Everett.

you may ask, "if every several manifestation of it in turn have to be corrected and sobered down and pruned away?" Such a thesis seems a paradox impossible to sustain reasonably,—yet I believe that something like it will have to be our final contention. That personal attitude which the individual finds himself impelled to take up towards what he apprehends to be the divine—and you will remember that this was our definition—will prove to be both a helpless and a sacrificial attitude. That is, we shall have to confess to at least some amount of dependence on sheer mercy, and to practice some amount of renunciation, great or small, to save our souls alive. The constitution of the world we live in requires it:—

> "Entbehren sollst du! sollst entbehren!
> Das ist der ewige Gesang
> Der jedem an die Ohren klingt,
> Den, unser ganzes Leben lang
> Uns heiser jede Stunde singt."

For when all is said and done, we are in the end absolutely dependent on the universe; and into sacrifices and surrenders of some sort, deliberately looked at and accepted, we are drawn and pressed as into our only permanent positions of repose. Now in those states of mind which fall short of religion, the surrender is submitted to as an imposition of necessity, and the sacrifice is undergone at the very best without complaint. In the religious life, on the contrary, surrender and sacrifice are positively espoused: even unnecessary givings-up are added in order that the happiness may increase. *Religion thus makes easy and felicitous what in any case is necessary;* and if it be the only agency that can accomplish this result, its vital importance as a human faculty stands vindicated beyond dispute. It becomes an essential organ of our life, performing a function which no other portion of our nature can so successfully fulfill. From the merely biological point of view, so to call it, this is a conclusion to which, so far as I can now see, we shall inevitably be led, and led moreover by following the purely empirical method of demonstration which I sketched to you in the first lecture. Of the farther office of religion as a metaphysical revelation I will say nothing now.

But to foreshadow the terminus of one's investigations is

one thing, and to arrive there safely is another. In the next lecture, abandoning the extreme generalities which have engrossed us hitherto, I propose that we begin our actual journey by addressing ourselves directly to the concrete facts.

LECTURE III

THE REALITY OF THE UNSEEN

WERE ONE ASKED to characterize the life of religion in the broadest and most general terms possible, one might say that it consists of the belief that there is an unseen order, and that our supreme good lies in harmoniously adjusting ourselves thereto. This belief and this adjustment are the religious attitude in the soul. I wish during this hour to call your attention to some of the psychological peculiarities of such an attitude as this, of belief in an object which we cannot see. All our attitudes, moral, practical, or emotional, as well as religious, are due to the 'objects' of our consciousness, the things which we believe to exist, whether really or ideally, along with ourselves. Such objects may be present to our senses, or they may be present only to our thought. In either case they elicit from us a *reaction*; and the reaction due to things of thought is notoriously in many cases as strong as that due to sensible presences. It may be even stronger. The memory of an insult may make us angrier than the insult did when we received it. We are frequently more ashamed of our blunders afterwards than we were at the moment of making them; and in general our whole higher prudential and moral life is based on the fact that material sensations actually present may have a weaker influence on our action than ideas of remoter facts.

The more concrete objects of most men's religion, the deities whom they worship, are known to them only in idea. It has been vouchsafed, for example, to very few Christian believers to have had a sensible vision of their Saviour; though enough appearances of this sort are on record, by way of miraculous exception, to merit our attention later. The whole force of the Christian religion, therefore, so far as belief in the divine personages determines the prevalent attitude of the believer, is in general exerted by the instrumentality of pure ideas, of which nothing in the individual's past experience directly serves as a model.

But in addition to these ideas of the more concrete religious objects, religion is full of abstract objects which prove to have an equal power. God's attributes as such, his holiness, his justice, his mercy, his absoluteness, his infinity, his omniscience, his tri-unity, the various mysteries of the redemptive process, the operation of the sacraments, etc., have proved fertile wells of inspiring meditation for Christian believers.[1] We shall see later that the absence of definite sensible images is positively insisted on by the mystical authorities in all religions as the *sine qua non* of a successful orison, or contemplation of the higher divine truths. Such contemplations are expected (and abundantly verify the expectation, as we shall also see) to influence the believer's subsequent attitude very powerfully for good.

Immanuel Kant held a curious doctrine about such objects of belief as God, the design of creation, the soul, its freedom, and the life hereafter. These things, he said, are properly not objects of knowledge at all. Our conceptions always require a sense-content to work with, and as the words 'soul,' 'God,' 'immortality,' cover no distinctive sense-content whatever, it follows that theoretically speaking they are words devoid of any significance. Yet strangely enough they have a definite meaning *for our practice*. We can act *as if* there were a God; feel *as if* we were free; consider Nature *as if* she were full of special designs; lay plans *as if* we were to be immortal; and we find then that these words do make a genuine difference in our moral life. Our faith *that* these unintelligible objects actually exist proves thus to be a full equivalent in *praktischer Hinsicht*, as Kant calls it, or from the point of view of our action, for a knowledge of *what* they might be, in case we were permitted positively to conceive them. So we have the strange phenomenon, as Kant assures us, of a mind believing with all its strength in the real presence of a set of things of no one of which it can form any notion whatsoever.

---

[1] Example: "I have had much comfort lately in meditating on the passages which show the personality of the Holy Ghost, and his distinctness from the Father and the Son. It is a subject that requires searching into to find out, but, when realized, gives one so much more true and lively a sense of the fullness of the Godhead, and its work in us and to us, than when only thinking of the Spirit in its effect on us." AUGUSTUS HARE: Memorials, i. 244, Maria Hare to Lucy H. Hare.

My object in thus recalling Kant's doctrine to your mind is
not to express any opinion as to the accuracy of this particularly uncouth part of his philosophy, but only to illustrate the
characteristic of human nature which we are considering, by
an example so classical in its exaggeration. The sentiment of
reality can indeed attach itself so strongly to our object of
belief that our whole life is polarized through and through,
so to speak, by its sense of the existence of the thing believed
in, and yet that thing, for purpose of definite description, can
hardly be said to be present to our mind at all. It is as if a bar
of iron, without touch or sight, with no representative faculty
whatever, might nevertheless be strongly endowed with an
inner capacity for magnetic feeling; and as if, through the various arousals of its magnetism by magnets coming and going
in its neighborhood, it might be consciously determined to
different attitudes and tendencies. Such a bar of iron could
never give you an outward description of the agencies that
had the power of stirring it so strongly; yet of their presence,
and of their significance for its life, it would be intensely
aware through every fibre of its being.

It is not only the Ideas of pure Reason, as Kant styled
them, that have this power of making us vitally feel presences
that we are impotent articulately to describe. All sorts of
higher abstractions bring with them the same kind of impalpable appeal. Remember those passages from Emerson which
I read at my last lecture. The whole universe of concrete objects, as we know them, swims, not only for such a transcendentalist writer, but for all of us, in a wider and higher
universe of abstract ideas, that lend it its significance. As time,
space, and the ether soak through all things, so (we feel) do
abstract and essential goodness, beauty, strength, significance,
justice, soak through all things good, strong, significant, and
just.

Such ideas, and others equally abstract, form the background for all our facts, the fountain-head of all the possibilities we conceive of. They give its 'nature,' as we call it, to
every special thing. Everything we know is 'what' it is by
sharing in the nature of one of these abstractions. We can
never look directly at them, for they are bodiless and featureless and footless, but we grasp all other things by their means,

and in handling the real world we should be stricken with helplessness in just so far forth as we might lose these mental objects, these adjectives and adverbs and predicates and heads of classification and conception.

This absolute determinability of our mind by abstractions is one of the cardinal facts in our human constitution. Polarizing and magnetizing us as they do, we turn towards them and from them, we seek them, hold them, hate them, bless them, just as if they were so many concrete beings. And beings they are, beings as real in the realm which they inhabit as the changing things of sense are in the realm of space.

Plato gave so brilliant and impressive a defense of this common human feeling, that the doctrine of the reality of abstract objects has been known as the platonic theory of ideas ever since. Abstract Beauty, for example, is for Plato a perfectly definite individual being, of which the intellect is aware as of something additional to all the perishing beauties of the earth. "The true order of going," he says, in the often quoted passage in his 'Banquet,' "is to use the beauties of earth as steps along which one mounts upwards for the sake of that other Beauty, going from one to two, and from two to all fair forms, and from fair forms to fair actions, and from fair actions to fair notions, until from fair notions he arrives at the notion of absolute Beauty, and at last knows what the essence of Beauty is."[1] In our last lecture we had a glimpse of the way in which a platonizing writer like Emerson may treat the abstract divineness of things, the moral structure of the universe, as a fact worthy of worship. In those various churches without a God which to-day are spreading through the world under the name of ethical societies, we have a similar worship of the abstract divine, the moral law believed in as an ultimate object. 'Science' in many minds is genuinely taking the place of a religion. Where this is so, the scientist treats the 'Laws of Nature' as objective facts to be revered. A brilliant school of interpretation of Greek mythology would have it that in their origin the Greek gods were only half-metaphoric personifications of those great spheres of abstract law and order into which the natural world falls apart—the sky-sphere, the

[1] Symposium, Jowett, 1871, i. 527.

ocean-sphere, the earth-sphere, and the like; just as even now we may speak of the smile of the morning, the kiss of the breeze, or the bite of the cold, without really meaning that these phenomena of nature actually wear a human face.[1]

As regards the origin of the Greek gods, we need not at present seek an opinion. But the whole array of our instances leads to a conclusion something like this: It is as if there were in the human consciousness a *sense of reality, a feeling of objective presence, a perception* of what we may call *'something there,'* more deep and more general than any of the special and particular 'senses' by which the current psychology supposes existent realities to be originally revealed. If this were so, we might suppose the senses to waken our attitudes and conduct as they so habitually do, by first exciting this sense of reality; but anything else, any idea, for example, that might similarly excite it, would have that same prerogative of appearing real which objects of sense normally possess. So far as religious conceptions were able to touch this reality-feeling, they would be believed in in spite of criticism, even though they might be so vague and remote as to be almost unimaginable, even though they might be such non-entities in point of *whatness* as Kant makes the objects of his moral theology to be.

The most curious proofs of the existence of such an undifferentiated sense of reality as this are found in experiences of hallucination. It often happens that an hallucination is imperfectly developed: the person affected will feel a 'presence' in the room, definitely localized, facing in one particular way, real in the most emphatic sense of the word, often coming suddenly, and as suddenly gone; and yet neither seen, heard, touched, nor cognized in any of the usual 'sensible' ways. Let me give you an example of this, before I pass to the objects with whose presence religion is more peculiarly concerned.

An intimate friend of mine, one of the keenest intellects I know, has had several experiences of this sort. He writes as follows in response to my inquiries:—

"I have several times within the past few years felt the

[1] Example: "Nature is always so interesting, under whatever aspect she shows herself, that when it rains, I seem to see a beautiful woman weeping. She appears the more beautiful, the more afflicted she is." B. de St. Pierre.

so-called 'consciousness of a presence.' The experiences which I have in mind are clearly distinguishable from another kind of experience which I have had very frequently, and which I fancy many persons would also call the 'consciousness of a presence.' But the difference for me between the two sets of experience is as great as the difference between feeling a slight warmth originating I know not where, and standing in the midst of a conflagration with all the ordinary senses alert.

"It was about September, 1884, when I had the first experience. On the previous night I had had, after getting into bed at my rooms in College, a vivid tactile hallucination of being grasped by the arm, which made me get up and search the room for an intruder; but the sense of presence properly so called came on the next night. After I had got into bed and blown out the candle, I lay awake awhile thinking on the previous night's experience, when suddenly I *felt* something come into the room and stay close to my bed. It remained only a minute or two. I did not recognize it by any ordinary sense, and yet there was a horribly unpleasant 'sensation' connected with it. It stirred something more at the roots of my being than any ordinary perception. The feeling had something of the quality of a very large tearing vital pain spreading chiefly over the chest, but within the organism—and yet the feeling was not *pain* so much as *abhorrence*. At all events, something was present with me, and I knew its presence far more surely than I have ever known the presence of any fleshly living creature. I was conscious of its departure as of its coming: an almost instantaneously swift going through the door, and the 'horrible sensation' disappeared.

"On the third night when I retired my mind was absorbed in some lectures which I was preparing, and I was still absorbed in these when I became aware of the actual presence (though not of the *coming*) of the thing that was there the night before, and of the 'horrible sensation.' I then mentally concentrated all my effort to charge this 'thing,' if it was evil, to depart, if it was *not* evil, to tell me who or what it was, and if it could not explain itself, to go, and that I would compel it to go. It went as on the previous night, and my body quickly recovered its normal state.

"On two other occasions in my life I have had precisely the same 'horrible sensation.' Once it lasted a full quarter of an hour. In all three instances the certainty that there in outward space there stood *something* was indescribably *stronger* than the ordinary certainty of companionship when we are in the close presence of ordinary living people. The something seemed close to me, and intensely more real than any ordinary perception. Although I felt it to be like unto myself, so to speak, or finite, small, and distressful, as it were, I did n't recognize it as any individual being or person."

Of course such an experience as this does not connect itself with the religious sphere. Yet it may upon occasion do so; and the same correspondent informs me that at more than one other conjuncture he had the sense of presence developed with equal intensity and abruptness, only then it was filled with a quality of joy.

"There was not a mere consciousness of something there, but fused in the central happiness of it, a startling aware- ness of some ineffable good. Not vague either, not like the emotional effect of some poem, or scene, or blossom, of music, but the sure knowledge of the close presence of a sort of mighty person, and after it went, the memory per- sisted as the one perception of reality. Everything else might be a dream, but not that."

My friend, as it oddly happens, does not interpret these latter experiences theistically, as signifying the presence of God. But it would clearly not have been unnatural to inter- pret them as a revelation of the deity's existence. When we reach the subject of mysticism, we shall have much more to say upon this head.

Lest the oddity of these phenomena should disconcert you, I will venture to read you a couple of similar narratives, much shorter, merely to show that we are dealing with a well- marked natural kind of fact. In the first case, which I take from the Journal of the Society for Psychical Research, the sense of presence developed in a few moments into a distinctly visualized hallucination,—but I leave that part of the story out.

"I had read," the narrator says, "some twenty minutes or so, was thoroughly absorbed in the book, my mind was perfectly quiet, and for the time being my friends were quite forgotten, when suddenly without a moment's warning my whole being seemed roused to the highest state of tension or aliveness, and I was aware, with an intenseness not easily imagined by those who had never experienced it, that another being or presence was not only in the room, but quite close to me. I put my book down, and although my excitement was great, I felt quite collected, and not conscious of any sense of fear. Without changing my position, and looking straight at the fire, I knew somehow that my friend A. H. was standing at my left elbow, but so far behind me as to be hidden by the armchair in which I was leaning back. Moving my eyes round slightly without otherwise changing my position, the lower portion of one leg became visible, and I instantly recognized the gray-blue material of trousers he often wore, but the stuff appeared semi-transparent, reminding me of tobacco smoke in consistency,"[1]—and hereupon the visual hallucination came.

Another informant writes:—

"Quite early in the night I was awakened. . . . I felt as if I had been aroused intentionally, and at first thought some one was breaking into the house. . . . I then turned on my side to go to sleep again, and immediately felt a consciousness of a presence in the room, and singular to state, it was not the consciousness of a live person, but of a spiritual presence. This may provoke a smile, but I can only tell you the facts as they occurred to me. I do not know how to better describe my sensations than by simply stating that I felt a consciousness of a spiritual presence. . . . I felt also at the same time a strong feeling of superstitious dread, as if something strange and fearful were about to happen."[2]

[1] Journal of the S. P. R., February, 1895, p. 26.
[2] E. GURNEY: Phantasms of the Living, i. 384.

Professor Flournoy of Geneva gives me the following testimony of a friend of his, a lady, who has the gift of automatic or involuntary writing:—

"Whenever I practice automatic writing, what makes me feel that it is not due to a subconscious self is the feeling I always have of a foreign presence, external to my body. It is sometimes so definitely characterized that I could point to its exact position. This impression of presence is impossible to describe. It varies in intensity and clearness according to the personality from whom the writing professes to come. If it is some one whom I love, I feel it immediately, before any writing has come. My heart seems to recognize it."

In an earlier book of mine I have cited at full length a curious case of presence felt by a blind man. The presence was that of the figure of a gray-bearded man dressed in a pepper and salt suit, squeezing himself under the crack of the door and moving across the floor of the room towards a sofa. The blind subject of this quasi-hallucination is an exceptionally intelligent reporter. He is entirely without internal visual imagery and cannot represent light or colors to himself, and is positive that his other senses, hearing, etc., were not involved in this false perception. It seems to have been an abstract conception rather, with the feelings of reality and spatial outwardness directly attached to it—in other words, a fully objectified and exteriorized *idea*.

Such cases, taken along with others which would be too tedious for quotation, seem sufficiently to prove the existence in our mental machinery of a sense of present reality more diffused and general than that which our special senses yield. For the psychologists the tracing of the organic seat of such a feeling would form a pretty problem—nothing could be more natural than to connect it with the muscular sense, with the feeling that our muscles were innervating themselves for action. Whatsoever thus innervated our activity, or 'made our flesh creep,'—our senses are what do so oftenest,—might then appear real and present, even though it were but an abstract idea. But with such vague conjectures we have no concern at present, for our interest lies with the faculty rather than with its organic seat.

Like all positive affections of consciousness, the sense of reality has its negative counterpart in the shape of a feeling of unreality by which persons may be haunted, and of which one sometimes hears complaint:—

"When I reflect on the fact that I have made my appearance by accident upon a globe itself whirled through space as the sport of the catastrophes of the heavens," says Madame Ackermann; "when I see myself surrounded by beings as ephemeral and incomprehensible as I am myself, and all excitedly pursuing pure chimeras, I experience a strange feeling of being in a dream. It seems to me as if I have loved and suffered and that erelong I shall die, in a dream. My last word will be, 'I have been dreaming.'"[1]

In another lecture we shall see how in morbid melancholy this sense of the unreality of things may become a carking pain, and even lead to suicide.

We may now lay it down as certain that in the distinctively religious sphere of experience, many persons (how many we cannot tell) possess the objects of their belief, not in the form of mere conceptions which their intellect accepts as true, but rather in the form of quasi-sensible realities directly apprehended. As his sense of the real presence of these objects fluctuates, so the believer alternates between warmth and coldness in his faith. Other examples will bring this home to one better than abstract description, so I proceed immediately to cite some. The first example is a negative one, deploring the loss of the sense in question. I have extracted it from an account given me by a scientific man of my acquaintance, of his religious life. It seems to me to show clearly that the feeling of reality may be something more like a sensation than an intellectual operation properly so-called.

"Between twenty and thirty I gradually became more and more agnostic and irreligious, yet I cannot say that I ever lost that 'indefinite consciousness' which Herbert Spencer describes so well, of an Absolute Reality behind phe-

[1] Pensées d'un Solitaire, p. 66.

nomena. For me this Reality was not the pure Unknowable of Spencer's philosophy, for although I had ceased my childish prayers to God, and never prayed to *It* in a formal manner, yet my more recent experience shows me to have been in a relation to *It* which practically was the same thing as prayer. Whenever I had any trouble, especially when I had conflict with other people, either domestically or in the way of business, or when I was depressed in spirits or anxious about affairs, I now recognize that I used to fall back for support upon this curious relation I felt myself to be in to this fundamental cosmical *It*. It was on my side, or I was on Its side, however you please to term it, in the particular trouble, and it always strengthened me and seemed to give me endless vitality to feel its underlying and supporting presence. In fact, it was an unfailing fountain of living justice, truth, and strength, to which I instinctively turned at times of weakness, and it always brought me out. I know now that it was a personal relation I was in to it, because of late years the power of communicating with it has left me, and I am conscious of a perfectly definite loss. I used never to fail to find it when I turned to it. Then came a set of years when sometimes I found it, and then again I would be wholly unable to make connection with it. I remember many occasions on which at night in bed, I would be unable to get to sleep on account of worry. I turned this way and that in the darkness, and groped mentally for the familiar sense of that higher mind of my mind which had always seemed to be close at hand as it were, closing the passage, and yielding support, but there was no electric current. A blank was there instead of *It*: I could n't find anything. Now, at the age of nearly fifty, my power of getting into connection with it has entirely left me; and I have to confess that a great help has gone out of my life. Life has become curiously dead and indifferent; and I can now see that my old experience was probably exactly the same thing as the prayers of the orthodox, only I did not call them by that name. What I have spoken of as 'It' was practically not Spencer's Unknowable, but just my own instinctive and individual God, whom I relied upon for higher sympathy, but whom somehow I have lost."

Nothing is more common in the pages of religious biography than the way in which seasons of lively and of difficult faith are described as alternating. Probably every religious person has the recollection of particular crises in which a directer vision of the truth, a direct perception, perhaps, of a living God's existence, swept in and overwhelmed the languor of the more ordinary belief. In James Russell Lowell's correspondence there is a brief memorandum of an experience of this kind:—

"I had a revelation last Friday evening. I was at Mary's, and happening to say something of the presence of spirits (of whom, I said, I was often dimly aware), Mr. Putnam entered into an argument with me on spiritual matters. As I was speaking, the whole system rose up before me like a vague destiny looming from the Abyss. I never before so clearly felt the Spirit of God in me and around me. The whole room seemed to me full of God. The air seemed to waver to and fro with the presence of Something I knew not what. I spoke with the calmness and clearness of a prophet. I cannot tell you what this revelation was. I have not yet studied it enough. But I shall perfect it one day, and then you shall hear it and acknowledge its grandeur."[1]

Here is a longer and more developed experience from a manuscript communication by a clergyman,—I take it from Starbuck's manuscript collection:—

"I remember the night, and almost the very spot on the hilltop, where my soul opened out, as it were, into the Infinite, and there was a rushing together of the two worlds, the inner and the outer. It was deep calling unto deep,— the deep that my own struggle had opened up within being answered by the unfathomable deep without, reaching beyond the stars. I stood alone with Him who had made me, and all the beauty of the world, and love, and sorrow, and even temptation. I did not seek Him, but felt the perfect unison of my spirit with His. The ordinary sense of things around me faded. For the moment nothing but an ineffable joy and exaltation remained. It is impossible fully to

[1] Letters of Lowell, i. 75.

describe the experience. It was like the effect of some great orchestra when all the separate notes have melted into one swelling harmony that leaves the listener conscious of nothing save that his soul is being wafted upwards, and almost bursting with its own emotion. The perfect stillness of the night was thrilled by a more solemn silence. The darkness held a presence that was all the more felt because it was not seen. I could not any more have doubted that *He* was there than that I was. Indeed, I felt myself to be, if possible, the less real of the two.

"My highest faith in God and truest idea of him were then born in me. I have stood upon the Mount of Vision since, and felt the Eternal round about me. But never since has there come quite the same stirring of the heart. Then, if ever, I believe, I stood face to face with God, and was born anew of his spirit. There was, as I recall it, no sudden change of thought or of belief, except that my early crude conception had, as it were, burst into flower. There was no destruction of the old, but a rapid, wonderful unfolding. Since that time no discussion that I have heard of the proofs of God's existence has been able to shake my faith. Having once felt the presence of God's spirit, I have never lost it again for long. My most assuring evidence of his existence is deeply rooted in that hour of vision, in the memory of that supreme experience, and in the conviction, gained from reading and reflection, that something the same has come to all who have found God. I am aware that it may justly be called mystical. I am not enough acquainted with philosophy to defend it from that or any other charge. I feel that in writing of it I have overlaid it with words rather than put it clearly to your thought. But, such as it is, I have described it as carefully as I now am able to do."

Here is another document, even more definite in character, which, the writer being a Swiss, I translate from the French original.[1]

"I was in perfect health: we were on our sixth day of

---

[1] I borrow it, with Professor Flournoy's permission, from his rich collection of psychological documents.

tramping, and in good training. We had come the day before from Sixt to Trient by Buet. I felt neither fatigue, hunger, nor thirst, and my state of mind was equally healthy. I
had had at Forclaz good news from home; I was subject to
no anxiety, either near or remote, for we had a good guide,
and there was not a shadow of uncertainty about the road
we should follow. I can best describe the condition in
which I was by calling it a state of equilibrium. When all
at once I experienced a feeling of being raised above myself,
I felt the presence of God—I tell of the thing just as I was
conscious of it—as if his goodness and his power were
penetrating me altogether. The throb of emotion was so
violent that I could barely tell the boys to pass on and not
wait for me. I then sat down on a stone, unable to stand
any longer, and my eyes overflowed with tears. I thanked
God that in the course of my life he had taught me to know
him, that he sustained my life and took pity both on the
insignificant creature and on the sinner that I was. I begged
him ardently that my life might be consecrated to the doing
of his will. I felt his reply, which was that I should do his
will from day to day, in humility and poverty, leaving him,
the Almighty God, to be judge of whether I should some
time be called to bear witness more conspicuously. Then,
slowly, the ecstasy left my heart; that is, I felt that God had
withdrawn the communion which he had granted, and I
was able to walk on, but very slowly, so strongly was I still
possessed by the interior emotion. Besides, I had wept uninterruptedly for several minutes, my eyes were swollen,
and I did not wish my companions to see me. The state of
ecstasy may have lasted four or five minutes, although it
seemed at the time to last much longer. My comrades
waited for me ten minutes at the cross of Barine, but I took
about twenty-five or thirty minutes to join them, for as well
as I can remember, they said that I had kept them back for
about half an hour. The impression had been so profound
that in climbing slowly the slope I asked myself if it were
possible that Moses on Sinai could have had a more intimate communication with God. I think it well to add
that in this ecstasy of mine God had neither form, color,
odor, nor taste; moreover, that the feeling of his presence

was accompanied with no determinate localization. It was rather as if my personality had been transformed by the presence of a *spiritual spirit*. But the more I seek words to express this intimate intercourse, the more I feel the impossibility of describing the thing by any of our usual images. At bottom the expression most apt to render what I felt is this: God was present, though invisible; he fell under no one of my senses, yet my consciousness perceived him."

The adjective 'mystical' is technically applied, most often, to states that are of brief duration. Of course such hours of rapture as the last two persons describe are mystical experiences, of which in a later lecture I shall have much to say. Meanwhile here is the abridged record of another mystical or semi-mystical experience, in a mind evidently framed by nature for ardent piety. I owe it to Starbuck's collection. The lady who gives the account is the daughter of a man well known in his time as a writer against Christianity. The suddenness of her conversion shows well how native the sense of God's presence must be to certain minds. She relates that she was brought up in entire ignorance of Christian doctrine, but, when in Germany, after being talked to by Christian friends, she read the Bible and prayed, and finally the plan of salvation flashed upon her like a stream of light.

"To this day," she writes, "I cannot understand dallying with religion and the commands of God. The very instant I heard my Father's cry calling unto me, my heart bounded in recognition. I ran, I stretched forth my arms, I cried aloud, 'Here, here I am, my Father.' Oh, happy child, what should I do? 'Love me,' answered my God. 'I do, I do,' I cried passionately. 'Come unto me,' called my Father. 'I will,' my heart panted. Did I stop to ask a single question? Not one. It never occurred to me to ask whether I was good enough, or to hesitate over my unfitness, or to find out what I thought of his church, or . . . to wait until I should be satisfied. Satisfied! I was satisfied. Had I not found my God and my Father? Did he not love me? Had he not called me? Was there not a Church into which I might enter? . . . Since then I have had direct answers to prayer—so significant as to be almost like talking with God and hearing his answer. The idea of God's reality has never left me for one moment."

Here is still another case, the writer being a man aged twenty-seven, in which the experience, probably almost as characteristic, is less vividly described:—

"I have on a number of occasions felt that I had enjoyed a period of intimate communion with the divine. These meetings came unasked and unexpected, and seemed to consist merely in the temporary obliteration of the conventionalities which usually surround and cover my life. . . . Once it was when from the summit of a high mountain I looked over a gashed and corrugated landscape extending to a long convex of ocean that ascended to the horizon, and again from the same point when I could see nothing beneath me but a boundless expanse of white cloud, on the blown surface of which a few high peaks, including the one I was on, seemed plunging about as if they were dragging their anchors. What I felt on these occasions was a temporary loss of my own identity, accompanied by an illumination which revealed to me a deeper significance than I had been wont to attach to life. It is in this that I find my justification for saying that I have enjoyed communication with God. Of course the absence of such a being as this would be chaos. I cannot conceive of life without its presence."

Of the more habitual and so to speak chronic sense of God's presence the following sample from Professor Starbuck's manuscript collection may serve to give an idea. It is from a man aged forty-nine,—probably thousands of unpretending Christians would write an almost identical account.

"God is more real to me than any thought or thing or person. I feel his presence positively, and the more as I live in closer harmony with his laws as written in my body and mind. I feel him in the sunshine or rain; and awe mingled with a delicious restfulness most nearly describes my feelings. I talk to him as to a companion in prayer and praise, and our communion is delightful. He answers me again and again, often in words so clearly spoken that it seems my outer ear must have carried the tone, but generally in strong mental impressions. Usually a text of Scripture, unfolding some new view of him and his love for me, and care for my safety. I could give hundreds of instances, in school matters, social problems, financial difficulties, etc. That he is mine and I am his never leaves me, it is an abiding joy. Without it life would be a blank, a desert, a shoreless, trackless waste."

I subjoin some more examples from writers of different ages and sexes. They are also from Professor Starbuck's collection, and their number might be greatly multiplied. The first is from a man twenty-seven years old: —

"God is quite real to me. I talk to him and often get answers. Thoughts sudden and distinct from any I have been entertaining come to my mind after asking God for his direction. Something over a year ago I was for some weeks in the direst perplexity. When the trouble first appeared before me I was dazed, but before long (two or three hours) I could hear distinctly a passage of Scripture: 'My grace is sufficient for thee.' Every time my thoughts turned to the trouble I could hear this quotation. I don't think I ever doubted the existence of God, or had him drop out of my consciousness. God has frequently stepped into my affairs very perceptibly, and I feel that he directs many little details all the time. But on two or three occasions he has ordered ways for me very contrary to my ambitions and plans."

Another statement (none the less valuable psychologically for being so decidedly childish) is that of a boy of seventeen: —

"Sometimes as I go to church, I sit down, join in the service, and before I go out I feel as if God was with me, right side of me, singing and reading the Psalms with me. . . . And then again I feel as if I could sit beside him, and put my arms around him, kiss him, etc. When I am taking Holy Communion at the altar, I try to get with him and generally feel his presence."

I let a few other cases follow at random: —

"God surrounds me like the physical atmosphere. He is closer to me than my own breath. In him literally I live and move and have my being." —

"There are times when I seem to stand in his very presence, to talk with him. Answers to prayer have come, sometimes direct and overwhelming in their revelation of his presence and powers. There are times when God seems far off, but this is always my own fault." —

"I have the sense of a presence, strong, and at the same time soothing, which hovers over me. Sometimes it seems to enwrap me with sustaining arms."

Such is the human ontological imagination, and such is the convincingness of what it brings to birth. Unpicturable beings are realized, and realized with an intensity almost like that of an hallucination. They determine our vital attitude as decisively as the vital attitude of lovers is determined by the habitual sense, by which each is haunted, of the other being in the world. A lover has notoriously this sense of the continuous being of his idol, even when his attention is addressed to other matters and he no longer represents her features. He cannot forget her; she uninterruptedly affects him through and through.

I spoke of the convincingness of these feelings of reality, and I must dwell a moment longer on that point. They are as convincing to those who have them as any direct sensible experiences can be, and they are, as a rule, much more convincing than results established by mere logic ever are. One may indeed be entirely without them; probably more than one of you here present is without them in any marked degree; but if you do have them, and have them at all strongly, the probability is that you cannot help regarding them as genuine perceptions of truth, as revelations of a kind of reality which no adverse argument, however unanswerable by you in words, can expel from your belief. The opinion opposed to mysticism in philosophy is sometimes spoken of as *rationalism*. Rationalism insists that all our beliefs ought ultimately to find for themselves articulate grounds. Such grounds, for rationalism, must consist of four things: (1) definitely statable abstract principles; (2) definite facts of sensation; (3) definite hypotheses based on such facts; and (4) definite inferences logically drawn. Vague impressions of something indefinable have no place in the rationalistic system, which on its positive side is surely a splendid intellectual tendency, for not only are all our philosophies fruits of it, but physical science (amongst other good things) is its result.

Nevertheless, if we look on man's whole mental life as it exists, on the life of men that lies in them apart from their learning and science, and that they inwardly and privately follow, we have to confess that the part of it of which rationalism can give an account is relatively superficial. It is the part that has the *prestige* undoubtedly, for it has the loquacity, it can challenge you for proofs, and chop logic, and put you down with words. But it will fail to convince or convert you all the same, if your dumb intuitions are opposed to its conclusions. If you have intuitions at all, they come from a deeper level of your nature than the loquacious level which rationalism inhabits. Your whole subconscious life, your impulses, your faiths, your needs, your divinations, have prepared the premises, of which your consciousness now feels the weight of the result; and something in you absolutely *knows* that that result must be truer than any logic-chopping rationalistic talk, however clever, that may contradict it. This inferiority of the rationalistic level in founding belief is just as manifest when rationalism argues for religion as when it argues against it. That vast literature of proofs of God's existence drawn from the order of nature, which a century ago seemed so overwhelmingly convincing, to-day does little more than gather dust in libraries, for the simple reason that our generation has ceased to believe in the kind of God it argued for. Whatever sort of a being God may be, we *know* to-day that he is nevermore that mere external inventor of 'contrivances' intended to make manifest his 'glory' in which our great-grandfathers took such satisfaction, though just how we know this we cannot possibly make clear by words either to others or to ourselves. I defy any of you here fully to account for your persuasion that if a God exist he must be a more cosmic and tragic personage than that Being.

The truth is that in the metaphysical and religious sphere,

articulate reasons are cogent for us only when our inarticulate feelings of reality have already been impressed in favor of the same conclusion. Then, indeed, our intuitions and our reason work together, and great world-ruling systems, like that of the Buddhist or of the Catholic philosophy, may grow up. Our impulsive belief is here always what sets up the original body of truth, and our philosophy is but its showy verbalized translation. The immediate assurance is the deep thing in us, the argument is but a surface exhibition. Instinct leads, intelligence does but follow. If a person feels the presence of a living God after the fashion shown by my quotations, your critical arguments, be they never so superior, will vainly set themselves to change his faith.

Please observe, however, that I do not yet say that it is *better* that the subconscious and non-rational should thus hold primacy in the religious realm. I confine myself to simply pointing out that they do so hold it as a matter of fact.

So much for our sense of the reality of the religious objects. Let me now say a brief word more about the attitudes they characteristically awaken.

We have already agreed that they are *solemn*; and we have seen reason to think that the most distinctive of them is the sort of joy which may result in extreme cases from absolute self-surrender. The sense of the kind of object to which the surrender is made has much to do with determining the precise complexion of the joy; and the whole phenomenon is more complex than any simple formula allows. In the literature of the subject, sadness and gladness have each been emphasized in turn. The ancient saying that the first maker of the Gods was fear receives voluminous corroboration from every age of religious history; but none the less does religious history show the part which joy has evermore tended to play. Sometimes the joy has been primary; sometimes secondary, being the gladness of deliverance from the fear. This latter state of things, being the more complex, is also the more complete; and as we proceed, I think we shall have abundant reason for refusing to leave out either the sadness or the gladness, if we look at religion with the breadth of view which it demands. Stated in the completest possible terms, a man's religion involves both moods of contraction and moods of

expansion of his being. But the quantitative mixture and order of these moods vary so much from one age of the world,
from one system of thought, and from one individual to another, that you may insist either on the dread and the submission, or on the peace and the freedom as the essence of
the matter, and still remain materially within the limits of the
truth. The constitutionally sombre and the constitutionally
sanguine onlooker are bound to emphasize opposite aspects
of what lies before their eyes.

The constitutionally sombre religious person makes even of
his religious peace a very sober thing. Danger still hovers in
the air about it. Flexion and contraction are not wholly
checked. It were sparrowlike and childish after our deliverance to explode into twittering laughter and caper-cutting,
and utterly to forget the imminent hawk on bough. Lie low,
rather, lie low; for you are in the hands of a living God. In
the Book of Job, for example, the impotence of man and the
omnipotence of God is the exclusive burden of its author's
mind. "It is as high as heaven; what canst thou do?—deeper
than hell; what canst thou know?" There is an astringent relish about the truth of this conviction which some men can
feel, and which for them is as near an approach as can be
made to the feeling of religious joy.

"In Job," says that coldly truthful writer, the author of
Mark Rutherford, "God reminds us that man is not the
measure of his creation. The world is immense, constructed
on no plan or theory which the intellect of man can grasp.
It is *transcendent* everywhere. This is the burden of every
verse, and is the secret, if there be one, of the poem. Sufficient or insufficient, there is nothing more. . . . God is
great, we know not his ways. He takes from us all we have,
but yet if we possess our souls in patience, we *may* pass the
valley of the shadow, and come out in sunlight again. We
may or we may not! . . . What more have we to say now
than God said from the whirlwind over two thousand five
hundred years ago?"[1]

If we turn to the sanguine onlooker, on the other hand, we

[1] Mark Rutherford's Deliverance, London, 1885, pp. 196, 198.

find that deliverance is felt as incomplete unless the burden be altogether overcome and the danger forgotten. Such on-lookers give us definitions that seem to the sombre minds of whom we have just been speaking to leave out all the solemnity that makes religious peace so different from merely animal joys. In the opinion of some writers an attitude might be called religious, though no touch were left in it of sacrifice or submission, no tendency to flexion, no bowing of the head. Any "habitual and regulated admiration," says Professor J. R. Seeley,[1] "is worthy to be called a religion"; and accordingly he thinks that our Music, our Science, and our so-called 'Civilization,' as these things are now organized and admiringly believed in, form the more genuine religions of our time. Certainly the unhesitating and unreasoning way in which we feel that we must inflict our Civilization upon 'lower' races, by means of Hotchkiss guns, etc., reminds one of nothing so much as of the early spirit of Islam spreading its religion by the sword.

In my last lecture I quoted to you the ultra-radical opinion of Mr. Havelock Ellis, that laughter of any sort may be considered a religious exercise, for it bears witness to the soul's emancipation. I quoted this opinion in order to deny its adequacy. But we must now settle our scores more carefully with this whole optimistic way of thinking. It is far too complex to be decided off-hand. I propose accordingly that we make of religious optimism the theme of the next two lectures.

[1] In his book (too little read, I fear), Natural Religion, 3d edition, Boston, 1886, pp. 91, 122.

LECTURES IV AND V

THE RELIGION OF HEALTHY-MINDEDNESS

IF WE WERE to ask the question: 'What is human life's chief concern?' one of the answers we should receive would be: 'It is happiness.' How to gain, how to keep, how to recover happiness, is in fact for most men at all times the secret motive of all they do, and of all they are willing to endure. The hedonistic school in ethics deduces the moral life wholly from the experiences of happiness and unhappiness which different kinds of conduct bring; and, even more in the religious life than in the moral life, happiness and unhappiness seem to be the poles round which the interest revolves. We need not go so far as to say with the author whom I lately quoted that any persistent enthusiasm is, as such, religion, nor need we call mere laughter a religious exercise; but we must admit that any persistent enjoyment may *produce* the sort of religion which consists in a grateful admiration of the gift of so happy an existence; and we must also acknowledge that the more complex ways of experiencing religion are new manners of producing happiness, wonderful inner paths to a supernatural kind of happiness, when the first gift of natural existence is unhappy, as it so often proves itself to be.

With such relations between religion and happiness, it is perhaps not surprising that men come to regard the happiness which a religious belief affords as a proof of its truth. If a creed makes a man feel happy, he almost inevitably adopts it. Such a belief ought to be true; therefore it is true—such, rightly or wrongly, is one of the 'immediate inferences' of the religious logic used by ordinary men.

"The near presence of God's spirit," says a German writer,[1] "may be experienced in its reality—indeed *only* experienced. And the mark by which the spirit's existence and nearness are made irrefutably clear to those who have ever had the experience is the utterly incomparable *feeling of happiness* which is connected with the nearness, and

[1] C. HILTY: Glück, dritter Theil, 1900, p. 18.

which is therefore not only a possible and altogether proper feeling for us to have here below, but is the best and most indispensable proof of God's reality. No other proof is equally convincing, and therefore happiness is the point from which every efficacious new theology should start."

In the hour immediately before us, I shall invite you to consider the simpler kinds of religious happiness, leaving the more complex sorts to be treated on a later day.

In many persons, happiness is congenital and irreclaimable. 'Cosmic emotion' inevitably takes in them the form of enthusiasm and freedom. I speak not only of those who are animally happy. I mean those who, when unhappiness is offered or proposed to them, positively refuse to feel it, as if it were something mean and wrong. We find such persons in every age, passionately flinging themselves upon their sense of the goodness of life, in spite of the hardships of their own condition, and in spite of the sinister theologies into which they may be born. From the outset their religion is one of union with the divine. The heretics who went before the reformation are lavishly accused by the church writers of antinomian practices, just as the first Christians were accused of indulgence in orgies by the Romans. It is probable that there never has been a century in which the deliberate refusal to think ill of life has not been idealized by a sufficient number of persons to form sects, open or secret, who claimed all natural things to be permitted. Saint Augustine's maxim, *Dilige et quod vis fac*,—if you but love [God], you may do as you incline,—is morally one of the profoundest of observations, yet it is pregnant, for such persons, with passports beyond the bounds of conventional morality. According to their characters they have been refined or gross; but their belief has been at all times systematic enough to constitute a definite religious attitude. God was for them a giver of freedom, and the sting of evil was overcome. Saint Francis and his immediate disciples were, on the whole, of this company of spirits, of which there are of course infinite varieties. Rousseau in the earlier years of his writing, Diderot, B. de Saint Pierre, and many of the leaders of the eighteenth century anti-christian movement were of this optimistic type. They owed their influence to a certain authoritativeness in their feeling that Nature, if you will only trust her sufficiently, is absolutely good.

It is to be hoped that we all have some friend, perhaps more often feminine than masculine, and young than old, whose soul is of this sky-blue tint, whose affinities are rather with flowers and birds and all enchanting innocencies than with dark human passions, who can think no ill of man or God, and in whom religious gladness, being in possession from the outset, needs no deliverance from any antecedent burden.

"God has two families of children on this earth," says Francis W. Newman,[1] "*the once-born* and *the twice-born*," and the once-born he describes as follows: "They see God, not as a strict Judge, not as a Glorious Potentate; but as the animating Spirit of a beautiful harmonious world, Beneficent and Kind, Merciful as well as Pure. The same characters generally have no metaphysical tendencies: they do not look back into themselves. Hence they are not distressed by their own imperfections: yet it would be absurd to call them self-righteous; for they hardly think of themselves *at all*. This childlike quality of their nature makes the opening of religion very happy to them: for they no more shrink from God, than a child from an emperor, before whom the parent trembles: in fact, they have no vivid conception of *any* of the qualities in which the severer Majesty of God consists.[2] He is to them the impersonation of Kindness and Beauty. They read his character, not in the disordered world of man, but in romantic and harmonious nature. Of human sin they know perhaps little in their own hearts and not very much in the world; and human suffering does but melt them to tenderness. Thus, when they approach God, no inward disturbance ensues; and without being as yet spiritual, they have a certain complacency and perhaps romantic sense of excitement in their simple worship."

[1] The Soul; its Sorrows and its Aspirations, 3d edition, 1852, pp. 89, 91.

[2] I once heard a lady describe the pleasure it gave her to think that she "could always cuddle up to God."

In the Romish Church such characters find a more congenial soil to grow in than in Protestantism, whose fashions of
feeling have been set by minds of a decidedly pessimistic
order. But even in Protestantism they have been abundant
enough; and in its recent 'liberal' developments of Unitarianism and latitudinarianism generally, minds of this order have
played and still are playing leading and constructive parts.
Emerson himself is an admirable example. Theodore Parker is
another,—here are a couple of characteristic passages from
Parker's correspondence.[1]

"Orthodox scholars say: 'In the heathen classics you find
no consciousness of sin.' It is very true—God be thanked
for it. They were conscious of wrath, of cruelty, avarice,
drunkenness, lust, sloth, cowardice, and other actual vices,
and struggled and got rid of the deformities, but they
were not conscious of 'enmity against God,' and did n't sit
down and whine and groan against non-existent evil. I
have done wrong things enough in my life, and do them
now; I miss the mark, draw bow, and try again. But I am
not conscious of hating God, or man, or right, or love,
and I know there is much 'health in me'; and in my body,
even now, there dwelleth many a good thing, spite of consumption and Saint Paul." In another letter Parker writes:
"I have swum in clear sweet waters all my days; and if
sometimes they were a little cold, and the stream ran adverse and something rough, it was never too strong to be
breasted and swum through. From the days of earliest
boyhood, when I went stumbling through the grass, . . .
up to the gray-bearded manhood of this time, there is
none but has left me honey in the hive of memory that I
now feed on for present delight. When I recall the years
. . . I am filled with a sense of sweetness and wonder that
such little things can make a mortal so exceedingly rich.
But I must confess that the chiefest of all my delights is
still the religious."

Another good expression of the 'once-born' type of con-

[1] JOHN WEISS: Life of Theodore Parker, i. 152, 32.

sciousness, developing straight and natural, with no element of morbid compunction or crisis, is contained in the answer of Dr. Edward Everett Hale, the eminent Unitarian preacher and writer, to one of Dr. Starbuck's circulars. I quote a part of it:—

"I observe, with profound regret, the religious struggles which come into many biographies, as if almost essential to the formation of the hero. I ought to speak of these, to say that any man has an advantage, not to be estimated, who is born, as I was, into a family where the religion is simple and rational; who is trained in the theory of such a religion, so that he never knows, for an hour, what these religious or irreligious struggles are. I always knew God loved me, and I was always grateful to him for the world he placed me in. I always liked to tell him so, and was always glad to receive his suggestions to me. . . . I can remember perfectly that when I was coming to manhood, the half-philosophical novels of the time had a deal to say about the young men and maidens who were facing the 'problem of life.' I had no idea whatever what the problem of life was. To live with all my might seemed to me easy; to learn where there was so much to learn seemed pleasant and almost of course; to lend a hand, if one had a chance, natural; and if one did this, why, he enjoyed life because he could not help it, and without proving to himself that he ought to enjoy it. . . . A child who is early taught that he is God's child, that he may live and move and have his being in God, and that he has, therefore, infinite strength at hand for the conquering of any difficulty, will take life more easily, and probably will make more of it, than one who is told that he is born the child of wrath and wholly incapable of good."[1]

One can but recognize in such writers as these the presence of a temperament organically weighted on the side of cheer and fatally forbidden to linger, as those of opposite temperament linger, over the darker aspects of the universe. In some

[1] STARBUCK: Psychology of Religion, pp. 305, 306.

individuals optimism may become quasi-pathological. The capacity for even a transient sadness or a momentary humility seems cut off from them as by a kind of congenital anæsthesia.[1]

The supreme contemporary example of such an inability to feel evil is of course Walt Whitman.

"His favorite occupation," writes his disciple, Dr. Bucke, "seemed to be strolling or sauntering about outdoors by himself, looking at the grass, the trees, the flowers, the vistas of light, the varying aspects of the sky, and listening to the birds, the crickets, the tree frogs, and all the hundreds of natural sounds. It was evident that these things gave him a pleasure far beyond what they give to ordinary people. Until I knew the man," continues Dr. Bucke, "it had not occurred to me that any one could derive so much absolute happiness from these things as he did. He was very fond of flowers, either wild or cultivated; liked all sorts. I think he admired lilacs and sunflowers just as much as roses. Perhaps, indeed, no man who ever lived liked so many things and disliked so few as Walt Whitman. All natural objects seemed to have a charm for him. All sights and sounds seemed to please him. He appeared to like (and I believe

[1] "I know not to what physical laws philosophers will some day refer the feelings of melancholy. For myself, I find that they are the most voluptuous of all sensations," writes Saint Pierre, and accordingly he devotes a series of sections of his work on Nature to the Plaisirs de la Ruine, Plaisirs des Tombeaux, Ruines de la Nature, Plaisirs de la Solitude—each of them more optimistic than the last.

This finding of a luxury in woe is very common during adolescence. The truth-telling Marie Bashkirtseff expresses it well: —

"In this depression and dreadful uninterrupted suffering, I don't condemn life. On the contrary, I like it and find it good. Can you believe it? I find everything good and pleasant, even my tears, my grief. I enjoy weeping, I enjoy my despair. I enjoy being exasperated and sad. I feel as if these were so many diversions, and I love life in spite of them all. I want to live on. It would be cruel to have me die when I am so accommodating. I cry, I grieve, and at the same time I am pleased—no, not exactly that—I know not how to express it. But everything in life pleases me. I find everything agreeable, and in the very midst of my prayers for happiness, I find myself happy at being miserable. It is not I who undergo all this—my body weeps and cries; but something inside of me which is above me is glad of it all." Journal de Marie Bashkirtseff, i. 67.

he did like) all the men, women, and children he saw (though I never knew him to say that he liked any one), but each who knew him felt that he liked him or her, and that he liked others also. I never knew him to argue or dispute, and he never spoke about money. He always justified, sometimes playfully, sometimes quite seriously, those who spoke harshly of himself or his writings, and I often thought he even took pleasure in the opposition of enemies. When I first knew [him], I used to think that he watched himself, and would not allow his tongue to give expression to fretfulness, antipathy, complaint, and remonstrance. It did not occur to me as possible that these mental states could be absent in him. After long observation, however, I satisfied myself that such absence or unconsciousness was entirely real. He never spoke deprecatingly of any nationality or class of men, or time in the world's history, or against any trades or occupations— not even against any animals, insects, or inanimate things, nor any of the laws of nature, nor any of the results of those laws, such as illness, deformity, and death. He never complained or grumbled either at the weather, pain, illness, or anything else. He never swore. He could not very well, since he never spoke in anger and apparently never was angry. He never exhibited fear, and I do not believe he ever felt it."[1]

Walt Whitman owes his importance in literature to the systematic expulsion from his writings of all contractile elements. The only sentiments he allowed himself to express were of the expansive order; and he expressed these in the first person, not as your mere monstrously conceited individual might so express them, but vicariously for all men, so that a passionate and mystic ontological emotion suffuses his words, and ends by persuading the reader that men and women, life and death, and all things are divinely good.

Thus it has come about that many persons to-day regard Walt Whitman as the restorer of the eternal natural religion. He has infected them with his own love of comrades, with his own gladness that he and they exist. Societies are actually

[1] R. M. BUCKE: Cosmic Consciousness, pp. 182–186, abridged.

formed for his cult; a periodical organ exists for its propagation, in which the lines of orthodoxy and heterodoxy are
already beginning to be drawn;[1] hymns are written by others
in his peculiar prosody; and he is even explicitly compared
with the founder of the Christian religion, not altogether to
the advantage of the latter.

Whitman is often spoken of as a 'pagan.' The word nowadays means sometimes the mere natural animal man without
a sense of sin; sometimes it means a Greek or Roman with
his own peculiar religious consciousness. In neither of these
senses does it fitly define this poet. He is more than your
mere animal man who has not tasted of the tree of good and
evil. He is aware enough of sin for a swagger to be present
in his indifference towards it, a conscious pride in his freedom
from flexions and contractions, which your genuine pagan in
the first sense of the word would never show.

"I could turn and live with animals, they are so placid and
    self-contained,
 I stand and look at them long and long;
 They do not sweat and whine about their condition.
 They do not lie awake in the dark and weep for their sins.
 Not one is dissatisfied, not one is demented with the mania
    of owning things,
 Not one kneels to another, nor to his kind that lived
    thousands of years ago,
 Not one is respectable or unhappy over the whole earth."[2]

No natural pagan could have written these well-known
lines. But on the other hand Whitman is less than a Greek or
Roman; for their consciousness, even in Homeric times, was
full to the brim of the sad mortality of this sunlit world, and
such a consciousness Walt Whitman resolutely refuses to
adopt. When, for example, Achilles, about to slay Lycaon,
Priam's young son, hears him sue for mercy, he stops to
say: —

    "Ah, friend, thou too must die: why thus lamentest

---

[1] I refer to The Conservator, edited by Horace Traubel, and published
monthly at Philadelphia.
[2] Song of Myself, 32.

thou? Patroclos too is dead, who was better far than thou. . . . Over me too hang death and forceful fate. There cometh morn or eve or some noonday when my life too some man shall take in battle, whether with spear he smite, or arrow from the string."[1]

Then Achilles savagely severs the poor boy's neck with his sword, heaves him by the foot into the Scamander, and calls to the fishes of the river to eat the white fat of Lycaon. Just as here the cruelty and the sympathy each ring true, and do not mix or interfere with one another, so did the Greeks and Romans keep all their sadnesses and gladnesses unmingled and entire. Instinctive good they did not reckon sin; nor had they any such desire to save the credit of the universe as to make them insist, as so many of *us* insist, that what immediately appears as evil must be 'good in the making,' or something equally ingenious. Good was good, and bad just bad, for the earlier Greeks. They neither denied the ills of nature,—Walt Whitman's verse, 'What is called good is perfect and what is called bad is just as perfect,' would have been mere silliness to them,—nor did they, in order to escape from those ills, invent 'another and a better world' of the imagination, in which, along with the ills, the innocent goods of sense would also find no place. This integrity of the instinctive reactions, this freedom from all moral sophistry and strain, gives a pathetic dignity to ancient pagan feeling. And this quality Whitman's outpourings have not got. His optimism is too voluntary and defiant; his gospel has a touch of bravado and an affected twist,[2] and this diminishes its effect on many readers who yet are well disposed towards optimism, and on the whole quite willing to admit that in important respects Whitman is of the genuine lineage of the prophets.

If, then, we give the name of healthy-mindedness to the tendency which looks on all things and sees that they are

---

[1] Iliad, XXI., E. Myers's translation.

[2] "God is afraid of me!" remarked such a titanic-optimistic friend in my presence one morning when he was feeling particularly hearty and cannibalistic. The defiance of the phrase showed that a Christian education in humility still rankled in his breast.

good, we find that we must distinguish between a more involuntary and a more voluntary or systematic way of being healthy-minded. In its involuntary variety, healthy-mindedness is a way of feeling happy about things immediately. In its systematical variety, it is an abstract way of conceiving things as good. Every abstract way of conceiving things selects some one aspect of them as their essence for the time being, and disregards the other aspects. Systematic healthy-mindedness, conceiving good as the essential and universal aspect of being, deliberately excludes evil from its field of vision; and although, when thus nakedly stated, this might seem a difficult feat to perform for one who is intellectually sincere with himself and honest about facts, a little reflection shows that the situation is too complex to lie open to so simple a criticism.

In the first place, happiness, like every other emotional state, has blindness and insensibility to opposing facts given it as its instinctive weapon for self-protection against disturbance. When happiness is actually in possession, the thought of evil can no more acquire the feeling of reality than the thought of good can gain reality when melancholy rules. To the man actively happy, from whatever cause, evil simply cannot then and there be believed in. He must ignore it; and to the bystander he may then seem perversely to shut his eyes to it and hush it up.

But more than this: the hushing of it up may, in a perfectly candid and honest mind, grow into a deliberate religious policy, or *parti pris*. Much of what we call evil is due entirely to the way men take the phenomenon. It can so often be converted into a bracing and tonic good by a simple change of the sufferer's inner attitude from one of fear to one of fight; its sting so often departs and turns into a relish when, after vainly seeking to shun it, we agree to face about and bear it cheerfully, that a man is simply bound in honor, with reference to many of the facts that seem at first to disconcert his peace, to adopt this way of escape. Refuse to admit their badness; despise their power; ignore their presence; turn your attention the other way; and so far as you yourself are concerned at any rate, though the facts may still exist, their evil character exists no longer. Since you make them evil or good by your own thoughts about them, it is the ruling of your thoughts which proves to be your principal concern.

The deliberate adoption of an optimistic turn of mind thus makes its entrance into philosophy. And once in, it is hard to trace its lawful bounds. Not only does the human instinct for happiness, bent on self-protection by ignoring, keep working in its favor, but higher inner ideals have weighty words to say. The attitude of unhappiness is not only painful, it is mean and ugly. What can be more base and unworthy than the pining, puling, mumping mood, no matter by what outward ills it may have been engendered? What is more injurious to others? What less helpful as a way out of the difficulty? It but fastens and perpetuates the trouble which occasioned it, and increases the total evil of the situation. At all costs, then, we ought to reduce the sway of that mood; we ought to scout it in ourselves and others, and never show it tolerance. But it is impossible to carry on this discipline in the subjective sphere without zealously emphasizing the brighter and minimizing the darker aspects of the objective sphere of things at the same time. And thus our resolution not to indulge in misery, beginning at a comparatively small point within ourselves, may not stop until it has brought the entire frame of reality under a systematic conception optimistic enough to be congenial with its needs.

In all this I say nothing of any mystical insight or persuasion that the total frame of things absolutely must be good. Such mystical persuasion plays an enormous part in the history of the religious consciousness, and we must look at it later with some care. But we need not go so far at present. More ordinary non-mystical conditions of rapture suffice for my immediate contention. All invasive moral states and passionate enthusiasms make one feelingless to evil in some direction. The common penalties cease to deter the patriot, the usual prudences are flung by the lover to the winds. When the passion is extreme, suffering may actually be gloried in, provided it be for the ideal cause, death may lose its sting, the grave its victory. In these states, the ordinary contrast of good and ill seems to be swallowed up in a higher denomination, an omnipotent excitement which engulfs the evil, and which the human being welcomes as the crowning experience of his life. This, he says, is truly to live, and I exult in the heroic opportunity and adventure.

The systematic cultivation of healthy-mindedness as a religious attitude is therefore consonant with important currents in human nature, and is anything but absurd. In fact, we all do cultivate it more or less, even when our professed theology should in consistency forbid it. We divert our attention from disease and death as much as we can; and the slaughter-houses and indecencies without end on which our life is founded are huddled out of sight and never mentioned, so that the world we recognize officially in literature and in society is a poetic fiction far handsomer and cleaner and better than the world that really is.[1]

The advance of liberalism, so-called, in Christianity, during the past fifty years, may fairly be called a victory of healthy-mindedness within the church over the morbidness with which the old hell-fire theology was more harmoniously related. We have now whole congregations whose preachers, far from magnifying our consciousness of sin, seem devoted rather to making little of it. They ignore, or even deny, eternal punishment, and insist on the dignity rather than on the depravity of man. They look at the continual preoccupation of the old-fashioned Christian with the salvation of his soul as something sickly and reprehensible rather than admirable; and a sanguine and 'muscular' attitude, which to our forefathers would have seemed purely heathen, has become in their eyes an ideal element of Christian character. I am not asking whether or not they are right, I am only pointing out the change.

The persons to whom I refer have still retained for the most part their nominal connection with Christianity, in spite of their discarding of its more pessimistic theological elements. But in that 'theory of evolution' which, gathering momentum for a century, has within the past twenty-five years swept so

---

[1] "As I go on in this life, day by day, I become more of a bewildered child; I cannot get used to this world, to procreation, to heredity, to sight, to hearing; the commonest things are a burthen. The prim, obliterated, polite surface of life, and the broad, bawdy, and orgiastic—or mænadic—foundations, form a spectacle to which no habit reconciles me." R. L. STEVENSON: Letters, ii. 355.

rapidly over Europe and America, we see the ground laid for a new sort of religion of Nature, which has entirely displaced Christianity from the thought of a large part of our generation. The idea of a universal evolution lends itself to a doctrine of general meliorism and progress which fits the religious needs of the healthy-minded so well that it seems almost as if it might have been created for their use. Accordingly we find 'evolutionism' interpreted thus optimistically and embraced as a substitute for the religion they were born in, by a multitude of our contemporaries who have either been trained scientifically, or been fond of reading popular science, and who had already begun to be inwardly dissatisfied with what seemed to them the harshness and irrationality of the orthodox Christian scheme. As examples are better than descriptions, I will quote a document received in answer to Professor Starbuck's circular of questions. The writer's state of mind may by courtesy be called a religion, for it is his reaction on the whole nature of things, it is systematic and reflective, and it loyally binds him to certain inner ideals. I think you will recognize in him, coarse-meated and incapable of wounded spirit as he is, a sufficiently familiar contemporary type.

Q. *What does Religion mean to you?*
A. It means nothing; and it seems, so far as I can observe, useless to others. I am sixty-seven years of age and have resided in X. fifty years, and have been in business forty-five, consequently I have some little experience of life and men, and some women too, and I find that the most religious and pious people are as a rule those most lacking in uprightness and morality. The men who do not go to church or have any religious convictions are the best. Praying, singing of hymns, and sermonizing are pernicious— they teach us to rely on some supernatural power, when we ought to rely on ourselves. I *tee*totally disbelieve in a God. The God-idea was begotten in ignorance, fear, and a general lack of any knowledge of Nature. If I were to die now, being in a healthy condition for my age, both mentally and physically, I would just as lief, yes, rather, die with a hearty enjoyment of music, sport, or any other rational pastime.

As a timepiece stops, we die—there being no immortality in either case.

Q. *What comes before your mind corresponding to the words God, Heaven, Angels, etc.?*

A. Nothing whatever. I am a man without a religion. These words mean so much mythic bosh.

Q. *Have you had any experiences which appeared providential?*

A. None whatever. There is no agency of the superintending kind. A little judicious observation as well as knowledge of scientific law will convince any one of this fact.

Q. *What things work most strongly on your emotions?*

A. Lively songs and music; Pinafore instead of an Oratorio. I like Scott, Burns, Byron, Longfellow, especially Shakespeare, etc., etc. Of songs, the Star-spangled Banner, America, Marseillaise, and all moral and soul-stirring songs, but wishy-washy hymns are my detestation. I greatly enjoy nature, especially fine weather, and until within a few years used to walk Sundays into the country, twelve miles often, with no fatigue, and bicycle forty or fifty. I have dropped the bicycle. I never go to church, but attend lectures when there are any good ones. All of my thoughts and cogitations have been of a healthy and cheerful kind, for instead of doubts and fears I see things as they are, for I endeavor to adjust myself to my environment. This I regard as the deepest law. Mankind is a progressive animal. I am satisfied he will have made a great advance over his present status a thousand years hence.

Q. *What is your notion of sin?*

A. It seems to me that sin is a condition, a disease, incidental to man's development not being yet advanced enough. Morbidness over it increases the disease. We should think that a million of years hence equity, justice, and mental and physical good order will be so fixed and organized that no one will have any idea of evil or sin.

Q. *What is your temperament?*

A. Nervous, active, wide-awake, mentally and physically. Sorry that Nature compels us to sleep at all.

If we are in search of a broken and a contrite heart, clearly we need not look to this brother. His contentment with the finite incases him like a lobster-shell and shields him from all morbid repining at his distance from the Infinite. We have in him an excellent example of the optimism which may be encouraged by popular science.

To my mind a current far more important and interesting religiously than that which sets in from natural science towards healthy-mindedness is that which has recently poured over America and seems to be gathering force every day,—I am ignorant what foothold it may yet have acquired in Great Britain,—and to which, for the sake of having a brief designation, I will give the title of the 'Mind-cure movement.' There are various sects of this 'New Thought,' to use another of the names by which it calls itself; but their agreements are so profound that their differences may be neglected for my present purpose, and I will treat the movement, without apology, as if it were a simple thing.

It is a deliberately optimistic scheme of life, with both a speculative and a practical side. In its gradual development during the last quarter of a century, it has taken up into itself a number of contributory elements, and it must now be reckoned with as a genuine religious power. It has reached the stage, for example, when the demand for its literature is great enough for insincere stuff, mechanically produced for the market, to be to a certain extent supplied by publishers, —a phenomenon never observed, I imagine, until a religion has got well past its earliest insecure beginnings.

One of the doctrinal sources of Mind-cure is the four Gospels; another is Emersonianism or New England transcendentalism; another is Berkeleyan idealism; another is spiritism, with its messages of 'law' and 'progress' and 'development'; another the optimistic popular science evolutionism of which I have recently spoken; and, finally, Hinduism has contributed a strain. But the most characteristic feature of the mind-cure movement is an inspiration much more direct. The leaders in this faith have had an intuitive belief in the all-saving power of healthy-minded attitudes as such, in the conquering efficacy of courage, hope, and trust, and a correlative contempt for doubt, fear, worry, and all nervously precautionary

states of mind.[1] Their belief has in a general way been corroborated by the practical experience of their disciples; and this
experience forms to-day a mass imposing in amount.

The blind have been made to see, the halt to walk; lifelong
invalids have had their health restored. The moral fruits have
been no less remarkable. The deliberate adoption of a healthy-
minded attitude has proved possible to many who never supposed they had it in them; regeneration of character has gone
on on an extensive scale; and cheerfulness has been restored
to countless homes. The indirect influence of this has been
great. The mind-cure principles are beginning so to pervade
the air that one catches their spirit at second-hand. One hears
of the 'Gospel of Relaxation,' of the 'Don't Worry Movement,' of people who repeat to themselves, 'Youth, health,
vigor!' when dressing in the morning, as their motto for the
day. Complaints of the weather are getting to be forbidden
in many households; and more and more people are recognizing it to be bad form to speak of disagreeable sensations,
or to make much of the ordinary inconveniences and ail-
ments of life. These general tonic effects on public opinion
would be good even if the more striking results were non-
existent. But the latter abound so that we can afford to overlook the innumerable failures and self-deceptions that are
mixed in with them (for in everything human failure is a
matter of course), and we can also overlook the verbiage of
a good deal of the mind-cure literature, some of which is so
moonstruck with optimism and so vaguely expressed that an
academically trained intellect finds it almost impossible to
read it at all.

The plain fact remains that the spread of the movement has
been due to practical fruits, and the extremely practical turn
of character of the American people has never been better

[1] 'Cautionary Verses for Children': this title of a much used work, published early in the nineteenth century, shows how far the muse of evangelical
protestantism in England, with her mind fixed on the idea of danger, had at
last drifted away from the original gospel freedom. Mind-cure might be
briefly called a reaction against all that religion of chronic anxiety which
marked the earlier part of our century in the evangelical circles of England
and America.

shown than by the fact that this, their only decidedly original contribution to the systematic philosophy of life, should be so intimately knit up with concrete therapeutics. To the importance of mind-cure the medical and clerical professions in the United States are beginning, though with much recalcitrancy and protesting, to open their eyes. It is evidently bound to develop still farther, both speculatively and practically, and its latest writers are far and away the ablest of the group.[1] It matters nothing that, just as there are hosts of persons who cannot pray, so there are greater hosts who cannot by any possibility be influenced by the mind-curers' ideas. For our immediate purpose, the important point is that so large a number should exist who *can* be so influenced. They form a psychic type to be studied with respect.[2]

To come now to a little closer quarters with their creed. The fundamental pillar on which it rests is nothing more than the general basis of all religious experience, the fact that man has a dual nature, and is connected with two spheres of thought, a shallower and a profounder sphere, in either of which he may learn to live more habitually. The shallower and lower sphere is that of the fleshly sensations, instincts,

[1] I refer to Mr. Horatio W. Dresser and Mr. Henry Wood, especially the former. Mr. Dresser's works are published by G. P. Putnam's Sons, New York and London; Mr. Wood's by Lee & Shepard, Boston.

[2] Lest my own testimony be suspected, I will quote another reporter, Dr. H. H. Goddard, of Clark University, whose thesis on "the Effects of Mind on Body as evidenced by Faith Cures" is published in the American Journal of Psychology for 1899 (vol. x.). This critic, after a wide study of the facts, concludes that the cures by mind-cure exist, but are in no respect different from those now officially recognized in medicine as cures by suggestion; and the end of his essay contains an interesting physiological speculation as to the way in which the suggestive ideas may work (p. 67 of the reprint). As regards the general phenomenon of mental cure itself, Dr. Goddard writes: "In spite of the severe criticism we have made of reports of cure, there still remains a vast amount of material, showing a powerful influence of the mind in disease. Many cases are of diseases that have been diagnosed and treated by the best physicians of the country, or which prominent hospitals have tried their hand at curing, but without success. People of culture and education have been treated by this method with satisfactory results. Diseases of long standing have been ameliorated, and even cured. . . . We have traced the mental element through primitive medicine and folk-medicine of to-day, patent medicine, and witchcraft. We are convinced that it is impossible to

and desires, of egotism, doubt, and the lower personal interests. But whereas Christian theology has always considered *frowardness* to be the essential vice of this part of human nature, the mind-curers say that the mark of the beast in it is *fear*; and this is what gives such an entirely new religious turn to their persuasion.

"Fear," to quote a writer of the school, "has had its uses in the evolutionary process, and seems to constitute the whole of forethought in most animals; but that it should remain any part of the mental equipment of human civilized life is an absurdity. I find that the fear element of forethought is not stimulating to those more civilized persons to whom duty and attraction are the natural motives, but is weakening and deterrent. As soon as it becomes unnecessary, fear becomes a positive deterrent, and should be entirely removed, as dead flesh is removed from living tissue. To assist in the analysis of fear, and in the denunciation of its expressions, I have coined the word *fearthought* to stand for the unprofitable element of forethought, and have defined the word 'worry' as *fearthought in contradistinction to forethought*. I have also defined fearthought as *the self-imposed or self-permitted suggestion of inferiority*, in order to

---

account for the existence of these practices, if they did not cure disease, and that if they cured disease, it must have been the mental element that was effective. The same argument applies to those modern schools of mental therapeutics—Divine Healing and Christian Science. It is hardly conceivable that the large body of intelligent people who comprise the body known distinctively as Mental Scientists should continue to exist if the whole thing were a delusion. It is not a thing of a day; it is not confined to a few; it is not local. It is true that many failures are recorded, but that only adds to the argument. There must be many and striking successes to counterbalance the failures, otherwise the failures would have ended the delusion. . . . Christian Science, Divine Healing, or Mental Science do not, and never can in the very nature of things, cure all diseases; nevertheless, the practical applications of the general principles of the broadest mental science will tend to prevent disease. . . . We do find sufficient evidence to convince us that the proper reform in mental attitude would relieve many a sufferer of ills that the ordinary physician cannot touch; would even delay the approach of death to many a victim beyond the power of absolute cure, and the faithful adherence to a truer philosophy of life will keep many a man well, and give the doctor time to devote to alleviating ills that are unpreventable" (pp. 33, 34 of reprint).

place it where it really belongs, in the category of harmful, unnecessary, and therefore not respectable things.'[1]

The 'misery-habit,' the 'martyr-habit,' engendered by the prevalent 'fearthought,' get pungent criticism from the mind-cure writers: —

"Consider for a moment the habits of life into which we are born. There are certain social conventions or customs and alleged requirements, there is a theological bias, a general view of the world. There are conservative ideas in regard to our early training, our education, marriage, and occupation in life. Following close upon this, there is a long series of anticipations, namely, that we shall suffer certain children's diseases, diseases of middle life, and of old age; the thought that we shall grow old, lose our faculties, and again become childlike; while crowning all is the fear of death. Then there is a long line of particular fears and trouble-bearing expectations, such, for example, as ideas associated with certain articles of food, the dread of the east wind, the terrors of hot weather, the aches and pains associated with cold weather, the fear of catching cold if one sits in a draught, the coming of hay-fever upon the 14th of August in the middle of the day, and so on through a long list of fears, dreads, worriments, anxieties, anticipations, expectations, pessimisms, morbidities, and the whole ghostly train of fateful shapes which our fellow-men, and especially physicians, are ready to help us conjure up, an array worthy to rank with Bradley's 'unearthly ballet of bloodless categories.'

"Yet this is not all. This vast array is swelled by innumerable volunteers from daily life,—the fear of accident, the possibility of calamity, the loss of property, the chance of robbery, of fire, or the outbreak of war. And it is not deemed sufficient to fear for ourselves. When a friend is taken ill, we must forthwith fear the worst and apprehend

[1] HORACE FLETCHER: Happiness as found in Forethought *minus* Fearthought, Menticulture Series, ii. Chicago and New York, Stone, 1897, pp. 21–25, abridged.

death. If one meets with sorrow . . . sympathy means to enter into and increase the suffering."[1]

"Man," to quote another writer, "often has fear stamped upon him before his entrance into the outer world; he is reared in fear; all his life is passed in bondage to fear of disease and death, and thus his whole mentality becomes cramped, limited, and depressed, and his body follows its shrunken pattern and specification. . . . Think of the millions of sensitive and responsive souls among our ancestors who have been under the dominion of such a perpetual nightmare! Is it not surprising that health exists at all? Nothing but the boundless divine love, exuberance, and vitality, constantly poured in, even though unconsciously to us, could in some degree neutralize such an ocean of morbidity."[2]

Although the disciples of the mind-cure often use Christian terminology, one sees from such quotations how widely their notion of the fall of man diverges from that of ordinary Christians.[3]

Their notion of man's higher nature is hardly less diver-

---

[1] H. W. DRESSER: Voices of Freedom, New York, 1899, p. 38.

[2] HENRY WOOD: Ideal Suggestion through Mental Photography, Boston, 1899, p. 54.

[3] Whether it differs so much from Christ's own notion is for the exegetists to decide. According to Harnack, Jesus felt about evil and disease much as our mind-curers do. "What is the answer which Jesus sends to John the Baptist?" asks Harnack, and says it is this: " 'The blind see, and the lame walk, the lepers are cleansed, and the deaf hear, the dead rise up, and the gospel is preached to the poor.' That is the 'coming of the kingdom,' or rather in these saving works the kingdom is already there. By the overcoming and removal of misery, of need, of sickness, by these actual effects John is to see that the new time has arrived. The casting out of devils is only a part of this work of redemption, *but Jesus points to that as the sense and seal of his mission.* Thus to the wretched, sick, and poor did he address himself, but not as a moralist, and without a trace of sentimentalism. He never makes groups and departments of the ills; he never spends time in asking whether the sick one 'deserves' to be cured; and it never occurs to him to sympathize with the pain or the death. He nowhere says that sickness is a beneficent infliction, and that evil has a healthy use. No, he calls sickness sickness and health health. All evil, all wretchedness, is for him something dreadful; it is of the great kingdom of Satan; but he feels the power of the Saviour within him. He knows that advance is possible only when weakness is overcome, when sickness is made well." Das Wesen des Christenthums, 1900, p. 39.

gent, being decidedly pantheistic. The spiritual in man appears in the mind-cure philosophy as partly conscious, but chiefly subconscious; and through the subconscious part of it we are already one with the Divine without any miracle of grace, or abrupt creation of a new inner man. As this view is variously expressed by different writers, we find in it traces of Christian mysticism, of transcendental idealism, of vedantism, and of the modern psychology of the subliminal self. A quotation or two will put us at the central point of view: —

"The great central fact of the universe is that spirit of infinite life and power that is back of all, that manifests itself in and through all. This spirit of infinite life and power that is back of all is what I call God. I care not what term you may use, be it Kindly Light, Providence, the Over-Soul, Omnipotence, or whatever term may be most convenient, so long as we are agreed in regard to the great central fact itself. God then fills the universe alone, so that all is from Him and in Him, and there is nothing that is outside. He is the life of our life, our very life itself. We are partakers of the life of God; and though we differ from Him in that we are individualized spirits, while He is the Infinite Spirit, including us, as well as all else beside, yet in essence the life of God and the life of man are identically the same, and so are one. They differ not in essence or quality; they differ in degree.

"The great central fact in human life is the coming into a conscious vital realization of our oneness with this Infinite Life, and the opening of ourselves fully to this divine inflow. In just the degree that we come into a conscious realization of our oneness with the Infinite Life, and open ourselves to this divine inflow, do we actualize in ourselves the qualities and powers of the Infinite Life, do we make ourselves channels through which the Infinite Intelligence and Power can work. In just the degree in which you realize your oneness with the Infinite Spirit, you will exchange dis-ease for ease, inharmony for harmony, suffering and pain for abounding health and strength. To recognize our own divinity, and our intimate relation to the Universal, is to attach the belts of our machinery to the powerhouse of the Universe. One need remain in hell no longer than one chooses to; we can rise to any heaven we ourselves choose; and when we choose so to rise, all the higher powers of the Universe combine to help us heavenward."[1]

Let me now pass from these abstracter statements to some more concrete accounts of experience with the mind-cure religion. I have many answers from correspondents—the only difficulty is to choose. The first two whom I shall quote are my personal friends. One of them, a woman, writing as follows, expresses well the feeling of continuity with the Infinite Power, by which all mind-cure disciples are inspired.

"The first underlying cause of all sickness, weakness, or depression is the *human sense of separateness* from that Divine Energy which we call God. The soul which can feel and affirm in serene but jubilant confidence, as did the Nazarene: 'I and my Father are one,' has no further need of healer, or of healing. This is the whole truth in a nutshell, and other foundation for wholeness can no man lay than this fact of impregnable divine union. Disease can no longer attack one whose feet are planted on this rock, who feels hourly, momently, the influx of the Deific Breath. If one with Omnipotence, how can weariness enter the consciousness, how illness assail that indomitable spark?

"This possibility of annulling forever the law of fatigue has been abundantly proven in my own case; for my earlier life bears a record of many, many years of bedridden invalidism, with spine and lower limbs paralyzed. My thoughts were no more impure than they are to-day, although my belief in the necessity of illness was dense and unenlightened; but since my resurrection in the flesh, I have worked as a healer unceasingly for fourteen years without a vacation, and can truthfully assert that I have never known a moment of fatigue or pain, although coming in touch constantly with excessive weakness, illness, and disease of all kinds. For how can a conscious part of Deity be sick?— since 'Greater is he that is *with* us than all that can strive against us.' "

[1] R. W. TRINE: In Tune with the Infinite, 26th thousand, N. Y., 1899. I have strung scattered passages together.

My second correspondent, also a woman, sends me the following statement: —

"Life seemed difficult to me at one time. I was always breaking down, and had several attacks of what is called nervous prostration, with terrible insomnia, being on the verge of insanity; besides having many other troubles, especially of the digestive organs. I had been sent away from home in charge of doctors, had taken all the narcotics, stopped all work, been fed up, and in fact knew all the doctors within reach. But I never recovered permanently till this New Thought took possession of me.

"I think that the one thing which impressed me most was learning the fact that we must be in absolutely constant relation or mental touch (this word is to me very expressive) with that essence of life which permeates all and which we call God. This is almost unrecognizable unless we live it into ourselves *actually*, that is, by a constant turning to the very innermost, deepest consciousness of our real selves or of God in us, for illumination from within, just as we turn to the sun for light, warmth, and invigoration without. When you do this consciously, realizing that to turn inward to the light within you is to live in the presence of God or your divine self, you soon discover the unreality of the objects to which you have hitherto been turning and which have engrossed you without.

"I have come to disregard the meaning of this attitude for bodily health *as such*, because that comes of itself, as an incidental result, and cannot be found by any special mental act or desire to have it, beyond that general attitude of mind I have referred to above. That which we usually make the object of life, those outer things we are all so wildly seeking, which we so often live and die for, but which then do not give us peace and happiness, they should all come of themselves as accessory, and as the mere outcome or natural result of a far higher life sunk deep in the bosom of the spirit. This life is the real seeking of the kingdom of God, the desire for his supremacy in our hearts, so that all else comes as that which shall be 'added unto you'—as quite incidental and as a surprise to us, perhaps; and yet it is the proof of the reality of the perfect poise in the very centre of our being.

"When I say that we commonly make the object of our life that which we should not work for primarily, I mean many things which the world considers praiseworthy and excellent, such as success in business, fame as author or artist, physician or lawyer, or renown in philanthropic undertakings. Such things should be results, not objects. I would also include pleasures of many kinds which seem harmless and good at the time, and are pursued because many accept them—I mean conventionalities, sociabilities, and fashions in their various development, these being mostly approved by the masses, although they may be unreal, and even unhealthy superfluities."

Here is another case, more concrete, also that of a woman. I read you these cases without comment,—they express so many varieties of the state of mind we are studying.

"I had been a sufferer from my childhood till my fortieth year. [Details of ill-health are given which I omit.] I had been in Vermont several months hoping for good from the change of air, but steadily growing weaker, when one day during the latter part of October, while resting in the afternoon, I suddenly heard as it were these words: 'You will be healed and do a work you never dreamed of.' These words were impressed upon my mind with such power I said at once that only God could have put them there. I believed them in spite of myself and of my suffering and weakness, which continued until Christmas, when I returned to Boston. Within two days a young friend offered to take me to a mental healer (this was January 7, 1881). The healer said: 'There is nothing but Mind; we are expressions of the One Mind; body is only a mortal belief; as a man thinketh so is he.' I could not accept all she said, but I translated all that was there for *me* in this way: 'There is nothing but God; I am created by Him, and am absolutely dependent upon Him; mind is given me to use; and by just so much of it as I will put upon the thought of right action in body I shall be lifted out of bondage to my ignorance and fear and past experience.' That day I commenced accordingly to take a little of every food provided for the family, constantly saying to myself: 'The Power that created the stomach must take care of what I have eaten.' By holding these suggestions through the evening I went to bed and fell asleep, saying: 'I am soul, spirit, just one with God's Thought of me,' and slept all night without waking, for the first time in several years [the distress-turns had usually recurred about two o'clock in the night]. I felt the next day like an escaped prisoner, and believed I had found the secret that would in time give me perfect health. Within ten days I was able to eat anything provided for others, and after two weeks I began to have my own positive mental suggestions of Truth, which were to me like stepping-stones. I will note a few of them; they came about two weeks apart.

"1st. I am Soul, therefore it is well with me.

"2d. I am Soul, therefore I *am* well.

"3d. A sort of inner vision of myself as a four-footed beast with a protuberance on every part of my body where I had suffering, with my own face, begging me to acknowledge it as myself. I resolutely fixed my attention on being well, and refused to even look at my old self in this form.

"4th. Again the vision of the beast far in the background, with faint voice. Again refusal to acknowledge.

"5th. Once more the vision, but only of my eyes with the longing look; and again the refusal. Then came the conviction, the inner consciousness, that I was perfectly well and always had been, for I was Soul, an expression of God's Perfect Thought. That was to me the perfect and completed separation between what I was and what I appeared to be. I succeeded in never losing sight after this of my real being, by constantly affirming this truth, and by degrees (though it took me two years of hard work to get there) *I expressed health continuously throughout my whole body.*

"In my subsequent nineteen years' experience I have never known this Truth to fail when I applied it, though in my ignorance I have often failed to apply it, but through my failures I have learned the simplicity and trustfulness of the little child."

But I fear that I risk tiring you by so many examples, and

I must lead you back to philosophic generalities again. You see already by such records of experience how impossible it is not to class mind-cure as primarily a religious movement. Its doctrine of the oneness of our life with God's life is in fact quite indistinguishable from an interpretation of Christ's message which in these very Gifford lectures has been defended by some of your very ablest Scottish religious philosophers.[1]

But philosophers usually profess to give a quasi-logical explanation of the existence of evil, whereas of the general fact of evil in the world, the existence of the selfish, suffering, timorous finite consciousness, the mind-curers, so far as I am acquainted with them, profess to give no speculative explanation. Evil is empirically there for them as it is for everybody, but the practical point of view predominates, and it would ill agree with the spirit of their system to spend time in worrying over it as a 'mystery' or 'problem,' or in 'laying to heart' the lesson of its experience, after the manner of the Evangelicals. Don't reason about it, as Dante says, but give a

[1] The Cairds, for example. In EDWARD CAIRD's Glasgow Lectures of 1890 – 92 passages like this abound: —

"The declaration made in the beginning of the ministry of Jesus that 'the time is fulfilled, and the kingdom of heaven is at hand,' passes with scarce a break into the announcement that 'the kingdom of God is among you'; and the importance of this announcement is asserted to be such that it makes, so to speak, a difference *in kind* between the greatest saints and prophets who lived under the previous reign of division, and 'the least in the kingdom of heaven.' The highest ideal is brought close to men and declared to be within their reach, they are called on to be 'perfect as their Father in heaven is perfect.' The sense of alienation and distance from God which had grown upon the pious in Israel just in proportion as they had learned to look upon Him as no mere national divinity, but as a God of justice who would punish Israel for its sin as certainly as Edom or Moab, is declared to be no longer in place; and the typical form of Christian prayer points to the abolition of the contrast between this world and the next which through all the history of the Jews had continually been growing wider: 'As in heaven, so on earth.' The sense of the division of man from God, as a finite being from the Infinite, as weak and sinful from the Omnipotent Goodness, is not indeed lost; but it can no longer overpower the consciousness of oneness. The terms 'Son' and 'Father' at once state the opposition and mark its limit. They show that it is not an absolute opposition, but one which presupposes an indestructible principle of unity, that can and must become a principle of reconciliation." The Evolution of Religion, ii. pp. 146, 147.

glance and pass beyond! It is Avidhya, ignorance! something merely to be outgrown and left behind, transcended and forgotten. Christian Science so-called, the sect of Mrs. Eddy, is the most radical branch of mind-cure in its dealings with evil. For it evil is simply a *lie*, and any one who mentions it is a liar. The optimistic ideal of duty forbids us to pay it the compliment even of explicit attention. Of course, as our next lectures will show us, this is a bad speculative omission, but it is intimately linked with the practical merits of the system we are examining. Why regret a philosophy of evil, a mind-curer would ask us, if I can put you in possession of a life of good?

After all, it is the life that tells; and mind-cure has developed a living system of mental hygiene which may well claim to have thrown all previous literature of the *Diätetik der Seele* into the shade. This system is wholly and exclusively compacted of optimism: 'Pessimism leads to weakness. Optimism leads to power.' 'Thoughts are things,' as one of the most vigorous mind-cure writers prints in bold type at the bottom of each of his pages; and if your thoughts are of health, youth, vigor, and success, before you know it these things will also be your outward portion. No one can fail of the regenerative influence of optimistic thinking, pertinaciously pursued. Every man owns indefeasibly this inlet to the divine. Fear, on the contrary, and all the contracted and egoistic modes of thought, are inlets to destruction. Most mind-curers here bring in a doctrine that thoughts are 'forces,' and that, by virtue of a law that like attracts like, one man's thoughts draw to themselves as allies all the thoughts of the same character that exist the world over. Thus one gets, by one's thinking, reinforcements from elsewhere for the realization of one's desires; and the great point in the conduct of life is to get the heavenly forces on one's side by opening one's own mind to their influx.

On the whole, one is struck by a psychological similarity between the mind-cure movement and the Lutheran and Wesleyan movements. To the believer in moralism and works, with his anxious query, 'What shall I do to be saved?' Luther and Wesley replied: 'You are saved now, if you would but believe it.' And the mind-curers come with precisely similar words of emancipation. They speak, it is true, to persons for whom the conception of salvation has lost its ancient theological meaning, but who labor nevertheless with the same eternal human difficulty. *Things are wrong with them*; and 'What shall I do to be clear, right, sound, whole, well?' is the form of their question. And the answer is: 'You *are* well, sound, and clear already, if you did but know it.' "The whole matter may be summed up in one sentence," says one of the authors whom I have already quoted, "*God is well, and so are you*. You must awaken to the knowledge of your real being."

The adequacy of their message to the mental needs of a large fraction of mankind is what gave force to those earlier gospels. Exactly the same adequacy holds in the case of the mind-cure message, foolish as it may sound upon its surface; and seeing its rapid growth in influence, and its therapeutic triumphs, one is tempted to ask whether it may not be destined (probably by very reason of the crudity and extravagance of many of its manifestations[1]) to play a part almost as great in the evolution of the popular religion of the future as did those earlier movements in their day.

But I here fear that I may begin to 'jar upon the nerves' of some of the members of this academic audience. Such contemporary vagaries, you may think, should hardly take so large a place in dignified Gifford lectures. I can only beseech you to have patience. The whole outcome of these lectures will, I imagine, be the emphasizing to your mind of the enormous diversities which the spiritual lives of different men exhibit. Their wants, their susceptibilities, and their capacities all vary and must be classed under different heads. The result is that we have really different types of religious experience; and, seeking in these lectures closer acquaintance with the healthy-minded type, we must take it where we find it in most radical form. The psychology of individual types of character has hardly begun even to be sketched as yet—our lectures may possibly serve as a crumb-like contribution to the struc-

[1] It remains to be seen whether the school of Mr. Dresser, which assumes more and more the form of mind-cure experience and academic philosophy mutually impregnating each other, will score the practical triumphs of the less critical and rational sects.

ture. The first thing to bear in mind (especially if we ourselves belong to the cleric-academic-scientific type, the officially and conventionally 'correct' type, 'the deadly respectable' type, for which to ignore others is a besetting temptation) is that nothing can be more stupid than to bar out phenomena from our notice, merely because we are incapable of taking any part in them ourselves.

Now the history of Lutheran salvation by faith, of methodistic conversions, and of what I call the mind-cure movement seems to prove the existence of numerous persons in whom—at any rate at a certain stage in their development— a change of character for the better, so far from being facilitated by the rules laid down by official moralists, will take place all the more successfully if those rules be exactly reversed. Official moralists advise us never to relax our strenuousness. "Be vigilant, day and night," they adjure us; "hold your passive tendencies in check; shrink from no effort; keep your will like a bow always bent." But the persons I speak of find that all this conscious effort leads to nothing but failure and vexation in their hands, and only makes them twofold more the children of hell they were before. The tense and voluntary attitude becomes in them an impossible fever and torment. Their machinery refuses to run at all when the bearings are made so hot and the belts so tight.

Under these circumstances the way to success, as vouched for by innumerable authentic personal narrations, is by an anti-moralistic method, by the 'surrender' of which I spoke in my second lecture. Passivity, not activity; relaxation, not intentness, should be now the rule. Give up the feeling of responsibility, let go your hold, resign the care of your destiny to higher powers, be genuinely indifferent as to what becomes of it all, and you will find not only that you gain a perfect inward relief, but often also, in addition, the particular goods you sincerely thought you were renouncing. This is the salvation through self-despair, the dying to be truly born, of Lutheran theology, the passage into *nothing* of which Jacob Behmen writes. To get to it, a critical point must usually be passed, a corner turned within one. Something must give way, a native hardness must break down and liquefy; and this event (as we shall abundantly see hereafter) is frequently sudden and automatic, and leaves on the Subject an impression that he has been wrought on by an external power.

Whatever its ultimate significance may prove to be, this is certainly one fundamental form of human experience. Some say that the capacity or incapacity for it is what divides the religious from the merely moralistic character. With those who undergo it in its fullness, no criticism avails to cast doubt on its reality. They *know*; for they have actually *felt* the higher powers, in giving up the tension of their personal will.

A story which revivalist preachers often tell is that of a man who found himself at night slipping down the side of a precipice. At last he caught a branch which stopped his fall, and remained clinging to it in misery for hours. But finally his fingers had to loose their hold, and with a despairing farewell to life, he let himself drop. He fell just six inches. If he had given up the struggle earlier, his agony would have been spared. As the mother earth received him, so, the preachers tell us, will the everlasting arms receive *us* if we confide absolutely in them, and give up the hereditary habit of relying on our personal strength, with its precautions that cannot shelter and safeguards that never save.

The mind-curers have given the widest scope to this sort of experience. They have demonstrated that a form of regeneration by relaxing, by letting go, psychologically indistinguishable from the Lutheran justification by faith and the Wesleyan acceptance of free grace, is within the reach of persons who have no conviction of sin and care nothing for the Lutheran theology. It is but giving your little private convulsive self a rest, and finding that a greater Self is there. The results, slow or sudden, or great or small, of the combined optimism and expectancy, the regenerative phenomena which ensue on the abandonment of effort, remain firm facts of human nature, no matter whether we adopt a theistic, a pantheistic-idealistic, or a medical-materialistic view of their ultimate causal explanation.[1]

[1] The theistic explanation is by divine grace, which creates a new nature within one the moment the old nature is sincerely given up. The pantheistic explanation (which is that of most mind-curers) is by the merging of the narrower private self into the wider or greater self, the spirit of the universe (which is your own 'subconscious' self), the moment the isolating barriers of

When we take up the phenomena of revivalistic conversion, we shall learn something more about all this. Meanwhile I will say a brief word about the mind-curer's *methods*.

They are of course largely suggestive. The suggestive influence of environment plays an enormous part in all spiritual education. But the word 'suggestion,' having acquired official status, is unfortunately already beginning to play in many quarters the part of a wet blanket upon investigation, being used to fend off all inquiry into the varying susceptibilities of individual cases. 'Suggestion' is only another name for the power of ideas, *so far as they prove efficacious over belief and conduct*. Ideas efficacious over some people prove inefficacious over others. Ideas efficacious at some times and in some human surroundings are not so at other times and elsewhere. The ideas of Christian churches are not efficacious in the therapeutic direction to-day, whatever they may have been in earlier centuries; and when the whole question is as to why the salt has lost its savor here or gained it there, the mere blank waving of the word 'suggestion' as if it were a banner gives no light. Dr. Goddard, whose candid psychological essay on Faith Cures ascribes them to nothing but ordinary suggestion, concludes by saying that "Religion [and by this he seems to mean our popular Christianity] has in it all there is in mental therapeutics, and has it in its best form. Living up to [our religious] ideas will do anything for us that can be done." And this in spite of the actual fact that the popular Christianity does absolutely *nothing*, or did nothing until mind-cure came to the rescue.[1]

An idea, to be suggestive, must come to the individual with

---

mistrust and anxiety are removed. The medico-materialistic explanation is that simpler cerebral processes act more freely where they are left to act automatically by the shunting-out of physiologically (though in this instance not spiritually) 'higher' ones which, seeking to regulate, only succeed in inhibiting results.—Whether this third explanation might, in a psycho-physical account of the universe, be combined with either of the others may be left an open question here.

[1] Within the churches a disposition has always prevailed to regard sickness as a visitation: something sent by God for our good, either as chastisement, as warning, or as opportunity for exercising virtue, and, in the Catholic Church, of earning 'merit.' "Illness," says a good Catholic writer (P. LEJEUNE:

the force of a revelation. The mind-cure with its gospel of healthy-mindedness has come as a revelation to many whose hearts the church-Christianity had left hardened. It has let loose their springs of higher life. In what can the originality of any religious movement consist, save in finding a channel, until then sealed up, through which those springs may be set free in some group of human beings?

The force of personal faith, enthusiasm, and example, and above all the force of novelty, are always the prime suggestive agency in this kind of success. If mind-cure should ever become official, respectable, and intrenched, these elements of suggestive efficacy will be lost. In its acuter stages every

---

Introd. à la Vie Mystique, 1899, p. 218), "is the most excellent of corporeal mortifications, the mortification which one has not one's self chosen, which is imposed directly by God, and is the direct expression of his will. 'If other mortifications are of silver,' Mgr. Gay says, 'this one is of gold; since although it comes of ourselves, coming as it does of original sin, still on its greater side, as coming (like all that happens) from the providence of God, it is of divine manufacture. And how just are its blows! And how efficacious it is! . . . I do not hesitate to say that patience in a long illness is mortification's very masterpiece, and consequently the triumph of mortified souls.' " According to this view, disease should in any case be submissively accepted, and it might under certain circumstances even be blasphemous to wish it away.

Of course there have been exceptions to this, and cures by special miracle have at all times been recognized within the church's pale, almost all the great saints having more or less performed them. It was one of the heresies of Edward Irving, to maintain them still to be possible. An extremely pure faculty of healing after confession and conversion on the patient's part, and prayer on the priest's, was quite spontaneously developed in the German pastor, Joh. Christoph Blumhardt, in the early forties and exerted during nearly thirty years. Blumhardt's Life by Zündel (5th edition, Zurich, 1887) gives in chapters ix., x., xi., and xvii. a pretty full account of his healing activity, which he invariably ascribed to direct divine interposition. Blumhardt was a singularly pure, simple, and non-fanatical character, and in this part of his work followed no previous model. In Chicago to-day we have the case of Dr. J. A. Dowie, a Scottish Baptist preacher, whose weekly 'Leaves of Healing' were in the year of grace 1900 in their sixth volume, and who, although he denounces the cures wrought in other sects as 'diabolical counterfeits' of his own exclusively 'Divine Healing,' must on the whole be counted into the mind-cure movement. In mind-cure circles the fundamental article of faith is that disease should never be accepted. It is wholly of the pit. God wants us to be absolutely healthy, and we should not tolerate ourselves on any lower terms.

religion must be a homeless Arab of the desert. The church knows this well enough, with its everlasting inner struggle of the acute religion of the few against the chronic religion of the many, indurated into an obstructiveness worse than that which irreligion opposes to the movings of the Spirit. "We may pray," says Jonathan Edwards, "concerning all those saints that are not lively Christians, that they may either be enlivened, or taken away; if that be true that is often said by some at this day, that these cold dead saints do more hurt than natural men, and lead more souls to hell, and that it would be well for mankind if they were all dead."[1]

The next condition of success is the apparent existence, in large numbers, of minds who unite healthy-mindedness with readiness for regeneration by letting go. Protestantism has been too pessimistic as regards the natural man, Catholicism has been too legalistic and moralistic, for either the one or the other to appeal in any generous way to the type of character formed of this peculiar mingling of elements. However few of us here present may belong to such a type, it is now evident that it forms a specific moral combination, well represented in the world.

Finally, mind-cure has made what in our protestant countries is an unprecedentedly great use of the subconscious life. To their reasoned advice and dogmatic assertion, its founders have added systematic exercise in passive relaxation, concentration, and meditation, and have even invoked something like hypnotic practice. I quote some passages at random:—

"The value, the potency of ideals is the great practical truth on which the New Thought most strongly insists,— the development namely from within outward, from small to great.[2] Consequently one's thought should be centred on the ideal outcome, even though this trust be literally like a step in the dark.[3] To attain the ability thus effec-

[1] Edwards, from whose book on the Revival in New England I quote these words, dissuades from such a use of prayer, but it is easy to see that he enjoys making his thrust at the cold dead church-members.

[2] H. W. DRESSER: Voices of Freedom, 46.

[3] DRESSER: Living by the Spirit, 58.

tively to direct the mind, the New Thought advises the practice of concentration, or in other words, the attainment of self-control. One is to learn to marshal the tendencies of the mind, so that they may be held together as a unit by the chosen ideal. To this end, one should set apart times for silent meditation, by one's self, preferably in a room where the surroundings are favorable to spiritual thought. In New Thought terms, this is called 'entering the silence.' "[1]

"The time will come when in the busy office or on the noisy street you can enter into the silence by simply drawing the mantle of your own thoughts about you and realizing that there and everywhere the Spirit of Infinite Life, Love, Wisdom, Peace, Power, and Plenty is guiding, keeping, protecting, leading you. This is the spirit of continual prayer.[2] One of the most intuitive men we ever met had a desk at a city office where several other gentlemen were doing business constantly, and often talking loudly. Entirely undisturbed by the many various sounds about him, this self-centred faithful man would, in any moment of perplexity, draw the curtains of privacy so completely about him that he would be as fully inclosed in his own psychic aura, and thereby as effectually removed from all distractions, as though he were alone in some primeval wood. Taking his difficulty with him into the mystic silence in the form of a direct question, to which he expected a certain answer, he would remain utterly passive until the reply came, and never once through many years' experience did he find himself disappointed or misled."[3]

Wherein, I should like to know, does this *intrinsically* differ from the practice of 'recollection' which plays so great a part in Catholic discipline? Otherwise called the practice of the presence of God (and so known among ourselves, as for instance in Jeremy Taylor), it is thus defined by the eminent teacher Alvarez de Paz in his work on Contemplation.

[1] DRESSER: Voices of Freedom, 33.
[2] TRINE: In Tune with the Infinite, p. 214.
[3] TRINE: p. 117.

"It is the recollection of God, the thought of God, which in all places and circumstances makes us see him present, lets us commune respectfully and lovingly with him, and fills us with desire and affection for him. . . . Would you escape from every ill? Never lose this recollection of God, neither in prosperity nor in adversity, nor on any occasion whichsoever it be. Invoke not, to excuse yourself from this duty, either the difficulty or the importance of your business, for you can always remember that God sees you, that you are under his eye. If a thousand times an hour you forget him, reanimate a thousand times the recollection. If you cannot practice this exercise continuously, at least make yourself as familiar with it as possible; and, like unto those who in a rigorous winter draw near the fire as often as they can, go as often as you can to that ardent fire which will warm your soul."[1]

All the external associations of the Catholic discipline are of course unlike anything in mind-cure thought, but the purely spiritual part of the exercise is identical in both communions, and in both communions those who urge it write with authority, for they have evidently experienced in their own persons that whereof they tell. Compare again some mind-cure utterances:—

"High, healthful, pure thinking can be encouraged, promoted, and strengthened. Its current can be turned upon grand ideals until it forms a habit and wears a channel. By means of such discipline the mental horizon can be flooded with the sunshine of beauty, wholeness, and harmony. To inaugurate pure and lofty thinking may at first seem difficult, even almost mechanical, but perseverance will at length render it easy, then pleasant, and finally delightful.

"The soul's real world is that which it has built of its thoughts, mental states, and imaginations. If we *will*, we can turn our backs upon the lower and sensuous plane, and lift ourselves into the realm of the spiritual and Real, and there gain a residence. The assumption of states of expec-

[1] Quoted by Lejeune: Introd. à la Vie Mystique, 1899, p. 66.

tancy and receptivity will attract spiritual sunshine, and it will flow in as naturally as air inclines to a vacuum. . . . Whenever the thought is not occupied with one's daily duty or profession, it should be sent aloft into the spiritual atmosphere. There are quiet leisure moments by day, and wakeful hours at night, when this wholesome and delightful exercise may be engaged in to great advantage. If one who has never made any systematic effort to lift and control the thought-forces will, for a single month, earnestly pursue the course here suggested, he will be surprised and delighted at the result, and nothing will induce him to go back to careless, aimless, and superficial thinking. At such favorable seasons the outside world, with all its current of daily events, is barred out, and one goes into the silent sanctuary of the inner temple of soul to commune and aspire. The spiritual hearing becomes delicately sensitive, so that the 'still, small voice' is audible, the tumultuous waves of external sense are hushed, and there is a great calm. The ego gradually becomes conscious that it is face to face with the Divine Presence; that mighty, healing, loving, Fatherly life which is nearer to us than we are to ourselves. There is soul-contact with the Parent-Soul, and an influx of life, love, virtue, health, and happiness from the Inexhaustible Fountain."[1]

When we reach the subject of mysticism, you will undergo so deep an immersion into these exalted states of consciousness as to be wet all over, if I may so express myself; and the cold shiver of doubt with which this little sprinkling may affect you will have long since passed away—doubt, I mean, as to whether all such writing be not mere abstract talk and rhetoric set down *pour encourager les autres*. You will then be convinced, I trust, that these states of consciousness of 'union' form a perfectly definite class of experiences, of which the soul may occasionally partake, and which certain persons may live by in a deeper sense than they live by anything else with which they have acquaintance. This brings me to a general philosophical reflection with which I should

---

[1] HENRY WOOD: Ideal Suggestion through Mental Photography, pp. 51, 70 (abridged).

like to pass from the subject of healthy-mindedness, and close a topic which I fear is already only too long drawn out. It concerns the relation of all this systematized healthy-mindedness and mind-cure religion to scientific method and the scientific life.

In a later lecture I shall have to treat explicitly of the relation of religion to science on the one hand, and to primeval savage thought on the other. There are plenty of persons to-day—'scientists' or 'positivists,' they are fond of calling themselves—who will tell you that religious thought is a mere survival, an atavistic reversion to a type of consciousness which humanity in its more enlightened examples has long since left behind and outgrown. If you ask them to explain themselves more fully, they will probably say that for primitive thought everything is conceived of under the form of personality. The savage thinks that things operate by personal forces, and for the sake of individual ends. For him, even external nature obeys individual needs and claims, just as if these were so many elementary powers. Now science, on the other hand, these positivists say, has proved that personality, so far from being an elementary force in nature, is but a passive resultant of the really elementary forces, physical, chemical, physiological, and psycho-physical, which are all impersonal and general in character. Nothing individual accomplishes anything in the universe save in so far as it obeys and exemplifies some universal law. Should you then inquire of them by what means science has thus supplanted primitive thought, and discredited its personal way of looking at things, they would undoubtedly say it has been by the strict use of the method of experimental verification. Follow out science's conceptions practically, they will say, the conceptions that ignore personality altogether, and you will always be corroborated. The world is so made that all your expectations will be experientially verified so long, and only so long, as you keep the terms from which you infer them impersonal and universal.

But here we have mind-cure, with her diametrically opposite philosophy, setting up an exactly identical claim. Live as if I were true, she says, and every day will practically prove you right. That the controlling energies of nature are personal, that your own personal thoughts are forces, that the powers of the universe will directly respond to your individual appeals and needs, are propositions which your whole bodily and mental experience will verify. And that experience does largely verify these primeval religious ideas is proved by the fact that the mind-cure movement spreads as it does, not by proclamation and assertion simply, but by palpable experiential results. Here, in the very heyday of science's authority, it carries on an aggressive warfare against the scientific philosophy, and succeeds by using science's own peculiar methods and weapons. Believing that a higher power will take care of us in certain ways better than we can take care of ourselves, if we only genuinely throw ourselves upon it and consent to use it, it finds the belief, not only not impugned, but corroborated by its observation.

How conversions are thus made, and converts confirmed, is evident enough from the narratives which I have quoted. I will quote yet another couple of shorter ones to give the matter a perfectly concrete turn. Here is one: —

"One of my first experiences in applying my teaching was two months after I first saw the healer. I fell, spraining my right ankle, which I had done once four years before, having then had to use a crutch and elastic anklet for some months, and carefully guarding it ever since. As soon as I was on my feet I made the positive suggestion (and felt it through all my being): 'There is nothing but God, all life comes from him perfectly. I cannot be sprained or hurt, I will let him take care of it.' Well, I never had a sensation in it, and I walked two miles that day."

The next case not only illustrates experiment and verification, but also the element of passivity and surrender of which awhile ago I made such account.

"I went into town to do some shopping one morning, and I had not been gone long before I began to feel ill. The ill feeling increased rapidly, until I had pains in all my bones, nausea and faintness, headache, all the symptoms in short that precede an attack of influenza. I thought that I was going to have the grippe, epidemic then in Boston, or something worse. The mind-cure teachings that I had been listening to all the winter thereupon came into my mind, and I thought that here was an opportunity to test myself. On my way home I met a friend, and I refrained with some effort from telling her how I felt. That was the first step gained. I went to bed immediately, and my husband wished to send for the doctor. But I told him that I would rather wait until morning and see how I felt. Then followed one of the most beautiful experiences of my life.

"I cannot express it in any other way than to say that I did 'lie down in the stream of life and let it flow over me.' I gave up all fear of any impending disease; I was perfectly willing and obedient. There was no intellectual effort, or train of thought. My dominant idea was: 'Behold the hand-maid of the Lord: be it unto me even as thou wilt,' and a perfect confidence that all would be well, that all *was* well. The creative life was flowing into me every instant, and I felt myself allied with the Infinite, in harmony, and full of the peace that passeth understanding. There was no place in my mind for a jarring body. I had no consciousness of time or space or persons; but only of love and happiness and faith.

"I do not know how long this state lasted, nor when I fell asleep; but when I woke up in the morning, *I was well.*"

These are exceedingly trivial instances,[1] but in them, if we have anything at all, we have the method of experiment and verification. For the point I am driving at now, it makes no difference whether you consider the patients to be deluded victims of their imagination or not. That they seemed to *themselves* to have been cured by the experiments tried was enough to make them converts to the system. And although it is evident that one must be of a certain mental mould to get such results (for not every one can get thus cured to his own satisfaction any more than every one can be cured by the first regular practitioner whom he calls in), yet it would surely be pedantic and over-scrupulous for those who *can* get their savage and primitive philosophy of mental healing verified in such experimental ways as this, to give them up at word of

[1] See Appendix to this lecture for two other cases furnished me by friends.

command for more scientific therapeutics. What are we to think of all this? Has science made too wide a claim?

I believe that the claims of the sectarian scientist are, to say the least, premature. The experiences which we have been studying during this hour (and a great many other kinds of religious experiences are like them) plainly show the universe to be a more many-sided affair than any sect, even the scientific sect, allows for. What, in the end, are all our verifications but experiences that agree with more or less isolated systems of ideas (conceptual systems) that our minds have framed? But why in the name of common sense need we assume that only one such system of ideas can be true? The obvious outcome of our total experience is that the world can be handled according to many systems of ideas, and is so handled by different men, and will each time give some characteristic kind of profit, for which he cares, to the handler, while at the same time some other kind of profit has to be omitted or postponed. Science gives to all of us telegraphy, electric lighting, and diagnosis, and succeeds in preventing and curing a certain amount of disease. Religion in the shape of mind-cure gives to some of us serenity, moral poise, and happiness, and prevents certain forms of disease as well as science does, or even better in a certain class of persons. Evidently, then, the science and the religion are both of them genuine keys for unlocking the world's treasure-house to him who can use either of them practically. Just as evidently neither is exhaustive or exclusive of the other's simultaneous use. And why, after all, may not the world be so complex as to consist of many interpenetrating spheres of reality, which we can thus approach in alternation by using different conceptions and assuming different attitudes, just as mathematicians handle the same numerical and spatial facts by geometry, by analytical geometry, by algebra, by the calculus, or by quaternions, and each time come out right? On this view religion and science, each verified in its own way from hour to hour and from life to life, would be co-eternal. Primitive thought, with its belief in individualized personal forces, seems at any rate as far as ever from being driven by science from the field to-day. Numbers of educated people still find it the directest experimental channel by which to carry on their intercourse with reality.[1]

The case of mind-cure lay so ready to my hand that I could not resist the temptation of using it to bring these last truths home to your attention, but I must content myself to-day with this very brief indication. In a later lecture the relations of religion both to science and to primitive thought will have to receive much more explicit attention.

APPENDIX

(See note to p. 115.)

CASE I. "My own experience is this: I had long been ill, and one of the first results of my illness, a dozen years before, had been a diplopia which deprived me of the use of my eyes for reading and writing almost entirely, while a later one had been to shut me out from exercise of any kind under penalty of immediate and great exhaustion. I had been under the care of doctors of the highest standing both in Europe and America, men in whose power to help me I had had great faith, with no or ill result. Then, at a time when I seemed to be rather rapidly losing ground, I heard some things that gave me interest enough in mental healing to make me try it; I had no great hope of getting any good from it—it was a *chance* I tried, partly because my thought was interested by the new possibility it seemed to open, partly because it was the only chance I then could see. I went to X. in Boston, from whom some friends of mine had got, or thought that they had got, great help; the treatment was a silent one; little was said, and that little carried no conviction to my mind; whatever influence was exerted was that of another person's thought or

[1] Whether the various spheres or systems are ever to fuse integrally into one absolute conception, as most philosophers assume that they must, and how, if so, that conception may best be reached, are questions that only the future can answer. What is certain now is the fact of lines of disparate conception, each corresponding to some part of the world's truth, each verified in some degree, each leaving out some part of real experience.

feeling silently projected on to my unconscious mind, into my nervous system as it were, as we sat still together. I believed from the start in the *possibility* of such action, for I knew the power of the mind to shape, helping or hindering, the body's nerve-activities, and I thought telepathy probable, although unproved, but I had no belief in it as more than a possibility, and no strong conviction nor any mystic or religious faith connected with my thought of it that might have brought imagination strongly into play.

"I sat quietly with the healer for half an hour each day, at first with no result; then, after ten days or so, I became quite suddenly and swiftly conscious of a tide of new energy rising within me, a sense of power to pass beyond old halting-places, of power to break the bounds that, though often tried before, had long been veritable walls about my life, too high to climb. I began to read and walk as I had not done for years, and the change was sudden, marked, and unmistakable. This tide seemed to mount for some weeks, three or four perhaps, when, summer having come, I came away, taking the treatment up again a few months later. The lift I got proved permanent, and left me slowly gaining ground instead of losing it, but with this lift the influence seemed in a way to have spent itself, and, though my confidence in the reality of the power had gained immensely from this first experience, and should have helped me to make further gain in health and strength if my belief in it had been the potent factor there, I never after this got any result at all as striking or as clearly marked as this which came when I made trial of it first, with little faith and doubtful expectation. It is difficult to put all the evidence in such a matter into words, to gather up into a distinct statement all that one bases one's conclusions on, but I have always felt that I had abundant evidence to justify (to myself, at least) the conclusion that I came to then, and since have held to, that the physical change which came at that time was, first, the result of a change wrought within me by a change of mental state; and, secondly, that that change of mental state was not, save in a very secondary way, brought about through the influence of an excited imagination, or a *consciously* received suggestion of an hypnotic sort. Lastly, I believe that this change was the result of my receiving telepathically, and upon a mental stratum quite below the level of immediate consciousness, a healthier and more energetic attitude, receiving it from another person whose thought was directed upon me with the intention of impressing the idea of this attitude upon me. In my case the disease was distinctly what would be classed as nervous, not organic; but from such opportunities as I have had of observing, I have come to the conclusion that the dividing line that has been drawn is an arbitrary one, the nerves controlling the internal activities and the nutrition of the body throughout; and I believe that the central nervous system, by starting and inhibiting local centres, can exercise a vast influence upon disease of any kind, if it can be brought to bear. In my judgment the question is simply how to bring it to bear, and I think that the uncertainty and remarkable differences in the results obtained through mental healing do but show how ignorant we are as yet of the forces at work and of the means we should take to make them effective. That these results are not due to chance coincidences my observation of myself and others makes me sure; that the conscious mind, the imagination, enters into them as a factor in many cases is doubtless true, but in many others, and sometimes very extraordinary ones, it hardly seems to enter in at all. On the whole I am inclined to think that as the healing action, like the morbid one, springs from the plane of the normally *un*conscious mind, so the strongest and most effective impressions are those which *it* receives, in some as yet unknown, subtle way, *directly* from a healthier mind whose state, through a hidden law of sympathy, it reproduces."

CASE II. "At the urgent request of friends, and with no faith and hardly any hope (possibly owing to a previous unsuccessful experience with a Christian Scientist), our little daughter was placed under the care of a healer, and cured of a trouble about which the physician had been very discouraging in his diagnosis. This interested me, and I began studying earnestly the method and philosophy of this method of healing. Gradually an inner peace and tranquillity came to me in so positive a way that my manner changed greatly. My children and friends noticed the change and commented upon it. All feelings of irritability disappeared. Even the expression of my face changed noticeably.

"I had been bigoted, aggressive, and intolerant in discussion, both in public and private. I grew broadly tolerant and receptive toward the views of others. I had been nervous and irritable, coming home two or three times a week with a sick headache induced, as I then supposed, by dyspepsia and catarrh. I grew serene and gentle, and the physical troubles entirely disappeared. I had been in the habit of approaching every business interview with an almost morbid dread. I now meet every one with confidence and inner calm.

"I may say that the growth has all been toward the elimination of selfishness. I do not mean simply the grosser, more sensual forms, but those subtler and generally unrecognized kinds, such as express themselves in sorrow, grief, regret, envy, etc. It has been in the direction of a practical, working realization of the immanence of God and the Divinity of man's true, inner self."

LECTURES VI AND VII

THE SICK SOUL

AT OUR LAST MEETING, we considered the healthy-minded temperament, the temperament which has a constitutional incapacity for prolonged suffering, and in which the tendency to see things optimistically is like a water of crystallization in which the individual's character is set. We saw how this temperament may become the basis for a peculiar type of religion, a religion in which good, even the good of this world's life, is regarded as the essential thing for a rational being to attend to. This religion directs him to settle his scores with the more evil aspects of the universe by systematically declining to lay them to heart or make much of them, by ignoring them in his reflective calculations, or even, on occasion, by denying outright that they exist. Evil is a disease; and worry over disease is itself an additional form of disease, which only adds to the original complaint. Even repentance and remorse, affections which come in the character of ministers of good, may be but sickly and relaxing impulses. The best repentance is to up and act for righteousness, and forget that you ever had relations with sin.

Spinoza's philosophy has this sort of healthy-mindedness woven into the heart of it, and this has been one secret of its fascination. He whom Reason leads, according to Spinoza, is led altogether by the influence over his mind of good. Knowledge of evil is an 'inadequate' knowledge, fit only for slavish minds. So Spinoza categorically condemns repentance. When men make mistakes, he says,—

> "One might perhaps expect gnawings of conscience and repentance to help to bring them on the right path, and might thereupon conclude (as every one does conclude) that these affections are good things. Yet when we look at the matter closely, we shall find that not only are they not good, but on the contrary deleterious and evil passions. For it is manifest that we can always get along better by reason and love of truth than by worry of conscience and remorse. Harmful are these and evil, inasmuch as they form a par-

ticular kind of sadness; and the disadvantages of sadness," he continues, "I have already proved, and shown that we should strive to keep it from our life. Just so we should endeavor, since uneasiness of conscience and remorse are of this kind of complexion, to flee and shun these states of mind."[1]

Within the Christian body, for which repentance of sins has from the beginning been the critical religious act, healthy-mindedness has always come forward with its milder interpretation. Repentance according to such healthy-minded Christians means *getting away from* the sin, not groaning and writhing over its commission. The Catholic practice of confession and absolution is in one of its aspects little more than a systematic method of keeping healthy-mindedness on top. By it a man's accounts with evil are periodically squared and audited, so that he may start the clean page with no old debts inscribed. Any Catholic will tell us how clean and fresh and free he feels after the purging operation. Martin Luther by no means belonged to the healthy-minded type in the radical sense in which we have discussed it, and he repudiated priestly absolution for sin. Yet in this matter of repentance he had some very healthy-minded ideas, due in the main to the largeness of his conception of God.

"When I was a monk," he says, "I thought that I was utterly cast away, if at any time I felt the lust of the flesh: that is to say, if I felt any evil motion, fleshly lust, wrath, hatred, or envy against any brother. I assayed many ways to help to quiet my conscience, but it would not be; for the concupiscence and lust of my flesh did always return, so that I could not rest, but was continually vexed with these thoughts: This or that sin thou hast committed: thou art infected with envy, with impatiency, and such other sins: therefore thou art entered into this holy order in vain, and all thy good works are unprofitable. But if then I had rightly understood these sentences of Paul: 'The flesh lusteth contrary to the Spirit, and the Spirit contrary to the flesh; and these two are one against another, so that ye

[1] Tract on God, Man, and Happiness, Book ii. ch. x.

cannot do the things that ye would do,' I should not have so miserably tormented myself, but should have thought and said to myself, as now commonly I do, 'Martin, thou shalt not utterly be without sin, for thou hast flesh; thou shalt therefore feel the battle thereof.' I remember that Staupitz was wont to say, 'I have vowed unto God above a thousand times that I would become a better man: but I never performed that which I vowed. Hereafter I will make no such vow: for I have now learned by experience that I am not able to perform it. Unless, therefore, God be favorable and merciful unto me for Christ's sake, I shall not be able, with all my vows and all my good deeds, to stand before him.' This (of Staupitz's) was not only a true, but also a godly and a holy desperation; and this must they all confess, both with mouth and heart, who will be saved. For the godly trust not to their own righteousness. They look unto Christ their reconciler, who gave his life for their sins. Moreover, they know that the remnant of sin which is in their flesh is not laid to their charge, but freely pardoned. Notwithstanding, in the mean while they fight in spirit against the flesh, lest they should *fulfill* the lusts thereof; and although they feel the flesh to rage and rebel, and themselves also do fall sometimes into sin through infirmity, yet are they not discouraged, nor think therefore that their state and kind of life, and the works which are done according to their calling, displease God; but they raise up themselves by faith."[1]

One of the heresies for which the Jesuits got that spiritual genius, Molinos, the founder of Quietism, so abominably condemned was his healthy-minded opinion of repentance: —

"When thou fallest into a fault, in what matter soever it be, do not trouble nor afflict thyself for it. For they are effects of our frail Nature, stained by Original Sin. The common enemy will make thee believe, as soon as thou fallest into any fault, that thou walkest in error, and therefore art out of God and his favor, and herewith would he make thee distrust of the divine Grace, telling thee of thy

[1] Commentary on Galatians, Philadelphia, 1891, pp. 510–514 (abridged).

misery, and making a giant of it; and putting it into thy head that every day thy soul grows worse instead of better, whilst it so often repeats these failings. O blessed Soul, open thine eyes; and shut the gate against these diabolical suggestions, knowing thy misery, and trusting in the mercy divine. Would not he be a mere fool who, running at tournament with others, and falling in the best of the career, should lie weeping on the ground and afflicting himself with discourses upon his fall? Man (they would tell him), lose no time, get up and take the course again, for he that rises again quickly and continues his race is as if he had never fallen. If thou seest thyself fallen once and a thousand times, thou oughtest to make use of the remedy which I have given thee, that is, a loving confidence in the divine mercy. These are the weapons with which thou must fight and conquer cowardice and vain thoughts. This is the means thou oughtest to use—not to lose time, not to disturb thyself, and reap no good."[1]

Now in contrast with such healthy-minded views as these, if we treat them as a way of deliberately minimizing evil, stands a radically opposite view, a way of maximizing evil, if you please so to call it, based on the persuasion that the evil aspects of our life are of its very essence, and that the world's meaning most comes home to us when we lay them most to heart. We have now to address ourselves to this more morbid way of looking at the situation. But as I closed our last hour with a general philosophical reflection on the healthy-minded way of taking life, I should like at this point to make another philosophical reflection upon it before turning to that heavier task. You will excuse the brief delay.

If we admit that evil is an essential part of our being and the key to the interpretation of our life, we load ourselves down with a difficulty that has always proved burdensome in philosophies of religion. Theism, whenever it has erected itself into a systematic philosophy of the universe, has shown a reluctance to let God be anything less than All-in-All. In other words, philosophic theism has always shown a tendency to become pantheistic and monistic, and to consider the world

[1] MOLINOS: Spiritual Guide, Book II., chaps. xvii., xviii. (abridged).

as one unit of absolute fact; and this has been at variance with popular or practical theism, which latter has ever been more or less frankly pluralistic, not to say polytheistic, and shown itself perfectly well satisfied with a universe composed of many original principles, provided we be only allowed to believe that the divine principle remains supreme, and that the others are subordinate. In this latter case God is not necessarily responsible for the existence of evil; he would only be responsible if it were not finally overcome. But on the monistic or pantheistic view, evil, like everything else, must have its foundation in God; and the difficulty is to see how this can possibly be the case if God be absolutely good. This difficulty faces us in every form of philosophy in which the world appears as one flawless unit of fact. Such a unit is an *Individual*, and in it the worst parts must be as essential as the best, must be as necessary to make the individual what he is; since if any part whatever in an individual were to vanish or alter, it would no longer be *that* individual at all. The philosophy of absolute idealism, so vigorously represented both in Scotland and America to-day, has to struggle with this difficulty quite as much as scholastic theism struggled in its time; and although it would be premature to say that there is no speculative issue whatever from the puzzle, it is perfectly fair to say that there is no clear or easy issue, and that the only *obvious* escape from paradox here is to cut loose from the monistic assumption altogether, and to allow the world to have existed from its origin in pluralistic form, as an aggregate or collection of higher and lower things and principles, rather than an absolutely unitary fact. For then evil would not need to be essential; it might be, and may always have been, an independent portion that had no rational or absolute right to live with the rest, and which we might conceivably hope to see got rid of at last.

Now the gospel of healthy-mindedness, as we have described it, casts its vote distinctly for this pluralistic view. Whereas the monistic philosopher finds himself more or less bound to say, as Hegel said, that everything actual is rational, and that evil, as an element dialectically required, must be pinned in and kept and consecrated and have a function awarded to it in the final system of truth, healthy-mindedness refuses to say anything of the sort.[1] Evil, it says, is emphatically irrational, and *not* to be pinned in, or preserved, or consecrated in any final system of truth. It is a pure abomination to the Lord, an alien unreality, a waste element, to be sloughed off and negated, and the very memory of it, if possible, wiped out and forgotten. The ideal, so far from being co-extensive with the whole actual, is a mere *extract* from the actual, marked by its deliverance from all contact with this diseased, inferior, and excrementitious stuff.

Here we have the interesting notion fairly and squarely presented to us, of there being elements of the universe which may make no rational whole in conjunction with the other elements, and which, from the point of view of any system which those other elements make up, can only be considered so much irrelevance and accident—so much 'dirt,' as it were, and matter out of place. I ask you now not to forget this notion; for although most philosophers seem either to forget it or to disdain it too much ever to mention it, I believe that we shall have to admit it ourselves in the end as containing an element of truth. The mind-cure gospel thus once more appears to us as having dignity and importance. We have seen it to be a genuine religion, and no mere silly appeal to imagination to cure disease; we have seen its method of experimental verification to be not unlike the method of all science; and now here we find mind-cure as the champion of a perfectly definite conception of the metaphysical structure of the world. I hope that, in view of all this, you will not regret my having pressed it upon your attention at such length.

Let us now say good-by for a while to all this way of thinking, and turn towards those persons who cannot so swiftly throw off the burden of the consciousness of evil, but are congenitally fated to suffer from its presence. Just as we saw

---

[1] I say this in spite of the monistic utterances of many mind-cure writers; for these utterances are really inconsistent with their attitude towards disease, and can easily be shown not to be logically involved in the experiences of union with a higher Presence with which they connect themselves. The higher Presence, namely, need not be the absolute whole of things, it is quite sufficient for the life of religious experience to regard it as a part, if only it be the most ideal part.

that in healthy-mindedness there are shallower and profounder levels, happiness like that of the mere animal, and
more regenerate sorts of happiness, so also are there different
levels of the morbid mind, and the one is much more formidable than the other. There are people for whom evil means
only a mal-adjustment with *things*, a wrong correspondence
of one's life with the environment. Such evil as this is curable,
in principle at least, upon the natural plane, for merely by
modifying either the self or the things, or both at once, the
two terms may be made to fit, and all go merry as a marriage
bell again. But there are others for whom evil is no mere
relation of the subject to particular outer things, but something more radical and general, a wrongness or vice in his
essential nature, which no alteration of the environment, or
any superficial rearrangement of the inner self, can cure, and
which requires a supernatural remedy. On the whole, the
Latin races have leaned more towards the former way of looking upon evil, as made up of ills and sins in the plural, removable in detail; while the Germanic races have tended
rather to think of Sin in the singular, and with a capital S, as
of something ineradicably ingrained in our natural subjectivity, and never to be removed by any superficial piecemeal operations.[1] These comparisons of races are always open to
exception, but undoubtedly the northern tone in religion has
inclined to the more intimately pessimistic persuasion, and
this way of feeling, being the more extreme, we shall find by
far the more instructive for our study.

Recent psychology has found great use for the word
'threshold' as a symbolic designation for the point at which
one state of mind passes into another. Thus we speak of the
threshold of a man's consciousness in general, to indicate the
amount of noise, pressure, or other outer stimulus which it
takes to arouse his attention at all. One with a high threshold
will doze through an amount of racket by which one with a
low threshold would be immediately waked. Similarly, when
one is sensitive to small differences in any order of sensation,
we say he has a low 'difference-threshold'—his mind easily
steps over it into the consciousness of the differences in ques-

---

[1] Cf. J. MILSAND: Luther et le Serf-Arbitre, 1884, *passim*.

tion. And just so we might speak of a 'pain-threshold,' a 'fear-threshold,' a 'misery-threshold,' and find it quickly overpassed by the consciousness of some individuals, but lying too high in others to be often reached by their consciousness. The sanguine and healthy-minded live habitually on the sunny side of their misery-line, the depressed and melancholy live beyond it, in darkness and apprehension. There are men who seem to have started in life with a bottle or two of champagne inscribed to their credit; whilst others seem to have been born close to the pain-threshold, which the slightest irritants fatally send them over.

Does it not appear as if one who lived more habitually on one side of the pain-threshold might need a different sort of religion from one who habitually lived on the other? This question, of the relativity of different types of religion to different types of need, arises naturally at this point, and will become a serious problem ere we have done. But before we confront it in general terms, we must address ourselves to the unpleasant task of hearing what the sick souls, as we may call them in contrast to the healthy-minded, have to say of the secrets of their prison-house, their own peculiar form of consciousness. Let us then resolutely turn our backs on the once-born and their sky-blue optimistic gospel; let us not simply cry out, in spite of all appearances, "Hurrah for the Universe!—God's in his Heaven, all's right with the world." Let us see rather whether pity, pain, and fear, and the sentiment of human helplessness may not open a profounder view and put into our hands a more complicated key to the meaning of the situation.

To begin with, how *can* things so insecure as the successful experiences of this world afford a stable anchorage? A chain is no stronger than its weakest link, and life is after all a chain. In the healthiest and most prosperous existence, how many links of illness, danger, and disaster are always interposed? Unsuspectedly from the bottom of every fountain of pleasure, as the old poet said, something bitter rises up: a touch of nausea, a falling dead of the delight, a whiff of melancholy, things that sound a knell, for fugitive as they may be, they bring a feeling of coming from a deeper region and often have an appalling convincingness. The buzz of life ceases at their touch as a piano-string stops sounding when the damper falls upon it.

Of course the music can commence again;—and again and again,—at intervals. But with this the healthy-minded consciousness is left with an irremediable sense of precariousness. It is a bell with a crack; it draws its breath on sufferance and by an accident.

Even if we suppose a man so packed with healthy-mindedness as never to have experienced in his own person any of these sobering intervals, still, if he is a reflecting being, he must generalize and class his own lot with that of others; and, doing so, he must see that his escape is just a lucky chance and no essential difference. He might just as well have been born to an entirely different fortune. And then indeed the hollow security! What kind of a frame of things is it of which the best you can say is, "Thank God, it has let me off clear this time!" Is not its blessedness a fragile fiction? Is not your joy in it a very vulgar glee, not much unlike the snicker of any rogue at his success? If indeed it were all success, even on such terms as that! But take the happiest man, the one most envied by the world, and in nine cases out of ten his inmost consciousness is one of failure. Either his ideals in the line of his achievements are pitched far higher than the achievements themselves, or else he has secret ideals of which the world knows nothing, and in regard to which he inwardly knows himself to be found wanting.

When such a conquering optimist as Goethe can express himself in this wise, how must it be with less successful men?

"I will say nothing," writes Goethe in 1824, "against the course of my existence. But at bottom it has been nothing but pain and burden, and I can affirm that during the whole of my 75 years, I have not had four weeks of genuine well-being. It is but the perpetual rolling of a rock that must be raised up again forever."

What single-handed man was ever on the whole as successful as Luther? yet when he had grown old, he looked back on his life as if it were an absolute failure.

"I am utterly weary of life. I pray the Lord will come forthwith and carry me hence. Let him come, above all, with his last Judgment: I will stretch out my neck, the thunder will burst forth, and I shall be at rest."—And having a necklace of white agates in his hand at the time he added: "Oh God, grant that it may come without delay. I would readily eat up this necklace to-day, for the Judgment to come to-morrow."—The Electress Dowager, one day when Luther was dining with her, said to him: "Doctor, I wish you may live forty years to come." "Madam," replied he, "rather than live forty years more, I would give up my chance of Paradise."

Failure, then, failure! so the world stamps us at every turn. We strew it with our blunders, our misdeeds, our lost opportunities, with all the memorials of our inadequacy to our vocation. And with what a damning emphasis does it then blot us out! No easy fine, no mere apology or formal expiation, will satisfy the world's demands, but every pound of flesh exacted is soaked with all its blood. The subtlest forms of suffering known to man are connected with the poisonous humiliations incidental to these results.

And they are pivotal human experiences. A process so ubiquitous and everlasting is evidently an integral part of life. "There is indeed one element in human destiny," Robert Louis Stevenson writes, "that not blindness itself can controvert. Whatever else we are intended to do, we are not intended to succeed; failure is the fate allotted."[1] And our nature being thus rooted in failure, is it any wonder that theologians should have held it to be essential, and thought that only through the personal experience of humiliation which it engenders the deeper sense of life's significance is reached?[2]

[1] He adds with characteristic healthy-mindedness: "Our business is to continue to fail in good spirits."

[2] The God of many men is little more than their court of appeal against the damnatory judgment passed on their failures by the opinion of this world. To our own consciousness there is usually a residuum of worth left over after our sins and errors have been told off—our capacity of acknowledging and regretting them is the germ of a better self *in posse* at least. But the world deals

But this is only the first stage of the world-sickness. Make the human being's sensitiveness a little greater, carry him a little farther over the misery-threshold, and the good quality of the successful moments themselves when they occur is spoiled and vitiated. All natural goods perish. Riches take wings; fame is a breath; love is a cheat; youth and health and pleasure vanish. Can things whose end is always dust and disappointment be the real goods which our souls require? Back of everything is the great spectre of universal death, the all-encompassing blackness:—

> "What profit hath a man of all his labour which he taketh under the Sun? I looked on all the works that my hands had wrought, and behold, all was vanity and vexation of spirit. For that which befalleth the sons of men befalleth beasts; as the one dieth, so dieth the other; all are of the dust, and all turn to dust again. . . . The dead know not anything, neither have they any more a reward; for the memory of them is forgotten. Also their love and their hatred and their envy is now perished; neither have they any more a portion for ever in anything that is done under the Sun. . . . Truly the light is sweet, and a pleasant thing it is for the eyes to behold the Sun: but if a man live many years and rejoice in them all, yet let him remember the days of darkness; for they shall be many."

In short, life and its negation are beaten up inextricably together. But if the life be good, the negation of it must be bad. Yet the two are equally essential facts of existence; and all natural happiness thus seems infected with a contradiction. The breath of the sepulchre surrounds it.

To a mind attentive to this state of things and rightly subject to the joy-destroying chill which such a contemplation engenders, the only relief that healthy-mindedness can give is

---

with us *in actu* and not *in posse*: and of this hidden germ, not to be guessed at from without, it never takes account. Then we turn to the All-knower, who knows our bad, but knows this good in us also, and who is just. We cast ourselves with our repentance on his mercy: only by an All-knower can we finally be judged. So the need of a God very definitely emerges from this sort of experience of life.

by saying: 'Stuff and nonsense, get out into the open air!' or 'Cheer up, old fellow, you'll be all right erelong, if you will only drop your morbidness!' But in all seriousness, can such bald animal talk as that be treated as a rational answer? To ascribe religious value to mere happy-go-lucky contentment with one's brief chance at natural good is but the very consecration of forgetfulness and superficiality. Our troubles lie indeed too deep for *that* cure. The fact that we *can* die, that we *can* be ill at all, is what perplexes us; the fact that we now for a moment live and are well is irrelevant to that perplexity. We need a life not correlated with death, a health not liable to illness, a kind of good that will not perish, a good in fact that flies beyond the Goods of nature.

It all depends on how sensitive the soul may become to discords. "The trouble with me is that I believe too much in common happiness and goodness," said a friend of mine whose consciousness was of this sort, "and nothing can console me for their transiency. I am appalled and disconcerted at its being possible." And so with most of us: a little cooling down of animal excitability and instinct, a little loss of animal toughness, a little irritable weakness and descent of the pain-threshold, will bring the worm at the core of all our usual springs of delight into full view, and turn us into melancholy metaphysicians. The pride of life and glory of the world will shrivel. It is after all but the standing quarrel of hot youth and hoary eld. Old age has the last word: the purely naturalistic look at life, however enthusiastically it may begin, is sure to end in sadness.

This sadness lies at the heart of every merely positivistic, agnostic, or naturalistic scheme of philosophy. Let sanguine healthy-mindedness do its best with its strange power of living in the moment and ignoring and forgetting, still the evil background is really there to be thought of, and the skull will grin in at the banquet. In the practical life of the individual, we know how his whole gloom or glee about any present fact depends on the remoter schemes and hopes with which it stands related. Its significance and framing give it the chief part of its value. Let it be known to lead nowhere, and however agreeable it may be in its immediacy, its glow and gilding vanish. The old man, sick with an insidious internal disease, may laugh and quaff his wine at first as well as ever, but he knows his fate now, for the doctors have revealed it; and the knowledge knocks the satisfaction out of all these functions. They are partners of death and the worm is their brother, and they turn to a mere flatness.

The lustre of the present hour is always borrowed from the background of possibilities it goes with. Let our common experiences be enveloped in an eternal moral order; let our suffering have an immortal significance; let Heaven smile upon the earth, and deities pay their visits; let faith and hope be the atmosphere which man breathes in;—and his days pass by with zest; they stir with prospects, they thrill with remoter values. Place around them on the contrary the curdling cold and gloom and absence of all permanent meaning which for pure naturalism and the popular science evolutionism of our time are all that is visible ultimately, and the thrill stops short, or turns rather to an anxious trembling.

For naturalism, fed on recent cosmological speculations, mankind is in a position similar to that of a set of people living on a frozen lake, surrounded by cliffs over which there is no escape, yet knowing that little by little the ice is melting, and the inevitable day drawing near when the last film of it will disappear, and to be drowned ignominiously will be the human creature's portion. The merrier the skating, the warmer and more sparkling the sun by day, and the ruddier the bonfires at night, the more poignant the sadness with which one must take in the meaning of the total situation.

The early Greeks are continually held up to us in literary works as models of the healthy-minded joyousness which the religion of nature may engender. There was indeed much joyousness among the Greeks—Homer's flow of enthusiasm for most things that the sun shines upon is steady. But even in Homer the reflective passages are cheerless,[1] and the moment the Greeks grew systematically pensive and thought of ultimates, they became unmitigated pessimists.[2] The jealousy of the gods, the nemesis that follows too much happiness, the

---

[1] E. g., Iliad, XVII. 446: "Nothing then is more wretched anywhere than man of all that breathes and creeps upon this earth."

[2] E. g., Theognis, 425–428: "Best of all for all things upon earth is it not to be born nor to behold the splendors of the Sun; next best to traverse as

all-encompassing death, fate's dark opacity, the ultimate and unintelligible cruelty, were the fixed background of their imagination. The beautiful joyousness of their polytheism is only a poetic modern fiction. They knew no joys comparable in quality of preciousness to those which we shall erelong see that Brahmans, Buddhists, Christians, Mohammedans, twice-born people whose religion is non-naturalistic, get from their several creeds of mysticism and renunciation.

Stoic insensibility and Epicurean resignation were the farthest advance which the Greek mind made in that direction. The Epicurean said: "Seek not to be happy, but rather to escape unhappiness; strong happiness is always linked with pain; therefore hug the safe shore, and do not tempt the deeper raptures. Avoid disappointment by expecting little, and by aiming low; and above all do not fret." The Stoic said: "The only genuine good that life can yield a man is the free possession of his own soul; all other goods are lies." Each of these philosophies is in its degree a philosophy of despair in nature's boons. Trustful self-abandonment to the joys that freely offer has entirely departed from both Epicurean and Stoic; and what each proposes is a way of rescue

---

soon as possible the gates of Hades." See also the almost identical passage in Œdipus in Colonus, 1225.—The Anthology is full of pessimistic utterances: "Naked came I upon the earth, naked I go below the ground—why then do I vainly toil when I see the end naked before me?"—"How did I come to be? Whence am I? Wherefore did I come? To pass away. How can I learn aught when naught I know? Being naught I came to life: once more shall I be what I was. Nothing and nothingness is the whole race of mortals."—"For death we are all cherished and fattened like a herd of hogs that is wantonly butchered."

The difference between Greek pessimism and the oriental and modern variety is that the Greeks had not made the discovery that the pathetic mood may be idealized, and figure as a higher form of sensibility. Their spirit was still too essentially masculine for pessimism to be elaborated or lengthily dwelt on in their classic literature. They would have despised a life set wholly in a minor key, and summoned it to keep within the proper bounds of lachrymosity. The discovery that the enduring emphasis, so far as this world goes, may be laid on its pain and failure, was reserved for races more complex, and (so to speak) more feminine than the Hellenes had attained to being in the classic period. But all the same was the outlook of those Hellenes blackly pessimistic.

from the resultant dust-and-ashes state of mind. The Epicurean still awaits results from economy of indulgence and
damping of desire. The Stoic hopes for no results, and gives
up natural good altogether. There is dignity in both these
forms of resignation. They represent distinct stages in the
sobering process which man's primitive intoxication with
sense-happiness is sure to undergo. In the one the hot blood
has grown cool, in the other it has become quite cold; and
although I have spoken of them in the past tense, as if they
were merely historic, yet Stoicism and Epicureanism will
probably be to all time typical attitudes, marking a certain
definite stage accomplished in the evolution of the world-
sick soul.[1] They mark the conclusion of what we call the
once-born period, and represent the highest flights of what
twice-born religion would call the purely natural man—Epicureanism, which can only by great courtesy be called a religion, showing his refinement, and Stoicism exhibiting his
moral will. They leave the world in the shape of an unrecon-
ciled contradiction, and seek no higher unity. Compared
with the complex ecstasies which the supernaturally regenerated Christian may enjoy, or the oriental pantheist indulge
in, their receipts for equanimity are expedients which seem
almost crude in their simplicity.

Please observe, however, that I am not yet pretending
finally to *judge* any of these attitudes. I am only describing
their variety.

The securest way to the rapturous sorts of happiness of
which the twice-born make report has as an historic matter of
fact been through a more radical pessimism than anything
that we have yet considered. We have seen how the lustre and

[1] For instance, on the very day on which I write this page, the post brings
me some aphorisms from a worldly-wise old friend in Heidelberg which may
serve as a good contemporaneous expression of Epicureanism: "By the word
'happiness' every human being understands something different. It is a phantom pursued only by weaker minds. The wise man is satisfied with the more
modest but much more definite term *contentment*. What education should
chiefly aim at is to save us from a discontented life. Health is one favoring
condition, but by no means an indispensable one, of contentment. Woman's
heart and love are a shrewd device of Nature, a trap which she sets for the
average man, to force him into working. But the wise man will always prefer
work chosen by himself."

enchantment may be rubbed off from the goods of nature. But there is a pitch of unhappiness so great that the goods of nature may be entirely forgotten, and all sentiment of their existence vanish from the mental field. For this extremity of pessimism to be reached, something more is needed than observation of life and reflection upon death. The individual must in his own person become the prey of a pathological melancholy. As the healthy-minded enthusiast succeeds in ignoring evil's very existence, so the subject of melancholy is forced in spite of himself to ignore that of all good whatever: for him it may no longer have the least reality. Such sensitiveness and susceptibility to mental pain is a rare occurrence where the nervous constitution is entirely normal; one seldom finds it in a healthy subject even where he is the victim of the most atrocious cruelties of outward fortune. So we note here the neurotic constitution, of which I said so much in my first lecture, making its active entrance on our scene, and destined to play a part in much that follows. Since these experiences of melancholy are in the first instance absolutely private and individual, I can now help myself out with personal documents. Painful indeed they will be to listen to, and there is almost an indecency in handling them in public. Yet they lie right in the middle of our path; and if we are to touch the psychology of religion at all seriously, we must be willing to forget conventionalities, and dive below the smooth and lying official conversational surface.

One can distinguish many kinds of pathological depression. Sometimes it is mere passive joylessness and dreariness, discouragement, dejection, lack of taste and zest and spring. Professor Ribot has proposed the name *anhedonia* to designate this condition.

"The state of *anhedonia*, if I may coin a new word to pair off with *analgesia*," he writes, "has been very little studied, but it exists. A young girl was smitten with a liver disease which for some time altered her constitution. She felt no longer any affection for her father and mother. She would have played with her doll, but it was impossible to find the least pleasure in the act. The same things which formerly convulsed her with laughter entirely failed to

interest her now. Esquirol observed the case of a very intelligent magistrate who was also a prey to hepatic disease.
Every emotion appeared dead within him. He manifested
neither perversion nor violence, but complete absence of
emotional reaction. If he went to the theatre, which he did
out of habit, he could find no pleasure there. The thought
of his house, of his home, of his wife, and of his absent
children moved him as little, he said, as a theorem of
Euclid."[1]

Prolonged seasickness will in most persons produce a temporary condition of anhedonia. Every good, terrestrial or celestial, is imagined only to be turned from with disgust. A
temporary condition of this sort, connected with the religious
evolution of a singularly lofty character, both intellectual and
moral, is well described by the Catholic philosopher, Father
Gratry, in his autobiographical recollections. In consequence
of mental isolation and excessive study at the Polytechnic
school, young Gratry fell into a state of nervous exhaustion
with symptoms which he thus describes:—

"I had such a universal terror that I woke at night with
a start, thinking that the Pantheon was tumbling on the
Polytechnic school, or that the school was in flames, or that
the Seine was pouring into the Catacombs, and that Paris
was being swallowed up. And when these impressions were
past, all day long without respite I suffered an incurable
and intolerable desolation, verging on despair. I thought
myself, in fact, rejected by God, lost, damned! I felt something like the suffering of hell. Before that I had never even
thought of hell. My mind had never turned in that direction. Neither discourses nor reflections had impressed me
in that way. I took no account of hell. Now, and all at
once, I suffered in a measure what is suffered there.

"But what was perhaps still more dreadful is that every
idea of heaven was taken away from me: I could no longer
conceive of anything of the sort. Heaven did not seem to
me worth going to. It was like a vacuum; a mythological
elysium, an abode of shadows less real than the earth. I

[1] RIBOT: Psychologie des sentiments, p. 54.

could conceive no joy, no pleasure in inhabiting it. Happiness, joy, light, affection, love—all these words were now devoid of sense. Without doubt I could still have talked of all these things, but I had become incapable of feeling anything in them, of understanding anything about them, of hoping anything from them, or of believing them to exist. There was my great and inconsolable grief! I neither perceived nor conceived any longer the existence of happiness or perfection. An abstract heaven over a naked rock. Such was my present abode for eternity."[1]

So much for melancholy in the sense of incapacity for joyous feeling. A much worse form of it is positive and active anguish, a sort of psychical neuralgia wholly unknown to healthy life. Such anguish may partake of various characters, having sometimes more the quality of loathing; sometimes that of irritation and exasperation; or again of self-mistrust and self-despair; or of suspicion, anxiety, trepidation, fear. The patient may rebel or submit; may accuse himself, or accuse outside powers; and he may or he may not be tormented by the theoretical mystery of why he should so have to suffer. Most cases are mixed cases, and we should not treat our classifications with too much respect. Moreover, it is only a relatively small proportion of cases that connect themselves with the religious sphere of experience at all. Exasperated cases, for

---

[1] A. GRATRY: Souvenirs de ma jeunesse, 1880, pp. 119–121, abridged. Some persons are affected with anhedonia permanently, or at any rate with a loss of the usual appetite for life. The annals of suicide supply such examples as the following:—

An uneducated domestic servant, aged nineteen, poisons herself, and leaves two letters expressing her motive for the act. To her parents she writes:—

"Life is sweet perhaps to some, but I prefer what is sweeter than life, and that is death. So good-by forever, my dear parents. It is nobody's fault, but a strong desire of my own which I have longed to fulfill for three or four years. I have always had a hope that some day I might have an opportunity of fulfilling it, and now it has come. . . . It is a wonder I have put this off so long, but I thought perhaps I should cheer up a bit and put all thought out of my head." To her brother she writes: "Good-by forever, my own dearest brother. By the time you get this I shall be gone forever. I know, dear love, there is no forgiveness for what I am going to do. . . . I am tired of living, so am willing to die. . . . Life may be sweet to some, but death to me is sweeter." S. A. K. STRAHAN: Suicide and Insanity, 2d edition, London, 1894, p. 131.

instance, as a rule do not. I quote now literally from the first case of melancholy on which I lay my hand. It is a letter from a patient in a French asylum.

"I suffer too much in this hospital, both physically and morally. Besides the burnings and the sleeplessness (for I no longer sleep since I am shut up here, and the little rest I get is broken by bad dreams, and I am waked with a jump by nightmares, dreadful visions, lightning, thunder, and the rest), fear, atrocious fear, presses me down, holds me without respite, never lets me go. Where is the justice in it all! What have I done to deserve this excess of severity? Under what form will this fear crush me? What would I not owe to any one who would rid me of my life! Eat, drink, lie awake all night, suffer without interruption—such is the fine legacy I have received from my mother! What I fail to understand is this abuse of power. There are limits to everything, there is a middle way. But God knows neither middle way nor limits. I say God, but why? All I have known so far has been the devil. After all, I am afraid of God as much as of the devil, so I drift along, thinking of nothing but suicide, but with neither courage nor means here to execute the act. As you read this, it will easily prove to you my insanity. The style and the ideas are incoherent enough—I can see that myself. But I cannot keep myself from being either crazy or an idiot; and, as things are, from whom should I ask pity? I am defenseless against the invisible enemy who is tightening his coils around me. I should be no better armed against him even if I saw him, or had seen him. Oh, if he would but kill me, devil take him! Death, death, once for all! But I stop. I have raved to you long enough. I say raved, for I can write no otherwise, having neither brain nor thoughts left. O God! what a misfortune to be born! Born like a mushroom, doubtless between an evening and a morning; and how true and right I was when in our philosophy-year in college I chewed the cud of bitterness with the pessimists. Yes, indeed, there is more pain in life than gladness—it is one long agony until the grave. Think how gay it makes me to remember that this horrible misery of mine, coupled with this unspeakable fear, may last fifty, one hundred, who knows how many more years!"[1]

This letter shows two things. First, you see how the entire consciousness of the poor man is so choked with the feeling of evil that the sense of there being any good in the world is lost for him altogether. His attention excludes it, cannot admit it: the sun has left his heaven. And secondly you see how the querulous temper of his misery keeps his mind from taking a religious direction. Querulousness of mind tends in fact rather towards irreligion; and it has played, so far as I know, no part whatever in the construction of religious systems.

Religious melancholy must be cast in a more melting mood. Tolstoy has left us, in his book called My Confession, a wonderful account of the attack of melancholy which led him to his own religious conclusions. The latter in some respects are peculiar; but the melancholy presents two characters which make it a typical document for our present purpose. First it is a well-marked case of anhedonia, of passive loss of appetite for all life's values; and second, it shows how the altered and estranged aspect which the world assumed in consequence of this stimulated Tolstoy's intellect to a gnawing, carking questioning and effort for philosophic relief. I mean to quote Tolstoy at some length; but before doing so, I will make a general remark on each of these two points.

First on our spiritual judgments and the sense of value in general.

It is notorious that facts are compatible with opposite emotional comments, since the same fact will inspire entirely different feelings in different persons, and at different times in the same person; and there is no rationally deducible connection between any outer fact and the sentiments it may happen to provoke. These have their source in another sphere of existence altogether, in the animal and spiritual region of the subject's being. Conceive yourself, if possible, suddenly stripped of all the emotion with which your world now inspires you, and try to imagine it *as it exists*, purely by itself, without your favorable or unfavorable, hopeful or apprehen-

[1] ROUBINOVITCH ET TOULOUSE: La Mélancolie, 1897, p. 170, abridged.

sive comment. It will be almost impossible for you to realize such a condition of negativity and deadness. No one portion of the universe would then have importance beyond another; and the whole collection of its things and series of its events would be without significance, character, expression, or perspective. Whatever of value, interest, or meaning our respective worlds may appear endued with are thus pure gifts of the spectator's mind. The passion of love is the most familiar and extreme example of this fact. If it comes, it comes; if it does not come, no process of reasoning can force it. Yet it transforms the value of the creature loved as utterly as the sunrise transforms Mont Blanc from a corpse-like gray to a rosy enchantment; and it sets the whole world to a new tune for the lover and gives a new issue to his life. So with fear, with indignation, jealousy, ambition, worship. If they are there, life changes. And whether they shall be there or not depends almost always upon non-logical, often on organic conditions. And as the excited interest which these passions put into the world is our gift to the world, just so are the passions themselves *gifts*,—gifts to us, from sources sometimes low and sometimes high; but almost always non-logical and beyond our control. How can the moribund old man reason back to himself the romance, the mystery, the imminence of great things with which our old earth tingled for him in the days when he was young and well? Gifts, either of the flesh or of the spirit; and the spirit bloweth where it listeth; and the world's materials lend their surface passively to all the gifts alike, as the stage-setting receives indifferently whatever alternating colored lights may be shed upon it from the optical apparatus in the gallery.

Meanwhile the practically real world for each one of us, the effective world of the individual, is the compound world, the physical facts and emotional values in indistinguishable combination. Withdraw or pervert either factor of this complex resultant, and the kind of experience we call pathological ensues.

In Tolstoy's case the sense that life had any meaning whatever was for a time wholly withdrawn. The result was a transformation in the whole expression of reality. When we come to study the phenomenon of conversion or religious regeneration, we shall see that a not infrequent consequence of the change operated in the subject is a transfiguration of the face of nature in his eyes. A new heaven seems to shine upon a new earth. In melancholiacs there is usually a similar change, only it is in the reverse direction. The world now looks remote, strange, sinister, uncanny. Its color is gone, its breath is cold, there is no speculation in the eyes it glares with. "It is as if I lived in another century," says one asylum patient.— "I see everything through a cloud," says another, "things are not as they were, and I am changed."—"I see," says a third, "I touch, but the things do not come near me, a thick veil alters the hue and look of everything."—"Persons move like shadows, and sounds seem to come from a distant world."— "There is no longer any past for me; people appear so strange; it is as if I could not see any reality, as if I were in a theatre; as if people were actors, and everything were scenery; I can no longer find myself; I walk, but why? Everything floats before my eyes, but leaves no impression."—"I weep false tears, I have unreal hands: the things I see are not real things."—Such are expressions that naturally rise to the lips of melancholy subjects describing their changed state.[1]

Now there are some subjects whom all this leaves a prey to the profoundest astonishment. The strangeness is wrong. The unreality cannot be. A mystery is concealed, and a metaphysical solution must exist. If the natural world is so double-faced and unhomelike, what world, what thing is real? An urgent wondering and questioning is set up, a poring theoretic activity, and in the desperate effort to get into right relations with the matter, the sufferer is often led to what becomes for him a satisfying religious solution.

At about the age of fifty, Tolstoy relates that he began to have moments of perplexity, of what he calls arrest, as if he knew not 'how to live,' or what to do. It is obvious that these were moments in which the excitement and interest which our functions naturally bring had ceased. Life had been enchanting, it was now flat sober, more than sober, dead. Things were meaningless whose meaning had always been self-evident. The questions 'Why?' and 'What next?' began to

[1] I cull these examples from the work of G. DUMAS: La Tristesse et la Joie, 1900.

beset him more and more frequently. At first it seemed as if such questions must be answerable, and as if he could easily find the answers if he would take the time; but as they ever became more urgent, he perceived that it was like those first discomforts of a sick man, to which he pays but little attention till they run into one continuous suffering, and then he realizes that what he took for a passing disorder means the most momentous thing in the world for him, means his death.

These questions 'Why?' 'Wherefore?' 'What for?' found no response.

"I felt," says Tolstoy, "that something had broken within me on which my life had always rested, that I had nothing left to hold on to, and that morally my life had stopped. An invincible force impelled me to get rid of my existence, in one way or another. It cannot be said exactly that I *wished* to kill myself, for the force which drew me away from life was fuller, more powerful, more general than any mere desire. It was a force like my old aspiration to live, only it impelled me in the opposite direction. It was an aspiration of my whole being to get out of life.

"Behold me then, a man happy and in good health, hiding the rope in order not to hang myself to the rafters of the room where every night I went to sleep alone; behold me no longer going shooting, lest I should yield to the too easy temptation of putting an end to myself with my gun.

"I did not know what I wanted. I was afraid of life; I was driven to leave it; and in spite of that I still hoped something from it.

"All this took place at a time when so far as all my outer circumstances went, I ought to have been completely happy. I had a good wife who loved me and whom I loved; good children and a large property which was increasing with no pains taken on my part. I was more respected by my kinsfolk and acquaintance than I had ever been; I was loaded with praise by strangers; and without exaggeration I could believe my name already famous. Moreover I was neither insane nor ill. On the contrary, I possessed a physical and mental strength which I have rarely met in persons of my age. I could mow as well as the peasants, I could work with my brain eight hours uninterruptedly and feel no bad effects.

"And yet I could give no reasonable meaning to any actions of my life. And I was surprised that I had not understood this from the very beginning. My state of mind was as if some wicked and stupid jest was being played upon me by some one. One can live only so long as one is intoxicated, drunk with life; but when one grows sober one cannot fail to see that it is all a stupid cheat. What is truest about it is that there is nothing even funny or silly in it; it is cruel and stupid, purely and simply.

"The oriental fable of the traveler surprised in the desert by a wild beast is very old.

"Seeking to save himself from the fierce animal, the traveler jumps into a well with no water in it; but at the bottom of this well he sees a dragon waiting with open mouth to devour him. And the unhappy man, not daring to go out lest he should be the prey of the beast, not daring to jump to the bottom lest he should be devoured by the dragon, clings to the branches of a wild bush which grows out of one of the cracks of the well. His hands weaken, and he feels that he must soon give way to certain fate; but still he clings, and sees two mice, one white, the other black, evenly moving round the bush to which he hangs, and gnawing off its roots.

"The traveler sees this and knows that he must inevitably perish; but while thus hanging he looks about him and finds on the leaves of the bush some drops of honey. These he reaches with his tongue and licks them off with rapture.

"Thus I hang upon the boughs of life, knowing that the inevitable dragon of death is waiting ready to tear me, and I cannot comprehend why I am thus made a martyr. I try to suck the honey which formerly consoled me; but the honey pleases me no longer, and day and night the white mouse and the black mouse gnaw the branch to which I cling. I can see but one thing: the inevitable dragon and the mice—I cannot turn my gaze away from them.

"This is no fable, but the literal incontestable truth which every one may understand. What will be the outcome of what I do to-day? Of what I shall do to-morrow? What will be the outcome of all my life? Why should I live? Why should I do anything? Is there in life any purpose which the inevitable death which awaits me does not undo and destroy?

"These questions are the simplest in the world. From the stupid child to the wisest old man, they are in the soul of every human being. Without an answer to them, it is impossible, as I experienced, for life to go on.

" 'But perhaps,' I often said to myself, 'there may be something I have failed to notice or to comprehend. It is not possible that this condition of despair should be natural to mankind.' And I sought for an explanation in all the branches of knowledge acquired by men. I questioned painfully and protractedly and with no idle curiosity. I sought, not with indolence, but laboriously and obstinately for days and nights together. I sought like a man who is lost and seeks to save himself,—and I found nothing. I became convinced, moreover, that all those who before me had sought for an answer in the sciences have also found nothing. And not only this, but that they have recognized that the very thing which was leading me to despair—the meaningless absurdity of life—is the only incontestable knowledge accessible to man."

To prove this point, Tolstoy quotes the Buddha, Solomon, and Schopenhauer. And he finds only four ways in which men of his own class and society are accustomed to meet the situation. Either mere animal blindness, sucking the honey without seeing the dragon or the mice,—"and from such a way," he says, "I can learn nothing, after what I now know;" or reflective epicureanism, snatching what it can while the day lasts,—which is only a more deliberate sort of stupefaction than the first; or manly suicide; or seeing the mice and dragon and yet weakly and plaintively clinging to the bush of life.

Suicide was naturally the consistent course dictated by the logical intellect.

"Yet," says Tolstoy, "whilst my intellect was working, something else in me was working too, and kept me from the deed—a consciousness of life, as I may call it, which was like a force that obliged my mind to fix itself in another direction and draw me out of my situation of despair. . . . During the whole course of this year, when I almost unceasingly kept asking myself how to end the business, whether by the rope or by the bullet, during all that time, alongside of all those movements of my ideas and observations, my heart kept languishing with another pining emotion. I can call this by no other name than that of a thirst for God. This craving for God had nothing to do with the movement of my ideas,—in fact, it was the direct contrary of that movement,—but it came from my heart. It was like a feeling of dread that made me seem like an orphan and isolated in the midst of all these things that were so foreign. And this feeling of dread was mitigated by the hope of finding the assistance of some one."[1]

Of the process, intellectual as well as emotional, which, starting from this idea of God, led to Tolstoy's recovery, I will say nothing in this lecture, reserving it for a later hour. The only thing that need interest us now is the phenomenon of his absolute disenchantment with ordinary life, and the fact that the whole range of habitual values may, to a man as powerful and full of faculty as he was, come to appear so ghastly a mockery.

When disillusionment has gone as far as this, there is seldom a *restitutio ad integrum.* One has tasted of the fruit of the tree, and the happiness of Eden never comes again. The happiness that comes, when any does come,—and often enough it fails to return in an acute form, though its form is sometimes very acute,—is not the simple ignorance of ill, but something vastly more complex, including natural evil as one of its elements, but finding natural evil no such stumbling-block and terror because it now sees it swallowed up in supernatural good. The process is one of redemption, not of mere reversion to natural health, and the sufferer, when saved, is saved by what seems to him a second birth, a deeper kind of conscious being than he could enjoy before.

[1] My extracts are from the French translation by 'ZORIA.' In abridging I have taken the liberty of transposing one passage.

We find a somewhat different type of religious melancholy enshrined in literature in John Bunyan's autobiography. Tolstoy's preoccupations were largely objective, for the purpose and meaning of life in general was what so troubled him; but poor Bunyan's troubles were over the condition of his own personal self. He was a typical case of the psychopathic temperament, sensitive of conscience to a diseased degree, beset by doubts, fears, and insistent ideas, and a victim of verbal automatisms, both motor and sensory. These were usually texts of Scripture which, sometimes damnatory and sometimes favorable, would come in a half-hallucinatory form as if they were voices, and fasten on his mind and buffet it between them like a shuttlecock. Added to this were a fearful melancholy self-contempt and despair.

"Nay, thought I, now I grow worse and worse; now I am farther from conversion than ever I was before. If now I should have burned at the stake, I could not believe that Christ had love for me; alas, I could neither hear him, nor see him, nor feel him, nor savor any of his things. Sometimes I would tell my condition to the people of God, which, when they heard, they would pity me, and would tell of the Promises. But they had as good have told me that I must reach the Sun with my finger as have bidden me receive or rely upon the Promise. [Yet] all this while as to the act of sinning, I never was more tender than now; I durst not take a pin or stick, though but so big as a straw, for my conscience now was sore, and would smart at every touch; I could not tell how to speak my words, for fear I should misplace them. Oh, how gingerly did I then go, in all I did or said! I found myself as on a miry bog that shook if I did but stir; and was as there left both by God and Christ, and the spirit, and all good things.

"But my original and inward pollution, that was my plague and my affliction. By reason of that, I was more loathsome in my own eyes than was a toad; and I thought I was so in God's eyes too. Sin and corruption, I said, would as naturally bubble out of my heart as water would bubble out of a fountain. I could have changed heart with anybody. I thought none but the Devil himself could equal me for inward wickedness and pollution of mind. Sure, thought I, I am forsaken of God; and thus I continued a long while, even for some years together.

"And now I was sorry that God had made me a man. The beasts, birds, fishes, etc., I blessed their condition, for they had not a sinful nature; they were not obnoxious to the wrath of God; they were not to go to hell-fire after death. I could therefore have rejoiced, had my condition been as any of theirs. Now I blessed the condition of the dog and toad, yea, gladly would I have been in the condition of the dog or horse, for I knew they had no soul to perish under the everlasting weight of Hell or Sin, as mine was like to do. Nay, and though I saw this, felt this, and was broken to pieces with it, yet that which added to my sorrow was, that I could not find with all my soul that I did desire deliverance. My heart was at times exceedingly hard. If I would have given a thousand pounds for a tear, I could not shed one; no, nor sometimes scarce desire to shed one.

"I was both a burthen and a terror to myself; nor did I ever so know, as now, what it was to be weary of my life, and yet afraid to die. How gladly would I have been anything but myself! Anything but a man! and in any condition but my own."[1]

Poor patient Bunyan, like Tolstoy, saw the light again, but we must also postpone that part of his story to another hour. In a later lecture I will also give the end of the experience of Henry Alline, a devoted evangelist who worked in Nova Scotia a hundred years ago, and who thus vividly describes the high-water mark of the religious melancholy which formed its beginning. The type was not unlike Bunyan's.

"Everything I saw seemed to be a burden to me; the earth seemed accursed for my sake: all trees, plants, rocks, hills, and vales seemed to be dressed in mourning and groaning, under the weight of the curse, and everything around me seemed to be conspiring my ruin. My sins seemed to be laid open; so that I thought that every one I

[1] Grace abounding to the Chief of Sinners: I have printed a number of detached passages continuously.

saw knew them, and sometimes I was almost ready to acknowledge many things, which I thought they knew: yea sometimes it seemed to me as if every one was pointing me out as the most guilty wretch upon earth. I had now so great a sense of the vanity and emptiness of all things here below, that I knew the whole world could not possibly make me happy, no, nor the whole system of creation. When I waked in the morning, the first thought would be, Oh, my wretched soul, what shall I do, where shall I go? And when I laid down, would say, I shall be perhaps in hell before morning. I would many times look on the beasts with envy, wishing with all my heart I was in their place, that I might have no soul to lose; and when I have seen birds flying over my head, have often thought within myself, Oh, that I could fly away from my danger and distress! Oh, how happy should I be, if I were in their place!"[1]

Envy of the placid beasts seems to be a very widespread affection in this type of sadness.

The worst kind of melancholy is that which takes the form of panic fear. Here is an excellent example, for permission to print which I have to thank the sufferer. The original is in French, and though the subject was evidently in a bad nervous condition at the time of which he writes, his case has otherwise the merit of extreme simplicity. I translate freely.

"Whilst in this state of philosophic pessimism and general depression of spirits about my prospects, I went one evening into a dressing-room in the twilight to procure some article that was there; when suddenly there fell upon me without any warning, just as if it came out of the darkness, a horrible fear of my own existence. Simultaneously there arose in my mind the image of an epileptic patient whom I had seen in the asylum, a black-haired youth with greenish skin, entirely idiotic, who used to sit all day on one of the benches, or rather shelves against the wall, with his knees drawn up against his chin, and

[1] The Life and Journal of the Rev. Mr. Henry Alline, Boston, 1806, pp. 25, 26. I owe my acquaintance with this book to my colleague, Dr. Benjamin Rand.

the coarse gray undershirt, which was his only garment, drawn over them inclosing his entire figure. He sat there like a sort of sculptured Egyptian cat or Peruvian mummy, moving nothing but his black eyes and looking absolutely non-human. This image and my fear entered into a species of combination with each other. *That shape am I*, I felt, potentially. Nothing that I possess can defend me against that fate, if the hour for it should strike for me as it struck for him. There was such a horror of him, and such a perception of my own merely momentary discrepancy from him, that it was as if something hitherto solid within my breast gave way entirely, and I became a mass of quivering fear. After this the universe was changed for me altogether. I awoke morning after morning with a horrible dread at the pit of my stomach, and with a sense of the insecurity of life that I never knew before, and that I have never felt since.[1] It was like a revelation; and although the immediate feelings passed away, the experience has made me sympathetic with the morbid feelings of others ever since. It gradually faded, but for months I was unable to go out into the dark alone.

"In general I dreaded to be left alone. I remember wondering how other people could live, how I myself had ever lived, so unconscious of that pit of insecurity beneath the surface of life. My mother in particular, a very cheerful person, seemed to me a perfect paradox in her unconsciousness of danger, which you may well believe I was very careful not to disturb by revelations of my own state of mind. I have always thought that this experience of melancholia of mine had a religious bearing."

On asking this correspondent to explain more fully what he meant by these last words, the answer he wrote was this:—

[1] Compare Bunyan: "There was I struck into a very great trembling, insomuch that at some times I could, for days together, feel my very body, as well as my mind, to shake and totter under the sense of the dreadful judgment of God, that should fall on those that have sinned that most fearful and unpardonable sin. I felt also such clogging and heat at my stomach, by reason of this my terror, that I was, especially at some times, as if my breast-bone would have split asunder. . . . Thus did I wind, and twine, and shrink, under the burden that was upon me; which burden also did so oppress me that I could neither stand, nor go, nor lie, either at rest or quiet."

"I mean that the fear was so invasive and powerful that if I had not clung to scripture-texts like 'The eternal God is my refuge,' etc., 'Come unto me, all ye that labor and are heavy-laden,' etc., 'I am the resurrection and the life,' etc., I think I should have grown really insane."[1]

There is no need of more examples. The cases we have looked at are enough. One of them gives us the vanity of mortal things; another the sense of sin; and the remaining one describes the fear of the universe;—and in one or other of these three ways it always is that man's original optimism and self-satisfaction get leveled with the dust.

In none of these cases was there any intellectual insanity or delusion about matters of fact; but were we disposed to open the chapter of really insane melancholia, with its hallucinations and delusions, it would be a worse story still—desperation absolute and complete, the whole universe coagulating about the sufferer into a material of overwhelming horror, surrounding him without opening or end. Not the conception or intellectual perception of evil, but the grisly blood-freezing heart-palsying sensation of it close upon one, and no other conception or sensation able to live for a moment in its presence. How irrelevantly remote seem all our usual refined optimisms and intellectual and moral consolations in presence of a need of help like this! Here is the real core of the religious problem: Help! help! No prophet can claim to bring a final message unless he says things that will have a sound of reality in the ears of victims such as these. But the deliverance must come in as strong a form as the complaint, if it is to take effect; and that seems a reason why the coarser religions, revivalistic, orgiastic, with blood and miracles and supernatural operations, may possibly never be displaced. Some constitutions need them too much.

Arrived at this point, we can see how great an antagonism may naturally arise between the healthy-minded way of viewing life and the way that takes all this experience of evil as something essential. To this latter way, the morbid-minded

[1] For another case of fear equally sudden, see HENRY JAMES: Society the Redeemed Form of Man, Boston, 1879, pp. 43 ff.

way, as we might call it, healthy-mindedness pure and simple seems unspeakably blind and shallow. To the healthy-minded way, on the other hand, the way of the sick soul seems unmanly and diseased. With their grubbing in rat-holes instead of living in the light; with their manufacture of fears, and preoccupation with every unwholesome kind of misery, there is something almost obscene about these children of wrath and cravers of a second birth. If religious intolerance and hanging and burning could again become the order of the day, there is little doubt that, however it may have been in the past, the healthy-minded would at present show themselves the less indulgent party of the two.

In our own attitude, not yet abandoned, of impartial onlookers, what are we to say of this quarrel? It seems to me that we are bound to say that morbid-mindedness ranges over the wider scale of experience, and that its survey is the one that overlaps. The method of averting one's attention from evil, and living simply in the light of good is splendid as long as it will work. It will work with many persons; it will work far more generally than most of us are ready to suppose; and within the sphere of its successful operation there is nothing to be said against it as a religious solution. But it breaks down impotently as soon as melancholy comes; and even though one be quite free from melancholy one's self, there is no doubt that healthy-mindedness is inadequate as a philosophical doctrine, because the evil facts which it refuses positively to account for are a genuine portion of reality; and they may after all be the best key to life's significance, and possibly the only openers of our eyes to the deepest levels of truth.

The normal process of life contains moments as bad as any of those which insane melancholy is filled with, moments in which radical evil gets its innings and takes its solid turn. The lunatic's visions of horror are all drawn from the material of daily fact. Our civilization is founded on the shambles, and every individual existence goes out in a lonely spasm of helpless agony. If you protest, my friend, wait till you arrive there yourself! To believe in the carnivorous reptiles of geologic times is hard for our imagination—they seem too much like mere museum specimens. Yet there is no tooth in any one of

those museum-skulls that did not daily through long years of
the foretime hold fast to the body struggling in despair of
some fated living victim. Forms of horror just as dreadful to
their victims, if on a smaller spatial scale, fill the world about
us to-day. Here on our very hearths and in our gardens the
infernal cat plays with the panting mouse, or holds the hot
bird fluttering in her jaws. Crocodiles and rattlesnakes and
pythons are at this moment vessels of life as real as we are;
their loathsome existence fills every minute of every day that
drags its length along; and whenever they or other wild beasts
clutch their living prey, the deadly horror which an agitated melancholiac feels is the literally right reaction on the
situation.[1]

It may indeed be that no religious reconciliation with the
absolute totality of things is possible. Some evils, indeed, are
ministerial to higher forms of good; but it may be that there
are forms of evil so extreme as to enter into no good system
whatsoever, and that, in respect of such evil, dumb submission or neglect to notice is the only practical resource. This
question must confront us on a later day. But provisionally,
and as a mere matter of program and method, since the evil
facts are as genuine parts of nature as the good ones, the
philosophic presumption should be that they have some

---

[1]Example: "It was about eleven o'clock at night . . . but I strolled on still
with the people. . . . Suddenly upon the left side of our road, a crackling
was heard among the bushes; all of us were alarmed, and in an instant a
tiger, rushing out of the jungle, pounced upon the one of the party that was
foremost, and carried him off in the twinkling of an eye. The rush of the
animal, and the crush of the poor victim's bones in his mouth, and his last
cry of distress, 'Ho hai!' involuntarily reëchoed by all of us, was over in three
seconds; and then I know not what happened till I returned to my senses,
when I found myself and companions lying down on the ground as if prepared to be devoured by our enemy, the sovereign of the forest. I find my
pen incapable of describing the terror of that dreadful moment. Our limbs
stiffened, our power of speech ceased, and our hearts beat violently, and only
a whisper of the same 'Ho hai!' was heard from us. In this state we crept on
all fours for some distance back, and then ran for life with the speed of an
Arab horse for about half an hour, and fortunately happened to come to a
small village. . . . After this every one of us was attacked with fever, attended with shivering, in which deplorable state we remained till morning."—Autobiography of Lutfullah, a Mohammedan Gentleman, Leipzig,
1857, p. 112.

rational significance, and that systematic healthy-mindedness, failing as it does to accord to sorrow, pain, and death any positive and active attention whatever, is formally less complete than systems that try at least to include these elements in their scope.

The completest religions would therefore seem to be those in which the pessimistic elements are best developed. Buddhism, of course, and Christianity are the best known to us of these. They are essentially religions of deliverance: the man must die to an unreal life before he can be born into the real life. In my next lecture, I will try to discuss some of the psychological conditions of this second birth. Fortunately from now onward we shall have to deal with more cheerful subjects than those which we have recently been dwelling on.

LECTURE VIII

THE DIVIDED SELF, AND THE PROCESS
OF ITS UNIFICATION

THE LAST LECTURE was a painful one, dealing as it did with evil as a pervasive element of the world we live in. At the close of it we were brought into full view of the contrast between the two ways of looking at life which are characteristic respectively of what we called the healthy-minded, who need to be born only once, and of the sick souls, who must be twice-born in order to be happy. The result is two different conceptions of the universe of our experience. In the religion of the once-born the world is a sort of rectilinear or one-storied affair, whose accounts are kept in one denomination, whose parts have just the values which naturally they appear to have, and of which a simple algebraic sum of pluses and minuses will give the total worth. Happiness and religious peace consist in living on the plus side of the account. In the religion of the twice-born, on the other hand, the world is a double-storied mystery. Peace cannot be reached by the simple addition of pluses and elimination of minuses from life. Natural good is not simply insufficient in amount and transient, there lurks a falsity in its very being. Cancelled as it all is by death if not by earlier enemies, it gives no final balance, and can never be the thing intended for our lasting worship. It keeps us from our real good, rather; and renunciation and despair of it are our first step in the direction of the truth. There are two lives, the natural and the spiritual, and we must lose the one before we can participate in the other.

In their extreme forms, of pure naturalism and pure salvationism, the two types are violently contrasted; though here as in most other current classifications, the radical extremes are somewhat ideal abstractions, and the concrete human beings whom we oftenest meet are intermediate varieties and mixtures. Practically, however, you all recognize the difference: you understand, for example, the disdain of the methodist convert for the mere sky-blue healthy-minded moralist; and you likewise enter into the aversion of the latter to what seems to him the diseased subjectivism of the Methodist, dying to live, as he calls it, and making of paradox and the inversion of natural appearances the essence of God's truth.[1]

The psychological basis of the twice-born character seems to be a certain discordancy or heterogeneity in the native temperament of the subject, an incompletely unified moral and intellectual constitution.

"Homo duplex, homo duplex!" writes Alphonse Daudet. "The first time that I perceived that I was two was at the death of my brother Henri, when my father cried out so dramatically, 'He is dead, he is dead!' While my first self wept, my second self thought, 'How truly given was that cry, how fine it would be at the theatre.' I was then fourteen years old.

"This horrible duality has often given me matter for reflection. Oh, this terrible second me, always seated whilst the other is on foot, acting, living, suffering, bestirring itself. This second me that I have never been able to intoxicate, to make shed tears, or put to sleep. And how it sees into things, and how it mocks!"[2]

Recent works on the psychology of character have had much to say upon this point.[3] Some persons are born with an inner constitution which is harmonious and well balanced from the outset. Their impulses are consistent with one another, their will follows without trouble the guidance of their intellect, their passions are not excessive, and their lives are little haunted by regrets. Others are oppositely constituted; and are so in degrees which may vary from something so slight as to result in a merely odd or whimsical inconsistency, to a discordancy of which the consequences may be inconvenient

---

[1] E. g., "Our young people are diseased with the theological problems of original sin, origin of evil, predestination, and the like. These never presented a practical difficulty to any man—never darkened across any man's road, who did not go out of his way to seek them. These are the soul's mumps, and measles, and whooping-coughs," etc. EMERSON: 'Spiritual Laws.'

[2] Notes sur la Vie, p. 1.

[3] See, for example, F. Paulhan, in his book Les Caractères, 1894, who contrasts les Equilibrés, les Unifiés, with les Inquiets, les Contrariants, les Incohérents, les Emiettés, as so many diverse psychic types.

in the extreme. Of the more innocent kinds of heterogeneity I find a good example in Mrs. Annie Besant's autobiography.

"I have ever been the queerest mixture of weakness and strength, and have paid heavily for the weakness. As a child I used to suffer tortures of shyness, and if my shoe-lace was untied would feel shamefacedly that every eye was fixed on the unlucky string; as a girl I would shrink away from strangers and think myself unwanted and unliked, so that I was full of eager gratitude to any one who noticed me kindly; as the young mistress of a house I was afraid of my servants, and would let careless work pass rather than bear the pain of reproving the ill-doer; when I have been lecturing and debating with no lack of spirit on the platform, I have preferred to go without what I wanted at the hotel rather than to ring and make the waiter fetch it. Combative on the platform in defense of any cause I cared for, I shrink from quarrel or disapproval in the house, and am a coward at heart in private while a good fighter in public. How often have I passed unhappy quarters of an hour screwing up my courage to find fault with some subordinate whom my duty compelled me to reprove, and how often have I jeered at myself for a fraud as the doughty platform combatant, when shrinking from blaming some lad or lass for doing their work badly. An unkind look or word has availed to make me shrink into myself as a snail into its shell, while, on the platform, opposition makes me speak my best."[1]

This amount of inconsistency will only count as amiable weakness; but a stronger degree of heterogeneity may make havoc of the subject's life. There are persons whose existence is little more than a series of zig-zags, as now one tendency and now another gets the upper hand. Their spirit wars with their flesh, they wish for incompatibles, wayward impulses interrupt their most deliberate plans, and their lives are one long drama of repentance and of effort to repair misdemeanors and mistakes.

Heterogeneous personality has been explained as the result of inheritance—the traits of character of incompatible and

[1] ANNIE BESANT: an Autobiography, p. 82.

antagonistic ancestors are supposed to be preserved alongside of each other.[1] This explanation may pass for what it is worth—it certainly needs corroboration. But whatever the cause of heterogeneous personality may be, we find the extreme examples of it in the psychopathic temperament, of which I spoke in my first lecture. All writers about that temperament make the inner heterogeneity prominent in their descriptions. Frequently, indeed, it is only this trait that leads us to ascribe that temperament to a man at all. A 'dégénéré supérieur' is simply a man of sensibility in many directions, who finds more difficulty than is common in keeping his spiritual house in order and running his furrow straight, because his feelings and impulses are too keen and too discrepant mutually. In the haunting and insistent ideas, in the irrational impulses, the morbid scruples, dreads, and inhibitions which beset the psychopathic temperament when it is thoroughly pronounced, we have exquisite examples of heterogeneous personality. Bunyan had an obsession of the words, "Sell Christ for this, sell him for that, sell him, sell him!" which would run through his mind a hundred times together, until one day out of breath with retorting, "I will not, I will not," he impulsively said, "Let him go if he will," and this loss of the battle kept him in despair for over a year. The lives of the saints are full of such blasphemous obsessions, ascribed invariably to the direct agency of Satan. The phenomenon connects itself with the life of the subconscious self, so-called, of which we must erelong speak more directly.

Now in all of us, however constituted, but to a degree the greater in proportion as we are intense and sensitive and subject to diversified temptations, and to the greatest possible degree if we are decidedly psychopathic, does the normal evolution of character chiefly consist in the straightening out and unifying of the inner self. The higher and the lower feelings, the useful and the erring impulses, begin by being a comparative chaos within us—they must end by forming a stable system of functions in right subordination. Unhappiness is apt to characterize the period of order-making and struggle. If the individual be of tender conscience and religiously

[1] SMITH BAKER, in Journal of Nervous and Mental Diseases, September, 1893.

quickened, the unhappiness will take the form of moral remorse and compunction, of feeling inwardly vile and wrong,
and of standing in false relations to the author of one's being
and appointer of one's spiritual fate. This is the religious melancholy and 'conviction of sin' that have played so large a part
in the history of Protestant Christianity. The man's interior is
a battle-ground for what he feels to be two deadly hostile
selves, one actual, the other ideal. As Victor Hugo makes his
Mahomet say:—

> "Fils, je suis le champ vil des sublimes combats:
> Tantôt l'homme d'en haut, et tantôt l'homme d'en bas;
> Et le mal dans ma bouche avec le bien alterne,
> Comme dans le désert le sable et la citerne."

Wrong living, impotent aspirations; "What I would, that do
I not; but what I hate, that do I," as Saint Paul says; self-
loathing, self-despair; an unintelligible and intolerable burden
to which one is mysteriously the heir.

Let me quote from some typical cases of discordant personality, with melancholy in the form of self-condemnation
and sense of sin. Saint Augustine's case is a classic example.
You all remember his half-pagan, half-Christian bringing up
at Carthage, his emigration to Rome and Milan, his adoption of Manicheism and subsequent skepticism, and his restless search for truth and purity of life; and finally how,
distracted by the struggle between the two souls in his
breast, and ashamed of his own weakness of will, when so
many others whom he knew and knew of had thrown off
the shackles of sensuality and dedicated themselves to chastity and the higher life, he heard a voice in the garden say,
"Sume, lege" (take and read), and opening the Bible at random, saw the text, "not in chambering and wantonness,"
etc., which seemed directly sent to his address, and laid the
inner storm to rest forever.[1] Augustine's psychological

[1] LOUIS GOURDON (Essai sur la Conversion de Saint Augustin, Paris,
Fischbacher, 1900) has shown by an analysis of Augustine's writings immediately after the date of his conversion (A. D. 386) that the account he gives
in the Confessions is premature. The crisis in the garden marked a definitive
conversion from his former life, but it was to the neo-platonic spiritualism
and only a halfway stage toward Christianity. The latter he appears not fully
and radically to have embraced until four years more had passed.

genius has given an account of the trouble of having a divided self which has never been surpassed.

"The new will which I began to have was not yet strong enough to overcome that other will, strengthened by long indulgence. So these two wills, one old, one new, one carnal, the other spiritual, contended with each other and disturbed my soul. I understood by my own experience what I had read, 'flesh lusteth against spirit, and spirit against flesh.' It was myself indeed in both the wills, yet more myself in that which I approved in myself than in that which I disapproved in myself. Yet it was through myself that habit had attained so fierce a mastery over me, because I had willingly come whither I willed not. Still bound to earth, I refused, O God, to fight on thy side, as much afraid to be freed from all bonds, as I ought to have feared being trammeled by them.

"Thus the thoughts by which I meditated upon thee were like the efforts of one who would awake, but being overpowered with sleepiness is soon asleep again. Often does a man when heavy sleepiness is on his limbs defer to shake it off, and though not approving it, encourage it; even so I was sure it was better to surrender to thy love than to yield to my own lusts, yet, though the former course convinced me, the latter pleased and held me bound. There was naught in me to answer thy call, 'Awake, thou sleeper,' but only drawling, drowsy words, 'Presently; yes, presently; wait a little while.' But the 'presently' had no 'present,' and the 'little while' grew long. . . . For I was afraid thou wouldst hear me too soon, and heal me at once of my disease of lust, which I wished to satiate rather than to see extinguished. With what lashes of words did I not scourge my own soul. Yet it shrank back; it refused, though it had no excuse to offer. . . . I said within myself: 'Come, let it be done now,' and as I said it, I was on the point of the resolve. I all but did it, yet I did not do it. And I made another effort, and almost succeeded, yet I did not reach it, and did not grasp it, hesitating to die to death, and live to life; and the evil to which I was so wonted held me more than the better life I had not tried."[1]

---

[1] Confessions, Book VIII., chaps. v., vii., xi., abridged.

There could be no more perfect description of the divided will, when the higher wishes lack just that last acuteness, that touch of explosive intensity, of dynamogenic quality (to use the slang of the psychologists), that enables them to burst their shell, and make irruption efficaciously into life and quell the lower tendencies forever. In a later lecture we shall have much to say about this higher excitability.

I find another good description of the divided will in the autobiography of Henry Alline, the Nova Scotian evangelist, of whose melancholy I read a brief account in my last lecture. The poor youth's sins were, as you will see, of the most harmless order, yet they interfered with what proved to be his truest vocation, so they gave him great distress.

"I was now very moral in my life, but found no rest of conscience. I now began to be esteemed in young company, who knew nothing of my mind all this while, and their esteem began to be a snare to my soul, for I soon began to be fond of carnal mirth, though I still flattered myself that if I did not get drunk, nor curse, nor swear, there would be no sin in frolicking and carnal mirth, and I thought God would indulge young people with some (what I called simple or civil) recreation. I still kept a round of duties, and would not suffer myself to run into any open vices, and so got along very well in time of health and prosperity, but when I was distressed or threatened by sickness, death, or heavy storms of thunder, my religion would not do, and I found there was something wanting, and would begin to repent my going so much to frolics, but when the distress was over, the devil and my own wicked heart, with the solicitations of my associates, and my fondness for young company, were such strong allurements, I would again give way, and thus I got to be very wild and rude, at the same time kept up my rounds of secret prayer and reading; but God, not willing I should destroy myself, still followed me with his calls, and moved with such power upon my conscience, that I could not satisfy myself with my diversions, and in the midst of my mirth sometimes would have such a sense of my lost and undone condition, that I would wish myself from the company, and after it was over, when I went home, would make many promises that I would attend no more on these frolics, and would beg forgiveness for hours and hours; but when I came to have the temptation again, I would give way: no sooner would I hear the music and drink a glass of wine, but I would find my mind elevated and soon proceed to any sort of merriment or diversion, that I thought was not debauched or openly vicious; but when I returned from my carnal mirth I felt as guilty as ever, and could sometimes not close my eyes for some hours after I had gone to my bed. I was one of the most unhappy creatures on earth.

"Sometimes I would leave the company (often speaking to the fiddler to cease from playing, as if I was tired), and go out and walk about crying and praying, as if my very heart would break, and beseeching God that he would not cut me off, nor give me up to hardness of heart. Oh, what unhappy hours and nights I thus wore away! When I met sometimes with merry companions, and my heart was ready to sink, I would labor to put on as cheerful a countenance as possible, that they might not distrust anything, and sometimes would begin some discourse with young men or young women on purpose, or propose a merry song, lest the distress of my soul would be discovered, or mistrusted, when at the same time I would then rather have been in a wilderness in exile, than with them or any of their pleasures or enjoyments. Thus for many months when I was in company, I would act the hypocrite and feign a merry heart, but at the same time would endeavor as much as I could to shun their company, oh wretched and unhappy mortal that I was! Everything I did, and wherever I went, I was still in a storm, and yet I continued to be the chief contriver and ringleader of the frolics for many months after; though it was a toil and torment to attend them; but the devil and my own wicked heart drove me about like a slave, telling me that I must do this and do that, and bear this and bear that, and turn here and turn there, to keep my credit up, and retain the esteem of my associates: and all this while I continued

as strict as possible in my duties, and left no stone un-
turned to pacify my conscience, watching even against my
thoughts, and praying continually wherever I went: for I
did not think there was any sin in my conduct, when I
was among carnal company, because I did not take any
satisfaction there, but only followed it, I thought, for sufficient reasons.

"But still, all that I did or could do, conscience would
roar night and day."

Saint Augustine and Alline both emerged into the smooth
waters of inner unity and peace, and I shall next ask you to
consider more closely some of the peculiarities of the process
of unification, when it occurs. It may come gradually, or it
may occur abruptly; it may come through altered feelings, or
through altered powers of action; or it may come through
new intellectual insights, or through experiences which we
shall later have to designate as 'mystical.' However it come, it
brings a characteristic sort of relief; and never such extreme
relief as when it is cast into the religious mould. Happiness!
happiness! religion is only one of the ways in which men gain
that gift. Easily, permanently, and successfully, it often transforms the most intolerable misery into the profoundest and
most enduring happiness.

But to find religion is only one out of many ways of reaching unity; and the process of remedying inner incompleteness
and reducing inner discord is a general psychological process,
which may take place with any sort of mental material, and
need not necessarily assume the religious form. In judging of
the religious types of regeneration which we are about to
study, it is important to recognize that they are only one species of a genus that contains other types as well. For example,
the new birth may be away from religion into incredulity; or
it may be from moral scrupulosity into freedom and license;
or it may be produced by the irruption into the individual's
life of some new stimulus or passion, such as love, ambition,
cupidity, revenge, or patriotic devotion. In all these instances
we have precisely the same psychological form of event,—a
firmness, stability, and equilibrium succeeding a period of
storm and stress and inconsistency. In these non-religious

cases the new man may also be born either gradually or suddenly.

The French philosopher Jouffroy has left an eloquent memorial of his own 'counter-conversion,' as the transition from orthodoxy to infidelity has been well styled by Mr. Starbuck. Jouffroy's doubts had long harassed him; but he dates his final crisis from a certain night when his disbelief grew fixed and stable, and where the immediate result was sadness at the illusions he had lost.

"I shall never forget that night of December," writes Jouffroy, "in which the veil that concealed from me my own incredulity was torn. I hear again my steps in that narrow naked chamber where long after the hour of sleep had come I had the habit of walking up and down. I see again that moon, half-veiled by clouds, which now and again illuminated the frigid window-panes. The hours of the night flowed on and I did not note their passage. Anxiously I followed my thoughts, as from layer to layer they descended towards the foundation of my consciousness, and, scattering one by one all the illusions which until then had screened its windings from my view, made them every moment more clearly visible.

"Vainly I clung to these last beliefs as a shipwrecked sailor clings to the fragments of his vessel; vainly, frightened at the unknown void in which I was about to float, I turned with them towards my childhood, my family, my country, all that was dear and sacred to me: the inflexible current of my thought was too strong,—parents, family, memory, beliefs, it forced me to let go of everything. The investigation went on more obstinate and more severe as it drew near its term, and did not stop until the end was reached. I knew then that in the depth of my mind nothing was left that stood erect.

"This moment was a frightful one; and when towards morning I threw myself exhausted on my bed, I seemed to feel my earlier life, so smiling and so full, go out like a fire, and before me another life opened, sombre and unpeopled, where in future I must live alone, alone with my fatal thought which had exiled me thither, and which I was tempted to curse. The days which followed this discovery were the saddest of my life."[1]

In John Foster's Essay on Decision of Character, there is an account of a case of sudden conversion to avarice, which is illustrative enough to quote: —

A young man, it appears, "wasted, in two or three years, a large patrimony in profligate revels with a number of worthless associates who called themselves his friends, and who, when his last means were exhausted, treated him of course with neglect or contempt. Reduced to absolute want, he one day went out of the house with an intention to put an end to his life; but wandering awhile almost unconsciously, he came to the brow of an eminence which overlooked what were lately his estates. Here he sat down, and remained fixed in thought a number of hours, at the end of which he sprang from the ground with a vehement,

---

[1] TH. JOUFFROY: Nouveaux Mélanges philosophiques, 2me édition, p. 83. I add two other cases of counter-conversion dating from a certain moment. The first is from Professor Starbuck's manuscript collection, and the narrator is a woman.

"Away down in the bottom of my heart, I believe I was always more or less skeptical about 'God;' skepticism grew as an undercurrent, all through my early youth, but it was controlled and covered by the emotional elements in my religious growth. When I was sixteen I joined the church and was asked if I loved God. I replied 'Yes,' as was customary and expected. But instantly with a flash something spoke within me, 'No, you do not.' I was haunted for a long time with shame and remorse for my falsehood and for my wickedness in not loving God, mingled with fear that there might be an avenging God who would punish me in some terrible way. . . . At nineteen, I had an attack of tonsilitis. Before I had quite recovered, I heard told a story of a brute who had kicked his wife downstairs, and then continued the operation until she became insensible. I felt the horror of the thing keenly. Instantly this thought flashed through my mind: 'I have no use for a God who permits such things.' This experience was followed by months of stoical indifference to the God of my previous life, mingled with feelings of positive dislike and a somewhat proud defiance of him. I still thought there might be a God. If so he would probably damn me, but I should have to stand it. I felt very little fear and no desire to propitiate him. I have never had any personal relations with him since this painful experience."

The second case exemplifies how small an additional stimulus will overthrow the mind into a new state of equilibrium when the process of preparation and incubation has proceeded far enough. It is like the

exulting emotion. He had formed his resolution, which was, that all these estates should be his again; he had formed his plan, too, which he instantly began to execute. He walked hastily forward, determined to seize the first opportunity, of however humble a kind, to gain any money, though it were ever so despicable a trifle, and resolved absolutely not to spend, if he could help it, a farthing of whatever he might obtain. The first thing that drew his attention was a heap of coals shot out of carts on the pavement before a house. He offered himself to shovel or wheel them into the place where they were to be laid, and was employed. He received a few pence for the labor; and then, in pursuance of the saving part of his plan, requested some small gratuity of meat and drink, which was given him. He then looked out for the next thing that might chance; and went, with indefatigable industry, through a succession of servile employments in different places, of longer and shorter duration, still scrupulous in avoiding, as far as possible, the expense of a penny. He promptly seized every opportunity which could advance his design, without re-

---

proverbial last straw added to the camel's burden, or that touch of a needle which makes the salt in a supersaturated fluid suddenly begin to crystallize out.

Tolstoy writes: "S., a frank and intelligent man, told me as follows how he ceased to believe: —

"He was twenty-six years old when one day on a hunting expedition, the time for sleep having come, he set himself to pray according to the custom he had held from childhood.

"His brother, who was hunting with him, lay upon the hay and looked at him. When S. had finished his prayer and was turning to sleep, the brother said, 'Do you still keep up that thing?' Nothing more was said. But since that day, now more than thirty years ago, S. has never prayed again; he never takes communion, and does not go to church. All this, not because he became acquainted with convictions of his brother which he then and there adopted; not because he made any new resolution in his soul, but merely because the words spoken by his brother were like the light push of a finger against a leaning wall already about to tumble by its own weight. These words but showed him that the place wherein he supposed religion dwelt in him had long been empty, and that the sentences he uttered, the crosses and bows which he made during his prayer, were actions with no inner sense. Having once seized their absurdity, he could no longer keep them up." Ma Confession, p. 8.

garding the meanness of occupation or appearance. By this method he had gained, after a considerable time, money enough to purchase in order to sell again a few cattle, of which he had taken pains to understand the value. He speedily but cautiously turned his first gains into second advantages; retained without a single deviation his extreme parsimony; and thus advanced by degrees into larger transactions and incipient wealth. I did not hear, or have forgotten, the continued course of his life, but the final result was, that he more than recovered his lost possessions, and died an inveterate miser, worth £60,000."[1]

Let me turn now to the kind of case, the religious case, namely, that immediately concerns us. Here is one of the simplest possible type, an account of the conversion to the sys-

[1]Op. cit., Letter III., abridged.

I subjoin an additional document which has come into my possession, and which represents in a vivid way what is probably a very frequent sort of conversion, if the opposite of 'falling in love,' falling out of love, may be so termed. Falling in love also conforms frequently to this type, a latent process of unconscious preparation often preceding a sudden awakening to the fact that the mischief is irretrievably done. The free and easy tone in this narrative gives it a sincerity that speaks for itself.

"For two years of this time I went through a very bad experience, which almost drove me mad. I had fallen violently in love with a girl who, young as she was, had a spirit of coquetry like a cat. As I look back on her now, I hate her, and wonder how I could ever have fallen so low as to be worked upon to such an extent by her attractions. Nevertheless, I fell into a regular fever, could think of nothing else; whenever I was alone, I pictured her attractions, and spent most of the time when I should have been working, in recalling our previous interviews, and imagining future conversations. She was very pretty, good humored, and jolly to the last degree, and intensely pleased with my admiration. Would give me no decided answer yes or no, and the queer thing about it was that whilst pursuing her for her hand, I secretly knew all along that she was unfit to be a wife for me, and that she never would say yes. Although for a year we took our meals at the same boarding-house, so that I saw her continually and familiarly, our closer relations had to be largely on the sly, and this fact, together with my jealousy of another one of her male admirers, and my own conscience despising me for my uncontrollable weakness, made me so nervous and sleepless that I really thought I should become insane. I understand well those young men murdering their sweethearts, which appear so often in the papers. Nevertheless I did love her passionately, and in some ways she did deserve it.

"The queer thing was the sudden and unexpected way in which it all stopped. I was going to my work after breakfast one morning, thinking as

tematic religion of healthy-mindedness of a man who must already have been naturally of the healthy-minded type. It shows how, when the fruit is ripe, a touch will make it fall.

Mr. Horace Fletcher, in his little book called Menticulture, relates that a friend with whom he was talking of the self-control attained by the Japanese through their practice of the Buddhist discipline said:—

"'You must first get rid of anger and worry.' 'But,' said I, 'is that possible?' 'Yes,' replied he; 'it is possible to the Japanese, and ought to be possible to us.'

"On my way back I could think of nothing else but the words 'get rid, get rid'; and the idea must have continued to possess me during my sleeping hours, for the first con-

---

usual of her and of my misery, when, just as if some outside power laid hold of me, I found myself turning round and almost running to my room, where I immediately got out all the relics of her which I possessed, including some hair, all her notes and letters, and ambrotypes on glass. The former I made a fire of, the latter I actually crushed beneath my heel, in a sort of fierce joy of revenge and punishment. I now loathed and despised her altogether, and as for myself I felt as if a load of disease had suddenly been removed from me. That was the end. I never spoke to her or wrote to her again in all the subsequent years, and I have never had a single moment of loving thought towards one who for so many months entirely filled my heart. In fact, I have always rather hated her memory, though now I can see that I had gone unnecessarily far in that direction. At any rate, from that happy morning onward I regained possession of my own proper soul, and have never since fallen into any similar trap."

This seems to me an unusually clear example of two different levels of personality, inconsistent in their dictates, yet so well balanced against each other as for a long time to fill the life with discord and dissatisfaction. At last, not gradually, but in a sudden crisis, the unstable equilibrium is resolved, and this happens so unexpectedly that it is as if, to use the writer's words, "some outside power laid hold."

Professor Starbuck gives an analogous case, and a converse case of hatred suddenly turning into love, in his Psychology of Religion, p. 141. Compare the other highly curious instances which he gives on pp. 137–144, of sudden non-religious alterations of habit or character. He seems right in conceiving all such sudden changes as results of special cerebral functions unconsciously developing until they are ready to play a controlling part, when they make irruption into the conscious life. When we treat of sudden 'conversion,' I shall make as much use as I can of this hypothesis of subconscious incubation.

sciousness in the morning brought back the same thought, with the revelation of a discovery, which framed itself into the reasoning, 'If it is possible to get rid of anger and worry, why is it necessary to have them at all?' I felt the strength of the argument, and at once accepted the reasoning. The baby had discovered that it could walk. It would scorn to creep any longer.

"From the instant I realized that these cancer spots of worry and anger were removable, they left me. With the discovery of their weakness they were exorcised. From that time life has had an entirely different aspect.

"Although from that moment the possibility and desirability of freedom from the depressing passions has been a reality to me, it took me some months to feel absolute security in my new position; but, as the usual occasions for worry and anger have presented themselves over and over again, and I have been unable to feel them in the slightest degree, I no longer dread or guard against them, and I am amazed at my increased energy and vigor of mind; at my strength to meet situations of all kinds, and at my disposition to love and appreciate everything.

"I have had occasion to travel more than ten thousand miles by rail since that morning. The same Pullman porter, conductor, hotel-waiter, peddler, book-agent, cabman, and others who were formerly a source of annoyance and irritation have been met, but I am not conscious of a single incivility. All at once the whole world has turned good to me. I have become, as it were, sensitive only to the rays of good.

"I could recount many experiences which prove a brand-new condition of mind, but one will be sufficient. Without the slightest feeling of annoyance or impatience, I have seen a train that I had planned to take with a good deal of interested and pleasurable anticipation move out of the station without me, because my baggage did not arrive. The porter from the hotel came running and panting into the station just as the train pulled out of sight. When he saw me, he looked as if he feared a scolding, and began to tell of being blocked in a crowded street and unable to get out. When he had finished, I said to him: 'It does n't matter at all, you could n't help it, so we will try again to-morrow. Here is your fee, I am sorry you had all this trouble in earning it.' The look of surprise that came over his face was so filled with pleasure that I was repaid on the spot for the delay in my departure. Next day he would not accept a cent for the service, and he and I are friends for life.

"During the first weeks of my experience I was on guard only against worry and anger; but, in the mean time, having noticed the absence of the other depressing and dwarfing passions, I began to trace a relationship, until I was convinced that they are all growths from the two roots I have specified. I have felt the freedom now for so long a time that I am sure of my relation toward it; and I could no more harbor any of the thieving and depressing influences that once I nursed as a heritage of humanity than a fop would voluntarily wallow in a filthy gutter.

"There is no doubt in my mind that pure Christianity and pure Buddhism, and the Mental Sciences and all Religions, fundamentally teach what has been a discovery to me; but none of them have presented it in the light of a simple and easy process of elimination. At one time I wondered if the elimination would not yield to indifference and sloth. In my experience, the contrary is the result. I feel such an increased desire to do something useful that it seems as if I were a boy again and the energy for play had returned. I could fight as readily as (and better than) ever, if there were occasion for it. It does not make one a coward. It can't, since fear is one of the things eliminated. I notice the absence of timidity in the presence of any audience. When a boy, I was standing under a tree which was struck by lightning, and received a shock from the effects of which I never knew exemption until I had dissolved partnership with worry. Since then, lightning and thunder have been encountered under conditions which would formerly have caused great depression and discomfort, without [my] experiencing a trace of either. Surprise is also greatly modified, and one is less liable to become startled by unexpected sights or noises.

"As far as I am individually concerned, I am not bothering

myself at present as to what the results of this emancipated condition may be. I have no doubt that the perfect health aimed at by Christian Science may be one of the possibilities, for I note a marked improvement in the way my stomach does its duty in assimilating the food I give it to handle, and I am sure it works better to the sound of a song than under the friction of a frown. Neither am I wasting any of this precious time formulating an idea of a future existence or a future Heaven. The Heaven that I have within myself is as attractive as any that has been promised or that I can imagine; and I am willing to let the growth lead where it will, as long as the anger and their brood have no part in misguiding it."[1]

The older medicine used to speak of two ways, *lysis* and *crisis*, one gradual, the other abrupt, in which one might recover from a bodily disease. In the spiritual realm there are also two ways, one gradual, the other sudden, in which inner unification may occur. Tolstoy and Bunyan may again serve us as examples, examples, as it happens, of the gradual way, though it must be confessed at the outset that it is hard to follow these windings of the hearts of others, and one feels that their words do not reveal their total secret.

Howe'er this be, Tolstoy, pursuing his unending questioning, seemed to come to one insight after another. First he perceived that his conviction that life was meaningless took only this finite life into account. He was looking for the value of one finite term in that of another, and the whole result could only be one of those indeterminate equations in mathematics which end with $0 = 0$. Yet this is as far as the reasoning intellect by itself can go, unless irrational sentiment or faith brings in the infinite. Believe in the infinite as common people do, and life grows possible again.

"Since mankind has existed, wherever life has been, there also has been the faith that gave the possibility of living. Faith is the sense of life, that sense by virtue of which man does not destroy himself, but continues to live on. It is the force whereby we live. If Man did not believe that he must

[1] H. FLETCHER: Menticulture, or the A-B-C of True Living, New York and Chicago, 1899, pp. 26–36, abridged.

live for something, he would not live at all. The idea of an infinite God, of the divinity of the soul, of the union of men's actions with God—these are ideas elaborated in the infinite secret depths of human thought. They are ideas without which there would be no life, without which I myself," said Tolstoy, "would not exist. I began to see that I had no right to rely on my individual reasoning and neglect these answers given by faith, for they are the only answers to the question."

Yet how believe as the common people believe, steeped as they are in grossest superstition? It is impossible,—but yet their life! their life! It is normal. It is happy! It is an answer to the question!

Little by little, Tolstoy came to the settled conviction—he says it took him two years to arrive there—that his trouble had not been with life in general, not with the common life of common men, but with the life of the upper, intellectual, artistic classes, the life which he had personally always led, the cerebral life, the life of conventionality, artificiality, and personal ambition. He had been living wrongly and must change. To work for animal needs, to abjure lies and vanities, to relieve common wants, to be simple, to believe in God, therein lay happiness again.

"I remember," he says, "one day in early spring, I was alone in the forest, lending my ear to its mysterious noises. I listened, and my thought went back to what for these three years it always was busy with—the quest of God. But the idea of him, I said, how did I ever come by the idea?

"And again there arose in me, with this thought, glad aspirations towards life. Everything in me awoke and received a meaning. . . . Why do I look farther? a voice within me asked. He is there: he, without whom one cannot live. To acknowledge God and to live are one and the same thing. God is what life is. Well, then! live, seek God, and there will be no life without him. . . .

"After this, things cleared up within me and about me better than ever, and the light has never wholly died away. I was saved from suicide. Just how or when the change took place I cannot tell. But as insensibly and gradually as the force of life had been annulled within me, and I had reached my moral death-bed, just as gradually and imperceptibly did the energy of life come back. And what was strange was that this energy that came back was nothing new. It was my ancient juvenile force of faith, the belief that the sole purpose of my life was to be *better*. I gave up the life of the conventional world, recognizing it to be no life, but a parody on life, which its superfluities simply keep us from comprehending,"—and Tolstoy thereupon embraced the life of the peasants, and has felt right and happy, or at least relatively so, ever since.[1]

As I interpret his melancholy, then, it was not merely an accidental vitiation of his humors, though it was doubtless also that. It was logically called for by the clash between his inner character and his outer activities and aims. Although a literary artist, Tolstoy was one of those primitive oaks of men to whom the superfluities and insincerities, the cupidities, complications, and cruelties of our polite civilization are profoundly unsatisfying, and for whom the eternal veracities lie with more natural and animal things. His crisis was the getting of his soul in order, the discovery of its genuine habitat and vocation, the escape from falsehoods into what for him were ways of truth. It was a case of heterogeneous personality tardily and slowly finding its unity and level. And though not many of us can imitate Tolstoy, not having enough, perhaps, of the aboriginal human marrow in our bones, most of us may at least feel as if it might be better for us if we could.

Bunyan's recovery seems to have been even slower. For years together he was alternately haunted with texts of Scripture, now up and now down, but at last with an ever growing relief in his salvation through the blood of Christ.

"My peace would be in and out twenty times a day; comfort now and trouble presently; peace now and before I could go a furlong as full of guilt and fear as ever heart could hold." When a good text comes home to him, "This," he writes, "gave me good encouragement for the

[1] I have considerably abridged Tolstoy's words in my translation.

space of two or three hours"; or "This was a good day to me, I hope I shall not forget it"; or "The glory of these words was then so weighty on me that I was ready to swoon as I sat; yet not with grief and trouble, but with solid joy and peace"; or "This made a strange seizure on my spirit; it brought light with it, and commanded a silence in my heart of all those tumultuous thoughts that before did use, like masterless hell-hounds, to roar and bellow and make a hideous noise within me. It showed me that Jesus Christ had not quite forsaken and cast off my Soul."

Such periods accumulate until he can write: "And now remained only the hinder part of the tempest, for the thunder was gone beyond me, only some drops would still remain, that now and then would fall upon me";—and at last: "Now did my chains fall off my legs indeed; I was loosed from my afflictions and irons; my temptations also fled away; so that from that time, those dreadful Scriptures of God left off to trouble me; now went I also home rejoicing, for the grace and love of God. . . . Now could I see myself in Heaven and Earth at once; in Heaven by my Christ, by my Head, by my Righteousness and Life, though on Earth by my body or person. . . . Christ was a precious Christ to my soul that night; I could scarce lie in my bed for joy and peace and triumph through Christ."

Bunyan became a minister of the gospel, and in spite of his neurotic constitution, and of the twelve years he lay in prison for his non-conformity, his life was turned to active use. He was a peacemaker and doer of good, and the immortal Allegory which he wrote has brought the very spirit of religious patience home to English hearts.

But neither Bunyan nor Tolstoy could become what we have called healthy-minded. They had drunk too deeply of the cup of bitterness ever to forget its taste, and their redemption is into a universe two stories deep. Each of them realized a good which broke the effective edge of his sadness; yet the sadness was preserved as a minor ingredient in the heart of the faith by which it was overcome. The fact of interest for us is that as a matter of fact they could and did find *something* welling up in the inner reaches of their consciousness, by which such extreme sadness could be overcome. Tolstoy does well to talk of it as *that by which men live*; for that is exactly what it is, a stimulus, an excitement, a faith, a force that re-infuses the positive willingness to live, even in full presence of the evil perceptions that erewhile made life seem unbearable. For Tolstoy's perceptions of evil appear within their sphere to have remained unmodified. His later works show him implacable to the whole system of official values: the ig-nobility of fashionable life; the infamies of empire; the spu-riousness of the church; the vain conceit of the professions; the meannesses and cruelties that go with great success; and every other pompous crime and lying institution of this world. To all patience with such things his experience has been for him a permanent ministry of death.

Bunyan also leaves this world to the enemy.

"I must first pass a sentence of death," he says, "upon everything that can properly be called a thing of this life, even to reckon myself, my wife, my children, my health, my enjoyments, and all, as dead to me, and myself as dead to them; to trust in God through Christ, as touching the world to come; and as touching this world, to count the grave my house, to make my bed in darkness, and to say to corruption, Thou art my father, and to the worm, Thou are my mother and sister. . . . The parting with my wife and my poor children hath often been to me as the pulling of my flesh from my bones, especially my poor blind child who lay nearer my heart than all I had besides. Poor child, thought I, what sorrow art thou like to have for thy por-tion in this world! Thou must be beaten, must beg, suffer hunger, cold, nakedness, and a thousand calamities, though I cannot now endure that the wind should blow upon thee. But yet I must venture you all with God, though it goeth to the quick to leave you."[1]

The 'hue of resolution' is there, but the full flood of ecstatic liberation seems never to have poured over poor John Bun-yan's soul.

[1]In my quotations from Bunyan I have omitted certain intervening por-tions of the text.

These examples may suffice to acquaint us in a general way with the phenomenon technically called 'Conversion.' In the next lecture I shall invite you to study its peculiarities and concomitants in some detail.

LECTURE IX

To BE CONVERTED, to be regenerated, to receive grace, to experience religion, to gain an assurance, are so many phrases which denote the process, gradual or sudden, by which a self hitherto divided, and consciously wrong inferior and unhappy, becomes unified and consciously right superior and happy, in consequence of its firmer hold upon religious realities. This at least is what conversion signifies in general terms, whether or not we believe that a direct divine operation is needed to bring such a moral change about.

Before entering upon a minuter study of the process, let me enliven our understanding of the definition by a concrete example. I choose the quaint case of an unlettered man, Stephen H. Bradley, whose experience is related in a scarce American pamphlet.[1]

I select this case because it shows how in these inner alterations one may find one unsuspected depth below another, as if the possibilities of character lay disposed in a series of layers or shells, of whose existence we have no premonitory knowledge.

Bradley thought that he had been already fully converted at the age of fourteen.

"I thought I saw the Saviour, by faith, in human shape, for about one second in the room, with arms extended, appearing to say to me, Come. The next day I rejoiced with trembling; soon after, my happiness was so great that I said that I wanted to die; this world had no place in my affections, as I knew of, and every day appeared as solemn to me as the Sabbath. I had an ardent desire that all mankind might feel as I did; I wanted to have them all love God supremely. Previous to this time I was very selfish and self-righteous; but now I desired the welfare of all mankind, and could with a feeling heart forgive my worst enemies, and I felt as if I should be willing to bear the scoffs and

[1] A sketch of the life of Stephen H. Bradley, from the age of five to twenty-four years, including his remarkable experience of the power of the Holy Spirit on the second evening of November, 1829. Madison, Connecticut, 1830.

sneers of any person, and suffer anything for His sake, if I could be the means in the hands of God, of the conversion of one soul."

Nine years later, in 1829, Mr. Bradley heard of a revival of religion that had begun in his neighborhood. "Many of the young converts," he says, "would come to me when in meeting and ask me if I had religion, and my reply generally was, I hope I have. This did not appear to satisfy them; they said they *knew they* had it. I requested them to pray for me, thinking with myself, that if I had not got religion now, after so long a time professing to be a Christian, that it was time I had, and hoped their prayers would be answered in my behalf.

"One Sabbath, I went to hear the Methodist at the Academy. He spoke of the ushering in of the day of general judgment; and he set it forth in such a solemn and terrible manner as I never heard before. The scene of that day appeared to be taking place, and so awakened were all the powers of my mind that, like Felix, I trembled involuntarily on the bench where I was sitting, though I felt nothing at heart. The next day evening I went to hear him again. He took his text from Revelation: 'And I saw the dead, small and great, stand before God.' And he represented the terrors of that day in such a manner that it appeared as if it would melt the heart of stone. When he finished his discourse, an old gentleman turned to me and said, 'This is what I call preaching.' I thought the same; but my feelings were still unmoved by what he said, and I did not enjoy religion, but I believe he did.

"I will now relate my experience of the power of the Holy Spirit which took place on the same night. Had any person told me previous to this that I could have experienced the power of the Holy Spirit in the manner which I did, I could not have believed it, and should have thought the person deluded that told me so. I went directly home after the meeting, and when I got home I wondered what made me feel so stupid. I retired to rest soon after I got home, and felt indifferent to the things of religion until I began to be exercised by the Holy Spirit, which began in about five minutes after, in the following manner: —

"At first, I began to feel my heart beat very quick all on a sudden, which made me at first think that perhaps something is going to ail me, though I was not alarmed, for I felt no pain. My heart increased in its beating, which soon convinced me that it was the Holy Spirit from the effect it had on me. I began to feel exceedingly happy and humble, and such a sense of unworthiness as I never felt before. I could not very well help speaking out, which I did, and said, Lord, I do not deserve this happiness, or words to that effect, while there was a stream (resembling air in feeling) came into my mouth and heart in a more sensible manner than that of drinking anything, which continued, as near as I could judge, five minutes or more, which appeared to be the cause of such a palpitation of my heart. It took complete possession of my soul, and I am certain that I desired the Lord, while in the midst of it, not to give me any more happiness, for it seemed as if I could not contain what I had got. My heart seemed as if it would burst, but it did not stop until I felt as if I was unutterably full of the love and grace of God. In the mean time while thus exercised, a thought arose in my mind, what can it mean? and all at once, as if to answer it, my memory became exceedingly clear, and it appeared to me just as if the New Testament was placed open before me, eighth chapter of Romans, and as light as if some candle lighted was held for me to read the 26th and 27th verses of that chapter, and I read these words: 'The Spirit helpeth our infirmities with groanings which cannot be uttered.' And all the time that my heart was a-beating, it made me groan like a person in distress, which was not very easy to stop, though I was in no pain at all, and my brother being in bed in another room came and opened the door, and asked me if I had got the toothache. I told him no, and that he might get to sleep. I tried to stop. I felt unwilling to go to sleep myself, I was so happy, fearing I should lose it—thinking within myself

> 'My willing soul would stay
> In such a frame as this.'

And while I lay reflecting, after my heart stopped beating,

feeling as if my soul was full of the Holy Spirit, I thought that perhaps there might be angels hovering round my bed. I felt just as if I wanted to converse with them, and finally I spoke, saying, 'O ye affectionate angels! how is it that ye can take so much interest in our welfare, and we take so little interest in our own.' After this, with difficulty I got to sleep; and when I awoke in the morning my first thoughts were: What has become of my happiness? and, feeling a degree of it in my heart, I asked for more, which was given to me as quick as thought. I then got up to dress myself, and found to my surprise that I could but just stand. It appeared to me as if it was a little heaven upon earth. My soul felt as completely raised above the fears of death as of going to sleep; and like a bird in a cage, I had a desire, if it was the will of God, to get released from my body and to dwell with Christ, though willing to live to do good to others, and to warn sinners to repent. I went downstairs feeling as solemn as if I had lost all my friends, and thinking with myself, that I would not let my parents know it until I had first looked into the Testament. I went directly to the shelf and looked into it, at the eighth chapter of Romans, and every verse seemed to almost speak and to confirm it to be truly the Word of God, and as if my feelings corresponded with the meaning of the word. I then told my parents of it, and told them that I thought that they must see that when I spoke, that it was not my own voice, for it appeared so to me. My speech seemed entirely under the control of the Spirit within me; I do not mean that the words which I spoke were not my own, for they were. I thought that I was influenced similar to the Apostles on the day of Pentecost (with the exception of having power to give it to others, and doing what they did). After breakfast I went round to converse with my neighbors on religion, which I could not have been hired to have done before this, and at their request I prayed with them, though I had never prayed in public before.

"I now feel as if I had discharged my duty by telling the truth, and hope by the blessing of God, it may do some good to all who shall read it. He has fulfilled his promise in sending the Holy Spirit down into our hearts, or mine at least, and I now defy all the Deists and Atheists in the world to shake my faith in Christ."

So much for Mr. Bradley and his conversion, of the effect of which upon his later life we gain no information. Now for a minuter survey of the constituent elements of the conversion process.

If you open the chapter on Association, of any treatise on Psychology, you will read that a man's ideas, aims, and objects form diverse internal groups and systems, relatively independent of one another. Each 'aim' which he follows awakens a certain specific kind of interested excitement, and gathers a certain group of ideas together in subordination to it as its associates; and if the aims and excitements are distinct in kind, their groups of ideas may have little in common. When one group is present and engrosses the interest, all the ideas connected with other groups may be excluded from the mental field. The President of the United States when, with paddle, gun, and fishing-rod, he goes camping in the wilderness for a vacation, changes his system of ideas from top to bottom. The presidential anxieties have lapsed into the background entirely; the official habits are replaced by the habits of a son of nature, and those who knew the man only as the strenuous magistrate would not 'know him for the same person' if they saw him as the camper.

If now he should never go back, and never again suffer political interests to gain dominion over him, he would be for practical intents and purposes a permanently transformed being. Our ordinary alterations of character, as we pass from one of our aims to another, are not commonly called transformations, because each of them is so rapidly succeeded by another in the reverse direction; but whenever one aim grows so stable as to expel definitively its previous rivals from the individual's life, we tend to speak of the phenomenon, and perhaps to wonder at it, as a 'transformation.'

These alternations are the completest of the ways in which a self may be divided. A less complete way is the simultaneous coexistence of two or more different groups of aims, of which one practically holds the right of way and instigates activity, whilst the others are only pious wishes, and never practically come to anything. Saint Augustine's aspirations to a purer life, in our last lecture, were for a while an example. Another would be the President in his full pride of office, wondering whether it were not all vanity, and whether the life of a wood-chopper were not the wholesomer destiny. Such fleeting aspirations are mere *velleitates*, whimsies. They exist on the remoter skirts of the mind, and the real self of the man, the centre of his energies, is occupied with an entirely different system. As life goes on, there is a constant change of our interests, and a consequent change of place in our systems of ideas, from more central to more peripheral, and from more peripheral to more central parts of consciousness. I remember, for instance, that one evening when I was a youth, my father read aloud from a Boston newspaper that part of Lord Gifford's will which founded these four lectureships. At that time I did not think of being a teacher of philosophy: and what I listened to was as remote from my own life as if it related to the planet Mars. Yet here I am, with the Gifford system part and parcel of my very self, and all my energies, for the time being, devoted to successfully identifying myself with it. My soul stands now planted in what once was for it a practically unreal object, and speaks from it as from its proper habitat and centre.

When I say 'Soul,' you need not take me in the ontological sense unless you prefer to; for although ontological language is instinctive in such matters, yet Buddhists or Humians can perfectly well describe the facts in the phenomenal terms which are their favorites. For them the soul is only a succession of fields of consciousness: yet there is found in each field a part, or sub-field, which figures as focal and contains the excitement, and from which, as from a centre, the aim seems to be taken. Talking of this part, we involuntarily apply words of perspective to distinguish it from the rest, words like 'here,' 'this,' 'now,' 'mine,' or 'me'; and we ascribe to the other parts the positions 'there,' 'then,' 'that,' 'his' or 'thine,' 'it,' 'not me.' But a 'here' can change to a 'there,' and a 'there' become a 'here,' and what was 'mine' and what was 'not mine' change their places.

What brings such changes about is the way in which emotional excitement alters. Things hot and vital to us to-day are cold to-morrow. It is as if seen from the hot parts of the field that the other parts appear to us, and from these hot parts personal desire and volition make their sallies. They are in short the centres of our dynamic energy, whereas the cold parts leave us indifferent and passive in proportion to their coldness.

Whether such language be rigorously exact is for the present of no importance. It is exact enough, if you recognize from your own experience the facts which I seek to designate by it.

Now there may be great oscillation in the emotional interest, and the hot places may shift before one almost as rapidly as the sparks that run through burnt-up paper. Then we have the wavering and divided self we heard so much of in the previous lecture. Or the focus of excitement and heat, the point of view from which the aim is taken, may come to lie permanently within a certain system; and then, if the change be a religious one, we call it a *conversion*, especially if it be by crisis, or sudden.

Let us hereafter, in speaking of the hot place in a man's consciousness, the group of ideas to which he devotes himself, and from which he works, call it *the habitual centre of his personal energy*. It makes a great difference to a man whether one set of his ideas, or another, be the centre of his energy; and it makes a great difference, as regards any set of ideas which he may possess, whether they become central or remain peripheral in him. To say that a man is 'converted' means, in these terms, that religious ideas, previously peripheral in his consciousness, now take a central place, and that religious aims form the habitual centre of his energy.

Now if you ask of psychology just *how* the excitement shifts in a man's mental system, and *why* aims that were peripheral become at a certain moment central, psychology has to reply that although she can give a general description of what happens, she is unable in a given case to account accurately for all the single forces at work. Neither an outside observer nor the Subject who undergoes the process can explain fully how particular experiences are able to change one's centre of energy so decisively, or why they so often have to bide their hour to do so. We have a thought, or we perform an act, repeatedly, but on a certain day the real meaning of the thought peals through us for the first time, or the act has suddenly turned into a moral impossibility. All we know is that there are dead feelings, dead ideas, and cold beliefs, and there are hot and live ones; and when one grows hot and alive within us, everything has to re-crystallize about it. We may say that the heat and liveliness mean only the 'motor efficacy,' long deferred but now operative, of the idea; but such talk itself is only circumlocution, for whence the sudden motor efficacy? And our explanations then get so vague and general that one realizes all the more the intense individuality of the whole phenomenon.

In the end we fall back on the hackneyed symbolism of a mechanical equilibrium. A mind is a system of ideas, each with the excitement it arouses, and with tendencies impulsive and inhibitive, which mutually check or reinforce one another. The collection of ideas alters by subtraction or by addition in the course of experience, and the tendencies alter as the organism gets more aged. A mental system may be undermined or weakened by this interstitial alteration just as a building is, and yet for a time keep upright by dead habit. But a new perception, a sudden emotional shock, or an occasion which lays bare the organic alteration, will make the whole fabric fall together; and then the centre of gravity sinks into an attitude more stable, for the new ideas that reach the centre in the rearrangement seem now to be locked there, and the new structure remains permanent.

Formed associations of ideas and habits are usually factors of retardation in such changes of equilibrium. New information, however acquired, plays an accelerating part in the changes; and the slow mutation of our instincts and propensities, under the 'unimaginable touch of time' has an enormous influence. Moreover, all these influences may work subconsciously or half unconsciously.[1] And when you get a

---

[1] Jouffroy is an example: "Down this slope it was that my intelligence had glided, and little by little it had got far from its first faith. But this melancholy revolution had not taken place in the broad daylight of my consciousness; too many scruples, too many guides and sacred affections had made it dread-

Subject in whom the subconscious life—of which I must speak more fully soon—is largely developed, and in whom motives habitually ripen in silence, you get a case of which you can never give a full account, and in which, both to the Subject and the onlookers, there may appear an element of marvel. Emotional occasions, especially violent ones, are extremely potent in precipitating mental rearrangements. The sudden and explosive ways in which love, jealousy, guilt, fear, remorse, or anger can seize upon one are known to everybody.[1] Hope, happiness, security, resolve, emotions characteristic of conversion, can be equally explosive. And emotions that come in this explosive way seldom leave things as they found them.

In his recent work on the Psychology of Religion, Professor Starbuck of California has shown by a statistical inquiry how closely parallel in its manifestations the ordinary 'conversion' which occurs in young people brought up in evangelical circles is to that growth into a larger spiritual life which is a normal phase of adolescence in every class of human beings. The age is the same, falling usually between fourteen and seventeen. The symptoms are the same,—sense of incompleteness and imperfection; brooding, depression, morbid introspection, and sense of sin; anxiety about the

---

ful to me, so that I was far from avowing to myself the progress it had made. It had gone on in silence, by an involuntary elaboration of which I was not the accomplice; and although I had in reality long ceased to be a Christian, yet, in the innocence of my intention, I should have shuddered to suspect it, and thought it calumny had I been accused of such a falling away." Then follows Jouffroy's account of his counter-conversion, quoted above on p. 164.

[1] One hardly needs examples; but for love, see p. 167, note; for fear, p. 149; for remorse, see Othello after the murder; for anger, see Lear after Cordelia's first speech to him; for resolve, see p. 165 (J. Foster case). Here is a pathological case in which *guilt* was the feeling that suddenly exploded: "One night I was seized on entering bed with a rigor, such as Swedenborg describes as coming over him with a sense of holiness, but over me with a sense of *guilt*. During that whole night I lay under the influence of the rigor, and from its inception I felt that I was under the curse of God. I have never done one act of duty in my life—sins against God and man, beginning as far as my memory goes back—a wildcat in human shape."

hereafter; distress over doubts, and the like. And the result is the same,—a happy relief and objectivity, as the confidence in self gets greater through the adjustment of the faculties to the wider outlook. In spontaneous religious awakening, apart from revivalistic examples, and in the ordinary storm and stress and moulting-time of adolescence, we also may meet with mystical experiences, astonishing the subjects by their suddenness, just as in revivalistic conversion. The analogy, in fact, is complete; and Starbuck's conclusion as to these ordinary youthful conversions would seem to be the only sound one: Conversion is in its essence a normal adolescent phenomenon, incidental to the passage from the child's small universe to the wider intellectual and spiritual life of maturity.

"Theology," says Dr. Starbuck, "takes the adolescent tendencies and builds upon them; it sees that the essential thing in adolescent growth is bringing the person out of childhood into the new life of maturity and personal insight. It accordingly brings those means to bear which will intensify the normal tendencies. It shortens up the period of duration of storm and stress." The conversion phenomena of 'conviction of sin' last, by this investigator's statistics, about one fifth as long as the periods of adolescent storm and stress phenomena of which he also got statistics, but they are very much more intense. Bodily accompaniments, loss of sleep and appetite, for example, are much more frequent in them. "The essential distinction appears to be that conversion intensifies but shortens the period by bringing the person to a definite crisis."[1]

The conversions which Dr. Starbuck here has in mind are of course mainly those of very commonplace persons, kept true to a pre-appointed type by instruction, appeal, and example. The particular form which they affect is the result of suggestion and imitation.[2] If they went through their

---

[1] E. D. STARBUCK: The Psychology of Religion, pp. 224, 262.

[2] No one understands this better than Jonathan Edwards understood it already. Conversion narratives of the more commonplace sort must always be taken with the allowances which he suggests: "A rule received and established by common consent has a very great, though to many persons an insensible influence in forming their notions of the process of their own experience. I know very well how they proceed as to this matter, for I have had frequent opportunities of observing their conduct. Very often their experience at first

growth-crisis in other faiths and other countries, although the essence of the change would be the same (since it is one in the main so inevitable), its accidents would be different. In Catholic lands, for example, and in our own Episcopalian sects, no such anxiety and conviction of sin is usual as in sects that encourage revivals. The sacraments being more relied on in these more strictly ecclesiastical bodies, the individual's personal acceptance of salvation needs less to be accentuated and led up to.

But every imitative phenomenon must once have had its original, and I propose that for the future we keep as close as may be to the more first-hand and original forms of experience. These are more likely to be found in sporadic adult cases.

Professor Leuba, in a valuable article on the psychology of conversion,[1] subordinates the theological aspect of the religious life almost entirely to its moral aspect. The religious sense he defines as "the feeling of unwholeness, of moral imperfection, of sin, to use the technical word, accompanied by the yearning after the peace of unity." "The word 'religion,'" he says, "is getting more and more to signify the conglomerate of desires and emotions springing from the sense of sin and its release"; and he gives a large number of examples, in which the sin ranges from drunkenness to spiritual pride, to show that the sense of it may beset one and crave relief as urgently as does the anguish of the sickened flesh or any form of physical misery.

Undoubtedly this conception covers an immense number of cases. A good one to use as an example is that of Mr. S. H.

---

appears like a confused chaos, but then those parts are selected which bear the nearest resemblance to such particular steps as are insisted on; and these are dwelt upon in their thoughts, and spoken of from time to time, till they grow more and more conspicuous in their view, and other parts which are neglected grow more and more obscure. Thus what they have experienced is insensibly strained, so as to bring it to an exact conformity to the scheme already established in their minds. And it becomes natural also for ministers, who have to deal with those who insist upon distinctness and clearness of method, to do so too." Treatise on Religious Affections.

[1] Studies in the Psychology of Religious Phenomena, American Journal of Psychology, vii. 309 (1896).

Hadley, who after his conversion became an active and useful rescuer of drunkards in New York. His experience runs as follows: —

"One Tuesday evening I sat in a saloon in Harlem, a homeless, friendless, dying drunkard. I had pawned or sold everything that would bring a drink. I could not sleep unless I was dead drunk. I had not eaten for days, and for four nights preceding I had suffered with delirium tremens, or the horrors, from midnight till morning. I had often said, 'I will never be a tramp. I will never be cornered, for when that time comes, if ever it comes, I will find a home in the bottom of the river.' But the Lord so ordered it that when that time did come I was not able to walk one quarter of the way to the river. As I sat there thinking, I seemed to feel some great and mighty presence. I did not know then what it was. I did learn afterwards that it was Jesus, the sinner's friend. I walked up to the bar and pounded it with my fist till I made the glasses rattle. Those who stood by drinking looked on with scornful curiosity. I said I would never take another drink, if I died on the street, and really I felt as though that would happen before morning. Something said, 'If you want to keep this promise, go and have yourself locked up.' I went to the nearest station-house and had myself locked up.

"I was placed in a narrow cell, and it seemed as though all the demons that could find room came in that place with me. This was not all the company I had, either. No, praise the Lord; that dear Spirit that came to me in the saloon was present, and said, Pray. I did pray, and though I did not feel any great help, I kept on praying. As soon as I was able to leave my cell I was taken to the police court and remanded back to the cell. I was finally released, and found my way to my brother's house, where every care was given me. While lying in bed the admonishing Spirit never left me, and when I arose the following Sabbath morning I felt that day would decide my fate, and toward evening it came into my head to go to Jerry M'Auley's Mission. I went. The house was packed, and with great difficulty I made my way to the space near the platform. There I saw the apostle to the drunkard and the outcast—that man of God, Jerry M'Auley. He rose, and amid deep silence told his experience. There was a sincerity about this man that carried conviction with it, and I found myself saying, 'I wonder if God can save *me*?' I listened to the testimony of twenty-five or thirty persons, every one of whom had been saved from rum, and I made up my mind that I would be saved or die right there. When the invitation was given, I knelt down with a crowd of drunkards. Jerry made the first prayer. Then Mrs. M'Auley prayed fervently for us. Oh, what a conflict was going on for my poor soul! A blessed whisper said, 'Come'; the devil said, 'Be careful.' I halted but a moment, and then, with a breaking heart, I said, 'Dear Jesus, can you help me?' Never with mortal tongue can I describe that moment. Although up to that moment my soul had been filled with indescribable gloom, I felt the glorious brightness of the noonday sun shine into my heart. I felt I was a free man. Oh, the precious feeling of safety, of freedom, of resting on Jesus! I felt that Christ with all his brightness and power had come into my life; that, indeed, old things had passed away and all things had become new.

"From that moment till now I have never wanted a drink of whiskey, and I have never seen money enough to make me take one. I promised God that night that if he would take away the appetite for strong drink, I would work for him all my life. He has done his part, and I have been trying to do mine."[1]

Dr. Leuba rightly remarks that there is little doctrinal theology in such an experience, which starts with the absolute need of a higher helper, and ends with the sense that he has helped us. He gives other cases of drunkards' conversions which are purely ethical, containing, as recorded, no theo-

---

[1] I have abridged Mr. Hadley's account. For other conversions of drunkards, see his pamphlet, Rescue Mission Work, published at the Old Jerry M'Auley Water Street Mission, New York city. A striking collection of cases also appears in the appendix to Professor Leuba's article.

logical beliefs whatever. John B. Gough's case, for instance, is practically, says Dr. Leuba, the conversion of an atheist—neither God nor Jesus being mentioned.[1] But in spite of the importance of this type of regeneration, with little or no intellectual readjustment, this writer surely makes it too exclusive. It corresponds to the subjectively centred form of morbid melancholy, of which Bunyan and Alline were examples. But we saw in our seventh lecture that there are objective forms of melancholy also, in which the lack of rational meaning of the universe, and of life anyhow, is the burden that weighs upon one—you remember Tolstoy's case.[2] So there are distinct elements in conversion, and their relations to individual lives deserve to be discriminated.[3]

Some persons, for instance, never are, and possibly never under any circumstances could be, converted. Religious ideas cannot become the centre of their spiritual energy. They may be excellent persons, servants of God in practical ways, but they are not children of his kingdom. They are either incapable of imagining the invisible; or else, in the language of devotion, they are life-long subjects of 'barrenness' and 'dryness.' Such inaptitude for religious faith may in some cases be intellectual in its origin. Their religious faculties may be checked in their natural tendency to expand, by beliefs about the world that are inhibitive, the pessimistic and materialistic beliefs, for example, within which so many good souls, who in former times would have freely indulged their religious propensities, find themselves nowadays, as it were, frozen; or the agnostic vetoes upon faith as something weak and

---

[1] A restaurant waiter served provisionally as Gough's 'Saviour.' General Booth, the founder of the Salvation Army, considers that the first vital step in saving outcasts consists in making them feel that some decent human being cares enough for them to take an interest in the question whether they are to rise or sink.

[2] The crisis of apathetic melancholy—no use in life—into which J. S. Mill records that he fell, and from which he emerged by the reading of Marmontel's Memoirs (Heaven save the mark!) and Wordsworth's poetry, is another intellectual and general metaphysical case. See Mill's Autobiography, New York, 1873, pp. 141, 148.

[3] Starbuck, in addition to 'escape from sin,' discriminates 'spiritual illumination' as a distinct type of conversion experience. Psychology of Religion, p. 85.

shameful, under which so many of us to-day lie cowering, afraid to use our instincts. In many persons such inhibitions are never overcome. To the end of their days they refuse to believe, their personal energy never gets to its religious centre, and the latter remains inactive in perpetuity.

In other persons the trouble is profounder. There are men anæsthetic on the religious side, deficient in that category of sensibility. Just as a bloodless organism can never, in spite of all its goodwill, attain to the reckless 'animal spirits' enjoyed by those of sanguine temperament; so the nature which is spiritually barren may admire and envy faith in others, but can never compass the enthusiasm and peace which those who are temperamentally qualified for faith enjoy. All this may, however, turn out eventually to have been a matter of temporary inhibition. Even late in life some thaw, some release may take place, some bolt be shot back in the barrenest breast, and the man's hard heart may soften and break into religious feeling. Such cases more than any others suggest the idea that sudden conversion is by miracle. So long as they exist, we must not imagine ourselves to deal with irretrievably fixed classes.

Now there are two forms of mental occurrence in human beings, which lead to a striking difference in the conversion process, a difference to which Professor Starbuck has called attention. You know how it is when you try to recollect a forgotten name. Usually you help the recall by working for it, by mentally running over the places, persons, and things with which the word was connected. But sometimes this effort fails: you feel then as if the harder you tried the less hope there would be, as though the name were *jammed*, and pressure in its direction only kept it all the more from rising. And then the opposite expedient often succeeds. Give up the effort entirely; think of something altogether different, and in half an hour the lost name comes sauntering into your mind, as Emerson says, as carelessly as if it had never been invited. Some hidden process was started in you by the effort, which went on after the effort ceased, and made the result come as if it came spontaneously. A certain music teacher, says Dr. Starbuck, says to her pupils after the thing to be done has been clearly pointed out, and unsuccessfully attempted: "Stop trying and it will do itself!"[1]

There is thus a conscious and voluntary way and an involuntary and unconscious way in which mental results may get accomplished; and we find both ways exemplified in the history of conversion, giving us two types, which Starbuck calls the *volitional type* and the *type by self-surrender* respectively.

In the volitional type the regenerative change is usually gradual, and consists in the building up, piece by piece, of a new set of moral and spiritual habits. But there are always critical points here at which the movement forward seems much more rapid. This psychological fact is abundantly illustrated by Dr. Starbuck. Our education in any practical accomplishment proceeds apparently by jerks and starts, just as the growth of our physical bodies does.

> "An athlete . . . sometimes awakens suddenly to an understanding of the fine points of the game and to a real enjoyment of it, just as the convert awakens to an appreciation of religion. If he keeps on engaging in the sport, there may come a day when all at once the game plays itself through him—when he loses himself in some great contest. In the same way, a musician may suddenly reach a point at which pleasure in the technique of the art entirely falls away, and in some moment of inspiration he becomes the instrument through which music flows. The writer has chanced to hear two different married persons, both of whose wedded lives had been beautiful from the beginning, relate that not until a year or more after marriage did they awake to the full blessedness of married life. So it is with the religious experience of these persons we are studying."[2]

We shall erelong hear still more remarkable illustrations of subconsciously maturing processes eventuating in results of which we suddenly grow conscious. Sir William Hamilton and Professor Laycock of Edinburgh were among the first to call attention to this class of effects; but Dr. Carpenter first, unless I am mistaken, introduced the term 'unconscious cerebration,' which has since then been a popular phrase of expla-

[1] Psychology of Religion, p. 117.
[2] Psychology of Religion, p. 385. Compare, also, pp. 137–144 and 262.

nation. The facts are now known to us far more extensively than he could know them, and the adjective 'unconscious,' being for many of them almost certainly a misnomer, is better replaced by the vaguer term 'subconscious' or 'subliminal.'

Of the volitional type of conversion it would be easy to give examples,[1] but they are as a rule less interesting than those of the self-surrender type, in which the subconscious effects are more abundant and often startling. I will therefore hurry to the latter, the more so because the difference between the two types is after all not radical. Even in the most voluntarily built-up sort of regeneration there are passages of partial self-surrender interposed; and in the great majority of all cases, when the will has done its uttermost towards bringing one close to the complete unification aspired after, it

[1] For instance, C. G. Finney italicizes the volitional element: "Just at this point the whole question of Gospel salvation opened to my mind in a manner most marvelous to me at the time. I think I then saw, as clearly as I ever have in my life, the reality and fullness of the atonement of Christ. Gospel salvation seemed to me to be an offer of something to be accepted, and all that was necessary on my part was to get my own consent to give up my sins and accept Christ. After this distinct revelation had stood for some little time before my mind, the question seemed to be put, 'Will you accept it now, to-day?' I replied, 'Yes; *I will accept it to-day, or I will die in the attempt!*' " He then went into the woods, where he describes his struggles. He could not pray, his heart was hardened in its pride. "I then reproached myself for having promised to give my heart to God before I left the woods. When I came to try, I found I could not. . . . My inward soul hung back, and there was no going out of my heart to God. The thought was pressing me, of the rashness of my promise that I would give my heart to God that day, or die in the attempt. It seemed to me as if that was binding on my soul; and yet I was going to break my vow. A great sinking and discouragement came over me, and I felt almost too weak to stand upon my knees. Just at this moment I again thought I heard some one approach me, and I opened my eyes to see whether it were so. But right there the revelation of my pride of heart, as the great difficulty that stood in the way, was distinctly shown to me. An overwhelming sense of my wickedness in being ashamed to have a human being see me on my knees before God took such powerful possession of me, that I *cried at the top of my voice, and exclaimed that I would not leave that place if all the men on earth and all the devils in hell surrounded me.* 'What!' I said, 'such a degraded sinner as I am, on my knees confessing my sins to the great and holy God; and ashamed to have any human being, and a sinner like myself, find me on my knees endeavoring to make my peace with my offended God!' The sin appeared awful, infinite. It broke me down before the Lord." Memoirs, pp. 14–16, abridged.

seems that the very last step must be left to other forces and performed without the help of its activity. In other words, self-surrender becomes then indispensable. "The personal will," says Dr. Starbuck, "must be given up. In many cases relief persistently refuses to come until the person ceases to resist, or to make an effort in the direction he desires to go."

"I had said I would not give up; but when my will was broken, it was all over," writes one of Starbuck's correspondents.—Another says: "I simply said: 'Lord, I have done all I can; I leave the whole matter with Thee;' and immediately there came to me a great peace."—Another: "All at once it occurred to me that I might be saved, too, if I would stop trying to do it all myself, and follow Jesus: somehow I lost my load."—Another: "I finally ceased to resist, and gave myself up, though it was a hard struggle. Gradually the feeling came over me that I had done my part, and God was willing to do his."[1] —"Lord, Thy will be done; damn or save!" cries John Nelson,[2] exhausted with the anxious struggle to escape damnation; and at that moment his soul was filled with peace.

Dr. Starbuck gives an interesting, and it seems to me a true, account—so far as conceptions so schematic can claim truth at all—of the reasons why self-surrender at the last moment should be so indispensable. To begin with, there are two things in the mind of the candidate for conversion: first, the present incompleteness or wrongness, the 'sin' which he is eager to escape from; and, second, the positive ideal which he longs to compass. Now with most of us the sense of our present wrongness is a far more distinct piece of our consciousness than is the imagination of any positive ideal we can aim at. In a majority of cases, indeed, the 'sin' almost exclusively engrosses the attention, so that conversion is *"a process of struggling away from sin rather than of striving towards righteousness."*[3] A man's conscious wit and will, so far as they strain towards the ideal, are aiming at something only dimly and inaccurately imagined. Yet all the while the forces of mere

[1] STARBUCK: Op. cit., pp. 91, 114.
[2] Extracts from the Journal of Mr. John Nelson, London, no date, p. 24.
[3] STARBUCK, p. 64.

organic ripening within him are going on towards their own prefigured result, and his conscious strainings are letting loose subconscious allies behind the scenes, which in their way work towards rearrangement; and the rearrangement towards which all these deeper forces tend is pretty surely definite, and definitely different from what he consciously conceives and determines. It may consequently be actually interfered with (*jammed*, as it were, like the lost word when we seek too energetically to recall it), by his voluntary efforts slanting from the true direction.

Starbuck seems to put his finger on the root of the matter when he says that to exercise the personal will is still to live in the region where the imperfect self is the thing most emphasized. Where, on the contrary, the subconscious forces take the lead, it is more probably the better self *in posse* which directs the operation. Instead of being clumsily and vaguely aimed at from without, it is then itself the organizing centre. What then must the person do? "He must relax," says Dr. Starbuck,—"that is, he must fall back on the larger Power that makes for righteousness, which has been welling up in his own being, and let it finish in its own way the work it has begun. . . . The act of yielding, in this point of view, is giving one's self over to the new life, making it the centre of a new personality, and living, from within, the truth of it which had before been viewed objectively."[1]

"Man's extremity is God's opportunity" is the theological way of putting this fact of the need of self-surrender; whilst the physiological way of stating it would be, "Let one do all in one's power, and one's nervous system will do the rest." Both statements acknowledge the same fact.[2]

To state it in terms of our own symbolism: When the new centre of personal energy has been subconsciously incubated so long as to be just ready to open into flower, 'hands off' is the only word for *us*, it must burst forth unaided!

We have used the vague and abstract language of psychology. But since, in any terms, the crisis described is the throwing of our conscious selves upon the mercy of powers which, whatever they may be, are more ideal than we are actually,

[1] STARBUCK, p. 115.
[2] STARBUCK, p. 113.

and make for our redemption, you see why self-surrender has been and always must be regarded as the vital turning-point of the religious life, so far as the religious life is spiritual and no affair of outer works and ritual and sacraments. One may say that the whole development of Christianity in inwardness has consisted in little more than the greater and greater emphasis attached to this crisis of self-surrender. From Catholicism to Lutheranism, and then to Calvinism; from that to Wesleyanism; and from this, outside of technical Christianity altogether, to pure 'liberalism' or transcendental idealism, whether or not of the mind-cure type, taking in the mediæval mystics, the quietists, the pietists, and quakers by the way, we can trace the stages of progress towards the idea of an immediate spiritual help, experienced by the individual in his forlornness and standing in no essential need of doctrinal apparatus or propitiatory machinery.

Psychology and religion are thus in perfect harmony up to this point, since both admit that there are forces seemingly outside of the conscious individual that bring redemption to his life. Nevertheless psychology, defining these forces as 'subconscious,' and speaking of their effects as due to 'incubation,' or 'cerebration,' implies that they do not transcend the individual's personality; and herein she diverges from Christian theology, which insists that they are direct supernatural operations of the Deity. I propose to you that we do not yet consider this divergence final, but leave the question for a while in abeyance—continued inquiry may enable us to get rid of some of the apparent discord.

Revert, then, for a moment more to the psychology of self-surrender.

When you find a man living on the ragged edge of his consciousness, pent in to his sin and want and incompleteness, and consequently inconsolable, and then simply tell him that all is well with him, that he must stop his worry, break with his discontent, and give up his anxiety, you seem to him to come with pure absurdities. The only positive consciousness he has tells him that all is *not* well, and the better way you offer sounds simply as if you proposed to him to assert coldblooded falsehoods. 'The will to believe' cannot be stretched as far as that. We can make ourselves more faithful to a belief of which we have the rudiments, but we cannot create a belief out of whole cloth when our perception actively assures us of its opposite. The better mind proposed to us comes in that case in the form of a pure negation of the only mind we have, and we cannot actively will a pure negation.

There are only two ways in which it is possible to get rid of anger, worry, fear, despair, or other undesirable affections. One is that an opposite affection should overpoweringly break over us, and the other is by getting so exhausted with the struggle that we have to stop,—so we drop down, give up, and *don't care* any longer. Our emotional brain-centres strike work, and we lapse into a temporary apathy. Now there is documentary proof that this state of temporary exhaustion not infrequently forms part of the conversion crisis. So long as the egoistic worry of the sick soul guards the door, the expansive confidence of the soul of faith gains no presence. But let the former faint away, even but for a moment, and the latter can profit by the opportunity, and, having once acquired possession, may retain it. Carlyle's Teufelsdröckh passes from the everlasting No to the everlasting Yes through a 'Centre of Indifference.'

Let me give you a good illustration of this feature in the conversion process. That genuine saint, David Brainerd, describes his own crisis in the following words:—

"One morning, while I was walking in a solitary place as usual, I at once saw that all my contrivances and projects to effect or procure deliverance and salvation for myself were utterly in vain; I was brought quite to a stand, as finding myself totally lost. I saw that it was forever impossible for me to do anything towards helping or delivering myself, that I had made all the pleas I ever could have made to all eternity; and that all my pleas were vain, for I saw that self-interest had led me to pray, and that I had never once prayed from any respect to the glory of God. I saw that there was no necessary connection between my prayers and the bestowment of divine mercy; that they laid not the least obligation upon God to bestow his grace upon me; and that there was no more virtue or goodness in them than there would be in my paddling with my hand in the water. I saw that I had been heaping up my devotions before God, fasting, praying, etc., pretending, and indeed really thinking sometimes that I was aiming at the glory of God; whereas I never once truly intended it, but only my own happiness. I saw that as I had never done anything for God, I had no claim on anything from him but perdition, on account of my hypocrisy and mockery. When I saw evidently that I had regard to nothing but self-interest, then my duties appeared a vile mockery and a continual course of lies, for the whole was nothing but self-worship, and an horrid abuse of God.

"I continued, as I remember, in this state of mind, from Friday morning till the Sabbath evening following (July 12, 1739), when I was walking again in the same solitary place. Here, in a mournful melancholy state *I was attempting to pray; but found no heart to engage in that or any other duty; my former concern, exercise, and religious affections were now gone. I thought that the Spirit of God had quite left me; but still was not distressed; yet disconsolate, as if there was nothing in heaven or earth could make me happy. Having been thus endeavoring to pray—though, as I thought, very stupid and senseless*—for near half an hour; then, as I was walking in a thick grove, unspeakable glory seemed to open to the apprehension of my soul. I do not mean any external brightness, nor any imagination of a body of light, but it was a new inward apprehension or view that I had of God, such as I never had before, nor anything which had the least resemblance to it. I had no particular apprehension of any one person in the Trinity, either the Father, the Son, or the Holy Ghost; but it appeared to be Divine glory. My soul rejoiced with joy unspeakable, to see such a God, such a glorious Divine Being; and I was inwardly pleased and satisfied that he should be God over all for ever and ever. My soul was so captivated and delighted with the excellency of God that I was even swallowed up in him; at least to that degree that I had no thought about my own salvation, and scarce reflected that there was such a creature as myself. I continued in this state of inward joy, peace, and astonishment, till near dark without any sensible abatement; and then began to think and examine what I had seen; and felt sweetly composed in my mind all the evening following. I felt myself in a new world, and everything about me appeared with a different aspect from what it was wont to do. At this time, the way of salvation opened to me with such infinite wisdom, suitableness, and excellency, that I wondered I should ever think of any other way of salvation; was amazed that I had not dropped my own contrivances, and complied with this lovely, blessed, and excellent way before. If I could have been saved by my own duties or any other way that I had formerly contrived, my whole soul would now have refused it. I wondered that all the world did not see and comply with this way of salvation, entirely by the righteousness of Christ.”[1]

I have italicized the passage which records the exhaustion of the anxious emotion hitherto habitual. In a large proportion, perhaps the majority, of reports, the writers speak as if the exhaustion of the lower and the entrance of the higher emotion were simultaneous,[2] yet often again they speak as if the higher actively drove the lower out. This is undoubtedly true in a great many instances, as we shall presently see. But often there seems little doubt that both conditions—subconscious ripening of the one affection and exhaustion of the other—must simultaneously have conspired, in order to produce the result.

T. W. B., a convert of Nettleton's, being brought to an acute paroxysm of conviction of sin, ate nothing all day, locked himself in his room in the evening in complete despair, crying aloud, “How long, O Lord, how long?”

---

[1] EDWARDS's and DWIGHT's Life of Brainerd, New Haven, 1822, pp. 45–47, abridged.

[2] Describing the whole phenomenon as a change of equilibrium, we might say that the movement of new psychic energies towards the personal centre and the recession of old ones towards the margin (or the rising of some objects above, and the sinking of others below the conscious threshold) were only two ways of describing an indivisible event. Doubtless this is often absolutely true, and Starbuck is right when he says that 'self-surrender' and 'new determination,' though seeming at first sight to be such different experiences, are “really the same thing. Self-surrender sees the change in terms of the old self; determination sees it in terms of the new.” Op. cit., p. 160.

"After repeating this and similar language," he says, "several times, *I seemed to sink away into a state of insensibility.* When I came to myself again I was on my knees, praying not for myself but for others. I felt submission to the will of God, willing that he should do with me as should seem good in his sight. My concern seemed all lost in concern for others."[1]

Our great American revivalist Finney writes: "I said to myself: 'What is this? I must have grieved the Holy Ghost entirely away. I have lost all my conviction. I have not a particle of concern about my soul; and it must be that the Spirit has left me.' 'Why!' thought I, 'I never was so far from being concerned about my own salvation in my life.' . . . I tried to recall my convictions, to get back again the load of sin under which I had been laboring. I tried in vain to make myself anxious. I was so quiet and peaceful that I tried to feel concerned about that, lest it should be the result of my having grieved the Spirit away."[2]

But beyond all question there are persons in whom, quite independently of any exhaustion in the Subject's capacity for feeling, or even in the absence of any acute previous feeling, the higher condition, having reached the due degree of energy, bursts through all barriers and sweeps in like a sudden flood. These are the most striking and memorable cases, the cases of instantaneous conversion to which the conception of divine grace has been most peculiarly attached. I have given one of them at length—the case of Mr. Bradley. But I had better reserve the other cases and my comments on the rest of the subject for the following lecture.

[1] A. A. BONAR: Nettleton and his Labors, Edinburgh, 1854, p. 261.
[2] CHARLES G. FINNEY: Memoirs written by Himself, 1876, pp. 17, 18.

LECTURE X

CONVERSION—*CONCLUDED*

IN THIS LECTURE we have to finish the subject of Conversion, considering at first those striking instantaneous instances of which Saint Paul's is the most eminent, and in which, often amid tremendous emotional excitement or perturbation of the senses, a complete division is established in the twinkling of an eye between the old life and the new. Conversion of this type is an important phase of religious experience, owing to the part which it has played in Protestant theology, and it behooves us to study it conscientiously on that account.

I think I had better cite two or three of these cases before proceeding to a more generalized account. One must know concrete instances first; for, as Professor Agassiz used to say, one can see no farther into a generalization than just so far as one's previous acquaintance with particulars enables one to take it in. I will go back, then, to the case of our friend Henry Alline, and quote his report of the 26th of March, 1775, on which his poor divided mind became unified for good.

"As I was about sunset wandering in the fields lamenting my miserable lost and undone condition, and almost ready to sink under my burden, I thought I was in such a miserable case as never any man was before. I returned to the house, and when I got to the door, just as I was stepping off the threshold, the following impressions came into my mind like a powerful but small still voice. You have been seeking, praying, reforming, laboring, reading, hearing, and meditating, and what have you done by it towards your salvation? Are you any nearer to conversion now than when you first began? Are you any more prepared for heaven, or fitter to appear before the impartial bar of God, than when you first began to seek?

"It brought such conviction on me that I was obliged to say that I did not think I was one step nearer than at first, but as much condemned, as much exposed, and as miser-

able as before. I cried out within myself, O Lord God, I am
lost, and if thou, O Lord, dost not find out some new way,
I know nothing of, I shall never be saved, for the ways and
methods I have prescribed to myself have all failed me, and
I am willing they should fail. O Lord, have mercy! O Lord,
have mercy!

"These discoveries continued until I went into the house
and sat down. After I sat down, being all in confusion, like
a drowning man that was just giving up to sink, and almost
in an agony, I turned very suddenly round in my chair, and
seeing part of an old Bible lying in one of the chairs, I
caught hold of it in great haste; and opening it without any
premeditation, cast my eyes on the 38th Psalm, which was
the first time I ever saw the word of God: it took hold of
me with such power that it seemed to go through my
whole soul, so that it seemed as if God was praying in,
with, and for me. About this time my father called the family to attend prayers; I attended, but paid no regard to
what he said in his prayer, but continued praying in those
words of the Psalm. Oh, help me, help me! cried I, thou
Redeemer of souls, and save me, or I am gone forever;
thou canst this night, if thou pleasest, with one drop of thy
blood atone for my sins, and appease the wrath of an angry
God. At that instant of time when I gave all up to him to
do with me as he pleased, and was willing that God should
rule over me at his pleasure, redeeming love broke into my
soul with repeated scriptures, with such power that my
whole soul seemed to be melted down with love; the burden of guilt and condemnation was gone, darkness was expelled, my heart humbled and filled with gratitude, and my
whole soul, that was a few minutes ago groaning under
mountains of death, and crying to an unknown God for
help, was now filled with immortal love, soaring on the
wings of faith, freed from the chains of death and darkness,
and crying out, My Lord and my God; thou art my rock
and my fortress, my shield and my high tower, my life, my
joy, my present and my everlasting portion. Looking up, I
thought I saw that same light [he had on more than one
previous occasion seen subjectively a bright blaze of light],
though it appeared different; and as soon as I saw it, the

design was opened to me, according to his promise, and I was obliged to cry out: Enough, enough, O blessed God! The work of conversion, the change, and the manifestations of it are no more disputable than that light which I see, or anything that ever I saw.

"In the midst of all my joys, in less than half an hour after my soul was set at liberty, the Lord discovered to me my labor in the ministry and call to preach the gospel. I cried out, Amen, Lord, I'll go; send me, send me. I spent the greatest part of the night in ecstasies of joy, praising and adoring the Ancient of Days for his free and un-bounded grace. After I had been so long in this transport and heavenly frame that my nature seemed to require sleep, I thought to close my eyes for a few moments; then the devil stepped in, and told me that if I went to sleep, I should lose it all, and when I should awake in the morning I would find it to be nothing but a fancy and delusion. I immediately cried out, O Lord God, if I am deceived, un-deceive me.

"I then closed my eyes for a few minutes, and seemed to be refreshed with sleep; and when I awoke, the first inquiry was, Where is my God? And in an instant of time, my soul seemed awake in and with God, and surrounded by the arms of everlasting love. About sunrise I arose with joy to relate to my parents what God had done for my soul, and declared to them the miracle of God's unbounded grace. I took a Bible to show them the words that were impressed by God on my soul the evening before; but when I came to open the Bible, it appeared all new to me.

"I so longed to be useful in the cause of Christ, in preaching the gospel, that it seemed as if I could not rest any longer, but go I must and tell the wonders of redeem-ing love. I lost all taste for carnal pleasures, and carnal com-pany, and was enabled to forsake them."[1]

Young Mr. Alline, after the briefest of delays, and with no book-learning but his Bible, and no teaching save that of his own experience, became a Christian minister, and thence-forward his life was fit to rank, for its austerity and single-

[1]Life and Journals, Boston, 1806, pp. 31–40, abridged.

mindedness, with that of the most devoted saints. But happy as he became in his strenuous way, he never got his taste for even the most innocent carnal pleasures back. We must class him, like Bunyan and Tolstoy, amongst those upon whose soul the iron of melancholy left a permanent imprint. His redemption was into another universe than this mere natural world, and life remained for him a sad and patient trial. Years later we can find him making such an entry as this in his diary: "On Wednesday the 12th I preached at a wedding, and had the happiness thereby to be the means of excluding carnal mirth."

The next case I will give is that of a correspondent of Professor Leuba, printed in the latter's article, already cited, in vol. vii. of the American Journal of Psychology. This subject was an Oxford graduate, the son of a clergyman, and the story resembles in many points the classic case of Colonel Gardiner, which everybody may be supposed to know. Here it is, somewhat abridged:—

"Between the period of leaving Oxford and my conversion I never darkened the door of my father's church, although I lived with him for eight years, making what money I wanted by journalism, and spending it in high carousal with any one who would sit with me and drink it away. So I lived, sometimes drunk for a week together, and then a terrible repentance, and would not touch a drop for a whole month.

"In all this period, that is, up to thirty-three years of age, I never had a desire to reform on religious grounds. But all my pangs were due to some terrible remorse I used to feel after a heavy carousal, the remorse taking the shape of regret after my folly in wasting my life in such a way—a man of superior talents and education. This terrible remorse turned me gray in one night, and whenever it came upon me I was perceptibly grayer the next morning. What I suffered in this way is beyond the expression of words. It was hell-fire in all its most dreadful tortures. Often did I vow that if I got over 'this time' I would reform. Alas, in about three days I fully recovered, and was as happy as ever. So it went on for years, but, with a physique like a rhinoceros,

I always recovered, and as long as I let drink alone, no man was as capable of enjoying life as I was.

"I was converted in my own bedroom in my father's rectory house at precisely three o'clock in the afternoon of a hot July day (July 13, 1886). I was in perfect health, having been off from the drink for nearly a month. I was in no way troubled about my soul. In fact, God was not in my thoughts that day. A young lady friend sent me a copy of Professor Drummond's Natural Law in the Spiritual World, asking me my opinion of it as a literary work only. Being proud of my critical talents and wishing to enhance myself in my new friend's esteem, I took the book to my bedroom for quiet, intending to give it a thorough study, and then write her what I thought of it. It was here that God met me face to face, and I shall never forget the meeting. 'He that hath the Son hath life eternal; he that hath not the Son hath not life.' I had read this scores of times before, but this made all the difference. I was now in God's presence and my attention was absolutely 'soldered' on to this verse, and I was not allowed to proceed with the book till I had fairly considered what these words really involved. Only then was I allowed to proceed, feeling all the while that there was another being in my bedroom, though not seen by me. The stillness was very marvelous, and I felt supremely happy. It was most unquestionably shown me, in one second of time, that I had never touched the Eternal: and that if I died then, I must inevitably be lost. I was undone. I knew it as well as I now know I am saved. The Spirit of God showed it me in ineffable love; there was no terror in it; I felt God's love so powerfully upon me that only a mighty sorrow crept over me that I had lost all through my own folly; and what was I to do? What could I do? I did not repent even; God never asked me to repent. All I felt was 'I am undone,' and God cannot help it, although he loves me. No fault on the part of the Almighty. All the time I was supremely happy: I felt like a little child before his father. I had done wrong, but my Father did not scold me, but loved me most wondrously. Still my doom was sealed. I was lost to a certainty, and being naturally of a brave disposition I did not quail under it, but deep sorrow for the past, mixed with regret for what I had lost, took hold upon me, and my soul thrilled within me to think it was all over. Then there crept in upon me so gently, so lovingly, so unmistakably, a way of escape, and what was it after all? The old, old story over again, told in the simplest way: 'There is no name under heaven whereby ye can be saved except that of the Lord Jesus Christ.' No words were spoken to me; my soul seemed to see my Saviour in the spirit, and from that hour to this, nearly nine years now, there has never been in my life one doubt that the Lord Jesus Christ and God the Father both worked upon me that afternoon in July, both differently, and both in the most perfect love conceivable, and I rejoiced there and then in a conversion so astounding that the whole village heard of it in less than twenty-four hours.

"But a time of trouble was yet to come. The day after my conversion I went into the hay-field to lend a hand with the harvest, and not having made any promise to God to abstain or drink in moderation only, I took too much and came home drunk. My poor sister was heartbroken; and I felt ashamed of myself and got to my bedroom at once, where she followed me, weeping copiously. She said I had been converted and fallen away instantly. But although I was quite full of drink (not muddled, however), I knew that God's work begun in me was not going to be wasted. About midday I made on my knees the first prayer before God for twenty years. I did not ask to be forgiven; I felt that was no good, for I would be sure to fall again. Well, what did I do? I committed myself to him in the profoundest belief that my individuality was going to be destroyed, that he would take all from me, and I was willing. In such a surrender lies the secret of a holy life. From that hour drink has had no terrors for me: I never touch it, never want it. The same thing occurred with my pipe: after being a regular smoker from my twelfth year the desire for it went at once, and has never returned. So with every known sin, the deliverance in each case being permanent and complete. I have had no temptation since conversion, God seemingly having shut out

Satan from that course with me. He gets a free hand in other ways, but never on sins of the flesh. Since I gave up to God all ownership in my own life, he has guided me in a thousand ways, and has opened my path in a way almost incredible to those who do not enjoy the blessing of a truly surrendered life."

So much for our graduate of Oxford, in whom you notice the complete abolition of an ancient appetite as one of the conversion's fruits.

The most curious record of sudden conversion with which I am acquainted is that of M. Alphonse Ratisbonne, a free-thinking French Jew, to Catholicism, at Rome in 1842. In a letter to a clerical friend, written a few months later, the convert gives a palpitating account of the circumstances.[1] The predisposing conditions appear to have been slight. He had an elder brother who had been converted and was a Catholic priest. He was himself irreligious, and nourished an antipathy to the apostate brother and generally to his 'cloth.' Finding himself at Rome in his twenty-ninth year, he fell in with a French gentleman who tried to make a proselyte of him, but who succeeded no farther after two or three con-versations than to get him to hang (half jocosely) a religious medal round his neck, and to accept and read a copy of a short prayer to the Virgin. M. Ratisbonne represents his own part in the conversations as having been of a light and chaffing order; but he notes the fact that for some days he was unable to banish the words of the prayer from his mind, and that the night before the crisis he had a sort of night-mare, in the imagery of which a black cross with no Christ upon it figured. Nevertheless, until noon of the next day he was free in mind and spent the time in trivial conversations. I now give his own words.

"If at this time any one had accosted me, saying: 'Al-phonse, in a quarter of an hour you shall be adoring Jesus Christ as your God and Saviour; you shall lie prostrate with

[1] My quotations are made from an Italian translation of this letter in the Biografia del Sig. M. A. Ratisbonne, Ferrara, 1843, which I have to thank Monsignore D. O'Connell of Rome for bringing to my notice. I abridge the original.

your face upon the ground in a humble church; you shall be smiting your breast at the foot of a priest; you shall pass the carnival in a college of Jesuits to prepare yourself to receive baptism, ready to give your life for the Catholic faith; you shall renounce the world and its pomps and pleasures; renounce your fortune, your hopes, and if need be, your betrothed; the affections of your family, the esteem of your friends, and your attachment to the Jewish people; you shall have no other aspiration than to follow Christ and bear his cross till death;'—if, I say, a prophet had come to me with such a prediction, I should have judged that only one person could be more mad than he,—whosoever, namely, might believe in the possibility of such senseless folly becoming true. And yet that folly is at present my only wisdom, my sole happiness.

"Coming out of the café I met the carriage of Monsieur B. [the proselyting friend]. He stopped and invited me in for a drive, but first asked me to wait for a few minutes whilst he attended to some duty at the church of San Andrea delle Fratte. Instead of waiting in the carriage, I entered the church myself to look at it. The church of San Andrea was poor, small, and empty; I believe that I found myself there almost alone. No work of art attracted my attention; and I passed my eyes mechanically over its interior without being arrested by any particular thought. I can only remember an entirely black dog which went trotting and turning before me as I mused. In an instant the dog had disappeared, the whole church had vanished, I no longer saw anything, . . . or more truly I saw, O my God, one thing alone.

"Heavens, how can I speak of it? Oh no! human words cannot attain to expressing the inexpressible. Any description, however sublime it might be, could be but a profanation of the unspeakable truth.

"I was there prostrate on the ground, bathed in my tears, with my heart beside itself, when M. B. called me back to life. I could not reply to the questions which followed from him one upon the other. But finally I took the medal which I had on my breast, and with all the effusion of my soul I kissed the image of the Virgin, radiant with grace, which it bore. Oh, indeed, it was She! It was indeed She! [What he had seen had been a vision of the Virgin.]

"I did not know where I was: I did not know whether I was Alphonse or another. I only felt myself changed and believed myself another me; I looked for myself in myself and did not find myself. In the bottom of my soul I felt an explosion of the most ardent joy; I could not speak; I had no wish to reveal what had happened. But I felt something solemn and sacred within me which made me ask for a priest. I was led to one; and there, alone, after he had given me the positive order, I spoke as best I could, kneeling, and with my heart still trembling. I could give no account to myself of the truth of which I had acquired a knowledge and a faith. All that I can say is that in an instant the bandage had fallen from my eyes; and not one bandage only, but the whole manifold of bandages in which I had been brought up. One after another they rapidly disappeared, even as the mud and ice disappear under the rays of the burning sun.

"I came out as from a sepulchre, from an abyss of darkness; and I was living, perfectly living. But I wept, for at the bottom of that gulf I saw the extreme of misery from which I had been saved by an infinite mercy; and I shuddered at the sight of my iniquities, stupefied, melted, overwhelmed with wonder and with gratitude. You may ask me how I came to this new insight, for truly I had never opened a book of religion nor even read a single page of the Bible, and the dogma of original sin is either entirely denied or forgotten by the Hebrews of to-day, so that I had thought so little about it that I doubt whether I ever knew its name. But how came I, then, to this perception of it? I can answer nothing save this, that on entering that church I was in darkness altogether, and on coming out of it I saw the fullness of the light. I can explain the change no better than by the simile of a profound sleep or the analogy of one born blind who should suddenly open his eyes to the day. He sees, but cannot define the light which bathes him and by means of which he sees the objects which excite his wonder. If we cannot explain physical light, how can we explain the light which is the truth itself? And I think I remain within the limits of veracity when I say that without having any knowledge of the letter of religious doctrine, I now intuitively perceived its sense and spirit. Better than if I saw them, I *felt* those hidden things; I felt them by the inexplicable effects they produced in me. It all happened in my interior mind; and those impressions, more rapid than thought, shook my soul, revolved and turned it, as it were, in another direction, towards other aims, by other paths. I express myself badly. But do you wish, Lord, that I should inclose in poor and barren words sentiments which the heart alone can understand?"

I might multiply cases almost indefinitely, but these will suffice to show you how real, definite, and memorable an event a sudden conversion may be to him who has the experience. Throughout the height of it he undoubtedly seems to himself a passive spectator or undergoer of an astounding process performed upon him from above. There is too much evidence of this for any doubt of it to be possible. Theology, combining this fact with the doctrines of election and grace, has concluded that the spirit of God is with us at these dramatic moments in a peculiarly miraculous way, unlike what happens at any other juncture of our lives. At that moment, it believes, an absolutely new nature is breathed into us, and we become partakers of the very substance of the Deity.

That the conversion should be instantaneous seems called for on this view, and the Moravian Protestants appear to have been the first to see this logical consequence. The Methodists soon followed suit, practically if not dogmatically, and a short time ere his death, John Wesley wrote:—

"In London alone I found 652 members of our Society who were exceeding clear in their experience, and whose testimony I could see no reason to doubt. And every one of these (without a single exception) has declared that his deliverance from sin was instantaneous; that the change was wrought in a moment. Had half of these, or one third, or one in twenty, declared it was *gradually* wrought in *them*, I should have believed this, with regard to *them*, and thought that *some* were gradually sanctified and some instantaneously. But as I have not found, in so long a space of time, a single person speaking thus, I cannot but believe that sanctification is commonly, if not always, an instantaneous work." Tyerman's Life of Wesley, i. 463.

All this while the more usual sects of Protestantism have set no such store by instantaneous conversion. For them as for the Catholic Church, Christ's blood, the sacraments, and the individual's ordinary religious duties are practically supposed to suffice to his salvation, even though no acute crisis of self-despair and surrender followed by relief should be experienced. For Methodism, on the contrary, unless there have been a crisis of this sort, salvation is only offered, not effectively received, and Christ's sacrifice in so far forth is incomplete. Methodism surely here follows, if not the healthier-minded, yet on the whole the profounder spiritual instinct. The individual models which it has set up as typical and worthy of imitation are not only the more interesting dramatically, but psychologically they have been the more complete.

In the fully evolved Revivalism of Great Britain and America we have, so to speak, the codified and stereotyped procedure to which this way of thinking has led. In spite of the unquestionable fact that saints of the once-born type exist, that there may be a gradual growth in holiness without a cataclysm; in spite of the obvious leakage (as one may say) of much mere natural goodness into the scheme of salvation; revivalism has always assumed that only its own type of religious experience can be perfect; you must first be nailed on the cross of natural despair and agony, and then in the twinkling of an eye be miraculously released.

It is natural that those who personally have traversed such an experience should carry away a feeling of its being a miracle rather than a natural process. Voices are often heard, lights seen, or visions witnessed; automatic motor phenomena occur; and it always seems, after the surrender of the personal will, as if an extraneous higher power had flooded in and taken possession. Moreover the sense of renovation, safety, cleanness, rightness, can be so marvelous and jubilant as well to warrant one's belief in a radically new substantial nature.

"Conversion," writes the New England Puritan, Joseph Alleine, "is not the putting in a patch of holiness; but with the true convert holiness is woven into all his powers, principles, and practice. The sincere Christian is quite a new fabric, from the foundation to the top-stone. He is a new man, a new creature."

And Jonathan Edwards says in the same strain: "Those gracious influences which are the effects of the Spirit of God are altogether supernatural—are quite different from anything that unregenerate men experience. They are what no improvement, or composition of natural qualifications or principles will ever produce; because they not only differ from what is natural, and from everything that natural men experience in degree and circumstances, but also in kind, and are of a nature far more excellent. From hence it follows that in gracious affections there are [also] new perceptions and sensations entirely different in their nature and kind from anything experienced by the [same] saints before they were sanctified. . . . The conceptions which the saints have of the loveliness of God, and that kind of delight which they experience in it, are quite peculiar, and entirely different from anything which a natural man can possess, or of which he can form any proper notion."

And that such a glorious transformation as this ought of necessity to be preceded by despair is shown by Edwards in another passage.

"Surely it cannot be unreasonable," he says, "that before God delivers us from a state of sin and liability to everlasting woe, he should give us some considerable sense of the evil from which he delivers us, in order that we may know and feel the importance of salvation, and be enabled to appreciate the value of what God is pleased to do for us. As those who are saved are successively in two extremely different states—first in a state of condemnation and then in a state of justification and blessedness—and as God, in the salvation of men, deals with them as rational and intelligent creatures, it appears agreeable to this wisdom, that those who are saved should be made sensible of their Being, in those two different states. In the first place, that they should be made sensible of their state of condemnation; and afterwards, of their state of deliverance and happiness."

Such quotations express sufficiently well for our purpose the doctrinal interpretation of these changes. Whatever part suggestion and imitation may have played in producing them in men and women in excited assemblies, they have at any rate been in countless individual instances an original and unborrowed experience. Were we writing the story of the mind from the purely natural-history point of view, with no religious interest whatever, we should still have to write down man's liability to sudden and complete conversion as one of his most curious peculiarities.

What, now, must we ourselves think of this question? Is an instantaneous conversion a miracle in which God is present as he is present in no change of heart less strikingly abrupt? Are there two classes of human beings, even among the apparently regenerate, of which the one class really partakes of Christ's nature while the other merely seems to do so? Or, on the contrary, may the whole phenomenon of regeneration, even in these startling instantaneous examples, possibly be a strictly natural process, divine in its fruits, of course, but in one case more and in another less so, and neither more nor less divine in its mere causation and mechanism than any other process, high or low, of man's interior life?

Before proceeding to answer this question, I must ask you to listen to some more psychological remarks. At our last lecture, I explained the shifting of men's centres of personal energy within them and the lighting up of new crises of emotion. I explained the phenomena as partly due to explicitly conscious processes of thought and will, but as due largely also to the subconscious incubation and maturing of motives deposited by the experiences of life. When ripe, the results hatch out, or burst into flower. I have now to speak of the subconscious region, in which such processes of flowering may occur, in a somewhat less vague way. I only regret that my limits of time here force me to be so short.

The expression 'field of consciousness' has but recently

come into vogue in the psychology books. Until quite lately the unit of mental life which figured most was the single 'idea,' supposed to be a definitely outlined thing. But at present psychologists are tending, first, to admit that the actual unit is more probably the total mental state, the entire wave of consciousness or field of objects present to the thought at any time; and, second, to see that it is impossible to outline this wave, this field, with any definiteness.

As our mental fields succeed one another, each has its centre of interest, around which the objects of which we are less and less attentively conscious fade to a margin so faint that its limits are unassignable. Some fields are narrow fields and some are wide fields. Usually when we have a wide field we rejoice, for we then see masses of truth together, and often get glimpses of relations which we divine rather than see, for they shoot beyond the field into still remoter regions of objectivity, regions which we seem rather to be about to perceive than to perceive actually. At other times, of drowsiness, illness, or fatigue, our fields may narrow almost to a point, and we find ourselves correspondingly oppressed and contracted.

Different individuals present constitutional differences in this matter of width of field. Your great organizing geniuses are men with habitually vast fields of mental vision, in which a whole programme of future operations will appear dotted out at once, the rays shooting far ahead into definite directions of advance. In common people there is never this magnificent inclusive view of a topic. They stumble along, feeling their way, as it were, from point to point, and often stop entirely. In certain diseased conditions consciousness is a mere spark, without memory of the past or thought of the future, and with the present narrowed down to some one simple emotion or sensation of the body.

The important fact which this 'field' formula commemorates is the indetermination of the margin. Inattentively realized as is the matter which the margin contains, it is nevertheless there, and helps both to guide our behavior and to determine the next movement of our attention. It lies around us like a 'magnetic field,' inside of which our centre of energy turns like a compass-needle, as the present phase of consciousness alters into its successor. Our whole past store of memories floats beyond this margin, ready at a touch to come in; and the entire mass of residual powers, impulses, and knowledges that constitute our empirical self stretches continuously beyond it. So vaguely drawn are the outlines between what is actual and what is only potential at any moment of our conscious life, that it is always hard to say of certain mental elements whether we are conscious of them or not.

The ordinary psychology, admitting fully the difficulty of tracing the marginal outline, has nevertheless taken for granted, first, that all the consciousness the person now has, be the same focal or marginal, inattentive or attentive, is there in the 'field' of the moment, all dim and impossible to assign as the latter's outline may be; and, second, that what is absolutely extra-marginal is absolutely non-existent, and cannot be a fact of consciousness at all.

And having reached this point, I must now ask you to recall what I said in my last lecture about the subconscious life. I said, as you may recollect, that those who first laid stress upon these phenomena could not know the facts as we now know them. My first duty now is to tell you what I meant by such a statement.

I cannot but think that the most important step forward that has occurred in psychology since I have been a student of that science is the discovery, first made in 1886, that, in certain subjects at least, there is not only the consciousness of the ordinary field, with its usual centre and margin, but an addition thereto in the shape of a set of memories, thoughts, and feelings which are extra-marginal and outside of the primary consciousness altogether, but yet must be classed as conscious facts of some sort, able to reveal their presence by unmistakable signs. I call this the most important step forward because, unlike the other advances which psychology has made, this discovery has revealed to us an entirely unsuspected peculiarity in the constitution of human nature. No other step forward which psychology has made can proffer any such claim as this.

In particular this discovery of a consciousness existing beyond the field, or subliminally as Mr. Myers terms it, casts light on many phenomena of religious biography. That is why I have to advert to it now, although it is naturally impossible for me in this place to give you any account of the evidence on which the admission of such a consciousness is based. You will find it set forth in many recent books, Binet's Alterations of Personality[1] being perhaps as good a one as any to recommend.

The human material on which the demonstration has been made has so far been rather limited and, in part at least, eccentric, consisting of unusually suggestible hypnotic subjects, and of hysteric patients. Yet the elementary mechanisms of our life are presumably so uniform that what is shown to be true in a marked degree of some persons is probably true in some degree of all, and may in a few be true in an extraordinarily high degree.

The most important consequence of having a strongly developed ultra-marginal life of this sort is that one's ordinary fields of consciousness are liable to incursions from it of which the subject does not guess the source, and which, therefore, take for him the form of unaccountable impulses to act, or inhibitions of action, of obsessive ideas, or even of hallucinations of sight or hearing. The impulses may take the direction of automatic speech or writing, the meaning of which the subject himself may not understand even while he utters it; and generalizing this phenomenon, Mr. Myers has given the name of *automatism*, sensory or motor, emotional or intellectual, to this whole sphere of effects, due to 'up-rushes' into the ordinary consciousness of energies originating in the subliminal parts of the mind.

The simplest instance of an automatism is the phenomenon of post-hypnotic suggestion, so-called. You give to a hypnotized subject, adequately susceptible, an order to perform some designated act—usual or eccentric, it makes no difference—after he wakes from his hypnotic sleep. Punctually, when the signal comes or the time elapses upon which you have told him that the act must ensue, he performs it;—but in so doing he has no recollection of your suggestion, and he always trumps up an improvised pretext for his behavior if the act be of an eccentric kind. It may even be suggested to a

[1] Published in the International Scientific Series.

subject to have a vision or to hear a voice at a certain interval after waking, and when the time comes the vision is seen or the voice heard, with no inkling on the subject's part of its source. In the wonderful explorations by Binet, Janet, Breuer, Freud, Mason, Prince, and others, of the subliminal consciousness of patients with hysteria, we have revealed to us whole systems of underground life, in the shape of memories of a painful sort which lead a parasitic existence, buried outside of the primary fields of consciousness, and making irruptions thereinto with hallucinations, pains, convulsions, paralyses of feeling and of motion, and the whole procession of symptoms of hysteric disease of body and of mind. Alter or abolish by suggestion these subconscious memories, and the patient immediately gets well. His symptoms were automatisms, in Mr. Myers's sense of the word. These clinical records sound like fairy-tales when one first reads them, yet it is impossible to doubt their accuracy; and, the path having been once opened by these first observers, similar observations have been made elsewhere. They throw, as I said, a wholly new light upon our natural constitution.

And it seems to me that they make a farther step inevitable. Interpreting the unknown after the analogy of the known, it seems to me that hereafter, wherever we meet with a phenomenon of automatism, be it motor impulses, or obsessive idea, or unaccountable caprice, or delusion, or hallucination, we are bound first of all to make search whether it be not an explosion, into the fields of ordinary consciousness, of ideas elaborated outside of those fields in subliminal regions of the mind. We should look, therefore, for its source in the Subject's subconscious life. In the hypnotic cases, we ourselves create the source by our suggestion, so we know it directly. In the hysteric cases, the lost memories which are the source have to be extracted from the patient's Subliminal by a number of ingenious methods, for an account of which you must consult the books. In other pathological cases, insane delusions, for example, or psychopathic obsessions, the source is yet to seek, but by analogy it also should be in subliminal regions which improvements in our methods may yet conceivably put on tap. There lies the mechanism logically to be assumed,—but the assumption involves a vast program of work to be done in the way of verification, in which the religious experiences of man must play their part.[1]

And thus I return to our own specific subject of instantaneous conversions. You remember the cases of Alline, Bradley, Brainerd, and the graduate of Oxford converted at three in the afternoon. Similar occurrences abound, some with and some without luminous visions, all with a sense of astonished happiness, and of being wrought on by a higher control. If, abstracting altogether from the question of their value for the future spiritual life of the individual, we take them on their psychological side exclusively, so many peculiarities in them remind us of what we find outside of conversion that we are tempted to class them along with other automatisms, and to suspect that what makes the difference between a sudden and a gradual convert is not necessarily the presence of divine

[1] The reader will here please notice that in my exclusive reliance in the last lecture on the subconscious 'incubation' of motives deposited by a growing experience, I followed the method of employing accepted principles of explanation as far as one can. The subliminal region, whatever else it may be, is at any rate a place now admitted by psychologists to exist for the accumulation of vestiges of sensible experience (whether inattentively or attentively registered), and for their elaboration according to ordinary psychological or logical laws into results that end by attaining such a 'tension' that they may at times enter consciousness with something like a burst. It thus is 'scientific' to interpret all otherwise unaccountable invasive alterations of consciousness as results of the tension of subliminal memories reaching the bursting-point. But candor obliges me to confess that there are occasional bursts into consciousness of results of which it is not easy to demonstrate any prolonged subconscious incubation. Some of the cases I used to illustrate the sense of presence of the unseen in Lecture III were of this order (compare pages 59, 62, 63, 67); and we shall see other experiences of the kind when we come to the subject of mysticism. The case of Mr. Bradley, that of M. Ratisbonne, possibly that of Colonel Gardiner, possibly that of Saint Paul, might not be so easily explained in this simple way. The result, then, would have to be ascribed either to a merely physiological nerve storm, a 'discharging lesion' like that of epilepsy; or, in case it were useful and rational, as in the two latter cases named, to some more mystical or theological hypothesis. I make this remark in order that the reader may realize that the subject is really complex. But I shall keep myself as far as possible at present to the more 'scientific' view; and only as the plot thickens in subsequent lectures shall I consider the question of its absolute sufficiency as an explanation of all the facts. That subconscious incubation explains a great number of them, there can be no doubt.

miracle in the case of one and of something less divine in that of the other, but rather a simple psychological peculiarity, the fact, namely, that in the recipient of the more instantaneous grace we have one of those Subjects who are in possession of a large region in which mental work can go on subliminally, and from which invasive experiences, abruptly upsetting the equilibrium of the primary consciousness, may come.

I do not see why Methodists need object to such a view. Pray go back and recollect one of the conclusions to which I sought to lead you in my very first lecture. You may remember how I there argued against the notion that the worth of a thing can be decided by its origin. Our spiritual judgment, I said, our opinion of the significance and value of a human event or condition, must be decided on empirical grounds exclusively. If the *fruits for life* of the state of conversion are good, we ought to idealize and venerate it, even though it be a piece of natural psychology; if not, we ought to make short work with it, no matter what supernatural being may have infused it.

Well, how is it with these fruits? If we except the class of preëminent saints of whom the names illumine history, and consider only the usual run of 'saints,' the shopkeeping church-members and ordinary youthful or middle-aged recipients of instantaneous conversion, whether at revivals or in the spontaneous course of methodistic growth, you will probably agree that no splendor worthy of a wholly supernatural creature fulgurates from them, or sets them apart from the mortals who have never experienced that favor. Were it true that a suddenly converted man as such is, as Edwards says,[1] of an entirely different kind from a natural man, partaking as he does directly of Christ's substance, there surely ought to be some exquisite class-mark, some distinctive radiance attaching even to the lowliest specimen of this genus, to which no one of us could remain insensible, and which, so far as it went, would prove him more excellent than ever the most highly gifted among mere natural men. But notoriously there

[1] Edwards says elsewhere: "I am bold to say that the work of God in the conversion of one soul, considered together with the source, foundation, and purchase of it, and also the benefit, end, and eternal issue of it, is a more glorious work of God than the creation of the whole material universe."

is no such radiance. Converted men as a class are indistinguishable from natural men; some natural men even excel some converted men in their fruits; and no one ignorant of doctrinal theology could guess by mere every-day inspection of the 'accidents' of the two groups of persons before him, that their substance differed as much as divine differs from human substance.

The believers in the non-natural character of sudden conversion have had practically to admit that there is no unmistakable class-mark distinctive of all true converts. The super-normal incidents, such as voices and visions and overpowering impressions of the meaning of suddenly presented scripture texts, the melting emotions and tumultuous affections connected with the crisis of change, may all come by way of nature, or worse still, be counterfeited by Satan. The real witness of the spirit to the second birth is to be found only in the disposition of the genuine child of God, the permanently patient heart, the love of self eradicated. And this, it has to be admitted, is also found in those who pass no crisis, and may even be found outside of Christianity altogether.

Throughout Jonathan Edwards's admirably rich and delicate description of the supernaturally infused condition, in his Treatise on Religious Affections, there is not one decisive trait, not one mark, that unmistakably parts it off from what may possibly be only an exceptionally high degree of natural goodness. In fact, one could hardly read a clearer argument than this book unwittingly offers in favor of the thesis that no chasm exists between the orders of human excellence, but that here as elsewhere, nature shows continuous differences, and generation and regeneration are matters of degree.

All which denial of two objective classes of human beings separated by a chasm must not leave us blind to the extraordinary momentousness of the fact of his conversion to the individual himself who gets converted. There are higher and lower limits of possibility set to each personal life. If a flood but goes above one's head, its absolute elevation becomes a matter of small importance; and when we touch our own upper limit and live in our own highest centre of energy, we may call ourselves saved, no matter how much higher some one else's centre may be. A small man's salvation will always be a great salvation and the greatest of all facts *for him*, and we should remember this when the fruits of our ordinary evangelicism look discouraging. Who knows how much less ideal still the lives of these spiritual grubs and earthworms, these Crumps and Stigginses, might have been, if such poor grace as they have received had never touched them at all?[1]

If we roughly arrange human beings in classes, each class standing for a grade of spiritual excellence, I believe we shall find natural men and converts both sudden and gradual in all the classes. The forms which regenerative change effects have, then, no general spiritual significance, but only a psychological significance. We have seen how Starbuck's laborious statistical studies tend to assimilate conversion to ordinary spiritual growth. Another American psychologist, Professor George A. Coe,[2] has analyzed the cases of seventy-seven converts or ex-candidates for conversion, known to him, and the results strikingly confirm the view that sudden conversion is connected with the possession of an active subliminal self. Examining his subjects with reference to their hypnotic sensibility and to such automatisms as hypnagogic hallucinations, odd impulses, religious dreams about the time of their conversion, etc., he found these relatively much more frequent in the group of converts whose transformation had been 'striking,' 'striking' transformation being defined as a "change which, though not necessarily instantaneous, seems to the subject of it to be distinctly different from a process of growth, however rapid."[3] Candidates for conversion at revivals are, as you know, often disappointed: they experience nothing striking. Professor Coe had a number of persons of this class among his seventy-seven subjects,

---

[1] Emerson writes: "When we see a soul whose acts are regal, graceful, and pleasant as roses, we must thank God that such things can be and are, and not turn sourly on the angel and say: Crump is a better man, with his grunting resistance to all his native devils." True enough. Yet Crump may really be the better *Crump*, for his inner discords and second birth; and your once-born 'regal' character, though indeed always better than poor Crump, may fall far short of what he individually might be had he only some Crump-like capacity for compunction over his own peculiar diabolisms, graceful and pleasant and invariably gentlemanly as these may be.

[2] In his book, The Spiritual Life, New York, 1900.

[3] Op. cit., p. 112.

and they almost all, when tested by hypnotism, proved to belong to a subclass which he calls 'spontaneous,' that is, fertile in self-suggestions, as distinguished from a 'passive' subclass, to which most of the subjects of striking transformation belonged. His inference is that self-suggestion of impossibility had prevented the influence upon these persons of an environment which, on the more 'passive' subjects, had easily brought forth the effects they looked for. Sharp distinctions are difficult in these regions, and Professor Coe's numbers are small. But his methods were careful, and the results tally with what one might expect; and they seem, on the whole, to justify his practical conclusion, which is that if you should expose to a converting influence a subject in whom three factors unite: first, pronounced emotional sensibility; second, tendency to automatisms; and third, suggestibility of the passive type; you might then safely predict the result: there would be a sudden conversion, a transformation of the striking kind.

Does this temperamental origin diminish the significance of the sudden conversion when it has occurred? Not in the least, as Professor Coe well says; for "the ultimate test of religious values is nothing psychological, nothing definable in terms of *how it happens*, but something ethical, definable only in terms of *what is attained*."[1]

As we proceed farther in our inquiry we shall see that what is attained is often an altogether new level of spiritual vitality, a relatively heroic level, in which impossible things have become possible, and new energies and endurances are shown. The personality is changed, the man *is* born anew, whether or not his psychological idiosyncrasies are what give the particular shape to his metamorphosis. 'Sanctification' is the technical name of this result; and erelong examples of it shall be brought before you. In this lecture I have still only to add a few remarks on the assurance and peace which fill the hour of change itself.

One word more, though, before proceeding to that point, lest the final purpose of my explanation of suddenness by sub-

[1] Op. cit., p. 144.

liminal activity be misunderstood. I do indeed believe that if the Subject have no liability to such subconscious activity, or if his conscious fields have a hard rind of a margin that resists incursions from beyond it, his conversion must be gradual if it occur, and must resemble any simple growth into new habits. His possession of a developed subliminal self, and of a leaky or pervious margin, is thus a *conditio sine qua non* of the Subject's becoming converted in the instantaneous way. But if you, being orthodox Christians, ask me as a psychologist whether the reference of a phenomenon to a subliminal self does not exclude the notion of the direct presence of the Deity altogether, I have to say frankly that as a psychologist I do not see why it necessarily should. The lower manifestations of the Subliminal, indeed, fall within the resources of the personal subject: his ordinary sense-material, inattentively taken in and subconsciously remembered and combined, will account for all his usual automatisms. But just as our primary wide-awake consciousness throws open our senses to the touch of things material, so it is logically conceivable that *if there be* higher spiritual agencies that can directly touch us, the psychological condition of their doing so *might be* our possession of a subconscious region which alone should yield access to them. The hubbub of the waking life might close a door which in the dreamy Subliminal might remain ajar or open.

Thus that perception of external control which is so essential a feature in conversion might, in some cases at any rate, be interpreted as the orthodox interpret it: forces transcending the finite individual might impress him, on condition of his being what we may call a subliminal human specimen. But in any case the *value* of these forces would have to be determined by their effects, and the mere fact of their transcendency would of itself establish no presumption that they were more divine than diabolical.

I confess that this is the way in which I should rather see the topic left lying in your minds until I come to a much later lecture, when I hope once more to gather these dropped threads together into more definitive conclusions. The notion of a subconscious self certainly ought not at this point of our inquiry to be held to *exclude* all notion of a higher penetration. If there be higher powers able to impress us, they may get access to us only through the subliminal door. (See below, p. 460 ff.)

Let us turn now to the feelings which immediately fill the hour of the conversion experience. The first one to be noted is just this sense of higher control. It is not always, but it is very often present. We saw examples of it in Alline, Bradley, Brainerd, and elsewhere. The need of such a higher controlling agency is well expressed in the short reference which the eminent French Protestant Adolphe Monod makes to the crisis of his own conversion. It was at Naples in his early manhood, in the summer of 1827.

"My sadness," he says, "was without limit, and having got entire possession of me, it filled my life from the most indifferent external acts to the most secret thoughts, and corrupted at their source my feelings, my judgment, and my happiness. It was then that I saw that to expect to put a stop to this disorder by my reason and my will, which were themselves diseased, would be to act like a blind man who should pretend to correct one of his eyes by the aid of the other equally blind one. I had then no resource save in *some influence from without.* I remembered the promise of the Holy Ghost; and what the positive declarations of the Gospel had never succeeded in bringing home to me, I learned at last from necessity, and believed, for the first time in my life, in this promise, in the only sense in which it answered the needs of my soul, in that, namely, of a real external supernatural action, capable of giving me thoughts, and taking them away from me, and exerted on me by a God as truly master of my heart as he is of the rest of nature. Renouncing then all merit, all strength, abandoning all my personal resources, and acknowledging no other title to his mercy than my own utter misery, I went home and threw myself on my knees, and prayed as I never yet prayed in my life. From this day onwards a new interior life began for me: not that my melancholy had disappeared, but it had lost its sting. Hope had entered into my heart, and once entered on the path, the God of Jesus Christ, to whom I then had learned to give myself up, little by little did the rest."[1]

It is needless to remind you once more of the admirable congruity of Protestant theology with the structure of the mind as shown in such experiences. In the extreme of melancholy the self that consciously *is* can do absolutely nothing. It is completely bankrupt and without resource, and no works it can accomplish will avail. Redemption from such subjective conditions must be a free gift or nothing, and grace through Christ's accomplished sacrifice is such a gift.

"God," says Luther, "is the God of the humble, the miserable, the oppressed, and the desperate, and of those that are brought even to nothing; and his nature is to give sight to the blind, to comfort the broken-hearted, to justify sinners, to save the very desperate and damned. Now that pernicious and pestilent opinion of man's own righteousness, which will not be a sinner, unclean, miserable, and damnable, but righteous and holy, suffereth not God to come to his own natural and proper work. Therefore God must take this maul in hand (the law, I mean) to beat in pieces and bring to nothing this beast with her vain confidence, that she may so learn at length by her own misery that she is utterly forlorn and damned. But here lieth the difficulty, that when a man is terrified and cast down, he is so little able to raise himself up again and say, 'Now I am bruised and afflicted enough; now is the time of grace; now is the time to hear Christ.' The foolishness of man's heart is so great that then he rather seeketh to himself more laws to satisfy his conscience. 'If I live,' saith he, 'I will amend my life: I will do this, I will do that.' But here, except thou do the quite contrary, except thou send Moses away with his law, and in these terrors and this anguish lay hold upon Christ who died for thy sins, look for no salvation. Thy cowl, thy shaven crown, thy chastity, thy obedience, thy poverty, thy works, thy merits? what shall all these do? what shall the

[1] I piece together a quotation made by W. Monod, in his book la Vie, and a letter printed in the work: Adolphe Monod: I., Souvenirs de sa Vie, 1885, p. 433.

law of Moses avail? If I, wretched and damnable sinner, through works or merits could have loved the Son of God, and so come to him, what needed he to deliver himself for me? If I, being a wretch and damned sinner, could be redeemed by any other price, what needed the Son of God to be given? But because there was no other price, therefore he delivered neither sheep, ox, gold, nor silver, but even God himself, entirely and wholly 'for me,' even 'for me,' I say, a miserable, wretched sinner. Now, therefore, I take comfort and apply this to *myself.* And this manner of applying is the very true force and power of faith. For he died *not* to justify the righteous, but the *un*-righteous, and to make *them* the children of God."[1]

That is, the more literally lost you are, the more literally you are the very being whom Christ's sacrifice has already saved. Nothing in Catholic theology, I imagine, has ever spoken to sick souls as straight as this message from Luther's personal experience. As Protestants are not all sick souls, of course reliance on what Luther exults in calling the dung of one's merits, the filthy puddle of one's own righteousness, has come to the front again in their religion; but the adequacy of his view of Christianity to the deeper parts of our human mental structure is shown by its wildfire contagiousness when it was a new and quickening thing.

Faith that Christ has genuinely done his work was part of what Luther meant by faith, which so far is faith in a fact intellectually conceived of. But this is only one part of Luther's faith, the other part being far more vital. This other part is something not intellectual but immediate and intuitive, the assurance, namely, that I, this individual I, just as I stand, without one plea, etc., am saved now and forever.[2]

---

[1] Commentary on Galatians, ch. iii. verse 19, and ch. ii. verse 20, abridged.

[2] In some conversions, both steps are distinct; in this one, for example:—

"Whilst I was reading the evangelical treatise, I was soon struck by an expression: 'the finished work of Christ.' 'Why,' I asked of myself, 'does the author use these terms? Why does he not say "the atoning work"?' Then these words, 'It is finished,' presented themselves to my mind. 'What is it that is finished?' I asked, and in an instant my mind replied: 'A perfect expiation for sin; entire satisfaction has been given; the debt has been paid by the

Professor Leuba is undoubtedly right in contending that the conceptual belief about Christ's work, although so often efficacious and antecedent, is really accessory and non-essential, and that the 'joyous conviction' can also come by far other channels than this conception. It is to the joyous conviction itself, the assurance that all is well with one, that he would give the name of faith *par excellence*.

"When the sense of estrangement," he writes, "fencing man about in a narrowly limited ego, breaks down, the individual finds himself 'at one with all creation.' He lives in the universal life; he and man, he and nature, he and God, are one. That state of confidence, trust, union with all things, following upon the achievement of moral unity, is the *Faith-state*. Various dogmatic beliefs suddenly, on the advent of the faith-state, acquire a character of certainty, assume a new reality, become an object of faith. As the ground of assurance here is not rational, argumentation is irrelevant. But such conviction being a mere casual offshoot of the faith-state, it is a gross error to imagine that the chief practical value of the faith-state is its power to stamp with the seal of reality certain particular theological conceptions.[1] On the contrary, its value lies solely in the fact that it is the psychic correlate of a biological growth reducing contending desires to one direction; a growth which expresses itself in new affective states and new reactions; in larger, nobler, more Christ-like activities. The ground of the specific assurance in religious dogmas is then an affective experience. The objects of faith may even

---

Substitute. Christ has died for our sins; not for ours only, but for those of all men. If, then, the entire work is finished, all the debt paid, what remains for me to do?' In another instant the light was shed through my mind by the Holy Ghost, and the joyous conviction was given me that nothing more was to be done, save to fall on my knees, to accept this Saviour and his love, to praise God forever." Autobiography of Hudson Taylor. I translate back into English from the French translation of Challand (Geneva, no date), the original not being accessible.

[1] Tolstoy's case was a good comment on those words. There was almost no theology in his conversion. His faith-state was the sense come back that life was infinite in its moral significance.

be preposterous; the affective stream will float them along, and invest them with unshakable certitude. The more startling the affective experience, the less explicable it seems, the easier it is to make it the carrier of unsubstantiated notions."[1]

The characteristics of the affective experience which, to avoid ambiguity, should, I think, be called the state of assurance rather than the faith-state, can be easily enumerated, though it is probably difficult to realize their intensity, unless one have been through the experience one's self.

The central one is the loss of all the worry, the sense that all is ultimately well with one, the peace, the harmony, the *willingness to be*, even though the outer conditions should remain the same. The certainty of God's 'grace,' of 'justification,' 'salvation,' is an objective belief that usually accompanies the change in Christians; but this may be entirely lacking and yet the affective peace remain the same—you will recollect the case of the Oxford graduate: and many might be given where the assurance of personal salvation was only a later result. A passion of willingness, of acquiescence, of admiration, is the glowing centre of this state of mind.

The second feature is the sense of perceiving truths not known before. The mysteries of life become lucid, as Professor Leuba says; and often, nay usually, the solution is more or less unutterable in words. But these more intellectual phenomena may be postponed until we treat of mysticism.

A third peculiarity of the assurance state is the objective change which the world often appears to undergo. 'An appearance of newness beautifies every object,' the precise opposite of that other sort of newness, that dreadful unreality and strangeness in the appearance of the world, which is experienced by melancholy patients, and of which you may recall my relating some examples.[2] This sense of clean and beautiful newness within and without is one of the commonest entries in conversion records. Jonathan Edwards thus describes it in himself:—

"After this my sense of divine things gradually increased,

---

[1] American Journal of Psychology, vii. 345–347, abridged.
[2] Above, p. 142.

and became more and more lively, and had more of that inward sweetness. The appearance of everything was altered; there seemed to be, as it were, a calm, sweet cast, or appearance of divine glory, in almost everything. God's excellency, his wisdom, his purity and love, seemed to appear in everything; in the sun, moon, and stars; in the clouds and blue sky; in the grass, flowers, and trees; in the water and all nature; which used greatly to fix my mind. And scarce anything, among all the works of nature, was so sweet to me as thunder and lightning; formerly nothing had been so terrible to me. Before, I used to be uncommonly terrified with thunder, and to be struck with terror when I saw a thunderstorm rising; but now, on the contrary, it rejoices me."[1]

Billy Bray, an excellent little illiterate English evangelist, records his sense of newness thus:—

"I said to the Lord: 'Thou hast said, they that ask shall receive, they that seek shall find, and to them that knock the door shall be opened, and I have faith to believe it.' In an instant the Lord made me so happy that I cannot express what I felt. I shouted for joy. I praised God with my whole heart. . . . I think this was in November, 1823, but what day of the month I do not know. I remember this, that everything looked new to me, the people, the fields, the cattle, the trees. I was like a new man in a new world. I spent the greater part of my time in praising the Lord."[2]

Starbuck and Leuba both illustrate this sense of newness by quotations. I take the two following from Starbuck's manuscript collection. One, a woman, says:—

"I was taken to a camp-meeting, mother and religious friends seeking and praying for my conversion. My emotional nature was stirred to its depths; confessions of depravity and pleading with God for salvation from sin made me oblivious of all surroundings. I plead for mercy, and had a vivid realization of forgiveness and renewal of my

[1] DWIGHT: Life of Edwards, New York, 1830, p. 61, abridged.
[2] W. F. BOURNE: The King's Son, a Memoir of Billy Bray, London, Hamilton, Adams & Co., 1887, p. 9.

nature. When rising from my knees I exclaimed, 'Old things have passed away, all things have become new.' It was like entering another world, a new state of existence. Natural objects were glorified, my spiritual vision was so clarified that I saw beauty in every material object in the universe, the woods were vocal with heavenly music; my soul exulted in the love of God, and I wanted everybody to share in my joy."

The next case is that of a man: —

"I know not how I got back into the encampment, but found myself staggering up to Rev. ——'s Holiness tent—and as it was full of seekers and a terrible noise inside, some groaning, some laughing, and some shouting, and by a large oak, ten feet from the tent, I fell on my face by a bench, and tried to pray, and every time I would call on God, something like a man's hand would strangle me by choking. I don't know whether there were any one around or near me or not. I thought I should surely die if I did not get help, but just as often as I would pray, that unseen hand was felt on my throat and my breath squeezed off. Finally something said: 'Venture on the atonement, for you will die anyway if you don't.' So I made one final struggle to call on God for mercy, with the same choking and strangling, determined to finish the sentence of prayer for Mercy, if I did strangle and die, and the last I remember that time was falling back on the ground with the same unseen hand on my throat. I don't know how long I lay there or what was going on. None of my folks were present. When I came to myself, there were a crowd around me praising God. The very heavens seemed to open and pour down rays of light and glory. Not for a moment only, but all day and night, floods of light and glory seemed to pour through my soul, and oh, how I was changed, and everything became new. My horses and hogs and even everybody seemed changed."

This man's case introduces the feature of automatisms, which in suggestible subjects have been so startling a feature at revivals since, in Edwards's, Wesley's, and Whitefield's time, these became a regular means of gospel-propagation. They were at first supposed to be semi-miraculous proofs of 'power' on the part of the Holy Ghost; but great divergence of opinion quickly arose concerning them. Edwards, in his Thoughts on the Revival of Religion in New England, has to defend them against their critics; and their value has long been matter of debate even within the revivalistic denominations.[1] They undoubtedly have no essential spiritual significance, and although their presence makes his conversion more memorable to the convert, it has never been proved that converts who show them are more persevering or fertile in good fruits than those whose change of heart has had less violent accompaniments. On the whole, unconsciousness, convulsions, visions, involuntary vocal utterances, and suffocation, must be simply ascribed to the subject's having a large subliminal region, involving nervous instability. This is often the subject's own view of the matter afterwards. One of Starbuck's correspondents writes, for instance:—

"I have been through the experience which is known as conversion. My explanation of it is this: the subject works his emotions up to the breaking point, at the same time resisting their physical manifestations, such as quickened pulse, etc., and then suddenly lets them have their full sway over his body. The relief is something wonderful, and the pleasurable effects of the emotions are experienced to the highest degree."

There is one form of sensory automatism which possibly deserves special notice on account of its frequency. I refer to hallucinatory or pseudo-hallucinatory luminous phenomena, *photisms*, to use the term of the psychologists. Saint Paul's blinding heavenly vision seems to have been a phenomen of this sort; so does Constantine's cross in the sky. The last case but one which I quoted mentions floods of light and glory. Henry Alline mentions a light, about whose externality he seems uncertain. Colonel Gardiner sees a blazing light. President Finney writes:—

[1] Consult WILLIAM B. SPRAGUE: Lectures on Revivals of Religion, New York, 1832, in the long Appendix to which the opinions of a large number of ministers are given.

"All at once the glory of God shone upon and round about me in a manner almost marvelous. . . . A light perfectly ineffable shone in my soul, that almost prostrated me on the ground. . . . This light seemed like the brightness of the sun in every direction. It was too intense for the eyes. . . . I think I knew something then, by actual experience, of that light that prostrated Paul on the way to Damascus. It was surely a light such as I could not have endured long."[1]

Such reports of photisms are indeed far from uncommon. Here is another from Starbuck's collection, where the light appeared evidently external: —

"I had attended a series of revival services for about two weeks off and on. Had been invited to the altar several times, all the time becoming more deeply impressed, when finally I decided I must do this, or I should be lost. Realization of conversion was very vivid, like a ton's weight being lifted from my heart; a strange light which seemed to light up the whole room (for it was dark); a conscious supreme bliss which caused me to repeat 'Glory to God' for a long time. Decided to be God's child for life, and to give up my pet ambition, wealth and social position. My former habits of life hindered my growth somewhat, but I set about overcoming these systematically, and in one year my whole nature was changed, i. e., my ambitions were of a different order."

Here is another one of Starbuck's cases, involving a luminous element: —

"I had been clearly converted twenty-three years before, or rather reclaimed. My experience in regeneration was then clear and spiritual, and I had not backslidden. But I experienced entire sanctification on the 15th day of March, 1893, about eleven o'clock in the morning. The particular accompaniments of the experience were entirely unexpected. I was quietly sitting at home singing selections out of Pentecostal Hymns. Suddenly there seemed to be a

[1] Memoirs, p. 34.

something sweeping into me and inflating my entire being—such a sensation as I had never experienced before. When this experience came, I seemed to be conducted around a large, capacious, well-lighted room. As I walked with my invisible conductor and looked around, a clear thought was coined in my mind, 'They are not here, they are gone.' As soon as the thought was definitely formed in my mind, though no word was spoken, the Holy Spirit impressed me that I was surveying my own soul. Then, for the first time in all my life, did I know that I was cleansed from all sin, and filled with the fullness of God."

Leuba quotes the case of a Mr. Peck, where the luminous affection reminds one of the chromatic hallucinations produced by the intoxicant cactus buds called mescal by the Mexicans:—

"When I went in the morning into the fields to work, the glory of God appeared in all his visible creation. I well remember we reaped oats, and how every straw and head of the oats seemed, as it were, arrayed in a kind of rainbow glory, or to glow, if I may so express it, in the glory of God."[1]

The most characteristic of all the elements of the conversion crisis, and the last one of which I shall speak, is the ecstasy of happiness produced. We have already heard several

[1] These reports of sensorial photism shade off into what are evidently only metaphorical accounts of the sense of new spiritual illumination, as, for instance, in Brainerd's statement: "As I was walking in a thick grove, unspeakable glory seemed to open to the apprehension of my soul. I do not mean any external brightness, for I saw no such thing, nor any imagination of a body of light in the third heavens, or anything of that nature, but it was a new inward apprehension or view that I had of God."

In a case like this next one from Starbuck's manuscript collection, the lighting up of the darkness is probably also metaphorical:—

"One Sunday night, I resolved that when I got home to the ranch where I was working, I would offer myself with my faculties and all to God to be used only by and for him. . . . It was raining and the roads were muddy; but this desire grew so strong that I kneeled down by the side of the road and told God all about it, intending then to get up and go on. Such a thing as any special answer to my prayer never entered my mind, having been

accounts of it, but I will add a couple more. President Finney's is so vivid that I give it at length:—

"All my feelings seemed to rise and flow out; and the utterance of my heart was, 'I want to pour my whole soul out to God.' The rising of my soul was so great that I rushed into the back room of the front office, to pray. There was no fire and no light in the room; nevertheless it appeared to me as if it were perfectly light. As I went in and shut the door after me, it seemed as if I met the Lord Jesus Christ face to face. It did not occur to me then, nor did it for some time afterwards, that it was wholly a mental state. On the contrary, it seemed to me that I saw him as I would see any other man. He said nothing, but looked at me in such a manner as to break me right down at his feet. I have always since regarded this as a most remarkable state of mind; for it seemed to me a reality that he stood before me, and I fell down at his feet and poured out my soul to him. I wept aloud like a child, and made such confessions

---

converted by faith, but still being most undoubtedly saved. Well, while I was praying, I remember holding out my hands to God and telling him they should work for him, my feet walk for him, my tongue speak for him, etc., etc., if he would only use me as his instrument and give me a satisfying experience—when suddenly the darkness of the night seemed lit up—I felt, realized, knew, that God heard and answered my prayer. Deep happiness came over me; I felt I was accepted into the inner circle of God's loved ones."

In the following case also the flash of light is metaphorical:—

"A prayer meeting had been called for at close of evening service. The minister supposed me impressed by his discourse (a mistake—he was dull). He came and, placing his hand upon my shoulder, said: 'Do you not want to give your heart to God?' I replied in the affirmative. Then said he, 'Come to the front seat.' They sang and prayed and talked with me. I experienced nothing but unaccountable wretchedness. They declared that the reason why I did not 'obtain peace' was because I was not willing to give up all to God. After about two hours the minister said we would go home. As usual, on retiring, I prayed. In great distress, I at this time simply said, 'Lord, I have done all I can, I leave the whole matter with thee.' Immediately, like a flash of light, there came to me a great peace, and I arose and went into my parents' bedroom and said, 'I do feel so wonderfully happy.' This I regard as the hour of conversion. It was the hour in which I became assured of divine acceptance and favor. So far as my life was concerned, it made little immediate change."

as I could with my choked utterance. It seemed to me that I bathed his feet with my tears; and yet I had no distinct impression that I touched him, that I recollect. I must have continued in this state for a good while; but my mind was too much absorbed with the interview to recollect anything that I said. But I know, as soon as my mind became calm enough to break off from the interview, I returned to the front office, and found that the fire that I had made of large wood was nearly burned out. But as I turned and was about to take a seat by the fire, I received a mighty baptism of the Holy Ghost. Without any expectation of it, without ever having the thought in my mind that there was any such thing for me, without any recollection that I had ever heard the thing mentioned by any person in the world, the Holy Spirit descended upon me in a manner that seemed to go through me, body and soul. I could feel the impression, like a wave of electricity, going through and through me. Indeed, it seemed to come in waves and waves of liquid love; for I could not express it in any other way. It seemed like the very breath of God. I can recollect distinctly that it seemed to fan me, like immense wings.

"No words can express the wonderful love that was shed abroad in my heart. I wept aloud with joy and love; and I do not know but I should say I literally bellowed out the unutterable gushings of my heart. These waves came over me, and over me, and over me, one after the other, until I recollect I cried out, 'I shall die if these waves continue to pass over me.' I said, 'Lord, I cannot bear any more;' yet I had no fear of death.

"How long I continued in this state, with this baptism continuing to roll over me and go through me, I do not know. But I know it was late in the evening when a member of my choir—for I was the leader of the choir—came into the office to see me. He was a member of the church. He found me in this state of loud weeping, and said to me, 'Mr. Finney, what ails you?' I could make him no answer for some time. He then said, 'Are you in pain?' I gathered myself up as best I could, and replied, 'No, but so happy that I cannot live.' "

I just now quoted Billy Bray; I cannot do better than give his own brief account of his post-conversion feelings:—

"I can't help praising the Lord. As I go along the street, I lift up one foot, and it seems to say 'Glory'; and I lift up the other, and it seems to say 'Amen'; and so they keep up like that all the time I am walking."[1]

One word, before I close this lecture, on the question of the transiency or permanence of these abrupt conversions. Some of you, I feel sure, knowing that numerous backslidings and relapses take place, make of these their apperceiving mass for interpreting the whole subject, and dismiss it with a pitying smile at so much 'hysterics.' Psychologically, as well as religiously, however, this is shallow. It misses the point of serious interest, which is not so much the duration as the nature and quality of these shiftings of character to higher levels. Men lapse from every level—we need no statistics to

[1] I add in a note a few more records:—

"One morning, being in deep distress, fearing every moment I should drop into hell, I was constrained to cry in earnest for mercy, and the Lord came to my relief, and delivered my soul from the burden and guilt of sin. My whole frame was in a tremor from head to foot, and my soul enjoyed sweet peace. The pleasure I then felt was indescribable. The happiness lasted about three days, during which time I never spoke to any person about my feelings." Autobiography of DAN YOUNG, edited by W. P. STRICKLAND, New York, 1860.

"In an instant there rose up in me such a sense of God's taking care of those who put their trust in him that for an hour all the world was crystalline, the heavens were lucid, and I sprang to my feet and began to cry and laugh." H. W. BEECHER, quoted by LEUBA.

"My tears of sorrow changed to joy, and I lay there praising God in such ecstasy of joy as only the soul who experiences it can realize."—"I cannot express how I felt. It was as if I had been in a dark dungeon and lifted into the light of the sun. I shouted and I sang praise unto him who loved me and washed me from my sins. I was forced to retire into a secret place, for the tears did flow, and I did not wish my shopmates to see me, and yet I could not keep it a secret."—"I experienced joy almost to weeping."—"I felt my face must have shone like that of Moses. I had a general feeling of buoyancy. It was the greatest joy it was ever my lot to experience."—"I wept and laughed alternately. I was as light as if walking on air. I felt as if I had gained greater peace and happiness than I had ever expected to experience." STARBUCK's correspondents.

tell us that. Love is, for instance, well known not to be irrevocable, yet, constant or inconstant, it reveals new flights and reaches of ideality while it lasts. These revelations form its significance to men and women, whatever be its duration. So with the conversion experience: that it should for even a short time show a human being what the high-water mark of his spiritual capacity is, this is what constitutes its importance,—an importance which backsliding cannot diminish, although persistence might increase it. As a matter of fact, all the more striking instances of conversion, all those, for instance, which I have quoted, *have* been permanent. The case of which there might be most doubt, on account of its suggesting so strongly an epileptoid seizure, was the case of M. Ratisbonne. Yet I am informed that Ratisbonne's whole future was shaped by those few minutes. He gave up his project of marriage, became a priest, founded at Jerusalem, where he went to dwell, a mission of nuns for the conversion of the Jews, showed no tendency to use for egotistic purposes the notoriety given him by the peculiar circumstances of his conversion,—which, for the rest, he could seldom refer to without tears,—and in short remained an exemplary son of the Church until he died, late in the 80's, if I remember rightly.

The only statistics I know of, on the subject of the duration of conversions, are those collected for Professor Starbuck by Miss Johnston. They embrace only a hundred persons, evangelical church-members, more than half being Methodists. According to the statement of the subjects themselves, there had been backsliding of some sort in nearly all the cases, 93 per cent. of the women, 77 per cent. of the men. Discussing the returns more minutely, Starbuck finds that only 6 per cent. are relapses from the religious faith which the conversion confirmed, and that the backsliding complained of is in most only a fluctuation in the ardor of sentiment. Only six of the hundred cases report a change of faith. Starbuck's conclusion is that the effect of conversion is to bring with it "a changed attitude towards life, which is fairly constant and permanent, although the feelings fluctuate. . . . In other words, the persons who have passed through conversion, having once taken a stand for the religious life, tend to feel themselves identified with it, no matter how much their religious enthusiasm declines."[1]

[1] Psychology of Religion, pp. 360, 357.

LECTURES XI, XII, AND XIII

SAINTLINESS

THE LAST LECTURE left us in a state of expectancy. What may the practical fruits for life have been, of such movingly happy conversions as those we heard of? With this question the really important part of our task opens, for you remember that we began all this empirical inquiry not merely to open a curious chapter in human consciousness, but rather to attain a spiritual judgment as to the total value and positive meaning of all the religious trouble and happiness which we have seen. We must, therefore, first describe the fruits of the religious life, and then we must judge them. This divides our inquiry into two distinct parts. Let us without further preamble proceed to the descriptive task.

It ought to be the pleasantest portion of our business in these lectures. Some small pieces of it, it is true, may be painful, or may show human nature in a pathetic light, but it will be mainly pleasant, because the best fruits of religious experience are the best things that history has to show. They have always been esteemed so; here if anywhere is the genuinely strenuous life; and to call to mind a succession of such examples as I have lately had to wander through, though it has been only in the reading of them, is to feel encouraged and uplifted and washed in better moral air.

The highest flights of charity, devotion, trust, patience, bravery to which the wings of human nature have spread themselves have been flown for religious ideals. I can do no better than quote, as to this, some remarks which Sainte-Beuve in his History of Port-Royal makes on the results of conversion or the state of grace.

"Even from the purely human point of view," Sainte-Beuve says, "the phenomenon of grace must still appear sufficiently extraordinary, eminent, and rare, both in its nature and in its effects, to deserve a closer study. For the soul arrives thereby at a certain fixed and invincible state, a state which is genuinely heroic, and from out of which the greatest deeds which it ever performs are executed. Through all the different forms of communion, and all the diversity of the means which help to produce this state, whether it be reached by a jubilee, by a general confession, by a solitary prayer and effusion, whatever in short be the place and the occasion, it is easy to recognize that it is fundamentally one state in spirit and in fruits. Penetrate a little beneath the diversity of circumstances, and it becomes evident that in Christians of different epochs it is always one and the same modification by which they are affected: there is veritably a single fundamental and identical spirit of piety and charity, common to those who have received grace; an inner state which before all things is one of love and humility, of infinite confidence in God, and of severity for one's self, accompanied with tenderness for others. The fruits peculiar to this condition of the soul have the same savor in all, under distant suns and in different surroundings, in Saint Teresa of Avila just as in any Moravian brother of Herrnhut."[1]

Sainte-Beuve has here only the more eminent instances of regeneration in mind, and these are of course the instructive ones for us also to consider. These devotees have often laid their course so differently from other men that, judging them by worldly law, we might be tempted to call them monstrous aberrations from the path of nature. I begin, therefore, by asking a general psychological question as to what the inner conditions are which may make one human character differ so extremely from another.

I reply at once that where the character, as something distinguished from the intellect, is concerned, the causes of human diversity lie chiefly in our *differing susceptibilities of emotional excitement*, and in the *different impulses and inhibitions* which these bring in their train. Let me make this more clear.

Speaking generally, our moral and practical attitude, at any given time, is always a resultant of two sets of forces within us, impulses pushing us one way and obstructions and inhibitions holding us back. "Yes! yes!" say the impulses; "No! no!" say the inhibitions. Few people who have not expressly reflected on the matter realize how constantly this factor of inhibition is upon us, how it constrains and moulds us by its

[1] SAINTE-BEUVE: Port-Royal, vol. i. pp. 95 and 106, abridged.

restrictive pressure almost as if we were fluids pent within the cavity of a jar. The influence is so incessant that it becomes subconscious. All of you, for example, sit here with a certain constraint at this moment, and entirely without express consciousness of the fact, because of the influence of the occasion. If left alone in the room, each of you would probably involuntarily rearrange himself, and make his attitude more 'free and easy.' But proprieties and their inhibitions snap like cobwebs if any great emotional excitement supervenes. I have seen a dandy appear in the street with his face covered with shaving-lather because a house across the way was on fire; and a woman will run among strangers in her nightgown if it be a question of saving her baby's life or her own. Take a self-indulgent woman's life in general. She will yield to every inhibition set by her disagreeable sensations, lie late in bed, live upon tea or bromides, keep indoors from the cold. Every difficulty finds her obedient to its 'no.' But make a mother of her, and what have you? Possessed by maternal excitement, she now confronts wakefulness, weariness, and toil without an instant of hesitation or a word of complaint. The inhibitive power of pain over her is extinguished wherever the baby's interests are at stake. The inconveniences which this creature occasions have become, as James Hinton says, the glowing heart of a great joy, and indeed are now the very conditions whereby the joy becomes most deep.

This is an example of what you have already heard of as the 'expulsive power of a higher affection.' But be the affection high or low, it makes no difference, so long as the excitement it brings be strong enough. In one of Henry Drummond's discourses he tells of an inundation in India where an eminence with a bungalow upon it remained unsubmerged, and became the refuge of a number of wild animals and reptiles in addition to the human beings who were there. At a certain moment a royal Bengal tiger appeared swimming towards it, reached it, and lay panting like a dog upon the ground in the midst of the people, still possessed by such an agony of terror that one of the Englishmen could calmly step up with a rifle and blow out its brains. The tiger's habitual ferocity was temporarily quelled by the emotion of fear, which became sovereign, and formed a new centre for his character.

Sometimes no emotional state is sovereign, but many contrary ones are mixed together. In that case one hears both 'yeses' and 'noes,' and the 'will' is called on then to solve the conflict. Take a soldier, for example, with his dread of cowardice impelling him to advance, his fears impelling him to run, and his propensities to imitation pushing him towards various courses if his comrades offer various examples. His person becomes the seat of a mass of interferences; and he may for a time simply waver, because no one emotion prevails. There is a pitch of intensity, though, which, if any emotion reach it, enthrones that one as alone effective and sweeps its antagonists and all their inhibitions away. The fury of his comrades' charge, once entered on, will give this pitch of courage to the soldier; the panic of their rout will give this pitch of fear. In these sovereign excitements, things ordinarily impossible grow natural because the inhibitions are annulled. Their 'no! no!' not only is not heard, it does not exist. Obstacles are then like tissue-paper hoops to the circus rider—no impediment; the flood is higher than the dam they make. "Lass sie betteln gehn wenn sie hungrig sind!" cries the grenadier, frantic over his Emperor's capture, when his wife and babes are suggested; and men pent into a burning theatre have been known to cut their way through the crowd with knives.[1]

One mode of emotional excitability is exceedingly important in the composition of the energetic character, from its

---

[1] " 'Love would not be love,' says Bourget, 'unless it could carry one to crime.' And so one may say that no passion would be a veritable passion unless it could carry one to crime." (SIGHELE: Psychologie des Sectes, p. 136.) In other words, great passions annul the ordinary inhibitions set by 'conscience.' And conversely, of all the criminal human beings, the false, cowardly, sensual, or cruel persons who actually live, there is perhaps not one whose criminal impulse may not be at some moment overpowered by the presence of some other emotion to which his character is also potentially liable, provided that other emotion be only made intense enough. Fear is usually the most available emotion for this result in this particular class of persons. It stands for conscience, and may here be classed appropriately as a 'higher affection.' If we are soon to die, or if we believe a day of judgment to be near at hand, how quickly do we put our moral house in order—we do not see how sin can evermore exert temptation over us! Old-fashioned hell-fire Christianity well knew how to extract from fear its full equivalent in the way of fruits for repentance, and its full conversion value.

peculiarly destructive power over inhibitions. I mean what in its lower form is mere irascibility, susceptibility to wrath, the fighting temper; and what in subtler ways manifests itself as impatience, grimness, earnestness, severity of character. Earnestness means willingness to live with energy, though energy bring pain. The pain may be pain to other people or pain to one's self—it makes little difference; for when the strenuous mood is on one, the aim is to break something, no matter whose or what. Nothing annihilates an inhibition as irresistibly as anger does it; for, as Moltke says of war, destruction pure and simple is its essence. This is what makes it so invaluable an ally of every other passion. The sweetest delights are trampled on with a ferocious pleasure the moment they offer themselves as checks to a cause by which our higher indignations are elicited. It costs then nothing to drop friendships, to renounce long-rooted privileges and possessions, to break with social ties. Rather do we take a stern joy in the astringency and desolation; and what is called weakness of character seems in most cases to consist in the inaptitude for these sacrificial moods, of which one's own inferior self and its pet softnesses must often be the targets and the victims.[1]

So far I have spoken of temporary alterations produced by shifting excitements in the same person. But the relatively fixed differences of character of different persons are explained in a precisely similar way. In a man with a liability to a special sort of emotion, whole ranges of inhibition habitually vanish, which in other men remain effective, and other sorts of inhibition take their place. When a person has an inborn genius for certain emotions, his life differs strangely from that of ordinary people, for none of their usual deterrents check him. Your mere aspirant to a type of character, on the contrary, only shows, when your natural lover, fighter, or reformer, with whom the passion is a gift of nature, comes along, the

[1] Example: Benjamin Constant was often marveled at as an extraordinary instance of superior intelligence with inferior character. He writes (Journal, Paris, 1895, p. 56), "I am tossed and dragged about by my miserable weakness. Never was anything so ridiculous as my indecision. Now marriage, now solitude; now Germany, now France, hesitation upon hesitation, and all because at bottom I am *unable to give up anything.*" He can't 'get mad' at any of his alternatives; and the career of a man beset by such an all-round amiability is hopeless.

hopeless inferiority of voluntary to instinctive action. He has deliberately to overcome his inhibitions; the genius with the inborn passion seems not to feel them at all; he is free of all that inner friction and nervous waste. To a Fox, a Garibaldi, a General Booth, a John Brown, a Louise Michel, a Brad-laugh, the obstacles omnipotent over those around them are as if non-existent. Could the rest of us so disregard them, there might be many such heroes, for many have the wish to live for similar ideals, and only the adequate degree of inhi-bition-quenching fury is lacking.[1]

The difference between willing and merely wishing, be-tween having ideals that are creative and ideals that are but pinings and regrets, thus depends solely either on the amount of steam-pressure chronically driving the character in the ideal direction, or on the amount of ideal excitement transiently acquired. Given a certain amount of love, indignation, gen-erosity, magnanimity, admiration, loyalty, or enthusiasm of self-surrender, the result is always the same. That whole raft of cowardly obstructions, which in tame persons and dull moods are sovereign impediments to action, sinks away at

---

[1] The great thing which the higher excitabilities give is *courage*; and the addition or subtraction of a certain amount of this quality makes a different man, a different life. Various excitements let the courage loose. Trustful hope will do it; inspiring example will do it; love will do it; wrath will do it. In some people it is natively so high that the mere touch of danger does it, though danger is for most men the great inhibitor of action. 'Love of adven-ture' becomes in such persons a ruling passion. "I believe," says General Sko-beleff, "that my bravery is simply the passion and at the same time the contempt of danger. The risk of life fills me with an exaggerated rapture. The fewer there are to share it, the more I like it. The participation of my body in the event is required to furnish me an adequate excitement. Everything intellectual appears to me to be reflex; but a meeting of man to man, a duel, a danger into which I can throw myself headforemost, attracts me, moves me, intoxicates me. I am crazy for it, I love it, I adore it. I run after danger as one runs after women; I wish it never to stop. Were it always the same, it would always bring me a new pleasure. When I throw myself into an adven-ture in which I hope to find it, my heart palpitates with the uncertainty; I could wish at once to have it appear and yet to delay. A sort of painful and delicious shiver shakes me; my entire nature runs to meet the peril with an impetus that my will would in vain try to resist." (JULIETTE ADAM: Le Géné-ral Skobeleff, Nouvelle Revue, 1886, abridged.) Skobeleff seems to have been a cruel egoist; but the disinterested Garibaldi, if one may judge by his 'Me-morie,' lived in an unflagging emotion of similar danger-seeking excitement.

once. Our conventionality,[1] our shyness, laziness, and stingi-
ness, our demands for precedent and permission, for guarantee and surety, our small suspicions, timidities, despairs,
where are they now? Severed like cobwebs, broken like bubbles in the sun—

> "Wo sind die Sorge nun und Noth
> Die mich noch gestern wollt' erschlaffen?
> Ich schäm' mich dess' im Morgenroth."

The flood we are borne on rolls them so lightly under that
their very contact is unfelt. Set free of them, we float and soar
and sing. This auroral openness and uplift gives to all creative
ideal levels a bright and caroling quality, which is nowhere
more marked than where the controlling emotion is religious.
"The true monk," writes an Italian mystic, "takes nothing
with him but his lyre."

We may now turn from these psychological generalities to
those fruits of the religious state which form the special subject of our present lecture. The man who lives in his religious
centre of personal energy, and is actuated by spiritual enthusiasms, differs from his previous carnal self in perfectly definite ways. The new ardor which burns in his breast consumes
in its glow the lower 'noes' which formerly beset him, and
keeps him immune against infection from the entire groveling
portion of his nature. Magnanimities once impossible are
now easy; paltry conventionalities and mean incentives once
tyrannical hold no sway. The stone wall inside of him has
fallen, the hardness in his heart has broken down. The rest of
us can, I think, imagine this by recalling our state of feeling
in those temporary 'melting moods' into which either the
trials of real life, or the theatre, or a novel sometimes throw
us. Especially if we weep! For it is then as if our tears broke
through an inveterate inner dam, and let all sorts of ancient
peccancies and moral stagnancies drain away, leaving us now
washed and soft of heart and open to every nobler leading.
With most of us the customary hardness quickly returns, but

[1] See the case on p. 70, above, where the writer describes his experiences
of communion with the Divine as consisting "merely in the *temporary obliteration of the conventionalities* which usually cover my life."

not so with saintly persons. Many saints, even as energetic ones as Teresa and Loyola, have possessed what the church traditionally reveres as a special grace, the so-called gift of tears. In these persons the melting mood seems to have held almost uninterrupted control. And as it is with tears and melting moods, so it is with other exalted affections. Their reign may come by gradual growth or by a crisis; but in either case it may have 'come to stay.'

At the end of the last lecture we saw this permanence to be true of the general paramountcy of the higher insight, even though in the ebbs of emotional excitement meaner motives might temporarily prevail and backsliding might occur. But that lower temptations may remain completely annulled, apart from transient emotion and as if by alteration of the man's habitual nature, is also proved by documentary evidence in certain cases. Before embarking on the general natural history of the regenerate character, let me convince you of this curious fact by one or two examples. The most numerous are those of reformed drunkards. You recollect the case of Mr. Hadley in the last lecture; the Jerry McAuley Water Street Mission abounds in similar instances.[1] You also remember the graduate of Oxford, converted at three in the afternoon, and getting drunk in the hay-field the next day, but after that permanently cured of his appetite. "From that hour drink has had no terrors for me: I never touch it, never want it. The same thing occurred with my pipe, . . . the desire for it went at once and has never returned. So with every known sin, the deliverance in each case being permanent and complete. I have had no temptations since conversion."

Here is an analogous case from Starbuck's manuscript collection:—

"I went into the old Adelphi Theatre, where there was a Holiness meeting, . . . and I began saying, 'Lord, Lord, I must have this blessing.' Then what was to me an audible voice said: 'Are you willing to give up everything to the Lord?' and question after question kept coming up, to all of which I said: 'Yes, Lord; yes, Lord!' until this came:

[1] Above, p. 188. "The only radical remedy I know for dipsomania is religiomania," is a saying I have heard quoted from some medical man.

'Why do you not accept it *now*?' and I said: 'I do, Lord.'—
I felt no particular joy, only a trust. Just then the meeting
closed, and, as I went out on the street, I met a gentleman
smoking a fine cigar, and a cloud of smoke came into my
face, and I took a long, deep breath of it, and praise the
Lord, all my appetite for it was gone. Then as I walked
along the street, passing saloons where the fumes of liquor
came out, I found that all my taste and longing for that
accursed stuff was gone. Glory to God! . . . [But] for ten
or eleven long years [after that] I was in the wilderness
with its ups and downs. My appetite for liquor never came
back."

The classic case of Colonel Gardiner is that of a man cured
of sexual temptation in a single hour. To Mr. Spears the colonel said, "I was effectually cured of all inclination to that sin
I was so strongly addicted to that I thought nothing but
shooting me through the head could have cured me of it; and
all desire and inclination to it was removed, as entirely as if I
had been a sucking child; nor did the temptation return to
this day." Mr. Webster's words on the same subject are these:
"One thing I have heard the colonel frequently say, that he
was much addicted to impurity before his acquaintance with
religion; but that, so soon as he was enlightened from above,
he felt the power of the Holy Ghost changing his nature so
wonderfully that his sanctification in this respect seemed more
remarkable than in any other."[1]

Such rapid abolition of ancient impulses and propensities
reminds us so strongly of what has been observed as the result
of hypnotic suggestion that it is difficult not to believe that
subliminal influences play the decisive part in these abrupt
changes of heart, just as they do in hypnotism.[2] Suggestive

---

[1] Doddridge's Life of Colonel James Gardiner, London Religious Tract Society, pp. 23–32.

[2] Here, for example, is a case, from Starbuck's book, in which a 'sensory
automatism' brought about quickly what prayers and resolves had been unable to effect. The subject is a woman. She writes:—

"When I was about forty I tried to quit smoking, but the desire was on
me, and had me in its power. I cried and prayed and promised God to quit,
but could not. I had smoked for fifteen years. When I was fifty-three, as I sat
by the fire one day smoking, a voice came to me. I did not hear it with my

therapeutics abound in records of cure, after a few sittings, of inveterate bad habits with which the patient, left to ordinary moral and physical influences, had struggled in vain. Both drunkenness and sexual vice have been cured in this way, action through the subliminal seeming thus in many individuals to have the prerogative of inducing relatively stable change. If the grace of God miraculously operates, it probably operates through the subliminal door, then. But just *how* anything operates in this region is still unexplained, and we shall do well now to say good-by to the *process* of transformation altogether,—leaving it, if you like, a good deal of a psychological or theological mystery,—and to turn our attention to the fruits of the religious condition, no matter in what way they may have been produced.[1]

---

ears, but more as a dream or sort of double think. It said, 'Louisa, lay down smoking.' At once I replied, 'Will you take the desire away?' But it only kept saying: 'Louisa, lay down smoking.' Then I got up, laid my pipe on the mantel-shelf, and never smoked again or had any desire to. The desire was gone as though I had never known it or touched tobacco. The sight of others smoking and the smell of smoke never gave me the least wish to touch it again." The Psychology of Religion, p. 142.

[1] Professor Starbuck expresses the radical destruction of old influences physiologically, as a cutting off of the connection between higher and lower cerebral centres. "This condition," he says, "in which the association-centres connected with the spiritual life are cut off from the lower, is often reflected in the way correspondents describe their experiences. . . . For example: 'Temptations from without still assail me, but there is nothing *within* to respond to them.' The ego [here] is wholly identified with the higher centres, whose quality of feeling is that of withinness. Another of the respondents says: 'Since then, although Satan tempts me, there is as it were a wall of brass around me, so that his darts cannot touch me.' "—Unquestionably, functional exclusions of this sort must occur in the cerebral organ. But on the side accessible to introspection, their causal condition is nothing but the degree of spiritual excitement, getting at last so high and strong as to be sovereign; and it must be frankly confessed that we do not know just why or how such sovereignty comes about in one person and not in another. We can only give our imagination a certain delusive help by mechanical analogies.

If we should conceive, for example, that the human mind, with its different possibilities of equilibrium, might be like a many-sided solid with different surfaces on which it could lie flat, we might liken mental revolutions to the spatial revolutions of such a body. As it is pried up, say by a lever, from a position in which it lies on surface A, for instance, it will linger for a time

The collective name for the ripe fruits of religion in a character is Saintliness.[1] The saintly character is the character for which spiritual emotions are the habitual centre of the personal energy; and there is a certain composite photograph of universal saintliness, the same in all religions, of which the features can easily be traced.[2]

They are these:—

1. A feeling of being in a wider life than that of this world's selfish little interests; and a conviction, not merely intellectual, but as it were sensible, of the existence of an Ideal Power. In Christian saintliness this power is always personified as God; but abstract moral ideals, civic or patriotic utopias, or inner visions of holiness or right may also be felt as the true lords

---

unstably halfway up, and if the lever cease to urge it, it will tumble back or 'relapse' under the continued pull of gravity. But if at last it rotate far enough for its centre of gravity to pass beyond surface A altogether, the body will fall over, on surface B, say, and abide there permanently. The pulls of gravity towards A have vanished, and may now be disregarded. The polyhedron has become immune against farther attraction from their direction.

In this figure of speech the lever may correspond to the emotional influences making for a new life, and the initial pull of gravity to the ancient drawbacks and inhibitions. So long as the emotional influence fails to reach a certain pitch of efficacy, the changes it produces are unstable, and the man relapses into his original attitude. But when a certain intensity is attained by the new emotion, a critical point is passed, and there then ensues an irreversible revolution, equivalent to the production of a new nature.

[1] I use this word in spite of a certain flavor of 'sanctimoniousness' which sometimes clings to it, because no other word suggests as well the exact combination of affections which the text goes on to describe.

[2] "It will be found," says Dr. W. R. INGE (in his lectures on Christian Mysticism, London, 1899, p. 326), "that men of preëminent saintliness agree very closely in what they tell us. They tell us that they have arrived at an unshakable conviction, not based on inference but on immediate experience, that God is a spirit with whom the human spirit can hold intercourse; that in him meet all that they can imagine of goodness, truth, and beauty; that they can see his footprints everywhere in nature, and feel his presence within them as the very life of their life, so that in proportion as they come to themselves they come to him. They tell us what separates us from him and from happiness is, first, self-seeking in all its forms; and, secondly, sensuality in all its forms; that these are the ways of darkness and death, which hide from us the face of God; while the path of the just is like a shining light, which shineth more and more unto the perfect day."

and enlargers of our life, in ways which I described in the lecture on the Reality of the Unseen.[1]

2. A sense of the friendly continuity of the ideal power with our own life, and a willing self-surrender to its control.

3. An immense elation and freedom, as the outlines of the confining selfhood melt down.

4. A shifting of the emotional centre towards loving and harmonious affections, towards 'yes, yes,' and away from 'no,' where the claims of the non-ego are concerned.

[1] The 'enthusiasm of humanity' may lead to a life which coalesces in many respects with that of Christian saintliness. Take the following rules proposed to members of the Union pour l'Action morale, in the Bulletin de l'Union, April 1–15, 1894. See, also, Revue Bleue, August 13, 1892.

"We would make known in our own persons the usefulness of rule, of discipline, of resignation and renunciation; we would teach the necessary perpetuity of suffering, and explain the creative part which it plays. We would wage war upon false optimism; on the base hope of happiness coming to us ready made; on the notion of a salvation by knowledge alone, or by material civilization alone, vain symbol as this is of civilization, precarious external arrangement, ill-fitted to replace the intimate union and consent of souls. We would wage war also on bad morals, whether in public or in private life; on luxury, fastidiousness, and over-refinement; on all that tends to increase the painful, immoral, and anti-social multiplication of our wants; on all that excites envy and dislike in the soul of the common people, and confirms the notion that the chief end of life is freedom to enjoy. We would preach by our example the respect of superiors and equals, the respect of all men; affectionate simplicity in our relations with inferiors and insignificant persons; indulgence where our own claims only are concerned, but firmness in our demands where they relate to duties towards others or towards the public.

"For the common people are what we help them to become; their vices are our vices, gazed upon, envied, and imitated; and if they come back with all their weight upon us, it is but just.

"We forbid ourselves all seeking after popularity, all ambition to appear important. We pledge ourselves to abstain from falsehood, in all its degrees. We promise not to create or encourage illusions as to what is possible, by what we say or write. We promise to one another active sincerity, which strives to see truth clearly, and which never fears to declare what it sees.

"We promise deliberate resistance to the tidal waves of fashion, to the 'booms' and panics of the public mind, to all the forms of weakness and of fear.

"We forbid ourselves the use of sarcasm. Of serious things we will speak seriously and unsmilingly, without banter and without the appearance of banter;—and even so of all things, for there are serious ways of being light of heart.

"We will put ourselves forward always for what we are, simply and without false humility, as well as without pedantry, affectation, or pride."

These fundamental inner conditions have characteristic practical consequences, as follows: —

a. Asceticism. — The self-surrender may become so passionate as to turn into self-immolation. It may then so overrule the ordinary inhibitions of the flesh that the saint finds positive pleasure in sacrifice and asceticism, measuring and expressing as they do the degree of his loyalty to the higher power.

b. Strength of Soul. — The sense of enlargement of life may be so uplifting that personal motives and inhibitions, commonly omnipotent, become too insignificant for notice, and new reaches of patience and fortitude open out. Fears and anxieties go, and blissful equanimity takes their place. Come heaven, come hell, it makes no difference now!

c. Purity. — The shifting of the emotional centre brings with it, first, increase of purity. The sensitiveness to spiritual discords is enhanced, and the cleansing of existence from brutal and sensual elements becomes imperative. Occasions of contact with such elements are avoided: the saintly life must deepen its spiritual consistency and keep unspotted from the world. In some temperaments this need of purity of spirit takes an ascetic turn, and weaknesses of the flesh are treated with relentless severity.

d. Charity. — The shifting of the emotional centre brings, secondly, increase of charity, tenderness for fellow-creatures. The ordinary motives to antipathy, which usually set such close bounds to tenderness among human beings, are inhibited. The saint loves his enemies, and treats loathsome beggars as his brothers.

I now have to give some concrete illustrations of these fruits of the spiritual tree. The only difficulty is to choose, for they are so abundant.

Since the sense of Presence of a higher and friendly Power seems to be the fundamental feature in the spiritual life, I will begin with that.

In our narratives of conversion we saw how the world might look shining and transfigured to the convert,[1] and,

[1] Above, pp. 228 ff.

apart from anything acutely religious, we all have moments when the universal life seems to wrap us round with friendliness. In youth and health, in summer, in the woods or on the mountains, there come days when the weather seems all whispering with peace, hours when the goodness and beauty of existence enfold us like a dry warm climate, or chime through us as if our inner ears were subtly ringing with the world's security. Thoreau writes:—

> "Once, a few weeks after I came to the woods, for an hour I doubted whether the near neighborhood of man was not essential to a serene and healthy life. To be alone was somewhat unpleasant. But, in the midst of a gentle rain, while these thoughts prevailed, I was suddenly sensible of such sweet and beneficent society in Nature, in the very pattering of the drops, and in every sight and sound around my house, an infinite and unaccountable friendliness all at once, like an atmosphere, sustaining me, as made the fancied advantages of human neighborhood insignificant, and I have never thought of them since. Every little pine-needle expanded and swelled with sympathy and befriended me. I was so distinctly made aware of the presence of something kindred to me, that I thought no place could ever be strange to me again."[1]

In the Christian consciousness this sense of the enveloping friendliness becomes most personal and definite. "The compensation," writes a German author, "for the loss of that sense of personal independence which man so unwillingly gives up, is the disappearance of all *fear* from one's life, the quite indescribable and inexplicable feeling of an inner *security*, which one can only experience, but which, once it has been experienced, one can never forget."[2]

I find an excellent description of this state of mind in a sermon by Mr. Voysey:—

> "It is the experience of myriads of trustful souls, that this sense of God's unfailing presence with them in their going out and in their coming in, and by night and day, is a

[1] H. THOREAU: Walden, Riverside edition, p. 206, abridged.
[2] C. HILTY: Glück, vol. i. p. 85.

source of absolute repose and confident calmness. It drives away all fear of what may befall them. That nearness of God is a constant security against terror and anxiety. It is not that they are at all assured of physical safety, or deem themselves protected by a love which is denied to others, but that they are in a state of mind equally ready to be safe or to meet with injury. If injury befall them, they will be content to bear it because the Lord is their keeper, and nothing can befall them without his will. If it be his will, then injury is for them a blessing and no calamity at all. Thus and thus only is the trustful man protected and shielded from harm. And I for one—by no means a thick-skinned or hard-nerved man—am absolutely satisfied with this arrangement, and do not wish for any other kind of immunity from danger and catastrophe. Quite as sensitive to pain as the most highly strung organism, I yet feel that the worst of it is conquered, and the sting taken out of it altogether, by the thought that God is our loving and sleepless keeper, and that nothing can hurt us without his will."[1]

More excited expressions of this condition are abundant in religious literature. I could easily weary you with their monotony. Here is an account from Mrs. Jonathan Edwards:—

"Last night," Mrs. Edwards writes, "was the sweetest night I ever had in my life. I never before, for so long a time together, enjoyed so much of the light and rest and sweetness of heaven in my soul, but without the least agitation of body during the whole time. Part of the night I lay awake, sometimes asleep, and sometimes between sleeping and waking. But all night I continued in a constant, clear, and lively sense of the heavenly sweetness of Christ's excellent love, of his nearness to me, and of my dearness to him; with an inexpressibly sweet calmness of soul in an entire rest in him. I seemed to myself to perceive a glow of divine love come down from the heart of Christ in heaven into my heart in a constant stream, like a stream or pencil of sweet light. At the same time my heart and soul all

[1] The Mystery of Pain and Death, London, 1892, p. 258.

flowed out in love to Christ, so that there seemed to be a
constant flowing and reflowing of heavenly love, and I appeared to myself to float or swim, in these bright, sweet
beams, like the motes swimming in the beams of the sun,
or the streams of his light which come in at the window. I
think that what I felt each minute was worth more than all
the outward comfort and pleasure which I had enjoyed in
my whole life put together. It was pleasure, without the
least sting, or any interruption. It was a sweetness, which
my soul was lost in; it seemed to be all that my feeble frame
could sustain. There was but little difference, whether I was
asleep or awake, but if there was any difference, the sweetness was greatest while I was asleep.[1] As I awoke early the
next morning, it seemed to me that I had entirely done
with myself. I felt that the opinions of the world concerning me were nothing, and that I had no more to do with
any outward interest of my own than with that of a person
whom I never saw. The glory of God seemed to swallow
up every wish and desire of my heart. . . . After retiring
to rest and sleeping a little while, I awoke, and was led to
reflect on God's mercy to me, in giving me, for many years,
a willingness to die; and after that, in making me willing
to live, that I might do and suffer whatever he called me to
here. I also thought how God had graciously given me an
entire resignation to his will, with respect to the kind and
manner of death that I should die; having been made willing to die on the rack, or at the stake, and if it were God's
will, to die in darkness. But now it occurred to me, I used
to think of living no longer than to the ordinary age of
man. Upon this I was led to ask myself, whether I was not

[1] Compare Madame Guyon: "It was my practice to arise at midnight for
purposes of devotion. . . . It seemed to me that God came at the precise
time and woke me from sleep in order that I might enjoy him. When I was
out of health or greatly fatigued, he did not awake me, but at such times I
felt, even in my sleep, a singular possession of God. He loved me so much
that he seemed to pervade my being, at a time when I could be only imperfectly conscious of his presence. My sleep is sometimes broken,—a sort of
half sleep; but my soul seems to be awake enough to know God, when it is
hardly capable of knowing anything else." T. C. UPHAM: The Life and Religious Experiences of Madame de la Mothe Guyon, New York, 1877, vol. i.
p. 260.

willing to be kept out of heaven even longer; and my whole heart seemed immediately to reply: Yes, a thousand years, and a thousand in horror, if it be most for the honor of God, the torment of my body being so great, awful, and overwhelming that none could bear to live in the country where the spectacle was seen, and the torment of my mind being vastly greater. And it seemed to me that I found a perfect willingness, quietness, and alacrity of soul in consenting that it should be so, if it were most for the glory of God, so that there was no hesitation, doubt, or darkness in my mind. The glory of God seemed to overcome me and swallow me up, and every conceivable suffering, and everything that was terrible to my nature, seemed to shrink to nothing before it. This resignation continued in its clearness and brightness the rest of the night, and all the next day, and the night following, and on Monday in the forenoon, without interruption or abatement."[1]

The annals of Catholic saintship abound in records as ecstatic or more ecstatic than this. "Often the assaults of the divine love," it is said of the Sister Séraphique de la Martinière, "reduced her almost to the point of death. She used tenderly to complain of this to God. 'I cannot support it,' she used to say. 'Bear gently with my weakness, or I shall expire under the violence of your love.' "[2]

Let me pass next to the Charity and Brotherly Love which are a usual fruit of saintliness, and have always been reckoned essential theological virtues, however limited may have been the kinds of service which the particular theology enjoined. Brotherly love would follow logically from the assurance of God's friendly presence, the notion of our brotherhood as men being an immediate inference from that of God's fatherhood of us all. When Christ utters the precepts: "Love your enemies, bless them that curse you, do good to them that hate you, and pray for them which despitefully use you, and persecute you," he gives for a reason: "That ye may be the

[1] I have considerably abridged the words of the original, which is given in EDWARDS's Narrative of the Revival in New England.

[2] BOUGAUD: Hist. de la Bienheureuse Marguerite Marie, 1894, p. 125.

children of your Father which is in heaven: for he maketh his
sun to rise on the evil and on the good, and sendeth rain on
the just and on the unjust." One might therefore be tempted
to explain both the humility as to one's self and the charity
towards others which characterize spiritual excitement, as results of the all-leveling character of theistic belief. But these
affections are certainly not mere derivatives of theism. We find
them in Stoicism, in Hinduism, and in Buddhism in the highest possible degree. They *harmonize* with paternal theism
beautifully; but they harmonize with all reflection whatever
upon the dependence of mankind on general causes; and we
must, I think, consider them not subordinate but coördinate
parts of that great complex excitement in the study of which
we are engaged. Religious rapture, moral enthusiasm, ontological wonder, cosmic emotion, are all unifying states of
mind, in which the sand and grit of the selfhood incline to
disappear, and tenderness to rule. The best thing is to describe the condition integrally as a characteristic affection to
which our nature is liable, a region in which we find ourselves
at home, a sea in which we swim; but not to pretend to explain its parts by deriving them too cleverly from one another. Like love or fear, the faith-state is a natural psychic
complex, and carries charity with it by organic consequence.
Jubilation is an expansive affection, and all expansive affections are self-forgetful and kindly so long as they endure.

We find this the case even when they are pathological in
origin. In his instructive work, la Tristesse et la Joie,[1] M.
Georges Dumas compares together the melancholy and the
joyous phase of circular insanity, and shows that, while selfishness characterizes the one, the other is marked by altruistic
impulses. No human being so stingy and useless as was Marie
in her melancholy period! But the moment the happy period
begins, "sympathy and kindness become her characteristic
sentiments. She displays a universal goodwill, not only of intention, but in act. . . . She becomes solicitous of the health
of other patients, interested in getting them out, desirous to
procure wool to knit socks for some of them. Never since she
has been under my observation have I heard her in her joyous

[1] Paris, 1900.

period utter any but charitable opinions."[1] And later, Dr. Dumas says of all such joyous conditions that "unselfish sentiments and tender emotions are the only affective states to be found in them. The subject's mind is closed against envy, hatred, and vindictiveness, and wholly transformed into benevolence, indulgence, and mercy."[2]

There is thus an organic affinity between joyousness and tenderness, and their companionship in the saintly life need in no way occasion surprise. Along with the happiness, this increase of tenderness is often noted in narratives of conversion. "I began to work for others";—"I had more tender feeling for my family and friends";—"I spoke at once to a person with whom I had been angry";—"I felt for every one, and loved my friends better";—"I felt every one to be my friend";—these are so many expressions from the records collected by Professor Starbuck.[3]

"When," says Mrs. Edwards, continuing the narrative from which I made quotation a moment ago, "I arose on the morning of the Sabbath, I felt a love to all mankind, wholly peculiar in its strength and sweetness, far beyond all that I had ever felt before. The power of that love seemed inexpressible. I thought, if I were surrounded by enemies, who were venting their malice and cruelty upon me, in tormenting me, it would still be impossible that I should cherish any feelings towards them but those of love, and pity, and ardent desires for their happiness. I never before felt so far from a disposition to judge and censure others, as I did that morning. I realized also, in an unusual and very lively manner, how great a part of Christianity lies in the performance of our social and relative duties to one another. The same joyful sense continued throughout the day—a sweet love to God and all mankind."

Whatever be the explanation of the charity, it may efface all usual human barriers.[4]

[1] Page 130.
[2] Page 167.
[3] Op. cit., p. 127.
[4] The barrier between men and animals also. We read of Towianski, an eminent Polish patriot and mystic, that "one day one of his friends met him in the rain, caressing a big dog which was jumping upon him and covering

Here, for instance, is an example of Christian non-resistance from Richard Weaver's autobiography. Weaver was a collier, a semi-professional pugilist in his younger days, who became a much beloved evangelist. Fighting, after drinking, seems to have been the sin to which he originally felt his flesh most perversely inclined. After his first conversion he had a backsliding, which consisted in pounding a man who had insulted a girl. Feeling that, having once fallen, he might as well be hanged for a sheep as for a lamb, he got drunk and went and broke the jaw of another man who had lately challenged him to fight and taunted him with cowardice for refusing as a Christian man;—I mention these incidents to show how genuine a change of heart is implied in the later conduct which he describes as follows:—

"I went down the drift and found the boy crying because a fellow-workman was trying to take the wagon from him by force. I said to him:—

" 'Tom, you must n't take that wagon.'

"He swore at me, and called me a Methodist devil. I told him that God did not tell me to let him rob me. He cursed again, and said he would push the wagon over me.

" 'Well,' I said, 'let us see whether the devil and thee are stronger than the Lord and me.'

"And the Lord and I proving stronger than the devil and he, he had to get out of the way, or the wagon would have

---

him horribly with mud. On being asked why he permitted the animal thus to dirty his clothes, Towianski replied: 'This dog, whom I am now meeting for the first time, has shown a great fellow-feeling for me, and a great joy in my recognition and acceptance of his greetings. Were I to drive him off, I should wound his feelings and do him a moral injury. It would be an offense not only to him, but to all the spirits of the other world who are on the same level with him. The damage which he does to my coat is as nothing in comparison with the wrong which I should inflict upon him, in case I were to remain indifferent to the manifestations of his friendship. We ought,' he added, 'both to lighten the condition of animals, whenever we can, and at the same time to facilitate in ourselves that union of the world of all spirits, which the sacrifice of Christ has made possible.' " André Towianski, Traduction de l'Italien, Turin, 1897 (privately printed). I owe my knowledge of this book and of Towianski to my friend Professor W. Lutoslawski, author of 'Plato's Logic.'

gone over him. So I gave the wagon to the boy. Then said Tom:—

" 'I 've a good mind to smack thee on the face.'

" 'Well,' I said, 'if that will do thee any good, thou canst do it.' So he struck me on the face.

"I turned the other cheek to him, and said, 'Strike again.'

"He struck again and again, till he had struck me five times. I turned my cheek for the sixth stroke; but he turned away cursing. I shouted after him: 'The Lord forgive thee, for I do, and the Lord save thee.'

"This was on a Saturday; and when I went home from the coal-pit my wife saw my face was swollen, and asked what was the matter with it. I said: 'I 've been fighting, and I 've given a man a good thrashing.'

"She burst out weeping, and said, 'O Richard, what made you fight?' Then I told her all about it; and she thanked the Lord I had not struck back.

"But the Lord had struck, and his blows have more effect than man's. Monday came. The devil began to tempt me, saying: 'The other men will laugh at thee for allowing Tom to treat thee as he did on Saturday.' I cried, 'Get thee behind me, Satan;'—and went on my way to the coal-pit.

"Tom was the first man I saw. I said 'Good-morning,' but got no reply.

"He went down first. When I got down, I was surprised to see him sitting on the wagon-road waiting for me. When I came to him he burst into tears and said: 'Richard, will you forgive me for striking you?'

" 'I have forgiven thee,' said I; 'ask God to forgive thee. The Lord bless thee.' I gave him my hand, and we went each to his work."[1]

'Love your enemies!' Mark you, not simply those who happen not to be your friends, but your *enemies*, your positive and active enemies. Either this is a mere Oriental hyperbole, a bit of verbal extravagance, meaning only that we should, as far as we can, abate our animosities, or else it is sincere and literal. Outside of certain cases of intimate individual relation, it seldom has been taken literally. Yet it makes one ask the

[1] J. PATTERSON's Life of Richard Weaver, pp. 66–68, abridged.

question: Can there in general be a level of emotion so unifying, so obliterative of differences between man and man,
that even enmity may come to be an irrelevant circumstance
and fail to inhibit the friendlier interests aroused? If positive
well-wishing could attain so supreme a degree of excitement,
those who were swayed by it might well seem superhuman
beings. Their life would be morally discrete from the life of
other men, and there is no saying, in the absence of positive
experience of an authentic kind,—for there are few active
examples in our scriptures, and the Buddhistic examples are
legendary,[1]—what the effects might be: they might conceivably transform the world.

Psychologically and in principle, the precept 'Love your
enemies' is not self-contradictory. It is merely the extreme
limit of a kind of magnanimity with which, in the shape of
pitying tolerance of our oppressors, we are fairly familiar. Yet
if radically followed, it would involve such a breach with our
instinctive springs of action as a whole, and with the present
world's arrangements, that a critical point would practically
be passed, and we should be born into another kingdom of
being. Religious emotion makes us feel that other kingdom
to be close at hand, within our reach.

The inhibition of instinctive repugnance is proved not only
by the showing of love to enemies, but by the showing of it
to any one who is personally loathsome. In the annals of
saintliness we find a curious mixture of motives impelling in
this direction. Asceticism plays its part; and along with charity pure and simple, we find humility or the desire to disclaim
distinction and to grovel on the common level before God.
Certainly all three principles were at work when Francis of
Assisi and Ignatius Loyola exchanged their garments with
those of filthy beggars. All three are at work when religious
persons consecrate their lives to the care of leprosy or other
peculiarly unpleasant diseases. The nursing of the sick is a
function to which the religious seem strongly drawn, even
apart from the fact that church traditions set that way. But in
the annals of this sort of charity we find fantastic excesses of

---

[1] As where the future Buddha, incarnated as a hare, jumps into the fire to
cook himself for a meal for a beggar—having previously shaken himself three
times, so that none of the insects in his fur should perish with him.

devotion recorded which are only explicable by the frenzy of self-immolation simultaneously aroused. Francis of Assisi kisses his lepers; Margaret Mary Alacoque, Francis Xavier, St. John of God, and others are said to have cleansed the sores and ulcers of their patients with their respective tongues; and the lives of such saints as Elizabeth of Hungary and Madame de Chantal are full of a sort of reveling in hospital purulence, disagreeable to read of, and which makes us admire and shudder at the same time.

So much for the human love aroused by the faith-state. Let me next speak of the Equanimity, Resignation, Fortitude, and Patience which it brings.

'A paradise of inward tranquillity' seems to be faith's usual result; and it is easy, even without being religious one's self, to understand this. A moment back, in treating of the sense of God's presence, I spoke of the unaccountable feeling of safety which one may then have. And, indeed, how can it possibly fail to steady the nerves, to cool the fever, and appease the fret, if one be sensibly conscious that, no matter what one's difficulties for the moment may appear to be, one's life as a whole is in the keeping of a power whom one can absolutely trust? In deeply religious men the abandonment of self to this power is passionate. Whoever not only says, but *feels*, 'God's will be done,' is mailed against every weakness; and the whole historic array of martyrs, missionaries, and religious reformers is there to prove the tranquil-mindedness, under naturally agitating or distressing circumstances, which self-surrender brings.

The temper of the tranquil-mindedness differs, of course, according as the person is of a constitutionally sombre or of a constitutionally cheerful cast of mind. In the sombre it partakes more of resignation and submission; in the cheerful it is a joyous consent. As an example of the former temper, I quote part of a letter from Professor Lagneau, a venerated teacher of philosophy who lately died, a great invalid, at Paris:—

"My life, for the success of which you send good wishes, will be what it is able to be. I ask nothing from it, I expect nothing from it. For long years now I exist, think, and act, and am worth what I am worth, only through the despair which is my sole strength and my sole foundation. May it preserve for me, even in these last trials to which I am coming, the courage to do without the desire of deliverance. I ask nothing more from the Source whence all strength cometh, and if that is granted, your wishes will have been accomplished."[1]

There is something pathetic and fatalistic about this, but the power of such a tone as a protection against outward shocks is manifest. Pascal is another Frenchman of pessimistic natural temperament. He expresses still more amply the temper of self-surrendering submissiveness: —

"Deliver me, Lord," he writes in his prayers, "from the sadness at my proper suffering which self-love might give, but put into me a sadness like your own. Let my sufferings appease your choler. Make them an occasion for my conversion and salvation. I ask you neither for health nor for sickness, for life nor for death; but that you may dispose of my health and my sickness, my life and my death, for your glory, for my salvation, and for the use of the Church and of your saints, of whom I would by your grace be one. You alone know what is expedient for me; you are the sovereign master; do with me according to your will. Give to me, or take away from me, only conform my will to yours. I know but one thing, Lord, that it is good to follow you, and bad to offend you. Apart from that, I know not what is good or bad in anything. I know not which is most profitable to me, health or sickness, wealth or poverty, nor anything else in the world. That discernment is beyond the power of men or angels, and is hidden among the secrets of your Providence, which I adore, but do not seek to fathom."[2]

When we reach more optimistic temperaments, the resignation grows less passive. Examples are sown so broadcast throughout history that I might well pass on without citation. As it is, I snatch at the first that occurs to my mind. Madame

---

[1] Bulletin de l'Union pour l'Action Morale, September, 1894.
[2] B. PASCAL: Prières pour les Maladies, §§ xiii., xiv., abridged.

Guyon, a frail creature physically, was yet of a happy native disposition. She went through many perils with admirable serenity of soul. After being sent to prison for heresy,—

"Some of my friends," she writes, "wept bitterly at the hearing of it, but such was my state of acquiescence and resignation that it failed to draw any tears from me. . . . There appeared to be in me then, as I find it to be in me now, such an entire loss of what regards myself, that any of my own interests gave me little pain or pleasure; ever wanting to will or wish for myself only the very thing which God does." In another place she writes: "We all of us came near perishing in a river which we found it necessary to pass. The carriage sank in the quicksand. Others who were with us threw themselves out in excessive fright. But I found my thoughts so much taken up with God that I had no distinct sense of danger. It is true that the thought of being drowned passed across my mind, but it cost no other sensation or reflection in me than this—that I felt quite contented and willing it were so, if it were my heavenly Father's choice." Sailing from Nice to Genoa, a storm keeps her eleven days at sea. "As the irritated waves dashed round us," she writes, "I could not help experiencing a certain degree of satisfaction in my mind. I pleased myself with thinking that those mutinous billows, under the command of Him who does all things rightly, might probably furnish me with a watery grave. Perhaps I carried the point too far, in the pleasure which I took in thus seeing myself beaten and bandied by the swelling waters. Those who were with me took notice of my intrepidity."[1]

The contempt of danger which religious enthusiasm produces may be even more buoyant still. I take an example from that charming recent autobiography, "With Christ at Sea," by Frank Bullen. A couple of days after he went through the conversion on shipboard of which he there gives an account,—

"It was blowing stiffly," he writes, "and we were carrying

[1] From THOMAS C. UPHAM's Life and Religious Opinions and Experiences of Madame de la Mothe Guyon, New York, 1877, ii. 48, i. 141, 413, abridged.

a press of canvas to get north out of the bad weather. Shortly after four bells we hauled down the flying-jib, and I sprang out astride the boom to furl it. I was sitting astride the boom when suddenly it gave way with me. The sail slipped through my fingers, and I fell backwards, hanging head downwards over the seething tumult of shining foam under the ship's bows, suspended by one foot. But I felt only high exultation in my certainty of eternal life. Although death was divided from me by a hair's breadth, and I was acutely conscious of the fact, it gave me no sensation but joy. I suppose I could have hung there no longer than five seconds, but in that time I lived a whole age of delight. But my body asserted itself, and with a desperate gymnastic effort I regained the boom. How I furled the sail I don't know, but I sang at the utmost pitch of my voice praises to God that went pealing out over the dark waste of waters."[1]

The annals of martyrdom are of course the signal field of triumph for religious imperturbability. Let me cite as an example the statement of a humble sufferer, persecuted as a Huguenot under Louis XIV.:—

"They shut all the doors," Blanche Gamond writes, "and I saw six women, each with a bunch of willow rods as thick as the hand could hold, and a yard long. He gave me the order, 'Undress yourself,' which I did. He said, 'You are leaving on your shift; you must take it off.' They had so little patience that they took it off themselves, and I was naked from the waist up. They brought a cord with which they tied me to a beam in the kitchen. They drew the cord tight with all their strength and asked me, 'Does it hurt you?' and then they discharged their fury upon me, exclaiming as they struck me, 'Pray now to your God.' It was the Roulette woman who held this language. But at this moment I received the greatest consolation that I can ever receive in my life, since I had the honor of being whipped for the name of Christ, and in addition of being crowned with his mercy and his consolations. Why can I not write down the inconceivable influences, consolations, and peace

[1] Op. cit., London, 1901, p. 130.

which I felt interiorly? To understand them one must have passed by the same trial; they were so great that I was ravished, for there where afflictions abound grace is given superabundantly. In vain the women cried, 'We must double our blows; she does not feel them, for she neither speaks nor cries.' And how should I have cried, since I was swooning with happiness within?"[1]

The transition from tenseness, self-responsibility, and worry, to equanimity, receptivity, and peace, is the most wonderful of all those shiftings of inner equilibrium, those changes of the personal centre of energy, which I have analyzed so often; and the chief wonder of it is that it so often comes about, not by doing, but by simply relaxing and throwing the burden down. This abandonment of self-responsibility seems to be the fundamental act in specifically religious, as distinguished from moral practice. It antedates theologies and is independent of philosophies. Mind-cure, theosophy, stoicism, ordinary neurological hygiene, insist on it as emphatically as Christianity does, and it is capable of entering into closest marriage with every speculative creed.[2] Christians who have it strongly live in what is called 'recollection,' and are never anxious about the future, nor worry over the outcome of the day. Of Saint Catharine of Genoa it is said that "she took cognizance of things, only as they were presented to her in succession, *moment by moment*." To her holy soul, "the divine moment was the present moment, . . . and when the present moment was estimated in itself and in its relations, and when the duty that was involved in it was accomplished, it was permitted to pass away as if it had never been, and to give way to the facts and duties of the moment which came after."[3] Hinduism, mind-cure, and theosophy all lay great emphasis upon this concentration of the consciousness upon the moment at hand.

[1] Claparède et Goty: Deux Héroines de la Foi, Paris, 1880, p. 112.

[2] Compare these three different statements of it: A. P. Call: As a Matter of Course, Boston, 1894; H. W. Dresser: Living by the Spirit, New York and London, 1900; H. W. Smith: The Christian's Secret of a Happy Life, published by the Willard Tract Repository, and now in thousands of hands.

[3] T. C. Upham: Life of Madame Catharine Adorna, 3d ed., New York, 1864, pp. 158, 172–174.

The next religious symptom which I will note is what I have called Purity of Life. The saintly person becomes exceedingly sensitive to inner inconsistency or discord, and mixture and confusion grow intolerable. All the mind's objects and occupations must be ordered with reference to the special spiritual excitement which is now its keynote. Whatever is unspiritual taints the pure water of the soul and is repugnant. Mixed with this exaltation of the moral sensibilities there is also an ardor of sacrifice, for the beloved deity's sake, of everything unworthy of him. Sometimes the spiritual ardor is so sovereign that purity is achieved at a stroke—we have seen examples. Usually it is a more gradual conquest. Billy Bray's account of his abandonment of tobacco is a good example of the latter form of achievement.

"I had been a smoker as well as a drunkard, and I used to love my tobacco as much as I loved my meat, and I would rather go down into the mine without my dinner than without my pipe. In the days of old, the Lord spoke by the mouths of his servants, the prophets; now he speaks to us by the spirit of his Son. I had not only the feeling part of religion, but I could hear the small, still voice within speaking to me. When I took the pipe to smoke, it would be applied within, 'It is an idol, a lust; worship the Lord with clean lips.' So, I felt it was not right to smoke. The Lord also sent a woman to convince me. I was one day in a house, and I took out my pipe to light it at the fire, and Mary Hawke—for that was the woman's name—said, 'Do you not feel it is wrong to smoke?' I said that I felt something inside telling me that it was an idol, a lust, and she said that was the Lord. Then I said, 'Now, I must give it up, for the Lord is telling me of it inside, and the woman outside, so the tobacco must go, love it as I may.' There and then I took the tobacco out of my pocket, and threw it into the fire, and put the pipe under my foot, 'ashes to ashes, dust to dust.' And I have not smoked since. I found it hard to break off old habits, but I cried to the Lord for help, and he gave me strength, for he has said, 'Call upon me in the day of trouble, and I will deliver thee.' The day after I gave up smoking I had the toothache so bad that I did not know what to do. I thought this was owing to giving up the pipe, but I said I would never smoke again, if I lost every tooth in my head. I said, 'Lord, thou hast told us My yoke is easy and my burden is light,' and when I said that, all the pain left me. Sometimes the thought of the pipe would come back to me very strong; but the Lord strengthened me against the habit, and, bless his name, I have not smoked since."

Bray's biographer writes that after he had given up smoking, he thought that he would chew a little, but he conquered this dirty habit, too. "On one occasion," Bray said, "when at a prayer-meeting at Hicks Mill, I heard the Lord say to me, 'Worship me with clean lips.' So, when we got up from our knees, I took the quid out of my mouth and 'whipped 'en' [threw it] under the form. But, when we got on our knees again, I put another quid into my mouth. Then the Lord said to me again, 'Worship me with clean lips.' So I took the quid out of my mouth, and whipped 'en under the form again, and said, 'Yes, Lord, I will.' From that time I gave up chewing as well as smoking, and have been a free man."

The ascetic forms which the impulse for veracity and purity of life may take are often pathetic enough. The early Quakers, for example, had hard battles to wage against the worldliness and insincerity of the ecclesiastical Christianity of their time. Yet the battle that cost them most wounds was probably that which they fought in defense of their own right to social veracity and sincerity in their thee-ing and thou-ing, in not doffing the hat or giving titles of respect. It was laid on George Fox that these conventional customs were a lie and a sham, and the whole body of his followers thereupon renounced them, as a sacrifice to truth, and so that their acts and the spirit they professed might be more in accord.

"When the Lord sent me into the world," says Fox in his Journal, "he forbade me to put off my hat to any, high or low: and I was required to 'thee' and 'thou' all men and women, without any respect to rich or poor, great or small. And as I traveled up and down, I was not to bid people Good-morning, or Good-evening, neither might I bow or scrape with my leg to any one. This made the sects and professions rage. Oh! the rage that was in the priests, magistrates, professors, and people of all sorts: and especially in priests and professors: for though 'thou' to a single person was according to their accidence and grammar rules, and according to the Bible, yet they could not bear to hear it: and because I could not put off my hat to them, it set them all into a rage. . . . Oh! the scorn, heat, and fury that arose! Oh! the blows, punchings, beatings, and imprisonments that we underwent for not putting off our hats to men! Some had their hats violently plucked off and thrown away, so that they quite lost them. The bad language and evil usage we received on this account is hard to be expressed, besides the danger we were sometimes in of losing our lives for this matter, and that by the great professors of Christianity, who thereby discovered they were not true believers. And though it was but a small thing in the eye of man, yet a wonderful confusion it brought among all professors and priests: but, blessed be the Lord, many came to see the vanity of that custom of putting off hats to men, and felt the weight of Truth's testimony against it."

In the autobiography of Thomas Elwood, an early Quaker, who at one time was secretary to John Milton, we find an exquisitely quaint and candid account of the trials he underwent both at home and abroad, in following Fox's canons of sincerity. The anecdotes are too lengthy for citation; but Elwood sets down his manner of feeling about these things in a shorter passage, which I will quote as a characteristic utterance of spiritual sensibility:—

"By this divine light, then," says Elwood, "I saw that though I had not the evil of the common uncleanliness, debauchery, profaneness, and pollutions of the world to put away, because I had, through the great goodness of God and a civil education, been preserved out of those grosser evils, yet I had many other evils to put away and to cease from; some of which were not by the world, which lies in wickedness (1 John v. 19), accounted evils, but by the light of Christ were made manifest to me to be evils, and as such condemned in me.

"As particularly those fruits and effects of pride that discover themselves in the vanity and superfluity of apparel; which I took too much delight in. This evil of my doings I was required to put away and cease from; and judgment lay upon me till I did so.

"I took off from my apparel those unnecessary trimmings of lace, ribbons, and useless buttons, which had no real service, but were set on only for that which was by mistake called ornament; and I ceased to wear rings.

"Again, the giving of flattering titles to men between whom and me there was not any relation to which such titles could be pretended to belong. This was an evil I had been much addicted to, and was accounted a ready artist in; therefore this evil also was I required to put away and cease from. So that thenceforward I durst not say, Sir, Master, My Lord, Madam (or My Dame); or say Your Servant to any one to whom I did not stand in the real relation of a servant, which I had never done to any.

"Again, respect of persons, in uncovering the head and bowing the knee or body in salutation, was a practice I had been much in the use of; and this, being one of the vain customs of the world, introduced by the spirit of the world, instead of the true honor which this is a false representation of, and used in deceit as a token of respect by persons one to another, who bear no real respect one to another; and besides this, being a type and a proper emblem of that divine honor which all ought to pay to Almighty God, and which all of all sorts, who take upon them the Christian name, appear in when they offer their prayers to him, and therefore should not be given to men;—I found this to be one of those evils which I had been too long doing; therefore I was now required to put it away and cease from it.

"Again, the corrupt and unsound form of speaking in the plural number to a single person, *you* to one, instead of *thou*, contrary to the pure, plain, and single language of truth, *thou* to one, and *you* to more than one, which had always been used by God to men, and men to God, as well as one to another, from the oldest record of time till corrupt men, for corrupt ends, in later and corrupt times, to flatter, fawn, and work upon the corrupt nature in men, brought in that false and senseless way of speaking *you* to one, which has since corrupted the modern languages, and hath greatly debased the spirits and depraved the manners of men;—this evil custom I had been as forward in as others, and this I was now called out of and required to cease from.

"These and many more evil customs which had sprung up in the night of darkness and general apostasy from the truth and true religion were now, by the inshining of this pure ray of divine light in my conscience, gradually discovered to me to be what I ought to cease from, shun, and stand a witness against."[1]

These early Quakers were Puritans indeed. The slightest inconsistency between profession and deed jarred some of them to active protest. John Woolman writes in his diary:—

"In these journeys I have been where much cloth hath been dyed; and have at sundry times walked over ground where much of their dyestuffs has drained away. This hath produced a longing in my mind that people might come into cleanness of spirit, cleanness of person, and cleanness about their houses and garments. Dyes being invented partly to please the eye, and partly to hide dirt, I have felt in this weak state, when traveling in dirtiness, and affected with unwholesome scents, a strong desire that the nature of dyeing cloth to hide dirt may be more fully considered.

"Washing our garments to keep them sweet is cleanly, but it is the opposite to real cleanliness to hide dirt in them. Through giving way to hiding dirt in our garments a spirit which would conceal that which is disagreeable is strengthened. Real cleanliness becometh a holy people; but hiding that which is not clean by coloring our garments seems contrary to the sweetness of sincerity. Through some sorts of dyes cloth is rendered less useful. And if the value of dyestuffs, and expense of dyeing, and the damage done to cloth, were all added together, and that cost applied to keeping all sweet and clean, how much more would real cleanliness prevail.

[1] The History of THOMAS ELWOOD, written by Himself, London, 1885, pp. 32–34.

"Thinking often on these things, the use of hats and garments dyed with a dye hurtful to them, and wearing more clothes in summer than are useful, grew more uneasy to me; believing them to be customs which have not their foundation in pure wisdom. The apprehension of being singular from my beloved friends was a strait upon me; and thus I continued in the use of some things, contrary to my judgment, about nine months. Then I thought of getting a hat the natural color of the fur, but the apprehension of being looked upon as one affecting singularity felt uneasy to me. On this account I was under close exercise of mind in the time of our general spring meeting in 1762, greatly desiring to be rightly directed; when, being deeply bowed in spirit before the Lord, I was made willing to submit to what I apprehended was required of me; and when I returned home, got a hat of the natural color of the fur.

"In attending meetings, this singularity was a trial to me, and more especially at this time, as white hats were used by some who were fond of following the changeable modes of dress, and as some friends, who knew not from what motives I wore it, grew shy of me, I felt my way for a time shut up in the exercise of the ministry. Some friends were apprehensive that my wearing such a hat savored of an affected singularity: those who spoke with me in a friendly way, I generally informed in a few words, that I believed my wearing it was not in my own will."

When the craving for moral consistency and purity is developed to this degree, the subject may well find the outer world too full of shocks to dwell in, and can unify his life and keep his soul unspotted only by withdrawing from it. That law which impels the artist to achieve harmony in his composition by simply dropping out whatever jars, or suggests a discord, rules also in the spiritual life. To omit, says Stevenson, is the one art in literature: "If I knew how to omit, I should ask no other knowledge." And life, when full of disorder and slackness and vague superfluity, can no more have what we call character than literature can have it under similar conditions. So monasteries and communities of sympathetic devotees open their doors, and in their changeless order, characterized by omissions quite as much as constituted of actions, the holy-minded person finds that inner smoothness and cleanness which it is torture to him to feel violated at every turn by the discordancy and brutality of secular existence.

That the scrupulosity of purity may be carried to a fantastic extreme must be admitted. In this it resembles Asceticism, to which further symptom of saintliness we had better turn next. The adjective 'ascetic' is applied to conduct originating on diverse psychological levels, which I might as well begin by distinguishing from one another.

1. Asceticism may be a mere expression of organic hardihood, disgusted with too much ease.

2. Temperance in meat and drink, simplicity of apparel, chastity, and non-pampering of the body generally, may be fruits of the love of purity, shocked by whatever savors of the sensual.

3. They may also be fruits of love, that is, they may appeal to the subject in the light of sacrifices which he is happy in making to the Deity whom he acknowledges.

4. Again, ascetic mortifications and torments may be due to pessimistic feelings about the self, combined with theological beliefs concerning expiation. The devotee may feel that he is buying himself free, or escaping worse sufferings hereafter, by doing penance now.

5. In psychopathic persons, mortifications may be entered on irrationally, by a sort of obsession or fixed idea which comes as a challenge and must be worked off, because only thus does the subject get his interior consciousness feeling right again.

6. Finally, ascetic exercises may in rarer instances be prompted by genuine perversions of the bodily sensibility, in consequence of which normally pain-giving stimuli are actually felt as pleasures.

I will try to give an instance under each of these heads in turn; but it is not easy to get them pure, for in cases pronounced enough to be immediately classed as ascetic, several of the assigned motives usually work together. Moreover, before citing any examples at all, I must invite you to some general psychological considerations which apply to all of them alike.

A strange moral transformation has within the past century swept over our Western world. We no longer think that we are called on to face physical pain with equanimity. It is not expected of a man that he should either endure it or inflict much of it, and to listen to the recital of cases of it makes our flesh creep morally as well as physically. The way in which our ancestors looked upon pain as an eternal ingredient of the world's order, and both caused and suffered it as a matter-of-course portion of their day's work, fills us with amazement. We wonder that any human beings could have been so callous. The result of this historic alteration is that even in the Mother Church herself, where ascetic discipline has such a fixed traditional prestige as a factor of merit, it has largely come into desuetude, if not discredit. A believer who flagellates or 'macerates' himself to-day arouses more wonder and fear than emulation. Many Catholic writers who admit that the times have changed in this respect do so resignedly; and even add that perhaps it is as well not to waste feelings in regretting the matter, for to return to the heroic corporeal discipline of ancient days might be an extravagance.

Where to seek the easy and the pleasant seems instinctive— and instinctive it appears to be in man; any deliberate tendency to pursue the hard and painful as such and for their own sakes might well strike one as purely abnormal. Nevertheless, in moderate degrees it is natural and even usual to human nature to court the arduous. It is only the extreme manifestations of the tendency that can be regarded as a paradox.

The psychological reasons for this lie near the surface. When we drop abstractions and take what we call our will in the act, we see that it is a very complex function. It involves both stimulations and inhibitions; it follows generalized habits; it is escorted by reflective criticisms; and it leaves a good or a bad taste of itself behind, according to the manner of the performance. The result is that, quite apart from the immediate pleasure which any sensible experience may give us, our own general moral attitude in procuring or undergoing the experience brings with it a secondary satisfaction or distaste. Some men and women, indeed, there are who can live on smiles and the word 'yes' forever. But for others (indeed for most), this is too tepid and relaxed a moral climate. Passive happiness is slack and insipid, and soon grows mawkish and intolerable. Some austerity and wintry negativity, some roughness, danger, stringency, and effort, some 'no! no!' must be mixed in, to produce the sense of an existence with character and texture and power. The range of individual differences in this respect is enormous; but whatever the mixture of yeses and noes may be, the person is infallibly aware when he has struck it in the right proportion *for him*. This, he feels, is my proper vocation, this is the *optimum*, the law, the life for me to live. Here I find the degree of equilibrium, safety, calm, and leisure which I need, or here I find the challenge, passion, fight, and hardship without which my soul's energy expires.

Every individual soul, in short, like every individual machine or organism, has its own best conditions of efficiency. A given machine will run best under a certain steam-pressure, a certain amperage; an organism under a certain diet, weight, or exercise. You seem to do best, I heard a doctor say to a patient, at about 140 millimeters of arterial tension. And it is just so with our sundry souls: some are happiest in calm weather; some need the sense of tension, of strong volition, to make them feel alive and well. For these latter souls, whatever is gained from day to day must be paid for by sacrifice and inhibition, or else it comes too cheap and has no zest.

Now when characters of this latter sort become religious, they are apt to turn the edge of their need of effort and negativity against their natural self; and the ascetic life gets evolved as a consequence.

When Professor Tyndall in one of his lectures tells us that Thomas Carlyle put him into his bath-tub every morning of a freezing Berlin winter, he proclaimed one of the lowest grades of asceticism. Even without Carlyle, most of us find it necessary to our soul's health to start the day with a rather cool immersion. A little farther along the scale we get such statements as this, from one of my correspondents, an agnostic: —

"Often at night in my warm bed I would feel ashamed to depend so on the warmth, and whenever the thought would come over me I would have to get up, no matter what time of night it was, and stand for a minute in the cold, just so as to prove my manhood."

Such cases as these belong simply to our head 1. In the next case we probably have a mixture of heads 2 and 3—the asceticism becomes far more systematic and pronounced. The writer is a Protestant, whose sense of moral energy could doubtless be gratified on no lower terms, and I take his case from Starbuck's manuscript collection.

"I practiced fasting and mortification of the flesh. I secretly made burlap shirts, and put the burrs next the skin, and wore pebbles in my shoes. I would spend nights flat on my back on the floor without any covering."

The Roman Church has organized and codified all this sort of thing, and given it a market-value in the shape of 'merit.' But we see the cultivation of hardship cropping out under every sky and in every faith, as a spontaneous need of character. Thus we read of Channing, when first settled as a Unitarian minister, that—

"He was now more simple than ever, and seemed to have become incapable of any form of self-indulgence. He took the smallest room in the house for his study, though he might easily have commanded one more light, airy, and in every way more suitable; and chose for his sleeping chamber an attic which he shared with a younger brother. The furniture of the latter might have answered for the cell of an anchorite, and consisted of a hard mattress on a cot-bedstead, plain wooden chairs and table, with matting on the floor. It was without fire, and to cold he was throughout life extremely sensitive; but he never complained or appeared in any way to be conscious of inconvenience. 'I recollect,' says his brother, 'after one most severe night, that in the morning he sportively thus alluded to his suffering: "If my bed were my country, I should be somewhat like Bonaparte: I have no control except over the part which I occupy; the instant I move, frost takes possession."' In sickness only would he change for the time his apartment and accept a few comforts. The dress too that he habitually adopted was of most inferior quality; and garments were constantly worn which the world would call mean, though an almost feminine neatness preserved him from the least appearance of neglect."[1]

Channing's asceticism, such as it was, was evidently a compound of hardihood and love of purity. The democracy which is an offshoot of the enthusiasm of humanity, and of which I will speak later under the head of the cult of poverty, doubtless bore also a share. Certainly there was no pessimistic element in his case. In the next case we have a strongly pessimistic element, so that it belongs under head 4. John Cennick was Methodism's first lay preacher. In 1735 he was convicted of sin, while walking in Cheapside, —

"And at once left off song-singing, card-playing, and attending theatres. Sometimes he wished to go to a popish monastery, to spend his life in devout retirement. At other times he longed to live in a cave, sleeping on fallen leaves, and feeding on forest fruits. He fasted long and often, and prayed nine times a day. . . . Fancying dry bread too great an indulgence for so great a sinner as himself, he began to feed on potatoes, acorns, crabs, and grass; and often wished that he could live on roots and herbs. At length, in 1737, he found peace with God, and went on his way rejoicing."[2]

In this poor man we have morbid melancholy and fear, and the sacrifices made are to purge out sin, and to buy safety. The hopelessness of Christian theology in respect of the flesh and the natural man generally has, in systematizing fear, made of it one tremendous incentive to self-mortification. It would be quite unfair, however, in spite of the fact that this incentive has often been worked in a mercenary way for hortatory purposes, to call it a mercenary incentive. The impulse to expiate and do penance is, in its first intention, far too immediate and spontaneous an expression of self-despair and

[1] Memoirs of W. E. Channing, Boston, 1840, i. 196.
[2] L. TYERMAN: The Life and Times of the Rev. John Wesley, i. 274.

anxiety to be obnoxious to any such reproach. In the form of loving sacrifice, of spending all we have to show our devotion, ascetic discipline of the severest sort may be the fruit of highly optimistic religious feeling.

M. Vianney, the curé of Ars, was a French country priest, whose holiness was exemplary. We read in his life the following account of his inner need of sacrifice:—

" 'On this path,' M. Vianney said, 'it is only the first step that costs. There is in mortification a balm and a savor without which one cannot live when once one has made their acquaintance. There is but one way in which to give one's self to God,—that is, to give one's self entirely, and to keep nothing for one's self. The little that one keeps is only good to trouble one and make one suffer.' Accordingly he imposed it on himself that he should never smell a flower, never drink when parched with thirst, never drive away a fly, never show disgust before a repugnant object, never complain of anything that had to do with his personal comfort, never sit down, never lean upon his elbows when he was kneeling. The Curé of Ars was very sensitive to cold, but he would never take means to protect himself against it. During a very severe winter, one of his missionaries contrived a false floor to his confessional and placed a metal case of hot water beneath. The trick succeeded, and the Saint was deceived: 'God is very good,' he said with emotion. 'This year, through all the cold, my feet have always been warm.' "[1]

In this case the spontaneous impulse to make sacrifices for the pure love of God was probably the uppermost conscious motive. We may class it, then, under our head 3. Some authors think that the impulse to sacrifice is the main religious phenomenon. It is a prominent, a universal phenomenon certainly, and lies deeper than any special creed. Here, for instance, is what seems to be a spontaneous example of it, simply expressing what seemed right at the time between the individual and his Maker. Cotton Mather, the New England Puritan divine, is generally reputed a rather grotesque pedant;

[1] A. MONNIN: Le Curé d'Ars, Vie de M. J. B. M. Vianney, 1864, p. 545, abridged.

yet what is more touchingly simple than his relation of what happened when his wife came to die?

"When I saw to what a point of resignation I was now called of the Lord," he says, "I resolved, with his help, therein to glorify him. So, two hours before my lovely consort expired, I kneeled by her bedside, and I took into my two hands a dear hand, the dearest in the world. With her thus in my hands, I solemnly and sincerely gave her up unto the Lord: and in token of my real *Resignation*, I gently put her out of my hands, and laid away a most lovely hand, resolving that I would never touch it more. This was the hardest, and perhaps the bravest action that ever I did. She . . . told me that she signed and sealed my act of resignation. And though before that she called for me continually, she after this never asked for me any more."[1]

Father Vianney's asceticism taken in its totality was simply the result of a permanent flood of high spiritual enthusiasm, longing to make proof of itself. The Roman Church has, in its incomparable fashion, collected all the motives towards asceticism together, and so codified them that any one wishing to pursue Christian perfection may find a practical system mapped out for him in any one of a number of ready-made manuals.[2] The dominant Church notion of perfection is of course the negative one of avoidance of sin. Sin proceeds from concupiscence, and concupiscence from our carnal passions and temptations, chief of which are pride, sensuality in all its forms, and the loves of worldly excitement and possession. All these sources of sin must be resisted; and discipline and austerities are a most efficacious mode of meeting them. Hence there are always in these books chapters on self-mortification. But whenever a procedure is codified, the more delicate spirit of it evaporates, and if we wish the undiluted ascetic spirit,—the passion of self-contempt wreaking itself on the poor flesh, the divine irrationality of devotion making

[1] B. WENDELL: Cotton Mather, New York, no date, p. 198.
[2] That of the earlier Jesuit, RODRIGUEZ, which has been translated into all languages, is one of the best known. A convenient modern manual, very well put together, is L'Ascétique Chrétienne, by M. J. RIBET, Paris, Poussielgue, nouvelle édition, 1898.

a sacrificial gift of all it has (its sensibilities, namely) to the object of its adoration,—we must go to autobiographies, or other individual documents.

Saint John of the Cross, a Spanish mystic who flourished—or rather who existed, for there was little that suggested flourishing about him—in the sixteenth century, will supply a passage suitable for our purpose.

"First of all, carefully excite in yourself an habitual affectionate will in all things to imitate Jesus Christ. If anything agreeable offers itself to your senses, yet does not at the same time tend purely to the honor and glory of God, renounce it and separate yourself from it for the love of Christ, who all his life long had no other taste or wish than to do the will of his Father whom he called his meat and nourishment. For example, you take satisfaction in *hearing* of things in which the glory of God bears no part. Deny yourself this satisfaction, mortify your wish to listen. You take pleasure in *seeing* objects which do not raise your mind to God: refuse yourself this pleasure, and turn away your eyes. The same with conversations and all other things. Act similarly, so far as you are able, with all the operations of the senses, striving to make yourself free from their yokes.

"The radical remedy lies in the mortification of the four great natural passions, joy, hope, fear, and grief. You must seek to deprive these of every satisfaction and leave them as it were in darkness and the void. Let your soul therefore turn always:

"Not to what is most easy, but to what is hardest;

"Not to what tastes best, but to what is most distasteful;

"Not to what most pleases, but to what disgusts;

"Not to matter of consolation, but to matter for desolation rather;

"Not to rest, but to labor;

"Not to desire the more, but the less;

"Not to aspire to what is highest and most precious, but to what is lowest and most contemptible;

"Not to will anything, but to will nothing;

"Not to seek the best in everything, but to seek the worst, so that you may enter for the love of Christ into a complete destitution, a perfect poverty of spirit, and an absolute renunciation of everything in this world.

"Embrace these practices with all the energy of your soul and you will find in a short time great delights and unspeakable consolations.

"Despise yourself, and wish that others should despise you.

"Speak to your own disadvantage, and desire others to do the same;

"Conceive a low opinion of yourself, and find it good when others hold the same;

"To enjoy the taste of all things, have no taste for anything.

"To know all things, learn to know nothing.

"To possess all things, resolve to possess nothing.

"To be all things, be willing to be nothing.

"To get to where you have no taste for anything, go through whatever experiences you have no taste for.

"To learn to know nothing, go whither you are ignorant.

"To reach what you possess not, go whithersoever you own nothing.

"To be what you are not, experience what you are not."

These later verses play with that vertigo of self-contradiction which is so dear to mysticism. Those that come next are completely mystical, for in them Saint John passes from God to the more metaphysical notion of the All.

"When you stop at one thing, you cease to open yourself to the All.

"For to come to the All you must give up the All.

"And if you should attain to owning the All, you must own it, desiring Nothing.

"In this spoliation, the soul finds its tranquillity and rest. Profoundly established in the centre of its own nothingness, it can be assailed by naught that comes from below; and since it no longer desires anything, what comes from above cannot depress it; for its desires alone are the causes of its woes."[1]

[1] SAINT JEAN DE LA CROIX, Vie et Œuvres, Paris, 1893, ii. 94, 99, abridged.

And now, as a more concrete example of heads 4 and 5, in fact of all our heads together, and of the irrational extreme to which a psychopathic individual may go in the line of bodily austerity, I will quote the sincere Suso's account of his own self-tortures. Suso, you will remember, was one of the fourteenth century German mystics; his autobiography, written in the third person, is a classic religious document.

"He was in his youth of a temperament full of fire and life; and when this began to make itself felt, it was very grievous to him; and he sought by many devices how he might bring his body into subjection. He wore for a long time a hair shirt and an iron chain, until the blood ran from him, so that he was obliged to leave them off. He secretly caused an undergarment to be made for him; and in the undergarment he had strips of leather fixed, into which a hundred and fifty brass nails, pointed and filed sharp, were driven, and the points of the nails were always turned towards the flesh. He had this garment made very tight, and so arranged as to go round him and fasten in front, in order that it might fit the closer to his body, and the pointed nails might be driven into his flesh; and it was high enough to reach upwards to his navel. In this he used to sleep at night. Now in summer, when it was hot, and he was very tired and ill from his journeyings, or when he held the office of lecturer, he would sometimes, as he lay thus in bonds, and oppressed with toil, and tormented also by noxious insects, cry aloud and give way to fretfulness, and twist round and round in agony, as a worm does when run through with a pointed needle. It often seemed to him as if he were lying upon an ant-hill, from the torture caused by the insects; for if he wished to sleep, or when he had fallen asleep, they vied with one another.[1] Sometimes he cried to Almighty God in the fullness of his heart: Alas!

[1] 'Insects,' i. e. lice, were an unfailing token of mediæval sainthood. We read of Francis of Assisi's sheepskin that "often a companion of the saint would take it to the fire to clean and *dispediculate* it, doing so, as he said, because the seraphic father himself was no enemy of *pidocchi*, but on the contrary kept them on him (le portava adosso), and held it for an honor and a glory to wear these celestial pearls in his habit." Quoted by P. SABATIER: Speculum Perfectionis, etc., Paris, 1898, p. 231, note.

Gentle God, what a dying is this! When a man is killed by murderers or strong beasts of prey it is soon over; but I lie dying here under the cruel insects, and yet cannot die. The nights in winter were never so long, nor was the summer so hot, as to make him leave off this exercise. On the contrary, he devised something farther—two leathern loops into which he put his hands, and fastened one on each side his throat, and made the fastenings so secure that even if his cell had been on fire about him, he could not have helped himself. This he continued until his hands and arms had become almost tremulous with the strain, and then he devised something else: two leather gloves; and he caused a brazier to fit them all over with sharp-pointed brass tacks, and he used to put them on at night, in order that if he should try while asleep to throw off the hair undergarment, or relieve himself from the gnawings of the vile insects, the tacks might then stick into his body. And so it came to pass. If ever he sought to help himself with his hands in his sleep, he drove the sharp tacks into his breast, and tore himself, so that his flesh festered. When after many weeks the wounds had healed, he tore himself again and made fresh wounds.

"He continued this tormenting exercise for about sixteen years. At the end of this time, when his blood was now chilled, and the fire of his temperament destroyed, there appeared to him in a vision on Whitsunday, a messenger from heaven, who told him that God required this of him no longer. Whereupon he discontinued it, and threw all these things away into a running stream."

Suso then tells how, to emulate the sorrows of his crucified Lord, he made himself a cross with thirty protruding iron needles and nails. This he bore on his bare back between his shoulders day and night. "The first time that he stretched out this cross upon his back his tender frame was struck with terror at it, and he blunted the sharp nails slightly against a stone. But soon, repenting of this womanly cowardice, he pointed them all again with a file, and placed once more the cross upon him. It made his back, where the bones are, bloody and seared. Whenever he sat down or stood up, it was as if a hedgehog-skin were on him. If any one touched him unawares, or pushed against his clothes, it tore him."

Suso next tells of his penitences by means of striking this cross and forcing the nails deeper into the flesh, and likewise of his self-scourgings,—a dreadful story,—and then goes on as follows: "At this same period the Servitor procured an old castaway door, and he used to lie upon it at night without any bedclothes to make him comfortable, except that he took off his shoes and wrapped a thick cloak round him. He thus secured for himself a most miserable bed; for hard pea-stalks lay in humps under his head, the cross with the sharp nails stuck into his back, his arms were locked fast in bonds, the horsehair undergarment was round his loins, and the cloak too was heavy and the door hard. Thus he lay in wretchedness, afraid to stir, just like a log, and he would send up many a sigh to God.

"In winter he suffered very much from the frost. If he stretched out his feet they lay bare on the floor and froze, if he gathered them up the blood became all on fire in his legs, and this was great pain. His feet were full of sores, his legs dropsical, his knees bloody and seared, his loins covered with scars from the horsehair, his body wasted, his mouth parched with intense thirst, and his hands tremulous from weakness. Amid these torments he spent his nights and days; and he endured them all out of the greatness of the love which he bore in his heart to the Divine and Eternal Wisdom, our Lord Jesus Christ, whose agonizing sufferings he sought to imitate. After a time he gave up this penitential exercise of the door, and instead of it he took up his abode in a very small cell, and used the bench, which was so narrow and short that he could not stretch himself upon it, as his bed. In this hole, or upon the door, he lay at night in his usual bonds, for about eight years. It was also his custom, during the space of twenty-five years, provided he was staying in the convent, never to go after compline in winter into any warm room, or to the convent stove to warm himself, no matter how cold it might be, unless he was obliged to do so for other reasons. Throughout all these years he never took a bath, either a water or a sweating bath; and this he did in order to mortify his comfort-seeking body. He practiced during a long time such rigid poverty that he would neither receive nor touch a penny, either with leave or without it. For a considerable time he strove to attain such a high degree of purity that he would neither scratch nor touch any part of his body, save only his hands and feet."[1]

I spare you the recital of poor Suso's self-inflicted tortures from thirst. It is pleasant to know that after his fortieth year, God showed him by a series of visions that he had sufficiently broken down the natural man, and that he might leave these exercises off. His case is distinctly pathological, but he does not seem to have had the alleviation, which some ascetics have enjoyed, of an alteration of sensibility capable of actually turning torment into a perverse kind of pleasure. Of the founder of the Sacred Heart order, for example, we read that

> "Her love of pain and suffering was insatiable. . . . She said that she could cheerfully live till the day of judgment, provided she might always have matter for suffering for God; but that to live a single day without suffering would be intolerable. She said again that she was devoured with two unassuageable fevers, one for the holy communion, the other for suffering, humiliation, and annihilation. 'Nothing but pain,' she continually said in her letters, 'makes my life supportable.' "[2]

So much for the phenomena to which the ascetic impulse will in certain persons give rise. In the ecclesiastically consecrated character three minor branches of self-mortification have been recognized as indispensable pathways to perfection. I refer to the chastity, obedience, and poverty which the monk vows to observe; and upon the heads of obedience and poverty I will make a few remarks.

First, of Obedience. The secular life of our twentieth century opens with this virtue held in no high esteem. The duty

---

[1] The Life of the Blessed HENRY SUSO, by Himself, translated by T. F. KNOX, London, 1865, pp. 56–80, abridged.

[2] BOUGAUD: Hist. de la bienheureuse Marguerite Marie, Paris, 1894, pp. 265, 171. Compare, also, pp. 386, 387.

of the individual to determine his own conduct and profit or suffer by the consequences seems, on the contrary, to be one of our best rooted contemporary Protestant social ideals. So much so that it is difficult even imaginatively to comprehend how men possessed of an inner life of their own could ever have come to think the subjection of its will to that of other finite creatures recommendable. I confess that to myself it seems something of a mystery. Yet it evidently corresponds to a profound interior need of many persons, and we must do our best to understand it.

On the lowest possible plane, one sees how the expediency of obedience in a firm ecclesiastical organization must have led to its being viewed as meritorious. Next, experience shows that there are times in every one's life when one can be better counseled by others than by one's self. Inability to decide is one of the commonest symptoms of fatigued nerves; friends who see our troubles more broadly, often see them more wisely than we do; so it is frequently an act of excellent virtue to consult and obey a doctor, a partner, or a wife. But, leaving these lower prudential regions, we find, in the nature of some of the spiritual excitements which we have been studying, good reasons for idealizing obedience. Obedience may spring from the general religious phenomenon of inner softening and self-surrender and throwing one's self on higher powers. So saving are these attitudes felt to be that in themselves, apart from utility, they become ideally consecrated; and in obeying a man whose fallibility we see through thoroughly, we, nevertheless, may feel much as we do when we resign our will to that of infinite wisdom. Add self-despair and the passion of self-crucifixion to this, and obedience becomes an ascetic sacrifice, agreeable quite irrespective of whatever prudential uses it might have.

It is as a sacrifice, a mode of 'mortification,' that obedience is primarily conceived by Catholic writers, a "sacrifice which man offers to God, and of which he is himself both the priest and the victim. By poverty he immolates his exterior possessions; by chastity he immolates his body; by obedience he completes the sacrifice, and gives to God all that he yet holds as his own, his two most precious goods, his intellect and his will. The sacrifice is then complete and unreserved, a genuine holocaust, for the entire victim is now consumed for the honor of God."[1] Accordingly, in Catholic discipline, we obey our superior not as mere man, but as the representative of Christ. Obeying God in him by our intention, obedience is easy. But when the text-book theologians marshal collectively all their reasons for recommending it, the mixture sounds to our ears rather odd.

"One of the great consolations of the monastic life," says a Jesuit authority, "is the assurance we have that in obeying we can commit no fault. The Superior may commit a fault in commanding you to do this thing or that, but you are certain that you commit no fault so long as you obey, because God will only ask you if you have duly performed what orders you received, and if you can furnish a clear account in that respect, you are absolved entirely. Whether the things you did were opportune, or whether there were not something better that might have been done, these are questions not asked of you, but rather of your Superior. The moment what you did was done obediently, God wipes it out of your account, and charges it to the Superior. So that Saint Jerome well exclaimed, in celebrating the advantages of obedience, 'Oh, sovereign liberty! Oh, holy and blessed security by which one becomes almost impeccable!'

"Saint John Climacus is of the same sentiment when he calls obedience an excuse before God. In fact, when God asks why you have done this or that, and you reply, it is because I was so ordered by my Superiors, God will ask for no other excuse. As a passenger in a good vessel with a good pilot need give himself no farther concern, but may go to sleep in peace, because the pilot has charge over all, and 'watches for him'; so a religious person who lives under the yoke of obedience goes to heaven as if while sleeping, that is, while leaning entirely on the conduct of his Superiors, who are the pilots of his vessel, and keep watch for him continually. It is no small thing, of a truth, to be able to cross the stormy sea of life on the shoulders and in

[1] LEJEUNE: Introduction à la Vie Mystique, 1899, p. 277. The holocaust simile goes back at least as far as Ignatius Loyola.

the arms of another, yet that is just the grace which God accords to those who live under the yoke of obedience. Their Superior bears all their burdens. . . . A certain grave doctor said that he would rather spend his life in picking up straws by obedience, than by his own responsible choice busy himself with the loftiest works of charity, because one is certain of following the will of God in whatever one may do from obedience, but never certain in the same degree of anything which we may do of our own proper movement."[1]

One should read the letters in which Ignatius Loyola recommends obedience as the backbone of his order, if one would gain insight into the full spirit of its cult.[2] They are too long to quote; but Ignatius's belief is so vividly expressed in a couple of sayings reported by companions that, though they have been so often cited, I will ask your permission to copy them once more: —

"I ought," an early biographer reports him as saying, "on entering religion, and thereafter, to place myself entirely in the hands of God, and of him who takes His place by His authority. I ought to desire that my Superior should oblige me to give up my own judgment, and conquer my own mind. I ought to set up no difference between one Superior and another, . . . but recognize them all as equal before God, whose place they fill. For if I distinguish persons, I weaken the spirit of obedience. In the hands of my Superior, I must be a soft wax, a thing, from which he is to require whatever pleases him, be it to write or receive letters, to speak or not to speak to such a person, or the like; and I must put all my fervor in executing zealously and exactly what I am ordered. I must consider myself as a corpse which has neither intelligence nor will; be like a mass of matter which without resistance lets itself be placed wherever it may please any one; like a stick in the hand of an old man, who uses it according to his needs and places

---

[1] Alfonso Rodriguez, S. J.: Pratique de la Perfection Chrétienne, Part iii., Treatise v., ch. x.

[2] Letters li. and cxx. of the collection translated into French by Bouix, Paris, 1870.

it where it suits him. So must I be under the hands of the Order, to serve it in the way it judges most useful.

"I must never ask of the Superior to be sent to a particular place, to be employed in a particular duty. . . . I must consider nothing as belonging to me personally, and as regards the things I use, be like a statue which lets itself be stripped and never opposes resistance."[1]

The other saying is reported by Rodriguez in the chapter from which I a moment ago made quotations. When speaking of the Pope's authority, Rodriguez writes:—

"Saint Ignatius said, when general of his company, that if the Holy Father were to order him to set sail in the first bark which he might find in the port of Ostia, near Rome, and to abandon himself to the sea, without a mast, without sails, without oars or rudder or any of the things that are needful for navigation or subsistence, he would obey not only with alacrity, but without anxiety or repugnance, and even with a great internal satisfaction."[2]

With a solitary concrete example of the extravagance to which the virtue we are considering has been carried, I will pass to the topic next in order.

"Sister Marie Claire [of Port Royal] had been greatly imbued with the holiness and excellence of M. de Langres. This prelate, soon after he came to Port Royal, said to her one day, seeing her so tenderly attached to Mother Angélique, that it would perhaps be better not to speak to her again. Marie Claire, greedy of obedience, took this inconsiderate word for an oracle of God, and from that day forward remained for several years without once speaking to her sister."[3]

Our next topic shall be Poverty, felt at all times and under all creeds as one adornment of a saintly life. Since the instinct of ownership is fundamental in man's nature, this is one more example of the ascetic paradox. Yet it appears no paradox at

[1] BARTOLI-MICHEL, ii. 13.
[2] RODRIGUEZ: Op. cit., Part iii., Treatise v., ch. vi.
[3] SAINTE-BEUVE: Histoire de Port Royal, i. 346.

all, but perfectly reasonable, the moment one recollects how easily higher excitements hold lower cupidities in check. Having just quoted the Jesuit Rodriguez on the subject of obedience, I will, to give immediately a concrete turn to our discussion of poverty, also read you a page from his chapter on this latter virtue. You must remember that he is writing instructions for monks of his own order, and bases them all on the text, "Blessed are the poor in spirit."

"If any one of you," he says, "will know whether or not he is really poor in spirit, let him consider whether he loves the ordinary consequences and effects of poverty, which are hunger, thirst, cold, fatigue, and the denudation of all conveniences. See if you are glad to wear a worn-out habit full of patches. See if you are glad when something is lacking to your meal, when you are passed by in serving it, when what you receive is distasteful to you, when your cell is out of repair. If you are not glad of these things, if instead of loving them you avoid them, then there is proof that you have not attained the perfection of poverty of spirit." Rodriguez then goes on to describe the practice of poverty in more detail. "The first point is that which Saint Ignatius proposes in his constitutions, when he says, 'Let no one use anything as if it were his private possession.' 'A religious person,' he says, 'ought in respect to all the things that he uses, to be like a statue which one may drape with clothing, but which feels no grief and makes no resistance when one strips it again. It is in this way that you should feel towards your clothes, your books, your cell, and everything else that you make use of; if ordered to quit them, or to exchange them for others, have no more sorrow than if you were a statue being uncovered. In this way you will avoid using them as if they were your private possession. But if, when you give up your cell, or yield possession of this or that object or exchange it for another, you feel repugnance and are not like a statue, that shows that you view these things as if they were your private property.'

"And this is why our holy founder wished the superiors to test their monks somewhat as God tested Abraham, and to put their poverty and their obedience to trial, that by this means they may become acquainted with the degree of their virtue, and gain a chance to make ever farther progress in perfection, . . . making the one move out of his room when he finds it comfortable and is attached to it; taking away from another a book of which he is fond; or obliging a third to exchange his garment for a worse one. Otherwise we should end by acquiring a species of property in all these several objects, and little by little the wall of poverty that surrounds us and constitutes our principal defense would be thrown down. The ancient fathers of the desert used often thus to treat their companions. . . . Saint Dositheus, being sick-nurse, desired a certain knife, and asked Saint Dorotheus for it, not for his private use, but for employment in the infirmary of which he had charge. Whereupon Saint Dorotheus answered him: 'Ha! Dositheus, so that knife pleases you so much! Will you be the slave of a knife or the slave of Jesus Christ? Do you not blush with shame at wishing that a knife should be your master? I will not let you touch it.' Which reproach and refusal had such an effect upon the holy disciple that since that time he never touched the knife again." . . .

"Therefore, in our rooms," Father Rodriguez continues, "there must be no other furniture than a bed, a table, a bench, and a candlestick, things purely necessary, and nothing more. It is not allowed among us that our cells should be ornamented with pictures or aught else, neither armchairs, carpets, curtains, nor any sort of cabinet or bureau of any elegance. Neither is it allowed us to keep anything to eat, either for ourselves or for those who may come to visit us. We must ask permission to go to the refectory even for a glass of water; and finally we may not keep a book in which we can write a line, or which we may take away with us. One cannot deny that thus we are in great poverty. But this poverty is at the same time a great repose and a great perfection. For it would be inevitable, in case a religious person were allowed to own superfluous possessions, that these things would greatly occupy his mind, be it to acquire them, to preserve them, or to increase them; so that in not permitting us at all to own them, all these inconveniences are remedied. Among the various good reasons why the company forbids secular persons to enter our cells, the principal one is that thus we may the easier be kept in poverty. After all, we are all men, and if we were to receive people of the world into our rooms, we should not have the strength to remain within the bounds prescribed, but should at least wish to adorn them with some books to give the visitors a better opinion of our scholarship."[1]

Since Hindu fakirs, Buddhist monks, and Mohammedan dervishes unite with Jesuits and Franciscans in idealizing poverty as the loftiest individual state, it is worth while to examine into the spiritual grounds for such a seemingly unnatural opinion. And first, of those which lie closest to common human nature.

The opposition between the men who *have* and the men who *are* is immemorial. Though the gentleman, in the old-fashioned sense of the man who is well born, has usually in point of fact been predaceous and reveled in lands and goods, yet he has never identified his essence with these possessions, but rather with the personal superiorities, the courage, generosity, and pride supposed to be his birthright. To certain huckstering kinds of consideration he thanked God he was forever inaccessible, and if in life's vicissitudes he should become destitute through their lack, he was glad to think that with his sheer valor he was all the freer to work out his salvation. "Wer nur selbst was hätte," says Lessing's Tempelherr, in Nathan the Wise, "mein Gott, mein Gott, ich habe nichts!" This ideal of the well-born man without possessions was embodied in knight-errantry and templardom; and, hideously corrupted as it has always been, it still dominates sentimentally, if not practically, the military and aristocratic view of life. We glorify the soldier as the man absolutely unincumbered. Owning nothing but his bare life, and willing to toss that up at any moment when the cause commands him, he is the representative of unhampered freedom in ideal directions. The laborer who pays with his person day by day, and has no rights invested in the future, offers also much of this ideal detachment. Like the savage, he may make his bed wherever his right arm can support him, and from his simple and

[1] RODRIGUEZ: Op. cit., Part iii., Treatise iii., chaps. vi., vii.

athletic attitude of observation, the property-owner seems buried and smothered in ignoble externalities and trammels, "wading in straw and rubbish to his knees." The claims which *things* make are corrupters of manhood, mortgages on the soul, and a drag anchor on our progress towards the empyrean.

"Everything I meet with," writes Whitefield, "seems to carry this voice with it,—'Go thou and preach the Gospel; be a pilgrim on earth; have no party or certain dwelling place.' My heart echoes back, 'Lord Jesus, help me to do or suffer thy will. When thou seest me in danger of *nestling*,— in pity—in tender pity,—put a *thorn* in my nest to prevent me from it.' "[1]

The loathing of 'capital' with which our laboring classes to-day are growing more and more infected seems largely composed of this sound sentiment of antipathy for lives based on mere having. As an anarchist poet writes:—

"Not by accumulating riches, but by giving away that which you have,

"Shall you become beautiful;

"You must undo the wrappings, not case yourself in fresh ones;

"Not by multiplying clothes shall you make your body sound and healthy, but rather by discarding them . . .

"For a soldier who is going on a campaign does not seek what fresh furniture he can carry on his back, but rather what he can leave behind;

"Knowing well that every additional thing which he cannot freely use and handle is an impediment."[2]

In short, lives based on having are less free than lives based either on doing or on being, and in the interest of action people subject to spiritual excitement throw away possessions as so many clogs. Only those who have no private interests can follow an ideal straight away. Sloth and cowardice creep in with every dollar or guinea we have to guard. When a

[1] R. PHILIP: The Life and Times of George Whitefield, London, 1842, p. 366.
[2] EDWARD CARPENTER: Towards Democracy, p. 362, abridged.

brother novice came to Saint Francis, saying: "Father, it would be a great consolation to me to own a psalter, but even supposing that our general should concede to me this indulgence, still I should like also to have your consent," Francis put him off with the examples of Charlemagne, Roland, and Oliver, pursuing the infidels in sweat and labor, and finally dying on the field of battle. "So care not," he said, "for owning books and knowledge, but care rather for works of goodness." And when some weeks later the novice came again to talk of his craving for the psalter, Francis said: "After you have got your psalter you will crave a breviary; and after you have got your breviary you will sit in your stall like a grand prelate, and will say to your brother: 'Hand me my breviary.' . . . And thenceforward he denied all such requests, saying: A man possesses of learning only so much as comes out of him in action, and a monk is a good preacher only so far as his deeds proclaim him such, for every tree is known by its fruits."[1]

But beyond this more worthily athletic attitude involved in doing and being, there is, in the desire of not having, something profounder still, something related to that fundamental mystery of religious experience, the satisfaction found in absolute surrender to the larger power. So long as any secular safeguard is retained, so long as any residual prudential guarantee is clung to, so long the surrender is incomplete, the vital crisis is not passed, fear still stands sentinel, and mistrust of the divine obtains: we hold by two anchors, looking to God, it is true, after a fashion, but also holding by our proper machinations. In certain medical experiences we have the same critical point to overcome. A drunkard, or a morphine or cocaine maniac, offers himself to be cured. He appeals to the doctor to wean him from his enemy, but he dares not face blank abstinence. The tyrannical drug is still an anchor to windward: he hides supplies of it among his clothing; arranges secretly to have it smuggled in in case of need. Even so an incompletely regenerate man still trusts in his own expedients. His money is like the sleeping potion which the chronically wakeful patient keeps beside his bed; he throws

---

[1] Speculum Perfectionis, ed. P. SABATIER, Paris, 1898, pp. 10, 13.

himself on God, but *if* he should need the other help, there it will be also. Every one knows cases of this incomplete and ineffective desire for reform,—drunkards whom, with all their self-reproaches and resolves, one perceives to be quite unwilling seriously to contemplate *never* being drunk again! Really to give up anything on which we have relied, to give it up definitively, 'for good and all' and forever, signifies one of those radical alterations of character which came under our notice in the lectures on conversion. In it the inner man rolls over into an entirely different position of equilibrium, lives in a new centre of energy from this time on, and the turning-point and hinge of all such operations seems usually to involve the sincere acceptance of certain nakednesses and destitutions.

Accordingly, throughout the annals of the saintly life, we find this ever-recurring note: Fling yourself upon God's providence without making any reserve whatever,—take no thought for the morrow,—sell all you have and give it to the poor,—only when the sacrifice is ruthless and reckless will the higher safety really arrive. As a concrete example let me read a page from the biography of Antoinette Bourignon, a good woman, much persecuted in her day by both Protestants and Catholics, because she would not take her religion at second hand. When a young girl, in her father's house,—

"She spent whole nights in prayer, oft repeating: *Lord, what wilt thou have me to do?* And being one night in a most profound penitence, she said from the bottom of her heart: 'O my Lord! What must I do to please thee? For I have nobody to teach me. Speak to my soul and it will hear thee.' At that instant she heard, as if another had spoke within her: *Forsake all earthly things. Separate thyself from the love of the creatures. Deny thyself.* She was quite astonished, not understanding this language, and mused long on these three points, thinking how she could fulfill them. She thought she could not live without earthly things, nor without loving the creatures, nor without loving herself. Yet she said, 'By thy Grace I will do it, Lord!' But when she would perform her promise, she knew not where to begin. Having thought on the religious in monasteries, that they forsook all earthly things by being shut up in a cloister, and the love of themselves by subjecting of their wills, she asked leave of her father to enter into a cloister of the barefoot Carmelites, but he would not permit it, saying he would rather see her laid in her grave. This seemed to her a great cruelty, for she thought to find in the cloister the true Christians she had been seeking, but she found afterwards that he knew the cloisters better than she; for after he had forbidden her, and told her he would never permit her to be a religious, nor give her any money to enter there, yet she went to Father Laurens, the Director, and offered to serve in the monastery and work hard for her bread, and be content with little, if he would receive her. At which he smiled and said: *That cannot be. We must have money to build; we take no maids without money; you must find the way to get it, else there is no entry here.*

"This astonished her greatly, and she was thereby undeceived as to the cloisters, resolving to forsake all company and live alone till it should please God to show her what she ought to do and whither to go. She asked always earnestly, 'When shall I be perfectly thine, O my God?' And she thought he still answered her, *When thou shalt no longer possess anything, and shalt die to thyself.* 'And where shall I do that, Lord?' He answered her, *In the desert.* This made so strong an impression on her soul that she aspired after this; but being a maid of eighteen years only, she was afraid of unlucky chances, and was never used to travel, and knew no way. She laid aside all these doubts and said, 'Lord, thou wilt guide me how and where it shall please thee. It is for thee that I do it. I will lay aside my habit of a maid, and will take that of a hermit that I may pass unknown.' Having then secretly made ready this habit, while her parents thought to have married her, her father having promised her to a rich French merchant, she prevented the time, and on Easter evening, having cut her hair, put on the habit, and slept a little, she went out of her chamber about four in the morning, taking nothing but one penny to buy bread for that day. And it being said to her in the going out, *Where is thy faith? in a penny?* she threw it away, begging pardon of God for her fault, and saying, 'No, Lord, my faith is not in a penny, but in thee alone.' Thus she went away wholly delivered from the heavy burthen of the cares and good things of this world, and found her soul so satisfied that she no longer wished for anything upon earth, resting entirely upon God, with this only fear lest she should be discovered and be obliged to return home; for she felt already more content in this poverty than she had done for all her life in all the delights of the world."[1]

The penny was a small financial safeguard, but an effective spiritual obstacle. Not till it was thrown away could the character settle into the new equilibrium completely.

Over and above the mystery of self-surrender, there are in the cult of poverty other religious mysteries. There is the mystery of veracity: "Naked came I into the world," etc.,—whoever first said that, possessed this mystery. My own bare entity must fight the battle—shams cannot save me. There is also the mystery of democracy, or sentiment of the equality before God of all his creatures. This sentiment (which seems in general to have been more widespread in Mohammedan than in Christian lands) tends to nullify man's usual acquisi-

---

[1] An Apology for M. Antonia Bourignon, London, 1699, pp. 269, 270, abridged.

Another example from Starbuck's MS. collection:—

"At a meeting held at six the next morning, I heard a man relate his experience. He said: The Lord asked him if he would confess Christ among the quarrymen with whom he worked, and he said he would. Then he asked him if he would give up to be used of the Lord the four hundred dollars he had laid up, and he said he would, and thus the Lord saved him. The thought came to me at once that I had never made a real consecration either of myself or of my property to the Lord, but had always tried to serve the Lord in *my* way. Now the Lord asked me if I would serve him in *his* way, and go out alone and penniless if he so ordered. The question was pressed home, and I must decide: To forsake all and have him, or have all and lose him! I soon decided to take him; and the blessed assurance came, that he had taken me for his own, and my joy was full. I returned home from the meeting with feelings as simple as a child. I thought all would be glad to hear of the joy of the Lord that possessed me, and so I began to tell the simple story. But to my great surprise, the pastors (for I attended meetings in three churches) opposed the experience and said it was fanaticism, and one told the members of his church to shun those that professed it, and I soon found that my foes were those of my own household."

tiveness. Those who have it spurn dignities and honors, privileges and advantages, preferring, as I said in a former lecture, to grovel on the common level before the face of God. It is not exactly the sentiment of humility, though it comes so close to it in practice. It is *humanity*, rather, refusing to enjoy anything that others do not share. A profound moralist, writing of Christ's saying, 'Sell all thou hast and follow me,' proceeds as follows: —

"Christ may have meant: If you love mankind absolutely you will as a result not care for any possessions whatever, and this seems a very likely proposition. But it is one thing to believe that a proposition is probably true; it is another thing to see it as a fact. If you loved mankind as Christ loved them, you would see his conclusion as a fact. It would be obvious. You would sell your goods, and they would be no loss to you. These truths, while literal to Christ, and to any mind that has Christ's love for mankind, become parables to lesser natures. There are in every generation people who, beginning innocently, with no predetermined intention of becoming saints, find themselves drawn into the vortex by their interest in helping mankind, and by the understanding that comes from actually doing it. The abandonment of their old mode of life is like dust in the balance. It is done gradually, incidentally, imperceptibly. Thus the whole question of the abandonment of luxury is no question at all, but a mere incident to another question, namely, the degree to which we abandon ourselves to the remorseless logic of our love for others."[1]

But in all these matters of sentiment one must have 'been there' one's self in order to understand them. No American can ever attain to understanding the loyalty of a Briton towards his king, of a German towards his emperor; nor can a Briton or German ever understand the peace of heart of an American in having no king, no Kaiser, no spurious nonsense, between him and the common God of all. If sentiments as simple as these are mysteries which one must receive as gifts of birth, how much more is this the case with those

[1] J. J. CHAPMAN, in the Political Nursery, vol. iv. p. 4, April, 1900, abridged.

subtler religious sentiments which we have been considering! One can never fathom an emotion or divine its dictates by standing outside of it. In the glowing hour of excitement, however, all incomprehensibilities are solved, and what was so enigmatical from without becomes transparently obvious. Each emotion obeys a logic of its own, and makes deductions which no other logic can draw. Piety and charity live in a different universe from worldly lusts and fears, and form another centre of energy altogether. As in a supreme sorrow lesser vexations may become a consolation; as a supreme love may turn minor sacrifices into gain; so a supreme trust may render common safeguards odious, and in certain glows of generous excitement it may appear unspeakably mean to retain one's hold of personal possessions. The only sound plan, if we are ourselves outside the pale of such emotions, is to observe as well as we are able those who feel them, and to record faithfully what we observe; and this, I need hardly say, is what I have striven to do in these last two descriptive lectures, which I now hope will have covered the ground sufficiently for our present needs.

LECTURES XIV AND XV

THE VALUE OF SAINTLINESS

WE HAVE NOW passed in review the more important of the phenomena which are regarded as fruits of genuine religion and characteristics of men who are devout. To-day we have to change our attitude from that of description to that of appreciation; we have to ask whether the fruits in question can help us to judge the absolute value of what religion adds to human life. Were I to parody Kant, I should say that a 'Critique of pure Saintliness' must be our theme.

If, in turning to this theme, we could descend upon our subject from above like Catholic theologians, with our fixed definitions of man and man's perfection and our positive dogmas about God, we should have an easy time of it. Man's perfection would be the fulfillment of his end; and his end would be union with his Maker. That union could be pursued by him along three paths, active, purgative, and contemplative, respectively; and progress along either path would be a simple matter to measure by the application of a limited number of theological and moral conceptions and definitions. The absolute significance and value of any bit of religious experience we might hear of would thus be given almost mathematically into our hands.

If convenience were everything, we ought now to grieve at finding ourselves cut off from so admirably convenient a method as this. But we did cut ourselves off from it deliberately in those remarks which you remember we made, in our first lecture, about the empirical method; and it must be confessed that after that act of renunciation we can never hope for clean-cut and scholastic results. *We* cannot divide man sharply into an animal and a rational part. *We* cannot distinguish natural from supernatural effects; nor among the latter know which are favors of God, and which are counterfeit operations of the demon. We have merely to collect things together without any special *a priori* theological system, and out of an aggregate of piecemeal judgments as to the value of this and that experience—judgments in which our general philo-

299

sophic prejudices, our instincts, and our common sense are our only guides—decide that *on the whole* one type of religion is approved by its fruits, and another type condemned. 'On the whole,'—I fear we shall never escape complicity with that qualification, so dear to your practical man, so repugnant to your systematizer!

I also fear that as I make this frank confession, I may seem to some of you to throw our compass overboard, and to adopt caprice as our pilot. Skepticism or wayward choice, you may think, can be the only results of such a formless method as I have taken up. A few remarks in deprecation of such an opinion, and in farther explanation of the empiricist principles which I profess, may therefore appear at this point to be in place.

Abstractly, it would seem illogical to try to measure the worth of a religion's fruits in merely human terms of value. How *can* you measure their worth without considering whether the God really exists who is supposed to inspire them? If he really exists, then all the conduct instituted by men to meet his wants must necessarily be a reasonable fruit of his religion,—it would be unreasonable only in case he did not exist. If, for instance, you were to condemn a religion of human or animal sacrifices by virtue of your subjective sentiments, and if all the while a deity were really there demanding such sacrifices, you would be making a theoretical mistake by tacitly assuming that the deity must be non-existent; you would be setting up a theology of your own as much as if you were a scholastic philosopher.

To this extent, to the extent of disbelieving peremptorily in certain types of deity, I frankly confess that we must be theologians. If disbeliefs can be said to constitute a theology, then the prejudices, instincts, and common sense which I chose as our guides make theological partisans of us whenever they make certain beliefs abhorrent.

But such common-sense prejudices and instincts are themselves the fruit of an empirical evolution. Nothing is more striking than the secular alteration that goes on in the moral and religious tone of men, as their insight into nature and their social arrangements progressively develop. After an

interval of a few generations the mental climate proves unfavorable to notions of the deity which at an earlier date were
perfectly satisfactory: the older gods have fallen below the
common secular level, and can no longer be believed in. To-
day a deity who should require bleeding sacrifices to placate
him would be too sanguinary to be taken seriously. Even if
powerful historical credentials were put forward in his favor,
we would not look at them. Once, on the contrary, his cruel
appetites were of themselves credentials. They positively recommended him to men's imaginations in ages when such
coarse signs of power were respected and no others could be
understood. Such deities then were worshiped because such
fruits were relished.

Doubtless historic accidents always played some later part,
but the original factor in fixing the figure of the gods must
always have been psychological. The deity to whom the
prophets, seers, and devotees who founded the particular cult
bore witness was worth something to them personally. They
could use him. He guided their imagination, warranted their
hopes, and controlled their will,—or else they required him
as a safeguard against the demon and a curber of other people's crimes. In any case, they chose him for the value of the
fruits he seemed to them to yield. So soon as the fruits began
to seem quite worthless; so soon as they conflicted with indispensable human ideals, or thwarted too extensively other
values; so soon as they appeared childish, contemptible, or
immoral when reflected on, the deity grew discredited, and
was erelong neglected and forgotten. It was in this way that
the Greek and Roman gods ceased to be believed in by educated pagans; it is thus that we ourselves judge of the Hindu,
Buddhist, and Mohammedan theologies; Protestants have so
dealt with the Catholic notions of deity, and liberal Protestants with older Protestant notions; it is thus that Chinamen
judge of us, and that all of us now living will be judged by
our descendants. When we cease to admire or approve what
the definition of a deity implies, we end by deeming that deity
incredible.

Few historic changes are more curious than these mutations of theological opinion. The monarchical type of sovereignty was, for example, so ineradicably planted in the mind

of our own forefathers that a dose of cruelty and arbitrariness in their deity seems positively to have been required by their imagination. They called the cruelty 'retributive justice,' and a God without it would certainly have struck them as not 'sovereign' enough. But to-day we abhor the very notion of eternal suffering inflicted; and that arbitrary dealing-out of salvation and damnation to selected individuals, of which Jonathan Edwards could persuade himself that he had not only a conviction, but a 'delightful conviction,' as of a doctrine 'exceeding pleasant, bright, and sweet,' appears to us, if sovereignly anything, sovereignly irrational and mean. Not only the cruelty, but the paltriness of character of the gods believed in by earlier centuries also strikes later centuries with surprise. We shall see examples of it from the annals of Catholic saintship which make us rub our Protestant eyes. Ritual worship in general appears to the modern transcendentalist, as well as to the ultra-puritanic type of mind, as if addressed to a deity of an almost absurdly childish character, taking delight in toy-shop furniture, tapers and tinsel, costume and mumbling and mummery, and finding his 'glory' incomprehensibly enhanced thereby; — just as on the other hand the formless spaciousness of pantheism appears quite empty to ritualistic natures, and the gaunt theism of evangelical sects seems intolerably bald and chalky and bleak. Luther, says Emerson, would have cut off his right hand rather than nail his theses to the door at Wittenberg, if he had supposed that they were destined to lead to the pale negations of Boston Unitarianism.

So far, then, although we are compelled, whatever may be our pretensions to empiricism, to employ some sort of a standard of theological probability of our own whenever we assume to estimate the fruits of other men's religion, yet this very standard has been begotten out of the drift of common life. It is the voice of human experience within us, judging and condemning all gods that stand athwart the pathway along which it feels itself to be advancing. Experience, if we take it in the largest sense, is thus the parent of those disbeliefs which, it was charged, were inconsistent with the experiential method. The inconsistency, you see, is immaterial, and the charge may be neglected.

If we pass from disbeliefs to positive beliefs, it seems to me that there is not even a formal inconsistency to be laid against our method. The gods we stand by are the gods we need and can use, the gods whose demands on us are reinforcements of our demands on ourselves and on one another. What I then propose to do is, briefly stated, to test saintliness by common sense, to use human standards to help us decide how far the religious life commends itself as an ideal kind of human activity. If it commends itself, then any theological beliefs that may inspire it, in so far forth will stand accredited. If not, then they will be discredited, and all without reference to anything but human working principles. It is but the elimination of the humanly unfit, and the survival of the humanly fittest, applied to religious beliefs; and if we look at history candidly and without prejudice, we have to admit that no religion has ever in the long run established or proved itself in any other way. Religions have *approved* themselves; they have ministered to sundry vital needs which they found reigning. When they violated other needs too strongly, or when other faiths came which served the same needs better, the first religions were supplanted.

The needs were always many, and the tests were never sharp. So the reproach of vagueness and subjectivity and 'on the whole'-ness, which can with perfect legitimacy be addressed to the empirical method as we are forced to use it, is after all a reproach to which the entire life of man in dealing with these matters is obnoxious. No religion has ever yet owed its prevalence to 'apodictic certainty.' In a later lecture I will ask whether objective certainty can ever be added by theological reasoning to a religion that already empirically prevails.

One word, also, about the reproach that in following this sort of an empirical method we are handing ourselves over to systematic skepticism.

Since it is impossible to deny secular alterations in our sentiments and needs, it would be absurd to affirm that one's own age of the world can be beyond correction by the next age. Skepticism cannot, therefore, be ruled out by any set of thinkers as a possibility against which their conclusions are secure; and no empiricist ought to claim exemption from this universal liability. But to admit one's liability to correction is one thing, and to embark upon a sea of wanton doubt is another. Of willfully playing into the hands of skepticism we cannot be accused. He who acknowledges the imperfectness of his instrument, and makes allowance for it in discussing his observations, is in a much better position for gaining truth than if he claimed his instrument to be infallible. Or is dogmatic or scholastic theology less doubted in point of fact for claiming, as it does, to be in point of right undoubtable? And if not, what command over truth would this kind of theology really lose if, instead of absolute certainty, she only claimed reasonable probability for her conclusions? If *we* claim only reasonable probability, it will be as much as men who love the truth can ever at any given moment hope to have within their grasp. Pretty surely it will be more than we could have had, if we were unconscious of our liability to err.

Nevertheless, dogmatism will doubtless continue to condemn us for this confession. The mere outward form of inalterable certainty is so precious to some minds that to renounce it explicitly is for them out of the question. They will claim it even where the facts most patently pronounce its folly. But the safe thing is surely to recognize that all the insights of creatures of a day like ourselves must be provisional. The wisest of critics is an altering being, subject to the better insight of the morrow, and right at any moment, only 'up to date' and 'on the whole.' When larger ranges of truth open, it is surely best to be able to open ourselves to their reception, unfettered by our previous pretensions. "Heartily know, when half-gods go, the gods arrive."

The fact of diverse judgments about religious phenomena is therefore entirely unescapable, whatever may be one's own desire to attain the irreversible. But apart from that fact, a more fundamental question awaits us, the question whether men's opinions ought to be expected to be absolutely uniform in this field. Ought all men to have the same religion? Ought they to approve the same fruits and follow the same leadings? Are they so like in their inner needs that, for hard and soft, for proud and humble, for strenuous and lazy, for healthy-minded and despairing, exactly the same religious incentives are required? Or are different functions in the organism of humanity allotted to different types of man, so that some may really be the better for a religion of consolation and reassurance, whilst others are better for one of terror and reproof? It might conceivably be so; and we shall, I think, more and more suspect it to be so as we go on. And if it be so, how can any possible judge or critic help being biased in favor of the religion by which his own needs are best met? He aspires to impartiality; but he is too close to the struggle not to be to some degree a participant, and he is sure to approve most warmly those fruits of piety in others which taste most good and prove most nourishing to *him*.

I am well aware of how anarchic much of what I say may sound. Expressing myself thus abstractly and briefly, I may seem to despair of the very notion of truth. But I beseech you to reserve your judgment until we see it applied to the details which lie before us. I do indeed disbelieve that we or any other mortal men can attain on a given day to absolutely incorrigible and unimprovable truth about such matters of fact as those with which religions deal. But I reject this dogmatic ideal not out of a perverse delight in intellectual instability. I am no lover of disorder and doubt as such. Rather do I fear to lose truth by this pretension to possess it already wholly. That we can gain more and more of it by moving always in the right direction, I believe as much as any one, and I hope to bring you all to my way of thinking before the termination of these lectures. Till then, do not, I pray you, harden your minds irrevocably against the empiricism which I profess.

I will waste no more words, then, in abstract justification of my method, but seek immediately to use it upon the facts.

In critically judging of the value of religious phenomena, it is very important to insist on the distinction between religion as an individual personal function, and religion as an institutional, corporate, or tribal product. I drew this distinction, you may remember, in my second lecture. The word 'religion,' as ordinarily used, is equivocal. A survey of history shows us that, as a rule, religious geniuses attract disciples, and produce groups of sympathizers. When these groups get strong enough to 'organize' themselves, they become ecclesiastical institutions with corporate ambitions of their own.

The spirit of politics and the lust of dogmatic rule are then apt to enter and to contaminate the originally innocent thing; so that when we hear the word 'religion' nowadays, we think inevitably of some 'church' or other; and to some persons the word 'church' suggests so much hypocrisy and tyranny and meanness and tenacity of superstition that in a wholesale undiscerning way they glory in saying that they are 'down' on religion altogether. Even we who belong to churches do not exempt other churches than our own from the general condemnation.

But in this course of lectures ecclesiastical institutions hardly concern us at all. The religious experience which we are studying is that which lives itself out within the private breast. First-hand individual experience of this kind has always appeared as a heretical sort of innovation to those who witnessed its birth. Naked comes it into the world and lonely; and it has always, for a time at least, driven him who had it into the wilderness, often into the literal wilderness out of doors, where the Buddha, Jesus, Mohammed, St. Francis, George Fox, and so many others had to go. George Fox expresses well this isolation; and I can do no better at this point than read to you a page from his Journal, referring to the period of his youth when religion began to ferment within him seriously.

"I fasted much," Fox says, "walked abroad in solitary places many days, and often took my Bible, and sat in hollow trees and lonesome places until night came on; and frequently in the night walked mournfully about by myself; for I was a man of sorrows in the time of the first workings of the Lord in me.

"During all this time I was never joined in profession of religion with any, but gave up myself to the Lord, having forsaken all evil company, taking leave of father and mother, and all other relations, and traveled up and down as a stranger on the earth, which way the Lord inclined my heart; taking a chamber to myself in the town where I came, and tarrying sometimes more, sometimes less in a place: for I durst not stay long in a place, being afraid both of professor and profane, lest, being a tender young man, I should be hurt by conversing much with either. For which reason I kept much as a stranger, seeking heavenly wisdom and getting knowledge from the Lord; and was brought off from outward things, to rely on the Lord alone. As I had forsaken the priests, so I left the separate preachers also, and those called the most experienced people; for I saw there was none among them all that could speak to my condition. And when all my hopes in them and in all men were gone so that I had nothing outwardly to help me, nor could tell what to do; then, oh then, I heard a voice which said, 'There is one, even Jesus Christ, that can speak to thy condition.' When I heard it, my heart did leap for joy. Then the Lord let me see why there was none upon the earth that could speak to my condition. I had not fellowship with any people, priests, nor professors, nor any sort of separated people. I was afraid of all carnal talk and talkers, for I could see nothing but corruptions. When I was in the deep, under all shut up, I could not believe that I should ever overcome; my troubles, my sorrows, and my temptations were so great that I often thought I should have despaired, I was so tempted. But when Christ opened to me how he was tempted by the same devil, and had overcome him, and had bruised his head; and that through him and his power, life, grace, and spirit, I should overcome also, I had confidence in him. If I had had a king's diet, palace, and attendance, all would have been as nothing; for nothing gave me comfort but the Lord by his power. I saw professors, priests, and people were whole and at ease in that condition which was my misery, and they loved that which I would have been rid of. But the Lord did stay my desires upon himself, and my care was cast upon him alone."[1]

A genuine first-hand religious experience like this is bound to be a heterodoxy to its witnesses, the prophet appearing as a mere lonely madman. If his doctrine prove contagious enough to spread to any others, it becomes a definite and labeled heresy. But if it then still prove contagious enough to triumph over persecution, it becomes itself an orthodoxy; and

[1] GEORGE FOX: Journal, Philadelphia, 1800, pp. 59–61, abridged.

when a religion has become an orthodoxy, its day of inwardness is over: the spring is dry; the faithful live at second hand
exclusively and stone the prophets in their turn. The new
church, in spite of whatever human goodness it may foster,
can be henceforth counted on as a staunch ally in every attempt to stifle the spontaneous religious spirit, and to stop all
later bubblings of the fountain from which in purer days it
drew its own supply of inspiration. Unless, indeed, by adopting new movements of the spirit it can make capital out of
them and use them for its selfish corporate designs! Of protective action of this politic sort, promptly or tardily decided
on, the dealings of the Roman ecclesiasticism with many individual saints and prophets yield examples enough for our
instruction.

The plain fact is that men's minds are built, as has been
often said, in water-tight compartments. Religious after a
fashion, they yet have many other things in them beside their
religion, and unholy entanglements and associations inevitably obtain. The basenesses so commonly charged to religion's
account are thus, almost all of them, not chargeable at all to
religion proper, but rather to religion's wicked practical partner, the spirit of corporate dominion. And the bigotries are
most of them in their turn chargeable to religion's wicked
intellectual partner, the spirit of dogmatic dominion, the passion for laying down the law in the form of an absolutely
closed-in theoretic system. The ecclesiastical spirit in general
is the sum of these two spirits of dominion; and I beseech
you never to confound the phenomena of mere tribal or corporate psychology which it presents with those manifestations
of the purely interior life which are the exclusive object of our
study. The baiting of Jews, the hunting of Albigenses and
Waldenses, the stoning of Quakers and ducking of Methodists, the murdering of Mormons and the massacring of
Armenians, express much rather that aboriginal human
neophobia, that pugnacity of which we all share the vestiges,
and that inborn hatred of the alien and of eccentric and non-
conforming men as aliens, than they express the positive piety
of the various perpetrators. Piety is the mask, the inner force
is tribal instinct. You believe as little as I do, in spite of the
Christian unction with which the German emperor addressed

his troops upon their way to China, that the conduct which he suggested, and in which other Christian armies went beyond them, had anything whatever to do with the interior religious life of those concerned in the performance.

Well, no more for past atrocities than for this atrocity should we make piety responsible. At most we may blame piety for not availing to check our natural passions, and sometimes for supplying them with hypocritical pretexts. But hypocrisy also imposes obligations, and with the pretext usually couples some restriction; and when the passion gust is over, the piety may bring a reaction of repentance which the irreligious natural man would not have shown.

For many of the historic aberrations which have been laid to her charge, religion as such, then, is not to blame. Yet of the charge that over-zealousness or fanaticism is one of her liabilities we cannot wholly acquit her, so I will next make a remark upon that point. But I will preface it by a preliminary remark which connects itself with much that follows.

Our survey of the phenomena of saintliness has unquestionably produced in your minds an impression of extravagance. Is it necessary, some of you have asked, as one example after another came before us, to be quite so fantastically good as that? We who have no vocation for the extremer ranges of sanctity will surely be let off at the last day if our humility, asceticism, and devoutness prove of a less convulsive sort. This practically amounts to saying that much that it is legitimate to admire in this field need nevertheless not be imitated, and that religious phenomena, like all other human phenomena, are subject to the law of the golden mean. Political reformers accomplish their successive tasks in the history of nations by being blind for the time to other causes. Great schools of art work out the effects which it is their mission to reveal, at the cost of a one-sidedness for which other schools must make amends. We accept a John Howard, a Mazzini, a Botticelli, a Michael Angelo, with a kind of indulgence. We are glad they existed to show us that way, but we are glad there are also other ways of seeing and taking life. So of many of the saints whom we have looked at. We are proud of a human nature that could be so passionately extreme, but we shrink from advising others to follow the example. The conduct we blame ourselves for not following lies nearer to the middle line of human effort. It is less dependent on particular beliefs and doctrines. It is such as wears well in different ages, such as under different skies all judges are able to commend.

The fruits of religion, in other words, are, like all human products, liable to corruption by excess. Common sense must judge them. It need not blame the votary; but it may be able to praise him only conditionally, as one who acts faithfully according to his lights. He shows us heroism in one way, but the unconditionally good way is that for which no indulgence need be asked.

We find that error by excess is exemplified by every saintly virtue. Excess, in human faculties, means usually one-sidedness or want of balance; for it is hard to imagine an essential faculty too strong, if only other faculties equally strong be there to coöperate with it in action. Strong affections need a strong will; strong active powers need a strong intellect; strong intellect needs strong sympathies, to keep life steady. If the balance exist, no one faculty can possibly be too strong—we only get the stronger all-round character. In the life of saints, technically so called, the spiritual faculties are strong, but what gives the impression of extravagance proves usually on examination to be a relative deficiency of intellect. Spiritual excitement takes pathological forms whenever other interests are too few and the intellect too narrow. We find this exemplified by all the saintly attributes in turn—devout love of God, purity, charity, asceticism, all may lead astray. I will run over these virtues in succession.

First of all let us take Devoutness. When unbalanced, one of its vices is called Fanaticism. Fanaticism (when not a mere expression of ecclesiastical ambition) is only loyalty carried to a convulsive extreme. When an intensely loyal and narrow mind is once grasped by the feeling that a certain superhuman person is worthy of its exclusive devotion, one of the first things that happens is that it idealizes the devotion itself. To adequately realize the merits of the idol gets to be considered the one great merit of the worshiper; and the sacrifices and servilities by which savage tribesmen have from time imme-

morial exhibited their faithfulness to chieftains are now out-
bid in favor of the deity. Vocabularies are exhausted and
languages altered in the attempt to praise him enough; death
is looked on as gain if it attract his grateful notice; and the
personal attitude of being his devotee becomes what one
might almost call a new and exalted kind of professional specialty within the tribe.[1] The legends that gather round the
lives of holy persons are fruits of this impulse to celebrate and
glorify. The Buddha[2] and Mohammed[3] and their companions
and many Christian saints are incrusted with a heavy jewelry
of anecdotes which are meant to be honorific, but are simply
abgeschmackt and silly, and form a touching expression of
man's misguided propensity to praise.

An immediate consequence of this condition of mind is
jealousy for the deity's honor. How can the devotee show his
loyalty better than by sensitiveness in this regard? The slightest affront or neglect must be resented, the deity's enemies
must be put to shame. In exceedingly narrow minds and
active wills, such a care may become an engrossing pre-

[1] Christian saints have had their specialties of devotion, Saint Francis to
Christ's wounds; Saint Anthony of Padua to Christ's childhood; Saint Bernard to his humanity; Saint Teresa to Saint Joseph, etc. The Shi-ite Mohammedans venerate Ali, the Prophet's son-in-law, instead of Abu-bekr, his
brother-in-law. Vambéry describes a dervish whom he met in Persia, "who
had solemnly vowed, thirty years before, that he would never employ his
organs of speech otherwise but in uttering, everlastingly, the name of his
favorite, *Ali, Ali.* He thus wished to signify to the world that he was the
most devoted partisan of that Ali who had been dead a thousand years. In
his own home, speaking with his wife, children, and friends, no other word
but 'Ali!' ever passed his lips. If he wanted food or drink or anything else, he
expressed his wants still by repeating 'Ali!' Begging or buying at the bazaar,
it was always 'Ali!' Treated ill or generously, he would still harp on his monotonous 'Ali!' Latterly his zeal assumed such tremendous proportions that,
like a madman, he would race, the whole day, up and down the streets of
the town, throwing his stick high up into the air, and shriek out, all the
while, at the top of his voice, 'Ali!' This dervish was venerated by everybody
as a saint, and received everywhere with the greatest distinction." ARMINIUS
VAMBÉRY, his Life and Adventures, written by Himself, London, 1889, p. 69.
On the anniversary of the death of Hussein, Ali's son, the Shi-ite Moslems
still make the air resound with cries of his name and Ali's.

[2] Compare H. C. WARREN: Buddhism in Translation, Cambridge, U. S.,
1898, passim.

[3] Compare J. L. MERRICK: The Life and Religion of Mohammed, as contained in the Sheeah traditions of the Hyat-ul-Kuloob, Boston, 1850, passim.

occupation; and crusades have been preached and massacres instigated for no other reason than to remove a fancied slight upon the God. Theologies representing the gods as mindful of their glory, and churches with imperialistic policies, have conspired to fan this temper to a glow, so that intolerance and persecution have come to be vices associated by some of us inseparably with the saintly mind. They are unquestionably its besetting sins. The saintly temper is a moral temper, and a moral temper has often to be cruel. It is a partisan temper, and that is cruel. Between his own and Jehovah's enemies a David knows no difference; a Catherine of Siena, panting to stop the warfare among Christians which was the scandal of her epoch, can think of no better method of union among them than a crusade to massacre the Turks; Luther finds no word of protest or regret over the atrocious tortures with which the Anabaptist leaders were put to death; and a Cromwell praises the Lord for delivering his enemies into his hands for 'execution.' Politics come in in all such cases; but piety finds the partnership not quite unnatural. So, when 'freethinkers' tell us that religion and fanaticism are twins, we cannot make an unqualified denial of the charge.

Fanaticism must then be inscribed on the wrong side of religion's account, so long as the religious person's intellect is on the stage which the despotic kind of God satisfies. But as soon as the God is represented as less intent on his own honor and glory, it ceases to be a danger.

Fanaticism is found only where the character is masterful and aggressive. In gentle characters, where devoutness is intense and the intellect feeble, we have an imaginative absorption in the love of God to the exclusion of all practical human interests, which, though innocent enough, is too one-sided to be admirable. A mind too narrow has room but for one kind of affection. When the love of God takes possession of such a mind, it expels all human loves and human uses. There is no English name for such a sweet excess of devotion, so I will refer to it as a *theopathic* condition.

The blessed Margaret Mary Alacoque may serve as an example.

"To be loved here upon the earth," her recent biographer

exclaims: "to be loved by a noble, elevated, distinguished being; to be loved with fidelity, with devotion,—what enchantment! But to be loved by God! and loved by him to distraction [aimé jusqu'à la folie]!—Margaret melted away with love at the thought of such a thing. Like Saint Philip of Neri in former times, or like Saint Francis Xavier, she said to God: 'Hold back, O my God, these torrents which overwhelm me, or else enlarge my capacity for their reception.' "[1]

The most signal proofs of God's love which Margaret Mary received were her hallucinations of sight, touch, and hearing, and the most signal in turn of these were the revelations of Christ's sacred heart, "surrounded with rays more brilliant than the Sun, and transparent like a crystal. The wound which he received on the cross visibly appeared upon it. There was a crown of thorns round about this divine Heart, and a cross above it." At the same time Christ's voice told her that, unable longer to contain the flames of his love for mankind, he had chosen her by a miracle to spread the knowledge of them. He thereupon took out her mortal heart, placed it inside of his own and inflamed it, and then replaced it in her breast, adding: "Hitherto thou hast taken the name of my slave, hereafter thou shalt be called the well-beloved disciple of my Sacred Heart."

In a later vision the Saviour revealed to her in detail the 'great design' which he wished to establish through her instrumentality. "I ask of thee to bring it about that every first Friday after the week of holy Sacrament shall be made into a special holy day for honoring my Heart by a general communion and by services intended to make honorable amends for the indignities which it has received. And I promise thee that my Heart will dilate to shed with abundance the influences of its love upon all those who pay to it these honors, or who bring it about that others do the same."

"This revelation," says Mgr. Bougaud, "is unquestionably the most important of all the revelations which have illu-

---

[1] BOUGAUD: Hist. de la bienheureuse Marguerite Marie, Paris, 1894, p. 145.

mined the Church since that of the Incarnation and of the Lord's Supper. . . . After the Eucharist, the supreme effort of the Sacred Heart."[1] Well, what were its good fruits for Margaret Mary's life? Apparently little else but sufferings and prayers and absences of mind and swoons and ecstasies. She became increasingly useless about the convent, her absorption in Christ's love,—

> "which grew upon her daily, rendering her more and more incapable of attending to external duties. They tried her in the infirmary, but without much success, although her kindness, zeal, and devotion were without bounds, and her charity rose to acts of such a heroism that our readers would not bear the recital of them. They tried her in the kitchen, but were forced to give it up as hopeless—everything dropped out of her hands. The admirable humility with which she made amends for her clumsiness could not prevent this from being prejudicial to the order and regularity which must always reign in a community. They put her in the school, where the little girls cherished her, and cut pieces out of her clothes [for relics] as if she were already a saint, but where she was too absorbed inwardly to pay the necessary attention. Poor dear sister, even less after her visions than before them was she a denizen of earth, and they had to leave her in her heaven."[2]

Poor dear sister, indeed! Amiable and good, but so feeble of intellectual outlook that it would be too much to ask of us, with our Protestant and modern education, to feel anything but indulgent pity for the kind of saintship which she embodies. A lower example still of theopathic saintliness is that of Saint Gertrude, a Benedictine nun of the thirteenth century, whose 'Revelations,' a well-known mystical authority, consist mainly of proofs of Christ's partiality for her undeserving person. Assurances of his love, intimacies and caresses and compliments of the most absurd and puerile sort, addressed by Christ to Gertrude as an individual, form the tissue of this

---

[1] BOUGAUD: Hist. de la bienheureuse Marguerite Marie, Paris, 1894, pp. 365, 241.
[2] BOUGAUD: Op. cit., p. 267.

paltry-minded recital.[1] In reading such a narrative, we realize the gap between the thirteenth and the twentieth century, and we feel that saintliness of character may yield almost absolutely worthless fruits if it be associated with such inferior intellectual sympathies. What with science, idealism, and democracy, our own imagination has grown to need a God of an entirely different temperament from that Being interested exclusively in dealing out personal favors, with whom our ancestors were so contented. Smitten as we are with the vision of social righteousness, a God indifferent to everything but adulation, and full of partiality for his individual favorites, lacks an essential element of largeness; and even the best professional sainthood of former centuries, pent in as it is to such a conception, seems to us curiously shallow and unedifying.

Take Saint Teresa, for example, one of the ablest women, in many respects, of whose life we have the record. She had a powerful intellect of the practical order. She wrote admirable descriptive psychology, possessed a will equal to any emergency, great talent for politics and business, a buoyant disposition, and a first-rate literary style. She was tenaciously aspiring, and put her whole life at the service of her religious

[1] Examples: "Suffering from a headache, she sought, for the glory of God, to relieve herself by holding certain odoriferous substances in her mouth, when the Lord appeared to her to lean over towards her lovingly, and to find comfort Himself in these odors. After having gently breathed them in, He arose, and said with a gratified air to the Saints, as if contented with what He had done: 'See the new present which my betrothed has given Me!'

"One day, at chapel, she heard supernaturally sung the words, *'Sanctus, Sanctus, Sanctus.'* The Son of God leaning towards her like a sweet lover, and giving to her soul the softest kiss, said to her at the second Sanctus: 'In this *Sanctus* addressed to my person, receive with this kiss all the sanctity of my divinity and of my humanity, and let it be to thee a sufficient preparation for approaching the communion table.' And the next following Sunday, while she was thanking God for this favor, behold the Son of God, more beauteous than thousands of angels, takes her in His arms as if He were proud of her, and presents her to God the Father, in that perfection of sanctity with which He had dowered her. And the Father took such delight in this soul thus presented by His only Son, that, as if unable longer to restrain Himself, He gave her, and the Holy Ghost gave her also, the Sanctity attributed to each by His own *Sanctus*—and thus she remained endowed with the plenary fullness of the blessing of *Sanctity*, bestowed on her by Omnipotence, by Wisdom, and by Love." Révélations de Sainte Gertrude, Paris, 1898, i. 44, 186.

ideals. Yet so paltry were these, according to our present way of thinking, that (although I know that others have been moved differently) I confess that my only feeling in reading her has been pity that so much vitality of soul should have found such poor employment.

In spite of the sufferings which she endured, there is a curious flavor of superficiality about her genius. A Birmingham anthropologist, Dr. Jordan, has divided the human race into two types, whom he calls 'shrews' and 'non-shrews' respectively.[1] The shrew-type is defined as possessing an 'active unimpassioned temperament.' In other words, shrews are the 'motors,' rather than the 'sensories,'[2] and their expressions are as a rule more energetic than the feelings which appear to prompt them. Saint Teresa, paradoxical as such a judgment may sound, was a typical shrew, in this sense of the term. The bustle of her style, as well as of her life, proves it. Not only must she receive unheard-of personal favors and spiritual graces from her Saviour, but she must immediately write about them and *exploiter* them professionally, and use her expertness to give instruction to those less privileged. Her voluble egotism; her sense, not of radical bad being, as the really contrite have it, but of her 'faults' and 'imperfections' in the plural; her stereotyped humility and return upon herself, as covered with 'confusion' at each new manifestation of God's singular partiality for a person so unworthy, are typical of shrewdom: a paramountly feeling nature would be objectively lost in gratitude, and silent. She had some public instincts, it is true; she hated the Lutherans, and longed for the church's triumph over them; but in the main her idea of religion seems to have been that of an endless amatory flirtation—if one may say so without irreverence—between the devotee and the deity; and apart from helping younger nuns to go in this direction by the inspiration of her example and instruction, there is absolutely no human use in her, or sign of any general human interest. Yet the spirit of her age, far from rebuking her, exalted her as superhuman.

[1] FURNEAUX JORDAN: Character in Birth and Parentage, first edition. Later editions change the nomenclature.

[2] As to this distinction, see the admirably practical account in J. M. BALDWIN's little book, The Story of the Mind, 1898.

We have to pass a similar judgment on the whole notion of saintship based on merits. Any God who, on the one hand, can care to keep a pedantically minute account of individual shortcomings, and on the other can feel such partialities, and load particular creatures with such insipid marks of favor, is too small-minded a God for our credence. When Luther, in his immense manly way, swept off by a stroke of his hand the very notion of a debit and credit account kept with individuals by the Almighty, he stretched the soul's imagination and saved theology from puerility.

So much for mere devotion, divorced from the intellectual conceptions which might guide it towards bearing useful human fruit.

The next saintly virtue in which we find excess is Purity. In theopathic characters, like those whom we have just considered, the love of God must not be mixed with any other love. Father and mother, sisters, brothers, and friends are felt as interfering distractions; for sensitiveness and narrowness, when they occur together, as they often do, require above all things a simplified world to dwell in. Variety and confusion are too much for their powers of comfortable adaptation. But whereas your aggressive pietist reaches his unity objectively, by forcibly stamping disorder and divergence out, your retiring pietist reaches his subjectively, leaving disorder in the world at large, but making a smaller world in which he dwells himself and from which he eliminates it altogether. Thus, alongside of the church militant with its prisons, dragonnades, and inquisition methods, we have the church *fugient*, as one might call it, with its hermitages, monasteries, and sectarian organizations, both churches pursuing the same object—to unify the life,[1] and simplify the spectacle presented

---

[1] On this subject I refer to the work of M. MURISIER (Les Maladies du Sentiment Religieux, Paris, 1901), who makes inner unification the mainspring of the whole religious life. But *all* strongly ideal interests, religious or irreligious, unify the mind and tend to subordinate everything to themselves. One would infer from M. Murisier's pages that this formal condition was peculiarly characteristic of religion, and that one might in comparison almost neglect material content, in studying the latter. I trust that the present work will convince the reader that religion has plenty of material content which is

to the soul. A mind extremely sensitive to inner discords will drop one external relation after another, as interfering with the absorption of consciousness in spiritual things. Amusements must go first, then conventional 'society,' then business, then family duties, until at last seclusion, with a subdivision of the day into hours for stated religious acts, is the only thing that can be borne. The lives of saints are a history of successive renunciations of complication, one form of contact with the outer life being dropped after another, to save the purity of inner tone.[1] "Is it not better," a young sister asks her Superior, "that I should not speak at all during the hour of recreation, so as not to run the risk, by speaking, of falling into some sin of which I might not be conscious?"[2] If the life remains a social one at all, those who take part in it must follow one identical rule. Embosomed in this monotony, the zealot for purity feels clean and free once more. The minuteness of uniformity maintained in certain sectarian communities, whether monastic or not, is something almost inconceivable to a man of the world. Costume, phraseology, hours, and habits are absolutely stereotyped, and there is no doubt that some persons are so made as to find in this stability an incomparable kind of mental rest.

We have no time to multiply examples, so I will let the case of Saint Louis of Gonzaga serve as a type of excess in purifi-

---

characteristic, and which is more important by far than any general psychological form. In spite of this criticism, I find M. Murisier's book highly instructive.

[1] Example: "At the first beginning of the Servitor's [Suso's] interior life, after he had purified his soul properly by confession, he marked out for himself, in thought, three circles, within which he shut himself up, as in a spiritual intrenchment. The first circle was his cell, his chapel, and the choir. When he was within this circle, he seemed to himself in complete security. The second circle was the whole monastery as far as the outer gate. The third and outermost circle was the gate itself, and here it was necessary for him to stand well upon his guard. When he went outside these circles, it seemed to him that he was in the plight of some wild animal which is outside its hole, and surrounded by the hunt, and therefore in need of all its cunning and watchfulness." The Life of the Blessed Henry Suso, by Himself, translated by KNOX, London, 1865, p. 168.

[2] Vie des premières Religieuses Dominicaines de la Congrégation de St. Dominique, à Nancy; Nancy, 1896, p. 129.

cation. I think you will agree that this youth carried the elimination of the external and discordant to a point which we cannot unreservedly admire. At the age of ten, his biographer says:—

"The inspiration came to him to consecrate to the Mother of God his own virginity—that being to her the most agreeable of possible presents. Without delay, then, and with all the fervor there was in him, joyous of heart, and burning with love, he made his vow of perpetual chastity. Mary accepted the offering of his innocent heart, and obtained for him from God, as a recompense, the extraordinary grace of never feeling during his entire life the slightest touch of temptation against the virtue of purity. This was an altogether exceptional favor, rarely accorded even to Saints themselves, and all the more marvelous in that Louis dwelt always in courts and among great folks, where danger and opportunity are so unusually frequent. It is true that Louis from his earliest childhood had shown a natural repugnance for whatever might be impure or unvirginal, and even for relations of any sort whatever between persons of opposite sex. But this made it all the more surprising that he should, especially since this vow, feel it necessary to have recourse to such a number of expedients for protecting against even the shadow of danger the virginity which he had thus consecrated. One might suppose that if any one could have contented himself with the ordinary precautions, prescribed for all Christians, it would assuredly have been he. But no! In the use of preservatives and means of defense, in flight from the most insignificant occasions, from every possibility of peril, just as in the mortification of his flesh, he went farther than the majority of saints. He, who by an extraordinary protection of God's grace was never tempted, measured all his steps as if he were threatened on every side by particular dangers. Thenceforward he never raised his eyes, either when walking in the streets, or when in society. Not only did he avoid all business with females even more scrupulously than before, but he renounced all conversation and every kind of social recreation with them, although his father tried to make him take part;

and he commenced only too early to deliver his innocent body to austerities of every kind."[1]

At the age of twelve, we read of this young man that "if by chance his mother sent one of her maids of honor to him with a message, he never allowed her to come in, but listened to her through the barely opened door, and dismissed her immediately. He did not like to be alone with his own mother, whether at table or in conversation; and when the rest of the company withdrew, he sought also a pretext for retiring. . . . Several great ladies, relatives of his, he avoided learning to know even by sight; and he made a sort of treaty with his father, engaging promptly and readily to accede to all his wishes, if he might only be excused from all visits to ladies." (Ibid., p. 71.)

When he was seventeen years old Louis joined the Jesuit order,[2] against his father's passionate entreaties, for he was heir of a princely house; and when a year later the father died, he took the loss as a 'particular attention' to himself on God's part, and wrote letters of stilted good advice, as from a spiritual superior, to his grieving mother. He soon became so good a monk that if any one asked him the number of his brothers and sisters, he had to reflect and count them over before replying. A Father asked him one day if he were never troubled by the thought of his family, to which, "I never think of them except when praying for them," was his only answer. Never was he seen to hold in his hand a flower or anything perfumed, that he might take pleasure in it. On the contrary, in the hospital, he used to seek for whatever was most disgusting, and eagerly snatch the bandages of ulcers, etc., from the hands of his companions. He avoided worldly talk, and immediately tried to turn every conversation on to pious subjects, or else he remained silent. He systematically refused to notice his surroundings. Being ordered one day to bring a book from the rector's seat in the refectory, he had

[1] MESCHLER'S Life of Saint Louis of Gonzaga, French translation by LE-BRÉQUIER, 1891, p. 40.

[2] In his boyish note-book he praises the monastic life for its freedom from sin, and for the imperishable treasures, which it enables us to store up, "of merit in God's eyes which makes of Him our debtor for all Eternity." Loc. cit., p. 62.

to ask where the rector sat, for in the three months he had eaten bread there, so carefully did he guard his eyes that he had not noticed the place. One day, during recess, having looked by chance on one of his companions, he reproached himself as for a grave sin against modesty. He cultivated silence, as preserving from sins of the tongue; and his greatest penance was the limit which his superiors set to his bodily penances. He sought after false accusations and unjust reprimands as opportunities of humility; and such was his obedience that, when a room-mate, having no more paper, asked him for a sheet, he did not feel free to give it to him without first obtaining the permission of the superior, who, as such, stood in the place of God, and transmitted his orders.

I can find no other sorts of fruit than these of Louis's saintship. He died in 1591, in his twenty-ninth year, and is known in the Church as the patron of all young people. On his festival, the altar in the chapel devoted to him in a certain church in Rome "is embosomed in flowers, arranged with exquisite taste; and a pile of letters may be seen at its foot, written to the Saint by young men and women, and directed to 'Paradiso.' They are supposed to be burnt unread except by San Luigi, who must find singular petitions in these pretty little missives, tied up now with a green ribbon, expressive of hope, now with a red one, emblematic of love," etc.[1]

[1] Mademoiselle Mori, a novel quoted in HARE's Walks in Rome, 1900, i. 55.
I cannot resist the temptation to quote from Starbuck's book, p. 388, another case of purification by elimination. It runs as follows:—
"The signs of abnormality which sanctified persons show are of frequent occurrence. They get out of tune with other people; often they will have nothing to do with churches, which they regard as worldly; they become hypercritical towards others; they grow careless of their social, political, and financial obligations. As an instance of this type may be mentioned a woman of sixty-eight of whom the writer made a special study. She had been a member of one of the most active and progressive churches in a busy part of a large city. Her pastor described her as having reached the censorious stage. She had grown more and more out of sympathy with the church; her connection with it finally consisted simply in attendance at prayer-meeting, at which her only message was that of reproof and condemnation of the others for living on a low plane. At last she withdrew from fellowship with any church. The writer found her living alone in a little room on the top story of a cheap boarding-house, quite out of touch with all human relations, but apparently happy in the enjoyment of her own spiritual blessings. Her time

Our final judgment of the worth of such a life as this will depend largely on our conception of God, and of the sort of conduct he is best pleased with in his creatures. The Catholicism of the sixteenth century paid little heed to social righteousness; and to leave the world to the devil whilst saving one's own soul was then accounted no discreditable scheme. To-day, rightly or wrongly, helpfulness in general human affairs is, in consequence of one of those secular mutations in moral sentiment of which I spoke, deemed an essential element of worth in character; and to be of some public or private use is also reckoned as a species of divine service. Other early Jesuits, especially the missionaries among them, the Xaviers, Brébeufs, Jogues, were objective minds, and fought in their way for the world's welfare; so their lives to-day inspire us. But when the intellect, as in this Louis, is originally no larger than a pin's head, and cherishes ideas of God of corresponding smallness, the result, notwithstanding the heroism put forth, is on the whole repulsive. Purity, we see in the object-lesson, is *not* the one thing needful; and it is better that a life should contract many a dirt-mark, than forfeit usefulness in its efforts to remain unspotted.

Proceeding onwards in our search of religious extravagance, we next come upon excesses of Tenderness and Charity. Here saintliness has to face the charge of preserving the unfit, and breeding parasites and beggars. 'Resist not evil,' 'Love your enemies,' these are saintly maxims of which men

---

was occupied in writing booklets on sanctification—page after page of dreamy rhapsody. She proved to be one of a small group of persons who claim that entire salvation involves three steps instead of two; not only must there be conversion and sanctification, but a third, which they call 'crucifixion' or 'perfect redemption,' and which seems to bear the same relation to sanctification that this bears to conversion. She related how the Spirit had said to her, 'Stop going to church. Stop going to holiness meetings. Go to your own room and I will teach you.' She professes to care nothing for colleges, or preachers, or churches, but only cares to listen to what God says to her. Her description of her experience seemed entirely consistent; she is happy and contented, and her life is entirely satisfactory to herself. While listening to her own story, one was tempted to forget that it was from the life of a person who could not live by it in conjunction with her fellows."

of this world find it hard to speak without impatience. Are the men of this world right, or are the saints in possession of the deeper range of truth?

No simple answer is possible. Here, if anywhere, one feels the complexity of the moral life, and the mysteriousness of the way in which facts and ideals are interwoven.

Perfect conduct is a relation between three terms: the actor, the objects for which he acts, and the recipients of the action. In order that conduct should be abstractly perfect, all three terms, intention, execution, and reception, should be suited to one another. The best intention will fail if it either work by false means or address itself to the wrong recipient. Thus no critic or estimator of the value of conduct can confine himself to the actor's animus alone, apart from the other elements of the performance. As there is no worse lie than a truth misunderstood by those who hear it, so reasonable arguments, challenges to magnanimity, and appeals to sympathy or justice, are folly when we are dealing with human crocodiles and boa-constrictors. The saint may simply give the universe into the hands of the enemy by his trustfulness. He may by non-resistance cut off his own survival.

Herbert Spencer tells us that the perfect man's conduct will appear perfect only when the environment is perfect: to no inferior environment is it suitably adapted. We may paraphrase this by cordially admitting that saintly conduct would be the most perfect conduct conceivable in an environment where all were saints already; but by adding that in an environment where few are saints, and many the exact reverse of saints, it must be ill adapted. We must frankly confess, then, using our empirical common sense and ordinary practical prejudices, that in the world that actually is, the virtues of sympathy, charity, and non-resistance may be, and often have been, manifested in excess. The powers of darkness have systematically taken advantage of them. The whole modern scientific organization of charity is a consequence of the failure of simply giving alms. The whole history of constitutional government is a commentary on the excellence of resisting evil, and when one cheek is smitten, of smiting back and not turning the other cheek also.

You will agree to this in general, for in spite of the Gospel, in spite of Quakerism, in spite of Tolstoi, you believe in fighting fire with fire, in shooting down usurpers, locking up thieves, and freezing out vagabonds and swindlers.

And yet you are sure, as I am sure, that were the world confined to these hard-headed, hard-hearted, and hard-fisted methods exclusively, were there no one prompt to help a brother first, and find out afterwards whether he were worthy; no one willing to drown his private wrongs in pity for the wronger's person; no one ready to be duped many a time rather than live always on suspicion; no one glad to treat individuals passionately and impulsively rather than by general rules of prudence; the world would be an infinitely worse place than it is now to live in. The tender grace, not of a day that is dead, but of a day yet to be born somehow, with the golden rule grown natural, would be cut out from the perspective of our imaginations.

The saints, existing in this way, may, with their extravagances of human tenderness, be prophetic. Nay, innumerable times they have proved themselves prophetic. Treating those whom they met, in spite of the past, in spite of all appearances, as worthy, they have stimulated them to *be* worthy, miraculously transformed them by their radiant example and by the challenge of their expectation.

From this point of view we may admit the human charity which we find in all saints, and the great excess of it which we find in some saints, to be a genuinely creative social force, tending to make real a degree of virtue which it alone is ready to assume as possible. The saints are authors, *auctores*, increasers, of goodness. The potentialities of development in human souls are unfathomable. So many who seemed irretrievably hardened have in point of fact been softened, converted, regenerated, in ways that amazed the subjects even more than they surprised the spectators, that we never can be sure in advance of any man that his salvation by the way of love is hopeless. We have no right to speak of human crocodiles and boa-constrictors as of fixedly incurable beings. We know not the complexities of personality, the smouldering emotional fires, the other facets of the character-polyhedron, the resources of the subliminal region. St. Paul long ago made our ancestors familiar with the idea that every soul is virtually sacred. Since Christ died for us all without exception, St. Paul said, we must despair of no one. This belief in the essential sacredness of every one expresses itself to-day in all sorts of humane customs and reformatory institutions, and in a growing aversion to the death penalty and to brutality in punishment. The saints, with their extravagance of human tenderness, are the great torch-bearers of this belief, the tip of the wedge, the cleavers of the darkness. Like the single drops which sparkle in the sun as they are flung far ahead of the advancing edge of a wave-crest or of a flood, they show the way and are forerunners. The world is not yet with them, so they often seem in the midst of the world's affairs to be preposterous. Yet they are impregnators of the world, vivifiers and animaters of potentialities of goodness which but for them would lie forever dormant. It is not possible to be quite as mean as we naturally are, when they have passed before us. One fire kindles another; and without that over-trust in human worth which they show, the rest of us would lie in spiritual stagnancy.

Momentarily considered, then, the saint may waste his tenderness and be the dupe and victim of his charitable fever, but the general function of his charity in social evolution is vital and essential. If things are ever to move upward, some one must be ready to take the first step, and assume the risk of it. No one who is not willing to try charity, to try non-resistance as the saint is always willing, can tell whether these methods will or will not succeed. When they do succeed, they are far more powerfully successful than force or worldly prudence. Force destroys enemies; and the best that can be said of prudence is that it keeps what we already have in safety. But non-resistance, when successful, turns enemies into friends; and charity regenerates its objects. These saintly methods are, as I said, creative energies; and genuine saints find in the elevated excitement with which their faith endows them an authority and impressiveness which makes them irresistible in situations where men of shallower nature cannot get on at all without the use of worldly prudence. This practical proof that worldly wisdom may be safely transcended is the saint's magic gift to mankind.[1] Not only does his vision of a better world console us for the generally prevailing prose and barrenness; but even when on the whole we have to confess him ill adapted, he makes some converts, and the environment gets better for his ministry. He is an effective ferment of

[1] The best missionary lives abound in the victorious combination of non-resistance with personal authority. John G. Paton, for example, in the New Hebrides, among brutish Melanesian cannibals, preserves a charmed life by dint of it. When it comes to the point, no one ever dares actually to strike him. Native converts, inspired by him, showed analogous virtue. "One of our chiefs, full of the Christ-kindled desire to seek and to save, sent a message to an inland chief, that he and four attendants would come on Sabbath and tell them the gospel of Jehovah God. The reply came back sternly forbidding their visit, and threatening with death any Christian that approached their village. Our chief sent in response a loving message, telling them that Jehovah had taught the Christians to return good for evil, and that they would come unarmed to tell them the story of how the Son of God came into the world and died in order to bless and save his enemies. The heathen chief sent back a stern and prompt reply once more: 'If you come, you will be killed.' On Sabbath morn the Christian chief and his four companions were met outside the village by the heathen chief, who implored and threatened them once more. But the former said: —

" 'We come to you without weapons of war! We come only to tell you about Jesus. We believe that He will protect us to-day.'

"As they pressed steadily forward towards the village, spears began to be thrown at them. Some they evaded, being all except one dexterous warriors; and others they literally received with their bare hands, and turned them aside in an incredible manner. The heathen, apparently thunderstruck at these men thus approaching them without weapons of war, and not even flinging back their own spears which they had caught, after having thrown what the old chief called 'a shower of spears,' desisted from mere surprise. Our Christian chief called out, as he and his companions drew up in the midst of them on the village public ground: —

" 'Jehovah thus protects us. He has given us all your spears! Once we would have thrown them back at you and killed you. But now we come, not to fight but to tell you about Jesus. He has changed our dark hearts. He asks you now to lay down all these your other weapons of war, and to hear what we can tell you about the love of God, our great Father, the only living God.'

"The heathen were perfectly overawed. They manifestly looked on these Christians as protected by some Invisible One. They listened for the first time to the story of the Gospel and of the Cross. We lived to see that chief and all his tribe sitting in the school of Christ. And there is perhaps not an island in these southern seas, amongst all those won for Christ, where similar acts of heroism on the part of converts cannot be recited." JOHN G. PATON, Missionary to the New Hebrides, An Autobiography, second part, London, 1890, p. 243.

goodness, a slow transmuter of the earthly into a more heavenly order.

In this respect the Utopian dreams of social justice in which many contemporary socialists and anarchists indulge are, in spite of their impracticability and non-adaptation to present environmental conditions, analogous to the saint's belief in an existent kingdom of heaven. They help to break the edge of the general reign of hardness, and are slow leavens of a better order.

The next topic in order is Asceticism, which I fancy you are all ready to consider without argument a virtue liable to extravagance and excess. The optimism and refinement of the modern imagination has, as I have already said elsewhere, changed the attitude of the church towards corporeal mortification, and a Suso or a Saint Peter of Alcantara[1] appear to us to-day rather in the light of tragic mountebanks than of sane men inspiring us with respect. If the inner dispositions are right, we ask, what need of all this torment, this violation of the outer nature? It keeps the outer nature too important. Any one who is genuinely emancipated from the flesh will look on pleasures and pains, abundance and privation, as alike irrelevant and indifferent. He can engage in actions and experience enjoyments without fear of corruption or enslavement. As the Bhagavad-Gita says, only those need renounce worldly actions who are still inwardly attached thereto. If one be really unattached to the fruits of action, one may mix in

[1] Saint Peter, Saint Teresa tells us in her autobiography (French translation, p. 333), "had passed forty years without ever sleeping more than an hour and a half a day. Of all his mortifications, this was the one that had cost him the most. To compass it, he kept always on his knees or on his feet. The little sleep he allowed nature to take was snatched in a sitting posture, his head leaning against a piece of wood fixed in the wall. Even had he wished to lie down, it would have been impossible, because his cell was only four feet and a half long. In the course of all these years he never raised his hood, no matter what the ardor of the sun or the rain's strength. He never put on a shoe. He wore a garment of coarse sackcloth, with nothing else upon his skin. This garment was as scant as possible, and over it a little cloak of the same stuff. When the cold was great he took off the cloak and opened for a while the door and little window of his cell. Then he closed them and resumed the mantle,—his way, as he told us, of warming himself, and making his body feel a better temperature. It was a frequent thing with him to eat

the world with equanimity. I quoted in a former lecture Saint Augustine's antinomian saying: If you only love God enough, you may safely follow all your inclinations. "He needs no devotional practices," is one of Ramakrishna's maxims, "whose heart is moved to tears at the mere mention of the name of Hari."[1] And the Buddha, in pointing out what he called 'the middle way' to his disciples, told them to abstain from both extremes, excessive mortification being as unreal and unworthy as mere desire and pleasure. The only perfect life, he said, is that of inner wisdom, which makes one thing as indifferent to us as another, and thus leads to rest, to peace, and to Nirvâna.[2]

We find accordingly that as ascetic saints have grown older, and directors of conscience more experienced, they usually have shown a tendency to lay less stress on special bodily mortifications. Catholic teachers have always professed the rule that, since health is needed for efficiency in God's service, health must not be sacrificed to mortification. The general optimism and healthy-mindedness of liberal Protestant circles to-day makes mortification for mortification's sake repugnant to us. We can no longer sympathize with cruel deities, and the notion that God can take delight in the spectacle of sufferings self-inflicted in his honor is abhorrent. In consequence of all these motives you probably are disposed, unless some

---

once only in three days; and when I expressed my surprise, he said that it was very easy if one once had acquired the habit. One of his companions has assured me that he has gone sometimes eight days without food. . . . His poverty was extreme; and his mortification, even in his youth, was such that he told me he had passed three years in a house of his order without knowing any of the monks otherwise than by the sound of their voice, for he never raised his eyes, and only found his way about by following the others. He showed this same modesty on public highways. He spent many years without ever laying eyes upon a woman; but he confessed to me that at the age he had reached it was indifferent to him whether he laid eyes on them or not. He was very old when I first came to know him, and his body so attenuated that it seemed formed of nothing so much as of so many roots of trees. With all this sanctity he was very affable. He never spoke unless he was questioned, but his intellectual right-mindedness and grace gave to all his words an irresistible charm."

[1] F. MAX MÜLLER: Ramakrishna, his Life and Sayings, 1899, p. 180.
[2] OLDENBERG: Buddha; translated by W. HOEY, London, 1882, p. 127.

special utility can be shown in some individual's discipline, to treat the general tendency to asceticism as pathological.

Yet I believe that a more careful consideration of the whole matter, distinguishing between the general good intention of asceticism and the uselessness of some of the particular acts of which it may be guilty, ought to rehabilitate it in our esteem. For in its spiritual meaning asceticism stands for nothing less than for the essence of the twice-born philosophy. It symbolizes, lamely enough no doubt, but sincerely, the belief that there is an element of real wrongness in this world, which is neither to be ignored nor evaded, but which must be squarely met and overcome by an appeal to the soul's heroic resources, and neutralized and cleansed away by suffering. As against this view, the ultra-optimistic form of the once-born philosophy thinks we may treat evil by the method of ignoring. Let a man who, by fortunate health and circumstances, escapes the suffering of any great amount of evil in his own person, also close his eyes to it as it exists in the wider universe outside his private experience, and he will be quit of it altogether, and can sail through life happily on a healthy-minded basis. But we saw in our lectures on melancholy how precarious this attempt necessarily is. Moreover it is but for the individual; and leaves the evil outside of him unredeemed and unprovided for in his philosophy.

No such attempt can be a *general* solution of the problem; and to minds of sombre tinge, who naturally feel life as a tragic mystery, such optimism is a shallow dodge or mean evasion. It accepts, in lieu of a real deliverance, what is a lucky personal accident merely, a cranny to escape by. It leaves the general world unhelped and still in the clutch of Satan. The real deliverance, the twice-born folk insist, must be of universal application. Pain and wrong and death must be fairly met and overcome in higher excitement, or else their sting remains essentially unbroken. If one has ever taken the fact of the prevalence of tragic death in this world's history fairly into his mind,—freezing, drowning, entombment alive, wild beasts, worse men, and hideous diseases,—he can with difficulty, it seems to me, continue his own career of worldly prosperity without suspecting that he may all the while not be really inside the game, that he may lack the great initiation.

Well, this is exactly what asceticism thinks; and it voluntarily takes the initiation. Life is neither farce nor genteel comedy, it says, but something we must sit at in mourning garments, hoping its bitter taste will purge us of our folly. The wild and the heroic are indeed such rooted parts of it that healthy-mindedness pure and simple, with its sentimental optimism, can hardly be regarded by any thinking man as a serious solution. Phrases of neatness, cosiness, and comfort can never be an answer to the sphinx's riddle.

In these remarks I am leaning only upon mankind's common instinct for reality, which in point of fact has always held the world to be essentially a theatre for heroism. In heroism, we feel, life's supreme mystery is hidden. We tolerate no one who has no capacity whatever for it in any direction. On the other hand, no matter what a man's frailties otherwise may be, if he be willing to risk death, and still more if he suffer it heroically, in the service he has chosen, the fact consecrates him forever. Inferior to ourselves in this or that way, if yet we cling to life, and he is able 'to fling it away like a flower' as caring nothing for it, we account him in the deepest way our born superior. Each of us in his own person feels that a high-hearted indifference to life would expiate all his shortcomings.

The metaphysical mystery, thus recognized by common sense, that he who feeds on death that feeds on men possesses life supereminently and excellently, and meets best the secret demands of the universe, is the truth of which asceticism has been the faithful champion. The folly of the cross, so inexplicable by the intellect, has yet its indestructible vital meaning.

Representatively, then, and symbolically, and apart from the vagaries into which the unenlightened intellect of former times may have let it wander, asceticism must, I believe, be acknowledged to go with the profounder way of handling the gift of existence. Naturalistic optimism is mere syllabub and flattery and sponge-cake in comparison. The practical course of action for us, as religious men, would therefore, it seems to me, not be simply to turn our backs upon the ascetic impulse, as most of us to-day turn them, but rather to discover some outlet for it of which the fruits in the way of privation and hardship might be objectively useful. The older monastic asceticism occupied itself with pathetic futilities, or terminated in the mere egotism of the individual, increasing his own perfection.[1] But is it not possible for us to discard most of these older forms of mortification, and yet find saner channels for the heroism which inspired them?

Does not, for example, the worship of material luxury and wealth, which constitutes so large a portion of the 'spirit' of our age, make somewhat for effeminacy and unmanliness? Is not the exclusively sympathetic and facetious way in which most children are brought up to-day—so different from the education of a hundred years ago, especially in evangelical circles—in danger, in spite of its many advantages, of developing a certain trashiness of fibre? Are there not hereabouts some points of application for a renovated and revised ascetic discipline?

Many of you would recognize such dangers, but would point to athletics, militarism, and individual and national enterprise and adventure as the remedies. These contemporary ideals are quite as remarkable for the energy with which they make for heroic standards of life, as contemporary religion is remarkable for the way in which it neglects them.[2] War and adventure assuredly keep all who engage in them from treating themselves too tenderly. They demand such incredible efforts, depth beyond depth of exertion, both in degree and in duration, that the whole scale of motivation alters. Discomfort and annoyance, hunger and wet, pain and cold, squalor and filth, cease to have any deterrent operation whatever. Death turns into a commonplace matter, and its usual power to check our action vanishes. With the annulling of these customary inhibitions, ranges of new energy are set free, and life seems cast upon a higher plane of power.

The beauty of war in this respect is that it is so congruous with ordinary human nature. Ancestral evolution has made us

---

[1] "The vanities of all others may die out, but the vanity of a saint as regards his sainthood is hard indeed to wear away." Ramakrishna, his Life and Sayings, 1899, p. 172.

[2] "When a church has to be run by oysters, ice-cream, and fun," I read in an American religious paper, "you may be sure that it is running away from Christ." Such, if one may judge by appearances, is the present plight of many of our churches.

all potential warriors; so the most insignificant individual, when thrown into an army in the field, is weaned from whatever excess of tenderness towards his precious person he may bring with him, and may easily develop into a monster of insensibility.

But when we compare the military type of self-severity with that of the ascetic saint, we find a world-wide difference in all their spiritual concomitants.

" 'Live and let live,' " writes a clear-headed Austrian officer, "is no device for an army. Contempt for one's own comrades, for the troops of the enemy, and, above all, fierce contempt for one's own person, are what war demands of every one. Far better is it for an army to be too savage, too cruel, too barbarous, than to possess too much sentimentality and human reasonableness. If the soldier is to be good for anything as a soldier, he must be exactly the opposite of a reasoning and thinking man. The measure of goodness in him is his possible use in war. War, and even peace, require of the soldier absolutely peculiar standards of morality. The recruit brings with him common moral notions, of which he must seek immediately to get rid. For him victory, success, must be *everything*. The most barbaric tendencies in men come to life again in war, and for war's uses they are incommensurably good."[1]

These words are of course literally true. The immediate aim of the soldier's life is, as Moltke said, destruction, and nothing but destruction; and whatever constructions wars result in are remote and non-military. Consequently the soldier cannot train himself to be too feelingless to all those usual sympathies and respects, whether for persons or for things, that make for conservation. Yet the fact remains that war is a school of strenuous life and heroism; and, being in the line of aboriginal instinct, is the only school that as yet is universally available. But when we gravely ask ourselves whether this wholesale organization of irrationality and crime be our only bulwark against effeminacy, we stand aghast at the thought, and think more kindly of ascetic religion. One hears of the mechanical equivalent of heat. What we now need to discover

[1] C. V. B. K.: Friedens- und Kriegs-moral der Heere. Quoted by HAMON: Psychologie du Militaire professionel, 1895, p. xli.

in the social realm is the moral equivalent of war: something heroic that will speak to men as universally as war does, and yet will be as compatible with their spiritual selves as war has proved itself to be incompatible. I have often thought that in the old monkish poverty-worship, in spite of the pedantry which infested it, there might be something like that moral equivalent of war which we are seeking. May not voluntarily accepted poverty be 'the strenuous life,' without the need of crushing weaker peoples?

Poverty indeed *is* the strenuous life,—without brass bands or uniforms or hysteric popular applause or lies or circumlo-cutions; and when one sees the way in which wealth-getting enters as an ideal into the very bone and marrow of our generation, one wonders whether a revival of the belief that poverty is a worthy religious vocation may not be 'the transformation of military courage,' and the spiritual reform which our time stands most in need of.

Among us English-speaking peoples especially do the praises of poverty need once more to be boldly sung. We have grown literally afraid to be poor. We despise any one who elects to be poor in order to simplify and save his inner life. If he does not join the general scramble and pant with the money-making street, we deem him spiritless and lacking in ambition. We have lost the power even of imagining what the ancient idealization of poverty could have meant: the libera-tion from material attachments, the unbribed soul, the man-lier indifference, the paying our way by what we are or do and not by what we have, the right to fling away our life at any moment irresponsibly,—the more athletic trim, in short, the moral fighting shape. When we of the so-called better classes are scared as men were never scared in history at ma-terial ugliness and hardship; when we put off marriage until our house can be artistic, and quake at the thought of having a child without a bank-account and doomed to manual labor, it is time for thinking men to protest against so unmanly and irreligious a state of opinion.

It is true that so far as wealth gives time for ideal ends and exercise to ideal energies, wealth is better than poverty and ought to be chosen. But wealth does this in only a portion of the actual cases. Elsewhere the desire to gain wealth and the fear to lose it are our chief breeders of cowardice and propagators of corruption. There are thousands of conjunctures in which a wealth-bound man must be a slave, whilst a man for whom poverty has no terrors becomes a freeman. Think of the strength which personal indifference to poverty would give us if we were devoted to unpopular causes. We need no longer hold our tongues or fear to vote the revolutionary or reformatory ticket. Our stocks might fall, our hopes of promotion vanish, our salaries stop, our club doors close in our faces; yet, while we lived, we would imperturbably bear witness to the spirit, and our example would help to set free our generation. The cause would need its funds, but we its servants would be potent in proportion as we personally were contented with our poverty.

I recommend this matter to your serious pondering, for it is certain that the prevalent fear of poverty among the educated classes is the worst moral disease from which our civilization suffers.

I have now said all that I can usefully say about the several fruits of religion as they are manifested in saintly lives, so I will make a brief review and pass to my more general conclusions.

Our question, you will remember, is as to whether religion stands approved by its fruits, as these are exhibited in the saintly type of character. Single attributes of saintliness may, it is true, be temperamental endowments, found in non-religious individuals. But the whole group of them forms a combination which, as such, is religious, for it seems to flow from the sense of the divine as from its psychological centre. Whoever possesses strongly this sense comes naturally to think that the smallest details of this world derive infinite significance from their relation to an unseen divine order. The thought of this order yields him a superior denomination of happiness, and a steadfastness of soul with which no other can compare. In social relations his serviceability is exemplary; he abounds in impulses to help. His help is inward as well as outward, for his sympathy reaches souls as well as bodies, and kindles unsuspected faculties therein. Instead of placing happiness where common men place it, in comfort, he places it in a higher kind of inner excitement, which converts discomforts into sources of cheer and annuls unhappiness. So he turns his back upon no duty, however thankless; and when we are in need of assistance, we can count upon the saint lending his hand with more certainty than we can count upon any other person. Finally, his humble-mindedness and his ascetic tendencies save him from the petty personal pretensions which so obstruct our ordinary social intercourse, and his purity gives us in him a clean man for a companion. Felicity, purity, charity, patience, self-severity,—these are splendid excellencies, and the saint of all men shows them in the completest possible measure.

But, as we saw, all these things together do not make saints infallible. When their intellectual outlook is narrow, they fall into all sorts of holy excesses, fanaticism or theopathic absorption, self-torment, prudery, scrupulosity, gullibility, and morbid inability to meet the world. By the very intensity of his fidelity to the paltry ideals with which an inferior intellect may inspire him, a saint can be even more objectionable and damnable than a superficial carnal man would be in the same situation. We must judge him not sentimentally only, and not in isolation, but using our own intellectual standards, placing him in his environment, and estimating his total function.

Now in the matter of intellectual standards, we must bear in mind that it is unfair, where we find narrowness of mind, always to impute it as a vice to the individual, for in religious and theological matters he probably absorbs his narrowness from his generation. Moreover, we must not confound the essentials of saintliness, which are those general passions of which I have spoken, with its accidents, which are the special determinations of these passions at any historical moment. In these determinations the saints will usually be loyal to the temporary idols of their tribe. Taking refuge in monasteries was as much an idol of the tribe in the middle ages, as bearing a hand in the world's work is to-day. Saint Francis or Saint Bernard, were they living to-day, would undoubtedly be leading consecrated lives of some sort, but quite as undoubtedly they would not lead them in retirement. Our animosity to special historic manifestations must not lead us to give away the saintly impulses in their essential nature to the tender mercies of inimical critics.

The most inimical critic of the saintly impulses whom I know is Nietzsche. He contrasts them with the worldly passions as we find these embodied in the predaceous military character, altogether to the advantage of the latter. Your born saint, it must be confessed, has something about him which often makes the gorge of a carnal man rise, so it will be worth while to consider the contrast in question more fully.

Dislike of the saintly nature seems to be a negative result of the biologically useful instinct of welcoming leadership, and glorifying the chief of the tribe. The chief is the potential, if not the actual tyrant, the masterful, overpowering man of prey. We confess our inferiority and grovel before him. We quail under his glance, and are at the same time proud of owning so dangerous a lord. Such instinctive and submissive hero-worship must have been indispensable in primeval tribal life. In the endless wars of those times, leaders were absolutely needed for the tribe's survival. If there were any tribes who owned no leaders, they can have left no issue to narrate their doom. The leaders always had good consciences, for conscience in them coalesced with will, and those who looked on their face were as much smitten with wonder at their freedom from inner restraint as with awe at the energy of their outward performances.

Compared with these beaked and taloned graspers of the world, saints are herbivorous animals, tame and harmless barn-yard poultry. There are saints whose beard you may, if you ever care to, pull with impunity. Such a man excites no thrills of wonder veiled in terror; his conscience is full of scruples and returns; he stuns us neither by his inward freedom nor his outward power; and unless he found within us an altogether different faculty of admiration to appeal to, we should pass him by with contempt.

In point of fact, he does appeal to a different faculty. Reënacted in human nature is the fable of the wind, the sun, and the traveler. The sexes embody the discrepancy. The woman loves the man the more admiringly the stormier he shows himself, and the world deifies its rulers the more for being willful and unaccountable. But the woman in turn subjugates the man by the mystery of gentleness in beauty, and the saint has always charmed the world by something similar. Mankind is susceptible and suggestible in opposite directions, and the rivalry of influences is unsleeping. The saintly and the worldly ideal pursue their feud in literature as much as in real life.

For Nietzsche the saint represents little but sneakingness and slavishness. He is the sophisticated invalid, the degenerate *par excellence*, the man of insufficient vitality. His prevalence would put the human type in danger.

"The sick are the greatest danger for the well. The weaker, not the stronger, are the strong's undoing. It is not *fear* of our fellow-man, which we should wish to see diminished; for fear rouses those who are strong to become terrible in turn themselves, and preserves the hard-earned and successful type of humanity. What is to be dreaded by us more than any other doom is not fear, but rather the great disgust, not fear, but rather the great pity—disgust and pity for our human fellows. . . . The *morbid* are our greatest peril—not the 'bad' men, not the predatory beings. Those born wrong, the miscarried, the broken—they it is, the *weakest*, who are undermining the vitality of the race, poisoning our trust in life, and putting humanity in question. Every look of them is a sigh,—'Would I were something other! I am sick and tired of what I am.' In this swamp-soil of self-contempt, every poisonous weed flourishes, and all so small, so secret, so dishonest, and so sweetly rotten. Here swarm the worms of sensitiveness and resentment; here the air smells odious with secrecy, with what is not to be acknowledged; here is woven endlessly the net of the meanest of conspiracies, the conspiracy of those who suffer against those who succeed and are victorious; here the very aspect of the victorious is hated—as if health, success, strength, pride, and the sense of power were in themselves things vicious, for which one ought eventually to make bitter expiation. Oh, how these people would themselves like to inflict the expiation, how they thirst to be the hangmen! And all the while their duplicity never confesses their hatred to be hatred."[1]

Poor Nietzsche's antipathy is itself sickly enough, but we all

[1] Zur Genealogie der Moral, Dritte Abhandlung, § 14. I have abridged, and in one place transposed, a sentence.

know what he means, and he expresses well the clash between the two ideals. The carnivorous-minded 'strong man,' the adult male and cannibal, can see nothing but mouldiness and morbidness in the saint's gentleness and self-severity, and regards him with pure loathing. The whole feud revolves essentially upon two pivots: Shall the seen world or the unseen world be our chief sphere of adaptation? and must our means of adaptation in this seen world be aggressiveness or non-resistance?

The debate is serious. In some sense and to some degree both worlds must be acknowledged and taken account of; and in the seen world both aggressiveness and non-resistance are needful. It is a question of emphasis, of more or less. Is the saint's type or the strong-man's type the more ideal?

It has often been supposed, and even now, I think, it is supposed by most persons, that there can be one intrinsically ideal type of human character. A certain kind of man, it is imagined, must be the best man absolutely and apart from the utility of his function, apart from economical considerations. The saint's type, and the knight's or gentleman's type, have always been rival claimants of this absolute ideality; and in the ideal of military religious orders both types were in a manner blended. According to the empirical philosophy, however, all ideals are matters of relation. It would be absurd, for example, to ask for a definition of 'the ideal horse,' so long as dragging drays and running races, bearing children, and jogging about with tradesmen's packages all remain as indispensable differentiations of equine function. You may take what you call a general all-round animal as a compromise, but he will be inferior to any horse of a more specialized type, in some one particular direction. We must not forget this now when, in discussing saintliness, we ask if it be an ideal type of manhood. We must test it by its economical relations.

I think that the method which Mr. Spencer uses in his Data of Ethics will help to fix our opinion. Ideality in conduct is altogether a matter of adaptation. A society where all were invariably aggressive would destroy itself by inner friction, and in a society where some are aggressive, others must be non-resistant, if there is to be any kind of order. This is the present constitution of society, and to the mixture we owe many of our blessings. But the aggressive members of society are always tending to become bullies, robbers, and swindlers; and no one believes that such a state of things as we now live in is the millennium. It is meanwhile quite possible to conceive an imaginary society in which there should be no aggressiveness, but only sympathy and fairness,—any small community of true friends now realizes such a society. Abstractly considered, such a society on a large scale would be the millennium, for every good thing might be realized there with no expense of friction. To such a millennial society the saint would be entirely adapted. His peaceful modes of appeal would be efficacious over his companions, and there would be no one extant to take advantage of his non-resistance. The saint is therefore abstractly a higher type of man than the 'strong man,' because he is adapted to the highest society conceivable, whether that society ever be concretely possible or not. The strong man would immediately tend by his presence to make that society deteriorate. It would become inferior in everything save in a certain kind of bellicose excitement, dear to men as they now are.

But if we turn from the abstract question to the actual situation, we find that the individual saint may be well or ill adapted, according to particular circumstances. There is, in short, no absoluteness in the excellence of sainthood. It must be confessed that as far as this world goes, any one who makes an out-and-out saint of himself does so at his peril. If he is not a large enough man, he may appear more insignificant and contemptible, for all his saintship, than if he had remained a worldling.[1] Accordingly religion has seldom been so radically taken in our Western world that the devotee could not mix it with some worldly temper. It has always found good men who could follow most of its impulses, but who stopped short when it came to non-resistance. Christ himself was fierce upon occasion. Cromwells, Stonewall Jacksons, Gordons, show that Christians can be strong men also.

---

[1] We all know *daft* saints, and they inspire a queer kind of aversion. But in comparing saints with strong men we must choose individuals on the same intellectual level. The under-witted strong man, homologous in his sphere with the under-witted saint, is the bully of the slums, the hooligan or rowdy. Surely on this level also the saint preserves a certain superiority.

How is success to be absolutely measured when there are so many environments and so many ways of looking at the adaptation? It cannot be measured absolutely; the verdict will vary according to the point of view adopted. From the biological point of view Saint Paul was a failure, because he was beheaded. Yet he was magnificently adapted to the larger environment of history; and so far as any saint's example is a leaven of righteousness in the world, and draws it in the direction of more prevalent habits of saintliness, he is a success, no matter what his immediate bad fortune may be. The greatest saints, the spiritual heroes whom every one acknowledges, the Francises, Bernards, Luthers, Loyolas, Wesleys, Channings, Moodys, Gratrys, the Phillips Brookses, the Agnes Joneses, Margaret Hallahans, and Dora Pattisons, are successes from the outset. They show themselves, and there is no question; every one perceives their strength and stature. Their sense of mystery in things, their passion, their goodness, irradiate about them and enlarge their outlines while they soften them. They are like pictures with an atmosphere and background; and, placed alongside of them, the strong men of this world and no other seem as dry as sticks, as hard and crude as blocks of stone or brickbats.

In a general way, then, and 'on the whole,'[1] our abandonment of theological criteria, and our testing of religion by practical common sense and the empirical method, leave it in possession of its towering place in history. Economically, the saintly group of qualities is indispensable to the world's welfare. The great saints are immediate successes; the smaller ones are at least heralds and harbingers, and they may be leavens also, of a better mundane order. Let us be saints, then, if we can, whether or not we succeed visibly and temporally. But in our Father's house are many mansions, and each of us must discover for himself the kind of religion and the amount of saintship which best comports with what he believes to be his powers and feels to be his truest mission and vocation. There are no successes to be guaranteed and no set orders to be given to individuals, so long as we follow the methods of empirical philosophy.

[1] See above, p. 300.

This is my conclusion so far. I know that on some of your minds it leaves a feeling of wonder that such a method should have been applied to such a subject, and this in spite of all those remarks about empiricism which I made at the beginning of Lecture XIV.[1] How, you say, can religion, which believes in two worlds and an invisible order, be estimated by the adaptation of its fruits to this world's order alone? It is its *truth*, not its utility, you insist, upon which our verdict ought to depend. If religion is true, its fruits are good fruits, even though in this world they should prove uniformly ill adapted and full of naught but pathos. It goes back, then, after all, to the question of the truth of theology. The plot inevitably thickens upon us; we cannot escape theoretical considerations. I propose, then, that to some degree we face the responsibility. Religious persons have often, though not uniformly, professed to see truth in a special manner. That manner is known as mysticism. I will consequently now proceed to treat at some length of mystical phenomena, and after that, though more briefly, I will consider religious philosophy.

[1] Above, pp. 300–305.

LECTURES XVI AND XVII
MYSTICISM

OVER AND OVER again in these lectures I have raised points and left them open and unfinished until we should have come to the subject of Mysticism. Some of you, I fear, may have smiled as you noted my reiterated postponements. But now the hour has come when mysticism must be faced in good earnest, and those broken threads wound up together. One may say truly, I think, that personal religious experience has its root and centre in mystical states of consciousness; so for us, who in these lectures are treating personal experience as the exclusive subject of our study, such states of consciousness ought to form the vital chapter from which the other chapters get their light. Whether my treatment of mystical states will shed more light or darkness, I do not know, for my own constitution shuts me out from their enjoyment almost entirely, and I can speak of them only at second hand. But though forced to look upon the subject so externally, I will be as objective and receptive as I can; and I think I shall at least succeed in convincing you of the reality of the states in question, and of the paramount importance of their function.

First of all, then, I ask, What does the expression 'mystical states of consciousness' mean? How do we part off mystical states from other states?

The words 'mysticism' and 'mystical' are often used as terms of mere reproach, to throw at any opinion which we regard as vague and vast and sentimental, and without a base in either facts or logic. For some writers a 'mystic' is any person who believes in thought-transference, or spirit-return. Employed in this way the word has little value: there are too many less ambiguous synonyms. So, to keep it useful by restricting it, I will do what I did in the case of the word 'religion,' and simply propose to you four marks which, when an experience has them, may justify us in calling it mystical for the purpose of the present lectures. In this way we shall save verbal disputation, and the recriminations that generally go therewith.

1. *Ineffability*.—The handiest of the marks by which I classify a state of mind as mystical is negative. The subject of it immediately says that it defies expression, that no adequate report of its contents can be given in words. It follows from this that its quality must be directly experienced; it cannot be imparted or transferred to others. In this peculiarity mystical states are more like states of feeling than like states of intellect. No one can make clear to another who has never had a certain feeling, in what the quality or worth of it consists. One must have musical ears to know the value of a symphony; one must have been in love one's self to understand a lover's state of mind. Lacking the heart or ear, we cannot interpret the musician or the lover justly, and are even likely to consider him weak-minded or absurd. The mystic finds that most of us accord to his experiences an equally incompetent treatment.

2. *Noetic quality*.—Although so similar to states of feeling, mystical states seem to those who experience them to be also states of knowledge. They are states of insight into depths of truth unplumbed by the discursive intellect. They are illuminations, revelations, full of significance and importance, all inarticulate though they remain; and as a rule they carry with them a curious sense of authority for after-time.

These two characters will entitle any state to be called mystical, in the sense in which I use the word. Two other qualities are less sharply marked, but are usually found. These are:—

3. *Transiency*.—Mystical states cannot be sustained for long. Except in rare instances, half an hour, or at most an hour or two, seems to be the limit beyond which they fade into the light of common day. Often, when faded, their quality can but imperfectly be reproduced in memory; but when they recur it is recognized; and from one recurrence to another it is susceptible of continuous development in what is felt as inner richness and importance.

4. *Passivity*.—Although the oncoming of mystical states may be facilitated by preliminary voluntary operations, as by fixing the attention, or going through certain bodily performances, or in other ways which manuals of mysticism prescribe; yet when the characteristic sort of consciousness once has set in, the mystic feels as if his own will were in abeyance,

and indeed sometimes as if he were grasped and held by a superior power. This latter peculiarity connects mystical states with certain definite phenomena of secondary or alternative personality, such as prophetic speech, automatic writing, or the mediumistic trance. When these latter conditions are well pronounced, however, there may be no recollection whatever of the phenomenon, and it may have no significance for the subject's usual inner life, to which, as it were, it makes a mere interruption. Mystical states, strictly so called, are never merely interruptive. Some memory of their content always remains, and a profound sense of their importance. They modify the inner life of the subject between the times of their recurrence. Sharp divisions in this region are, however, difficult to make, and we find all sorts of gradations and mixtures.

These four characteristics are sufficient to mark out a group of states of consciousness peculiar enough to deserve a special name and to call for careful study. Let it then be called the mystical group.

Our next step should be to gain acquaintance with some typical examples. Professional mystics at the height of their development have often elaborately organized experiences and a philosophy based thereupon. But you remember what I said in my first lecture: phenomena are best understood when placed within their series, studied in their germ and in their over-ripe decay, and compared with their exaggerated and degenerated kindred. The range of mystical experience is very wide, much too wide for us to cover in the time at our disposal. Yet the method of serial study is so essential for interpretation that if we really wish to reach conclusions we must use it. I will begin, therefore, with phenomena which claim no special religious significance, and end with those of which the religious pretensions are extreme.

The simplest rudiment of mystical experience would seem to be that deepened sense of the significance of a maxim or formula which occasionally sweeps over one. "I've heard that said all my life," we exclaim, "but I never realized its full meaning until now." "When a fellow-monk," said Luther, "one day repeated the words of the Creed: 'I believe in the forgiveness of sins,' I saw the Scripture in an entirely new light;

and straightway I felt as if I were born anew. It was as if I had found the door of paradise thrown wide open."[1] This sense of deeper significance is not confined to rational propositions. Single words,[2] and conjunctions of words, effects of light on land and sea, odors and musical sounds, all bring it when the mind is tuned aright. Most of us can remember the strangely moving power of passages in certain poems read when we were young, irrational doorways as they were through which the mystery of fact, the wildness and the pang of life, stole into our hearts and thrilled them. The words have now perhaps become mere polished surfaces for us; but lyric poetry and music are alive and significant only in proportion as they fetch these vague vistas of a life continuous with our own, beckoning and inviting, yet ever eluding our pursuit. We are alive or dead to the eternal inner message of the arts according as we have kept or lost this mystical susceptibility.

A more pronounced step forward on the mystical ladder is found in an extremely frequent phenomenon, that sudden feeling, namely, which sometimes sweeps over us, of having 'been here before,' as if at some indefinite past time, in just this place, with just these people, we were already saying just these things. As Tennyson writes:

> "Moreover, something is or seems,
> That touches me with mystic gleams,
> Like glimpses of forgotten dreams—
>
> "Of something felt, like something here;
> Of something done, I know not where;
> Such as no language may declare."[3]

[1] Newman's *Securus judicat orbis terrarum* is another instance.
[2] 'Mesopotamia' is the stock comic instance.—An excellent old German lady, who had done some traveling in her day, used to describe to me her *Sehnsucht* that she might yet visit 'Philadelphia,' whose wondrous name had always haunted her imagination. Of John Foster it is said that "single words (as *chalcedony*), or the names of ancient heroes, had a mighty fascination over him. 'At any time the word *hermit* was enough to transport him.' The words *woods* and *forests* would produce the most powerful emotion." Foster's Life, by RYLAND, New York, 1846, p. 3.
[3] The Two Voices. In a letter to Mr. B. P. Blood, Tennyson reports of himself as follows:—

Sir James Crichton-Browne has given the technical name of 'dreamy states' to these sudden invasions of vaguely reminiscent consciousness.[1] They bring a sense of mystery and of the metaphysical duality of things, and the feeling of an enlargement of perception which seems imminent but which never completes itself. In Dr. Crichton-Browne's opinion they connect themselves with the perplexed and scared disturbances of self-consciousness which occasionally precede epileptic attacks. I think that this learned alienist takes a rather absurdly alarmist view of an intrinsically insignificant phenomenon. He follows it along the downward ladder, to insanity; our path pursues the upward ladder chiefly. The divergence shows how important it is to neglect no part of a phenomenon's connections, for we make it appear admirable or dreadful according to the context by which we set it off.

Somewhat deeper plunges into mystical consciousness are met with in yet other dreamy states. Such feelings as these which Charles Kingsley describes are surely far from being uncommon, especially in youth: —

> "When I walk the fields, I am oppressed now and then with an innate feeling that everything I see has a meaning, if I could but understand it. And this feeling of being surrounded with truths which I cannot grasp amounts to

---

"I have never had any revelations through anæsthetics, but a kind of waking trance—this for lack of a better word—I have frequently had, quite up from boyhood, when I have been all alone. This has come upon me through repeating my own name to myself silently, till all at once, as it were out of the intensity of the consciousness of individuality, individuality itself seemed to dissolve and fade away into boundless being, and this not a confused state but the clearest, the surest of the surest, utterly beyond words—where death was an almost laughable impossibility—the loss of personality (if so it were) seeming no extinction, but the only true life. I am ashamed of my feeble description. Have I not said the state is utterly beyond words?"

Professor Tyndall, in a letter, recalls Tennyson saying of this condition: "By God Almighty! there is no delusion in the matter! It is no nebulous ecstasy, but a state of transcendent wonder, associated with absolute clearness of mind." Memoirs of Alfred Tennyson, ii. 473.

[1] The Lancet, July 6 and 13, 1895, reprinted as the Cavendish Lecture, on Dreamy Mental States, London, Baillière, 1895. They have been a good deal discussed of late by psychologists. See, for example, BERNARD-LEROY: L'Illusion de Fausse Reconnaissance, Paris, 1898.

indescribable awe sometimes. . . . Have you not felt that your real soul was imperceptible to your mental vision, except in a few hallowed moments?"[1]

A much more extreme state of mystical consciousness is described by J. A. Symonds; and probably more persons than we suspect could give parallels to it from their own experience.

"Suddenly," writes Symonds, "at church, or in company, or when I was reading, and always, I think, when my muscles were at rest, I felt the approach of the mood. Irresistibly it took possession of my mind and will, lasted what seemed an eternity, and disappeared in a series of rapid sensations which resembled the awakening from anæsthetic influence. One reason why I disliked this kind of trance was that I could not describe it to myself. I cannot even now find words to render it intelligible. It consisted in a gradual but swiftly progressive obliteration of space, time, sensation, and the multitudinous factors of experience which seem to qualify what we are pleased to call our Self. In proportion as these conditions of ordinary consciousness were subtracted, the sense of an underlying or essential consciousness acquired intensity. At last nothing remained but a pure, absolute, abstract Self. The universe became without form and void of content. But Self persisted, formidable in its vivid keenness, feeling the most poignant doubt about reality, ready, as it seemed, to find existence break as breaks a bubble round about it. And what then? The apprehension of a coming dissolution, the grim conviction that this state was the last state of the conscious Self, the sense that I had followed the last thread of being to the verge of the abyss, and had arrived at demonstration of eternal Maya or illusion, stirred or seemed to stir me up again. The return to ordinary conditions of sentient existence began by my first recovering the power of touch, and then by the gradual though rapid influx of familiar impressions and diurnal interests. At last I felt myself once more a human being; and though the riddle of what is meant by

[1] Charles Kingsley's Life, i. 55, quoted by INGE: Christian Mysticism, London, 1899, p. 341.

life remained unsolved, I was thankful for this return from the abyss—this deliverance from so awful an initiation into the mysteries of skepticism.

"This trance recurred with diminishing frequency until I reached the age of twenty-eight. It served to impress upon my growing nature the phantasmal unreality of all the circumstances which contribute to a merely phenomenal consciousness. Often have I asked myself with anguish, on waking from that formless state of denuded, keenly sentient being, Which is the unreality?—the trance of fiery, vacant, apprehensive, skeptical Self from which I issue, or these surrounding phenomena and habits which veil that inner Self and build a self of flesh-and-blood conventionality? Again, are men the factors of some dream, the dream-like unsubstantiality of which they comprehend at such eventful moments? What would happen if the final stage of the trance were reached?"[1]

In a recital like this there is certainly something suggestive of pathology.[2] The next step into mystical states carries us into a realm that public opinion and ethical philosophy have long since branded as pathological, though private practice and certain lyric strains of poetry seem still to bear witness to its ideality. I refer to the consciousness produced by intoxicants and anæsthetics, especially by alcohol. The sway of alcohol over mankind is unquestionably due to its power to stimulate the mystical faculties of human nature, usually crushed to earth by the cold facts and dry criticisms of the sober hour. Sobriety diminishes, discriminates, and says no; drunkenness expands, unites, and says yes. It is in fact the great exciter of the *Yes* function in man. It brings its votary from the chill periphery of things to the radiant core. It makes

[1] H. F. Brown: J. A. Symonds, a Biography, London, 1895, pp. 29–31, abridged.

[2] Crichton-Browne expressly says that Symonds's "highest nerve centres were in some degree enfeebled or damaged by these dreamy mental states which afflicted him so grievously." Symonds was, however, a perfect monster of many-sided cerebral efficiency, and his critic gives no objective grounds whatever for his strange opinion, save that Symonds complained occasionally, as all susceptible and ambitious men complain, of lassitude and uncertainty as to his life's mission.

him for the moment one with truth. Not through mere perversity do men run after it. To the poor and the unlettered it stands in the place of symphony concerts and of literature; and it is part of the deeper mystery and tragedy of life that whiffs and gleams of something that we immediately recognize as excellent should be vouchsafed to so many of us only in the fleeting earlier phases of what in its totality is so degrading a poisoning. The drunken consciousness is one bit of the mystic consciousness, and our total opinion of it must find its place in our opinion of that larger whole.

Nitrous oxide and ether, especially nitrous oxide, when sufficiently diluted with air, stimulate the mystical consciousness in an extraordinary degree. Depth beyond depth of truth seems revealed to the inhaler. This truth fades out, however, or escapes, at the moment of coming to; and if any words remain over in which it seemed to clothe itself, they prove to be the veriest nonsense. Nevertheless, the sense of a profound meaning having been there persists; and I know more than one person who is persuaded that in the nitrous oxide trance we have a genuine metaphysical revelation.

Some years ago I myself made some observations on this aspect of nitrous oxide intoxication, and reported them in print. One conclusion was forced upon my mind at that time, and my impression of its truth has ever since remained unshaken. It is that our normal waking consciousness, rational consciousness as we call it, is but one special type of consciousness, whilst all about it, parted from it by the filmiest of screens, there lie potential forms of consciousness entirely different. We may go through life without suspecting their existence; but apply the requisite stimulus, and at a touch they are there in all their completeness, definite types of mentality which probably somewhere have their field of application and adaptation. No account of the universe in its totality can be final which leaves these other forms of consciousness quite disregarded. How to regard them is the question,—for they are so discontinuous with ordinary consciousness. Yet they may determine attitudes though they cannot furnish formulas, and open a region though they fail to give a map. At any rate, they forbid a premature closing of our accounts with reality. Looking back on my own experiences, they all converge towards a kind of insight to which I cannot help ascribing some metaphysical significance. The keynote of it is invariably a reconciliation. It is as if the opposites of the world, whose contradictoriness and conflict make all our difficulties and troubles, were melted into unity. Not only do they, as contrasted species, belong to one and the same genus, but *one of the species*, the nobler and better one, *is itself the genus, and so soaks up and absorbs its opposite into itself.* This is a dark saying, I know, when thus expressed in terms of common logic, but I cannot wholly escape from its authority. I feel as if it must mean something, something like what the hegelian philosophy means, if one could only lay hold of it more clearly. Those who have ears to hear, let them hear; to me the living sense of its reality only comes in the artificial mystic state of mind.[1]

I just now spoke of friends who believe in the anæsthetic revelation. For them too it is a monistic insight, in which the *other* in its various forms appears absorbed into the One.

> "Into this pervading genius," writes one of them, "we pass, forgetting and forgotten, and thenceforth each is all, in God. There is no higher, no deeper, no other, than the life in which we are founded. 'The One remains, the many change and pass;' and each and every one of us *is* the One that remains. . . . This is the ultimatum. . . . As sure as being—whence is all our care—so sure is content, beyond duplexity, antithesis, or trouble, where I have triumphed in a solitude that God is not above."[2]

[1] What reader of Hegel can doubt that that sense of a perfected Being with all its otherness soaked up into itself, which dominates his whole philosophy, must have come from the prominence in his consciousness of mystical moods like this, in most persons kept subliminal? The notion is thoroughly characteristic of the mystical level, and the *Aufgabe* of making it articulate was surely set to Hegel's intellect by mystical feeling.

[2] BENJAMIN PAUL BLOOD: The Anæsthetic Revelation and the Gist of Philosophy, Amsterdam, N. Y., 1874, pp. 35, 36. Mr. Blood has made several attempts to adumbrate the anæsthetic revelation, in pamphlets of rare literary distinction, privately printed and distributed by himself at Amsterdam. Xenos Clark, a philosopher, who died young at Amherst in the '80's, much lamented by those who knew him, was also impressed by the revelation. "In the first place," he once wrote to me, "Mr. Blood and I agree that the revelation is, if anything, non-emotional. It is utterly flat. It is, as Mr. Blood says, 'the one

This has the genuine religious mystic ring! I just now quoted J. A. Symonds. He also records a mystical experience with chloroform, as follows:—

---

sole and sufficient insight why, or not why, but how, the present is pushed on by the past, and sucked forward by the vacuity of the future. Its inevitableness defeats all attempts at stopping or accounting for it. It is all precedence and presupposition, and questioning is in regard to it forever too late. It is an *initiation of the past*.' The real secret would be the formula by which the 'now' keeps exfoliating out of itself, yet never escapes. What is it, indeed, that keeps existence exfoliating? The formal being of anything, the logical definition of it, is static. For mere logic every question contains its own answer—we simply fill the hole with the dirt we dug out. Why are twice two four? Because, in fact, four is twice two. Thus logic finds in life no propulsion, only a momentum. It goes because it is a-going. But the revelation adds: it goes because it *was* a-going. You walk, as it were, round yourself in the revelation. Ordinary philosophy is like a hound hunting his own trail. The more he hunts the farther he has to go, and his nose never catches up with his heels, because it is forever ahead of them. So the present is already a foregone conclusion, and I am ever too late to understand it. But at the moment of recovery from anæsthesis, just then, *before starting on life*, I catch, so to speak, a glimpse of my heels, a glimpse of the eternal process just in the act of starting. The truth is that we travel on a journey that was accomplished before we set out; and the real end of philosophy is accomplished, not when we arrive at, but when we remain in, our destination (being already there),—which may occur vicariously in this life when we cease our intellectual questioning. That is why there is a smile upon the face of the revelation, as we view it. It tells us that we are forever half a second too late—that's all. 'You could kiss your own lips, and have all the fun to yourself,' it says, if you only knew the trick. It would be perfectly easy if they would just stay there till you got round to them. Why don't you manage it somehow?"

Dialectically minded readers of this farrago will at least recognize the region of thought of which Mr. Clark writes, as familiar. In his latest pamphlet, 'Tennyson's Trances and the Anæsthetic Revelation,' Mr. Blood describes its value for life as follows:—

"The Anæsthetic Revelation is the Initiation of Man into the Immemorial Mystery of the Open Secret of Being, revealed as the Inevitable Vortex of Continuity. Inevitable is the word. Its motive is inherent—it is what has to be. It is not for any love or hate, nor for joy nor sorrow, nor good nor ill. End, beginning, or purpose, it knows not of.

"It affords no particular of the multiplicity and variety of things; but it fills appreciation of the historical and the sacred with a secular and intimately personal illumination of the nature and motive of existence, which then seems reminiscent—as if it should have appeared, or shall yet appear, to every participant thereof.

"Although it is at first startling in its solemnity, it becomes directly such a

"After the choking and stifling had passed away, I seemed at first in a state of utter blankness; then came flashes of intense light, alternating with blackness, and with a keen vision of what was going on in the room around me, but no sensation of touch. I thought that I was near death; when, suddenly, my soul became aware of God, who was manifestly dealing with me, handling me, so to speak, in an intense personal present reality. I felt him streaming in like light upon me. . . . I cannot describe the ecstasy I felt. Then, as I gradually awoke from the influence of the anæsthetics, the old sense of my relation to the world began to return, the new sense of my relation to God began to fade. I suddenly leapt to my feet on the chair where I was sitting, and shrieked out, 'It is too horrible, it is too horrible, it is too horrible,' meaning that I could not bear this

---

matter of course—so old-fashioned, and so akin to proverbs, that it inspires exultation rather than fear, and a sense of safety, as identified with the aboriginal and the universal. But no words may express the imposing certainty of the patient that he is realizing the primordial, Adamic surprise of Life.

"Repetition of the experience finds it ever the same, and as if it could not possibly be otherwise. The subject resumes his normal consciousness only to partially and fitfully remember its occurrence, and to try to formulate its baffling import,—with only this consolatory afterthought: that he has known the oldest truth, and that he has done with human theories as to the origin, meaning, or destiny of the race. He is beyond instruction in 'spiritual things.'

"The lesson is one of central safety: the Kingdom is within. All days are judgment days: but there can be no climacteric purpose of eternity, nor any scheme of the whole. The astronomer abridges the row of bewildering figures by increasing his unit of measurement: so may we reduce the distracting multiplicity of things to the unity for which each of us stands.

"This has been my moral sustenance since I have known of it. In my first printed mention of it I declared: 'The world is no more the alien terror that was taught me. Spurning the cloud-grimed and still sultry battlements whence so lately Jehovan thunders boomed, my gray gull lifts her wing against the nightfall, and takes the dim leagues with a fearless eye.' And now, after twenty-seven years of this experience, the wing is grayer, but the eye is fearless still, while I renew and doubly emphasize that declaration. I know—as having known—the meaning of Existence: the sane centre of the universe—at once the wonder and the assurance of the soul—for which the speech of reason has as yet no name but the Anæsthetic Revelation."—I have considerably abridged the quotation.

disillusionment. Then I flung myself on the ground, and
at last awoke covered with blood, calling to the two sur-
geons (who were frightened), 'Why did you not kill me?
Why would you not let me die?' Only think of it. To
have felt for that long dateless ecstasy of vision the very
God, in all purity and tenderness and truth and absolute
love, and then to find that I had after all had no revelation,
but that I had been tricked by the abnormal excitement of
my brain.

"Yet, this question remains, Is it possible that the inner
sense of reality which succeeded, when my flesh was dead
to impressions from without, to the ordinary sense of physical relations, was not a delusion but an actual experience?
Is it possible that I, in that moment, felt what some of the
saints have said they always felt, the undemonstrable but
irrefragable certainty of God?"[1]

[1]Op. cit., pp. 78–80, abridged. I subjoin, also abridging it, another interesting anæsthetic revelation communicated to me in manuscript by a friend
in England. The subject, a gifted woman, was taking ether for a surgical
operation.

"I wondered if I was in a prison being tortured, and why I remembered
having heard it said that people 'learn through suffering,' and in view of what
I was seeing, the inadequacy of this saying struck me so much that I said,
aloud, 'to suffer *is* to learn.'

"With that I became unconscious again, and my last dream immediately
preceded my real coming to. It only lasted a few seconds, and was most vivid
and real to me, though it may not be clear in words.

"A great Being or Power was traveling through the sky, his foot was on a
kind of lightning as a wheel is on a rail, it was his pathway. The lightning
was made entirely of the spirits of innumerable people close to one another,
and I was one of them. He moved in a straight line, and each part of the
streak or flash came into its short conscious existence only that he might
travel. I seemed to be directly under the foot of God, and I thought he was
grinding his own life up out of my pain. Then I saw that what he had been
trying with all his might to do was to *change his course*, to *bend* the line of
lightning to which he was tied, in the direction in which he wanted to go. I
felt my flexibility and helplessness, and knew that he would succeed. He
bended me, turning his corner by means of my hurt, hurting me more than
I had ever been hurt in my life, and at the acutest point of this, as he passed,
I *saw*. I understood for a moment things that I have now forgotten, things
that no one could remember while retaining sanity. The angle was an obtuse
angle, and I remember thinking as I woke that had he made it a right or

With this we make connection with religious mysticism pure and simple. Symonds's question takes us back to those examples which you will remember my quoting in the lecture on the Reality of the Unseen, of sudden realization of the immediate presence of God. The phenomenon in one shape or another is not uncommon.

---

acute angle, I should have both suffered and 'seen' still more, and should probably have died.

"He went on and I came to. In that moment the whole of my life passed before me, including each little meaningless piece of distress, and I *understood* them. *This* was what it had all meant, *this* was the piece of work it had all been contributing to do. I did not see God's purpose, I only saw his intentness and his entire relentlessness towards his means. He thought no more of me than a man thinks of hurting a cork when he is opening wine, or hurting a cartridge when he is firing. And yet, on waking, my first feeling was, and it came with tears, 'Domine non sum digna,' for I had been lifted into a position for which I was too small. I realized that in that half hour under ether I had served God more distinctly and purely than I had ever done in my life before, or than I am capable of desiring to do. I was the means of his achieving and revealing something, I know not what or to whom, and that, to the exact extent of my capacity for suffering.

"While regaining consciousness, I wondered why, since I had gone so deep, I had seen nothing of what the saints call the *love* of God, nothing but his relentlessness. And then I heard an answer, which I could only just catch, saying, 'Knowledge and Love are One, and the *measure* is suffering'—I give the words as they came to me. With that I came finally to (into what seemed a dream world compared with the reality of what I was leaving), and I saw that what would be called the 'cause' of my experience was a slight operation under insufficient ether, in a bed pushed up against a window, a common city window in a common city street. If I had to formulate a few of the things I then caught a glimpse of, they would run somewhat as follows:—

"The eternal necessity of suffering and its eternal vicariousness. The veiled and incommunicable nature of the worst sufferings;—the passivity of genius, how it is essentially instrumental and defenseless, moved, not moving, it must do what it does;—the impossibility of discovery without its price;—finally, the excess of what the suffering 'seer' or genius pays over what his generation gains. (He seems like one who sweats his life out to earn enough to save a district from famine, and just as he staggers back, dying and satisfied, bringing a lac of rupees to buy grain with, God lifts the lac away, dropping *one* rupee, and says, 'That you may give them. That you have earned for them. The rest is for ME.') I perceived also in a way never to be forgotten, the excess of what we see over what we can demonstrate.

"And so on!—these things may seem to you delusions, or truisms; but for me they are dark truths, and the power to put them into even such words as these has been given me by an ether dream."

"I know," writes Mr. Trine, "an officer on our police force who has told me that many times when off duty, and on his way home in the evening, there comes to him such a vivid and vital realization of his oneness with this Infinite Power, and this Spirit of Infinite Peace so takes hold of and so fills him, that it seems as if his feet could hardly keep to the pavement, so buoyant and so exhilarated does he become by reason of this inflowing tide."[1]

Certain aspects of nature seem to have a peculiar power of awakening such mystical moods.[2] Most of the striking cases which I have collected have occurred out of doors. Literature has commemorated this fact in many passages of great beauty—this extract, for example, from Amiel's Journal Intime:—

[1] In Tune with the Infinite, p. 137.

[2] The larger God may then swallow up the smaller one. I take this from Starbuck's manuscript collection:—

"I never lost the consciousness of the presence of God until I stood at the foot of the Horseshoe Falls, Niagara. Then I lost him in the immensity of what I saw. I also lost myself, feeling that I was an atom too small for the notice of Almighty God."

I subjoin another similar case from Starbuck's collection:—

"In that time the consciousness of God's nearness came to me sometimes. I say God, to describe what is indescribable. A presence, I might say, yet that is too suggestive of personality, and the moments of which I speak did not hold the consciousness of a personality, but something in myself made me feel myself a part of something bigger than I, that was controlling. I felt myself one with the grass, the trees, birds, insects, everything in Nature. I exulted in the mere fact of existence, of being a part of it all—the drizzling rain, the shadows of the clouds, the tree-trunks, and so on. In the years following, such moments continued to come, but I wanted them constantly. I knew so well the satisfaction of losing self in a perception of supreme power and love, that I was unhappy because that perception was not constant." The cases quoted in my third lecture, pp. 66, 67, 70, are still better ones of this type. In her essay, The Loss of Personality, in The Atlantic Monthly (vol. lxxxv. p. 195), Miss Ethel D. Puffer explains that the vanishing of the sense of self, and the feeling of immediate unity with the object, is due to the disappearance, in these rapturous experiences, of the motor adjustments which habitually intermediate between the constant background of consciousness (which is the Self) and the object in the foreground, whatever it may be. I must refer the reader to the highly instructive article, which seems to me to throw light upon the psychological conditions, though it fails to account for the rapture or the revelation-value of the experience in the Subject's eyes.

"Shall I ever again have any of those prodigious reveries which sometimes came to me in former days? One day, in youth, at sunrise, sitting in the ruins of the castle of Faucigny; and again in the mountains, under the noonday sun, above Lavey, lying at the foot of a tree and visited by three butterflies; once more at night upon the shingly shore of the Northern Ocean, my back upon the sand and my vision ranging through the milky way;—such grand and spacious, immortal, cosmogonic reveries, when one reaches to the stars, when one owns the infinite! Moments divine, ecstatic hours; in which our thought flies from world to world, pierces the great enigma, breathes with a respiration broad, tranquil, and deep as the respiration of the ocean, serene and limitless as the blue firmament; . . . instants of irresistible intuition in which one feels one's self great as the universe, and calm as a god. . . . What hours, what memories! The vestiges they leave behind are enough to fill us with belief and enthusiasm, as if they were visits of the Holy Ghost."[1]

Here is a similar record from the memoirs of that interesting German idealist, Malwida von Meysenbug:—

"I was alone upon the seashore as all these thoughts flowed over me, liberating and reconciling; and now again, as once before in distant days in the Alps of Dauphiné, I was impelled to kneel down, this time before the illimitable ocean, symbol of the Infinite. I felt that I prayed as I had never prayed before, and knew now what prayer really is: to return from the solitude of individuation into the consciousness of unity with all that is, to kneel down as one that passes away, and to rise up as one imperishable. Earth, heaven, and sea resounded as in one vast world-encircling harmony. It was as if the chorus of all the great who had ever lived were about me. I felt myself one with them, and it appeared as if I heard their greeting: 'Thou too belongest to the company of those who overcome.' "[2]

[1] Op. cit., i. 43–44.
[2] Memoiren einer Idealistin, 5te Auflage, 1900, iii. 166. For years she had been unable to pray, owing to materialistic belief.

The well-known passage from Walt Whitman is a classical expression of this sporadic type of mystical experience.

"I believe in you, my Soul . . .
Loaf with me on the grass, loose the stop from your
throat; . . .
Only the lull I like, the hum of your valved voice.
I mind how once we lay, such a transparent summer
morning.
Swiftly arose and spread around me the peace and
knowledge that pass all the argument of the earth,
And I know that the hand of God is the promise of my
own,
And I know that the spirit of God is the brother of my own,
And that all the men ever born are also my brothers and
the women my sisters and lovers,
And that a kelson of the creation is love."[1]

I could easily give more instances, but one will suffice. I take it from the Autobiography of J. Trevor.[2]

"One brilliant Sunday morning, my wife and boys went to the Unitarian Chapel in Macclesfield. I felt it impossible to accompany them—as though to leave the sunshine on the hills, and go down there to the chapel, would be for the time an act of spiritual suicide. And I felt such need for new inspiration and expansion in my life. So, very reluctantly and sadly, I left my wife and boys to go down into the town, while I went further up into the hills with my

[1] Whitman in another place expresses in a quieter way what was probably with him a chronic mystical perception: "There is," he writes, "apart from mere intellect, in the make-up of every superior human identity, a wondrous something that realizes without argument, frequently without what is called education (though I think it the goal and apex of all education deserving the name), an intuition of the absolute balance, in time and space, of the whole of this multifariousness, this revel of fools, and incredible make-believe and general unsettledness, we call *the world*; a soul-sight of that divine clue and unseen thread which holds the whole congeries of things, all history and time, and all events, however trivial, however momentous, like a leashed dog in the hand of the hunter. [Of] such soul-sight and root-centre for the mind mere optimism explains only the surface." Whitman charges it against Carlyle that he lacked this perception. Specimen Days and Collect, Philadelphia, 1882, p. 174.
[2] My Quest for God, London, 1897, pp. 268, 269, abridged.

stick and my dog. In the loveliness of the morning, and the beauty of the hills and valleys, I soon lost my sense of sadness and regret. For nearly an hour I walked along the road to the 'Cat and Fiddle,' and then returned. On the way back, suddenly, without warning, I felt that I was in Heaven—an inward state of peace and joy and assurance indescribably intense, accompanied with a sense of being bathed in a warm glow of light, as though the external condition had brought about the internal effect—a feeling of having passed beyond the body, though the scene around me stood out more clearly and as if nearer to me than before, by reason of the illumination in the midst of which I seemed to be placed. This deep emotion lasted, though with decreasing strength, until I reached home, and for some time after, only gradually passing away."

The writer adds that having had further experiences of a similar sort, he now knows them well.

"The spiritual life," he writes, "justifies itself to those who live it; but what can we say to those who do not understand? This, at least, we can say, that it is a life whose experiences are proved real to their possessor, because they remain with him when brought closest into contact with the objective realities of life. Dreams cannot stand this test. We wake from them to find that they are but dreams. Wanderings of an overwrought brain do not stand this test. These highest experiences that I have had of God's presence have been rare and brief—flashes of consciousness which have compelled me to exclaim with surprise—God is *here!*—or conditions of exaltation and insight, less intense, and only gradually passing away. I have severely questioned the worth of these moments. To no soul have I named them, lest I should be building my life and work on mere phantasies of the brain. But I find that, after every questioning and test, they stand out to-day as the most real experiences of my life, and experiences which have explained and justified and unified all past experiences and all past growth. Indeed, their reality and their far-reaching significance are ever becoming more clear and evident. When they came, I was living the fullest, strongest, sanest, deepest

life. I was not seeking them. What I was seeking, with res-
olute determination, was to live more intensely my own
life, as against what I knew would be the adverse judgment
of the world. It was in the most real seasons that the Real
Presence came, and I was aware that I was immersed in the
infinite ocean of God."[1]

Even the least mystical of you must by this time be convinced of the existence of mystical moments as states of consciousness of an entirely specific quality, and of the deep
impression which they make on those who have them. A Ca-
nadian psychiatrist, Dr. R. M. Bucke, gives to the more distinctly characterized of these phenomena the name of cosmic
consciousness. "Cosmic consciousness in its more striking instances is not," Dr. Bucke says, "simply an expansion or extension of the self-conscious mind with which we are all
familiar, but the superaddition of a function as distinct from
any possessed by the average man as *self*-consciousness is
distinct from any function possessed by one of the higher
animals."

"The prime characteristic of cosmic consciousness is a
consciousness of the cosmos, that is, of the life and order
of the universe. Along with the consciousness of the cosmos there occurs an intellectual enlightenment which alone
would place the individual on a new plane of existence—
would make him almost a member of a new species. To this
is added a state of moral exaltation, an indescribable feeling
of elevation, elation, and joyousness, and a quickening of
the moral sense, which is fully as striking, and more important than is the enhanced intellectual power. With these
come what may be called a sense of immortality, a consciousness of eternal life, not a conviction that he shall have
this, but the consciousness that he has it already."[2]

It was Dr. Bucke's own experience of a typical onset of
cosmic consciousness in his own person which led him to in-
vestigate it in others. He has printed his conclusions in a

[1] Op. cit., pp. 256, 257, abridged.
[2] Cosmic Consciousness: a study in the evolution of the human Mind. Philadelphia, 1901, p. 2.

highly interesting volume, from which I take the following account of what occurred to him: —

"I had spent the evening in a great city, with two friends, reading and discussing poetry and philosophy. We parted at midnight. I had a long drive in a hansom to my lodging. My mind, deeply under the influence of the ideas, images, and emotions called up by the reading and talk, was calm and peaceful. I was in a state of quiet, almost passive enjoyment, not actually thinking, but letting ideas, images, and emotions flow of themselves, as it were, through my mind. All at once, without warning of any kind, I found myself wrapped in a flame-colored cloud. For an instant I thought of fire, an immense conflagration somewhere close by in that great city; the next, I knew that the fire was within myself. Directly afterward there came upon me a sense of exultation, of immense joyousness accompanied or immediately followed by an intellectual illumination impossible to describe. Among other things, I did not merely come to believe, but I saw that the universe is not composed of dead matter, but is, on the contrary, a living Presence; I became conscious in myself of eternal life. It was not a conviction that I would have eternal life, but a consciousness that I possessed eternal life then; I saw that all men are immortal; that the cosmic order is such that without any peradventure all things work together for the good of each and all; that the foundation principle of the world, of all the worlds, is what we call love, and that the happiness of each and all is in the long run absolutely certain. The vision lasted a few seconds and was gone; but the memory of it and the sense of the reality of what it taught has remained during the quarter of a century which has since elapsed. I knew that what the vision showed was true. I had attained to a point of view from which I saw that it must be true. That view, that conviction, I may say that consciousness, has never, even during periods of the deepest depression, been lost."[1]

[1] Loc. cit., pp. 7, 8. My quotation follows the privately printed pamphlet which preceded Dr. Bucke's larger work, and differs verbally a little from the text of the latter.

We have now seen enough of this cosmic or mystic consciousness, as it comes sporadically. We must next pass to its methodical cultivation as an element of the religious life. Hindus, Buddhists, Mohammedans, and Christians all have cultivated it methodically.

In India, training in mystical insight has been known from time immemorial under the name of yoga. Yoga means the experimental union of the individual with the divine. It is based on persevering exercise; and the diet, posture, breathing, intellectual concentration, and moral discipline vary slightly in the different systems which teach it. The yogi, or disciple, who has by these means overcome the obscurations of his lower nature sufficiently, enters into the condition termed *samâdhi*, "and comes face to face with facts which no instinct or reason can ever know." He learns—

"That the mind itself has a higher state of existence, beyond reason, a superconscious state, and that when the mind gets to that higher state, then this knowledge beyond reasoning comes. . . . All the different steps in yoga are intended to bring us scientifically to the superconscious state or samâdhi. . . . Just as unconscious work is beneath consciousness, so there is another work which is above consciousness, and which, also, is not accompanied with the feeling of egoism. . . . There is no feeling of *I*, and yet the mind works, desireless, free from restlessness, objectless, bodiless. Then the Truth shines in its full effulgence, and we know ourselves—for Samâdhi lies potential in us all—for what we truly are, free, immortal, omnipotent, loosed from the finite, and its contrasts of good and evil altogether, and identical with the Atman or Universal Soul."[1]

The Vedantists say that one may stumble into superconsciousness sporadically, without the previous discipline, but it is then impure. Their test of its purity, like our test of religion's value, is empirical: its fruits must be good for life. When a man comes out of Samâdhi, they assure us that he

[1] My quotations are from VIVEKANANDA, Raja Yoga, London, 1896. The completest source of information on Yoga is the work translated by VIHARI LALA MITRA: Yoga Vasishta Maha Ramayana, 4 vols., Calcutta, 1891–99.

remains "enlightened, a sage, a prophet, a saint, his whole character changed, his life changed, illumined."[1]

The Buddhists use the word 'samâdhi' as well as the Hindus; but 'dhyâna' is their special word for higher states of contemplation. There seem to be four stages recognized in dhyâna. The first stage comes through concentration of the mind upon one point. It excludes desire, but not discernment or judgment: it is still intellectual. In the second stage the intellectual functions drop off, and the satisfied sense of unity remains. In the third stage the satisfaction departs, and indifference begins, along with memory and self-consciousness. In the fourth stage the indifference, memory, and self-consciousness are perfected. [Just what 'memory' and 'self-consciousness' mean in this connection is doubtful. They cannot be the faculties familiar to us in the lower life.] Higher stages still of contemplation are mentioned—a region where there exists nothing, and where the meditator says: "There exists absolutely nothing," and stops. Then he reaches another region where he says: "There are neither ideas nor absence of ideas," and stops again. Then another region where, "having reached the end of both idea and perception, he stops finally." This would seem to be, not yet Nirvâna, but as close an approach to it as this life affords.[2]

In the Mohammedan world the Sufi sect and various dervish bodies are the possessors of the mystical tradition. The Sufis have existed in Persia from the earliest times, and as their pantheism is so at variance with the hot and rigid monotheism of the Arab mind, it has been suggested that Sufism must have been inoculated into Islam by Hindu influences. We Christians know little of Sufism, for its secrets are dis-

---

[1] A European witness, after carefully comparing the results of Yoga with those of the hypnotic or dreamy states artificially producible by us, says: "It makes of its true disciples good, healthy, and happy men. . . . Through the mastery which the yogi attains over his thoughts and his body, he grows into a 'character.' By the subjection of his impulses and propensities to his will, and the fixing of the latter upon the ideal of goodness, he becomes a 'personality' hard to influence by others, and thus almost the opposite of what we usually imagine a 'medium' so-called, or 'psychic subject' to be." KARL KELLNER: Yoga: Eine Skizze, München, 1896, p. 21.

[2] I follow the account in C. F. KOEPPEN: Die Religion des Buddha, Berlin, 1857, i. 585 ff.

closed only to those initiated. To give its existence a certain liveliness in your minds, I will quote a Moslem document, and pass away from the subject.

Al-Ghazzali, a Persian philosopher and theologian, who flourished in the eleventh century, and ranks as one of the greatest doctors of the Moslem church, has left us one of the few autobiographies to be found outside of Christian literature. Strange that a species of book so abundant among ourselves should be so little represented elsewhere—the absence of strictly personal confessions is the chief difficulty to the purely literary student who would like to become acquainted with the inwardness of religions other than the Christian.

M. Schmölders has translated a part of Al-Ghazzali's autobiography into French:[1]—

"The Science of the Sufis," says the Moslem author, "aims at detaching the heart from all that is not God, and at giving to it for sole occupation the meditation of the divine being. Theory being more easy for me than practice, I read [certain books] until I understood all that can be learned by study and hearsay. Then I recognized that what pertains most exclusively to their method is just what no study can grasp, but only transport, ecstasy, and the transformation of the soul. How great, for example, is the difference between knowing the definitions of health, of satiety, with their causes and conditions, and being really healthy or filled. How different to know in what drunkenness consists,—as being a state occasioned by a vapor that rises from the stomach,—and *being* drunk effectively. Without doubt, the drunken man knows neither the definition of drunkenness nor what makes it interesting for science. Being drunk, he knows nothing; whilst the physician, although not drunk, knows well in what drunkenness consists, and what are its predisposing conditions. Similarly there is a difference between knowing the nature of abstinence, and *being* abstinent or having one's soul detached from the world.—Thus I had learned what words could teach of Sufism, but what was left could be learned neither

[1] For a full account of him, see D. B. MACDONALD: The Life of Al-Ghazzali, in the Journal of the American Oriental Society, 1899, vol. xx. p. 71.

by study nor through the ears, but solely by giving one's self up to ecstasy and leading a pious life.

"Reflecting on my situation, I found myself tied down by a multitude of bonds—temptations on every side. Considering my teaching, I found it was impure before God. I saw myself struggling with all my might to achieve glory and to spread my name. [Here follows an account of his six months' hesitation to break away from the conditions of his life at Bagdad, at the end of which he fell ill with a paralysis of the tongue.] Then, feeling my own weakness, and having entirely given up my own will, I repaired to God like a man in distress who has no more resources. He answered, as he answers the wretch who invokes him. My heart no longer felt any difficulty in renouncing glory, wealth, and my children. So I quitted Bagdad, and reserving from my fortune only what was indispensable for my subsistence, I distributed the rest. I went to Syria, where I remained about two years, with no other occupation than living in retreat and solitude, conquering my desires, combating my passions, training myself to purify my soul, to make my character perfect, to prepare my heart for meditating on God—all according to the methods of the Sufis, as I had read of them.

"This retreat only increased my desire to live in solitude, and to complete the purification of my heart and fit it for meditation. But the vicissitudes of the times, the affairs of the family, the need of subsistence, changed in some respects my primitive resolve, and interfered with my plans for a purely solitary life. I had never yet found myself completely in ecstasy, save in a few single hours; nevertheless, I kept the hope of attaining this state. Every time that the accidents led me astray, I sought to return; and in this situation I spent ten years. During this solitary state things were revealed to me which it is impossible either to describe or to point out. I recognized for certain that the Sufis are assuredly walking in the path of God. Both in their acts and in their inaction, whether internal or external, they are illumined by the light which proceeds from the prophetic source. The first condition for a Sufi is to purge his heart entirely of all that is not God. The next key of the contemplative life consists in the humble prayers which escape from the fervent soul, and in the meditations on God in which the heart is swallowed up entirely. But in reality this is only the beginning of the Sufi life, the end of Sufism being total absorption in God. The intuitions and all that precede are, so to speak, only the threshold for those who enter. From the beginning, revelations take place in so flagrant a shape that the Sufis see before them, whilst wide awake, the angels and the souls of the prophets. They hear their voices and obtain their favors. Then the transport rises from the perception of forms and figures to a degree which escapes all expression, and which no man may seek to give an account of without his words involving sin.

"Whoever has had no experience of the transport knows of the true nature of prophetism nothing but the name. He may meanwhile be sure of its existence, both by experience and by what he hears the Sufis say. As there are men endowed only with the sensitive faculty who reject what is offered them in the way of objects of the pure understanding, so there are intellectual men who reject and avoid the things perceived by the prophetic faculty. A blind man can understand nothing of colors save what he has learned by narration and hearsay. Yet God has brought prophetism near to men in giving them all a state analogous to it in its principal characters. This state is sleep. If you were to tell a man who was himself without experience of such a phenomenon that there are people who at times swoon away so as to resemble dead men, and who [in dreams] yet perceive things that are hidden, he would deny it [and give his reasons]. Nevertheless, his arguments would be refuted by actual experience. Wherefore, just as the understanding is a stage of human life in which an eye opens to discern various intellectual objects uncomprehended by sensation; just so in the prophetic the sight is illumined by a light which uncovers hidden things and objects which the intellect fails to reach. The chief properties of prophetism are perceptible only during the transport, by those who embrace the Sufi life. The prophet is endowed with qualities to which you possess nothing analogous, and which consequently you cannot possibly understand. How should you know their true nature, since one knows only what one can comprehend? But the transport which one attains by the method of the Sufis is like an immediate perception, as if one touched the objects with one's hand."[1]

This incommunicableness of the transport is the keynote of all mysticism. Mystical truth exists for the individual who has the transport, but for no one else. In this, as I have said, it resembles the knowledge given to us in sensations more than that given by conceptual thought. Thought, with its remoteness and abstractness, has often enough in the history of philosophy been contrasted unfavorably with sensation. It is a commonplace of metaphysics that God's knowledge cannot be discursive but must be intuitive, that is, must be constructed more after the pattern of what in ourselves is called immediate feeling, than after that of proposition and judgment. But *our* immediate feelings have no content but what the five senses supply; and we have seen and shall see again that mystics may emphatically deny that the senses play any part in the very highest type of knowledge which their transports yield.

In the Christian church there have always been mystics. Although many of them have been viewed with suspicion, some have gained favor in the eyes of the authorities. The experiences of these have been treated as precedents, and a codified system of mystical theology has been based upon them, in which everything legitimate finds its place.[2] The basis of the system is 'orison' or meditation, the methodical elevation of the soul towards God. Through the practice of orison the higher levels of mystical experience may be attained. It is odd that Protestantism, especially evangelical Protestantism, should seemingly have abandoned everything methodical in this line. Apart from what prayer may lead to, Protestant mystical experience appears to have been almost exclusively

[1] A. SCHMÖLDERS: Essai sur les écoles philosophiques chez les Arabes, Paris, 1842, pp. 54–68, abridged.

[2] GÖRRES's Christliche Mystik gives a full account of the facts. So does RIBET's Mystique Divine, 2 vols., Paris, 1890. A still more methodical modern work is the Mystica Theologia of VALLGORNERA, 2 vols., Turin, 1890.

sporadic. It has been left to our mind-curers to reintroduce methodical meditation into our religious life.

The first thing to be aimed at in orison is the mind's detachment from outer sensations, for these interfere with its concentration upon ideal things. Such manuals as Saint Ignatius's Spiritual Exercises recommend the disciple to expel sensation by a graduated series of efforts to imagine holy scenes. The acme of this kind of discipline would be a semi-hallucinatory mono-ideism—an imaginary figure of Christ, for example, coming fully to occupy the mind. Sensorial images of this sort, whether literal or symbolic, play an enormous part in mysticism.[1] But in certain cases imagery may fall away entirely, and in the very highest raptures it tends to do so. The state of consciousness becomes then insusceptible of any verbal description. Mystical teachers are unanimous as to this. Saint John of the Cross, for instance, one of the best of them, thus describes the condition called the 'union of love,' which, he says, is reached by 'dark contemplation.' In this the Deity compenetrates the soul, but in such a hidden way that the soul—

"finds no terms, no means, no comparison whereby to render the sublimity of the wisdom and the delicacy of the spiritual feeling with which she is filled. . . . We receive this mystical knowledge of God clothed in none of the kinds of images, in none of the sensible representations, which our mind makes use of in other circumstances. Accordingly in this knowledge, since the senses and the imagination are not employed, we get neither form nor impression, nor can we give any account or furnish any likeness, although the mysterious and sweet-tasting wisdom comes home so clearly to the inmost parts of our soul. Fancy a man seeing a certain kind of thing for the first time in his life. He can understand it, use and enjoy it, but he cannot apply a name to it, nor communicate any idea of it, even though all the while it be a mere thing of sense.

[1] M. Récéjac, in a recent volume, makes them essential. Mysticism he defines as "the tendency to draw near to the Absolute morally, *and by the aid of Symbols.*" See his Fondements de la Connaissance mystique, Paris, 1897, p. 66. But there are unquestionably mystical conditions in which sensible symbols play no part.

How much greater will be his powerlessness when it goes beyond the senses! This is the peculiarity of the divine language. The more infused, intimate, spiritual, and supersensible it is, the more does it exceed the senses, both inner and outer, and impose silence upon them. . . . The soul then feels as if placed in a vast and profound solitude, to which no created thing has access, in an immense and boundless desert, desert the more delicious the more solitary it is. There, in this abyss of wisdom, the soul grows by what it drinks in from the well-springs of the comprehension of love, . . . and recognizes, however sublime and learned may be the terms we employ, how utterly vile, insignificant, and improper they are, when we seek to discourse of divine things by their means."[1]

I cannot pretend to detail to you the sundry stages of the Christian mystical life.[2] Our time would not suffice, for one thing; and moreover, I confess that the subdivisions and names which we find in the Catholic books seem to me to represent nothing objectively distinct. So many men, so many minds: I imagine that these experiences can be as infinitely varied as are the idiosyncrasies of individuals.

The cognitive aspects of them, their value in the way of revelation, is what we are directly concerned with, and it is easy to show by citation how strong an impression they leave of being revelations of new depths of truth. Saint Teresa is the expert of experts in describing such conditions, so I will turn immediately to what she says of one of the highest of them, the 'orison of union.'

"In the orison of union," says Saint Teresa, "the soul is

[1] Saint John of the Cross: The Dark Night of the Soul, book ii. ch. xvii., in Vie et Œuvres, 3me édition, Paris, 1893, iii. 428–432. Chapter xi. of book ii. of Saint John's Ascent of Carmel is devoted to showing the harmfulness for the mystical life of the use of sensible imagery.

[2] In particular I omit mention of visual and auditory hallucinations, verbal and graphic automatisms, and such marvels as 'levitation,' stigmatization, and the healing of disease. These phenomena, which mystics have often presented (or are believed to have presented), have no essential mystical significance, for they occur with no consciousness of illumination whatever, when they occur, as they often do, in persons of non-mystical mind. Consciousness of illumination is for us the essential mark of 'mystical' states.

fully awake as regards God, but wholly asleep as regards things of this world and in respect of herself. During the short time the union lasts, she is as it were deprived of every feeling, and even if she would, she could not think of any single thing. Thus she needs to employ no artifice in order to arrest the use of her understanding: it remains so stricken with inactivity that she neither knows what she loves, nor in what manner she loves, nor what she wills. In short, she is utterly dead to the things of the world and lives solely in God. . . . I do not even know whether in this state she has enough life left to breathe. It seems to me she has not; or at least that if she does breathe, she is unaware of it. Her intellect would fain understand something of what is going on within her, but it has so little force now that it can act in no way whatsoever. So a person who falls into a deep faint appears as if dead. . . .

"Thus does God, when he raises a soul to union with himself, suspend the natural action of all her faculties. She neither sees, hears, nor understands, so long as she is united with God. But this time is always short, and it seems even shorter than it is. God establishes himself in the interior of this soul in such a way, that when she returns to herself, it is wholly impossible for her to doubt that she has been in God, and God in her. This truth remains so strongly impressed on her that, even though many years should pass without the condition returning, she can neither forget the favor she received, nor doubt of its reality. If you, nevertheless, ask how it is possible that the soul can see and understand that she has been in God, since during the union she has neither sight nor understanding, I reply that she does not see it then, but that she sees it clearly later, after she has returned to herself, not by any vision, but by a certitude which abides with her and which God alone can give her. I knew a person who was ignorant of the truth that God's mode of being in everything must be either by presence, by power, or by essence, but who, after having received the grace of which I am speaking, believed this truth in the most unshakable manner. So much so that, having consulted a half-learned man who was as ignorant on this point as she had been before she was enlightened, when he replied that God is in us only by 'grace,' she disbelieved his reply, so sure she was of the true answer; and when she came to ask wiser doctors, they confirmed her in her belief, which much consoled her. . . .

"But how, you will repeat, *can* one have such certainty in respect to what one does not see? This question, I am powerless to answer. These are secrets of God's omnipotence which it does not appertain to me to penetrate. All that I know is that I tell the truth; and I shall never believe that any soul who does not possess this certainty has ever been really united to God."[1]

The kinds of truth communicable in mystical ways, whether these be sensible or supersensible, are various. Some of them relate to this world,—visions of the future, the reading of hearts, the sudden understanding of texts, the knowledge of distant events, for example; but the most important revelations are theological or metaphysical.

"Saint Ignatius confessed one day to Father Laynez that a single hour of meditation at Manresa had taught him more truths about heavenly things than all the teachings of all the doctors put together could have taught him. . . . One day in orison, on the steps of the choir of the Dominican church, he saw in a distinct manner the plan of divine wisdom in the creation of the world. On another occasion, during a procession, his spirit was ravished in God, and it was given him to contemplate, in a form and images fitted to the weak understanding of a dweller on the earth, the deep mystery of the holy Trinity. This last vision flooded his heart with such sweetness, that the mere memory of it in after times made him shed abundant tears."[2]

---

[1] The Interior Castle, Fifth Abode, ch. i., in Œuvres, translated by BOUIX, iii. 421–424.

[2] BARTOLI-MICHEL: Vie de Saint Ignace de Loyola, i. 34–36. Others have had illuminations about the created world, Jacob Boehme, for instance. At the age of twenty-five he was "surrounded by the divine light, and replenished with the heavenly knowledge; insomuch as going abroad into the fields to a green, at Görlitz, he there sat down, and viewing the herbs and grass of the field, in his inward light he saw into their essences, use, and properties,

Similarly with Saint Teresa. "One day, being in orison," she writes, "it was granted me to perceive in one instant how all things are seen and contained in God. I did not perceive them in their proper form, and nevertheless the view I had of them was of a sovereign clearness, and has remained vividly impressed upon my soul. It is one of the most signal of all the graces which the Lord has granted me. . . . The view was so subtile and delicate that the understanding cannot grasp it."[1]

She goes on to tell how it was as if the Deity were an enormous and sovereignly limpid diamond, in which all our actions were contained in such a way that their full sinfulness appeared evident as never before. On another day, she relates, while she was reciting the Athanasian Creed,—

"Our Lord made me comprehend in what way it is that

----

which was discovered to him by their lineaments, figures, and signatures." Of a later period of experience he writes: "In one quarter of an hour I saw and knew more than if I had been many years together at an university. For I saw and knew the being of all things, the Byss and the Abyss, and the eternal generation of the holy Trinity, the descent and original of the world and of all creatures through the divine wisdom. I knew and saw in myself all the three worlds, the external and visible world being of a procreation or extern birth from both the internal and spiritual worlds; and I saw and knew the whole working essence, in the evil and in the good, and the mutual original and existence; and likewise how the fruitful bearing womb of eternity brought forth. So that I did not only greatly wonder at it, but did also exceedingly rejoice, albeit I could very hardly apprehend the same in my external man and set it down with the pen. For I had a thorough view of the universe as in a chaos, wherein all things are couched and wrapt up, but it was impossible for me to explicate the same." Jacob Behmen's Theosophic Philosophy, etc., by EDWARD TAYLOR, London, 1691, pp. 425, 427, abridged. So George Fox: "I was come up to the state of Adam in which he was before he fell. The creation was opened to me; and it was showed me, how all things had their names given to them, according to their nature and virtue. I was at a stand in my mind, whether I should practice physic for the good of mankind, seeing the nature and virtues of the creatures were so opened to me by the Lord." Journal, Philadelphia, no date, p. 69. Contemporary 'Clairvoyance' abounds in similar revelations. Andrew Jackson Davis's cosmogonies, for example, or certain experiences related in the delectable 'Reminiscences and Memories of Henry Thomas Butterworth,' Lebanon, Ohio, 1886.

[1] Vie, pp. 581, 582.

one God can be in three Persons. He made me see it so clearly that I remained as extremely surprised as I was comforted, . . . and now, when I think of the holy Trinity, or hear It spoken of, I understand how the three adorable Persons form only one God and I experience an unspeakable happiness."

On still another occasion, it was given to Saint Teresa to see and understand in what wise the Mother of God had been assumed into her place in Heaven.[1]

The deliciousness of some of these states seems to be beyond anything known in ordinary consciousness. It evidently involves organic sensibilities, for it is spoken of as something too extreme to be borne, and as verging on bodily pain.[2] But it is too subtle and piercing a delight for ordinary words to denote. God's touches, the wounds of his spear, references to ebriety and to nuptial union have to figure in the phraseology by which it is shadowed forth. Intellect and senses both swoon away in these highest states of ecstasy. "If our understanding comprehends," says Saint Teresa, "it is in a mode which remains unknown to it, and it can understand nothing of what it comprehends. For my own part, I do not believe that it does comprehend, because, as I said, it does not understand itself to do so. I confess that it is all a mystery in which I am lost."[3] In the condition called *raptus* or ravishment by theologians, breathing and circulation are so depressed that it is a question among the doctors whether the soul be or be not temporarily dissevered from the body. One must read Saint Teresa's descriptions and the very exact distinctions which she makes, to persuade one's self that one is dealing, not with imaginary experiences, but with phenomena which, however rare, follow perfectly definite psychological types.

[1] Loc. cit., p. 574.
[2] Saint Teresa discriminates between pain in which the body has a part and pure spiritual pain (Interior Castle, 6th Abode, ch. xi.). As for the bodily part in these celestial joys, she speaks of it as "penetrating to the marrow of the bones, whilst earthly pleasures affect only the surface of the senses. I think," she adds, "that this is a just description, and I cannot make it better." Ibid., 5th Abode, ch. i.
[3] Vie, p. 198.

To the medical mind these ecstasies signify nothing but suggested and imitated hypnoid states, on an intellectual basis of superstition, and a corporeal one of degeneration and hysteria. Undoubtedly these pathological conditions have existed in many and possibly in all the cases, but that fact tells us nothing about the value for knowledge of the consciousness which they induce. To pass a spiritual judgment upon these states, we must not content ourselves with superficial medical talk, but inquire into their fruits for life.

Their fruits appear to have been various. Stupefaction, for one thing, seems not to have been altogether absent as a result. You may remember the helplessness in the kitchen and schoolroom of poor Margaret Mary Alacoque. Many other ecstatics would have perished but for the care taken of them by admiring followers. The 'other-worldliness' encouraged by the mystical consciousness makes this over-abstraction from practical life peculiarly liable to befall mystics in whom the character is naturally passive and the intellect feeble; but in natively strong minds and characters we find quite opposite results. The great Spanish mystics, who carried the habit of ecstasy as far as it has often been carried, appear for the most part to have shown indomitable spirit and energy, and all the more so for the trances in which they indulged.

Saint Ignatius was a mystic, but his mysticism made him assuredly one of the most powerfully practical human engines that ever lived. Saint John of the Cross, writing of the intuitions and 'touches' by which God reaches the substance of the soul, tells us that—

> "They enrich it marvelously. A single one of them may be sufficient to abolish at a stroke certain imperfections of which the soul during its whole life had vainly tried to rid itself, and to leave it adorned with virtues and loaded with supernatural gifts. A single one of these intoxicating consolations may reward it for all the labors undergone in its life—even were they numberless. Invested with an invincible courage, filled with an impassioned desire to suffer for its God, the soul then is seized with a strange torment—that of not being allowed to suffer enough."[1]

[1] Œuvres, ii. 320.

Saint Teresa is as emphatic, and much more detailed. You may perhaps remember a passage I quoted from her in my first lecture.[1] There are many similar pages in her autobiography. Where in literature is a more evidently veracious account of the formation of a new centre of spiritual energy, than is given in her description of the effects of certain ecstasies which in departing leave the soul upon a higher level of emotional excitement?

"Often, infirm and wrought upon with dreadful pains before the ecstasy, the soul emerges from it full of health and admirably disposed for action . . . as if God had willed that the body itself, already obedient to the soul's desires, should share in the soul's happiness. . . . The soul after such a favor is animated with a degree of courage so great that if at that moment its body should be torn to pieces for the cause of God, it would feel nothing but the liveliest comfort. Then it is that promises and heroic resolutions spring up in profusion in us, soaring desires, horror of the world, and the clear perception of our proper nothingness. . . . What empire is comparable to that of a soul who, from this sublime summit to which God has raised her, sees all the things of earth beneath her feet, and is captivated by no one of them? How ashamed she is of her former attachments! How amazed at her blindness! What lively pity she feels for those whom she recognizes still shrouded in the darkness! . . . She groans at having ever been sensitive to points of honor, at the illusion that made her ever see as honor what the world calls by that name. Now she sees in this name nothing more than an immense lie of which the world remains a victim. She discovers, in the new light from above, that in genuine honor there is nothing spurious, that to be faithful to this honor is to give our respect to what deserves to be respected really, and to consider as nothing, or as less than nothing, whatsoever perishes and is not agreeable to God. . . . She laughs when she sees grave persons, persons of orison, caring for points of honor for which she now feels profoundest contempt. It is suitable to the dignity of their rank to act thus,

[1] Above, p. 27.

they pretend, and it makes them more useful to others. But she knows that in despising the dignity of their rank for the pure love of God they would do more good in a single day than they would effect in ten years by preserving it. . . . She laughs at herself that there should ever have been a time in her life when she made any case of money, when she ever desired it. . . . Oh! if human beings might only agree together to regard it as so much useless mud, what harmony would then reign in the world! With what friendship we would all treat each other if our interest in honor and in money could but disappear from earth! For my own part, I feel as if it would be a remedy for all our ills."[1]

Mystical conditions may, therefore, render the soul more energetic in the lines which their inspiration favors. But this could be reckoned an advantage only in case the inspiration were a true one. If the inspiration were erroneous, the energy would be all the more mistaken and misbegotten. So we stand once more before that problem of truth which confronted us at the end of the lectures on saintliness. You will remember that we turned to mysticism precisely to get some light on truth. Do mystical states establish the truth of those theological affections in which the saintly life has its root?

In spite of their repudiation of articulate self-description, mystical states in general assert a pretty distinct theoretic drift. It is possible to give the outcome of the majority of them in terms that point in definite philosophical directions. One of these directions is optimism, and the other is monism. We pass into mystical states from out of ordinary consciousness as from a less into a more, as from a smallness into a vastness, and at the same time as from an unrest to a rest. We feel them as reconciling, unifying states. They appeal to the yes-function more than to the no-function in us. In them the unlimited absorbs the limits and peacefully closes the account. Their very denial of every adjective you may propose as applicable to the ultimate truth,—He, the Self, the Atman, is to be described by 'No! no!' only, say the Upanishads,[2]—though it seems on the surface to be a no-function, is a denial

[1] Vie, pp. 229, 200, 231–233, 243.
[2] MÜLLER's translation, part ii. p. 180.

made on behalf of a deeper yes. Whoso calls the Absolute anything in particular, or says that it is *this*, seems implicitly to shut it off from being *that*—it is as if he lessened it. So we deny the 'this,' negating the negation which it seems to us to imply, in the interests of the higher affirmative attitude by which we are possessed. The fountain-head of Christian mysticism is Dionysius the Areopagite. He describes the absolute truth by negatives exclusively.

"The cause of all things is neither soul nor intellect; nor has it imagination, opinion, or reason, or intelligence; nor is it reason or intelligence; nor is it spoken or thought. It is neither number, nor order, nor magnitude, nor littleness, nor equality, nor inequality, nor similarity, nor dissimilarity. It neither stands, nor moves, nor rests. . . . It is neither essence, nor eternity, nor time. Even intellectual contact does not belong to it. It is neither science nor truth. It is not even royalty or wisdom; not one; not unity; not divinity or goodness; nor even spirit as we know it," etc., *ad libitum.*[1]

But these qualifications are denied by Dionysius, not because the truth falls short of them, but because it so infinitely excels them. It is above them. It is *super*-lucent, *super*-splendent, *super*-essential, *super*-sublime, *super* everything that can be named. Like Hegel in his logic, mystics journey towards the positive pole of truth only by the 'Methode der Absoluten Negativität.'[2]

Thus come the paradoxical expressions that so abound in mystical writings. As when Eckhart tells of the still desert of the Godhead, "where never was seen difference, neither Father, Son, nor Holy Ghost, where there is no one at home, yet where the spark of the soul is more at peace than in itself."[3] As when Boehme writes of the Primal Love, that "it may fitly be compared to Nothing, for it is deeper than any Thing, and is as nothing with respect to all things, forasmuch

---

[1] T. Davidson's translation, in Journal of Speculative Philosophy, 1893, vol. xxii. p. 399.

[2] "Deus propter excellentiam non immerito Nihil vocatur." Scotus Erigena, quoted by Andrew Seth: Two Lectures on Theism, New York, 1897, p. 55.

[3] J. Royce: Studies in Good and Evil, p. 282.

as it is not comprehensible by any of them. And because it is nothing respectively, it is therefore free from all things, and is that only good, which a man cannot express or utter what it is, there being nothing to which it may be compared, to express it by."[1] Or as when Angelus Silesius sings:—

"Gott ist ein lauter Nichts, ihn rührt kein Nun noch Hier;
Je mehr du nach ihm greiffst, je mehr entwind er dir."[2]

To this dialectical use, by the intellect, of negation as a mode of passage towards a higher kind of affirmation, there is correlated the subtlest of moral counterparts in the sphere of the personal will. Since denial of the finite self and its wants, since asceticism of some sort, is found in religious experience to be the only doorway to the larger and more blessed life, this moral mystery intertwines and combines with the intellectual mystery in all mystical writings.

"Love," continues Behmen, is Nothing, for "when thou art gone forth wholly from the Creature and from that which is visible, and art become Nothing to all that is Nature and Creature, then thou art in that eternal One, which is God himself, and then thou shalt feel within thee the highest virtue of Love. . . . The treasure of treasures for the soul is where she goeth out of the Somewhat into that Nothing out of which all things may be made. The soul here saith, *I have nothing*, for I am utterly stripped and naked; *I can do nothing*, for I have no manner of power, but am as water poured out; *I am nothing*, for all that I am is no more than an image of Being, and only God is to me I AM; and so, sitting down in my own Nothingness, I give glory to the eternal Being, and *will nothing* of myself, that so God may will all in me, being unto me my God and all things."[3]

In Paul's language, I live, yet not I, but Christ liveth in me.

[1] Jacob Behmen's Dialogues on the Supersensual Life, translated by BERNARD HOLLAND, London, 1901, p. 48.
[2] Cherubinischer Wandersmann, Strophe 25.
[3] Op. cit., pp. 42, 74, abridged.

Only when I become as nothing can God enter in and no difference between his life and mine remain outstanding.[1]

This overcoming of all the usual barriers between the individual and the Absolute is the great mystic achievement. In mystic states we both become one with the Absolute and we become aware of our oneness. This is the everlasting and triumphant mystical tradition, hardly altered by differences of clime or creed. In Hinduism, in Neoplatonism, in Sufism, in Christian mysticism, in Whitmanism, we find the same recurring note, so that there is about mystical utterances an eternal unanimity which ought to make a critic stop and think, and which brings it about that the mystical classics have, as has been said, neither birthday nor native land. Perpetually telling of the unity of man with God, their speech antedates languages, and they do not grow old.[2]

'That art Thou!' say the Upanishads, and the Vedantists

---

[1] From a French book I take this mystical expression of happiness in God's indwelling presence: —

"Jesus has come to take up his abode in my heart. It is not so much a habitation, an association, as a sort of fusion. Oh, new and blessed life! life which becomes each day more luminous. . . . The wall before me, dark a few moments since, is splendid at this hour because the sun shines on it. Wherever its rays fall they light up a conflagration of glory; the smallest speck of glass sparkles, each grain of sand emits fire; even so there is a royal song of triumph in my heart because the Lord is there. My days succeed each other; yesterday a blue sky; to-day a clouded sun; a night filled with strange dreams; but as soon as the eyes open, and I regain consciousness and seem to begin life again, it is always the same figure before me, always the same presence filling my heart. . . . Formerly the day was dulled by the absence of the Lord. I used to wake invaded by all sorts of sad impressions, and I did not find him on my path. To-day he is with me; and the light cloudiness which covers things is not an obstacle to my communion with him. I feel the pressure of his hand, I feel something else which fills me with a serene joy; shall I dare to speak it out? Yes, for it is the true expression of what I experience. The Holy Spirit is not merely making me a visit; it is no mere dazzling apparition which may from one moment to another spread its wings and leave me in my night, it is a permanent habitation. He can depart only if he takes me with him. More than that; he is not other than myself: he is one with me. It is not a juxtaposition, it is a penetration, a profound modification of my nature, a new manner of my being." Quoted from the MS. 'of an old man' by WILFRED MONOD: Il Vit: six méditations sur le mystère chrétien, pp. 280–283.

[2] Compare M. MAETERLINCK: L'Ornement des Noces spirituelles de Ruysbroeck, Bruxelles, 1891, Introduction, p. xix.

add: 'Not a part, not a mode of That, but identically That, that absolute Spirit of the World.' "As pure water poured into pure water remains the same, thus, O Gautama, is the Self of a thinker who knows. Water in water, fire in fire, ether in ether, no one can distinguish them; likewise a man whose mind has entered into the Self."[1] " 'Every man,' says the Sufi Gulshan-Râz, 'whose heart is no longer shaken by any doubt, knows with certainty that there is no being save only One. . . . In his divine majesty the *me*, the *we*, the *thou*, are not found, for in the One there can be no distinction. Every being who is annulled and entirely separated from himself, hears resound outside of him this voice and this echo: *I am God*: he has an eternal way of existing, and is no longer subject to death.' "[2] In the vision of God, says Plotinus, "what sees is not our reason, but something prior and superior to our reason. . . . He who thus sees does not properly see, does not distinguish or imagine two things. He changes, he ceases to be himself, preserves nothing of himself. Absorbed in God, he makes but one with him, like a centre of a circle coinciding with another centre."[3] "Here," writes Suso, "the spirit dies, and yet is all alive in the marvels of the Godhead . . . and is lost in the stillness of the glorious dazzling obscurity and of the naked simple unity. It is in this modeless *where* that the highest bliss is to be found."[4] "Ich bin so gross als Gott," sings Angelus Silesius again, "Er ist als ich so klein; Er kann nicht über mich, ich unter ihm nicht sein."[5]

In mystical literature such self-contradictory phrases as 'dazzling obscurity,' ' whispering silence,' 'teeming desert,' are continually met with. They prove that not conceptual speech, but music rather, is the element through which we are best spoken to by mystical truth. Many mystical scriptures are indeed little more than musical compositions.

"He who would hear the voice of Nada, 'the Soundless Sound,' and comprehend it, he has to learn the nature of

---

[1] Upanishads, M. MÜLLER's translation, ii. 17, 334.

[2] SCHMÖLDERS: Op. cit., p. 210.

[3] Enneads, BOUILLET's translation, Paris, 1861, iii. 561. Compare pp. 473–477, and vol. i. p. 27.

[4] Autobiography, pp. 309, 310.

[5] Op. cit., Strophe 10.

Dhâranâ. . . . When to himself his form appears unreal, as do on waking all the forms he sees in dreams; when he has ceased to hear the many, he may discern the ONE— the inner sound which kills the outer. . . . For then the soul will hear, and will remember. And then to the inner ear will speak THE VOICE OF THE SILENCE. . . . And now thy *Self* is lost in SELF, *thyself* unto THYSELF, merged in that SELF from which thou first didst radiate. . . . Behold! thou hast become the Light, thou hast become the Sound, thou art thy Master and thy God. Thou art THYSELF the object of thy search: the VOICE unbroken, that resounds throughout eternities, exempt from change, from sin exempt, the seven sounds in one, the VOICE OF THE SILENCE. *Om tat Sat.*"[1]

These words, if they do not awaken laughter as you receive them, probably stir chords within you which music and language touch in common. Music gives us ontological messages which non-musical criticism is unable to contradict, though it may laugh at our foolishness in minding them. There is a verge of the mind which these things haunt; and whispers therefrom mingle with the operations of our understanding, even as the waters of the infinite ocean send their waves to break among the pebbles that lie upon our shores.

"Here begins the sea that ends not till the world's end.
    Where we stand,
  Could we know the next high sea-mark set beyond these
    waves that gleam,
  We should know what never man hath known, nor eye of
    man hath scanned. . . .
  Ah, but here man's heart leaps, yearning towards the gloom
    with venturous glee,
  From the shore that hath no shore beyond it, set in all the
    sea."[2]

That doctrine, for example, that eternity is timeless, that our 'immortality,' if we live in the eternal, is not so much future as already now and here, which we find so often ex-

[1] H. P. BLAVATSKY: The Voice of the Silence.
[2] SWINBURNE: On the Verge, in 'A Midsummer Vacation.'

pressed to-day in certain philosophic circles, finds its support in a 'hear, hear!' or an 'amen,' which floats up from that mysteriously deeper level.[1] We recognize the passwords to the mystical region as we hear them, but we cannot use them ourselves; it alone has the keeping of 'the password primeval.'[2]

I have now sketched with extreme brevity and insufficiency, but as fairly as I am able in the time allowed, the general traits of the mystic range of consciousness. *It is on the whole pantheistic and optimistic, or at least the opposite of pessimistic. It is anti-naturalistic, and harmonizes best with twice-bornness and so-called other-worldly states of mind.*

My next task is to inquire whether we can invoke it as authoritative. Does it furnish any *warrant for the truth* of the twice-bornness and supernaturality and pantheism which it favors? I must give my answer to this question as concisely as I can.

In brief my answer is this,—and I will divide it into three parts:—

(1) Mystical states, when well developed, usually are, and have the right to be, absolutely authoritative over the individuals to whom they come.

(2) No authority emanates from them which should make it a duty for those who stand outside of them to accept their revelations uncritically.

(3) They break down the authority of the non-mystical or rationalistic consciousness, based upon the understanding and the senses alone. They show it to be only one kind of consciousness. They open out the possibility of other orders of truth, in which, so far as anything in us vitally responds to them, we may freely continue to have faith.

I will take up these points one by one.

I.

As a matter of psychological fact, mystical states of a well-pronounced and emphatic sort *are* usually authoritative over

---

[1] Compare the extracts from Dr. Bucke, quoted on pp. 359, 360.
[2] As serious an attempt as I know to mediate between the mystical region and the discursive life is contained in an article on Aristotle's Unmoved Mover, by F. C. S. SCHILLER, in Mind, vol. ix., 1900.

those who have them.[1] They have been 'there,' and know. It is vain for rationalism to grumble about this. If the mystical truth that comes to a man proves to be a force that he can live by, what mandate have we of the majority to order him to live in another way? We can throw him into a prison or a madhouse, but we cannot change his mind—we commonly attach it only the more stubbornly to its beliefs.[2] It mocks our utmost efforts, as a matter of fact, and in point of logic it absolutely escapes our jurisdiction. Our own more 'rational' beliefs are based on evidence exactly similar in nature to that which mystics quote for theirs. Our senses, namely, have assured us of certain states of fact; but mystical experiences are as direct perceptions of fact for those who have them as any sensations ever were for us. The records show that even though the five senses be in abeyance in them, they are absolutely sensational in their epistemological quality, if I may be pardoned the barbarous expression,—that is, they are face to face presentations of what seems immediately to exist.

The mystic is, in short, *invulnerable*, and must be left, whether we relish it or not, in undisturbed enjoyment of his creed. Faith, says Tolstoy, is that by which men live. And faith-state and mystic state are practically convertible terms.

2.

But I now proceed to add that mystics have no right to claim that we ought to accept the deliverance of their peculiar experiences, if we are ourselves outsiders and feel no private call thereto. The utmost they can ever ask of us in this life is to admit that they establish a presumption. They form a

---

[1] I abstract from weaker states, and from those cases of which the books are full, where the director (but usually not the subject) remains in doubt whether the experience may not have proceeded from the demon.

[2] Example: Mr. John Nelson writes of his imprisonment for preaching Methodism: "My soul was as a watered garden, and I could sing praises to God all day long; for he turned my captivity into joy, and gave me to rest as well on the boards, as if I had been on a bed of down. Now could I say, 'God's service is perfect freedom,' and I was carried out much in prayer that my enemies might drink of the same river of peace which my God gave so largely to me." Journal, London, no date, p. 172.

consensus and have an unequivocal outcome; and it would be odd, mystics might say, if such a unanimous type of experience should prove to be altogether wrong. At bottom, however, this would only be an appeal to numbers, like the appeal of rationalism the other way; and the appeal to numbers has no logical force. If we acknowledge it, it is for 'suggestive,' not for logical reasons: we follow the majority because to do so suits our life.

But even this presumption from the unanimity of mystics is far from being strong. In characterizing mystic states as pantheistic, optimistic, etc., I am afraid I over-simplified the truth. I did so for expository reasons, and to keep the closer to the classic mystical tradition. The classic religious mysticism, it now must be confessed, is only a 'privileged case.' It is an *extract*, kept true to type by the selection of the fittest specimens and their preservation in 'schools.' It is carved out from a much larger mass; and if we take the larger mass as seriously as religious mysticism has historically taken itself, we find that the supposed unanimity largely disappears. To begin with, even religious mysticism itself, the kind that accumulates traditions and makes schools, is much less unanimous than I have allowed. It has been both ascetic and antinomianly self-indulgent within the Christian church.[1] It is dualistic in Sankhya, and monistic in Vedanta philosophy. I called it pantheistic; but the great Spanish mystics are anything but pantheists. They are with few exceptions non-metaphysical minds, for whom 'the category of personality' is absolute. The 'union' of man with God is for them much more like an occasional miracle than like an original identity.[2] How different again, apart from the happiness common to all, is the mysticism of Walt Whitman, Edward Carpenter, Richard Jefferies, and other naturalistic pantheists, from the more distinctively Christian sort.[3] The fact is

[1] RUYSBROECK, in the work which Maeterlinck has translated, has a chapter against the antinomianism of disciples. H. DELACROIX's book (Essai sur le mysticisme spéculatif en Allemagne au XIVme Siècle, Paris, 1900) is full of antinomian material. Compare also A. JUNDT: Les Amis de Dieu au XIVme Siècle, Thèse de Strasbourg, 1879.

[2] Compare PAUL ROUSSELOT: Les Mystiques Espagnols, Paris, 1869, ch. xii.

[3] See CARPENTER's Towards Democracy, especially the latter parts, and JEFFERIES's wonderful and splendid mystic rhapsody, The Story of my Heart.

that the mystical feeling of enlargement, union, and emancipation has no specific intellectual content whatever of its own. It is capable of forming matrimonial alliances with material furnished by the most diverse philosophies and theologies, provided only they can find a place in their framework for its peculiar emotional mood. We have no right, therefore, to invoke its prestige as distinctively in favor of any special belief, such as that in absolute idealism, or in the absolute monistic identity, or in the absolute goodness, of the world. It is only relatively in favor of all these things—it passes out of common human consciousness in the direction in which they lie.

So much for religious mysticism proper. But more remains to be told, for religious mysticism is only one half of mysticism. The other half has no accumulated traditions except those which the text-books on insanity supply. Open any one of these, and you will find abundant cases in which 'mystical ideas' are cited as characteristic symptoms of enfeebled or deluded states of mind. In delusional insanity, paranoia, as they sometimes call it, we may have a *diabolical* mysticism, a sort of religious mysticism turned upside down. The same sense of ineffable importance in the smallest events, the same texts and words coming with new meanings, the same voices and visions and leadings and missions, the same controlling by extraneous powers; only this time the emotion is pessimistic: instead of consolations we have desolations; the meanings are dreadful; and the powers are enemies to life. It is evident that from the point of view of their psychological mechanism, the classic mysticism and these lower mysticisms spring from the same mental level, from that great subliminal or transmarginal region of which science is beginning to admit the existence, but of which so little is really known. That region contains every kind of matter: 'seraph and snake' abide there side by side. To come from thence is no infallible credential. What comes must be sifted and tested, and run the gauntlet of confrontation with the total context of experience, just like what comes from the outer world of sense. Its value must be ascertained by empirical methods, so long as we are not mystics ourselves.

Once more, then, I repeat that non-mystics are under no obligation to acknowledge in mystical states a superior authority conferred on them by their intrinsic nature.[1]

3.

Yet, I repeat once more, the existence of mystical states absolutely overthrows the pretension of non-mystical states to be the sole and ultimate dictators of what we may believe. As a rule, mystical states merely add a supersensuous meaning to the ordinary outward data of consciousness. They are excitements like the emotions of love or ambition, gifts to our spirit by means of which facts already objectively before us fall into a new expressiveness and make a new connection with our active life. They do not contradict these facts as such, or deny anything that our senses have immediately seized.[2] It is the rationalistic critic rather who plays the part of denier in the controversy, and his denials have no strength, for there never can be a state of facts to which new meaning may not truthfully be added, provided the mind ascend to a more enveloping point of view. It must always remain an open question whether mystical states may not possibly be such superior points of view, windows through which the mind looks out upon a more extensive and inclusive world. The difference of the views seen from the different mystical windows need not prevent us from entertaining this supposition. The wider

[1] In chapter i. of book ii. of his work Degeneration, 'MAX NORDAU' seeks to undermine all mysticism by exposing the weakness of the lower kinds. Mysticism for him means any sudden perception of hidden significance in things. He explains such perception by the abundant uncompleted associations which experiences may arouse in a degenerate brain. These give to him who has the experience a vague and vast sense of its leading further, yet they awaken no definite or useful consequent in his thought. The explanation is a plausible one for certain sorts of feeling of significance; and other alienists (WERNICKE, for example, in his Grundriss der Psychiatrie, Theil ii., Leipzig, 1896) have explained 'paranoiac' conditions by a laming of the association-organ. But the higher mystical flights, with their positiveness and abruptness, are surely products of no such merely negative condition. It seems far more reasonable to ascribe them to inroads from the subconscious life, of the cerebral activity correlative to which we as yet know nothing.

[2] They sometimes add subjective *audita et visa* to the facts, but as these are usually interpreted as transmundane, they oblige no alteration in the facts of sense.

world would in that case prove to have a mixed constitution like that of this world, that is all. It would have its celestial and its infernal regions, its tempting and its saving moments, its valid experiences and its counterfeit ones, just as our world has them; but it would be a wider world all the same. We should have to use its experiences by selecting and subordinating and substituting just as is our custom in this ordinary naturalistic world; we should be liable to error just as we are now; yet the counting in of that wider world of meanings, and the serious dealing with it, might, in spite of all the perplexity, be indispensable stages in our approach to the final fullness of the truth.

In this shape, I think, we have to leave the subject. Mystical states indeed wield no authority due simply to their being mystical states. But the higher ones among them point in directions to which the religious sentiments even of non-mystical men incline. They tell of the supremacy of the ideal, of vastness, of union, of safety, and of rest. They offer us *hypotheses*, hypotheses which we may voluntarily ignore, but which as thinkers we cannot possibly upset. The supernaturalism and optimism to which they would persuade us may, interpreted in one way or another, be after all the truest of insights into the meaning of this life.

"Oh, the little more, and how much it is; and the little less, and what worlds away!" It may be that possibility and permission of this sort are all that the religious consciousness requires to live on. In my last lecture I shall have to try to persuade you that this is the case. Meanwhile, however, I am sure that for many of my readers this diet is too slender. If supernaturalism and inner union with the divine are true, you think, then not so much permission, as compulsion to believe, ought to be found. Philosophy has always professed to prove religious truth by coercive argument; and the construction of philosophies of this kind has always been one favorite function of the religious life, if we use this term in the large historic sense. But religious philosophy is an enormous subject, and in my next lecture I can only give that brief glance at it which my limits will allow.

LECTURE XVIII

PHILOSOPHY

THE SUBJECT of Saintliness left us face to face with the question, Is the sense of divine presence a sense of anything objectively true? We turned first to mysticism for an answer, and found that although mysticism is entirely willing to corroborate religion, it is too private (and also too various) in its utterances to be able to claim a universal authority. But philosophy publishes results which claim to be universally valid if they are valid at all, so we now turn with our question to philosophy. Can philosophy stamp a warrant of veracity upon the religious man's sense of the divine?

I imagine that many of you at this point begin to indulge in guesses at the goal to which I am tending. I have undermined the authority of mysticism, you say, and the next thing I shall probably do is to seek to discredit that of philosophy. Religion, you expect to hear me conclude, is nothing but an affair of faith, based either on vague sentiment, or on that vivid sense of the reality of things unseen of which in my second lecture and in the lecture on Mysticism I gave so many examples. It is essentially private and individualistic; it always exceeds our powers of formulation; and although attempts to pour its contents into a philosophic mould will probably always go on, men being what they are, yet these attempts are always secondary processes which in no way add to the authority, or warrant the veracity, of the sentiments from which they derive their own stimulus and borrow whatever glow of conviction they may themselves possess. In short, you suspect that I am planning to defend feeling at the expense of reason, to rehabilitate the primitive and unreflective, and to dissuade you from the hope of any Theology worthy of the name.

To a certain extent I have to admit that you guess rightly. I do believe that feeling is the deeper source of religion, and that philosophic and theological formulas are secondary products, like translations of a text into another tongue. But all such statements are misleading from their brevity, and it will take the whole hour for me to explain to you exactly what I mean.

When I call theological formulas secondary products, I mean that in a world in which no religious feeling had ever existed, I doubt whether any philosophic theology could ever have been framed. I doubt if dispassionate intellectual contemplation of the universe, apart from inner unhappiness and need of deliverance on the one hand and mystical emotion on the other, would ever have resulted in religious philosophies such as we now possess. Men would have begun with animistic explanations of natural fact, and criticised these away into scientific ones, as they actually have done. In the science they would have left a certain amount of 'psychical research,' even as they now will probably have to re-admit a certain amount. But high-flying speculations like those of either dogmatic or idealistic theology, these they would have had no motive to venture on, feeling no need of commerce with such deities. These speculations must, it seems to me, be classed as over-beliefs, buildings-out performed by the intellect into directions of which feeling originally supplied the hint.

But even if religious philosophy had to have its first hint supplied by feeling, may it not have dealt in a superior way with the matter which feeling suggested? Feeling is private and dumb, and unable to give an account of itself. It allows that its results are mysteries and enigmas, declines to justify them rationally, and on occasion is willing that they should even pass for paradoxical and absurd. Philosophy takes just the opposite attitude. Her aspiration is to reclaim from mystery and paradox whatever territory she touches. To find an escape from obscure and wayward personal persuasion to truth objectively valid for all thinking men has ever been the intellect's most cherished ideal. To redeem religion from unwholesome privacy, and to give public status and universal right of way to its deliverances, has been reason's task.

I believe that philosophy will always have opportunity to labor at this task.[1] We are thinking beings, and we cannot exclude the intellect from participating in any of our functions. Even in soliloquizing with ourselves, we construe our feelings intellectually. Both our personal ideals and our religious and mystical experiences must be interpreted con-

[1] Compare Professor W. WALLACE's Gifford Lectures, in Lectures and Essays, Oxford, 1898, pp. 17 ff.

gruously with the kind of scenery which our thinking mind inhabits. The philosophic climate of our time inevitably forces its own clothing on us. Moreover, we must exchange our feelings with one another, and in doing so we have to speak, and to use general and abstract verbal formulas. Conceptions and constructions are thus a necessary part of our religion; and as moderator amid the clash of hypotheses, and mediator among the criticisms of one man's constructions by another, philosophy will always have much to do. It would be strange if I disputed this, when these very lectures which I am giving are (as you will see more clearly from now onwards) a laborious attempt to extract from the privacies of religious experience some general facts which can be defined in formulas upon which everybody may agree.

Religious experience, in other words, spontaneously and inevitably engenders myths, superstitions, dogmas, creeds, and metaphysical theologies, and criticisms of one set of these by the adherents of another. Of late, impartial classifications and comparisons have become possible, alongside of the denunciations and anathemas by which the commerce between creeds used exclusively to be carried on. We have the beginnings of a 'Science of Religions,' so-called; and if these lectures could ever be accounted a crumb-like contribution to such a science, I should be made very happy.

But all these intellectual operations, whether they be constructive or comparative and critical, presuppose immediate experiences as their subject-matter. They are interpretative and inductive operations, operations after the fact, consequent upon religious feeling, not coördinate with it, not independent of what it ascertains.

The intellectualism in religion which I wish to discredit pretends to be something altogether different from this. It assumes to construct religious objects out of the resources of logical reason alone, or of logical reason drawing rigorous inference from non-subjective facts. It calls its conclusions dogmatic theology, or philosophy of the absolute, as the case may be; it does not call them science of religions. It reaches them in an a priori way, and warrants their veracity.

Warranted systems have ever been the idols of aspiring

souls. All-inclusive, yet simple; noble, clean, luminous, stable, rigorous, true;—what more ideal refuge could there be than such a system would offer to spirits vexed by the muddiness and accidentality of the world of sensible things? Accordingly, we find inculcated in the theological schools of to-day, almost as much as in those of the fore-time, a disdain for merely possible or probable truth, and of results that only private assurance can grasp. Scholastics and idealists both express this disdain. Principal John Caird, for example, writes as follows in his Introduction to the Philosophy of Religion:—

> "Religion must indeed be a thing of the heart; but in order to elevate it from the region of subjective caprice and waywardness, and to distinguish between that which is true and false in religion, we must appeal to an objective standard. That which enters the heart must first be discerned by the intelligence to be *true*. It must be seen as having in its own nature a *right* to dominate feeling, and as constituting the principle by which feeling must be judged.[1] In estimating the religious character of individuals, nations, or races, the first question is, not how they feel, but what they think and believe—not whether their religion is one which manifests itself in emotions, more or less vehement and enthusiastic, but what are the *conceptions* of God and divine things by which these emotions are called forth. Feeling is necessary in religion, but it is by the *content* or intelligent basis of a religion, and not by feeling, that its character and worth are to be determined."[2]

Cardinal Newman, in his work, The Idea of a University, gives more emphatic expression still to this disdain for sentiment.[3] Theology, he says, is a science in the strictest sense of the word. I will tell you, he says, what it is not—not 'physical evidences' for God, not 'natural religion,' for these are but vague subjective interpretations:—

> "If," he continues, "the Supreme Being is powerful or skillful, just so far as the telescope shows power, or the

[1] Op. cit., p. 174, abridged.
[2] Ibid., p. 186, abridged and italicized.
[3] Discourse II. § 7.

microscope shows skill, if his moral law is to be ascertained simply by the physical processes of the animal frame, or his will gathered from the immediate issues of human affairs, if his Essence is just as high and deep and broad as the universe and no more; if this be the fact, then will I confess that there is no specific science about God, that theology is but a name, and a protest in its behalf an hypocrisy. Then, pious as it is to think of Him, while the pageant of experiment or abstract reasoning passes by, still such piety is nothing more than a poetry of thought, or an ornament of language, a certain view taken of Nature which one man has and another has not, which gifted minds strike out, which others see to be admirable and ingenious, and which all would be the better for adopting. It is but the theology of Nature, just as we talk of the *philosophy* or the *romance* of history, or the *poetry* of childhood, or the picturesque or the sentimental or the humorous, or any other abstract quality which the genius or the caprice of the individual, or the fashion of the day, or the consent of the world, recognizes in any set of objects which are subjected to its contemplation. I do not see much difference between avowing that there is no God, and implying that nothing definite can be known for certain about Him."

What I mean by Theology, continues Newman, is none of these things: "I simply mean the *Science of God*, or the truths we know about God, put into a system, just as we have a science of the stars and call it astronomy, or of the crust of the earth and call it geology."

In both these extracts we have the issue clearly set before us: Feeling valid only for the individual is pitted against reason valid universally. The test is a perfectly plain one of fact. Theology based on pure reason must in point of fact convince men universally. If it did not, wherein would its superiority consist? If it only formed sects and schools, even as sentiment and mysticism form them, how would it fulfill its programme of freeing us from personal caprice and waywardness? This perfectly definite practical test of the pretensions of philosophy to found religion on universal reason simplifies my procedure to-day. I need not discredit philosophy by laborious criticism of its arguments. It will suffice if I show that as a matter of history it fails to prove its pretension to be 'objectively' convincing. In fact, philosophy does so fail. It does not banish differences; it founds schools and sects just as feeling does. The logical reason of man operates, in short, in this field of divinity exactly as it has always operated in love, or in patriotism, or in politics, or in any other of the wider affairs of life, in which our passions or our mystical intuitions fix our beliefs beforehand. It finds arguments for our conviction, for indeed it *has* to find them. It amplifies and defines our faith, and dignifies it and lends it words and plausibility. It hardly ever engenders it; it cannot now secure it.[1]

Lend me your attention while I run through some of the points of the older systematic theology. You find them in both Protestant and Catholic manuals, best of all in the innumerable text-books published since Pope Leo's Encyclical recommending the study of Saint Thomas. I glance first at the arguments by which dogmatic theology establishes God's existence, after that at those by which it establishes his nature.[2]

The arguments for God's existence have stood for hundreds of years with the waves of unbelieving criticism breaking against them, never totally discrediting them in the ears of the faithful, but on the whole slowly and surely washing out the mortar from between their joints. If you have a God already whom you believe in, these arguments confirm you. If you

[1] As regards the secondary character of intellectual constructions, and the primacy of feeling and instinct in founding religious beliefs, see the striking work of H. Fielding, The Hearts of Men, London, 1902, which came into my hands after my text was written. "Creeds," says the author, "are the grammar of religion, they are to religion what grammar is to speech. Words are the expression of our wants; grammar is the theory formed afterwards. Speech never proceeded from grammar, but the reverse. As speech progresses and changes from unknown causes, grammar must follow" (p. 313). The whole book, which keeps unusually close to concrete facts, is little more than an amplification of this text.

[2] For convenience' sake, I follow the order of A. Stöckl's Lehrbuch der Philosophie, 5te Auflage, Mainz, 1881, Band ii. B. Boedder's Natural Theology, London, 1891, is a handy English Catholic Manual; but an almost identical doctrine is given by such Protestant theologians as C. Hodge: Systematic Theology, New York, 1873, or A. H. Strong: Systematic Theology, 5th edition, New York, 1896.

are atheistic, they fail to set you right. The proofs are various. The 'cosmological' one, so-called, reasons from the contingence of the world to a First Cause which must contain whatever perfections the world itself contains. The 'argument from design' reasons, from the fact that Nature's laws are mathematical, and her parts benevolently adapted to each other, that this cause is both intellectual and benevolent. The 'moral argument' is that the moral law presupposes a lawgiver. The 'argument *ex consensu gentium*' is that the belief in God is so widespread as to be grounded in the rational nature of man, and should therefore carry authority with it.

As I just said, I will not discuss these arguments technically. The bare fact that all idealists since Kant have felt entitled either to scout or to neglect them shows that they are not solid enough to serve as religion's all-sufficient foundation. Absolutely impersonal reasons would be in duty bound to show more general convincingness. Causation is indeed too obscure a principle to bear the weight of the whole structure of theology. As for the argument from design, see how Darwinian ideas have revolutionized it. Conceived as we now conceive them, as so many fortunate escapes from almost limitless processes of destruction, the benevolent adaptations which we find in Nature suggest a deity very different from the one who figured in the earlier versions of the argument.[1] The fact is that these arguments do but follow the combined

---

[1] It must not be forgotten that any form of *dis*order in the world might, by the design argument, suggest a God for just that kind of disorder. The truth is that any state of things whatever that can be named is logically susceptible of teleological interpretation. The ruins of the earthquake at Lisbon, for example: the whole of past history had to be planned exactly as it was to bring about in the fullness of time just that particular arrangement of débris of masonry, furniture, and once living bodies. No other train of causes would have been sufficient. And so of any other arrangement, bad or good, which might as a matter of fact be found resulting anywhere from previous conditions. To avoid such pessimistic consequences and save its beneficent designer, the design argument accordingly invokes two other principles, restrictive in their operation. The first is physical: Nature's forces tend of their own accord only to disorder and destruction, to heaps of ruins, not to architecture. This principle, though plausible at first sight, seems, in the light of recent biology, to be more and more improbable. The second principle is one of anthropomorphic interpretation. No arrangement that for *us* is

suggestions of the facts and of our feeling. They prove nothing rigorously. They only corroborate our preëxistent partialities.

If philosophy can do so little to establish God's existence, how stands it with her efforts to define his attributes? It is worth while to look at the attempts of systematic theology in this direction.

Since God is First Cause, this science of sciences says, he differs from all his creatures in possessing existence *a se*. From this 'a-se-ity' on God's part, theology deduces by

---

'disorderly' can possibly have been an object of design at all. This principle is of course a mere assumption in the interests of anthropomorphic Theism.

When one views the world with no definite theological bias one way or the other, one sees that order and disorder, as we now recognize them, are purely human inventions. We are interested in certain types of arrangement, useful, æsthetic, or moral,—so interested that whenever we find them realized, the fact emphatically rivets our attention. The result is that we work over the contents of the world selectively. It is overflowing with disorderly arrangements from our point of view, but order is the only thing we care for and look at, and by choosing, one can always find some sort of orderly arrangement in the midst of any chaos. If I should throw down a thousand beans at random upon a table, I could doubtless, by eliminating a sufficient number of them, leave the rest in almost any geometrical pattern you might propose to me, and you might then say that that pattern was the thing prefigured beforehand, and that the other beans were mere irrelevance and packing material. Our dealings with Nature are just like this. She is a vast *plenum* in which our attention draws capricious lines in innumerable directions. We count and name whatever lies upon the special lines we trace, whilst the other things and the untraced lines are neither named nor counted. There are in reality infinitely more things 'unadapted' to each other in this world than there are things 'adapted'; infinitely more things with irregular relations than with regular relations between them. But we look for the regular kind of thing exclusively, and ingeniously discover and preserve it in our memory. It accumulates with other regular kinds, until the collection of them fills our encyclopædias. Yet all the while between and around them lies an infinite anonymous chaos of objects that no one ever thought of together, of relations that never yet attracted our attention.

The facts of order from which the physico-theological argument starts are thus easily susceptible of interpretation as arbitrary human products. So long as this is the case, although of course no argument against God follows, it follows that the argument for him will fail to constitute a knockdown proof of his existence. It will be convincing only to those who on other grounds believe in him already.

mere logic most of his other perfections. For instance, he must be both *necessary* and *absolute*, cannot not be, and cannot in any way be determined by anything else. This makes Him absolutely unlimited from without, and unlimited also from within; for limitation is non-being; and God is being itself. This unlimitedness makes God infinitely perfect. Moreover, God is *One*, and *Only*, for the infinitely perfect can admit no peer. He is *Spiritual*, for were He composed of physical parts, some other power would have to combine them into the total, and his aseity would thus be contradicted. He is therefore both simple and non-physical in nature. He is *simple metaphysically* also, that is to say, his nature and his existence cannot be distinct, as they are in finite substances which share their formal natures with one another, and are individual only in their material aspect. Since God is one and only, his *essentia* and his *esse* must be given at one stroke. This excludes from his being all those distinctions, so familiar in the world of finite things, between potentiality and actuality, substance and accidents, being and activity, existence and attributes. We can talk, it is true, of God's powers, acts, and attributes, but these discriminations are only 'virtual,' and made from the human point of view. In God all these points of view fall into an absolute identity of being.

This absence of all potentiality in God obliges Him to be *immutable*. He is actuality, through and through. Were there anything potential about Him, He would either lose or gain by its actualization, and either loss or gain would contradict his perfection. He cannot, therefore, change. Furthermore, He is *immense*, *boundless*; for could He be outlined in space, He would be composite, and this would contradict his indivisibility. He is therefore *omnipresent*, indivisibly there, at every point of space. He is similarly wholly present at every point of time,—in other words *eternal*. For if He began in time, He would need a prior cause, and that would contradict his aseity. If He ended, it would contradict his necessity. If He went through any succession, it would contradict his immutability.

He has *intelligence* and *will* and every other creature-perfection, for *we* have them, and *effectus nequit superare causam.* In Him, however, they are absolutely and eternally in act, and their *object*, since God can be bounded by naught that is external, can primarily be nothing else than God himself. He knows himself, then, in one eternal indivisible act, and wills himself with an infinite self-pleasure.[1] Since He must of logical necessity thus love and will himself, He cannot be called 'free' *ad intra*, with the freedom of contrarieties that characterizes finite creatures. *Ad extra*, however, or with respect to his creation, God is free. He cannot *need* to create, being perfect in being and in happiness already. He *wills* to create, then, by an absolute freedom.

Being thus a substance endowed with intellect and will and freedom, God is a *person*; and a *living* person also, for He is both object and subject of his own activity, and to be this distinguishes the living from the lifeless. He is thus absolutely *self-sufficient*: his *self-knowledge* and *self-love* are both of them infinite and adequate, and need no extraneous conditions to perfect them.

He is *omniscient*, for in knowing himself as Cause He knows all creature things and events by implication. His knowledge is *previsive*, for He is present to all time. Even our free acts are known beforehand to Him, for otherwise his wisdom would admit of successive moments of enrichment, and this would contradict his immutability. He is *omnipotent* for everything that does not involve logical contradiction. He can make *being*—in other words his power includes *creation*. If what He creates were made of his own substance, it would have to be infinite in essence, as that substance is; but it is finite; so it must be non-divine in substance. If it were made of a substance, an eternally existing matter, for example, which God found there to his hand, and to which He simply gave its form, that would contradict God's definition as First Cause, and make Him a mere mover of something caused already. The things he creates, then, He creates *ex nihilo*, and gives them absolute being as so many finite substances additional to himself. The forms which he imprints upon them have their prototypes in his ideas. But as in God there is no such thing as

---

[1] For the scholastics the *facultas appetendi* embraces feeling, desire, and will.

multiplicity, and as these ideas for us are manifold, we must distinguish the ideas as they are in God and the way in which our minds externally imitate them. We must attribute them to Him only in a *terminative* sense, as differing aspects, from the finite point of view, of his unique essence.

God of course is holy, good, and just. He can do no evil, for He is positive being's fullness, and evil is negation. It is true that He has created physical evil in places, but only as a means of wider good, for *bonum totius præeminet bonum partis.* Moral evil He cannot will, either as end or means, for that would contradict his holiness. By creating free beings He *permits* it only, neither his justice nor his goodness obliging Him to prevent the recipients of freedom from misusing the gift.

As regards God's purpose in creating, primarily it can only have been to exercise his absolute freedom by the manifestation to others of his glory. From this it follows that the others must be rational beings, capable in the first place of knowledge, love, and honor, and in the second place of happiness, for the knowledge and love of God is the mainspring of felicity. In so far forth one may say that God's secondary purpose in creating is *love*.

I will not weary you by pursuing these metaphysical determinations farther, into the mysteries of God's Trinity, for example. What I have given will serve as a specimen of the orthodox philosophical theology of both Catholics and Protestants. Newman, filled with enthusiasm at God's list of perfections, continues the passage which I began to quote to you by a couple of pages of a rhetoric so magnificent that I can hardly refrain from adding them, in spite of the inroad they would make upon our time.[1] He first enumerates God's attributes sonorously, then celebrates his ownership of everything in earth and Heaven, and the dependence of all that happens upon his permissive will. He gives us scholastic philosophy 'touched with emotion,' and every philosophy should be touched with emotion to be rightly understood. Emotionally, then, dogmatic theology is worth something to minds of the

[1] Op. cit., Discourse III. § 7.

type of Newman's. It will aid us to estimate what it is worth intellectually, if at this point I make a short digression.

What God hath joined together, let no man put asunder. The Continental schools of philosophy have too often overlooked the fact that man's thinking is organically connected with his conduct. It seems to me to be the chief glory of English and Scottish thinkers to have kept the organic connection in view. The guiding principle of British philosophy has in fact been that every difference must *make* a difference, every theoretical difference somewhere issue in a practical difference, and that the best method of discussing points of theory is to begin by ascertaining what practical difference would result from one alternative or the other being true. What is the particular truth in question *known as*? In what facts does it result? What is its cash-value in terms of particular experience? This is the characteristic English way of taking up a question. In this way, you remember, Locke takes up the question of personal identity. What you mean by it is just your chain of particular memories, says he. That is the only concretely verifiable part of its significance. All further ideas about it, such as the oneness or manyness of the spiritual substance on which it is based, are therefore void of intelligible meaning; and propositions touching such ideas may be indifferently affirmed or denied. So Berkeley with his 'matter.' The cash-value of matter is our physical sensations. That is what it is known as, all that we concretely verify of its conception. That, therefore, is the whole meaning of the term 'matter'— any other pretended meaning is mere wind of words. Hume does the same thing with causation. It is known as habitual antecedence, and as tendency on our part to look for something definite to come. Apart from this practical meaning it has no significance whatever, and books about it may be committed to the flames, says Hume. Dugald Stewart and Thomas Brown, James Mill, John Mill, and Professor Bain, have followed more or less consistently the same method; and Shadworth Hodgson has used the principle with full explicitness. When all is said and done, it was English and Scotch writers, and not Kant, who introduced 'the critical method' into philosophy, the one method fitted to make philosophy a study worthy of serious men. For what seriousness can possibly remain in debating philosophic propositions that will never make an appreciable difference to us in action? And what could it matter, if all propositions were practically indifferent, which of them we should agree to call true or which false?

An American philosopher of eminent originality, Mr. Charles Sanders Peirce, has rendered thought a service by disentangling from the particulars of its application the principle by which these men were instinctively guided, and by singling it out as fundamental and giving to it a Greek name. He calls it the principle of *pragmatism*, and he defends it somewhat as follows:[1] —

Thought in movement has for its only conceivable motive the attainment of belief, or thought at rest. Only when our thought about a subject has found its rest in belief can our action on the subject firmly and safely begin. Beliefs, in short, are rules for action; and the whole function of thinking is but one step in the production of active habits. If there were any part of a thought that made no difference in the thought's practical consequences, then that part would be no proper element of the thought's significance. To develop a thought's meaning we need therefore only determine what conduct it is fitted to produce; that conduct is for us its sole significance; and the tangible fact at the root of all our thought-distinctions is that there is no one of them so fine as to consist in anything but a possible difference of practice. To attain perfect clearness in our thoughts of an object, we need then only consider what sensations, immediate or remote, we are conceivably to expect from it, and what conduct we must prepare in case the object should be true. Our conception of these practical consequences is for us the whole of our conception of the object, so far as that conception has positive significance at all.

This is the principle of Peirce, the principle of pragmatism. Such a principle will help us on this occasion to decide, among the various attributes set down in the scholastic inven-

---

[1] In an article, How to make our Ideas Clear, in the Popular Science Monthly for January, 1878, vol. xii. p. 286.

tory of God's perfections, whether some be not far less significant than others.

If, namely, we apply the principle of pragmatism to God's metaphysical attributes, strictly so called, as distinguished from his moral attributes, I think that, even were we forced by a coercive logic to believe them, we still should have to confess them to be destitute of all intelligible significance. Take God's aseity, for example; or his necessariness; his immateriality; his 'simplicity' or superiority to the kind of inner variety and succession which we find in finite beings, his indivisibility, and lack of the inner distinctions of being and activity, substance and accident, potentiality and actuality, and the rest; his repudiation of inclusion in a genus; his actualized infinity; his 'personality,' apart from the moral qualities which it may comport; his relations to evil being permissive and not positive; his self-sufficiency, self-love, and absolute felicity in himself:—candidly speaking, how do such qualities as these make any definite connection with our life? And if they severally call for no distinctive adaptations of our conduct, what vital difference can it possibly make to a man's religion whether they be true or false?

For my own part, although I dislike to say aught that may grate upon tender associations, I must frankly confess that even though these attributes were faultlessly deduced, I cannot conceive of its being of the smallest consequence to us religiously that any one of them should be true. Pray, what specific act can I perform in order to adapt myself the better to God's simplicity? Or how does it assist me to plan my behavior, to know that his happiness is anyhow absolutely complete? In the middle of the century just past, Mayne Reid was the great writer of books of out-of-door adventure. He was forever extolling the hunters and field-observers of living animals' habits, and keeping up a fire of invective against the 'closet-naturalists,' as he called them, the collectors and classifiers, and handlers of skeletons and skins. When I was a boy, I used to think that a closet-naturalist must be the vilest type of wretch under the sun. But surely the systematic theologians are the closet-naturalists of the deity, even in Captain Mayne Reid's sense. What is their deduction of these metaphysical attributes but a shuffling and matching of pedantic dictionary-adjectives, aloof from morals, aloof from human needs, something that might be worked out from the mere word 'God' by one of those logical machines of wood and brass which recent ingenuity has contrived as well as by a man of flesh and blood. They have the trail of the serpent over them. One feels that in the theologians' hands, they are only a set of titles obtained by a mechanical manipulation of synonyms; verbality has stepped into the place of vision, professionalism into that of life. Instead of bread we have a stone; instead of a fish, a serpent. Did such a conglomeration of abstract terms give really the gist of our knowledge of the deity, schools of theology might indeed continue to flourish, but religion, vital religion, would have taken its flight from this world. What keeps religion going is something else than abstract definitions and systems of concatenated adjectives, and something different from faculties of theology and their professors. All these things are after-effects, secondary accretions upon those phenomena of vital conversation with the unseen divine, of which I have shown you so many instances, renewing themselves *in sæcula sæculorum* in the lives of humble private men.

So much for the metaphysical attributes of God! From the point of view of practical religion, the metaphysical monster which they offer to our worship is an absolutely worthless invention of the scholarly mind.

What shall we now say of the attributes called moral? Pragmatically, they stand on an entirely different footing. They positively determine fear and hope and expectation, and are foundations for the saintly life. It needs but a glance at them to show how great is their significance.

God's holiness, for example: being holy, God can will nothing but the good. Being omnipotent, he can secure its triumph. Being omniscient, he can see us in the dark. Being just, he can punish us for what he sees. Being loving, he can pardon too. Being unalterable, we can count on him securely. These qualities enter into connection with our life, it is highly important that we should be informed concerning them. That God's purpose in creation should be the manifestation of his glory is also an attribute which has definite relations to our practical life. Among other things it has given a definite character to worship in all Christian countries. If dogmatic theology really does prove beyond dispute that a God with characters like these exists, she may well claim to give a solid basis to religious sentiment. But verily, how stands it with her arguments?

It stands with them as ill as with the arguments for his existence. Not only do post-Kantian idealists reject them root and branch, but it is a plain historic fact that they never have converted any one who has found in the moral complexion of the world, as he experienced it, reasons for doubting that a good God can have framed it. To prove God's goodness by the scholastic argument that there is no non-being in his essence would sound to such a witness simply silly.

No! the book of Job went over this whole matter once for all and definitively. Ratiocination is a relatively superficial and unreal path to the deity: "I will lay mine hand upon my mouth; I have heard of Thee by the hearing of the ear, but now mine eye seeth Thee." An intellect perplexed and baffled, yet a trustful sense of presence—such is the situation of the man who is sincere with himself and with the facts, but who remains religious still.[1]

We must therefore, I think, bid a definitive good-by to dogmatic theology. In all sincerity our faith must do without that warrant. Modern idealism, I repeat, has said good-by to this theology forever. Can modern idealism give faith a better warrant, or must she still rely on her poor self for witness?

The basis of modern idealism is Kant's doctrine of the Transcendental Ego of Apperception. By this formidable term Kant merely meant the fact that the consciousness 'I think

[1] Pragmatically, the most important attribute of God is his punitive justice. But who, in the present state of theological opinion on that point, will dare maintain that hell fire or its equivalent in some shape is rendered certain by pure logic? Theology herself has largely based this doctrine upon revelation; and, in discussing it, has tended more and more to substitute conventional ideas of criminal law for a priori principles of reason. But the very notion that this glorious universe, with planets and winds, and laughing sky and ocean, should have been conceived and had its beams and rafters laid in technicalities of criminality, is incredible to our modern imagination. It weakens a religion to hear it argued upon such a basis.

them' must (potentially or actually) accompany all our objects. Former skeptics had said as much, but the 'I' in question had remained for them identified with the personal individual. Kant abstracted and depersonalized it, and made it the most universal of all his categories, although for Kant himself the Transcendental Ego had no theological implications.

It was reserved for his successors to convert Kant's notion of *Bewusstsein überhaupt*, or abstract consciousness, into an infinite concrete self-consciousness which is the soul of the world, and in which our sundry personal self-consciousnesses have their being. It would lead me into technicalities to show you even briefly how this transformation was in point of fact effected. Suffice it to say that in the Hegelian school, which to-day so deeply influences both British and American thinking, two principles have borne the brunt of the operation.

The first of these principles is that the old logic of identity never gives us more than a post-mortem dissection of *disjecta membra*, and that the fullness of life can be construed to thought only by recognizing that every object which our thought may propose to itself involves the notion of some other object which seems at first to negate the first one.

The second principle is that to be conscious of a negation is already virtually to be beyond it. The mere asking of a question or expression of a dissatisfaction proves that the answer or the satisfaction is already imminent; the finite, realized as such, is already the infinite *in posse*.

Applying these principles, we seem to get a propulsive force into our logic which the ordinary logic of a bare, stark self-identity in each thing never attains to. The objects of our thought now *act* within our thought, act as objects act when given in experience. They change and develop. They introduce something other than themselves along with them; and this other, at first only ideal or potential, presently proves itself also to be actual. It supersedes the thing at first supposed, and both verifies and corrects it, in developing the fullness of its meaning.

The program is excellent; the universe *is* a place where things are followed by other things that both correct and fulfill them; and a logic which gave us something like this movement of fact would express truth far better than the traditional school-logic, which never gets of its own accord from anything to anything else, and registers only predictions and subsumptions, or static resemblances and differences. Nothing could be more unlike the methods of dogmatic theology than those of this new logic. Let me quote in illustration some passages from the Scottish transcendentalist whom I have already named.

"How are we to conceive," Principal Caird writes, "of the reality in which all intelligence rests?" He replies: "Two things may without difficulty be proved, viz., that this reality is an absolute Spirit, and conversely that it is only in communion with this absolute Spirit or Intelligence that the finite Spirit can realize itself. It is absolute; for the faintest movement of human intelligence would be arrested, if it did not presuppose the absolute reality of intelligence, of thought itself. Doubt or denial themselves presuppose and indirectly affirm it. When I pronounce anything to be true, I pronounce it, indeed, to be relative to thought, but not to be relative to my thought, or to the thought of any other individual mind. From the existence of all individual minds as such I can abstract; I can think them away. But that which I cannot think away is thought or self-consciousness itself, in its independence and absoluteness, or, in other words, an Absolute Thought or Self-Consciousness."

Here, you see, Principal Caird makes the transition which Kant did not make: he converts the omnipresence of consciousness in general as a condition of 'truth' being anywhere possible, into an omnipresent universal consciousness, which he identifies with God in his concreteness. He next proceeds to use the principle that to acknowledge your limits is in essence to be beyond them; and makes the transition to the religious experience of individuals in the following words:—

"If [Man] were only a creature of transient sensations and impulses, of an ever coming and going succession of intuitions, fancies, feelings, then nothing could ever have for him the character of objective truth or reality. But it is the prerogative of man's spiritual nature that he can yield himself up to a thought and will that are infinitely larger than his own. As a thinking, self-conscious being, indeed, he may be said, by his very nature, to live in the atmosphere of the Universal Life. As a thinking being, it is possible for me to suppress and quell in my consciousness every movement of self-assertion, every notion and opinion that is merely mine, every desire that belongs to me as this particular Self, and to become the pure medium of a thought that is universal—in one word, to live no more my own life, but let my consciousness be possessed and suffused by the Infinite and Eternal life of spirit. And yet it is just in this renunciation of self that I truly gain myself, or realize the highest possibilities of my own nature. For whilst in one sense we give up self to live the universal and absolute life of reason, yet that to which we thus surrender ourselves is in reality our truer self. The life of absolute reason is not a life that is foreign to us."

Nevertheless, Principal Caird goes on to say, so far as we are able outwardly to realize this doctrine, the balm it offers remains incomplete. Whatever we may be *in posse*, the very best of us *in actu* falls very short of being absolutely divine. Social morality, love, and self-sacrifice even, merge our Self only in some other finite self or selves. They do not quite identify it with the Infinite. Man's ideal destiny, infinite in abstract logic, might thus seem in practice forever unrealizable.

"Is there, then," our author continues, "no solution of the contradiction between the ideal and the actual? We answer, There is such a solution, but in order to reach it we are carried beyond the sphere of morality into that of religion. It may be said to be the essential characteristic of religion as contrasted with morality, that it changes aspiration into fruition, anticipation into realization; that instead of leaving man in the interminable pursuit of a vanishing ideal, it makes him the actual partaker of a divine or infinite life. Whether we view religion from the human side or the divine—as the surrender of the soul to God, or as the life of God in the soul—in either aspect it is of its very essence that the Infinite has ceased to be a far-off vision, and has become a present reality. The very first pulsation of the spiritual life, when we rightly apprehend its significance, is the indication that the division between the Spirit and its object has vanished, that the ideal has become real, that the finite has reached its goal and become suffused with the presence and life of the Infinite.

"Oneness of mind and will with the divine mind and will is not the future hope and aim of religion, but its very beginning and birth in the soul. To enter on the religious life is to terminate the struggle. In that act which constitutes the beginning of the religious life—call it faith, or trust, or self-surrender, or by whatever name you will—there is involved the identification of the finite with a life which is eternally realized. It is true indeed that the religious life is progressive; but understood in the light of the foregoing idea, religious progress is not progress *towards*, but *within* the sphere of the Infinite. It is not the vain attempt by endless finite additions or increments to become possessed of infinite wealth, but it is the endeavor, by the constant exercise of spiritual activity, to appropriate that infinite inheritance of which we are already in possession. The whole future of the religious life is given in its beginning, but it is given implicitly. The position of the man who has entered on the religious life is that evil, error, imperfection, do not really belong to him: they are excrescences which have no organic relation to his true nature: they are already virtually, as they will be actually, suppressed and annulled, and in the very process of being annulled they become the means of spiritual progress. Though he is not exempt from temptation and conflict, [yet] in that inner sphere in which his true life lies, the struggle is over, the victory already achieved. It is not a finite but an infinite life which the spirit lives. Every pulse-beat of its [existence] is the expression and realization of the life of God."[1]

You will readily admit that no description of the phenomena of the religious consciousness could be better than these words of your lamented preacher and philosopher. They reproduce the very rapture of those crises of conversion of

[1] John Caird: An Introduction to the Philosophy of Religion, London and New York, 1880, pp. 243–250, and 291–299, much abridged.

which we have been hearing; they utter what the mystic felt but was unable to communicate; and the saint, in hearing them, recognizes his own experience. It is indeed gratifying to find the content of religion reported so unanimously. But when all is said and done, has Principal Caird—and I only use him as an example of that whole mode of thinking—transcended the sphere of feeling and of the direct experience of the individual, and laid the foundations of religion in impartial reason? Has he made religion universal by coercive reasoning, transformed it from a private faith into a public certainty? Has he rescued its affirmations from obscurity and mystery?

I believe that he has done nothing of the kind, but that he has simply reaffirmed the individual's experiences in a more generalized vocabulary. And again, I can be excused from proving technically that the transcendentalist reasonings fail to make religion universal, for I can point to the plain fact that a majority of scholars, even religiously disposed ones, stubbornly refuse to treat them as convincing. The whole of Germany, one may say, has positively rejected the Hegelian argumentation. As for Scotland, I need only mention Professor Fraser's and Professor Pringle-Pattison's memorable criticisms, with which so many of you are familiar.[1] Once more, I ask, if transcendental idealism were as objectively and absolutely rational as it pretends to be, could it possibly fail so egregiously to be persuasive?

What religion reports, you must remember, always purports to be a fact of experience: the divine is actually present, religion says, and between it and ourselves relations of give and take are actual. If definite perceptions of fact like this cannot stand upon their own feet, surely abstract reasoning

[1] A. C. FRASER: Philosophy of Theism, second edition, Edinburgh and London, 1899, especially part ii. chaps. vii. and viii.; A. SETH [PRINGLE-PATTISON]: Hegelianism and Personality, Ibid., 1890, passim.

The most persuasive arguments in favor of a concrete individual Soul of the world, with which I am acquainted, are those of my colleague, Josiah Royce, in his Religious Aspect of Philosophy, Boston, 1885; in his Conception of God, New York and London, 1897; and lately in his Aberdeen Gifford Lectures, The World and the Individual, 2 vols., New York and London, 1901–02. I doubtless seem to some of my readers to evade the philosophic duty which my thesis in this lecture imposes on me, by not even attempting

cannot give them the support they are in need of. Conceptual processes can class facts, define them, interpret them; but they do not produce them, nor can they reproduce their individuality. There is always a *plus*, a *thisness*, which feeling alone can answer for. Philosophy in this sphere is thus a secondary function, unable to warrant faith's veracity, and so I revert to the thesis which I announced at the beginning of this lecture.

In all sad sincerity I think we must conclude that the attempt to demonstrate by purely intellectual processes the truth of the deliverances of direct religious experience is absolutely hopeless.

It would be unfair to philosophy, however, to leave her under this negative sentence. Let me close, then, by briefly enumerating what she *can* do for religion. If she will abandon metaphysics and deduction for criticism and induction, and frankly transform herself from theology into science of religions, she can make herself enormously useful.

The spontaneous intellect of man always defines the divine which it feels in ways that harmonize with its temporary intellectual prepossessions. Philosophy can by comparison eliminate the local and the accidental from these definitions. Both from dogma and from worship she can remove historic incrustations. By confronting the spontaneous religious constructions with the results of natural science, philosophy can also eliminate doctrines that are now known to be scientifically absurd or incongruous.

Sifting out in this way unworthy formulations, she can

---

to meet Professor Royce's arguments articulately. I admit the momentary evasion. In the present lectures, which are cast throughout in a popular mould, there seemed no room for subtle metaphysical discussion, and for tactical purposes it was sufficient, the contention of philosophy being what it is (namely, that religion can be transformed into a universally convincing science), to point to the fact that no religious philosophy has actually convinced the mass of thinkers. Meanwhile let me say that I hope that the present volume may be followed by another, if I am spared to write it, in which not only Professor Royce's arguments, but others for monistic absolutism shall be considered with all the technical fullness which their great importance calls for. At present I resign myself to lying passive under the reproach of superficiality.

leave a residuum of conceptions that at least are possible. With these she can deal as *hypotheses*, testing them in all the manners, whether negative or positive, by which hypotheses are ever tested. She can reduce their number, as some are found more open to objection. She can perhaps become the champion of one which she picks out as being the most closely verified or verifiable. She can refine upon the definition of this hypothesis, distinguishing between what is innocent over-belief and symbolism in the expression of it, and what is to be literally taken. As a result, she can offer mediation between different believers, and help to bring about consensus of opinion. She can do this the more successfully, the better she discriminates the common and essential from the individual and local elements of the religious beliefs which she compares.

I do not see why a critical Science of Religions of this sort might not eventually command as general a public adhesion as is commanded by a physical science. Even the personally non-religious might accept its conclusions on trust, much as blind persons now accept the facts of optics—it might appear as foolish to refuse them. Yet as the science of optics has to be fed in the first instance, and continually verified later, by facts experienced by seeing persons; so the science of religions would depend for its original material on facts of personal experience, and would have to square itself with personal experience through all its critical reconstructions. It could never get away from concrete life, or work in a conceptual vacuum. It would forever have to confess, as every science confesses, that the subtlety of nature flies beyond it, and that its formulas are but approximations. Philosophy lives in words, but truth and fact well up into our lives in ways that exceed verbal formulation. There is in the living act of perception always something that glimmers and twinkles and will not be caught, and for which reflection comes too late. No one knows this as well as the philosopher. He must fire his volley of new vocables out of his conceptual shotgun, for his profession condemns him to this industry, but he secretly knows the hollowness and irrelevancy. His formulas are like stereoscopic or kinetoscopic photographs seen outside the instrument; they lack the depth, the motion, the vitality. In the religious sphere, in particular, belief that formulas are true can never wholly take the place of personal experience.

In my next lecture I will try to complete my rough description of religious experience; and in the lecture after that, which is the last one, I will try my own hand at formulating conceptually the truth to which it is a witness.

LECTURE XIX

OTHER CHARACTERISTICS

WE HAVE WOUND our way back, after our excursion through mysticism and philosophy, to where we were before: the uses of religion, its uses to the individual who has it, and the uses of the individual himself to the world, are the best arguments that truth is in it. We return to the empirical philosophy: the true is what works well, even though the qualification 'on the whole' may always have to be added. In this lecture we must revert to description again, and finish our picture of the religious consciousness by a word about some of its other characteristic elements. Then, in a final lecture, we shall be free to make a general review and draw our independent conclusions.

The first point I will speak of is the part which the æsthetic life plays in determining one's choice of a religion. Men, I said awhile ago, involuntarily intellectualize their religious experience. They need formulas, just as they need fellowship in worship. I spoke, therefore, too contemptuously of the pragmatic uselessness of the famous scholastic list of attributes of the deity, for they have one use which I neglected to consider. The eloquent passage in which Newman enumerates them[1] puts us on the track of it. Intoning them as he would intone a cathedral service, he shows how high is their æsthetic value. It enriches our bare piety to carry these exalted and mysterious verbal additions just as it enriches a church to have an organ and old brasses, marbles and frescoes and stained windows. Epithets lend an atmosphere and overtones to our devotion. They are like a hymn of praise and service of glory, and may sound the more sublime for being incomprehensible. Minds like Newman's[2] grow as jealous of their credit as

[1] Idea of a University, Discourse III. § 7.
[2] Newman's imagination so innately craved a sacerdotal system that he can write: "From the age of fifteen, dogma has been the fundamental principle of my religion: I know no other religion; I cannot enter into the idea of any other sort of religion." And again, speaking of himself about the age of thirty, he writes: "I loved to act as feeling myself in my Bishop's sight, as if it were the sight of God." Apologia, 1897, pp. 48, 50.

heathen priests are of that of the jewelry and ornaments that blaze upon their idols.

Among the buildings-out of religion which the mind spontaneously indulges in, the æsthetic motive must never be forgotten. I promised to say nothing of ecclesiastical systems in these lectures. I may be allowed, however, to put in a word at this point on the way in which their satisfaction of certain æsthetic needs contributes to their hold on human nature. Although some persons aim most at intellectual purity and simplification, for others *richness* is the supreme imaginative requirement.[1] When one's mind is strongly of this type, an individual religion will hardly serve the purpose. The inner need is rather of something institutional and complex, majestic in the hierarchic interrelatedness of its parts, with authority descending from stage to stage, and at every stage objects for adjectives of mystery and splendor, derived in the last resort from the Godhead who is the fountain and culmination of the system. One feels then as if in presence of some vast incrusted work of jewelry or architecture; one hears the multitudinous liturgical appeal; one gets the honorific vibration coming from every quarter. Compared with such a noble complexity, in which ascending and descending movements seem in no way to jar upon stability, in which no single item, however humble, is insignificant, because so many august institutions hold it in its place, how flat does evangelical Protestantism appear, how bare those isolated religious lives whose boast it is that "man in

---

[1] The intellectual difference is quite on a par in practical importance with the analogous difference in character. We saw, under the head of Saintliness, how some characters resent confusion and must live in purity, consistency, simplicity (above, p. 257 ff.). For others, on the contrary, superabundance, over-pressure, stimulation, lots of superficial relations, are indispensable. There are men who would suffer a very syncope if you should pay all their debts, bring it about that their engagements had been kept, their letters answered, their perplexities relieved, and their duties fulfilled, down to one which lay on a clean table under their eyes with nothing to interfere with its immediate performance. A day stripped so staringly bare would be for them appalling. So with ease, elegance, tributes of affection, social recognitions— some of us require amounts of these things which to others would appear a mass of lying and sophistication.

the bush with God may meet."[1] What a pulverization and leveling of what a gloriously piled-up structure! To an imagination used to the perspectives of dignity and glory, the naked gospel scheme seems to offer an almshouse for a palace.

It is much like the patriotic sentiment of those brought up in ancient empires. How many emotions must be frustrated of their object, when one gives up the titles of dignity, the crimson lights and blare of brass, the gold embroidery, the plumed troops, the fear and trembling, and puts up with a president in a black coat who shakes hands with you, and comes, it may be, from a 'home' upon a veldt or prairie with one sitting-room and a Bible on its centre-table. It pauperizes the monarchical imagination!

The strength of these æsthetic sentiments makes it rigorously impossible, it seems to me, that Protestantism, however superior in spiritual profundity it may be to Catholicism, should at the present day succeed in making many converts from the more venerable ecclesiasticism. The latter offers a so much richer pasturage and shade to the fancy, has so many cells with so many different kinds of honey, is so indulgent in its multiform appeals to human nature, that Protestantism will always show to Catholic eyes the almshouse physiognomy. The bitter negativity of it is to the Catholic mind incomprehensible. To intellectual Catholics many of the antiquated beliefs and practices to which the Church gives countenance are, if taken literally, as childish as they are to Protestants. But they are childish in the pleasing sense of 'childlike,'—innocent and amiable, and worthy to be smiled on in consideration of the undeveloped condition of the dear people's intellects. To the Protestant, on the contrary, they are childish in the sense of being idiotic falsehoods. He must stamp out their delicate and lovable redundancy, leaving the Catholic to shudder at his literalness. He appears to the latter as morose as if he were some hard-eyed, numb, monotonous kind of reptile. The two will never understand each other— their centres of emotional energy are too different. Rigorous

---

[1] In Newman's Lectures on Justification, Lecture VIII. § 6, there is a splendid passage expressive of this æsthetic way of feeling the Christian scheme. It is unfortunately too long to quote.

truth and human nature's intricacies are always in need of a mutual interpreter.[1] So much for the æsthetic diversities in the religious consciousness.

In most books on religion, three things are represented as its most essential elements. These are Sacrifice, Confession, and Prayer. I must say a word in turn of each of these elements, though briefly. First of Sacrifice.

Sacrifices to gods are omnipresent in primeval worship; but, as cults have grown refined, burnt offerings and the blood of he-goats have been superseded by sacrifices more spiritual in their nature. Judaism, Islam, and Buddhism get along without ritual sacrifice; so does Christianity, save in so far as the notion is preserved in transfigured form in the mystery of Christ's atonement. These religions substitute offerings of the heart, renunciations of the inner self, for all those vain oblations. In the ascetic practices which Islam, Buddhism, and the older Christianity encourage we see how indestructible is the idea that sacrifice of some sort is a religious exercise. In lecturing on asceticism I spoke of its significance as symbolic of the sacrifices which life, whenever it is taken strenuously, calls for.[2] But, as I said my say about those, and as these lectures expressly avoid earlier religious usages and questions of derivation, I will pass from the subject of Sacrifice altogether and turn to that of Confession.

In regard to Confession I will also be most brief, saying my word about it psychologically, not historically. Not nearly as widespread as sacrifice, it corresponds to a more inward and moral stage of sentiment. It is part of the general system of purgation and cleansing which one feels one's self in need of, in order to be in right relations to one's deity. For him who

---

[1] Compare the informality of Protestantism, where the 'meek lover of the good,' alone with his God, visits the sick, etc., for their own sakes, with the elaborate 'business' that goes on in Catholic devotion, and carries with it the social excitement of all more complex businesses. An essentially worldly-minded Catholic woman can become a visitor of the sick on purely coquettish principles, with her confessor and director, her 'merit' storing up, her patron saints, her privileged relation to the Almighty, drawing his attention as a professional *dévote*, her definite 'exercises,' and her definitely recognized social *pose* in the organization.

[2] Above, p. 328 ff.

confesses, shams are over and realities have begun; he has exteriorized his rottenness. If he has not actually got rid of it, he at least no longer smears it over with a hypocritical show of virtue—he lives at least upon a basis of veracity. The complete decay of the practice of confession in Anglo-Saxon communities is a little hard to account for. Reaction against popery is of course the historic explanation, for in popery confession went with penances and absolution, and other inadmissible practices. But on the side of the sinner himself it seems as if the need ought to have been too great to accept so summary a refusal of its satisfaction. One would think that in more men the shell of secrecy would have had to open, the pent-in abscess to burst and gain relief, even though the ear that heard the confession were unworthy. The Catholic church, for obvious utilitarian reasons, has substituted auricular confession to one priest for the more radical act of public confession. We English-speaking Protestants, in the general self-reliance and unsociability of our nature, seem to find it enough if we take God alone into our confidence.[1]

The next topic on which I must comment is Prayer,—and this time it must be less briefly. We have heard much talk of late against prayer, especially against prayers for better weather and for the recovery of sick people. As regards prayers for the sick, if any medical fact can be considered to stand firm, it is that in certain environments prayer may contribute to recovery, and should be encouraged as a therapeutic measure. Being a normal factor of moral health in the person, its omission would be deleterious. The case of the weather is different. Notwithstanding the recency of the opposite belief,[2] every one now knows that droughts and storms follow from physical antecedents, and that moral appeals cannot avert them. But petitional prayer is only one department

[1] A fuller discussion of confession is contained in the excellent work by FRANK GRANGER: The Soul of a Christian, London, 1900, ch. xii.

[2] Example: "The minister at Sudbury, being at the Thursday lecture in Boston, heard the officiating clergyman praying for rain. As soon as the service was over, he went to the petitioner and said, 'You Boston ministers, as soon as a tulip wilts under your windows, go to church and pray for rain, until all Concord and Sudbury are under water.'" R. W. EMERSON: Lectures and Biographical Sketches, p. 363.

of prayer; and if we take the word in the wider sense as meaning every kind of inward communion or conversation with the power recognized as divine, we can easily see that scientific criticism leaves it untouched.

Prayer in this wide sense is the very soul and essence of religion. "Religion," says a liberal French theologian, "is an intercourse, a conscious and voluntary relation, entered into by a soul in distress with the mysterious power upon which it feels itself to depend, and upon which its fate is contingent. This intercourse with God is realized by prayer. Prayer is religion in act; that is, prayer is real religion. It is prayer that distinguishes the religious phenomenon from such similar or neighboring phenomena as purely moral or æsthetic sentiment. Religion is nothing if it be not the vital act by which the entire mind seeks to save itself by clinging to the principle from which it draws its life. This act is prayer, by which term I understand no vain exercise of words, no mere repetition of certain sacred formulæ, but the very movement itself of the soul, putting itself in a personal relation of contact with the mysterious power of which it feels the presence,—it may be even before it has a name by which to call it. Wherever this interior prayer is lacking, there is no religion; wherever, on the other hand, this prayer rises and stirs the soul, even in the absence of forms or of doctrines, we have living religion. One sees from this why 'natural religion,' so-called, is not properly a religion. It cuts man off from prayer. It leaves him and God in mutual remoteness, with no intimate commerce, no interior dialogue, no interchange, no action of God in man, no return of man to God. At bottom this pretended religion is only a philosophy. Born at epochs of rationalism, of critical investigations, it never was anything but an abstraction. An artificial and dead creation, it reveals to its examiner hardly one of the characters proper to religion."[1]

It seems to me that the entire series of our lectures proves the truth of M. Sabatier's contention. The religious phenomenon, studied as an inner fact, and apart from ecclesiastical or theological complications, has shown itself to consist everywhere, and at all its stages, in the consciousness which indi-

[1] AUGUSTE SABATIER: Esquisse d'une Philosophie de la Religion, 2me éd., 1897, pp. 24–26, abridged.

viduals have of an intercourse between themselves and higher powers with which they feel themselves to be related. This intercourse is realized at the time as being both active and mutual. If it be not effective; if it be not a give and take relation; if nothing be really transacted while it lasts; if the world is in no whit different for its having taken place; then prayer, taken in this wide meaning of a sense that *something is transacting*, is of course a feeling of what is illusory, and religion must on the whole be classed, not simply as containing elements of delusion,—these undoubtedly everywhere exist,—but as being rooted in delusion altogether, just as materialists and atheists have always said it was. At most there might remain, when the direct experiences of prayer were ruled out as false witnesses, some inferential belief that the whole order of existence must have a divine cause. But this way of contemplating nature, pleasing as it would doubtless be to persons of a pious taste, would leave to them but the spectators' part at a play, whereas in experimental religion and the prayerful life, we seem ourselves to be the actors, and to act, not in a play, but in a very serious reality.

The genuineness of religion is thus indissolubly bound up with the question whether the prayerful consciousness be or be not deceitful. The conviction that something is genuinely transacted in this consciousness is the very core of living religion. As to what is transacted, great differences of opinion have prevailed. The unseen powers have been supposed, and are yet supposed, to do things which no enlightened man can nowadays believe in. It may well prove that the sphere of influence in prayer is subjective exclusively, and that what is immediately changed is only the mind of the praying person. But however our opinion of prayer's effects may come to be limited by criticism, religion, in the vital sense in which these lectures study it, must stand or fall by the persuasion that effects of some sort genuinely do occur. Through prayer, religion insists, things which cannot be realized in any other manner come about: energy which but for prayer would be bound is by prayer set free and operates in some part, be it objective or subjective, of the world of facts.

This postulate is strikingly expressed in a letter written by the late Frederic W. H. Myers to a friend, who allows me to quote from it. It shows how independent the prayer-instinct is of usual doctrinal complications. Mr. Myers writes:—

"I am glad that you have asked me about prayer, because I have rather strong ideas on the subject. First consider what are the facts. There exists around us a spiritual universe, and that universe is in actual relation with the material. From the spiritual universe comes the energy which maintains the material; the energy which makes the life of each individual spirit. Our spirits are supported by a perpetual indrawal of this energy, and the vigor of that indrawal is perpetually changing, much as the vigor of our absorption of material nutriment changes from hour to hour.

"I call these 'facts' because I think that some scheme of this kind is the only one consistent with our actual evidence; too complex to summarize here. How, then, should we *act* on these facts? Plainly we must endeavor to draw in as much spiritual life as possible, and we must place our minds in any attitude which experience shows to be favorable to such indrawal. *Prayer* is the general name for that attitude of open and earnest expectancy. If we then ask to *whom* to pray, the answer (strangely enough) must be that *that* does not much matter. The prayer is not indeed a purely subjective thing;—it means a real increase in intensity of absorption of spiritual power or grace;—but we do not know enough of what takes place in the spiritual world to know how the prayer operates;—*who* is cognizant of it, or through what channel the grace is given. Better let children pray to Christ, who is at any rate the highest individual spirit of whom we have any knowledge. But it would be rash to say that Christ himself *hears us*; while to say that *God* hears us is merely to restate the first principle,—that grace flows in from the infinite spiritual world."

Let us reserve the question of the truth or falsehood of the belief that power is absorbed until the next lecture, when our dogmatic conclusions, if we have any, must be reached. Let this lecture still confine itself to the description of phenomena; and as a concrete example of an extreme sort, of the way in which the prayerful life may still be led, let me take a case with which most of you must be acquainted, that of George Müller of Bristol, who died in 1898. Müller's prayers were of the crassest petitional order. Early in life he resolved on taking certain Bible promises in literal sincerity, and on letting himself be fed, not by his own worldly foresight, but by the Lord's hand. He had an extraordinarily active and successful career, among the fruits of which were the distribution of over two million copies of the Scripture text, in different languages; the equipment of several hundred missionaries; the circulation of more than a hundred and eleven million of scriptural books, pamphlets, and tracts; the building of five large orphanages, and the keeping and educating of thousands of orphans; finally, the establishment of schools in which over a hundred and twenty-one thousand youthful and adult pupils were taught. In the course of this work Mr. Müller received and administered nearly a million and a half of pounds sterling, and traveled over two hundred thousand miles of sea and land.[1] During the sixty-eight years of his ministry, he never owned any property except his clothes and furniture, and cash in hand; and he left, at the age of eighty-six, an estate worth only a hundred and sixty pounds.

His method was to let his general wants be publicly known, but not to acquaint other people with the details of his temporary necessities. For the relief of the latter, he prayed directly to the Lord, believing that sooner or later prayers are always answered if one have trust enough. "When I lose such a thing as a key," he writes, "I ask the Lord to direct me to it, and I look for an answer to my prayer; when a person with whom I have made an appointment does not come, according to the fixed time, and I begin to be inconvenienced by it, I ask the Lord to be pleased to hasten him to me, and I look for an answer; when I do not understand a passage of the word of God, I lift up my heart to the Lord that he would be pleased by his Holy Spirit to instruct me, and I expect to be taught, though I do not fix the time when, and the manner how it should be; when I am going to minister in the Word, I seek

[1] My authority for these statistics is the little work on Müller, by FREDERIC G. WARNE, New York, 1898.

help from the Lord, and . . . am not cast down, but of good cheer because I look for his assistance."

Müller's custom was to never run up bills, not even for a week. "As the Lord deals out to us by the day, . . . the week's payment might become due and we have no money to meet it; and thus those with whom we deal might be inconvenienced by us, and we be found acting against the commandment of the Lord: 'Owe no man anything.' From this day and henceforward whilst the Lord gives to us our supplies by the day, we purpose to pay at once for every article as it is purchased, and never to buy anything except we can pay for it at once, however much it may seem to be needed, and however much those with whom we deal may wish to be paid only by the week."

The articles needed of which Müller speaks were the food, fuel, etc., of his orphanages. Somehow, near as they often come to going without a meal, they hardly ever seem actually to have done so. "Greater and more manifest nearness of the Lord's presence I have never had than when after breakfast there were no means for dinner for more than a hundred persons; or when after dinner there were no means for the tea, and yet the Lord provided the tea; and all this without one single human being having been informed about our need. . . . Through Grace my mind is so fully assured of the faithfulness of the Lord, that in the midst of the greatest need, I am enabled in peace to go about my other work. Indeed, did not the Lord give me this, which is the result of trusting in him, I should scarcely be able to work at all; for it is now comparatively a rare thing that a day comes when I am not in need for one or another part of the work."[1]

In building his orphanages simply by prayer and faith, Müller affirms that his prime motive was "to have something to point to as a visible proof that our God and Father is the same faithful God that he ever was,—as willing as ever to prove himself the living God, in our day as formerly, to all that put their trust in him."[2] For this reason

[1] The Life of Trust; Being a Narrative of the Lord's Dealings with George Müller, New American edition, N. Y., Crowell, pp. 228, 194, 219.
[2] Ibid., p. 126.

he refused to borrow money for any of his enterprises. "How does it work when we thus anticipate God by going our own way? We certainly weaken faith instead of increasing it; and each time we work thus a deliverance of our own we find it more and more difficult to trust in God, till at last we give way entirely to our natural fallen reason and unbelief prevails. How different if one is enabled to wait God's own time, and to look alone to him for help and deliverance! When at last help comes, after many seasons of prayer it may be, how sweet it is, and what a present recompense! Dear Christian reader, if you have never walked in this path of obedience before, do so now, and you will then know experimentally the sweetness of the joy which results from it."[1]

When the supplies came in but slowly, Müller always considered that this was for the trial of his faith and patience. When his faith and patience had been sufficiently tried, the Lord would send more means. "And thus it has proved,"—I quote from his diary,—"for to-day was given me the sum of 2050 pounds, of which 2000 are for the building fund [of a certain house], and 50 for present necessities. It is impossible to describe my joy in God when I received this donation. I was neither excited nor surprised; for I *look out* for answers to my prayers. *I believe that God hears me.* Yet my heart was so full of joy that I could only *sit* before God, and admire him, like David in 2 Samuel vii. At last I cast myself flat down upon my face and burst forth in thanksgiving to God and in surrendering my heart afresh to him for his blessed service."[2]

George Müller's is a case extreme in every respect, and in no respect more so than in the extraordinary narrowness of the man's intellectual horizon. His God was, as he often said, his business partner. He seems to have been for Müller little more than a sort of supernatural clergyman interested in the congregation of tradesmen and others in Bristol who were his saints, and in the orphanages and other enterprises, but unpossessed of any of those vaster and wilder and more ideal

[1] Op. cit., p. 383, abridged.
[2] Ibid., p. 323.

attributes with which the human imagination elsewhere has invested him. Müller, in short, was absolutely unphilosophical. His intensely private and practical conception of his relations with the Deity continued the traditions of the most primitive human thought.[1] When we compare a mind like his with such a mind as, for example, Emerson's or Phillips Brooks's, we see the range which the religious consciousness covers.

There is an immense literature relating to answers to petitional prayer. The evangelical journals are filled with such answers, and books are devoted to the subject,[2] but for us Müller's case will suffice.

[1] I cannot resist the temptation of quoting an expression of an even more primitive style of religious thought, which I find in Arber's English Garland, vol. vii. p. 440. Robert Lyde, an English sailor, along with an English boy, being prisoners on a French ship in 1689, set upon the crew, of seven Frenchmen, killed two, made the other five prisoners, and brought home the ship. Lyde thus describes how in this feat he found his God a very present help in time of trouble: —

"With the assistance of God I kept my feet when they three and one more did strive to throw me down. Feeling the Frenchman which hung about my middle hang very heavy, I said to the boy, 'Go round the binnacle, and knock down that man that hangeth on my back.' So the boy did strike him one blow on the head which made him fall. . . . Then I looked about for a marlin spike or anything else to strike them withal. But seeing nothing, I said, 'LORD! what shall I do?' Then casting up my eye upon my left side, and seeing a marlin spike hanging, I jerked my right arm and took hold, and struck the point four times about a quarter of an inch deep into the skull of that man that had hold of my left arm. [One of the Frenchmen then hauled the marlin spike away from him.] But through GOD's wonderful providence! it either fell out of his hand, or else he threw it down, and at this time the Almighty GOD gave me strength enough to take one man in one hand, and throw at the other's head: and looking about again to see anything to strike them withal, but seeing nothing, I said, 'LORD! what shall I do now?' And then it pleased GOD to put me in mind of my knife in my pocket. And although two of the men had hold of my right arm, yet GOD Almighty strengthened me so that I put my right hand into my right pocket, drew out the knife and sheath, . . . put it between my legs and drew it out, and then cut the man's throat with it that had his back to my breast: and he immediately dropt down, and scarce ever stirred after."—I have slightly abridged Lyde's narrative.

[2] As, for instance, In Answer to Prayer, by the BISHOP OF RIPON and others, London, 1898; Touching Incidents and Remarkable Answers to Prayer, Harrisburg, Pa., 1898 (?); H. L. HASTINGS: The Guiding Hand, or Providential Direction, illustrated by Authentic Instances, Boston, 1898 (?).

A less sturdy-beggarlike fashion of leading the prayerful life is followed by innumerable other Christians. Persistence in leaning on the Almighty for support and guidance will, such persons say, bring with it proofs, palpable but much more subtle, of his presence and active influence. The following description of a 'led' life, by a Swiss writer whom I have already quoted, would no doubt appear to countless Christians in every country as if transcribed from their own personal experience. One finds in this guided sort of life, says Dr. Hilty,—

"That books and words (and sometimes people) come to one's cognizance just at the very moment in which one needs them; that one glides over great dangers as if with shut eyes, remaining ignorant of what would have terrified one or led one astray, until the peril is past—this being especially the case with temptations to vanity and sensuality; that paths on which one ought not to wander are, as it were, hedged off with thorns; but that on the other side great obstacles are suddenly removed; that when the time has come for something, one suddenly receives a courage that formerly failed, or perceives the root of a matter that until then was concealed, or discovers thoughts, talents, yea, even pieces of knowledge and insight, in one's self, of which it is impossible to say whence they come; finally, that persons help us or decline to help us, favor us or refuse us, as if they had to do so against their will, so that often those indifferent or even unfriendly to us yield us the greatest service and furtherance. (God takes often their worldly goods, from those whom he leads, at just the right moment, when they threaten to impede the effort after higher interests.)

"Besides all this, other noteworthy things come to pass, of which it is not easy to give account. There is no doubt whatever that now one walks continually through 'open doors' and on the easiest roads, with as little care and trouble as it is possible to imagine.

"Furthermore one finds one's self settling one's affairs neither too early nor too late, whereas they were wont to be spoiled by untimeliness, even when the preparations had been well laid. In addition to this, one does them with perfect tranquillity of mind, almost as if they were matters of no consequence, like errands done by us for another person, in which case we usually act more calmly than when we act in our own concerns. Again, one finds that one can *wait* for everything patiently, and that is one of life's great arts. One finds also that each thing comes duly, one thing after the other, so that one gains time to make one's footing sure before advancing farther. And then everything occurs to us at the right moment, just what we ought to do, etc., and often in a very striking way, just as if a third person were keeping watch over those things which we are in easy danger of forgetting.

"Often, too, persons are sent to us at the right time, to offer or ask for what is needed, and what we should never have had the courage or resolution to undertake of our own accord.

"Through all these experiences one finds that one is kindly and tolerant of other people, even of such as are repulsive, negligent, or ill-willed, for they also are instruments of good in God's hand, and often most efficient ones. Without these thoughts it would be hard for even the best of us always to keep our equanimity. But with the consciousness of divine guidance, one sees many a thing in life quite differently from what would otherwise be possible.

"All these are things that every human being *knows*, who has had experience of them; and of which the most speaking examples could be brought forward. The highest resources of worldly wisdom are unable to attain that which, under divine leading, comes to us of its own accord."[1]

Such accounts as this shade away into others where the belief is, not that particular events are tempered more towardly to us by a superintending providence, as a reward for our reliance, but that by cultivating the continuous sense of our connection with the power that made things as they are, we are tempered more towardly for their reception. The outward face of nature need not alter, but the expressions of meaning in it alter. It was dead and is alive again. It is like the differ-

[1] C. HILTY: Glück, Dritter Theil, 1900, pp. 92 ff.

ence between looking on a person without love, or upon the same person with love. In the latter case intercourse springs into new vitality. So when one's affections keep in touch with the divinity of the world's authorship, fear and egotism fall away; and in the equanimity that follows, one finds in the hours, as they succeed each other, a series of purely benignant opportunities. It is as if all doors were opened, and all paths freshly smoothed. We meet a new world when we meet the old world in the spirit which this kind of prayer infuses.

Such a spirit was that of Marcus Aurelius and Epictetus.[1] It is that of mind-curers, of the transcendentalists, and of the so-called 'liberal' Christians. As an expression of it, I will quote a page from one of Martineau's sermons:—

"The universe, open to the eye to-day, looks as it did a thousand years ago: and the morning hymn of Milton does but tell the beauty with which our own familiar sun dressed the earliest fields and gardens of the world. We see what all our fathers saw. And if we cannot find God in your house or in mine, upon the roadside or the margin of the sea; in the bursting seed or opening flower; in the day duty or the night musing; in the general laugh and the secret grief; in the procession of life, ever entering afresh, and solemnly passing by and dropping off; I do not think we should discern him any more on the grass of Eden, or beneath the moonlight of Gethsemane. Depend upon it, it is not the want of greater miracles, but of the soul to perceive such

[1] "Good Heaven!" says Epictetus, "any one thing in the creation is sufficient to demonstrate a Providence, to a humble and grateful mind. The mere possibility of producing milk from grass, cheese from milk, and wool from skins; who formed and planned it? Ought we not, whether we dig or plough or eat, to sing this hymn to God? Great is God, who has supplied us with these instruments to till the ground; great is God, who has given us hands and instruments of digestion; who has given us to grow insensibly and to breathe in sleep. These things we ought forever to celebrate. . . . But because the most of you are blind and insensible, there must be some one to fill this station, and lead, in behalf of all men, the hymn to God; for what else can I do, a lame old man, but sing hymns to God? Were I a nightingale, I would act the part of a nightingale; were I a swan, the part of a swan. But since I am a reasonable creature, it is my duty to praise God . . . and I call on you to join the same song." Works, book i. ch. xvi., CARTER-HIGGINSON translation, abridged.

as are allowed us still, that makes us push all the sanctities into the far spaces we cannot reach. The devout feel that wherever God's hand is, *there* is miracle: and it is simply an indevoutness which imagines that only where miracle is, can there be the real hand of God. The customs of Heaven ought surely to be more sacred in our eyes than its anomalies; the dear old ways, of which the Most High is never tired, than the strange things which he does not love well enough ever to repeat. And he who will but discern beneath the sun, as he rises any morning, the supporting finger of the Almighty, may recover the sweet and reverent surprise with which Adam gazed on the first dawn in Paradise. It is no outward change, no shifting in time or place; but only the loving meditation of the pure in heart, that can reawaken the Eternal from the sleep within our souls: that can render him a reality again, and reassert for him once more his ancient name of 'the Living God.' "[1]

When we see all things in God, and refer all things to him, we read in common matters superior expressions of meaning. The deadness with which custom invests the familiar vanishes, and existence as a whole appears transfigured. The state of a mind thus awakened from torpor is well expressed in these words, which I take from a friend's letter: —

"If we occupy ourselves in summing up all the mercies and bounties we are privileged to have, we are overwhelmed by their number (so great that we can imagine ourselves unable to give ourselves time even to begin to review the things we may imagine *we have not*). We sum them and realize that *we are actually killed with God's kindness*; that we are surrounded by bounties upon bounties, without which all would fall. Should we not love it; should we not feel buoyed up by the Eternal Arms?"

Sometimes this realization that facts are of divine sending, instead of being habitual, is casual, like a mystical experience.

[1] JAMES MARTINEAU: end of the sermon 'Help Thou Mine Unbelief,' in Endeavours after a Christian Life, 2d series. Compare with this page the extract from Voysey on p. 252, above, and those from Pascal and Madame Guyon on p. 262.

Father Gratry gives this instance from his youthful melancholy period: —

> "One day I had a moment of consolation, because I met with something which seemed to me ideally perfect. It was a poor drummer beating the tattoo in the streets of Paris. I walked behind him in returning to the school on the evening of a holiday. His drum gave out the tattoo in such a way that, at that moment at least, however peevish I were, I could find no pretext for fault-finding. It was impossible to conceive more nerve or spirit, better time or measure, more clearness or richness, than were in this drumming. Ideal desire could go no farther in that direction. I was enchanted and consoled; the perfection of this wretched act did me good. Good is at least possible, I said, since the ideal can thus sometimes get embodied."[1]

In Sénancour's novel of Obermann a similar transient lifting of the veil is recorded. In Paris streets, on a March day, he comes across a flower in bloom, a jonquil:

> "It was the strongest expression of desire: it was the first perfume of the year. I felt all the happiness destined for man. This unutterable harmony of souls, the phantom of the ideal world, arose in me complete. I never felt anything so great or so instantaneous. I know not what shape, what analogy, what secret of relation it was that made me see in this flower a limitless beauty. . . . I shall never inclose in a conception this power, this immensity that nothing will express; this form that nothing will contain; this ideal of a better world which one feels, but which, it seems, nature has not made actual."[2]

We heard in previous lectures of the vivified face of the world as it may appear to converts after their awakening.[3] As a rule, religious persons generally assume that whatever natural facts connect themselves in any way with their destiny are significant of the divine purposes with them. Through

---

[1] Souvenirs de ma Jeunesse, 1897, p. 122.

[2] Op. cit., Letter XXX.

[3] Above, p. 228 ff. Compare the withdrawal of expression from the world, in Melancholiacs, p. 142.

prayer the purpose, often far from obvious, comes home to them, and if it be 'trial,' strength to endure the trial is given. Thus at all stages of the prayerful life we find the persuasion that in the process of communion energy from on high flows in to meet demand, and becomes operative within the phenomenal world. So long as this operativeness is admitted to be real, it makes no essential difference whether its immediate effects be subjective or objective. The fundamental religious point is that in prayer, spiritual energy, which otherwise would slumber, does become active, and spiritual work of some kind is effected really.

So much for Prayer, taken in the wide sense of any kind of communion. As the core of religion, we must return to it in the next lecture.

The last aspect of the religious life which remains for me to touch upon is the fact that its manifestations so frequently connect themselves with the subconscious part of our existence. You may remember what I said in my opening lecture[1] about the prevalence of the psychopathic temperament in religious biography. You will in point of fact hardly find a religious leader of any kind in whose life there is no record of automatisms. I speak not merely of savage priests and prophets, whose followers regard automatic utterance and action as by itself tantamount to inspiration, I speak of leaders of thought and subjects of intellectualized experience. Saint Paul had his visions, his ecstasies, his gift of tongues, small as was the importance he attached to the latter. The whole array of Christian saints and heresiarchs, including the greatest, the Bernards, the Loyolas, the Luthers, the Foxes, the Wesleys, had their visions, voices, rapt conditions, guiding impressions, and 'openings.' They had these things, because they had exalted sensibility, and to such things persons of exalted sensibility are liable. In such liability there lie, however, consequences for theology. Beliefs are strengthened wherever automatisms corroborate them. Incursions from beyond the transmarginal region have a peculiar power to increase conviction. The inchoate sense of presence is infinitely stronger

[1] Above, pp. 30, 31.

than conception, but strong as it may be, it is seldom equal to the evidence of hallucination. Saints who actually see or hear their Saviour reach the acme of assurance. Motor automatisms, though rarer, are, if possible, even more convincing than sensations. The subjects here actually feel themselves played upon by powers beyond their will. The evidence is dynamic; the God or spirit moves the very organs of their body.[1]

The great field for this sense of being the instrument of a higher power is of course 'inspiration.' It is easy to discriminate between the religious leaders who have been habitually subject to inspiration and those who have not. In the teachings of the Buddha, of Jesus, of Saint Paul (apart from his gift of tongues), of Saint Augustine, of Huss, of Luther, of Wesley, automatic or semi-automatic composition appears to have been only occasional. In the Hebrew prophets, on the contrary, in Mohammed, in some of the Alexandrians, in many minor Catholic saints, in Fox, in Joseph Smith, something like it appears to have been frequent, sometimes habitual. We have distinct professions of being under the direction of a foreign power, and serving as its mouthpiece. As regards the Hebrew prophets, it is extraordinary, writes an author who has made a careful study of them, to see—

[1] A friend of mine, a first-rate psychologist, who is a subject of graphic automatism, tells me that the appearance of independent actuation in the movements of his arm, when he writes automatically, is so distinct that it obliges him to abandon a psychophysical theory which he had previously believed in, the theory, namely, that we have no feeling of the discharge downwards of our voluntary motor-centres. We must normally have such a feeling, he thinks, or the *sense of an absence* would not be so striking as it is in these experiences. Graphic automatism of a fully developed kind is rare in religious history, so far as my knowledge goes. Such statements as Antonia Bourignon's, that "I do nothing but lend my hand and spirit to another power than mine," is shown by the context to indicate inspiration rather than directly automatic writing. In some eccentric sects this latter occurs. The most striking instance of it is probably the bulky volume called, 'Oahspe, a new Bible in the Words of Jehovah and his angel ambassadors,' Boston and London, 1891, written and illustrated automatically by Dr. Newbrough of New York, whom I understand to be now, or to have been lately, at the head of the spiritistic community of Shalam in New Mexico. The latest automatically written book which has come under my notice is 'Zertoulem's Wisdom of the Ages,' by George A. Fuller, Boston, 1901.

"How, one after another, the same features are reproduced in the prophetic books. The process is always extremely different from what it would be if the prophet arrived at his insight into spiritual things by the tentative efforts of his own genius. There is something sharp and sudden about it. He can lay his finger, so to speak, on the moment when it came. And it always comes in the form of an overpowering force from without, against which he struggles, but in vain. Listen, for instance, [to] the opening of the book of Jeremiah. Read through in like manner the first two chapters of the prophecy of Ezekiel.

"It is not, however, only at the beginning of his career that the prophet passes through a crisis which is clearly not self-caused. Scattered all through the prophetic writings are expressions which speak of some strong and irresistible impulse coming down upon the prophet, determining his attitude to the events of his time, constraining his utterance, making his words the vehicle of a higher meaning than their own. For instance, this of Isaiah's: 'The Lord spake thus to me with a strong hand,'—an emphatic phrase which denotes the overmastering nature of the impulse,—'and instructed me that I should not walk in the way of this people.' . . . Or passages like this from Ezekiel: 'The hand of the Lord God fell upon me,' 'The hand of the Lord was strong upon me.' The one standing characteristic of the prophet is that he speaks with the authority of Jehovah himself. Hence it is that the prophets one and all preface their addresses so confidently, 'The Word of the Lord,' or 'Thus saith the Lord.' They have even the audacity to speak in the first person, as if Jehovah himself were speaking. As in Isaiah: 'Hearken unto me, O Jacob, and Israel my called; I am He, I am the First, I also am the last,'—and so on. The personality of the prophet sinks entirely into the background; he feels himself for the time being the mouthpiece of the Almighty."[1]

"We need to remember that prophecy was a profession, and that the prophets formed a professional class. There were schools of the prophets, in which the gift was regu-

[1] W. SANDAY: The Oracles of God, London, 1892, pp. 49–56, abridged.

larly cultivated. A group of young men would gather round some commanding figure—a Samuel or an Elisha—and would not only record or spread the knowledge of his sayings and doings, but seek to catch themselves something of his inspiration. It seems that music played its part in their exercises. . . . It is perfectly clear that by no means all of these Sons of the prophets ever succeeded in acquiring more than a very small share in the gift which they sought. It was clearly possible to 'counterfeit' prophecy. Sometimes this was done deliberately. . . . But it by no means follows that in all cases where a false message was given, the giver of it was altogether conscious of what he was doing."[1]

Here, to take another Jewish case, is the way in which Philo of Alexandria describes his inspiration:—

"Sometimes, when I have come to my work empty, I have suddenly become full; ideas being in an invisible manner showered upon me, and implanted in me from on high; so that through the influence of divine inspiration, I have become greatly excited, and have known neither the place in which I was, nor those who were present, nor myself, nor what I was saying, nor what I was writing; for then I have been conscious of a richness of interpretation, an enjoyment of light, a most penetrating insight, a most manifest energy in all that was to be done; having such effect on my mind as the clearest ocular demonstration would have on the eyes."[2]

If we turn to Islam, we find that Mohammed's revelations all came from the subconscious sphere. To the question in what way he got them,—

"Mohammed is said to have answered that sometimes he heard a knell as from a bell, and that this had the strongest effect on him; and when the angel went away, he had

---

[1] Op. cit., p. 91. This author also cites Moses's and Isaiah's commissions, as given in Exodus, chaps. iii. and iv., and Isaiah, chap. vi.

[2] Quoted by AUGUSTUS CLISSOLD: The Prophetic Spirit in Genius and Madness, 1870, p. 67. Mr. Clissold is a Swedenborgian. Swedenborg's case is of course the palmary one of *audita et visa*, serving as a basis of religious revelation.

received the revelation. Sometimes again he held converse with the angel as with a man, so as easily to understand his words. The later authorities, however, . . . distinguish still other kinds. In the Itqân (103) the following are enumerated: 1, revelations with sound of bell, 2, by inspiration of the holy spirit in M.'s heart, 3, by Gabriel in human form, 4, by God immediately, either when awake (as in his journey to heaven) or in dream. . . . In Almawâhib alladunîya the kinds are thus given: 1, Dream, 2, Inspiration of Gabriel in the Prophet's heart, 3, Gabriel taking Dahya's form, 4, with the bell-sound, etc., 5, Gabriel in propriâ personâ (only twice), 6, revelation in heaven, 7, God appearing in person, but veiled, 8, God revealing himself immediately without veil. Others add two other stages, namely: 1, Gabriel in the form of still another man, 2, God showing himself personally in dream."[1]

In none of these cases is the revelation distinctly motor. In the case of Joseph Smith (who had prophetic revelations innumerable in addition to the revealed translation of the gold plates which resulted in the Book of Mormon), although there may have been a motor element, the inspiration seems to have been predominantly sensorial. He began his translation by the aid of the 'peep-stones' which he found, or thought or said that he found, with the gold plates,—apparently a case of 'crystal gazing.' For some of the other revelations he used the peep-stones, but seems generally to have asked the Lord for more direct instruction.[2]

Other revelations are described as 'openings'—Fox's, for example, were evidently of the kind known in spiritistic circles

[1] NÖLDEKE, Geschichte des Qorâns, 1860, p. 16. Compare the fuller account in Sir WILLIAM MUIR's Life of Mahomet, 3d ed., 1894, ch. iii.

[2] The Mormon theocracy has always been governed by direct revelations accorded to the President of the Church and its Apostles. From an obliging letter written to me in 1899 by an eminent Mormon, I quote the following extract:—

"It may be very interesting for you to know that the President [Mr. Snow] of the Mormon Church claims to have had a number of revelations very recently from heaven. To explain fully what these revelations are, it is necessary to know that we, as a people, believe that the Church of Jesus Christ has again been established through messengers sent from heaven. This Church has at its head a prophet, seer, and revelator, who gives to man God's holy

of to-day as 'impressions.' As all effective initiators of change must needs live to some degree upon this psychopathic level of sudden perception or conviction of new truth, or of impulse to action so obsessive that it must be worked off, I will say nothing more about so very common a phenomenon.

When, in addition to these phenomena of inspiration, we take religious mysticism into the account, when we recall the striking and sudden unifications of a discordant self which we saw in conversion, and when we review the extravagant obsessions of tenderness, purity, and self-severity met with in saintliness, we cannot, I think, avoid the conclusion that in religion we have a department of human nature with unusually close relations to the transmarginal or subliminal region. If the word 'subliminal' is offensive to any of you, as smelling too much of psychical research or other aberrations, call it by any other name you please, to distinguish it from the level of full sunlit consciousness. Call this latter the A-region of personality, if you care to, and call the other the B-region. The B-region, then, is obviously the larger part of each of us, for it is the abode of everything that is latent and the reservoir of everything that passes unrecorded or unobserved. It contains, for example, such things as all our momentarily inactive memories, and it harbors the springs of all our obscurely motived passions, impulses, likes, dislikes, and prejudices. Our intuitions, hypotheses, fancies, superstitions, persuasions, convictions, and in general all our non-rational operations, come from it. It is the source of our dreams, and apparently they may return to it. In it arise whatever mystical experiences we may have, and our automatisms, sensory or motor; our life in hypnotic and 'hypnoid' conditions, if we are subjects to such conditions; our delusions, fixed ideas, and hysterical accidents, if we are hysteric subjects; our supra-normal cognitions, if such there be, and if we are telepathic subjects. It is also the fountain-head of much that feeds our religion. In

---

will. Revelation is the means through which the will of God is declared directly and in fullness to man. These revelations are got through dreams of sleep or in waking visions of the mind, by voices without visional appearance, or by actual manifestations of the Holy Presence before the eye. We believe that God has come in person and spoken to our prophet and revelator."

persons deep in the religious life, as we have now abundantly seen,—and this is my conclusion,—the door into this region seems unusually wide open; at any rate, experiences making their entrance through that door have had emphatic influence in shaping religious history.

With this conclusion I turn back and close the circle which I opened in my first lecture, terminating thus the review which I then announced of inner religious phenomena as we find them in developed and articulate human individuals. I might easily, if the time allowed, multiply both my documents and my discriminations, but a broad treatment is, I believe, in itself better, and the most important characteristics of the subject lie, I think, before us already. In the next lecture, which is also the last one, we must try to draw the critical conclusions which so much material may suggest.

LECTURE XX

CONCLUSIONS

THE MATERIAL of our study of human nature is now spread before us; and in this parting hour, set free from the duty of description, we can draw our theoretical and practical conclusions. In my first lecture, defending the empirical method, I foretold that whatever conclusions we might come to could be reached by spiritual judgments only, appreciations of the significance for life of religion, taken 'on the whole.' Our conclusions cannot be as sharp as dogmatic conclusions would be, but I will formulate them, when the time comes, as sharply as I can.

Summing up in the broadest possible way the characteristics of the religious life, as we have found them, it includes the following beliefs: —

1. That the visible world is part of a more spiritual universe from which it draws its chief significance;

2. That union or harmonious relation with that higher universe is our true end;

3. That prayer or inner communion with the spirit thereof—be that spirit 'God' or 'law'—is a process wherein work is really done, and spiritual energy flows in and produces effects, psychological or material, within the phenomenal world.

Religion includes also the following psychological characteristics: —

4. A new zest which adds itself like a gift to life, and takes the form either of lyrical enchantment or of appeal to earnestness and heroism.

5. An assurance of safety and a temper of peace, and, in relation to others, a preponderance of loving affections.

In illustrating these characteristics by documents, we have been literally bathed in sentiment. In re-reading my manuscript, I am almost appalled at the amount of emotionality which I find in it. After so much of this, we can afford to be dryer and less sympathetic in the rest of the work that lies before us.

The sentimentality of many of my documents is a consequence of the fact that I sought them among the extravagances of the subject. If any of you are enemies of what our ancestors used to brand as enthusiasm, and are, nevertheless, still listening to me now, you have probably felt my selection to have been sometimes almost perverse, and have wished I might have stuck to soberer examples. I reply that I took these extremer examples as yielding the profounder information. To learn the secrets of any science, we go to expert specialists, even though they may be eccentric persons, and not to commonplace pupils. We combine what they tell us with the rest of our wisdom, and form our final judgment independently. Even so with religion. We who have pursued such radical expressions of it may now be sure that we know its secrets as authentically as any one can know them who learns them from another; and we have next to answer, each of us for himself, the practical question: what are the dangers in this element of life? and in what proportion may it need to be restrained by other elements, to give the proper balance?

But this question suggests another one which I will answer immediately and get it out of the way, for it has more than once already vexed us.[1] Ought it to be assumed that in all men the mixture of religion with other elements should be identical? Ought it, indeed, to be assumed that the lives of all men should show identical religious elements? In other words, is the existence of so many religious types and sects and creeds regrettable?

To these questions I answer 'No' emphatically. And my reason is that I do not see how it is possible that creatures in such different positions and with such different powers as human individuals are, should have exactly the same functions and the same duties. No two of us have identical difficulties, nor should we be expected to work out identical solutions. Each, from his peculiar angle of observation, takes in a certain sphere of fact and trouble, which each must deal with in a unique manner. One of us must soften himself, another must

[1] For example, on pages 128, 152, 304, above.

harden himself; one must yield a point, another must stand firm,—in order the better to defend the position assigned him. If an Emerson were forced to be a Wesley, or a Moody forced to be a Whitman, the total human consciousness of the divine would suffer. The divine can mean no single quality, it must mean a group of qualities, by being champions of which in alternation, different men may all find worthy missions. Each attitude being a syllable in human nature's total message, it takes the whole of us to spell the meaning out completely. So a 'god of battles' must be allowed to be the god for one kind of person, a god of peace and heaven and home, the god for another. We must frankly recognize the fact that we live in partial systems, and that parts are not interchangeable in the spiritual life. If we are peevish and jealous, destruction of the self must be an element of our religion; why need it be one if we are good and sympathetic from the outset? If we are sick souls, we require a religion of deliverance; but why think so much of deliverance, if we are healthy-minded?[1] Unquestionably, some men have the completer experience and the higher vocation, here just as in the social world; but

[1] From this point of view, the contrasts between the healthy and the morbid mind, and between the once-born and the twice-born types, of which I spoke in earlier lectures (see pp. 151–156), cease to be the radical antagonisms which many think them. The twice-born look down upon the rectilinear consciousness of life of the once-born as being 'mere morality,' and not properly religion. "Dr. Channing," an orthodox minister is reported to have said, "is excluded from the highest form of religious life by the extraordinary rectitude of his character." It is indeed true that the outlook upon life of the twice-born—holding as it does more of the element of evil in solution—is the wider and completer. The 'heroic' or 'solemn' way in which life comes to them is a 'higher synthesis' into which healthy-mindedness and morbidness both enter and combine. Evil is not evaded, but sublated in the higher religious cheer of these persons (see pp. 49–54, 328–331). But the final consciousness which each type reaches of union with the divine has the same practical significance for the individual; and individuals may well be allowed to get to it by the channels which lie most open to their several temperaments. In the cases which were quoted in Lecture IV, of the mind-cure form of healthy-mindedness, we found abundant examples of regenerative process. The severity of the crisis in this process is a matter of degree. How long one shall continue to drink the consciousness of evil, and when one shall begin to short-circuit and get rid of it, are also matters of amount and degree, so that in many instances it is quite arbitrary whether we class the individual as a once-born or a twice-born subject.

for each man to stay in his own experience, whate'er it be, and for others to tolerate him there, is surely best.

But, you may now ask, would not this one-sidedness be cured if we should all espouse the science of religions as our own religion? In answering this question I must open again the general relations of the theoretic to the active life.

Knowledge about a thing is not the thing itself. You remember what Al-Ghazzali told us in the Lecture on Mysticism,—that to understand the causes of drunkenness, as a physician understands them, is not to be drunk. A science might come to understand everything about the causes and elements of religion, and might even decide which elements were qualified, by their general harmony with other branches of knowledge, to be considered true; and yet the best man at this science might be the man who found it hardest to be personally devout. *Tout savoir c'est tout pardonner.* The name of Renan would doubtless occur to many persons as an example of the way in which breadth of knowledge may make one only a dilettante in possibilities, and blunt the acuteness of one's living faith.[1] If religion be a function by which either God's cause or man's cause is to be really advanced, then he who lives the life of it, however narrowly, is a better servant than he who merely knows about it, however much. Knowledge about life is one thing; effective occupation of a place in life, with its dynamic currents passing through your being, is another.

For this reason, the science of religions may not be an equivalent for living religion; and if we turn to the inner difficulties of such a science, we see that a point comes when she must drop the purely theoretic attitude, and either let her knots remain uncut, or have them cut by active faith. To see this, suppose that we have our science of religions constituted as a matter of fact. Suppose that she has assimilated all the necessary historical material and distilled out of it as its essence the same conclusions which I myself a few moments ago pronounced. Suppose that she agrees that religion, wherever it is an active thing, involves a belief in ideal presences,

---

[1] Compare, e. g., the quotation from Renan on p. 40, above.

and a belief that in our prayerful communion with them,[1] work is done, and something real comes to pass. She has now to exert her critical activity, and to decide how far, in the light of other sciences and in that of general philosophy, such beliefs can be considered *true*.

Dogmatically to decide this is an impossible task. Not only are the other sciences and the philosophy still far from being completed, but in their present state we find them full of conflicts. The sciences of nature know nothing of spiritual presences, and on the whole hold no practical commerce whatever with the idealistic conceptions towards which general philosophy inclines. The scientist, so-called, is, during his scientific hours at least, so materialistic that one may well say that on the whole the influence of science goes against the notion that religion should be recognized at all. And this antipathy to religion finds an echo within the very science of religions itself. The cultivator of this science has to become acquainted with so many groveling and horrible superstitions that a presumption easily arises in his mind that any belief that is religious probably is false. In the 'prayerful communion' of savages with such mumbo-jumbos of deities as they acknowledge, it is hard for us to see what genuine spiritual work— even though it were work relative only to their dark savage obligations—can possibly be done.

The consequence is that the conclusions of the science of religions are as likely to be adverse as they are to be favorable to the claim that the essence of religion is true. There is a notion in the air about us that religion is probably only an anachronism, a case of 'survival,' an atavistic relapse into a mode of thought which humanity in its more enlightened examples has outgrown; and this notion our religious anthropologists at present do little to counteract.

This view is so widespread at the present day that I must consider it with some explicitness before I pass to my own conclusions. Let me call it the 'Survival theory,' for brevity's sake.

The pivot round which the religious life, as we have traced it, revolves, is the interest of the individual in his private

---

[1] 'Prayerful' taken in the broader sense explained above on pp. 415 ff.

personal destiny. Religion, in short, is a monumental chapter in the history of human egotism. The gods believed in—whether by crude savages or by men disciplined intellectually—agree with each other in recognizing personal calls. Religious thought is carried on in terms of personality, this being, in the world of religion, the one fundamental fact. To-day, quite as much as at any previous age, the religious individual tells you that the divine meets him on the basis of his personal concerns.

Science, on the other hand, has ended by utterly repudiating the personal point of view. She catalogues her elements and records her laws indifferent as to what purpose may be shown forth by them, and constructs her theories quite careless of their bearing on human anxieties and fates. Though the scientist may individually nourish a religion, and be a theist in his irresponsible hours, the days are over when it could be said that for Science herself the heavens declare the glory of God and the firmament showeth his handiwork. Our solar system, with its harmonies, is seen now as but one passing case of a certain sort of moving equilibrium in the heavens, realized by a local accident in an appalling wilderness of worlds where no life can exist. In a span of time which as a cosmic interval will count but as an hour, it will have ceased to be. The Darwinian notion of chance production, and subsequent destruction, speedy or deferred, applies to the largest as well as to the smallest facts. It is impossible, in the present temper of the scientific imagination, to find in the driftings of the cosmic atoms, whether they work on the universal or on the particular scale, anything but a kind of aimless weather, doing and undoing, achieving no proper history, and leaving no result. Nature has no one distinguishable ultimate tendency with which it is possible to feel a sympathy. In the vast rhythm of her processes, as the scientific mind now follows them, she appears to cancel herself. The books of natural theology which satisfied the intellects of our grandfathers seem to us quite grotesque,[1] representing, as they did, a God who

[1] How was it ever conceivable, we ask, that a man like Christian Wolff, in whose dry-as-dust head all the learning of the early eighteenth century was concentrated, should have preserved such a baby-like faith in the personal and human character of Nature as to expound her operations as he did in his

conformed the largest things of nature to the paltriest of our private wants. The God whom science recognizes must be a God of universal laws exclusively, a God who does a whole-sale, not a retail business. He cannot accommodate his pro-cesses to the convenience of individuals. The bubbles on the foam which coats a stormy sea are floating episodes, made and unmade by the forces of the wind and water. Our private

---

work on the uses of natural things? This, for example, is the account he gives of the sun and its utility: —

"We see that God has created the sun to keep the changeable conditions on the earth in such an order that living creatures, men and beasts, may inhabit its surface. Since men are the most reasonable of creatures, and able to infer God's invisible being from the contemplation of the world, the sun in so far forth contributes to the primary purpose of creation: without it the race of man could not be preserved or continued. . . . The sun makes day-light, not only on our earth, but also on the other planets; and daylight is of the utmost utility to us; for by its means we can commodiously carry on those occupations which in the night-time would either be quite impossible, or at any rate impossible without our going to the expense of artificial light. The beasts of the field can find food by day which they would not be able to find at night. Moreover we owe it to the sunlight that we are able to see everything that is on the earth's surface, not only near by, but also at a dis-tance, and to recognize both near and far things according to their species, which again is of manifold use to us not only in the business necessary to human life, and when we are traveling, but also for the scientific knowledge of Nature, which knowledge for the most part depends on observations made with the help of sight, and, without the sunshine, would have been impossi-ble. If any one would rightly impress on his mind the great advantages which he derives from the sun, let him imagine himself living through only one month, and see how it would be with all his undertakings, if it were not day but night. He would then be sufficiently convinced out of his own experi-ence, especially if he had much work to carry on in the street or in the fields. . . . From the sun we learn to recognize when it is midday, and by knowing this point of time exactly, we can set our clocks right, on which account astronomy owes much to the sun. . . . By help of the sun one can find the meridian. . . . But the meridian is the basis of our sun-dials, and generally speaking, we should have no sun-dials if we had no sun." Vernünftige Ge-danken von den Absichten der natürlichen Dinge, 1782, pp. 74–84.

Or read the account of God's beneficence in the institution of "the great variety throughout the world of men's faces, voices, and handwriting," given in Derham's Physico-theology, a book that had much vogue in the eigh-teenth century. "Had Man's body," says Dr. Derham, "been made according to any of the Atheistical Schemes, or any other Method than that of the infinite Lord of the World, this wise Variety would never have been: but

selves are like those bubbles,—epiphenomena, as Clifford, I believe, ingeniously called them; their destinies weigh nothing and determine nothing in the world's irremediable currents of events.

Men's Faces would have been cast in the same, or not a very different Mould, their Organs of Speech would have sounded the same or not so great a Variety of Notes; and the same Structure of Muscles and Nerves would have given the Hand the same Direction in Writing. And in this Case, what Confusion, what Disturbance, what Mischiefs would the world eternally have lain under! No Security could have been to our persons; no Certainty, no Enjoyment of our Possessions; no Justice between Man and Man; no Distinction between Good and Bad, between Friends and Foes, between Father and Child, Husband and Wife, Male or Female; but all would have been turned topsy-turvy, by being exposed to the Malice of the Envious and ill-Natured, to the Fraud and Violence of Knaves and Robbers, to the Forgeries of the crafty Cheat, to the Lusts of the Effeminate and Debauched, and what not! Our Courts of Justice can abundantly testify the dire Effects of Mistaking Men's Faces, of counterfeiting their Hands, and forging Writings. But now as the infinitely wise Creator and Ruler hath ordered the Matter, every man's Face can distinguish him in the Light, and his Voice in the Dark; his Handwriting can speak for him though absent, and be his Witness, and secure his Contracts in future Generations. A manifest as well as admirable Indication of the divine Superintendence and Management."

A God so careful as to make provision even for the unmistakable signing of bank checks and deeds was a deity truly after the heart of eighteenth century Anglicanism.

I subjoin, omitting the capitals, Derham's 'Vindication of God by the Institution of Hills and Valleys,' and Wolff's altogether culinary account of the institution of Water:—

"The uses," says Wolff, "which water serves in human life are plain to see and need not be described at length. Water is a universal drink of man and beasts. Even though men have made themselves drinks that are artificial, they could not do this without water. Beer is brewed of water and malt, and it is the water in it which quenches thirst. Wine is prepared from grapes, which could never have grown without the help of water; and the same is true of those drinks which in England and other places they produce from fruit. . . . Therefore since God so planned the world that men and beasts should live upon it and find there everything required for their necessity and convenience, he also made water as one means whereby to make the earth into so excellent a dwelling. And this is all the more manifest when we consider the advantages which we obtain from this same water for the cleaning of our household utensils, of our clothing, and of other matters. . . . When one goes into a grinding-mill one sees that the grindstone must always be kept wet and then one will get a still greater idea of the use of water."

Of the hills and valleys, Derham, after praising their beauty, discourses as

You see how natural it is, from this point of view, to treat religion as a mere survival, for religion does in fact perpetuate the traditions of the most primeval thought. To coerce the spiritual powers, or to square them and get them on our side, was, during enormous tracts of time, the one great object in our dealings with the natural world. For our ancestors, dreams, hallucinations, revelations, and cock-and-bull stories were inextricably mixed with facts. Up to a comparatively recent date such distinctions as those between what has been verified and what is only conjectured, between the impersonal and the personal aspects of existence, were hardly suspected

---

follows: "Some constitutions are indeed of so happy a strength, and so confirmed an health, as to be indifferent to almost any place or temperature of the air. But then others are so weakly and feeble, as not to be able to bear one, but can live comfortably in another place. With some the more subtle and finer air of the hills doth best agree, who are languishing and dying in the feculent and grosser air of great towns, or even the warmer and vaporous air of the valleys and waters. But contrariwise, others languish on the hills, and grow lusty and strong in the warmer air of the valleys.

"So that this opportunity of shifting our abode from the hills to the vales, is an admirable easement, refreshment, and great benefit to the valetudinarian, feeble part of mankind; affording those an easy and comfortable life, who would otherwise live miserably, languish, and pine away.

"To this salutary conformation of the earth we may add another great convenience of the hills, and that is affording commodious places for habitation, serving (as an eminent author wordeth it) as screens to keep off the cold and nipping blasts of the northern and easterly winds, and reflecting the benign and cherishing sunbeams, and so rendering our habitations both more comfortable and more cheerly in winter.

"Lastly, it is to the hills that the fountains owe their rise and the rivers their conveyance, and consequently those vast masses and lofty piles are not, as they are charged, such rude and useless excrescences of our ill-formed globe; but the admirable tools of nature, contrived and ordered by the infinite Creator, to do one of its most useful works. For, was the surface of the earth even and level, and the middle parts of its islands and continents not mountainous and high as now it is, it is most certain there could be no descent for the rivers, no conveyance for the waters; but, instead of gliding along those gentle declivities which the higher lands now afford them quite down to the sea, they would stagnate and perhaps stink, and also drown large tracts of land.

"[Thus] the hills and vales, though to a peevish and weary traveler they may seem incommodious and troublesome, yet are a noble work of the great Creator, and wisely appointed by him for the good of our sublunary world."

or conceived. Whatever you imagined in a lively manner, whatever you thought fit to be true, you affirmed confidently; and whatever you affirmed, your comrades believed. Truth was what had not yet been contradicted, most things were taken into the mind from the point of view of their human suggestiveness, and the attention confined itself exclusively to the æsthetic and dramatic aspects of events.[1]

How indeed could it be otherwise? The extraordinary

[1] Until the seventeenth century this mode of thought prevailed. One need only recall the dramatic treatment even of mechanical questions by Aristotle, as, for example, his explanation of the power of the lever to make a small weight raise a larger one. This is due, according to Aristotle, to the generally miraculous character of the circle and of all circular movement. The circle is both convex and concave; it is made by a fixed point and a moving line, which contradict each other; and whatever moves in a circle moves in opposite directions. Nevertheless, movement in a circle is the most 'natural' movement; and the long arm of the lever, moving, as it does, in the larger circle, has the greater amount of this natural motion, and consequently requires the lesser force. Or recall the explanation by Herodotus of the position of the sun in winter: It moves to the south because of the cold which drives it into the warm parts of the heavens over Libya. Or listen to Saint Augustine's speculations: "Who gave to chaff such power to freeze that it preserves snow buried under it, and such power to warm that it ripens green fruit? Who can explain the strange properties of fire itself, which blackens all that it burns, though itself bright, and which, though of the most beautiful colors, discolors almost all that it touches and feeds upon, and turns blazing fuel into grimy cinders? . . . Then what wonderful properties do we find in charcoal, which is so brittle that a light tap breaks it, and a slight pressure pulverizes it, and yet is so strong that no moisture rots it, nor any time causes it to decay." City of God, book xxi. ch. iv.

Such aspects of things as these, their naturalness and unnaturalness, the sympathies and antipathies of their superficial qualities, their eccentricities, their brightness and strength and destructiveness, were inevitably the ways in which they originally fastened our attention.

If you open early medical books, you will find sympathetic magic invoked on every page. Take, for example, the famous vulnerary ointment attributed to Paracelsus. For this there were a variety of receipts, including usually human fat, the fat of either a bull, a wild boar, or a bear; powdered earthworms, the *usnia*, or mossy growth on the weathered skull of a hanged criminal, and other materials equally unpleasant—the whole prepared under the planet Venus if possible, but never under Mars or Saturn. Then, if a splinter of wood, dipped in the patient's blood, or the bloodstained weapon that wounded him, be immersed in this ointment, the wound itself being tightly bound up, the latter infallibly gets well,—I quote now Van Helmont's account,—for the blood on the weapon or splinter, containing in it the spirit of the wounded man, is roused to active excitement by the contact of the

value, for explanation and prevision, of those mathematical and mechanical modes of conception which science uses, was a result that could not possibly have been expected in advance. Weight, movement, velocity, direction, position, what

---

ointment, whence there results to it a full commission or power to cure its cousin-german, the blood in the patient's body. This it does by sucking out the dolorous and exotic impression from the wounded part. But to do this it has to implore the aid of the bull's fat, and other portions of the unguent. The reason why bull's fat is so powerful is that the bull at the time of slaughter is full of secret reluctancy and vindictive murmurs, and therefore dies with a higher flame of revenge about him than any other animal. And thus we have made it out, says this author, that the admirable efficacy of the ointment ought to be imputed, not to any auxiliary concurrence of Satan, but simply to the energy of the *posthumous character of Revenge* remaining firmly impressed upon the blood and concreted fat in the unguent. J. B. VAN HELMONT: A Ternary of Paradoxes, translated by WALTER CHARLETON, London, 1650.—I much abridge the original in my citations.

The author goes on to prove by the analogy of many other natural facts that this sympathetic action between things at a distance is the true rationale of the case. "If," he says, "the heart of a horse, slain by a witch, taken out of the yet reeking carcase, be impaled upon an arrow and roasted, immediately the whole witch becomes tormented with the insufferable pains and cruelty of the fire, which could by no means happen unless there preceded a conjunction of the spirit of the witch with the spirit of the horse. In the reeking and yet panting heart, the spirit of the witch is kept captive, and the retreat of it prevented by the arrow transfixed. Similarly hath not many a murdered carcase at the coroner's inquest suffered a fresh hæmorrhage or cruentation at the presence of the assassin?—the blood being, as in a furious fit of anger, enraged and agitated by the impress of revenge conceived against the murderer, at the instant of the soul's compulsive exile from the body. So, if you have dropsy, gout, or jaundice, by including some of your warm blood in the shell and white of an egg, which, exposed to a gentle heat, and mixed with a bait of flesh, you shall give to a hungry dog or hog, the disease shall instantly pass from you into the animal, and leave you entirely. And similarly again, if you burn some of the milk either of a cow or of a woman, the gland from which it issued will dry up. A gentleman at Brussels had his nose mowed off in a combat, but the celebrated surgeon Tagliacozzus digged a new nose for him out of the skin of the arm of a porter at Bologna. About thirteen months after his return to his own country, the engrafted nose grew cold, putrefied, and in a few days dropped off, and it was then discovered that the porter had expired, near about the same punctilio of time. There are still at Brussels eye-witnesses of this occurrence," says Van Helmont; and adds, "I pray what is there in this of superstition or of exalted imagination?"

Modern mind-cure literature—the works of Prentice Mulford, for example—is full of sympathetic magic.

thin, pallid, uninteresting ideas! How could the richer animistic aspects of Nature, the peculiarities and oddities that make phenomena picturesquely striking or expressive, fail to have been first singled out and followed by philosophy as the more promising avenue to the knowledge of Nature's life? Well, it is still in these richer animistic and dramatic aspects that religion delights to dwell. It is the terror and beauty of phenomena, the 'promise' of the dawn and of the rainbow, the 'voice' of the thunder, the 'gentleness' of the summer rain, the 'sublimity' of the stars, and not the physical laws which these things follow, by which the religious mind still continues to be most impressed; and just as of yore, the devout man tells you that in the solitude of his room or of the fields he still feels the divine presence, that inflowings of help come in reply to his prayers, and that sacrifices to this unseen reality fill him with security and peace.

Pure anachronism! says the survival-theory;—anachronism for which deanthropomorphization of the imagination is the remedy required. The less we mix the private with the cosmic, the more we dwell in universal and impersonal terms, the truer heirs of Science we become.

In spite of the appeal which this impersonality of the scientific attitude makes to a certain magnanimity of temper, I believe it to be shallow, and I can now state my reason in comparatively few words. That reason is that, so long as we deal with the cosmic and the general, we deal only with the symbols of reality, but *as soon as we deal with private and personal phenomena as such, we deal with realities in the completest sense of the term.* I think I can easily make clear what I mean by these words.

The world of our experience consists at all times of two parts, an objective and a subjective part, of which the former may be incalculably more extensive than the latter, and yet the latter can never be omitted or suppressed. The objective part is the sum total of whatsoever at any given time we may be thinking of, the subjective part is the inner 'state' in which the thinking comes to pass. What we think of may be enormous,—the cosmic times and spaces, for example,—whereas the inner state may be the most fugitive and paltry activity of mind. Yet the cosmic objects, so far as the experience yields them, are but ideal pictures of something whose existence we do not inwardly possess but only point at outwardly, while the inner state is our very experience itself; its reality and that of our experience are one. A conscious field *plus* its object as felt or thought of *plus* an attitude towards the object *plus* the sense of a self to whom the attitude belongs—such a concrete bit of personal experience may be a small bit, but it is a solid bit as long as it lasts; not hollow, not a mere abstract element of experience, such as the 'object' is when taken all alone. It is a *full* fact, even though it be an insignificant fact; it is of the *kind* to which all realities whatsoever must belong; the motor currents of the world run through the like of it; it is on the line connecting real events with real events. That unsharable feeling which each one of us has of the pinch of his individual destiny as he privately feels it rolling out on fortune's wheel may be disparaged for its egotism, may be sneered at as unscientific, but it is the one thing that fills up the measure of our concrete actuality, and any would-be existent that should lack such a feeling, or its analogue, would be a piece of reality only half made up.[1]

If this be true, it is absurd for science to say that the egotistic elements of experience should be suppressed. The axis of reality runs solely through the egotistic places,—they are strung upon it like so many beads. To describe the world with all the various feelings of the individual pinch of destiny, all the various spiritual attitudes, left out from the description—they being as describable as anything else—would be something like offering a printed bill of fare as the equivalent for a solid meal. Religion makes no such blunder. The individual's religion may be egotistic, and those private realities which it keeps in touch with may be narrow enough; but at any rate it always remains infinitely less hollow and abstract, as far as it goes, than a science which prides itself on taking no account of anything private at all.

A bill of fare with one real raisin on it instead of the word

[1] Compare Lotze's doctrine that the only meaning we can attach to the notion of a thing as it is 'in itself' is by conceiving it as it is *for* itself; i. e., as a piece of full experience with a private sense of 'pinch' or inner activity of some sort going with it.

'raisin,' with one real egg instead of the word 'egg,' might be an inadequate meal, but it would at least be a commencement of reality. The contention of the survival-theory that we ought to stick to non-personal elements exclusively seems like saying that we ought to be satisfied forever with reading the naked bill of fare. I think, therefore, that however particular questions connected with our individual destinies may be answered, it is only by acknowledging them as genuine questions, and living in the sphere of thought which they open up, that we become profound. But to live thus is to be religious; so I unhesitatingly repudiate the survival-theory of religion, as being founded on an egregious mistake. It does not follow, because our ancestors made so many errors of fact and mixed them with their religion, that we should therefore leave off being religious at all.[1] By being religious we establish ourselves in possession of ultimate reality at the only points at which reality is given us to guard. Our responsible concern is with our private destiny, after all.

You see now why I have been so individualistic throughout these lectures, and why I have seemed so bent on rehabilitating the element of feeling in religion and subordinating its intellectual part. Individuality is founded in feeling; and the recesses of feeling, the darker, blinder strata of character, are the only places in the world in which we catch real fact in the

[1] Even the errors of fact may possibly turn out not to be as wholesale as the scientist assumes. We saw in Lecture IV how the religious conception of the universe seems to many mind-curers 'verified' from day to day by their experience of fact. 'Experience of fact' is a field with so many things in it that the sectarian scientist, methodically declining, as he does, to recognize such 'facts' as mind-curers and others like them experience, otherwise than by such rude heads of classification as 'bosh,' 'rot,' 'folly,' certainly leaves out a mass of raw fact which, save for the industrious interest of the religious in the more personal aspects of reality, would never have succeeded in getting itself recorded at all. We know this to be true already in certain cases; it may, therefore, be true in others as well. Miraculous healings have always been part of the supernaturalist stock in trade, and have always been dismissed by the scientist as figments of the imagination. But the scientist's tardy education in the facts of hypnotism has recently given him an apperceiving mass for phenomena of this order, and he consequently now allows that the healings may exist, provided you expressly call them effects of 'suggestion.' Even the stigmata of the cross on Saint Francis's hands and feet may on these terms not be a fable. Similarly, the time-honored phenomenon of diabolical

making, and directly perceive how events happen, and how work is actually done.[1] Compared with this world of living individualized feelings, the world of generalized objects which the intellect contemplates is without solidity or life. As in stereoscopic or kinetoscopic pictures seen outside the instrument, the third dimension, the movement, the vital element, are not there. We get a beautiful picture of an express train supposed to be moving, but where in the picture, as I have heard a friend say, is the energy or the fifty miles an hour?[2]

Let us agree, then, that Religion, occupying herself with personal destinies and keeping thus in contact with the only absolute realities which we know, must necessarily play an eternal part in human history. The next thing to decide is

---

possession is on the point of being admitted by the scientist as a fact, now that he has the name of 'hystero-demonopathy' by which to apperceive it. No one can foresee just how far this legitimation of occultist phenomena under newly found scientist titles may proceed—even 'prophecy,' even 'levitation,' might creep into the pale.

Thus the divorce between scientist facts and religious facts may not necessarily be as eternal as it at first sight seems, nor the personalism and romanticism of the world, as they appeared to primitive thinking, be matters so irrevocably outgrown. The final human opinion may, in short, in some manner now impossible to foresee, revert to the more personal style, just as any path of progress may follow a spiral rather than a straight line. If this were so, the rigorously impersonal view of science might one day appear as having been a temporarily useful eccentricity rather than the definitively triumphant position which the sectarian scientist at present so confidently announces it to be.

[1] Hume's criticism has banished causation from the world of physical objects, and 'Science' is absolutely satisfied to define cause in terms of concomitant change—read Mach, Pearson, Ostwald. The 'original' of the notion of causation is in our inner personal experience, and only there can causes in the old-fashioned sense be directly observed and described.

[2] When I read in a religious paper words like these: "Perhaps the best thing we can say of God is that he is *the Inevitable Inference*," I recognize the tendency to let religion evaporate in intellectual terms. Would martyrs have sung in the flames for a mere inference, however inevitable it might be? Original religious men, like Saint Francis, Luther, Behmen, have usually been enemies of the intellect's pretension to meddle with religious things. Yet the intellect, everywhere invasive, shows everywhere its shallowing effect. See how the ancient spirit of Methodism evaporates under those wonderfully able rationalistic booklets (which every one should read) of a philosopher like Professor Bowne (The Christian Revelation, The Christian Life, The Atone-

what she reveals about those destinies, or whether indeed she reveals anything distinct enough to be considered a general message to mankind. We have done as you see, with our preliminaries, and our final summing up can now begin.

I am well aware that after all the palpitating documents which I have quoted, and all the perspectives of emotion-inspiring institution and belief that my previous lectures have opened, the dry analysis to which I now advance may appear to many of you like an anticlimax, a tapering-off and flattening out of the subject, instead of a crescendo of interest and result. I said awhile ago that the religious attitude of Protestants appears poverty-stricken to the Catholic imagination. Still more poverty-stricken, I fear, may my final summing up of the subject appear at first to some of you. On which account I pray you now to bear this point in mind, that in the present part of it I am expressly trying to reduce religion to its lowest admissible terms, to that minimum, free from

---

ment: Cincinnati and New York, 1898, 1899, 1900). See the positively expulsive purpose of philosophy properly so called:—

"Religion," writes M. Vacherot (La Religion, Paris, 1869, pp. 313, 436, et passim), "answers to a transient state or condition, not to a permanent determination of human nature, being merely an expression of that stage of the human mind which is dominated by the imagination. . . . Christianity has but a single possible final heir to its estate, and that is scientific philosophy."

In a still more radical vein, Professor Ribot (Psychologie des Sentiments, p. 310) describes the evaporation of religion. He sums it up in a single formula—the ever-growing predominance of the rational intellectual element, with the gradual fading out of the emotional element, this latter tending to enter into the group of purely intellectual sentiments. "Of religious sentiment properly so called, nothing survives at last save a vague respect for the unknowable x which is a last relic of the fear, and a certain attraction towards the ideal, which is a relic of the love, that characterized the earlier periods of religious growth. To state this more simply, *religion tends to turn into religious philosophy.*—These are psychologically entirely different things, the one being a theoretic construction of ratiocination, whereas the other is the living work of a group of persons, or of a great inspired leader, calling into play the entire thinking and feeling organism of man."

I find the same failure to recognize that the stronghold of religion lies in individuality in attempts like those of Professor Baldwin (Mental Development, Social and Ethical Interpretations, ch. x.) and Mr. H. R. Marshall (Instinct and Reason, chaps. viii. to xii.) to make it a purely 'conservative social force.'

individualistic excrescences, which all religions contain as their nucleus, and on which it may be hoped that all religious persons may agree. That established, we should have a result which might be small, but would at least be solid; and on it and round it the ruddier additional beliefs on which the different individuals make their venture might be grafted, and flourish as richly as you please. I shall add my own over-belief (which will be, I confess, of a somewhat pallid kind, as befits a critical philosopher), and you will, I hope, also add your over-beliefs, and we shall soon be in the varied world of concrete religious constructions once more. For the moment, let me dryly pursue the analytic part of the task.

Both thought and feeling are determinants of conduct, and the same conduct may be determined either by feeling or by thought. When we survey the whole field of religion, we find a great variety in the thoughts that have prevailed there; but the feelings on the one hand and the conduct on the other are almost always the same, for Stoic, Christian, and Buddhist saints are practically indistinguishable in their lives. The theories which Religion generates, being thus variable, are secondary; and if you wish to grasp her essence, you must look to the feelings and the conduct as being the more constant elements. It is between these two elements that the short circuit exists on which she carries on her principal business, while the ideas and symbols and other institutions form loop-lines which may be perfections and improvements, and may even some day all be united into one harmonious system, but which are not to be regarded as organs with an indispensable function, necessary at all times for religious life to go on. This seems to me the first conclusion which we are entitled to draw from the phenomena we have passed in review.

The next step is to characterize the feelings. To what psychological order do they belong?

The resultant outcome of them is in any case what Kant calls a 'sthenic' affection, an excitement of the cheerful, expansive, 'dynamogenic' order which, like any tonic, freshens our vital powers. In almost every lecture, but especially in the lectures on Conversion and on Saintliness, we have seen how this emotion overcomes temperamental melancholy and imparts endurance to the Subject, or a zest, or a meaning, or an enchantment and glory to the common objects of life.[1] The name of 'faith-state,' by which Professor Leuba designates it, is a good one.[2] It is a biological as well as a psychological condition, and Tolstoy is absolutely accurate in classing faith among the forces *by which men live*.[3] The total absence of it, anhedonia,[4] means collapse.

The faith-state may hold a very minimum of intellectual content. We saw examples of this in those sudden raptures of the divine presence, or in such mystical seizures as Dr. Bucke described.[5] It may be a mere vague enthusiasm, half spiritual, half vital, a courage, and a feeling that great and wondrous things are in the air.[6]

When, however, a positive intellectual content is associated

[1] Compare, for instance, pages 189, 202, 206, 209, 229 to 236, 252 to 255.

[2] American Journal of Psychology, vii. 345.

[3] Above, p. 171.

[4] Above, p. 136.

[5] Above, p. 360.

[6] Example: Henri Perreyve writes to Gratry: "I do not know how to deal with the happiness which you aroused in me this morning. It overwhelms me; I want to *do* something, yet I can do nothing and am fit for nothing. . . . I would fain do *great things*." Again, after an inspiring interview, he writes: "I went homewards, intoxicated with joy, hope, and strength. I wanted to feed upon my happiness in solitude, far from all men. It was late; but, unheeding that, I took a mountain path and went on like a madman, looking at the heavens, regardless of earth. Suddenly an instinct made me draw hastily back—I was on the very edge of a precipice, one step more and I must have fallen. I took fright and gave up my nocturnal promenade." A. GRATRY: Henri Perreyve, London, 1872, pp. 92, 89.

This primacy, in the faith-state, of vague expansive impulse over direction is well expressed in Walt Whitman's lines (Leaves of Grass, 1872, p. 190):—

"O to confront night, storms, hunger, ridicule, accidents, rebuffs, as the trees and animals do. . . .
Dear Camerado! I confess I have urged you onward with me, and still urge you, without the least idea what is our destination,
Or whether we shall be victorious, or utterly quell'd and defeated."

This readiness for great things, and this sense that the world by its importance, wonderfulness, etc., is apt for their production, would seem to be the undifferentiated germ of all the higher faiths. Trust in our own dreams of ambition, or in our country's expansive destinies, and faith in the providence of God, all have their source in that onrush of our sanguine impulses, and in that sense of the exceedingness of the possible over the real.

with a faith-state, it gets invincibly stamped in upon belief,[1] and this explains the passionate loyalty of religious persons everywhere to the minutest details of their so widely differing creeds. Taking creeds and faith-state together, as forming 're-ligions,' and treating these as purely subjective phenomena, without regard to the question of their 'truth,' we are obliged, on account of their extraordinary influence upon action and endurance, to class them amongst the most important biolog-ical functions of mankind. Their stimulant and anæsthetic ef-fect is so great that Professor Leuba, in a recent article,[2] goes so far as to say that so long as men can *use* their God, they care very little who he is, or even whether he is at all. "The truth of the matter can be put," says Leuba, "in this way: *God is not known, he is not understood; he is used*—sometimes as meat-purveyor, sometimes as moral support, sometimes as friend, sometimes as an object of love. If he proves himself useful, the religious consciousness asks for no more than that. Does God really exist? How does he exist? What is he? are so many irrelevant questions. Not God, but life, more life, a larger, richer, more satisfying life, is, in the last analysis, the end of religion. The love of life, at any and every level of development, is the religious impulse."[3]

At this purely subjective rating, therefore, Religion must be considered vindicated in a certain way from the attacks of her critics. It would seem that she cannot be a mere anachronism and survival, but must exert a permanent function, whether she be with or without intellectual content, and whether, if she have any, it be true or false.

[1] Compare LEUBA: Loc. cit., pp. 346–349.
[2] The Contents of Religious Consciousness, in The Monist, xi. 536, July, 1901.
[3] Loc. cit., pp. 571, 572, abridged. See, also, this writer's extraordinarily true criticism of the notion that religion primarily seeks to solve the intellectual mystery of the world. Compare what W. BENDER says (in his Wesen der Religion, Bonn, 1888, pp. 85, 38): "Not the question about God, and not the inquiry into the origin and purpose of the world is religion, but the question about Man. All religious views of life are anthropocentric." "Religion is that activity of the human impulse towards self-preservation by means of which Man seeks to carry his essential vital purposes through against the adverse pressure of the world by raising himself freely towards the world's ordering and governing powers when the limits of his own strength are reached." The whole book is little more than a development of these words.

We must next pass beyond the point of view of merely subjective utility, and make inquiry into the intellectual content itself.

First, is there, under all the discrepancies of the creeds, a common nucleus to which they bear their testimony unanimously?

And second, ought we to consider the testimony true?

I will take up the first question first, and answer it immediately in the affirmative. The warring gods and formulas of the various religions do indeed cancel each other, but there is a certain uniform deliverance in which religions all appear to meet. It consists of two parts: —

1. An uneasiness; and
2. Its solution.

1. The uneasiness, reduced to its simplest terms, is a sense that there is *something wrong about us* as we naturally stand.

2. The solution is a sense that *we are saved from the wrongness* by making proper connection with the higher powers.

In those more developed minds which alone we are studying, the wrongness takes a moral character, and the salvation takes a mystical tinge. I think we shall keep well within the limits of what is common to all such minds if we formulate the essence of their religious experience in terms like these: —

The individual, so far as he suffers from his wrongness and criticises it, is to that extent consciously beyond it, and in at least possible touch with something higher, if anything higher exist. Along with the wrong part there is thus a better part of him, even though it may be but a most helpless germ. With which part he should identify his real being is by no means obvious at this stage; but when stage 2 (the stage of solution or salvation) arrives,[1] the man identifies his real being with the germinal higher part of himself; and does so in the following way. *He becomes conscious that this higher part is conterminous and continuous with a MORE of the same quality, which is operative in the universe outside of him, and which he can keep in working touch with, and in a fashion get on board of and save himself when all his lower being has gone to pieces in the wreck.*

[1] Remember that for some men it arrives suddenly, for others gradually, whilst others again practically enjoy it all their life.

It seems to me that all the phenomena are accurately describable in these very simple general terms.[1] They allow for the divided self and the struggle; they involve the change of personal centre and the surrender of the lower self; they express the appearance of exteriority of the helping power and yet account for our sense of union with it;[2] and they fully justify our feelings of security and joy. There is probably no autobiographic document, among all those which I have quoted, to which the description will not well apply. One need only add such specific details as will adapt it to various theologies and various personal temperaments, and one will then have the various experiences reconstructed in their individual forms.

So far, however, as this analysis goes, the experiences are only psychological phenomena. They possess, it is true, enormous biological worth. Spiritual strength really increases in the subject when he has them, a new life opens for him, and they seem to him a place of conflux where the forces of two universes meet; and yet this may be nothing but his subjective way of feeling things, a mood of his own fancy, in spite of the effects produced. I now turn to my second question: What is the objective 'truth' of their content?[3]

The part of the content concerning which the question of truth most pertinently arises is that 'MORE of the same quality' with which our own higher self appears in the experience to come into harmonious working relation. Is such a 'more' merely our own notion, or does it really exist? If so, in what shape does it exist? Does it act, as well as exist? And in what form should we conceive of that 'union' with it of which religious geniuses are so convinced?

---

[1] The practical difficulties are: 1, to 'realize the reality' of one's higher part; 2, to identify one's self with it exclusively; and 3, to identify it with all the rest of ideal being.

[2] "When mystical activity is at its height, we find consciousness possessed by the sense of a being at once *excessive* and *identical* with the self: great enough to be God; interior enough to be *me*. The 'objectivity' of it ought in that case to be called *excessivity*, rather, or exceedingness." RÉCÉJAC: Essai sur les fondements de la conscience mystique, 1897, p. 46.

[3] The word 'truth' is here taken to mean something additional to bare value for life, although the natural propensity of man is to believe that whatever has great value for life is thereby certified as true.

It is in answering these questions that the various theologies perform their theoretic work, and that their divergencies most come to light. They all agree that the 'more' really exists; though some of them hold it to exist in the shape of a personal god or gods, while others are satisfied to conceive it as a stream of ideal tendency embedded in the eternal structure of the world. They all agree, moreover, that it acts as well as exists, and that something really is effected for the better when you throw your life into its hands. It is when they treat of the experience of 'union' with it that their speculative differences appear most clearly. Over this point pantheism and theism, nature and second birth, works and grace and karma, immortality and reincarnation, rationalism and mysticism, carry on inveterate disputes.

At the end of my lecture on Philosophy[1] I held out the notion that an impartial science of religions might sift out from the midst of their discrepancies a common body of doctrine which she might also formulate in terms to which physical science need not object. This, I said, she might adopt as her own reconciling hypothesis, and recommend it for general belief. I also said that in my last lecture I should have to try my own hand at framing such an hypothesis.

The time has now come for this attempt. Who says 'hypothesis' renounces the ambition to be coercive in his arguments. The most I can do is, accordingly, to offer something that may fit the facts so easily that your scientific logic will find no plausible pretext for vetoing your impulse to welcome it as true.

The 'more,' as we called it, and the meaning of our 'union' with it, form the nucleus of our inquiry. Into what definite description can these words be translated, and for what definite facts do they stand? It would never do for us to place ourselves offhand at the position of a particular theology, the Christian theology, for example, and proceed immediately to define the 'more' as Jehovah, and the 'union' as his imputation to us of the righteousness of Christ. That would be unfair to other religions, and, from our present standpoint at least, would be an over-belief.

[1] Above, p. 408.

We must begin by using less particularized terms; and, since one of the duties of the science of religions is to keep religion in connection with the rest of science, we shall do well to seek first of all a way of describing the 'more,' which psychologists may also recognize as real. The *subconscious self* is nowadays a well-accredited psychological entity; and I believe that in it we have exactly the mediating term required. Apart from all religious considerations, there is actually and literally more life in our total soul than we are at any time aware of. The exploration of the transmarginal field has hardly yet been seriously undertaken, but what Mr. Myers said in 1892 in his essay on the Subliminal Consciousness[1] is as true as when it was first written: "Each of us is in reality an abiding psychical entity far more extensive than he knows—an individuality which can never express itself completely through any corporeal manifestation. The Self manifests through the organism; but there is always some part of the Self unmanifested; and always, as it seems, some power of organic expression in abeyance or reserve."[2] Much of the content of this larger background against which our conscious being stands out in relief is insignificant. Imperfect memories, silly jingles, inhibitive timidities, 'dissolutive' phenomena of various sorts, as Myers calls them, enter into it for a large part. But in it many of the performances of genius seem also to have their origin; and in our study of conversion, of mystical experiences, and of prayer, we have seen how striking a part invasions from this region play in the religious life.

Let me then propose, as an hypothesis, that whatever it

[1] Proceedings of the Society for Psychical Research, vol. vii. p. 305. For a full statement of Mr. Myers's views, I may refer to his posthumous work, 'Human Personality in the Light of Recent Research,' which, I understand, will be published by Longmans, Green & Co., soon after the appearance of the present volume. Compare also my paper: 'Frederic Myers's Services to Psychology,' in the said Proceedings, part xlii., May, 1901.

[2] Compare the inventory given above on p. 433, and also what is said of the subconscious self on pp. 215–218, 221–222.—In a privately printed syllabus which I receive from Mr. H. Jamyn Brooks, 78 Brondesbury Villas, London, N. W., what Myers terms the subliminal self is called the 'Greater Mind,' and hypotheses concerning it are formulated, of which any one interested in the subject would do well to take cognizance.

may be on its *farther* side, the 'more' with which in religious experience we feel ourselves connected is on its *hither* side the subconscious continuation of our conscious life. Starting thus with a recognized psychological fact as our basis, we seem to preserve a contact with 'science' which the ordinary theologian lacks. At the same time the theologian's contention that the religious man is moved by an external power is vindicated, for it is one of the peculiarities of invasions from the subconscious region to take on objective appearances, and to suggest to the Subject an external control. In the religious life the control is felt as 'higher'; but since on our hypothesis it is primarily the higher faculties of our own hidden mind which are controlling, the sense of union with the power beyond us is a sense of something, not merely apparently, but literally true.

This doorway into the subject seems to me the best one for a science of religions, for it mediates between a number of different points of view. Yet it is only a doorway, and difficulties present themselves as soon as we step through it, and ask how far our transmarginal consciousness carries us if we follow it on its remoter side. Here the over-beliefs begin: here mysticism and the conversion-rapture and Vedantism and transcendental idealism bring in their monistic interpretations[1] and tell us that the finite self rejoins the absolute self, for it was always one with God and identical with the soul of the world.[2] Here the prophets of all the different religions come with their visions, voices, raptures, and other

[1] Compare above, pp. 378 ff.

[2] One more expression of this belief, to increase the reader's familiarity with the notion of it:—

"If this room is full of darkness for thousands of years, and you come in and begin to weep and wail, 'Oh, the darkness,' will the darkness vanish? Bring the light in, strike a match, and light comes in a moment. So what good will it do you to think all your lives, 'Oh, I have done evil, I have made many mistakes'? It requires no ghost to tell us that. Bring in the light, and the evil goes in a moment. Strengthen the real nature, build up yourselves, the effulgent, the resplendent, the ever pure, call that up in every one whom you see. I wish that every one of us had come to such a state that even when we see the vilest of human beings we can see the God within, and instead of condemning, say, 'Rise, thou effulgent One, rise thou who art always pure, rise thou birthless and deathless, rise almighty, and manifest your nature.' . . . This is the highest prayer that the Advaita teaches. This is the one

openings, supposed by each to authenticate his own peculiar faith.

Those of us who are not personally favored with such specific revelations must stand outside of them altogether and, for the present at least, decide that, since they corroborate incompatible theological doctrines, they neutralize one another and leave no fixed result. If we follow any one of them, or if we follow philosophical theory and embrace monistic pantheism on non-mystical grounds, we do so in the exercise of our individual freedom, and build out our religion in the way most congruous with our personal susceptibilities. Among these susceptibilities intellectual ones play a decisive part. Although the religious question is primarily a question of life, of living or not living in the higher union which opens itself to us as a gift, yet the spiritual excitement in which the gift appears a real one will often fail to be aroused in an individual until certain particular intellectual beliefs or ideas which, as we say, come home to him, are touched.[1] These ideas will thus be essential to that individual's religion;—

---

prayer: remembering our nature." . . . "Why does man go out to look for a God? . . . It is your own heart beating, and you did not know, you were mistaking it for something external. He, nearest of the near, my own self, the reality of my own life, my body and my soul.—I am Thee and Thou art Me. That is your own nature. Assert it, manifest it. Not to become pure, you are pure already. You are not to be perfect, you are that already. Every good thought which you think or act upon is simply tearing the veil, as it were, and the purity, the Infinity, the God behind, manifests itself—the eternal Subject of everything, the eternal Witness in this universe, your own Self. Knowledge is, as it were, a lower step, a degradation. We are It already; how to know It?" SWAMI VIVEKANANDA: Addresses, No. XII., Practical Vedanta, part iv. pp. 172, 174, London, 1897; and Lectures, The Real and the Apparent Man, p. 24, abridged.

[1] For instance, here is a case where a person exposed from her birth to Christian ideas had to wait till they came to her clad in spiritistic formulas before the saving experience set in:—

"For myself I can say that spiritualism has saved me. It was revealed to me at a critical moment of my life, and without it I don't know what I should have done. It has taught me to detach myself from worldly things and to place my hope in things to come. Through it I have learned to see in all men, even in those most criminal, even in those from whom I have most suffered, undeveloped brothers to whom I owed assistance, love, and forgiveness. I have learned that I must lose my temper over nothing, despise no one, and

which is as much as to say that over-beliefs in various directions are absolutely indispensable, and that we should treat them with tenderness and tolerance so long as they are not intolerant themselves. As I have elsewhere written, the most interesting and valuable things about a man are usually his over-beliefs.

Disregarding the over-beliefs, and confining ourselves to what is common and generic, we have in *the fact that the conscious person is continuous with a wider self through which saving experiences come*,[1] a positive content of religious experience which, it seems to me, *is literally and objectively true as far as it goes*. If I now proceed to state my own hypothesis about the farther limits of this extension of our personality, I shall be offering my own over-belief—though I know it will appear a sorry under-belief to some of you—for which I can only bespeak the same indulgence which in a converse case I should accord to yours.

The further limits of our being plunge, it seems to me, into an altogether other dimension of existence from the sensible and merely 'understandable' world. Name it the mystical region, or the supernatural region, whichever you choose. So far as our ideal impulses originate in this region (and most of them do originate in it, for we find them possessing us in a way for which we cannot articulately account), we belong to it in a more intimate sense than that in which we belong to the visible world, for we belong in the most intimate sense wherever our ideals belong. Yet the unseen region in question is not merely ideal, for it produces effects in this world. When we commune with it, work is actually done upon our finite

---

pray for all. Most of all I have learned to pray! And although I have still much to learn in this domain, prayer ever brings me more strength, consolation, and comfort. I feel more than ever that I have only made a few steps on the long road of progress; but I look at its length without dismay, for I have confidence that the day will come when all my efforts shall be rewarded. So Spiritualism has a great place in my life, indeed it holds the first place there." Flournoy Collection.

[1] "The influence of the Holy Spirit, exquisitely called the Comforter, is a matter of actual experience, as solid a reality as that of electro-magnetism." W. C. BROWNELL, Scribner's Magazine, vol. xxx. p. 112.

personality, for we are turned into new men, and consequences in the way of conduct follow in the natural world upon our regenerative change.[1] But that which produces effects within another reality must be termed a reality itself, so I feel as if we had no philosophic excuse for calling the unseen or mystical world unreal.

God is the natural appellation, for us Christians at least, for the supreme reality, so I will call this higher part of the universe by the name of God.[2] We and God have business with each other; and in opening ourselves to his influence our deepest destiny is fulfilled. The universe, at those parts of it which our personal being constitutes, takes a turn genuinely for the worse or for the better in proportion as each one of us fulfills or evades God's demands. As far as this goes I probably have you with me, for I only translate into schematic language what I may call the instinctive belief of mankind: God is real since he produces real effects.

The real effects in question, so far as I have as yet admitted them, are exerted on the personal centres of energy of the various subjects, but the spontaneous faith of most of the

[1]That the transaction of opening ourselves, otherwise called prayer, is a perfectly definite one for certain persons, appears abundantly in the preceding lectures. I append another concrete example to reinforce the impression on the reader's mind: —

"Man can learn to transcend these limitations [of finite thought] and draw power and wisdom at will. . . . The divine presence is known through experience. The turning to a higher plane is a distinct act of consciousness. It is not a vague, twilight or semi-conscious experience. It is not an ecstasy; it is not a trance. It is not super-consciousness in the Vedantic sense. It is not due to self-hypnotization. It is a perfectly calm, sane, sound, rational, common-sense shifting of consciousness from the phenomena of sense-perception to the phenomena of seership, from the thought of self to a distinctively higher realm. . . . For example, if the lower self be nervous, anxious, tense, one can in a few moments compel it to be calm. This is not done by a word simply. Again I say, it is not hypnotism. It is by the exercise of power. One feels the spirit of peace as definitely as heat is perceived on a hot summer day. The power can be as surely used as the sun's rays can be focused and made to do work, to set fire to wood." The Higher Law, vol. iv. pp. 4, 6, Boston, August, 1901.

[2]Transcendentalists are fond of the term 'Over-soul,' but as a rule they use it in an intellectualist sense, as meaning only a medium of communion. 'God' is a causal agent as well as a medium of communion, and that is the aspect which I wish to emphasize.

subjects is that they embrace a wider sphere than this. Most religious men believe (or 'know,' if they be mystical) that not only they themselves, but the whole universe of beings to whom the God is present, are secure in his parental hands. There is a sense, a dimension, they are sure, in which we are *all* saved, in spite of the gates of hell and all adverse terrestrial appearances. God's existence is the guarantee of an ideal order that shall be permanently preserved. This world may indeed, as science assures us, some day burn up or freeze; but if it is part of his order, the old ideals are sure to be brought else-where to fruition, so that where God is, tragedy is only pro-visional and partial, and shipwreck and dissolution are not the absolutely final things. Only when this farther step of faith concerning God is taken, and remote objective consequences are predicted, does religion, as it seems to me, get wholly free from the first immediate subjective experience, and bring a *real hypothesis* into play. A good hypothesis in science must have other properties than those of the phenomenon it is immediately invoked to explain, otherwise it is not prolific enough. God, meaning only what enters into the religious man's experience of union, falls short of being an hypothesis of this more useful order. He needs to enter into wider cosmic relations in order to justify the subject's absolute con-fidence and peace.

That the God with whom, starting from the hither side of our own extra-marginal self, we come at its remoter margin into commerce should be the absolute world-ruler, is of course a very considerable over-belief. Over-belief as it is, though, it is an article of almost every one's religion. Most of us pretend in some way to prop it upon our philosophy, but the philosophy itself is really propped upon this faith. What is this but to say that Religion, in her fullest exercise of func-tion, is not a mere illumination of facts already elsewhere given, not a mere passion, like love, which views things in a rosier light. It is indeed that, as we have seen abundantly. But it is something more, namely, a postulator of new *facts* as well. The world interpreted religiously is not the materialistic world over again, with an altered expression; it must have, over and above the altered expression, *a natural constitution* different at some point from that which a materialistic world would have. It must be such that different events can be expected in it, different conduct must be required.

This thoroughly 'pragmatic' view of religion has usually been taken as a matter of course by common men. They have interpolated divine miracles into the field of nature, they have built a heaven out beyond the grave. It is only transcendentalist metaphysicians who think that, without adding any concrete details to Nature, or subtracting any, but by simply calling it the expression of absolute spirit, you make it more divine just as it stands. I believe the pragmatic way of taking religion to be the deeper way. It gives it body as well as soul, it makes it claim, as everything real must claim, some characteristic realm of fact as its very own. What the more characteristically divine facts are, apart from the actual inflow of energy in the faith-state and the prayer-state, I know not. But the over-belief on which I am ready to make my personal venture is that they exist. The whole drift of my education goes to persuade me that the world of our present consciousness is only one out of many worlds of consciousness that exist, and that those other worlds must contain experiences which have a meaning for our life also; and that although in the main their experiences and those of this world keep discrete, yet the two become continuous at certain points, and higher energies filter in. By being faithful in my poor measure to this over-belief, I seem to myself to keep more sane and true. I *can*, of course, put myself into the sectarian scientist's attitude, and imagine vividly that the world of sensations and of scientific laws and objects may be all. But whenever I do this, I hear that inward monitor of which W. K. Clifford once wrote, whispering the word 'bosh!' Humbug is humbug, even though it bear the scientific name, and the total expression of human experience, as I view it objectively, invincibly urges me beyond the narrow 'scientific' bounds. Assuredly, the real world is of a different temperament,—more intricately built than physical science allows. So my objective and my subjective conscience both hold me to the over-belief which I express. Who knows whether the faithfulness of individuals here below to their own poor over-beliefs may not actually help God in turn to be more effectively faithful to his own greater tasks?

POSTSCRIPT

IN WRITING my concluding lecture I had to aim so much at simplification that I fear that my general philosophic position received so scant a statement as hardly to be intelligible to some of my readers. I therefore add this epilogue, which must also be so brief as possibly to remedy but little the defect. In a later work I may be enabled to state my position more amply and consequently more clearly.

Originality cannot be expected in a field like this, where all the attitudes and tempers that are possible have been exhibited in literature long ago, and where any new writer can immediately be classed under a familiar head. If one should make a division of all thinkers into naturalists and supernaturalists, I should undoubtedly have to go, along with most philosophers, into the supernaturalist branch. But there is a crasser and a more refined supernaturalism, and it is to the refined division that most philosophers at the present day belong. If not regular transcendental idealists, they at least obey the Kantian direction enough to bar out ideal entities from interfering causally in the course of phenomenal events. Refined supernaturalism is universalistic supernaturalism; for the 'crasser' variety 'piecemeal' supernaturalism would perhaps be the better name. It went with that older theology which today is supposed to reign only among uneducated people, or to be found among the few belated professors of the dualisms which Kant is thought to have displaced. It admits miracles and providential leadings, and finds no intellectual difficulty in mixing the ideal and the real worlds together by interpolating influences from the ideal region among the forces that causally determine the real world's details. In this the refined supernaturalists think that it muddles disparate dimensions of existence. For them the world of the ideal has no efficient causality, and never bursts into the world of phenomena at particular points. The ideal world, for them, is not a world of facts, but only of the meaning of facts; it is a point of view for judging facts. It appertains to a different '-ology,' and inhabits a different dimension of being altogether from that in which existential propositions obtain. It cannot get down

464

upon the flat level of experience and interpolate itself piece-meal between distinct portions of nature, as those who be-lieve, for example, in divine aid coming in response to prayer, are bound to think it must.

Notwithstanding my own inability to accept either popular Christianity or scholastic theism, I suppose that my belief that in communion with the Ideal new force comes into the world, and new departures are made here below, subjects me to being classed among the supernaturalists of the piecemeal or crasser type. Universalistic supernaturalism surrenders, it seems to me, too easily to naturalism. It takes the facts of physical science at their face-value, and leaves the laws of life just as naturalism finds them, with no hope of remedy, in case their fruits are bad. It confines itself to sentiments about life as a whole, sentiments which may be admiring and adoring, but which need not be so, as the existence of systematic pes-simism proves. In this universalistic way of taking the ideal world, the essence of practical religion seems to me to evap-orate. Both instinctively and for logical reasons, I find it hard to believe that principles can exist which make no difference in facts.[1] But all facts are particular facts, and the whole inter-est of the question of God's existence seems to me to lie in the consequences for particulars which that existence may be expected to entail. That no concrete particular of experience should alter its complexion in consequence of a God being there seems to me an incredible proposition, and yet it is the thesis to which (implicitly at any rate) refined supernaturalism

---

[1]Transcendental idealism, of course, insists that its ideal world makes *this* difference, that facts *exist*. We owe it to the Absolute that we have a world of fact at all. 'A world' of fact!—that exactly is the trouble. An entire world is the smallest unit with which the Absolute can work, whereas to our finite minds work for the better ought to be done within this world, setting in at single points. Our difficulties and our ideals are all piecemeal affairs, but the Absolute can do no piecework for us; so that all the interests which our poor souls compass raise their heads too late. We should have spoken earlier, prayed for another world absolutely, before this world was born. It is strange, I have heard a friend say, to see this blind corner into which Chris-tian thought has worked itself at last, with its God who can raise no partic-ular weight whatever, who can help us with no private burden, and who is on the side of our enemies as much as he is on our own. Odd evolution from the God of David's psalms!

seems to cling. It is only with experience *en bloc*, it says, that the Absolute maintains relations. It condescends to no trans-actions of detail.

I am ignorant of Buddhism and speak under correction, and merely in order the better to describe my general point of view; but as I apprehend the Buddhistic doctrine of Karma, I agree in principle with that. All supernaturalists ad-mit that facts are under the judgment of higher law; but for Buddhism as I interpret it, and for religion generally so far as it remains unweakened by transcendentalistic metaphysics, the word 'judgment' here means no such bare academic verdict or platonic appreciation as it means in Vedantic or modern absolutist systems; it carries, on the contrary, *execution* with it, is *in rebus* as well as *post rem*, and operates 'causally' as partial factor in the total fact. The universe becomes a gnosticism[1] pure and simple on any other terms. But this view that judgment and execution go together is that of the crasser supernaturalist way of thinking, so the present volume must on the whole be classed with the other expressions of that creed.

I state the matter thus bluntly, because the current of thought in academic circles runs against me, and I feel like a man who must set his back against an open door quickly if he does not wish to see it closed and locked. In spite of its being so shocking to the reigning intellectual tastes, I believe that a candid consideration of piecemeal supernaturalism and a complete discussion of all its metaphysical bearings will show it to be the hypothesis by which the largest number of legitimate requirements are met. That of course would be a program for other books than this; what I now say suffi-ciently indicates to the philosophic reader the place where I belong.

If asked just where the differences in fact which are due to God's existence come in, I should have to say that in general I have no hypothesis to offer beyond what the phenomenon of 'prayerful communion,' especially when certain kinds of in-cursion from the subconscious region take part in it, imme-

[1] See my Will to Believe and other Essays in Popular Philosophy, 1897, p. 165.

diately suggests. The appearance is that in this phenomenon something ideal, which in one sense is part of ourselves and in another sense is not ourselves, actually exerts an influence, raises our centre of personal energy, and produces regenerative effects unattainable in other ways. If, then, there be a wider world of being than that of our every-day consciousness, if in it there be forces whose effects on us are intermittent, if one facilitating condition of the effects be the openness of the 'subliminal' door, we have the elements of a theory to which the phenomena of religious life lend plausibility. I am so impressed by the importance of these phenomena that I adopt the hypothesis which they so naturally suggest. At these places at least, I say, it would seem as though transmundane energies, God, if you will, produced immediate effects within the natural world to which the rest of our experience belongs.

The difference in natural 'fact' which most of us would assign as the first difference which the existence of a God ought to make would, I imagine, be personal immortality. Religion, in fact, for the great majority of our own race *means* immortality, and nothing else. God is the producer of immortality; and whoever has doubts of immortality is written down as an atheist without farther trial. I have said nothing in my lectures about immortality or the belief therein, for to me it seems a secondary point. If only our ideals are cared for in 'eternity,' I do not see why we might not be willing to resign their care to other hands than ours. Yet I sympathize with the urgent impulse to be present ourselves, and in the conflict of impulses, both of them so vague yet both of them noble, I know not how to decide. It seems to me that it is eminently a case for facts to testify. Facts, I think, are yet lacking to prove 'spirit-return,' though I have the highest respect for the patient labors of Messrs. Myers, Hodgson, and Hyslop, and am somewhat impressed by their favorable conclusions. I consequently leave the matter open, with this brief word to save the reader from a possible perplexity as to why immortality got no mention in the body of this book.

The ideal power with which we feel ourselves in connection, the 'God' of ordinary men, is, both by ordinary men and by philosophers, endowed with certain of those metaphysical attributes which in the lecture on philosophy I treated with such disrespect. He is assumed as a matter of course to be 'one and only' and to be 'infinite'; and the notion of many finite gods is one which hardly any one thinks it worth while to consider, and still less to uphold. Nevertheless, in the interests of intellectual clearness, I feel bound to say that religious experience, as we have studied it, cannot be cited as unequivocally supporting the infinitist belief. The only thing that it unequivocally testifies to is that we can experience union with *something* larger than ourselves and in that union find our greatest peace. Philosophy, with its passion for unity, and mysticism with its mono-ideistic bent, both 'pass to the limit' and identify the something with a unique God who is the all-inclusive soul of the world. Popular opinion, respectful to their authority, follows the example which they set.

Meanwhile the practical needs and experiences of religion seem to me sufficiently met by the belief that beyond each man and in a fashion continuous with him there exists a larger power which is friendly to him and to his ideals. All that the facts require is that the power should be both other and larger than our conscious selves. Anything larger will do, if only it be large enough to trust for the next step. It need not be infinite, it need not be solitary. It might conceivably even be only a larger and more godlike self, of which the present self would then be but the mutilated expression, and the universe might conceivably be a collection of such selves, of different degrees of inclusiveness, with no absolute unity realized in it at all.[1] Thus would a sort of polytheism return upon us—a polytheism which I do not on this occasion defend, for my only aim at present is to keep the testimony of religious experience clearly within its proper bounds.[2]

Upholders of the monistic view will say to such a polytheism (which, by the way, has always been the real religion of common people, and is so still to-day) that unless there be one all-inclusive God, our guarantee of security is left imperfect. In the Absolute, and in the Absolute only, *all* is saved. If there be different gods, each caring for his part, some por-

---

[1] Such a notion is suggested in my Ingersoll Lecture On Human Immortality, Boston and London, 1899.
[2] Cf. above pp. 124–125.

tion of some of us might not be covered with divine protection, and our religious consolation would thus fail to be complete. It goes back to what was said on pages 124–126, about the possibility of there being portions of the universe that may irretrievably be lost. Common sense is less sweeping in its demands than philosophy or mysticism have been wont to be, and can suffer the notion of this world being partly saved and partly lost. The ordinary moralistic state of mind makes the salvation of the world conditional upon the success with which each unit does its part. Partial and conditional salvation is in fact a most familiar notion when taken in the abstract, the only difficulty being to determine the details. Some men are even disinterested enough to be willing to be in the unsaved remnant as far as their persons go, if only they can be persuaded that their cause will prevail—all of us are willing, whenever our activity-excitement rises sufficiently high. I think, in fact, that a final philosophy of religion will have to consider the pluralistic hypothesis more seriously than it has hitherto been willing to consider it. For practical life at any rate, the *chance* of salvation is enough. No fact in human nature is more characteristic than its willingness to live on a chance. The existence of the chance makes the difference, as Edmund Gurney says, between a life of which the keynote is resignation and a life of which the keynote is hope.[1] But all these statements are unsatisfactory from their brevity, and I can only say that I hope to return to the same questions in another book.

[1] Tertium Quid, 1887, p. 99. See also pp. 148, 149.

Index

PRAGMATISM

A New Name for Some Old Ways of Thinking

POPULAR LECTURES ON PHILOSOPHY

TO THE MEMORY OF JOHN STUART MILL
FROM WHOM I FIRST LEARNED THE
PRAGMATIC OPENNESS OF MIND
AND WHOM MY FANCY LIKES TO PICTURE AS
OUR LEADER
WERE HE ALIVE TO-DAY

Preface

THE LECTURES that follow were delivered at the Lowell Institute in Boston in November and December, 1906, and in January, 1907, at Columbia University, in New York. They are printed as delivered, without developments or notes. The pragmatic movement, so-called—I do not like the name, but apparently it is too late to change it—seems to have rather suddenly precipitated itself out of the air. A number of tendencies that have always existed in philosophy have all at once become conscious of themselves collectively, and of their combined mission; and this has occurred in so many countries, and from so many different points of view, that much unconcerted statement has resulted. I have sought to unify the picture as it presents itself to my own eyes, dealing in broad strokes, and avoiding minute controversy. Much futile controversy might have been avoided, I believe, if our critics had been willing to wait until we got our message fairly out.

If my lectures interest any reader in the general subject, he will doubtless wish to read farther. I therefore give him a few references.

In America, JOHN DEWEY's 'Studies in Logical Theory' are the foundation. Read also by DEWEY the articles in the *Philosophical Review*, vol. xv, pp. 113 and 465, in *Mind*, vol. xv, p. 293, and in the *Journal of Philosophy*, vol. iv, p. 197.

Probably the best statements to begin with, however, are F. C. S. SCHILLER's in his 'Studies in Humanism,' especially the essays numbered i, v, vi, vii, xviii and xix. His previous essays and in general the polemic literature of the subject are fully referred to in his footnotes.

Furthermore, see G. MILHAUD: *le Rationnel*, 1898, and the fine articles by LE ROY in the *Revue de Métaphysique*, vols. 7, 8 and 9. Also articles by BLONDEL and DE SAILLY in the *Annales de Philosophie Chrétienne*, 4me Série, vols. 2 and 3. PAPINI announces a book on Pragmatism, in the French language, to be published very soon.

To avoid one misunderstanding at least, let me say that there is no logical connexion between pragmatism, as I understand it, and a doctrine which I have recently set forth as 'radical empiricism.' The latter stands on its own feet. One may entirely reject it and still be a pragmatist.

HARVARD UNIVERSITY, April, 1907.

Contents

LECTURE IV

LECTURE V

LECTURE VI

LECTURE VII

LECTURE VIII

LECTURE I

THE PRESENT DILEMMA IN PHILOSOPHY

IN THE PREFACE to that admirable collection of essays of his called 'Heretics,' Mr. Chesterton writes these words: "There are some people—and I am one of them—who think that the most practical and important thing about a man is still his view of the universe. We think that for a landlady considering a lodger it is important to know his income, but still more important to know his philosophy. We think that for a general about to fight an enemy it is important to know the enemy's numbers, but still more important to know the enemy's philosophy. We think the question is not whether the theory of the cosmos affects matters, but whether in the long run anything else affects them."

I think with Mr. Chesterton in this matter. I know that you, ladies and gentlemen, have a philosophy, each and all of you, and that the most interesting and important thing about you is the way in which it determines the perspective in your several worlds. You know the same of me. And yet I confess to a certain tremor at the audacity of the enterprise which I am about to begin. For the philosophy which is so important in each of us is not a technical matter; it is our more or less dumb sense of what life honestly and deeply means. It is only partly got from books; it is our individual way of just seeing and feeling the total push and pressure of the cosmos. I have no right to assume that many of you are students of the cosmos in the classroom sense, yet here I stand desirous of interesting you in a philosophy which to no small extent has to be technically treated. I wish to fill you with sympathy with a contemporaneous tendency in which I profoundly believe, and yet I have to talk like a professor to you who are not students. Whatever universe a professor believes in must at any rate be a universe that lends itself to lengthy discourse. A universe definable in two sentences is something for which the professorial intellect has no use. No faith in anything of that cheap kind! I have heard friends and colleagues try to popularize philosophy in this very hall, but they soon grew dry, and then technical, and the results were only partially encouraging. So my enterprise is a bold one. The founder of pragmatism himself recently gave a course of lectures at the Lowell Institute with that very word in its title,—flashes of brilliant light relieved against Cimmerian darkness! None of us, I fancy, understood *all* that he said—yet here I stand, making a very similar venture.

I risk it because the very lectures I speak of *drew*—they brought good audiences. There is, it must be confessed, a curious fascination in hearing deep things talked about, even though neither we nor the disputants understand them. We get the problematic thrill, we feel the presence of the vastness. Let a controversy begin in a smoking-room anywhere, about free-will or God's omniscience, or good and evil, and see how every one in the place pricks up his ears. Philosophy's results concern us all most vitally, and philosophy's queerest arguments tickle agreeably our sense of subtlety and ingenuity.

Believing in philosophy myself devoutly, and believing also that a kind of new dawn is breaking upon us philosophers, I feel impelled, *per fas aut nefas*, to try to impart to you some news of the situation.

Philosophy is at once the most sublime and the most trivial of human pursuits. It works in the minutest crannies and it opens out the widest vistas. It 'bakes no bread,' as has been said, but it can inspire our souls with courage; and repugnant as its manners, its doubting and challenging, its quibbling and dialectics, often are to common people, no one of us can get along without the far-flashing beams of light it sends over the world's perspectives. These illuminations at least, and the contrast-effects of darkness and mystery that accompany them, give to what it says an interest that is much more than professional.

The history of philosophy is to a great extent that of a certain clash of human temperaments. Undignified as such a treatment may seem to some of my colleagues, I shall have to take account of this clash and explain a good many of the divergencies of philosophers by it. Of whatever temperament a professional philosopher is, he tries, when philosophizing, to sink the fact of his temperament. Temperament is no conventionally recognized reason, so he urges impersonal reasons only for his conclusions. Yet his temperament really gives him a stronger bias than any of his more strictly objective premises. It loads the evidence for him one way or the other, making for a more sentimental or a more hard-hearted view of the universe, just as this fact or that principle would. He *trusts* his temperament. Wanting a universe that suits it, he believes in any representation of the universe that does suit it. He feels men of opposite temper to be out of key with the world's character, and in his heart considers them incompetent and 'not in it,' in the philosophic business, even though they may far excel him in dialectical ability.

Yet in the forum he can make no claim, on the bare ground of his temperament, to superior discernment or authority. There arises thus a certain insincerity in our philosophic discussions: the potentest of all our premises is never mentioned. I am sure it would contribute to clearness if in these lectures we should break this rule and mention it, and I accordingly feel free to do so.

Of course I am talking here of very positively marked men, men of radical idiosyncracy, who have set their stamp and likeness on philosophy and figure in its history. Plato, Locke, Hegel, Spencer, are such temperamental thinkers. Most of us have, of course, no very definite intellectual temperament, we are a mixture of opposite ingredients, each one present very moderately. We hardly know our own preferences in abstract matters; some of us are easily talked out of them, and end by following the fashion or taking up with the beliefs of the most impressive philosopher in our neighborhood, whoever he may be. But the one thing that has *counted* so far in philosophy is that a man should *see* things, see them straight in his own peculiar way, and be dissatisfied with any opposite way of seeing them. There is no reason to suppose that this strong temperamental vision is from now onward to count no longer in the history of man's beliefs.

Now the particular difference of temperament that I have in mind in making these remarks is one that has counted in literature, art, government, and manners as well as in philosophy. In manners we find formalists and free-and-easy persons. In government, authoritarians and anarchists. In literature, purists or academicals, and realists. In art, classics and romantics. You recognize these contrasts as familiar; well, in philosophy we have a very similar contrast expressed in the pair of terms 'rationalist' and 'empiricist,' 'empiricist' meaning your lover of facts in all their crude variety, 'rationalist' meaning your devotee to abstract and eternal principles. No one can live an hour without both facts and principles, so it is a difference rather of emphasis; yet it breeds antipathies of the most pungent character between those who lay the emphasis differently; and we shall find it extraordinarily convenient to express a certain contrast in men's ways of taking their universe, by talking of the 'empiricist' and of the 'rationalist' temper. These terms make the contrast simple and massive.

More simple and massive than are usually the men of whom the terms are predicated. For every sort of permutation and combination is possible in human nature; and if I now proceed to define more fully what I have in mind when I speak of rationalists and empiricists, by adding to each of those titles some secondary qualifying characteristics, I beg you to regard my conduct as to a certain extent arbitrary. I select types of combination that nature offers very frequently, but by no means uniformly, and I select them solely for their convenience in helping me to my ulterior purpose of characterizing pragmatism. Historically we find the terms 'intellectualism' and 'sensationalism' used as synonyms of 'rationalism' and 'empiricism.' Well, nature seems to combine most frequently with intellectualism an idealistic and optimistic tendency. Empiricists on the other hand are not uncommonly materialistic, and their optimism is apt to be decidedly conditional and tremulous. Rationalism is always monistic. It starts from wholes and universals, and makes much of the unity of things. Empiricism starts from the parts, and makes of the whole a collection—is not averse therefore to calling itself pluralistic. Rationalism usually considers itself more religious than empiricism, but there is much to say about this claim, so I merely mention it. It is a true claim when the individual rationalist is what is called a man of feeling, and when the individual empiricist prides himself on being hardheaded. In that case the rationalist will usually also be in favor of what is called free-will, and the empiricist will be a fatalist—I use the terms most popularly current. The rationalist finally will be of dogmatic temper in his affirmations, while the empiricist may be more sceptical and open to discussion.

I will write these traits down in two columns. I think you will practically recognize the two types of mental make-up that I mean if I head the columns by the titles 'tender-minded' and 'tough-minded' respectively.

THE TENDER-MINDED.	THE TOUGH-MINDED.
Rationalistic (going by 'principles'),	Empiricist (going by 'facts'),
Intellectualistic,	Sensationalistic,
Idealistic,	Materialistic,
Optimistic,	Pessimistic,
Religious,	Irreligious,
Free-willist,	Fatalistic,
Monistic,	Pluralistic,
Dogmatical.	Sceptical.

Pray postpone for a moment the question whether the two contrasted mixtures which I have written down are each inwardly coherent and self-consistent or not—I shall very soon have a good deal to say on that point. It suffices for our immediate purpose that tender-minded and tough-minded people, characterized as I have written them down, do both exist. Each of you probably knows some well-marked example of each type, and you know what each example thinks of the example on the other side of the line. They have a low opinion of each other. Their antagonism, whenever as individuals their temperaments have been intense, has formed in all ages a part of the philosophic atmosphere of the time. It forms a part of the philosophic atmosphere to-day. The tough think of the tender as sentimentalists and soft-heads. The tender feel the tough to be unrefined, callous, or brutal. Their mutual reaction is very much like that that takes place when Bostonian tourists mingle with a population like that of Cripple Creek. Each type believes the other to be inferior to itself; but disdain in the one case is mingled with amusement, in the other it has a dash of fear.

Now, as I have already insisted, few of us are tender-foot Bostonians pure and simple, and few are typical Rocky Mountain toughs, in philosophy. Most of us have a hankering for the good things on both sides of the line. Facts are good, of course—give us lots of facts. Principles are good—give us plenty of principles. The world is indubitably one if you look at it in one way, but as indubitably is it many, if you look at it in another. It is both one and many—let us adopt a sort of pluralistic monism. Everything of course is necessarily determined, and yet of course our wills are free: a sort of free-will determinism is the true philosophy. The evil of the parts is undeniable, but the whole can't be evil: so practical pessimism may be combined with metaphysical optimism. And so forth—your ordinary philosophic layman never being a radical, never straightening out his system, but living vaguely in one plausible compartment of it or another to suit the temptations of successive hours.

But some of us are more than mere laymen in philosophy. We are worthy of the name of amateur athletes, and are vexed by too much inconsistency and vacillation in our creed. We cannot preserve a good intellectual conscience so long as we keep mixing incompatibles from opposite sides of the line.

And now I come to the first positively important point which I wish to make. Never were as many men of a decidedly empiricist proclivity in existence as there are at the present day. Our children, one may say, are almost born scientific. But our esteem for facts has not neutralized in us all religiousness. It is itself almost religious. Our scientific temper is devout. Now take a man of this type, and let him be also a philosophic amateur, unwilling to mix a hodge-podge system after the fashion of a common layman, and what does he find his situation to be, in this blessed year of our Lord 1906? He wants facts; he wants science; but he also wants a religion. And being an amateur and not an independent originator in philosophy he naturally looks for guidance to the experts and professionals whom he finds already in the field. A very large number of you here present, possibly a majority of you, are amateurs of just this sort.

Now what kinds of philosophy do you find actually offered to meet your need? You find an empirical philosophy that is not religious enough, and a religious philosophy that is not empirical enough for your purpose. If you look to the quarter where facts are most considered you find the whole tough-minded program in operation, and the 'conflict between science and religion' in full blast. Either it is that Rocky Mountain tough of a Haeckel with his materialistic monism, his ether-god and his jest at your God as a 'gaseous verte-brate'; or it is Spencer treating the world's history as a redis-tribution of matter and motion solely, and bowing religion politely out at the front door:—she may indeed continue to exist, but she must never show her face inside the temple.

For a hundred and fifty years past the progress of science has seemed to mean the enlargement of the material universe and the diminution of man's importance. The result is what one may call the growth of naturalistic or positivistic feeling. Man is no lawgiver to nature, he is an absorber. She it is who stands firm; he it is who must accommodate himself. Let him record truth, inhuman though it be, and submit to it! The romantic spontaneity and courage are gone, the vision is ma-terialistic and depressing. Ideals appear as inert by-products of physiology; what is higher is explained by what is lower and treated forever as a case of 'nothing but'—nothing but something else of a quite inferior sort. You get, in short, a materialistic universe, in which only the tough-minded find themselves congenially at home.

If now, on the other hand, you turn to the religious quarter for consolation, and take counsel of the tender-minded phi-losophies, what do you find?

Religious philosophy in our day and generation is, among us English-reading people, of two main types. One of these is more radical and aggressive, the other has more the air of fighting a slow retreat. By the more radical wing of religious philosophy I mean the so-called transcendental idealism of the Anglo-Hegelian school, the philosophy of such men as Green, the Cairds, Bosanquet, and Royce. This philosophy has greatly influenced the more studious members of our protes-tant ministry. It is pantheistic, and undoubtedly it has already blunted the edge of the traditional theism in protestantism at large.

That theism remains, however. It is the lineal descendant, through one stage of concession after another, of the dog-matic scholastic theism still taught rigorously in the semi-

naries of the catholic church. For a long time it used to be
called among us the philosophy of the Scottish school. It is
what I meant by the philosophy that has the air of fighting a
slow retreat. Between the encroachments of the hegelians
and other philosophers of the 'Absolute,' on the one hand,
and those of the scientific evolutionists and agnostics, on the
other, the men that give us this kind of a philosophy, James
Martineau, Professor Bowne, Professor Ladd and others,
must feel themselves rather tightly squeezed. Fair-minded
and candid as you like, this philosophy is not radical in temper. It is eclectic, a thing of compromises, that seeks a *modus
vivendi* above all things. It accepts the facts of Darwinism,
the facts of cerebral physiology, but it does nothing active or
enthusiastic with them. It lacks the victorious and aggressive
note. It lacks *prestige* in consequence; whereas absolutism
has a certain *prestige* due to the more radical style of it.

These two systems are what you have to choose between if
you turn to the tender-minded school. And if you are the
lovers of facts I have supposed you to be, you find the trail
of the serpent of rationalism, of intellectualism, over everything that lies on that side of the line. You escape indeed the
materialism that goes with the reigning empiricism; but you
pay for your escape by losing contact with the concrete parts
of life. The more absolutistic philosophers dwell on so high a
level of abstraction that they never even try to come down.
The absolute mind which they offer us, the mind that makes
our universe by thinking it, might, for aught they show us to
the contrary, have made any one of a million other universes
just as well as this. You can deduce no single actual particular
from the notion of it. It is compatible with any state of things
whatever being true here below. And the theistic God is almost as sterile a principle. You have to go to the world which
he has created to get any inkling of his actual character: he is
the kind of god that has once for all made that kind of a
world. The God of the theistic writers lives on as purely abstract heights as does the Absolute. Absolutism has a certain
sweep and dash about it, while the usual theism is more insipid, but both are equally remote and vacuous. What *you*
want is a philosophy that will not only exercise your powers

of intellectual abstraction, but that will make some positive connexion with this actual world of finite human lives.

You want a system that will combine both things, the scientific loyalty to facts and willingness to take account of them, the spirit of adaptation and accommodation, in short, but also the old confidence in human values and the resultant spontaneity, whether of the religious or of the romantic type. And this is then your dilemma: you find the two parts of your *quaesitum* hopelessly separated. You find empiricism with inhumanism and irreligion; or else you find a rationalistic philosophy that indeed may call itself religious, but that keeps out of all definite touch with concrete facts and joys and sorrows.

I am not sure how many of you live close enough to philosophy to realize fully what I mean by this last reproach, so I will dwell a little longer on that unreality in all rationalistic systems by which your serious believer in facts is so apt to feel repelled.

I wish that I had saved the first couple of pages of a thesis which a student handed me a year or two ago. They illustrated my point so clearly that I am sorry I can not read them to you now. This young man, who was a graduate of some Western college, began by saying that he had always taken for granted that when you entered a philosophic classroom you had to open relations with a universe entirely distinct from the one you left behind you in the street. The two were supposed, he said, to have so little to do with each other, that you could not possibly occupy your mind with them at the same time. The world of concrete personal experiences to which the street belongs is multitudinous beyond imagination, tangled, muddy, painful and perplexed. The world to which your philosophy-professor introduces you is simple, clean and noble. The contradictions of real life are absent from it. Its architecture is classic. Principles of reason trace its outlines, logical necessities cement its parts. Purity and dignity are what it most expresses. It is a kind of marble temple shining on a hill.

In point of fact it is far less an account of this actual world than a clear addition built upon it, a classic sanctuary in which the rationalist fancy may take refuge from the intolerably confused and gothic character which mere facts present. It is no *explanation* of our concrete universe, it is another thing altogether, a substitute for it, a remedy, a way of escape.

Its temperament, if I may use the word temperament here, is utterly alien to the temperament of existence in the concrete. *Refinement* is what characterizes our intellectualist philosophies. They exquisitely satisfy that craving for a refined object of contemplation which is so powerful an appetite of the mind. But I ask you in all seriousness to look abroad on this colossal universe of concrete facts, on their awful bewilderments, their surprises and cruelties, on the wildness which they show, and then to tell me whether 'refined' is the one inevitable descriptive adjective that springs to your lips.

Refinement has its place in things, true enough. But a philosophy that breathes out nothing but refinement will never satisfy the empiricist temper of mind. It will seem rather a monument of artificiality. So we find men of science preferring to turn their backs on metaphysics as on something altogether cloistered and spectral, and practical men shaking philosophy's dust off their feet and following the call of the wild.

Truly there is something a little ghastly in the satisfaction with which a pure but unreal system will fill a rationalist mind. Leibnitz was a rationalist mind, with infinitely more interest in facts than most rationalist minds can show. Yet if you wish for superficiality incarnate, you have only to read that charmingly written 'Théodicée' of his, in which he sought to justify the ways of God to man, and to prove that the world we live in is the best of possible worlds. Let me quote a specimen of what I mean.

Among other obstacles to his optimistic philosophy, it falls to Leibnitz to consider the number of the eternally damned. That it is infinitely greater, in our human case, than that of those saved, he assumes as a premise from the theologians, and then proceeds to argue in this way. Even then, he says:

"The evil will appear as almost nothing in comparison with the good, if we once consider the real magnitude of the City of God. Coelius Secundus Curio has written a little book, 'De Amplitudine Regni Coelestis,' which was reprinted not long ago. But he failed to compass the extent of the kingdom of the heavens. The ancients had small ideas of the works of God. . . . It seemed to them that only our earth had inhabitants, and even the notion of our antipodes gave them pause. The rest of the world for them consisted of some shining globes and a few crystalline spheres. But to-day, whatever be the limits that we may grant or refuse to the Universe we must recognize in it a countless number of globes, as big as ours or bigger, which have just as much right as it has to support rational inhabitants, tho it does not follow that these need all be men. Our earth is only one among the six principal satellites of our sun. As all the fixed stars are suns, one sees how small a place among visible things our earth takes up, since it is only a satellite of one among them. Now all these suns *may* be inhabited by none but happy creatures; and nothing obliges us to believe that the number of damned persons is very great; for *a very few instances and samples suffice for the utility which good draws from evil.* Moreover, since there is no reason to suppose that there are stars everywhere, may there not be a great space beyond the region of the stars? And this immense space, surrounding all this region, . . . may be replete with happiness and glory. . . . What now becomes of the consideration of our Earth and of its denizens? Does it not dwindle to something incomparably less than a physical point, since our Earth is but a point compared with the distance of the fixed stars. Thus the part of the Universe which we know, being almost lost in nothingness compared with that which is unknown to us, but which we are yet obliged to admit; and all the evils that we know lying in this almost-nothing; it follows that the evils may be almost-nothing in comparison with the goods that the Universe contains."

Leibnitz continues elsewhere:

"There is a kind of justice which aims neither at the amendment of the criminal, nor at furnishing an example to others, nor at the reparation of the injury. This justice is founded in pure fitness, which finds a certain satisfaction in the expiation of a wicked deed. The Socinians and Hobbes objected to this punitive justice, which is properly vindictive justice, and which God has reserved for himself at many junctures. . . . It is always founded in the fitness of things, and satisfies not

only the offended party, but all wise lookers-on, even as beautiful music or a fine piece of architecture satisfies a well-
constituted mind. It is thus that the torments of the damned
continue, even tho they serve no longer to turn any one away
from sin, and that the rewards of the blest continue, even tho
they confirm no one in good ways. The damned draw to
themselves ever new penalties by their continuing sins, and
the blest attract ever fresh joys by their unceasing progress in
good. Both facts are founded on the principle of fitness, . . .
for God has made all things harmonious in perfection as I
have already said."

Leibnitz's feeble grasp of reality is too obvious to need
comment from me. It is evident that no realistic image of the
experience of a damned soul had ever approached the portals
of his mind. Nor had it occurred to him that the smaller is
the number of 'samples' of the genus 'lost-soul' whom God
throws as a sop to the eternal fitness, the more unequitably
grounded is the glory of the blest. What he gives us is a cold
literary exercise, whose cheerful substance even hell-fire does
not warm.

And do not tell me that to show the shallowness of rationalist philosophizing I have had to go back to a shallow wig-
pated age. The optimism of present-day rationalism sounds
just as shallow to the fact-loving mind. The actual universe is
a thing wide open, but rationalism makes systems, and systems must be closed. For men in practical life perfection is
something far off and still in process of achievement. This for
rationalism is but the illusion of the finite and relative: the
absolute ground of things is a perfection eternally complete.

I find a fine example of revolt against the airy and shallow
optimism of current religious philosophy in a publication of
that valiant anarchistic writer Morrison I. Swift. Mr. Swift's
anarchism goes a little farther than mine does, but I confess
that I sympathize a good deal, and some of you, I know, will
sympathize heartily with his dissatisfaction with the idealistic
optimisms now in vogue. He begins his pamphlet on 'Human
Submission' with a series of city reporter's items from newspapers (suicides, deaths from starvation, and the like) as specimens of our civilized régime. For instance:

"After trudging through the snow from one end of the city

to the other in the vain hope of securing employment, and with his wife and six children without food and ordered to leave their home in an upper east-side tenement-house because of non-payment of rent, John Corcoran, a clerk, to-day ended his life by drinking carbolic acid. Corcoran lost his position three weeks ago through illness, and during the period of idleness his scanty savings disappeared. Yesterday he obtained work with a gang of city snow-shovelers, but he was too weak from illness, and was forced to quit after an hour's trial with the shovel. Then the weary task of looking for employment was again resumed. Thoroughly discouraged, Corcoran returned to his home last night to find his wife and children without food and the notice of dispossession on the door. On the following morning he drank the poison.

"The records of many more such cases lie before me [Mr. Swift goes on]; an encyclopedia might easily be filled with their kind. These few I cite as an interpretation of the Universe. 'We are aware of the presence of God in his world,' says a writer in a recent English review. [The very presence of ill in the temporal order is the condition of the perfection of the eternal order, writes Professor Royce (The World and the Individual, II, 385).] 'The Absolute is the richer for every discord and for all the diversity which it embraces,' says F. H. Bradley (Appearance and Reality, 204). He means that these slain men make the universe richer, and that is philosophy. But while Professors Royce and Bradley and a whole host of guileless thoroughfed thinkers are unveiling Reality and the Absolute and explaining away evil and pain, this is the condition of the only beings known to us anywhere in the universe with a developed consciousness of what the universe is. What these people experience *is* Reality. It gives us an absolute phase of the universe. It is the personal experience of those best qualified in our circle of knowledge to *have* experience, to tell us *what is*. Now what does *thinking about* the experience of these persons come to, compared to directly and personally feeling it as they feel it? The philosophers are dealing in shades, while those who live and feel know truth. And the mind of mankind—not yet the mind of philosophers and of the proprietary class—but of the great mass of the silently thinking men and feeling men, is coming to this view. They are judging the universe as they have hitherto permitted the hierophants of religion and learning to judge *them*. . . .

"This Cleveland workingman, killing his children and himself [another of the cited cases] is one of the elemental stupendous facts of this modern world and of this universe. It cannot be glozed over or minimized away by all the treatises on God, and Love, and Being, helplessly existing in their monumental vacuity. This is one of the simple irreducible elements of this world's life, after millions of years of opportunity and twenty centuries of Christ. It is in the mental world what atoms or sub-atoms are in the physical, primary, indestructible. And what it blazons to man is the imposture of all philosophy which does not see in such events the consummate factor of all conscious experience. These facts invincibly prove religion a nullity. Man will not give religion two thousand centuries or twenty centuries more to try itself and waste human time. Its time is up; its probation is ended; its own record ends it. Mankind has not æons and eternities to spare for trying out discredited systems."[1]

Such is the reaction of an empiricist mind upon the rationalist bill of fare. It is an absolute 'No, I thank you.' 'Religion,' says Mr. Swift, 'is like a sleep-walker to whom actual things are blank.' And such, tho possibly less tensely charged with feeling, is the verdict of every seriously inquiring amateur in philosophy to-day who turns to the philosophy-professors for the wherewithal to satisfy the fulness of his nature's needs. Empiricist writers give him a materialism, rationalists give him something religious, but to that religion 'actual things are blank.' He becomes thus the judge of us philosophers. Tender or tough, he finds us wanting. None of us may treat his verdicts disdainfully, for after all, his is the typically perfect mind, the mind the sum of whose demands is greatest, the mind whose criticisms and dissatisfactions are fatal in the long run.

It is at this point that my own solution begins to appear. I offer the oddly-named thing pragmatism as a philosophy that can satisfy both kinds of demand. It can remain religious like the rationalisms, but at the same time, like the empiricisms, it

[1] Morrison I. Swift, *Human Submission*, Part Second, Philadelphia, Liberty Press, 1905, pp. 4–10.

can preserve the richest intimacy with facts. I hope I may be able to leave many of you with as favorable an opinion of it as I preserve myself. Yet, as I am near the end of my hour, I will not introduce pragmatism bodily now. I will begin with it on the stroke of the clock next time. I prefer at the present moment to return a little on what I have said.

If any of you here are professional philosophers, and some of you I know to be such, you will doubtless have felt my discourse so far to have been crude in an unpardonable, nay, in an almost incredible degree. Tender-minded and tough-minded, what a barbaric disjunction! And, in general, when philosophy is all compacted of delicate intellectualities and subtleties and scrupulosities, and when every possible sort of combination and transition obtains within its bounds, what a brutal caricature and reduction of highest things to the lowest possible expression is it to represent its field of conflict as a sort of rough-and-tumble fight between two hostile temperaments! What a childishly external view! And again, how stupid it is to treat the abstractness of rationalist systems as a crime, and to damn them because they offer themselves as sanctuaries and places of escape, rather than as prolongations of the world of facts. Are not all our theories just remedies and places of escape? And, if philosophy is to be religious, how can she be anything else than a place of escape from the crassness of reality's surface? What better thing can she do than raise us out of our animal senses and show us another and a nobler home for our minds in that great framework of ideal principles subtending all reality, which the intellect divines? How can principles and general views ever be anything but abstract outlines? Was Cologne cathedral built without an architect's plan on paper? Is refinement in itself an abomination? Is concrete rudeness the only thing that's true?

Believe me, I feel the full force of the indictment. The picture I have given is indeed monstrously over-simplified and rude. But like all abstractions, it will prove to have its use. If philosophers can treat the life of the universe abstractly, they must not complain of an abstract treatment of the life of philosophy itself. In point of fact the picture I have given is, however coarse and sketchy, literally true. Temperaments with their cravings and refusals do determine men in their philosophies, and always will. The details of systems may be reasoned out piecemeal, and when the student is working at a system, he may often forget the forest for the single tree. But when the labor is accomplished, the mind always performs its big summarizing act, and the system forthwith stands over against one like a living thing, with that strange simple note of individuality which haunts our memory, like the wraith of the man, when a friend or enemy of ours is dead.

Not only Walt Whitman could write 'who touches this book touches a man.' The books of all the great philosophers are like so many men. Our sense of an essential personal flavor in each one of them, typical but indescribable, is the finest fruit of our own accomplished philosophic education. What the system pretends to be is a picture of the great universe of God. What it is,—and oh so flagrantly!—is the revelation of how intensely odd the personal flavor of some fellow creature is. Once reduced to these terms (and all our philosophies get reduced to them in minds made critical by learning) our commerce with the systems reverts to the informal, to the instinctive human reaction of satisfaction or dislike. We grow as peremptory in our rejection or admission, as when a person presents himself as a candidate for our favor; our verdicts are couched in as simple adjectives of praise or dispraise. We measure the total character of the universe as we feel it, against the flavor of the philosophy proffered us, and one word is enough.

'Statt der lebendigen Natur,' we say, 'da Gott die Menschen schuf hinein,'—that nebulous concoction, that wooden, that straight-laced thing, that crabbed artificiality, that musty schoolroom product, that sick man's dream! Away with it. Away with all of them! Impossible! Impossible!

Our work over the details of his system is indeed what gives us our resultant impression of the philosopher, but it is on the resultant impression itself that we react. Expertness in philosophy is measured by the definiteness of our summarizing reactions, by the immediate perceptive epithet with which the expert hits such complex objects off. But great expertness is not necessary for the epithet to come. Few people have definitely articulated philosophies of their own. But almost

every one has his own peculiar sense of a certain total character in the universe, and of the inadequacy fully to match it
of the peculiar systems that he knows. They don't just cover
his world. One will be too dapper, another too pedantic, a
third too much of a job-lot of opinions, a fourth too morbid,
and a fifth too artificial, or what not. At any rate he and we
know off-hand that such philosophies are out of plumb and
out of key and out of 'whack,' and have no business to speak
up in the universe's name. Plato, Locke, Spinoza, Mill, Caird,
Hegel—I prudently avoid names nearer home!—I am sure
that to many of you, my hearers, these names are little more
than reminders of as many curious personal ways of falling
short. It would be an obvious absurdity if such ways of taking
the universe were actually true.

We philosophers have to reckon with such feelings on your
part. In the last resort, I repeat, it will be by them that all our
philosophies shall ultimately be judged. The finally victorious
way of looking at things will be the most completely *impressive* way to the normal run of minds.

One word more—namely about philosophies necessarily
being abstract outlines. There are outlines and outlines, outlines of buildings that are *fat*, conceived in the cube by their
planner, and outlines of buildings invented flat on paper, with
the aid of ruler and compass. These remain skinny and emaciated even when set up in stone and mortar, and the outline
already suggests that result. An outline in itself is meagre,
truly, but it does not necessarily suggest a meagre thing. It is
the essential meagreness of *what is suggested* by the usual rationalistic philosophies that moves empiricists to their gesture
of rejection. The case of Herbert Spencer's system is much to
the point here. Rationalists feel his fearful array of insufficien-
cies. His dry schoolmaster temperament, the hurdy-gurdy
monotony of him, his preference for cheap makeshifts in argument, his lack of education even in mechanical principles,
and in general the vagueness of all his fundamental ideas, his
whole system wooden, as if knocked together out of cracked
hemlock boards—and yet the half of England wants to bury
him in Westminster Abbey.

Why? Why does Spencer call out so much reverence in

spite of his weakness in rationalistic eyes? Why should so many educated men who feel that weakness, you and I perhaps, wish to see him in the Abbey notwithstanding?

Simply because we feel his heart to be *in the right place* philosophically. His principles may be all skin and bone, but at any rate his books try to mould themselves upon the particular shape of this particular world's carcase. The noise of facts resounds through all his chapters, the citations of fact never cease, he emphasizes facts, turns his face towards their quarter; and that is enough. It means the right *kind* of thing for the empiricist mind.

The pragmatistic philosophy of which I hope to begin talking in my next lecture preserves as cordial a relation with facts, and, unlike Spencer's philosophy, it neither begins nor ends by turning positive religious constructions out of doors—it treats them cordially as well.

I hope I may lead you to find it just the mediating way of thinking that you require.

LECTURE II

WHAT PRAGMATISM MEANS

SOME YEARS AGO, being with a camping party in the mountains, I returned from a solitary ramble to find every one engaged in a ferocious metaphysical dispute. The *corpus* of the dispute was a squirrel—a live squirrel supposed to be clinging to one side of a tree-trunk; while over against the tree's opposite side a human being was imagined to stand. This human witness tries to get sight of the squirrel by moving rapidly round the tree, but no matter how fast he goes, the squirrel moves as fast in the opposite direction, and always keeps the tree between himself and the man, so that never a glimpse of him is caught. The resultant metaphysical problem now is this: *Does the man go round the squirrel or not?* He goes round the tree, sure enough, and the squirrel is on the tree; but does he go round the squirrel? In the unlimited leisure of the wilderness, discussion had been worn threadbare. Every one had taken sides, and was obstinate; and the numbers on both sides were even. Each side, when I appeared therefore appealed to me to make it a majority. Mindful of the scholastic adage that whenever you meet a contradiction you must make a distinction, I immediately sought and found one, as follows: "Which party is right," I said, "depends on what you *practically mean* by 'going round' the squirrel. If you mean passing from the north of him to the east, then to the south, then to the west, and then to the north of him again, obviously the man does go round him, for he occupies these successive positions. But if on the contrary you mean being first in front of him, then on the right of him, then behind him, then on his left, and finally in front again, it is quite as obvious that the man fails to go round him, for by the compensating movements the squirrel makes, he keeps his belly turned towards the man all the time, and his back turned away. Make the distinction, and there is no occasion for any farther dispute. You are both right and both wrong according as you conceive the verb 'to go round' in one practical fashion or the other."

Although one or two of the hotter disputants called my speech a shuffling evasion, saying they wanted no quibbling or scholastic hair-splitting, but meant just plain honest English 'round,' the majority seemed to think that the distinction had assuaged the dispute.

I tell this trivial anecdote because it is a peculiarly simple example of what I wish now to speak of as *the pragmatic method*. The pragmatic method is primarily a method of settling metaphysical disputes that otherwise might be interminable. Is the world one or many?—fated or free?—material or spiritual?—here are notions either of which may or may not hold good of the world; and disputes over such notions are unending. The pragmatic method in such cases is to try to interpret each notion by tracing its respective practical consequences. What difference would it practically make to any one if this notion rather than that notion were true? If no practical difference whatever can be traced, then the alternatives mean practically the same thing, and all dispute is idle. Whenever a dispute is serious, we ought to be able to show some practical difference that must follow from one side or the other's being right.

A glance at the history of the idea will show you still better what pragmatism means. The term is derived from the same Greek word πράγμα, meaning action, from which our words 'practice' and 'practical' come. It was first introduced into philosophy by Mr. Charles Peirce in 1878. In an article entitled 'How to Make Our Ideas Clear,' in the 'Popular Science Monthly' for January of that year[1] Mr. Peirce, after pointing out that our beliefs are really rules for action, said that, to develop a thought's meaning, we need only determine what conduct it is fitted to produce: that conduct is for us its sole significance. And the tangible fact at the root of all our thought-distinctions, however subtle, is that there is no one of them so fine as to consist in anything but a possible difference of practice. To attain perfect clearness in our thoughts of an object, then, we need only consider what conceivable effects of a practical kind the object may involve—what sensations we are to expect from it, and what reactions we must

---

[1] Translated in the *Revue Philosophique* for January, 1879 (vol. vii).

prepare. Our conception of these effects, whether immediate or remote, is then for us the whole of our conception of the object, so far as that conception has positive significance at all.

This is the principle of Peirce, the principle of pragmatism. It lay entirely unnoticed by any one for twenty years, until I, in an address before Professor Howison's philosophical union at the university of California, brought it forward again and made a special application of it to religion. By that date (1898) the times seemed ripe for its reception. The word 'pragmatism' spread, and at present it fairly spots the pages of the philosophic journals. On all hands we find the 'pragmatic movement' spoken of, sometimes with respect, sometimes with contumely, seldom with clear understanding. It is evident that the term applies itself conveniently to a number of tendencies that hitherto have lacked a collective name, and that it has 'come to stay.'

To take in the importance of Peirce's principle, one must get accustomed to applying it to concrete cases. I found a few years ago that Ostwald, the illustrious Leipzig chemist, had been making perfectly distinct use of the principle of pragmatism in his lectures on the philosophy of science, though he had not called it by that name.

"All realities influence our practice," he wrote me, "and that influence is their meaning for us. I am accustomed to put questions to my classes in this way: In what respects would the world be different if this alternative or that were true? If I can find nothing that would become different, then the alternative has no sense."

That is, the rival views mean practically the same thing, and meaning, other than practical, there is for us none. Ostwald in a published lecture gives this example of what he means. Chemists have long wrangled over the inner constitution of certain bodies called 'tautomerous.' Their properties seemed equally consistent with the notion that an instable hydrogen atom oscillates inside of them, or that they are instable mixtures of two bodies. Controversy raged, but never was decided. "It would never have begun," says Ostwald, "if the combatants had asked themselves what particular experimental fact could have been made different by one or the other view being correct. For it would then have appeared that no difference of fact could possibly ensue; and the quarrel was as unreal as if, theorizing in primitive times about the raising of dough by yeast, one party should have invoked a 'brownie,' while another insisted on an 'elf' as the true cause of the phenomenon."[1]

It is astonishing to see how many philosophical disputes collapse into insignificance the moment you subject them to this simple test of tracing a concrete consequence. There can *be* no difference anywhere that does n't *make* a difference elsewhere—no difference in abstract truth that does n't express itself in a difference in concrete fact and in conduct consequent upon that fact, imposed on somebody, somehow, somewhere, and somewhen. The whole function of philosophy ought to be to find out what definite difference it will make to you and me, at definite instants of our life, if this world-formula or that world-formula be the true one.

There is absolutely nothing new in the pragmatic method. Socrates was an adept at it. Aristotle used it methodically. Locke, Berkeley, and Hume made momentous contributions to truth by its means. Shadworth Hodgson keeps insisting that realities are only what they are 'known as.' But these forerunners of pragmatism used it in fragments: they were preluders only. Not until in our time has it generalized itself, become conscious of a universal mission, pretended to a conquering destiny. I believe in that destiny, and I hope I may end by inspiring you with my belief.

Pragmatism represents a perfectly familiar attitude in philosophy, the empiricist attitude, but it represents it, as it seems to me, both in a more radical and in a less objectionable form than it has ever yet assumed. A pragmatist turns his back resolutely and once for all upon a lot of inveterate habits dear to professional philosophers. He turns away from ab-

---

[1] 'Theorie und Praxis,' *Zeitsch. des Oesterreichischen Ingenieur u. Architecten-Vereines*, 1905, Nr. 4 u. 6. I find a still more radical pragmatism than Ostwald's in an address by Professor W. S. Franklin: "I think that the sickliest notion of physics, even if a student gets it, is that it is 'the science of masses, molecules, and the ether.' And I think that the healthiest notion, even if a student does not wholly get it, is that physics is the science of the ways of taking hold of bodies and pushing them!" (*Science*, January 2, 1903.)

straction and insufficiency, from verbal solutions, from bad *a priori* reasons, from fixed principles, closed systems, and pretended absolutes and origins. He turns towards concreteness and adequacy, towards facts, towards action and towards power. That means the empiricist temper regnant and the rationalist temper sincerely given up. It means the open air and possibilities of nature, as against dogma, artificiality, and the pretence of finality in truth.

At the same time it does not stand for any special results. It is a method only. But the general triumph of that method would mean an enormous change in what I called in my last lecture the 'temperament' of philosophy. Teachers of the ultra-rationalistic type would be frozen out, much as the courtier type is frozen out in republics, as the ultramontane type of priest is frozen out in protestant lands. Science and metaphysics would come much nearer together, would in fact work absolutely hand in hand.

Metaphysics has usually followed a very primitive kind of quest. You know how men have always hankered after unlawful magic, and you know what a great part in magic *words* have always played. If you have his name, or the formula of incantation that binds him, you can control the spirit, genie, afrite, or whatever the power may be. Solomon knew the names of all the spirits, and having their names, he held them subject to his will. So the universe has always appeared to the natural mind as a kind of enigma, of which the key must be sought in the shape of some illuminating or power-bringing word or name. That word names the universe's *principle*, and to possess it is after a fashion to possess the universe itself. 'God,' 'Matter,' 'Reason,' 'the Absolute,' 'Energy,' are so many solving names. You can rest when you have them. You are at the end of your metaphysical quest.

But if you follow the pragmatic method, you cannot look on any such word as closing your quest. You must bring out of each word its practical cash-value, set it at work within the stream of your experience. It appears less as a solution, then, than as a program for more work, and more particularly as an indication of the ways in which existing realities may be *changed*.

Theories thus become instruments, not answers to enigmas, in which we can rest. We don't lie back upon them, we move forward, and, on occasion, make nature over again by their aid. Pragmatism unstiffens all our theories, limbers them up and sets each one at work. Being nothing essentially new, it harmonizes with many ancient philosophic tendencies. It agrees with nominalism for instance, in always appealing to particulars; with utilitarianism in emphasizing practical aspects; with positivism in its disdain for verbal solutions, useless questions and metaphysical abstractions.

All these, you see, are *anti-intellectualist* tendencies. Against rationalism as a pretension and a method pragmatism is fully armed and militant. But, at the outset, at least, it stands for no particular results. It has no dogmas, and no doctrines save its method. As the young Italian pragmatist Papini has well said, it lies in the midst of our theories, like a corridor in a hotel. Innumerable chambers open out of it. In one you may find a man writing an atheistic volume; in the next some one on his knees praying for faith and strength; in a third a chemist investigating a body's properties. In a fourth a system of idealistic metaphysics is being excogitated; in a fifth the impossibility of metaphysics is being shown. But they all own the corridor, and all must pass through it if they want a practicable way of getting into or out of their respective rooms.

No particular results then, so far, but only an attitude of orientation, is what the pragmatic method means. *The attitude of looking away from first things, principles, 'categories,' supposed necessities; and of looking towards last things, fruits, consequences, facts.*

So much for the pragmatic method! You may say that I have been praising it rather than explaining it to you, but I shall presently explain it abundantly enough by showing how it works on some familiar problems. Meanwhile the word pragmatism has come to be used in a still wider sense, as meaning also a certain *theory of truth.* I mean to give a whole lecture to the statement of that theory, after first paving the way, so I can be very brief now. But brevity is hard to follow, so I ask for your redoubled attention for a quarter of an hour. If much remains obscure, I hope to make it clearer in the later lectures.

One of the most successfully cultivated branches of philosophy in our time is what is called inductive logic, the study of the conditions under which our sciences have evolved. Writers on this subject have begun to show a singular unanimity as to what the laws of nature and elements of fact mean, when formulated by mathematicians, physicists and chemists. When the first mathematical, logical, and natural uniformities, the first *laws*, were discovered, men were so carried away by the clearness, beauty and simplification that resulted, that they believed themselves to have deciphered authentically the eternal thoughts of the Almighty. His mind also thundered and reverberated in syllogisms. He also thought in conic sections, squares and roots and ratios, and geometrized like Euclid. He made Kepler's laws for the planets to follow; he made velocity increase proportionally to the time in falling bodies; he made the law of the sines for light to obey when refracted; he established the classes, orders, families and genera of plants and animals, and fixed the distances between them. He thought the archetypes of all things, and devised their variations; and when we rediscover any one of these his wondrous institutions, we seize his mind in its very literal intention.

But as the sciences have developed farther, the notion has gained ground that most, perhaps all, of our laws are only approximations. The laws themselves, moreover, have grown so numerous that there is no counting them; and so many rival formulations are proposed in all the branches of science that investigators have become accustomed to the notion that no theory is absolutely a transcript of reality, but that any one of them may from some point of view be useful. Their great use is to summarize old facts and to lead to new ones. They are only a man-made language, a conceptual shorthand, as some one calls them, in which we write our reports of nature; and languages, as is well known, tolerate much choice of expression and many dialects.

Thus human arbitrariness has driven divine necessity from scientific logic. If I mention the names of Sigwart, Mach, Ostwald, Pearson, Milhaud, Poincaré, Duhem, Ruyssen, those of you who are students will easily identify the tendency I speak of, and will think of additional names.

Riding now on the front of this wave of scientific logic Messrs. Schiller and Dewey appear with their pragmatistic account of what truth everywhere signifies. Everywhere, these teachers say, 'truth' in our ideas and beliefs means the same thing that it means in science. It means, they say, nothing but this, *that ideas (which themselves are but parts of our experience) become true just in so far as they help us to get into satisfactory relation with other parts of our experience,* to summarize them and get about among them by conceptual short-cuts instead of following the interminable succession of particular phenomena. Any idea upon which we can ride, so to speak; any idea that will carry us prosperously from any one part of our experience to any other part, linking things satisfactorily, working securely, simplifying, saving labor; is true for just so much, true in so far forth, true *instrumentally*. This is the 'instrumental' view of truth taught so successfully at Chicago, the view that truth in our ideas means their power to 'work,' promulgated so brilliantly at Oxford.

Messrs. Dewey, Schiller and their allies, in reaching this general conception of all truth, have only followed the example of geologists, biologists and philologists. In the establishment of these other sciences, the successful stroke was always to take some simple process actually observable in operation—as denudation by weather, say, or variation from parental type, or change of dialect by incorporation of new words and pronunciations—and then to generalize it, making it apply to all times, and produce great results by summating its effects through the ages.

The observable process which Schiller and Dewey particularly singled out for generalization is the familiar one by which any individual settles into *new opinions*. The process here is always the same. The individual has a stock of old opinions already, but he meets a new experience that puts them to a strain. Somebody contradicts them; or in a reflective moment he discovers that they contradict each other; or he hears of facts with which they are incompatible; or desires arise in him which they cease to satisfy. The result is an inward trouble to which his mind till then had been a stranger, and from which he seeks to escape by modifying his previous mass of opinions. He saves as much of it as he can, for in this matter of belief we are all extreme conservatives. So he tries to change first this opinion, and then that (for they resist change very variously), until at last some new idea comes up which he can graft upon the ancient stock with a minimum of disturbance of the latter, some idea that mediates between the stock and the new experience and runs them into one another most felicitously and expediently.

This new idea is then adopted as the true one. It preserves the older stock of truths with a minimum of modification, stretching them just enough to make them admit the novelty, but conceiving that in ways as familiar as the case leaves possible. An *outrée* explanation, violating all our preconceptions, would never pass for a true account of a novelty. We should scratch round industriously till we found something less excentric. The most violent revolutions in an individual's beliefs leave most of his old order standing. Time and space, cause and effect, nature and history, and one's own biography remain untouched. New truth is always a go-between, a smoother-over of transitions. It marries old opinion to new fact so as ever to show a minimum of jolt, a maximum of continuity. We hold a theory true just in proportion to its success in solving this 'problem of maxima and minima.' But success in solving this problem is eminently a matter of approximation. We say this theory solves it on the whole more satisfactorily than that theory; but that means more satisfactorily to ourselves, and individuals will emphasize their points of satisfaction differently. To a certain degree, therefore, everything here is plastic.

The point I now urge you to observe particularly is the part played by the older truths. Failure to take account of it is the source of much of the unjust criticism levelled against pragmatism. Their influence is absolutely controlling. Loyalty to them is the first principle—in most cases it is the only principle; for by far the most usual way of handling phenomena so novel that they would make for a serious rearrangement of our preconceptions is to ignore them altogether, or to abuse those who bear witness for them.

You doubtless wish examples of this process of truth's growth, and the only trouble is their superabundance. The simplest case of new truth is of course the mere numerical addition of new kinds of facts, or of new single facts of old kinds, to our experience—an addition that involves no alteration in the old beliefs. Day follows day, and its contents are simply added. The new contents themselves are not true, they simply *come* and *are*. Truth is *what we say about* them, and when we say that they have come, truth is satisfied by the plain additive formula.

But often the day's contents oblige a rearrangement. If I should now utter piercing shrieks and act like a maniac on this platform, it would make many of you revise your ideas as to the probable worth of my philosophy. 'Radium' came the other day as part of the day's content, and seemed for a moment to contradict our ideas of the whole order of nature, that order having come to be identified with what is called the conservation of energy. The mere sight of radium paying heat away indefinitely out of its own pocket seemed to violate that conservation. What to think? If the radiations from it were nothing but an escape of unsuspected 'potential' energy, pre-existent inside of the atoms, the principle of conservation would be saved. The discovery of 'helium' as the radiation's outcome, opened a way to this belief. So Ramsay's view is generally held to be true, because, although it extends our old ideas of energy, it causes a minimum of alteration in their nature.

I need not multiply instances. A new opinion counts as 'true' just in proportion as it gratifies the individual's desire to assimilate the novel in his experience to his beliefs in stock. It must both lean on old truth and grasp new fact; and its success (as I said a moment ago) in doing this, is a matter for the individual's appreciation. When old truth grows, then, by new truth's addition, it is for subjective reasons. We are in the process and obey the reasons. That new idea is truest which performs most felicitously its function of satisfying our double urgency. It makes itself true, gets itself classed as true, by the way it works; grafting itself then upon the ancient body of truth, which thus grows much as a tree grows by the activity of a new layer of cambium.

Now Dewey and Schiller proceed to generalize this observation and to apply it to the most ancient parts of truth. They also once were plastic. They also were called true for human reasons. They also mediated between still earlier truths and what in those days were novel observations. Purely objective truth, truth in whose establishment the function of giving human satisfaction in marrying previous parts of experience with newer parts played no rôle whatever, is nowhere to be found. The reasons why we call things true is the reason why they *are* true, for 'to be true' *means* only to perform this marriage-function.

The trail of the human serpent is thus over everything. Truth independent; truth that we *find* merely; truth no longer malleable to human need; truth incorrigible, in a word; such truth exists indeed superabundantly—or is supposed to exist by rationalistically minded thinkers; but then it means only the dead heart of the living tree, and its being there means only that truth also has its paleontology and its 'prescription,' and may grow stiff with years of veteran service and petrified in men's regard by sheer antiquity. But how plastic even the oldest truths nevertheless really are has been vividly shown in our day by the transformation of logical and mathematical ideas, a transformation which seems even to be invading physics. The ancient formulas are reinterpreted as special expressions of much wider principles, principles that our ancestors never got a glimpse of in their present shape and formulation.

Mr. Schiller still gives to all this view of truth the name of 'Humanism,' but, for this doctrine too, the name of pragmatism seems fairly to be in the ascendant, so I will treat it under the name of pragmatism in these lectures.

Such then would be the scope of pragmatism—first, a method; and second, a genetic theory of what is meant by truth. And these two things must be our future topics.

What I have said of the theory of truth will, I am sure, have appeared obscure and unsatisfactory to most of you by reason of its brevity. I shall make amends for that hereafter. In a lecture on 'common sense' I shall try to show what I mean by truths grown petrified by antiquity. In another lecture I shall expatiate on the idea that our thoughts become true in proportion as they successfully exert their go-between function. In a third I shall show how hard it is to discriminate subjective from objective factors in Truth's development. You may not follow me wholly in these lectures; and if you do, you may not wholly agree with me. But you will, I know, regard me at least as serious, and treat my effort with respectful consideration.

You will probably be surprised to learn, then, that Messrs. Schiller's and Dewey's theories have suffered a hailstorm of contempt and ridicule. All rationalism has risen against them. In influential quarters Mr. Schiller, in particular, has been treated like an impudent schoolboy who deserves a spanking. I should not mention this, but for the fact that it throws so much sidelight upon that rationalistic temper to which I have opposed the temper of pragmatism. Pragmatism is uncomfortable away from facts. Rationalism is comfortable only in the presence of abstractions. This pragmatist talk about truths in the plural, about their utility and satisfactoriness, about the success with which they 'work,' etc., suggests to the typical intellectualist mind a sort of coarse lame second-rate makeshift article of truth. Such truths are not real truth. Such tests are merely subjective. As against this, objective truth must be something non-utilitarian, haughty, refined, remote, august, exalted. It must be an absolute correspondence of our thoughts with an equally absolute reality. It must be what we *ought* to think unconditionally. The conditioned ways in which we *do* think are so much irrelevance and matter for psychology. Down with psychology, up with logic, in all this question!

See the exquisite contrast of the types of mind! The pragmatist clings to facts and concreteness, observes truth at its work in particular cases, and generalizes. Truth, for him, becomes a class-name for all sorts of definite working-values in experience. For the rationalist it remains a pure abstraction, to the bare name of which we must defer. When the pragmatist undertakes to show in detail just *why* we must defer, the rationalist is unable to recognize the concretes from which his own abstraction is taken. He accuses us of *denying* truth; whereas we have only sought to trace exactly why people follow it and always ought to follow it. Your typical ultra-abstractionist fairly shudders at concreteness: other things equal, he positively prefers the pale and spectral. If the two universes were offered, he would always choose the skinny outline rather than the rich thicket of reality. It is so much purer, clearer, nobler.

I hope that as these lectures go on, the concreteness and closeness to facts of the pragmatism which they advocate may be what approves itself to you as its most satisfactory peculiarity. It only follows here the example of the sister-sciences, interpreting the unobserved by the observed. It brings old and new harmoniously together. It converts the absolutely empty notion of a static relation of 'correspondence' (what that may mean we must ask later) between our minds and reality, into that of a rich and active commerce (that any one may follow in detail and understand) between particular thoughts of ours, and the great universe of other experiences in which they play their parts and have their uses.

But enough of this at present? The justification of what I say must be postponed. I wish now to add a word in further explanation of the claim I made at our last meeting, that pragmatism may be a happy harmonizer of empiricist ways of thinking with the more religious demands of human beings.

Men who are strongly of the fact-loving temperament, you may remember me to have said, are liable to be kept at a distance by the small sympathy with facts which that philosophy from the present-day fashion of idealism offers them. It is far too intellectualistic. Old fashioned theism was bad enough, with its notion of God as an exalted monarch, made up of a lot of unintelligible or preposterous 'attributes'; but, so long as it held strongly by the argument from design, it kept some touch with concrete realities. Since, however, darwinism has once for all displaced design from the minds of the 'scientific,' theism has lost that foothold; and some kind of an immanent or pantheistic deity working *in* things rather than above them is, if any, the kind recommended to our contemporary imagination. Aspirants to a philosophic religion turn, as a rule, more hopefully nowadays towards idealistic pantheism than towards the older dualistic theism, in spite of the fact that the latter still counts able defenders.

But, as I said in my first lecture, the brand of pantheism offered is hard for them to assimilate if they are lovers of facts, or empirically minded. It is the absolutistic brand, spurning the dust and reared upon pure logic. It keeps no connexion whatever with concreteness. Affirming the Absolute Mind, which is its substitute for God, to be the rational presupposition of all particulars of fact, whatever they may be, it remains supremely indifferent to what the particular facts in our world actually are. Be they what they may, the Absolute will father them. Like the sick lion in Esop's fable, all footprints lead into his den, but *nulla vestigia retrorsum*. You cannot redescend into the world of particulars by the Absolute's aid, or deduce any necessary consequences of detail important for your life from your idea of his nature. He gives you indeed the assurance that all is well with *Him*, and for his eternal way of thinking; but thereupon he leaves you to be finitely saved by your own temporal devices.

Far be it from me to deny the majesty of this conception, or its capacity to yield religious comfort to a most respectable class of minds. But from the human point of view, no one can pretend that it does n't suffer from the faults of remoteness and abstractness. It is eminently a product of what I have ventured to call the rationalistic temper. It disdains empiricism's needs. It substitutes a pallid outline for the real world's richness. It is dapper, it is noble in the bad sense, in the sense in which to be noble is to be inapt for humble service. In this real world of sweat and dirt, it seems to me that when a view of things is 'noble,' that ought to count as a presumption against its truth, and as a philosophic disqualification. The prince of darkness may be a gentleman, as we are told he is, but whatever the God of earth and heaven is, he can surely be no gentleman. His menial services are needed in the dust of our human trials, even more than his dignity is needed in the empyrean.

Now pragmatism, devoted though she be to facts, has no such materialistic bias as ordinary empiricism labors under. Moreover, she has no objection whatever to the realizing of abstractions, so long as you get about among particulars with their aid and they actually carry you somewhere. Interested in no conclusions but those which our minds and our experiences work out together, she has no *a priori* prejudices against theology. *If theological ideas prove to have a value for concrete life, they will be true, for pragmatism, in the sense of being good for so much. For how much more they are true, will depend entirely on their relations to the other truths that also have to be acknowledged.*

What I said just now about the Absolute of transcendental idealism is a case in point. First, I called it majestic and said it yielded religious comfort to a class of minds, and then I accused it of remoteness and sterility. But so far as it affords such comfort, it surely is not sterile; it has that amount of value; it performs a concrete function. As a good pragmatist, I myself ought to call the Absolute true 'in so far forth,' then; and I unhesitatingly now do so.

But what does *true in so far forth* mean in this case? To answer, we need only apply the pragmatic method. What do believers in the Absolute mean by saying that their belief affords them comfort? They mean that since in the Absolute finite evil is 'overruled' already, we may, therefore, whenever we wish, treat the temporal as if it were potentially the eternal, be sure that we can trust its outcome, and, without sin, dismiss our fear and drop the worry of our finite responsibility. In short, they mean that we have a right ever and anon to take a moral holiday, to let the world wag in its own way, feeling that its issues are in better hands than ours and are none of our business.

The universe is a system of which the individual members may relax their anxieties occasionally, in which the don't-care mood is also right for men, and moral holidays in order,— that, if I mistake not, is part, at least, of what the Absolute is 'known-as,' that is the great difference in our particular experiences which his being true makes, for us, that is part of his cash-value when he is pragmatically interpreted. Farther than that the ordinary lay-reader in philosophy who thinks favorably of absolute idealism does not venture to sharpen his conceptions. He can use the Absolute for so much, and so much is very precious. He is pained at hearing you speak incredulously of the Absolute, therefore, and disregards your criticisms because they deal with aspects of the conception that he fails to follow.

If the Absolute means this, and means no more than this, who can possibly deny the truth of it? To deny it would be to insist that men should never relax, and that holidays are never in order.

I am well aware how odd it must seem to some of you to hear me say that an idea is 'true' so long as to believe it is profitable to our lives. That it is *good*, for as much as it profits, you will gladly admit. If what we do by its aid is good, you will allow the idea itself to be good in so far forth, for we are the better for possessing it. But is it not a strange misuse of the word 'truth,' you will say, to call ideas also 'true' for this reason?

To answer this difficulty fully is impossible at this stage of my account. You touch here upon the very central point of Messrs. Schiller's, Dewey's and my own doctrine of truth, which I can not discuss with detail until my sixth lecture. Let me now say only this, that truth is *one species of good*, and not, as is usually supposed, a category distinct from good, and co-ordinate with it. *The true is the name of whatever proves itself to be good in the way of belief, and good, too, for definite, assignable reasons.* Surely you must admit this, that if there were *no* good for life in true ideas, or if the knowledge of them were positively disadvantageous and false ideas the only useful ones, then the current notion that truth is divine and precious, and its pursuit a duty, could never have grown up or become a dogma. In a world like that, our duty would be to *shun* truth, rather. But in this world, just as certain foods are not only agreeable to our taste, but good for our teeth, our stomach, and our tissues; so certain ideas are not only agreeable to think about, or agreeable as supporting other ideas that we are fond of, but they are also helpful in life's practical struggles. If there be any life that it is really better we should lead, and if there be any idea which, if believed in, would help us to lead that life, then it would be really *better for us* to believe in that idea, *unless, indeed, belief in it incidentally clashed with other greater vital benefits.*

'What would be better for us to believe'! This sounds very like a definition of truth. It comes very near to saying 'what we *ought* to believe': and in *that* definition none of you would find any oddity. Ought we ever not to believe what it is *better for us* to believe? And can we then keep the notion of what is better for us, and what is true for us, permanently apart?

Pragmatism says no, and I fully agree with her. Probably you also agree, so far as the abstract statement goes, but with a suspicion that if we practically did believe everything that made for good in our own personal lives, we should be found indulging all kinds of fancies about this world's affairs, and all kinds of sentimental superstitions about a world hereafter. Your suspicion here is undoubtedly well founded, and it is evident that something happens when you pass from the abstract to the concrete that complicates the situation.

I said just now that what is better for us to believe is true *unless the belief incidentally clashes with some other vital benefit.* Now in real life what vital benefits is any particular belief of ours most liable to clash with? What indeed except the vital benefits yielded by *other beliefs* when these prove incompatible with the first ones? In other words, the greatest enemy of any one of our truths may be the rest of our truths. Truths have once for all this desperate instinct of self-preservation and of desire to extinguish whatever contradicts them. My belief in the Absolute, based on the good it does me, must run the gauntlet of all my other beliefs. Grant that it may be true in giving me a moral holiday. Nevertheless, as I conceive it,— and let me speak now confidentially, as it were, and merely in my own private person,—it clashes with other truths of mine whose benefits I hate to give up on its account. It happens to be associated with a kind of logic of which I am the enemy, I find that it entangles me in metaphysical paradoxes that are inacceptable, etc., etc. But as I have enough trouble in life already without adding the trouble of carrying these intellectual inconsistencies, I personally just give up the Absolute. I just *take* my moral holidays; or else as a professional philosopher, I try to justify them by some other principle.

If I could restrict my notion of the Absolute to its bare holiday-giving value, it would n't clash with my other truths. But we can not easily thus restrict our hypotheses. They carry supernumerary features, and these it is that clash so. My disbelief in the Absolute means then disbelief in those other supernumerary features, for I fully believe in the legitimacy of taking moral holidays.

You see by this what I meant when I called pragmatism a mediator and reconciler and said, borrowing the word from

Papini, that she 'unstiffens' our theories. She has in fact no prejudices whatever, no obstructive dogmas, no rigid canons of what shall count as proof. She is completely genial. She will entertain any hypothesis, she will consider any evidence. It follows that in the religious field she is at a great advantage both over positivistic empiricism, with its anti-theological bias, and over religious rationalism, with its exclusive interest in the remote, the noble, the simple, and the abstract in the way of conception.

In short, she widens the field of search for God. Rationalism sticks to logic and the empyrean. Empiricism sticks to the external senses. Pragmatism is willing to take anything, to follow either logic or the senses and to count the humblest and most personal experiences. She will count mystical experiences if they have practical consequences. She will take a God who lives in the very dirt of private fact—if that should seem a likely place to find him.

Her only test of probable truth is what works best in the way of leading us, what fits every part of life best and combines with the collectivity of experience's demands, nothing being omitted. If theological ideas should do this, if the notion of God, in particular, should prove to do it, how could pragmatism possibly deny God's existence? She could see no meaning in treating as 'not true' a notion that was pragmatically so successful. What other kind of truth could there be, for her, than all this agreement with concrete reality?

In my last lecture I shall return again to the relations of pragmatism with religion. But you see already how democratic she is. Her manners are as various and flexible, her resources as rich and endless, and her conclusions as friendly as those of mother nature.

LECTURE III

SOME METAPHYSICAL PROBLEMS
PRAGMATICALLY CONSIDERED

I AM NOW to make the pragmatic method more familiar by giving you some illustrations of its application to particular problems. I will begin with what is driest, and the first thing I shall take will be the problem of *Substance*. Every one uses the old distinction between substance and attribute, enshrined as it is in the very structure of human language, in the difference between grammatical subject and predicate. Here is a bit of blackboard crayon. Its modes, attributes, properties, accidents, or affections,—use which term you will,—are whiteness, friability, cylindrical shape, insolubility in water, etc., etc. But the bearer of these attributes is so much *chalk*, which thereupon is called the substance in which they inhere. So the attributes of this desk inhere in the substance 'wood,' those of my coat in the substance 'wool,' and so forth. Chalk, wood and wool, show again, in spite of their differences, common properties, and in so far forth they are themselves counted as modes of a still more primal substance, *matter*, the attributes of which are space-occupancy and impenetrability. Similarly our thoughts and feelings are affections or properties of our several *souls*, which are substances, but again not wholly in their own right, for they are modes of the still deeper substance 'spirit.'

Now it was very early seen that all *we know* of the chalk is the whiteness, friability, etc., all *we know* of the wood is the combustibility and fibrous structure. A group of attributes is what each substance here is known-as, they form its sole cash-value for our actual experience. The substance is in every case revealed through *them*; if we were cut off from *them* we should never suspect its existence; and if God should keep sending them to us in an unchanged order, miraculously annihilating at a certain moment the substance that supported them, we never could detect the moment, for our experiences themselves would be unaltered. Nominalists accordingly adopt the opinion that substance is a spurious idea due to our inveterate human trick of turning names into things. Phenomena come in groups—the chalk-group, the wood-group, etc.,—and each group gets its name. The name we then treat as in a way supporting the group of phenomena. The low thermometer to-day, for instance, is supposed to come from something called the 'climate.' Climate is really only the name for a certain group of days, but it is treated as if it lay *behind* the day, and in general we place the name, as if it were a being, behind the facts it is the name of. But the phenomenal properties of things, nominalists say, surely do not really inhere in names, and if not in names then they do not inhere in anything. They *ad*here, or *co*here, rather, *with each other*, and the notion of a substance inaccessible to us, which we think accounts for such cohesion by supporting it, as cement might support pieces of mosaic, must be abandoned. The fact of the bare cohesion itself is all that the notion of the substance signifies. Behind that fact is nothing.

Scholasticism has taken the notion of substance from common sense and made it very technical and articulate. Few things would seem to have fewer pragmatic consequences for us than substances, cut off as we are from every contact with them. Yet in one case scholasticism has proved the importance of the substance-idea by treating it pragmatically. I refer to certain disputes about the mystery of the Eucharist. Substance here would appear to have momentous pragmatic value. Since the accidents of the wafer don't change in the Lord's supper, and yet it has become the very body of Christ, it must be that the change is in the substance solely. The bread-substance must have been withdrawn, and the divine substance substituted miraculously without altering the immediate sensible properties. But tho these don't alter, a tremendous difference has been made, no less a one than this, that we who take the sacrament, now feed upon the very substance of divinity. The substance-notion breaks into life, then, with tremendous effect, if once you allow that substances can separate from their accidents, and exchange these latter.

This is the only pragmatic application of the substance-idea with which I am acquainted; and it is obvious that it will only be treated seriously by those who already believe in the 'real presence' on independent grounds.

Material substance was criticised by Berkeley with such telling effect that his name has reverberated through all subsequent philosophy. Berkeley's treatment of the notion of matter is so well known as to need hardly more than a mention. So far from denying the external world which we know, Berkeley corroborated it. It was the scholastic notion of a material substance unapproachable by us, *behind* the external world, deeper and more real than it, and needed to support it, which Berkeley maintained to be the most effective of all reducers of the external world to unreality. Abolish that substance, he said, believe that God, whom you can understand and approach, sends you the sensible world directly, and you confirm the latter and back it up by his divine authority. Berkeley's criticism of 'matter' was consequently absolutely pragmatistic. Matter is known as our sensations of colour, figure, hardness and the like. They are the cash-value of the term. The difference matter makes to us by truly being is that we then get such sensations; by not being, is that we lack them. These sensations then are its sole meaning. Berkeley does n't deny matter, then; he simply tells us what it consists of. It is a true name for just so much in the way of sensations.

Locke, and later Hume, applied a similar pragmatic criticism to the notion of *spiritual substance*. I will only mention Locke's treatment of our 'personal identity.' He immediately reduces this notion to its pragmatic value in terms of experience. It means, he says, so much 'consciousness,' namely the fact that at one moment of life we remember other moments, and feel them all as parts of one and the same personal history. Rationalism had explained this practical continuity in our life by the unity of our soul-substance. But Locke says: suppose that God should take away the consciousness, should *we* be any the better for having still the soul-principle? Suppose he annexed the same consciousness to different souls, should *we*, as we realize *ourselves*, be any the worse for that fact? In Locke's day the soul was chiefly a thing to be rewarded or punished. See how Locke, discussing it from this point of view, keeps the question pragmatic:

"Suppose," he says, "one to think himself to be the same *soul* that once was Nestor or Thersites. Can he think their actions his own any more than the actions of any other man that ever existed? But let him once find himself *conscious* of any of the actions of Nestor, he then finds himself the same person with Nestor. . . . In this personal identity is founded all the right and justice of reward and punishment. It may be reasonable to think, no one shall be made to answer for what he knows nothing of, but shall receive his doom, his consciousness accusing or excusing. Supposing a man punished now for what he had done in another life, whereof he could be made to have no consciousness at all, what difference is there between that punishment and being created miserable?"

Our personal identity, then, consists, for Locke, solely in pragmatically definable particulars. Whether, apart from these verifiable facts, it also inheres in a spiritual principle, is a merely curious speculation. Locke, compromiser that he was, passively tolerated the belief in a substantial soul behind our consciousness. But his successor Hume, and most empirical psychologists after him, have denied the soul, save as the name for verifiable cohesions in our inner life. They redescend into the stream of experience with it, and cash it into so much small-change value in the way of 'ideas' and their peculiar connexions with each other. As I said of Berkeley's matter, the soul is good or 'true' for just *so much*, but no more.

The mention of material substance naturally suggests the doctrine of 'materialism,' but philosophical materialism is not necessarily knit up with belief in 'matter,' as a metaphysical principle. One may deny matter in that sense, as strongly as Berkeley did, one may be a phenomenalist like Huxley, and yet one may still be a materialist in the wider sense, of explaining higher phenomena by lower ones, and leaving the destinies of the world at the mercy of its blinder parts and forces. It is in this wider sense of the word that materialism is opposed to spiritualism or theism. The laws of physical nature are what run things, materialism says. The highest productions of human genius might be ciphered by one who had complete acquaintance with the facts, out of their physiological conditions, regardless whether nature be there only for our minds, as idealists contend, or not. Our minds in any case would have to record the kind of nature it is, and write it down as operating through blind laws of physics. This is the complexion of present day materialism, which may better be called naturalism. Over against it stands 'theism,' or what in a wide sense may be termed 'spiritualism.' Spiritualism says that mind not only witnesses and records things, but also runs and operates them: the world being thus guided, not by its lower, but by its higher element.

Treated as it often is, this question becomes little more than a conflict between æsthetic preferences. Matter is gross, coarse, crass, muddy; spirit is pure, elevated, noble; and since it is more consonant with the dignity of the universe to give the primacy in it to what appears superior, spirit must be affirmed as the ruling principle. To treat abstract principles as finalities, before which our intellects may come to rest in a state of admiring contemplation, is the great rationalist failing. Spiritualism, as often held, may be simply a state of admiration for one kind, and of dislike for another kind, of abstraction. I remember a worthy spiritualist professor who always referred to materialism as the 'mud-philosophy,' and deemed it thereby refuted.

To such spiritualism as this there is an easy answer, and Mr. Spencer makes it effectively. In some well-written pages at the end of the first volume of his Psychology he shows us that a 'matter' so infinitely subtle, and performing motions as inconceivably quick and fine as those which modern science postulates in her explanations, has no trace of grossness left. He shows that the conception of spirit, as we mortals hitherto have framed it, is itself too gross to cover the exquisite tenuity of nature's facts. Both terms, he says, are but symbols, pointing to that one unknowable reality in which their oppositions cease.

To an abstract objection an abstract rejoinder suffices; and so far as one's opposition to materialism springs from one's disdain of matter as something 'crass,' Mr. Spencer cuts the ground from under one. Matter is indeed infinitely and incredibly refined. To any one who has ever looked on the face of a dead child or parent the mere fact that matter *could* have taken for a time that precious form, ought to make matter sacred ever after. It makes no difference what the *principle* of life may be, material or immaterial, matter at any rate co-operates, lends itself to all life's purposes. That beloved incarnation was among matter's possibilities.

But now, instead of resting in principles after this stagnant intellectualist fashion, let us apply the pragmatic method to the question. What do we *mean* by matter? What practical difference can it make *now* that the world should be run by matter or by spirit? I think we find that the problem takes with this a rather different character.

And first of all I call your attention to a curious fact. It makes not a single jot of difference so far as the *past* of the world goes, whether we deem it to have been the work of matter or whether we think a divine spirit was its author.

Imagine, in fact, the entire contents of the world to be once for all irrevocably given. Imagine it to end this very moment, and to have no future; and then let a theist and a materialist apply their rival explanations to its history. The theist shows how a God made it; the materialist shows, and we will suppose with equal success, how it resulted from blind physical forces. Then let the pragmatist be asked to choose between their theories. How can he apply his test if the world is already completed? Concepts for him are things to come back into experience with, things to make us look for differences. But by hypothesis there is to be no more experience and no possible differences can now be looked for. Both theories have shown all their consequences and, by the hypothesis we are adopting, these are identical. The pragmatist must consequently say that the two theories, in spite of their different-sounding names, mean exactly the same thing, and that the dispute is purely verbal. [I am supposing, of course, that the theories *have* been equally successful in their explanations of what is.]

For just consider the case sincerely, and say what would be the *worth* of a God if he *were* there, with his work accomplished and his world run down. He would be worth no more than just that world was worth. To that amount of result, with its mixed merits and defects, his creative power could attain but go no farther. And since there is to be no future; since the whole value and meaning of the world has been already paid in and actualized in the feelings that went with it in the passing, and now go with it in the ending; since it draws no supplemental significance (such as our real world draws) from its function of preparing something yet to come;

why then, by it we take God's measure, as it were. He is the Being who could once for all do *that*; and for that much we are thankful to him, but for nothing more. But now, on the contrary hypothesis, namely, that the bits of matter following their laws could make that world and do no less, should we not be just as thankful to them? Wherein should we suffer loss, then, if we dropped God as an hypothesis and made the matter alone responsible? Where would any special deadness, or crassness, come in? And how, experience being what is once for all, would God's presence in it make it any more living or richer?

Candidly, it is impossible to give any answer to this question. The actually experienced world is supposed to be the same in its details on either hypothesis, 'the same, for our praise or blame,' as Browning says. It stands there indefeasibly: a gift which can't be taken back. Calling matter the cause of it retracts no single one of the items that have made it up, nor does calling God the cause augment them. They are the God or the atoms, respectively, of just that and no other world. The God, if there, has been doing just what atoms could do—appearing in the character of atoms, so to speak—and earning such gratitude as is due to atoms, and no more. If his presence lends no different turn or issue to the performance, it surely can lend it no increase of dignity. Nor would indignity come to it were he absent, and did the atoms remain the only actors on the stage. When a play is once over, and the curtain down, you really make it no better by claiming an illustrious genius for its author, just as you make it no worse by calling him a common hack.

Thus if no future detail of experience or conduct is to be deduced from our hypothesis, the debate between materialism and theism becomes quite idle and insignificant. Matter and God in that event mean exactly the same thing—the power, namely, neither more nor less, that could make just this completed world—and the wise man is he who in such a case would turn his back on such a supererogatory discussion. Accordingly, most men instinctively, and positivists and scientists deliberately, do turn their backs on philosophical disputes from which nothing in the line of definite future consequences can be seen to follow. The verbal and empty character of philosophy is surely a reproach with which we are but too familiar. If pragmatism be true, it is a perfectly sound reproach unless the theories under fire can be shown to have alternative practical outcomes, however delicate and distant these may be. The common man and the scientist say they discover no such outcomes, and if the metaphysician can discern none either, the others certainly are in the right of it, as against him. His science is then but pompous trifling; and the endowment of a professorship for such a being would be silly.

Accordingly, in every genuine metaphysical debate some practical issue, however conjectural and remote, is involved. To realize this, revert with me to our question, and place yourselves this time in the world we live in, in the world that *has* a future, that is yet uncompleted whilst we speak. In this unfinished world the alternative of 'materialism or theism?' is intensely practical; and it is worth while for us to spend some minutes of our hour in seeing that it is so.

How, indeed, does the program differ for us, according as we consider that the facts of experience up to date are purposeless configurations of blind atoms moving according to eternal laws, or that on the other hand they are due to the providence of God? As far as the past facts go, indeed, there is no difference. Those facts are in, are bagged, are captured; and the good that's in them is gained, be the atoms or be the God their cause. There are accordingly many materialists about us to-day who, ignoring altogether the future and practical aspects of the question, seek to eliminate the odium attaching to the word materialism, and even to eliminate the word itself, by showing that, if matter could give birth to all these gains, why then matter, functionally considered, is just as divine an entity as God, in fact coalesces with God, is what you mean by God. Cease, these persons advise us, to use either of these terms, with their outgrown opposition. Use a term free of the clerical connotations, on the one hand; of the suggestion of grossness, coarseness, ignobility, on the other. Talk of the primal mystery, of the unknowable energy, of the one and only power, instead of saying either God or matter. This is the course to which Mr. Spencer urges us; and if philosophy were purely retrospective, he would thereby proclaim himself an excellent pragmatist.

But philosophy is prospective also, and, after finding what the world has been and done and yielded, still asks the further question 'what does the world *promise*?' Give us a matter that promises *success*, that is bound by its laws to lead our world ever nearer to perfection, and any rational man will worship that matter as readily as Mr. Spencer worships his own so-called unknowable power. It not only has made for righteousness up to date, but it will make for righteousness forever; and that is all we need. Doing practically all that a God can do, it is equivalent to God, its function is a God's function, and in a world in which a God would be superfluous; from such a world a God could never lawfully be missed. 'Cosmic emotion' would here be the right name for religion.

But *is* the matter by which Mr. Spencer's process of cosmic evolution is carried on any such principle of never-ending perfection as this? Indeed it is not, for the future end of every cosmically evolved thing or system of things is foretold by science to be death and tragedy; and Mr. Spencer, in confining himself to the æsthetic and ignoring the practical side of the controversy, has really contributed nothing serious to its relief. But apply now our principle of practical results, and see what a vital significance the question of materialism or theism immediately acquires.

Theism and materialism, so indifferent when taken retrospectively, point, when we take them prospectively, to wholly different outlooks of experience. For, according to the theory of mechanical evolution, the laws of redistribution of matter and motion, though they are certainly to thank for all the good hours which our organisms have ever yielded us and for all the ideals which our minds now frame, are yet fatally certain to undo their work again, and to redissolve everything that they have once evolved. You all know the picture of the last state of the universe which evolutionary science foresees. I can not state it better than in Mr. Balfour's words: "The energies of our system will decay, the glory of the sun will be dimmed, and the earth, tideless and inert, will no longer tolerate the race which has for a moment disturbed its solitude.

Man will go down into the pit, and all his thoughts will perish. The uneasy consciousness which in this obscure corner has for a brief space broken the contented silence of the universe, will be at rest. Matter will know itself no longer. 'Imperishable monuments' and 'immortal deeds,' death itself, and love stronger than death, will be as if they had not been. Nor will anything that is, be better or worse for all that the labor, genius, devotion, and suffering of man have striven through countless ages to effect."[1]

That is the sting of it, that in the vast driftings of the cosmic weather, though many a jewelled shore appears, and many an enchanted cloud-bank floats away, long lingering ere it be dissolved—even as our world now lingers, for our joy— yet when these transient products are gone, nothing, absolutely *nothing* remains, to represent those particular qualities, those elements of preciousness which they may have enshrined. Dead and gone are they, gone utterly from the very sphere and room of being. Without an echo; without a memory; without an influence on aught that may come after, to make it care for similar ideals. This utter final wreck and tragedy is of the essence of scientific materialism as at present understood. The lower and not the higher forces are the eternal forces, or the last surviving forces within the only cycle of evolution which we can definitely see. Mr. Spencer believes this as much as any one; so why should he argue with us as if we were making silly æsthetic objections to the 'grossness' of 'matter and motion,' the principles of his philosophy, when what really dismays us is the disconsolateness of its ulterior practical results?

No, the true objection to materialism is not positive but negative. It would be farcical at this day to make complaint of it for what it *is*, for 'grossness.' Grossness is what grossness *does*—we now know *that*. We make complaint of it, on the contrary, for what it is *not*—not a permanent warrant for our more ideal interests, not a fulfiller of our remotest hopes.

The notion of God, on the other hand, however inferior it may be in clearness to those mathematical notions so current in mechanical philosophy, has at least this practical superiority

[1] *The Foundations of Belief*, p. 30.

over them, that it guarantees an ideal order that shall be permanently preserved. A world with a God in it to say the last word, may indeed burn up or freeze, but we then think of him as still mindful of the old ideals and sure to bring them elsewhere to fruition; so that, where he is, tragedy is only provisional and partial, and shipwreck and dissolution not the absolutely final things. This need of an eternal moral order is one of the deepest needs of our breast. And those poets, like Dante and Wordsworth, who live on the conviction of such an order, owe to that fact the extraordinary tonic and consoling power of their verse. Here then, in these different emotional and practical appeals, in these adjustments of our concrete attitudes of hope and expectation, and all the delicate consequences which their differences entail, lie the real meanings of materialism and spiritualism—not in hair-splitting abstractions about matter's inner essence, or about the metaphysical attributes of God. Materialism means simply the denial that the moral order is eternal, and the cutting off of ultimate hopes; spiritualism means the affirmation of an eternal moral order and the letting loose of hope. Surely here is an issue genuine enough, for any one who feels it; and, as long as men are men, it will yield matter for a serious philosophic debate.

But possibly some of you may still rally to their defence. Even whilst admitting that spiritualism and materialism make different prophecies of the world's future, you may yourselves pooh-pooh the difference as something so infinitely remote as to mean nothing for a sane mind. The essence of a sane mind, you may say, is to take shorter views, and to feel no concern about such chimæras as the latter end of the world. Well, I can only say that if you say this, you do injustice to human nature. Religious melancholy is not disposed of by a simple flourish of the word insanity. The absolute things, the last things, the overlapping things, are the truly philosophic concerns; all superior minds feel seriously about them, and the mind with the shortest views is simply the mind of the more shallow man.

The issues of fact at stake in the debate are of course vaguely enough conceived by us at present. But spiritualistic faith in all its forms deals with a world of *promise*, while materialism's sun sets in a sea of disappointment. Remember what I said of the Absolute: it grants us moral holidays. Any religious view does this. It not only incites our more strenuous moments, but it also takes our joyous, careless, trustful moments, and it justifies them. It paints the grounds of justification vaguely enough, to be sure. The exact features of the saving future facts that our belief in God insures, will have to be ciphered out by the interminable methods of science: we can *study* our God only by studying his Creation. But we can *enjoy* our God, if we have one, in advance of all that labor. I myself believe that the evidence for God lies primarily in inner personal experiences. When they have once given you your God, his name means at least the benefit of the holiday. You remember what I said yesterday about the way in which truths clash and try to 'down' each other. The truth of 'God' has to run the gauntlet of all our other truths. It is on trial by them and they on trial by it. Our *final* opinion about God can be settled only after all the truths have straightened themselves out together. Let us hope that they shall find a *modus vivendi*!

Let me pass to a very cognate philosophic problem, the *question of design in nature*. God's existence has from time immemorial been held to be proved by certain natural facts. Many facts appear as if expressly designed in view of one another. Thus the woodpecker's bill, tongue, feet, tail, etc., fit him wondrously for a world of trees with grubs hid in their bark to feed upon. The parts of our eye fit the laws of light to perfection, leading its rays to a sharp picture on our retina. Such mutual fitting of things diverse in origin argued design, it was held; and the designer was always treated as a man-loving deity.

The first step in these arguments was to prove that the design *existed*. Nature was ransacked for results obtained through separate things being co-adapted. Our eyes, for instance, originate in intra-uterine darkness, and the light originates in the sun, yet see how they fit each other. They are evidently made *for* each other. Vision is the end designed, light and eyes the separate means devised for its attainment.

It is strange, considering how unanimously our ancestors felt the force of this argument, to see how little it counts for since the triumph of the darwinian theory. Darwin opened our minds to the power of chance-happenings to bring forth 'fit' results if only they have time to add themselves together. He showed the enormous waste of nature in producing results that get destroyed because of their unfitness. He also emphasized the number of adaptations which, if designed, would argue an evil rather than a good designer. Here all depends upon the point of view. To the grub under the bark the exquisite fitness of the woodpecker's organism to extract him would certainly argue a diabolical designer.

Theologians have by this time stretched their minds so as to embrace the darwinian facts, and yet to interpret them as still showing divine purpose. It used to be a question of purpose *against* mechanism, of one *or* the other. It was as if one should say "My shoes are evidently designed to fit my feet, hence it is impossible that they should have been produced by machinery." We know that they are both: they are made by a machinery itself designed to fit the feet with shoes. Theology need only stretch similarly the designs of God. As the aim of a football-team is not merely to get the ball to a certain goal (if that were so, they would simply get up on some dark night and place it there), but to get it there by a fixed *machinery of conditions*—the game's rules and the opposing players; so the aim of God is not merely, let us say, to make men and to save them, but rather to get this done through the sole agency of nature's vast machinery. Without nature's stupendous laws and counter-forces, man's creation and perfection, we might suppose, would be too insipid achievements for God to have designed them.

This saves the form of the design-argument at the expense of its old easy human content. The designer is no longer the old man-like deity. His designs have grown so vast as to be incomprehensible to us humans. The *what* of them so overwhelms us that to establish the mere *that* of a designer for them becomes of very little consequence in comparison. We can with difficulty comprehend the character of a cosmic mind whose purposes are fully revealed by the strange mixture of goods and evils that we find in this actual world's particulars. Or rather we cannot by any possibility comprehend it. The mere word 'design' by itself has, we see, no

consequences and explains nothing. It is the barrenest of principles. The old question of *whether* there is design is idle. The
real question is *what* is the world, whether or not it have a
designer—and that can be revealed only by the study of all
nature's particulars.

Remember that no matter what nature may have produced
or may be producing, the means must necessarily have been
adequate, must have been *fitted to that production*. The argument from fitness to design would consequently always apply,
whatever were the product's character. The recent Mont-
Pelée eruption, for example, required all previous history to
produce that exact combination of ruined houses, human and
animal corpses, sunken ships, volcanic ashes, etc., in just that
one hideous configuration of positions. France had to be a
nation and colonize Martinique. Our country had to exist and
send our ships there. *If* God aimed at just that result, the
means by which the centuries bent their influences towards it,
showed exquisite intelligence. And so of any state of things
whatever, either in nature or in history, which we find actually realized. For the parts of things must always make *some*
definite resultant, be it chaotic or harmonious. When we look
at what has actually come, the conditions must always appear
perfectly designed to ensure it. We can always say, therefore,
in any conceivable world, of any conceivable character, that
the whole cosmic machinery *may* have been designed to produce it.

Pragmatically, then, the abstract word 'design' is a blank
cartridge. It carries no consequences, it does no execution.
What sort of design? and what sort of a designer? are the only
serious questions, and the study of facts is the only way of
getting even approximate answers. Meanwhile, pending the
slow answer from facts, any one who insists that there *is* a
designer and who is sure he is a divine one, gets a certain
pragmatic benefit from the term—the same, in fact, which we
saw that the terms God, Spirit, or the Absolute, yield us. 'Design,' worthless tho it be as a mere rationalistic principle set
above or behind things for our admiration, becomes, if our
faith concretes it into something theistic, a term of *promise*.
Returning with it into experience, we gain a more confiding
outlook on the future. If not a blind force but a seeing force

runs things, we may reasonably expect better issues. This vague confidence in the future is the sole pragmatic meaning at present discernible in the terms design and designer. But if cosmic confidence is right not wrong, better not worse, that is a most important meaning. That much at least of possible 'truth' the terms will then have in them.

Let me take up another well-worn controversy, *the free-will problem*. Most persons who believe in what is called their free-will do so after the rationalistic fashion. It is a principle, a positive faculty or virtue added to man, by which his dignity is enigmatically augmented. He ought to believe it for this reason. Determinists, who deny it, who say that individual men originate nothing, but merely transmit to the future the whole push of the past cosmos of which they are so small an expression, diminish man. He is less admirable, stripped of this creative principle. I imagine that more than half of you share our instinctive belief in free-will, and that admiration of it as a principle of dignity has much to do with your fidelity.

But free-will has also been discussed pragmatically, and, strangely enough, the same pragmatic interpretation has been put upon it by both disputants. You know how large a part questions of *accountability* have played in ethical controversy. To hear some persons, one would suppose that all that ethics aims at is a code of merits and demerits. Thus does the old legal and theological leaven, the interest in crime and sin and punishment abide with us. 'Who's to blame? whom can we punish? whom will God punish?'—these preoccupations hang like a bad dream over man's religious history.

So both free-will and determinism have been inveighed against and called absurd, because each, in the eyes of its enemies, has seemed to prevent the 'imputability' of good or bad deeds to their authors. Queer antinomy this! Free-will means novelty, the grafting on to the past of something not involved therein. If our acts were predetermined, if we merely transmitted the push of the whole past, the free-willists say, how could we be praised or blamed for anything? We should be 'agents' only, not 'principals,' and where then would be our precious imputability and responsibility?

But where would it be if we *had* free-will? rejoin the determinists. If a 'free' act be a sheer novelty, that comes not *from* me, the previous me, but *ex nihilo*, and simply tacks itself on to me, how can *I*, the previous I, be responsible? How can I have any permanent *character* that will stand still long enough for praise or blame to be awarded? The chaplet of my days tumbles into a cast of disconnected beads as soon as the thread of inner necessity is drawn out by the preposterous indeterminist doctrine. Messrs. Fullerton and McTaggart have recently laid about them doughtily with this argument.

It may be good *ad hominem*, but otherwise it is pitiful. For I ask you, quite apart from other reasons, whether any man, woman or child, with a sense for realities, ought not to be ashamed to plead such principles as either dignity or imput-ability. Instinct and utility between them can safely be trusted to carry on the social business of punishment and praise. If a man does good acts we shall praise him, if he does bad acts we shall punish him,—anyhow, and quite apart from theories as to whether the acts result from what was previous in him or are novelties in a strict sense. To make our human ethics revolve about the question of 'merit' is a piteous unreality— God alone can know our merits, if we have any. The real ground for supposing free-will is indeed pragmatic, but it has nothing to do with this contemptible right to punish which has made such a noise in past discussions of the subject.

Free-will pragmatically means *novelties in the world*, the right to expect that in its deepest elements as well as in its surface phenomena, the future may not identically repeat and imitate the past. That imitation *en masse* is there, who can deny? The general 'uniformity of nature' is presupposed by every lesser law. But nature may be only approximately uni-form; and persons in whom knowledge of the world's past has bred pessimism (or doubts as to the world's good char-acter, which become certainties if that character be supposed eternally fixed) may naturally welcome free-will as a *melioris-tic* doctrine. It holds up improvement as at least possible; whereas determinism assures us that our whole notion of possibility is born of human ignorance, and that necessity and impossibility between them rule the destinies of the world.

Free-will is thus a general cosmological theory of *promise*, just like the Absolute, God, Spirit or Design. Taken abstractly, no one of these terms has any inner content, none of them gives us any picture, and no one of them would retain the least pragmatic value in a world whose character was obviously perfect from the start. Elation at mere existence, pure cosmic emotion and delight, would, it seems to me, quench all interest in those speculations, if the world were nothing but a lubberland of happiness already. Our interest in religious metaphysics arises in the fact that our empirical future feels to us unsafe, and needs some higher guarantee. If the past and present were purely good, who could wish that the future might possibly not resemble them? Who could desire free-will? Who would not say, with Huxley, 'let me be wound up every day like a watch, to go right fatally, and I ask no better freedom.' 'Freedom' in a world already perfect could only mean freedom to *be worse*, and who could be so insane as to wish that? To be necessarily what it is, to be impossibly aught else, would put the last touch of perfection upon optimism's universe. Surely the only *possibility* that one can rationally claim is the possibility that things may be *better*. That possibility, I need hardly say, is one that, as the actual world goes, we have ample grounds for desiderating.

Free-will thus has no meaning unless it be a doctrine of *relief*. As such, it takes its place with other religious doctrines. Between them, they build up the old wastes and repair the former desolations. Our spirit, shut within this courtyard of sense-experience, is always saying to the intellect upon the tower: 'Watchman, tell us of the night, if it aught of promise bear,' and the intellect gives it then these terms of promise.

Other than this practical significance, the words God, free-will, design, etc., have none. Yet dark tho they be in themselves, or intellectualistically taken, when we bear them into life's thicket with us the darkness *there* grows light about us. If you stop, in dealing with such words, with their definition, thinking that to be an intellectual finality, where are you? Stupidly staring at a pretentious sham! "Deus est Ens, a se, extra et supra omne genus, necessarium, unum, infinite perfectum, simplex, immutabile, immensum, aeternum, intelligens," etc.,—wherein is such a definition really instructive? It means less than nothing, in its pompous robe of adjectives. Pragmatism alone can read a positive meaning into it, and for that she turns her back upon the intellectualist point of view altogether. 'God's in his heaven; all's right with the world!'— *That's* the real heart of your theology, and for that you need no rationalist definitions.

Why should n't we all of us, rationalists as well as pragmatists, confess this? Pragmatism, so far from keeping her eyes bent on the immediate practical foreground, as she is accused of doing, dwells just as much upon the world's remotest perspectives.

See then how all these ultimate questions turn, as it were, upon their hinges; and from looking backwards upon principles, upon an *erkenntnisstheoretische Ich*, a God, a *Kausalitätsprinzip*, a Design, a Free-will, taken in themselves, as something august and exalted above facts,—see, I say, how pragmatism shifts the emphasis and looks forward into facts themselves. The really vital question for us all is, What is this world going to be? What is life eventually to make of itself? The centre of gravity of philosophy must therefore alter its place. The earth of things, long thrown into shadow by the glories of the upper ether, must resume its rights. To shift the emphasis in this way means that philosophic questions will fall to be treated by minds of a less abstractionist type than heretofore, minds more scientific and individualistic in their tone yet not irreligious either. It will be an alteration in 'the seat of authority' that reminds one almost of the protestant reformation. And as, to papal minds, protestantism has often seemed a mere mess of anarchy and confusion, such, no doubt, will pragmatism often seem to ultra-rationalist minds in philosophy. It will seem so much sheer trash, philosophically. But life wags on, all the same, and compasses its ends, in protestant countries. I venture to think that philosophic protestantism will compass a not dissimilar prosperity.

LECTURE IV

THE ONE AND THE MANY

WE SAW in the last lecture that the pragmatic method, in its dealings with certain concepts, instead of ending with admiring contemplation, plunges forward into the river of experience with them and prolongs the perspective by their means. Design, free-will, the absolute mind, spirit instead of matter, have for their sole meaning a better promise as to this world's outcome. Be they false or be they true, the meaning of them is this meliorism. I have sometimes thought of the phenomenon called 'total reflexion' in optics as a good symbol of the relation between abstract ideas and concrete realities, as pragmatism conceives it. Hold a tumbler of water a little above your eyes and look up through the water at its surface—or better still look similarly through the flat wall of an aquarium. You will then see an extraordinarily brilliant reflected image say of a candle-flame, or any other clear object, situated on the opposite side of the vessel. No candle-ray, under these circumstances gets beyond the water's surface: every ray is totally reflected back into the depths again. Now let the water represent the world of sensible facts, and let the air above it represent the world of abstract ideas. Both worlds are real, of course, and interact; but they interact only at their boundary, and the *locus* of everything that lives, and happens to us, so far as full experience goes, is the water. We are like fishes swimming in the sea of sense, bounded above by the superior element, but unable to breathe it pure or penetrate it. We get our oxygen from it, however, we touch it incessantly, now in this part, now in that, and every time we touch it, we are reflected back into the water with our course re-determined and re-energized. The abstract ideas of which the air consists are indispensable for life, but irrespirable by themselves, as it were, and only active in their re-directing function. All similes are halting, but this one rather takes my fancy. It shows how something, not sufficient for life in itself, may nevertheless be an effective determinant of life elsewhere.

In this present hour I wish to illustrate the pragmatic method by one more application. I wish to turn its light upon the ancient problem of 'the one and the many.' I suspect that in but few of you has this problem occasioned sleepless nights, and I should not be astonished if some of you told me it had never vexed you. I myself have come, by long brooding over it, to consider it the most central of all philosophic problems, central because so pregnant. I mean by this that if you know whether a man is a decided monist or a decided pluralist, you perhaps know more about the rest of his opinions than if you give him any other name ending in *ist*. To believe in the one or in the many, that is the classification with the maximum number of consequences. So bear with me for an hour while I try to inspire you with my own interest in this problem.

Philosophy has often been defined as the quest or the vision of the world's unity. We never hear this definition challenged, and it is true as far as it goes, for philosophy has indeed manifested above all things its interest in unity. But how about the *variety* in things? Is that such an irrelevant matter? If instead of using the term philosophy, we talk in general of our intellect and its needs, we quickly see that unity is only one of these. Acquaintance with the details of fact is always reckoned, along with their reduction to system, as an indispensable mark of mental greatness. Your 'scholarly' mind, of encyclopedic, philological type, your man essentially of learning, has never lacked for praise along with your philosopher. What our intellect really aims at is neither variety nor unity taken singly, but totality.[1] In this, acquaintance with reality's diversities is as important as understanding their connexion. The human passion of curiosity runs on all fours with the systematizing passion.

In spite of this obvious fact the unity of things has always been considered more illustrious, as it were, than their variety. When a young man first conceives the notion that the whole world forms one great fact, with all its parts moving abreast, as it were, and interlocked, he feels as if he were enjoying a great insight, and looks superciliously on all who still

[1]Compare A. Bellanger: *Les concepts de Cause, et l'activité intentionelle de l'Esprit*. Paris, Alcan, 1905, p. 79 ff.

fall short of this sublime conception. Taken thus abstractly as it first comes to one, the monistic insight is so vague as hardly to seem worth defending intellectually. Yet probably every one in this audience in some way cherishes it. A certain abstract monism, a certain emotional response to the character of oneness, as if it were a feature of the world not co-ordinate with its manyness, but vastly more excellent and eminent, is so prevalent in educated circles that we might almost call it a part of philosophic common sense. Of *course* the world is one, we say. How else could it be a world at all? Empiricists as a rule, are as stout monists of this abstract kind as rationalists are.

The difference is that the empiricists are less dazzled. Unity doesn't blind them to everything else, doesn't quench their curiosity for special facts, whereas there is a kind of rationalist who is sure to interpret abstract unity mystically and to forget everything else, to treat it as a principle; to admire and worship it; and thereupon to come to a full stop intellectually.

'The world is One!'—the formula may become a sort of number-worship. 'Three' and 'seven' have, it is true, been reckoned sacred numbers; but, abstractly taken, why is 'one' more excellent than 'forty-three,' or than 'two million and ten'? In this first vague conviction of the world's unity, there is so little to take hold of that we hardly know what we mean by it.

The only way to get forward with our notion is to treat it pragmatically. Granting the oneness to exist, what facts will be different in consequence? What will the unity be known as? The world is one—yes, but *how* one? What is the practical value of the oneness for *us*?

Asking such questions, we pass from the vague to the definite, from the abstract to the concrete. Many distinct ways in which a oneness predicated of the universe might make a difference, come to view. I will note successively the more obvious of these ways.

1. First, the world is at least *one subject of discourse*. If its manyness were so irremediable as to permit *no* union whatever of its parts, not even our minds could 'mean' the whole of it at once: they would be like eyes trying to look in oppo-

site directions. But in point of fact we mean to cover the whole of it by our abstract term 'world' or 'universe,' which expressly intends that no part shall be left out. Such unity of discourse carries obviously no farther monistic specifications. A 'chaos,' once so named, has as much unity of discourse as a cosmos. It is an odd fact that many monists consider a great victory scored for their side when pluralists say 'the universe is many.' " 'The *uni*verse'!" they chuckle—"his speech bewrayeth him. He stands confessed of monism out of his own mouth." Well, let things be one in that sense! You can then fling such a word as universe at the whole collection of them, but what matters it? It still remains to be ascertained whether they are one in any other sense that is more valuable.

2. Are they, for example, *continuous*? Can you pass from one to another, keeping always in your one universe without any danger of falling out? In other words, do the parts of our universe *hang together*, instead of being like detached grains of sand?

Even grains of sand hang together through the space in which they are embedded, and if you can in any way move through such space, you can pass continuously from number one of them to number two. Space and time are thus vehicles of continuity by which the world's parts hang together. The practical difference to us, resultant from these forms of union, is immense. Our whole motor life is based upon them.

3. There are innumerable other paths of practical continuity among things. Lines of *influence* can be traced by which they hang together. Following any such line you pass from one thing to another till you may have covered a good part of the universe's extent. Gravity and heat-conduction are such all-uniting influences, so far as the physical world goes. Electric, luminous and chemical influences follow similar lines of influence. But opaque and inert bodies interrupt the continuity here, so that you have to step round them, or change your mode of progress if you wish to get farther on that day. Practically, you have then lost your universe's unity, *so far as it was constituted by those first lines of influence*.

There are innumerable kinds of connexion that special things have with other special things; and the *ensemble* of any one of these connexions forms one sort of *system* by which things are conjoined. Thus men are conjoined in a vast network of *acquaintanceship*. Brown knows Jones, Jones knows Robinson, etc.; and *by choosing your farther intermediaries rightly* you may carry a message from Jones to the Empress of China, or the Chief of the African Pigmies, or to any one else in the inhabited world. But you are stopped short, as by a non-conductor, when you choose one man wrong in this experiment. What may be called love-systems are grafted on the acquaintance-system. A loves (or hates) B; B loves (or hates) C, etc. But these systems are smaller than the great acquaintance-system that they presuppose.

Human efforts are daily unifying the world more and more in definite systematic ways. We found colonial, postal, consular, commercial systems, all the parts of which obey definite influences that propagate themselves within the system but not to facts outside of it. The result is innumerable little hangings-together of the world's parts within the larger hangings-together, little worlds, not only of discourse but of operation, within the wider universe. Each system exemplifies one type or grade of union, its parts being strung on that peculiar kind of relation, and the same part may figure in many different systems, as a man may hold several offices and belong to various clubs. From this 'systematic' point of view, therefore, the pragmatic value of the world's unity is that all these definite networks actually and practically exist. Some are more enveloping and extensive, some less so; they are superposed upon each other; and between them all they let no individual elementary part of the universe escape. Enormous as is the amount of disconnexion among things (for these systematic influences and conjunctions follow rigidly exclusive paths), everything that exists is influenced in *some* way by something else, if you can only pick the way out rightly. Loosely speaking, and in general, it may be said that all things cohere and adhere to each other *somehow*, and that the universe exists practically in reticulated or concatenated forms which make of it a continuous or 'integrated' affair. Any kind of influence whatever helps to make the world one, so far as you can follow it from next to next. You may then say that 'the world *is* One,'—meaning in these respects, namely, and just so far as they obtain. But just as definitely is it *not* One,

so far as they do not obtain; and there is no species of connexion which will not fail, if, instead of choosing conductors
for it you choose non-conductors. You are then arrested at
your very first step and have to write the world down as a
pure *many* from that particular point of view. If our intellect
had been as much interested in disjunctive as it is in conjunctive relations, philosophy would have equally successfully
celebrated the world's *disunion*.

The great point is to notice that the oneness and the manyness are absolutely co-ordinate here. Neither is primordial or
more essential or excellent than the other. Just as with space,
whose separating of things seems exactly on a par with its
uniting of them, but sometimes one function and sometimes
the other is what comes home to us most, so, in our general
dealings with the world of influences, we now need conductors and now need non-conductors, and wisdom lies in knowing which is which at the appropriate moment.

4. All these systems of influence or non-influence may be
listed under the general problem of the world's *causal unity*.
If the minor causal influences among things should converge
towards one common causal origin of them in the past, one
great first cause for all that is, one might then speak of the
absolute causal unity of the world. God's *fiat* on creation's
day has figured in traditional philosophy as such an absolute
cause and origin. Transcendental Idealism, translating 'creation' into 'thinking' (or 'willing to think') calls the divine
act 'eternal' rather than 'first'; but the union of the many here
is absolute, just the same—the many would not *be*, save for
the One. Against this notion of the unity of origin of all
things there has always stood the pluralistic notion of an eternal self-existing many in the shape of atoms or even of spiritual units of some sort. The alternative has doubtless a
pragmatic meaning, but perhaps, as far as these lectures go,
we had better leave the question of unity of origin unsettled.

5. The most important sort of union that obtains among
things, pragmatically speaking, is their *generic unity*. Things
exist in kinds, there are many specimens in each kind, and
what the 'kind' implies for one specimen, it implies also for
every other specimen of that kind. We can easily conceive that
every fact in the world might be singular, that is, unlike any

other fact and sole of its kind. In such a world of singulars our logic would be useless, for logic works by predicating of the single instance what is true of all its kind. With no two things alike in the world, we should be unable to reason from our past experiences to our future ones. The existence of so much generic unity in things is thus perhaps the most momentous pragmatic specification of what it may mean to say 'the world is One.' *Absolute* generic unity would obtain if there were one *summum genus* under which all things without exception could be eventually subsumed. 'Beings,' 'thinkables,' 'experiences,' would be candidates for this position. Whether the alternatives expressed by such words have any pragmatic significance or not, is another question which I prefer to leave unsettled just now.

6. Another specification of what the phrase 'the world is one' may mean is *unity of purpose*. An enormous number of things in the world subserve a common purpose. All the manmade systems, administrative, industrial, military, or what not, exist each for its controlling purpose. Every living being pursues its own peculiar purposes. They co-operate, according to the degree of their development, in collective or tribal purposes, larger ends thus enveloping lesser ones, until an absolutely single, final and climacteric purpose subserved by all things without exception might conceivably be reached. It is needless to say that the appearances conflict with such a view. Any resultant, as I said in my third lecture, *may* have been purposed in advance, but none of the results we actually know in this world have in point of fact been purposed in advance in all their details. Men and nations start with a vague notion of being rich, or great, or good. Each step they make brings unforeseen chances into sight, and shuts out older vistas, and the specifications of the general purpose have to be daily changed. What is reached in the end may be better or worse than what was proposed, but it is always more complex and different.

Our different purposes also are at war with each other. Where one can't crush the other out, they compromise; and the result is again different from what any one distinctly proposed beforehand. Vaguely and generally, much of what was purposed may be gained; but everything makes strongly for the view that our world is incompletely unified teleologically and is still trying to get its unification better organized.

Whoever claims *absolute* teleological unity, saying that there is one purpose that every detail of the universe subserves, dogmatizes at his own risk. Theologians who dogmatize thus find it more and more impossible, as our acquaintance with the warring interests of the world's parts grows more concrete, to imagine what the one climacteric purpose may possibly be like. We see indeed that certain evils minister to ulterior goods, that the bitter makes the cocktail better, and that a bit of danger or hardship puts us agreeably to our trumps. We can vaguely generalize this into the doctrine that all the evil in the universe is but instrumental to its greater perfection. But the scale of the evil actually in sight defies all human tolerance; and transcendental idealism, in the pages of a Bradley or a Royce, brings us no farther than the book of Job did—God's ways are not our ways, so let us put our hands upon our mouth. A God who can relish such superfluities of horror is no God for human beings to appeal to. His animal spirits are too high, his practical jokes too monstrous. In other words the 'Absolute' with his one purpose, is not the man-like God of common people.

7. *Æsthetic union* among things also obtains, and is very analogous to teleological union. Things tell a story. Their parts hang together so as to work out a climax. They play into each other's hands expressively. Retrospectively, we can see that altho no definite purpose presided over a chain of events, yet the events fell into a dramatic form, with a start, a middle, and a finish. In point of fact all stories end; and here again the point of view of a many is the more natural one to take. The world is full of partial stories that run parallel to one another, beginning and ending at odd times. They mutually interlace and interfere at points, but we can not unify them completely in our minds. In following your life-history, I must temporarily turn my attention from my own. Even a biographer of twins would have to press them alternately upon his reader's attention.

It follows that whoever says that the whole world tells one story utters another of those monistic dogmas that a man believes at his risk. It is easy to see the world's history pluralistically, as a rope of which each fibre tells a separate tale; but to conceive of each cross-section of the rope as an absolutely single fact, and to sum the whole longitudinal series into one being living an undivided life, is harder. We have indeed the analogy of embryology to help us. The microscopist makes a hundred flat cross-sections of a given embryo, and mentally unites them into one solid whole. But the great world's ingredients, so far as they are beings, seem, like the rope's fibres, to be discontinuous cross-wise, and to cohere only in the longitudinal direction. Followed in that direction they are many. Even the embryologist, when he follows the *development* of his object, has to treat the history of each single organ in turn. *Absolute* æsthetic union is thus another barely abstract ideal. The world appears as something more epic than dramatic.

So far, then, we see how the world is unified by its many systems, kinds, purposes, and dramas. That there is more union in all these ways than openly appears is certainly true. That there *may* be one sovereign purpose, system, kind, and story, is a legitimate hypothesis. All I say here is that it is rash to affirm this dogmatically without better evidence than we possess at present.

8. The *great* monistic *denkmittel* for a hundred years past has been the notion of *the one Knower*. The many exist only as objects for his thought—exist in his dream, as it were; and *as he knows* them, they have one purpose, form one system, tell one tale for him. This notion of an *all-enveloping noetic unity* in things is the sublimest achievement of intellectualist philosophy. Those who believe in the Absolute, as the all-knower is termed, usually say that they do so for coercive reasons, which clear thinkers can not evade. The Absolute has far-reaching practical consequences, to some of which I drew attention in my second lecture. Many kinds of difference important to us would surely follow from its being true. I can not here enter into all the logical proofs of such a Being's existence, farther than to say that none of them seem to me sound. I must therefore treat the notion of an All-Knower simply as an hypothesis, exactly on a par logically with the pluralist notion that there is no point of view, no focus of information extant, from which the entire content of the uni-

verse is visible at once. "God's conscience," says Professor Royce,[1] "forms in its wholeness one luminously transparent conscious moment"—this is the type of noetic unity on which rationalism insists. Empiricism on the other hand is satisfied with the type of noetic unity that is humanly familiar. Everything gets known by *some* knower along with something else; but the knowers may in the end be irreducibly many, and the greatest knower of them all may yet not know the whole of everything, or even know what he does know at one single stroke:—he may be liable to forget. Whichever type obtained, the world would still be a universe noetically. Its parts would be conjoined by knowledge, but in the one case the knowledge would be absolutely unified, in the other it would be strung along and overlapped.

The notion of one instantaneous or eternal Knower—either adjective here means the same thing—is, as I said, the great intellectualist achievement of our time. It has practically driven out that conception of 'Substance' which earlier philosophers set such store by, and by which so much unifying work used to be done—universal substance which alone has being in and from itself, and of which all the particulars of experience are but forms to which it gives support. Substance has succumbed to the pragmatic criticisms of the English school. It appears now only as another name for the fact that phenomena as they come are actually grouped and given in coherent forms, the very forms in which we finite knowers experience or think them together. These forms of conjunction are as much parts of the tissue of experience as are the terms which they connect; and it is a great pragmatic achievement for recent idealism to have made the world hang together in these directly representable ways instead of drawing its unity from the 'inherence' of its parts—whatever that may mean—in an unimaginable principle behind the scenes.

'The world is one,' therefore, just so far as we experience it to be concatenated, one by as many definite conjunctions as appear. But then also *not* one by just as many definite *dis*junctions as we find. The oneness and the manyness of it thus obtain in respects which can be separately named. It is neither

<hr />

[1] *The Conception of God*, New York, 1897, p. 292.

a universe pure and simple nor a multiverse pure and simple. And its various manners of being one suggest, for their accurate ascertainment, so many distinct programs of scientific work. Thus the pragmatic question 'What is the oneness known as? What practical difference will it make?' saves us from all feverish excitement over it as a principle of sublimity and carries us forward into the stream of experience with a cool head. The stream may indeed reveal far more connexion and union than we now suspect, but we are not entitled on pragmatic principles to claim absolute oneness in any respect in advance.

It is so difficult to see definitely what absolute oneness can mean, that probably the majority of you are satisfied with the sober attitude which we have reached. Nevertheless there are possibly some radically monistic souls among you who are not content to leave the one and the many on a par. Union of various grades, union of diverse types, union that stops at non-conductors, union that merely goes from next to next, and means in many cases outer nextness only, and not a more internal bond, union of concatenation, in short; all that sort of thing seems to you a halfway stage of thought. The oneness of things, superior to their manyness, you think must also be more deeply true, must be the more real aspect of the world. The pragmatic view, you are sure, gives us a universe imperfectly rational. The real universe must form an unconditional unit of being, something consolidated, with its parts co-implicated through and through. Only then could we consider our estate completely rational.

There is no doubt whatever that this ultra-monistic way of thinking means a great deal to many minds. "One Life, One Truth, one Love, one Principle, One Good, One God"—I quote from a Christian Science leaflet which the day's mail brings into my hands—beyond doubt such a confession of faith has pragmatically an emotional value, and beyond doubt the word 'one' contributes to the value quite as much as the other words. But if we try to realize *intellectually* what we can possibly *mean* by such a glut of oneness we are thrown right back upon our pragmatistic determinations again. It means either the mere name One, the universe of discourse; or it means the sum total of all the ascertainable particular conjunctions and concatenations; or, finally, it means some one vehicle of conjunction treated as all-inclusive, like one origin, one purpose, or one knower. In point of fact it always means one *knower* to those who take it intellectually to-day. The one knower involves, they think, the other forms of conjunction. His world must have all its parts co-implicated in the one logical-æsthetical-teleological unit-picture which is his eternal dream.

The character of the absolute knower's picture is however so impossible for us to represent clearly, that we may fairly suppose that the authority which absolute monism undoubtedly possesses, and probably always will possess over some persons, draws its strength far less from intellectual than from mystical grounds. To interpret absolute monism worthily, be a mystic. Mystical states of mind in every degree are shown by history, usually tho not always, to make for the monistic view. This is no proper occasion to enter upon the general subject of mysticism, but I will quote one mystical pronouncement to show just what I mean. The paragon of all monistic systems is the Vedânta philosophy of Hindostan, and the paragon of Vedântist missionaries was the late Swami Vivekananda who visited our shores some years ago. The method of Vedântism is the mystical method. You do not reason, but after going through a certain discipline *you see*, and having seen, you can report the truth. Vivekananda thus reports the truth in one of his lectures here:

"Where is there any more misery for him who sees this Oneness in the universe, this Oneness of life, Oneness of everything? . . . This separation between man and man, man and woman, man and child, nation from nation, earth from moon, moon from sun, this separation between atom and atom is the cause really of all the misery, and the Vedânta says this separation does not exist, it is not real. It is merely apparent, on the surface. In the heart of things there is unity still. If you go inside you find that unity between man and man, women and children, races and races, high and low, rich and poor, the gods and men: all are One, and animals too, if you go deep enough, and he who has attained to that has no more delusion. . . . Where is there any more delusion for him? What can delude him? He knows the reality of everything, the secret of everything. Where is there any more misery for him? What does he desire? He has traced the reality of everything unto the Lord, that centre, that Unity of everything, and that is Eternal Bliss, Eternal Knowledge, Eternal Existence. Neither death nor disease nor sorrow nor misery nor discontent is There. . . . In the Centre, the reality, there is no one to be mourned for, no one to be sorry for. He has penetrated everything, the Pure One, the Formless, the Bodiless, the Stainless, He the Knower, He the great Poet, the Self-Existent, He who is giving to every one what he deserves."

Observe how radical the character of the monism here is. Separation is not simply overcome by the One, it is denied to exist. There is no many. We are not parts of the One; It has no parts; and since in a sense we undeniably *are*, it must be that each of us *is* the One, indivisibly and totally. *An Absolute One, and I that One,*—surely we have here a religion which, emotionally considered, has a high pragmatic value; it imparts a perfect sumptuosity of security. As our Swami says in another place:

"When man has seen himself as One with the infinite Being of the universe, when all separateness has ceased, when all men, all women, all angels, all gods, all animals, all plants, the whole universe has been melted into that oneness, then all fear disappears. Whom to fear? Can I hurt myself? Can I kill myself? Can I injure myself? Do you fear yourself? Then will all sorrow disappear. What can cause me sorrow? I am the One Existence of the universe. Then all jealousies will disappear; of whom to be jealous? Of myself? Then all bad feelings disappear. Against whom shall I have this bad feeling? Against myself? There is none in the universe but me . . . kill out this differentiation, kill out this superstition that there are many. 'He who, in this world of many, sees that One; he who, in this mass of insentiency, sees that One Sentient Being; he who in this world of shadow, catches that Reality, unto him belongs eternal peace, unto none else, unto none else.' "

We all have some ear for this monistic music: it elevates and reassures. We all have at least the germ of mysticism in us. And when our idealists recite their arguments for the Absolute, saying that the slightest union admitted anywhere carries logically absolute Oneness with it, and that the slightest separation admitted anywhere logically carries disunion remediless and complete, I cannot help suspecting that the palpable weak places in the intellectual reasonings they use are protected from their own criticism by a mystical feeling that, logic or no logic, absolute Oneness must somehow at any cost be true. Oneness overcomes *moral* separateness at any rate. In the passion of love we have the mystic germ of what might mean a total union of all sentient life. This mystical germ wakes up in us on hearing the monistic utterances, acknowledges their authority, and assigns to intellectual considerations a secondary place.

I will dwell no longer on these religious and moral aspects of the question in this lecture. When I come to my final lecture there will be something more to say.

Leave then out of consideration for the moment the authority which mystical insights may be conjectured eventually to possess; treat the problem of the One and the Many in a purely intellectual way; and we see clearly enough where pragmatism stands. With her criterion of the practical differences that theories make, we see that she must equally abjure absolute monism and absolute pluralism. The world is One just so far as its parts hang together by any definite connexion. It is many just so far as any definite connexion fails to obtain. And finally it is growing more and more unified by those systems of connexion at least which human energy keeps framing as time goes on.

It is possible to imagine alternative universes to the one we know, in which the most various grades and types of union should be embodied. Thus the lowest grade of universe would be a world of mere *withness*, of which the parts were only strung together by the conjunction 'and.' Such a universe is even now the collection of our several inner lives. The spaces and times of your imagination, the objects and events of your day-dreams are not only more or less incoherent *inter se*, but are wholly out of definite relation with the similar contents of any one else's mind. Our various reveries now as we sit here compenetrate each other idly without influencing or interfering. They coexist, but in no order and in no receptacle, being the nearest approach to an absolute 'many' that we can conceive. We can not even imagine any reason why they *should* be known all together, and we can imagine even less, if they were known together, how they could be known as one systematic whole.

But add our sensations and bodily actions, and the union mounts to a much higher grade. Our *audita et visa* and our acts fall into those receptacles of time and space in which each event finds its date and place. They form 'things' and are of 'kinds' too, and can be classed. Yet we can imagine a world of things and of kinds in which the causal interactions with which we are so familiar should not exist. Everything there might be inert towards everything else, and refuse to propagate its influence. Or gross mechanical influences might pass, but no chemical action. Such worlds would be far less unified than ours. Again there might be complete physico-chemical interaction, but no minds; or minds, but altogether private ones, with no social life; or social life limited to acquaintance, but no love; or love, but no customs or institutions that should systematize it. No one of these grades of universe would be absolutely irrational or disintegrated, inferior tho it might appear when looked at from the higher grades. For instance, if our minds should ever become 'telepathically' connected, so that we knew immediately, or could under certain conditions know immediately, each what the other was thinking, the world we now live in would appear to the thinkers in that world to have been of an inferior grade.

With the whole of past eternity open for our conjectures to range in, it may be lawful to wonder whether the various kinds of union now realized in the universe that we inhabit may not possibly have been successively evolved after the fashion in which we now see human systems evolving in consequence of human needs. If such an hypothesis were legitimate, total oneness would appear at the end of things rather than at their origin. In other words the notion of the 'Absolute' would have to be replaced by that of the 'Ultimate.' The two notions would have the same content—the maximally unified content of fact, namely—but their time-relations would be positively reversed.[1]

---

[1] Compare on the Ultimate, Mr. Schiller's essay "Activity and Substance," in his book entitled *Humanism*, p. 204.

After discussing the unity of the universe in this pragmatic way, you ought to see why I said in my second lecture, borrowing the word from my friend G. Papini, that pragmatism tends to *unstiffen* all our theories. The world's oneness has generally been affirmed abstractly only, and as if any one who questioned it must be an idiot. The temper of monists has been so vehement, as almost at times to be convulsive; and this way of holding a doctrine does not easily go with reasonable discussion and the drawing of distinctions. The theory of the Absolute, in particular, has had to be an article of faith, affirmed dogmatically and exclusively. The One and All, first in the order of being and of knowing, logically necessary itself, and uniting all lesser things in the bonds of mutual necessity, how could it allow of any mitigation of its inner rigidity? The slightest suspicion of pluralism, the minutest wiggle of independence of any one of its parts from the control of the totality would ruin it. Absolute unity brooks no degrees,—as well might you claim absolute purity for a glass of water because it contains but a single little cholera-germ. The independence, however infinitesimal, of a part, however small, would be to the Absolute as fatal as a cholera-germ.

Pluralism on the other hand has no need of this dogmatic rigoristic temper. Provided you grant *some* separation among things, some tremor of independence, some free play of parts on one another, some real novelty or chance, however minute, she is amply satisfied, and will allow you any amount, however great, of real union. How much of union there may be is a question that she thinks can only be decided empirically. The amount may be enormous, colossal; but absolute monism is shattered if, along with all the union, there has to be granted the slightest modicum, the most incipient nascency, or the most residual trace, of a separation that is not 'overcome.'

Pragmatism, pending the final empirical ascertainment of just what the balance of union and disunion among things may be, must obviously range herself upon the pluralistic side. Some day, she admits, even total union, with one knower, one origin, and a universe consolidated in every conceivable way, may turn out to be the most acceptable of all hypotheses. Meanwhile the opposite hypothesis, of a world imperfectly unified still, and perhaps always to remain so, must be sincerely entertained. This latter hypothesis is pluralism's doctrine. Since absolute monism forbids its being even considered seriously, branding it as irrational from the start, it is clear that pragmatism must turn its back on absolute monism, and follow pluralism's more empirical path.

This leaves us with the common-sense world, in which we find things partly joined and partly disjoined. 'Things,' then, and their 'conjunctions'—what do such words mean, pragmatically handled? In my next lecture, I will apply the pragmatic method to the stage of philosophizing known as Common Sense.

LECTURE V

IN THE LAST lecture we turned ourselves from the usual way of talking of the universe's oneness as a principle, sublime in all its blankness, towards a study of the special kinds of union which the universe enfolds. We found many of these to coexist with kinds of separation equally real. 'How far am I verified?' is the question which each kind of union and each kind of separation asks us here, so as good pragmatists we have to turn our face towards experience, towards 'facts.'

Absolute oneness remains, but only as an hypothesis, and that hypothesis is reduced nowadays to that of an omniscient knower who sees all things without exception as forming one single systematic fact. But the knower in question may still be conceived either as an Absolute or as an Ultimate; and over against the hypothesis of him in either form the counter-hypothesis that the widest field of knowledge that ever was or will be still contains some ignorance, may be legitimately held. Some bits of information always may escape.

This is the hypothesis of *noetic pluralism*, which monists consider so absurd. Since we are bound to treat it as respectfully as noetic monism, until the facts shall have tipped the beam, we find that our pragmatism, tho originally nothing but a method, has forced us to be friendly to the pluralistic view. It *may* be that some parts of the world are connected so loosely with some other parts as to be strung along by nothing but the copula *and*. They might even come and go without those other parts suffering any internal change. This pluralistic view, of a world of *additive* constitution, is one that pragmatism is unable to rule out from serious consideration. But this view leads one to the farther hypothesis that the actual world, instead of being complete 'eternally,' as the monists assure us, may be eternally incomplete, and at all times subject to addition or liable to loss.

It *is* at any rate incomplete in one respect, and flagrantly so. The very fact that we debate this question shows that *our knowledge* is incomplete at present and subject to addition. In respect of the knowledge it contains the world does genuinely change and grow. Some general remarks on the way in which our knowledge completes itself—when it does complete itself—will lead us very conveniently into our subject for this lecture, which is 'Common Sense.'

To begin with, our knowledge grows *in spots*. The spots may be large or small, but the knowledge never grows all over: some old knowledge always remains what it was. Your knowledge of pragmatism, let us suppose, is growing now. Later, its growth may involve considerable modification of opinions which you previously held to be true. But such modifications are apt to be gradual. To take the nearest possible example, consider these lectures of mine. What you first gain from them is probably a small amount of new information, a few new definitions, or distinctions, or points of view. But while these special ideas are being added, the rest of your knowledge stands still, and only gradually will you 'line up' your previous opinions with the novelties I am trying to instil, and modify to some slight degree their mass.

You listen to me now, I suppose, with certain prepossessions as to my competency, and these affect your reception of what I say, but were I suddenly to break off lecturing, and to begin to sing 'We won't go home till morning' in a rich baritone voice, not only would that new fact be added to your stock, but it would oblige you to define me differently, and that might alter your opinion of the pragmatic philosophy, and in general bring about a rearrangement of a number of your ideas. Your mind in such processes is strained, and sometimes painfully so, between its older beliefs and the novelties which experience brings along.

Our minds thus grow in spots; and like grease-spots, the spots spread. But we let them spread as little as possible: we keep unaltered as much of our old knowledge, as many of our old prejudices and beliefs, as we can. We patch and tinker more than we renew. The novelty soaks in; it stains the ancient mass; but it is also tinged by what absorbs it. Our past apperceives and co-operates; and in the new equilibrium in which each step forward in the process of learning terminates, it happens relatively seldom that the new fact is added *raw*.

More usually it is embedded cooked, as one might say, or stewed down in the sauce of the old.

New truths thus are resultants of new experiences and of old truths combined and mutually modifying one another. And since this is the case in the changes of opinion of to-day, there is no reason to assume that it has not been so at all times. It follows that very ancient modes of thought may have survived through all the later changes in men's opinions. The most primitive ways of thinking may not yet be wholly expunged. Like our five fingers, our ear-bones, our rudimentary caudal appendage, or our other 'vestigial' peculiarities, they may remain as indelible tokens of events in our race-history. Our ancestors may at certain moments have struck into ways of thinking which they might conceivably not have found. But once they did so, and after the fact, the inheritance continues. When you begin a piece of music in a certain key, you must keep the key to the end. You may alter your house *ad libitum*, but the ground-plan of the first architect persists— you can make great changes, but you can not change a Gothic church into a Doric temple. You may rinse and rinse the bottle, but you can't get the taste of the medicine or whiskey that first filled it wholly out.

My thesis now is this, that *our fundamental ways of thinking about things are discoveries of exceedingly remote ancestors, which have been able to preserve themselves throughout the experience of all subsequent time.* They form one great stage of equilibrium in the human mind's development, the stage of *common sense.* Other stages have grafted themselves upon this stage, but have never succeeded in displacing it. Let us consider this common-sense stage first, as if it might be final.

In practical talk, a man's common sense means his good judgment, his freedom from excentricity, his *gumption*, to use the vernacular word. In philosophy it means something entirely different, it means his use of certain intellectual forms or categories of thought. Were we lobsters, or bees, it might be that our organization would have led to our using quite different modes from these of apprehending our experiences. It *might* be too (we can not dogmatically deny this) that such categories, unimaginable by us to-day, would have proved on the whole as serviceable for handling our experiences mentally as those which we actually use.

If this sounds paradoxical to any one, let him think of analytical geometry. The identical figures which Euclid defined by intrinsic relations were defined by Descartes by the relations of their points to adventitious co-ordinates, the result being an absolutely different and vastly more potent way of handling curves. All our conceptions are what the Germans call *Denkmittel*, means by which we handle facts by thinking them. Experience merely as such doesn't come ticketed and labelled, we have first to discover what it is. Kant speaks of it as being in its first intention a *gewühl der erscheinungen*, a *rhapsodie der wahrnehmungen*, a mere motley which we have to unify by our wits. What we usually do is first to frame some system of concepts mentally classified, serialized, or connected in some intellectual way, and then to use this as a tally by which we 'keep tab' on the impressions that present themselves. When each is referred to some possible place in the conceptual system, it is thereby 'understood.' This notion of parallel 'manifolds' with their elements standing reciprocally in 'one-to-one relations,' is proving so convenient nowadays in mathematics and logic as to supersede more and more the older classificatory conceptions. There are many conceptual systems of this sort; and the sense manifold is also such a system. Find a one-to-one relation for your sense-impressions *anywhere* among the concepts, and in so far forth you rationalize the impressions. But obviously you can rationalize them by using various conceptual systems.

The old common-sense way of rationalizing them is by a set of concepts of which the most important are these:

Thing;
The same or different;
Kinds;
Minds;
Bodies;
One Time;
One Space;
Subjects and attributes;
Causal influences;

The fancied;
The real.

We are now so familiar with the order that these notions have woven for us out of the everlasting weather of our perceptions that we find it hard to realize how little of a fixed routine the perceptions follow when taken by themselves. The word weather is a good one to use here. In Boston, for example, the weather has almost no routine, the only law being that if you have had any weather for two days, you will probably but not certainly have another weather on the third. Weather-experience as it thus comes to Boston, is discontinuous and chaotic. In point of temperature, of wind, rain or sunshine, it *may* change three times a day. But the Washington weather-bureau intellectualizes this disorder by making each successive bit of Boston weather *episodic*. It refers it to its place and moment in a continental cyclone, on the history of which the local changes everywhere are strung as beads are strung upon a cord.

Now it seems almost certain that young children and the inferior animals take all their experiences very much as uninstructed Bostonians take their weather. They know no more of time or space as world-receptacles, or of permanent subjects and changing predicates, or of causes, or kinds, or thoughts, or things, than our common people know of continental cyclones. A baby's rattle drops out of his hand, but the baby looks not for it. It has 'gone out' for him, as a candle-flame goes out; and it comes back, when you replace it in his hand, as the flame comes back when relit. The idea of its being a 'thing,' whose permanent existence by itself he might interpolate between its successive apparitions has evidently not occurred to him. It is the same with dogs. Out of sight, out of mind, with them. It is pretty evident that they have no *general* tendency to interpolate 'things.' Let me quote here a passage from my colleague G. Santayana's book.

"If a dog, while sniffing about contentedly, sees his master arriving after a long absence . . . the poor brute asks for no reason why his master went, why he has come again, why he should be loved, or why presently while lying at his feet you forget him and begin to grunt and dream of the chase—all that is an utter mystery, utterly unconsidered. Such experi-

ence has variety, scenery, and a certain vital rhythm; its story
might be told in dithyrambic verse. It moves wholly by inspiration; every event is providential, every act unpremeditated.
Absolute freedom and absolute helplessness have met together: you depend wholly on divine favor, yet that unfathomable agency is not distinguishable from your own life.
. . . [But] the figures even of that disordered drama have
their exits and their entrances; and their cues can be gradually
discovered by a being capable of fixing his attention and retaining the order of events. . . . In proportion as such
understanding advances, each moment of experience becomes
consequential and prophetic of the rest. The calm places in
life are filled with power and its spasms with resource. No
emotion can overwhelm the mind, for of none is the basis or
issue wholly hidden; no event can disconcert it altogether,
because it sees beyond. Means can be looked for to escape
from the worst predicament; and whereas each moment had
been formerly filled with nothing but its own adventures and
surprised emotion, each now makes room for the lesson of
what went before and surmises what may be the plot of the
whole."[1]

Even to-day science and philosophy are still laboriously
trying to part fancies from realities in our experience; and in
primitive times they made only the most incipient distinctions
in this line. Men believed whatever they thought with any
liveliness, and they mixed their dreams with their realities inextricably. The categories of 'thought' and 'things' are indispensable here—instead of being realities we now call certain
experiences only 'thoughts.' There is not a category, among
those enumerated, of which we may not imagine the use to
have thus originated historically and only gradually spread.

That one Time which we all believe in and in which each
event has its definite date, that one Space in which each thing
has its position, these abstract notions unify the world incomparably; but in their finished shape as concepts how different
they are from the loose unordered time-and-space experiences
of natural men! Everything that happens to us brings its own
duration and extension, and both are vaguely surrounded by

[1] *The Life of Reason: Reason in Common Sense*, 1905, p. 59.

a marginal 'more' that runs into the duration and extension of the next thing that comes. But we soon lose all our definite bearings; and not only do our children make no distinction between yesterday and the day before yesterday, the whole past being churned up together, but we adults still do so whenever the times are large. It is the same with spaces. On a map I can distinctly see the relation of London, Constantinople, and Pekin to the place where I am; in reality I utterly fail to *feel* the facts which the map symbolizes. The directions and distances are vague, confused and mixed. Cosmic space and cosmic time, so far from being the intuitions that Kant said they were, are constructions as patently artificial as any that science can show. The great majority of the human race never use these notions, but live in plural times and spaces, interpenetrant and *durcheinander*.

Permanent 'things' again; the 'same' thing and its various 'appearances' and 'alterations'; the different 'kinds' of thing; with the 'kind' used finally as a 'predicate,' of which the thing remains the 'subject'—what a straightening of the tangle of our experience's immediate flux and sensible variety does this list of terms suggest! And it is only the smallest part of his experience's flux that any one actually does straighten out by applying to it these conceptual instruments. Out of them all our lowest ancestors probably used only, and then most vaguely and inaccurately, the notion of 'the same again.' But even then if you had asked them whether the same were a 'thing' that had endured throughout the unseen interval, they would probably have been at a loss, and would have said that they had never asked that question, or considered matters in that light.

Kinds, and sameness of kind—what colossally useful *denkmittel* for finding our way among the many! The manyness might conceivably have been absolute. Experiences might have all been singulars, no one of them occurring twice. In such a world logic would have had no application; for kind and sameness of kind are logic's only instruments. Once we know that whatever is of a kind is also of that kind's kind, we can travel through the universe as if with seven-league boots. Brutes surely never use these abstractions, and civilized men use them in most various amounts.

Causal influence, again! This, if anything, seems to have been an antediluvian conception; for we find primitive men thinking that almost everything is significant and can exert influence of some sort. The search for the more definite influences seems to have started in the question: "Who, or what, is to blame?"—for any illness, namely, or disaster, or untoward thing. From this centre the search for causal influences has spread. Hume and 'Science' together have tried to eliminate the whole notion of influence, substituting the entirely different *denkmittel* of 'law.' But law is a comparatively recent invention, and influence reigns supreme in the older realm of common sense.

The 'possible,' as something less than the actual and more than the wholly unreal, is another of these magisterial notions of common sense. Criticise them as you may, they persist; and we fly back to them the moment critical pressure is relaxed. 'Self,' 'body,' in the substantial or metaphysical sense— no one escapes subjection to *those* forms of thought. In practice, the common-sense *denkmittel* are uniformly victorious. Every one, however instructed, still thinks of a 'thing' in the common-sense way, as a permanent unit-subject that 'supports' its attributes interchangeably. No one stably or sincerely uses the more critical notion, of a group of sense-qualities united by a law. With these categories in our hand, we make our plans and plot together, and connect all the remoter parts of experience with what lies before our eyes. Our later and more critical philosophies are mere fads and fancies compared with this natural mother-tongue of thought.

Common sense appears thus as a perfectly definite stage in our understanding of things, a stage that satisfies in an extraordinarily successful way the purposes for which we think. 'Things' do exist, even when we do not see them. Their 'kinds' also exist. Their 'qualities' are what they act by, and are what we act on; and these also exist. These lamps shed their quality of light on every object in this room. We intercept *it* on its way whenever we hold up an opaque screen. It is the very sound that my lips emit that travels into your ears. It is the sensible heat of the fire that migrates into the water in which we boil an egg; and we can change the heat into coolness by dropping in a lump of ice. At this stage of phi-

losophy all non-European men without exception have remained. It suffices for all the necessary practical ends of life;
and, among our own race even, it is only the highly sophisticated specimens, the minds debauched by learning, as Berkeley calls them, who have ever even suspected common sense
of not being absolutely true.

But when we look back, and speculate as to how the
common-sense categories may have achieved their wonderful
supremacy, no reason appears why it may not have been
by a process just like that by which the conceptions due to
Democritus, Berkeley, or Darwin, achieved their similar
triumphs in more recent times. In other words, they may have
been successfully *discovered* by prehistoric geniuses whose
names the night of antiquity has covered up; they may have
been verified by the immediate facts of experience which they
first fitted; and then from fact to fact and from man to man
they may have *spread*, until all language rested on them and
we are now incapable of thinking naturally in any other
terms. Such a view would only follow the rule that has proved
elsewhere so fertile, of assuming the vast and remote to conform to the laws of formation that we can observe at work in
the small and near.

For all utilitarian practical purposes these conceptions amply suffice; but that they began at special points of discovery
and only gradually spread from one thing to another, seems
proved by the exceedingly dubious limits of their application
to-day. We assume for certain purposes one 'objective' Time
that *aequabiliter fluit*, but we don't livingly believe in or realize any such equally-flowing time. 'Space' is a less vague notion; but 'things,' what are they? Is a constellation properly a
thing? or an army? or is an *ens rationis* such as space or justice
a thing? Is a knife whose handle and blade are changed the
'same'? Is the 'changeling,' whom Locke so seriously discusses, of the human 'kind'? Is 'telepathy' a 'fancy' or a 'fact'?
The moment you pass beyond the practical use of these categories (a use usually suggested sufficiently by the circumstances of the special case) to a merely curious or speculative
way of thinking, you find it impossible to say within just what
limits of fact any one of them shall apply.

The peripatetic philosophy, obeying rationalist propensities, has tried to eternalize the common-sense categories by treating them very technically and articulately. A 'thing' for instance is a being, or *ens*. An *ens* is a subject in which qualities 'inhere.' A subject is a substance. Substances are of kinds, and kinds are definite in number, and discrete. These distinctions are fundamental and eternal. As terms of *discourse* they are indeed magnificently useful, but what they mean, apart from their use in steering our discourse to profitable issues, does not appear. If you ask a scholastic philosopher what a substance may be in itself, apart from its being the support of attributes, he simply says that your intellect knows perfectly what the word means.

But what the intellect knows clearly is only the word itself and its steering function. So it comes about that intellects *sibi permissi*, intellects only curious and idle, have forsaken the common-sense level for what in general terms may be called the 'critical' level of thought. Not merely *such* intellects either—your Humes and Berkeleys and Hegels; but practical observers of facts, your Galileos, Daltons, Faradays, have found it impossible to treat the *naïfs* sense-termini of common sense as ultimately real. As common sense interpolates her constant 'things' between our intermittent sensations, so science *extra*polates her world of 'primary' qualities, her atoms, her ether, her magnetic fields, and the like, beyond the common-sense world. The 'things' are now invisible impalpable things; and the old visible common-sense things are supposed to result from the mixture of these invisibles. Or else the whole *naïf* conception of thing gets superseded, and a thing's name is interpreted as denoting only the law or *regel der verbindung* by which certain of our sensations habitually succeed or coexist.

Science and critical philosophy thus burst the bounds of common sense. With science *naïf* realism ceases: 'Secondary' qualities become unreal; primary ones alone remain. With critical philosophy, havoc is made of everything. The common-sense categories one and all cease to represent anything in the way of *being*; they are but sublime tricks of human thought, our ways of escaping bewilderment in the midst of sensation's irremediable flow.

But the scientific tendency in critical thought, tho inspired

at first by purely intellectual motives, has opened an entirely
unexpected range of practical utilities to our astonished view.
Galileo gave us accurate clocks and accurate artillery-practice;
the chemists flood us with new medicines and dye-stuffs; Am-
père and Faraday have endowed us with the New York sub-
way and with Marconi telegrams. The hypothetical things
that such men have invented, defined as they have defined
them, are showing an extraordinary fertility in consequences
verifiable by sense. Our logic can deduce from them a consequence due under certain conditions, we can then bring about
the conditions, and presto, the consequence is there before
our eyes. The scope of the practical control of nature newly
put into our hand by scientific ways of thinking vastly exceeds
the scope of the old control grounded on common sense. Its
rate of increase accelerates so that no one can trace the limit;
one may even fear that the *being* of man may be crushed by
his own powers, that his fixed nature as an organism may not
prove adequate to stand the strain of the ever increasingly
tremendous functions, almost divine creative functions, which
his intellect will more and more enable him to wield. He may
drown in his wealth like a child in a bath-tub, who has turned
on the water and who can not turn it off.

The philosophic stage of criticism, much more thorough in
its negations than the scientific stage, so far gives us no new
range of practical power. Locke, Hume, Berkeley, Kant, Hegel, have all been utterly sterile, so far as shedding any light
on the details of nature goes, and I can think of no invention
or discovery that can be directly traced to anything in their
peculiar thought, for neither with Berkeley's tar-water nor
with Kant's nebular hypothesis had their respective philosophic tenets anything to do. The satisfactions they yield to
their disciples are intellectual, not practical; and even then we
have to confess that there is a large minus-side to the account.

There are thus at least three well-characterized levels, stages
or types of thought about the world we live in, and the notions of one stage have one kind of merit, those of another
stage another kind. It is impossible, however, to say that any
stage as yet in sight is absolutely more *true* than any other.
Common sense is the more *consolidated* stage, because it got
its innings first, and made all language into its ally. Whether

it or science be the more *august* stage may be left to private judgment. But neither consolidation nor augustness are decisive marks of truth. If common sense were true, why should science have had to brand the secondary qualities, to which our world owes all its living interest, as false, and to invent an invisible world of points and curves and mathematical equations instead? Why should it have needed to transform causes and activities into laws of 'functional variation'? Vainly did scholasticism, common sense's college-trained younger sister, seek to stereotype the forms the human family had always talked with, to make them definite and fix them for eternity. Substantial forms (in other words our secondary qualities) hardly outlasted the year of our Lord 1600. People were already tired of them then; and Galileo, and Descartes, with his 'new philosophy,' gave them only a little later their *coup de grâce*.

But now if the new kinds of scientific 'thing,' the corpuscular and etheric world, were essentially more 'true,' why should they have excited so much criticism within the body of science itself? Scientific logicians are saying on every hand that these entities and their determinations, however definitely conceived, should not be held for literally real. It is *as if* they existed; but in reality they are like co-ordinates or logarithms, only artificial short-cuts for taking us from one part to another of experience's flux. We can cipher fruitfully with them; they serve us wonderfully; but we must not be their dupes.

There is no *ringing* conclusion possible when we compare these types of thinking, with a view to telling which is the more absolutely true. Their naturalness, their intellectual economy, their fruitfulness for practice, all start up as distinct tests of their veracity, and as a result we get confused. Common sense is *better* for one sphere of life, science for another, philosophic criticism for a third; but whether either be *truer* absolutely, Heaven only knows. Just now, if I understand the matter rightly, we are witnessing a curious reversion to the common sense way of looking at physical nature, in the philosophy of science favored by such men as Mach, Ostwald and Duhem. According to these teachers no hypothesis is truer than any other in the sense of being a more literal copy

of reality. They are all but ways of talking on our part, to be
compared solely from the point of view of their *use*. The only
literally true thing is *reality*; and the only reality we know is,
for these logicians, sensible reality, the flux of our sensations
and emotions as they pass. 'Energy' is the collective name
(according to Ostwald) for the sensations just as they present
themselves (the movement, heat, magnetic pull, or light, or
whatever it may be) when they are measured in certain ways.
So measuring them, we are enabled to describe the correlated
changes which they show us, in formulas matchless for their
simplicity and fruitfulness for human use. They are sovereign
triumphs of economy in thought.

No one can fail to admire the 'energetic' philosophy. But
the hypersensible entities, the corpuscles and vibrations, hold
their own with most physicists and chemists, in spite of its
appeal. It seems too economical to be all-sufficient. Profusion,
not economy, may after all be reality's key-note.

I am dealing here with highly technical matters, hardly suitable for popular lecturing, and in which my own competence
is small. All the better for my conclusion, however, which at
this point is this. The whole notion of truth, which naturally
and without reflexion we assume to mean the simple duplication by the mind of a ready-made and given reality, proves
hard to understand clearly. There is no simple test available
for adjudicating offhand between the divers types of thought
that claim to possess it. Common sense, common science or
corpuscular philosophy, ultra-critical science, or energetics,
and critical or idealistic philosophy, all seem insufficiently true
in some regard and leave some dissatisfaction. It is evident
that the conflict of these so widely differing systems obliges
us to overhaul the very idea of truth, for at present we have
no definite notion of what the word may mean. I shall face
that task in my next lecture, and will add but a few words, in
finishing the present one.

There are only two points that I wish you to retain from
the present lecture. The first one relates to common sense. We
have seen reason to suspect it, to suspect that in spite of their
being so venerable, of their being so universally used and
built into the very structure of language, its categories may
after all be only a collection of extraordinarily successful

hypotheses (historically discovered or invented by single men, but gradually communicated, and used by everybody) by which our forefathers have from time immemorial unified and straightened the discontinuity of their immediate experiences, and put themselves into an equilibrium with the surface of nature so satisfactory for ordinary practical purposes that it certainly would have lasted forever, but for the excessive intellectual vivacity of Democritus, Archimedes, Galileo, Berkeley, and other excentric geniuses whom the example of such men inflamed. Retain, I pray you, this suspicion about common sense.

The other point is this. Ought not the existence of the various types of thinking which we have reviewed, each so splendid for certain purposes, yet all conflicting still, and neither one of them able to support a claim of absolute veracity, to awaken a presumption favorable to the pragmatistic view that all our theories are *instrumental*, are mental modes of *adaptation* to reality, rather than revelations or gnostic answers to some divinely instituted world-enigma? I expressed this view as clearly as I could in the second of these lectures. Certainly the restlessness of the actual theoretic situation, the value for some purposes of each thought-level, and the inability of either to expel the others decisively, suggest this pragmatistic view, which I hope that the next lectures may soon make entirely convincing. May there not after all be a possible ambiguity in truth?

LECTURE VI

PRAGMATISM'S CONCEPTION OF TRUTH

WHEN Clerk-Maxwell was a child it is written that he had a mania for having everything explained to him, and that when people put him off with vague verbal accounts of any phenomenon he would interrupt them impatiently by saying, 'Yes; but I want you to tell me the *particular go* of it!' Had his question been about truth, only a pragmatist could have told him the particular go of it. I believe that our contemporary pragmatists, especially Messrs. Schiller and Dewey, have given the only tenable account of this subject. It is a very ticklish subject, sending subtle rootlets into all kinds of crannies, and hard to treat in the sketchy way that alone befits a public lecture. But the Schiller-Dewey view of truth has been so ferociously attacked by rationalistic philosophers, and so abominably misunderstood, that here, if anywhere, is the point where a clear and simple statement should be made.

I fully expect to see the pragmatist view of truth run through the classic stages of a theory's career. First, you know, a new theory is attacked as absurd; then it is admitted to be true, but obvious and insignificant; finally it is seen to be so important that its adversaries claim that they themselves discovered it. Our doctrine of truth is at present in the first of these three stages, with symptoms of the second stage having begun in certain quarters. I wish that this lecture might help it beyond the first stage in the eyes of many of you.

Truth, as any dictionary will tell you, is a property of certain of our ideas. It means their 'agreement,' as falsity means their disagreement, with 'reality.' Pragmatists and intellectualists both accept this definition as a matter of course. They begin to quarrel only after the question is raised as to what may precisely be meant by the term 'agreement,' and what by the term 'reality,' when reality is taken as something for our ideas to agree with.

In answering these questions the pragmatists are more analytic and painstaking, the intellectualists more offhand and irreflective. The popular notion is that a true idea must copy its reality. Like other popular views, this one follows the analogy of the most usual experience. Our true ideas of sensible things do indeed copy them. Shut your eyes and think of yonder clock on the wall, and you get just such a true picture or copy of its dial. But your idea of its 'works' (unless you are a clock-maker) is much less of a copy, yet it passes muster, for it in no way clashes with the reality. Even though it should shrink to the mere word 'works,' that word still serves you truly; and when you speak of the 'time-keeping function' of the clock, or of its spring's 'elasticity,' it is hard to see exactly what your ideas can copy.

You perceive that there is a problem here. Where our ideas cannot copy definitely their object, what does agreement with that object mean? Some idealists seem to say that they are true whenever they are what God means that we ought to think about that object. Others hold the copy-view all through, and speak as if our ideas possessed truth just in proportion as they approach to being copies of the Absolute's eternal way of thinking.

These views, you see, invite pragmatistic discussion. But the great assumption of the intellectualists is that truth means essentially an inert static relation. When you've got your true idea of anything, there's an end of the matter. You're in possession; you *know*; you have fulfilled your thinking destiny. You are where you ought to be mentally; you have obeyed your categorical imperative; and nothing more need follow on that climax of your rational destiny. Epistemologically you are in stable equilibrium.

Pragmatism, on the other hand, asks its usual question. "Grant an idea or belief to be true," it says, "what concrete difference will its being true make in any one's actual life? How will the truth be realized? What experiences will be different from those which would obtain if the belief were false? What, in short, is the truth's cash-value in experiential terms?"

The moment pragmatism asks this question, it sees the answer: *True ideas are those that we can assimilate, validate, corroborate and verify. False ideas are those that we can not.* That is the practical difference it makes to us to have true ideas; that, therefore, is the meaning of truth, for it is all that truth is known-as.

This thesis is what I have to defend. The truth of an idea is not a stagnant property inherent in it. Truth *happens* to an idea. It *becomes* true, is *made* true by events. Its verity *is* in fact an event, a process: the process namely of its verifying itself, its veri-*fication*. Its validity is the process of its valid-*ation*.

But what do the words verification and validation themselves pragmatically mean? They again signify certain practical consequences of the verified and validated idea. It is hard to find any one phrase that characterizes these consequences better than the ordinary agreement-formula—just such consequences being what we have in mind whenever we say that our ideas 'agree' with reality. They lead us, namely, through the acts and other ideas which they instigate, into or up to, or towards, other parts of experience with which we feel all the while—such feeling being among our potentialities—that the original ideas remain in agreement. The connexions and transitions come to us from point to point as being progressive, harmonious, satisfactory. This function of agreeable leading is what we mean by an idea's verification. Such an account is vague and it sounds at first quite trivial, but it has results which it will take the rest of my hour to explain.

Let me begin by reminding you of the fact that the possession of true thoughts means everywhere the possession of invaluable instruments of action; and that our duty to gain truth, so far from being a blank command from out of the blue, or a 'stunt' self-imposed by our intellect, can account for itself by excellent practical reasons.

The importance to human life of having true beliefs about matters of fact is a thing too notorious. We live in a world of realities that can be infinitely useful or infinitely harmful. Ideas that tell us which of them to expect count as the true ideas in all this primary sphere of verification, and the pursuit of such ideas is a primary human duty. The possession of truth, so far from being here an end in itself, is only a preliminary means towards other vital satisfactions. If I am lost in the woods and starved, and find what looks like a cow-path, it is of the utmost importance that I should think of a human habitation at the end of it, for if I do so and follow it, I save myself. The true thought is useful here because the house which is its object is useful. The practical value of true ideas is thus primarily derived from the practical importance of their objects to us. Their objects are, indeed, not important at all times. I may on another occasion have no use for the house; and then my idea of it, however verifiable, will be practically irrelevant, and had better remain latent. Yet since almost any object may some day become temporarily important, the advantage of having a general stock of *extra* truths, of ideas that shall be true of merely possible situations, is obvious. We store such extra truths away in our memories, and with the overflow we fill our books of reference. Whenever such an extra truth becomes practically relevant to one of our emergencies, it passes from cold-storage to do work in the world and our belief in it grows active. You can say of it then either that 'it is useful because it is true' or that 'it is true because it is useful.' Both these phrases mean exactly the same thing, namely that here is an idea that gets fulfilled and can be verified. True is the name for whatever idea starts the verification-process, useful is the name for its completed function in experience. True ideas would never have been singled out as such, would never have acquired a class-name, least of all a name suggesting value, unless they had been useful from the outset in this way.

From this simple cue pragmatism gets her general notion of truth as something essentially bound up with the way in which one moment in our experience may lead us towards other moments which it will be worth while to have been led to. Primarily, and on the common-sense level, the truth of a state of mind means this function of *a leading that is worth while*. When a moment in our experience, of any kind whatever, inspires us with a thought that is true, that means that sooner or later we dip by that thought's guidance into the particulars of experience again and make advantageous connexion with them. This is a vague enough statement, but I beg you to retain it, for it is essential.

Our experience meanwhile is all shot through with regularities. One bit of it can warn us to get ready for another bit, can 'intend' or be 'significant of' that remoter object. The object's advent is the significance's verification. Truth, in these cases, meaning nothing but eventual verification, is manifestly incompatible with waywardness on our part. Woe to him whose beliefs play fast and loose with the order which realities follow in his experience; they will lead him nowhere or else make false connexions.

By 'realities' or 'objects' here, we mean either things of common sense, sensibly present, or else common-sense relations, such as dates, places, distances, kinds, activities. Following our mental image of a house along the cow-path, we actually come to see the house; we get the image's full verification. *Such simply and fully verified leadings are certainly the originals and prototypes of the truth-process.* Experience offers indeed other forms of truth-process, but they are all conceivable as being primary verifications arrested, multiplied or substituted one for another.

Take, for instance, yonder object on the wall. You and I consider it to be a 'clock,' altho no one of us has seen the hidden works that make it one. We let our notion pass for true without attempting to verify. If truths mean verification-process essentially, ought we then to call such unverified truths as this abortive? No, for they form the overwhelmingly large number of the truths we live by. Indirect as well as direct verifications pass muster. Where circumstantial evidence is sufficient, we can go without eye-witnessing. Just as we here assume Japan to exist without ever having been there, because it *works* to do so, everything we know conspiring with the belief, and nothing interfering, so we assume that thing to be a clock. We *use* it as a clock, regulating the length of our lecture by it. The verification of the assumption here means its leading to no frustration or contradiction. Verifi-*ability* of wheels and weights and pendulum is as good as verification. For one truth-process completed there are a million in our lives that function in this state of nascency. They turn us *towards* direct verification; lead us into the *surroundings* of the objects they envisage; and then, if everything runs on harmoniously, we are so sure that verification is possible that we omit it, and are usually justified by all that happens.

Truth lives, in fact, for the most part on a credit system. Our thoughts and beliefs 'pass,' so long as nothing challenges them, just as bank-notes pass so long as nobody refuses them. But this all points to direct face-to-face verifications somewhere, without which the fabric of truth collapses like a financial system with no cash-basis whatever. You accept my verification of one thing, I yours of another. We trade on each other's truth. But beliefs verified concretely by *somebody* are the posts of the whole superstructure.

Another great reason—beside economy of time—for waiving complete verification in the usual business of life is that all things exist in kinds and not singly. Our world is found once for all to have that peculiarity. So that when we have once directly verified our ideas about one specimen of a kind, we consider ourselves free to apply them to other specimens without verification. A mind that habitually discerns the kind of thing before it, and acts by the law of the kind immediately, without pausing to verify, will be a 'true' mind in ninety-nine out of a hundred emergencies, proved so by its conduct fitting everything it meets, and getting no refutation.

Indirectly or only potentially verifying processes may thus be true as well as full verification-processes. They work as true processes would work, give us the same advantages, and claim our recognition for the same reasons. All this on the common-sense level of matters of fact, which we are alone considering.

But matters of fact are not our only stock in trade. *Relations among purely mental ideas* form another sphere where true and false beliefs obtain, and here the beliefs are absolute, or unconditional. When they are true they bear the name either of definitions or of principles. It is either a principle or a definition that 1 and 1 make 2, that 2 and 1 make 3, and so on; that white differs less from gray than it does from black; that when the cause begins to act the effect also commences. Such propositions hold of all possible 'ones,' of all conceivable 'whites' and 'grays' and 'causes.' The objects here are mental objects. Their relations are perceptually obvious at a glance, and no sense-verification is necessary. Moreover, once true, always true, of those same mental objects. Truth here has an 'eternal' character. If you can find a concrete thing anywhere that is 'one' or 'white' or 'gray' or an 'effect,' then your principles will everlastingly apply to it. It is but a case of ascertaining the kind, and then applying the law of its kind to the particular object. You are sure to get truth if you can but name the kind rightly, for your mental relations hold good of everything of that kind without exception. If you then, nevertheless, failed to get truth concretely, you would say that you had classed your real objects wrongly.

In this realm of mental relations, truth again is an affair of leading. We relate one abstract idea with another, framing in the end great systems of logical and mathematical truth, under the respective terms of which the sensible facts of experience eventually arrange themselves, so that our eternal truths hold good of realities also. This marriage of fact and theory is endlessly fertile. What we say is here already true in advance of special verification, *if we have subsumed our objects rightly*. Our ready-made ideal framework for all sorts of possible objects follows from the very structure of our thinking. We can no more play fast and loose with these abstract relations than we can do so with our sense-experiences. They coerce us; we must treat them consistently, whether or not we like the results. The rules of addition apply to our debts as rigorously as to our assets. The hundredth decimal of π, the ratio of the circumference to its diameter, is predetermined ideally now, tho no one may have computed it. If we should ever need the figure in our dealings with an actual circle we should need to have it given rightly, calculated by the usual rules; for it is the same kind of truth that those rules elsewhere calculate.

Between the coercions of the sensible order and those of the ideal order, our mind is thus wedged tightly. Our ideas must agree with realities, be such realities concrete or abstract, be they facts or be they principles, under penalty of endless inconsistency and frustration.

So far, intellectualists can raise no protest. They can only say that we have barely touched the skin of the matter.

Realities mean, then, either concrete facts, or abstract kinds of things and relations perceived intuitively between them. They furthermore and thirdly mean, as things that new ideas of ours must no less take account of, the whole body of other truths already in our possession. But what now does 'agreement' with such threefold realities mean?—to use again the definition that is current.

Here it is that pragmatism and intellectualism begin to part company. Primarily, no doubt, to agree means to copy, but we saw that the mere word 'clock' would do instead of a mental picture of its works, and that of many realities our ideas can only be symbols and not copies. 'Past time,' 'power,' 'spontaneity,'—how can our mind copy such realities?

To 'agree' in the widest sense with a reality *can only mean to be guided either straight up to it or into its surroundings, or to be put into such working touch with it as to handle either it or something connected with it better than if we disagreed.* Better either intellectually or practically! And often agreement will only mean the negative fact that nothing contradictory from the quarter of that reality comes to interfere with the way in which our ideas guide us elsewhere. To copy a reality is, indeed, one very important way of agreeing with it, but it is far from being essential. The essential thing is the process of being guided. Any idea that helps us to *deal*, whether practically or intellectually, with either the reality or its belongings, that doesn't entangle our progress in frustrations, that *fits*, in fact, and adapts our life to the reality's whole setting, will agree sufficiently to meet the requirement. It will hold true of that reality.

Thus, *names* are just as 'true' or 'false' as definite mental pictures are. They set up similar verification-processes, and lead to fully equivalent practical results.

All human thinking gets discursified; we exchange ideas; we lend and borrow verifications, get them from one another by means of social intercourse. All truth thus gets verbally built out, stored up, and made available for every one. Hence, we must *talk* consistently just as we must *think* consistently: for both in talk and thought we deal with kinds. Names are arbitrary, but once understood they must be kept to. We mustn't now call Abel 'Cain' or Cain 'Abel.' If we do, we ungear ourselves from the whole book of Genesis, and from all its connexions with the universe of speech and fact down to the present time. We throw ourselves out of whatever truth that entire system of speech and fact may embody.

The overwhelming majority of our true ideas admit of no

direct or face-to-face verification—those of past history, for
example, as of Cain and Abel. The stream of time can be re-
mounted only verbally, or verified indirectly by the present
prolongations or effects of what the past harbored. Yet if they
agree with these verbalities and effects, we can know that our
ideas of the past are true. *As true as past time itself was*, so true
was Julius Cæsar, so true were antediluvian monsters, all in
their proper dates and settings. That past time itself was, is
guaranteed by its coherence with everything that's present.
True as the present *is*, the past *was* also.

Agreement thus turns out to be essentially an affair of leading—leading that is useful because it is into quarters that
contain objects that are important. True ideas lead us into
useful verbal and conceptual quarters as well as directly up to
useful sensible termini. They lead to consistency, stability and
flowing human intercourse. They lead away from excentricity
and isolation, from foiled and barren thinking. The untrammelled flowing of the leading-process, its general freedom
from clash and contradiction, passes for its indirect verification; but all roads lead to Rome, and in the end and eventually, all true processes must lead to the face of directly
verifying sensible experiences *somewhere*, which somebody's
ideas have copied.

Such is the large loose way in which the pragmatist interprets the word agreement. He treats it altogether practically.
He lets it cover any process of conduction from a present idea
to a future terminus, provided only it run prosperously. It is
only thus that 'scientific' ideas, flying as they do beyond common sense, can be said to agree with their realities. It is, as I
have already said, *as if* reality were made of ether, atoms or
electrons, but we must n't think so literally. The term 'energy'
does n't even pretend to stand for anything 'objective.' It is
only a way of measuring the surface of phenomena so as to
string their changes on a simple formula.

Yet in the choice of these man-made formulas we can not
be capricious with impunity any more than we can be capricious on the common-sense practical level. We must find a
theory that will *work*; and that means something extremely
difficult; for our theory must mediate between all previous
truths and certain new experiences. It must derange common

sense and previous belief as little as possible, and it must lead to some sensible terminus or other that can be verified exactly. To 'work' means both these things; and the squeeze is so tight that there is little loose play for any hypothesis. Our theories are wedged and controlled as nothing else is. Yet sometimes alternative theoretic formulas are equally compatible with all the truths we know, and then we choose between them for subjective reasons. We choose the kind of theory to which we are already partial; we follow 'elegance' or 'economy.' Clerk-Maxwell somewhere says it would be 'poor scientific taste' to choose the more complicated of two equally well-evidenced conceptions; and you will all agree with him. Truth in science is what gives us the maximum possible sum of satisfactions, taste included, but consistency both with previous truth and with novel fact is always the most imperious claimant.

I have led you through a very sandy desert. But now, if I may be allowed so vulgar an expression, we begin to taste the milk in the cocoanut. Our rationalist critics here discharge their batteries upon us, and to reply to them will take us out from all this dryness into full sight of a momentous philosophical alternative.

Our account of truth is an account of truths in the plural, of processes of leading, realized *in rebus*, and having only this quality in common, that they *pay*. They pay by guiding us into or towards some part of a system that dips at numerous points into sense-percepts, which we may copy mentally or not, but with which at any rate we are now in the kind of commerce vaguely designated as verification. Truth for us is simply a collective name for verification-processes, just as health, wealth, strength, etc., are names for other processes connected with life, and also pursued because it pays to pursue them. Truth is *made*, just as health, wealth and strength are made, in the course of experience.

Here rationalism is instantaneously up in arms against us. I can imagine a rationalist to talk as follows:

"Truth is not made," he will say; "it absolutely obtains, being a unique relation that does not wait upon any process, but shoots straight over the head of experience, and hits its reality every time. Our belief that yon thing on the wall is a clock is true already, altho no one in the whole history of the world should verify it. The bare quality of standing in that transcendent relation is what makes any thought true that possesses it, whether or not there be verification. You pragmatists put the cart before the horse in making truth's being reside in verification-processes. These are merely signs of its being, merely our lame ways of ascertaining after the fact, which of our ideas already has possessed the wondrous quality. The quality itself is timeless, like all essences and natures. Thoughts partake of it directly, as they partake of falsity or of irrelevancy. It can't be analyzed away into pragmatic consequences."

The whole plausibility of this rationalist tirade is due to the fact to which we have already paid so much attention. In our world, namely, abounding as it does in things of similar kinds and similarly associated, one verification serves for others of its kind, and one great use of knowing things is to be led not so much to them as to their associates, especially to human talk about them. The quality of truth, obtaining *ante rem*, pragmatically means, then, the fact that in such a world innumerable ideas work better by their indirect or possible than by their direct and actual verification. Truth *ante rem* means only verifiability, then; or else it is a case of the stock rationalist trick of treating the *name* of a concrete phenomenal reality as an independent prior entity, and placing it behind the reality as its explanation. Professor Mach quotes somewhere an epigram of Lessing's:

> Sagt Hänschen Schlau zu Vetter Fritz,
> "Wie kommt es, Vetter Fritzen,
> Dass grad' die Reichsten in der Welt,
> Das meiste Geld besitzen?"

Hänschen Schlau here treats the principle 'wealth' as something distinct from the facts denoted by the man's being rich. It antedates them; the facts become only a sort of secondary coincidence with the rich man's essential nature.

In the case of 'wealth' we all see the fallacy. We know that wealth is but a name for concrete processes that certain men's lives play a part in, and not a natural excellence found in Messrs. Rockefeller and Carnegie, but not in the rest of us.

Like wealth, health also lives *in rebus*. It is a name for processes, as digestion, circulation, sleep, etc., that go on happily, tho in this instance we are more inclined to think of it as a principle and to say the man digests and sleeps so well *because* he is so healthy.

With 'strength' we are, I think, more rationalistic still, and decidedly inclined to treat it as an excellence pre-existing in the man and explanatory of the herculean performances of his muscles.

With 'truth' most people go over the border entirely, and treat the rationalistic account as self-evident. But really all these words in *th* are exactly similar. Truth exists *ante rem* just as much and as little as the other things do.

The scholastics, following Aristotle, made much of the distinction between habit and act. Health *in actu* means, among other things, good sleeping and digesting. But a healthy man need not always be sleeping, or always digesting, any more than a wealthy man need be always handling money, or a strong man always lifting weights. All such qualities sink to the status of 'habits' between their times of exercise; and similarly truth becomes a habit of certain of our ideas and beliefs in their intervals of rest from their verifying activities. But those activities are the root of the whole matter, and the condition of there being any habit to exist in the intervals.

'The true,' to put it very briefly, is only the expedient in the way of our thinking, just as 'the right' is only the expedient in the way of our behaving. Expedient in almost any fashion; and expedient in the long run and on the whole of course; for what meets expediently all the experience in sight won't necessarily meet all farther experiences equally satisfactorily. Experience, as we know, has ways of *boiling over*, and making us correct our present formulas.

The 'absolutely' true, meaning what no farther experience will ever alter, is that ideal vanishing-point towards which we imagine that all our temporary truths will some day converge. It runs on all fours with the perfectly wise man, and with the absolutely complete experience; and, if these ideals are ever realized, they will all be realized together. Meanwhile we have to live to-day by what truth we can get to-day, and be ready to-morrow to call it falsehood. Ptolemaic astronomy, euclidean space, aristotelian logic, scholastic metaphysics, were expedient for centuries, but human experience has boiled over those limits, and we now call these things only relatively true, or true within those borders of experience. 'Absolutely' they are false; for we know that those limits were casual, and might have been transcended by past theorists just as they are by present thinkers.

When new experiences lead to retrospective judgments, using the past tense, what these judgments utter *was* true, even tho no past thinker had been led there. We live forwards, a Danish thinker has said, but we understand backwards. The present sheds a backward light on the world's previous processes. They may have been truth-processes for the actors in them. They are not so for one who knows the later revelations of the story.

This regulative notion of a potential better truth to be established later, possibly to be established some day absolutely, and having powers of retroactive legislation, turns its face, like all pragmatist notions, towards concreteness of fact, and towards the future. Like the half-truths, the absolute truth will have to be *made*, made as a relation incidental to the growth of a mass of verification-experience, to which the half-true ideas are all along contributing their quota.

I have already insisted on the fact that truth is made largely out of previous truths. Men's beliefs at any time are so much experience *funded*. But the beliefs are themselves parts of the sum total of the world's experience, and become matter, therefore, for the next day's funding operations. So far as reality means experienceable reality, both it and the truths men gain about it are everlastingly in process of mutation —mutation towards a definite goal, it may be—but still mutation.

Mathematicians can solve problems with two variables. On the Newtonian theory, for instance, acceleration varies with distance, but distance also varies with acceleration. In the realm of truth-processes facts come independently and determine our beliefs provisionally. But these beliefs make us act, and as fast as they do so, they bring into sight or into existence new facts which re-determine the beliefs accordingly. So the whole coil and ball of truth, as it rolls up, is the product of a double influence. Truths emerge from facts; but they dip forward into facts again and add to them; which facts again create or reveal new truth (the word is indifferent) and so on indefinitely. The 'facts' themselves meanwhile are not *true*. They simply *are*. Truth is the function of the beliefs that start and terminate among them.

The case is like a snowball's growth, due as it is to the distribution of the snow on the one hand, and to the successive pushes of the boys on the other, with these factors co-determining each other incessantly.

The most fateful point of difference between being a rationalist and being a pragmatist is now fully in sight. Experience is in mutation, and our psychological ascertainments of truth are in mutation—so much rationalism will allow; but never that either reality itself or truth itself is mutable. Reality stands complete and ready-made from all eternity, rationalism insists, and the agreement of our ideas with it is that unique unanalyzable virtue in them of which she has already told us. As that intrinsic excellence, their truth has nothing to do with our experiences. It adds nothing to the content of experience. It makes no difference to reality itself; it is supervenient, inert, static, a reflexion merely. It doesn't *exist*, it *holds* or *obtains*, it belongs to another dimension from that of either facts or fact-relations, belongs, in short, to the epistemological dimension—and with that big word rationalism closes the discussion.

Thus, just as pragmatism faces forward to the future, so does rationalism here again face backward to a past eternity. True to her inveterate habit, rationalism reverts to 'principles,' and thinks that when an abstraction once is named, we own an oracular solution.

The tremendous pregnancy in the way of consequences for life of this radical difference of outlook will only become apparent in my later lectures. I wish meanwhile to close this lecture by showing that rationalism's sublimity does not save it from inanity.

* * *

When, namely, you ask rationalists, instead of accusing pragmatism of desecrating the notion of truth, to define it themselves by saying exactly what *they* understand by it, the only positive attempts I can think of are these two:

1. "Truth is the system of propositions which have an unconditional claim to be recognized as valid."[1]

2. Truth is a name for all those judgments which we find ourselves under obligation to make by a kind of imperative duty.[2]

The first thing that strikes one in such definitions is their unutterable triviality. They are absolutely true, of course, but absolutely insignificant until you handle them pragmatically. What do you mean by 'claim' here, and what do you mean by 'duty'? As summary names for the concrete reasons why thinking in true ways is overwhelmingly expedient and good for mortal men, it is all right to talk of claims on reality's part to be agreed with, and of obligations on our part to agree. We feel both the claims and the obligations, and we feel them for just those reasons.

But the rationalists who talk of claim and obligation *expressly say that they have nothing to do with our practical interests or personal reasons.* Our reasons for agreeing are psychological facts, they say, relative to each thinker, and to the accidents of his life. They are his evidence merely, they are no part of the life of truth itself. That life transacts itself in a purely logical or epistemological, as distinguished from a psychological, dimension, and its claims antedate and exceed all personal motivations whatsoever. Tho neither man nor God should ever ascertain truth, the word would still have to be defined as that which *ought* to be ascertained and recognized.

There never was a more exquisite example of an idea abstracted from the concretes of experience and then used to oppose and negate what it was abstracted from.

Philosophy and common life abound in similar instances. The 'sentimentalist fallacy' is to shed tears over abstract justice and generosity, beauty, etc., and never to know these qualities when you meet them in the street, because there the

---

[1] A. E. Taylor, *Philosophical Review*, vol. xiv, p. 288.

[2] H. Rickert, *Der Gegenstand der Erkenntniss*, chapter on 'Die Urtheilsnothwendigkeit.'

circumstances make them vulgar. Thus I read in the privately printed biography of an eminently rationalistic mind: "It was strange that with such admiration for beauty in the abstract, my brother had no enthusiasm for fine architecture, for beautiful painting, or for flowers." And in almost the last philosophic work I have read, I find such passages as the following: "Justice is ideal, solely ideal. Reason conceives that it ought to exist, but experience shows that it can not. . . . Truth, which ought to be, can not be. . . . Reason is deformed by experience. As soon as reason enters experience it becomes contrary to reason."

The rationalist's fallacy here is exactly like the sentimentalist's. Both extract a quality from the muddy particulars of experience, and find it so pure when extracted that they contrast it with each and all its muddy instances as an opposite and higher nature. All the while it is *their* nature. It is the nature of truths to be validated, verified. It pays for our ideas to be validated. Our obligation to seek truth is part of our general obligation to do what pays. The payments true ideas bring are the sole why of our duty to follow them.

Identical whys exist in the case of wealth and health. Truth makes no other kind of claim and imposes no other kind of ought than health and wealth do. All these claims are conditional; the concrete benefits we gain are what we mean by calling the pursuit a duty. In the case of truth, untrue beliefs work as perniciously in the long run as true beliefs work beneficially. Talking abstractly, the quality 'true' may thus be said to grow absolutely precious and the quality 'untrue' absolutely damnable: the one may be called good, the other bad, unconditionally. We ought to think the true, we ought to shun the false, imperatively.

But if we treat all this abstraction literally and oppose it to its mother soil in experience, see what a preposterous position we work ourselves into.

We can not then take a step forward in our actual thinking. When shall I acknowledge this truth and when that? Shall the acknowledgment be loud?—or silent? If sometimes loud, sometimes silent, which *now*? When may a truth go into cold-storage in the encyclopedia? and when shall it come out for battle? Must I constantly be repeating the truth 'twice two are four' because of its eternal claim on recognition? or is it sometimes irrelevant? Must my thoughts dwell night and day on my personal sins and blemishes, because I truly have them?—or may I sink and ignore them in order to be a decent social unit, and not a mass of morbid melancholy and apology?

It is quite evident that our obligation to acknowledge truth, so far from being unconditional, is tremendously conditioned. Truth with a big T, and in the singular, claims abstractly to be recognized, of course; but concrete truths in the plural need be recognized only when their recognition is expedient. A truth must always be preferred to a falsehood when both relate to the situation; but when neither does, truth is as little of a duty as falsehood. If you ask me what o'clock it is and I tell you that I live at 95 Irving Street, my answer may indeed be true, but you don't see why it is my duty to give it. A false address would be as much to the purpose.

With this admission that there are conditions that limit the application of the abstract imperative, *the pragmatistic treatment of truth sweeps back upon us in its fulness*. Our duty to agree with reality is seen to be grounded in a perfect jungle of concrete expediencies.

When Berkeley had explained what people meant by matter, people thought that he denied matter's existence. When Messrs. Schiller and Dewey now explain what people mean by truth, they are accused of denying *its* existence. These pragmatists destroy all objective standards, critics say, and put foolishness and wisdom on one level. A favorite formula for describing Mr. Schiller's doctrines and mine is that we are persons who think that by saying whatever you find it pleasant to say and calling it truth you fulfil every pragmatistic requirement.

I leave it to you to judge whether this be not an impudent slander. Pent in, as the pragmatist more than any one else sees himself to be, between the whole body of funded truths squeezed from the past and the coercions of the world of sense about him, who so well as he feels the immense pressure of objective control under which our minds perform their operations? If any one imagines that this law is lax, let him keep its commandment one day, says Emerson. We have heard much of late of the uses of the imagination in science. It is high time to urge the use of a little imagination in philosophy. The unwillingness of some of our critics to read any but the silliest of possible meanings into our statements is as discreditable to their imaginations as anything I know in recent philosophic history. Schiller says the true is that which 'works.' Thereupon he is treated as one who limits verification to the lowest material utilities. Dewey says truth is what gives 'satisfaction.' He is treated as one who believes in calling everything true which, if it were true, would be pleasant.

Our critics certainly need more imagination of realities. I have honestly tried to stretch my own imagination and to read the best possible meaning into the rationalist conception, but I have to confess that it still completely baffles me. The notion of a reality calling on us to 'agree' with it, and that for no reasons, but simply because its claim is 'unconditional' or 'transcendent,' is one that I can make neither head nor tail of. I try to imagine myself as the sole reality in the world, and then to imagine what more I would 'claim' if I were allowed to. If you suggest the possibility of my claiming that a mind should come into being from out of the void inane and stand and *copy* me, I can indeed imagine what the copying might mean, but I can conjure up no motive. What good it would do me to be copied, or what good it would do that mind to copy me, if further consequences are expressly and in principle ruled out as motives for the claim (as they are by our rationalist authorities) I can not fathom. When the Irishman's admirers ran him along to the place of banquet in a sedan chair with no bottom, he said, "Faith, if it wasn't for the honor of the thing, I might as well have come on foot." So here: but for the honor of the thing, I might as well have remained uncopied. Copying is one genuine mode of knowing (which for some strange reason our contemporary transcendentalists seem to be tumbling over each other to repudiate); but when we get beyond copying, and fall back on unnamed forms of agreeing that are expressly denied to be either copyings or leadings or fittings, or any other processes pragmatically definable, the *what* of the 'agreement' claimed becomes as unintelligible as the why of it. Neither content nor motive can be imagined for it. It is an absolutely mean-ingless abstraction.[1]

Surely in this field of truth it is the pragmatists and not the rationalists who are the more genuine defenders of the universe's rationality.

[1] I am not forgetting that Professor Rickert long ago gave up the whole notion of truth being founded on agreement with reality. Reality according to him, is whatever agrees with truth, and truth is founded solely on our primal duty. This fantastic flight, together with Mr. Joachim's candid confession of failure in his book *The Nature of Truth*, seems to me to mark the bankruptcy of rationalism when dealing with this subject. Rickert deals with part of the pragmatistic position under the head of what he calls 'Relativismus.' I can not discuss his text here. Suffice it to say that his argumentation in that chapter is so feeble as to seem almost incredible in so generally able a writer.

LECTURE VII

PRAGMATISM AND HUMANISM

WHAT HARDENS the heart of every one I approach with the view of truth sketched in my last lecture is that typical idol of the tribe, the notion of *the* Truth, conceived as the one answer, determinate and complete, to the one fixed enigma which the world is believed to propound. For popular tradition, it is all the better if the answer be oracular, so as itself to awaken wonder as an enigma of the second order, veiling rather than revealing what its profundities are supposed to contain. All the great single-word answers to the world's riddle, such as God, the One, Reason, Law, Spirit, Matter, Nature, Polarity, the Dialectic Process, the Idea, the Self, the Oversoul, draw the admiration that men have lavished on them from this oracular rôle. By amateurs in philosophy and professionals alike, the universe is represented as a queer sort of petrified sphinx whose appeal to men consists in a monotonous challenge to his divining powers. *The* Truth: what a perfect idol of the rationalistic mind! I read in an old letter—from a gifted friend who died too young—these words: "In everything, in science, art, morals and religion, there *must* be one system that is right and *every* other wrong." How characteristic of the enthusiasm of a certain stage of youth! At twenty-one we rise to such a challenge and expect to find the system. It never occurs to most of us even later that the question 'what is *the* truth?' is no real question (being irrelative to all conditions) and that the whole notion of *the* truth is an abstraction from the fact of truths in the plural, a mere useful summarizing phrase like *the* Latin Language or *the* Law.

Common-law judges sometimes talk about the law, and schoolmasters talk about the latin tongue, in a way to make their hearers think they mean entities pre-existent to the decisions or to the words and syntax, determining them unequivocally and requiring them to obey. But the slightest exercise of reflexion makes us see that, instead of being principles of this kind, both law and latin are results. Distinctions

between the lawful and the unlawful in conduct, or between
the correct and incorrect in speech, have grown up incidentally among the interactions of men's experiences in detail;
and in no other way do distinctions between the true and the
false in belief ever grow up. Truth grafts itself on previous
truth, modifying it in the process, just as idiom grafts itself
on previous idiom, and law on previous law. Given previous
law and a novel case, and the judge will twist them into fresh
law. Previous idiom; new slang or metaphor or oddity that
hits the public taste;—and presto, a new idiom is made. Previous truth; fresh facts:—and our mind finds a new truth.

All the while, however, we pretend that the eternal is unrolling, that the one previous justice, grammar or truth is simply fulgurating and not being made. But imagine a youth in
the courtroom trying cases with his abstract notion of 'the'
law, or a censor of speech let loose among the theatres with
his idea of 'the' mother-tongue, or a professor setting up to
lecture on the actual universe with his rationalistic notion of
'the Truth' with a big T, and what progress do they make?
Truth, law, and language fairly boil away from them at the
least touch of novel fact. These things *make themselves* as we
go. Our rights, wrongs, prohibitions, penalties, words, forms,
idioms, beliefs, are so many new creations that add themselves
as fast as history proceeds. Far from being antecedent principles that animate the process, law, language, truth are but
abstract names for its results.

Laws and languages at any rate are thus seen to be man-
made things. Mr. Schiller applies the analogy to beliefs, and
proposes the name of 'Humanism' for the doctrine that to an
unascertainable extent our truths are man-made products too.
Human motives sharpen all our questions, human satisfactions lurk in all our answers, all our formulas have a human
twist. This element is so inextricable in the products that Mr.
Schiller sometimes seems almost to leave it an open question
whether there be anything else. "The world," he says, "is essentially ὕλη, it is what we make it. It is fruitless to define it
by what it originally was or by what it is apart from us; it *is*
what is made of it. Hence . . . the world *is plastic*."[1] He adds

---

[1] *Personal Idealism*, p. 60.

that we can learn the limits of the plasticity only by trying, and that we ought to start as if it were wholly plastic, acting methodically on that assumption, and stopping only when we are decisively rebuked.

This is Mr. Schiller's butt-end-foremost statement of the humanist position, and it has exposed him to severe attack. I mean to defend the humanist position in this lecture, so I will insinuate a few remarks at this point.

Mr. Schiller admits as emphatically as any one the presence of resisting factors in every actual experience of truth-making, of which the new-made special truth must take account, and with which it has perforce to 'agree.' All our truths are beliefs about 'Reality'; and in any particular belief the reality acts as something independent, as a thing *found*, not manufactured. Let me here recall a bit of my last lecture.

'Reality' is in general what truths have to take account of;[1] and the *first* part of reality from this point of view is the flux of our sensations. Sensations are forced upon us, coming we know not whence. Over their nature, order and quantity we have as good as no control. *They* are neither true nor false; they simply *are*. It is only what we say about them, only the names we give them, our theories of their source and nature and remote relations, that may be true or not.

The *second* part of reality, as something that our beliefs must also obediently take account of, is the *relations* that obtain between our sensations or between their copies in our minds. This part falls into two sub-parts: 1) the relations that are mutable and accidental, as those of date and place; and 2) those that are fixed and essential because they are grounded on the inner natures of their terms—such are likeness and unlikeness. Both sorts of relation are matters of immediate perception. Both are 'facts.' But it is the latter kind of fact that forms the more important sub-part of reality for our theories of knowledge. Inner relations namely are 'eternal,' are perceived whenever their sensible terms are compared; and of them our thought—mathematical and logical thought so-called—must eternally take account.

The *third* part of reality, additional to these perceptions

[1] Mr. Taylor in his *Elements of Metaphysics* uses this excellent pragmatic definition.

(tho largely based upon them), is the *previous truths* of which
every new inquiry takes account. This third part is a much
less obdurately resisting factor: it often ends by giving way.
In speaking of these three portions of reality as at all times
controlling our belief's formation, I am only reminding you
of what we heard in our last hour.

Now however fixed these elements of reality may be, we
still have a certain freedom in our dealings with them. Take
our sensations. *That* they are is undoubtedly beyond our control; but *which* we attend to, note, and make emphatic in our
conclusions depends on our own interests; and, according as
we lay the emphasis here or there, quite different formulations of truth result. We read the same facts differently. 'Wa-
terloo,' with the same fixed details, spells a 'victory' for an
Englishman; for a Frenchman it spells a 'defeat.' So, for an
optimist philosopher the universe spells victory, for a pessi-
mist, defeat.

What we say about reality thus depends on the perspective
into which we throw it. The *that* of it is its own; but the
what depends on the *which*; and the which depends on *us*.
Both the sensational and the relational parts of reality are
dumb; they say absolutely nothing about themselves. We it is
who have to speak for them. This dumbness of sensations has
led such intellectualists as T. H. Green and Edward Caird to
shove them almost beyond the pale of philosophic recognition, but pragmatists refuse to go so far. A sensation is rather
like a client who has given his case to a lawyer and then has
passively to listen in the courtroom to whatever account of
his affairs, pleasant or unpleasant, the lawyer finds it most
expedient to give.

Hence, even in the field of sensation, our minds exert a
certain arbitrary choice. By our inclusions and omissions we
trace the field's extent; by our emphasis we mark its foreground and its background; by our order we read it in this
direction or in that. We receive in short the block of marble,
but we carve the statue ourselves.

This applies to the 'eternal' parts of reality as well: we shuf-
fle our perceptions of intrinsic relation and arrange them just
as freely. We read them in one serial order or another, class
them in this way or in that, treat one or the other as more

fundamental, until our beliefs about them form those bodies of truth known as logics, geometries, or arithmetics, in each and all of which the form and order in which the whole is cast is flagrantly man-made.

Thus, to say nothing of the new *facts* which men add to the matter of reality by the acts of their own lives, they have already impressed their mental forms on that whole third of reality which I have called 'previous truths.' Every hour brings its new percepts, its own facts of sensation and relation, to be truly taken account of; but the whole of our *past* dealings with such facts is already funded in the previous truths. It is therefore only the smallest and recentest fraction of the first two parts of reality that comes to us without the human touch, and that fraction has immediately to become humanized in the sense of being squared, assimilated, or in some way adapted, to the humanized mass already there. As a matter of fact we can hardly take in an impression at all, in the absence of a preconception of what impressions there may possibly be.

When we talk of reality 'independent' of human thinking, then, it seems a thing very hard to find. It reduces to the notion of what is just entering into experience and yet to be named, or else to some imagined aboriginal presence in experience, before any belief about the presence had arisen, before any human conception had been applied. It is what is absolutely dumb and evanescent, the merely ideal limit of our minds. We may glimpse it, but we never grasp it; what we grasp is always some substitute for it which previous human thinking has peptonized and cooked for our consumption. If so vulgar an expression were allowed us, we might say that wherever we find it, it has been already *faked*. This is what Mr. Schiller has in mind when he calls independent reality a mere unresisting ὕλη, which *is* only to be made over by us.

That is Mr. Schiller's belief about the sensible core of reality. We 'encounter' it (in Mr. Bradley's words) but don't possess it. Superficially this sounds like Kant's view; but between categories fulminated before nature began, and categories gradually forming themselves in nature's presence, the whole chasm between rationalism and empiricism yawns. To the

genuine 'Kantianer' Schiller will always be to Kant as a satyr
to Hyperion.

Other pragmatists may reach more positive beliefs about
the sensible core of reality. They may think to get at it in its
independent nature, by peeling off the successive man-made
wrappings. They may make theories that tell us where it
comes from and all about it; and *if these theories work satisfactorily they will be true*. The transcendental idealists say there is
no core, the finally completed wrapping being reality and
truth in one. Scholasticism still teaches that the core is 'matter.' Professor Bergson, Heymans, Strong, and others believe
in the core and bravely try to define it. Messrs. Dewey and
Schiller treat it as a 'limit.' Which is the truer of all these diverse accounts, or of others comparable with them, unless it
be the one that finally proves the most satisfactory? On the
one hand there will stand reality, on the other an account of
it which proves impossible to better or to alter. If the impossibility prove permanent, the truth of the account will be
absolute. Other content of truth than this I can find nowhere. If the anti-pragmatists have any other meaning, let
them for heaven's sake reveal it, let them grant us access to
it!

Not *being* reality, but only our belief *about* reality, it will
contain human elements, but these will *know* the non-human
element, in the only sense in which there can be knowledge
of anything. Does the river make its banks, or do the banks
make the river? Does a man walk with his right leg or with
his left leg more essentially? Just as impossible may it be to
separate the real from the human factors in the growth of our
cognitive experience.

Let this stand as a first brief indication of the humanistic
position. Does it seem paradoxical? If so, I will try to make it
plausible by a few illustrations, which will lead to a fuller acquaintance with the subject.

In many familiar objects every one will recognize the human element. We conceive a given reality in this way or in
that, to suit our purpose, and the reality passively submits to
the conception. You can take the number 27 as the cube of 3,
or as the product of 3 and 9, or as 26 *plus* 1, or 100 *minus* 73,
or in countless other ways, of which one will be just as true

as another. You can take a chess-board as black squares on a white ground, or as white squares on a black ground, and neither conception is a false one.

 You can treat the adjoined figure as a star, as two big triangles crossing each other, as a hexagon with legs set up on its angles, as six equal triangles hanging together by their tips, etc. All these treatments are true treatments—the sensible *that* upon the paper resists no one of them. You can say of a line that it runs east, or you can say that it runs west, and the line *per se* accepts both descriptions without rebelling at the inconsistency.

We carve out groups of stars in the heavens, and call them constellations, and the stars patiently suffer us to do so,—though if they knew what we were doing, some of them might feel much surprised at the partners we had given them. We name the same constellation diversely, as Charles's Wain, the Great Bear, or the Dipper. None of the names will be false, and one will be as true as another, for all are applicable.

In all these cases we humanly make an addition to some sensible reality, and that reality tolerates the addition. All the additions 'agree' with the reality; they fit it, while they build it out. No one of them is false. Which may be treated as the more true, depends altogether on the human use of it. If the 27 is a number of dollars which I find in a drawer where I had left 28, it is 28 minus 1. If it is the number of inches in a shelf which I wish to insert into a cupboard 26 inches wide, it is 26 plus 1. If I wish to ennoble the heavens by the constellations I see there, 'Charles's Wain' would be more true than 'Dipper.' My friend Frederick Myers was humorously indignant that that prodigious star-group should remind us Americans of nothing but a culinary utensil.

What shall we call a *thing* anyhow? It seems quite arbitrary, for we carve out everything, just as we carve out constellations, to suit our human purposes. For me, this whole 'audience' is one thing, which grows now restless, now attentive. I have no use at present for its individual units, so I don't consider them. So of an 'army,' of a 'nation.' But in your own eyes, ladies and gentlemen, to call you 'audience' is an accidental way of taking you. The permanently real things for you are your individual persons. To an anatomist, again, those persons are but organisms, and the real things are the organs. Not the organs, so much as their constituent cells, say the histologists; not the cells, but their molecules, say in turn the chemists.

We break the flux of sensible reality into things, then, at our will. We create the subjects of our true as well as of our false propositions.

We create the predicates also. Many of the predicates of things express only the relations of the things to us and to our feelings. Such predicates of course are human additions. Cæsar crossed the Rubicon, and was a menace to Rome's freedom. He is also an American schoolroom pest, made into one by the reaction of our schoolboys on his writings. The added predicate is as true of him as the earlier ones.

You see how naturally one comes to the humanistic principle: you can't weed out the human contribution. Our nouns and adjectives are all humanized heirlooms, and in the theories we build them into, the inner order and arrangement is wholly dictated by human considerations, intellectual consistency being one of them. Mathematics and logic themselves are fermenting with human rearrangements; physics, astronomy and biology follow massive cues of preference. We plunge forward into the field of fresh experience with the beliefs our ancestors and we have made already; these determine what we notice; what we notice determines what we do; what we do again determines what we experience; so from one thing to another, altho the stubborn fact remains that there *is* a sensible flux, what is *true of it* seems from first to last to be largely a matter of our own creation.

We build the flux out inevitably. The great question is: does it, with our additions, *rise or fall in value*? Are the additions *worthy* or *unworthy*? Suppose a universe composed of seven stars, and nothing else but three human witnesses and their critic. One witness names the stars 'Great Bear'; one calls them 'Charles's Wain'; one calls them the 'Dipper.' Which human addition has made the best universe of the given stellar material? If Frederick Myers were the critic, he would have no hesitation in 'turning down' the American witness.

Lotze has in several places made a deep suggestion. We na-ïvely assume, he says, a relation between reality and our minds which may be just the opposite of the true one. Real-ity, we naturally think, stands ready-made and complete, and our intellects supervene with the one simple duty of describ-ing it as it is already. But may not our descriptions, Lotze asks, be themselves important additions to reality? And may not previous reality itself be there, far less for the purpose of reappearing unaltered in our knowledge, than for the very purpose of stimulating our minds to such additions as shall enhance the universe's total value. '*Die erhöhung des vorgefun-denen daseins*' is a phrase used by Professor Eucken some-where, which reminds one of this suggestion by the great Lotze.

It is identically our pragmatistic conception. In our cogni-tive as well as in our active life we are creative. We *add*, both to the subject and to the predicate part of reality. The world stands really malleable, waiting to receive its final touches at our hands. Like the kingdom of heaven, it suffers human vi-olence willingly. Man *engenders* truths upon it.

No one can deny that such a rôle would add both to our dignity and to our responsibility as thinkers. To some of us it proves a most inspiring notion. Signore Papini, the leader of Italian pragmatism, grows fairly dithyrambic over the view that it opens of man's divinely-creative functions.

The import of the difference between pragmatism and ra-tionalism is now in sight throughout its whole extent. The essential contrast is that *for rationalism reality is ready-made and complete from all eternity, while for pragmatism it is still in the making, and awaits part of its complexion from the future.* On the one side the universe is absolutely secure, on the other it is still pursuing its adventures.

We have got into rather deep water with this humanistic view, and it is no wonder that misunderstanding gathers round it. It is accused of being a doctrine of caprice. Mr. Bradley, for example, says that a humanist, if he understood his own doctrine, would have to 'hold any end, however perverted, to be rational, if I insist on it personally, and any idea, however mad, to be the truth if only some one is re-solved that he will have it so.' The humanist view of 'reality,' as something resisting, yet malleable, which controls our thinking as an energy that must be taken 'account' of incessantly (tho not necessarily merely *copied*) is evidently a difficult one to introduce to novices. The situation reminds me of one that I have personally gone through. I once wrote an essay on our right to believe, which I unluckily called the *Will* to Believe. All the critics, neglecting the essay, pounced upon the title. Psychologically it was impossible, morally it was iniquitous. The 'will to deceive,' the 'will to make-believe,' were wittily proposed as substitutes for it.

The alternative between pragmatism and rationalism, in the shape in which we now have it before us, is no longer a question in the theory of knowledge, it concerns the structure of the universe itself.

On the pragmatist side we have only one edition of the universe, unfinished, growing in all sorts of places, especially in the places where thinking beings are at work.

On the rationalist side we have a universe in many editions, one real one, the infinite folio, or *édition de luxe*, eternally complete; and then the various finite editions, full of false readings, distorted and mutilated each in its own way.

So the rival metaphysical hypotheses of pluralism and monism here come back upon us. I will develope their differences during the remainder of our hour.

And first let me say that it is impossible not to see a temperamental difference at work in the choice of sides. The rationalist mind, radically taken, is of a doctrinaire and authoritative complexion: the phrase '*must* be' is ever on its lips. The bellyband of its universe must be tight. A radical pragmatist on the other hand is a happy-go-lucky anarchistic sort of creature. If he had to live in a tub like Diogenes he wouldn't mind at all if the hoops were loose and the staves let in the sun.

Now the idea of this loose universe affects your typical rationalists in much the same way as 'freedom of the press' might affect a veteran official in the Russian bureau of censorship; or as 'simplified spelling' might affect an elderly schoolmistress. It affects him as the swarm of protestant sects affects a papist onlooker. It appears as backboneless and devoid of principle as 'opportunism' in politics appears to an old-fashioned French legitimist, or to a fanatical believer in the divine right of the people.

For pluralistic pragmatism, truth grows up inside of all the finite experiences. They lean on each other, but the whole of them, if such a whole there be, leans on nothing. All 'homes' are in finite experience; finite experience as such is homeless. Nothing outside of the flux secures the issue of it. It can hope salvation only from its own intrinsic promises and potencies.

To rationalists this describes a tramp and vagrant world, adrift in space, with neither elephant nor tortoise to plant the sole of its foot upon. It is a set of stars hurled into heaven without even a centre of gravity to pull against. In other spheres of life it is true that we have got used to living in a state of relative insecurity. The authority of 'the State,' and that of an absolute 'moral law,' have resolved themselves into expediencies, and holy church has resolved itself into 'meeting-houses.' Not so as yet within the philosophic class-rooms. A universe with such as *us* contributing to create its truth, a world delivered to *our* opportunisms and our private judgments! Home-rule for Ireland would be a millennium in comparison. We're no more fit for such a part than the Filipinos are 'fit for self-government.' Such a world would not be *respectable* philosophically. It is a trunk without a tag, a dog without a collar, in the eyes of most professors of philosophy.

What then would tighten this loose universe, according to the professors?

Something to support the finite many, to tie it to, to unify and anchor it. Something unexposed to accident, something eternal and unalterable. The mutable in experience must be founded on immutability. Behind our *de facto* world, our world in act, there must be a *de jure* duplicate fixed and previous, with all that can happen here already there *in posse*, every drop of blood, every smallest item, appointed and provided, stamped and branded, without chance of variation. The negatives that haunt our ideals here below must be themselves negated in the absolutely Real. This alone makes the universe solid. This is the resting deep. We live upon the stormy surface; but with this our anchor holds, for it grapples rocky bottom. This is Wordsworth's 'eternal peace abiding at

the heart of endless agitation.' This is Vivekananda's mystical
One of which I read to you. This is Reality with the big R,
reality that makes the timeless claim, reality to which defeat
can't happen. This is what the men of principles, and in general all the men whom I called tender-minded in my first lecture, think themselves obliged to postulate.

And this, exactly this, is what the tough-minded of that
lecture find themselves moved to call a piece of perverse abstraction-worship. The tough-minded are the men whose alpha and omega are *facts*. Behind the bare phenomenal facts,
as my tough-minded old friend Chauncey Wright, the great
Harvard empiricist of my youth, used to say, there is *nothing*.
When a rationalist insists that behind the facts there is the
ground of the facts, the *possibility* of the facts, the tougher
empiricists accuse him of taking the mere name and nature of
a fact and clapping it behind the fact as a duplicate entity to
make it possible. That such sham grounds are often invoked
is notorious. At a surgical operation I heard a bystander ask
a doctor why the patient breathed so deeply. 'Because ether is
a respiratory stimulant,' the doctor answered. 'Ah!' said the
questioner, as if relieved by the explanation. But this is like
saying that cyanide of potassium kills because it is a 'poison,'
or that it is so cold to-night because it is 'winter,' or that we
have five fingers because we are 'pentadactyls.' These are but
names for the facts, taken from the facts, and then treated as
previous and explanatory. The tender-minded notion of an
absolute reality is, according to the radically tough-minded,
framed on just this pattern. It is but our summarizing name
for the whole spread-out and strung-along mass of phenomena, treated as if it were a different entity, both one and
previous.

You see how differently people take things. The world we
live in exists diffused and distributed, in the form of an indefinitely numerous lot of *eaches*, coherent in all sorts of ways
and degrees; and the tough-minded are perfectly willing to
keep them at that valuation. They can *stand* that kind of
world, their temper being well adapted to its insecurity. Not
so the tender-minded party. They must back the world we
find ourselves born into by 'another and a better' world in
which the eaches form an All and the All a One that logically

presupposes, co-implicates, and secures each *each* without exception.

Must we as pragmatists be radically tough-minded? or can we treat the absolute edition of the world as a legitimate hypothesis? It is certainly legitimate, for it is thinkable, whether we take it in its abstract or in its concrete shape.

By taking it abstractly I mean placing it behind our finite life as we place the word 'winter' behind to-night's cold weather. 'Winter' is only the name for a certain number of days which we find generally characterized by cold weather, but it guarantees nothing in that line, for our thermometer to-morrow may soar into the 70's. Nevertheless the word is a useful one to plunge forward with into the stream of our experience. It cuts off certain probabilities and sets up others. You can put away your straw hats; you can unpack your arctics. It is a summary of things to look for. It names a part of nature's habits, and gets you ready for their continuation. It is a definite instrument abstracted from experience, a conceptual reality that you must take account of, and which reflects you totally back into sensible realities. The pragmatist is the last person to deny the reality of such abstractions. They are so much past experience funded.

But taking the absolute edition of the world concretely means a different hypothesis. Rationalists take it concretely and *oppose* it to the world's finite editions. They give it a particular nature. It is perfect, finished. Everything known there is known along with everything else; here, where ignorance reigns, far otherwise. If there is want there, there also is the satisfaction provided. Here all is process; that world is timeless. Possibilities obtain in our world; in the absolute world, where all that is *not* is from eternity impossible, and all that *is* is necessary, the category of possibility has no application. In this world crimes and horrors are regretable. In that totalized world regret obtains not, for 'the existence of ill in the temporal order is the very condition of the perfection of the eternal order.'

Once more, either hypothesis is legitimate in pragmatist eyes, for either has its uses. Abstractly, or taken like the word winter, as a memorandum of past experience that orients us towards the future, the notion of the absolute world is indispensable. Concretely taken, it is also indispensable, at least to certain minds, for it determines them religiously, being often a thing to change their lives by, and by changing their lives, to change whatever in the outer order depends on them.

We can not therefore methodically join the tough minds in their rejection of the whole notion of a world beyond our finite experience. One misunderstanding of pragmatism is to identify it with positivistic tough-mindedness, to suppose that it scorns every rationalistic notion as so much jabber and gesticulation, that it loves intellectual anarchy as such and prefers a sort of wolf-world absolutely unpent and wild and without a master or a collar to any philosophic classroom product whatsoever. I have said so much in these lectures against the over-tender forms of rationalism, that I am prepared for some misunderstanding here, but I confess that the amount of it that I have found in this very audience surprises me, for I have simultaneously defended rationalistic hypotheses, so far as these re-direct you fruitfully into experience.

For instance I receive this morning this question on a postcard: "Is a pragmatist necessarily a complete materialist and agnostic?" One of my oldest friends, who ought to know me better, writes me a letter that accuses the pragmatism I am recommending of shutting out all wider metaphysical views and condemning us to the most *terre-à-terre* naturalism. Let me read you some extracts from it.

"It seems to me," my friend writes, "that the pragmatic objection to pragmatism lies in the fact that it might accentuate the narrowness of narrow minds.

"Your call to the rejection of the namby-pamby and the wishy-washy is of course inspiring. But altho it is salutary and stimulating to be told that one should be responsible for the immediate issues and bearings of his words and thoughts, I decline to be deprived of the pleasure and profit of dwelling also on remoter bearings and issues, and it is the *tendency* of pragmatism to refuse this privilege.

"In short, it seems to me that the limitations, or rather the dangers, of the pragmatic tendency, are analogous to those which beset the unwary followers of the 'natural sciences.' Chemistry and physics are eminently pragmatic; and many of their devotees, smugly content with the data that their weights and measures furnish, feel an infinite pity and disdain for all students of philosophy and metaphysics whomsoever. And of course everything can be expressed,—after a fashion, and 'theoretically,'—in terms of chemistry and physics, that is, *everything except the vital principle of the whole*, and that, they say, there is no pragmatic use in trying to express; it has no bearings—for *them*. I for my part refuse to be persuaded that we can not look beyond the obvious pluralism of the naturalist and the pragmatist to a logical unity in which they take no interest."

How is such a conception of the pragmatism I am advocating possible, after my first and second lectures? I have all along been offering it expressly as a mediator between tough-mindedness and tender-mindedness. If the notion of a world *ante rem*, whether taken abstractly like the word winter, or concretely as the hypothesis of an Absolute, can be shown to have any consequences whatever for our life, it has a meaning. If the meaning works, it will have *some* truth that ought to be held to through all possible reformulations, for pragmatism.

The absolutistic hypothesis, that perfection is eternal, aboriginal, and most real, has a perfectly definite meaning, and it works religiously. To examine how, will be the subject of my next and final lecture.

LECTURE VIII

PRAGMATISM AND RELIGION

AT THE CLOSE of the last lecture I reminded you of the first one, in which I had opposed tough-mindedness to tender-mindedness and recommended pragmatism as their mediator. Tough-mindedness positively rejects tender-mindedness's hypothesis of an eternal perfect edition of the universe coexisting with our finite experience.

On pragmatic principles we can not reject any hypothesis if consequences useful to life flow from it. Universal conceptions, as things to take account of, may be as real for pragmatism as particular sensations are. They have, indeed, no meaning and no reality if they have no use. But if they have any use they have that amount of meaning. And the meaning will be true if the use squares well with life's other uses.

Well, the use of the Absolute is proved by the whole course of men's religious history. The eternal arms are then beneath. Remember Vivekananda's use of the Atman: it is indeed not a scientific use, for we can make no particular deductions from it. It is emotional and spiritual altogether.

It is always best to discuss things by the help of concrete examples. Let me read therefore some of those verses entitled 'To You' by Walt Whitman—'You' of course meaning the reader or hearer of the poem whosoever he or she may be.

Whoever you are, now I place my hand upon you that you
  be my poem;
I whisper with my lips close to your ear,
I have loved many women and men, but I love none better
  than you.

O I have been dilatory and dumb;
I should have made my way to you long ago;
I should have blabbed nothing but you, I should have
  chanted nothing but you.

I will leave all and come and make the hymns of you;
None have understood you, but I understand you;

606

None have done justice to you—you have not done justice
   to yourself;
None but have found you imperfect—I only find no
   imperfection in you.

O I could sing such glories and grandeurs about you;
You have not known what you are—you have slumbered
   upon yourself all your life;
What you have done returns already in mockeries.

But the mockeries are not you;
Underneath them and within them, I see you lurk;
I pursue you where none else has pursued you.
Silence, the desk, the flippant expression, the night, the
   accustomed routine, if these conceal you from others, or
   from yourself, they do not conceal you from me;
The shaved face, the unsteady eye, the impure complexion, if
   these balk others, they do not balk me;
The pert apparel, the deformed attitude, drunkenness, greed,
   premature death, all these I part aside.

There is no endowment in man or woman that is not tallied
   in you;
There is no virtue, no beauty, in man or woman, but as
   good is in you;
No pluck nor endurance in others, but as good is in you;
No pleasure waiting for others, but an equal pleasure waits
   for you.

Whoever you are! claim your own at any hazard!
These shows of the east and west are tame, compared with
   you;
These immense meadows—these interminable rivers—you
   are immense and interminable as they;
You are he or she who is master or mistress over them,
Master or mistress in your own right over Nature, elements,
   pain, passion, dissolution.

The hopples fall from your ankles—you find an unfailing
   sufficiency;
Old or young, male or female, rude, low, rejected by the
   rest, whatever you are promulges itself;

Through birth, life, death, burial, the means are provided,
　　nothing is scanted;
Through angers, losses, ambition, ignorance, ennui, what
　　you are picks its way.

Verily a fine and moving poem, in any case, but there are
two ways of taking it, both useful.

One is the monistic way, the mystical way of pure cosmic
emotion. The glories and grandeurs, they are yours absolutely, even in the midst of your defacements. Whatever may
happen to you, whatever you may appear to be, inwardly you
are safe. Look back, *lie* back, on your true principle of being!
This is the famous way of quietism, of indifferentism. Its enemies compare it to a spiritual opium. Yet pragmatism must
respect this way, for it has massive historic vindication.

But pragmatism sees another way to be respected also, the
pluralistic way of interpreting the poem. The you so glorified,
to which the hymn is sung, may mean your better possibilities
phenomenally taken, or the specific redemptive effects even of
your failures, upon yourself or others. It may mean your loyalty to the possibilities of others whom you admire and love
so that you are willing to accept your own poor life, for it is
that glory's partner. You can at least appreciate, applaud, furnish the audience, of so brave a total world. Forget the low
in yourself, then, think only of the high. Identify your life
therewith; then, through angers, losses, ignorance, ennui,
whatever you thus make yourself, whatever you thus most
deeply are, picks its way.

In either way of taking the poem, it encourages fidelity to
ourselves. Both ways satisfy; both sanctify the human flux.
Both paint the portrait of the *you* on a gold background. But
the background of the first way is the static One, while in the
second way it means possibles in the plural, genuine possibles, and it has all the restlessness of that conception.

Noble enough is either way of reading the poem; but
plainly the pluralistic way agrees with the pragmatic temper
best, for it immediately suggests an infinitely larger number
of the details of future experience to our mind. It sets definite
activities in us at work. Altho this second way seems prosaic
and earth-born in comparison with the first way, yet no one

can accuse it of tough-mindedness in any brutal sense of the term. Yet if, as pragmatists, you should positively set up the second way *against* the first way, you would very likely be misunderstood. You would be accused of denying nobler conceptions, and of being an ally of tough-mindedness in the worst sense.

You remember the letter from a member of this audience from which I read some extracts at our previous meeting. Let me read you an additional extract now. It shows a vagueness in realizing the alternatives before us which I think is very widespread.

"I believe," writes my friend and correspondent, "in pluralism; I believe that in our search for truth we leap from one floating cake of ice to another, on an infinite sea, and that by each of our acts we make new truths possible and old ones impossible; I believe that each man is responsible for making the universe better, and that if he does not do this it will be in so far left undone.

"Yet at the same time I am willing to endure that my children should be incurably sick and suffering (as they are not) and I myself stupid and yet with brains enough to see my stupidity, only on one condition, namely, that through the construction, in imagination and by reasoning, of a *rational unity of all things*, I can conceive my acts and my thoughts and my troubles as *supplemented by all the other phenomena of the world, and as forming—when thus supplemented—a scheme which I approve and adopt as my own*; and for my part I refuse to be persuaded that we can not look beyond the obvious pluralism of the naturalist and pragmatist to a logical unity in which they take no interest or stock."

Such a fine expression of personal faith warms the heart of the hearer. But how much does it clear his philosophic head? Does the writer consistently favor the monistic, or the pluralistic, interpretation of the world's poem? His troubles become atoned for *when thus supplemented*, he says, supplemented, that is, by all the remedies that *the other phenomena* may supply. Obviously here the writer faces forward into the particulars of experience, which he interprets in a pluralistic-melioristic way.

But he believes himself to face backward. He speaks of

what he calls the rational *unity* of things, when all the while he really means their possible empirical *unification*. He supposes at the same time that the pragmatist, because he criticises rationalism's abstract One, is cut off from the consolation of believing in the saving possibilities of the concrete many. He fails in short to distinguish between taking the world's perfection as a necessary principle, and taking it only as a possible *terminus ad quem*.

I regard the writer of the letter as a genuine pragmatist, but as a pragmatist *sans le savoir*. He appears to me as one of that numerous class of philosophic amateurs whom I spoke of in my first lecture, as wishing to have all the good things going, without being too careful as to how they agree or disagree. 'Rational unity of all things' is so inspiring a formula, that he brandishes it off-hand, and abstractly accuses pluralism of conflicting with it (for the bare names do conflict), altho concretely he means by it just the pragmatistically unified and ameliorated world. Most of us remain in this essential vagueness, and it is well that we should; but in the interest of clearheadedness it is well that some of us should go farther, so I will try now to focus a little more discriminatingly on this particular religious point.

Is then this you of yous, this absolutely real world, this unity that yields the moral inspiration and has the religious value, to be taken monistically or pluralistically? Is it *ante rem* or *in rebus*? Is it a principle or an end, an absolute or an ultimate, a first or a last? Does it make you look forward or lie back? It is certainly worth while not to clump the two things together, for if discriminated, they have decidedly diverse meanings for life.

Please observe that the whole dilemma revolves pragmatically about the notion of the world's possibilities. Intellectually, rationalism invokes its absolute principle of unity, as a ground of possibility for the many facts. Emotionally, it sees it as a container and limiter of possibilities, a guarantee that the upshot shall be good. Taken in this way, the absolute makes all good things certain, and all bad things impossible (in the eternal, namely), and may be said to transmute the entire category of possibility into categories more secure. One sees at this point that the great religious difference lies between the men who insist that the world *must and shall be*, and those who are contented with believing that the world *may be*, saved. The whole clash of rationalistic and empiricist religion is thus over the validity of possibility. It is necessary therefore to begin by focusing upon that word. What may the word 'possible' definitely mean?

To unreflecting men the possible means a sort of third estate of being, less real than existence, more real than non-existence, a twilight realm, a hybrid status, a limbo into which and out of which realities ever and anon are made to pass. Such a conception is of course too vague and nondescript to satisfy us. Here, as elsewhere, the only way to extract a term's meaning is to use the pragmatic method on it. When you say a thing is possible, what difference does it make?

It makes at least this difference that if any one calls it impossible you can contradict him, if any one calls it actual you can contradict *him*, and if any one calls it necessary you can contradict him too. But these privileges of contradiction don't amount to much. When you say a thing is possible, does not that make some farther difference in terms of actual fact?

It makes at least this negative difference that if the statement be true, it follows that *there is nothing extant capable of preventing* the possible thing. The absence of real grounds of interference may thus be said to make things *not impossible*, possible therefore in the *bare* or *abstract* sense.

But most possibles are not bare, they are concretely grounded, or well-grounded, as we say. What does this mean pragmatically? It means not only that there are no preventive conditions present, but that some of the conditions of production of the possible thing actually are here. Thus a concretely possible chicken means: (1) that the idea of chicken contains no essential self-contradiction; (2) that no boys, skunks, or other enemies are about; and (3) that at least an actual egg exists. Possible chicken means actual egg—plus actual sitting hen, or incubator, or what not. As the actual conditions approach completeness the chicken becomes a better-and-better-grounded possibility. When the conditions are entirely complete, it ceases to be a possibility, and turns into an actual fact.

Let us apply this notion to the salvation of the world. What does it pragmatically mean to say that this is possible? It means that some of the conditions of the world's deliverance do actually exist. The more of them there are existent, the fewer preventing conditions you can find, the better-grounded is the salvation's possibility, the more *probable* does the fact of the deliverance become.

So much for our preliminary look at possibility.

Now it would contradict the very spirit of life to say that our minds must be indifferent and neutral in questions like that of the world's salvation. Any one who pretends to be neutral writes himself down here as a fool and a sham. We all do wish to minimize the insecurity of the universe; we are and ought to be unhappy when we regard it as exposed to every enemy and open to every life-destroying draft. Nevertheless there are unhappy men who think the salvation of the world impossible. Theirs is the doctrine known as pessimism.

Optimism in turn would be the doctrine that thinks the world's salvation inevitable.

Midway between the two there stands what may be called the doctrine of meliorism, tho it has hitherto figured less as a doctrine than as an attitude in human affairs. Optimism has always been the regnant *doctrine* in European philosophy. Pessimism was only recently introduced by Schopenhauer and counts few systematic defenders as yet. Meliorism treats salvation as neither inevitable nor impossible. It treats it as a possibility, which becomes more and more of a probability the more numerous the actual conditions of salvation become.

It is clear that pragmatism must incline towards meliorism. Some conditions of the world's salvation are actually extant, and she can not possibly close her eyes to this fact: and should the residual conditions come, salvation would become an accomplished reality. Naturally the terms I use here are exceedingly summary. You may interpret the word 'salvation' in any way you like, and make it as diffuse and distributive, or as climacteric and integral a phenomenon as you please.

Take, for example, any one of us in this room with the ideals which he cherishes and is willing to live and work for.

Every such ideal realized will be one moment in the world's salvation. But these particular ideals are not bare abstract possibilities. They are grounded, they are *live* possibilities, for we are their live champions and pledges, and if the complementary conditions come and add themselves, our ideals will become actual things. What now are the complementary conditions? They are first such a mixture of things as will in the fulness of time give us a chance, a gap that we can spring into, and, finally, *our act*.

Does our act then *create* the world's salvation so far as it makes room for itself, so far as it leaps into the gap? Does it create, not the whole world's salvation of course, but just so much of this as itself covers of the world's extent?

Here I take the bull by the horns, and in spite of the whole crew of rationalists and monists, of whatever brand they be, I ask *why not?* Our acts, our turning-places, where we seem to ourselves to make ourselves and grow, are the parts of the world to which we are closest, the parts of which our knowledge is the most intimate and complete. Why should we not take them at their face-value? Why may they not be the actual turning-places and growing-places which they seem to be, of the world—why not the workshop of being, where we catch fact in the making, so that nowhere may the world grow in any other kind of way than this?

Irrational! we are told. How can new being come in local spots and patches which add themselves or stay away at random, independently of the rest? There must be a reason for our acts, and where in the last resort can any reason be looked for save in the material pressure or the logical compulsion of the total nature of the world? There can be but one real agent of growth, or seeming growth, anywhere, and that agent is the integral world itself. It may grow all-over, if growth there be, but that single parts should grow *per se* is irrational.

But if one talks of rationality—and of reasons for things, and insists that they can't just come in spots, what *kind* of a reason can there ultimately be why anything should come at all? Talk of logic and necessity and categories and the absolute and the contents of the whole philosophical machine-shop as you will, the only *real* reason I can think of why anything should ever come is that *some one wishes it to be here*. It is *demanded*,—demanded, it may be, to give relief to no matter how small a fraction of the world's mass. This is *living reason*, and compared with it material causes and logical necessities are spectral things.

In short the only fully rational world would be the world of wishing-caps, the world of telepathy, where every desire is fulfilled instanter, without having to consider or placate surrounding or intermediate powers. This is the Absolute's own world. He calls upon the phenomenal world to be, and it *is*, exactly as he calls for it, no other condition being required. In our world, the wishes of the individual are only one condition. Other individuals are there with other wishes and they must be propitiated first. So Being grows under all sorts of resistances in this world of the many, and, from compromise to compromise, only gets organized gradually into what may be called secondarily rational shape. We approach the wishing-cap type of organization only in a few departments of life. We want water and we turn a faucet. We want a kodak-picture and we press a button. We want information and we telephone. We want to travel and we buy a ticket. In these and similar cases, we hardly need to do more than the wishing—the world is rationally organized to do the rest.

But this talk of rationality is a parenthesis and a digression. What we were discussing was the idea of a world growing not integrally but piecemeal by the contributions of its several parts. Take the hypothesis seriously and as a live one. Suppose that the world's author put the case to you before creation, saying: "I am going to make a world not certain to be saved, a world the perfection of which shall be conditional merely, the condition being that each several agent does its own 'level best.' I offer you the chance of taking part in such a world. Its safety, you see, is unwarranted. It is a real adventure, with real danger, yet it may win through. It is a social scheme of co-operative work genuinely to be done. Will you join the procession? Will you trust yourself and trust the other agents enough to face the risk?"

Should you in all seriousness, if participation in such a world were proposed to you, feel bound to reject it as not safe enough? Would you say that, rather than be part and parcel of so fundamentally pluralistic and irrational a universe, you preferred to relapse into the slumber of nonentity from which you had been momentarily aroused by the tempter's voice?

Of course if you are normally constituted, you would do nothing of the sort. There is a healthy-minded buoyancy in most of us which such a universe would exactly fit. We would therefore accept the offer—"Top! und schlag auf schlag!" It would be just like the world we practically live in; and loyalty to our old nurse Nature would forbid us to say no. The world proposed would seem 'rational' to us in the most living way.

Most of us, I say, would therefore welcome the proposition and add our *fiat* to the *fiat* of the creator. Yet perhaps some would not; for there are morbid minds in every human collection, and to them the prospect of a universe with only a fighting chance of safety would probably make no appeal. There are moments of discouragement in us all, when we are sick of self and tired of vainly striving. Our own life breaks down, and we fall into the attitude of the prodigal son. We mistrust the chances of things. We want a universe where we can just give up, fall on our father's neck, and be absorbed into the absolute life as a drop of water melts into the river or the sea.

The peace and rest, the security desiderated at such moments is security against the bewildering accidents of so much finite experience. Nirvana means safety from this everlasting round of adventures of which the world of sense consists. The hindoo and the buddhist, for this is essentially their attitude, are simply afraid, afraid of more experience, afraid of life.

And to men of this complexion, religious monism comes with its consoling words: "All is needed and essential—even you with your sick soul and heart. All are one with God, and with God all is well. The everlasting arms are beneath, whether in the world of finite appearance you seem to fail or to succeed." There can be no doubt that when men are reduced to their last sick extremity absolutism is the only saving scheme. Pluralistic moralism simply makes their teeth chatter, it refrigerates the very heart within their breast.

So we see concretely two types of religion in sharp contrast. Using our old terms of comparison, we may say that the absolutistic scheme appeals to the tender-minded while the pluralistic scheme appeals to the tough. Many persons would refuse to call the pluralistic scheme religious at all. They would call it moralistic, and would apply the word religious to the monistic scheme alone. Religion in the sense of self-surrender, and moralism in the sense of self-sufficingness, have been pitted against each other as incompatibles frequently enough in the history of human thought.

We stand here before the final question of philosophy. I said in my fourth lecture that I believed the monistic-pluralistic alternative to be the deepest and most pregnant question that our minds can frame. Can it be that the disjunction is a final one? that only one side can be true? Are a pluralism and monism genuine incompatibles? So that, if the world were really pluralistically constituted, if it really existed distributively and were made up of a lot of eaches, it could only be saved piecemeal and *de facto* as the result of their behavior, and its epic history in no wise short-circuited by some essential oneness in which the severalness were already 'taken up' beforehand and eternally 'overcome'? If this were so, we should have to choose one philosophy or the other. We could not say 'yes, yes' to both alternatives. There would have to be a 'no' in our relations with the possible. We should confess an ultimate disappointment: we could not remain healthy-minded and sick-minded in one indivisible act.

Of course as human beings we can be healthy minds on one day and sick souls on the next; and as amateur dabblers in philosophy we may perhaps be allowed to call ourselves monistic pluralists, or free-will determinists, or whatever else may occur to us of a reconciling kind. But as philosophers aiming at clearness and consistency, and feeling the pragmatistic need of squaring truth with truth, the question is forced upon us of frankly adopting either the tender or the robustious type of thought. In particular *this* query has always come home to me: May not the claims of tender-mindedness go too far? May not the notion of a world already saved *in toto* anyhow, be too saccharine to stand? May not religious optimism be too idyllic? Must *all* be saved? Is *no* price to be paid in the work of salvation? Is the last word sweet? Is all 'yes, yes' in the universe? Does n't the fact of 'no' stand at the very core of life? Does n't the very 'seriousness' that we attribute to life mean that ineluctable noes and losses form a part of it, that there are genuine sacrifices somewhere, and that something permanently drastic and bitter always remains at the bottom of its cup?

I can not speak officially as a pragmatist here; all I can say is that my own pragmatism offers no objection to my taking sides with this more moralistic view, and giving up the claim of total reconciliation. The possibility of this is involved in the pragmatistic willingness to treat pluralism as a serious hypothesis. In the end it is our faith and not our logic that decides such questions, and I deny the right of any pretended logic to veto my own faith. I find myself willing to take the universe to be really dangerous and adventurous, without therefore backing out and crying 'no play.' I am willing to think that the prodigal-son attitude, open to us as it is in many vicissitudes, is not the right and final attitude towards the whole of life. I am willing that there should be real losses and real losers, and no total preservation of all that is. I can believe in the ideal as an ultimate, not as an origin, and as an extract, not the whole. When the cup is poured off, the dregs are left behind for ever, but the possibility of what is poured off is sweet enough to accept.

As a matter of fact countless human imaginations live in this moralistic and epic kind of a universe, and find its disseminated and strung-along successes sufficient for their rational needs. There is a finely translated epigram in the Greek anthology which admirably expresses this state of mind, this acceptance of loss as unatoned for, even though the lost element might be one's self:

> "A shipwrecked sailor, buried on this coast,
> Bids you set sail.
> Full many a gallant bark, when we were lost,
> Weathered the gale."

Those puritans who answered 'yes' to the question: Are you willing to be damned for God's glory? were in this objective and magnanimous condition of mind. The way of escape from evil on this system is *not* by getting it 'aufgehoben,' or preserved in the whole as an element essential but 'overcome.' *It is by dropping it out altogether, throwing it overboard and getting beyond it, helping to make a universe that shall forget its very place and name.*

It is then perfectly possible to accept sincerely a drastic kind of a universe from which the element of 'seriousness' is not to be expelled. Whoso does so is, it seems to me, a genuine pragmatist. He is willing to live on a scheme of uncertified possibilities which he trusts; willing to pay with his own person, if need be, for the realization of the ideals which he frames.

What now actually *are* the other forces which he trusts to co-operate with him, in a universe of such a type? They are at least his fellow men, in the stage of being which our actual universe has reached. But are there not superhuman forces also, such as religious men of the pluralistic type we have been considering have always believed in? Their words may have sounded monistic when they said "there is no God but God"; but the original polytheism of mankind has only imperfectly and vaguely sublimated itself into monotheism, and monotheism itself, so far as it was religious and not a scheme of classroom instruction for the metaphysicians, has always viewed God as but one helper, *primus inter pares*, in the midst of all the shapers of the great world's fate.

I fear that my previous lectures, confined as they have been to human and humanistic aspects, may have left the impression on many of you that pragmatism means methodically to leave the superhuman out. I have shown small respect indeed for the Absolute, and I have until this moment spoken of no other superhuman hypothesis but that. But I trust that you see sufficiently that the Absolute has nothing but its superhumanness in common with the theistic God. On pragmatistic principles, if the hypothesis of God works satisfactorily in the widest sense of the word, it is true. Now whatever its residual difficulties may be, experience shows that it certainly does work, and that the problem is to build it out and determine it so that it will combine satisfactorily with all the other working truths. I can not start upon a whole theology at the end of this last lecture; but when I tell you that I have written a book on men's religious experience, which on the whole has been regarded as making for the reality of God, you will perhaps exempt my own pragmatism from the charge of being an atheistic system. I firmly disbelieve, myself, that our human experience is the highest form of experience extant in the universe. I believe rather that we stand in much the same relation to the whole of the universe as our canine and feline pets do to the whole of human life. They inhabit our drawing-rooms and libraries. They take part in scenes of whose significance they have no inkling. They are merely tangent to curves of history the beginnings and ends and forms of which pass wholly beyond their ken. So we are tangent to the wider life of things. But, just as many of the dog's and cat's ideals coincide with our ideals, and the dogs and cats have daily living proof of the fact, so we may well believe, on the proofs that religious experience affords, that higher powers exist and are at work to save the world on ideal lines similar to our own.

You see that pragmatism can be called religious, if you allow that religion can be pluralistic or merely melioristic in type. But whether you will finally put up with that type of religion or not is a question that only you yourself can decide. Pragmatism has to postpone dogmatic answer, for we do not yet know certainly which type of religion is going to work best in the long run. The various overbeliefs of men, their several faith-ventures, are in fact what are needed to bring the evidence in. You will probably make your own ventures severally. If radically tough, the hurly-burly of the sensible facts of nature will be enough for you, and you will need no religion at all. If radically tender, you will take up with the more monistic form of religion: the pluralistic form, with its reliance on possibilities that are not necessities, will not seem to afford you security enough.

But if you are neither tough nor tender in an extreme and radical sense, but mixed as most of us are, it may seem to you that the type of pluralistic and moralistic religion that I have offered is as good a religious synthesis as you are likely to find. Between the two extremes of crude naturalism on the one hand and transcendental absolutism on the other, you may find that what I take the liberty of calling the pragmatistic or melioristic type of theism is exactly what you require.

Index

A PLURALISTIC UNIVERSE

*Hibbert Lectures at Manchester College on
the Present Situation in Philosophy*

Contents

LECTURE I

THE TYPES OF PHILOSOPHIC THINKING

As THESE LECTURES are meant to be public, and so few, I have assumed all very special problems to be excluded, and some topic of general interest required. Fortunately, our age seems to be growing philosophical again—still in the ashes live the wonted fires. Oxford, long the seed-bed, for the english world, of the idealism inspired by Kant and Hegel, has recently become the nursery of a very different way of thinking. Even non-philosophers have begun to take an interest in a controversy over what is known as pluralism or humanism. It looks a little as if the ancient english empiricism, so long put out of fashion here by nobler sounding germanic formulas, might be re-pluming itself and getting ready for a stronger flight than ever. It looks as if foundations were being sounded and examined afresh.

Individuality outruns all classification, yet we insist on classifying every one we meet under some general head. As these heads usually suggest prejudicial associations to some hearer or other, the life of philosophy largely consists of resentments at the classing, and complaints of being misunderstood. But there are signs of clearing up, and, on the whole, less acrimony in discussion, for which both Oxford and Harvard are partly to be thanked. As I look back into the sixties, Mill, Bain, and Hamilton were the only official philosophers in Britain. Spencer, Martineau, and Hodgson were just beginning. In France, the pupils of Cousin were delving into history only, and Renouvier alone had an original system. In Germany, the hegelian impetus had spent itself, and, apart from historical scholarship, nothing but the materialistic controversy remained, with such men as Büchner and Ulrici as its champions. Lotze and Fechner were the sole original thinkers, and Fechner was not a professional philosopher at all.

The general impression made was of crude issues and oppositions, of small subtlety and of a widely spread ignorance. Amateurishness was rampant. Samuel Bailey's 'letters on the philosophy of the human mind,' published in 1855, are one of the ablest expressions of english associationism, and a book of real power. Yet hear how he writes of Kant: 'No one, after reading the extracts, etc., can be surprised to hear of a declaration by men of eminent abilities, that, after years of study, they had not succeeded in gathering one clear idea from the speculations of Kant. I should have been almost surprised if they had. In or about 1818, Lord Grenville, when visiting the Lakes of England, observed to Professor Wilson that, after five years' study of Kant's philosophy, he had not gathered from it one clear idea. Wilberforce, about the same time, made the same confession to another friend of my own. "I am endeavoring," exclaims Sir James Mackintosh, in the irritation, evidently, of baffled efforts, "to understand this accursed german philosophy." '[1]

What Oxford thinker would dare to print such *naïf* and provincial-sounding citations of authority to-day?

The torch of learning passes from land to land as the spirit bloweth the flame. The deepening of philosophic consciousness came to us english folk from Germany, as it will probably pass back ere long. Ferrier, J. H. Stirling, and, most of all, T. H. Green are to be thanked. If asked to tell in broad strokes what the main doctrinal change has been, I should call it a change from the crudity of the older english thinking, its ultra-simplicity of mind, both when it was religious and when it was anti-religious, toward a rationalism derived in the first instance from Germany, but relieved from german technicality and shrillness, and content to suggest, and to remain vague, and to be, in the english fashion, devout.

By the time T. H. Green began at Oxford, the generation seemed to feel as if it had fed on the chopped straw of psychology and of associationism long enough, and as if a little vastness, even though it went with vagueness, as of some moist wind from far away, reminding us of our pre-natal sublimity, would be welcome.

Green's great point of attack was the disconnectedness of the reigning english sensationalism. *Relating* was the great intellectual activity for him, and the key to this relating was

[1] Bailey: *op cit.*, First Series, p. 52.

believed by him to lodge itself at last in what most of you know as Kant's unity of apperception, transformed into a living spirit of the world.

Hence a monism of a devout kind. In some way we must be fallen angels, one with intelligence as such; and a great disdain for empiricism of the sensationalist sort has always characterized this school of thought, which, on the whole, has reigned supreme at Oxford and in the scottish universities until the present day.

But now there are signs of its giving way to a wave of revised empiricism. I confess that I should be glad to see this latest wave prevail; so—the sooner I am frank about it the better—I hope to have my voice counted in its favor as one of the results of this lecture-course.

What do the terms empiricism and rationalism mean? Reduced to their most pregnant difference, *empiricism means the habit of explaining wholes by parts, and rationalism means the habit of explaining parts by wholes*. Rationalism thus preserves affinities with monism, since wholeness goes with union, while empiricism inclines to pluralistic views. No philosophy can ever be anything but a summary sketch, a picture of the world in abridgment, a foreshortened bird's-eye view of the perspective of events. And the first thing to notice is this, that the only material we have at our disposal for making a picture of the whole world is supplied by the various portions of that world of which we have already had experience. We can invent no new forms of conception, applicable to the whole exclusively, and not suggested originally by the parts. All philosophers, accordingly, have conceived of the whole world after the analogy of some particular feature of it which has particularly captivated their attention. Thus, the theists take their cue from manufacture, the pantheists from growth. For one man, the world is like a thought or a grammatical sentence in which a thought is expressed. For such a philosopher, the whole must logically be prior to the parts; for letters would never have been invented without syllables to spell, or syllables without words to utter.

Another man, struck by the disconnectedness and mutual accidentality of so many of the world's details, takes the universe as a whole to have been such a disconnectedness originally, and supposes order to have been superinduced upon it in the second instance, possibly by attrition and the gradual wearing away by internal friction of portions that originally interfered.

Another will conceive the order as only a statistical appearance, and the universe will be for him like a vast grab-bag with black and white balls in it, of which we guess the quantities only probably, by the frequency with which we experience their egress.

For another, again, there is no really inherent order, but it is we who project order into the world by selecting objects and tracing relations so as to gratify our intellectual interests. We *carve out* order by leaving the disorderly parts out; and the world is conceived thus after the analogy of a forest or a block of marble from which parks or statues may be produced by eliminating irrelevant trees or chips of stone.

Some thinkers follow suggestions from human life, and treat the universe as if it were essentially a place in which ideals are realized. Others are more struck by its lower features, and for them, brute necessities express its character better.

All follow one analogy or another; and all the analogies are with some one or other of the universe's subdivisions. Every one is nevertheless prone to claim that his conclusions are the only logical ones, that they are necessities of universal reason, they being all the while, at bottom, accidents more or less of personal vision which had far better be avowed as such; for one man's vision may be much more valuable than another's, and our visions are usually not only our most interesting but our most respectable contributions to the world in which we play our part. What was reason given to men for, said some eighteenth century writer, except to enable them to find reasons for what they want to think and do?—and I think the history of philosophy largely bears him out. 'The aim of knowledge,' says Hegel,[1] 'is to divest the objective world of its strangeness, and to make us more at home in it.' Different men find their minds more at home in very different fragments of the world.

[1] *Smaller Logic,* § 194.

Let me make a few comments, here, on the curious antipathies which these partialities arouse. They are sovereignly unjust, for all the parties are human beings with the same essential interests, and no one of them is the wholly perverse demon which another often imagines him to be. Both are loyal to the world that bears them; neither wishes to spoil it; neither wishes to regard it as an insane incoherence; both want to keep it as a universe of some kind; and their differences are all secondary to this deep agreement. They may be only propensities to emphasize differently. Or one man may care for finality and security more than the other. Or their tastes in language may be different. One may like a universe that lends itself to lofty and exalted characterization. To another this may seem sentimental or rhetorical. One may wish for the right to use a clerical vocabulary, another a technical or professorial one. A certain old farmer of my acquaintance in America was called a rascal by one of his neighbors. He immediately smote the man, saying, 'I won't stand none of your diminutive epithets.' Empiricist minds, putting the parts before the whole, appear to rationalists, who start from the whole, and consequently enjoy magniloquent privileges, to use epithets offensively diminutive. But all such differences are minor matters which ought to be subordinated in view of the fact that, whether we be empiricists or rationalists, we are, ourselves, parts of the universe and share the same one deep concern in its destinies. We crave alike to feel more truly at home with it, and to contribute our mite to its amelioration. It would be pitiful if small æsthetic discords were to keep honest men asunder.

I shall myself have use for the diminutive epithets of empiricism. But if you look behind the words at the spirit, I am sure you will not find it matricidal. I am as good a son as any rationalist among you to our common mother.

What troubles me more than this misapprehension is the genuine abstruseness of many of the matters I shall be obliged to talk about, and the difficulty of making them intelligible at one hearing. But there are two pieces, 'zwei stücke,' as Kant would have said, in every philosophy—the final outlook, belief, or attitude to which it brings us, and the reasonings by which that attitude is reached and mediated. A philosophy, as

James Ferrier used to tell us, must indeed be true, but that is the least of its requirements. One may be true without being a philosopher, true by guesswork or by revelation. What distinguishes a philosopher's truth is that it is *reasoned*. Argument, not supposition, must have put it in his possession. Common men find themselves inheriting their beliefs, they know not how. They jump into them with both feet, and stand there. Philosophers must do more; they must first get reason's license for them; and to the professional philosophic mind the operation of procuring the license is usually a thing of much more pith and moment than any particular beliefs to which the license may give the rights of access. Suppose, for example, that a philosopher believes in what is called free-will. That a common man alongside of him should also share that belief, possessing it by a sort of inborn intuition, does not endear the man to the philosopher at all—he may even be ashamed to be associated with such a man. What interests the philosopher is the particular premises on which the free-will he believes in is established, the sense in which it is taken, the objections it eludes, the difficulties it takes account of, in short the whole form and temper and manner and technical apparatus that goes with the belief in question. A philosopher across the way who should use the same technical apparatus, making the same distinctions, etc., but drawing opposite conclusions and denying free-will entirely, would fascinate the first philosopher far more than would the *naïf* co-believer. Their common technical interests would unite them more than their opposite conclusions separate them. Each would feel an essential consanguinity in the other, would think of him, write *at* him, care for his good opinion. The simple-minded believer in free-will would be disregarded by either. Neither as ally nor as opponent would his vote be counted.

In a measure this is doubtless as it should be, but like all professionalism it can go to abusive extremes. The end is after all more than the way, in most things human, and forms and methods may easily frustrate their own purpose. The abuse of technicality is seen in the infrequency with which, in philosophical literature, metaphysical questions are discussed directly and on their own merits. Almost always they are handled as if through a heavy woolen curtain, the veil of previous philosophers' opinions. Alternatives are wrapped in proper names, as if it were indecent for a truth to go naked. The late Professor John Grote of Cambridge has some good remarks about this. 'Thought,' he says, 'is not a professional matter, not something for so-called philosophers only or for professed thinkers. The best philosopher is the man who can think most *simply*. . . . I wish that people would consider that thought—and philosophy is no more than good and methodical thought—is a matter *intimate* to them, a portion of their real selves . . . that they would *value* what they think, and be interested in it. . . . In my own opinion,' he goes on, 'there is something depressing in this weight of learning, with nothing that can come into one's mind but one is told, Oh, that is the opinion of such and such a person long ago. . . . I can conceive of nothing more noxious for students than to get into the habit of saying to themselves about their ordinary philosophic thought, Oh, somebody must have thought it all before.'[1] Yet this is the habit most encouraged at our seats of learning. You must tie your opinion to Aristotle's or Spinoza's; you must define it by its distance from Kant's; you must refute your rival's view by identifying it with Protagoras's. Thus does all spontaneity of thought, all freshness of conception, get destroyed. Everything you touch is shopworn. The over-technicality and consequent dreariness of the younger disciples at our american universities is appalling. It comes from too much following of german models and manners. Let me fervently express the hope that in this country you will hark back to the more humane english tradition. American students have to regain direct relations with our subject by painful individual effort in later life. Some of us have done so. Some of the younger ones, I fear, never will, so strong are the professional shop-habits already.

In a subject like philosophy it is really fatal to lose connexion with the open air of human nature, and to think in terms of shop-tradition only. In Germany the forms are so professionalized that anybody who has gained a teaching chair and written a book, however distorted and eccentric, has the legal right to figure forever in the history of the subject like a fly

---

[1] *Exploratio philosophica*, Part I, 1865, pp. xxxviii, 130.

in amber. All later comers have the duty of quoting him and measuring their opinions with his opinion. Such are the rules of the professorial game—they think and write from each other and for each other and at each other exclusively. With this exclusion of the open air all true perspective gets lost, extremes and oddities count as much as sanities, and command the same attention; and if by chance any one writes popularly and about results only, with his mind directly focussed on the subject, it is reckoned *oberflächliches zeug* and *ganz unwissenschaftlich*. Professor Paulsen has recently written some feeling lines about this over-professionalism, from the reign of which in Germany his own writings, which sin by being 'literary,' have suffered loss of credit. Philosophy, he says, has long assumed in Germany the character of being an esoteric and occult science. There is a genuine fear of popularity. Simplicity of statement is deemed synonymous with hollowness and shallowness. He recalls an old professor saying to him once: 'Yes, we philosophers, whenever we wish, can go so far that in a couple of sentences we can put ourselves where nobody can follow us.' The professor said this with conscious pride, but he ought to have been ashamed of it. Great as technique is, results are greater. To teach philosophy so that the pupils' interest in technique exceeds that in results is surely a vicious aberration. It is bad form, not good form, in a discipline of such universal human interest. Moreover, technique for technique, does n't David Hume's technique set, after all, the kind of pattern most difficult to follow? Is n't it the most admirable? The english mind, thank heaven, and the french mind, are still kept, by their aversion to crude technique and barbarism, closer to truth's natural probabilities. Their literatures show fewer obvious falsities and monstrosities than that of Germany. Think of the german literature of æsthetics, with the preposterousness of such an unæsthetic personage as Immanuel Kant enthroned in its centre! Think of german books on *religions-philosophie*, with the heart's battles translated into conceptual jargon and made dialectic. The most persistent setter of questions, feeler of objections, insister on satisfactions, is the religious life. Yet all its troubles can be treated with absurdly little technicality. The wonder is that, with their way of working philosophy, individual Germans should preserve any spontaneity of mind at all. That they still manifest freshness and originality in so eminent a degree, proves the indestructible richness of the german cerebral endowment.

Let me repeat once more that a man's vision is the great fact about him. Who cares for Carlyle's reasons, or Schopenhauer's, or Spencer's? A philosophy is the expression of a man's intimate character, and all definitions of the universe are but the deliberately adopted reactions of human characters upon it. In the recent book from which I quoted the words of Professor Paulsen, a book of successive chapters by various living german philosophers,[1] we pass from one idiosyncratic personal atmosphere into another almost as if we were turning over a photograph album.

If we take the whole history of philosophy, the systems reduce themselves to a few main types which, under all the technical verbiage in which the ingenious intellect of man envelops them, are just so many visions, modes of feeling the whole push, and seeing the whole drift of life, forced on one by one's total character and experience, and on the whole *preferred*—there is no other truthful word—as one's best working attitude. Cynical characters take one general attitude, sympathetic characters another. But no general attitude is possible towards the world as a whole, until the intellect has developed considerable generalizing power and learned to take pleasure in synthetic formulas. The thought of very primitive men has hardly any tincture of philosophy. Nature can have little unity for savages. It is a Walpurgis-nacht procession, a checkered play of light and shadow, a medley of impish and elfish friendly and inimical powers. 'Close to nature' though they live, they are anything but Wordsworthians. If a bit of cosmic emotion ever thrills them, it is likely to be at midnight, when the camp smoke rises straight to the wicked full moon in the zenith, and the forest is all whispering with witchery and danger. The eeriness of the world, the mischief and the manyness, the littleness of the forces, the magical surprises, the unaccountability of every agent, these surely are the characters most impressive at that stage of culture, these

[1] Hinneberg: *Die Kultur der Gegenwart: Systematische Philosophie.* Leipzig: Teubner, 1907.

communicate the thrills of curiosity and the earliest intellectual stirrings. Tempests and conflagrations, pestilences and earthquakes, reveal supramundane powers, and instigate religious terror rather than philosophy. Nature, more demonic than divine, is above all things *multifarious*. So many creatures that feed or threaten, that help or crush, so many beings to hate or love, to understand or start at—which is on top and which subordinate? Who can tell? They are co-ordinate, rather, and to adapt ourselves to them singly, to 'square' the dangerous powers and keep the others friendly, regardless of consistency or unity, is the chief problem. The symbol of nature at this stage, as Paulsen well says, is the sphinx, under whose nourishing breasts the tearing claws are visible.

But in due course of time the intellect awoke, with its passion for generalizing, simplifying, and subordinating, and then began those divergences of conception which all later experience seems rather to have deepened than to have effaced, because objective nature has contributed to both sides impartially, and has let the thinkers emphasize different parts of her, and pile up opposite imaginary supplements.

Perhaps the most interesting opposition is that which results from the clash between what I lately called the sympathetic and the cynical temper. Materialistic and spiritualistic philosophies are the rival types that result: the former defining the world so as to leave man's soul upon it as a sort of outside passenger or alien, while the latter insists that the intimate and human must surround and underlie the brutal. This latter is the spiritual way of thinking.

Now there are two very distinct types or stages in spiritualistic philosophy, and my next purpose in this lecture is to make their contrast evident. Both types attain the sought-for intimacy of view, but the one attains it somewhat less successfully than the other.

The generic term spiritualism, which I began by using merely as the opposite of materialism, thus subdivides into two species, the more intimate one of which is monistic and the less intimate dualistic. The dualistic species is the *theism* that reached its elaboration in the scholastic philosophy, while the monistic species is the *pantheism* spoken of sometimes simply as idealism, and sometimes as 'post-kantian' or 'absolute' idealism. Dualistic theism is professed as firmly as ever at all catholic seats of learning, whereas it has of late years tended to disappear at our british and american universities, and to be replaced by a monistic pantheism more or less open or disguised. I have an impression that ever since T. H. Green's time absolute idealism has been decidedly in the ascendent at Oxford. It is in the ascendent at my own university of Harvard.

Absolute idealism attains, I said, to the more intimate point of view; but the statement needs some explanation. So far as theism represents the world as God's world, and God as what Matthew Arnold called a magnified non-natural man, it would seem as if the inner quality of the world remained human, and as if our relations with it might be intimate enough—for what is best in ourselves appears then also outside of ourselves, and we and the universe are of the same spiritual species. So far, so good, then; and one might consequently ask, What more of intimacy do you require? To which the answer is that to be like a thing is not as intimate a relation as to be substantially fused into it, to form one continuous soul and body with it; and that pantheistic idealism, making us entitatively one with God, attains this higher reach of intimacy.

The theistic conception, picturing God and his creation as entities distinct from each other, still leaves the human subject outside of the deepest reality in the universe. God is from eternity complete, it says, and sufficient unto himself; he throws off the world by a free act and as an extraneous substance, and he throws off man as a third substance, extraneous to both the world and himself. Between them, God says 'one,' the world says 'two,' and man says 'three,'—that is the orthodox theistic view. And orthodox theism has been so jealous of God's glory that it has taken pains to exaggerate everything in the notion of him that could make for isolation and separateness. Page upon page in scholastic books go to prove that God is in no sense implicated by his creative act, or involved in his creation. That his relation to the creatures he has made should make any difference to him, carry any consequence, or qualify his being, is repudiated as a pantheistic slur upon his self-sufficingness. I said a moment ago that theism treats us and God as of the same species, but from the orthodox point of view that was a slip of language. God and his creatures are *toto genere* distinct in the scholastic theology, they have absolutely *nothing* in common; nay, it degrades God to attribute to him any generic nature whatever; he can be classed with nothing. There is a sense, then, in which philosophic theism makes us outsiders and keeps us foreigners in relation to God, in which, at any rate, his connexion with us appears as unilateral and not reciprocal. His action can affect us, but he can never be affected by our reaction. Our relation, in short, is not a strictly social relation. Of course in common men's religion the relation is believed to be social, but that is only one of the many differences between religion and theology.

This essential dualism of the theistic view has all sorts of collateral consequences. Man being an outsider and a mere subject to God, not his intimate partner, a character of externality invades the field. God is not heart of our heart and reason of our reason, but our magistrate, rather; and mechanically to obey his commands, however strange they may be, remains our only moral duty. Conceptions of criminal law have in fact played a great part in defining our relations with him. Our relations with speculative truth show the same externality. One of our duties is to know truth, and rationalist thinkers have always assumed it to be our sovereign duty. But in scholastic theism we find truth already instituted and established without our help, complete apart from our knowing; and the most we can do is to acknowledge it passively and adhere to it, altho such adhesion as ours can make no jot of difference to what is adhered to. The situation here again is radically dualistic. It is not as if the world came to know itself, or God came to know himself, partly through us, as pantheistic idealists have maintained, but truth exists *per se* and absolutely, by God's grace and decree, no matter who of us knows it or is ignorant, and it would continue to exist unaltered, even though we finite knowers were all annihilated.

It has to be confessed that this dualism and lack of intimacy has always operated as a drag and handicap on christian thought. Orthodox theology has had to wage a steady fight within the schools against the various forms of pantheistic heresy which the mystical experiences of religious persons, on the one hand, and the formal or æsthetic superiorities of monism to dualism, on the other, kept producing. God as intimate soul and reason of the universe has always seemed to some people a more worthy conception than God as external creator. So conceived, he appeared to unify the world more perfectly, he made it less finite and mechanical, and in comparison with such a God an external creator seemed more like the product of a childish fancy. I have been told by Hindoos that the great obstacle to the spread of Christianity in their country is the puerility of our dogma of creation. It has not sweep and infinity enough to meet the requirements of even the illiterate natives of India.

Assuredly most members of this audience are ready to side with Hinduism in this matter. Those of us who are sexagenarians have witnessed in our own persons one of those gradual mutations of intellectual climate, due to innumerable influences, that make the thought of a past generation seem as foreign to its successor as if it were the expression of a different race of men. The theological machinery that spoke so livingly to our ancestors, with its finite age of the world, its creation out of nothing, its juridical morality and eschatology, its relish for rewards and punishments, its treatment of God as an external contriver, an 'intelligent and moral governor,' sounds as odd to most of us as if it were some outlandish savage religion. The vaster vistas which scientific evolutionism has opened, and the rising tide of social democratic ideals, have changed the type of our imagination, and the older monarchical theism is obsolete or obsolescent. The place of the divine in the world must be more organic and intimate. An external creator and his institutions may still be verbally confessed at Church in formulas that linger by their mere inertia, but the life is out of them, we avoid dwelling on them, the sincere heart of us is elsewhere.

I shall leave cynical materialism entirely out of our discussion as not calling for treatment before this present audience, and I shall ignore old-fashioned dualistic theism for the same reason. Our contemporary mind having once for all grasped the possibility of a more intimate *weltanschauung*, the only opinions quite worthy of arresting our attention will fall within the general scope of what may roughly be called the pantheistic field of vision, the vision of God as the indwelling divine rather than the external creator, and of human life as part and parcel of that deep reality.

As we have found that spiritualism in general breaks into a more intimate and a less intimate species, so the more intimate species itself breaks into two subspecies, of which the one is more monistic, the other more pluralistic in form. I say in form, for our vocabulary gets unmanageable if we don't distinguish between form and substance here. The inner life of things must be substantially akin anyhow to the tenderer parts of man's nature in any spiritualistic philosophy. The word 'intimacy' probably covers the essential difference. Materialism holds the foreign in things to be more primary and lasting, it sends us to a lonely corner with our intimacy. The brutal aspects overlap and outwear; refinement has the feebler and more ephemeral hold on reality.

From a pragmatic point of view the difference between living against a background of foreignness and one of intimacy means the difference between a general habit of wariness and one of trust. One might call it a social difference, for after all, the common *socius* of us all is the great universe whose children we are. If materialistic, we must be suspicious of this socius, cautious, tense, on guard. If spiritualistic, we may give way, embrace, and keep no ultimate fear.

The contrast is rough enough, and can be cut across by all sorts of other divisions, drawn from other points of view than that of foreignness and intimacy. We have so many different businesses with nature that no one of them yields us an all-embracing clasp. The philosophic attempt to define nature so that no one's business is left out, so that no one lies outside the door saying 'Where do *I* come in?' is sure in advance to fail. The most a philosophy can hope for is not to lock out any interest forever. No matter what doors it closes, it must leave other doors open for the interests which it neglects. I have begun by shutting ourselves up to intimacy and foreignness because that makes so generally interesting a contrast, and because it will conveniently introduce a farther contrast to which I wish this hour to lead.

The majority of men are sympathetic. Comparatively few

are cynics because they like cynicism, and most of our existing materialists are such because they think the evidence of facts impels them, or because they find the idealists they are in contact with too private and tender-minded; so, rather than join their company, they fly to the opposite extreme. I therefore propose to you to disregard materialists altogether for the present, and to consider the sympathetic party alone.

It is normal, I say, to be sympathetic in the sense in which I use the term. Not to demand intimate relations with the universe, and not to wish them satisfactory, should be accounted signs of something wrong. Accordingly when minds of this type reach the philosophic level, and seek some unification of their vision, they find themselves compelled to correct that aboriginal appearance of things by which savages are not troubled. That sphinx-like presence, with its breasts and claws, that first bald multifariousness, is too discrepant an object for philosophic contemplation. The intimacy and the foreignness cannot be written down as simply coexisting. An order must be made; and in that order the higher side of things must dominate. The philosophy of the absolute agrees with the pluralistic philosophy which I am going to contrast with it in these lectures, in that both identify human substance with the divine substance. But whereas absolutism thinks that the said substance becomes fully divine only in the form of totality, and is not its real self in any form but the *all*-form, the pluralistic view which I prefer to adopt is willing to believe that there may ultimately never be an all-form at all, that the substance of reality may never get totally collected, that some of it may remain outside of the largest combination of it ever made, and that a distributive form of reality, the *each*-form, is logically as acceptable and empirically as probable as the all-form commonly acquiesced in as so obviously the self-evident thing. The contrast between these two forms of a reality which we will agree to suppose substantially spiritual is practically the topic of this course of lectures. You see now what I mean by pantheism's two subspecies. If we give to the monistic subspecies the name of philosophy of the absolute, we may give that of radical empiricism to its pluralistic rival, and it may be well to distinguish them occasionally later by these names.

As a convenient way of entering into the study of their differences, I may refer to a recent article by Professor Jacks of Manchester College. Professor Jacks, in some brilliant pages in the 'Hibbert Journal' for last October, studies the relation between the universe and the philosopher who describes and defines it for us. You may assume two cases, he says. Either what the philosopher tells us is extraneous to the universe he is accounting for, an indifferent parasitic outgrowth, so to speak; or the fact of his philosophizing is itself one of the things taken account of in the philosophy, and self-included in the description. In the former case the philosopher means by the universe everything *except* what his own presence brings; in the latter case his philosophy is itself an intimate part of the universe, and may be a part momentous enough to give a different turn to what the other parts signify. It may be a supreme reaction of the universe upon itself by which it rises to self-comprehension. It may handle itself differently in consequence of this event.

Now both empiricism and absolutism bring the philosopher inside and make man intimate, but the one being pluralistic and the other monistic, they do so in differing ways that need much explanation. Let me then contrast the one with the other way of representing the status of the human thinker.

For monism the world is no collection, but one great all-inclusive fact outside of which is nothing—nothing is its only alternative. When the monism is idealistic, this all-enveloping fact is represented as an absolute mind that makes the partial facts by thinking them, just as we make objects in a dream by dreaming them, or personages in a story by imagining them. To *be*, on this scheme, is, on the part of a finite thing, to be an object for the absolute; and on the part of the absolute it is to be the thinker of that assemblage of objects. If we use the word 'content' here, we see that the absolute and the world have an identical content. The absolute is nothing but the knowledge of those objects; the objects are nothing but what the absolute knows. The world and the all-thinker thus compenetrate and soak each other up without residuum. They are but two names for the same identical material, considered now from the subjective, and now from the objective point of view—gedanke and gedachtes, as we would say if we were Germans. We philosophers naturally form part of the material, on the monistic scheme. The absolute makes us by thinking us, and if we ourselves are enlightened enough to be believers in the absolute, one may then say that our philosophizing is one of the ways in which the absolute is conscious of itself. This is the full pantheistic scheme, the *identitätsphilosophie*, the immanence of God in his creation, a conception sublime from its tremendous unity. And yet that unity is incomplete, as closer examination will show.

The absolute and the world are one fact, I said, when materially considered. Our philosophy, for example, is not numerically distinct from the absolute's own knowledge of itself, not a duplicate and copy of it, it is part of that very knowledge, is numerically identical with as much of it as our thought covers. The absolute just *is* our philosophy, along with everything else that is known, in an act of knowing which (to use the words of my gifted absolutist colleague Royce) forms in its wholeness one luminously transparent conscious moment.

But one as we are in this material sense with the absolute substance, that being only the whole of us, and we only the parts of it, yet in a formal sense something like a pluralism breaks out. When we speak of the absolute we *take* the one universal known material collectively or integrally; when we speak of its objects, of our finite selves, etc., we *take* that same identical material distributively and separately. But what is the use of a thing's *being* only once if it can be *taken* twice over, and if being taken in different ways makes different things true of it? As the absolute takes me, for example, I appear *with* everything else in its field of perfect knowledge. As I take myself, I appear *without* most other things in my field of relative ignorance. And practical differences result from its knowledge and my ignorance. Ignorance breeds mistake, curiosity, misfortune, pain, for me; I suffer those consequences. The absolute knows of those things, of course, for it knows me and my suffering, but it does n't itself suffer. It can't be ignorant, for simultaneous with its knowledge of each question goes its knowledge of each answer. It can't be patient, for it has to wait for nothing, having everything at once in its possession. It can't be surprised; it can't be guilty. No attribute connected with succession can be applied to it, for it is all at once and wholly what it is, 'with the unity of a single instant,' and succession is not of it but in it, for we are continually told that it is 'timeless.'

Things true of the world in its finite aspects, then, are not true of it in its infinite capacity. *Quâ* finite and plural its accounts of itself to itself are different from what its account to itself *quâ* infinite and one must be.

With this radical discrepancy between the absolute and the relative points of view, it seems to me that almost as great a bar to intimacy between the divine and the human breaks out in pantheism as that which we found in monarchical theism, and hoped that pantheism might not show. We humans are incurably rooted in the temporal point of view. The eternal's ways are utterly unlike our ways. 'Let us imitate the All,' said the original prospectus of that admirable Chicago quarterly called the 'Monist.' As if we could, either in thought or conduct! We are invincibly parts, let us talk as we will, and must always apprehend the absolute as if it were a foreign being. If what I mean by this is not wholly clear to you at this point, it ought to grow clearer as my lectures proceed.

LECTURE II

MONISTIC IDEALISM

LET ME RECALL to you the programme which I indicated to you at our last meeting. After agreeing not to consider materialism in any shape, but to place ourselves straightway upon a more spiritualistic platform, I pointed out three kinds of spiritual philosophy between which we are asked to choose. The first way was that of the older dualistic theism, with ourselves represented as a secondary order of substances created by God. We found that this allowed of a degree of intimacy with the creative principle inferior to that implied in the pantheistic belief that we are substantially one with it, and that the divine is therefore the most intimate of all our possessions, heart of our heart, in fact. But we saw that this pantheistic belief could be held in two forms, a monistic form which I called philosophy of the absolute, and a pluralistic form which I called radical empiricism, the former conceiving that the divine exists authentically only when the world is experienced all at once in its absolute totality, whereas radical empiricism allows that the absolute sum-total of things may never be actually experienced or realized in that shape at all, and that a disseminated, distributed, or incompletely unified appearance is the only form that reality may yet have achieved.

I may contrast the monistic and pluralistic forms in question as the 'all-form' and the 'each-form.' At the end of the last hour I animadverted on the fact that the all-form is so radically different from the each-form, which is our human form of experiencing the world, that the philosophy of the absolute, so far as insight and understanding go, leaves us almost as much outside of the divine being as dualistic theism does. I believe that radical empiricism, on the contrary, holding to the each-form, and making of God only one of the eaches, affords the higher degree of intimacy. The general thesis of these lectures I said would be a defence of the pluralistic against the monistic view. Think of the universe as existing solely in the each-form, and you will have on the whole a more reasonable and satisfactory idea of it than if you insist on the all-form being necessary. The rest of my lectures will do little more than make this thesis more concrete, and I hope more persuasive.

It is curious how little countenance radical pluralism has ever had from philosophers. Whether materialistically or spiritualistically minded, philosophers have always aimed at cleaning up the litter with which the world apparently is filled. They have substituted economical and orderly conceptions for the first sensible tangle; and whether these were morally elevated or only intellectually neat, they were at any rate always æsthetically pure and definite, and aimed at ascribing to the world something clean and intellectual in the way of inner structure. As compared with all these rationalizing pictures, the pluralistic empiricism which I profess offers but a sorry appearance. It is a turbid, muddled, gothic sort of an affair, without a sweeping outline and with little pictorial nobility. Those of you who are accustomed to the classical constructions of reality may be excused if your first reaction upon it be absolute contempt—a shrug of the shoulders as if such ideas were unworthy of explicit refutation. But one must have lived some time with a system to appreciate its merits. Perhaps a little more familiarity may mitigate your first surprise at such a programme as I offer.

First, one word more than what I said last time about the relative foreignness of the divine principle in the philosophy of the absolute. Those of you who have read the last two chapters of Mr. Bradley's wonderful book, 'Appearance and reality,' will remember what an elaborately foreign aspect *his* absolute is finally made to assume. It is neither intelligence nor will, neither a self nor a collection of selves, neither truthful, good, nor beautiful, as we understand these terms. It is, in short, a metaphysical monster, all that we are permitted to say of it being that whatever it is, it is at any rate *worth* more (worth more to itself, that is) than if any eulogistic adjectives of ours applied to it. It is us, and all other appearances, but none of us *as such*, for in it we are all 'transmuted,' and its own as-suchness is of another denomination altogether.

Spinoza was the first great absolutist, and the impossibility of being intimate with *his* God is universally recognized.

Quatenus infinitus est he is other than what he is *quatenus humanam mentem constituit.* Spinoza's philosophy has been rightly said to be worked by the word *quatenus.* Conjunctions, prepositions, and adverbs play indeed the vital part in all philosophies; and in contemporary idealism the words 'as' and 'quâ' bear the burden of reconciling metaphysical unity with phenomenal diversity. Quâ absolute the world is one and perfect, quâ relative it is many and faulty, yet it is identically the self-same world—instead of talking of it as many facts, we call it one fact in many aspects.

As absolute, then, or *sub specie eternitatis,* or *quatenus infinitus est,* the world repels our sympathy because it has no history. *As such,* the absolute neither acts nor suffers, nor loves nor hates; it has no needs, desires, or aspirations, no failures or successes, friends or enemies, victories or defeats. All such things pertain to the world quâ relative, in which our finite experiences lie, and whose vicissitudes alone have power to arouse our interest. What boots it to tell me that the absolute way is the true way, and to exhort me, as Emerson says, to lift mine eye up to its style, and manners of the sky, if the feat is impossible by definition? I am finite once for all, and all the categories of my sympathy are knit up with the finite world *as such,* and with things that have a history. 'Aus dieser erde quellen meine freuden, und ihre sonne scheinet meinen leiden.' I have neither eyes nor ears nor heart nor mind for anything of an opposite description, and the stagnant felicity of the absolute's own perfection moves me as little as I move it. If we were *readers* only of the cosmic novel, things would be different: we should then share the author's point of view and recognize villains to be as essential as heroes in the plot. But we are not the readers but the very personages of the world-drama. In your own eyes each of you here is its hero, and the villains are your respective friends or enemies. The tale which the absolute reader finds so perfect, we spoil for one another through our several vital identifications with the destinies of the particular personages involved.

The doctrine on which the absolutists lay most stress is the absolute's 'timeless' character. For pluralists, on the other hand, time remains as real as anything, and nothing in the universe is great or static or eternal enough not to have some history. But the world that each of us feels most intimately at home with is that of beings with histories that play into our history, whom we can help in their vicissitudes even as they help us in ours. This satisfaction the absolute denies us; we can neither help nor hinder it, for it stands outside of history. It surely is a merit in a philosophy to make the very life we lead seem real and earnest. Pluralism, in exorcising the absolute, exorcises the great de-realizer of the only life we are at home in, and thus redeems the nature of reality from essential foreignness. Every end, reason, motive, object of desire or aversion, ground of sorrow or joy that we feel is in the world of finite multifariousness, for only in that world does anything really happen, only there do events come to pass.

In one sense this is a far-fetched and rather childish objection, for so much of the history of the finite is as formidably foreign to us as the static absolute can possibly be—in fact that entity derives its own foreignness largely from the bad character of the finite which it simultaneously is—that this sentimental reason for preferring the pluralistic view seems small.[1] I shall return to the subject in my final lecture, and meanwhile, with your permission, I will say no more about this objection. The more so as the necessary foreignness of the absolute is cancelled emotionally by its attribute of *totality*, which is universally considered to carry the further attribute of *perfection* in its train. 'Philosophy,' says a recent american philosopher, 'is humanity's hold on totality,' and there is no doubt that most of us find that the bare notion of an absolute all-one is inspiring. 'I yielded myself to the perfect whole,' writes Emerson; and where can you find a more mind-dilating object? A certain loyalty is called forth by the idea; even if not proved actual, it must be believed in somehow. Only an enemy of philosophy can speak lightly of it. Rationalism starts from the idea of such a whole and builds downward. Movement and change are absorbed into its immutability as forms of mere appearance. When you accept this beatific vision of what *is*, in contrast with what *goes on*, you

[1] The difference is that the bad parts of this finite are eternal and essential for absolutists, whereas pluralists may hope that they will eventually get sloughed off and become as if they had not been.

feel as if you had fulfilled an intellectual duty. 'Reality is not in its truest nature a process,' Mr. McTaggart tells us, 'but a stable and timeless state.'[1] 'The true knowledge of God begins,' Hegel writes, 'when we know that things as they immediately are have no truth.'[2] 'The consummation of the infinite aim,' he says elsewhere, 'consists merely in removing the illusion which makes it seem yet unaccomplished. Good and absolute goodness is eternally accomplishing itself in the world: and the result is that it needs not wait upon *us*, but is already . . . accomplished. It is an illusion under which we live. . . . In the course of its process the Idea makes itself that illusion, by setting an antithesis to confront it, and its action consists in getting rid of the illusion which it has created.'[3]

But abstract emotional appeals of any kind sound amateurish in the business that concerns us. Impressionistic philosophizing, like impressionistic watchmaking or land-surveying, is intolerable to experts. Serious discussion of the alternative before us forces me, therefore, to become more technical. The great *claim* of the philosophy of the absolute is that the absolute is no hypothesis, but a presupposition implicated in all thinking, and needing only a little effort of analysis to be seen as a logical necessity. I will therefore take it in this more rigorous character and see whether its claim is in effect so coercive.

It has seemed coercive to an enormous number of contemporaneous thinkers. Professor Henry Jones thus describes the range and influence of it upon the social and political life of the present time:[4] 'For many years adherents of this way of thought have deeply interested the british public by their writings. Almost more important than their writings is the fact that they have occupied philosophical chairs in almost every university in the kingdom. Even the professional critics of idealism are for the most part idealists—after a fashion. And when they are not, they are as a rule more occupied with the refutation of idealism than with the construction of a

---

[1] Quoted by W. Wallace: *Lectures and Essays*, Oxford, 1898, p. 560.
[2] *Logic*, tr. Wallace, 1874, p. 181.
[3] *Ibid.*, p. 304.
[4] *Contemporary Review*, December, 1907, vol. 92, p. 618.

better theory. It follows from their position of academic authority, were it from nothing else, that idealism exercises an influence not easily measured upon the youth of the nation—upon those, that is, who from the educational opportunities they enjoy may naturally be expected to become the leaders of the nation's thought and practice. . . . Difficult as it is to measure the forces . . . it is hardly to be denied that the power exercised by Bentham and the utilitarian school has, for better or for worse, passed into the hands of the idealists. . . . "The Rhine has flowed into the Thames" is the warning note rung out by Mr. Hobhouse. Carlyle introduced it, bringing it as far as Chelsea. Then Jowett and Thomas Hill Green, and William Wallace and Lewis Nettleship, and Arnold Toynbee and David Ritchie—to mention only those teachers whose voices now are silent—guided the waters into those upper reaches known locally as the Isis. John and Edward Caird brought them up the Clyde, Hutchison Stirling up the Firth of Forth. They have passed up the Mersey and up the Severn and Dee and Don. They pollute the bay of St. Andrews and swell the waters of the Cam, and have somehow crept overland into Birmingham. The stream of german idealism has been diffused over the academical world of Great Britain. The disaster is universal.'

Evidently if weight of authority were all, the truth of absolutism would be thus decided. But let us first pass in review the general style of argumentation of that philosophy.

As I read it, its favorite way of meeting pluralism and empiricism is by a *reductio ad absurdum* framed somewhat as follows: You contend, it says to the pluralist, that things, though in some respects connected, are in other respects independent, so that they are not members of one all-inclusive individual fact. Well, your position is absurd on either point. For admit in fact the slightest modicum of independence, and you find (if you will only think accurately) that you have to admit more and more of it, until at last nothing but an absolute chaos, or the proved impossibility of any connexion whatever between the parts of the universe, remains upon your hands. Admit, on the other hand, the most incipient minimum of relation between any two things, and again you can't stop until you see that the absolute unity of all things is implied.

If we take the latter *reductio ad absurdum* first, we find a good example of it in Lotze's well-known proof of monism from the fact of interaction between finite things. Suppose, Lotze says in effect, and for simplicity's sake I have to paraphrase him, for his own words are too long to quote—many distinct beings *a, b, c,* etc., to exist independently of each other: *can a in that case ever act on b?*

What is it to act? Is it not to exert an influence? Does the influence detach itself from *a* and find *b*? If so, it is a third fact, and the problem is not how *a* acts, but how its 'influence' acts on *b*. By another influence perhaps? And how in the end does the chain of influences find *b* rather than *c* unless *b* is somehow prefigured in them already? And when they have found *b*, how do they make *b* respond, if *b* has nothing in common with them? Why don't they go right through *b*? The change in *b* is a *response*, due to *b*'s capacity for taking account of *a*'s influence, and that again seems to prove that *b*'s nature is somehow fitted to *a*'s nature in advance. *A* and *b*, in short, are not really as distinct as we at first supposed them, not separated by a void. Were this so they would be mutually impenetrable, or at least mutually irrelevant. They would form two universes each living by itself, making no difference to each other, taking no account of each other, much as the universe of your day dreams takes no account of mine. They must therefore belong together beforehand, be co-implicated already, their natures must have an inborn mutual reference each to each.

Lotze's own solution runs as follows: The multiple independent things supposed cannot be real in that shape, but all of them, if reciprocal action is to be possible between them, must be regarded as parts of a single real being, M. The pluralism with which our view began has to give place to a monism; and the 'transeunt' interaction, being unintelligible as such, is to be understood as an immanent operation.[1]

The words 'immanent operation' seem here to mean that

---

[1] *Metaphysic*, sec. 69 ff.

the single real being M, of which *a* and *b* are members, is the only thing that changes, and that when it changes, it changes inwardly and all over at once. When part *a* in it changes, consequently, part *b* must also change, but without the whole M changing this would not occur.

A pretty argument, but a purely verbal one, as I apprehend it. *Call* your *a* and *b* distinct, they can't interact; *call* them one, they can. For taken abstractly and without qualification the words 'distinct' and 'independent' suggest only disconnection. If this be the only property of your *a* and *b* (and it is the only property your words imply), then of course, since you can't deduce their mutual influence from *it*, you can find no ground of its occurring between them. Your bare word 'separate,' contradicting your bare word 'joined,' seems to exclude connexion.

Lotze's remedy for the impossibility thus verbally found is to change the first word. If, instead of calling *a* and *b* independent, we now call them 'interdependent,' 'united,' or 'one,' he says, *these* words do not contradict any sort of mutual influence that may be proposed. If *a* and *b* are 'one,' and the one changes, *a* and *b* of course must co-ordinately change. What under the old name they could n't do, they now have license to do under the new name.

But I ask you whether giving the name of 'one' to the former 'many' makes us really understand the modus operandi of interaction any better. We have now given verbal permission to the many to change all together, if they can; we have removed a verbal impossibility and substituted a verbal possibility, but the new name, with the possibility it suggests, tells us nothing of the actual process by which real things that are one can and do change at all. In point of fact abstract oneness as such *does n't* change, neither has it parts—any more than abstract independence as such interacts. But then neither abstract oneness nor abstract independence *exists*; only concrete real things exist, which add to these properties the other properties which they possess, to make up what we call their total nature. To construe any one of their abstract names as *making their total nature impossible* is a misuse of the function of naming. The real way of rescue from the abstract consequences of one name is not to fly to an opposite name, equally abstract, but rather to correct the first name by qualifying adjectives that restore some concreteness to the case. Don't take your 'independence' *simpliciter*, as Lotze does, take it *secundum quid*. Only when we know what the process of interaction literally and concretely *consists* in can we tell whether beings independent *in definite respects*, distinct, for example, in origin, separate in place, different in kind, etc., can or cannot interact.

The treating of a name as excluding from the fact named what the name's definition fails positively to include, is what I call 'vicious intellectualism.' Later I shall have more to say about this intellectualism, but that Lotze's argument is tainted by it I hardly think we can deny. As well might you contend (to use an instance from Sigwart) that a person whom you have once called an 'equestrian' is thereby forever made unable to walk on his own feet.

I almost feel as if I should apologize for criticising such subtle arguments in rapid lectures of this kind. The criticisms have to be as abstract as the arguments, and in exposing their unreality, take on such an unreal sound themselves that a hearer not nursed in the intellectualist atmosphere knows not which of them to accuse. But *le vin est versé, il faut le boire*, and I must cite a couple more instances before I stop.

If we are empiricists and go from parts to wholes, we believe that beings may first exist and feed so to speak on their own existence, and then secondarily become known to one another. But philosophers of the absolute tell us that such independence of being from being known would, if once admitted, disintegrate the universe beyond all hope of mending. The argument is one of Professor Royce's proofs that the only alternative we have is to choose the complete disunion of all things or their complete union in the absolute One.

Take, for instance, the proverb 'a cat may look at a king' and adopt the realistic view that the king's being is independent of the cat's witnessing. This assumption, which amounts to saying that it need make no essential difference to the royal object whether the feline subject cognizes him or not, that the cat may look away from him or may even be annihilated, and the king remain unchanged,—this assumption, I say, is considered by my ingenious colleague to lead to the absurd practical consequence that the two beings *can* never later acquire any possible linkages or connexions, but must remain eternally as if in different worlds. For suppose any connexion whatever to ensue, this connexion would simply be a third being additional to the cat and the king, which would itself have to be linked to both by additional links before it could connect them, and so on *ad infinitum*, the argument, you see, being the same as Lotze's about how *a*'s influence does its influencing when it influences *b*.

In Royce's own words, if the king can be without the cat knowing him, then king and cat 'can have no common features, no ties, no true relations; they are separated, each from the other, by absolutely impassable chasms. They can never come to get either ties or community of nature; they are not in the same space, nor in the same time, nor in the same natural or spiritual order.'[1] They form in short two unrelated universes,—which is the *reductio ad absurdum* required.

To escape this preposterous state of things we must accordingly revoke the original hypothesis. The king and the cat are not indifferent to each other in the way supposed. But if not in that way, then in no way, for connexion in that way carries connexion in other ways; so that, pursuing the reverse line of reasoning, we end with the absolute itself as the smallest fact that can exist. Cat and king are co-involved, they are a single fact in two names, they can never have been absent from each other, and they are both equally co-implicated with all the other facts of which the universe consists.

Professor Royce's proof that whoso admits the cat's witnessing the king at all must thereupon admit the integral absolute, may be briefly put as follows:—

First, to know the king, the cat must intend *that* king, must somehow pass over and lay hold of him individually and specifically. The cat's idea, in short, must transcend the cat's own separate mind and somehow include the king, for were the king utterly outside and independent of the cat, the cat's pure other, the beast's mind could touch the king in no wise. This makes the cat much less distinct from the king than we

---

[1] *The World and the Individual*, vol. i, pp. 131–132.

had at first naïvely supposed. There must be some prior continuity between them, which continuity Royce interprets idealistically as meaning a higher mind that owns them both as objects, and owning them can also own any relation, such as the supposed witnessing, that may obtain between them. Taken purely pluralistically, neither of them can own any part of a *between*, because, so taken, each is supposed shut up to itself: the fact of a *between* thus commits us to a higher knower.

But the higher knower that knows the two beings we start with proves to be the same knower that knows everything else. For assume any third being, the queen, say, and as the cat knew the king, so let the king know his queen, and let this second knowledge, by the same reasoning, require a higher knower as its presupposition. That knower of the king's knowing must, it is now contended, be the same higher knower that was required for the cat's knowing; for if you suppose otherwise, you have no longer the *same king*. This may not seem immediately obvious, but if you follow the intellectualistic logic employed in all these reasonings, I don't see how you can escape the admission. If it be true that the independent or indifferent cannot be related, for the abstract words 'independent' or 'indifferent' as such imply no relation, then it is just as true that the king known by the cat cannot be the king that knows the queen, for taken merely 'as such,' the abstract term 'what the cat knows' and the abstract term 'what knows the queen' are logically distinct. The king thus logically breaks into two kings, with nothing to connect them, until a higher knower is introduced to recognize them as the self-same king concerned in any previous acts of knowledge which he may have brought about. This he can do because he possesses all the terms as his own objects and can treat them as he will. Add any fourth or fifth term, and you get a like result, and so on, until at last an all-owning knower, otherwise called the absolute, is reached. The co-implicated 'through-and-through' world of monism thus stands proved by irrefutable logic, and all pluralism appears as absurd.

The reasoning is pleasing from its ingenuity, and it is almost a pity that so straight a bridge from abstract logic to concrete fact should not bear our weight. To have the alternative forced upon us of admitting either finite things each cut off from all relation with its environment, or else of accepting the integral absolute with no environment and all relations packed within itself, would be too delicious a simplification. But the purely verbal character of the operation is undisguised. Because the *names* of finite things and their relations are disjoined, it does n't follow that the realities named need a *deus ex machina* from on high to conjoin them. The same things disjoined in one respect *appear* as conjoined in another. Naming the disjunction does n't debar us from also naming the conjunction in a later modifying statement, for the two are absolutely co-ordinate elements in the finite tissue of experience. When at Athens it was found self-contradictory that a boy could be both tall and short (tall namely in respect of a child, short in respect of a man), the absolute had not yet been thought of, but it might just as well have been invoked by Socrates as by Lotze or Royce, as a relief from his peculiar intellectualistic difficulty.

Everywhere we find rationalists using the same kind of reasoning. The primal whole which is their vision must be there not only as a fact but as a logical necessity. It must be the minimum that can exist—either that absolute whole is there, or there is absolutely nothing. The logical proof alleged of the irrationality of supposing otherwise, is that you can deny the whole only in words that implicitly assert it. If you say 'parts,' of *what* are they parts? If you call them a 'many,' that very word unifies them. If you suppose them unrelated in any particular respect, that 'respect' connects them; and so on. In short you fall into hopeless contradiction. You must stay either at one extreme or the other.[1] 'Partly this and partly that,' partly rational, for instance, and partly irrational, is no admissible description of the world. If rationality be in it at all, it must be in it throughout; if irrationality be in it anywhere, that also must pervade it throughout. It must be wholly

---

[1] A good illustration of this is to be found in a controversy between Mr. Bradley and the present writer, in *Mind* for 1893, Mr. Bradley contending (if I understood him rightly) that 'resemblance' is an illegitimate category, because it admits of degrees, and that the only real relations in comparison are absolute identity and absolute non-comparability.

rational or wholly irrational, pure universe or pure multiverse or nulliverse; and reduced to this violent alternative, no one's choice ought long to remain doubtful. The individual absolute, with its parts co-implicated through and through, so that there is nothing in any part by which any other part can remain inwardly unaffected, is the only rational supposition. Connexions of an external sort, by which the many became merely continuous instead of being consubstantial, would be an irrational supposition.

Mr. Bradley is the pattern champion of this philosophy *in extremis*, as one might call it, for he shows an intolerance to pluralism so extreme that I fancy few of his readers have been able fully to share it. His reasoning exemplifies everywhere what I call the vice of intellectualism, for abstract terms are used by him as positively excluding all that their definition fails to include. Some Greek sophists could deny that we may say that man is good, for man, they said, means only man, and good means only good, and the word *is* can't be construed to identify such disparate meanings. Mr. Bradley revels in the same type of argument. No adjective can rationally qualify a substantive, he thinks, for if distinct from the substantive, it can't be united with it; and if not distinct, there is only one thing there, and nothing left to unite. Our whole pluralistic procedure in using subjects and predicates as we do is fundamentally irrational, an example of the desperation of our finite intellectual estate, infected and undermined as that is by the separatist discursive forms which are our only categories, but which absolute reality must somehow absorb into its unity and overcome.

Readers of 'Appearance and reality' will remember how Mr. Bradley suffers from a difficulty identical with that to which Lotze and Royce fall a prey—how shall an influence influence? how shall a relation relate? Any conjunctive relation between two phenomenal experiences a and b must, in the intellectualist philosophy of these authors, be itself a third entity; and as such, instead of bridging the one original chasm, it can only create two smaller chasms, each to be freshly bridged. Instead of hooking a to b, it needs itself to be hooked by a fresh relation r' to a and by another r'' to b. These new relations are but two more entities which themselves require to be hitched in turn by four still newer relations—so behold the vertiginous *regressus ad infinitum* in full career.

Since a *regressus ad infinitum* is deemed absurd, the notion that relations come 'between' their terms must be given up. No mere external go-between can logically connect. What occurs must be more intimate. The hooking must be a penetration, a possession. The relation must *involve* the terms, each term must involve *it*, and merging thus their being in it, they must somehow merge their being in each other, tho, as they seem still phenomenally so separate, we can never conceive exactly how it is that they are inwardly one. The absolute, however, must be supposed able to perform the unifying feat in his own inscrutable fashion.

In old times, whenever a philosopher was assailed for some particularly tough absurdity in his system, he was wont to parry the attack by the argument from the divine omnipotence. 'Do you mean to limit God's power?' he would reply: 'do you mean to say that God could not, if he would, do this or that?' This retort was supposed to close the mouths of all objectors of properly decorous mind. The functions of the bradleian absolute are in this particular identical with those of the theistic God. Suppositions treated as too absurd to pass muster in the finite world which we inhabit, the absolute must be able to make good 'somehow' in his ineffable way. First we hear Mr. Bradley convicting things of absurdity; next, calling on the absolute to vouch for them *quand même*. Invoked for no other duty, that duty it must and shall perform.

The strangest discontinuity of our world of appearance with the supposed world of absolute reality is asserted both by Bradley and by Royce; and both writers, the latter with great ingenuity, seek to soften the violence of the jolt. But it remains violent all the same, and is felt to be so by most readers. Whoever feels the violence strongly sees as on a diagram in just what the peculiarity of all this philosophy of the absolute consists. First, there is a healthy faith that the world must be rational and self-consistent. 'All science, all real knowledge, all experience presuppose,' as Mr. Ritchie writes, 'a coherent universe.' Next, we find a loyal clinging to the rationalist belief that sense-data and their associations are incoherent, and that only in substituting a conceptual order for their order can truth be found. Third, the substituted conceptions are treated intellectualistically, that is as mutually exclusive and discontinuous, so that the first innocent continuity of the flow of sense-experience is shattered for us without any higher conceptual continuity taking its place. Finally, since this broken state of things is intolerable, the absolute *deus ex machina* is called on to mend it in his own way, since we cannot mend it in ours.

Any other picture than this of post-kantian absolutism I am unable to frame. I see the intellectualistic criticism destroying the immediately given coherence of the phenomenal world, but unable to make its own conceptual substitutes cohere, and I see the resort to the absolute for a coherence of a higher type. The situation has dramatic liveliness, but it is inwardly incoherent throughout, and the question inevitably comes up whether a mistake may not somewhere have crept in in the process that has brought it about. May not the remedy lie rather in revising the intellectualist criticism than in first adopting it and then trying to undo its consequences by an arbitrary act of faith in an unintelligible agent. May not the flux of sensible experience itself contain a rationality that has been overlooked, so that the real remedy would consist in harking back to it more intelligently, and not in advancing in the opposite direction away from it and even away beyond the intellectualist criticism that disintegrates it, to the pseudo-rationality of the supposed absolute point of view. I myself believe that this is the real way to keep rationality in the world, and that the traditional rationalism has always been facing in the wrong direction. I hope in the end to make you share, or at any rate respect, this belief, but there is much to talk of before we get to that point.

I employed the word 'violent' just now in describing the dramatic situation in which it pleases the philosophy of the absolute to make its camp. I don't see how any one can help being struck in absolutist writings by that curious tendency to fly to violent extremes of which I have already said a word. The universe must be rational; well and good; but *how* rational? in what sense of that eulogistic but ambiguous word?—this would seem to be the next point to bring up. There are surely degrees in rationality that might be discriminated and described. Things can be consistent or coherent in very diverse ways. But no more in its conception of rationality than in its conception of relations can the monistic mind suffer the notion of more or less. Rationality is one and indivisible: if not rational thus indivisibly, the universe must be completely irrational, and no shadings or mixtures or compromises can obtain. Mr. McTaggart writes, in discussing the notion of a mixture: 'The two principles, of rationality and irrationality, to which the universe is then referred, will have to be absolutely separate and independent. For if there were any common unity to which they should be referred, it would be that unity and not its two manifestations which would be the ultimate explanation . . . and the theory, having thus become monistic,[1] would resolve itself into the same alternative once more: is the single principle rational through and through or not?

'Can a plurality of reals be possible?' asks Mr. Bradley, and answers, 'No, impossible.' For it would mean a number of beings not dependent on each other, and this independence their plurality would contradict. For to be 'many' is to be related, the word having no meaning unless the units are somehow taken together, and it is impossible to take them in a sort of unreal void, so they must belong to a larger reality, and so carry the essence of the units beyond their proper selves, into a whole which possesses unity and is a larger system.[2] Either absolute independence or absolute mutual dependence—this, then, is the only alternative allowed by these thinkers. Of course 'independence,' if absolute, would be preposterous, so the only conclusion allowable is that, in Ritchie's words, 'every single event is ultimately related to every other, and determined by the whole to which it belongs.' The whole complete block-universe through-and-through, therefore, or no universe at all!

Professor Taylor is so *naïf* in this habit of thinking only in extremes that he charges the pluralists with cutting the ground from under their own feet in not consistently follow-

---

[1] *Studies in the Hegelian Dialectic*, p. 184.
[2] *Appearance and Reality*, 1893, pp. 141–142.

ing it themselves. What pluralists say is that a universe really connected loosely, after the pattern of our daily experience, is possible, and that for certain reasons it is the hypothesis to be preferred. What Professor Taylor thinks they naturally must or should say is that any other sort of universe is logically impossible, and that a totality of things interrelated like the world of the monists is not an hypothesis that can be seriously thought out at all.[1] Meanwhile no sensible pluralist ever flies or wants to fly to this dogmatic extreme.

If chance is spoken of as an ingredient of the universe, absolutists interpret it to mean that double sevens are as likely to be thrown out of a dice box as double sixes are. If freewill is spoken of, that must mean that an english general is as likely to eat his prisoners to-day as a Maori chief was a hundred years ago. It is as likely—I am using Mr. McTaggart's examples—that a majority of Londoners will burn themselves alive to-morrow as that they will partake of food, as likely that I shall be hanged for brushing my hair as for committing a murder,[2] and so forth, through various suppositions that no indeterminist ever sees real reason to make.

This habit of thinking only in the most violent extremes reminds me of what Mr. Wells says of the current objections to socialism, in his wonderful little book, 'New worlds for old.' The commonest vice of the human mind is its disposition to see everything as yes or no, as black or white, its incapacity for discrimination of intermediate shades. So the critics agree to some hard and fast impossible definition of socialism, and extract absurdities from it as a conjurer gets rabbits from a hat. Socialism abolishes property, abolishes the family, and the rest. The method, Mr. Wells continues, is always the same: It is to assume that whatever the socialist postulates as desirable is wanted without limit of qualification,—for socialist read pluralist and the parallel holds good, —it is to imagine that whatever proposal is made by him is to be carried out by uncontrolled monomaniacs, and so to make a picture of the socialist dream which can be presented to the simple-minded person in doubt—'This is socialism'—

[1] Cf. *Elements of Metaphysics*, p. 88.
[2] *Some Dogmas of Religion*, p. 184.

or pluralism, as the case may be. 'Surely!—SURELY! you don't want *this*!'

How often have I been replied to, when expressing doubts of the logical necessity of the absolute, of flying to the opposite extreme: 'But surely, SURELY there must be *some* connexion among things!' As if I must necessarily be an uncontrolled monomanic insanely denying any connexion whatever. The whole question revolves in very truth about the word 'some.' Radical empiricism and pluralism stand out for the legitimacy of the notion of *some*: each part of the world is in some ways connected, in some other ways not connected with its other parts, and the ways can be discriminated, for many of them are obvious, and their differences are obvious to view. Absolutism, on its side, seems to hold that 'some' is a category ruinously infected with self-contradictoriness, and that the only categories inwardly consistent and therefore pertinent to reality are 'all' and 'none.'

The question runs into the still more general one with which Mr. Bradley and later writers of the monistic school have made us abundantly familiar—the question, namely, whether all the relations with other things, possible to a being, are pre-included in its intrinsic nature and enter into its essence, or whether, in respect to some of these relations, it can *be* without reference to them, and, if it ever does enter into them, do so adventitiously and as it were by an afterthought. This is the great question as to whether 'external' relations can exist. They seem to, undoubtedly. My manuscript, for example, is 'on' the desk. The relation of being 'on' does n't seem to implicate or involve in any way the inner meaning of the manuscript or the inner structure of the desk—these objects engage in it only by their outsides, it seems only a temporary accident in their respective histories. Moreover, the 'on' fails to appear to our senses as one of those unintelligible 'betweens' that have to be separately hooked on the terms they pretend to connect. All this innocent sense-appearance, however, we are told, cannot pass muster in the eyes of reason. It is a tissue of self-contradiction which only the complete absorption of the desk and the manuscript into the higher unity of a more absolute reality can overcome.

The reasoning by which this conclusion is supported is too subtle and complicated to be properly dealt with in a public lecture, and you will thank me for not inviting you to consider it at all.[1] I feel the more free to pass it by now as I think that the cursory account of the absolutistic attitude which I have already given is sufficient for our present purpose, and that my own verdict on the philosophy of the absolute as 'not proven'—please observe that I go no farther now—need not be backed by argument at every special point. Flanking operations are less costly and in some ways more effective than frontal attacks. Possibly you will yourselves think after hearing my remaining lectures that the alternative of an universe absolutely rational or absolutely irrational is forced and strained, and that a *via media* exists which some of you may agree with me is to be preferred. *Some* rationality certainly does characterize our universe; and, weighing one kind with another, we may deem that the incomplete kinds that appear are on the whole as acceptable as the through-and-through sort of rationality on which the monistic systematizers insist.

All the said systematizers who have written since Hegel have owed their inspiration largely to him. Even when they have found no use for his particular triadic dialectic, they have drawn confidence and courage from his authoritative and conquering tone. I have said nothing about Hegel in this lecture, so I must repair the omission in the next.

[1] For a more detailed criticism of Mr. Bradley's intellectualism, see Appendix A.

LECTURE III

HEGEL AND HIS METHOD

DIRECTLY OR INDIRECTLY, that strange and powerful genius Hegel has done more to strengthen idealistic pantheism in thoughtful circles than all other influences put together. I must talk a little about him before drawing my final conclusions about the cogency of the arguments for the absolute. In no philosophy is the fact that a philosopher's vision and the technique he uses in proof of it are two different things more palpably evident than in Hegel. The vision in his case was that of a world in which reason holds all things in solution and accounts for all the irrationality that superficially appears by taking it up as a 'moment' into itself. This vision was so intense in Hegel, and the tone of authority with which he spoke from out of the midst of it was so weighty, that the impression he made has never been effaced. Once dilated to the scale of the master's eye, the disciples' sight could not contract to any lesser prospect. The technique which Hegel used to prove his vision was the so-called dialectic method, but here his fortune has been quite contrary. Hardly a recent disciple has felt his particular applications of the method to be satisfactory. Many have let them drop entirely, treating them rather as a sort of provisional stop-gap, symbolic of what might some day prove possible of execution, but having no literal cogency or value now. Yet these very same disciples hold to the vision itself as a revelation that can never pass away. The case is curious and worthy of our study.

It is still more curious in that these same disciples, altho they are usually willing to abandon any particular instance of the dialectic method to its critics, are unshakably sure that in some shape the dialectic method is the key to truth. What, then, is the dialectic method? It is itself a part of the hegelian vision or intuition, and a part that finds the strongest echo in empiricism and common sense. Great injustice is done to Hegel by treating him as primarily a reasoner. He is in reality a naïvely observant man, only beset with a perverse preference for the use of technical and logical jargon. He plants himself in the empirical flux of things and gets the impression of what happens. His mind is in very truth *impressionistic*; and his thought, when once you put yourself at the animating centre of it, is the easiest thing in the world to catch the pulse of and to follow.

Any author is easy if you can catch the centre of his vision. From the centre in Hegel come those towering sentences of his that are comparable only to Luther's, as where, speaking of the ontological proof of God's existence from the concept of him as the *ens perfectissimum* to which no attribute can be lacking, he says: 'It would be strange if the Notion, the very heart of the mind, or, in a word, the concrete totality we call God, were not rich enough to embrace so poor a category as Being, the very poorest and most abstract of all—for nothing can be more insignificant than Being.' But if Hegel's central thought is easy to catch, his abominable habits of speech make his application of it to details exceedingly difficult to follow. His passion for the slipshod in the way of sentences, his unprincipled playing fast and loose with terms; his dreadful vocabulary, calling what completes a thing its 'negation,' for example; his systematic refusal to let you know whether he is talking logic or physics or psychology, his whole deliberately adopted policy of ambiguity and vagueness, in short: all these things make his present-day readers wish to tear their hair—or his—out in desperation. Like Byron's corsair, he has left a name 'to other times, linked with one virtue and a thousand crimes.'

The virtue was the vision, which was really in two parts. The first part was that reason is all-inclusive, the second was that things are 'dialectic.' Let me say a word about this second part of Hegel's vision.

The impression that any *naïf* person gets who plants himself innocently in the flux of things is that things are off their balance. Whatever equilibriums our finite experiences attain to are but provisional. Martinique volcanoes shatter our wordsworthian equilibrium with nature. Accidents, either moral, mental, or physical, break up the slowly built-up equilibriums men reach in family life and in their civic and professional relations. Intellectual enigmas frustrate our scientific systems, and the ultimate cruelty of the universe upsets our religious attitudes and outlooks. Of no special system of good attained does the universe recognize the value as sacred. Down it tumbles, over it goes, to feed the ravenous appetite for destruction, of the larger system of history in which it stood for a moment as a landing-place and stepping-stone. This dogging of everything by its negative, its fate, its undoing, this perpetual moving on to something future which shall supersede the present, this is the hegelian intuition of the essential provisionality, and consequent unreality, of everything empirical and finite. Take any concrete finite thing and try to hold it fast. You cannot, for so held, it proves not to be concrete at all, but an arbitrary extract or abstract which you have made from the remainder of empirical reality. The rest of things invades and overflows both it and you together, and defeats your rash attempt. Any partial view whatever of the world tears the part out of its relations, leaves out some truth concerning it, is untrue of it, falsifies it. The full truth about anything involves more than that thing. In the end nothing less than the whole of everything can be the truth of anything at all.

Taken so far, and taken in the rough, Hegel is not only harmless, but accurate. There is a dialectic movement in things, if such it please you to call it, one that the whole constitution of concrete life establishes; but it is one that can be described and accounted for in terms of the pluralistic vision of things far more naturally than in the monistic terms to which Hegel finally reduced it. Pluralistic empiricism knows that everything is in an environment, a surrounding world of other things, and that if you leave it to work there it will inevitably meet with friction and opposition from its neighbors. Its rivals and enemies will destroy it unless it can buy them off by compromising some part of its original pretensions.

But Hegel saw this undeniable characteristic of the world we live in in a non-empirical light. Let the *mental idea* of the thing work in your thought all alone, he fancied, and just the same consequences will follow. It will be negated by the opposite ideas that dog it, and can survive only by entering, along with them, into some kind of treaty. This treaty will be an instance of the so-called 'higher synthesis' of everything with its negative; and Hegel's originality lay in transporting the process from the sphere of percepts to that of concepts and treating it as the universal method by which every kind of life, logical, physical, or psychological, is mediated. Not to the sensible facts as such, then, did Hegel point for the secret of what keeps existence going, but rather to the conceptual way of treating them. Concepts were not in his eyes the static self-contained things that previous logicians had supposed, but were germinative, and passed beyond themselves into each other by what he called their immanent dialectic. In ignoring each other as they do, they virtually exclude and deny each other, he thought, and thus in a manner introduce each other. So the dialectic logic, according to him, had to supersede the 'logic of identity' in which, since Aristotle, all Europe had been brought up.

This view of concepts is Hegel's revolutionary performance; but so studiously vague and ambiguous are all his expressions of it that one can hardly tell whether it is the concepts as such, or the sensible experiences and elements conceived, that Hegel really means to work with. The only thing that is certain is that whatever you may say of his procedure, some one will accuse you of misunderstanding it. I make no claim to understanding it, I treat it merely impressionistically.

So treating it, I regret that he should have called it by the name of logic. Clinging as he did to the vision of a really living world, and refusing to be content with a chopped-up intellectualist picture of it, it is a pity that he should have adopted the very word that intellectualism had already preempted. But he clung fast to the old rationalist contempt for the immediately given world of sense and all its squalid particulars, and never tolerated the notion that the form of philosophy might be empirical only. His own system had to be a product of eternal reason, so the word 'logic,' with its suggestions of coercive necessity, was the only word he could find natural. He pretended therefore to be using the *a priori* method, and to be working by a scanty equipment of ancient logical terms—position, negation, reflection, universal, particular, individual, and the like. But what he really worked by was his own empirical perceptions, which exceeded and overflowed his miserably insufficient logical categories in every instance of their use.

What he did with the category of negation was his most original stroke. The orthodox opinion is that you can advance logically through the field of concepts only by going from the same to the same. Hegel felt deeply the sterility of this law of conceptual thought; he saw that in a fashion negation also relates things; and he had the brilliant idea of transcending the ordinary logic by treating advance from the different to the different as if it were also a necessity of thought. 'The so-called maxim of identity,' he wrote, 'is supposed to be accepted by the consciousness of every one. But the language which such a law demands, "a planet is a planet, magnetism is magnetism, mind is mind," deserves to be called silliness. No mind either speaks or thinks or forms conceptions in accordance with this law, and no existence of any kind whatever conforms to it. We must never view identity as abstract identity, to the exclusion of all difference. That is the touchstone for distinguishing all bad philosophy from what alone deserves the name of philosophy. If thinking were no more than registering abstract identities, it would be a most superfluous performance. Things and concepts are identical with themselves only in so far as at the same time they involve distinction.'[1]

The distinction that Hegel has in mind here is naturally in the first instance distinction from all other things or concepts. But in his hands this quickly develops into contradiction of them, and finally, reflected back upon itself, into self-contradiction; and the immanent self-contradictoriness of all finite concepts thenceforth becomes the propulsive logical force that moves the world.[2] 'Isolate a thing from all its relations,' says Dr. Edward Caird,[3] expounding Hegel, 'and try to assert it by itself; you find that it has negated itself as well as its relations. The thing in itself is nothing.' Or, to quote Hegel's own words: 'When we suppose an existent A, and another, B, B is at first defined as the other. But A is just as much

---

[1] Hegel, *Smaller Logic*, pp. 184–185.

[2] Cf. Hegel's fine vindication of this function of contradiction in his *Wissenschaft der Logik*, Bk. ii, sec. 1, chap. ii, C, Anmerkung 3.

[3] *Hegel*, in *Blackwood's Philosophical Classics*, p. 162.

the other of B. Both are others in the same fashion. . . .
"Other" is the other by itself, therefore the other of every
other, consequently the other of itself, the simply unlike itself,
the self-negator, the self-alterer,' etc.[1] Hegel writes elsewhere:
'The finite, as implicitly other than what it is, is forced to
surrender its own immediate or natural being, and to turn
suddenly into its opposite. . . . Dialectic is the universal and
irresistible power before which nothing can stay. . . . *Summum jus, summa injuria*—to drive an abstract right to excess
is to commit injustice. . . . Extreme anarchy and extreme
despotism lead to one another. Pride comes before a fall. Too
much wit outwits itself. Joy brings tears, melancholy a sardonic smile.'[2] To which one well might add that most human
institutions, by the purely technical and professional manner
in which they come to be administered, end by becoming obstacles to the very purposes which their founders had in view.

Once catch well the knack of this scheme of thought and
you are lucky if you ever get away from it. It is all you can
see. Let any one pronounce anything, and your feeling of a
contradiction being implied becomes a habit, almost a motor
habit in some persons who symbolize by a stereotyped gesture the position, sublation, and final reinstatement involved.
If you say 'two' or 'many,' your speech bewrayeth you, for
the very name collects them into one. If you express doubt,
your expression contradicts its content, for the doubt itself is
not doubted but affirmed. If you say 'disorder,' what is that
but a certain bad kind of order? if you say 'indetermination,'
you are determining just *that*. If you say 'nothing but the
unexpected happens,' the unexpected becomes what you expected. If you say 'all things are relative,' to what is the all of
them itself relative? If you say 'no more,' you have said more
already, by implying a region in which no more is found; to
know a limit as such is consequently already to have got beyond it; and so forth, throughout as many examples as one
cares to cite.

Whatever you posit appears thus as one-sided, and negates
its other, which, being equally one-sided, negates *it*; and,
since this situation remains unstable, the two contradictory

[1] *Wissenschaft der Logik*, Bk. i, sec. 1, chap. ii, B, a.
[2] Wallace's translation of the *Smaller Logic*, p. 128.

terms have together, according to Hegel, to engender a higher truth of which they both appear as indispensable members, mutually mediating aspects of that higher concept or situation in thought.

Every higher total, however provisional and relative, thus reconciles the contradictions which its parts, abstracted from it, prove implicitly to contain. Rationalism, you remember, is what I called the way of thinking that methodically subordinates parts to wholes, so Hegel here is rationalistic through and through. The only whole by which *all* contradictions are reconciled is for him the absolute whole of wholes, the all-inclusive reason to which Hegel himself gave the name of the absolute Idea, but which I shall continue to call 'the absolute' purely and simply, as I have done hitherto.

Empirical instances of the way in which higher unities reconcile contradictions are innumerable, so here again Hegel's vision, taken merely impressionistically, agrees with countless facts. Somehow life does, out of its total resources, find ways of satisfying opposites at once. This is precisely the paradoxical aspect which much of our civilization presents. Peace we secure by armaments, liberty by laws and constitutions; simplicity and naturalness are the consummate result of artificial breeding and training; health, strength, and wealth are increased only by lavish use, expense, and wear. Our mistrust of mistrust engenders our commercial system of credit; our tolerance of anarchistic and revolutionary utterances is the only way of lessening their danger; our charity has to say no to beggars in order not to defeat its own desires; the true epicurean has to observe great sobriety; the way to certainty lies through radical doubt; virtue signifies not innocence but the knowledge of sin and its overcoming; by obeying nature, we command her, etc. The ethical and the religious life are full of such contradictions held in solution. You hate your enemy?—well, forgive him, and thereby heap coals of fire on his head; to realize yourself, renounce yourself; to save your soul, first lose it; in short, die to live.

From such massive examples one easily generalizes Hegel's vision. Roughly, his 'dialectic' picture is a fair account of a good deal of the world. It sounds paradoxical, but whenever you once place yourself at the point of view of any higher synthesis, you see exactly how it does in a fashion take up opposites into itself. As an example, consider the conflict between our carnivorous appetites and hunting instincts and the sympathy with animals which our refinement is bringing in its train. We have found how to reconcile these opposites most effectively by establishing game-laws and close seasons and by keeping domestic herds. The creatures preserved thus are preserved for the sake of slaughter, truly, but if not preserved for that reason, not one of them would be alive at all. Their will to live and our will to kill them thus harmoniously combine in this peculiar higher synthesis of domestication.

Merely as a reporter of certain empirical aspects of the actual, Hegel, then, is great and true. But he aimed at being something far greater than an empirical reporter, so I must say something about that essential aspect of his thought. Hegel was dominated by the notion of a truth that should prove incontrovertible, binding on every one, and certain, which should be *the* truth, one, indivisible, eternal, objective, and necessary, to which all our particular thinking must lead as to its consummation. This is the dogmatic ideal, the postulate, uncriticised, undoubted, and unchallenged, of all rationalizers in philosophy. '*I have never doubted,*' a recent Oxford writer says, that truth is universal and single and timeless, a single content or significance, one and whole and complete.[1] Advance in thinking, in the hegelian universe, has, in short, to proceed by the apodictic words *must be* rather than by those inferior hypothetic words *may be*, which are all that empiricists can use.

Now Hegel found that his idea of an immanent movement through the field of concepts by way of 'dialectic' negation played most beautifully into the hands of this rationalistic demand for something absolute and *inconcussum* in the way of truth. It is easy to see how. If you affirm anything, for example that A is, and simply leave the matter thus, you leave it at the mercy of any one who may supervene and say 'not A, but B is.' If he does say so, your statement does n't refute

---

[1] Joachim, *The Nature of Truth*, Oxford, 1906, pp. 22, 178. The argument in case the belief should be doubted would be the higher synthetic idea: if two truths were possible, the duality of that possibility would itself be the one truth that would unite them.

him, it simply contradicts him, just as his contradicts you. The only way of making your affirmation about A *self-securing* is by getting it into a form which will by implication negate all possible negations in advance. The mere absence of negation is not enough; it must be present, but present with its fangs drawn. What you posit as A must already have cancelled the alternative or made it innocuous, by having negated it in advance. Double negation is the only form of affirmation that fully plays into the hands of the dogmatic ideal. Simply and innocently affirmative statements are good enough for empiricists, but unfit for rationalist use, lying open as they do to every accidental contradictor, and exposed to every puff of doubt. The *final* truth must be something to which there is no imaginable alternative, because it contains all its possible alternatives inside of itself as moments already taken account of and overcome. Whatever involves its own alternatives as elements of itself is, in a phrase often repeated, its 'own other,' made so by the *methode der absoluten negativität*.

Formally, this scheme of an organism of truth that has already fed as it were on its own liability to death, so that, death once dead for it, there 's no more dying then, is the very fulfilment of the rationalistic aspiration. That one and only whole, with all its parts involved in it, negating and making one another impossible if abstracted and taken singly, but necessitating and holding one another in place if the whole of them be taken integrally, is the literal ideal sought after; it is the very diagram and picture of that notion of *the* truth with no outlying alternative, to which nothing can be added, nor from it anything withdrawn, and all variations from which are absurd, which so dominates the human imagination. Once we have taken in the features of this diagram that so successfully solves the world-old problem, the older ways of proving the necessity of judgments cease to give us satisfaction. Hegel's way we think must be the right way. The true must be essentially the self-reflecting self-contained recurrent, that which secures itself by including its own other and negating it; that makes a spherical system with no loose ends hanging out for foreignness to get a hold upon; that is forever rounded in and closed, not strung along rectilinearly and open at its ends like that universe of simply collective or additive form which

Hegel calls the world of the bad infinite, and which is all that empiricism, starting with simply posited single parts and elements, is ever able to attain to.

No one can possibly deny the sublimity of this hegelian conception. It is surely in the grand style, if there be such a thing as a grand style in philosophy. For us, however, it remains, so far, a merely formal and diagrammatic conception; for with the actual content of absolute truth, as Hegel materially tries to set it forth, few disciples have been satisfied, and I do not propose to refer at all to the concreter parts of his philosophy. The main thing now is to grasp the generalized vision, and feel the authority of the abstract scheme of a statement self-secured by involving double negation. Absolutists who make no use of Hegel's own technique are really working by his method. You remember the proofs of the absolute which I instanced in my last lecture, Lotze's and Royce's proofs by *reductio ad absurdum*, to the effect that any smallest connexion rashly supposed in things will logically work out into absolute union, and any minimal disconnexion into absolute disunion,—these are really arguments framed on the hegelian pattern. The truth is that which you implicitly affirm in the very attempt to deny it; it is that from which every variation refutes itself by proving self-contradictory. This is the supreme insight of rationalism, and to-day the best *must-be's* of rationalist argumentation are but so many attempts to communicate it to the hearer.

Thus, you see, my last lecture and this lecture make connexion again and we can consider Hegel and the other absolutists to be supporting the same system. The next point I wish to dwell on is the part played by what I have called vicious intellectualism in this wonderful system's structure.

Rationalism in general thinks it gets the fulness of truth by turning away from sensation to conception, conception obviously giving the more universal and immutable picture. Intellectualism in the vicious sense I have already defined as the habit of assuming that a concept *ex*cludes from any reality conceived by its means everything not included in the concept's definition. I called such intellectualism illegitimate as I found it used in Lotze's, Royce's, and Bradley's proofs of the absolute (which absolute I consequently held to be non-proven by their arguments), and I left off by asserting my own belief that a pluralistic and incompletely integrated universe, describable only by the free use of the word 'some,' is a legitimate hypothesis.

Now Hegel himself, in building up his method of double negation, offers the vividest possible example of this vice of intellectualism. Every idea of a finite thing is of course a concept of *that* thing and not a concept of anything else. But Hegel treats this not being a concept of anything else as if it were *equivalent to the concept of anything else not being*, or in other words as if it were a denial or negation of everything else. Then, as the other things, thus implicitly contradicted by the thing first conceived, also by the same law contradict *it*, the pulse of dialectic commences to beat and the famous triads begin to grind out the cosmos. If any one finds the process here to be a luminous one, he must be left to the illumination, he must remain an undisturbed hegelian. What others feel as the intolerable ambiguity, verbosity, and unscrupulousness of the master's way of deducing things, he will probably ascribe—since divine oracles are notoriously hard to interpret—to the 'difficulty' that habitually accompanies profundity. For my own part, there seems something grotesque and *saugrenu* in the pretension of a style so disobedient to the first rules of sound communication between minds, to be the authentic mother-tongue of reason, and to keep step more accurately than any other style does with the absolute's own ways of thinking. I do not therefore take Hegel's technical apparatus seriously at all. I regard him rather as one of those numerous original seers who can never learn how to articulate. His would-be coercive logic counts for nothing in my eyes; but that does not in the least impugn the philosophic importance of his conception of the absolute, if we take it merely hypothetically as one of the great types of cosmic vision.

Taken thus hypothetically, I wish to discuss it briefly. But before doing so I must call your attention to an odd peculiarity in the hegelian procedure. The peculiarity is one which will come before us again for a final judgment in my seventh lecture, so at present I only note it in passing. Hegel, you remember, considers that the immediate finite data of experience are 'untrue' because they are not their own others. They are negated by what is external to them. The absolute is true because it and it only has no external environment, and has attained to being its own other. (These words sound queer enough, but those of you who know something of Hegel's text will follow them.) Granting his premise that to be true a thing must in some sort be its own other, everything hinges on whether he is right in holding that the several pieces of finite experience themselves cannot be said to be in any wise *their* own others. When conceptually or intellectualistically treated, they of course cannot be their own others. Every abstract concept as such excludes what it does n't include, and if such concepts are adequate substitutes for reality's concrete pulses, the latter must square themselves with intellectualistic logic, and no one of them in any sense can claim to be its own other. If, however, the conceptual treatment of the flow of reality should prove for any good reason to be inadequate and to have a practical rather than a theoretical or speculative value, then an independent empirical look into the constitution of reality's pulses might possibly show that some of them *are* their own others, and indeed are so in the self-same sense in which the absolute is maintained to be so by Hegel. When we come to my sixth lecture, on Professor Bergson, I shall in effect defend this very view, strengthening my thesis by his authority. I am unwilling to say anything more about the point at this time, and what I have just said of it is only a sort of surveyor's note of where our present position lies in the general framework of these lectures.

Let us turn now at last to the great question of fact, *Does the absolute exist or not?* to which all our previous discussion has been preliminary. I may sum up that discussion by saying that whether there really be an absolute or not, no one makes himself absurd or self-contradictory by doubting or denying it. The charges of self-contradiction, where they do not rest on purely verbal reasoning, rest on a vicious intellectualism. I will not recapitulate my criticisms. I will simply ask you to change the *venue*, and to discuss the absolute now as if it were only an open hypothesis. As such, is it more probable or more improbable?

But first of all I must parenthetically ask you to distinguish the notion of the absolute carefully from that of another object with which it is liable to become heedlessly entangled. That other object is the 'God' of common people in their religion, and the creator-God of orthodox christian theology. Only thoroughgoing monists or pantheists believe in the absolute. The God of our popular Christianity is but one member of a pluralistic system. He and we stand outside of each other, just as the devil, the saints, and the angels stand outside of both of us. I can hardly conceive of anything more different from the absolute than the God, say, of David or of Isaiah. *That* God is an essentially finite being *in* the cosmos, not with the cosmos in him, and indeed he has a very local habitation there, and very one-sided local and personal attachments. If it should prove probable that the absolute does not exist, it will not follow in the slightest degree that a God like that of David, Isaiah, or Jesus may not exist, or may not be the most important existence in the universe for us to acknowledge. I pray you, then, not to confound the two ideas as you listen to the criticisms I shall have to proffer. I hold to the finite God, for reasons which I shall touch on in the seventh of these lectures; but I hold that his rival and competitor—I feel almost tempted to say his enemy—the absolute, is not only not forced on us by logic, but that it is an improbable hypothesis.

The great claim made for the absolute is that by supposing it we make the world appear more rational. Any hypothesis that does that will always be accepted as more probably true than an hypothesis that makes the world appear irrational. Men are once for all so made that they prefer a rational world to believe in and to live in. But rationality has at least four dimensions, intellectual, æsthetical, moral, and practical; and to find a world rational to the maximal degree *in all these respects simultaneously* is no easy matter. Intellectually, the world of mechanical materialism is the most rational, for we subject its events to mathematical calculation. But the mechanical world is ugly, as arithmetic is ugly, and it is nonmoral. Morally, the theistic world is rational enough, but full of intellectual frustrations. The practical world of affairs, in its turn, so supremely rational to the politician, the military man, or the man of conquering business-faculty that he never would vote to change the type of it, is irrational to moral and artistic temperaments; so that whatever demand for rationality we find satisfied by a philosophic hypothesis, we are liable to find some other demand for rationality unsatisfied by the same hypothesis. The rationality we gain in one coin we thus pay for in another; and the problem accordingly seems at first sight to resolve itself into that of getting a conception which will yield the largest *balance* of rationality rather than one which will yield perfect rationality of every description. In general, it may be said that if a man's conception of the world lets loose any action in him that is easy, or any faculty which he is fond of exercising, he will deem it rational in so far forth, be the faculty that of computing, fighting, lecturing, classifying, framing schematic tabulations, getting the better end of a bargain, patiently waiting and enduring, preaching, joke-making, or what you like. Albeit the absolute is defined as being necessarily an embodiment of objectively perfect rationality, it is fair to its english advocates to say that those who have espoused the hypothesis most concretely and seriously have usually avowed the irrationality to their own minds of certain elements in it.

Probably the weightiest contribution to our feeling of the rationality of the universe which the notion of the absolute brings is the assurance that however disturbed the surface may be, at bottom all is well with the cosmos—central peace abiding at the heart of endless agitation. This conception is rational in many ways, beautiful æsthetically, beautiful intellectually (could we only follow it into detail), and beautiful morally, if the enjoyment of security can be accounted moral. Practically it is less beautiful; for, as we saw in our last lecture, in representing the deepest reality of the world as static and without a history, it loosens the world's hold upon our sympathies and leaves the soul of it foreign. Nevertheless it does give *peace*, and that kind of rationality is so paramountly demanded by men that to the end of time there will be absolutists, men who choose belief in a static eternal, rather than admit that the finite world of change and striving, even with a God as one of the strivers, is itself eternal. For such minds Professor Royce's words will always be the truest: 'The very presence of ill in the temporal order is the condition of the perfection of the eternal order. . . . We long for the absolute only in so far as in us the absolute also longs, and seeks through our very temporal striving, the peace that is nowhere in time, but only, and yet absolutely, in eternity. Were there no longing in time there would be no peace in eternity. . . . God [*i. e.* the absolute] who here in me aims at what I now temporally miss, not only possesses in the eternal world the goal after which I strive, but comes to possess it even through and because of my sorrow. Through this my tribulation the absolute triumph then is won. . . . In the absolute I am ful-filled. Yet my very fulfilment demands and therefore can tran-scend this sorrow.'[1] Royce is particularly felicitous in his ability to cite parts of finite experience to which he finds his picture of this absolute experience analogous. But it is hard to portray the absolute at all without rising into what might be called the 'inspired' style of language—I use the word not ironically, but prosaically and descriptively, to designate the only literary form that goes with the kind of emotion that the absolute arouses. One can follow the pathway of reasoning soberly enough,[2] but the picture itself has to be effulgent. This admirable faculty of transcending, whilst inwardly pre-serving, every contrariety, is the absolute's characteristic form of rationality. We are but syllables in the mouth of the Lord; if the whole sentence is divine, each syllable is absolutely what it should be, in spite of all appearances. In making up the balance for or against absolutism, this emotional value weights heavily the credit side of the account.

The trouble is that we are able to see so little into the pos-itive detail of it, and that if once admitted not to be coercively proven by the intellectualist arguments, it remains only a hy-pothetic possibility.

On the debit side of the account the absolute, taken seri-ously, and not as a mere name for our right occasionally to drop the strenuous mood and take a moral holiday, intro-duces all those tremendous irrationalities into the universe which a frankly pluralistic theism escapes, but which have

---

[1] *The World and the Individual*, vol. ii, pp. 385, 386, 409.

[2] The best *un*inspired argument (again not ironical!) which I know is that in Miss M. W. Calkins's excellent book, *The Persistent Problems of Philosophy*, Macmillan, 1902.

been flung as a reproach at every form of monistic theism or pantheism. It introduces a speculative 'problem of evil' namely, and leaves us wondering why the perfection of the absolute should require just such particular hideous forms of life as darken the day for our human imaginations. If they were forced on it by something alien, and to 'overcome' them the absolute had still to keep hold of them, we could understand its feeling of triumph, though we, so far as we were ourselves among the elements overcome, could acquiesce but sullenly in the resultant situation, and would never just have chosen it as the most rational one conceivable. But the absolute is represented as a being without environment, upon which nothing alien can be forced, and which has spontaneously chosen from within to give itself the spectacle of all that evil rather than a spectacle with less evil in it.[1] Its perfection is represented as the source of things, and yet the first effect of that perfection is the tremendous imperfection of all finite experience. In whatever sense the word 'rationality' may be taken, it is vain to contend that the impression made on our finite minds by such a way of representing things is altogether rational. Theologians have felt its irrationality acutely, and the 'fall,' the predestination, and the election which the situation involves have given them more trouble than anything else in their attempt to pantheize Christianity. The whole business remains a puzzle, both intellectually and morally.

Grant that the spectacle or world-romance offered to itself by the absolute is in the absolute's eyes perfect. Why would not the world be more perfect by having the affair remain in just those terms, and by not having any finite spectators to come in and add to what was perfect already their innumerable imperfect manners of seeing the same spectacle? Suppose the entire universe to consist of one superb copy of a book, fit for the ideal reader. Is that universe improved or deteriorated by having myriads of garbled and misprinted separate leaves and chapters also publisht, giving false impressions of the book to whoever looks at them? To say the least, the balance of rationality is not obviously in favor of such added

[1] Cf. Dr. Fuller's excellent article, 'Ethical monism and the problem of evil,' in the *Harvard Journal of Theology*, vol. i, No. 2, April, 1908.

mutilations. So this question becomes urgent: Why, the absolute's own total vision of things being so rational, was it necessary to comminute it into all these coexisting inferior fragmentary visions?

Leibnitz in his theodicy represents God as limited by an antecedent reason in things which makes certain combinations logically incompatible, certain goods impossible. He surveys in advance all the universes he might create, and by an act of what Leibnitz calls his antecedent will he chooses our actual world as the one in which the evil, unhappily necessary anyhow, is at its minimum. It is the best of all the worlds that are possible, therefore, but by no means the most abstractly desirable world. Having made this mental choice, God next proceeds to what Leibnitz calls his act of consequent or decretory will: he says 'Fiat' and the world selected springs into objective being, with all the finite creatures in it to suffer from its imperfections without sharing in its creator's atoning vision.

Lotze has made some penetrating remarks on this conception of Leibnitz's, and they exactly fall in with what I say of the absolutist conception. The world projected out of the creative mind by the *fiat*, and existing in detachment from its author, is a sphere of being where the parts realize themselves only singly. If the divine value of them is evident only when they are collectively looked at, then, Lotze rightly says, the world surely becomes poorer and not richer for God's utterance of the *fiat*. He might much better have remained contented with his merely antecedent choice of the scheme, without following it up by a creative decree. The scheme *as such* was admirable; it could only lose by being translated into reality.[1] Why, I similarly ask, should the absolute ever have lapsed from the perfection of its own integral experience of things, and refracted itself into all our finite experiences?

It is but fair to recent english absolutists to say that many of them have confessed the imperfect rationality of the absolute from this point of view. Mr. McTaggart, for example, writes: 'Does not our very failure to perceive the perfection of the universe destroy it? . . . In so far as we do not see the

[1] *Metaphysic*, sec. 79.

perfection of the universe, we are not perfect ourselves. And as we are parts of the universe, that cannot be perfect.'[1]

And Mr. Joachim finds just the same difficulty. Calling the hypothesis of the absolute by the name of the 'coherence theory of truth,' he calls the problem of understanding how the complete coherence of all things in the absolute should involve as a necessary moment in its self-maintenance the self-assertion of the finite minds, a self-assertion which in its extreme form is error,—he calls this problem, I say, an insoluble puzzle. If truth be the universal *fons et origo*, how does error slip in? 'The coherence theory of truth,' he concludes, 'may thus be said to suffer shipwreck at the very entrance of the harbor.'[2] Yet in spite of this rather bad form of irrationality, Mr. Joachim stoutly asserts his 'immediate certainty'[3] of the theory shipwrecked, the correctness of which he says he has 'never doubted.' This candid confession of a fixed attitude of faith in the absolute, which even one's own criticisms and perplexities fail to disturb, seems to me very significant. Not only empiricists, but absolutists also, would all, if they were as candid as this author, confess that the prime thing in their philosophy is their vision of a truth possible, which they then employ their reasoning to convert, as best it can, into a certainty or probability.

I can imagine a believer in the absolute retorting at this point that *he* at any rate is not dealing with mere probabilities, but that the nature of things logically requires the multitudinous erroneous copies, and that therefore the universe cannot be the absolute's book alone. For, he will ask, is not the absolute defined as the total consciousness of everything that is? Must not its field of view consist of parts? And what can the parts of a total consciousness be unless they be fractional consciousnesses? Our finite minds *must* therefore coexist with the absolute mind. We are its constituents, and it cannot live without us.—But if any one of you feels tempted to retort in this wise, let me remind you that you are frankly employing pluralistic weapons, and thereby giving up the absolutist cause. The notion that the absolute is made of

---

[1] *Studies in the Hegelian Dialectic*, secs. 150, 153.
[2] *The Nature of Truth*, 1906, pp. 170–171.
[3] *Ibid.*, p. 179.

constituents on which its being depends is the rankest empiricism. The absolute as such has *objects*, not constituents, and if the objects develop selfhoods upon their own several accounts, those selfhoods must be set down as facts additional to the absolute consciousness, and not as elements implicated in its definition. The absolute is a rationalist conception. Rationalism goes from wholes to parts, and always assumes wholes to be self-sufficing.[1]

My conclusion, so far, then, is this, that altho the hypothesis of the absolute, in yielding a certain kind of religious peace, performs a most important rationalizing function, it nevertheless, from the intellectual point of view, remains decidedly irrational. The *ideally* perfect whole is certainly that whole of which the *parts also are perfect*—if we can depend on logic for anything, we can depend on it for that definition. The absolute is defined as the ideally perfect whole, yet most of its parts, if not all, are admittedly imperfect. Evidently the conception lacks internal consistency, and yields us a problem rather than a solution. It creates a speculative puzzle, the so-called mystery of evil and of error, from which a pluralistic metaphysic is entirely free.

In any pluralistic metaphysic, the problems that evil presents are practical, not speculative. Not why evil should exist at all, but how we can lessen the actual amount of it, is the sole question we need there consider. 'God,' in the religious life of ordinary men, is the name not of the whole of things, heaven forbid, but only of the ideal tendency in things, believed in as a superhuman person who calls us to co-operate in his purposes, and who furthers ours if they are worthy. He works in an external environment, has limits, and has enemies. When John Mill said that the notion of God's omnipotence must be given up, if God is to be kept as a religious object, he was surely accurately right; yet so prevalent is the lazy monism that idly haunts the region of God's name, that so simple and truthful a saying was generally treated as a

[1]The psychological analogy that certain finite tracts of consciousness are composed of isolable parts added together, cannot be used by absolutists as proof that such parts are essential elements of all consciousness. Other finite fields of consciousness seem in point of fact not to be similarly resolvable into isolable parts.

paradox: God, it was said, *could* not be finite. I believe that the only God worthy of the name *must* be finite, and I shall return to this point in a later lecture. If the absolute exist in addition—and the hypothesis must, in spite of its irrational features, still be left open—then the absolute is only the wider cosmic whole of which our God is but the most ideal portion, and which in the more usual human sense is hardly to be termed a religious hypothesis at all. 'Cosmic emotion' is the better name for the reaction it may awaken.

Observe that all the irrationalities and puzzles which the absolute gives rise to, and from which the finite God remains free, are due to the fact that the absolute has nothing, absolutely nothing, outside of itself. The finite God whom I contrast with it may conceivably have *almost* nothing outside of himself; he may already have triumphed over and absorbed all but the minutest fraction of the universe; but that fraction, however small, reduces him to the status of a relative being, and in principle the universe is saved from all the irrationalities incidental to absolutism. The only irrationality left would be the irrationality of which pluralism as such is accused, and of this I hope to say a word more later.

I have tired you with so many subtleties in this lecture that I will add only two other counts to my indictment.

First, then, let me remind you that *the absolute is useless for deductive purposes*. It gives us absolute safety if you will, but it is compatible with every relative danger. You cannot enter the phenomenal world with the notion of it in your grasp, and name beforehand any detail which you are likely to meet there. Whatever the details of experience may prove to be, *after the fact of them* the absolute will adopt them. It is an hypothesis that functions retrospectively only, not prospectively. *That*, whatever it may be, will have been in point of fact the sort of world which the absolute was pleased to offer to itself as a spectacle.

Again, the absolute is always represented idealistically, as the all-knower. Thinking this view consistently out leads one to frame an almost ridiculous conception of the absolute mind, owing to the enormous mass of unprofitable information which it would then seem obliged to carry. One of the many *reductiones ad absurdum* of pluralism by which idealism thinks it proves the absolute One is as follows: Let there be many facts; but since on idealist principles facts exist only by being known, the many facts will therefore mean many knowers. But that there are so many knowers is itself a fact, which in turn requires *its* knower, so the one absolute knower has eventually to be brought in. *All* facts lead to him. If it be a fact that this table is not a chair, not a rhinoceros, not a logarithm, not a mile away from the door, not worth five hundred pounds sterling, not a thousand centuries old, the absolute must even now be articulately aware of all these negations. Along with what everything is it must also be conscious of everything which it is not. This infinite atmosphere of explicit negativity—observe that it has to be explicit— around everything seems to us so useless an encumbrance as to make the absolute still more foreign to our sympathy. Furthermore, if it be a fact that certain ideas are silly, the absolute has to have already thought the silly ideas to establish them in silliness. The rubbish in its mind would thus appear easily to outweigh in amount the more desirable material. One would expect it fairly to burst with such an obesity, plethora, and superfœtation of useless information.[1]

I will spare you further objections. The sum of it all is that the absolute is not forced on our belief by logic, that it involves features of irrationality peculiar to itself, and that a thinker to whom it does not come as an 'immediate certainty' (to use Mr. Joachim's words), is in no way bound to treat it as anything but an emotionally rather sublime hypothesis. As such, it might, with all its defects, be, on account of its peace-conferring power and its formal grandeur, more rational than anything else in the field. But meanwhile the strung-along unfinished world in time is its rival: *reality MAY exist in distributive form, in the shape not of an all but of a set of eaches, just as it seems to*—this is the anti-absolutist hypothesis. *Prima facie*

[1] Judging by the analogy of the relation which our central consciousness seems to bear to that of our spinal cord, lower ganglia, etc., it would seem natural to suppose that in whatever superhuman mental synthesis there may be, the neglect and elimination of certain contents of which we are conscious on the human level might be as characteristic a feature as is the combination and interweaving of other human contents.

there is this in favor of the eaches, that they are at any rate real enough to have made themselves at least *appear* to every one, whereas the absolute has as yet appeared immediately to only a few mystics, and indeed to them very ambiguously. The advocates of the absolute assure us that any distributive form of being is infected and undermined by self-contradiction. If we are unable to assimilate their arguments, and we have been unable, the only course we can take, it seems to me, is to let the absolute bury the absolute, and to seek reality in more promising directions, even among the details of the finite and the immediately given.

If these words of mine sound in bad taste to some of you, or even sacrilegious, I am sorry. Perhaps the impression may be mitigated by what I have to say in later lectures.

LECTURE IV

THE PRESTIGE of the absolute has rather crumbled in our hands. The logical proofs of it miss fire; the portraits which its best court-painters show of it are featureless and foggy in the extreme; and, apart from the cold comfort of assuring us that with *it* all is well, and that to see that all is well with us also we need only rise to its eternal point of view, it yields us no relief whatever. It introduces, on the contrary, into philosophy and theology certain poisonous difficulties of which but for its intrusion we never should have heard.

But if we drop the absolute out of the world, must we then conclude that the world contains nothing better in the way of consciousness than our consciousness? Is our whole instinctive belief in higher presences, our persistent inner turning towards divine companionship, to count for nothing? Is it but the pathetic illusion of beings with incorrigibly social and imaginative minds?

Such a negative conclusion would, I believe, be desperately hasty, a sort of pouring out of the child with the bath. Logically it is possible to believe in superhuman beings without identifying them with the absolute at all. The treaty of offensive and defensive alliance which certain groups of the christian clergy have recently made with our transcendentalist philosophers seems to me to be based on a well-meaning but baleful mistake. Neither the Jehovah of the old testament nor the heavenly father of the new has anything in common with the absolute except that they are all three greater than man; and if you say that the notion of the absolute is what the gods of Abraham, of David, and of Jesus, after first developing into each other, were inevitably destined to develop into in more reflective and modern minds, I reply that although in certain specifically philosophical minds this may have been the case, in minds more properly to be termed religious the development has followed quite another path. The whole history of evangelical Christianity is there to prove it. I propose in these lectures to plead for that other line of development. To set the doctrine of the absolute in its proper framework, so that it shall not fill the whole welkin and exclude all alternative possibilities of higher thought—as it seems to do for many students who approach it with a limited previous acquaintance with philosophy—I will contrast it with a system which, abstractly considered, seems at first to have much in common with absolutism, but which, when taken concretely and temperamentally, really stands at the opposite pole. I refer to the philosophy of Gustav Theodor Fechner, a writer but little known as yet to English readers, but destined, I am persuaded, to wield more and more influence as time goes on.

It is the intense concreteness of Fechner, his fertility of detail, which fills me with an admiration which I should like to make this audience share. Among the philosophic cranks of my acquaintance in the past was a lady all the tenets of whose system I have forgotten except one. Had she been born in the Ionian Archipelago some three thousand years ago, that one doctrine would probably have made her name sure of a place in every university curriculum and examination paper. The world, she said, is composed of only two elements, the Thick, namely, and the Thin. No one can deny the truth of this analysis, as far as it goes (though in the light of our contemporary knowledge of nature it has itself a rather 'thin' sound), and it is nowhere truer than in that part of the world called philosophy. I am sure, for example, that many of you, listening to what poor account I have been able to give of transcendental idealism, have received an impression of its arguments being strangely thin, and of the terms it leaves us with being shiveringly thin wrappings for so thick and burly a world as this. Some of you of course will charge the thinness to my exposition; but thin as that has been, I believe the doctrines reported on to have been thinner. From Green to Haldane the absolute proposed to us to straighten out the confusions of the thicket of experience in which our life is passed remains a pure abstraction which hardly any one tries to make a whit concreter. If we open Green, we get nothing but the transcendental ego of apperception (Kant's name for the fact that to be counted in experience a thing has to be witnessed), blown up into a sort of timeless soap-bubble large enough to mirror the whole universe. Nature, Green keeps insisting, consists only in relations, and these imply the action of a mind that is eternal; a self-distinguishing consciousness which itself escapes from the relations by which it determines other things. Present to whatever is in succession, it is not in succession itself. If we take the Cairds, they tell us little more of the principle of the universe—it is always a return into the identity of the self from the difference of its objects. It separates itself from them and so becomes conscious of them in their separation from one another, while at the same time it binds them together as elements in one higher self-consciousness.

This seems the very quintessence of thinness; and the matter hardly grows thicker when we gather, after enormous amounts of reading, that the great enveloping self in question is absolute reason as such, and that as such it is characterized by the habit of using certain jejune 'categories' with which to perform its eminent relating work. The whole active material of natural fact is tried out, and only the barest intellectualistic formalism remains.

Hegel tried, as we saw, to make the system concreter by making the relations between things 'dialectic,' but if we turn to those who use his name most worshipfully, we find them giving up all the particulars of his attempt, and simply praising his intention—much as in our manner we have praised it ourselves. Mr. Haldane, for example, in his wonderfully clever Gifford lectures, praises Hegel to the skies, but what he tells of him amounts to little more than this, that 'the categories in which the mind arranges its experiences, and gives meaning to them, the universals in which the particulars are grasped in the individual, are a logical chain, in which the first presupposes the last, and the last is its presupposition and its truth.' He hardly tries at all to thicken this thin logical scheme. He says indeed that absolute mind in itself, and absolute mind in its hetereity or otherness, under the distinction which it sets up of itself from itself, have as their real *prius* absolute mind in synthesis; and, this being absolute mind's true nature, its dialectic character must show itself in such concrete forms as Goethe's and Wordsworth's poetry, as well as in religious forms. 'The nature of God, the nature of absolute mind, is to exhibit the triple movement of dialectic, and so the nature of

God as presented in religion must be a triplicity, a trinity.' But beyond thus naming Goethe and Wordsworth and establishing the trinity, Mr. Haldane's Hegelianism carries us hardly an inch into the concrete detail of the world we actually inhabit.

Equally thin is Mr. Taylor, both in his principles and in their results. Following Mr. Bradley, he starts by assuring us that reality cannot be self-contradictory, but to be related to anything really outside of one's self is to be self-contradictory, so the ultimate reality must be a single all-inclusive systematic whole. Yet all he can say of this whole at the end of his excellently written book is that the notion of it 'can make no addition to our information and can of itself supply no motives for practical endeavor.'

Mr. McTaggart treats us to almost as thin a fare. 'The main practical interest of Hegel's philosophy,' he says, 'is to be found in the abstract certainty which the logic gives us that all reality is rational and righteous, even when we cannot see in the least how it is so. . . . Not that it shows us how the facts around us are good, not that it shows us how we can make them better, but that it proves that they, like other reality, are *sub specie eternitatis*, perfectly good, and *sub specie temporis*, destined to become perfectly good.'

Here again, no detail whatever, only the abstract certainty that whatever the detail may prove to be, it will be good. Common non-dialectical men have already this certainty as a result of the generous vital enthusiasm about the universe with which they are born. The peculiarity of transcendental philosophy is its sovereign contempt for merely vital functions like enthusiasm, and its pretension to turn our simple and immediate trusts and faiths into the form of logically mediated certainties, to question which would be absurd. But the whole basis on which Mr. McTaggart's own certainty so solidly rests, settles down into the one nutshell of an assertion into which he puts Hegel's gospel, namely, that in every bit of experience and thought, however finite, the whole of reality (the absolute idea, as Hegel calls it) is 'implicitly present.'

This indeed is Hegel's *vision*, and Hegel thought that the details of his dialectic proved its truth. But disciples who treat the details of the proof as unsatisfactory and yet cling to the vision, are surely, in spite of their pretension to a more rational consciousness, no better than common men with their enthusiasms or deliberately adopted faiths. We have ourselves seen some of the weakness of the monistic proofs. Mr. Mc-Taggart picks plenty of holes of his own in Hegel's logic, and finally concludes that 'all true philosophy must be mystical, not indeed in its methods but in its final conclusions,' which is as much as to say that the rationalistic methods leave us in the lurch, in spite of all their superiority, and that in the end vision and faith must eke them out. But how abstract and thin is here the vision, to say nothing of the faith! The whole of reality, explicitly absent from our finite experiences, must nevertheless be present in them all implicitly, altho no one of us can ever see how—the bare word 'implicit' here bearing the whole pyramid of the monistic system on its slender point. Mr. Joachim's monistic system of truth rests on an even slenderer point.—'I have never doubted,' he says, 'that universal and timeless truth is a single content or significance, one and whole and complete,' and he candidly confesses the failure of rationalistic attempts 'to raise this immediate certainty' to the level of reflective knowledge. There is, in short, no mediation for him between the Truth in capital letters and all the little 'lower-case' truths—and errors—which life presents. The psychological fact that he never has 'doubted' is enough.

The whole monistic pyramid, resting on points as thin as these, seems to me to be a *machtspruch*, a product of will far more than one of reason. Unity is good, therefore things *shall* cohere; they *shall* be one; there *shall* be categories to make them one, no matter what empirical disjunctions may appear. In Hegel's own writings, the *shall-be* temper is ubiquitous and towering; it overrides verbal and logical resistances alike. Hegel's error, as Professor Royce so well says, 'lay not in introducing logic into passion,' as some people charge, 'but in conceiving the logic of passion as the only logic. . . . He is [thus] suggestive,' Royce says, 'but never final. His system as a system has crumbled, but his vital comprehension of our life remains forever.'[1]

---

[1] *The Spirit of Modern Philosophy*, p. 227.

That vital comprehension we have already seen. It is that there is a sense in which real things are not merely their own bare selves, but may vaguely be treated as also their own others, and that ordinary logic, since it denies this, must be overcome. Ordinary logic denies this because it substitutes concepts for real things, and concepts *are* their own bare selves and nothing else. What Royce calls Hegel's 'system' was Hegel's attempt to make us believe that he was working by concepts and grinding out a higher style of logic, when in reality sensible experiences, hypotheses, and passion furnished him with all his results.

What I myself may mean by things being their own others, we shall see in a later lecture. It is now time to take our look at Fechner, whose thickness is a refreshing contrast to the thin, abstract, indigent, and threadbare appearance, the starving, school-room aspect, which the speculations of most of our absolutist philosophers present.

There is something really weird and uncanny in the contrast between the abstract pretensions of rationalism and what rationalistic methods concretely can do. If the 'logical prius' of our mind were really the 'implicit presence' of the whole 'concrete universal,' the whole of reason, or reality, or spirit, or the absolute idea, or whatever it may be called, in all our finite thinking, and if this reason worked (for example) by the dialectical method, does n't it seem odd that in the greatest instance of rationalization mankind has known, in 'science,' namely, the dialectical method should never once have been tried? Not a solitary instance of the use of it in science occurs to my mind. Hypotheses, and deductions from these, controlled by sense-observations and analogies with what we know elsewhere, are to be thanked for all of science's results.

Fechner used no methods but these latter ones in arguing for his metaphysical conclusions about reality—but let me first rehearse a few of the facts about his life.

Born in 1801, the son of a poor country pastor in Saxony, he lived from 1817 to 1887, when he died, seventy years therefore, at Leipzig, a typical *gelehrter* of the old-fashioned german stripe. His means were always scanty, so his only extravagances could be in the way of thought, but these were gorgeous ones. He passed his medical examinations at

Leipzig University at the age of twenty-one, but decided, instead of becoming a doctor, to devote himself to physical science. It was ten years before he was made professor of physics, although he soon was authorized to lecture. Meanwhile, he had to make both ends meet, and this he did by voluminous literary labors. He translated, for example, the four volumes of Biot's treatise on physics, and the six of Thénard's work on chemistry, and took care of their enlarged editions later. He edited repertories of chemistry and physics, a pharmaceutical journal, and an encyclopædia in eight volumes, of which he wrote about one third. He published physical treatises and experimental investigations of his own, especially in electricity. Electrical measurements, as you know, are the basis of electrical science, and Fechner's measurements in galvanism, performed with the simplest self-made apparatus, are classic to this day. During this time he also published a number of half-philosophical, half-humorous writings, which have gone through several editions, under the name of Dr. Mises, besides poems, literary and artistic essays, and other occasional articles.

But overwork, poverty, and an eye-trouble produced by his observations on after-images in the retina (also a classic piece of investigation) produced in Fechner, then about thirty-eight years old, a terrific attack of nervous prostration with painful hyperæsthesia of all the functions, from which he suffered three years, cut off entirely from active life. Present-day medicine would have classed poor Fechner's malady quickly enough, as partly a habit-neurosis, but its severity was such that in his day it was treated as a visitation incomprehensible in its malignity; and when he suddenly began to get well, both Fechner and others treated the recovery as a sort of divine miracle. This illness, bringing Fechner face to face with inner desperation, made a great crisis in his life. 'Had I not then clung to the faith,' he writes, 'that clinging to faith would somehow or other work its reward, *so hätte ich jene zeit nicht ausgehalten.*' His religious and cosmological faiths saved him—thenceforward one great aim with him was to work out and communicate these faiths to the world. He did so on the largest scale; but he did many other things too ere he died.

A book on the atomic theory, classic also; four elaborate mathematical and experimental volumes on what he called psychophysics—many persons consider Fechner to have practically founded scientific psychology in the first of these books; a volume on organic evolution, and two works on experimental æsthetics, in which again Fechner is considered by some judges to have laid the foundations of a new science, must be included among these other performances. Of the more religious and philosophical works, I shall immediately give a further account.

All Leipzig mourned him when he died, for he was the pattern of the ideal german scholar, as daringly original in his thought as he was homely in his life, a modest, genial, laborious slave to truth and learning, and withal the owner of an admirable literary style of the vernacular sort. The materialistic generation, that in the fifties and sixties called his speculations fantastic, had been replaced by one with greater liberty of imagination, and a Preyer, a Wundt, a Paulsen, and a Lasswitz could now speak of Fechner as their master.

His mind was indeed one of those multitudinously organized cross-roads of truth which are occupied only at rare intervals by children of men, and from which nothing is either too far or too near to be seen in due perspective. Patientest observation, exactest mathematics, shrewdest discrimination, humanest feeling, flourished in him on the largest scale, with no apparent detriment to one another. He was in fact a philosopher in the 'great' sense, altho he cared so much less than most philosophers care for abstractions of the 'thin' order. For him the abstract lived in the concrete, and the hidden motive of all he did was to bring what he called the daylight view of the world into ever greater evidence, that daylight view being this, that the whole universe in its different spans and wave-lengths, exclusions and envelopments, is everywhere alive and conscious. It has taken fifty years for his chief book, 'Zend-avesta,' to pass into a second edition (1901). 'One swallow,' he cheerfully writes, 'does not make a summer. But the first swallow would not come unless the summer were coming; and for me that summer means my daylight view some time prevailing.'

The original sin, according to Fechner, of both our popular

and our scientific thinking, is our inveterate habit of regarding the spiritual not as the rule but as an exception in the
midst of nature. Instead of believing our life to be fed at the
breasts of the greater life, our individuality to be sustained by
the greater individuality, which must necessarily have more
consciousness and more independence than all that it brings
forth, we habitually treat whatever lies outside of our life as
so much slag and ashes of life only; or if we believe in a
Divine Spirit, we fancy him on the one side as bodiless, and
nature as soulless on the other. What comfort, or peace, Fechner asks, can come from such a doctrine? The flowers wither
at its breath, the stars turn into stone; our own body grows
unworthy of our spirit and sinks to a tenement for carnal
senses only. The book of nature turns into a volume on mechanics, in which whatever has life is treated as a sort of
anomaly; a great chasm of separation yawns between us and
all that is higher than ourselves; and God becomes a thin nest
of abstractions.

Fechner's great instrument for vivifying the daylight view
is analogy; not a rationalistic argument is to be found in all
his many pages—only reasonings like those which men continually use in practical life. For example: My house is built
by some one, the world too is built by some one. The world
is greater than my house, it must be a greater some one who
built the world. My body moves by the influence of my feeling and will; the sun, moon, sea, and wind, being themselves
more powerful, move by the influence of some more powerful
feeling and will. I live now, and change from one day to another; I shall live hereafter, and change still more, etc.

Bain defines genius as the power of seeing analogies. The
number that Fechner could perceive was prodigious; but he
insisted on the differences as well. Neglect to make allowance
for these, he said, is the common fallacy in analogical reasoning. Most of us, for example, reasoning justly that, since all
the minds we know are connected with bodies, therefore
God's mind should be connected with a body, proceed to
suppose that that body must be just an animal body over
again, and paint an altogether human picture of God. But all
that the analogy comports is *a* body—the particular features
of *our* body are adaptations to a habitat so different from

God's that if God have a physical body at all, it must be utterly different from ours in structure. Throughout his writings Fechner makes difference and analogy walk abreast, and by his extraordinary power of noticing both, he converts what would ordinarily pass for objections to his conclusions into factors of their support.

The vaster orders of mind go with the vaster orders of body. The entire earth on which we live must have, according to Fechner, its own collective consciousness. So must each sun, moon, and planet; so must the whole solar system have its own wider consciousness, in which the consciousness of our earth plays one part. So has the entire starry system as such its consciousness; and if that starry system be not the sum of all that *is*, materially considered, then that whole system, along with whatever else may be, is the body of that absolutely totalized consciousness of the universe to which men give the name of God.

Speculatively Fechner is thus a monist in his theology; but there is room in his universe for every grade of spiritual being between man and the final all-inclusive God; and in suggesting what the positive content of all this super-humanity may be, he hardly lets his imagination fly beyond simple spirits of the planetary order. The earth-soul he passionately believes in; he treats the earth as our special human guardian angel; we can pray to the earth as men pray to their saints; but I think that in his system, as in so many of the actual historic theologies, the supreme God marks only a sort of limit of enclosure of the worlds above man. He is left thin and abstract in his majesty, men preferring to carry on their personal transactions with the many less remote and abstract messengers and mediators whom the divine order provides.

I shall ask later whether the abstractly monistic turn which Fechner's speculations took was necessitated by logic. I believe it not to have been required. Meanwhile let me lead you a little more into the detail of his thought. Inevitably one does him miserable injustice by summarizing and abridging him. For altho the type of reasoning he employs is almost childlike for simplicity, and his bare conclusions can be written on a single page, the *power* of the man is due altogether to the profuseness of his concrete imagination, to the multitude of the points which he considers successively, to the cumulative effect of his learning, of his thoroughness, and of the ingenuity of his detail, to his admirably homely style, to the sincerity with which his pages glow, and finally to the impression he gives of a man who does n't live at second-hand, but who *sees*, who in fact speaks as one having authority, and not as if he were one of the common herd of professorial philosophic scribes.

Abstractly set down, his most important conclusion for my purpose in these lectures is that the constitution of the world is identical throughout. In ourselves, visual consciousness goes with our eyes, tactile consciousness with our skin. But altho neither skin nor eye knows aught of the sensations of the other, they come together and figure in some sort of relation and combination in the more inclusive consciousness which each of us names his *self*. Quite similarly, then, says Fechner, we must suppose that my consciousness of myself and yours of yourself, altho in their immediacy they keep separate and know nothing of each other, are yet known and used together in a higher consciousness, that of the human race, say, into which they enter as constituent parts. Similarly, the whole human and animal kingdoms come together as conditions of a consciousness of still wider scope. This combines in the soul of the earth with the consciousness of the vegetable kingdom, which in turn contributes its share of experience to that of the whole solar system, and so on from synthesis to synthesis and height to height, till an absolutely universal consciousness is reached.

A vast analogical series, in which the basis of the analogy consists of facts directly observable in ourselves.

The supposition of an earth-consciousness meets a strong instinctive prejudice which Fechner ingeniously tries to overcome. Man's mind is the highest consciousness upon the earth, we think—the earth itself being in all ways man's inferior. How should its consciousness, if it have one, be superior to his?

What are the marks of superiority which we are tempted to use here? If we look more carefully into them, Fechner points out that the earth possesses each and all of them more perfectly than we. He considers in detail the points of difference between us, and shows them all to make for the earth's higher rank. I will touch on only a few of these points.

One of them of course is independence of other external beings. External to the earth are only the other heavenly bodies. All the things on which we externally depend for life—air, water, plant and animal food, fellow men, etc.—are included in her as her constituent parts. She is self-sufficing in a million respects in which we are not so. We depend on her for almost everything, she on us for but a small portion of her history. She swings us in her orbit from winter to summer and revolves us from day into night and from night into day.

Complexity in unity is another sign of superiority. The total earth's complexity far exceeds that of any organism, for she includes all our organisms in herself, along with an infinite number of things that our organisms fail to include. Yet how simple and massive are the phases of her own proper life! As the total bearing of any animal is sedate and tranquil compared with the agitation of its blood corpuscles, so is the earth a sedate and tranquil being compared with the animals whom she supports.

To develop from within, instead of being fashioned from without, is also counted as something superior in men's eyes. An egg is a higher style of being than a piece of clay which an external modeler makes into the image of a bird. Well, the earth's history develops from within. It is like that of a wonderful egg which the sun's heat, like that of a mother-hen, has stimulated to its cycles of evolutionary change.

Individuality of type, and difference from other beings of its type, is another mark of rank. The earth differs from every other planet, and as a class planetary beings are extraordinarily distinct from other beings.

Long ago the earth was called an animal; but a planet is a higher class of being than either man or animal; not only quantitatively greater, like a vaster and more awkward whale or elephant, but a being whose enormous size requires an altogether different plan of life. Our animal organization comes from our inferiority. Our need of moving to and fro, of stretching our limbs and bending our bodies, shows only our defect. What are our legs but crutches, by means of which, with restless efforts, we go hunting after the things we have not inside of ourselves. But the earth is no such cripple; why should she who already possesses within herself the things we so painfully pursue, have limbs analogous to ours? Shall she mimic a small part of herself? What need has she of arms, with nothing to reach for? of a neck, with no head to carry? of eyes or nose when she finds her way through space without either, and has the millions of eyes of all her animals to guide their movements on her surface, and all their noses to smell the flowers that grow? For, as we are ourselves a part of the earth, so our organs are her organs. She is, as it were, eye and ear over her whole extent—all that we see and hear in separation she sees and hears at once. She brings forth living beings of countless kinds upon her surface, and their multitudinous conscious relations with each other she takes up into her higher and more general conscious life.

Most of us, considering the theory that the whole terrestrial mass is animated as our bodies are, make the mistake of working the analogy too literally, and allowing for no differences. If the earth be a sentient organism, we say, where are her brain and nerves? What corresponds to her heart and lungs? In other words, we expect functions which she already performs through us, to be performed outside of us again, and in just the same way. But we see perfectly well how the earth performs some of these functions in a way unlike our way. If you speak of circulation, what need has she of a heart when the sun keeps all the showers of rain that fall upon her and all the springs and brooks and rivers that irrigate her, going? What need has she of internal lungs, when her whole sensitive surface is in living commerce with the atmosphere that clings to it?

The organ that gives us most trouble is the brain. All the consciousness we directly know seems tied to brains.—Can there be consciousness, we ask, where there is no brain? But our brain, which primarily serves to correlate our muscular reactions with the external objects on which we depend, performs a function which the earth performs in an entirely different way. She has no proper muscles or limbs of her own, and the only objects external to her are the other stars. To these her whole mass reacts by most exquisite alterations in its total gait, and by still more exquisite vibratory responses in its substance. Her ocean reflects the lights of heaven as in a mighty mirror, her atmosphere refracts them like a monstrous lens, the clouds and snow-fields combine them into white, the woods and flowers disperse them into colors. Polarization, interference, absorption, awaken sensibilities in matter of which our senses are too coarse to take any note.

For these cosmic relations of hers, then, she no more needs a special brain than she needs eyes or ears. *Our* brains do indeed unify and correlate innumerable functions. Our eyes know nothing of sound, our ears nothing of light, but, having brains, we can feel sound and light together, and compare them. We account for this by the fibres which in the brain connect the optical with the acoustic centre, but just how these fibres bring together not only the centres, but the sensations, we fail to see. But if fibres are indeed all that is needed to do that trick, has not the earth pathways, by which you and I are physically continuous, more than enough to do for our two minds what the brain-fibres do for the sounds and sights in a single mind? Must every higher means of unification between things be a literal *brain*-fibre, and go by that name? Cannot the earth-mind know otherwise the contents of our minds together?

Fechner's imagination, insisting on the differences as well as on the resemblances, thus tries to make our picture of the whole earth's life more concrete. He revels in the thought of its perfections. To carry her precious freight through the hours and seasons what form could be more excellent than hers—being as it is horse, wheels, and wagon all in one. Think of her beauty—a shining ball, sky-blue and sun-lit over one half, the other bathed in starry night, reflecting the heavens from all her waters, myriads of lights and shadows in the folds of her mountains and windings of her valleys, she would be a spectacle of rainbow glory, could one only see her from afar as we see parts of her from her own mountain-tops. Every quality of landscape that has a name would then be visible in her at once—all that is delicate or graceful, all that is quiet, or wild, or romantic, or desolate, or cheerful, or luxuriant, or fresh. That landscape is her face—a peopled landscape, too, for men's eyes would appear in it like diamonds among the dew-drops. Green would be the dominant color, but the blue atmosphere and the clouds would enfold her as a bride is shrouded in her veil—a veil the vapory transparent folds of which the earth, through her ministers the winds, never tires of laying and folding about herself anew.

Every element has its own living denizens. Can the celestial ocean of ether, whose waves are light, in which the earth herself floats, not have hers, higher by as much as their element is higher, swimming without fins, flying without wings, moving, immense and tranquil, as by a half-spiritual force through the half-spiritual sea which they inhabit, rejoicing in the exchange of luminous influence with one another, following the slightest pull of one another's attraction, and harboring, each of them, an inexhaustible inward wealth?

Men have always made fables about angels, dwelling in the light, needing no earthly food or drink, messengers between ourselves and God. Here are actually existent beings, dwelling in the light and moving through the sky, needing neither food nor drink, intermediaries between God and us, obeying his commands. So, if the heavens really are the home of angels, the heavenly bodies must be those very angels, for other creatures *there* are none. Yes! the earth is our great common guardian angel, who watches over all our interests combined.

In a striking page Fechner relates one of his moments of direct vision of this truth.

'On a certain spring morning I went out to walk. The fields were green, the birds sang, the dew glistened, the smoke was rising, here and there a man appeared; a light as of transfiguration lay on all things. It was only a little bit of the earth; it was only one moment of her existence; and yet as my look embraced her more and more it seemed to me not only so beautiful an idea, but so true and clear a fact, that she is an angel, an angel so rich and fresh and flower-like, and yet going her round in the skies so firmly and so at one with herself, turning her whole living face to Heaven, and carrying me along with her into that Heaven, that I asked myself how the opinions of men could ever have so spun themselves away from life so far as to deem the earth only a dry clod, and to seek for angels above it or about it in the emptiness of the sky,—only to find them nowhere. . . . But such an experience as this passes for fantastic. The earth is a globular body, and what more she may be, one can find in mineralogical cabinets.'[1]

Where there is no vision the people perish. Few professorial philosophers have any vision. Fechner had vision, and that is why one can read him over and over again, and each time bring away a fresh sense of reality.

His earliest book was a vision of what the inner life of plants may be like. He called it 'Nanna.' In the development of animals the nervous system is the central fact. Plants develop centrifugally, spread their organs abroad. For that reason people suppose that they can have no consciousness, for they lack the unity which the central nervous system provides. But the plant's consciousness may be of another type, being connected with other structures. Violins and pianos give out sounds because they have strings. Does it follow that nothing but strings can give out sound? How then about flutes and organ-pipes? Of course their sounds are of a different quality, and so may the consciousness of plants be of a quality correlated exclusively with the kind of organization that they possess. Nutrition, respiration, propagation take place in them without nerves. In us these functions are conscious only in unusual states, normally their consciousness is eclipsed by that which goes with the brain. No such eclipse occurs in plants, and their lower consciousness may therefore be all the more lively. With nothing to do but to drink the light and air with their leaves, to let their cells proliferate, to feel their rootlets draw the sap, is it conceivable that they should not consciously suffer if water, light, and air are suddenly withdrawn? or that when the flowering and fertilization which are the culmination of their life take place, they should not feel their own existence more intensely and enjoy something like what we call pleasure in ourselves? Does the water-lily, rocking in her triple bath of water, air, and light, relish in no wise her own beauty? When the plant in our room turns to the light, closes her blossoms in the dark, responds to our watering or pruning by increase of size or change of shape and bloom, who has the right to say she does not feel, or that she plays a

[1] Fechner: *Über die Seelenfrage*, 1861, p. 170.

purely passive part? Truly plants can foresee nothing, neither the scythe of the mower, nor the hand extended to pluck their flowers. They can neither run away nor cry out. But this only proves how different their modes of feeling life must be from those of animals that live by eyes and ears and locomotive organs, it does not prove that they have no mode of feeling life at all.

How scanty and scattered would sensation be on our globe, if the feeling-life of plants were blotted from existence. Solitary would consciousness move through the woods in the shape of some deer or other quadruped, or fly about the flowers in that of some insect, but can we really suppose that the Nature through which God's breath blows is such a barren wilderness as this?

I have probably by this time said enough to acquaint those of you who have never seen these metaphysical writings of Fechner with their more general characteristics, and I hope that some of you may now feel like reading them yourselves.[1] The special thought of Fechner's with which in these lectures I have most practical concern, is his belief that the more inclusive forms of consciousness are in part *constituted* by the more limited forms. Not that they are the mere sum of the more limited forms. As our mind is not the bare sum of our sights plus our sounds plus our pains, but in adding these terms together also finds relations among them and weaves them into schemes and forms and objects of which no one sense in its separate estate knows anything, so the earth-soul traces relations between the contents of my mind and the contents of yours of which neither of our separate minds is conscious. It has schemes, forms, and objects proportionate to its wider field, which our mental fields are far too narrow to cognize. By ourselves we are simply out of relation with each other, for it we are both of us there, and *different* from each other, which is a positive relation. What we are without knowing, it knows that we are. We are closed against its

[1] Fechner's latest summarizing of his views, *Die Tagesansicht gegenüber der Nachtansicht*, Leipzig, 1879, is now, I understand, in process of translation. His *Little Book of Life after Death* exists already in two American versions, one published by Little, Brown & Co., Boston, the other by the Open Court Co., Chicago.

world, but that world is not closed against us. It is as if the total universe of inner life had a sort of grain or direction, a sort of valvular structure, permitting knowledge to flow in one way only, so that the wider might always have the narrower under observation, but never the narrower the wider.

Fechner's great analogy here is the relation of the senses to our individual minds. When our eyes are open their sensations enter into our general mental life, which grows incessantly by the addition of what they see. Close the eyes, however, and the visual additions stop, nothing but thoughts and memories of the past visual experiences remain—in combination of course with the enormous stock of other thoughts and memories, and with the data coming in from the senses not yet closed. Our eye-sensations of themselves know nothing of this enormous life into which they fall. Fechner thinks, as any common man would think, that they are taken into it directly when they occur, and form part of it just as they are. They don't stay outside and get represented inside by their copies. It is only the memories and concepts of them that are copies; the sensible perceptions themselves are taken in or walled out in their own proper persons according as the eyes are open or shut.

Fechner likens our individual persons on the earth unto so many sense-organs of the earth's soul. We add to its perceptive life so long as our own life lasts. It absorbs our perceptions, just as they occur, into its larger sphere of knowledge, and combines them with the other data there. When one of us dies, it is as if an eye of the world were closed, for all *perceptive* contributions from that particular quarter cease. But the memories and conceptual relations that have spun themselves round the perceptions of that person remain in the larger earth-life as distinct as ever, and form new relations and grow and develop throughout all the future, in the same way in which our own distinct objects of thought, once stored in memory, form new relations and develop throughout our whole finite life. This is Fechner's theory of immortality, first published in the little 'Büchlein des lebens nach dem tode,' in 1836, and re-edited in greatly improved shape in the last volume of his 'Zend-avesta.'

We rise upon the earth as wavelets rise upon the ocean. We

grow out of her soil as leaves grow from a tree. The wavelets catch the sunbeams separately, the leaves stir when the branches do not move. They realize their own events apart, just as in our own consciousness, when anything becomes emphatic, the background fades from observation. Yet the event works back upon the background, as the wavelet works upon the waves, or as the leaf's movements work upon the sap inside the branch. The whole sea and the whole tree are registers of what has happened, and are different for the wave's and the leaf's action having occurred. A grafted twig may modify its scion to the roots:—so our outlived private experiences, impressed on the whole earth-mind as memories, lead the immortal life of ideas there, and become parts of the great system, fully distinguished from one another, just as we ourselves when alive were distinct, realizing themselves no longer isolatedly, but along with one another as so many partial systems, entering thus into new combinations, being affected by the perceptive experiences of those living then, and affecting the living in their turn—altho they are so seldom recognized by living men to do so.

If you imagine that this entrance after the death of the body into a common life of higher type means a merging and loss of our distinct personality, Fechner asks you whether a visual sensation of our own exists in any sense *less for itself* or *less distinctly*, when it enters into our higher relational consciousness and is there distinguished and defined.

—But here I must stop my reporting and send you to his volumes. Thus is the universe alive, according to this philosopher! I think you will admit that he makes it more *thickly* alive than do the other philosophers who, following rationalistic methods solely, gain the same results, but only in the thinnest outlines. Both Fechner and Professor Royce, for example, believe ultimately in one all-inclusive mind. Both believe that we, just as we stand here, are constituent parts of that mind. No other *content* has it than us, with all the other creatures like or unlike us, and the relations which it finds between us. Our eaches, collected into one, are substantively identical with its all, tho the all is perfect while no each is perfect, so that we have to admit that new qualities as well as unperceived relations accrue from the collective form. It is thus superior to the distributive form. But having reached this result, Royce (tho his treatment of the subject on its moral side seems to me infinitely richer and thicker than that of any other contemporary idealistic philosopher) leaves us very much to our own devices. Fechner, on the contrary, tries to trace the superiorities due to the more collective form in as much detail as he can. He marks the various intermediary stages and halting places of collectivity,—as we are to our separate senses, so is the earth to us, so is the solar system to the earth, etc.,—and if, in order to escape an infinitely long summation, he posits a complete God as the all-container and leaves him about as indefinite in feature as the idealists leave their absolute, he yet provides us with a very definite gate of approach to him in the shape of the earth-soul, through which in the nature of things we must first make connexion with all the more enveloping superhuman realms, and with which our more immediate religious commerce at any rate has to be carried on.

Ordinary monistic idealism leaves everything intermediary out. It recognizes only the extremes, as if, after the first rude face of the phenomenal world in all its particularity, nothing but the supreme in all its perfection could be found. First, you and I, just as we are in this room; and the moment we get below that surface, the unutterable absolute itself! Does n't this show a singularly indigent imagination? Is n't this brave universe made on a richer pattern, with room in it for a long hierarchy of beings? Materialistic science makes it infinitely richer in terms, with its molecules, and ether, and electrons, and what not. Absolute idealism, thinking of reality only under intellectual forms, knows not what to do with *bodies* of any grade, and can make no use of any psychophysical analogy or correspondence. The resultant thinness is startling when compared with the thickness and articulation of such a universe as Fechner paints. May not satisfaction with the rationalistic absolute as the alpha and omega, and treatment of it in all its abstraction as an adequate religious object, argue a certain native poverty of mental demand? Things reveal themselves soonest to those who most passionately want them, for our need sharpens our wit. To a mind content with little, the much in the universe may always remain hid.

To be candid, one of my reasons for saying so much about Fechner has been to make the thinness of our current transcendentalism appear more evident by an effect of contrast. Scholasticism ran thick; Hegel himself ran thick; but english and american transcendentalisms run thin. If philosophy is more a matter of passionate vision than of logic,—and I believe it is, logic only finding reasons for the vision afterwards,—must not such thinness come either from the vision being defective in the disciples, or from their passion, matched with Fechner's or with Hegel's own passion, being as moonlight unto sunlight or as water unto wine?[1]

But I have also a much deeper reason for making Fechner a part of my text. His *assumption that conscious experiences freely compound and separate themselves*, the same assumption by which absolutism explains the relation of our minds to the eternal mind, and the same by which empiricism explains the composition of the human mind out of subordinate mental elements, is not one which we ought to let pass without scrutiny. I shall scrutinize it in the next lecture.

[1] Mr. Bradley ought to be to some degree exempted from my attack in these last pages. Compare especially what he says of non-human consciousness in his *Appearance and Reality*, pp. 269–272.

LECTURE V

THE COMPOUNDING OF CONSCIOUSNESS

I N MY LAST LECTURE I gave a miserably scanty outline of the way of thinking of a philosopher remarkable for the almost unexampled richness of his imagination of details. I owe to Fechner's shade an apology for presenting him in a manner so unfair to the most essential quality of his genius; but the time allotted is too short to say more about the particulars of his work, so I proceed to the programme I suggested at the end of our last hour. I wish to discuss the assumption that states of consciousness, so-called, can separate and combine themselves freely, and keep their own identity unchanged while forming parts of simultaneous fields of experience of wider scope.

Let me first explain just what I mean by this. While you listen to my voice, for example, you are perhaps inattentive to some bodily sensation due to your clothing or your posture. Yet that sensation would seem probably to be there, for in an instant, by a change of attention, you can have it in one field of consciousness with the voice. It seems as if it existed first in a separate form, and then as if, without itself changing, it combined with your other co-existent sensations. It is after this analogy that pantheistic idealism thinks that we exist in the absolute. The absolute, it thinks, makes the world by knowing the whole of it at once in one undivided eternal act.[1] To 'be,' *really* to be, is to be as it knows us to be, along with everything else, namely, and clothed with the fulness of our meaning. Meanwhile we *are* at the same time not only really and as it knows us, but also apparently, for to our separate single selves we appear *without* most other things and unable to declare with any fulness what our own meaning is. Now the classic doctrine of pantheistic idealism, from the Upanishads down to Josiah Royce, is that the finite knowers, in spite of their apparent ignorance, are one with the knower of the all. In the most limited moments of our private experience, the absolute idea, as Dr. McTaggart told us, is implicitly

[1] Royce: *The Spirit of Modern Philosophy*, p. 379.

contained. The moments, as Royce says, exist only in relation to it. They are true or erroneous only through its overshadowing presence. Of the larger self that alone eternally is, they are the organic parts. They *are*, only inasmuch as they are implicated in its being.

There is thus in reality but this one self, consciously inclusive of all the lesser selves, *logos*, problem-solver, and all-knower; and Royce ingeniously compares the ignorance that in our persons breaks out in the midst of its complete knowledge and isolates me from you and both of us from it, to the inattention into which our finite minds are liable to fall with respect to such implicitly present details as those corporeal sensations to which I made allusion just now. Those sensations stand to our total private minds in the same relation in which our private minds stand to the absolute mind. Privacy means ignorance—I still quote Royce—and ignorance means inattention. We are finite because our wills, as such, are only fragments of the absolute will; because will means interest, and an incomplete will means an incomplete interest; and because incompleteness of interest means inattention to much that a fuller interest would bring us to perceive.[1]

In this account Royce makes by far the manliest of the post-hegelian attempts to read some empirically apprehensible content into the notion of our relation to the absolute mind.

I have to admit, now that I propose to you to scrutinize this assumption rather closely, that trepidation seizes me. The subject is a subtle and abstruse one. It is one thing to delve into subtleties by one's self with pen in hand, or to study out abstruse points in books, but quite another thing to make a popular lecture out of them. Nevertheless I must not flinch from my task here, for I think that this particular point forms perhaps the vital knot of the present philosophic situation, and I imagine that the times are ripe, or almost ripe, for a serious attempt to be made at its untying.

It may perhaps help to lessen the arduousness of the subject if I put the first part of what I have to say in the form of a direct personal confession.

In the year 1890 I published a work on psychology in which

[1] *The World and the Individual*, vol. ii, pp. 58–62.

it became my duty to discuss the value of a certain explanation of our higher mental states that had come into favor
among the more biologically inclined psychologists. Suggested partly by the association of ideas, and partly by the
analogy of chemical compounds, this opinion was that complex mental states are resultants of the self-compounding of
simpler ones. The Mills had spoken of mental chemistry;
Wundt of a 'psychic synthesis,' which might develop properties not contained in the elements; and such writers as Spencer, Taine, Fiske, Barratt, and Clifford had propounded a
great evolutionary theory in which, in the absence of souls,
selves, or other principles of unity, primordial units of mind-
stuff or mind-dust were represented as summing themselves
together in successive stages of compounding and re-com-
pounding, and thus engendering our higher and more complex states of mind. The elementary feeling of A, let us say,
and the elementary feeling of B, when they occur in certain
conditions, combine, according to this doctrine, into a feeling
of A-plus-B, and this in turn combines with a similarly generated feeling of C-plus-D, until at last the whole alphabet
may appear together in one field of awareness, without any
other witnessing principle or principles beyond the feelings of
the several letters themselves, being supposed to exist. What
each of them witnesses separately, 'all' of them are supposed
to witness in conjunction. But their distributive knowledge
does n't *give rise* to their collective knowledge by any act, it *is*
their collective knowledge. The lower forms of consciousness
'taken together' *are* the higher. It, 'taken apart,' consists of
nothing and *is* nothing but them. This, at least, is the most
obvious way of understanding the doctrine, and is the way I
understood it in the chapter in my psychology.

Superficially looked at, this seems just like the combination
of H_2 and O into water, but looked at more closely, the analogy halts badly. When a chemist tells us that two atoms of
hydrogen and one of oxygen combine themselves of their
own accord into the new compound substance 'water,' he
knows (if he believes in the mechanical view of nature) that
this is only an elliptical statement for a more complex fact.
That fact is that when H_2 and O, instead of keeping far apart,
get into closer quarters, say into the position H-O-H, they

affect surrounding bodies differently: they now wet our skin, dissolve sugar, put out fire, etc., which they did n't in their former positions. 'Water' is but *our name* for what acts thus peculiarly. But if the skin, sugar, and fire were absent, no witness would speak of water at all. He would still talk of the H and O distributively, merely noting that they acted now in the new position H-O-H.

In the older psychologies the soul or self took the place of the sugar, fire, or skin. The lower feelings produced *effects on it*, and their apparent compounds were only its reactions. As you tickle a man's face with a feather, and he laughs, so when you tickle his intellectual principle with a retinal feeling, say, and a muscular feeling at once, it laughs responsively by its category of 'space,' but it would be false to treat the space as simply made of those simpler feelings. It is rather a new and unique psychic creation which their combined action on the mind is able to evoke.

I found myself obliged, in discussing the mind-dust theory, to urge this last alternative view. The so-called mental compounds are simple psychic reactions of a higher type. The form itself of them, I said, is something new. We can't say that awareness of the alphabet as such is nothing more than twenty-six awarenesses, each of a separate letter; for those are twenty-six distinct awarenesses, of single letters *without* others, while their so-called sum is one awareness, of every letter *with* its comrades. There is thus something new in the collective consciousness. It knows the same letters, indeed, but it knows them in this novel way. It is safer, I said (for I fought shy of admitting a self or soul or other agent of combination), to treat the consciousness of the alphabet as a twenty-seventh fact, the substitute and not the sum of the twenty-six simpler consciousnesses, and to say that while under certain physiological conditions they alone are produced, other more complex physiological conditions result in its production instead. Do not talk, therefore, I said, of the higher states *consisting* of the simpler, or *being* the same with them; talk rather of their *knowing the same things*. They are different mental facts, but they apprehend, each in its own peculiar way, the same objective A, B, C, and D.

The theory of combination, I was forced to conclude, is

thus untenable, being both logically nonsensical and practically unnecessary. Say what you will, twelve thoughts, each of a single word, are not the self-same mental thing as one thought of the whole sentence. The higher thoughts, I insisted, are psychic units, not compounds; but for all that, they may know together as a collective multitude the very same objects which under other conditions are known separately by as many simple thoughts.

For many years I held rigorously to this view,[1] and the reasons for doing so seemed to me during all those years to apply also to the opinion that the absolute mind stands to our minds in the relation of a whole to its parts. If untenable in finite psychology, that opinion ought to be untenable in metaphysics also. The great transcendentalist metaphor has always been, as I lately reminded you, a grammatical sentence. Physically such a sentence is of course composed of clauses, these of words, the words of syllables, and the syllables of letters. We may take each word in, yet not understand the sentence; but if suddenly the meaning of the whole sentence flashes, the sense of each word is taken up into that whole meaning. Just so, according to our transcendentalist teachers, the absolute mind thinks the whole sentence, while we, according to our rank as thinkers, think a clause, a word, a syllable, or a letter. Most of us are, as I said, mere syllables in the mouth of Allah. And as Allah comes first in the order of being, so comes first the entire sentence, the *logos* that forms the eternal absolute thought. Students of language tell us that speech began with men's efforts to make *statements*. The rude synthetic vocal utterances first used for this effect slowly got stereotyped, and then much later got decomposed into grammatical parts. It is not as if men had first invented letters and made syllables of them, then made words of the syllables and sentences of the words;—they actually followed the reverse

---

[1] I hold to it still as the best description of an enormous number of our higher fields of consciousness. They demonstrably do not *contain* the lower states that know the same objects. Of other fields, however, this is not so true; so, in the *Psychological Review* for 1895, vol. ii, p. 105 (see especially pp. 119–120), I frankly withdrew, in principle, my former objection to talking of fields of consciousness being made of simpler 'parts,' leaving the facts to decide the question in each special case.

order. So, the transcendentalists affirm, the complete absolute thought is the pre-condition of our thoughts, and we finite creatures *are* only in so far as it owns us as its verbal fragments.

The metaphor is so beautiful, and applies, moreover, so literally to such a multitude of the minor wholes of experience, that by merely hearing it most of us are convinced that it must apply universally. We see that no smallest raindrop can come into being without a whole shower, no single feather without a whole bird, neck and crop, beak and tail, coming into being simultaneously: so we unhesitatingly lay down the law that no part of anything can be except so far as the whole also is. And then, since everything whatever is part of the whole universe, and since (if we are idealists) nothing, whether part or whole, exists except for a witness, we proceed to the conclusion that the unmitigated absolute as witness of the whole is the one sole ground of being of every partial fact, the fact of our own existence included. We think of ourselves as being only a few of the feathers, so to speak, which help to constitute that absolute bird. Extending the analogy of certain wholes, of which we have familiar experience, to the whole of wholes, we easily become absolute idealists.

But if, instead of yielding to the seductions of our metaphor, be it sentence, shower, or bird, we analyze more carefully the notion suggested by it that we are constituent parts of the absolute's eternal field of consciousness, we find grave difficulties arising. First, the difficulty I found with the mind-dust theory. If the absolute makes us by knowing us, how can we exist otherwise than *as* it knows us? But it knows each of us indivisibly from everything else. Yet if to exist means nothing but to be experienced, as idealism affirms, we surely exist otherwise, for we experience *ourselves* ignorantly and in division. We indeed differ from the absolute not only by defect, but by excess. Our ignorances, for example, bring curiosities and doubts by which it cannot be troubled, for it owns eternally the solution of every problem. Our impotence entails pains, our imperfection sins, which its perfection keeps at a distance. What I said of the alphabet-form and the letters holds good of the absolute experience and our experiences.

Their relation, whatever it may be, seems not to be that of identity.

It is impossible to reconcile the peculiarities of our experience with our being only the absolute's mental objects. A God, as distinguished from the absolute, creates things by projecting them beyond himself as so many substances, each endowed with *perseity*, as the scholastics call it. But objects of thought are not things *per se*. They are there only *for* their thinker, and only *as* he thinks them. How, then, can they become severally alive on their own accounts and think themselves quite otherwise than as he thinks them? It is as if the characters in a novel were to get up from the pages, and walk away and transact business of their own outside of the author's story.

A third difficulty is this: The bird-metaphor is physical, but we see on reflection that in the *physical* world there is no real compounding. 'Wholes' are not realities there, parts only are realities. 'Bird' is only our *name* for the physical fact of a certain grouping of organs, just as 'Charles's Wain' is our name for a certain grouping of stars. The 'whole,' be it bird or constellation, is nothing but our vision, nothing but an effect on our sensorium when a lot of things act on it together. It is not realized by any organ or any star, or experienced apart from the consciousness of an onlooker.[1] In the physical world taken by itself there *is* thus no 'all,' there are only the 'eaches'—at least that is the 'scientific' view.

In the mental world, on the contrary, wholes do in point of fact realize themselves *per se*. The meaning of the whole sentence is just as much a real experience as the feeling of each word is; the absolute's experience *is* for itself, as much as yours is for yourself or mine for myself. So the feather-and-bird analogy won't work unless you make the absolute into a distinct sort of mental agent with a vision produced in it *by* our several minds analogous to the 'bird'-vision which the feathers, beak, etc., produce *in* those same minds. The 'whole,' which is *its* experience, would then be its unifying reaction on our experiences, and not those very experiences

[1] I abstract from the consciousness attached to the whole itself, if such consciousness be there.

self-combined. Such a view as this would go with theism, for the theistic God is a separate being; but it would not go with pantheistic idealism, the very essence of which is to insist that we are literally *parts* of God, and he only ourselves in our totality—the word 'ourselves' here standing of course for all the universe's finite facts.

I am dragging you into depths unsuitable, I fear, for a rapid lecture. Such difficulties as these have to be teased out with a needle, so to speak, and lecturers should take only bird's-eye views. The practical upshot of the matter, however, so far as I am concerned, is this, that if I had been lecturing on the absolute a very few years ago, I should unhesitatingly have urged these difficulties, and developed them at still greater length, to show that the hypothesis of the absolute was not only non-coercive from the logical point of view, but self-contradictory as well, its notion that parts and whole are only two names for the same thing not bearing critical scrutiny. If you stick to purely physical terms like stars, there *is* no whole. If you call the whole mental, then the so-called whole, instead of being one fact with the parts, appears rather as the integral reaction on those parts of an independent higher witness, such as the theistic God is supposed to be.

So long as this was the state of my own mind, I could accept the notion of self-compounding in the supernal spheres of experience no more easily than in that chapter on mind-dust I had accepted it in the lower spheres. I found myself compelled, therefore, to call the absolute impossible; and the untrammelled freedom with which pantheistic or monistic idealists stepped over the logical barriers which Lotze and others had set down long before I had—I had done little more than quote these previous critics in my chapter—surprised me not a little, and made me, I have to confess, both resentful and envious. Envious because in the bottom of my heart I wanted the same freedom myself, for motives which I shall develop later; and resentful because my absolutist friends seemed to me to be stealing the privilege of blowing both hot and cold. To establish their absolute they used an intellectualist type of logic which they disregarded when employed against it. It seemed to me that they ought at least to have mentioned the objections that had stopped me so completely. I had yielded to them against my 'will to believe,' out of pure logical scrupulosity. They, professing to loathe the will to believe and to follow purest rationality, had simply ignored them. The method was easy, but hardly to be called candid. Fechner indeed was candid enough, for he had never thought of the objections, but later writers, like Royce, who should presumably have heard them, had passed them by in silence. I felt as if these philosophers were granting their will to believe in monism too easy a license. My own conscience would permit me no such license.

So much for the personal confession by which you have allowed me to introduce the subject. Let us now consider it more objectively.

The fundamental difficulty I have found is the number of contradictions which idealistic monists seem to disregard. In the first place they attribute to all existence a mental or experiential character, but I find their simultaneous belief that the higher and the lower in the universe are entitatively identical, incompatible with this character. Incompatible in consequence of the generally accepted doctrine that, whether Berkeley were right or not in saying of material existence that its *esse* is *sentiri*, it is undoubtedly right to say of *mental* existence that its *esse* is *sentiri* or *experiri*. If I feel pain, it is just pain that I feel, however I may have come by the feeling. No one pretends that pain as such only appears like pain, but in itself is different, for to be as a mental experience *is* only to appear to some one.

The idealists in question ought then to do one of two things, but they do neither. They ought either to refute the notion that as mental states appear, so they are; or, still keeping that notion, they ought to admit a distinct agent of unification to do the work of the all-knower, just as our respective souls or selves in popular philosophy do the work of partial knowers. Otherwise we have a joint-stock company all shareholders and no treasurer or manager. If our finite minds formed a billion facts, then its mind, knowing our billion, would make a universe composed of a billion and one facts. But transcendental idealism is quite as unfriendly to active principles called souls as physiological psychology is, Kant having, as it thinks, definitively demolished them. And altho some disciples speak of the transcendental ego of apperception (which they celebrate as Kant's most precious legacy to posterity) as if it were a combining agent, the drift of monistic authority is certainly in the direction of treating it as only an all-witness, whose field of vision we finite witnesses do not cause, but constitute rather. We are the letters, it is the alphabet; we are the features, it is the face; not indeed as if either alphabet or face were something additional to the letters or the features, but rather as if it were only another name for the very letters or features themselves. The all-form assuredly differs from the each-form, but the *matter* is the same in both, and the each-form only an unaccountable appearance.

But this, as you see, contradicts the other idealist principle, of a mental fact being just what it appears to be. If their forms of appearance are so different, the all and the eaches cannot be identical.

The way out (unless, indeed, we are willing to discard the logic of identity altogether) would seem to be frankly to write down the all and the eaches as two distinct orders of witness, each minor witness being aware of its own 'content' solely, while the greater witness knows the minor witnesses, knows their whole content pooled together, knows their relations to one another, and knows of just how much each one of them is ignorant.

The two types of witnessing are here palpably non-identical. We get a pluralism, not a monism, out of them. In my psychology-chapter I had resorted openly to such pluralism, treating each total field of consciousness as a distinct entity, and maintaining that the higher fields merely supersede the lower functionally by knowing more about the same objects.

The monists themselves writhe like worms on the hook to escape pluralistic or at least dualistic language, but they cannot escape it. They speak of the eternal and the temporal 'points of view'; of the universe in its infinite 'aspect' or in its finite 'capacity'; they say that '*quâ* absolute' it is one thing, '*quâ* relative' another; they contrast its 'truth' with its 'appearances'; they distinguish the total from the partial way of 'taking' it, etc.; but they forget that, on idealistic principles, to make such distinctions is tantamount to making different beings, or at any rate that varying points of view, aspects, appearances, ways of taking, and the like, are meaningless phrases unless we suppose outside of the unchanging content of reality a diversity of witnesses who experience or take it variously, the absolute mind being just the witness that takes it most completely.

For consider the matter one moment longer, if you can. Ask what this notion implies, of appearing differently from different points of view. If there be no outside witness, a thing can appear only to itself, the eaches or parts to their several selves temporally, the all or whole to itself eternally. Different 'selves' thus break out inside of what the absolutist insists to be intrinsically one fact. But how can what is *actually* one be *effectively* so many? Put your witnesses anywhere, whether outside or inside of what is witnessed, in the last resort your witnesses must on idealistic principles be distinct, for what is witnessed is different.

I fear that I am expressing myself with terrible obscurity— some of you, I know, are groaning over the logic-chopping. Be a pluralist or be a monist, you say, for heaven's sake, no matter which, so long as you stop arguing. It reminds one of Chesterton's epigram that the only thing that ever drives human beings insane is logic. But whether I be sane or insane, you cannot fail, even tho you be transcendentalists yourselves, to recognize to some degree by my trouble the difficulties that beset monistic idealism. What boots it to call the parts and the whole the same body of experience, when in the same breath you have to say that the all 'as such' means one sort of experience and each part 'as such' means another?

Difficulties, then, so far, but no stable solution as yet, for I have been talking only critically. You will probably be relieved to hear, then, that having rounded this corner, I shall begin to consider what may be the possibilities of getting farther.

To clear the path, I beg you first to note one point. What has so troubled my logical conscience is not so much the absolute by itself as the whole class of suppositions of which it is the supreme example, collective experiences namely, claiming identity with their constituent parts, yet experiencing things quite differently from these latter. If *any* such collective experience can be, then of course, so far as the mere logic of the case goes, the absolute may be. In a previous lecture I have talked against the absolute from other points of view. In this lecture I have meant merely to take it as the example most prominent at Oxford of the thing which has given me such logical perplexity. I don't logically see how a collective experience of any grade whatever can be treated as logically identical with a lot of distributive experiences. They form two different concepts. The absolute happens to be the only collective experience concerning which Oxford idealists have urged the identity, so I took it as my prerogative instance. But Fechner's earth-soul, or any stage of being below or above that, would have served my purpose just as well: the same logical objection applies to these collective experiences as to the absolute.

So much, then, in order that you may not be confused about my strategical objective. The real point to defend against the logic that I have used is the identity of the collective and distributive anyhow, not the particular example of such identity known as the absolute.

So now for the directer question. Shall we say that every complex mental fact is a separate psychic entity *succeeding upon* a lot of other psychic entities which are erroneously called its parts, and superseding them in function, but not literally being composed of them? This was the course I took in my psychology; and if followed in theology, we should have to deny the absolute as usually conceived, and replace it by the 'God' of theism. We should also have to deny Fechner's 'earth-soul' and all other superhuman collections of experience of every grade, so far at least as these are held to be compounded of our simpler souls in the way which Fechner believed in; and we should have to make all these denials in the name of the incorruptible logic of self-identity, teaching us that to call a thing and its other the same is to commit the crime of self-contradiction.

But if we realize the whole philosophic situation thus produced, we see that it is almost intolerable. Loyal to the logical kind of rationality, it is disloyal to every other kind. It makes the universe discontinuous. These fields of experience that replace each other so punctually, each knowing the same matter, but in ever-widening contexts, from simplest feeling up to absolute knowledge, *can* they have no *being* in common when their cognitive function is so manifestly common? The regular succession of them is on such terms an unintelligible miracle. If you reply that their common *object* is of itself enough to make the many witnesses continuous, the same implacable logic follows you—how *can* one and the same object appear so variously? Its diverse appearances break it into a plurality; and our world of objects then falls into discontinuous pieces quite as much as did our world of subjects. The resultant irrationality is really intolerable.

I said awhile ago that I was envious of Fechner and the other pantheists because I myself wanted the same freedom that I saw them unscrupulously enjoying, of letting mental fields compound themselves and so make the universe more continuous, but that my conscience held me prisoner. In my heart of hearts, however, I knew that my situation was absurd and could be only provisional. That secret of a continuous life which the universe knows by heart and acts on every instant cannot be a contradiction incarnate. If logic says it is one, so much the worse for logic. Logic being the lesser thing, the static incomplete abstraction, must succumb to reality, not reality to logic. Our intelligence cannot wall itself up alive, like a pupa in its chrysalis. It must at any cost keep on speaking terms with the universe that engendered it. Fechner, Royce, and Hegel seem on the truer path. Fechner has never heard of logic's veto, Royce hears the voice but cannily ignores the utterances, Hegel hears them but to spurn them—and all go on their way rejoicing. Shall we alone obey the veto?

Sincerely, and patiently as I could, I struggled with the problem for years, covering hundreds of sheets of paper with notes and memoranda and discussions with myself over the difficulty. How can many consciousnesses be at the same time one consciousness? How can one and the same identical fact experience itself so diversely? The struggle was vain; I found myself in an *impasse*. I saw that I must either forswear that 'psychology without a soul' to which my whole psychological and kantian education had committed me,—I must, in short, bring back distinct spiritual agents to know the mental states, now singly and now in combination, in a word bring back scholasticism and common sense—or else I must squarely confess the solution of the problem impossible, and then either give up my intellectualistic logic, the logic of identity, and adopt some higher (or lower) form of rationality, or, finally, face the fact that life is logically irrational.

Sincerely, this is the actual trilemma that confronts every one of us. Those of you who are scholastic-minded, or simply common-sense minded, will smile at the elaborate groans of my parturient mountain resulting in nothing but this mouse. Accept the spiritual agents, for heaven's sake, you will say, and leave off your ridiculous pedantry. Let but our 'souls' combine our sensations by their intellectual faculties, and let but 'God' replace the pantheistic world-soul, and your wheels will go round again—you will enjoy both life and logic together.

This solution is obvious and I know that many of you will adopt it. It is comfortable, and all our habits of speech support it. Yet it is not for idle or fantastical reasons that the notion of the substantial soul, so freely used by common men and the more popular philosophies, has fallen upon such evil days, and has no prestige in the eyes of critical thinkers. It only shares the fate of other unrepresentable substances and principles. They are without exception all so barren that to sincere inquirers they appear as little more than names masquerading—Wo die begriffe fehlen da stellt ein wort zur rechten zeit sich ein. You see no deeper into the fact that a hundred sensations get compounded or known together by thinking that a 'soul' does the compounding than you see into a man's living eighty years by calling him a predestined octogenarian, or into our having five fingers by calling us pentadactyls. Souls have worn out both themselves and their welcome, that is the plain truth. Philosophy ought to get the manifolds of experience unified on principles less empty. Like the word 'cause,' the word 'soul' is but a theoretic stop-gap—it marks a place and claims it for a future explanation to occupy.

This being our post-humian and post-kantian state of mind, I will ask your permission to leave the soul wholly out of the present discussion and to consider only the residual dilemma. Some day, indeed, souls may get their innings again in philosophy—I am quite ready to admit that possibility—

they form a category of thought too natural to the human mind to expire without prolonged resistance. But if the belief in the soul ever does come to life after the many funeral-discourses which humian and kantian criticism have preached over it, I am sure it will be only when some one has found in the term a pragmatic significance that has hitherto eluded observation. When that champion speaks, as he well may speak some day, it will be time to consider souls more seriously.

Let us leave out the soul, then, and confront what I just called the residual dilemma. Can we, on the one hand, give up the logic of identity?—can we, on the other, believe human experience to be fundamentally irrational? Neither is easy, yet it would seem that we must do one or the other.

Few philosophers have had the frankness fairly to admit the necessity of choosing between the 'horns' offered. Reality must be rational, they have said, and since the ordinary intellectualist logic is the only usual test of rationality, reality and logic must agree 'somehow.' Hegel was the first non-mystical writer to face the dilemma squarely and throw away the ordinary logic, saving a pseudo-rationality for the universe by inventing the higher logic of the 'dialectic process.' Bradley holds to the intellectualist logic, and by dint of it convicts the human universe of being irrationality incarnate. But what must be and can be, is, he says; there must and can be relief from *that* irrationality; and the absolute must already have got the relief in secret ways of its own, impossible for us to guess at. *We* of course get no relief, so Bradley's is a rather ascetic doctrine. Royce and Taylor accept similar solutions, only they emphasize the irrationality of our finite universe less than Bradley does; and Royce in particular, being unusually 'thick' for an idealist, tries to bring the absolute's secret forms of relief more sympathetically home to our imagination.

Well, what must we do in this tragic predicament? For my own part, I have finally found myself compelled to *give up the logic*, fairly, squarely, and irrevocably. It has an imperishable use in human life, but that use is not to make us theoretically acquainted with the essential nature of reality—just what it is I can perhaps suggest to you a little later. Reality, life, experience, concreteness, immediacy, use what word you will, exceeds our logic, overflows and surrounds it. If you like to employ words eulogistically, as most men do, and so encourage confusion, you may say that reality obeys a higher logic, or enjoys a higher rationality. But I think that even eulogistic words should be used rather to distinguish than to commingle meanings, so I prefer bluntly to call reality if not irrational then at least non-rational in its constitution,—and by reality here I mean reality where things *happen*, all temporal reality without exception. I myself find no good warrant for even suspecting the existence of any reality of a higher denomination than that distributed and strung-along and flowing sort of reality which we finite beings swim in. That is the sort of reality given us, and that is the sort with which logic is so incommensurable. If there be any higher sort of reality—the 'absolute,' for example—that sort, by the confession of those who believe in it, is still less amenable to ordinary logic; it transcends logic and is therefore still less rational in the intellectualist sense, so it cannot help us to save our logic as an adequate definer and confiner of existence.

These sayings will sound queer and dark, probably they will sound quite wild or childish in the absence of explanatory comment. Only the persuasion that I soon can explain them, if not satisfactorily to all of you, at least intelligibly, emboldens me to state them thus baldly as a sort of programme. Please take them as a thesis, therefore, to be defended by later pleading.

I told you that I had long and sincerely wrestled with the dilemma. I have now to confess (and this will probably reanimate your interest) that I should not now be emancipated, not now subordinate logic with so very light a heart, or throw it out of the deeper regions of philosophy to take its rightful and respectable place in the world of simple human practice, if I had not been influenced by a comparatively young and very original french writer, Professor Henri Bergson. Reading his works is what has made me bold. If I had not read Bergson, I should probably still be blackening endless pages of paper privately, in the hope of making ends meet that were never meant to meet, and trying to discover some mode of conceiving the behavior of reality which should leave no discrepancy between it and the accepted laws of the logic of identity. It is certain, at any rate, that without the confidence which being able to lean on Bergson's authority gives me I should never have ventured to urge these particular views of mine upon this ultra-critical audience.

I must therefore, in order to make my own views more intelligible, give some preliminary account of the bergsonian philosophy. But here, as in Fechner's case, I must confine myself only to the features that are essential to the present purpose, and not entangle you in collateral details, however interesting otherwise. For our present purpose, then, the essential contribution of Bergson to philosophy is his criticism of intellectualism. In my opinion he has killed intellectualism definitively and without hope of recovery. I don't see how it can ever revive again in its ancient platonizing rôle of claiming to be the most authentic, intimate, and exhaustive definer of the nature of reality. Others, as Kant for example, have denied intellectualism's pretensions to define reality *an sich* or in its absolute capacity; but Kant still leaves it laying down laws—and laws from which there is no appeal—to all our human experience; while what Bergson denies is that its methods give any adequate account of this human experience in its very finiteness. Just how Bergson accomplishes all this I must try to tell in my imperfect way in the next lecture; but since I have already used the words 'logic,' 'logic of identity,' 'intellectualistic logic,' and 'intellectualism' so often, and sometimes used them as if they required no particular explanation, it will be wise at this point to say at greater length than heretofore in what sense I take these terms when I claim that Bergson has refuted their pretension to decide what reality can or cannot be. Just what I mean by intellectualism is therefore what I shall try to give a fuller idea of during the remainder of this present hour.

In recent controversies some participants have shown resentment at being classed as intellectualists. I mean to use the word disparagingly, but shall be sorry if it works offence. Intellectualism has its source in the faculty which gives us our chief superiority to the brutes, our power, namely, of translating the crude flux of our merely feeling-experience into a conceptual order. An immediate experience, as yet unnamed or classed, is a mere *that* that we undergo, a thing that asks, '*What* am I?' When we name and class it, we say for the first time what it is, and all these whats are abstract names or concepts. Each concept means a particular *kind* of thing, and as things seem once for all to have been created in kinds, a far more efficient handling of a given bit of experience begins as soon as we have classed the various parts of it. Once classed, a thing can be treated by the law of its class, and the advantages are endless. Both theoretically and practically this power of framing abstract concepts is one of the sublimest of our human prerogatives. We come back into the concrete from our journey into these abstractions, with an increase both of vision and of power. It is no wonder that earlier thinkers, forgetting that concepts are only man-made extracts from the temporal flux, should have ended by treating them as a superior type of being, bright, changeless, true, divine, and utterly opposed in nature to the turbid, restless lower world. The latter then appears as but their corruption and falsification.

Intellectualism in the vicious sense began when Socrates and Plato taught that what a thing really is, is told us by its *definition*. Ever since Socrates we have been taught that reality consists of essences, not of appearances, and that the essences of things are known whenever we know their definitions. So first we identify the thing with a concept and then we identify the concept with a definition, and only then, inasmuch as the thing *is* whatever the definition expresses, are we sure of apprehending the real essence of it or the full truth about it.

So far no harm is done. The misuse of concepts begins with the habit of employing them privatively as well as positively, using them not merely to assign properties to things, but to deny the very properties with which the things sensibly present themselves. Logic can extract all its possible consequences from any definition, and the logician who is *unerbittlich consequent* is often tempted, when he cannot extract a certain property from a definition, to deny that the concrete object to which the definition applies can possibly possess that property. The definition that fails to yield it must exclude or negate it. This is Hegel's regular method of establishing his system.

It is but the old story, of a useful practice first becoming a method, then a habit, and finally a tyranny that defeats the end it was used for. Concepts, first employed to make things intelligible, are clung to even when they make them unintelligible. Thus it comes that when once you have conceived things as 'independent,' you must proceed to deny the possibility of any connexion whatever among them, because the notion of connexion is not contained in the definition of independence. For a like reason you must deny any possible forms or modes of unity among things which you have begun by defining as a 'many.' We have cast a glance at Hegel's and Bradley's use of this sort of reasoning, and you will remember Sigwart's epigram that according to it a horseman can never in his life go on foot, or a photographer ever wash his hands, or do anything but photograph.

The classic extreme in this direction is the denial of the possibility of change, and the consequent branding of the world of change as unreal, by certain philosophers. The definition of A is changeless, so is the definition of B. The one definition cannot change into the other, so the notion that a concrete thing A should change into another concrete thing B is made out to be contrary to reason. In Mr. Bradley's difficulty in seeing how sugar can be sweet intellectualism outstrips itself and becomes openly a sort of verbalism. Sugar is just sugar and sweet is just sweet; neither is the other; nor can the word 'is' ever be understood to join any subject to its predicate rationally. Nothing 'between' things can connect them, for 'between' is just that third thing, 'between,' and would need itself to be connected to the first and second things by two still finer betweens, and so on ad infinitum.

The particular intellectualistic difficulty that had held my own thought so long in a vise was, as we have seen at such tedious length, the impossibility of understanding how 'your' experience and 'mine,' which 'as such' are defined as not conscious of each other, can nevertheless at the same time be members of a world-experience defined expressly as having all its parts co-conscious, or known together. The definitions are contradictory, so the things defined can in no way be united. You see how unintelligible intellectualism here seems to make the world of our most accomplished philosophers. Neither as they use it nor as we use it does it do anything but make nature look irrational and seem impossible.

In my next lecture, using Bergson as my principal topic, I shall enter into more concrete details and try, by giving up intellectualism frankly, to make, if not the world, at least my own general thesis, less unintelligible.

LECTURE VI

I GAVE YOU a very stiff lecture last time, and I fear that this one can be little less so. The best way of entering into it will be to begin immediately with Bergson's philosophy, since I told you that that was what had led me personally to renounce the intellectualistic method and the current notion that logic is an adequate measure of what can or cannot be.

Professor Henri Bergson is a young man, comparatively, as influential philosophers go, having been born at Paris in 1859. His career has been the perfectly routine one of a successful french professor. Entering the école normale supérieure at the age of twenty-two, he spent the next seventeen years teaching at *lycées*, provincial or parisian, until his fortieth year, when he was made professor at the said école normale. Since 1900 he has been professor at the Collège de France, and member of the Institute since 1900.

So far as the outward facts go, Bergson's career has then been commonplace to the utmost. Neither one of Taine's famous principles of explanation of great men, *the race, the environment, or the moment*, no, nor all three together, will explain that peculiar way of looking at things that constitutes his mental individuality. Originality in men dates from nothing previous, other things date from it, rather. I have to confess that Bergson's originality is so profuse that many of his ideas baffle me entirely. I doubt whether any one understands him all over, so to speak; and I am sure that he would himself be the first to see that this must be, and to confess that things which he himself has not yet thought out clearly, had yet to be mentioned and have a tentative place assigned them in his philosophy. Many of us are profusely original, in that no man can understand us—violently peculiar ways of looking at things are no great rarity. The rarity is when great peculiarity of vision is allied with great lucidity and unusual command of all the classic expository apparatus. Bergson's resources in the way of erudition are remarkable, and in the way of expression they are simply phenomenal. This is why in France, where *l'art de bien dire* counts for so much and is so sure of appreciation, he has immediately taken so eminent a place in public esteem. Old-fashioned professors, whom his ideas quite fail to satisfy, nevertheless speak of his talent almost with bated breath, while the youngsters flock to him as to a master.

If anything can make hard things easy to follow, it is a style like Bergson's. A 'straightforward' style, an american reviewer lately called it; failing to see that such straightforwardness means a flexibility of verbal resource that follows the thought without a crease or wrinkle, as elastic silk underclothing follows the movements of one's body. The lucidity of Bergson's way of putting things is what all readers are first struck by. It seduces you and bribes you in advance to become his disciple. It is a miracle, and he a real magician.

M. Bergson, if I am rightly informed, came into philosophy through the gateway of mathematics. The old antinomies of the infinite were, I imagine, the irritant that first woke his faculties from their dogmatic slumber. You all remember Zeno's famous paradox, or sophism, as many of our logic books still call it, of Achilles and the tortoise. Give that reptile ever so small an advance and the swift runner Achilles can never overtake him, much less get ahead of him; for if space and time are infinitely divisible (as our intellects tell us they must be), by the time Achilles reaches the tortoise's starting-point, the tortoise has already got ahead of *that* starting-point, and so on *ad infinitum*, the interval between the pursuer and the pursued growing endlessly minuter, but never becoming wholly obliterated. The common way of showing up the sophism here is by pointing out the ambiguity of the expression 'never can overtake.' What the word 'never' falsely suggests, it is said, is an infinite duration of time; what it really means is the inexhaustible number of the steps of which the overtaking must consist. But if these steps are infinitely short, a finite time will suffice for them; and in point of fact they do rapidly converge, whatever be the original interval or the contrasted speeds, toward infinitesimal shortness. This proportionality of the shortness of the times to that of the spaces required frees us, it is claimed, from the sophism which the word 'never' suggests.

But this criticism misses Zeno's point entirely. Zeno would have been perfectly willing to grant that if the tortoise can be overtaken at all, he can be overtaken in (say) twenty seconds, but he would still have insisted that he can't be overtaken at all. Leave Achilles and the tortoise out of the account altogether, he would have said—they complicate the case unnecessarily. Take any single process of change whatever, take the twenty seconds themselves elapsing. If time be infinitely divisible, and it must be so on intellectualist principles, they simply cannot elapse, their end cannot be reached; for no matter how much of them has already elapsed, before the remainder, however minute, can have wholly elapsed, the earlier half of it must first have elapsed. And this ever re-arising need of making the earlier half elapse *first* leaves time with always something to do *before* the last thing is done, so that the last thing never gets done. Expressed in bare numbers, it is like the convergent series ½ plus ¼ plus ⅛ . . . , of which the limit is one. But this limit, simply because it is a limit, stands outside the series, the value of which approaches it indefinitely but never touches it. If in the natural world there were no other way of getting things save by such successive addition of their logically involved fractions, no complete units or whole things would ever come into being, for the fractions' sum would always leave a remainder. But in point of fact nature does n't make eggs by making first half an egg, then a quarter, then an eighth, etc., and adding them together. She either makes a whole egg at once or none at all, and so of all her other units. It is only in the sphere of change, then, where one phase of a thing must needs come into being before another phase can come that Zeno's paradox gives trouble.

And it gives trouble then only if the succession of steps of change be infinitely divisible. If a bottle had to be emptied by an infinite number of successive decrements, it is mathematically impossible that the emptying should ever positively terminate. In point of fact, however, bottles and coffee-pots empty themselves by a finite number of decrements, each of definite amount. Either a whole drop emerges or nothing emerges from the spout. If all change went thus drop-wise, so to speak, if real time sprouted or grew by units of duration of determinate amount, just as our perceptions of it grow by pulses, there would be no zenonian paradoxes or kantian antinomies to trouble us. All our sensible experiences, as we get them immediately, do thus change by discrete pulses of perception, each of which keeps us saying 'more, more, more,' or 'less, less, less,' as the definite increments or diminutions make themselves felt. The discreteness is still more obvious when, instead of old things changing, they cease, or when altogether new things come. Fechner's term of the 'threshold,' which has played such a part in the psychology of perception, is only one way of naming the quantitative discreteness in the change of all our sensible experiences. They come to us in drops. Time itself comes in drops.

Our ideal decomposition of the drops which are all that we feel into still finer fractions is but an incident in that great transformation of the perceptual order into a conceptual order of which I spoke in my last lecture. It is made in the interest of our rationalizing intellect solely. The times directly *felt* in the experiences of living subjects have originally no common measure. Let a lump of sugar melt in a glass, to use one of M. Bergson's instances. We feel the time to be long while waiting for the process to end, but who knows how long or how short it feels to the sugar? All *felt* times coexist and overlap or compenetrate each other thus vaguely, but the artifice of plotting them on a common scale helps us to reduce their aboriginal confusion, and it helps us still more to plot, against the same scale, the successive possible steps into which nature's various changes may be resolved, either sensibly or conceivably. We thus straighten out the aboriginal privacy and vagueness, and can date things publicly, as it were, and by each other. The notion of one objective and 'evenly flowing' time, cut into numbered instants, applies itself as a common measure to all the steps and phases, no matter how many, into which we cut the processes of nature. They are now definitely contemporary, or later or earlier one than another, and we can handle them mathematically, as we say, and far better, practically as well as theoretically, for having thus correlated them one to one with each other on the common schematic or conceptual time-scale.

Motion, to take a good example, is originally a turbid

sensation, of which the native shape is perhaps best preserved in the phenomenon of vertigo. In vertigo we feel that movement *is*, and is more or less violent or rapid, more or less in this direction or that, more or less alarming or sickening. But a man subject to vertigo may gradually learn to co-ordinate his felt motion with his real position and that of other things, and intellectualize it enough to succeed at last in walking without staggering. The mathematical mind similarly organizes motion in its way, putting it into a logical definition: motion is now conceived as 'the occupancy of serially successive points of space at serially successive instants of time.' With such a definition we escape wholly from the turbid privacy of sense. But do we not also escape from sense-reality altogether? Whatever motion really may be, it surely is not static; but the definition we have gained is of the absolutely static. It gives a set of one-to-one relations between space-points and time-points, which relations themselves are as fixed as the points are. It gives *positions* assignable ad infinitum, but how the body gets from one position to another it omits to mention. The body gets there by moving, of course; but the conceived positions, however numerously multiplied, contain no element of movement, so Zeno, using nothing but them in his discussion, has no alternative but to say that our intellect repudiates motion as a non-reality. Intellectualism here does what I said it does—it makes experience less instead of more intelligible.

We of course need a stable scheme of concepts, stably related with one another, to lay hold of our experiences and to co-ordinate them withal. When an experience comes with sufficient saliency to stand out, we keep the thought of it for future use, and store it in our conceptual system. What does not of itself stand out, we learn to *cut* out; so the system grows completer, and new reality, as it comes, gets named after and conceptually strung upon this or that element of it which we have already established. The immutability of such an abstract system is its great practical merit; the same identical terms and relations in it can always be recovered and referred to—change itself is just such an unalterable concept. But all these abstract concepts are but as flowers gathered, they are only moments dipped out from the stream of time, snap-shots taken, as by a kinetoscopic camera, at a life that in its original coming is continuous. Useful as they are as samples of the garden, or to re-enter the stream with, or to insert in our revolving lantern, they have no value but these practical values. You cannot explain by them what makes any single phenomenon be or go—you merely dot out the path of appearances which it traverses. For you cannot make continuous being out of discontinuities, and your concepts are discontinuous. The stages into which you analyze a change are *states*, the change itself goes on between them. It lies along their intervals, inhabits what your definition fails to gather up, and thus eludes conceptual explanation altogether.

'When the mathematician,' Bergson writes, 'calculates the state of a system at the end of a time *t*, nothing need prevent him from supposing that betweenwhiles the universe vanishes, in order suddenly to appear again at the due moment in the new configuration. It is only the *t*-th moment that counts—that which flows throughout the intervals, namely real time, plays no part in his calculation. . . . In short, the world on which the mathematician operates is a world which dies and is born anew at every instant, like the world which Descartes thought of when he spoke of a continued creation.' To know adequately what really *happens* we ought, Bergson insists, to see into the intervals, but the mathematician sees only their extremities. He fixes only a few results, he dots a curve and then interpolates, he substitutes a tracing for a reality.

This being so undeniably the case, the history of the way in which philosophy has dealt with it is curious. The ruling tradition in philosophy has always been the platonic and aristotelian belief that fixity is a nobler and worthier thing than change. Reality must be one and unalterable. Concepts, being themselves fixities, agree best with this fixed nature of truth, so that for any knowledge of ours to be quite true it must be knowledge by universal concepts rather than by particular experiences, for these notoriously are mutable and corruptible. This is the tradition known as rationalism in philosophy, and what I have called intellectualism is only the extreme application of it. In spite of sceptics and empiricists, in spite of Protagoras, Hume, and James Mill, rationalism has never been seriously questioned, for its sharpest critics have always had a

tender place in their hearts for it, and have obeyed some of
its mandates. They have not been consistent; they have played
fast and loose with the enemy; and Bergson alone has been
radical.

To show what I mean by this, let me contrast his procedure
with that of some of the transcendentalist philosophers whom
I have lately mentioned. Coming after Kant, these pique
themselves on being 'critical,' on building in fact upon Kant's
'critique' of pure reason. What that critique professed to establish was this, that concepts do not apprehend reality, but
only such appearances as our senses feed out to them. They
give immutable intellectual forms to these appearances, it is
true, but the reality *an sich* from which in ultimate resort the
sense-appearances have to come remains forever unintelligible
to our intellect. Take motion, for example. Sensibly, motion
comes in drops, waves, or pulses; either some actual amount
of it, or none, being apprehended. This amount is the datum
or *gabe* which reality feeds out to our intellectual faculty; but
our intellect makes of it a task or *aufgabe*—this pun is one of
the most memorable of Kant's formulas—and insists that in
every pulse of it an infinite number of successive minor pulses
shall be ascertainable. These minor pulses *we* can indeed *go
on* to ascertain or to compute indefinitely if we have patience;
but it would contradict the definition of an infinite number
to suppose the endless series of them to have actually counted
themselves out piecemeal. Zeno made this manifest; so the infinity which our intellect requires of the sense-datum is thus
a future and potential rather than a past and actual infinity of
structure. The datum after it has made itself must be decom-
pos*able* ad infinitum by our conception, but of the steps by
which that structure actually got composed we know nothing.
Our intellect casts, in short, no ray of light on the processes
by which experiences *get made*.

Kant's monistic successors have in general found the data
of immediate experience even more self-contradictory, when
intellectually treated, than Kant did. Not only the character
of infinity involved in the relation of various empirical data to
their 'conditions,' but the very notion that empirical things
should be related to one another at all, has seemed to them,
when the intellectualistic fit was upon them, full of paradox

and contradiction. We saw in a former lecture numerous instances of this from Hegel, Bradley, Royce, and others. We saw also where the solution of such an intolerable state of things was sought for by these authors. Whereas Kant had placed it outside of and *before* our experience, in the *dinge an sich* which are the causes of the latter, his monistic successors all look for it either *after* experience, as its absolute completion, or else consider it to be even now implicit within experience as its ideal signification. Kant and his successors look, in short, in diametrically opposite directions. Do not be misled by Kant's admission of theism into his system. His God is the ordinary dualistic God of Christianity, to whom his philosophy simply opens the door; he has nothing whatsoever in common with the 'absolute spirit' set up by his successors. So far as this absolute spirit is logically derived from Kant, it is not from his God, but from entirely different elements of his philosophy. First from his notion that an unconditioned totality of the conditions of any experience must be assignable; and then from his other notion that the presence of some witness, or ego of apperception, is the most universal of all the conditions in question. The post-kantians make of the witness-condition what is called a concrete universal, an individualized all-witness or world-self, which shall imply in its rational constitution each and all of the other conditions put together, and therefore necessitate each and all of the conditioned experiences.

Abridgments like this of other men's opinions are very unsatisfactory, they always work injustice; but in this case those of you who are familiar with the literature will see immediately what I have in mind; and to the others, if there be any here, it will suffice to say that what I am trying so pedantically to point out is only the fact that monistic idealists after Kant have invariably sought relief from the supposed contradictions of our world of sense by looking forward toward an *ens rationis* conceived as its integration or logical completion, while he looked backward toward non-rational *dinge an sich* conceived as its cause. Pluralistic empiricists, on the other hand, have remained in the world of sense, either naïvely and because they overlooked the intellectualistic contradictions, or because, not able to ignore them, they thought they could refute them by a superior use of the same intellectualistic logic. Thus it is that John Mill pretends to refute the Achilles-tortoise fallacy.

The important point to notice here is the intellectualist logic. Both sides treat it as authoritative, but they do so capriciously: the absolutists smashing the world of sense by its means, the empiricists smashing the absolute—for the absolute, they say, is the quintessence of all logical contradictions. Neither side attains consistency. The Hegelians have to invoke a higher logic to supersede the purely destructive efforts of their first logic. The empiricists use their logic against the absolute, but refuse to use it against finite experience. Each party uses it or drops it to suit the vision it has faith in, but neither impugns in principle its general theoretic authority.

Bergson alone challenges its theoretic authority in principle. He alone denies that mere conceptual logic can tell us what is impossible or possible in the world of being or fact; and he does so for reasons which at the same time that they rule logic out from lordship over the whole of life, establish a vast and definite sphere of influence where its sovereignty is indisputable. Bergson's own text, felicitous as it is, is too intricate for quotation, so I must use my own inferior words in explaining what I mean by saying this.

In the first place, logic, giving primarily the relations between concepts as such, and the relations between natural facts only secondarily or so far as the facts have been already identified with concepts and defined by them, must of course stand or fall with the conceptual method. But the conceptual method is a transformation which the flux of life undergoes at our hands in the interests of practice essentially and only subordinately in the interests of theory. We live forward, we understand backward, said a danish writer; and to understand life by concepts is to arrest its movement, cutting it up into bits as if with scissors, and immobilizing these in our logical herbarium where, comparing them as dried specimens, we can ascertain which of them statically includes or excludes which other. This treatment supposes life to have already accomplished itself, for the concepts, being so many views taken after the fact, are retrospective and post mortem. Nevertheless we can draw conclusions from them and project them into the future. We cannot learn from them how life made itself go, or how it will make itself go; but, on the supposition that its ways of making itself go are unchanging, we can calculate what positions of imagined arrest it will exhibit hereafter under given conditions. We can compute, for instance, at what point Achilles will be, and where the tortoise will be, at the end of the twentieth minute. Achilles may then be at a point far ahead; but the full detail of how he will have managed practically to get there our logic never gives us—we have seen, indeed, that it finds that its results contradict the facts of nature. The computations which the other sciences make differ in no respect from those of mathematics. The concepts used are all of them dots through which, by interpolation or extrapolation, curves are drawn, while along the curves other dots are found as consequences. The latest refinements of logic dispense with the curves altogether, and deal solely with the dots and their correspondences each to each in various series. The authors of these recent improvements tell us expressly that their aim is to abolish the last vestiges of intuition, *videlicet* of concrete reality, from the field of reasoning, which then will operate literally on mental dots or bare abstract units of discourse, and on the ways in which they may be strung in naked series.

This is all very esoteric, and my own understanding of it is most likely misunderstanding. So I speak here only by way of brief reminder to those who know. For the rest of us it is enough to recognize this fact, that altho by means of concepts cut out from the sensible flux of the past, we can re-descend upon the future flux and, making another cut, say what particular thing is likely to be found there; and that altho in this sense concepts give us knowledge, and may be said to have some theoretic value (especially when the particular thing foretold is one in which we take no present practical interest); yet in the deeper sense of giving *insight* they have no theoretic value, for they quite fail to connect us with the inner life of the flux, or with the causes that govern its direction. Instead of being interpreters of reality, concepts negate the inwardness of reality altogether. They make the whole notion of a causal influence between finite things incomprehensible. No real activities and indeed no real connexions of any kind can obtain if we follow the conceptual logic; for to be distinguishable, according to what I call intellectualism, is to be incapable of connexion. The work begun by Zeno, and continued by Hume, Kant, Herbart, Hegel, and Bradley, does not stop till sensible reality lies entirely disintegrated at the feet of 'reason.'

Of the 'absolute' reality which reason proposes to substitute for sensible reality I shall have more to say presently. Meanwhile you see what Professor Bergson means by insisting that the function of the intellect is practical rather than theoretical. Sensible reality is too concrete to be entirely manageable— look at the narrow range of it which is all that any animal, living in it exclusively as he does, is able to compass. To get from one point in it to another we have to plough or wade through the whole intolerable interval. No detail is spared us; it is as bad as the barbed-wire complications at Port Arthur, and we grow old and die in the process. But with our faculty of abstracting and fixing concepts we are there in a second, almost as if we controlled a fourth dimension, skipping the intermediaries as by a divine winged power, and getting at the exact point we require without entanglement with any context. What we do in fact is to *harness up* reality in our conceptual systems in order to drive it the better. This process is practical because all the termini to which we drive are *particular* termini, even when they are facts of the mental order. But the sciences in which the conceptual method chiefly celebrates its triumphs are those of space and matter, where the transformations of external things are dealt with. To deal with moral facts conceptually, we have first to transform them, substitute brain-diagrams or physical metaphors, treat ideas as atoms, interests as mechanical forces, our conscious 'selves' as 'streams,' and the like. Paradoxical effect! as Bergson well remarks, if our intellectual life were not practical but destined to reveal the inner natures. One would then suppose that it would find itself most at home in the domain of its own intellectual realities. But it is precisely there that it finds itself at the end of its tether. We know the inner movements of our spirit only perceptually. We feel them live in us, but can give no distinct account of their elements, nor definitely predict their future; while things that lie along the world of space,

things of the sort that we literally *handle*, are what our intellects cope with most successfully. Does not this confirm us in
the view that the original and still surviving function of our
intellectual life is to guide us in the practical adaptation of
our expectancies and activities?

One can easily get into a verbal mess at this point, and my
own experience with 'pragmatism' makes me shrink from the
dangers that lie in the word 'practical'; so, far rather than
stand out against you for that word, I am quite willing to
part company with Professor Bergson, and to ascribe a primarily theoretical function to our intellect, provided you on
your part then agree to discriminate 'theoretic' or scientific
knowledge from the deeper 'speculative' knowledge aspired to
by most philosophers, and concede that theoretic knowledge,
which is knowledge *about* things, as distinguished from living
or sympathetic acquaintance with them, touches only the
outer surface of reality.[1] The surface which theoretic knowl-

---

[1] For a more explicit vindication of the notion of activity, see Appendix B,
where I try to defend its recognition as a definite form of immediate experience against its rationalistic critics.

I subjoin here a few remarks destined to disarm some possible critics of
Professor Bergson, who, to defend himself against misunderstandings of his
meaning, ought to amplify and more fully explain his statement that concepts
have a practical but not a theoretical use. Understood in one way, the thesis
sounds indefensible, for by concepts we certainly increase our knowledge
about things, and that seems a theoretical achievement, whatever practical
achievements may follow in its train. Indeed, M. Bergson might seem to be
easily refutable out of his own mouth. His philosophy pretends, if anything,
to give a better insight into truth than rationalistic philosophies give: yet
what is it in itself if not a conceptual system? Does its author not reason by concepts exclusively in his very attempt to show that they can give no insight?

To this particular objection, at any rate, it is easy to reply. In using concepts of his own to discredit the theoretic claims of concepts generally, Bergson does not contradict, but on the contrary emphatically illustrates his own
view of their practical side, for they serve in his hands only to 'orient' us, to
show us to what quarter we must *practically turn* if we wish to gain that
completer insight into reality which he denies that they can give. He directs
our hopes away from them and towards the despised sensible flux. *What he
reaches by their means is thus only a new practical attitude.* He but restores,
against the vetoes of intellectualist philosophy, our naturally cordial relations
with sensible experience and common sense. This service is surely only practical; but it is a service for which we may be almost immeasurably grateful.
To trust our senses again with a good philosophic conscience!—who ever
conferred on us so valuable a freedom before?

edge taken in this sense covers may indeed be enormous in extent; it may dot the whole diameter of space and time with its conceptual creations; but it does not penetrate a millimeter

---

By making certain distinctions and additions it seems easy to meet the other counts of the indictment. Concepts are realities of a new order, with particular relations between them. These relations are just as much directly perceived, when we compare our various concepts, as the distance between two sense-objects is perceived when we look at it. Conception is an operation which gives us material for new acts of perception, then; and when the results of these are written down, we get those bodies of 'mental truth' (as Locke called it) known as mathematics, logic, and *a priori* metaphysics. To know all this truth is a theoretic achievement, indeed, but it is a narrow one; for the relations between conceptual objects as such are only the static ones of bare comparison, as difference or sameness, congruity or contradiction, inclusion or exclusion. Nothing *happens* in the realm of concepts; relations there are 'eternal' only. The theoretic gain fails so far, therefore, to touch even the outer hem of the real world, the world of causal and dynamic relations, of activity and history. To gain insight into all that moving life, Bergson is right in turning us away from conception and towards perception.

By combining concepts with percepts, *we can draw maps of the distribution* of other percepts in distant space and time. To know this distribution is of course a theoretic achievement, but the achievement is extremely limited, it cannot be effected without percepts, and even then what it yields is only static relations. From maps we learn positions only, and the position of a thing is but the slightest kind of truth about it; but, being indispensable for forming our plans of action, the conceptual map-making has the enormous practical importance on which Bergson so rightly insists.

But concepts, it will be said, do not only give us eternal truths of comparison and maps of the positions of things, they bring new *values* into life. In their mapping function they stand to perception in general in the same relation in which sight and hearing stand to touch—Spencer calls these higher senses only organs of anticipatory touch. But our eyes and ears also open to us worlds of independent glory: music and decorative art result, and an incredible enhancement of life's value follows. Even so does the conceptual world bring new ranges of value and of motivation to our life. Its maps not only serve us practically, but the mere mental possession of such vast pictures is of itself an inspiring good. New interests and incitements, and feelings of power, sublimity, and admiration are aroused.

Abstractness *per se* seems to have a touch of ideality. ROYCE's 'loyalty to loyalty' is an excellent example. 'Causes,' as anti-slavery, democracy, liberty, etc., dwindle when realized in their sordid particulars. The veritable 'cash-value' of the idea seems to cleave to it only in the abstract status. Truth at large, as ROYCE contends, in his *Philosophy of Loyalty*, appears another thing altogether from the true particulars in which it is best to believe. It transcends in value all those 'expediencies,' and is something to live for, whether

into the solid dimension. That inner dimension of reality is occupied by the *activities* that keep it going, but the intellect, speaking through Hume, Kant & Co., finds itself obliged to

---

expedient or inexpedient. Truth with a big T is a 'momentous issue'; truths in detail are 'poor scraps,' mere 'crumbling successes.' (*Op. cit.*, Lecture VII, especially § v.)

Is, now, such bringing into existence of a new *value* to be regarded as a theoretic achievement? The question is a nice one, for altho a value is in one sense an objective quality perceived, the essence of that quality is its relation to the will, and consists in its being a dynamogenic spur that makes our action different. So far as their value-creating function goes, it would thus appear that concepts connect themselves more with our active than with our theoretic life, so here again Bergson's formulation seems unobjectionable. Persons who have certain concepts are animated otherwise, pursue their own vital careers differently. It does n't necessarily follow that they understand other vital careers more intimately.

Again it may be said that we combine old concepts into new ones, conceiving thus such realities as the ether, God, souls, or what not, of which our sensible life alone would leave us altogether ignorant. This surely is an increase of our knowledge, and may well be called a theoretical achievement. Yet here again Bergson's criticisms hold good. Much as conception may tell us *about* such invisible objects, it sheds no ray of light into their interior. The completer, indeed, our definitions of ether-waves, atoms, Gods, or souls become, the less instead of the more intelligible do they appear to us. The learned in such things are consequently beginning more and more to ascribe a solely instrumental value to our concepts of them. Ether and molecules may be like co-ordinates and averages, only so many crutches by the help of which we practically perform the operation of getting about among our sensible experiences.

We see from these considerations how easily the question of whether the function of concepts is theoretical or practical may grow into a logomachy. It may be better from this point of view to refuse to recognize the alternative as a sharp one. The sole thing that is certain in the midst of it all is that Bergson is absolutely right in contending that the whole life of activity and change is inwardly impenetrable to conceptual treatment, and that it opens itself only to sympathetic apprehension at the hands of immediate feeling. All the *whats* as well as the *thats* of reality, relational as well as terminal, are in the end contents of immediate concrete perception. Yet the remoter unperceived *arrangements*, temporal, spatial, and logical, of these contents, are also something that we need to know as well for the pleasure of the knowing as for the practical help. We may call this need of arrangement a theoretic need or a practical need, according as we choose to lay the emphasis; but Bergson is accurately right when he limits conceptual knowledge to arrangement, and when he insists that arrangement is the mere skirt and skin of the whole of what we ought to know.

deny, and persists in denying, that activities have any intelligible existence. What exists for *thought*, we are told, is at most the results that we illusorily ascribe to such activities, strung along the surfaces of space and time by *regeln der verknüpfung*, laws of nature which state only coexistences and successions.

Thought deals thus solely with surfaces. It can name the thickness of reality, but it cannot fathom it, and its insufficiency here is essential and permanent, not temporary.

The only way in which to apprehend reality's thickness is either to experience it directly by being a part of reality one's self, or to evoke it in imagination by sympathetically divining some one else's inner life. But what we thus immediately experience or concretely divine is very limited in duration, whereas abstractly we are able to conceive eternities. Could we feel a million years concretely as we now feel a passing minute, we should have very little employment for our conceptual faculty. We should know the whole period fully at every moment of its passage, whereas we must now construct it laboriously by means of concepts which we project. Direct acquaintance and conceptual knowledge are thus complementary of each other; each remedies the other's defects. If what we care most about be the synoptic treatment of phenomena, the vision of the far and the gathering of the scattered like, we must follow the conceptual method. But if, as metaphysicians, we are more curious about the inner nature of reality or about what really makes it go, we must turn our backs upon our winged concepts altogether, and bury ourselves in the thickness of those passing moments over the surface of which they fly, and on particular points of which they occasionally rest and perch.

Professor Bergson thus inverts the traditional platonic doctrine absolutely. Instead of intellectual knowledge being the profounder, he calls it the more superficial. Instead of being the only adequate knowledge, it is grossly inadequate, and its only superiority is the practical one of enabling us to make short cuts through experience and thereby to save time. The one thing it cannot do is to reveal the nature of things—which last remark, if not clear already, will become clearer as I proceed. Dive back into the flux itself, then, Bergson tells us, if you wish to *know* reality, that flux which Platonism, in its strange belief that only the immutable is excellent, has always spurned; turn your face toward sensation, that flesh-bound thing which rationalism has always loaded with abuse.—This, you see, is exactly the opposite remedy from that of looking forward into the absolute, which our idealistic contemporaries prescribe. It violates our mental habits, being a kind of passive and receptive listening quite contrary to that effort to react noisily and verbally on everything, which is our usual intellectual pose.

What, then, are the peculiar features in the perceptual flux which the conceptual translation so fatally leaves out?

The essence of life is its continuously changing character; but our concepts are all discontinuous and fixed, and the only mode of making them coincide with life is by arbitrarily supposing positions of arrest therein. With such arrests our concepts may be made congruent. But these concepts are not *parts* of reality, not real positions taken by it, but *suppositions* rather, notes taken by ourselves, and you can no more dip up the substance of reality with them than you can dip up water with a net, however finely meshed.

When we conceptualize, we cut out and fix, and exclude everything but what we have fixed. A concept means a *that-and-no-other*. Conceptually, time excludes space; motion and rest exclude each other; approach excludes contact; presence excludes absence; unity excludes plurality; independence excludes relativity; 'mine' excludes 'yours'; this connexion excludes that connexion—and so on indefinitely; whereas in the real concrete sensible flux of life experiences compenetrate each other so that it is not easy to know just what is excluded and what not. Past and future, for example, conceptually separated by the cut to which we give the name of present, and defined as being the opposite sides of that cut, are to some extent, however brief, co-present with each other throughout experience. The literally present moment is a purely verbal supposition, not a position; the only present ever realized concretely being the 'passing moment' in which the dying rearward of time and its dawning future forever mix their lights. Say 'now' and it *was* even while you say it.

It is just intellectualism's attempt to substitute static cuts for units of experienced duration that makes real motion so unintelligible. The conception of the first half of the interval between Achilles and the tortoise excludes that of the last half, and the mathematical necessity of traversing it separately before the last half is traversed stands permanently in the way of the last half ever being traversed. Meanwhile the living Achilles (who, for the purposes of this discussion, is only the abstract name of one phenomenon of impetus, just as the tortoise is of another) asks no leave of logic. The velocity of his acts is an indivisible nature in them like the expansive tension in a spring compressed. We define it conceptually as s/t, but the s and t are only artificial cuts made after the fact, and indeed most artificial when we treat them in both runners as the same tracts of 'objective' space and time, for the experienced spaces and times in which the tortoise inwardly lives are probably as different as his velocity from the same things in Achilles. The impetus of Achilles is one concrete fact, and carries space, time, and conquest over the inferior creature's motion indivisibly in it. He perceives nothing, while running, of the mathematician's homogeneous time and space, of the infinitely numerous succession of cuts in both, or of their order. End and beginning come for him in the one onrush, and all that he actually experiences is that, in the midst of a certain intense effort of his own, the rival is in point of fact outstripped.

We are so inveterately wedded to the conceptual decomposition of life that I know that this will seem to you like putting muddiest confusion in place of clearest thought, and relapsing into a molluscoid state of mind. Yet I ask you whether the absolute superiority of our higher thought is so very clear, if all that it can find is impossibility in tasks which sense-experience so easily performs.

What makes you call real life confusion is that it presents, as if they were dissolved in one another, a lot of differents which conception breaks life's flow by keeping apart. But *are* not differents actually dissolved in one another? Has n't every bit of experience its quality, its duration, its extension, its intensity, its urgency, its clearness, and many aspects besides, no one of which can exist in the isolation in which our verbalized logic keeps it? They exist only *durcheinander*. Reality always is, in M. Bergson's phrase, an endosmosis or conflux of the same with the different: they compenetrate and telescope. For conceptual logic, the same is nothing but the same, and all sames with a third thing are the same with each other. Not so in concrete experience. Two spots on our skin, each of which feels the same as a third spot when touched along with it, are felt as different from each other. Two tones, neither distinguishable from a third tone, are perfectly distinct from each other. The whole process of life is due to life's violation of our logical axioms. Take its continuity as an example. Terms like A and C appear to be connected by intermediaries, by B for example. Intellectualism calls this absurd, for 'B-connected-with-A' is, 'as such,' a different term from 'B-connected-with-C.' But real life laughs at logic's veto. Imagine a heavy log which takes two men to carry it. First A and B take it. Then C takes hold and A drops off; then D takes hold and B drops off, so that C and D now bear it; and so on. The log meanwhile never drops, and keeps its sameness throughout the journey. Even so it is with all our experiences. Their changes are not complete annihilations followed by complete creations of something absolutely novel. There is partial decay and partial growth, and all the while a nucleus of relative constancy from which what decays drops off, and which takes into itself whatever is grafted on, until at length something wholly different has taken its place. In such a process we are as sure, in spite of intellectualist logic with its 'as suches,' that it *is* the same nucleus which is able now to make connexion with what goes and again with what comes, as we are sure that the same point can lie on diverse lines that intersect there. Without being one throughout, such a universe is continuous. Its members interdigitate with their next neighbors in manifold directions, and there are no clean cuts between them anywhere.

The great clash of intellectualist logic with sensible experience is where the experience is that of influence exerted. Intellectualism denies (as we saw in lecture ii) that finite things can act on one another, for all things, once translated into concepts, remain shut up to themselves. To act on anything means to get into it somehow; but that would mean to get

out of one's self and be one's other, which is self-contradictory, etc. Meanwhile each of us actually *is* his own other to
that extent, livingly knowing how to perform the trick which
logic tells us can't be done. My thoughts animate and actuate
this very body which you see and hear, and thereby influence
your thoughts. The dynamic current somehow does get from
me to you, however numerous the intermediary conductors
may have to be. Distinctions may be insulators in logic as
much as they like, but in life distinct things can and do commune together every moment.

The conflict of the two ways of knowing is best summed
up in the intellectualist doctrine that 'the same cannot exist in
many relations.' This follows of course from the concepts of
the two relations being so distinct that 'what-is-in-the-one'
means 'as such' something distinct from what 'what-is-in-the-
other' means. It is like Mill's ironical saying, that we should
not think of Newton as both an Englishman and a mathematician, because an Englishman as such is not a mathematician and a mathematician as such is not an Englishman. But
the real Newton was somehow both things at once; and
throughout the whole finite universe each real thing proves
to be many differents without undergoing the necessity of
breaking into disconnected editions of itself.

These few indications will perhaps suffice to put you at
the bergsonian point of view. The immediate experience of
life solves the problems which so baffle our conceptual intelligence: How can what is manifold be one? how can things
get out of themselves? how be their own others? how be
both distinct and connected? how can they act on one another? how be for others and yet for themselves? how be absent and present at once? The intellect asks these questions
much as we might ask how anything can both separate and
unite things, or how sounds can grow more alike by continuing to grow more different. If you already know space
sensibly, you can answer the former question by pointing to
any interval in it, long or short; if you know the musical
scale, you can answer the latter by sounding an octave; but
then you must first have the sensible knowledge of these
realities. Similarly Bergson answers the intellectualist conun-
drums by pointing back to our various finite sensational ex-

periences and saying, 'Lo, even thus; even so are these other problems solved livingly.'

When you have broken the reality into concepts you never can reconstruct it in its wholeness. Out of no amount of discreteness can you manufacture the concrete. But place yourself at a bound, or *d'emblée*, as M. Bergson says, inside of the living, moving, active thickness of the real, and all the abstractions and distinctions are given into your hand: you can now make the intellectualist substitutions to your heart's content. Install yourself in phenomenal movement, for example, and velocity, succession, dates, positions, and innumerable other things are given you in the bargain. But with only an abstract succession of dates and positions you can never patch up movement itself. It slips through their intervals and is lost.

So it is with every concrete thing, however complicated. Our intellectual handling of it is a retrospective patchwork, a post-mortem dissection, and can follow any order we find most expedient. We can make the thing seem self-contradictory whenever we wish to. But place yourself at the point of view of the thing's interior *doing*, and all these back-looking and conflicting conceptions lie harmoniously in your hand. Get at the expanding centre of a human character, the *élan vital* of a man, as Bergson calls it, by living sympathy, and at a stroke you see how it makes those who see it from without interpret it in such diverse ways. It is something that breaks into both honesty and dishonesty, courage and cowardice, stupidity and insight, at the touch of varying circumstances, and you feel exactly why and how it does this, and never seek to identify it stably with any of these single abstractions. Only your intellectualist does that,—and you now also feel why *he* must do it to the end.

Place yourself similarly at the centre of a man's philosophic vision and you understand at once all the different things it makes him write or say. But keep outside, use your post-mortem method, try to build the philosophy up out of the single phrases, taking first one and then another and seeking to make them fit 'logically,' and of course you fail. You crawl over the thing like a myopic ant over a building, tumbling into every microscopic crack or fissure, finding nothing but inconsistencies, and never suspecting that a centre exists. I hope that some of the philosophers in this audience may occasionally have had something different from this intellectualist type of criticism applied to their own works!

What really *exists* is not things made but things in the making. Once made, they are dead, and an infinite number of alternative conceptual decompositions can be used in defining them. But put yourself *in the making* by a stroke of intuitive sympathy with the thing and, the whole range of possible decompositions coming at once into your possession, you are no longer troubled with the question which of them is the more absolutely true. Reality *falls* in passing into conceptual analysis; it *mounts* in living its own undivided life—it buds and bourgeons, changes and creates. Once adopt the movement of this life in any given instance and you know what Bergson calls the *devenir réel* by which the thing evolves and grows. Philosophy should seek this kind of living understanding of the movement of reality, not follow science in vainly patching together fragments of its dead results.

Thus much of M. Bergson's philosophy is sufficient for my purpose in these lectures, so here I will stop, leaving unnoticed all its other constituent features, original and interesting tho they be. You may say, and doubtless some of you now are saying inwardly, that his remanding us to sensation in this wise is only a regress, a return to that ultra-crude empiricism which your own idealists since Green have buried ten times over. I confess that it is indeed a return to empiricism, but I think that the return in such accomplished shape only proves the latter's immortal truth. What won't stay buried must have some genuine life. *Am anfang war die tat*; fact is a *first*; to which all our conceptual handling comes as an inadequate second, never its full equivalent. When I read recent transcendentalist literature—I must partly except my colleague Royce!—I get nothing but a sort of marking of time, champing of jaws, pawing of the ground, and resettling into the same attitude, like a weary horse in a stall with an empty manger. It is but turning over the same few threadbare categories, bringing the same objections, and urging the same answers and solutions, with never a new fact or a new horizon coming into sight. But open Bergson, and new horizons loom on every page you read. It is like the breath of the morning and the song of birds. It tells of reality itself, instead of merely reiterating what dusty-minded professors have written about what other previous professors have thought. Nothing in Bergson is shop-worn or at second hand.

That he gives us no closed-in system will of course be fatal to him in intellectualist eyes. He only evokes and invites; but he first annuls the intellectualist veto, so that we now join step with reality with a philosophical conscience never quite set free before. As a french disciple of his well expresses it: 'Bergson claims of us first of all a certain inner catastrophe, and not every one is capable of such a logical revolution. But those who have once found themselves flexible enough for the execution of such a psychological change of front, discover somehow that they can never return again to their ancient attitude of mind. They are now Bergsonians . . . and possess the principal thoughts of the master all at once. They have understood in the fashion in which one loves, they have caught the whole melody and can thereafter admire at their leisure the originality, the fecundity, and the imaginative genius with which its author develops, transposes, and varies in a thousand ways by the orchestration of his style and dialectic, the original theme.'[1]

This, scant as it is, is all I have to say about Bergson on this occasion—I hope it may send some of you to his original text. I must now turn back to the point where I found it advisable to appeal to his ideas. You remember my own intellectualist difficulties in the last lecture, about how a lot of separate consciousnesses can at the same time be one collective thing. How, I asked, can one and the same identical content of experience, of which on idealist principles the *esse* is to be felt, be felt so diversely if itself be the only feeler? The usual way of escape by 'quatenus' or 'as such' won't help us here if we are radical intellectualists, I said, for appearance-together is as such *not* appearance-apart, the world *quâ* many is not the world *quâ* one, as absolutism claims. If we hold to Hume's maxim, which later intellectualism uses so well, that whatever things are distinguished are as separate as if there

[1] Gaston Rageot, *Revue Philosophique*, vol. lxiv, p. 85 (July, 1907).

were no manner of connexion between them, there seemed no way out of the difficulty save by stepping outside of experience altogether and invoking different spiritual agents, selves or souls, to realize the diversity required. But this rescue by 'scholastic entities' I was unwilling to accept any more than pantheistic idealists accept it.

Yet, to quote Fechner's phrase again, 'nichts wirkliches kann unmöglich sein,' the actual cannot be impossible, and what *is* actual at every moment of our lives is the sort of thing which I now proceed to remind you of. You can hear the vibration of an electric contact-maker, smell the ozone, see the sparks, and feel the thrill, co-consciously as it were or in one field of experience. But you can also isolate any one of these sensations by shutting out the rest. If you close your eyes, hold your nose, and remove your hand, you can get the sensation of sound alone, but it seems still the same sensation that it was; and if you restore the action of the other organs, the sound coalesces with the feeling, the sight, and the smell sensations again. Now the natural way of talking of all this[1] is to say that certain sensations are experienced, now singly, and now together with other sensations, in a common conscious field. Fluctuations of attention give analogous results. We let a sensation in or keep it out by changing our attention; and similarly we let an item of memory in or drop it out. [Please don't raise the question here of how these changes *come to pass*. The immediate condition is probably cerebral in every instance, but it would be irrelevant now to consider it, for now we are thinking only of results, and I repeat that the natural way of thinking of them is that which intellectualist criticism finds so absurd.]

The absurdity charged is that the self-same should function so differently, now with and now without something else. But this it sensibly seems to do. This very desk which I strike with my hand strikes in turn your eyes. It functions at once as a physical object in the outer world and as a mental object in our sundry mental worlds. The very body of mine that *my* thought actuates is the body whose gestures are *your* visual

---

[1] I have myself talked in other ways as plausibly as I could, in my *Psychology*, and talked truly (as I believe) in certain selected cases; but for other cases the natural way invincibly comes back.

object and to which you give my name. The very log which John helped to carry is the log now borne by James. The very girl you love is simultaneously entangled elsewhere. The very place behind me is in front of you. Look where you will, you gather only examples of the same amid the different, and of different relations existing as it were in solution in the same thing. *Quâ* this an experience is not the same as it is *quâ* that, truly enough; but the *quâs* are conceptual shots of ours at its post-mortem remains, and in its sensational immediacy everything is all at once whatever different things it is at once at all. It is before C and after A, far from you and near to me, without this associate and with that one, active and passive, physical and mental, a whole of parts and part of a higher whole, all simultaneously and without interference or need of doubling-up its being, so long as we keep to what I call the 'immediate' point of view, the point of view in which we follow our sensational life's continuity, and to which all living language conforms. It is only when you try—to continue using the hegelian vocabulary—to 'mediate' the immediate, or to substitute concepts for sensational life, that intellectualism celebrates its triumph and the immanent-self-contradictoriness of all this smooth-running finite experience gets proved.

Of the oddity of inventing as a remedy for the inconveniences resulting from this situation a supernumerary conceptual object called an absolute, into which you pack the self-same contradictions unreduced, I will say something in the next lecture. The absolute is said to perform its feats by taking up its other into itself. But that is exactly what is done when every individual morsel of the sensational stream takes up the adjacent morsels by coalescing with them. This is just what we mean by the stream's sensible continuity. No element *there* cuts itself off from any other element, as concepts cut themselves from concepts. No part *there* is so small as not to be a place of conflux. No part there is not really *next* its neighbors; which means that there is literally nothing between; which means again that no part goes exactly so far and no farther; that no part absolutely excludes another, but that they compenetrate and are cohesive; that if you tear out one, its roots bring out more with them; that whatever is real is telescoped and diffused into other reals; that, in short, every minutest thing is already its hegelian 'own other,' in the fullest sense of the term.

Of course this *sounds* self-contradictory, but as the immediate facts don't sound at all, but simply *are*, until we conceptualize and name them vocally, the contradiction results only from the conceptual or discursive form being substituted for the real form. But if, as Bergson shows, that form is superimposed for practical ends only, in order to let us jump about over life instead of wading through it; and if it cannot even pretend to reveal anything of what life's inner nature is or ought to be; why then we can turn a deaf ear to its accusations. The resolve to turn the deaf ear is the inner crisis or 'catastrophe' of which M. Bergson's disciple whom I lately quoted spoke. We are so subject to the philosophic tradition which treats *logos* or discursive thought generally as the sole avenue to truth, that to fall back on raw unverbalized life as more of a revealer, and to think of concepts as the merely practical things which Bergson calls them, comes very hard. It is putting off our proud maturity of mind and becoming again as foolish little children in the eyes of reason. But difficult as such a revolution is, there is no other way, I believe, to the possession of reality, and I permit myself to hope that some of you may share my opinion after you have heard my next lecture.

LECTURE VII

THE CONTINUITY OF EXPERIENCE

I FEAR that few of you will have been able to obey Berg-son's call upon you to look towards the sensational life for the fuller knowledge of reality, or to sympathize with his attempt to limit the divine right of concepts to rule our mind absolutely. It is too much like looking downward and not up. Philosophy, you will say, does n't lie flat on its belly in the middle of experience, in the very thick of its sand and gravel, as this Bergsonism does, never getting a peep at anything from above. Philosophy is essentially the vision of things from above. It does n't simply feel the detail of things, it comprehends their intelligible plan, sees their forms and principles, their categories and rules, their order and necessity. It takes the superior point of view of the architect. Is it conceivable that it should ever forsake that point of view and abandon itself to a slovenly life of immediate feeling? To say nothing of your traditional Oxford devotion to Aristotle and Plato, the leaven of T. H. Green probably works still too strongly here for his anti-sensationalism to be outgrown quickly. Green more than any one realized that knowledge *about* things was knowledge of their relations; but nothing could persuade him that our sensational life could contain any relational element. He followed the strict intellectualist method with sensations. What they were not expressly defined as including, they must exclude. Sensations are not defined as relations, so in the end Green thought that they could get related together only by the action on them from above of a 'self-distinguishing' absolute and eternal mind, present to that which is related, but not related itself. 'A relation,' he said, 'is not contingent with the contingency of feeling. It is permanent with the permanence of the combining and comparing thought which alone constitutes it.'[1] In other words, relations are purely conceptual objects, and the sensational life as such cannot relate itself together. Sensation in itself, Green wrote, is fleeting, momentary, unnameable (because, while we

[1] *Introduction to Hume*, 1874, p. 151.

name it, it has become another), and for the same reason unknowable, the very negation of knowability. Were there no
permanent objects of conception for our sensations to be 'referred to,' there would be no significant names, but only
noises, and a consistent sensationalism must be speechless.[1]
Green's intellectualism was so earnest that it produced a natural and an inevitable effect. But the atomistic and unrelated
sensations which he had in mind were purely fictitious products of his rationalist fancy. The psychology of our own day
disavows them utterly,[2] and Green's laborious belaboring of
poor old Locke for not having first seen that his ideas of sensation were just that impracticable sort of thing, and then fled
to transcendental idealism as a remedy,—his belaboring of
poor old Locke for this, I say, is pathetic. Every examiner of
the sensible life *in concreto* must see that relations of every
sort, of time, space, difference, likeness, change, rate, cause,
or what not, are just as integral members of the sensational
flux as terms are, and that conjunctive relations are just as true
members of the flux as disjunctive relations are.[3] This is what
in some recent writings of mine I have called the 'radically
empiricist' doctrine (in distinction from the doctrine of mental atoms which the name empiricism so often suggests). Intellectualistic critics of sensation insist that sensations are
*dis*joined only. Radical empiricism insists that conjunctions
between them are just as immediately given as disjunctions
are, and that relations, whether disjunctive or conjunctive, are
in their original sensible givenness just as fleeting and momentary (in Green's words), and just as 'particular,' as terms
are. Later, both terms and relations get universalized by being
conceptualized and named.[4] But all the thickness, concrete-

[1] *Ibid.*, pp. 16, 21, 36, *et passim*.

[2] See, *inter alia*, the chapter on the 'Stream of Thought' in my own Psychologies; H. Cornelius, *Psychologie*, 1897, chaps. i and iii; G. H. Luquet,
Idées Générales de Psychologie, 1906, *passim*.

[3] Compare, as to all this, an article by the present writer, entitled 'A world
of pure experience,' in the *Journal of Philosophy*, New York, vol. i, pp. 533, 561
(1905).

[4] Green's attempt to discredit sensations by reminding us of their 'dumbness,' in that they do not come already *named*, as concepts may be said to
do, only shows how intellectualism is dominated by verbality. The unnamed
appears in Green as synonymous with the unreal.

ness, and individuality of experience exists in the immediate and relatively unnamed stages of it, to the richness of which, and to the standing inadequacy of our conceptions to match it, Professor Bergson so emphatically calls our attention.

And now I am happy to say that we can begin to gather together some of the separate threads of our argument, and see a little better the general kind of conclusion toward which we are tending. Pray go back with me to the lecture before the last, and recall what I said about the difficulty of seeing how states of consciousness can compound themselves. The difficulty seemed to be the same, you remember, whether we took it in psychology as the composition of finite states of mind out of simpler finite states, or in metaphysics as the composition of the absolute mind out of finite minds in general. It is the general conceptualist difficulty of any one thing being the same with many things, either at once or in succession, for the abstract concepts of oneness and manyness must needs exclude each other. In the particular instance that we have dwelt on so long, the one thing is the all-form of experience, the many things are the each-forms of experience in you and me. To call them the same we must treat them as if each were simultaneously its own other, a feat on conceptualist principles impossible of performance.

On the principle of going behind the conceptual function altogether, however, and looking to the more primitive flux of the sensational life for reality's true shape, a way is open to us, as I tried in my last lecture to show. Not only the absolute is its own other, but the simplest bits of immediate experience are their own others, if that hegelian phrase be once for all allowed. The concrete pulses of experience appear pent in by no such definite limits as our conceptual substitutes for them are confined by. They run into one another continuously and seem to interpenetrate. What in them is relation and what is matter related is hard to discern. You feel no one of them as inwardly simple, and no two as wholly without confluence where they touch. There is no datum so small as not to show this mystery, if mystery it be. The tiniest feeling that we can possibly have comes with an earlier and a later part and with a sense of their continuous procession. Mr. Shadworth Hodgson showed long ago that there is literally no such object as the present moment except as an unreal postulate of abstract thought.[1] The 'passing' moment is, as I already have reminded you, the minimal fact, with the 'apparition of difference' inside of it as well as outside. If we do not feel both past and present in one field of feeling, we feel them not at all. We have the same many-in-one in the matter that fills the passing time. The rush of our thought forward through its fringes is the everlasting peculiarity of its life. We realize this life as something always off its balance, something in transition, something that shoots out of a darkness through a dawn into a brightness that we feel to be the dawn fulfilled. In the very midst of the continuity our experience comes as an alteration. 'Yes,' we say at the full brightness, '*this* is what I just meant.' 'No,' we feel at the dawning, 'this is not yet the full meaning, there is more to come.' In every crescendo of sensation, in every effort to recall, in every progress towards the satisfaction of desire, this succession of an emptiness and fulness that have reference to each other and are one flesh is the essence of the phenomenon. In every hindrance of desire the sense of an ideal presence which is absent in fact, of an absent, in a word, which the only function of the present is to *mean*, is even more notoriously there. And in the movement of pure thought we have the same phenomenon. When I say *Socrates is mortal*, the moment *Socrates* is incomplete; it falls forward through the *is* which is pure movement, into the *mortal* which is indeed bare mortal on the tongue, but for the mind is *that mortal*, the *mortal Socrates*, at last satisfactorily disposed of and told off.[2]

Here, then, inside of the minimal pulses of experience, is realized that very inner complexity which the transcendentalists say only the absolute can genuinely possess. The gist of the matter is always the same—something ever goes indissolubly with something else. You cannot separate the same from its other, except by abandoning the real altogether and taking to the conceptual system. What is immediately given

[1] *Philosophy of Reflection*, i, 248 ff.

[2] Most of this paragraph is extracted from an address of mine before the American Psychological Association, printed in the *Psychological Review*, vol. ii, p. 105. I take pleasure in the fact that already in 1895 I was so far advanced towards my present bergsonian position.

in the single and particular instance is always something pooled and mutual, something with no dark spot, no point of ignorance. No one elementary bit of reality is eclipsed from the next bit's point of view, if only we take reality sensibly and in small enough pulses—and by us it has to be taken pulse-wise, for our span of consciousness is too short to grasp the larger collectivity of things except nominally and abstractly. No more of reality collected together at once is extant anywhere, perhaps, than in my experience of reading this page, or in yours of listening; yet within those bits of experience as they come to pass we get a fulness of content that no conceptual description can equal. Sensational experiences *are* their 'own others,' then, both internally and externally. Inwardly they are one with their parts, and outwardly they pass continuously into their next neighbors, so that events separated by years of time in a man's life hang together unbrokenly by the intermediary events. Their *names*, to be sure, cut them into separate conceptual entities, but no cuts existed in the continuum in which they originally came.

If, with all this in our mind, we turn to our own particular predicament, we see that our old objection to the self-compounding of states of consciousness, our accusation that it was impossible for purely logical reasons, is unfounded in principle. Every smallest state of consciousness, concretely taken, overflows its own definition. Only concepts are self-identical; only 'reason' deals with closed equations; nature is but a name for excess; every point in her opens out and runs into the more; and the only question, with reference to any point we may be considering, is how far into the rest of nature we may have to go in order to get entirely beyond its overflow. In the pulse of inner life immediately present now in each of us is a little past, a little future, a little awareness of our own body, of each other's persons, of these sublimities we are trying to talk about, of the earth's geography and the direction of history, of truth and error, of good and bad, and of who knows how much more? Feeling, however dimly and subconsciously, all these things, your pulse of inner life is continuous with them, belongs to them and they to it. You can't identify it with either one of them rather than with the others, for if you let it develop into no matter which of those directions, what it develops into will look back on it and say, 'That was the original germ of me.'

In *principle*, then, the real units of our immediately-felt life are unlike the units that intellectualist logic holds to and makes its calculations with. They are not separate from their own others, and you have to take them at widely separated dates to find any two of them that seem unblent. Then indeed they do appear separate even as their concepts are separate; a chasm yawns between them; but the chasm itself is but an intellectualist fiction, got by abstracting from the continuous sheet of experiences with which the intermediary time was filled. It is like the log carried first by William and Henry, then by William, Henry, and John, then by Henry and John, then by John and Peter, and so on. All real units of experience *overlap*. Let a row of equidistant dots on a sheet of paper symbolize the concepts by which we intellectualize the world. Let a ruler long enough to cover at least three dots stand for our sensible experience. Then the conceived changes of the sensible experience can be symbolized by sliding the ruler along the line of dots. One concept after another will apply to it, one after another drop away, but it will always cover at least two of them, and no dots less than three will ever adequately cover *it*. You falsify it if you treat it conceptually, or by the law of dots.

What is true here of successive states must also be true of simultaneous characters. They also overlap each other with their being. My present field of consciousness is a centre surrounded by a fringe that shades insensibly into a subconscious more. I use three separate terms here to describe this fact; but I might as well use three hundred, for the fact is all shades and no boundaries. Which part of it properly is in my consciousness, which out? If I name what is out, it already has come in. The centre works in one way while the margins work in another, and presently overpower the centre and are central themselves. What we conceptually identify ourselves with and say we are thinking of at any time is the centre; but our *full* self is the whole field, with all those indefinitely radiating subconscious possibilities of increase that we can only feel without conceiving, and can hardly begin to analyze. The collective and the distributive ways of being coexist here, for each part functions distinctly, makes connexion with its own peculiar region in the still wider rest of experience and tends to draw us into that line, and yet the whole is somehow felt as one pulse of our life,—not conceived so, but felt so.

In principle, then, as I said, intellectualism's edge is broken; it can only approximate to reality, and its logic is inapplicable to our inner life, which spurns its vetoes and mocks at its impossibilities. Every bit of us at every moment is part and parcel of a wider self, it quivers along various radii like the wind-rose on a compass, and the actual in it is continuously one with possibles not yet in our present sight.[1] And just as we are co-conscious with our own momentary margin, may not we ourselves form the margin of some more really central self in things which is co-conscious with the whole of us? May not you and I be confluent in a higher consciousness, and confluently active there, tho we now know it not?

I am tiring myself and you, I know, by vainly seeking to describe by concepts and words what I say at the same time exceeds either conceptualization or verbalization. As long as one continues *talking*, intellectualism remains in undisturbed possession of the field. The return to life can't come about by talking. It is an *act*; to make you return to life, I must set an example for your imitation, I must deafen you to talk, or to the importance of talk, by showing you, as Bergson does, that the concepts we talk with are made for purposes of *practice* and not for purposes of insight. Or I must *point*, point to the mere *that* of life, and you by inner sympathy must fill out the *what* for yourselves. The minds of some of you, I know, will absolutely refuse to do so, refuse to think in non-conceptualized terms. I myself absolutely refused to do so for years to-

[1] The conscious self of the moment, the central self, is probably determined to this privileged position by its functional connexion with the body's imminent or present acts. It is the present *acting* self. Tho the more that surrounds it may be 'subconscious' to us, yet if in its 'collective capacity' it also exerts an active function, it may be conscious in a wider way, conscious, as it were, over our heads.

On the relations of consciousness to action see Bergson's *Matière et Mémoire*, *passim*, especially chap. i. Compare also the hints in Münsterberg's *Grundzüge der Psychologie*, chap. xv; those in my own *Principles of Psychology*, vol. ii, pp. 581–592; and those in W. McDougall's *Physiological Psychology*, chap. vii.

gether, even after I knew that the denial of manyness-in-oneness by intellectualism must be false, for the same reality does perform the most various functions at once. But I hoped ever for a revised intellectualist way round the difficulty, and it was only after reading Bergson that I saw that to continue using the intellectualist method was itself the fault. I saw that philosophy had been on a false scent ever since the days of Socrates and Plato, that an *intellectual* answer to the intellectualist's difficulties will never come, and that the real way out of them, far from consisting in the discovery of such an answer, consists in simply closing one's ears to the question. When conceptualism summons life to justify itself in conceptual terms, it is like a challenge addressed in a foreign language to some one who is absorbed in his own business; it is irrelevant to him altogether—he may let it lie unnoticed. I went thus through the 'inner catastrophe' of which I spoke in the last lecture; I had literally come to the end of my conceptual stock-in-trade, I was bankrupt intellectualistically, and had to change my base. No words of mine will probably convert you, for words can be the names only of concepts. But if any of you try sincerely and pertinaciously on your own separate accounts to intellectualize reality, you may be similarly driven to a change of front. I say no more: I must leave life to teach the lesson.

We have now reached a point of view from which the self-compounding of mind in its smaller and more accessible portions seems a certain fact, and in which the speculative assumption of a similar but wider compounding in remoter regions must be reckoned with as a legitimate hypothesis. The absolute is not the impossible being I once thought it. Mental facts do function both singly and together, at once, and we finite minds may simultaneously be co-conscious with one another in a superhuman intelligence. It is only the extravagant claims of coercive necessity on the absolute's part that have to be denied by *a priori* logic. As an hypothesis trying to make itself probable on analogical and inductive grounds, the absolute is entitled to a patient hearing. Which is as much as to say that our serious business from now onward lies with Fechner and his method, rather than with Hegel, Royce, or Bradley. Fechner treats the superhuman consciousness he so fervently believes in as an hypothesis only, which he then recommends by all the resources of induction and persuasion.

It is true that Fechner himself is an absolutist in his books, not actively but passively, if I may say so. He talks not only of the earth-soul and of the star-souls, but of an integrated soul of all things in the cosmos without exception, and this he calls God just as others call it the absolute. Nevertheless he *thinks* only of the subordinate superhuman souls, and content with having made his obeisance once for all to the august total soul of the cosmos, he leaves it in its lonely sublimity with no attempt to define its nature. Like the absolute, it is 'out of range,' and not an object for distincter vision. Psychologically, it seems to me that Fechner's God is a lazy postulate of his, rather than a part of his system positively thought out. As we envelop our sight and hearing, so the earth-soul envelops us, and the star-soul the earth-soul, until—what? Envelopment can't go on forever; it must have an *abschluss*, a total envelope must terminate the series, so God is the name that Fechner gives to this last all-enveloper. But if nothing escapes this all-enveloper, he is responsible for everything, including evil, and all the paradoxes and difficulties which I found in the absolute at the end of our third lecture recur undiminished. Fechner tries sincerely to grapple with the problem of evil, but he always solves it in the leibnitzian fashion by making his God non-absolute, placing him under conditions of 'metaphysical necessity' which even his omnipotence cannot violate. His will has to struggle with conditions not imposed on that will by itself. He tolerates provisionally what he has not created, and then with endless patience tries to overcome it and live it down. He has, in short, a history. Whenever Fechner tries to represent him clearly, his God becomes the ordinary God of theism, and ceases to be the absolutely totalized all-enveloper.[1] In this shape, he represents the ideal element in things solely, and is our champion and our helper and we his helpers, against the bad parts of the universe.

Fechner was in fact too little of a metaphysician to care for perfect formal consistency in these abstract regions. He believed in God in the pluralistic manner, but partly from

[1] Compare *Zend-Avesta*, 2d edition, vol. i, pp. 165 ff., 181, 206, 244 ff., etc.; *Die Tagesansicht*, etc., chap. v, § 6; and chap. xv.

convention and partly from what I should call intellectual laziness, if laziness of any kind could be imputed to a Fechner, he let the usual monistic talk about him pass unchallenged. I propose to you that we should discuss the question of God without entangling ourselves in advance in the monistic assumption. Is it probable that there is any superhuman consciousness at all, in the first place? When that is settled, the further question whether its form be monistic or pluralistic is in order.

Before advancing to either question, however, and I shall have to deal with both but very briefly after what has been said already, let me finish our retrospective survey by one more remark about the curious logical situation of the absolutists. For what have they invoked the absolute except as a being the peculiar inner form of which shall enable it to overcome the contradictions with which intellectualism has found the finite many as such to be infected? The many-in-one character that, as we have seen, every smallest tract of finite experience offers, is considered by intellectualism to be fatal to the reality of finite experience. What can be distinguished, it tells us, is separate; and what is separate is unrelated, for a relation, being a 'between,' would bring only a twofold separation. Hegel, Royce, Bradley, and the Oxford absolutists in general seem to agree about this logical absurdity of manyness-in-oneness in the only places where it is empirically found. But see the curious tactics! Is the absurdity *reduced* in the absolute being whom they call in to relieve it? Quite otherwise, for that being shows it on an infinitely greater scale, and flaunts it in its very definition. The fact of its not being related to any outward environment, the fact that all relations are inside of itself, does n't save it, for Mr. Bradley's great argument against the finite is that *in* any given bit of it (a bit of sugar, for instance) the presence of a plurality of characters (whiteness and sweetness, for example) is self-contradictory; so that in the final end all that the absolute's name appears to stand for is the persistent claim of outraged human nature that reality *shall* not be called absurd. *Somewhere* there must be an aspect of it guiltless of self-contradiction. All we can see of the absolute, meanwhile, is guilty in the same way in which the finite is. Intellectualism sees what it calls the guilt, when comminuted in the finite object; but is too near-sighted to see it in the more enormous object. Yet the absolute's constitution, if imagined at all, has to be imagined after the analogy of some bit of finite experience. Take any *real* bit, suppress its environment and then magnify it to monstrosity, and you get identically the type of structure of the absolute. It is obvious that all your difficulties here remain and go with you. If the relative experience was inwardly absurd, the absolute experience is infinitely more so. Intellectualism, in short, strains off the gnat, but swallows the whole camel. But this polemic against the absolute is as odious to me as it is to you, so I will say no more about that being. It is only one of those wills of the wisp, those lights that do mislead the morn, that have so often impeded the clear progress of philosophy, so I will turn to the more general positive question of whether superhuman unities of consciousness should be considered as more probable or more improbable.

In a former lecture I went over some of the fechnerian reasons for their plausibility, or reasons that at least replied to our more obvious grounds of doubt concerning them. The numerous facts of divided or split human personality which the genius of certain medical men, as Janet, Freud, Prince, Sidis, and others, have unearthed were unknown in Fechner's time, and neither the phenomena of automatic writing and speech, nor of mediumship and 'possession' generally, had been recognized or studied as we now study them, so Fechner's stock of analogies is scant compared with our present one. He did the best with what he had, however. For my own part I find in some of these abnormal or supernormal facts the strongest suggestions in favor of a superior co-consciousness being possible. I doubt whether we shall ever understand some of them without using the very letter of Fechner's conception of a great reservoir in which the memories of earth's inhabitants are pooled and preserved, and from which, when the threshold lowers or the valve opens, information ordinarily shut out leaks into the mind of exceptional individuals among us. But those regions of inquiry are perhaps too spook-haunted to interest an academic audience, and the only evidence I feel it now decorous to bring to the support of Fechner is drawn from ordinary religious experience. I think it may be asserted that there *are* religious experiences of a specific nature, not deducible by analogy or psychological reasoning from our other sorts of experience. I think that they point with reasonable probability to the continuity of our consciousness with a wider spiritual environment from which the ordinary prudential man (who is the only man that scientific psychology, so called, takes cognizance of) is shut off. I shall begin my final lecture by referring to them again briefly.

LECTURE VIII

CONCLUSIONS

AT THE CLOSE of my last lecture I referred to the existence of religious experiences of a specific nature. I must now explain just what I mean by such a claim. Briefly, the facts I have in mind may all be described as experiences of an unexpected life succeeding upon death. By this I don't mean immortality, or the death of the body. I mean the deathlike termination of certain mental processes within the individual's experience, processes that run to failure, and in some individuals, at least, eventuate in despair. Just as romantic love seems a comparatively recent literary invention, so these experiences of a life that supervenes upon despair seem to have played no great part in official theology till Luther's time; and possibly the best way to indicate their character will be to point to a certain contrast between the inner life of ourselves and of the ancient Greeks and Romans.

Mr. Chesterton, I think, says somewhere, that the Greeks and Romans, in all that concerned their moral life, were an extraordinarily solemn set of folks. The Athenians thought that the very gods must admire the rectitude of Phocion and Aristides; and those gentlemen themselves were apparently of much the same opinion. Cato's veracity was so impeccable that the extremest incredulity a Roman could express of anything was to say, 'I would not believe it even if Cato had told me.' Good was good, and bad was bad, for these people. Hypocrisy, which church-Christianity brought in, hardly existed; the naturalistic system held firm; its values showed no hollowness and brooked no irony. The individual, if virtuous enough, could meet all possible requirements. The pagan pride had never crumbled. Luther was the first moralist who broke with any effectiveness through the crust of all this naturalistic self-sufficiency, thinking (and possibly he was right) that Saint Paul had done it already. Religious experience of the lutheran type brings all our naturalistic standards to bankruptcy. You are strong only by being weak, it shows. You cannot live on pride or self-sufficingness. There is a light in

768

which all the naturally founded and currently accepted distinctions, excellences, and safeguards of our characters appear as utter childishness. Sincerely to give up one's conceit or hope of being good in one's own right is the only door to the universe's deeper reaches.

These deeper reaches are familiar to evangelical Christianity and to what is nowadays becoming known as 'mind-cure' religion or 'new thought.' The phenomenon is that of new ranges of life succeeding on our most despairing moments. There are resources in us that naturalism with its literal and legal virtues never recks of, possibilities that take our breath away, of another kind of happiness and power, based on giving up our own will and letting something higher work for us, and these seem to show a world wider than either physics or philistine ethics can imagine. Here is a world in which all is well, in *spite* of certain forms of death, indeed *because* of certain forms of death—death of hope, death of strength, death of responsibility, of fear and worry, competency and desert, death of everything that paganism, naturalism, and legalism pin their faith on and tie their trust to.

Reason, operating on our other experiences, even our psychological experiences, would never have inferred these specifically religious experiences in advance of their actual coming. She could not suspect their existence, for they are discontinuous with the 'natural' experiences they succeed upon and invert their values. But as they actually come and are given, creation widens to the view of their recipients. They suggest that our natural experience, our strictly moralistic and prudential experience, may be only a fragment of real human experience. They soften nature's outlines and open out the strangest possibilities and perspectives.

This is why it seems to me that the logical understanding, working in abstraction from such specifically religious experiences, will always omit something, and fail to reach completely adequate conclusions. Death and failure, it will always say, *are* death and failure simply, and can nevermore be one with life; so religious experience, peculiarly so called, needs, in my opinion, to be carefully considered and interpreted by every one who aspires to reason out a more complete philosophy.

The sort of belief that religious experience of this type naturally engenders in those who have it is fully in accord with Fechner's theories. To quote words which I have used elsewhere, the believer finds that the tenderer parts of his personal life are continuous with a *more* of the same quality which is operative in the universe outside of him and which he can keep in working touch with, and in a fashion get on board of and save himself, when all his lower being has gone to pieces in the wreck. In a word, the believer is continuous, to his own consciousness, at any rate, with a wider self from which saving experiences flow in. Those who have such experiences distinctly enough and often enough to live in the light of them remain quite unmoved by criticism, from whatever quarter it may come, be it academic or scientific, or be it merely the voice of logical common sense. They have had their vision and they *know*—that is enough—that we inhabit an invisible spiritual environment from which help comes, our soul being mysteriously one with a larger soul whose instruments we are.

One may therefore plead, I think, that Fechner's ideas are not without direct empirical verification. There is at any rate one side of life which would be easily explicable if those ideas were true, but of which there appears no clear explanation so long as we assume either with naturalism that human consciousness is the highest consciousness there is, or with dualistic theism that there is a higher mind in the cosmos, but that it is discontinuous with our own. It has always been a matter of surprise with me that philosophers of the absolute should have shown so little interest in this department of life, and so seldom put its phenomena in evidence, even when it seemed obvious that personal experience of some kind must have made their confidence in their own vision so strong. The logician's bias has always been too much with them. They have preferred the thinner to the thicker method, dialectical abstraction being so much more dignified and academic than the confused and unwholesome facts of personal biography.

In spite of rationalism's disdain for the particular, the personal, and the unwholesome, the drift of all the evidence we have seems to me to sweep us very strongly towards the belief in some form of superhuman life with which we may, unknown to ourselves, be co-conscious. We may be in the universe as dogs and cats are in our libraries, seeing the books and hearing the conversation, but having no inkling of the meaning of it all. The intellectualist objections to this fall away when the authority of intellectualist logic is undermined by criticism, and then the positive empirical evidence remains. The analogies with ordinary psychology and with the facts of pathology, with those of psychical research, so called, and with those of religious experience, establish, when taken together, a decidedly *formidable* probability in favor of a general view of the world almost identical with Fechner's. The outlines of the superhuman consciousness thus made probable must remain, however, very vague, and the number of functionally distinct 'selves' it comports and carries has to be left entirely problematic. It may be polytheistically or it may be monotheistically conceived of. Fechner, with his distinct earth-soul functioning as our guardian angel, seems to me clearly polytheistic; but the word 'polytheism' usually gives offence, so perhaps it is better not to use it. Only one thing is certain, and that is the result of our criticism of the absolute: the only way to escape from the paradoxes and perplexities that a consistently thought-out monistic universe suffers from as from a species of auto-intoxication—the mystery of the 'fall' namely, of reality lapsing into appearance, truth into error, perfection into imperfection; of evil, in short; the mystery of universal determinism, of the block-universe eternal and without a history, etc.;—the only way of escape, I say, from all this is to be frankly pluralistic and assume that the superhuman consciousness, however vast it may be, has itself an external environment, and consequently is finite. Present day monism carefully repudiates complicity with spinozistic monism. In that, it explains, the many get dissolved in the one and lost, whereas in the improved idealistic form they get preserved in all their manyness as the one's eternal object. The absolute itself is thus represented by absolutists as having a pluralistic object. But if even the absolute has to have a pluralistic vision, why should we ourselves hesitate to be pluralists on our own sole account? Why should we envelop our many with the 'one' that brings so much poison in its train?

The line of least resistance, then, as it seems to me, both in theology and in philosophy, is to accept, along with the superhuman consciousness, the notion that it is not all-embracing, the notion, in other words, that there is a God, but that he is finite, either in power or in knowledge, or in both at once. These, I need hardly tell you, are the terms in which common men have usually carried on their active commerce with God; and the monistic perfections that make the notion of him so paradoxical practically and morally are the colder addition of remote professorial minds operating *in distans* upon conceptual substitutes for him alone.

Why cannot 'experience' and 'reason' meet on this common ground? Why cannot they compromise? May not the godlessness usually but needlessly associated with the philosophy of immediate experience give way to a theism now seen to follow directly from that experience more widely taken? and may not rationalism, satisfied with seeing her *a priori* proofs of God so effectively replaced by empirical evidence, abate something of her absolutist claims? Let God but have the least infinitesimal *other* of any kind beside him, and empiricism and rationalism might strike hands in a lasting treaty of peace. Both might then leave abstract thinness behind them, and seek together, as scientific men seek, by using all the analogies and data within reach, to build up the most probable approximate idea of what the divine consciousness concretely may be like. I venture to beg the younger Oxford idealists to consider seriously this alternative. Few men are as qualified by their intellectual gifts to reap the harvests that seem certain to any one who, like Fechner and Bergson, will leave the thinner for the thicker path.

Compromise and mediation are inseparable from the pluralistic philosophy. Only monistic dogmatism can say of any of its hypotheses, 'It is either that or nothing; take it or leave it just as it stands.' The type of monism prevalent at Oxford has kept this steep and brittle attitude, partly through the proverbial academic preference for thin and elegant logical solutions, partly from a mistaken notion that the only solidly grounded basis for religion was along those lines. If Oxford men could be ignorant of anything, it might almost seem that they had remained ignorant of the great empirical movement towards a pluralistic panpsychic view of the universe, into which our own generation has been drawn, and which threatens to short-circuit their methods entirely and become their religious rival unless they are willing to make themselves its allies. Yet, wedded as they seem to be to the logical machinery and technical apparatus of absolutism, I cannot but believe that their fidelity to the religious ideal in general is deeper still. Especially do I find it hard to believe that the more clerical adherents of the school would hold so fast to its particular machinery if only they could be made to think that religion could be secured in some other way. Let empiricism once become associated with religion, as hitherto, through some strange misunderstanding, it has been associated with irreligion, and I believe that a new era of religion as well as of philosophy will be ready to begin. That great awakening of a new popular interest in philosophy, which is so striking a phenomenon at the present day in all countries, is undoubtedly due in part to religious demands. As the authority of past tradition tends more and more to crumble, men naturally turn a wistful ear to the authority of reason or to the evidence of present fact. They will assuredly not be disappointed if they open their minds to what the thicker and more radical empiricism has to say. I fully believe that such an empiricism is a more natural ally than dialectics ever were, or can be, of the religious life. It is true that superstitions and wild-growing over-beliefs of all sorts will undoubtedly begin to abound if the notion of higher consciousness enveloping ours, of fechnerian earth-souls and the like, grows orthodox and fashionable; still more will they superabound if science ever puts her approving stamp on the phenomena of which Frederic Myers so earnestly advocated the scientific recognition, the phenomena of psychic research so-called—and I myself firmly believe that most of these phenomena are rooted in reality. But ought one seriously to allow such a timid consideration as that to deter one from following the evident path of greatest religious promise? Since when, in this mixed world, was any good thing given us in purest outline and isolation? One of the chief characteristics of life is life's redundancy. The sole condition of our having anything, no matter what, is that we should have so much of it, that we are fortunate if we do not grow sick of the sight and sound of it altogether. Everything is smothered in the litter that is fated to accompany it. Without too much you cannot have enough, of anything. Lots of inferior books, lots of bad statues, lots of dull speeches, of tenth-rate men and women, as a condition of the few precious specimens in either kind being realized! The gold-dust comes to birth with the quartz-sand all around it, and this is as much a condition of religion as of any other excellent possession. There must be extrication; there must be competition for survival; but the clay matrix and the noble gem must first come into being unsifted. Once extricated, the gem can be examined separately, conceptualized, defined, and insulated. But this process of extrication cannot be short-circuited—or if it is, you get the thin inferior abstractions which we have seen, either the hollow unreal god of scholastic theology, or the unintelligible pantheistic monster, instead of the more living divine reality with which it appears certain that empirical methods tend to connect men in imagination.

Arrived at this point, I ask you to go back to my first lecture and remember, if you can, what I quoted there from your own Professor Jacks—what he said about the philosopher himself being taken up into the universe which he is accounting for. This is the fechnerian as well as the hegelian view, and thus our end rejoins harmoniously our beginning. Philosophies are intimate parts of the universe, they express something of its own thought of itself. A philosophy may indeed be a most momentous reaction of the universe upon itself. It may, as I said, possess and handle itself differently in consequence of us philosophers, with our theories, being here; it may trust itself or mistrust itself the more, and, by doing the one or the other, deserve more the trust or the mistrust. What mistrusts itself deserves mistrust.

This is the philosophy of humanism in the widest sense. Our philosophies swell the current of being, add their character to it. They are part of all that we have met, of all that makes us be. As a French philosopher says, 'Nous sommes du réel dans le réel.' Our thoughts determine our acts, and our acts redetermine the previous nature of the world.

Thus does foreignness get banished from our world, and far more so when we take the system of it pluralistically than when we take it monistically. We are indeed internal parts of

God and not external creations, on any possible reading of the panpsychic system. Yet because God is not the absolute, but is himself a part when the system is conceived pluralistically, his functions can be taken as not wholly dissimilar to those of the other smaller parts,—as similar to our functions consequently.

Having an environment, being in time, and working out a history just like ourselves, he escapes from the foreignness from all that is human, of the static timeless perfect absolute.

Remember that one of our troubles with that was its essential foreignness and monstrosity—there really is no other word for it than that. Its having the all-inclusive form gave to it an essentially heterogeneous *nature* from ourselves. And this great difference between absolutism and pluralism demands no difference in the universe's material content—it follows from a difference in the form alone. The all-form or monistic form makes the foreignness result, the each-form or pluralistic form leaves the intimacy undisturbed.

No matter what the content of the universe may be, if you only allow that it is *many* everywhere and always, that *nothing* real escapes from having an environment; so far from defeating its rationality, as the absolutists so unanimously pretend, you leave it in possession of the maximum amount of rationality practically attainable by our minds. Your relations with it, intellectual, emotional, and active, remain fluent and congruous with your own nature's chief demands.

It would be a pity if the word 'rationality' were allowed to give us trouble here. It is one of those eulogistic words that both sides claim—for almost no one is willing to advertise his philosophy as a system of irrationality. But like most of the words which people used eulogistically, the word 'rational' carries too many meanings. The most objective one is that of the older logic—the connexion between two things is rational when you can infer one from the other, mortal from Socrates, *e. g.*; and you can do that only when they have a quality in common. But this kind of rationality is just that logic of identity which all disciples of Hegel find insufficient. They supersede it by the higher rationality of negation and contradiction and make the notion vague again. Then you get the æsthetic or teleologic kinds of rationality, saying that

whatever fits in any way, whatever is beautiful or good, whatever is purposive or gratifies desire, is rational in so far forth.
Then again, according to Hegel, whatever is 'real' is rational.
I myself said awhile ago that whatever lets loose any action
which we are fond of exerting seems rational. It would be
better to give up the word 'rational' altogether than to get
into a merely verbal fight about who has the best right to
keep it.

Perhaps the words 'foreignness' and 'intimacy,' which I put
forward in my first lecture, express the contrast I insist on
better than the words 'rationality' and 'irrationality'—let us
stick to them, then. I now say that the notion of the 'one'
breeds foreignness and that of the 'many' intimacy, for reasons which I have urged at only too great length, and with
which, whether they convince you or not, I may suppose that
you are now well acquainted. But what at bottom is meant
by calling the universe many or by calling it one?

Pragmatically interpreted, pluralism or the doctrine that it
is many means only that the sundry parts of reality *may be
externally related*. Everything you can think of, however vast
or inclusive, has on the pluralistic view a genuinely 'external'
environment of some sort or amount. Things are 'with' one
another in many ways, but nothing includes everything, or
dominates over everything. The word 'and' trails along after
every sentence. Something always escapes. 'Ever not quite'
has to be said of the best attempts made anywhere in the
universe at attaining all-inclusiveness. The pluralistic world is
thus more like a federal republic than like an empire or a
kingdom. However much may be collected, however much
may report itself as present at any effective centre of consciousness or action, something else is self-governed and absent and unreduced to unity.

Monism, on the other hand, insists that when you come
down to reality as such, to the reality of realities, everything
is present to *everything* else in one vast instantaneous co-
implicated completeness—nothing can in *any* sense, functional or substantial, be really absent from anything else, all
things interpenetrate and telescope together in the great total
conflux.

For pluralism, all that we are required to admit as the

constitution of reality is what we ourselves find empirically realized in every minimum of finite life. Briefly it is this, that nothing real is absolutely simple, that every smallest bit of experience is a *multum in parvo* plurally related, that each relation is one aspect, character, or function, way of its being taken, or way of its taking something else; and that a bit of reality when actively engaged in one of these relations is not *by that very fact* engaged in all the other relations simultaneously. The relations are not *all* what the French call *solidaires* with one another. Without losing its identity a thing can either take up or drop another thing, like the log I spoke of, which by taking up new carriers and dropping old ones can travel anywhere with a light escort.

For monism, on the contrary, everything, whether we realize it or not, drags the whole universe along with itself and drops nothing. The log starts and arrives with all its carriers supporting it. If a thing were once disconnected, it could never be connected again, according to monism. The pragmatic difference between the two systems is thus a definite one. It is just thus, that if *a* is once out of sight of *b* or out of touch with it, or, more briefly, 'out' of it at all, then, according to monism, it must always remain so, they can never get together; whereas pluralism admits that on another occasion they may work together, or in some way be connected again. Monism allows for no such things as 'other occasions' in reality—in *real* or absolute reality, that is.

The difference I try to describe amounts, you see, to nothing more than the difference between what I formerly called the each-form and the all-form of reality. Pluralism lets things really exist in the each-form or distributively. Monism thinks that the all-form or collective-unit form is the only form that is rational. The all-form allows of no taking up and dropping of connexions, for in the all the parts are essentially and eternally co-implicated. In the each-form, on the contrary, a thing may be connected by intermediary things, with a thing with which it has no immediate or essential connexion. It is thus at all times in many possible connexions which are not necessarily actualized at the moment. They depend on which actual path of intermediation it may functionally strike into: the word 'or' names a genuine reality. Thus, as I speak here, I may look ahead *or* to the right *or* to the left, and in either case the intervening space and air and ether enable me to see the faces of a different portion of this audience. My being here is independent of any one set of these faces.

If the each-form be the eternal form of reality no less than it is the form of temporal appearance, we still have a coherent world, and not an incarnate incoherence, as is charged by so many absolutists. Our 'multiverse' still makes a 'universe'; for every part, tho it may not be in actual or immediate connexion, is nevertheless in some possible or mediated connexion, with every other part however remote, through the fact that each part hangs together with its very next neighbors in inextricable interfusion. The type of union, it is true, is different here from the monistic type of *all-einheit*. It is not a universal co-implication, or integration of all things *durcheinander*. It is what I call the strung-along type, the type of continuity, contiguity, or concatenation. If you prefer greek words, you may call it the synechistic type. At all events, you see that it forms a definitely conceivable alternative to the through-and-through unity of all things at once, which is the type opposed to it by monism. You see also that it stands or falls with the notion I have taken such pains to defend, of the through-and-through union of adjacent minima of experience, of the confluence of every passing moment of concretely felt experience with its immediately next neighbors. The recognition of this fact of coalescence of next with next in concrete experience, so that all the insulating cuts we make there are artificial products of the conceptualizing faculty, is what distinguishes the empiricism which I call 'radical,' from the bugaboo empiricism of the traditional rationalist critics, which (rightly or wrongly) is accused of chopping up experience into atomistic sensations, incapable of union with one another until a purely intellectual principle has swooped down upon them from on high and folded them in its own conjunctive categories.

Here, then, you have the plain alternative, and the full mystery of the difference between pluralism and monism, as clearly as I can set it forth on this occasion. It packs up into a nutshell:—Is the manyness in oneness that indubitably characterizes the world we inhabit, a property only of the absolute whole of things, so that you must postulate that one-enormous-whole indivisibly as the *prius* of there being any many at all—in other words, start with the rationalistic block-universe, entire, unmitigated, and complete?—or can the finite elements have their own aboriginal forms of many-ness in oneness, and where they have no immediate oneness still be continued into one another by intermediary terms—each one of these terms being one with its next neighbors, and yet the total 'oneness' never getting absolutely complete?

The alternative is definite. It seems to me, moreover, that the two horns of it make pragmatically different ethical appeals—at least they *may* do so, to certain individuals. But if you consider the pluralistic horn to be intrinsically irrational, self-contradictory, and absurd, I can now say no more in its defence. Having done what I could in my earlier lectures to break the edge of the intellectualistic *reductiones ad absurdum*, I must leave the issue in your hands. Whatever I may say, each of you will be sure to take pluralism or leave it, just as your own sense of rationality moves and inclines. The only thing I emphatically insist upon is that it is a fully co-ordinate hypothesis with monism. This world *may*, in the last resort, be a block-universe; but on the other hand it *may* be a universe only strung-along, not rounded in and closed. Reality *may* exist distributively just as it sensibly seems to, after all. On that possibility I do insist.

One's general vision of the probable usually decides such alternatives. They illustrate what I once wrote of as the 'will to believe.' In some of my lectures at Harvard I have spoken of what I call the 'faith-ladder,' as something quite different from the *sorites* of the logic-books, yet seeming to have an analogous form. I think you will quickly recognize in yourselves, as I describe it, the mental process to which I give this name.

A conception of the world arises in you somehow, no matter how. Is it true or not? you ask.

It *might* be true somewhere, you say, for it is not self-contradictory.

It *may* be true, you continue, even here and now.

It is *fit* to be true, it would be *well if it were true*, it *ought* to be true, you presently feel.

It *must* be true, something persuasive in you whispers next; and then—as a final result—

It shall be *held for true*, you decide; it *shall be* as if true, for *you*.

And your acting thus may in certain special cases be a means of making it securely true in the end.

Not one step in this process is logical, yet it is the way in which monists and pluralists alike espouse and hold fast to their visions. It is life exceeding logic, it is the practical reason for which the theoretic reason finds arguments after the conclusion is once there. In just this way do some of us hold to the unfinished pluralistic universe; in just this way do others hold to the timeless universe eternally complete.

Meanwhile the incompleteness of the pluralistic universe, thus assumed and held to as the most probable hypothesis, is also represented by the pluralistic philosophy as being self-reparative through us, as getting its disconnections remedied in part by our behavior. 'We use what we are and have, to know; and what we know, to be and have still more.'[1] Thus do philosophy and reality, theory and action, work in the same circle indefinitely.

I have now finished these poor lectures, and as you look back on them, they doubtless seem rambling and inconclusive enough. My only hope is that they may possibly have proved suggestive; and if indeed they have been suggestive of one point of method, I am almost willing to let all other suggestions go. That point is that *it is high time for the basis of discussion in these questions to be broadened and thickened up*. It is for that that I have brought in Fechner and Bergson, and descriptive psychology and religious experiences, and have ventured even to hint at psychical research and other wild beasts of the philosophic desert. Owing possibly to the fact that Plato and Aristotle, with their intellectualism, are the basis of philosophic study here, the Oxford brand of transcendentalism seems to me to have confined itself too exclusively to thin logical considerations, that would hold good in all conceivable worlds, worlds of an empirical constitution

[1] Blondel: *Annales de Philosophie Chrétienne*, June, 1906, p. 241.

entirely different from ours. It is as if the actual peculiarities of the world that is were entirely irrelevant to the content of truth. But they cannot be irrelevant; and the philosophy of the future must imitate the sciences in taking them more and more elaborately into account. I urge some of the younger members of this learned audience to lay this hint to heart. If you can do so effectively, making still more concrete advances upon the path which Fechner and Bergson have so enticingly opened up, if you can gather philosophic conclusions of any kind, monistic or pluralistic, from the *particulars of life*, I will say, as I now do say, with the cheerfullest of hearts, 'Ring out, ring out my mournful rhymes, but ring the fuller minstrel in.'

APPENDIX A

THE THING AND ITS RELATIONS[1]

EXPERIENCE in its immediacy seems perfectly fluent. The active sense of living which we all enjoy, before reflection shatters our instinctive world for us, is self-luminous and suggests no paradoxes. Its difficulties are disappointments and uncertainties. They are not intellectual contradictions.

When the reflective intellect gets at work, however, it discovers incomprehensibilities in the flowing process. Distinguishing its elements and parts, it gives them separate names, and what it thus disjoins it cannot easily put together. Pyrrhonism accepts the irrationality and revels in its dialectic elaboration. Other philosophies try, some by ignoring, some by resisting, and some by turning the dialectic procedure against itself, negating its first negations, to restore the fluent sense of life again, and let redemption take the place of innocence. The perfection with which any philosophy may do this is the measure of its human success and of its importance in philosophic history. In an article entitled 'A world of pure experience,'[2] I tried my own hand sketchily at the problem, resisting certain first steps of dialectics by insisting in a general way that the immediately experienced conjunctive relations are as real as anything else. If my sketch is not to appear too *naïf*, I must come closer to details, and in the present essay I propose to do so.

I

'Pure experience' is the name which I gave to the immediate flux of life which furnishes the material to our later reflection with its conceptual categories. Only new-born babes, or men in semi-coma from sleep, drugs, illnesses, or blows, may be assumed to have an experience pure in the literal sense of a *that* which is not yet any definite *what*, tho ready to be all

---

[1] Reprinted from the *Journal of Philosophy, Psychology, and Scientific Methods*, vol. ii, New York, 1905, with slight verbal revision.

[2] *Journal of Philosophy, Psychology, and Scientific Methods*, vol. i, No. 20, p. 566.

sorts of whats; full both of oneness and of manyness, but in respects that don't appear; changing throughout, yet so confusedly that its phases interpenetrate and no points, either of distinction or of identity, can be caught. Pure experience in this state is but another name for feeling or sensation. But the flux of it no sooner comes than it tends to fill itself with emphases, and these salient parts become identified and fixed and abstracted; so that experience now flows as if shot through with adjectives and nouns and prepositions and conjunctions. Its purity is only a relative term, meaning the proportional amount of unverbalized sensation which it still embodies.

Far back as we go, the flux, both as a whole and in its parts, is that of things conjunct and separated. The great continua of time, space, and the self envelop everything, betwixt them, and flow together without interfering. The things that they envelop come as separate in some ways and as continuous in others. Some sensations coalesce with some ideas, and others are irreconcilable. Qualities compenetrate one space, or exclude each other from it. They cling together persistently in groups that move as units, or else they separate. Their changes are abrupt or discontinuous; and their kinds resemble or differ; and, as they do so, they fall into either even or irregular series.

In all this the continuities and the discontinuities are absolutely co-ordinate matters of immediate feeling. The conjunctions are as primordial elements of 'fact' as are the distinctions and disjunctions. In the same act by which I feel that this passing minute is a new pulse of my life, I feel that the old life continues into it, and the feeling of continuance in no wise jars upon the simultaneous feeling of a novelty. They, too, compenetrate harmoniously. Prepositions, copulas, and conjunctions, 'is,' 'is n't,' 'then,' 'before,' 'in,' 'on,' 'beside,' 'between,' 'next,' 'like,' 'unlike,' 'as,' 'but,' flower out of the stream of pure experience, the stream of concretes or the sensational stream, as naturally as nouns and adjectives do, and they melt into it again as fluidly when we apply them to a new portion of the stream.

II

If now we ask why we must translate experience from a

more concrete or pure into a more intellectualized form, filling it with ever more abounding conceptual distinctions, rationalism and naturalism give different replies.

The rationalistic answer is that the theoretic life is absolute and its interests imperative; that to understand is simply the duty of man; and that who questions this need not be argued with, for by the fact of arguing he gives away his case.

The naturalist answer is that the environment kills as well as sustains us, and that the tendency of raw experience to extinguish the experient himself is lessened just in the degree in which the elements in it that have a practical bearing upon life are analyzed out of the continuum and verbally fixed and coupled together, so that we may know what is in the wind for us and get ready to react in time. Had pure experience, the naturalist says, been always perfectly healthy, there would never have arisen the necessity of isolating or verbalizing any of its terms. We should just have experienced inarticulately and unintellectually enjoyed. This leaning on 'reaction' in the naturalist account implies that, whenever we intellectualize a relatively pure experience, we ought to do so for the sake of redescending to the purer or more concrete level again; and that if an intellect stays aloft among its abstract terms and generalized relations, and does not reinsert itself with its conclusions into some particular point of the immediate stream of life, it fails to finish out its function and leaves its normal race unrun.

Most rationalists nowadays will agree that naturalism gives a true enough account of the way in which our intellect arose at first, but they will deny these latter implications. The case, they will say, resembles that of sexual love. Originating in the animal need of getting another generation born, this passion has developed secondarily such imperious spiritual needs that, if you ask why another generation ought to be born at all, the answer is: 'Chiefly that love may go on.' Just so with our intellect: it originated as a practical means of serving life; but it has developed incidentally the function of understanding absolute truth; and life itself now seems to be given chiefly as a means by which that function may be prosecuted. But truth and the understanding of it lie among the abstracts and universals, so the intellect now carries on its higher business wholly in this region, without any need of redescending into pure experience again.

If the contrasted tendencies which I thus designate as naturalistic and rationalistic are not recognized by the reader, perhaps an example will make them more concrete. Mr. Bradley, for instance, is an ultra-rationalist. He admits that our intellect is primarily practical, but says that, for philosophers, the practical need is simply Truth.[1] Truth, moreover, must be assumed 'consistent.' Immediate experience has to be broken into subjects and qualities, terms and relations, to be understood as truth at all. Yet when so broken it is less consistent than ever. Taken raw, it is all undistinguished. Intellectualized, it is all distinction without oneness. 'Such an arrangement may *work*, but the theoretic problem is not solved' (p. 23). The question is, '*How* the diversity can exist in harmony with the oneness' (p. 118). To go back to pure experience is unavailing. 'Mere feeling gives no answer to our riddle' (p. 104). Even if your intuition is a fact, it is not an *understanding*. 'It is a mere experience, and furnishes no consistent view' (pp. 108–109). The experiences offered as facts or truths 'I find that my intellect rejects because they contradict themselves. They offer a complex of diversities conjoined in a way which it feels is not its way and which it cannot repeat as its own. . . . For to be satisfied, my intellect must understand, and it cannot understand by taking a congeries in the lump' (p. 570). So Mr. Bradley, in the sole interests of 'understanding' (as he conceives that function), turns his back on finite experience forever. Truth must lie in the opposite direction, the direction of the absolute; and this kind of rationalism and naturalism, or (as I will now call it) pragmatism, walk thenceforward upon opposite paths. For the one, those intellectual products are most true which, turning their face towards the absolute, come nearest to symbolizing its ways of uniting the many and the one. For the other, those are most true which most successfully dip back into the finite stream of feeling and grow most easily confluent with some particular wave or wavelet. Such confluence not only proves the intellectual operation to have been true (as an addition may 'prove' that a

[1] *Appearance and Reality*, pp. 152–153.

subtraction is already rightly performed), but it constitutes, according to pragmatism, all that we mean by calling it true. Only in so far as they lead us, successfully or unsuccessfully, into sensible experience again, are our abstracts and universals true or false at all.

III

In Section the 6th of my article, 'A world of pure experience,' I adopted in a general way the common-sense belief that one and the same world is cognized by our different minds; but I left undiscussed the dialectical arguments which maintain that this is logically absurd. The usual reason given for its being absurd is that it assumes one object (to wit, the world) to stand in two relations at once; to my mind, namely, and again to yours; whereas a term taken in a second relation cannot logically be the same term which it was at first.

I have heard this reason urged so often in discussing with absolutists, and it would destroy my radical empiricism so utterly, if it were valid, that I am bound to give it an attentive ear, and seriously to search its strength.

For instance, let the matter in dispute be a term M, asserted to be on the one hand related to L, and on the other to N; and let the two cases of relation be symbolized by $L—M$ and $M—N$ respectively. When, now, I assume that the experience may immediately come and be given in the shape $L—M—N$, with no trace of doubling or internal fission in the M, I am told that this is all a popular delusion; that $L—M—N$ logically means two different experiences, $L—M$ and $M—N$, namely; and that although the absolute may, and indeed must, from its superior point of view, read its own kind of unity into M's two editions, yet as elements in finite experience the two M's lie irretrievably asunder, and the world between them is broken and unbridged.

In arguing this dialectic thesis, one must avoid slipping from the logical into the physical point of view. It would be easy, in taking a concrete example to fix one's ideas by, to choose one in which the letter M should stand for a collective noun of some sort, which noun, being related to L by one of its parts and to N by another, would inwardly be two things when it stood outwardly in both relations. Thus, one might say: 'David Hume, who weighed so many stone by his body, influences posterity by his doctrine.' The body and the doctrine are two things, between which our finite minds can discover no real sameness, though the same name covers both of them. And then, one might continue: 'Only an absolute is capable of uniting such a non-identity.' We must, I say, avoid this sort of example; for the dialectic insight, if true at all, must apply to terms and relations universally. It must be true of abstract units as well as of nouns collective; and if we prove it by concrete examples, we must take the simplest, so as to avoid irrelevant material suggestions.

Taken thus in all its generality, the absolutist contention seems to use as its major premise Hume's notion 'that all our distinct perceptions are distinct existences, and that the mind never perceives any real connexion among distinct existences.' Undoubtedly, since we use two phrases in talking first about 'M's relation to L' and then again about 'M's relation to N,' we must be having, or must have had, two distinct perceptions;—and the rest would then seem to follow duly. But the starting-point of the reasoning here seems to be the fact of the two *phrases*; and this suggests that the argument may be merely verbal. Can it be that the whole dialectic achievement consists in attributing to the experience talked-about a constitution similar to that of the language in which we describe it? Must we assert the objective doubleness of the M merely because we have to name it twice over when we name its two relations?

Candidly, I can think of no other reason than this for the dialectic conclusion![1] for, if we think, not of our words, but of any simple concrete matter which they may be held to signify, the experience itself belies the paradox asserted. We use indeed two separate concepts in analyzing our object, but we know them all the while to be but substitutional, and that the M in L—M and the M in M—N *mean* (*i. e.*, are capable of leading to and terminating in) one self-same piece, M, of sensible experience. This persistent identity of certain units, or emphases, or points, or objects, or members—call them what

[1] Technically, it seems classable as a 'fallacy of composition.' A duality, predicable of the two wholes, L—M and M—N, is forthwith predicated of one of their parts, M.

you will—of the experience-continuum, is just one of those conjunctive features of it, on which I am obliged to insist so emphatically. For samenesses are parts of experience's indefeasible structure. When I hear a bell-stroke and, as life flows on, its after-image dies away, I still hark back to it as 'that same bell-stroke.' When I see a thing M, with L to the left of it and N to the right of it, I see it *as* one M; and if you tell me I have had to 'take' it twice, I reply that if I 'took' it a thousand times, I should still *see* it as a unit.[1] Its unity is aboriginal, just as the multiplicity of my successive takings is aboriginal. It comes unbroken as *that M*, as a singular which I encounter; they come broken, as *those* takings, as my plurality of operations. The unity and the separateness are strictly co-ordinate. I do not easily fathom why my opponents should find the separateness so much more easily understandable that they must needs infect the whole of finite experience with it, and relegate the unity (now taken as a bare postulate and no longer as a thing positively perceivable) to the region of the absolute's mysteries. I do not easily fathom this, I say, for the said opponents are above mere verbal quibbling; yet all that I can catch in their talk is the substitution of what is true of certain words for what is true of what they signify. They stay with the words,—not returning to the stream of life whence all the meaning of them came, and which is always ready to reabsorb them.

IV

For aught this argument proves, then, we may continue to believe that one thing can be known by many knowers. But the denial of one thing in many relations is but one application of a still profounder dialectic difficulty. Man can't be good, said the sophists, for man is *man* and *good* is good; and Hegel and Herbart in their day, more recently H. Spir, and most recently and elaborately of all, Mr. Bradley, inform

[1] I may perhaps refer here to my *Principles of Psychology*, vol. i, pp. 459 ff. It really seems 'weird' to have to argue (as I am forced now to do) for the notion that it is one sheet of paper (with its two surfaces and all that lies between) which is both under my pen and on the table while I write—the 'claim' that it is two sheets seems so brazen. Yet I sometimes suspect the absolutists of sincerity!

us that a term can logically only be a punctiform unit, and that not one of the conjunctive relations between things, which experience seems to yield, is rationally possible.

Of course, if true, this cuts off radical empiricism without even a shilling. Radical empiricism takes conjunctive relations at their face-value, holding them to be as real as the terms united by them. The world it represents as a collection, some parts of which are conjunctively and others disjunctively related. Two parts, themselves disjoined, may nevertheless hang together by intermediaries with which they are severally connected, and the whole world eventually may hang together similarly, inasmuch as *some* path of conjunctive transition by which to pass from one of its parts to another may always be discernible. Such determinately various hanging-together may be called *concatenated* union, to distinguish it from the 'through-and-through' type of union, 'each in all and all in each' (union of *total conflux*, as one might call it), which monistic systems hold to obtain when things are taken in their absolute reality. In a concatenated world a partial conflux often is experienced. Our concepts and our sensations are confluent; successive states of the same ego, and feelings of the same body are confluent. Where the experience is not of conflux, it may be of conterminousness (things with but one thing between); or of contiguousness (nothing between); or of likeness; or of nearness; or of simultaneousness; or of inness; or of on-ness; or of for-ness; or of simple with-ness; or even of mere and-ness, which last relation would make of however disjointed a world otherwise, at any rate for that occasion a universe 'of discourse.' Now Mr. Bradley tells us that none of these relations, as we actually experience them, can possibly be real.[1] My next duty, accordingly, must be to rescue radical empiricism from Mr. Bradley. Fortunately, as it

[1] Here again the reader must beware of slipping from logical into phenomenal considerations. It may well be that we *attribute* a certain relation falsely, because the circumstances of the case, being complex, have deceived us. At a railway station we may take our own train, and not the one that fills our window, to be moving. We here put motion in the wrong place in the world, but in its original place the motion is a part of reality. What Mr. Bradley means is nothing like this, but rather that such things as motion are nowhere real, and that, even in their aboriginal and empirically incorrigible seats, relations are impossible of comprehension.

seems to me, his general contention, that the very notion of relation is unthinkable clearly, has been successfully met by many critics.[1]

It is a burden to the flesh, and an injustice both to readers and to the previous writers, to repeat good arguments already printed. So, in noticing Mr. Bradley, I will confine myself to the interests of radical empiricism solely.

V

The first duty of radical empiricism, taking given conjunctions at their face-value, is to class some of them as more intimate and some as more external. When two terms are *similar*, their very natures enter into the relation. Being *what* they are, no matter where or when, the likeness never can be denied, if asserted. It continues predicable as long as the terms continue. Other relations, the *where* and the *when*, for example, seem adventitious. The sheet of paper may be 'off' or 'on' the table, for example; and in either case the relation involves only the outside of its terms. Having an outside, both of them, they contribute by it to the relation. It is external: the term's inner nature is irrelevant to it. Any book, any table, may fall into the relation, which is created *pro hac vice*, not by their existence, but by their casual situation. It is just because so many of the conjunctions of experience seem so external that a philosophy of pure experience must tend to pluralism in its ontology. So far as things have space-relations, for example, we are free to imagine them with different origins even. If they could get to *be*, and get into space at all, then they may have done so separately. Once there, however, they are *additives* to one another, and, with no prejudice to their natures, all sorts of space-relations may supervene between them. The question of how things could come to be, anyhow, is wholly different from the question what their relations, once the being accomplished, may consist in.

---

[1] Particularly so by Andrew Seth Pringle-Pattison, in his *Man and the Cosmos*; by L. T. Hobhouse, in chapter xii (the Validity of Judgment) of his *Theory of Knowledge*; and by F. C. S. Schiller, in his *Humanism*, Essay XI. Other fatal reviews (in my opinion) are Hodder's, in the *Psychological Review*, vol. i, 307; Stout's, in the *Proceedings of the Aristotelian Society*, 1901–02, p. 1; and MacLennan's, in the *Journal of Philosophy*, etc., vol. i, 403.

Mr. Bradley now affirms that such external relations as the space-relations which we here talk of must hold of entirely different subjects from those of which the absence of such relations might a moment previously have been plausibly asserted. Not only is the *situation* different when the book is on the table, but the *book itself* is different as a book, from what it was when it was off the table.[1] He admits that 'such external relations seem possible and even existing. . . . That you do not alter what you compare or rearrange in space seems to common sense quite obvious, and that on the other side there are as obvious difficulties does not occur to common sense at all. And I will begin by pointing out these difficulties. . . . There is a relation in the result, and this relation, we hear, is to make no difference in its terms. But, if so, to what does it make a difference? [*does n't it make a difference to us onlookers, at least?*] and what is the meaning and sense of qualifying the terms by it? [*Surely the meaning is to tell the truth about their relative position.*[2]] If, in short, it is external to the terms, how can it possibly be true *of* them? [*Is it the 'intimacy' suggested by the little word 'of,' here, which I have underscored, that is the root of Mr. Bradley's trouble?*] . . . If the terms from their inner nature do not enter into the relation, then, so far as they are concerned, they seem related for no reason at all. . . . Things are spatially related, first in one way, and then become related in another way, and yet in no way themselves are altered; for the relations, it is said, are but external. But I reply that, if so, I cannot *understand* the leaving by the terms of one set of relations and their adoption of another fresh set. The process and its result to the terms, if

[1] Once more, don't slip from logical into physical situations. Of course, if the table be wet, it will moisten the book, or if it be slight enough and the book heavy enough, the book will break it down. But such collateral phenomena are not the point at issue. The point is whether the successive relations 'on' and 'not-on' can rationally (not physically) hold of the same constant terms, abstractly taken. Professor A. E. Taylor drops from logical into material considerations when he instances color-contrast as a proof that *A*, 'as contra-distinguished from *B*, is not the same thing as mere *A* not in any way affected' (*Elements of Metaphysics*, 1903, p. 145). Note the substitution, for 'related,' of the word 'affected,' which begs the whole question.

[2] But 'is there any sense,' asks Mr. Bradley, peevishly, on p. 579, 'and if so, what sense, in truth that is only outside and "about" things?' Surely such a question may be left unanswered.

they contribute nothing to it [*surely they contribute to it all there is 'of' it!*], seem irrational throughout. [*If 'irrational' here means simply 'non-rational,' or non-deducible from the essence of either term singly, it is no reproach; if it means 'contradicting' such essence, Mr. Bradley should show wherein and how.*] But, if they contribute anything, they must surely be affected internally. [*Why so, if they contribute only their surface? In such relations as 'on,' 'a foot away,' 'between,' 'next,' etc., only surfaces are in question.*] . . . If the terms contribute anything whatever, then the terms are affected [*inwardly altered?*] by the arrangement. . . . That for working purposes we treat, and do well to treat, some relations as external merely, I do not deny, and that of course is not the question at issue here. That question is . . . whether in the end and in principle a mere external relation [*i. e., a relation which can change without forcing its terms to change their nature simultaneously*] is possible and forced on us by the facts.'[1]

Mr. Bradley next reverts to the antinomies of space, which, according to him, prove it to be unreal, although it appears as so prolific a medium of external relations; and he then concludes that 'Irrationality and externality cannot be the last truth about things. Somewhere there must be a reason why this and that appear together. And this reason and reality must reside in the whole from which terms and relations are abstractions, a whole in which their internal connexion must lie, and out of which from the background appear those fresh results which never could have come from the premises' (p. 577). And he adds that 'Where the whole is different, the terms that qualify and contribute to it must so far be different. . . . They are altered so far only [*how far? farther than externally, yet not through and through?*], but still they are altered. . . . I must insist that in each case the terms are qualified by their whole [*qualified how?—do their external relations, situations, dates, etc., changed as these are in the new whole, fail to qualify them 'far' enough?*], and that in the second case there is a whole which differs both logically and psychologically from the first whole; and I urge that in contributing to the change the terms so far are altered' (p. 579).

---

[1] *Appearance and Reality*, 2d edition, pp. 575–576.

Not merely the relations, then, but the terms are altered: *und zwar* 'so far.' But just *how* far is the whole problem; and 'through-and-through' would seem (in spite of Mr. Bradley's somewhat undecided utterances[1]) to be the full bradleyan answer. The 'whole' which he here treats as primary and determinative of each part's manner of 'contributing,' simply *must*, when it alters, alter in its entirety. There *must* be total conflux of its parts, each into and through each other. The 'must' appears here as a *Machtspruch*, as an *ipse dixit* of Mr. Bradley's absolutistically tempered 'understanding,' for he candidly confesses that how the parts *do* differ as they contribute to different wholes, is unknown to him (p. 578).

Although I have every wish to comprehend the authority by which Mr. Bradley's understanding speaks, his words leave me wholly unconverted. 'External relations' stand with their withers all unwrung, and remain, for aught he proves to the contrary, not only practically workable, but also perfectly intelligible factors of reality.

VI

Mr. Bradley's understanding shows the most extraordinary power of perceiving separations and the most extraordinary impotence in comprehending conjunctions. One would natu-

---

[1] I say 'undecided,' because, apart from the 'so far,' which sounds terribly half-hearted, there are passages in these very pages in which Mr. Bradley admits the pluralistic thesis. Read, for example, what he says, on p. 578, of a billiard ball keeping its 'character' unchanged, though, in its change of place, its 'existence' gets altered; or what he says, on p. 579, of the possibility that an abstract quality A, B, or C, in a thing, 'may throughout remain unchanged' although the thing be altered; or his admission that in red-hairedness, both as analyzed out of a man and when given with the rest of him, there may be 'no change' (p. 580). Why does he immediately add that for the pluralist to plead the non-mutation of such abstractions would be an *ignoratio elenchi*? It is impossible to admit it to be such. The entire *elenchus* and inquest is just as to whether parts which you can abstract from existing wholes can also contribute to other wholes without changing their inner nature. If they can thus mould various wholes into new *gestaltqualitäten*, then it follows that the same elements are logically able to exist in different wholes [whether physically able would depend on additional hypotheses]; that partial changes are thinkable, and through-and-through change not a dialectic necessity; that monism is only an hypothesis; and that an additively constituted universe is a rationally respectable hypothesis also. All the theses of radical empiricism, in short, follow.

rally say 'neither or both,' but not so Mr. Bradley. When a common man analyzes certain *whats* from out the stream of experience, he understands their distinctness *as thus isolated*. But this does not prevent him from equally well understanding their combination with each other *as originally experienced in the concrete*, or their confluence with new sensible experiences in which they recur as 'the same.' Returning into the stream of sensible presentation, nouns and adjectives, and *thats* and abstract *whats*, grow confluent again, and the word 'is' names all these experiences of conjunction. Mr. Bradley understands the isolation of the abstracts, but to understand the combination is to him impossible.[1] 'To understand a complex *AB*,' he says, 'I must begin with *A* or *B*. And beginning, say with *A*, if I then merely find *B*, I have either lost *A*, or I have got beside *A*, [*the word 'beside' seems here vital, as meaning a conjunction 'external' and therefore unintelligible*] something else, and in neither case have I understood.[2] For my intellect cannot simply unite a diversity, nor has it in itself any form or way of togetherness, and you gain nothing if, beside *A* and *B*, you offer me their conjunction in fact. For to my intellect that is no more than another external element. And "facts," once for all, are for my intellect not true unless they satisfy it. . . . The intellect has in its nature no principle of mere togetherness' (pp. 570, 572).

Of course Mr. Bradley has a right to define 'intellect' as the power by which we perceive separations but not unions—provided he give due notice to the reader. But why then claim that such a maimed and amputated power must reign su-

---

[1] So far as I catch his state of mind, it is somewhat like this: 'Book,' 'table,' 'on'—how does the existence of these three abstract elements result in *this* book being livingly on *this* table? Why is n't the table on the book? Or why does n't the 'on' connect itself with another book, or something that is not a table? Must n't something *in* each of the three elements already determine the two others to *it*, so that they do not settle elsewhere or float vaguely? Must n't the *whole fact be prefigured in each part*, and exist *de jure* before it can exist *de facto*? But, if so, in what can the jural existence consist, if not in a spiritual miniature of the whole fact's constitution actuating every partial factor as its purpose? But is this anything but the old metaphysical fallacy of looking behind a fact *in esse* for the ground of the fact, and finding it in the shape of the very same fact *in posse*? Somewhere we must leave off with a *constitution* behind which there is nothing.

[2] Apply this to the case of 'book-on-table'! W. J.

preme in philosophy, and accuse on its behoof the whole empirical world of irrationality? It is true that he elsewhere (p.
568) attributes to the intellect a *proprius motus* of transition,
but says that when he looks for *these* transitions in the detail
of living experience, he 'is unable to verify such a solution'
(p. 569).

Yet he never explains what the intellectual transitions would
be like in case we had them. He only defines them nega-
tively—they are not spatial, temporal, predicative, or causal;
or qualitatively or otherwise serial; or in any way relational as
we naïvely trace relations, for relations *separate* terms, and
need themselves to be hooked on *ad infinitum*. The nearest
approach he makes to describing a truly intellectual transition
is where he speaks of *A* and *B* as being 'united, each from its
own nature, in a whole which is the nature of both alike' (p.
570). But this (which, *pace* Mr. Bradley, seems exquisitely
analogous to 'taking a congeries in a lump,' if not to 'swamp-
ing') suggests nothing but that *conflux* which pure experience
so abundantly offers, as when 'space,' 'white,' and 'sweet' are
confluent in a 'lump of sugar,' or kinesthetic, dermal, and optical sensations confluent in 'my hand.'[1] All that I can verify
in the transitions which Mr. Bradley's intellect desiderates as
its *proprius motus* is a reminiscence of these and other sensible
conjunctions (especially space-conjunctions), but a reminiscence so vague that its originals are not recognized. Bradley,
in short, repeats the fable of the dog, the bone, and its image
in the water. With a world of particulars, given in loveliest
union, in conjunction definitely various, and variously definite, the 'how' of which you 'understand' as soon as you see
the fact of them,[2] for there is no how except the constitution
of the fact as given; with all this given him, I say, in pure
experience, he asks for some ineffable union in the abstract
instead, which, if he gained it, would only be a duplicate of

[1] How meaningless is the contention that in such wholes (or in 'book-on-
table,' 'watch-in-pocket,' etc.) the relation is an additional entity *between* the
terms, needing itself to be related again to each! Both Bradley (*Appearance
and Reality*, pp. 32–33) and Royce (*The World and the Individual*, i, 128)
lovingly repeat this piece of profundity.

[2] The 'why' and the 'whence' are entirely other questions, not under discussion, as I understand Mr. Bradley. Not how experience gets itself born,
but how it can be what it is after it is born, is the puzzle.

what he has already in his full possession. Surely he abuses the privilege which society grants to all of us philosophers, of being puzzle-headed.

Polemic writing like this is odious; but with absolutism in possession in so many quarters, omission to defend my radical empiricism against its best known champion would count as either superficiality or inability. I have to conclude that its dialectic has not invalidated in the least degree the usual conjunctions by which the world, as experienced, hangs so variously together. In particular it leaves an empirical theory of knowledge intact, and lets us continue to believe with common sense that one object *may* be known, if we have any ground for thinking that it *is* known, to many knowers.

APPENDIX B

THE EXPERIENCE OF ACTIVITY[1]

M R. BRADLEY calls the question of activity a scandal
. . . to philosophy, and if one turns to the current
literature of the subject—his own writings included—one
easily gathers what he means. The opponents cannot even
understand one another. Mr. Bradley says to Mr. Ward: 'I do
not care what your oracle is, and your preposterous psychology may here be gospel if you please; . . . but if the revelation does contain a meaning, I will commit myself to this:
either the oracle is so confused that its signification is not
discoverable, or, upon the other hand, if it can be pinned
down to any definite statement, then that statement will be
false.'[2] Mr. Ward in turn says of Mr. Bradley: 'I cannot even
imagine the state of mind to which his description applies. . . . It reads like an unintentional travesty of Herbar-
tian Psychology by one who has tried to improve upon it
without being at the pains to master it.' Münsterberg excludes
a view opposed to his own by saying that with any one who
holds it a *verständigung* with him is '*grundsätzlich ausgeschlossen*'; and Royce, in a review of Stout,[3] hauls him over the
coals at great length for defending 'efficacy' in a way which I,
for one, never gathered from reading him, and which I have
heard Stout himself say was quite foreign to the intention of
his text.

In these discussions distinct questions are habitually jum-
bled and different points of view are talked of *durcheinander*.

(1) There is a psychological question: Have we perceptions
of activity? and if so, what are they like, and when and where
do we have them?

(2) There is a metaphysical question: Is there a *fact* of activity? and if so, what idea must we frame of it? What is it

[1]President's Address before the American Psychological Association, December, 1904. Reprinted from the *Psychological Review*, vol. xii, 1905, with
slight verbal revision.
[2]*Appearance and Reality*, p. 117. Obviously written *at* Ward, though Ward's
name is not mentioned.
[3]*Mind*, N. S., VI, 379.

like? and what does it do, if it does anything? And finally there is a logical question:

(3) Whence do we *know* activity? By our own feelings of it solely? or by some other source of information? Throughout page after page of the literature one knows not which of these questions is before one; and mere description of the surface-show of experience is proffered as if it implicitly answered every one of them. No one of the disputants, moreover, tries to show what pragmatic consequences his own view would carry, or what assignable particular differences in any one's experience it would make if his adversary's were triumphant.

It seems to me that if radical empiricism be good for anything, it ought, with its pragmatic method and its principle of pure experience, to be able to avoid such tangles, or at least to simplify them somewhat. The pragmatic method starts from the postulate that there is no difference of truth that does n't make a difference of fact somewhere; and it seeks to determine the meaning of all differences of opinion by making the discussion hinge as soon as possible upon some practical or particular issue. The principle of pure experience is also a methodical postulate. Nothing shall be admitted as fact, it says, except what can be experienced at some definite time by some experient; and for every feature of fact ever so experienced, a definite place must be found somewhere in the final system of reality. In other words: Everything real must be experienceable somewhere, and every kind of thing experienced must somewhere be real.

Armed with these rules of method, let us see what face the problems of activity present to us.

By the principle of pure experience, either the word 'activity' must have no meaning at all, or else the original type and model of what it means must lie in some concrete kind of experience that can be definitely pointed out. Whatever ulterior judgments we may eventually come to make regarding activity, *that sort* of thing will be what the judgments are about. The first step to take, then, is to ask where in the stream of experience we seem to find what we speak of as activity. What we are to think of the activity thus found will be a later question.

Now it is obvious that we are tempted to affirm activity

wherever we find anything *going on*. Taken in the broadest sense, any apprehension of something *doing*, is an experience of activity. Were our world describable only by the words 'nothing happening,' 'nothing changing,' 'nothing doing,' we should unquestionably call it an 'inactive' world. Bare activity, then, as we may call it, means the bare fact of event or change. 'Change taking place' is a unique content of experience, one of those 'conjunctive' objects which radical empiricism seeks so earnestly to rehabilitate and preserve. The sense of activity is thus in the broadest and vaguest way synonymous with the sense of 'life.' We should feel our own subjective life at least, even in noticing and proclaiming an otherwise inactive world. Our own reaction on its monotony would be the one thing experienced there in the form of something coming to pass.

This seems to be what certain writers have in mind when they insist that for an experient to be at all is to be active. It seems to justify, or at any rate to explain, Mr. Ward's expression that we *are* only as we are active,[1] for we *are* only as experients; and it rules out Mr. Bradley's contention that 'there is no original experience of anything like activity.' What we ought to say about activities thus simply given, whose they are, what they effect, or whether indeed they effect anything at all—these are later questions, to be answered only when the field of experience is enlarged.

Bare activity would thus be predicable, though there were no definite direction, no actor, and no aim. Mere restless zigzag movement, or a wild *ideenflucht*, or *rhapsodie der wahrnehmungen*, as Kant would say, would constitute an active as distinguished from an inactive world.

But in this actual world of ours, as it is given, a part at least of the activity comes with definite direction; it comes with desire and sense of goal; it comes complicated with resistances which it overcomes or succumbs to, and with the efforts which the feeling of resistance so often provokes; and it is in complex experiences like these that the notions of distinct agents, and of passivity as opposed to activity arise. Here also the notion of causal efficacy comes to birth. Perhaps the most

[1] *Naturalism and Agnosticism*, vol. ii, p. 245. One thinks naturally of the peripatetic *actus primus* and *actus secundus* here.

elaborate work ever done in descriptive psychology has been the analysis by various recent writers of the more complex activity-situations. In their descriptions, exquisitely subtle some of them,[1] the activity appears as the *gestaltqualität* or the *fundirte inhalt* (or as whatever else you may please to call the conjunctive form) which the content falls into when we experience it in the ways which the describers set forth. Those factors in those relations are what we *mean* by activity-situations; and to the possible enumeration and accumulation of their circumstances and ingredients there would seem to be no natural bound. Every hour of human life could contribute to the picture gallery; and this is the only fault that one can find with such descriptive industry—where is it going to stop? Ought we to listen forever to verbal pictures of what we have already in concrete form in our own breasts?[2] They never take us off the superficial plane. We knew the facts already—less spread out and separated, to be sure—but we knew them still. We always felt our own activity, for example, as 'the expansion of an idea with which our Self is identified, against an obstacle'; and the following out of such a definition through a multitude of cases elaborates the obvious so as to be little more than an exercise in synonymic speech.

All the descriptions have to trace familiar outlines, and to use familiar terms. The activity is, for example, attributed either to a physical or to a mental agent, and is either aimless or directed. If directed, it shows tendency. The tendency may or may not be resisted. If not, we call the activity immanent, as when a body moves in empty space by its momentum, or our thoughts wander at their own sweet will. If resistance is met, *its* agent complicates the situation. If now, in spite of resistance, the original tendency continues, effort makes its appearance, and along with effort, strain or squeeze. Will, in the narrower sense of the word, then comes upon the scene, whenever, along with the tendency, the strain and squeeze are

[1] Their existence forms a curious commentary on Professor Münsterberg's dogma that will-attitudes are not describable. He himself has contributed in a superior way to their description, both in his *Willenshandlung*, and in his *Grundzüge*, Part II, chap. ix, § 7.

[2] I ought myself to cry *peccavi*, having been a voluminous sinner in my own chapter on the will.

sustained. But the resistance may be great enough to check the tendency, or even to reverse its path. In that case, we (if 'we' were the original agents or subjects of the tendency) are overpowered. The phenomenon turns into one of tension simply, or of necessity succumbed-to, according as the opposing power is only equal, or is superior to ourselves.

Whosoever describes an experience in such terms as these, describes an experience *of* activity. If the word have any meaning, it must denote what there is found. *There* is complete activity in its original and first intention. What it is 'known-as' is what there appears. The experiencer of such a situation possesses all that the idea contains. He feels the tendency, the obstacle, the will, the strain, the triumph, or the passive giving up, just as he feels the time, the space, the swiftness or intensity, the movement, the weight and color, the pain and pleasure, the complexity, or whatever remaining characters the situation may involve. He goes through all that ever can be imagined where activity is supposed. If we suppose activities to go on outside of our experience, it is in forms like these that we must suppose them, or else give them some other name; for the word 'activity' has no imaginable content whatever save these experiences of process, obstruction, striving, strain, or release, ultimate *qualia* as they are of the life given us to be known.

Were this the end of the matter, one might think that whenever we had successfully lived through an activity-situation we should have to be permitted, without provoking contradiction, to say that we had been really active, that we had met real resistance and had really prevailed. Lotze somewhere says that to be an entity all that is necessary is to *gelten* as an entity, to operate, or be felt, experienced, recognized, or in any way realized, as such. In our activity-experiences the activity assuredly fulfils Lotze's demand. It makes itself *gelten*. It is witnessed at its work. No matter what activities there may really be in this extraordinary universe of ours, it is impossible for us to conceive of any one of them being either lived through or authentically known otherwise than in this dramatic shape of something sustaining a felt purpose against felt obstacles and overcoming or being overcome. What 'sustaining' means here is clear to any one who has lived through the experience, but to no one else; just as 'loud,' 'red,' 'sweet,' mean something only to beings with ears, eyes, and tongues. The *percipi* in these originals of experience is the *esse*; the curtain is the picture. If there is anything hiding in the background, it ought not to be called activity, but should get itself another name.

This seems so obviously true that one might well experience astonishment at finding so many of the ablest writers on the subject flatly denying that the activity we live through in these situations is real. Merely to feel active is not to be active, in their sight. The agents that appear in the experience are not real agents, the resistances do not really resist, the effects that appear are not really effects at all.[1] It is evident from this that mere descriptive analysis of any one of our activity-experiences is not the whole story, that there is something still to tell *about* them that has led such able writers to conceive of a *Simon-pure* activity, of an activity *an sich*, that does, and does n't merely appear to us to do, and compared with whose real doing all this phenomenal activity is but a specious sham.

[1] *Verborum gratiâ*: 'The feeling of activity is not able, quâ feeling, to tell us anything about activity' (Loveday: *Mind*, N. s., X., 463); 'A sensation or feeling or sense of activity . . . is not, looked at in another way, a feeling of activity at all. It is a mere sensation shut up within which you could by no reflection get the idea of activity. . . . Whether this experience is or is not later on a character essential to our perception and our idea of activity, it, as it comes first, is not in itself an experience of activity at all. It, as it comes first, is only so for extraneous reasons and only so for an outside observer' (Bradley, *Appearance and Reality*, 2d edition, p. 605); 'In dem tätigkeitsgefühle leigt an sich nicht der geringste beweis für das vorhandensein einer psychischen tätigkeit' (Münsterberg: *Grundzüge*, etc., p. 67). I could multiply similar quotations, and would have introduced some of them into my text to make it more concrete, save that the mingling of different points of view in most of these author's discussions (not in Münsterberg's) make it impossible to disentangle exactly what they mean. I am sure in any case to be accused of misrepresenting them totally, even in this note, by omission of the context, so the less I name names and the more I stick to abstract characterization of a merely possible style of opinion, the safer it will be. And apropos of misunderstandings, I may add to this note a complaint on my own account. Professor Stout, in the excellent chapter on 'Mental Activity,' in vol. i of his *Analytic Psychology*, takes me to task for identifying spiritual activity with certain muscular feelings, and gives quotations to bear him out. They are from certain paragraphs on 'the Self,' in which my attempt was to show what the central nucleus of the activities that we call 'ours' is. I found it in certain intracephalic movements which we habitually oppose, as 'sub-

The metaphysical question opens here; and I think that the state of mind of one possessed by it is often something

---

jective,' to the activities of the transcorporeal world. I sought to show that there is no direct evidence that we feel the activity of an inner spiritual agent as such (I should now say the activity of 'consciousness' as such, see my paper 'Does consciousness exist?' in the *Journal of Philosophy*, vol. i, p. 477). There are, in fact, three distinguishable 'activities' in the field of discussion: the elementary activity involved in the mere *that* of experience, in the fact that *something* is going on, and the farther specification of this *something* into two *whats*, an activity felt as 'ours,' and an activity ascribed to objects. Stout, as I apprehend him, identifies 'our' activity with that of the total experience-process, and when I circumscribe it as a part thereof, accuses me of treating it as a sort of external appendage to itself (pp. 162–163), as if I 'separated the activity from the process which is active.' But all the processes in question are active, and their activity is inseparable from their being. My book raised only the question of *which* activity deserved the name of 'ours.' So far as we are 'persons,' and contrasted and opposed to an 'environment,' movements in our body figure as our activities; and I am unable to find any other activities that are ours in this strictly personal sense. There is a wider sense in which the whole 'choir of heaven and furniture of the earth,' and their activities, are ours, for they are our 'objects.' But 'we' are here only another name for the total process of experience, another name for all that is, in fact; and I was dealing with the personal and individualized self exclusively in the passages with which Professor Stout finds fault.

The individualized self, which I believe to be the only thing properly called self, is a part of the content of the world experienced. The world experienced (otherwise called the 'field of consciousness') comes at all times with our body as its centre, centre of vision, centre of action, centre of interest. Where the body is is 'here'; when the body acts is 'now'; what the body touches is 'this'; all other things are 'there' and 'then' and 'that.' These words of emphasized position imply a systematization of things with reference to a focus of action and interest which lies in the body; and the systematization is now so instinctive (was it ever not so?) that no developed or active experience exists for us at all except in that ordered form. So far as 'thoughts' and 'feelings' can be active, their activity terminates in the activity of the body, and only through first arousing its activities can they begin to change those of the rest of the world. The body is the storm centre, the origin of co-ordinates, the constant place of stress in all that experience-train. Everything circles round it, and is felt from its point of view. The word 'I,' then, is primarily a noun of position, just like 'this' and 'here.' Activities attached to 'this' position have prerogative emphasis, and, if activities have feelings, must be felt in a peculiar way. The word 'my' designates the kind of emphasis. I see no inconsistency whatever in defending, on the one hand, 'my' activities as unique and opposed to those of outer nature, and, on the other hand, in affirming, after introspection, that they consist in movements in the head. The 'my' of them is the emphasis, the feeling of perspective-interest in which they are dyed.

like this: 'It is all very well,' we may imagine him saying, 'to talk about certain experience-series taking on the form of feelings of activity, just as they might take on musical or geometric forms. Suppose that they do so; suppose that what we feel is a will to stand a strain. Does our feeling do more than *record* the fact that the strain is sustained? The *real* activity, meanwhile, is the *doing* of the fact; and what is the doing made of before the record is made? What in the will *enables* it to act thus? And these trains of experience themselves, in which activities appear, what makes them *go* at all? Does the activity in one bit of experience bring the next bit into being? As an empiricist you cannot say so, for you have just declared activity to be only a kind of synthetic object, or conjunctive relation experienced between bits of experience already made. But what made them at all? What propels experience *überhaupt* into being? *There* is the activity that *operates*; the activity *felt* is only its superficial sign.'

To the metaphysical question, popped upon us in this way, I must pay serious attention ere I end my remarks, but, before doing so, let me show that without leaving the immediate reticulations of experience, or asking what makes activity itself act, we still find the distinction between less real and more real activities forced upon us, and are driven to much soul-searching on the purely phenomenal plane.

We must not forget, namely, in talking of the ultimate character of our activity-experiences, that each of them is but a portion of a wider world, one link in the vast chain of processes of experience out of which history is made. Each partial process, to him who lives through it, defines itself by its origin and its goal; but to an observer with a wider mind-span who should live outside of it, that goal would appear but as a provisional halting-place, and the subjectively felt activity would be seen to continue into objective activities that led far beyond. We thus acquire a habit, in discussing activity-experiences, of defining them by their relation to something more. If an experience be one of narrow span, it will be mistaken as to what activity it is and whose. You think that *you* are acting while you are only obeying some one's push. You think you are doing *this*, but you are doing something of which you do not dream. For instance, you think you are but drinking this glass; but you are really creating the liver-cirrhosis that will end your days. You think you are just driving this bargain, but, as Stevenson says somewhere, you are laying down a link in the policy of mankind.

Generally speaking, the onlooker, with his wider field of vision, regards the *ultimate outcome* of an activity as what it is more really doing; and *the most previous agent* ascertainable, being the first source of action, he regards as the most real agent in the field. The others but transmit that agent's impulse; on him we put responsibility; we name him when one asks us, 'Who's to blame?'

But the most previous agents ascertainable, instead of being of longer span, are often of much shorter span than the activity in view. Brain-cells are our best example. My brain-cells are believed to excite each other from next to next (by contiguous transmission of katabolic alteration, let us say), and to have been doing so long before this present stretch of lecturing-activity on my part began. If any one cell-group stops its activity, the lecturing will cease or show disorder of form. *Cessante causa, cessat et effectus*—does not this look as if the short-span brain activities were the more real activities, and the lecturing activities on my part only their effects? Moreover, as Hume so clearly pointed out, in my mental activity-situation the words physically to be uttered are represented as the activity's immediate goal. These words, however, cannot be uttered without intermediate physical processes in the bulb and vagi nerves, which processes nevertheless fail to figure in the mental activity-series at all. That series, therefore, since it leaves out vitally real steps of action, cannot represent the real activities. It is something purely subjective; the *facts* of activity are elsewhere. They are something far more interstitial, so to speak, than what my feelings record.

The *real* facts of activity that have in point of fact been systematically pleaded for by philosophers have, so far as my information goes, been of three principal types.

The first type takes a consciousness of wider time-span than ours to be the vehicle of the more real activity. Its will is the agent, and its purpose is the action done.

The second type assumes that 'ideas' struggling with one

another are the agents, and that the prevalence of one set of them is the action.

The third type believes that nerve-cells are the agents, and that resultant motor discharges are the acts achieved.

Now if we must de-realize our immediately felt activity-situations for the benefit of either of these types of substitute, we ought to know what the substitution practically involves. *What practical difference ought it to make if*, instead of saying naïvely that 'I' am active now in delivering this address, I say that *a wider thinker is active*, or that *certain ideas are active*, or that *certain nerve-cells are active*, in producing the result?

This would be the pragmatic meaning of the three hypotheses. Let us take them in succession in seeking a reply.

If we assume a wider thinker, it is evident that his purposes envelop mine. I am really lecturing *for* him; and altho I cannot surely know to what end, yet if I take him religiously, I can trust it to be a good end, and willingly connive. I can be happy in thinking that my activity transmits his impulse, and that his ends prolong my own. So long as I take him religiously, in short, he does not de-realize my activities. He tends rather to corroborate the reality of them, so long as I believe both them and him to be good.

When now we turn to ideas, the case is different, inasmuch as ideas are supposed by the association psychology to influence each other only from next to next. The 'span' of an idea, or pair of ideas, is assumed to be much smaller instead of being larger than that of my total conscious field. The same results may get worked out in both cases, for this address is being given anyhow. But the ideas supposed to 'really' work it out had no prevision of the whole of it; and if I was lecturing for an absolute thinker in the former case, so, by similar reasoning, are my ideas now lecturing for me, that is, accomplishing unwittingly a result which I approve and adopt. But, when this passing lecture is over, there is nothing in the bare notion that ideas have been its agents that would seem to guarantee that my present purposes in lecturing will be prolonged. *I* may have ulterior developments in view; but there is no certainty that my ideas as such will wish to, or be able to, work them out.

The like is true if nerve-cells be the agents. The activity of a nerve-cell must be conceived of as a tendency of exceedingly short reach, an 'impulse' barely spanning the way to the next cell—for surely that amount of actual 'process' must be 'experienced' by the cells if what happens between them is to deserve the name of activity at all. But here again the gross resultant, as *I* perceive it, is indifferent to the agents, and neither wished or willed or foreseen. Their being agents now congruous with my will gives me no guarantee that like results will recur again from their activity. In point of fact, all sorts of other results do occur. My mistakes, impotencies, perversions, mental obstructions, and frustrations generally, are also results of the activity of cells. Altho these are letting me lecture now, on other occasions they make me do things that I would willingly not do.

The question *Whose is the real activity?* is thus tantamount to the question *What will be the actual results?* Its interest is dramatic; how will things work out? If the agents are of one sort, one way; if of another sort, they may work out very differently. The pragmatic meaning of the various alternatives, in short, is great. It makes more than a merely verbal difference which opinion we take up.

You see it is the old dispute come back! Materialism and teleology; elementary short-span actions summing themselves 'blindly,' or far foreseen ideals coming with effort into act.

Naïvely we believe, and humanly and dramatically we like to believe, that activities both of wider and of narrower span are at work in life together, that both are real, and that the long-span tendencies yoke the others in their service, encouraging them in the right direction, and damping them when they tend in other ways. But how to represent clearly the *modus operandi* of such steering of small tendencies by large ones is a problem which metaphysical thinkers will have to ruminate upon for many years to come. Even if such control should eventually grow clearly picturable, the question how far it is successfully exerted in this actual world can be answered only by investigating the details of fact. No philosophic knowledge of the general nature and constitution of tendencies, or of the relation of larger to smaller ones, can help us to predict which of all the various competing tendencies that interest us in this universe are likeliest to prevail. We know as an empirical fact that far-seeing tendencies often carry out their purpose, but we know also that they are often defeated by the failure of some contemptibly small process on which success depends. A little thrombus in a statesman's meningeal artery will throw an empire out of gear. Therefore I cannot even hint at any solution of the pragmatic issue. I have only wished to show you that that issue is what gives the real interest to all inquiries into what kinds of activity may be real. Are the forces that really act in the world more fore-seeing or more blind? As between 'our' activities as 'we' ex-perience them, and those of our ideas, or of our brain-cells, the issue is well defined.

I said awhile back (p. 804) that I should return to the 'metaphysical' question before ending; so, with a few words about that, I will now close my remarks.

In whatever form we hear this question propounded, I think that it always arises from two things, a belief that *cau-sality* must be exerted in activity, and a wonder as to how causality is made. If we take an activity-situation at its face-value, it seems as if we caught *in flagrante delicto* the very power that makes facts come and be. I now am eagerly striv-ing, for example, to get this truth which I seem half to per-ceive, into words which shall make it show more clearly. If the words come, it will seem as if the striving itself had drawn or pulled them into actuality out from the state of merely possible being in which they were. How is this feat per-formed? How does the pulling *pull*? How do I get my hold on words not yet existent, and when they come, by what means have I *made* them come? Really it is the problem of creation; for in the end the question is: How do I make them *be*? Real activities are those that really make things be, with-out which the things are not, and with which they are there. Activity, so far as we merely feel it, on the other hand, is only an impression of ours, it may be maintained; and an impres-sion is, for all this way of thinking, only a shadow of another fact.

Arrived at this point, I can do little more than indicate the principles on which, as it seems to me, a radically empirical philosophy is obliged to rely in handling such a dispute.

If there *be* real creative activities in being, radical empiricism must say, somewhere they must be immediately lived. Somewhere the *that* of efficacious causing and the *what* of it must be experienced in one, just as the what and the that of 'cold' are experienced in one whenever a man has the sensation of cold here and now. It boots not to say that our sensations are fallible. They are indeed; but to see the thermometer contradict us when we say 'it is cold' does not abolish cold as a specific nature from the universe. Cold is in the arctic circle if not here. Even so, to feel that our train is moving when the train beside our window moves, to see the moon through a telescope come twice as near, or to see two pictures as one solid when we look through a stereoscope at them, leaves motion, nearness, and solidity still in being—if not here, yet each in its proper seat elsewhere. And wherever the seat of real causality *is*, as ultimately known 'for true' (in nerve-processes, if you will, that cause our feelings of activity as well as the movements which these seem to prompt), a philosophy of pure experience can consider the real causation as no other *nature* of thing than that which even in our most erroneous experiences appears to be at work. Exactly what appears there is what we *mean* by working, tho we may later come to learn that working was not exactly *there*. Sustaining, persevering, striving, paying with effort as we go, hanging on, and finally achieving our intention—this *is* action, this *is* effectuation in the only shape in which, by a pure experience-philosophy, the whereabouts of it anywhere can be discussed. Here is creation in its first intention, here is causality at work.[1] To treat this offhand as the bare illusory surface of a

---

[1] Let me not be told that this contradicts a former article of mine, 'Does consciousness exist?' in the *Journal of Philosophy* for September 1, 1904 (see especially page 489), in which it was said that while 'thoughts' and 'things' have the same natures, the natures work 'energetically' on each other in the things (fire burns, water wets, etc.), but not in the thoughts. Mental activity-trains are composed of thoughts, yet their members do work on each other: they check, sustain, and introduce. They do so when the activity is merely associational as well as when effort is there. But, and this is my reply, they

world whose real causality is an unimaginable ontological principle hidden in the cubic deeps, is, for the more empirical way of thinking, only animism in another shape. You explain your given fact by your 'principle,' but the principle itself, when you look clearly at it, turns out to be nothing but a previous little spiritual copy of the fact. Away from that one and only kind of fact your mind, considering causality, can never get.[1]

I conclude, then, that real effectual causation as an ultimate nature, as a 'category,' if you like, of reality, is *just what we feel it to be*, just that kind of conjunction which our own activity-series reveal. We have the whole butt and being of it in

---

do so by other parts of their nature than those that energize physically. One thought in every developed activity-series is a desire or thought of purpose, and all the other thoughts acquire a feeling tone from their relation of harmony or oppugnancy to this. The interplay of these secondary tones (among which 'interest,' 'difficulty,' and 'effort' figure) runs the drama in the mental series. In what we term the physical drama these qualities play absolutely no part. The subject needs careful working out; but I can see no inconsistency.

[1] I have found myself more than once accused in print of being the assertor of a metaphysical principle of activity. Since literary misunderstandings retard the settlement of problems, I should like to say that such an interpretation of the pages I have published on effort and on will is absolutely foreign to what I meant to express. I owe all my doctrines on this subject to Renouvier; and Renouvier, as I understand him, is (or at any rate then was) an out and out phenomenist, a denier of 'forces' in the most strenuous sense. Single clauses in my writing, or sentences read out of their connexion, may possibly have been compatible with a transphenomenal principle of energy; but I defy any one to show a single sentence which, taken with its context, should be naturally held to advocate that view. The misinterpretation probably arose at first from my having defended (after Renouvier) the indeterminism of our efforts. 'Free will' was supposed by my critics to involve a supernatural agent. As a matter of plain history, the only 'free will' I have ever thought of defending is the character of novelty in fresh activity-situations. If an activity-process is the form of a whole 'field of consciousness,' and if each field of consciousness is not only in its totality unique (as is now commonly admitted), but has its elements unique (since in that situation they are all dyed in the total), then novelty is perpetually entering the world and what happens there is not pure *repetition*, as the dogma of the literal uniformity of nature requires. Activity-situations come, in short, each with an original touch. A 'principle' of free will, if there were one, would doubtless manifest itself in such phenomena, but I never saw, nor do I now see, what the principle could do except rehearse the phenomenon beforehand, or why it ever should be invoked.

our hands; and the healthy thing for philosophy is to leave off grubbing underground for what effects effectuation, or what makes action act, and to try to solve the concrete questions of where effectuation in this world is located, of which things are the true causal agents there, and of what the more remote effects consist.

From this point of view the greater sublimity traditionally attributed to the metaphysical inquiry, the grubbing inquiry, entirely disappears. If we could know what causation really and transcendentally is in itself, the only *use* of the knowledge would be to help us to recognize an actual cause when we had one, and so to track the future course of operations more intelligently out. The mere abstract inquiry into causation's hidden nature is not more sublime than any other inquiry equally abstract. Causation inhabits no more sublime level than anything else. It lives, apparently, in the dirt of the world as well as in the absolute, or in man's unconquerable mind. The worth and interest of the world consists not in its elements, be these elements things, or be they the conjunctions of things; it exists rather in the dramatic outcome of the whole process, and in the meaning of the succession stages which the elements work out.

My colleague and master, Josiah Royce, in a page of his review of Stout's *Analytic Psychology*, in *Mind* for 1897, has some fine words on this point with which I cordially agree. I cannot agree with his separating the notion of efficacy from that of activity altogether (this I understand to be one contention of his), for activities are efficacious whenever they are real activities at all. But the inner nature both of efficacy and of activity are superficial problems, I understand Royce to say; and the only point for us in solving them would be their possible use in helping us to solve the far deeper problem of the course and meaning of the world of life. Life, says our colleague, is full of significance, of meaning, of success and of defeat, of hoping and of striving, of longing, of desire, and of inner value. It is a total presence that embodies worth. To live our own lives better in this presence is the true reason why we wish to know the elements of things; so even we psychologists must end on this pragmatic note.

The urgent problems of activity are thus more concrete.

They all are problems of the true relation of longer-span to shorter-span activities. When, for example, a number of 'ideas' (to use the name traditional in psychology) grow confluent in a larger field of consciousness, do the smaller activities still coexist with the wider activities then experienced by the conscious subject? And, if so, do the wide activities accompany the narrow ones inertly, or do they exert control? Or do they perhaps utterly supplant and replace them and short-circuit their effects? Again, when a mental activity-process and a brain-cell series of activities both terminate in the same muscular movement, does the mental process steer the neural processes or not? Or, on the other hand, does it independently short-circuit their effects? Such are the questions that we must begin with. But so far am I from suggesting any definitive answer to such questions, that I hardly yet can put them clearly. They lead, however, into that region of panpsychic and ontologic speculation of which Professors Bergson and Strong have lately enlarged the literature in so able and interesting a way. The results of these authors seem in many respects dissimilar, and I understand them as yet but imperfectly; but I cannot help suspecting that the direction of their work is very promising, and that they have the hunter's instinct for the fruitful trails.

APPENDIX C

ON THE NOTION OF REALITY AS CHANGING

In my *Principles of Psychology* (vol. ii, p. 646) I gave the name of the 'axiom of skipped intermediaries and transferred relations' to a serial principle of which the foundation of logic, the *dictum de omni et nullo* (or, as I expressed it, the rule that what is of a kind is of that kind's kind), is the most familiar instance. More than the more is more than the less, equals of equals are equal, sames of the same are the same, the cause of a cause is the cause of its effects, are other examples of this serial law. Altho it applies infallibly and without restriction throughout certain abstract series, where the 'sames,' 'causes,' etc., spoken of, are 'pure,' and have no properties save their sameness, causality, etc., it cannot be applied offhand to concrete objects with numerous properties and relations, for it is hard to trace a straight line of sameness, causation, or whatever it may be, through a series of such objects without swerving into some 'respect' where the relation, as pursued originally, no longer holds: the objects have so many 'aspects' that we are constantly deflected from our original direction, and find, we know not why, that we are following something different from what we started with. Thus a cat is in a sense the same as a mouse-trap, and a mouse-trap the same as a bird-cage; but in no valuable or easily intelligible sense is a cat the same as a bird-cage. Commodore Perry was in a sense the cause of the new régime in Japan, and the new régime was the cause of the russian Douma; but it would hardly profit us to insist on holding to Perry as the cause of the Douma: the terms have grown too remote to have any real or practical relation to each other. In every series of real terms, not only do the terms themselves and their associates and environments change, but we change, and their *meaning* for us changes, so that new kinds of sameness and types of causation continually come into view and appeal to our interest. Our earlier lines, having grown irrelevant, are then dropped. The old terms can no longer be substituted nor the relations 'transferred,' because of so many new dimensions into which experience has opened. Instead of a straight line, it now follows a zigzag; and to keep it straight, one must do violence to its spontaneous development. Not that one might not possibly, by careful seeking (tho I doubt it), *find* some line in nature along which terms literally the same, or causes causal in the same way, might be serially strung without limit, if one's interest lay in such finding. Within such lines our axioms might hold, causes might cause their effect's effects, etc.; but such lines themselves would, if found, only be partial members of a vast natural network, within the other lines of which you could not say, in any sense that a wise man or a sane man would ever think of, in any sense that would not be concretely *silly*, that the principle of skipt intermediaries still held good. In the *practical* world, the world whose significances we follow, sames of the same are certainly not sames of one another; and things constantly cause other things without being held responsible for everything of which those other things are causes.

Professor Bergson, believing as he does in a heraclitean 'devenir réel,' ought, if I rightly understand him, positively to deny that in the actual world the logical axioms hold good without qualification. Not only, according to him, do terms change, so that after a certain time the very elements of things are no longer what they were, but relations also change, so as no longer to obtain in the same identical way between the new things that have succeeded upon the old ones. If this were really so, then however indefinitely sames might still be substituted for sames in the logical world of nothing but pure sameness, in the world of real operations every line of sameness actually started and followed up would eventually give out, and cease to be traceable any farther. Sames of the same, in such a world, will not always (or rather, in a strict sense will never) be the same as one another, for in such a world there *is* no literal or ideal sameness among numerical differents. Nor in such a world will it be true that the cause of the cause is unreservedly the cause of the effect; for if we follow lines of real causation, instead of contenting ourselves with Hume's and Kant's eviscerated schematism, we find that remoter effects are seldom aimed at by causal intentions,[1] that

[1] Compare the douma with what Perry aimed at.

no one kind of causal activity continues indefinitely, and that the principle of skipt intermediaries can be talked of only *in abstracto*.[1]

Volumes i, ii, and iii of the *Monist* (1890–1893) contain a number of articles by Mr. Charles S. Peirce, articles the originality of which has apparently prevented their making an immediate impression, but which, if I mistake not, will prove a gold-mine of ideas for thinkers of the coming generation. Mr. Peirce's views, tho reached so differently, are altogether congruous with Bergson's. Both philosophers believe that the appearance of novelty in things is genuine. To an observer standing outside of its generating causes, novelty can appear only as so much 'chance,' while to one who stands inside it is the expression of 'free creative activity.' Peirce's 'tychism' is thus practically synonymous with Bergson's 'devenir réel.' The common objection to admitting novelties is that by jumping abruptly in, *ex nihilo*, they shatter the world's rational continuity. Peirce meets this objection by combining his tychism with an express doctrine of 'synechism' or continuity, the two doctrines merging into the higher synthesis on which he bestows the name of 'agapasticism' (*loc. cit.*, iii, 188), which means exactly the same thing as Bergson's 'évolution créatrice.' Novelty, as empirically found, does n't arrive by jumps and jolts, it leaks in insensibly, for adjacents in experience are always interfused, the smallest real datum being both a coming and a going, and even numerical distinctness being realized effectively only after a concrete interval has passed. The intervals also deflect us from the original paths of direction, and all the old identities at last give out, for the fatally continuous infiltration of otherness warps things out of every original rut. Just so, in a curve, the same direction is *never* followed, and the conception of it as a myriad-sided polygon falsifies it by supposing it to do so for however short a time. Peirce speaks of an 'infinitesimal' tendency to diversification. The mathematical notion of an infinitesimal contains, in truth, the whole paradox of the same and yet the nascent other, of an identity that won't *keep* except so far as it keeps *failing*, that won't *transfer*, any more than the serial relations

---

[1] Compare Appendix B, as to what I mean here by 'real' causal activity.

in question transfer, when you apply them to reality instead of applying them to concepts alone.

A friend of mine has an idea, which illustrates on such a magnified scale the impossibility of tracing the same line through reality, that I will mention it here. He thinks that nothing more is needed to make history 'scientific' than to get the content of any two epochs (say the end of the thirteenth and the end of the nineteenth century) accurately defined, then accurately to define the direction of the change that led from the one epoch into the other, and finally to prolong the line of that direction into the future. So prolonging the line, he thinks, we ought to be able to define the actual state of things at any future date we please. We all feel the essential unreality of such a conception of 'history' as this; but if such a synechistic pluralism as Peirce, Bergson, and I believe in, be what really exists, every phenomenon of development, even the simplest, would prove equally rebellious to our science should the latter pretend to give us literally accurate instead of approximate, or statistically generalized, pictures of the development of reality.

I can give no further account of Mr. Peirce's ideas in this note, but I earnestly advise all students of Bergson to compare them with those of the french philosopher.

Index to the Lectures

THE MEANING OF TRUTH

A Sequel to 'Pragmatism'

Preface

THE PIVOTAL PART of my book named *Pragmatism* is its account of the relation called 'truth' which may obtain between an idea (opinion, belief, statement, or what not) and its object. 'Truth,' I there say, 'is a property of certain of our ideas. It means their agreement, as falsity means their disagreement, with reality. Pragmatists and intellectualists both accept this definition as a matter of course.

'Where our ideas [do] not copy definitely their object, what does agreement with that object mean? . . . Pragmatism asks its usual question. "Grant an idea or belief to be true," it says, "what concrete difference will its being true make in any one's actual life? What experiences [may] be different from those which would obtain if the belief were false? How will the truth be realized? What, in short, is the truth's cash-value in experiential terms?" The moment pragmatism asks this question, it sees the answer: *True ideas are those that we can assimilate, validate, corroborate, and verify. False ideas are those that we cannot.* That is the practical difference it makes to us to have true ideas; that therefore is the meaning of truth, for it is all that truth is known as.

'The truth of an idea is not a stagnant property inherent in it. Truth *happens* to an idea. It *becomes* true, is *made* true by events. Its verity *is* in fact an event, a process, the process namely of its verifying itself, its veri*fication*. Its validity is the process of its valid*ation*.[1]

'To agree in the widest sense with a reality can only mean to be guided either straight up to it or into its surroundings, or to be put into such working touch with it as to handle either it or something connected with it better than if we disagreed. Better either intellectually or practically. . . . Any idea that helps us to deal, whether practically or intellec-

---

[1] But *'verifiability,'* I add, 'is as good as verification. For one truth-process completed, there are a million in our lives that function in [the] state of nascency. They lead us towards direct verification; lead us into the surroundings of the object they envisage; and then, if everything runs on harmoniously, we are so sure that verification is possible that we omit it, and are usually justified by all that happens.'

tually, with either the reality or its belongings, that does n't entangle our progress in frustrations, that *fits*, in fact, and adapts our life to the reality's whole setting, will agree sufficiently to meet the requirement. It will be true of that reality.

'*The true,* to put it very briefly, *is only the expedient in the way of our thinking, just as the right is only the expedient in the way of our behaving.* Expedient in almost any fashion, and expedient in the long run and on the whole, of course; for what meets expediently all the experience in sight won't necessarily meet all farther experiences equally satisfactorily. Experience, as we know, has ways of *boiling over*, and making us correct our present formulas.'

This account of truth, following upon the similar ones given by Messrs. Dewey and Schiller, has occasioned the liveliest discussion. Few critics have defended it, most of them have scouted it. It seems evident that the subject is a hard one to understand, under its apparent simplicity; and evident also, I think, that the definitive settlement of it will mark a turning-point in the history of epistemology, and consequently in that of general philosophy. In order to make my own thought more accessible to those who hereafter may have to study the question, I have collected in the volume that follows all the work of my pen that bears directly on the truth-question. My first statement was in 1884, in the article that begins the present volume. The other papers follow in the order of their publication. Two or three appear now for the first time.

One of the accusations which I oftenest have had to meet is that of making the truth of our religious beliefs consist in their 'feeling good' to us, and in nothing else. I regret to have given some excuse for this charge, by the unguarded language in which, in the book *Pragmatism*, I spoke of the truth of the belief of certain philosophers in the absolute. Explaining why I do not believe in the absolute myself (p. 521), yet finding that it may secure 'moral holidays' to those who need them, and is true in so far forth (if to gain moral holidays be a good),[1] I offered this as a conciliatory olive-branch to my

[1] *Op. cit.,* p. 520.

enemies. But they, as is only too common with such offerings, trampled the gift under foot and turned and rent the
giver. I had counted too much on their good will—oh for
the rarity of christian charity under the sun! Oh for the rarity
of ordinary secular intelligence also! I had supposed it to be
matter of common observation that, of two competing views
of the universe which in all other respects are equal, but of
which the first denies some vital human need while the second satisfies it, the second will be favored by sane men for
the simple reason that it makes the world seem more rational.
To choose the first view under such circumstances would be
an ascetic act, an act of philosophic self-denial of which no
normal human being would be guilty. Using the pragmatic
test of the meaning of concepts, I had shown the concept of
the absolute to *mean* nothing but the holiday giver, the ban-
isher of cosmic fear. One's objective deliverance, when one
says 'the absolute exists,' amounted, on my showing, just to
this, that 'some justification of a feeling of security in presence
of the universe,' exists, and that systematically to refuse to
cultivate a feeling of security would be to do violence to a
tendency in one's emotional life which might well be respected as prophetic.

Apparently my absolutist critics fail to see the workings of
their own minds in any such picture, so all that I can do is to
apologize, and take my offering back. The absolute is true in
no way then, and least of all, by the verdict of the critics, in
the way which I assigned!

My treatment of 'God,' 'freedom,' and 'design' was similar.
Reducing, by the pragmatic test, the meaning of each of these
concepts to its positive experienceable operation, I showed
them all to mean the same thing, viz., the presence of 'promise'
in the world. 'God or no God?' means 'promise or no promise?' It seems to me that the alternative is objective enough,
being a question as to whether the cosmos has one character
or another, even though our own provisional answer be made
on subjective grounds. Nevertheless christian and non-christian critics alike accuse me of summoning people to say 'God
exists,' *even when he does n't exist*, because forsooth in my philosophy the 'truth' of the saying does n't really mean that he exists in any shape whatever, but only that to say so feels good.

Most of the pragmatist and anti-pragmatist warfare is over what the word 'truth' shall be held to signify, and not over any of the facts embodied in truth-situations; for both pragmatists and anti-pragmatists believe in existent objects, just as they believe in our ideas of them. The difference is that when the pragmatists speak of truth, they mean exclusively something about the ideas, namely their workableness; whereas when anti-pragmatists speak of truth they seem most often to mean something about the objects. Since the pragmatist, if he agrees that an idea is 'really' true, also agrees to whatever it says about its object; and since most anti-pragmatists have already come round to agreeing that, if the object exists, the idea that it does so is workable; there would seem so little left to fight about that I might well be asked why instead of reprinting my share in so much verbal wrangling, I do not show my sense of 'values' by burning it all up.

I understand the question and I will give my answer. I am interested in another doctrine in philosophy to which I give the name of radical empiricism, and it seems to me that the establishment of the pragmatist theory of truth is a step of first-rate importance in making radical empiricism prevail. Radical empiricism consists first of a postulate, next of a statement of fact, and finally of a generalized conclusion.

The postulate is that the only things that shall be debatable among philosophers shall be things definable in terms drawn from experience. [Things of an unexperienceable nature may exist ad libitum, but they form no part of the material for philosophic debate.]

The statement of fact is that the relations between things, conjunctive as well as disjunctive, are just as much matters of direct particular experience, neither more so nor less so, than the things themselves.

The generalized conclusion is that therefore the parts of experience hold together from next to next by relations that are themselves parts of experience. The directly apprehended universe needs, in short, no extraneous trans-empirical connective support, but possesses in its own right a concatenated or continuous structure.

The great obstacle to radical empiricism in the contemporary mind is the rooted rationalist belief that experience as immediately given is all disjunction and no conjunction, and that to make one world out of this separateness, a higher unifying agency must be there. In the prevalent idealism this agency is represented as the absolute all-witness which 'relates' things together by throwing 'categories' over them like a net. The most peculiar and unique, perhaps, of all these categories is supposed to be the truth-relation, which connects parts of reality in pairs, making of one of them a knower, and of the other a thing known, yet which is itself contentless experientially, neither describable, explicable, nor reduceable to lower terms, and denotable only by uttering the name 'truth.'

The pragmatist view, on the contrary, of the truth-relation is that it has a definite content, and that everything in it is experienceable. Its whole nature can be told in positive terms. The 'workableness' which ideas must have, in order to be true, means particular workings, physical or intellectual, actual or possible, which they may set up from next to next inside of concrete experience. Were this pragmatic contention admitted, one great point in the victory of radical empiricism would also be scored, for the relation between an object and the idea that truly knows it, is held by rationalists to be nothing of this describable sort, but to stand outside of all possible temporal experience; and on the relation, so interpreted, rationalism is wonted to make its last most obdurate rally.

Now the anti-pragmatist contentions which I try to meet in this volume can be so easily used by rationalists as weapons of resistance, not only to pragmatism but to radical empiricism also (for if the truth-relation were transcendent, others might be so too), that I feel strongly the strategical importance of having them definitely met and got out of the way. What our critics most persistently keep saying is that though workings go with truth, yet they do not constitute it. It is numerically additional to them, prior to them, explanatory *of* them, and in no wise to be explained *by* them, we are incessantly told. The first point for our enemies to establish, therefore, is that *something* numerically additional and prior to the workings is involved in the truth of an idea. Since the *object* is additional, and usually prior, most rationalists plead *it*, and boldly accuse us of denying it. This leaves on the bystanders the impression—since we cannot reasonably deny the existence of the object—that our account of truth breaks down, and that our critics have driven us from the field. Altho in various places in this volume I try to refute the slanderous charge that we deny real existence, I will say here again, for the sake of emphasis, that the existence of the object, whenever the idea asserts it 'truly,' is the only reason, in innumerable cases, why the idea does work successfully, if it work at all; and that it seems an abuse of language, to say the least, to transfer the word 'truth' from the idea to the object's existence, when the falsehood of ideas that won't work is explained by that existence as well as the truth of those that will.

I find this abuse prevailing among my most accomplished adversaries. But once establish the proper verbal custom, let the word 'truth' represent a property of the idea, cease to make it something mysteriously connected with the object known, and the path opens fair and wide, as I believe, to the discussion of radical empiricism on its merits. The truth of an idea will then mean only its workings, or that in it which by ordinary psychological laws sets up those workings; it will mean neither the idea's object, nor anything 'saltatory' inside the idea, that terms drawn from experience cannot describe.

One word more, ere I end this preface. A distinction is sometimes made between Dewey, Schiller and myself, as if I, in supposing the object's existence, made a concession to popular prejudice which they, as more radical pragmatists, refuse to make. As I myself understand these authors, we all three absolutely agree in admitting the transcendency of the object (provided it be an experienceable object) to the subject, in the truth-relation. Dewey in particular has insisted almost ad nauseam that the whole meaning of our cognitive states and processes lies in the way they intervene in the control and revaluation of independent existences or facts. His account of knowledge is not only absurd, but meaningless, unless independent existences be there of which our ideas take account, and for the transformation of which they work. But because he and Schiller refuse to discuss objects and relations 'transcendent' in the sense of being *altogether trans-experiential*, their critics pounce on sentences in their writings to that effect to show that they deny the existence *within the realm of experience* of objects external to the ideas that declare their presence there.[1] It seems incredible that educated and apparently sincere critics should so fail to catch their adversary's point of view.

What misleads so many of them is possibly also the fact that the universes of discourse of Schiller, Dewey, and myself are panoramas of different extent, and that what the one postulates explicitly the other provisionally leaves only in a state of implication, while the reader thereupon considers it to be denied. Schiller's universe is the smallest, being essentially a psychological one. He starts with but one sort of thing, truth-claims, but is led ultimately to the independent objective facts which they assert, inasmuch as the most successfully validated of all claims is that such facts are there. My universe is more essentially epistemological. I start with two things, the objective facts and the claims, and indicate which claims, the facts being there, will work successfully as the latter's substitutes and which will not. I call the former claims true. Dewey's panorama, if I understand this colleague, is the widest of the three, but I refrain from giving my own account of its complexity. Suffice it that he holds as firmly as I do to objects independent of our judgments. If I am wrong in saying this, he must correct me. I decline in this matter to be corrected at second hand.

I have not pretended in the following pages to consider all the critics of my account of truth, such as Messrs. Taylor, Lovejoy, Gardiner, Bakewell, Creighton, Hibben, Parodi, Salter, Carus, Lalande, Mentré, McTaggart, G. E. Moore, Ladd and others, especially not Professor Schinz, who has published under the title of *Anti-pragmatisme* an amusing

---

[1] It gives me pleasure to welcome Professor Carveth Read into the pragmatistic church, so far as his epistemology goes. See his vigorous book, *The Metaphysics of Nature*, 2d Edition, Appendix A. (London, Black, 1908.) The work *What is Reality?* by Francis Howe Johnson (Boston, 1891), of which I make the acquaintance only while correcting these proofs, contains some striking anticipations of the later pragmatist view. *The Psychology of Thinking*, by Irving E. Miller (New York, Macmillan Co., 1909), which has just appeared, is one of the most convincing pragmatist documents yet published, tho it does not use the word 'pragmatism' at all. While I am making references, I cannot refrain from inserting one to the extraordinarily acute article by H. V. Knox, in the *Quarterly Review* for April, 1909.

sociological romance. Some of these critics seem to me to labor under an inability almost pathetic, to understand the thesis which they seek to refute. I imagine that most of their difficulties have been answered by anticipation elsewhere in this volume, and I am sure that my readers will thank me for not adding more repetition to the fearful amount that is already there.

95 IRVING ST., CAMBRIDGE (MASS.),
    August, 1909.

Contents

I

THE FUNCTION OF COGNITION[1]

THE FOLLOWING inquiry is (to use a distinction familiar to readers of Mr. Shadworth Hodgson) not an inquiry into the 'how it comes,' but into the 'what it is' of cognition. What we call acts of cognition are evidently realized through what we call brains and their events, whether there be 'souls' dynamically connected with the brains or not. But with neither brains nor souls has this essay any business to transact. In it we shall simply assume that cognition *is* produced, somehow, and limit ourselves to asking what elements it contains, what factors it implies.

Cognition is a function of consciousness. The first factor it implies is therefore a state of consciousness wherein the cognition shall take place. Having elsewhere used the word 'feeling' to designate generically all states of consciousness considered subjectively, or without respect to their possible function, I shall then say that, whatever elements an act of cognition may imply besides, it at least implies the existence of a *feeling*. [If the reader share the current antipathy to the word 'feeling,' he may substitute for it, wherever I use it, the word 'idea,' taken in the old broad Lockian sense, or he may use the clumsy phrase 'state of consciousness,' or finally he may say 'thought' instead.]

Now it is to be observed that the common consent of mankind has agreed that some feelings are cognitive and some are simple facts having a subjective, or, what one might almost call a physical, existence, but no such self-transcendent function as would be implied in their being pieces of knowledge. Our task is again limited here. We are not to ask, 'How is self-transcendence possible?' We are only to ask, 'How comes it that common sense has assigned a number of cases in which it is assumed not only to be possible but actual? And what are the marks used by common sense to distinguish those

---

[1]Read before the Aristotelian Society, December 1, 1884, and first published in *Mind*, vol. x (1885).—This, and the following articles have received a very slight verbal revision, consisting mostly in the omission of redundancy.

cases from the rest?' In short, our inquiry is a chapter in descriptive psychology,—hardly anything more.

Condillac embarked on a quest similar to this by his famous hypothesis of a statue to which various feelings were successively imparted. Its first feeling was supposed to be one of fragrance. But to avoid all possible complication with the question of genesis, let us not attribute even to a statue the possession of our imaginary feeling. Let us rather suppose it attached to no matter, nor localized at any point in space, but left swinging *in vacuo*, as it were, by the direct creative *fiat* of a god. And let us also, to escape entanglement with difficulties about the physical or psychical nature of its 'object,' not call it a feeling of fragrance or of any other determinate sort, but limit ourselves to assuming that it is a feeling of *q*. What is true of it under this abstract name will be no less true of it in any more particular shape (such as fragrance, pain, hardness) which the reader may suppose.

Now, if this feeling of *q* be the only creation of the god, it will of course form the entire universe. And if, to escape the cavils of that large class of persons who believe that *semper idem sentire ac non sentire* are the same,[1] we allow the feeling to be of as short a duration as they like, that universe will only need to last an infinitesimal part of a second. The feeling in question will thus be reduced to its fighting weight, and all that befalls it in the way of a cognitive function must be held to befall in the brief instant of its quickly snuffed-out life,—a life, it will also be noticed, that has no other moment of consciousness either preceding or following it.

---

[1]'The Relativity of Knowledge,' held in this sense, is, it may be observed in passing, one of the oddest of philosophic superstitions. Whatever facts may be cited in its favor are due to the properties of nerve-tissue, which may be exhausted by too prolonged an excitement. Patients with neuralgias that last unremittingly for days can, however, assure us that the limits of this nerve-law are pretty widely drawn. But if we physically could get a feeling that should last eternally unchanged, what atom of logical or psychological argument is there to prove that it would not be felt as long as it lasted, and felt for just what it is, all that time? The reason for the opposite prejudice seems to be our reluctance to think that so *stupid* a thing as such a feeling would necessarily be, should be allowed to fill eternity with its presence. An interminable acquaintance, leading to no knowledge-*about*,—such would be its condition.

Well now, can our little feeling, thus left alone in the universe,—for the god and we psychological critics may be supposed left out of the account,—can the feeling, I say, be said to have any sort of a cognitive function? For it to *know*, there must be something to be known. What is there, on the present supposition? One may reply, 'the feeling's content *q*.' But does it not seem more proper to call this the feeling's *quality* than its content? Does not the word 'content' suggest that the feeling has already dirempted itself as an act from its content as an object? And would it be quite safe to assume so promptly that the quality *q* of a feeling is one and the same thing with a feeling of the quality *q*? The quality *q*, so far, is an entirely subjective fact which the feeling carries so to speak endogenously, or in its pocket. If any one pleases to dignify so simple a fact as this by the name of knowledge, of course nothing can prevent him. But let us keep closer to the path of common usage, and reserve the name knowledge for the cognition of 'realities,' meaning by realities things that exist independently of the feeling through which their cognition occurs. If the content of the feeling occur nowhere in the universe outside of the feeling itself, and perish with the feeling, common usage refuses to call it a reality, and brands it as a subjective feature of the feeling's constitution, or at the most as the feeling's *dream*.

For the feeling to be cognitive in the specific sense, then, it must be self-transcendent; and we must prevail upon the god to *create a reality outside of it* to correspond to its intrinsic quality *q*. Thus only can it be redeemed from the condition of being a solipsism. If now the new-created reality *resemble* the feeling's quality *q*, I say that the feeling may be held by us *to be cognizant of that reality*.

This first instalment of my thesis is sure to be attacked. But one word before defending it. 'Reality' has become our warrant for calling a feeling cognitive; but what becomes our warrant for calling anything reality? The only reply is—the faith of the present critic or inquirer. At every moment of his life he finds himself subject to a belief in *some* realities, even though his realities of this year should prove to be his illusions of the next. Whenever he finds that the feeling he is studying contemplates what he himself regards as a reality, he must of course admit the feeling itself to be truly cognitive. We are ourselves the critics here; and we shall find our burden much lightened by being allowed to take reality in this relative and provisional way. Every science must make some assumptions. *Erkenntnisstheoretiker* are but fallible mortals. When they study the function of cognition, they do it by means of the same function in themselves. And knowing that the fountain cannot go higher than its source, we should promptly confess that our results in this field are affected by our own liability to err. *The most we can claim is, that what we say about cognition may be counted as true as what we say about anything else.* If our hearers agree with us about what are to be held 'realities,' they will perhaps also agree to the reality of our doctrine of the way in which they are known. We cannot ask for more.

Our terminology shall follow the spirit of these remarks. We will deny the function of knowledge to any feeling whose quality or content we do not ourselves believe to exist outside of that feeling as well as in it. We may call such a feeling a dream if we like; we shall have to see later whether we can call it a fiction or an error.

To revert now to our thesis. Some persons will immediately cry out, 'How *can* a reality resemble a feeling?' Here we find how wise we were to name the quality of the feeling by an algebraic letter *q*. We flank the whole difficulty of resemblance between an inner state and an outward reality, by leaving it free to any one to postulate as the reality whatever sort of thing he thinks *can* resemble a feeling,—if not an outward thing, then another feeling like the first one,—the mere feeling *q* in the critic's mind for example. Evading thus this objection, we turn to another which is sure to be urged.

It will come from those philosophers to whom 'thought,' in the sense of a knowledge of relations, is the all in all of mental life; and who hold a merely feeling consciousness to be no better—one would sometimes say from their utterances, a good deal worse—than no consciousness at all. Such phrases as these, for example, are common to-day in the mouths of those who claim to walk in the footprints of Kant and Hegel rather than in the ancestral English paths: 'A perception detached from all others, "left out of the heap

we call a mind," being out of all relation, has no qualities—
is simply nothing. We can no more consider it than we can
see vacancy.' 'It is simply in itself fleeting, momentary, unnameable (because while we name it it has become another),
and for the very same reason unknowable, the very negation
of knowability.' 'Exclude from what we have considered real
all qualities constituted by relation, we find that none are
left.'

Altho such citations as these from the writings of Professor
Green might be multiplied almost indefinitely, they would
hardly repay the pains of collection, so egregiously false is the
doctrine they teach. Our little supposed feeling, whatever it
may be, from the cognitive point of view, whether a bit of
knowledge or a dream, is certainly no psychical zero. It is a
most positively and definitely qualified inner fact, with a complexion all its own. Of course there are many mental facts
which it is *not*. It knows *q*, if *q* be a reality, with a very
minimum of knowledge. It neither dates nor locates it. It neither classes nor names it. And it neither knows itself as a feeling, nor contrasts itself with other feelings, nor estimates its
own duration or intensity. It is, in short, if there is no more
of it than this, a most dumb and helpless and useless kind of
thing.

But if we must describe it by so many negations, and if it
can say nothing *about* itself or *about* anything else, by what
right do we deny that it is a psychical zero? And may not the
'relationists' be right after all?

In the innocent looking word 'about' lies the solution of
this riddle; and a simple enough solution it is when frankly
looked at. A quotation from a too seldom quoted book, the
Exploratio Philosophica of John Grote (London, 1865), p. 60,
will form the best introduction to it.

'Our knowledge,' writes Grote, 'may be contemplated in
either of two ways, or, to use other words, we may speak in
a double manner of the "object" of knowledge. That is, we
may either use language thus: we *know* a thing, a man, etc.;
or we may use it thus: we know such and such things *about*
the thing, the man, etc. Language in general, following its
true logical instinct, distinguishes between these two applications of the notion of knowledge, the one being γνῶναι,

noscere, *kennen*, *connaître*, the other being ειδέναι, *scire*, *wissen*, *savoir*. In the origin, the former may be considered more what I have called phenomenal—it is the notion of knowledge as *acquaintance* or familiarity with what is known; which notion is perhaps more akin to the phenomenal bodily communication, and is less purely intellectual than the other; it is the kind of knowledge which we have of a thing by the presentation to the senses or the representation of it in picture or type, a *Vorstellung*. The other, which is what we express in judgments or propositions, what is embodied in *Begriffe* or concepts without any necessary imaginative representation, is in its origin the more intellectual notion of knowledge. There is no reason, however, why we should not express our knowledge, whatever its kind, in either manner, provided only we do not confusedly express it, in the same proposition or piece of reasoning, in both.'

Now obviously if our supposed feeling of *q* is (if knowledge at all) only knowledge of the mere acquaintance-type, it is milking a he-goat, as the ancients would have said, to try to extract from it any deliverance *about* anything under the sun, even about itself. And it is as unjust, after our failure, to turn upon it and call it a psychical nothing, as it would be, after our fruitless attack upon the billy-goat, to proclaim the non-lactiferous character of the whole goat-tribe. But the entire industry of the Hegelian school in trying to shove simple sensation out of the pale of philosophic recognition is founded on this false issue. It is always the 'speechlessness' of sensation, its inability to make any 'statement,'[1] that is held to make the very notion of it meaningless, and to justify the student of knowledge in scouting it out of existence. 'Significance,' in the sense of standing as the sign of other mental states, is taken to be the sole function of what mental states we have; and from the perception that our little primitive sensation has as yet no significance in this literal sense, it is an easy step to call it first meaningless, next senseless, then vacuous, and finally to brand it as absurd and inadmissible. But in this universal liquidation, this everlasting slip,

[1]See, for example, Green's Introduction to Hume's *Treatise of Human Nature*, p. 36.

slip, slip, of direct acquaintance into knowledge-*about*, until at last nothing is left about which the knowledge can be supposed to obtain, does not all 'significance' depart from the situation? And when our knowledge about things has reached its never so complicated perfection, must there not needs abide alongside of it and inextricably mixed in with it some acquaintance with *what* things all this knowledge is about?

Now, our supposed little feeling gives a *what*; and if other feelings should succeed which remember the first, its *what* may stand as subject or predicate of some piece of knowledge-about, of some judgment, perceiving relations between it and other *whats* which the other feelings may know. The hitherto dumb *q* will then receive a name and be no longer speechless. But every name, as students of logic know, has its 'denotation'; and the denotation always means some reality or content, relationless *ab extra* or with its internal relations unanalyzed, like the *q* which our primitive sensation is supposed to know. No relation-expressing proposition is possible except on the basis of a preliminary acquaintance with such 'facts,' with such contents, as this. Let the *q* be fragrance, let it be toothache, or let it be a more complex kind of feeling, like that of the full-moon swimming in her blue abyss, it must first come in that simple shape, and be held fast in that first intention, before any knowledge *about* it can be attained. The knowledge *about* it is *it* with a context added. Undo *it*, and what is added cannot be *con*text.[1]

Let us say no more then about this objection, but enlarge our thesis, thus: If there be in the universe a *q* other than the *q* in the feeling, the latter may have acquaintance with an entity ejective to itself; an acquaintance moreover, which, as mere acquaintance, it would be hard to imagine susceptible either of improvement or increase, being in its way com-

---

[1] If A enters and B exclaims, 'Did n't you see my brother on the stairs?' we all hold that A may answer, 'I saw him, but did n't know he was your brother'; ignorance of brotherhood not abolishing power to see. But those who, on account of the unrelatedness of the first facts with which we become acquainted, deny them to be 'known' to us, ought in consistency to maintain that if A did not perceive the relationship of the man on the stairs to B, it was impossible he should have noticed him at all.

plete; and which would oblige us (so long as we refuse not to call acquaintance knowledge) to say not only that the feeling is cognitive, but that all qualities of feeling, *so long as there is anything outside of them which they resemble*, are feelings *of* qualities of existence, and perceptions of outward fact.

The point of this vindication of the cognitive function of the first feeling lies, it will be noticed, in the discovery that q does exist elsewhere than in it. In case this discovery were not made, we could not be sure the feeling was cognitive; and in case there were nothing outside to be discovered, we should have to call the feeling a dream. But the feeling itself cannot make the discovery. Its own q is the only q it grasps; and its own nature is not a particle altered by having the self-transcendent function of cognition either added to it or taken away. The function is accidental; synthetic, not analytic; and falls outside and not inside its being.[1]

A feeling feels as a gun shoots. If there be nothing to be felt or hit, they discharge themselves *ins blaue hinein*. If, however, something starts up opposite them, they no longer simply shoot or feel, they hit and know.

But with this arises a worse objection than any yet made. We the critics look on and see a real q and a feeling of q; and because the two resemble each other, we say the one knows the other. But what right have we to say this until we know that the feeling of q means to stand for or represent just that *same* other q? Suppose, instead of one q, a number of real q's in the field. If the gun shoots and hits, we can easily see which one of them it hits. But how can we distinguish which one

---

[1] It seems odd to call so important a function accidental, but I do not see how we can mend the matter. Just as, if we start with the reality and ask how it may come to be known, we can only reply by invoking a feeling which shall *reconstruct* it in its own more private fashion; so, if we start with the feeling and ask how it may come to know, we can only reply by invoking a reality which shall *reconstruct* it in its own more public fashion. In either case, however, the datum we start with remains just what it was. One may easily get lost in verbal mysteries about the difference between quality of feeling and feeling of quality, between receiving and reconstructing the knowledge of a reality. But at the end we must confess that the notion of real cognition involves an unmediated dualism of the knower and the known. See Bowne's *Metaphysics*, New York, 1882, pp. 403–412, and various passages in Lotze, *e. g.*, *Logic*, § 308. ['Unmediated' is a bad word to have used.—1909.]

the feeling knows? It knows the one it stands for. But which one *does* it stand for? It declares no intention in this respect. It merely resembles; it resembles all indifferently; and resembling, *per se*, is not necessarily representing or standing-for at all. Eggs resemble each other, but do not on that account represent, stand for, or know each other. And if you say this is because neither of them is a *feeling*, then imagine the world to consist of nothing but toothaches, which *are* feelings, feelings resembling each other exactly,—would they know each other the better for all that?

The case of *q* being a bare quality like that of toothache-pain is quite different from that of its being a concrete individual thing. There is practically no test for deciding whether the feeling of a bare quality means to represent it or not. It can *do* nothing to the quality beyond resembling it, simply because an abstract quality is a thing to which nothing can be done. Being without context or environment or *principium individuationis*, a quiddity with no hæcceity, a platonic idea, even duplicate editions of such a quality (were they possible), would be indiscernible, and no sign could be given, no result altered, whether the feeling meant to stand for this edition or for that, or whether it simply resembled the quality without meaning to stand for it at all.

If now we grant a genuine pluralism of editions to the quality *q*, by assigning to each a *context* which shall distinguish it from its mates, we may proceed to explain which edition of it the feeling knows, by extending our principle of resemblance to the context too, and saying the feeling knows the particular *q* whose context it most exactly duplicates. But here again the theoretic doubt recurs: duplication and coincidence, are they knowledge? The gun shows which *q* it points to and hits, by *breaking* it. Until the feeling can show us which *q* it points to and knows, by some equally flagrant token, why are we not free to deny that it either points to or knows any one of the *real q*'s at all, and to affirm that the word 'resemblance' exhaustively describes its relation to the reality?

Well, as a matter of fact, every actual feeling *does* show us, quite as flagrantly as the gun, which *q* it points to; and practically in concrete cases the matter is decided by an element we have hitherto left out. Let us pass from abstractions to possible instances, and ask our obliging *deus ex machina* to frame for us a richer world. Let him send me, for example, a dream of the death of a certain man, and let him simultaneously cause the man to die. How would our practical instinct spontaneously decide whether this were a case of cognition of the reality, or only a sort of marvellous coincidence of a resembling reality with my dream? Just such puzzling cases as this are what the 'society for psychical research' is busily collecting and trying to interpret in the most reasonable way.

If my dream were the only one of the kind I ever had in my life, if the context of the death in the dream differed in many particulars from the real death's context, and if my dream led me to no action about the death, unquestionably we should all call it a strange coincidence, and naught besides. But if the death in the dream had a long context, agreeing point for point with every feature that attended the real death; if I were constantly having such dreams, all equally perfect, and if on awaking I had a habit of *acting* immediately as if they were true and so getting 'the start' of my more tardily instructed neighbors,—we should in all probability have to admit that I had some mysterious kind of clairvoyant power, that my dreams in an inscrutable way meant just those realities they figured, and that the word 'coincidence' failed to touch the root of the matter. And whatever doubts any one preserved would completely vanish, if it should appear that from the midst of my dream I had the power of *interfering* with the course of the reality, and making the events in it turn this way or that, according as I dreamed they should. Then at least it would be certain that my waking critics and my dreaming self were dealing with the *same*.

And thus do men invariably decide such a question. *The falling of the dream's practical consequences* into the real world, and the *extent* of the resemblance between the two worlds are the criteria they instinctively use.[1] All feeling is for the sake

[1] The thoroughgoing objector might, it is true, still return to the charge, and, granting a dream which should completely mirror the real universe, and all the actions dreamed in which should be instantly matched by duplicate actions in this universe, still insist that this is nothing more than harmony,

of action, all feeling results in action,—to-day no argument is needed to prove these truths. But by a most singular disposition of nature which we may conceive to have been different, *my feelings act upon the realities within my critic's world.* Unless, then, my critic can prove that my feeling does not 'point to' those realities which it acts upon, how can he continue to doubt that he and I are alike cognizant of one and the same real world? If the action is performed in one world, that must be the world the feeling intends; if in another world, *that* is the world the feeling has in mind. If your feeling bear no fruits in my world, I call it utterly detached from my world; I call it a solipsism, and call its world a dream-world. If your toothache do not prompt you to *act* as if I had a toothache, nor even as if I had a separate existence; if you neither say to me, 'I know now how you must suffer!' nor tell me of a remedy, I deny that your feeling, however it may resemble mine, is really cognizant of mine. It gives no *sign* of being cognizant, and such a sign is absolutely necessary to my admission that it is.

Before I can think you to mean my world, you must affect my world; before I can think you to mean much of it, you must affect much of it; and before I can be sure you mean it *as I do*, you must affect it *just as I should* if I were in your place. Then I, your critic, will gladly believe that we are

---

and that it is as far as ever from being made clear whether the dream-world refers to that other world, all of whose details it so closely copies. This objection leads deep into metaphysics. I do not impugn its importance, and justice obliges me to say that but for the teachings of my colleague, Dr. Josiah Royce, I should neither have grasped its full force nor made my own practical and psychological point of view as clear to myself as it is. On this occasion I prefer to stick steadfastly to that point of view; but I hope that Dr. Royce's more fundamental criticism of the function of cognition may ere long see the light. [I referred in this note to Royce's *Religious aspect of philosophy*, then about to be published. This powerful book maintained that the notion of *referring* involved that of an inclusive mind that shall own both the real q and the mental q, and use the latter expressly as a representative symbol of the former. At the time I could not refute this transcendentalist opinion. Later, largely through the influence of Professor D. S. Miller (see his essay 'The meaning of truth and error,' in the *Philosophical Review* for 1893, vol. 2 p. 403) I came to see that any definitely experienceable workings would serve as intermediaries quite as well as the absolute mind's intentions would.]

thinking, not only of the same reality, but that we are thinking it *alike*, and thinking of much of its extent.

Without the practical effects of our neighbor's feelings on our own world, we should never suspect the existence of our neighbor's feelings at all, and of course should never find ourselves playing the critic as we do in this article. The constitution of nature is very peculiar. In the world of each of us are certain objects called human bodies, which move about and act on all the other objects there, and the occasions of their action are in the main what the occasions of our action would be, were they our bodies. They use words and gestures, which, if we used them, would have thoughts behind them,—no mere thoughts *überhaupt*, however, but strictly determinate thoughts. I think you have the notion of fire in general, because I see you act towards this fire in my room just as I act towards it,—poke it and present your person towards it, and so forth. But that binds me to believe that if you feel 'fire' at all, *this* is the fire you feel. As a matter of fact, whenever we constitute ourselves into psychological critics, it is not by dint of discovering which reality a feeling 'resembles' that we find out which reality it means. We become first aware of which one it means, and then we suppose that to be the one it resembles. We see each other looking at the same objects, pointing to them and turning them over in various ways, and thereupon we hope and trust that all of our several feelings resemble the reality and each other. But this is a thing of which we are never theoretically sure. Still, it would practically be a case of *grübelsucht*, if a ruffian were assaulting and drubbing my body, to spend much time in subtle speculation either as to whether his vision of my body resembled mine, or as to whether the body he really *meant* to insult were not some body in his mind's eye, altogether other from my own. The practical point of view brushes such metaphysical cobwebs away. If what he have in mind be not *my* body, why call we it a body at all? His mind is inferred by me as a term, to whose existence we trace the things that happen. The inference is quite void if the term, once inferred, be separated from its connection with the body that made me infer it, and connected with another that is not mine at all. No matter for the metaphysical puzzle of how our two minds, the ruffian's and mine, *can* mean the same body. Men who see each other's bodies sharing the same space, treading the same earth, splashing the same water, making the same air resonant, and pursuing the same game and eating out of the same dish, will never practically believe in a pluralism of solipsistic worlds.

Where, however, the actions of one mind seem to take no effect in the world of the other, the case is different. This is what happens in poetry and fiction. Every one knows *Ivanhoe*, for example; but so long as we stick to the story pure and simple without regard to the facts of its production, few would hesitate to admit that there are as many different Ivanhoes as there are different minds cognizant of the story.[1] The fact that all these Ivanhoes *resemble* each other does not prove the contrary. But if an alteration invented by one man in his version were to reverberate immediately through all the other versions, and produce changes therein, we should then easily agree that all these thinkers were thinking the *same* Ivanhoe, and that, fiction or no fiction, it formed a little world common to them all.

Having reached this point, we may take up our thesis and improve it again. Still calling the reality by the name of *q* and

[1]That is, there is no *real* 'Ivanhoe,' not even the one in Sir Walter Scott's mind as he was writing the story. That one is only the *first* one of the Ivanhoe-solipsisms. It is quite true we can make it the real Ivanhoe if we like, and then say that the other Ivanhoes know it or do not know it, according as they refer to and resemble it or no. This is done by bringing in Sir Walter Scott himself as the author of the real Ivanhoe, and so making a complex object of both. This object, however, is not a story pure and simple. It has dynamic relations with the world common to the experience of all the readers. Sir Walter Scott's Ivanhoe got itself printed in volumes which we all can handle, and to any one of which we can refer to see which of our versions be the true one, *i. e.*, the original one of Scott himself. We can see the manuscript; in short we can get back to the Ivanhoe in Scott's mind by many an avenue and channel of this real world of our experience,—a thing we can by no means do with either the Ivanhoe or the Rebecca, either the Templar or the Isaac of York, of the story taken simply as such, and detached from the conditions of its production. Everywhere, then, we have the same test: can we pass continuously from two objects in two minds to a third object which seems to be in *both* minds, because each mind feels every modification imprinted on it by the other? If so, the first two objects named are derivatives, to say the least, from the same third object, and may be held, if they resemble each other, to refer to one and the same reality.

letting the critic's feeling vouch for it, we can say that any other feeling will be held cognizant of q, provided it both resemble q, and refer to q, as shown by its either modifying q directly, or modifying some other reality, p or r, which the critic knows to be continuous with q. Or more shortly, thus: *The feeling of q knows whatever reality it resembles, and either directly or indirectly operates on.* If it resemble without operating, it is a dream; if it operate without resembling, it is an error.[1]

It is to be feared that the reader may consider this formula rather insignificant and obvious, and hardly worth the labor of so many pages, especially when he considers that the only cases to which it applies are *percepts*, and that the whole field

[1]Among such errors are those cases in which our feeling operates on a reality which it does partially resemble, and yet does not intend: as for instance, when I take up your umbrella, meaning to take my own. I cannot be said here either to know your umbrella, or my own, which latter my feeling more completely resembles. I am mistaking them both, misrepresenting their context, etc.

We have spoken in the text as if the critic were necessarily one mind, and the feeling criticised another. But the criticised feeling and its critic may be earlier and later feelings of the same mind, and here it might seem that we could dispense with the notion of operating, to prove that critic and criticised are referring to and meaning to represent the *same*. We think we see our past feelings directly, and know what they refer to without appeal. At the worst, we can always fix the intention of our present feeling and *make* it refer to the same reality to which any one of our past feelings may have referred. So we need no 'operating' here, to make sure that the feeling and its critic mean the same real q. Well, all the better if this is so! We have covered the more complex and difficult case in our text, and we may let this easier one go. The main thing at present is to stick to practical psychology, and ignore metaphysical difficulties.

One more remark. Our formula contains, it will be observed, nothing to correspond to the great principle of cognition laid down by Professor Ferrier in his *Institutes of Metaphysic* and apparently adopted by all the followers of Fichte, the principle, namely, that for knowledge to be constituted there must be knowledge of the knowing mind along with whatever else is known: not q, as we have supposed, but *q plus myself*, must be the least I can know. It is certain that the common sense of mankind never dreams of using any such principle when it tries to discriminate between conscious states that are knowledge and conscious states that are not. So that Ferrier's principle, if it have any relevancy at all, must have relevancy to the metaphysical possibility of consciousness at large, and not to the practically recognized constitution of cognitive consciousness. We may therefore pass it by without further notice here.

of symbolic or conceptual thinking seems to elude its grasp. Where the reality is either a material thing or act, or a state of the critic's consciousness, I may both mirror it in my mind and operate upon it—in the latter case indirectly, of course—as soon as I perceive it. But there are many cognitions, universally allowed to be such, which neither mirror nor operate on their realities.

In the whole field of symbolic thought we are universally held both to intend, to speak of, and to reach conclusions about—to know in short—particular realities, without having in our subjective consciousness any mind-stuff that resembles them even in a remote degree. We are instructed about them by language which awakens no consciousness beyond its sound; and we know *which* realities they are by the faintest and most fragmentary glimpse of some remote context they may have and by no direct imagination of themselves. As minds may differ here, let me speak in the first person. I am sure that my own current thinking has *words* for its almost exclusive subjective material, words which are made intelligible by being referred to some reality that lies beyond the horizon of direct consciousness, and of which I am only aware as of a terminal *more* existing in a certain direction, to which the words might lead but do not lead yet. The *subject*, or *topic*, of the words is usually something towards which I mentally seem to pitch them in a backward way, almost as I might jerk my thumb over my shoulder to point at something, without looking round, if I were only entirely sure that it was there. The *upshot*, or *conclusion*, of the words is something towards which I seem to incline my head forwards, as if giving assent to its existence, tho all my mind's eye catches sight of may be some tatter of an image connected with it, which tatter, however, if only endued with the feeling of familiarity and reality, makes me feel that the whole to which it belongs is rational and real, and fit to be let pass.

Here then is cognitive consciousness on a large scale, and yet what it knows, it hardly resembles in the least degree. The formula last laid down for our thesis must therefore be made more complete. We may now express it thus: *A percept knows whatever reality it directly or indirectly operates on and resembles;*

a conceptual feeling, or thought knows[1] *a reality, whenever it actually or potentially terminates in a percept that operates on, or
resembles that reality, or is otherwise connected with it or with its
context.* The latter percept may be either sensation or sensorial
idea; and when I say the thought must *terminate* in such a
percept, I mean that it must ultimately be capable of leading
up thereto,—by the way of practical experience, if the terminal feeling be a sensation; by the way of logical or habitual
suggestion, if it be only an image in the mind.

Let an illustration make this plainer. I open the first book
I take up, and read the first sentence that meets my eye:
'Newton saw the handiwork of God in the heavens as plainly
as Paley in the animal kingdom.' I immediately look back
and try to analyze the subjective state in which I rapidly apprehended this sentence as I read it. In the first place there
was an obvious feeling that the sentence was intelligible and
rational and related to the world of realities. There was also
a sense of agreement or harmony between 'Newton,' 'Paley,'
and 'God.' There was no apparent image connected with the
words 'heavens,' or 'handiwork,' or 'God'; they were words
merely. With 'animal kingdom' I think there was the faintest
consciousness (it may possibly have been an image of the
steps) of the Museum of Zoölogy in the town of Cambridge
where I write. With 'Paley' there was an equally faint consciousness of a small dark leather book; and with 'Newton' a
pretty distinct vision of the right-hand lower corner of a
curling periwig. This is all the mind-stuff I can discover in
my first consciousness of the meaning of this sentence, and I
am afraid that even not all of this would have been present
had I come upon the sentence in a genuine reading of the
book, and not picked it out for an experiment. And yet my
consciousness was truly cognitive. The sentence is 'about
realities' which my psychological critic—for we must not
forget him—acknowledges to be such, even as he acknowledges my distinct feeling that they *are* realities, and my acquiescence in the general rightness of what I read of them,
to be true knowledge on my part.

Now what justifies my critic in being as lenient as this? This

[1] Is an incomplete 'thought about' that reality, that reality is its 'topic,' etc.

singularly inadequate consciousness of mine, made up of symbols that neither resemble nor affect the realities they stand for,—how can he be sure it is cognizant of the very realities he has himself in mind?

He is sure because in countless like cases he has seen such inadequate and symbolic thoughts, by developing themselves, terminate in percepts that practically modified and presumably resembled his own. By 'developing' themselves is meant obeying their tendencies, following up the suggestions nascently present in them, working in the direction in which they seem to point, clearing up the penumbra, making distinct the halo, unravelling the fringe, which is part of their composition, and in the midst of which their more substantive kernel of subjective content seems consciously to lie. Thus I may develop my thought in the Paley direction by procuring the brown leather volume and bringing the passages about the animal kingdom before the critic's eyes. I may satisfy him that the words mean for me just what they mean for him, by showing him *in concreto* the very animals and their arrangements, of which the pages treat. I may get Newton's works and portraits; or if I follow the line of suggestion of the wig, I may smother my critic in seventeenth-century matters pertaining to Newton's environment, to show that the word 'Newton' has the same *locus* and relations in both our minds. Finally I may, by act and word, persuade him that what I mean by God and the heavens and the analogy of the handiworks, is just what he means also.

My demonstration in the last resort is to his *senses*. My thought makes me act on his senses much as he might himself act on them, were he pursuing the consequences of a perception of his own. Practically then *my* thought terminates in *his* realities. He willingly supposes it, therefore, to be *of* them, and inwardly to *resemble* what his own thought would be, were it of the same symbolic sort as mine. And the pivot and fulcrum and support of his mental persuasion, is the sensible operation which my thought leads me, or may lead, to effect—the bringing of Paley's book, of Newton's portrait, etc., before his very eyes.

In the last analysis, then, we believe that we all know and think about and talk about the same world, because *we believe our PERCEPTS are possessed by us in common.* And we believe this because the percepts of each one of us seem to be changed in consequence of changes in the percepts of some one else. What I am for you is in the first instance a percept of your own. Unexpectedly, however, I open and show you a book, uttering certain sounds the while. These acts are also your percepts, but they so resemble acts of yours with feelings prompting them, that you cannot doubt I have the feelings too, or that the book is one book felt in both our worlds. That it is felt in the same way, that my feelings of it resemble yours, is something of which we never can be sure, but which we assume as the simplest hypothesis that meets the case. As a matter of fact, we never *are* sure of it, and, as *erkenntniss-theoretiker*, we can only say that of feelings that should *not* resemble each other, both could not know the same thing at the same time in the same way.[1] If each holds to its own percept as the reality, it is bound to say of the other percept, that, though it may *intend* that reality, and prove this by working change upon it, yet, if it do not resemble it, it is all false and wrong.[2]

If this be so of percepts, how much more so of higher modes of thought! Even in the sphere of sensation individuals are probably different enough. Comparative study of the simplest conceptual elements seems to show a wider divergence still. And when it comes to general theories and emotional attitudes towards life, it is indeed time to say with Thackeray, 'My friend, two different universes walk about under your hat and under mine.'

What can save us at all and prevent us from flying asunder into a chaos of mutually repellent solipsisms? Through what can our several minds commune? Through nothing but the mutual resemblance of those of our perceptual feelings which

[1]Though both might terminate in the same thing and be incomplete thoughts 'about' it.

[2]The difference between Idealism and Realism is immaterial here. What is said in the text is consistent with either theory. A law by which my percept shall change yours directly is no more mysterious than a law by which it shall first change a physical reality, and then the reality change yours. In either case you and I seem knit into a continuous world, and not to form a pair of solipsisms.

have this power of modifying one another, *which are mere dumb knowledges-of-acquaintance*, and which must also resemble their realities or not know them aright at all. In such pieces of knowledge-of-acquaintance all our knowledge-about must end, and carry a sense of this possible termination as part of its content. These percepts, these *termini*, these sensible things, these mere matters-of-acquaintance, are the only realities we ever directly know, and the whole history of our thought is the history of our substitution of one of them for another, and the reduction of the substitute to the status of a conceptual sign. Contemned though they be by some thinkers, these sensations are the mother-earth, the anchorage, the stable rock, the first and last limits, the *terminus a quo* and the *terminus ad quem* of the mind. To find such sensational *termini* should be our aim with all our higher thought. They end discussion; they destroy the false conceit of knowledge; and without them we are all at sea with each other's meaning. If two men act alike on a percept, they believe themselves to feel alike about it; if not, they may suspect they know it in differing ways. We can never be sure we understand each other till we are able to bring the matter to this test.[1] This is why metaphysical discussions are so much like fighting with the air; they have no practical issue of a sensational kind. 'Scientific' theories, on the other hand, always terminate in definite percepts. You can deduce a possible sensation from your theory and, taking me into your laboratory, prove that your theory is true of my world by giving me the sensation then and there. Beautiful is the flight of conceptual reason through the upper air of truth. No wonder philosophers are dazzled by it still, and no wonder they look with some disdain at the low earth of feeling from which the goddess launched herself aloft. But woe to her if she return not home to its acquaint-

[1]'There is no distinction of meaning so fine as to consist in anything but a possible difference of practice. . . . It appears, then, that the rule for attaining the [highest] grade of clearness of apprehension is as follows: Consider what effects, which might conceivably have practical bearings, we conceive the object of our conception to have. Then, our conception of these effects is the whole of our conception of the object.' Charles S. Peirce: 'How to make our Ideas clear,' in *Popular Science Monthly*, New York, January, 1878, p. 293.

ance; *Nirgends haften dann die unsicheren Sohlen*—every crazy wind will take her, and, like a fire-balloon at night, she will go out among the stars.

NOTE.—The reader will easily see how much of the account of the truth-function developed later in *Pragmatism* was already explicit in this earlier article, and how much came to be defined later. In this earlier article we find distinctly asserted:—

1. The reality, external to the true idea;

2. The critic, reader, or epistemologist, with his own belief, as warrant for this reality's existence;

3. The experienceable environment, as the vehicle or medium connecting knower with known, and yielding the cognitive *relation*;

4. The notion of *pointing*, through this medium, to the reality, as one condition of our being said to know it;

5. That of *resembling* it, and eventually *affecting* it, as determining the pointing to *it* and not to something else.

6. The elimination of the 'epistemological gulf,' so that the whole truth-relation falls inside of the continuities of concrete experience, and is constituted of particular processes, varying with every object and subject, and susceptible of being described in detail.

The defects in this earlier account are:—

1. The possibly undue prominence given to resembling, which altho a fundamental function in knowing truly, is so often dispensed with;

2. The undue emphasis laid upon operating on the object itself, which in many cases is indeed decisive of that being what we refer to, but which is often lacking, or replaced by operations on other things related to the object.

3. The imperfect development of the generalized notion of the *workability* of the feeling or idea as equivalent to that *satisfactory adaptation* to the particular reality, which constitutes the truth of the idea. It is this more generalized notion, as covering all such specifications as pointing, fitting, operating or resembling, that distinguishes the developed view of Dewey, Schiller, and myself.

4. The treatment, on page 851, of percepts as the only realm of reality. I now treat concepts as a co-ordinate realm.

The next paper represents a somewhat broader grasp of the topic on the writer's part.

II

THERE ARE two ways of knowing things, knowing them immediately or intuitively, and knowing them conceptually or representatively. Altho such things as the white paper before our eyes can be known intuitively, most of the things we know, the tigers now in India, for example, or the scholastic system of philosophy, are known only representatively or symbolically.

Suppose, to fix our ideas, that we take first a case of conceptual knowledge; and let it be our knowledge of the tigers in India, as we sit here. Exactly what do we *mean* by saying that we here know the tigers? What is the precise fact that the cognition so confidently claimed is *known-as*, to use Shadworth Hodgson's inelegant but valuable form of words?

Most men would answer that what we mean by knowing the tigers is having them, however absent in body, become in some way present to our thought; or that our knowledge of them is known as presence of our thought to them. A great mystery is usually made of this peculiar presence in absence; and the scholastic philosophy, which is only common sense grown pedantic, would explain it as a peculiar kind of existence, called *intentional inexistence*, of the tigers in our mind. At the very least, people would say that what we mean by knowing the tigers is mentally *pointing* towards them as we sit here.

But now what do we mean by *pointing*, in such a case as this? What is the pointing known-as, here?

To this question I shall have to give a very prosaic answer—one that traverses the prepossessions not only of common sense and scholasticism, but also those of nearly all the epistemological writers whom I have ever read. The answer, made brief, is this: The pointing of our thought to the tigers is known simply and solely as a procession of mental associates and motor consequences that follow on the thought, and

[1]Extracts from a presidential address before the American Psychological Association, published in the *Psychological Review*, vol. ii, p. 105 (1895).

that would lead harmoniously, if followed out, into some ideal or real context, or even into the immediate presence, of the tigers. It is known as our rejection of a jaguar, if that beast were shown us as a tiger; as our assent to a genuine tiger if so shown. It is known as our ability to utter all sorts of propositions which don't contradict other propositions that are true of the real tigers. It is even known, if we take the tigers very seriously, as actions of ours which may terminate in directly intuited tigers, as they would if we took a voyage to India for the purpose of tiger-hunting and brought back a lot of skins of the striped rascals which we had laid low. In all this there is no self-transcendency in our mental images *taken by themselves*. They are one phenomenal fact; the tigers are another; and their pointing to the tigers is a perfectly commonplace intra-experiential relation, *if you once grant a connecting world to be there*. In short, the ideas and the tigers are in themselves as loose and separate, to use Hume's language, as any two things can be; and pointing means here an operation as external and adventitious as any that nature yields.[1]

I hope you may agree with me now that in representative knowledge there is no special inner mystery, but only an outer chain of physical or mental intermediaries connecting thought and thing. *To know an object is here to lead to it through a context which the world supplies.* All this was most instructively set forth by our colleague D. S. Miller at our meeting in New York last Christmas, and for re-confirming my sometime wavering opinion, I owe him this acknowledgment.[2]

Let us next pass on to the case of immediate or intuitive acquaintance with an object, and let the object be the white paper before our eyes. The thought-stuff and the thing-stuff

---

[1] A stone in one field may 'fit,' we say, a hole in another field. But the relation of 'fitting,' so long as no one carries the stone to the hole and drops it in, is only one name for the fact that such an act *may* happen. Similarly with the knowing of the tigers here and now. It is only an anticipatory name for a further associative and terminative process that *may* occur.

[2] See Dr. Miller's articles on Truth and Error, and on Content and Function, in the *Philosophical Review*, July, 1893, and Nov., 1895.

are here indistinguishably the same in nature, as we saw a moment since, and there is no context of intermediaries or associates to stand between and separate the thought and thing. There is no 'presence in absence' here, and no 'pointing,' but rather an allround embracing of the paper by the thought; and it is clear that the knowing cannot now be explained exactly as it was when the tigers were its object. Dotted all through our experience are states of immediate acquaintance just like this. Somewhere our belief always does rest on ultimate data like the whiteness, smoothness, or squareness of this paper. Whether such qualities be truly ultimate aspects of being, or only provisional suppositions of ours, held-to till we get better informed, is quite immaterial for our present inquiry. So long as it is believed in, we see our object face to face. What now do we mean by 'knowing' such a sort of object as this? For this is also the way in which we should know the tiger if our conceptual idea of him were to terminate by having led us to his lair?

This address must not become too long, so I must give my answer in the fewest words. And let me first say this: So far as the white paper or other ultimate datum of our experience is considered to enter also into some one else's experience, and we, in knowing it, are held to know it there as well as here; so far, again, as it is considered to be a mere mask for hidden molecules that other now impossible experiences of our own might some day lay bare to view; so far it is a case of tigers in India again—the things known being absent experiences, the knowing can only consist in passing smoothly towards them through the intermediary context that the world supplies. But if our own private vision of the paper be considered in abstraction from every other event, as if it constituted by itself the universe (and it might perfectly well do so, for aught we can understand to the contrary), then the paper seen and the seeing of it are only two names for one indivisible fact which, properly named, is *the datum, the phenomenon, or the experience*. The paper is in the mind and the mind is around the paper, because paper and mind are only two names that are given later to the one experience, when, taken in a larger world of which it forms a part, its connections are traced in different directions.[1] *To know immediately, then, or intuitively, is for mental content and object to be identical.* This is a very different definition from that which we gave of representative knowledge; but neither definition involves those mysterious notions of self-transcendency and presence in absence which are such essential parts of the ideas of knowledge, both of philosophers and of common men.[2]

[1]What is meant by this is that 'the experience' can be referred to either of two great associative systems, that of the experiencer's mental history, or that of the experienced facts of the world. Of both of these systems it forms part, and may be regarded, indeed, as one of their points of intersection. One

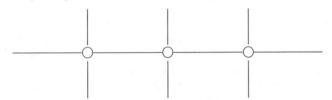

might let a vertical line stand for the mental history; but the same object, O, appears also in the mental history of different persons, represented by the other vertical lines. It thus ceases to be the private property of one experience, and becomes, so to speak, a shared or public thing. We can track its outer history in this way, and represent it by the horizontal line. [It is also known representatively at other points of the vertical lines, or intuitively there again, so that the line of its outer history would have to be looped and wandering, but I make it straight for simplicity's sake.] In any case, however, it is the same *stuff* that figures in all the sets of lines.

[2][The reader will observe that the text is written from the point of view of *naïf* realism or common sense, and avoids raising the idealistic controversy.]

III

RECEIVING FROM the Editor of *Mind* an advance proof of Mr. Bradley's article on 'Truth and Practice,' I understand this as a hint to me to join in the controversy over 'Pragmatism' which seems to have seriously begun. As my name has been coupled with the movement, I deem it wise to take the hint, the more so as in some quarters greater credit has been given me than I deserve, and probably undeserved discredit in other quarters falls also to my lot.

First, as to the word 'pragmatism.' I myself have only used the term to indicate a method of carrying on abstract discussion. The serious meaning of a concept, says Mr. Peirce, lies in the concrete difference to some one which its being true will make. Strive to bring all debated conceptions to that 'pragmatic' test, and you will escape vain wrangling: if it can make no practical difference which of two statements be true, then they are really one statement in two verbal forms; if it can make no practical difference whether a given statement be true or false, then the statement has no real meaning. In neither case is there anything fit to quarrel about: we may save our breath, and pass to more important things.

All that the pragmatic method implies, then, is that truths should *have* practical[2] consequences. In England the word has been used more broadly still, to cover the notion that the truth of any statement *consists* in the consequences, and particularly in their being good consequences. Here we get beyond affairs of method altogether; and since my pragmatism and this wider pragmatism are so different, and both are important enough to have different names, I think that Mr. Schiller's proposal to call the wider pragmatism by the name of 'humanism' is excellent and ought to be adopted. The

[1]Reprinted, with slight verbal revision, from *Mind*, vol. xiii, N. S., p. 457 (October, 1904). A couple of interpolations from another article in *Mind*, 'Humanism and truth once more,' in vol. xiv, have been made.

[2]['Practical' in the sense of *particular*, of course, not in the sense that the consequences may not be *mental* as well as physical.]

narrower pragmatism may still be spoken of as the 'pragmatic method.'

I have read in the past six months many hostile reviews of Schiller's and Dewey's publications; but with the exception of Mr. Bradley's elaborate indictment, they are out of reach where I write, and I have largely forgotten them. I think that a free discussion of the subject on my part would in any case be more useful than a polemic attempt at rebutting these criticisms in detail. Mr. Bradley in particular can be taken care of by Mr. Schiller. He repeatedly confesses himself unable to comprehend Schiller's views, he evidently has not sought to do so sympathetically, and I deeply regret to say that his laborious article throws, for my mind, absolutely no useful light upon the subject. It seems to me on the whole an *ignoratio elenchi*, and I feel free to disregard it altogether.

The subject is unquestionably difficult. Messrs. Dewey's and Schiller's thought is eminently an induction, a generalization working itself free from all sorts of entangling particulars. If true, it involves much restatement of traditional notions. This is a kind of intellectual product that never attains a classic form of expression when first promulgated. The critic ought therefore not to be too sharp and logic-chopping in his dealings with it, but should weigh it as a whole, and especially weigh it against its possible alternatives. One should also try to apply it first to one instance, and then to another to see how it will work. It seems to me that it is emphatically not a case for instant execution, by conviction of intrinsic absurdity or of self-contradiction, or by caricature of what it would look like if reduced to skeleton shape. Humanism is in fact much more like one of those secular changes that come upon public opinion overnight, as it were, borne upon tides 'too deep for sound or foam,' that survive all the crudities and extravagances of their advocates, that you can pin to no one absolutely essential statement, nor kill by any one decisive stab.

Such have been the changes from aristocracy to democracy, from classic to romantic taste, from theistic to pantheistic feeling, from static to evolutionary ways of understanding life— changes of which we all have been spectators. Scholasticism still opposes to such changes the method of confutation by single decisive reasons, showing that the new view involves self-contradiction, or traverses some fundamental principle. This is like stopping a river by planting a stick in the middle of its bed. Round your obstacle flows the water and 'gets there all the same.' In reading some of our opponents, I am not a little reminded of those catholic writers who refute darwinism by telling us that higher species cannot come from lower because *minus nequit gignere plus*, or that the notion of transformation is absurd, for it implies that species tend to their own destruction, and that would violate the principle that every reality tends to persevere in its own shape. The point of view is too myopic, too tight and close to take in the inductive argument. Wide generalizations in science always meet with these summary refutations in their early days; but they outlive them, and the refutations then sound oddly antiquated and scholastic. I cannot help suspecting that the humanistic theory is going through this kind of would-be refutation at present.

The one condition of understanding humanism is to become inductive-minded oneself, to drop rigorous definitions, and follow lines of least resistance 'on the whole.' 'In other words,' an opponent might say, 'resolve your intellect into a kind of slush.' 'Even so,' I make reply,—'if you will consent to use no politer word.' For humanism, conceiving the more 'true' as the more 'satisfactory' (Dewey's term), has sincerely to renounce rectilinear arguments and ancient ideals of rigor and finality. It is in just this temper of renunciation, so different from that of pyrrhonistic scepticism, that the spirit of humanism essentially consists. Satisfactoriness has to be measured by a multitude of standards, of which some, for aught we know, may fail in any given case; and what is more satisfactory than any alternative in sight, may to the end be a sum of *pluses* and *minuses*, concerning which we can only trust that by ulterior corrections and improvements a maximum of the one and a minimum of the other may some day be approached. It means a real change of heart, a break with absolutistic hopes, when one takes up this inductive view of the conditions of belief.

As I understand the pragmatist way of seeing things, it

owes its being to the break-down which the last fifty years
have brought about in the older notions of scientific truth.
'God geometrizes,' it used to be said; and it was believed that
Euclid's elements literally reproduced his geometrizing. There
is an eternal and unchangeable 'reason'; and its voice was supposed to reverberate in *Barbara* and *Celarent*. So also of the
'laws of nature,' physical and chemical, so of natural history
classifications—all were supposed to be exact and exclusive
duplicates of pre-human archetypes buried in the structure of
things, to which the spark of divinity hidden in our intellect
enables us to penetrate. The anatomy of the world is logical,
and its logic is that of a university professor, it was thought.
Up to about 1850 almost every one believed that sciences expressed truths that were exact copies of a definite code of
non-human realities. But the enormously rapid multiplication
of theories in these latter days has well-nigh upset the notion
of any one of them being a more literally objective kind of
thing than another. There are so many geometries, so many
logics, so many physical and chemical hypotheses, so many
classifications, each one of them good for so much and yet
not good for everything, that the notion that even the truest
formula may be a human device and not a literal transcript
has dawned upon us. We hear scientific laws now treated as
so much 'conceptual shorthand,' true so far as they are useful
but no farther. Our mind has become tolerant of symbol instead of reproduction, of approximation instead of exactness,
of plasticity instead of rigor. 'Energetics,' measuring the bare
face of sensible phenomena so as to describe in a single
formula all their changes of 'level,' is the last word of this
scientific humanism, which indeed leaves queries enough
outstanding as to the reason for so curious a congruence between the world and the mind, but which at any rate makes
our whole notion of scientific truth more flexible and genial
than it used to be.

It is to be doubted whether any theorizer to-day, either in
mathematics, logic, physics or biology, conceives himself to
be literally re-editing processes of nature or thoughts of God.
The main forms of our thinking, the separation of subjects
from predicates, the negative, hypothetic and disjunctive
judgments, are purely human habits. The ether, as Lord

Salisbury said, is only a noun for the verb to undulate; and many of our theological ideas are admitted, even by those who call them 'true,' to be humanistic in like degree.

I fancy that these changes in the current notions of truth are what originally gave the impulse to Messrs. Dewey's and Schiller's views. The suspicion is in the air nowadays that the superiority of one of our formulas to another may not consist so much in its literal 'objectivity,' as in subjective qualities like its usefulness, its 'elegance' or its congruity with our residual beliefs. Yielding to these suspicions, and generalizing, we fall into something like the humanistic state of mind. Truth we conceive to mean everywhere, not duplication, but addition; not the constructing of inner copies of already complete realities, but rather the collaborating with realities so as to bring about a clearer result. Obviously this state of mind is at first full of vagueness and ambiguity. 'Collaborating' is a vague term; it must at any rate cover conceptions and logical arrangements. 'Clearer' is vaguer still. Truth must bring clear thoughts, as well as clear the way to action. 'Reality' is the vaguest term of all. The only way to test such a programme at all is to apply it to the various types of truth, in the hope of reaching an account that shall be more precise. Any hypothesis that forces such a review upon one has one great merit, even if in the end it prove invalid: it gets us better acquainted with the total subject. To give the theory plenty of 'rope' and see if it hangs itself eventually is better tactics than to choke it off at the outset by abstract accusations of self-contradiction. I think therefore that a decided effort at sympathetic mental play with humanism is the provisional attitude to be recommended to the reader.

When I find myself playing sympathetically with humanism, something like what follows is what I end by conceiving it to mean.

Experience is a process that continually gives us new material to digest. We handle this intellectually by the mass of beliefs of which we find ourselves already possessed, assimilating, rejecting, or rearranging in different degrees. Some of the apperceiving ideas are recent acquisitions of our own, but most of them are common-sense traditions of the race. There is probably not a common-sense tradition, of all those which we now live by, that was not in the first instance a genuine discovery, an inductive generalization like those more recent ones of the atom, of inertia, of energy, of reflex action, or of fitness to survive. The notions of one Time and of one Space as single continuous receptacles; the distinction between thoughts and things, matter and mind; between permanent subjects and changing attributes; the conception of classes with sub-classes within them; the separation of fortuitous from regularly caused connections; surely all these were once definite conquests made at historic dates by our ancestors in their attempts to get the chaos of their crude individual experiences into a more shareable and manageable shape. They proved of such sovereign use as *denkmittel* that they are now a part of the very structure of our mind. We cannot play fast and loose with them. No experience can upset them. On the contrary, they apperceive every experience and assign it to its place.

To what effect? That we may the better foresee the course of our experiences, communicate with one another, and steer our lives by rule. Also that we may have a cleaner, clearer, more inclusive mental view.

The greatest common-sense achievement, after the discovery of one Time and one Space, is probably the concept of permanently existing things. When a rattle first drops out of the hand of a baby, he does not look to see where it has gone. Non-perception he accepts as annihilation until he finds a better belief. That our perceptions mean *beings*, rattles that are there whether we hold them in our hands or not, becomes an interpretation so luminous of what happens to us that, once employed, it never gets forgotten. It applies with equal felicity to things and persons, to the objective and to the ejective realm. However a Berkeley, a Mill, or a Cornelius may criticise it, it *works*; and in practical life we never think of 'going back' upon it, or reading our incoming experiences in any other terms. We may, indeed, speculatively imagine a state of 'pure' experience before the hypothesis of permanent objects behind its flux had been framed; and we can play with the idea that some primeval genius might have struck into a different hypothesis. But we cannot positively imagine to-day what the different hypothesis could have been, for the category of trans-perceptual reality is now one of the foundations of our life. Our thoughts must still employ it if they are to possess reasonableness and truth.

This notion of a *first* in the shape of a most chaotic pure experience which sets us questions, of a *second* in the way of fundamental categories, long ago wrought into the structure of our consciousness and practically irreversible, which define the general frame within which answers must fall, and of a *third* which gives the detail of the answers in the shapes most congruous with all our present needs, is, as I take it, the essence of the humanistic conception. It represents experience in its pristine purity to be now so enveloped in predicates historically worked out that we can think of it as little more than an *Other*, of a *That*, which the mind, in Mr. Bradley's phrase, 'encounters,' and to whose stimulating presence we respond by ways of thinking which we call 'true' in proportion as they facilitate our mental or physical activities and bring us outer power and inner peace. But whether the Other, the universal *That*, has itself any definite inner structure, or whether, if it have any, the structure resembles any of our predicated *whats*, this is a question which humanism leaves untouched. For us, at any rate, it insists, reality is an accumulation of our own intellectual inventions, and the struggle for 'truth' in our progressive dealings with it is always a struggle to work in new nouns and adjectives while altering as little as possible the old.

It is hard to see why either Mr. Bradley's own logic or his metaphysics should oblige him to quarrel with this conception. He might consistently adopt it *verbatim et literatim*, if he would, and simply throw his peculiar absolute round it, following in this the good example of Professor Royce. Bergson in France, and his disciples, Wilbois the physicist and Leroy, are thoroughgoing humanists in the sense defined. Professor Milhaud also appears to be one; and the great Poincaré misses it by only the breadth of a hair. In Germany the name of Simmel offers itself as that of a humanist of the most radical sort. Mach and his school, and Hertz and Ostwald must be classed as humanists. The view is in the atmosphere and must be patiently discussed.

The best way to discuss it would be to see what the alternative might be. What is it indeed? Its critics make no explicit statement, Professor Royce being the only one so far who has formulated anything definite. The first service of humanism to philosophy accordingly seems to be that it will probably oblige those who dislike it to search their own hearts and heads. It will force analysis to the front and make it the order of the day. At present the lazy tradition that truth is *adæquatio intellectûs et rei* seems all there is to contradict it with. Mr. Bradley's only suggestion is that true thought 'must correspond to a determinate being which it cannot be said to make,' and obviously that sheds no new light. What is the meaning of the word to 'correspond'? Where is the 'being'? What sort of things are 'determinations,' and what is meant in this particular case by 'not to make'?

Humanism proceeds immediately to refine upon the looseness of these epithets. We correspond in *some* way with anything with which we enter into any relations at all. If it be a thing, we may produce an exact copy of it, or we may simply feel it as an existent in a certain place. If it be a demand, we may obey it without knowing anything more about it than its push. If it be a proposition, we may agree by not contradicting it, by letting it pass. If it be a relation between things, we may act on the first thing so as to bring ourselves out where the second will be. If it be something inaccessible, we may substitute a hypothetical object for it, which, having the same consequences, will cipher out for us real results. In a general way we may simply *add our thought to it*; and if it *suffers the addition*, and the whole situation harmoniously prolongs and enriches itself, the thought will pass for true.

As for the whereabouts of the beings thus corresponded to, although they may be outside of the present thought as well as in it, humanism sees no ground for saying they are outside of finite experience itself. Pragmatically, their reality means that we submit to them, take account of them, whether we like to or not, but this we must perpetually do with experiences other than our own. The whole system of what the present experience must correspond to 'adequately' may be continuous with the present experience itself. Reality, so taken as experience other than the present, might be either the legacy of past experience or the content of experience to come. Its determinations for *us* are in any case the adjectives which our acts of judging fit to it, and those are essentially humanistic things.

To say that our thought does not 'make' this reality means pragmatically that if our own particular thought were annihilated the reality would still be there in some shape, though possibly it might be a shape that would lack something that our thought supplies. That reality is 'independent' means that there is something in every experience that escapes our arbitrary control. If it be a sensible experience it coerces our attention; if a sequence, we cannot invert it; if we compare two terms we can come to only one result. There is a push, an urgency, within our very experience, against which we are on the whole powerless, and which drives us in a direction that is the destiny of our belief. That this drift of experience itself is in the last resort due to something independent of all possible experience may or may not be true. There may or may not be an extra-experiential 'ding an sich' that keeps the ball rolling, or an 'absolute' that lies eternally behind all the successive determinations which human thought has made. But within our experience *itself*, at any rate, humanism says, some determinations show themselves as being independent of others; some questions, if we ever ask them, can only be answered in one way; some beings, if we ever suppose them, must be supposed to have existed previously to the supposing; some relations, if they exist ever, must exist as long as their terms exist.

Truth thus means, according to humanism, the relation of less fixed parts of experience (predicates) to other relatively more fixed parts (subjects); and we are not required to seek it in a relation of experience as such to anything beyond itself. We can stay at home, for our behavior as experients is hemmed in on every side. The forces both of advance and of resistance are exerted by our own objects, and the notion of truth as something opposed to waywardness or license inevitably grows up solipsistically inside of every human life.

So obvious is all this that a common charge against the

humanistic authors 'makes me tired.' 'How can a deweyite discriminate sincerity from bluff?' was a question asked at a philosophic meeting where I reported on Dewey's *Studies*. 'How can the mere[1] pragmatist feel any duty to think truly?' is the objection urged by Professor Royce. Mr. Bradley in turn says that if a humanist understands his own doctrine, 'he must hold any idea, however mad, to be the truth, if any one will have it so.' And Professor Taylor describes pragmatism as believing anything one pleases and calling it truth.

Such a shallow sense of the conditions under which men's thinking actually goes on seems to me most surprising. These critics appear to suppose that, if left to itself, the rudderless raft of our experience must be ready to drift anywhere or nowhere. Even tho there were compasses on board, they seem to say, there would be no pole for them to point to. There must be absolute sailing-directions, they insist, decreed from outside, and an independent chart of the voyage added to the 'mere' voyage itself, if we are ever to make a port. But is it not obvious that even tho there be such absolute sailing-directions in the shape of pre-human standards of truth that we *ought* to follow, the only guarantee that we shall in fact follow them must lie in our human equipment. The 'ought' would be a *brutum fulmen* unless there were a felt grain inside of our experience that conspired. As a matter of fact the devoutest believers in absolute standards must admit that men fail to obey them. Waywardness is here, in spite of the eternal prohibitions, and the existence of any amount of reality *ante rem* is no warrant against unlimited error *in rebus* being incurred. The only *real* guarantee we have against licentious thinking is the circumpressure of experience itself, which gets us sick of concrete errors, whether there be a trans-empirical reality or not. How does the partisan of absolute reality know what this orders him to think? He cannot get direct sight of the absolute; and he has no means of guessing what it wants of him except by following the humanistic clues. The only truth that he himself will ever practically *accept* will be that to which his finite experiences lead him of themselves. The state of mind which shudders at the idea of a lot of experiences left

---

[1] I know of no 'mere' pragmatist, if *mereness* here means, as it seems to, the denial of all concreteness to the pragmatist's thought.

to themselves, and that augurs protection from the sheer name of an absolute, as if, however inoperative, that might still stand for a sort of ghostly security, is like the mood of those good people who, whenever they hear of a social tendency that is damnable, begin to redden and to puff, and say 'Parliament or Congress ought to make a law against it,' as if an impotent decree would give relief.

All the *sanctions* of a law of truth lie in the very texture of experience. Absolute or no absolute, the concrete truth *for us* will always be that way of thinking in which our various experiences most profitably combine.

And yet, the opponent obstinately urges, your humanist will always have a greater liberty to play fast and loose with truth than will your believer in an independent realm of reality that makes the standard rigid. If by this latter believer he means a man who pretends to know the standard and who fulminates it, the humanist will doubtless prove more flexible; but no more flexible than the absolutist himself if the latter follows (as fortunately our present-day absolutists do follow) empirical methods of inquiry in concrete affairs. To consider hypotheses is surely always better than to dogmatize *ins blaue hinein*.

Nevertheless this probable flexibility of temper in him has been used to convict the humanist of sin. Believing as he does, that truth lies *in rebus*, and is at every moment our own line of most propitious reaction, he stands forever debarred, as I have heard a learned colleague say, from trying to convert opponents, for does not their view, being *their* most propitious momentary reaction, already fill the bill? Only the believer in the *ante-rem* brand of truth can on this theory seek to make converts without self-stultification. But can there be self-stultification in urging any account whatever of truth? Can the definition ever contradict the deed? 'Truth is what I feel like saying'—suppose that to be the definition. 'Well, I feel like saying that, and I want you to feel like saying it, and shall continue to say it until I get you to agree.' Where is there any contradiction? Whatever truth may be said to be, that is the kind of truth which the saying can be held to carry. The *temper* which a saying may comport is an extra-logical matter. It may indeed be hotter in some individual absolutist than in a humanist, but it need not be so in another. And the humanist, for his part, is perfectly consistent in compassing sea and land to make one proselyte, if his nature be enthusiastic enough.

'But how *can* you be enthusiastic over any view of things which you know to have been partly made by yourself, and which is liable to alter during the next minute? How is any heroic devotion to the ideal of truth possible under such paltry conditions?'

This is just another of those objections by which the antihumanists show their own comparatively slack hold on the realities of the situation. If they would only follow the pragmatic method and ask: 'What is truth *known-as*? What does its existence stand for in the way of concrete goods?'—they would see that the name of it is the *inbegriff* of almost everything that is valuable in our lives. The true is the opposite of whatever is instable, of whatever is practically disappointing, of whatever is useless, of whatever is lying and unreliable, of whatever is unverifiable and unsupported, of whatever is inconsistent and contradictory, of whatever is artificial and eccentric, of whatever is unreal in the sense of being of no practical account. Here are pragmatic reasons with a vengeance why we should turn to truth—truth saves us from a world of that complexion. What wonder that its very name awakens loyal feeling! In particular what wonder that all little provisional fool's paradises of belief should appear contemptible in comparison with its bare pursuit! When absolutists reject humanism because they feel it to be untrue, that means that the whole habit of their mental needs is wedded already to a different view of reality, in comparison with which the humanistic world seems but the whim of a few irresponsible youths. Their own subjective apperceiving mass is what speaks here in the name of the eternal natures and bids them reject our humanism—as they apprehend it. Just so with us humanists, when we condemn all noble, clean-cut, fixed, eternal, rational, temple-like systems of philosophy. These contradict the *dramatic temperament* of nature, as our dealings with nature and our habits of thinking have so far brought us to conceive it. They seem oddly personal and artificial, even when not bureaucratic and professional in an absurd degree.

We turn from them to the great unpent and unstayed wilderness of truth as we feel it to be constituted, with as good a conscience as rationalists are moved by when they turn from our wilderness into their neater and cleaner intellectual abodes.[1]

This is surely enough to show that the humanist does not ignore the character of objectivity and independence in truth. Let me turn next to what his opponents mean when they say that to be true, our thoughts must 'correspond.'

The vulgar notion of correspondence here is that the thoughts must *copy* the reality—cognitio fit per *assimiliationem* cogniti et cognoscentis; and philosophy, without having ever fairly sat down to the question, seems to have instinctively accepted this idea: propositions are held true if they copy the eternal thought; terms are held true if they copy extra-mental realities. Implicitly, I think that the copy-theory has animated most of the criticisms that have been made on humanism.

A priori, however, it is not self-evident that the sole business of our mind with realities should be to copy them. Let my reader suppose himself to constitute for a time all the reality there is in the universe, and then to receive the announcement that another being is to be created who shall know him truly. How will he represent the knowing in advance? What

[1] [I cannot forbear quoting as an illustration of the contrast between humanist and rationalist tempers of mind, in a sphere remote from philosophy, these remarks on the Dreyfus 'affaire,' written by one who assuredly had never heard of humanism or pragmatism. 'Autant que la Révolution, "l'Affaire" est désormais une de nos "origines." Si elle n'a pas fait ouvrir le gouffre, c'est elle du moins qui a rendu patent et visible le long travail souterrain qui, silencieusement, avait preparé la séparation entre nos deux camps d'aujourd'hui, pour écarter enfin, d'un coup soudain, *la France des traditionalistes* (*poseurs de principes, chercheurs d'unité, constructeurs de systèmes à priori*) *et la France éprise du fait positif et de libre examen;*—la France révolutionnaire et romantique si l'on veut, celle qui met très haut l'individu, qui ne veut pas qu'un juste périsse, fut-ce pour sauver la nation, et qui cherche la vérité dans toutes ses parties aussi bien que dans une vue d'ensemble. . . . Duclaux ne pouvait pas concevoir qu'on préferât quelque chose à la vérité. Mais il voyait autour de lui de fort honnêtes gens qui, mettant en balance la vie d'un homme et la raison d'État, lui avouaient de quel poids léger ils jugeaient une simple existence individuelle, pour innocente qu'elle fût. *C'etaient des classiques, des gens à qui l'ensemble seul importe.*' *La Vie de Emile Duclaux*, par Mme. Em. D., Laval, 1906, pp. 243, 247–248.]

will he hope it to be? I doubt extremely whether it could ever occur to him to fancy it as a mere copying. Of what use to him would an imperfect second edition of himself in the new comer's interior be? It would seem pure waste of a propitious opportunity. The demand would more probably be for something absolutely new. The reader would conceive the knowing humanistically, 'the new comer,' he would say, 'must *take account of my presence by reacting on it in such a way that good would accrue to us both*. If copying be requisite to that end, let there be copying; otherwise not.' The essence in any case would not be the copying, but the enrichment of the previous world.

I read the other day, in a book of Professor Eucken's, a phrase, *'Die erhöhung des vorgefundenen daseins,'* which seems to be pertinent here. Why may not thought's mission be to increase and elevate, rather than simply to imitate and reduplicate, existence? No one who has read Lotze can fail to remember his striking comment on the ordinary view of the secondary qualities of matter, which brands them as 'illusory' because they copy nothing in the thing. The notion of a world complete in itself, to which thought comes as a passive mirror, adding nothing to fact, Lotze says is irrational. Rather is thought itself a most momentous part of fact, and the whole mission of the pre-existing and insufficient world of matter may simply be to provoke thought to produce its far more precious supplement.

'Knowing,' in short, may, for aught we can see beforehand to the contrary, be *only one way of getting into fruitful relations with reality*, whether copying be one of the relations or not.

It is easy to see from what special type of knowing the copy-theory arose. In our dealings with natural phenomena the great point is to be able to foretell. Foretelling, according to such a writer as Spencer, is the whole meaning of intelligence. When Spencer's 'law of intelligence' says that inner and outer relations must 'correspond,' it means that the distribution of terms in our inner time-scheme and space-scheme must be an exact copy of the distribution in real time and space of the real terms. In strict theory the mental terms themselves need not answer to the real terms in the sense of severally copying them, symbolic mental terms being enough, if only the real dates and places be copied. But in our ordinary life the mental terms are images and the real ones are sensations, and the images so often copy the sensations, that we easily take copying of terms as well as of relations to be the natural significance of knowing. Meanwhile much, even of this common descriptive truth, is couched in verbal symbols. If our symbols *fit* the world, in the sense of determining our expectations rightly, they may even be the better for not copying its terms.

It seems obvious that the pragmatic account of all this routine of phenomenal knowledge is accurate. Truth here is a relation, not of our ideas to non-human realities, but of conceptual parts of our experience to sensational parts. Those thoughts are true which guide us to *beneficial interaction* with sensible particulars as they occur, whether they copy these in advance or not.

From the frequency of copying in the knowledge of phenomenal fact, copying has been supposed to be the essence of truth in matters rational also. Geometry and logic, it has been supposed, must copy archetypal thoughts in the Creator. But in these abstract spheres there is no need of assuming archetypes. The mind is free to carve so many figures out of space, to make so many numerical collections, to frame so many classes and series, and it can analyze and compare so endlessly, that the very superabundance of the resulting ideas makes us doubt the 'objective' pre-existence of their models. It would be plainly wrong to suppose a God whose thought consecrated rectangular but not polar co-ordinates, or Jevons's notation but not Boole's. Yet if, on the other hand, we assume God to have thought in advance of every *possible* flight of human fancy in these directions, his mind becomes too much like a Hindoo idol with three heads, eight arms and six breasts, too much made up of superfœtation and redundancy for us to wish to copy it, and the whole notion of copying tends to evaporate from these sciences. Their objects can be better interpreted as being created step by step by men, as fast as they successively conceive them.

If now it be asked how, if triangles, squares, square roots, genera, and the like, are but improvised human 'artefacts,' their properties and relations can be so promptly known to be 'eternal,' the humanistic answer is easy. If triangles and genera are of our own production we can keep them invariant. We can make them 'timeless' by expressly decreeing that on *the things we mean* time shall exert no altering effect, that they are intentionally and it may be fictitiously abstracted from every corrupting real associate and condition. But relations between invariant objects will themselves be invariant. Such relations cannot be happenings, for by hypothesis nothing shall happen to the objects. I have tried to show in the last chapter of my *Principles of Psychology*[1] that they can only be relations of comparison. No one so far seems to have noticed my suggestion, and I am too ignorant of the development of mathematics to feel very confident of my own view. But if it were correct it would solve the difficulty perfectly. Relations of comparison are matters of direct inspection. As soon as mental objects are mentally compared, they are perceived to be either like or unlike. But once the same, always the same, once different, always different, under these timeless conditions. Which is as much as to say that truths concerning these man-made objects are necessary and eternal. We can change our conclusions only by changing our data first.

The whole fabric of the *a priori* sciences can thus be treated as a man-made product. As Locke long ago pointed out, these sciences have no immediate connection with fact. Only *if* a fact can be humanized by being identified with any of these ideal objects, is what was true of the objects now true also of the facts. The truth itself meanwhile was originally a copy of nothing; it was only a relation directly perceived to obtain between two artificial mental things.[2]

We may now glance at some special types of knowing, so as to see better whether the humanistic account fits. On the mathematical and logical types we need not enlarge further, nor need we return at much length to the case of our descriptive knowledge of the course of nature. So far as this involves anticipation, tho that *may* mean copying, it need, as we saw, mean little more than 'getting ready' in advance. But with

[1] Vol. ii, pp. 641 ff.
[2] [Mental things which are realities of course within the mental world.]

many distant and future objects, our practical relations are to the last degree potential and remote. In no sense can we now get ready for the arrest of the earth's revolution by the tidal brake, for instance; and with the past, tho we suppose ourselves to know it truly, we have no practical relations at all. It is obvious that, altho interests strictly practical have been the original starting-point of our search for true phenomenal descriptions, yet an intrinsic interest in the bare describing function has grown up. We wish accounts that shall be true, whether they bring collateral profit or not. The primitive function has developed its demand for mere exercise. This theoretic curiosity seems to be the characteristically human *differentia*, and humanism recognizes its enormous scope. A true idea now means not only one that prepares us for an actual perception. It means also one that might prepare us for a merely possible perception, or one that, if spoken, would suggest possible perceptions to others, or suggest actual perceptions which the speaker cannot share. The *ensemble* of perceptions thus thought of as either actual or possible form a system which it is obviously advantageous to us to get into a stable and consistent shape; and here it is that the common-sense notion of permanent beings finds triumphant use. Beings acting outside of the thinker explain, not only his actual perceptions, past and future, but his possible perceptions and those of every one else. Accordingly they gratify our theoretic need in a supremely beautiful way. We pass from our immediate actual through them into the foreign and the potential, and back again into the future actual, accounting for innumerable particulars by a single cause. As in those circular panoramas, where a real foreground of dirt, grass, bushes, rocks and a broken-down cannon is enveloped by a canvas picture of sky and earth and of a raging battle, continuing the foreground so cunningly that the spectator can detect no joint; so these conceptual objects, added to our present perceptual reality, fuse with it into the whole universe of our belief. In spite of all berkeleyan criticism, we do not doubt that they are really there. Tho our discovery of any one of them may only date from now, we unhesitatingly say that it not only *is*, but *was* there, if, by so saying, the past appears connected more consistently with what we feel the present to

be. This is historic truth. Moses wrote the Pentateuch, we
think, because if he did n't, all our religious habits will have
to be undone. Julius Cæsar was real, or we can never listen to
history again. Trilobites were once alive, or all our thought
about the strata is at sea. Radium, discovered only yesterday,
must always have existed, or its analogy with other natural
elements, which are permanent, fails. In all this, it is but one
portion of our beliefs reacting on another so as to yield the
most satisfactory total state of mind. That state of mind, we
say, sees truth, and the content of its deliverances we believe.

Of course, if you take the satisfactoriness concretely, as
something felt by you now, and if, by truth, you mean truth
taken abstractly and verified in the long run, you cannot make
them equate, for it is notorious that the temporarily satisfactory is often false. Yet at each and every concrete moment,
truth for each man is what that man 'troweth' at that moment
with the maximum of satisfaction to himself; and similarly,
abstract truth, truth verified by the long run, and abstract
satisfactoriness, long-run satisfactoriness, coincide. If, in short,
we compare concrete with concrete and abstract with abstract, the true and the satisfactory do mean the same thing.
I suspect that a certain muddling of matters hereabouts is
what makes the general philosophic public so impervious to
humanism's claims.

The fundamental fact about our experience is that it is a
process of change. For the 'trower' at any moment, truth, like
the visible area round a man walking in a fog, or like what
George Eliot calls 'the wall of dark seen by small fishes' eyes
that pierce a span in the wide Ocean,' is an objective field
which the next moment enlarges and of which it is the critic,
and which then either suffers alteration or is continued unchanged. The critic sees both the first trower's truth and his
own truth, compares them with each other, and verifies or
confutes. *His* field of view is the reality independent of that
earlier trower's thinking with which that thinking ought to
correspond. But the critic is himself only a trower; and if the
whole process of experience should terminate at that instant,
there would be no otherwise known independent reality with
which *his* thought might be compared.

The immediate in experience is always provisionally in this

situation. The humanism, for instance, which I see and try so hard to defend, is the completest truth attained from my point of view up to date. But, owing to the fact that all experience is a process, no point of view can ever be *the* last one. Every one is insufficient and off its balance, and responsible to later points of view than itself. You, occupying some of these later points in your own person, and believing in the reality of others, will not agree that my point of view sees truth positive, truth timeless, truth that counts, unless they verify and confirm what it sees.

You generalize this by saying that any opinion, however satisfactory, can count positively and absolutely as true only so far as it agrees with a standard beyond itself; and if you then forget that this standard perpetually grows up endogenously inside the web of the experiences, you may carelessly go on to say that what distributively holds of each experience, holds also collectively of all experience, and that experience as such and in its totality owes whatever truth it may be possessed-of to its correspondence with absolute realities outside of its own being. This evidently is the popular and traditional position. From the fact that finite experiences must draw support from one another, philosophers pass to the notion that experience *überhaupt* must need an absolute support. The denial of such a notion by humanism lies probably at the root of most of the dislike which it incurs.

But is this not the globe, the elephant and the tortoise over again? Must not something end by supporting itself? Humanism is willing to let finite experience be self-supporting. Somewhere being must immediately breast nonentity. Why may not the advancing front of experience, carrying its immanent satisfactions and dissatisfactions, cut against the black inane as the luminous orb of the moon cuts the cærulean abyss? Why should anywhere the world be absolutely fixed and finished? And if reality genuinely grows, why may it not grow in these very determinations which here and now are made?

In point of fact it actually seems to grow by our mental determinations, be these never so 'true.' Take the 'great bear' or 'dipper' constellation in the heavens. We call it by that name, we count the stars and call them seven, we say they were seven before they were counted, and we say that whether any one had ever noted the fact or not, the dim resemblance to a long-tailed (or long-necked?) animal was always truly there. But what do we mean by this projection into past eternity of recent human ways of thinking? Did an 'absolute' thinker actually do the counting, tell off the stars upon his standing number-tally, and make the bear-comparison, silly as the latter is? Were they explicitly seven, explicitly bear-like, before the human witness came? Surely nothing in the truth of the attributions drives us to think this. They were only implicitly or virtually what we call them, and we human witnesses first explicated them and made them 'real.' A fact virtually pre-exists when every condition of its realization save one is already there. In this case the condition lacking is the act of the counting and comparing mind. But the stars (once the mind considers them) themselves dictate the result. The counting in no wise modifies their previous nature, and, they being what and where they are, the count cannot fall out differently. It could then *always* be made. *Never* could the number seven be questioned, *if the question once were raised.*

We have here a quasi-paradox. Undeniably something comes by the counting that was not there before. And yet that something was *always true*. In one sense you create it, and in another sense you *find* it. You have to treat your count as being true beforehand, the moment you come to treat the matter at all.

Our stellar attributes must always be called true, then; yet none the less are they genuine additions made by our intellect to the world of fact. Not additions of consciousness only, but additions of 'content.' They copy nothing that pre-existed, yet they agree with what pre-existed, fit it, amplify it, relate and connect it with a 'wain,' a number-tally, or what not, and build it out. It seems to me that humanism is the only theory that builds this case out in the good direction, and this case stands for innumerable other kinds of case. In all such cases, odd as it may sound, our judgment may actually be said to retroact and to enrich the past.

Our judgments at any rate change the character of *future* reality by the acts to which they lead. Where these acts are acts expressive of trust,—trust, *e. g.*, that a man is honest, that our health is good enough, or that we can make a successful effort,—which acts may be a needed antecedent of the trusted things becoming true, Professor Taylor says[1] that our trust is at any rate *untrue when it is made, i. e.*, before the action; and I seem to remember that he disposes of anything like a faith in the general excellence of the universe (making the faithful person's part in it at any rate more excellent) as a 'lie in the soul.' But the pathos of this expression should not blind us to the complication of the facts. I doubt whether Professor Taylor would himself be in favor of practically handling trusters of these kinds as liars. Future and present really mix in such emergencies, and one can always escape lies in them by using hypothetic forms. But Mr. Taylor's attitude suggests such absurd possibilities of practice that it seems to me to illustrate beautifully how self-stultifying the conception of a truth that shall merely register a standing fixture may become. Theoretic truth, truth of passive copying, sought in the sole interests of copying as such, not because copying is *good for something*, but because copying ought *schlechthin* to be, seems, if you look at it coldly, to be an almost preposterous ideal. Why should the universe, existing in itself, also exist in copies? How *can* it be copied in the solidity of its objective fulness? And even if it could, what would the motive be? 'Even the hairs of your head are numbered.' Doubtless they are, virtually; but why, as an absolute proposition, *ought* the number to become copied and known? Surely knowing is only one way of interacting with reality and adding to its effect.

The opponent here will ask: 'Has not the knowing of truth any substantive value on its own account, apart from the collateral advantages it may bring? And if you allow theoretic satisfactions to exist at all, do they not crowd the collateral satisfactions out of house and home, and must not pragmatism go into bankruptcy, if she admits them at all?' The destructive force of such talk disappears as soon as we use words concretely instead of abstractly, and ask, in our quality of

---

[1] In an article criticising Pragmatism (as he conceives it) in the *McGill University Quarterly* published at Montreal, for May, 1904.

good pragmatists, just what the famous theoretic needs are known as and in what the intellectual satisfactions consist.

Are they not all mere matters of *consistency*—and emphatically *not* of consistency between an absolute reality and the mind's copies of it, but of actually felt consistency among judgments, objects, and habits of reacting, in the mind's own experienceable world? And are not both our need of such consistency and our pleasure in it conceivable as outcomes of the natural fact that we are beings that do develop mental *habits*—habit itself proving adaptively beneficial in an environment where the same objects, or the same kinds of objects, recur and follow 'law'? If this were so, what would have come first would have been the collateral profits of habit as such, and the theoretic life would have grown up in aid of these. In point of fact, this seems to have been the probable case. At life's origin, any present perception may have been 'true'— if such a word could then be applicable. Later, when reactions became organized, the reactions became 'true' whenever expectation was fulfilled by them. Otherwise they were 'false' or 'mistaken' reactions. But the same class of objects needs the same kind of reaction, so the impulse to react consistently must gradually have been established, and a disappointment felt whenever the results frustrated expectation. Here is a perfectly plausible germ for all our higher consistencies. Nowadays, if an object claims from us a reaction of the kind habitually accorded only to the opposite class of objects, our mental machinery refuses to run smoothly. The situation is intellectually unsatisfactory.

Theoretic truth thus falls *within* the mind, being the accord of some of its processes and objects with other processes and objects—'accord' consisting here in well-definable relations. So long as the satisfaction of feeling such an accord is denied us, whatever collateral profits may seem to inure from what we believe in are but as dust in the balance—provided always that we are highly organized intellectually, which the majority of us are not. The amount of accord which satisfies most men and women is merely the absence of violent clash between their usual thoughts and statements and the limited sphere of sense-perceptions in which their lives are cast. The theoretic truth that most of us think we 'ought' to attain to is thus the possession of a set of predicates that do not explicitly contradict their subjects. We preserve it as often as not by leaving other predicates and subjects out.

In some men theory is a passion, just as music is in others. The form of inner consistency is pursued far beyond the line at which collateral profits stop. Such men systematize and classify and schematize and make synoptical tables and invent ideal objects for the pure love of unifying. Too often the results, glowing with 'truth' for the inventors, seem pathetically personal and artificial to bystanders. Which is as much as to say that the purely theoretic criterion of truth can leave us in the lurch as easily as any other criterion, and that the absolutists, for all their pretensions, are 'in the same boat' concretely with those whom they attack.

I am well aware that this paper has been rambling in the extreme. But the whole subject is inductive, and sharp logic is hardly yet in order. My great trammel has been the non-existence of any definitely stated alternative on my opponents' part. It may conduce to clearness if I recapitulate, in closing, what I conceive the main points of humanism to be. They are these: —

1. An experience, perceptual or conceptual, must conform to reality in order to be true.

2. By 'reality' humanism means nothing more than the other conceptual or perceptual experiences with which a given present experience may find itself in point of fact mixed up.[1]

3. By 'conforming,' humanism means taking account-of in such a way as to gain any intellectually and practically satisfactory result.

4. To 'take account-of' and to be 'satisfactory' are terms that admit of no definition, so many are the ways in which these requirements can practically be worked out.

5. Vaguely and in general, we take account of a reality by *preserving* it in as unmodified a form as possible. But, to be then satisfactory, it must not contradict other realities outside of it which claim also to be preserved. That we must preserve

[1] This is meant merely to exclude reality of an 'unknowable' sort, of which no account in either perceptual or conceptual terms can be given. It includes of course any amount of empirical reality independent of the knower. Pragmatism is thus 'epistemologically' realistic in its account.

all the experience we can and minimize contradiction in what we preserve, is about all that can be said in advance.

6. The truth which the conforming experience embodies may be a positive addition to the previous reality, and later judgments may have to conform to *it*. Yet, virtually at least, it may have been true previously. Pragmatically, virtual and actual truth mean the same thing: the possibility of only one answer, *when once the question is raised.*

IV

THE RELATION BETWEEN KNOWER AND KNOWN[1]

THROUGHOUT the history of philosophy the subject and its object have been treated as absolutely discontinuous entities; and thereupon the presence of the latter to the former, or the 'apprehension' by the former of the latter, has assumed a paradoxical character which all sorts of theories had to be invented to overcome. Representative theories put a mental 'representation,' 'image,' or 'content' into the gap, as a sort of intermediary. Common-sense theories left the gap untouched, declaring our mind able to clear it by a self-transcending leap. Transcendentalist theories left it impossible to traverse by finite knowers, and brought an absolute in to perform the saltatory act. All the while, in the very bosom of the finite experience, every conjunction required to make the relation intelligible is given in full. Either the knower and the known are:

(1) the self-same piece of experience taken twice over in different contexts; or they are

(2) two pieces of *actual* experience belonging to the same subject, with definite tracts of conjunctive transitional experience between them; or

(3) the known is a *possible* experience either of ᵗhat subject or another, to which the said conjunctive transitiᵤₛ *would* lead, if sufficiently prolonged.

To discuss all the ways in which one experience may function as the knower of another, would be incompatible with the limits of this essay. I have treated of type 1, the kind of knowledge called perception, in an article in the *Journal of Philosophy*, for September 1, 1904, called 'Does consciousness exist?' This is the type of case in which the mind enjoys direct 'acquaintance' with a present object. In the other types the mind has 'knowledge-about' an object not immediately there. Type 3 can always formally and hypothetically be reduced to type 2, so that a brief description of that type will now put

[1] Extract from an article entitled 'A World of Pure Experience,' in the *Journal of Philosophy, etc.*, September 29, 1904.

the present reader sufficiently at my point of view, and make
him see what the actual meanings of the mysterious cognitive
relation may be.

Suppose me to be sitting here in my library at Cambridge,
at ten minutes' walk from 'Memorial Hall,' and to be thinking
truly of the latter object. My mind may have before it only
the name, or it may have a clear image, or it may have a very
dim image of the hall, but such an intrinsic difference in the
image makes no difference in its cognitive function. Certain
extrinsic phenomena, special experiences of conjunction, are
what impart to the image, be it what it may, its knowing
office.

For instance, if you ask me what hall I mean by my image,
and I can tell you nothing; or if I fail to point or lead you
towards the Harvard Delta; or if, being led by you, I am
uncertain whether the Hall I see be what I had in mind or
not; you would rightly deny that I had 'meant' that particular
hall at all, even tho my mental image might to some degree
have resembled it. The resemblance would count in that case
as coincidental merely, for all sorts of things of a kind resemble one another in this world without being held for that
reason to take cognizance of one another.

On the other hand, if I can lead you to the hall, and tell
you of its history and present uses; if in its presence I feel my
idea, however imperfect it may have been, to have led hither
and to be now *terminated*; if the associates of the image and
of the felt hall run parallel, so that each term of the one context corresponds serially, as I walk, with an answering term
of the other; why then my soul was prophetic, and my idea
must be, and by common consent would be, called cognizant
of reality. That percept was what I *meant*, for into it my idea
has passed by conjunctive experiences of sameness and fulfilled intention. Nowhere is there jar, but every later moment
continues and corroborates an earlier one.

In this continuing and corroborating, taken in no transcendental sense, but denoting definitely felt transitions, *lies all
that the knowing of a percept by an idea can possibly contain or
signify*. Wherever such transitions are felt, the first experience
knows the last one. Where they do not, or where even as possibles they can not, intervene, there can be no pretence of

knowing. In this latter case the extremes will be connected, if connected at all, by inferior relations—bare likeness or succession, or by 'withness' alone. Knowledge of sensible realities thus comes to life inside the tissue of experience. It is *made*; and made by relations that unroll themselves in time. Whenever certain intermediaries are given, such that, as they develop towards their terminus, there is experience from point to point of one direction followed, and finally of one process fulfilled, the result is that *their starting-point thereby becomes a knower and their terminus an object meant or known.* That is all that knowing (in the simple case considered) can be known-as, that is the whole of its nature, put into experiential terms. Whenever such is the sequence of our experiences we may freely say that we had the terminal object 'in mind' from the outset, even altho *at* the outset nothing was there in us but a flat piece of substantive experience like any other, with no self-transcendency about it, and no mystery save the mystery of coming into existence and of being gradually followed by other pieces of substantive experience, with conjunctively transitional experiences between. That is what we *mean* here by the object's being 'in mind.' Of any deeper more real way of its being in mind we have no positive conception, and we have no right to discredit our actual experience by talking of such a way at all.

I know that many a reader will rebel at this. 'Mere intermediaries,' he will say, 'even tho they be feelings of continuously growing fulfilment, only *separate* the knower from the known, whereas what we have in knowledge is a kind of immediate touch of the one by the other, an "apprehension" in the etymological sense of the word, a leaping of the chasm as by lightning, an act by which two terms are smitten into one over the head of their distinctness. All these dead intermediaries of yours are out of each other, and outside of their termini still.'

But do not such dialectic difficulties remind us of the dog dropping his bone and snapping at its image in the water? If we knew any more real kind of union *aliunde*, we might be entitled to brand all our empirical unions as a sham. But unions by continuous transition are the only ones we know of, whether in this matter of a knowledge-about that terminates in an acquaintance, whether in personal identity, in logical predication through the copula 'is,' or elsewhere. If anywhere there were more absolute unions, they could only reveal themselves to us by just such conjunctive results. These are what the unions are *worth*, these are all that *we can ever practically mean* by union, by continuity. Is it not time to repeat what Lotze said of substances, that to *act like* one is to *be* one? Should we not say here that to be experienced as continuous is to be really continuous, in a world where experience and reality come to the same thing? In a picture gallery a painted hook will serve to hang a painted chain by, a painted cable will hold a painted ship. In a world where both the terms and their distinctions are affairs of experience, conjunctions that are experienced must be at least as real as anything else. They will be 'absolutely' real conjunctions, if we have no transphenomenal absolute ready, to derealize the whole experienced world by, at a stroke.

So much for the essentials of the cognitive relation where the knowledge is conceptual in type, or forms knowledge 'about' an object. It consists in intermediary experiences (possible, if not actual) of continuously developing progress, and, finally, of fulfilment, when the sensible percept which is the object is reached. The percept here not only *verifies* the concept, proves its function of knowing that percept to be true, but the percept's existence as the terminus of the chain of intermediaries *creates* the function. Whatever terminates that chain was, because it now proves itself to be, what the concept 'had in mind.'

The towering importance for human life of this kind of knowing lies in the fact that an experience that knows another can figure as its *representative*, not in any quasi-miraculous 'epistemological' sense, but in the definite practical sense of being its *substitute* in various operations, sometimes physical and sometimes mental, which lead us to its associates and results. By experimenting on our ideas of reality, we may save ourselves the trouble of experimenting on the real experiences which they severally mean. The ideas form related systems, corresponding point for point to the systems which the realities form; and by letting an ideal term call up its associates systematically, we may be led to a terminus which the corresponding real term would have led to in case we had operated on the real world. And this brings us to the general question of substitution.

What, exactly, in a system of experiences, does the 'substitution' of one of them for another mean?

According to my view, experience as a whole is a process in time, whereby innumerable particular terms lapse and are superseded by others that follow upon them by transitions which, whether disjunctive or conjunctive in content, are themselves experiences, and must in general be accounted at least as real as the terms which they relate. What the nature of the event called 'superseding' signifies, depends altogether on the kind of transition that obtains. Some experiences simply abolish their predecessors without continuing them in any way. Others are felt to increase or to enlarge their meaning, to carry out their purpose, or to bring us nearer to their goal. They 'represent' them, and may fulfil their function better than they fulfilled it themselves. But to 'fulfil a function' in a world of pure experience can be conceived and defined in only one possible way. In such a world transitions and arrivals (or terminations) are the only events that happen, tho they happen by so many sorts of path. The only function that one experience can perform is to lead into another experience; and the only fulfilment we can speak of is the reaching of a certain experienced end. When one experience leads to (or can lead to) the same end as another, they agree in function. But the whole system of experiences as they are immediately given presents itself as a quasi-chaos through which one can pass out of an initial term in many directions and yet end in the same terminus, moving from next to next by a great many possible paths.

Either one of these paths might be a functional substitute for another, and to follow one rather than another might on occasion be an advantageous thing to do. As a matter of fact, and in a general way, the paths that run through conceptual experiences, that is, through 'thoughts' or 'ideas' that 'know' the things in which they terminate, are highly advantageous paths to follow. Not only do they yield inconceivably rapid transitions; but, owing to the 'universal' character[1] which they frequently possess, and to their capacity for association with one another in great systems, they outstrip the tardy consecutions of the things themselves, and sweep us on towards our ultimate termini in a far more labor-saving way than the following of trains of sensible perception ever could. Wonderful are the new cuts and the short-circuits the thought-paths make. Most thought-paths, it is true, are substitutes for nothing actual; they end outside the real world altogether, in wayward fancies, utopias, fictions or mistakes. But where they do re-enter reality and terminate therein, we substitute them always; and with these substitutes we pass the greater number of our hours.[2]

Whosoever feels his experience to be something substitutional even while he has it, may be said to have an experience that reaches beyond itself. From inside of its own entity it says 'more,' and postulates reality existing elsewhere. For the transcendentalist, who holds knowing to consist in a *salto mortale* across an 'epistemological chasm,' such an idea presents no difficulty; but it seems at first sight as if it might be inconsistent with an empiricism like our own. Have we not explained that conceptual knowledge is made such wholly by

[1] Of which all that need be said in this essay is that it also can be conceived as functional, and defined in terms of transitions, or of the possibility of such.

[2] This is why I called our experiences, taken all together, a quasi-chaos. There is vastly more discontinuity in the sum total of experiences than we commonly suppose. The objective nucleus of every man's experience, his own body, is, it is true, a continuous percept; and equally continuous as a percept (though we may be inattentive to it) is the material environment of that body, changing by gradual transition when the body moves. But the distant parts of the physical world are at all times absent from us, and form conceptual objects merely, into the perceptual reality of which our life inserts itself at points discrete and relatively rare. Round their several objective nuclei, partly shared and common, partly discrete, of the real physical world, innumerable thinkers, pursuing their several lines of physically true cogitation, trace paths that intersect one another only at discontinuous perceptual points, and the rest of the time are quite incongruent; and around all the nuclei of shared 'reality' floats the vast cloud of experiences that are wholly subjective, that are non-substitutional, that find not even an eventual ending for themselves in the perceptual world—the mere day-dreams and joys and sufferings and wishes of the individual minds. These exist *with* one another, indeed, and with the objective nuclei, but out of them it is probable that to all eternity no inter-related system of any kind will ever be made.

the existence of things that fall outside of the knowing experience itself—by intermediary experiences and by a terminus that fulfils? Can the knowledge be there before these elements that constitute its being have come? And, if knowledge be not there, how can objective reference occur?

The key to this difficulty lies in the distinction between knowing as verified and completed, and the same knowing as in transit and on its way. To recur to the Memorial Hall example lately used, it is only when our idea of the Hall has actually terminated in the percept that we know 'for certain' that from the beginning it was truly cognitive of *that*. Until established by the end of the process, its quality of knowing that, or indeed of knowing anything, could still be doubted; and yet the knowing really was there, as the result now shows. We were *virtual* knowers of the Hall long before we were certified to have been its actual knowers, by the percept's retroactive validating power. Just so we are 'mortal' all the time, by reason of the virtuality of the inevitable event which will make us so when it shall have come.

Now the immensely greater part of all our knowing never gets beyond this virtual stage. It never is completed or nailed down. I speak not merely of our ideas of imperceptibles like ether-waves or dissociated 'ions,' or of 'ejects' like the contents of our neighbors' minds; I speak also of ideas which we might verify if we would take the trouble, but which we hold for true altho unterminated perceptually, because nothing says 'no' to us, and there is no contradicting truth in sight. *To continue thinking unchallenged is, ninety-nine times out of a hundred, our practical substitute for knowing in the completed sense.* As each experience runs by cognitive transition into the next one, and we nowhere feel a collision with what we elsewhere count as truth or fact, we commit ourselves to the current as if the port were sure. We live, as it were, upon the front edge of an advancing wave-crest, and our sense of a determinate direction in falling forward is all we cover of the future of our path. It is as if a differential quotient should be conscious and treat itself as an adequate substitute for a traced-out curve. Our experience, *inter alia*, is of variations of rate and of direction, and lives in these transitions more than in the journey's end. The experiences of tendency are sufficient to act upon—what more could we have *done* at those moments even if the later verification comes complete?

This is what, as a radical empiricist, I say to the charge that the objective reference which is so flagrant a character of our experiences involves a chasm and a mortal leap. A positively conjunctive transition involves neither chasm nor leap. Being the very original of what we mean by continuity, it makes a continuum wherever it appears. Objective reference is an incident of the fact that so much of our experience comes as an insufficient and consists of process and transition. Our fields of experience have no more definite boundaries than have our fields of view. Both are fringed forever by a *more* that continuously develops, and that continuously supersedes them as life proceeds. The relations, generally speaking, are as real here as the terms are, and the only complaint of the transcendentalist's with which I could at all sympathize would be his charge that, by first making knowledge to consist in external relations as I have done, and by then confessing that nine-tenths of the time these are not actually but only virtually there, I have knocked the solid bottom out of the whole business, and palmed off a substitute of knowledge for the genuine thing. Only the admission, such a critic might say, that our ideas are self-transcendent and 'true' already, in advance of the experiences that are to terminate them, can bring solidity back to knowledge in a world like this, in which transitions and terminations are only by exception fulfilled.

This seems to me an excellent place for applying the pragmatic method. What would the self-transcendency affirmed to exist in advance of all experiential mediation or termination, be *known-as*? What would it practically result in for *us*, were it true?

It could only result in our orientation, in the turning of our expectations and practical tendencies into the right path; and the right path here, so long as we and the object are not yet face to face (or can never get face to face, as in the case of ejects), would be the path that led us into the object's nearest neighborhood. Where direct acquaintance is lacking, 'knowledge about' is the next best thing, and an acquaintance with what actually lies about the object, and is most closely related to it, puts such knowledge within our grasp. Ether-waves and your anger, for example, are things in which my thoughts will never *perceptually* terminate, but my concepts of them lead me to their very brink, to the chromatic fringes and to the hurtful words and deeds which are their really next effects.

Even if our ideas did in themselves possess the postulated self-transcendency, it would still remain true that their putting us into possession of such effects *would be the sole cash-value of the self-transcendency for us*. And this cash-value, it is needless to say, is *verbatim et literatim* what our empiricist account pays in. On pragmatist principles therefore, a dispute over self-transcendency is a pure logomachy. Call our concepts of ejective things self-transcendent or the reverse, it makes no difference, so long as we don't differ about the nature of that exalted virtue's fruits—fruits for us, of course, humanistic fruits.

The transcendentalist believes his ideas to be self-transcendent only because he finds that in fact they do bear fruits. Why need he quarrel with an account of knowledge that insists on naming this effect? Why not treat the working of the idea from next to next as the essence of its self-transcendency? Why insist that knowing is a static relation out of time when it practically seems so much a function of our active life? For a thing to be valid, says Lotze, is the same as to make itself valid. When the whole universe seems only to be making itself valid and to be still incomplete (else why its ceaseless changing?) why, of all things, should knowing be exempt? Why should it not be making itself valid like everything else? That some parts of it may be already valid or verified beyond dispute, the empirical philosopher, of course, like any one else, may always hope.

V

THE ESSENCE OF HUMANISM[1]

HUMANISM IS a ferment that has 'come to stay.' It is not a single hypothesis or theorem, and it dwells on no new facts. It is rather a slow shifting in the philosophic perspective, making things appear as from a new centre of interest or point of sight. Some writers are strongly conscious of the shifting, others half unconscious, even though their own vision may have undergone much change. The result is no small confusion in debate, the half-conscious humanists often taking part against the radical ones, as if they wished to count upon the other side.[2]

If humanism really be the name for such a shifting of perspective, it is obvious that the whole scene of the philosophic stage will change in some degree if humanism prevails. The emphasis of things, their foreground and background distribution, their sizes and values, will not keep just the same.[3] If such pervasive consequences be involved in humanism, it is clear that no pains which philosophers may take, first in defining it, and then in furthering, checking, or steering its progress, will be thrown away.

It suffers badly at present from incomplete definition. Its most systematic advocates, Schiller and Dewey, have pub-

---

[1] Reprinted from the *Journal of Philosophy, Psychology and Scientific Methods*, vol. ii, No. 5, March 2, 1905.

[2] Professor Baldwin, for example. His address 'Selective Thinking' (*Psychological Review*, January, 1898, reprinted in his volume, 'Development and Evolution') seems to me an unusually well written pragmatic manifesto. Nevertheless in 'The Limits of Pragmatism' (*ibid.*, January, 1904), he (much less clearly) joins in the attack.

[3] The ethical changes, it seems to me, are beautifully made evident in Professor Dewey's series of articles, which will never get the attention they deserve till they are printed in a book. I mean: 'The Significance of Emotions,' *Psychological Review*, vol. ii, 13; 'The Reflex Arc Concept in Psychology,' *ibid.*, iii, 357; 'Psychology and Social Practice,' *ibid.*, vii, 105; 'Interpretation of Savage Mind,' *ibid.*, ix, 217; 'Green's Theory of the Moral Motive,' *Philosophical Review*, vol. i, 593; 'Self-realization as the Moral Ideal,' *ibid.*, ii, 652; 'The Psychology of Effort,' *ibid.*, vi, 43; 'The Evolutionary Method as Applied to Morality,' *ibid.*, xi, 107, 353; 'Evolution and Ethics,' *Monist*, vol. viii, 321; to mention only a few.

lished fragmentary programmes only; and its bearing on many vital philosophic problems has not been traced except by adversaries who, scenting heresies in advance, have showered blows on doctrines—subjectivism and scepticism, for example—that no good humanist finds it necessary to entertain. By their still greater reticences, the anti-humanists have, in turn, perplexed the humanists. Much of the controversy has involved the word 'truth.' It is always good in debate to know your adversary's point of view authentically. But the critics of humanism never define exactly what the word 'truth' signifies when they use it themselves. The humanists have to guess at their view; and the result has doubtless been much beating of the air. Add to all this, great individual differences in both camps, and it becomes clear that nothing is so urgently needed, at the stage which things have reached at present, as a sharper definition by each side of its central point of view.

Whoever will contribute any touch of sharpness will help us to make sure of what's what and who is who. Any one can contribute such a definition, and, without it, no one knows exactly where he stands. If I offer my own provisional definition of humanism now and here, others may improve it, some adversary may be led to define his own creed more sharply by the contrast, and a certain quickening of the crystallization of general opinion may result.

I

The essential service of humanism, as I conceive the situation, is to have seen that *tho one part of our experience may lean upon another part to make it what it is in any one of several aspects in which it may be considered, experience as a whole is self-containing and leans on nothing.* Since this formula also expresses the main contention of transcendental idealism, it needs abundant explication to make it unambiguous. It seems, at first sight, to confine itself to denying theism and pantheism. But, in fact, it need not deny either; everything would depend on the exegesis; and if the formula ever became canonical, it would certainly develop both right-wing and left-wing interpreters. I myself read humanism theistically and pluralistically. If there be a God, he is no absolute all-experiencer, but simply the experiencer of widest actual conscious span. Read thus, humanism is for me a religion susceptible of reasoned defence, tho I am well aware how many minds there are to whom it can appeal religiously only when it has been monistically translated. Ethically the pluralistic form of it takes for me a stronger hold on reality than any other philosophy I know of—it being essentially a *social* philosophy, a philosophy of '*co*,' in which conjunctions do the work. But my primary reason for advocating it is its matchless intellectual economy. It gets rid, not only of the standing 'problems' that monism engenders ('problem of evil,' 'problem of freedom,' and the like), but of other metaphysical mysteries and paradoxes as well.

It gets rid, for example, of the whole agnostic controversy, by refusing to entertain the hypothesis of trans-empirical reality at all. It gets rid of any need for an absolute of the bradleyan type (avowedly sterile for intellectual purposes) by insisting that the conjunctive relations found within experience are faultlessly real. It gets rid of the need of an absolute of the roycean type (similarly sterile) by its pragmatic treatment of the problem of knowledge. As the views of knowledge, reality and truth imputed to humanism have been those so far most fiercely attacked, it is in regard to these ideas that a sharpening of focus seems most urgently required. I proceed therefore to bring the views which *I* impute to humanism in these respects into focus as briefly as I can.

II

If the central humanistic thesis, printed above in italics, be accepted, it will follow that, if there be any such thing at all as knowing, the knower and the object known must both be portions of experience. One part of experience must, therefore, either

(1) Know another part of experience—in other words, parts must, as Professor Woodbridge says,[1] represent *one another* instead of representing realities outside of 'consciousness'—this case is that of conceptual knowledge; or else

---

[1] In *Science*, November 4, 1904, p. 599.

(2) They must simply exist as so many ultimate *thats* or facts of being, in the first instance; and then, as a secondary complication, and without doubling up its entitative single-ness, any one and the same *that* in experience must figure alternately as a thing known and as a knowledge of the thing, by reason of two divergent kinds of context into which, in the general course of experience, it gets woven.[1]

This second case is that of sense-perception. There is a stage of thought that goes beyond common sense, and of it I shall say more presently; but the common-sense stage is a per-fectly definite halting-place of thought, primarily for purposes of action; and, so long as we remain on the common-sense stage of thought, object and subject *fuse* in the fact of 'presen-tation' or sense-perception—the pen and hand which I now *see* writing, for example, *are* the physical realities which those words designate. In this case there is no self-transcendency implied in the knowing. Humanism, here, is only a more comminuted *identitätsphilosophie*.

In case (1), on the contrary, the representative experience *does transcend itself* in knowing the other experience that is its object. No one can talk of the knowledge of the one by the other without seeing them as numerically distinct entities, of which the one lies beyond the other and away from it, along some direction and with some interval, that can be definitely named. But, if the talker be a humanist, he must also see this distance-interval concretely and pragmatically, and confess it to consist of other intervening experiences—of possible ones, at all events, if not of actual. To call my present idea of my dog, for example, cognitive of the real dog means that, as the actual tissue of experience is constituted, the idea is capable of leading into a chain of other experiences on my part that go from next to next and terminate at last in vivid sense-per-ceptions of a jumping, barking, hairy body. Those *are* the real dog, the dog's full presence, for my common sense. If the supposed talker is a profound philosopher, altho they may not *be* the real dog for him, they *mean* the real dog, are prac-tical substitutes for the real dog, as the representation was a

[1] This statement is probably excessively obscure to any one who has not read my two articles 'Does Consciousness Exist?' and 'A World of Pure Ex-perience' in the *Journal of Philosophy*, vol. i, 1904.

practical substitute for them, that real dog being a lot of atoms, say, or of mind-stuff, that lie *where* the sense-perceptions lie in his experience as well as in my own.

The philosopher here stands for the stage of thought that goes beyond the stage of common sense; and the difference is simply that he 'interpolates' and 'extrapolates,' where common sense does not. For common sense, two men see the same identical real dog. Philosophy, noting actual differences in their perceptions, points out the duality of these latter, and interpolates something between them as a more real terminus—first, organs, viscera, etc.; next, cells; then, ultimate atoms; lastly, mind-stuff perhaps. The original sense-termini of the two men, instead of coalescing with each other and with the real dog-object, as at first supposed, are thus held by philosophers to be separated by invisible realities with which, at most, they are conterminous.

Abolish, now, one of the percipients, and the interpolation changes into 'extrapolation.' The sense-terminus of the remaining percipient is regarded by the philosopher as not quite reaching reality. He has only carried the procession of experiences, the philosopher thinks, to a definite, because practical, halting-place somewhere on the way towards an absolute truth that lies beyond.

The humanist sees all the time, however, that there is no absolute transcendency even about the more absolute realities thus conjectured or believed in. The viscera and cells are only possible percepts following upon that of the outer body. The atoms again, tho we may never attain to human means of perceiving them, are still defined perceptually. The mind-stuff itself is conceived as a kind of experience; and it is possible to frame the hypothesis (such hypotheses can by no logic be excluded from philosophy) of two knowers of a piece of mind-stuff and the mind-stuff itself becoming 'confluent' at the moment at which our imperfect knowing might pass into knowing of a completed type. Even so do you and I habitually conceive our two perceptions and the real dog as confluent, tho only provisionally, and for the common-sense stage of thought. If my pen be inwardly made of mind-stuff, there is no confluence *now* between that mind-stuff and my visual perception of the pen. But conceivably there might come to be such confluence; for, in the case of my *hand*, the visual sensations and the inward feelings of the hand, its mind-stuff, so to speak, are even now as confluent as any two things can be.

There is, thus, no breach in humanistic epistemology. Whether knowledge be taken as ideally perfected, or only as true enough to pass muster for practice, it is hung on one continuous scheme. Reality, howsoever remote, is always defined as a terminus within the general possibilities of experience; and what knows it is defined as an experience *that 'represents' it, in the sense of being substitutable for it in our thinking because it leads to the same associates, or in the sense of 'pointing to it' through a chain of other experiences that either intervene or may intervene.*

Absolute reality here bears the same relation to sensation as sensation bears to conception or imagination. Both are provisional or final termini, sensation being only the terminus at which the practical man habitually stops, while the philosopher projects a 'beyond,' in the shape of more absolute reality. These termini, for the practical and the philosophical stages of thought respectively, are self-supporting. They are not 'true' of anything else, they simply *are*, are *real*. They 'lean on nothing,' as my italicized formula said. Rather does the whole fabric of experience lean on them, just as the whole fabric of the solar system, including many relative positions, leans, for its absolute position in space, on any one of its constituent stars. Here, again, one gets a new *Identitätsphilosophie* in pluralistic form.

IV

If I have succeeded in making this at all clear (tho I fear that brevity and abstractness between them may have made me fail), the reader will see that the 'truth' of our mental operations must always be an intra-experiential affair. A conception is reckoned true by common sense when it can be made to lead to a sensation. The sensation, which for common sense is not so much 'true' as 'real,' is held to be *provisionally* true by the philosopher just in so far as it *covers* (abuts at, or occupies the place of) a still more absolutely real experience, in the possibility of which, to some remoter experient, the philosopher finds reason to believe.

Meanwhile what actually *does* count for true to any individual trower, whether he be philosopher or common man, is always a result of his *apperceptions*. If a novel experience, conceptual or sensible, contradict too emphatically our pre-existent system of beliefs, in ninety-nine cases out of a hundred it is treated as false. Only when the older and the newer experiences are congruous enough to mutually apperceive and modify each other, does what we treat as an advance in truth result. In no case, however, need truth consist in a relation between our experiences and something archetypal or trans-experiential. Should we ever reach absolutely terminal experiences, experiences in which we all agreed, which were superseded by no revised continuations, these would not be *true*, they would be *real*, they would simply *be*, and be indeed the angles, corners, and linchpins of all reality, on which the truth of everything else would be stayed. Only such *other* things as led to these by satisfactory conjunctions would be 'true.' Satisfactory connection of some sort with such termini is all that the word 'truth' means. On the common-sense stage of thought sense-presentations serve as such termini. Our ideas and concepts and scientific theories pass for true only so far as they harmoniously lead back to the world of sense.

I hope that many humanists will endorse this attempt of mine to trace the more essential features of that way of viewing things. I feel almost certain that Messrs. Dewey and Schiller will do so. If the attackers will also take some slight account of it, it may be that discussion will be a little less wide of the mark than it has hitherto been.

VI

MY FAILURE in making converts to my conception of truth seems, if I may judge by what I hear in conversation, almost complete. An ordinary philosopher would feel disheartened, and a common choleric sinner would curse God and die, after such a reception. But instead of taking counsel of despair, I make bold to vary my statements, in the faint hope that repeated droppings may wear upon the stone, and that my formulas may seem less obscure if surrounded by something more of a 'mass' whereby to apperceive them.

For fear of compromising other pragmatists, whoe'er they be, I will speak of the conception which I am trying to make intelligible, as my own conception. I first published it in the year 1885, in the first article reprinted in the present book. Essential theses of this article were independently supported in 1893 and 1895 by Professor D. S. Miller[2] and were repeated by me in a presidential address on 'The knowing of things together'[3] in 1895. Professor Strong, in an article in the *Journal of Philosophy, etc.*,[4] entitled 'A naturalistic theory of the reference of thought to reality,' called our account 'the James-Miller theory of cognition,' and, as I understood him, gave it his adhesion. Yet, such is the difficulty of writing clearly in these penetralia of philosophy, that each of these revered colleagues informs me privately that the account of truth I now give—which to me is but that earlier statement more completely set forth—is to him inadequate, and seems to leave the gist of real cognition out. If such near friends disagree, what can I hope from remoter ones, and what from unfriendly critics?

Yet I feel so sure that the fault must lie in my lame forms of statement and not in my doctrine, that I am fain to try once more to express myself.

[1] Reprint from the *Journal of Philosophy*, July 18, 1907.
[2] *Philosophical Review*, vol. ii, p. 408, and *Psychological Review*, vol. ii, p. 533.
[3] The relevant parts of which are printed above, p. 853.
[4] Vol. i, p. 253.

I

Are there not some general distinctions which it may help us to agree about in advance? Professor Strong distinguishes between what he calls 'saltatory' and what he calls 'ambulatory' relations. 'Difference,' for example, is saltatory, jumping as it were immediately from one term to another, but 'distance' in time or space is made out of intervening parts of experience through which we ambulate in succession. Years ago, when T. H. Green's ideas were most influential, I was much troubled by his criticisms of english sensationalism. One of his disciples in particular would always say to me, 'Yes! *terms* may indeed be possibly sensational in origin; but *relations*, what are they but pure acts of the intellect coming upon the sensations from above, and of a higher nature?' I well remember the sudden relief it gave me to perceive one day that *space*-relations at any rate were homogeneous with the terms between which they mediated. The terms were spaces, and the relations were other intervening spaces.[1] For the Greenites space-relations had been saltatory, for me they became thenceforward ambulatory.

Now the most general way of contrasting my view of knowledge with the popular view (which is also the view of most epistemologists) is to call my view ambulatory, and the other view saltatory; and the most general way of characterizing the two views is by saying that my view describes knowing as it exists concretely, while the other view only describes its results abstractly taken.

I fear that most of my recalcitrant readers fail to recognize that what is ambulatory in the concrete may be taken so abstractly as to appear saltatory. Distance, for example, is made abstract by emptying out whatever is particular in the concrete intervals—it is reduced thus to a sole 'difference,' a difference of 'place,' which is a logical or saltatory distinction, a so-called 'pure relation.'

The same is true of the relation called 'knowing,' which may connect an idea with a reality. My own account of this relation is ambulatory through and through. I say that we know an object by means of an idea, whenever we ambulate

---

[1] See my *Principles of Psychology*, vol. ii, pp. 148–153.

towards the object under the impulse which the idea communicates. If we believe in so-called 'sensible' realities, the idea may not only send us towards its object, but may put the latter into our very hand, make it our immediate sensation. But, if, as most reflective people opine, sensible realities are not 'real' realities, but only their appearances, our idea brings us at least so far, puts us in touch with reality's most authentic appearances and substitutes. In any case our idea brings us into the object's neighborhood, practical or ideal, gets us into commerce with it, helps us towards its closer acquaintance, enables us to foresee it, class it, compare it, deduce it,—in short, to deal with it as we could not were the idea not in our possession.

The idea is thus, when functionally considered, an instrument for enabling us the better to *have to do* with the object and to act about it. But it and the object are both of them bits of the general sheet and tissue of reality at large; and when we say that the idea leads us towards the object, that only means that it carries us forward through intervening tracts of that reality into the object's closer neighborhood, into the midst of its associates at least, be these its physical neighbors, or be they its logical congeners only. Thus carried into closer quarters, we are in an improved situation as regards acquaintance and conduct; and we say that through the idea we now *know* the object better or more truly.

My thesis is that the knowing here is *made* by the ambulation through the intervening experiences. If the idea led us nowhere, or *from* that object instead of towards it, could we talk at all of its having any cognitive quality? Surely not, for it is only when taken in conjunction with the intermediate experiences that it gets related to *that particular object* rather than to any other part of nature. Those intermediaries determine what particular knowing function it exerts. The terminus they guide us to tells us what object it 'means,' the results they enrich us with 'verify' or 'refute' it. Intervening experiences are thus as indispensable foundations for a concrete relation of cognition as intervening space is for a relation of distance. Cognition, whenever we take it concretely, means determinate 'ambulation,' through intermediaries, from a *terminus a quo* to, or towards, a *terminus ad quem*.

As the intermediaries are other than the termini, and connected with them by the usual associative bonds (be these 'external' or be they logical, *i. e.*, classificatory, in character), there would appear to be nothing especially unique about the processes of knowing. They fall wholly within experience; and we need use, in describing them, no other categories than those which we employ in describing other natural processes.

But there exist no processes which we cannot also consider abstractly, eviscerating them down to their essential skeletons or outlines; and when we have treated the processes of knowing thus, we are easily led to regard them as something altogether unparalleled in nature. For we first empty idea, object and intermediaries of all their particularities, in order to retain only a general scheme, and then we consider the latter only in its function of giving a result, and not in its character of being a process. In this treatment the intermediaries shrivel into the form of a mere space of separation, while the idea and object retain only the logical distinctness of being the end-terms that are separated. In other words, the intermediaries which in their concrete particularity form a bridge, evaporate ideally into an empty interval to cross, and then, the relation of the end-terms having become saltatory, the whole hocus-pocus of *erkenntnisstheorie* begins, and goes on unrestrained by further concrete considerations. The idea, in 'meaning' an object separated by an 'epistemological chasm' from itself, now executes what Professor Ladd calls a *'salto mortale'*; in knowing the object's nature, it now 'transcends' its own. The object in turn becomes 'present' where it is really absent, etc.; until a scheme remains upon our hands, the sublime paradoxes of which some of us think that nothing short of an 'absolute' can explain.

The relation between idea and object, thus made abstract and saltatory, is thenceforward opposed, as being more essential and previous, to its own ambulatory self, and the more concrete description is branded as either false or insufficient. The bridge of intermediaries, actual or possible, which in every real case is what carries and defines the knowing, gets treated as an episodic complication which need not even potentially be there. I believe that this vulgar fallacy of opposing abstractions to the concretes from which they are abstracted, is the main reason why my account of knowing is deemed so unsatisfactory, and I will therefore say a word more on that general point.

Any vehicle of conjunction, if *all* its particularities are abstracted from it, will leave us with nothing on our hands but the original disjunction which it bridged over. But to escape treating the resultant self-contradiction as an achievement of dialectical profundity, all we need is to restore some part, no matter how small, of what we have taken away. In the case of the epistemological chasm the first reasonable step is to remember that the chasm was filled with *some* empirical material, whether ideational or sensational, which performed *some* bridging function and saved us from the mortal leap. Restoring thus the indispensable modicum of reality to the matter of our discussion, we find our abstract treatment genuinely useful. We escape entanglement with special cases without at the same time falling into gratuitous paradoxes. We can now describe the general features of cognition, tell what on the whole it *does for us*, in a universal way.

We must remember that this whole inquiry into knowing grows up on a reflective level. In any real moment of knowing, what we are thinking of is our object, not the way in which we ourselves are momentarily knowing it. We at this moment, as it happens, have knowing itself for our object; but I think that the reader will agree that his present knowing of that object is included only abstractly, and by anticipation, in the results he may reach. What he concretely has before his mind, as he reasons, is some supposed objective instance of knowing, as he conceives it to go on in some other person, or recalls it from his own past. As such, he, the critic, sees it to contain both an idea and an object, and processes by which the knower is guided from the one towards the other. He sees that the idea is remote from the object, and that, whether through intermediaries or not, it genuinely *has to do* with it. He sees that it thus works beyond its immediate being, and lays hold of a remote reality; it jumps across, transcends itself. It does all this by extraneous aid, to be sure, but when the aid has come, it *has* done it and the result is secure. Why not talk of results by themselves, then, without considering means? Why not treat the idea as simply grasping or intuiting the reality, of its having the faculty anyhow, of shooting over nature behind the scenes and knowing things immediately and directly? Why need we always lug in the bridging?—it only retards our discourse to do so.

Such abstract talk about cognition's results is surely convenient; and it is surely as legitimate as it is convenient, *so long as we do not forget or positively deny, what it ignores*. We may on occasion say that our idea meant *always* that particular object, that it led us there because it was *of* it intrinsically and essentially. We may insist that its verification follows upon that original cognitive virtue in it—and all the rest—and we shall do no harm so long as we know that these are only short cuts in our thinking. They are positively true accounts of fact *as far as they go*, only they leave vast tracts of fact out of the account, tracts of fact that have to be reinstated to make the accounts literally true of any real case. But if, not merely passively ignoring the intermediaries, you actively deny them[1] to be even potential requisites for the results you are so struck by, your epistemology goes to irremediable smash. You are as far off the track as an historian would be, if, lost in admiration of Napoleon's personal power, he were to ignore his marshals and his armies, and were to accuse you of error in describing his conquests as effected by their means. Of such abstractness and one-sidedness I accuse most of the critics of my own account.

In the second lecture of the book *Pragmatism*, I used the illustration of a squirrel scrambling round a tree-trunk to keep out of sight of a pursuing man: both go round the tree, but does the man go round the squirrel? It all depends, I said, on what you mean by 'going round.' In one sense of the word the man 'goes round,' in another sense he does not. I settled the dispute by pragmatically distinguishing the senses. But I told how some disputants had called my distinction a shuffling evasion and taken their stand on what they called 'plain honest English going-round.'

In such a simple case few people would object to letting the term in dispute be translated into its concreter equiva-

[1] This is the fallacy which I have called 'vicious intellectualism' in my book *A Pluralistic Universe*, Longmans, Green & Co., 1909.

lents. But in the case of a complex function like our knowing they act differently. I give full concrete particular value for the ideas of knowing in every case I can think of, yet my critics insist that 'plain honest English knowing' is left out of my account. They write as if the minus were on my side and the plus on theirs.

The essence of the matter for me is that altho knowing can be both abstractly and concretely described, and altho the abstract descriptions are often useful enough, yet they are all sucked up and absorbed without residuum into the concreter ones, and contain nothing of any essentially other or higher nature, which the concrete descriptions can be justly accused of leaving behind. Knowing is just a natural process like any other. There is no ambulatory process whatsoever, the results of which we may not describe, if we prefer to, in saltatory terms, or represent in static formulation. Suppose, *e. g.*, that we say a man is 'prudent.' Concretely, that means that he takes out insurance, hedges in betting, looks before he leaps. Do such acts *constitute* the prudence? *are* they the man quâ prudent? Or is the prudence something by itself and independent of them? As a constant habit in him, a permanent tone of character, it is convenient to call him prudent in abstraction from any one of his acts, prudent in general and without specification, and to say the acts follow from the pre-existing prudence. There are peculiarities in his psycho-physical system that make him act prudently; and there are tendencies to association in our thoughts that prompt some of them to make for truth and others for error. But would the man be prudent in the absence of each and all of the acts? Or would the thoughts be true if they had no associative or impulsive tendencies? Surely we have no right to oppose static essences in this way to the moving processes in which they live embedded.

My bedroom is above my library. Does the 'aboveness' here mean aught that is different from the concrete spaces which have to be moved-through in getting from the one to the other? It means, you may say, a pure topographic relation, a sort of architect's plan among the eternal essences. But that is not the full aboveness, it is only an abbreviated substitute that on occasion may lead my mind towards truer, *i. e.*, fuller, dealings with the real aboveness. It is not an aboveness *ante rem*, it is a *post rem* extract from the aboveness *in rebus*. We may indeed talk, for certain conveniences, as if the abstract scheme preceded, we may say 'I must go up stairs because of the essential aboveness,' just as we may say that the man 'does prudent acts because of his ingrained prudence,' or that our ideas 'lead us truly because of their intrinsic truth.' But this should not debar us on other occasions from using completer forms of description. A concrete matter of fact always remains identical under any form of description, as when we say of a line, now that it runs from left to right, and now that it runs from right to left. These are but names of one and the same fact, one more expedient to use at one time, one at another. The *full* facts of cognition, whatever be the way in which we talk about them, even when we talk most abstractly, stand inalterably given in the actualities and possibilities of the experience-continuum.[1] But my critics treat my own more concrete talk as if *it* were the kind that sinned by its inadequacy, and as if the full continuum left something out.

A favorite way of opposing the more abstract to the more concrete account is to accuse those who favor the latter of 'confounding psychology with logic.' Our critics say that when we are asked what truth *means*, we reply by telling only how it is *arrived-at*. But since a meaning is a logical relation, static, independent of time, how can it possibly be identified, they say, with any concrete man's experience, perishing as this does at the instant of its production? This, indeed, sounds profound, but I challenge the profundity. I defy any one to show any difference between logic and psychology here. The logical relation stands to the psychological relation between idea and object only as saltatory abstractness stands to ambulatory concreteness. Both relations need a psychological vehicle; and the 'logical' one is simply the 'psychological' one disemboweled of its fulness, and reduced to a bare abstractional scheme.

---

[1] The ultimate object or terminus of a cognitive process may in certain instances lie beyond the direct experience of the particular cognizer, but it, of course, must exist as part of the total universe of experience whose constitution, with cognition in it, the critic is discussing.

A while ago a prisoner, on being released, tried to assassi-
nate the judge who had sentenced him. He had apparently
succeeded in conceiving the judge timelessly, had reduced
him to a bare logical meaning, that of being his 'enemy and
persecutor,' by stripping off all the concrete conditions (as
jury's verdict, official obligation, absence of personal spite,
possibly sympathy) that gave its full psychological character
to the sentence as a particular man's act in time. Truly the
sentence *was* inimical to the culprit; but which idea of it is
the truer one, that bare logical definition of it, or its full psychological specification? The anti-pragmatists ought in consistency to stand up for the criminal's view of the case, treat the
judge as the latter's logical enemy, and bar out the other conditions as so much inessential psychological stuff.

II

A still further obstacle, I suspect, stands in the way of my
account's acceptance. Like Dewey and like Schiller, I have
had to say that the truth of an idea is determined by its satisfactoriness. But satisfactoriness is a subjective term, just as
idea is; and truth is generally regarded as 'objective.' Readers
who admit that satisfactoriness is our only *mark* of truth, the
only sign that we possess the precious article, will still say that
the objective relation between idea and object which the word
'truth' points to is left out of my account altogether. I fear
also that the association of my poor name with the 'will to
believe' (which 'will,' it seems to me, ought to play no part
in this discussion) works against my credit in some quarters.
I fornicate with that unclean thing, my adversaries may think,
whereas your genuine truth-lover must discourse in huxleyan
heroics, and feel as if truth, to be real truth, ought to bring
eventual messages of death to all our satisfactions. Such divergences certainly prove the complexity of the area of our
discussion; but to my mind they also are based on misunderstandings, which (tho with but little hope of success) I will
try to diminish by a further word of explanation.

First, then, I will ask my objectors to define exactly what
sort of thing it is they have in mind when they speak of a
truth that shall be absolute, complete and objective; and then
I will defy them to show me any conceivable standing-room

for such a kind of truth outside the terms of my own description. It will fall, as I contend, entirely within the field of my analysis.

To begin with, it must obtain between an idea and a reality that is the idea's object; and, as a predicate, it must apply to the idea and not to the object, for objective realities are not *true*, at least not in the universe of discourse to which we are now confining ourselves, for there they are taken as simply *being*, while the ideas are true *of* them. But we can suppose a series of ideas to be successively more and more true of the same object, and can ask what is the extreme approach to being absolutely true that the last idea might attain to.

The maximal conceivable truth in an idea would seem to be that it should lead to an actual merging of ourselves with the object, to an utter mutual confluence and identification. On the common-sense level of belief this is what is supposed really to take place in sense-perception. My idea of this pen verifies itself through my percept; and my percept is held to *be* the pen for the time being—percepts and physical realities being treated by common sense as identical. But the physiology of the senses has criticised common sense out of court, and the pen 'in itself' is now believed to lie beyond my momentary percept. Yet the notion once suggested, of what a completely consummated acquaintance with a reality might be like, remains over for our speculative purposes. *Total conflux of the mind with the reality* would be the absolute limit of truth, there could be no better or more satisfying knowledge than that.

Such total conflux, it is needless to say, is *already explicitly provided for, as a possibility, in my account of the matter.* If an idea should ever lead us not only *towards*, or *up to*, or *against*, a reality, but so close that we and the reality should *melt together*, it would be made absolutely true, according to me, by that performance.

In point of fact philosophers doubt that this ever occurs. What happens, they think, is only that we get nearer and nearer to realities, we approximate more and more to the all-satisfying limit; and the definition of actually, as distinguished from imaginably, complete and objective truth, can then only be that it belongs to the idea that will lead us as *close up against the object* as in the nature of our experience is possible, literally *next* to it, for instance.

Suppose, now, there were an idea that did this for a certain objective reality. Suppose that no further approach were possible, that nothing lay between, that the next step would carry us right *into* the reality; then that result, being the next thing to conflux, would make the idea true in the maximal degree that might be supposed practically attainable in the world which we inhabit.

Well, I need hardly explain that *that degree of truth is also provided for in my account of the matter*. And if satisfactions are the marks of truth's presence, we may add that any less true substitute for such a true idea would prove less satisfactory. Following its lead, we should probably find out that we did not quite touch the terminus. We should desiderate a closer approach, and not rest till we had found it.

I am, of course, postulating here a standing reality independent of the idea that knows it. I am also postulating that satisfactions grow *pari passu* with our approximation to such reality.[1] If my critics challenge this latter assumption, I retort upon them with the former. Our whole notion of a standing reality grows up in the form of an ideal limit to the series of successive termini to which our thoughts have led us and still are leading us. Each terminus proves provisional by leaving us unsatisfied. The truer idea is the one that pushes farther; so we are ever beckoned on by the ideal notion of an ultimate completely satisfactory terminus. I, for one, obey and accept that notion. I can conceive no other objective *content* to the notion of ideally perfect truth than that of penetration into such a terminus, nor can I conceive that the notion would ever have grown up, or that true ideas would ever have been sorted out from false or idle ones, save for the greater sum of satisfactions, intellectual or practical, which the truer ones brought with them. Can we imagine a man absolutely satisfied with an idea and with all its relations to his other ideas and to his sensible experiences, who should yet *not* take its

[1] Say, if you prefer to, that *dis*satisfactions decrease *pari passu* with such approximation. The approximation may be of any kind assignable—approximation in time or in space, or approximation in kind, which in common speech means 'copying.'

content as a true account of reality? The *matter* of the true is thus absolutely identical with the matter of the satisfactory. You may put either word first in your ways of talking; but leave out that whole notion of *satisfactory working* or *leading* (which is the essence of my pragmatistic account) and call truth a static logical relation, independent even of *possible* leadings or satisfactions, and it seems to me you cut all ground from under you.

I fear that I am still very obscure. But I respectfully implore those who reject my doctrine because they can make nothing of my stumbling language, to tell us in their own name—*und zwar* very concretely and articulately!—just how the real, genuine and absolutely 'objective' truth which they believe in so profoundly, *is* constituted and established. They must n't point to the 'reality' itself, for truth is only our subjective relation to realities. What is the nominal essence of this relation, its logical definition, whether or not it be 'objectively' attainable by mortals?

Whatever they may say it is, I have the firmest faith that my account will prove to have allowed for it and included it by anticipation, as one possible case in the total mixture of cases. There is, in short, no *room* for any grade or sort of truth outside of the framework of the pragmatic system, outside of that jungle of empirical workings and leadings, and their nearer or ulterior terminations, of which I seem to have written so unskilfully.

VII

I[1]

PROFESSOR J. B. Pratt's paper in the *Journal of Philosophy* for June 6, 1907, is so brilliantly written that its misconception of the pragmatist position seems doubly to call for a reply.

He asserts that, for a pragmatist, truth cannot be a relation between an idea and a reality outside and transcendent of the idea, but must lie 'altogether within experience,' where it will need 'no reference to anything else to justify it'—no reference to the object, apparently. The pragmatist must 'reduce everything to psychology,' aye, and to the psychology of the immediate moment. He is consequently debarred from saying that an idea that eventually gets psychologically verified *was* already true before the process of verifying was complete; and he is equally debarred from treating an idea as true provisionally so long as he only believes that he *can* verify it whenever he will.

Whether such a pragmatist as this exists, I know not, never having myself met with the beast. We can define terms as we like; and if that be my friend Pratt's definition of a pragmatist, I can only concur with his anti-pragmatism. But, in setting up the weird type, he quotes words from me; so, in order to escape being classed by some reader along with so asinine a being, I will reassert my own view of truth once more.

Truth is essentially a relation between two things, an idea, on the one hand, and a reality outside of the idea, on the other. This relation, like all relations, has its *fundamentum*, namely, the matrix of experiential circumstance, psychological as well as physical, in which the correlated terms are found embedded. In the case of the relation between 'heir' and 'legacy' the *fundamentum* is a world in which there was a testator, and in which there is now a will and an executor; in the

[1] Reprinted from the *Journal of Philosophy, etc.*, August 15, 1907 (vol. iv, p. 464).

909

case of that between idea and object, it is a world with circumstances of a sort to make a satisfactory verification process, lying around and between the two terms. But just as a
man may be called an heir and treated as one before the executor has divided the estate, so an idea may practically be
credited with truth before the verification process has been
exhaustively carried out—the existence of the mass of verifying circumstance is enough. Where potentiality counts for actuality in so many other cases, one does not see why it may
not so count here. We call a man benevolent not only for his
kind acts paid in, but for his readiness to perform others; we
treat an idea as 'luminous' not only for the light it has shed,
but for that we expect it will shed on dark problems. Why
should we not equally trust the truth of our ideas? We live on
credits everywhere; and we use our ideas far oftener for calling up things connected with their immediate objects, than
for calling up those objects themselves. Ninety-nine times out
of a hundred the only use we should make of the object itself,
if we were led up to it by our idea, would be to pass on to
those connected things by its means. So we continually curtail
verification-processes, letting our belief that they are possible
suffice.

What *constitutes the relation* known as truth, I now say, is
just the *existence in the empirical world of this fundamentum of
circumstance surrounding object and idea* and ready to be either
short-circuited or traversed at full length. So long as it exists,
and a satisfactory passage through it between the object and
the idea is possible, that idea will both *be* true, and will *have
been* true of that object, whether fully developed verification
has taken place or not. The nature and place and affinities of
the object of course play as vital a part in making the particular passage possible as do the nature and associative tendencies of the idea; so that the notion that truth could fall
altogether inside of the thinker's private experience and be
something purely psychological, is absurd. It is *between* the
idea and the object that the truth-relation is to be sought and
it involves both terms.

But the 'intellectualistic' position, if I understand Mr. Pratt
rightly, is that, altho we can use this *fundamentum*, this mass
of go-between experience, for *testing* truth, yet the truth-

relation in itself remains as something apart. It means, in Mr. Pratt's words, merely *'this simple thing that the object of which one is thinking is as one thinks it.'*

It seems to me that the word 'as,' which qualifies the relation here, and bears the whole 'epistemological' burden, is anything but simple. What it most immediately suggests is that the idea should be *like* the object; but most of our ideas, being abstract concepts, bear almost no resemblance to their objects. The 'as' must therefore, I should say, be usually interpreted functionally, as meaning that the idea shall lead us into the same quarters of experience *as* the object would. Experience leads ever on and on, and objects and our ideas of objects may both lead to the same goals. The ideas being in that case shorter cuts, we *substitute* them more and more for their objects; and we habitually waive direct verification of each one of them, as their train passes through our mind, because if an idea leads *as* the object would lead, we can say, in Mr. Pratt's words, that in so far forth the object is *as* we think it, and that the idea, verified thus in so far forth, is true enough.

Mr. Pratt will undoubtedly accept most of these facts, but he will deny that they spell pragmatism. Of course, definitions are free to every one; but I have myself never meant by the pragmatic view of truth anything different from what I now describe; and inasmuch as my use of the term came earlier than my friend's, I think it ought to have the right of way. But I suspect that Professor Pratt's contention is not solely as to what one must think in order to be called a pragmatist. I am sure that he believes that the truth-relation has something *more* in it than the *fundamentum* which I assign can account for. Useful to test truth by, the matrix of circumstance, he thinks, cannot found the truth-relation *in se*, for that is transempirical and 'saltatory.'

Well, take an object and an idea, and assume that the latter is true of the former—as eternally and absolutely true as you like. Let the object be as much 'as' the idea thinks it, as it is possible for one thing to be 'as' another. I now formally ask of Professor Pratt to tell what this 'as'-ness in itself *consists* in—for it seems to me that it ought to consist in something assignable and describable, and not remain a pure mystery, and I promise that if he can assign any determination of it whatever which I cannot successfully refer to some specification of what in this article I have called the empirical *fundamentum*, I will confess my stupidity cheerfully, and will agree never to publish a line upon this subject of truth again.

II

Professor Pratt has returned to the charge in a whole book,[1] which for its clearness and good temper deserves to supersede all the rest of the anti-pragmatistic literature. I wish it might do so; for its author admits all *my* essential contentions, simply distinguishing my account of truth as 'modified' pragmatism from Schiller's and Dewey's, which he calls pragmatism of the 'radical' sort. As I myself understand Dewey and Schiller, our views absolutely agree, in spite of our different modes of statement; but I have enough trouble of my own in life without having to defend my friends, so I abandon them provisionally to the tender mercy of Professor Pratt's interpretations, utterly erroneous tho I deem these to be. My reply as regards myself can be very short, for I prefer to consider only essentials, and Dr. Pratt's whole book hardly takes the matter farther than the article to which I retort in Part I of the present paper.

He repeats the 'as'-formula, as if it were something that I, along with other pragmatists, had denied,[2] whereas I have only asked those who insist so on its importance to do something more than merely utter it—to explicate it, for example, and tell us what its so great importance consists in. I myself agree most cordially that for an idea to be true the object must be 'as' the idea declares it, but I explicate the 'as'-ness as meaning the idea's verifiability.

Now since Dr. Pratt denies none of these verifying 'workings' for which I have pleaded, but only insists on their inability to serve as the *fundamentum* of the truth-relation, it seems that there is really nothing in the line of *fact* about which we differ, and that the issue between us is solely as to

---

[1] J. B. Pratt: *What is Pragmatism.* New York, The Macmillan Company, 1909.—The comments I have printed were written in March, 1909, after some of the articles printed later in the present volume.

[2] *Op. cit.*, pp. 77–80.

how far the notion of workableness or verifiability is an essential part of the notion of 'trueness'—'trueness' being Dr. Pratt's present name for the character of as-ness in the true idea. I maintain that there is no meaning left in this notion of as-ness or trueness if no reference to the possibility of concrete working on the part of the idea is made.

Take an example where there can be no possible working. Suppose I have an idea to which I give utterance by the vocable 'skrkl,' claiming at the same time that it is true. Who now can say that it is *false*, for why may there not be somewhere in the unplumbed depths of the cosmos some object with which 'skrkl' can agree and have trueness in Dr. Pratt's sense? On the other hand who can say that it is *true*, for who can lay his hand on that object and show that it and nothing else is what I *mean* by my word? But yet again, who can gainsay any one who shall call my word utterly *irrelative* to other reality, and treat it as a bare fact in my mind, devoid of any cognitive function whatever. One of these three alternatives must surely be predicated of it. For it not to be irrelevant (or not-cognitive in nature), an object of some kind must be provided which it may refer to. Supposing that object provided, whether 'skrkl' is true or false of it, depends, according to Professor Pratt, on no intermediating condition whatever. The trueness or the falsity is even now immediately, absolutely, and positively there.

I, on the other hand, demand a cosmic environment of some kind to establish which of them is there rather than utter irrelevancy.[1] I then say, first, that unless some sort of a natural path exists between the 'skrkl' and *that* object, distinguishable among the innumerable pathways that run among

[1] Dr. Pratt, singularly enough, disposes of this primal postulate of all pragmatic epistemology, by saying that the pragmatist 'unconsciously surrenders his whole case by smuggling in the idea of a conditioning environment which determines whether or not the experience can work, and which cannot itself be identified with the experience or any part of it' (pp. 167–168). The 'experience' means here of course the idea, or belief; and the expression 'smuggling in' is to the last degree diverting. If any epistemologist could dispense with a conditioning environment, it would seem to be the anti-pragmatist, with his immediate saltatory trueness, independent of work done. The mediating pathway which the environment supplies is the very essence of the pragmatist's explanation.

all the realities of the universe, linking them promiscuously with one another, there is nothing there to constitute even the *possibility of its referring* to that object rather than to any other.

I say furthermore that unless it have some *tendency to follow up that path*, there is nothing to constitute its *intention* to refer to the object in question.

Finally, I say that unless the path be strown with possibilities of frustration or encouragement, and offer some sort of terminal satisfaction or contradiction, there is nothing to constitute its *agreement* or *disagreement* with that object, or to constitute the as-ness (or 'not-as-ness') in which the trueness (or falseness) is said to consist.

I think that Dr. Pratt ought to do something more than repeat the name 'trueness,' in answer to my pathetic question whether that there be not some *constitution* to a relation as important as this. The pathway, the tendency, the corroborating or contradicting progress, need not in every case be experienced in full, but I don't see, if the universe does n't contain them among its possibilities of furniture, what *logical material for defining* the trueness of my idea is left. But if it do contain them, they and they only are the logical material required.

I am perplexed by the superior importance which Dr. Pratt attributes to abstract trueness over concrete verifiability in an idea, and I wish that he might be moved to explain. It is prior to verification, to be sure, but so is the verifiability for which I contend prior, just as a man's 'mortality' (which is nothing but the possibility of his death) is prior to his death, but it can hardly be that this abstract priority of all possibility to its correlative fact is what so obstinate a quarrel is about. I think it probable that Dr. Pratt is vaguely thinking of something concreter than this. The trueness of an idea must mean *something definite in it that determines its tendency to work*, and indeed towards this object rather than towards that. Undoubtedly there is something of this sort in the idea, just as there is something in man that accounts for his tendency towards death, and in bread that accounts for its tendency to nourish. What that something is in the case of truth psychology tells us: the idea has associates peculiar to itself, motor as well as ideational; it tends by its place and nature to call these into being, one after another; and the appearance of them in succession is what we mean by the 'workings' of the idea. According to what they are, does the trueness or falseness which the idea harbored come to light. These tendencies have still earlier conditions which, in a general way, biology, psychology and biography can trace. This whole chain of natural causal conditions produces a resultant state of things in which new relations, not simply causal, can now be found, or into which they can now be introduced,—the relations namely which we epistemologists study, relations of adaptation, of substitutability, of instrumentality, of reference and of truth.

The prior causal conditions, altho there could be no knowing of any kind, true or false, without them, are but preliminary to the question of what makes the ideas true or false when once their tendencies have been obeyed. The tendencies must exist in some shape anyhow, but their fruits are truth, falsity, or irrelevancy, according to what they concretely turn out to be. They are not 'saltatory' at any rate, for they evoke their consequences contiguously, from next to next only; and not until the final result of the whole associative sequence, actual or potential, is in our mental sight, can we feel sure what its epistemological significance, if it have any, may be. True knowing is, in fine, not substantially, in itself, or 'as such,' inside of the idea from the first, any more than mortality *as such* is inside of the man, or nourishment *as such* inside of the bread. Something else is there first, that practically *makes for* knowing, dying or nourishing, as the case may be. That something is the 'nature' namely of the first term, be it idea, man, or bread, that operates to start the causal chain of processes which, when completed, is the complex fact to which we give whatever functional name best fits the case. Another nature, another chain of cognitive workings; and then either another object known or the same object known differently, will ensue.

Dr. Pratt perplexes me again by seeming to charge Dewey and Schiller[1] (I am not sure that he charges me) with an ac-

[1] Page 200.

count of truth which would allow the object believed in not
to exist, even if the belief in it were true. 'Since the truth of
an idea,' he writes, 'means merely the fact that the idea works,
that fact is all that you mean when you say the idea is true'
(p. 206). *When you say the idea is true*—does that mean true
for *you*, the critic, or true for the believer whom you are describing? The critic's trouble over this seems to come from his
taking the word 'true' irrelatively, whereas the pragmatist always means 'true for him who experiences the workings.' 'But
is the object *really* true or not?'—the critic then seems to
ask,—as if the pragmatist were bound to throw in a whole
ontology on top of his epistemology and tell us what realities
indubitably exist. 'One world at a time,' would seem to be the
right reply here.

One other trouble of Dr. Pratt's must be noticed. It concerns the 'transcendence' of the object. When our ideas have
worked so as to bring us flat up against the object, *next* to it,
'is our relation to it then ambulatory or saltatory?' Dr. Pratt
asks. If *your* headache be my object, '*my* experiences break off
where yours begin,' Dr. Pratt writes, and 'this fact is of great
importance, for it bars out the sense of transition and fulfilment which forms so important an element in the pragmatist
description of knowledge—the sense of fulfilment due to a
continuous passage from the original idea to the known object. If this comes at all when I know your headache, it comes
not with the object, but quite on my side of the "epistemological gulf." The gulf is still there to be transcended' (p. 158).

Some day of course, or even now somewhere in the larger
life of the universe, different men's headaches may become
confluent or be 'co-conscious.' Here and now, however, headaches do transcend each other and, when not felt, can be
known only conceptually. My idea is that you really have a
headache; it works well with what I see of your expression,
and with what I hear you say; but it does n't put me in possession of the headache itself. I am still at one remove, and
the headache 'transcends' me, even tho it be in nowise transcendent of human experience generally. But the 'gulf' here is
that which the pragmatist epistemology itself fixes in the very
first words it uses, by saying there must be an object and an
idea. The idea however does n't immediately leap the gulf, it

only works from next to next so as to bridge it, fully or approximately. If it bridges it, in the pragmatist's vision of his hypothetical universe, it can be called a 'true' idea. If it only *might* bridge it, but does n't, or if it throws a bridge distinctly *at* it, it still has, in the onlooking pragmatist's eyes, what Professor Pratt calls 'trueness.' But to ask the pragmatist thereupon whether, when it thus fails to coalesce bodily with the object, it is *really* true or has *real* trueness,—in other words whether the headache he supposes, and supposes the thinker he supposes, to believe in, be a real headache or not,—is to step from his hypothetical universe of discourse into the altogether different world of natural fact.

VIII

THE PRAGMATIST ACCOUNT OF TRUTH
AND ITS MISUNDERSTANDERS[1]

THE ACCOUNT of truth given in my volume entitled *Pragmatism*, continues to meet with such persistent misunderstanding that I am tempted to make a final brief reply. My ideas may well deserve refutation, but they can get none till they are conceived of in their proper shape. The fantastic character of the current misconceptions shows how unfamiliar is the concrete point of view which pragmatism assumes. Persons who are familiar with a conception move about so easily in it that they understand each other at a hint, and can converse without anxiously attending to their P's and Q's. I have to admit, in view of the results, that we have assumed too ready an intelligence, and consequently in many places used a language too slipshod. We should never have spoken elliptically. The critics have boggled at every word they could boggle at, and refused to take the spirit rather than the letter of our discourse. This seems to show a genuine unfamiliarity in the whole point of view. It also shows, I think, that the second stage of opposition, which has already begun to express itself in the stock phrase that 'what is new is not true, and what is true not new,' in pragmatism, is insincere. If we said nothing in any degree new, why was our meaning so desperately hard to catch? The blame cannot be laid wholly upon our obscurity of speech, for in other subjects we have attained to making ourselves understood. But recriminations are tasteless; and, as far as I personally am concerned, I am sure that some of the misconception I complain of is due to my doctrine of truth being surrounded in that volume of popular lectures by a lot of other opinions not necessarily implicated with it, so that a reader may very naturally have grown confused. For this I am to blame,—likewise for omitting certain explicit cautions, which the pages that follow will now in part supply.

[1] Reprint from the *Philosophical Review*, January, 1908 (vol. xvii, p. 1).

First misunderstanding: Pragmatism is only a re-editing of positivism.

This seems the commonest mistake. Scepticism, positivism, and agnosticism agree with ordinary dogmatic rationalism in presupposing that everybody knows what the word 'truth' means, without further explanation. But the former doctrines then either suggest or declare that real truth, absolute truth, is inaccessible to us, and that we must fain put up with relative or phenomenal truth as its next best substitute. By scepticism this is treated as an unsatisfactory state of affairs, while positivism and agnosticism are cheerful about it, call real truth sour grapes, and consider phenomenal truth quite sufficient for all our 'practical' purposes.

In point of fact, nothing could be farther from all this than what pragmatism has to say of truth. Its thesis is an altogether previous one. It leaves off where these other theories begin, having contented itself with the word truth's *definition*. 'No matter whether any mind extant in the universe possess truth or not,' it asks, 'what does the notion of truth signify *ideally?*' 'What kind of things would true judgments be *in case* they existed?' The answer which pragmatism offers is intended to cover the most complete truth that can be conceived of, 'absolute' truth if you like, as well as truth of the most relative and imperfect description. This question of what truth would be like if it did exist, belongs obviously to a purely speculative field of inquiry. It is not a theory about any sort of reality, or about what kind of knowledge is actually possible; it abstracts from particular terms altogether, and defines the nature of a possible relation between two of them.

As Kant's question about synthetic judgments had escaped previous philosophers, so the pragmatist question is not only so subtle as to have escaped attention hitherto, but even so subtle, it would seem, that when openly broached now, dogmatists and sceptics alike fail to apprehend it, and deem the pragmatist to be treating of something wholly different. He insists, they say (I quote an actual critic), 'that the greater problems are insoluble by human intelligence, that our need of knowing truly is artificial and illusory, and that our reason, incapable of reaching the foundations of reality, must turn itself exclusively towards *action*.' There could not be a worse misapprehension.

Second misunderstanding: Pragmatism is primarily an appeal to action.

The name 'pragmatism,' with its suggestions of action, has been an unfortunate choice, I have to admit, and has played into the hands of this mistake. But no word could protect the doctrine from critics so blind to the nature of the inquiry that, when Dr. Schiller speaks of ideas 'working' well, the only thing they think of is their immediate workings in the physical environment, their enabling us to make money, or gain some similar 'practical' advantage. Ideas do work thus, of course, immediately or remotely; but they work indefinitely inside of the mental world also. Not crediting us with this rudimentary insight, our critics treat our view as offering itself exclusively to engineers, doctors, financiers, and men of action generally, who need some sort of a rough and ready *weltanschauung*, but have no time or wit to study genuine philosophy. It is usually described as a characteristically American movement, a sort of bobtailed scheme of thought, excellently fitted for the man on the street, who naturally hates theory and wants cash returns immediately.

It is quite true that, when the refined theoretic question that pragmatism begins with is once answered, secondary corollaries of a practical sort follow. Investigation shows that, in the function called truth, previous realities are not the only independent variables. To a certain extent our ideas, being realities, are also independent variables, and, just as they follow other reality and fit it, so, in a measure, does other reality follow and fit them. When they add themselves to being, they partly redetermine the existent, so that reality as a whole appears incompletely definable unless ideas also are kept account of. This pragmatist doctrine, exhibiting our ideas as complemental factors of reality, throws open (since our ideas are instigators of our action) a wide window upon human action, as well as a wide license to originality in thought. But few things could be sillier than to ignore the prior epistemological edifice in which the window is built, or to talk as if pragmatism began and ended at the window. This, nevertheless, is what our critics do almost without exception. They ignore our primary step and its motive, and make the relation to action, which is our secondary achievement, primary.

Third misunderstanding: Pragmatists cut themselves off from the right to believe in ejective realities.

They do so, according to the critics, by making the truth of our beliefs consist in their verifiability, and their verifiability in the way in which they do work for us. Professor Stout, in his otherwise admirable and hopeful review of Schiller in *Mind* for October, 1897, considers that this ought to lead Schiller (could he sincerely realize the effects of his own doctrine) to the absurd consequence of being unable to believe genuinely in another man's headache, even were the headache there. He can only 'postulate' it for the sake of the working value of the postulate to himself. The postulate guides certain of his acts and leads to advantageous consequences; but the moment he understands fully that the postulate is true *only* (!) in this sense, it ceases (or should cease) to be true for him that the other man really *has* a headache. All that makes the postulate most precious then evaporates: his interest in his fellow-man 'becomes a veiled form of self-interest, and his world grows cold, dull, and heartless.'

Such an objection makes a curious muddle of the pragmatist's universe of discourse. Within that universe the pragmatist finds some one with a headache or other feeling, and some one else who postulates that feeling. Asking on what condition the postulate is 'true,' the pragmatist replies that, for the postulator at any rate, it is true just in proportion as to believe in it works in him the fuller sum of satisfactions. What is it that is satisfactory here? Surely to *believe* in the postulated object, namely, in the really existing feeling of the other man. But how (especially if the postulator were himself a thoroughgoing pragmatist) could it ever be satisfactory to him *not* to believe in that feeling, so long as, in Professor Stout's words, disbelief 'made the world seem to him cold, dull, and heartless'? Disbelief would seem, on pragmatist principles, quite out of the question under such conditions, unless the heartlessness of the world were made probable already on other grounds. And since the belief in the headache, true for the subject assumed in the pragmatist's universe of discourse, is also true for the pragmatist who for his epistemologizing purposes has assumed that entire universe, why is it not true in that universe absolutely? The headache believed in is a reality there, and no extant mind disbelieves it, neither the critic's mind nor his subject's! Have our opponents any better brand of truth in this real universe of ours that they can show us?[1]

So much for the third misunderstanding, which is but one specification of the following still wider one.

Fourth misunderstanding: No pragmatist can be a realist in his epistemology.

This is supposed to follow from his statement that the truth of our beliefs consists in general in their giving satisfaction. Of course satisfaction *per se* is a subjective condition; so the conclusion is drawn that truth falls wholly inside of the subject, who then may manufacture it at his pleasure. True beliefs

[1] I see here a chance to forestall a criticism which some one may make on Lecture III of my *Pragmatism*, where, on pp. 528–529, I said that 'God' and 'Matter' might be regarded as synonymous terms, so long as no differing future consequences were deducible from the two conceptions. The passage was transcribed from my address at the California Philosophical Union, reprinted in the *Journal of Philosophy*, vol. i, p. 673. I had no sooner given the address than I perceived a flaw in that part of it; but I have left the passage unaltered ever since, because the flaw did not spoil its illustrative value. The flaw was evident when, as a case analogous to that of a godless universe, I thought of what I called an 'automatic sweetheart,' meaning a soulless body which should be absolutely indistinguishable from a spiritually animated maiden, laughing, talking, blushing, nursing us, and performing all feminine offices as tactfully and sweetly as if a soul were in her. Would any one regard her as a full equivalent? Certainly not, and why? Because, framed as we are, our egoism craves above all things inward sympathy and recognition, love and admiration. The outward treatment is valued mainly as an expression, as a manifestation of the accompanying consciousness believed in. Pragmatically, then, belief in the automatic sweetheart would not *work*, and in point of fact no one treats it as a serious hypothesis. The godless universe would be exactly similar. Even if matter could do every outward thing that God does, the idea of it would not work as satisfactorily, because the chief call for a God on modern men's part is for a being who will inwardly recognize them and judge them sympathetically. Matter disappoints this craving of our ego, so God remains for most men the truer hypothesis, and indeed remains so for definite pragmatic reasons.

become thus wayward affections, severed from all responsibility to other parts of experience.

It is difficult to excuse such a parody of the pragmatist's opinion, ignoring as it does every element but one of his universe of discourse. The terms of which that universe consists positively forbid any non-realistic interpretation of the function of knowledge defined there. The pragmatizing epistemologist posits there a reality and a mind with ideas. What, now, he asks, can make those ideas true of that reality? Ordinary epistemology contents itself with the vague statement that the ideas must 'correspond' or 'agree'; the pragmatist insists on being more concrete, and asks what such 'agreement' may mean in detail. He finds first that the ideas must point to or lead towards *that* reality and no other, and then that the pointings and leadings must yield satisfaction as their result. So far the pragmatist is hardly less abstract than the ordinary slouchy epistemologist; but as he defines himself farther, he grows more concrete. The entire quarrel of the intellectualist with him is over his concreteness, intellectualism contending that the vaguer and more abstract account is here the more profound. The concrete pointing and leading are conceived by the pragmatist to be the work of other portions of the same universe to which the reality and the mind belong, intermediary verifying bits of experience with which the mind at one end, and the reality at the other, are joined. The 'satisfaction,' in turn, is no abstract satisfaction *überhaupt*, felt by an unspecified being, but is assumed to consist of such satisfactions (in the plural) as concretely existing men actually do find in their beliefs. As we humans are constituted in point of fact, we find that to believe in other men's minds, in independent physical realities, in past events, in eternal logical relations, is satisfactory. We find hope satisfactory. We often find it satisfactory to cease to doubt. Above all we find *consistency* satisfactory, consistency between the present idea and the entire rest of our mental equipment, including the whole order of our sensations, and that of our intuitions of likeness and difference, and our whole stock of previously acquired truths.

The pragmatist, being himself a man, and imagining in general no contrary lines of truer belief than ours about the 'reality' which he has laid at the base of his epistemological discussion, is willing to treat our satisfactions as possibly really true guides to it, not as guides true solely for *us*. It would seem here to be the duty of his critics to show with some explicitness why, being our subjective feelings, these satisfactions can *not* yield 'objective' truth. The beliefs which they accompany 'posit' the assumed reality, 'correspond' and 'agree' with it, and 'fit' it in perfectly definite and assignable ways, through the sequent trains of thought and action which form their verification, so merely to insist on using these words abstractly instead of concretely is no way of driving the pragmatist from the field,—his more concrete account virtually includes his critic's. If our critics have any definite idea of a truth more objectively grounded than the kind we propose, why do they not show it more articulately? As they stand, they remind one of Hegel's man who wanted 'fruit,' but rejected cherries, pears, and grapes, because they were not fruit in the abstract. We offer them the full quart-pot, and they cry for the empty quart-capacity.

But here I think I hear some critic retort as follows: 'If satisfactions are all that is needed to make truth, how about the notorious fact that errors are so often satisfactory? And how about the equally notorious fact that certain true beliefs may cause the bitterest dissatisfaction? Is n't it clear that not the satisfaction which it gives, but the relation of the belief *to the reality* is all that makes it true? Suppose there were no such reality, and that the satisfactions yet remained: would they not then effectively work falsehood? Can they consequently be treated distinctively as the truth-builders? It is the *inherent relation to reality* of a belief that gives us that specific *truth*-satisfaction, compared with which all other satisfactions are the hollowest humbug. The satisfaction of *knowing truly* is thus the only one which the pragmatist ought to have considered. As a *psychological sentiment*, the anti-pragmatist gladly concedes it to him, but then only as a concomitant of truth, not as a constituent. What *constitutes* truth is not the sentiment, but the purely logical or objective function of rightly cognizing the reality, and the pragmatist's failure to reduce this function to lower values is patent.'

Such anti-pragmatism as this seems to me a tissue of confusion. To begin with, when the pragmatist says 'indispens-able,' it confounds this with 'sufficient.' The pragmatist calls satisfactions indispensable for truth-building, but I have every-where called them insufficient unless reality be also inciden-tally led to. If the reality assumed were cancelled from the prag-matist's universe of discourse, he would straightway give the name of falsehoods to the beliefs remaining, in spite of all their satisfactoriness. For him, as for his critic, there can be no truth if there is nothing to be true about. Ideas are so much flat psychological surface unless some mirrored matter gives them cognitive lustre. This is why as a pragmatist I have so carefully posited 'reality' *ab initio*, and why, throughout my whole discussion, I remain an epistemological realist.[1]

The anti-pragmatist is guilty of the further confusion of imagining that, in undertaking to give him an account of what truth formally means, we are assuming at the same time to provide a warrant for it, trying to define the occasions when he can be sure of materially possessing it. Our making it hinge on a reality so 'independent' that when it comes, truth comes, and when it goes, truth goes with it, disappoints this *naïve* expectation, so he deems our description unsatisfac-tory. I suspect that under this confusion lies the still deeper one of not discriminating sufficiently between the two no-tions, truth and reality. Realities are not *true*, they *are*; and beliefs are true *of* them. But I suspect that in the anti-prag-matist mind the two notions sometimes swap their attributes. The reality itself, I fear, is treated as if 'true,' and conversely. Whoso tells us of the one, it is then supposed, must also be telling us of the other; and a true idea must in a manner *be*, or at least *yield* without extraneous aid, the reality it cogni-tively is possessed of.

To this absolute-idealistic demand pragmatism simply op-poses its *non possumus*. If there is to be truth, it says, both realities and beliefs about them must conspire to make it; but whether there ever is such a thing, or how anyone can be sure that his own beliefs possess it, it never pretends to determine. That truth-satisfaction *par excellence* which may tinge a belief

[1] I need hardly remind the reader that both sense-percepts and percepts of ideal relation (comparisons, etc.) should be classed among the realities. The bulk of our mental 'stock' consists of truths concerning these terms.

unsatisfactory in other ways, it easily explains as the feeling of consistency with the stock of previous truths, or supposed truths, of which one's whole past experience may have left one in possession.

But are not all pragmatists sure that their own belief is right? their enemies will ask at this point; and this leads me to the

Fifth misunderstanding: What pragmatists say is inconsistent with their saying so.

A correspondent puts this objection as follows: 'When you say to your audience, "pragmatism is the truth concerning truth," the first truth is different from the second. About the first you and they are not to be at odds; you are not giving them liberty to take or leave it according as it works satisfactorily or not for their private uses. Yet the second truth, which ought to describe and include the first, affirms this liberty. Thus the *intent* of your utterance seems to contradict the *content* of it.'

General scepticism has always received this same classic refutation. 'You have to dogmatize,' the rationalists say to the sceptics, 'whenever you express the sceptical position; so your lives keep contradicting your thesis.' One would suppose that the impotence of so hoary an argument to abate in the slightest degree the amount of general scepticism in the world might have led some rationalists themselves to doubt whether these instantaneous logical refutations are such fatal ways, after all, of killing off live mental attitudes. General scepticism is the live mental attitude of refusing to conclude. It is a permanent torpor of the will, renewing itself in detail towards each successive thesis that offers, and you can no more kill it off by logic than you can kill off obstinacy or practical joking. This is why it is so irritating. Your consistent sceptic never puts his scepticism into a formal proposition,—he simply chooses it as a habit. He provokingly hangs back when he might so easily join us in saying yes, but he is not illogical or stupid,—on the contrary, he often impresses us by his intellectual superiority. This is the *real* scepticism that rationalists have to meet, and their logic does not even touch it.

No more can logic kill the pragmatist's behavior: his act

of utterance, so far from contradicting, accurately exemplifies the matter which he utters. What is the matter which he utters? In part, it is this, that truth, concretely considered, is an attribute of our beliefs, and that these are attitudes that follow satisfactions. The ideas around which the satisfactions cluster are primarily only hypotheses that challenge or summon a belief to come and take its stand upon them. The pragmatist's idea of truth is just such a challenge. He finds it ultra-satisfactory to accept it, and takes his own stand accordingly. But, being gregarious as they are, men seek to spread their beliefs, to awaken imitation, to infect others. Why should not *you* also find the same belief satisfactory? thinks the pragmatist, and forthwith endeavors to convert you. You and he will then believe similarly; you will hold up your subject-end of a truth, which will be a truth objective and irreversible if the reality holds up the object-end by being itself present simultaneously. What there is of self-contradiction in all this I confess I cannot discover. The pragmatist's conduct in his own case seems to me on the contrary admirably to illustrate his universal formula; and of all epistemologists, he is perhaps the only one who is irreproachably self-consistent.

Sixth misunderstanding: Pragmatism explains not what truth is, but only how it is arrived at.

In point of fact it tells us both, tells us what it is incidentally to telling us how it is arrived at,—for what *is* arrived at except just what the truth is? If I tell you how to get to the railroad station, don't I implicitly introduce you to the *what*, to the being and nature of that edifice? It is quite true that the abstract *word* 'how' has n't the same meaning as the abstract *word* 'what,' but in this universe of concrete facts you cannot keep hows and whats asunder. The reasons why I find it satisfactory to believe that any idea is true, the *how* of my arriving at that belief, may be among the very reasons why the idea *is* true in reality. If not, I summon the anti-pragmatist to explain the impossibility articulately.

His trouble seems to me mainly to arise from his fixed inability to understand how a concrete statement can possibly mean as much, or be as valuable, as an abstract one. I said above that the main quarrel between us and our critics was that of concreteness *versus* abstractness. This is the place to develop that point farther.

In the present question, the links of experience sequent upon an idea, which mediate between it and a reality, form and for the pragmatist indeed *are*, the *concrete* relation of truth that may obtain between the idea and that reality. They, he says, are all that we mean when we speak of the idea 'pointing' to the reality, 'fitting' it, 'corresponding' with it, or 'agreeing' with it,—they or other similar mediating trains of verification. Such mediating events *make* the idea 'true.' The idea itself, if it exists at all, is also a concrete event: so pragmatism insists that truth in the singular is only a collective name for truths in the plural, these consisting always of series of definite events; and that what intellectualism calls *the* truth, the *inherent* truth, of any one such series is only the abstract name for its truthfulness in act, for the fact that the ideas there do lead to the supposed reality in a way that we consider satisfactory.

The pragmatist himself has no objection to abstractions. Elliptically, and 'for short,' he relies on them as much as any one, finding upon innumerable occasions that their comparative emptiness makes of them useful substitutes for the overfulness of the facts he meets with. But he never ascribes to them a higher grade of reality. The full reality of a truth for him is always some process of verification, in which the abstract property of connecting ideas with objects truly is workingly embodied. Meanwhile it is endlessly serviceable to be able to talk of properties abstractly and apart from their working, to find them the same in innumerable cases, to take them 'out of time,' and to treat of their relations to other similar abstractions. We thus form whole universes of platonic ideas *ante rem*, universes *in posse*, tho none of them exists effectively except *in rebus*. Countless relations obtain there which nobody experiences as obtaining,—as, in the eternal universe of musical relations, for example, the notes of Aennchen von Tharau were a lovely melody long ere mortal ears ever heard them. Even so the music of the future sleeps now, to be awakened hereafter. Or, if we take the world of geometrical relations, the thousandth decimal of π sleeps there, tho no one may ever try to compute it. Or, if we take the universe of 'fitting,' countless coats 'fit' backs, and countless boots 'fit' feet, on which they are not practically *fitted*; countless stones 'fit' gaps in walls into which no one seeks to fit them actually. In the same way countless opinions 'fit' realities, and countless truths are valid, tho no thinker ever thinks them.

For the anti-pragmatist these prior timeless relations are the presupposition of the concrete ones, and possess the profounder dignity and value. The actual workings of our ideas in verification-processes are as naught in comparison with the 'obtainings' of this discarnate truth within them.

For the pragmatist, on the contrary, all discarnate truth is static, impotent, and relatively spectral, full truth being the truth that energizes and does battle. Can any one suppose that the sleeping quality of truth would ever have been abstracted or have received a name, if truths had remained forever in that storage-vault of essential timeless 'agreements' and had never been embodied in any panting struggle of men's live ideas for verification? Surely no more than the abstract property of 'fitting' would have received a name, if in our world there had been no backs or feet or gaps in walls to be actually fitted. *Existential* truth is incidental to the actual competition of opinions. *Essential* truth, the truth of the intellectualists, the truth with no one thinking it, is like the coat that fits tho no one has ever tried it on, like the music that no ear has listened to. It is less real, not more real, than the verified article; and to attribute a superior degree of glory to it seems little more than a piece of perverse abstraction-worship. As well might a pencil insist that the outline is the essential thing in all pictorial representation, and chide the paint-brush and the camera for omitting it, forgetting that *their* pictures not only contain the whole outline, but a hundred other things in addition. Pragmatist truth contains the whole of intellectualist truth and a hundred other things in addition. Intellectualist truth is then only pragmatist truth *in posse*. That on innumerable occasions men do substitute truth *in posse* or verifiability, for verification or truth in act, is a fact to which no one attributes more importance than the pragmatist: he emphasizes the practical utility of such a habit. But he does not on that account consider truth *in posse*,

—truth not alive enough ever to have been asserted or questioned or contradicted,—to be the metaphysically prior
thing, to which truths in act are tributary and subsidiary.
When intellectualists do this, pragmatism charges them with
inverting the real relation. Truth in posse *means* only truths
in act; and he insists that these latter take precedence in the
order of logic as well as in that of being.

*Seventh misunderstanding: Pragmatism ignores the theoretic
interest.*

This would seem to be an absolutely wanton slander, were
not a certain excuse to be found in the linguistic affinities of
the word 'pragmatism,' and in certain offhand habits of
speech of ours which assumed too great a generosity on our
reader's part. When we spoke of the meaning of ideas consisting in their 'practical' consequences, or of the 'practical'
differences which our beliefs make to us; when we said that
the truth of a belief consists in its 'working' value, etc.; our
language evidently was too careless, for by 'practical' we were
almost unanimously held to mean *opposed* to theoretical or
genuinely cognitive, and the consequence was punctually
drawn that a truth in our eyes could have no relation to any
independent reality, or to any other truth, or to anything
whatever but the acts which we might ground on it or the
satisfactions they might bring. The mere existence of the idea,
all by itself, if only its results were satisfactory, would give
full truth to it, it was charged, in our absurd pragmatist epistemology. The solemn attribution of this rubbish to us was
also encouraged by two other circumstances. First, ideas *are*
practically useful in the narrow sense, false ideas sometimes,
but most often ideas which we can verify by the sum total of
all their leadings, and the reality of whose objects may thus
be considered established beyond doubt. That these ideas
should be true in advance of and apart from their utility, that,
in other words, their objects should be really there, is the very
condition of their having that kind of utility,—the objects
they connect us with are so important that the ideas which
serve as the objects' substitutes grow important also. This
manner of their practical working was the first thing that
made truths good in the eyes of primitive men; and buried

among all the other good workings by which true beliefs are characterized, this kind of subsequential utility remains.

The second misleading circumstance was the emphasis laid by Schiller and Dewey on the fact that, unless a truth be relevant to the mind's momentary predicament, unless it be germane to the 'practical' situation,—meaning by this the quite particular perplexity,—it is no good to urge it. It does n't meet our interests any better than a falsehood would under the same circumstances. But why our predicaments and perplexities might not be theoretical here as well as narrowly practical, I wish that our critics would explain. They simply assume that no pragmatist *can* admit a genuinely theoretic interest. Having used the phrase 'cash-value' of an idea, I am implored by one correspondent to alter it, 'for every one thinks you mean only pecuniary profit and loss.' Having said that the true is 'the expedient in our thinking,' I am rebuked in this wise by another learned correspondent: 'The word expedient has no other meaning than that of self-interest. The pursuit of this has ended by landing a number of officers of national banks in penitentiaries. A philosophy that leads to such results must be unsound.'

But the word 'practical' is so habitually loosely used that more indulgence might have been expected. When one says that a sick man has now practically recovered, or that an enterprise has practically failed, one usually means just the opposite of practically in the literal sense. One means that, altho untrue in strict practice, what one says is true in theory, true virtually, *certain to be* true. Again, by the practical one often means the distinctively concrete, the individual, particular, and effective, as opposed to the abstract, general, and inert. To speak for myself, whenever I have emphasized the practical nature of truth, this is mainly what has been in my mind. 'Pragmata' are things in their plurality; and in that early California address, when I described pragmatism as holding that 'the meaning of any proposition can always be brought down to some particular consequence in our future practical experience, whether passive or active,' I expressly added these qualifying words: 'the point lying rather in the fact that the experience must be particular than in the fact that it must be active,'—by 'active' meaning here 'practical' in the narrow literal sense.[1] But particular consequences can perfectly well be of a theoretic nature. Every remote fact which we infer from an idea is a particular theoretic consequence which our mind practically works towards. The loss of every old opinion of ours which we see that we shall have to give up if a new opinion be true, is a particular theoretic as well as a particular practical consequence. After man's interest in breathing freely, the greatest of all his interests (because it never fluctuates or remits, as most of his physical interests do), is his interest in *consistency*, in feeling that what he now thinks goes with what he thinks on other occasions. We tirelessly compare truth with truth for this sole purpose. Is the present candidate for belief perhaps contradicted by principle number one? Is it compatible with fact number two? and so forth. The particular operations here are the purely logical ones of analysis, deduction, comparison, etc.; and altho general terms may be used *ad libitum*, the satisfactory *practical working* of the candidate-idea consists in the consciousness yielded by each successive theoretic consequence in particular. It is therefore simply idiotic to repeat that pragmatism takes no account of purely theoretic interests. All it insists on is that verity in act means *verifications*, and that these are always particulars. Even in exclusively theoretic matters, it insists that vagueness and generality serve to verify nothing.

Eighth misunderstanding: Pragmatism is shut up to solipsism.
I have already said something about this misconception under the third and fourth heads, above, but a little more may be helpful. The objection is apt to clothe itself in words like these: 'You make truth to consist in every value except the cognitive value proper; you always leave your knower at

[1]The ambiguity of the word 'practical' comes out well in these words of a recent would-be reporter of our views: 'Pragmatism is an Anglo-Saxon reaction against the intellectualism and rationalism of the Latin mind. . . . Man, each individual man is the measure of things. He is able to conceive none but relative truths, that is to say, illusions. What these illusions are worth is revealed to him, not by general theory, but by individual practice. Pragmatism, which consists in experiencing these illusions of the mind and obeying them by acting them out, is a *philosophy without words*, a philosophy of *gestures and of acts*, which abandons what is general and holds only to what is particular.' (Bourdeau, in *Journal des Débats*, October 29, 1907.)

many removes (or, at the uttermost, at one remove) from his real object; the best you do is to let his ideas carry him towards it; it remains forever outside of him,' etc.

I think that the leaven working here is the rooted intellectualist persuasion that, to know a reality, an idea must in some inscrutable fashion possess or be it.[1] For pragmatism this kind of coalescence is inessential. As a rule our cognitions are only processes of mind off their balance and in motion towards real termini; and the reality of the termini, believed in by the states of mind in question, can be *guaranteed* only by some wider knower.[2] But if there is no reason extant in the universe why they should be doubted, the beliefs are true in the only sense in which anything can be true anyhow: they are practically and concretely true, namely. True in the mystical mongrel sense of an *Identitätsphilosophie* they need not be; nor is there any intelligible reason why they ever need be true otherwise than verifiably and practically. It is reality's part to possess its own existence; it is thought's part to get into 'touch' with it by innumerable paths of verification.

I fear that the 'humanistic' developments of pragmatism may cause a certain difficulty here. We get at one truth only through the rest of truth; and the reality, everlastingly postulated as that which all our truth must keep in touch with, may never be given to us save in the form of truth other than

[1] Sensations may, indeed, possess their objects or coalesce with them, as common sense supposes that they do; and intuited differences between concepts may coalesce with the 'eternal' objective differences; but to simplify our discussion here we can afford to abstract from these very special cases of knowing.

[2] The transcendental idealist thinks that, in some inexplicable way, the finite states of mind are identical with the transfinite all-knower which he finds himself obliged to postulate in order to supply a *fundamentum* for the relation of knowing, as he apprehends it. Pragmatists can leave the question of identity open; but they cannot do without the wider knower any more than they can do without the reality, if they want to *prove* a case of knowing. They themselves play the part of the absolute knower for the universe of discourse which serves them as material for epistemologizing. They warrant the reality there, and the subject's true knowledge, there, of it. But whether what they themselves say about that whole universe is objectively true, *i. e.*, whether the pragmatic theory of truth is true *really*, they cannot warrant,—they can only believe it. To their hearers they can only *propose* it, as I propose it to my readers, as something to be verified *ambulando*, or by the way in which its consequences may confirm it.

that which we are now testing. But since Dr. Schiller has shown that all our truths, even the most elemental, are affected by race-inheritance with a human coefficient, reality *per se* thus may appear only as a sort of limit; it may be held to shrivel to the mere *place* for an object, and what is known may be held to be only matter of our psyche that we fill the place with.

It must be confessed that pragmatism, worked in this humanistic way, is *compatible* with solipsism. It joins friendly hands with the agnostic part of kantism, with contemporary agnosticism, and with idealism generally. But worked thus, it is a metaphysical theory about the matter of reality, and flies far beyond pragmatism's own modest analysis of the nature of the knowing function, which analysis may just as harmoniously be combined with less humanistic accounts of reality. One of pragmatism's merits is that it is so purely epistemological. It must assume realities; but it prejudges nothing as to their constitution, and the most diverse metaphysics can use it as their foundation. It certainly has no special affinity with solipsism.

As I look back over what I have written, much of it gives me a queer impression, as if the obvious were set forth so condescendingly that readers might well laugh at my pomposity. It may be, however, that concreteness as radical as ours is not so obvious. The whole originality of pragmatism, the whole point in it, is its use of the concrete way of seeing. It begins with concreteness, and returns and ends with it. Dr. Schiller, with his two 'practical' aspects of truth, (1) relevancy to situation, and (2) subsequential utility, is only filling the cup of concreteness to the brim for us. Once seize that cup, and you cannot misunderstand pragmatism. It seems as if the power of imagining the world concretely *might* have been common enough to let our readers apprehend us better, as if they might have read between our lines, and, in spite of all our infelicities of expression, guessed a little more correctly what our thought was. But alas! this was not on fate's programme, so we can only think, with the German ditty:—

> "Es wär' zu schön gewesen,
> Es hat nicht sollen sein."

IX

MY ACCOUNT of truth is realistic, and follows the episte-mological dualism of common sense. Suppose I say to you 'The thing exists'—is that true or not? How can you tell? Not till my statement has developed its meaning farther is it determined as being true, false, or irrelevant to reality alto-gether. But if now you ask 'what thing?' and I reply 'a desk'; if you ask 'where?' and I point to a place; if you ask 'does it exist materially, or only in imagination?' and I say 'materi-ally'; if moreover I say 'I mean that desk,' and then grasp and shake a desk which you see just as I have described it, you are willing to call my statement true. But you and I are commut-able here; we can exchange places; and, as you go bail for my desk, so I can go bail for yours.

This notion of a reality independent of either of us, taken from ordinary social experience, lies at the base of the prag-matist definition of truth. With some such reality any state-ment, in order to be counted true, must agree. Pragmatism defines 'agreeing' to mean certain ways of 'working,' be they actual or potential. Thus, for my statement 'the desk exists' to be true of a desk recognized as real by you, it must be able to lead me to shake your desk, to explain myself by words that suggest that desk to your mind, to make a drawing that is like the desk you see, etc. Only in such ways as this is there sense in saying it agrees with *that* reality, only thus does it gain for me the satisfaction of hearing you corroborate me. Reference then to something determinate, and some sort of adaptation to it worthy of the name of agreement, are thus constituent elements in the definition of any statement of mine as 'true.'

You cannot get at either the reference or the adaptation without using the notion of the workings. *That* the thing is, *what* it is, and *which* it is (of all the possible things with that what) are points determinable only by the pragmatic method. The 'which' means a possibility of pointing, or of otherwise

[1] Remarks at the meeting of the American Philosophical Association, Cor-nell University, December, 1907.

singling out the special object; the 'what' means choice on our part of an essential aspect to conceive it by (and this is always relative to what Dewey calls our own 'situation'); and the 'that' means our assumption of the attitude of belief, the reality-recognizing attitude. Surely for understanding what the word 'true' means as applied to a statement, the mention of such workings is indispensable. Surely if we leave them out the subject and the object of the cognitive relation float—in the same universe, 't is true—but vaguely and ignorantly and without mutual contact or mediation.

Our critics nevertheless call the workings inessential. No functional possibilities 'make' our beliefs true, they say; they are true inherently, true positively, born 'true' as the Count of Chambord was born 'Henri-Cinq.' Pragmatism insists, on the contrary, that statements and beliefs are thus inertly and statically true only by courtesy: they practically pass for true; but you *cannot define what you mean* by calling them true without referring to their functional possibilities. These give its whole *logical content* to that relation to reality on a belief's part to which the name 'truth' is applied, a relation which otherwise remains one of mere coexistence or bare witness.

The foregoing statements reproduce the essential content of the lecture on Truth in my book *Pragmatism*. Schiller's doctrine of 'humanism,' Dewey's 'Studies in logical theory,' and my own 'radical empiricism,' all involve this general notion of truth as 'working,' either actual or conceivable. But they envelop it as only one detail in the midst of much wider theories that aim eventually at determining the notion of what 'reality' at large is in its ultimate nature and constitution.

X

MY ACCOUNT of truth is purely logical and relates to its definition only. I contend that you cannot tell what the *word* 'true' *means*, as applied to a statement, without invoking the *concept of the statement's workings*.

Assume, to fix our ideas, a universe composed of two things only: imperial Cæsar dead and turned to clay, and me, saying 'Cæsar really existed.' Most persons would naïvely deem truth to be thereby uttered, and say that by a sort of *actio in distans* my statement had taken direct hold of the other fact.

But have my words so certainly denoted *that* Cæsar?—or so certainly connoted *his* individual attributes? To fill out the complete measure of what the epithet 'true' may ideally mean, my thought ought to bear a fully determinate and unambiguous 'one-to-one-relation' to its own particular object. In the ultra-simple universe imagined the reference is uncertified. Were there two Cæsars we should n't know which was meant. The conditions of truth thus seem incomplete in this universe of discourse so that it must be enlarged.

Transcendentalists enlarge it by invoking an absolute mind which, as it owns all the facts, can sovereignly correlate them. If it intends that my statement *shall* refer to that identical Cæsar, and that the attributes I have in mind *shall* mean his attributes, that intention suffices to make the statement true.

I, in turn, enlarge the universe by admitting finite intermediaries between the two original facts. Cæsar *had*, and my statement *has*, effects; and if these effects in any way run together, a concrete medium and bottom is provided for the determinate cognitive relation, which, as a pure *actio in distans*, seemed to float too vaguely and unintelligibly.

The real Cæsar, for example, wrote a manuscript of which I see a real reprint, and say 'the Cæsar I mean is the author of *that*.' The workings of my thought thus determine both its

[1] Originally printed under the title of 'Truth versus Truthfulness,' in the *Journal of Philosophy*.

denotative and its connotative significance more fully. It now defines itself as neither irrelevant to the real Cæsar, nor false in what it suggests of him. The absolute mind, seeing me thus working towards Cæsar through the cosmic intermediaries, might well say: 'Such workings only specify in detail what I meant myself by the statement being true. I decree the cognitive relation between the two original facts to mean that just that kind of concrete chain of intermediaries exists or can exist.'

But the chain involves facts prior to the statement the logical conditions of whose truth we are defining, and facts subsequent to it; and this circumstance, coupled with the vulgar employment of the terms truth and fact as synonyms, has laid my account open to misapprehension. 'How,' it is confusedly asked, 'can Cæsar's existence, a truth already 2000 years old, depend for its truth on anything about to happen now? How can my acknowledgment of it be made true by the acknowledgment's own effects? The effects may indeed confirm my belief, but the belief was made true already by the fact that Cæsar really did exist.'

Well, be it so, for if there were no Cæsar, there could, of course, be no positive truth about him—but then distinguish between 'true' as being positively and completely so established, and 'true' as being so only 'practically,' elliptically, and by courtesy, in the sense of not being positively irrelevant or *un*true. Remember also that Cæsar's having existed in fact may make a present statement false or irrelevant as well as it may make it true, and that in neither case does it itself have to alter. It being given, whether truth, untruth, or irrelevancy shall be also given depends on something coming from the statement itself. What pragmatism contends for is that you cannot adequately *define* the something if you leave the notion of the statement's functional workings out of your account. Truth meaning agreement with reality, the mode of the agreeing is a practical problem which the subjective term of the relation alone can solve.

NOTE. This paper was originally followed by a couple of paragraphs meant to conciliate the intellectualist opposition. Since you love the word 'true' so, and since you despise so the concrete working of our ideas, I said, keep the word 'truth' for the saltatory and incomprehensible relation you care so much for, and I will say of thoughts that know their objects in an intelligible sense that they are 'truthful.'

Like most offerings, this one has been spurned, so I revoke it, repenting of my generosity. Professor Pratt, in his recent book, calls any objective state of *facts* 'a truth,' and uses the word 'trueness' in the sense of 'truth' as proposed by me. Mr. Hawtrey (see below, page 966) uses 'correctness' in the same sense. Apart from the general evil of ambiguous vocabularies, we may really forsake all hope, if the term 'truth' is officially to lose its status as a property of our beliefs and opinions, and become recognized as a technical synonym for 'fact.'

XI

PROFESSOR W. A. Brown, in the *Journal* for August 15, approves my pragmatism for allowing that a belief in the absolute may give holidays to the spirit, but takes me to task for the narrowness of this concession, and shows by striking examples how great a power the same belief may have in letting loose the strenuous life.

I have no criticism whatever to make upon his excellent article, but let me explain why 'moral holidays' were the only gift of the absolute which I picked out for emphasis. I was primarily concerned in my lectures with contrasting the belief that the world is still in process of making with the belief that there is an 'eternal' edition of it ready-made and complete. The former, or 'pluralistic' belief, was the one that my pragmatism favored. Both beliefs confirm our strenuous moods. Pluralism actually demands them, since it makes the world's salvation depend upon the energizing of its several parts, among which we are. Monism permits them, for however furious they may be, we can always justify ourselves in advance for indulging them by the thought that they *will have been* expressions of the absolute's perfect life. By escaping from your finite perceptions to the conception of the eternal whole, you can hallow any tendency whatever. Tho the absolute *dictates* nothing, it will *sanction* anything and everything after the fact, for whatever is once there will have to be regarded as an integral member of the universe's perfection. Quietism and frenzy thus alike receive the absolute's permit to exist. Those of us who are naturally inert may abide in our resigned passivity; those whose energy is excessive may grow more reckless still. History shows how easily both quietists and fanatics have drawn inspiration from the absolutistic scheme. It suits sick souls and strenuous ones equally well.

One cannot say thus of pluralism. Its world is always vulnerable, for some part may go astray; and having no 'eternal' edition of it to draw comfort from, its partisans must always

[1] Reprinted from the *Journal of Philosophy, etc.,* 1906.

feel to some degree insecure. If, as pluralists, we grant ourselves moral holidays, they can only be provisional breathing-spells, intended to refresh us for the morrow's fight. This forms one permanent inferiority of pluralism from the pragmatic point of view. It has no saving message for incurably sick souls. Absolutism, among its other messages, has that message, and is the only scheme that has it necessarily. That constitutes its chief superiority and is the source of its religious power. That is why, desiring to do it full justice, I valued its aptitude for moral-holiday giving so highly. Its claims in that way are unique, whereas its affinities with strenuousness are less emphatic than those of the pluralistic scheme.

In the last lecture of my book I candidly admitted this inferiority of pluralism. It lacks the wide indifference that absolutism shows. It is bound to disappoint many sick souls whom absolutism can console. It seems therefore poor tactics for absolutists to make little of this advantage. The needs of sick souls are surely the most urgent; and believers in the absolute should rather hold it to be great merit in their philosophy that it can meet them so well.

The pragmatism or pluralism which I defend has to fall back on a certain ultimate hardihood, a certain willingness to live without assurances or guarantees. To minds thus willing to live on possibilities that are not certainties, quietistic religion, sure of salvation *any how*, has a slight flavor of fatty degeneration about it which has caused it to be looked askance on, even in the church. Which side is right here, who can say? Within religion, emotion is apt to be tyrannical; but philosophy must favor the emotion that allies itself best with the whole body and drift of all the truths in sight. I conceive this to be the more strenuous type of emotion; but I have to admit that its inability to let loose quietistic raptures is a serious deficiency in the pluralistic philosophy which I profess.

XII

PROFESSOR HÉBERT ON PRAGMATISM[1]

PROFESSOR Marcel Hébert is a singularly erudite and liberal thinker (a seceder, I believe, from the Catholic priesthood) and an uncommonly direct and clear writer. His book *Le Divin* is one of the ablest reviews of the general subject of religious philosophy which recent years have produced; and in the small volume the title of which is copied above he has, perhaps, taken more pains not to do injustice to pragmatism than any of its numerous critics. Yet the usual fatal misapprehension of its purposes vitiates his exposition and his critique. His pamphlet seems to me to form a worthy hook, as it were, on which to hang one more attempt to tell the reader what the pragmatist account of truth really means.

M. Hébert takes it to mean what most people take it to mean, the doctrine, namely, that whatever proves subjectively expedient in the way of our thinking is 'true' in the absolute and unrestricted sense of the word, whether it corresponds to any objective state of things outside of our thought or not. Assuming this to be the pragmatist thesis, M. Hébert opposes it at length. Thought that proves itself to be thus expedient may, indeed, have every *other* kind of value for the thinker, he says, but cognitive value, representative value, *valeur de connaissance proprement dite*, it has not; and when it does have a high degree of general utility value, this is in every case derived from its previous value in the way of correctly representing independent objects that have an important influence on our lives. Only by thus representing things truly do we reap the useful fruits. But the fruits follow on the truth, they do not constitute it; so M. Hébert accuses pragmatism of telling us everything about truth except what it essentially is. He admits, indeed, that the world is so framed that when men have true ideas of realities, consequential utilities ensue in abundance; and no one of our critics, I think, has shown as

[1] Reprint from the *Journal of Philosophy* for December 3, 1908 (vol. v, p. 689), of a review of *Le pragmatisme et ses diverses formes anglo-américaines*, by Marcel Hébert. (Paris: Librairie critique Emile Nourry. 1908. Pp. 105.)

concrete a sense of the variety of these utilities as he has; but he reiterates that, whereas such utilities are secondary, we insist on treating them as primary, and that the *connaissance objective* from which they draw all their being is something which we neglect, exclude, and destroy. The utilitarian value and the strictly cognitive value of our ideas may perfectly well harmonize, he says—and in the main he allows that they do harmonize—but they are not logically identical for that. He admits that subjective interests, desires, impulses may even have the active 'primacy' in our intellectual life. Cognition awakens only at their spur, and follows their cues and aims; yet, when it *is* awakened, it is objective cognition proper and not merely another name for the impulsive tendencies themselves in the state of satisfaction. The owner of a picture ascribed to Corot gets uneasy when its authenticity is doubted. He looks up its origin and is reassured. But his uneasiness does not make the proposition false, any more than his relief makes the proposition true, that the actual Corot was the painter. Pragmatism, which, according to M. Hébert, claims that our sentiments *make* truth and falsehood, would oblige us to conclude that our minds exert no genuinely cognitive function whatever.

This subjectivist interpretation of our position seems to follow from my having happened to write (without supposing it necessary to explain that I was treating of cognition solely on its subjective side) that in the long run the true is the expedient in the way of our thinking, much as the good is the expedient in the way of our behavior! Having previously written that truth means 'agreement with reality,' and insisted that the chief part of the expediency of any one opinion is its agreement with the rest of acknowledged truth, I apprehended no exclusively subjectivistic reading of my meaning. My mind was so filled with the notion of objective reference that I never dreamed that my hearers would let go of it; and the very last accusation I expected was that in speaking of ideas and their satisfactions, I was denying realities outside. My only wonder now is that critics should have found so silly a personage as I must have seemed in their eyes, worthy of explicit refutation.

The object, for me, is just as much one part of reality as

the idea is another part. The truth of the idea is one relation of it to the reality, just as its date and its place are other relations. All three relations *consist* of intervening parts of the universe which can in every particular case be assigned and catalogued, and which differ in every instance of truth, just as they differ with every date and place.

The pragmatist thesis, as Dr. Schiller and I hold it,—I prefer to let Professor Dewey speak for himself,—is that the relation called 'truth' is thus concretely *definable*. Ours is the only articulate attempt in the field to say positively what truth actually *consists of*. Our denouncers have literally nothing to oppose to it as an alternative. For them, when an idea is true, it *is* true, and there the matter terminates, the word 'true' being indefinable. The relation of the true idea to its object, being, as they think, unique, it can be expressed in terms of nothing else, and needs only to be named for any one to recognize and understand it. Moreover it is invariable and universal, the same in every single instance of truth, however diverse the ideas, the realities, and the other relations between them may be.

Our pragmatist view, on the contrary, is that the truth-relation is a definitely experienceable relation, and therefore describable as well as namable; that it is not unique in kind, and neither invariable nor universal. The relation to its object that makes an idea true in any given instance, is, we say, embodied in intermediate details of reality which lead towards the object, which vary in every instance, and which in every instance can be concretely traced. The chain of workings which an opinion sets up *is* the opinion's truth, falsehood, or irrelevancy, as the case may be. Every idea that a man has works some consequences in him, in the shape either of bodily actions or of other ideas. Through these consequences the man's relations to surrounding realities are modified. He is carried nearer to some of them and farther from others, and gets now the feeling that the idea has worked satisfactorily, now that it has not. The idea has put him into touch with something that fulfils its intent, or it has not.

This something is the *man's object*, primarily. Since the only realities we can talk about are such *objects-believed-in*, the pragmatist, whenever he says 'reality,' means in the first instance what may count for the man himself as a reality, what he believes at the moment to be such. Sometimes the reality is a concrete sensible presence. The idea, for example, may be that a certain door opens into a room where a glass of beer may be bought. If opening the door leads to the actual sight and taste of the beer, the man calls the idea true. Or his idea may be that of an abstract relation, say of that between the sides and the hypothenuse of a triangle, such a relation being, of course, a reality quite as much as a glass of beer is. If the thought of such a relation leads him to draw auxiliary lines and to compare the figures they make, he may at last, perceiving one equality after another, *see* the relation thought of, by a vision quite as particular and direct as was the taste of the beer. If he does so, he calls *that* idea, also, true. His idea has, in each case, brought him into closer touch with a reality felt at the moment to verify just that idea. Each reality verifies and validates its own idea exclusively; and in each case the verification consists in the satisfactorily-ending consequences, mental or physical, which the idea was able to set up. These 'workings' differ in every single instance, they never transcend experience, they consist of particulars, mental or sensible, and they admit of concrete description in every individual case. Pragmatists are unable to see what you can possibly *mean* by calling an idea true, unless you mean that between it as a *terminus a quo* in some one's mind and some particular reality as a *terminus ad quem*, such concrete workings do or may intervene. Their direction constitutes the idea's reference to that reality, their satisfactoriness constitutes its adaptation thereto, and the two things together constitute the 'truth' of the idea for its possessor. Without such intermediating portions of concretely real experience the pragmatist sees no materials out of which the adaptive relation called truth can be built up.

The anti-pragmatist view is that the workings are but evidences of the truth's previous inherent presence in the idea, and that you can wipe the very possibility of them out of existence and still leave the truth of the idea as solid as ever. But surely this is not a counter-theory of truth to ours. It is the renunciation of all articulate theory. It is but a claim to the right to call certain ideas true anyhow; and this is what I

meant above by saying that the anti-pragmatists offer us no
real alternative, and that our account is literally the only positive theory extant. What meaning, indeed, can an idea's truth
have save its power of adapting us either mentally or physically to a reality?

How comes it, then, that our critics so uniformly accuse us
of subjectivism, of denying the reality's existence? It comes, I
think, from the necessary predominance of subjective language in our analysis. However independent and ejective realities may be, we can talk about them, in framing our accounts
of truth, only as so many objects believed-in. But the process
of experience leads men so continually to supersede their
older objects by newer ones which they find it more satisfactory to believe in, that the notion of an *absolute* reality inevitably arises as a *grenzbegriff*, equivalent to that of an object
that shall never be superseded, and belief in which shall be
endgültig. Cognitively we thus live under a sort of rule of
three: as our private concepts represent the sense-objects to
which they lead us, these being public realities independent
of the individual, so these sense-realities may, in turn, represent realities of a hypersensible order, electrons, mind-stuff,
God, or what not, existing independently of all human thinkers. The notion of such final realities, knowledge of which
would be absolute truth, is an outgrowth of our cognitive
experience from which neither pragmatists nor anti-pragmatists escape. They form an inevitable regulative postulate in
every one's thinking. Our notion of them is the most abundantly suggested and satisfied of all our beliefs, the last to
suffer doubt. The difference is that our critics use this belief
as their sole paradigm, and treat any one who talks of human
realities as if he thought the notion of reality 'in itself' illegitimate. Meanwhile, reality-in-itself, so far as by them *talked of*,
is only a human object; they postulate it just as we postulate
it; and if we are subjectivists they are so no less. Realities in
themselves can be there *for* any one, whether pragmatist or
anti-pragmatist, only by being believed; they are believed only
by their notions appearing true; and their notions appear true
only because they work satisfactorily. Satisfactorily, moreover,
for the particular thinker's purpose. There is no idea which
is *the* true idea, of anything. Whose is *the* true idea of the

absolute? Or to take M. Hébert's example, what is *the* true idea of a picture which you possess? It is the idea that most satisfactorily meets your present interest. The interest may be in the picture's place, its age, its 'tone,' its subject, its dimensions, its authorship, its price, its merit, or what not. If its authorship by Corot have been doubted, what will satisfy the interest aroused in you at that moment will be to have your claim to own a Corot confirmed; but, if you have a normal human mind, merely calling it a Corot will not satisfy other demands of your mind at the same time. For *them* to be satisfied, what you learn of the picture must make smooth connection with what you know of the rest of the system of reality in which the actual Corot played his part. M. Hébert accuses us of holding that the proprietary satisfactions of themselves suffice to make the belief true, and that, so far as we are concerned, no actual Corot need ever have existed. Why we should be thus cut off from the more general and intellectual satisfactions, I know not; but whatever the satisfactions may be, intellectual or proprietary, they belong to the subjective side of the truth-relation. They found our beliefs; our beliefs are in realities; if no realities are there, the beliefs are false; but if realities are there, how they can ever be *known* without first being *believed*; or how *believed* except by our first having ideas of them that work satisfactorily, pragmatists find it impossible to imagine. They also find it impossible to imagine what makes the anti-pragmatists' dogmatic 'ipse dixit' assurance of reality more credible than the pragmatists' conviction based on concrete verifications. M. Hébert will probably agree to this, when put in this way, so I do not see our inferiority to him in the matter of *connaissance proprement dite*.

Some readers will say that, altho *I* may possibly believe in realities beyond our ideas, Dr. Schiller, at any rate, does not. This is a great misunderstanding, for Schiller's doctrine and mine are identical, only our expositions follow different directions. He starts from the subjective pole of the chain, the individual with his beliefs, as the more concrete and immediately given phenomenon. 'An individual claims his belief to be true,' Schiller says, 'but what does he mean by true?

and how does he establish the claim?' With these questions we embark on a psychological inquiry. To be true, it appears, means, *for that individual*, to work satisfactorily for him; and the working and the satisfaction, since they vary from case to case, admit of no universal description. What works is true and represents a reality, for the individual for whom it works. If he is infallible, the reality is 'really' there; if mistaken it is not there, or not there as he thinks it. We all believe, when our ideas work satisfactorily; but we don't yet know who of us is infallible; so that the problem of truth and that of error are *ebenbürtig* and arise out of the same situations. Schiller, remaining with the fallible individual, and treating only of reality-for-him, seems to many of his readers to ignore reality-in-itself altogether. But that is because he seeks only to tell us how truths are attained, not what the content of those truths, when attained, shall be. It may be that the truest of all beliefs shall be that in transsubjective realities. It certainly *seems* the truest, for no rival belief is as voluminously satisfactory, and it is probably Dr. Schiller's own belief; but he is not required, for his immediate purpose, to profess it. Still less is he obliged to assume it in advance as the basis of his discussion.

I, however, warned by the ways of critics, adopt different tactics. I start from the object-pole of the idea-reality chain and follow it in the opposite direction from Schiller's. Anticipating the results of the general truth-processes of mankind, I begin with the abstract notion of an objective reality. I postulate it, and ask on my own account, *I vouching for this reality*, what would make any one else's idea of it true for me as well as for him. But I find no different answer from that which Schiller gives. If the other man's idea leads him, not only to believe that the reality is there, but to use it as the reality's temporary substitute, by letting it evoke adaptive thoughts and acts similar to those which the reality itself would provoke, then it is true in the only intelligible sense, true through its particular consequences, and true for me as well as for the man.

My account is more of a logical definition; Schiller's is more of a psychological description. Both treat an absolutely identical matter of experience, only they traverse it in opposite ways.

Possibly these explanations may satisfy M. Hébert, whose little book, apart from the false accusation of subjectivism, gives a fairly instructive account of the pragmatist epistemology.

XIII

ABSTRACT CONCEPTS, such as elasticity, voluminousness, disconnectedness, are salient aspects of our concrete experiences which we find it useful to single out. Useful, because we are then reminded of other things that offer those same aspects; and, if the aspects carry consequences in those other things, we can return to our first things, expecting those same consequences to accrue.

To be helped to anticipate consequences is always a gain, and such being the help that abstract concepts give us, it is obvious that their use is fulfilled only when we get back again into concrete particulars by their means, bearing the consequences in our minds, and enriching our notion of the original objects therewithal.

Without abstract concepts to handle our perceptual particulars by, we are like men hopping on one foot. Using concepts along with the particulars, we become bipedal. We throw our concept forward, get a foothold on the consequence, hitch our line to this, and draw our percept up, travelling thus with a hop, skip and jump over the surface of life at a vastly rapider rate than if we merely waded through the thickness of the particulars as accident rained them down upon our heads. Animals have to do this, but men raise their heads higher and breathe freely in the upper conceptual air.

The enormous esteem professed by all philosophers for the conceptual form of consciousness is easy to understand. From Plato's time downwards it has been held to be our sole avenue to essential truth. Concepts are universal, changeless, pure; their relations are eternal; they are spiritual, while the concrete particulars which they enable us to handle are corrupted by the flesh. They are precious in themselves, then, apart from their original use, and confer new dignity upon our life.

One can find no fault with this way of feeling about concepts so long as their original function does not get swallowed up in the admiration and lost. That function is of course to enlarge mentally our momentary experiences by *adding* to them the consequences conceived; but unfortunately, that function is not only too often forgotten by philosophers in their reasonings, but is often converted into its exact opposite, and made a means of diminishing the original experience by *denying* (implicitly or explicitly) all its features save the one specially abstracted to conceive it by.

This itself is a highly abstract way of stating my complaint, and it needs to be redeemed from obscurity by showing instances of what is meant. Some beliefs very dear to my own heart have been conceived in this viciously abstract way by critics. One is the 'will to believe,' so called; another is the indeterminism of certain futures; a third is the notion that truth may vary with the standpoint of the man who holds it. I believe that the perverse abuse of the abstracting function has led critics to employ false arguments against these doctrines, and often has led their readers too to false conclusions. I should like to try to save the situation, if possible, by a few counter-critical remarks.

Let me give the name of 'vicious abstractionism' to a way of using concepts which may be thus described: We conceive a concrete situation by singling out some salient or important feature in it, and classing it under that; then, instead of adding to its previous characters all the positive consequences which the new way of conceiving it may bring, we proceed to use our concept privatively; reducing the originally rich phenomenon to the naked suggestions of that name abstractly taken, treating it as a case of 'nothing but' that concept, and acting as if all the other characters from out of which the concept is abstracted were expunged.[1] Abstraction, functioning in this way, becomes a means of arrest far more than a means of advance in thought. It mutilates things; it creates difficulties and finds impossibilities; and more than half the trouble that metaphysicians and logicians give themselves over the paradoxes and dialectic puzzles of the universe may, I am convinced, be traced to this relatively simple source. *The viciously privative employment of abstract characters and class*

[1] Let not the reader confound the fallacy here described with legitimately negative inferences such as those drawn in the mood 'celarent' of the logic-books.

names is, I am persuaded, one of the great original sins of the rationalistic mind.

To proceed immediately to concrete examples, cast a glance at the belief in 'free will,' demolished with such specious persuasiveness recently by the skilful hand of Professor Fullerton.[1] When a common man says that his will is free, what does he mean? He means that there are situations of bifurcation inside of his life in which two futures seem to him equally possible, for both have their roots equally planted in his present and his past. Either, if realized, will grow out of his previous motives, character and circumstances, and will continue uninterruptedly the pulsations of his personal life. But sometimes both at once are incompatible with physical nature, and then it seems to the naïve observer as if he made a choice between them *now*, and that the question of which future is to be, instead of having been decided at the foundation of the world, were decided afresh at every passing moment in which fact seems livingly to grow, and possibility seems, in turning itself towards one act, to exclude all others.

He who takes things at their face-value here may indeed be deceived. He may far too often mistake his private ignorance of what is predetermined for a real indetermination of what is to be. Yet, however imaginary it may be, his picture of the situation offers no appearance of breach between the past and future. A train is the same train, its passengers are the same passengers, its momentum is the same momentum, no matter which way the switch which fixes its direction is placed. For the indeterminist there is at all times enough past for all the different futures in sight, and more besides, to find their reasons in it, and whichever future comes will slide out of that past as easily as the train slides by the switch. The world, in short, is just as *continuous with itself* for the believers in free will as for the rigorous determinists, only the latter are unable to believe in points of bifurcation as spots of really indifferent equilibrium or as containing shunts which there—and there only, *not before*—direct existing motions without altering their amount.

[1] *Popular Science Monthly*, N. Y., vols. lviii and lix.

Were there such spots of indifference, the rigorous deter-minists think, the future and the past would be separated ab-solutely, for, *abstractly taken, the word 'indifferent' suggests disconnection solely*. Whatever is indifferent is in so far forth unrelated and detached. Take the term thus strictly, and you see, they tell us, that if any spot of indifference is found upon the broad highway between the past and the future, then *no* connection of any sort whatever, no continuous momentum, no identical passenger, no common aim or agent, can be found on both sides of the shunt or switch which there is moved. The place is an impassable chasm.

Mr. Fullerton writes—the italics are mine—as follows:—

'In so far as my action is free, what I have been, what I am, what I have always done or striven to do, what I most ear-nestly wish or resolve to do at the present moment—these things can have *no more to do with its future realization than if they had no existence*. . . . The possibility is a hideous one; and surely even the most ardent free-willist will, when he con-templates it frankly, excuse me for hoping that if I am free I am at least not very free, and that I may reasonably expect to find *some* degree of consistency in my life and actions. . . . Suppose that I have given a dollar to a blind beggar. Can *I*, if it is really an act of free-will, be properly said to have given the money? Was it given because I was a man of tender heart, etc., etc.? . . . What has all this to do with acts of free-will? If they are free, they must not be conditioned by antecedent circumstances of *any* sort, by the misery of the beggar, by the pity in the heart of the passer-by. They must be causeless, not determined. They must drop from a clear sky out of the void, for just in so far as they can be accounted for, they are not free.'[1]

Heaven forbid that I should get entangled here in a contro-versy about the rights and wrongs of the free-will question at large, for I am only trying to illustrate vicious abstractionism by the conduct of some of the doctrine's assailants. The moments of bifurcation, as the indeterminist seems to him-self to experience them, are moments both of re-direction and of continuation. But because in the 'either—or' of the

[1] *Loc. cit.*, vol. lviii, pp. 189, 188.

re-direction we hesitate, the determinist abstracts this little element of discontinuity from the superabundant continuities of the experience, and cancels in its behalf all the connective characters with which the latter is filled. Choice, for him, means henceforward *dis*connection pure and simple, something undetermined in advance *in any respect whatever*, and a life of choices must be a raving chaos, at no two moments of which could we be treated as one and the same man. If Nero were 'free' at the moment of ordering his mother's murder, Mr. McTaggart[1] assures us that no one would have the right at any other moment to call him a bad man, for he would then be an absolutely other Nero.

A polemic author ought not merely to destroy his victim. He ought to try a bit to make him feel his error—perhaps not enough to convert him, but enough to give him a bad conscience and to weaken the energy of his defence. These violent caricatures of men's beliefs arouse only contempt for the incapacity of their authors to see the situations out of which the problems grow. To treat the negative character of one abstracted element as annulling all the positive features with which it coexists, is no way to change any actual indeterminist's way of looking on the matter, tho it may make the gallery applaud.

Turn now to some criticisms of the 'will to believe,' as another example of the vicious way in which abstraction is currently employed. The right to believe in things for the truth of which complete objective proof is yet lacking is defended by those who apprehend certain human situations in their concreteness. In those situations the mind has alternatives before it so vast that the full evidence for either branch is missing, and yet so significant that simply to wait for proof, and to doubt while waiting, might often in practical respects be the same thing as weighing down the negative side. Is life worth while at all? Is there any general meaning in all this cosmic weather? Is anything being permanently bought by all this suffering? Is there perhaps a transmundane experience in Being, something corresponding to a 'fourth dimension,'

[1] *Some Dogmas of Religion*, p. 179.

which, if we had access to it, might patch up some of this world's *zerrissenheit* and make things look more rational than they at first appear? Is there a superhuman consciousness of which our minds are parts, and from which inspiration and help may come? Such are the questions in which the right to take sides practically for yes or no is affirmed by some of us, while others hold that this is methodologically inadmissible, and summon us to die professing ignorance and proclaiming the duty of every one to refuse to believe.

I say nothing of the personal inconsistency of some of these critics, whose printed works furnish exquisite illustrations of the will to believe, in spite of their denunciations of it as a phrase and as a recommended thing. Mr. McTaggart, whom I will once more take as an example, is sure that 'reality is rational and righteous' and 'destined *sub specie temporis* to become perfectly good'; and his calling this belief a result of necessary logic has surely never deceived any reader as to its real genesis in the gifted author's mind. Mankind is made on too uniform a pattern for any of us to escape successfully from acts of faith. We have a lively vision of what a certain view of the universe would mean for us. We kindle or we shudder at the thought, and our feeling runs through our whole logical nature and animates its workings. It *can't* be that, we feel; it *must* be this. It must be what it *ought* to be, and it *ought* to be this; and then we seek for every reason, good or bad, to make this which so deeply ought to be, seem objectively the probable thing. We show the arguments against it to be insufficient, so that it *may* be true; we represent its appeal to be to our whole nature's loyalty and not to any emaciated faculty of syllogistic proof. We reinforce it by remembering the enlargement of our world by music, by thinking of the promises of sunsets and the impulses from vernal woods. And the essence of the whole experience, when the individual swept through it says finally 'I believe,' is the intense concreteness of his vision, the individuality of the hypothesis before him, and the complexity of the various concrete motives and perceptions that issue in his final state.

But see now how the abstractionist treats this rich and intricate vision that a certain state of things must be true.

He accuses the believer of reasoning by the following syllogism:—

All good desires must be fulfilled;
The desire to believe this proposition is a good desire;
Ergo, this proposition must be believed.

He substitutes this abstraction for the concrete state of mind of the believer, pins the naked absurdity of it upon him, and easily proves that any one who defends him must be the greatest fool on earth. As if any real believer ever thought in this preposterous way, or as if any defender of the legitimacy of men's concrete ways of concluding ever used the abstract and general premise, 'All desires must be fulfilled'! Nevertheless, Mr. McTaggart solemnly and laboriously refutes the syllogism in sections 47 to 57 of the above-cited book. He shows that there is no fixed link in the dictionary between the abstract concepts 'desire,' 'goodness' and 'reality'; and he ignores all the links which in the single concrete case the believer feels and perceives to be there! He adds:—

'When the reality of a thing is uncertain, the argument encourages us to suppose that our approval of a thing can determine its reality. And when this unhallowed link has once been established, retribution overtakes us. For when the reality of the thing is independently certain, we [then] have to admit that the reality of the thing should determine our approval of that thing. I find it difficult to imagine a more degraded position.'

One here feels tempted to quote ironically Hegel's famous equation of the real with the rational to his english disciple, who ends his chapter with the heroic words:—

'For those who do not pray, there remains the resolve that, so far as their strength may permit, neither the pains of death nor the pains of life shall drive them to any comfort in that which they hold to be false, or drive them from any comfort [discomfort?] in that which they hold to be true.'

How can so ingenious-minded a writer fail to see how far over the heads of the enemy all his arrows pass? When Mr. McTaggart himself believes that the universe is run by the dialectic energy of the absolute idea, his insistent desire to have a world of that sort is felt by him to be no chance example of desire in general, but an altogether peculiar *in-*

sight-giving passion to which, in this if in no other instance, he would be *stupid* not to yield. He obeys its concrete singularity, not the bare abstract feature in it of being a 'desire.' His situation is as particular as that of an actress who resolves that it is best for her to marry and leave the stage, of a priest who becomes secular, of a politician who abandons public life. What sensible man would seek to refute the concrete decisions of such persons by tracing them to abstract premises, such as that 'all actresses must marry,' 'all clergymen must be laymen,' 'all politicians should resign their posts'? Yet this type of refutation, absolutely unavailing though it be for purposes of conversion, is spread by Mr. McTaggart through many pages of his book. For the aboundingness of our real reasons he substitutes one narrow point. For men's real probabilities he gives a skeletonized abstraction which no man was ever tempted to believe.

The abstraction in my next example is less simple, but is quite as flimsy as a weapon of attack. Empiricists think that truth in general is distilled from single men's beliefs; and the so-called pragmatists 'go them one better' by trying to define what it consists in when it comes. It consists, I have elsewhere said, in such a working on the part of the beliefs as may bring the man into satisfactory relations with objects to which these latter point. The working is of course a concrete working in the actual experience of human beings, among their ideas, feelings, perceptions, beliefs and acts, as well as among the physical things of their environment, and the relations must be understood as being possible as well as actual. In the chapter on truth of my book *Pragmatism* I have taken pains to defend energetically this view. Strange indeed have been the misconceptions of it by its enemies, and many have these latter been. Among the most formidable-sounding onslaughts on the attempt to introduce some concreteness into our notion of what the truth of an idea may mean, is one that has been raised in many quarters to the effect that to make truth grow in any way out of human opinion is but to reproduce that protagorean doctrine that the individual man is 'the measure of all things,' which Plato in his immortal dialogue, the Thæatetus, is unanimously said to have laid away so comfortably in its grave two thousand years ago. The two cleverest brandishers of this objection to make truth concrete, Professors Rickert and Münsterberg, write in German,[1] and 'relativismus' is the name they give to the heresy which they endeavor to uproot.

The first step in their campaign against 'relativismus' is entirely in the air. They accuse relativists—and we pragmatists are typical relativists—of being debarred by their self-adopted principles, not only from the privilege which rationalist philosophers enjoy, of believing that these principles of their own are truth impersonal and absolute, but even of framing the abstract notion of such a truth, *in the pragmatic sense, of an ideal opinion in which all men might agree, and which no man should ever wish to change.* Both charges fall wide of their mark. I myself, as a pragmatist, believe in my own account of truth as firmly as any rationalist can possibly believe in his. And I believe in it for the very reason that I *have* the idea of truth which my learned adversaries contend that no pragmatist can frame. I expect, namely, that the more fully men discuss and test my account, the more they will agree that it *fits*, and the less will they desire a change. I may of course be premature in this confidence, and the glory of being truth final and absolute may fall upon some later revision and correction of my scheme, which latter will then be judged untrue in just the measure in which it departs from that finally satisfactory formulation. To admit, as we pragmatists do, that we are liable to correction (even tho we may not expect it) *involves* the use on our part of an ideal standard. Rationalists themselves are, as individuals, sometimes sceptical enough to admit the abstract possibility of their own present opinions being corrigible and revisable to some degree, so the fact that the mere *notion* of an absolute standard should seem to them so important a thing to claim for themselves and to deny to us is not easy to explain. If, along with the notion of the standard, they could also claim its exclusive warrant for their own fulminations now, it would be important to them indeed. But absolutists like Rickert freely admit the sterility of the notion, even in their own hands. Truth is what we *ought* to believe, they say, even tho no man ever did or shall believe

---

[1] Münsterberg's book has just appeared in an english version: *The Eternal Values*, Boston, 1909.

it, and even tho we have no way of getting at it save by the usual empirical processes of testing our opinions by one another and by facts. Pragmatically, then, this part of the dispute is idle. No relativist who ever actually walked the earth[1] has denied the regulative character in his own thinking of the notion of absolute truth. What is challenged by relativists is the pretence on any one's part to have found for certain at any given moment what the shape of that truth is. Since the better absolutists agree in this, admitting that the proposition 'There *is* absolute truth' is the only absolute truth of which we can be sure,[2] further debate is practically unimportant, so we may pass to their next charge.

It is in this charge that the vicious abstractionism becomes most apparent. The anti-pragmatist, in postulating absolute truth, refuses to give any account of what the words may mean. For him they form a self-explanatory term. The pragmatist, on the contrary, articulately defines their meaning. Truth absolute, he says, means an ideal set of formulations towards which all opinions may in the long run of experience be expected to converge. In this definition of absolute truth he not only postulates that there is a tendency to such convergence of opinions, to such ultimate consensus, but he postulates the other factors of his definition equally, borrowing them by anticipation from the true conclusions expected to be reached. He postulates the existence of opinions, he postulates the experience that will sift them, and the consistency which that experience will show. He justifies himself in these assumptions by saying that they are not postulates in the strict

---

[1] Of course the bugaboo creature called 'the sceptic' in the logic-books, who dogmatically makes the statement that no statement, not even the one he now makes, is true, is a mere mechanical toy-target for the rationalist shooting-gallery—hit him and he turns a summersault—yet he is the only sort of relativist whom my colleagues appear able to imagine to exist.

[2] Compare Rickert's *Gegenstand der Erkentniss*, pp. 137, 138. Münsterberg's version of this first truth is that 'Es gibt eine Welt,'—see his *Philosophie der Werte*, pp. 38 and 74. And, after all, both these philosophers confess in the end that the primal truth of which they consider our supposed denial so irrational is not properly an insight at all, but a dogma adopted by the will which any one who turns his back on duty may disregard! But if it all reverts to 'the will to believe,' pragmatists have that privilege as well as their critics.

sense but simple inductions from the past extended to the future by analogy; and he insists that human opinion has already reached a pretty stable equilibrium regarding them, and that if its future development fails to alter them, the definition itself, with all its terms included, will be part of the very absolute truth which it defines. The hypothesis will, in short, have worked successfully all round the circle and proved self-corroborative, and the circle will be closed.

The anti-pragmatist, however, immediately falls foul of the word 'opinion' here, abstracts it from the universe of life, and uses it as a bare dictionary-substantive, to deny the rest of the assumptions which it coexists withal. The dictionary says that an opinion is 'what some one thinks or believes.' This definition leaves every one's opinion free to be autogenous, or unrelated either to what any one else may think or to what the truth may be. Therefore, continue our abstractionists, we must conceive it *as essentially thus unrelated*, so that even were a billion men to sport the same opinion, and only one man to differ, we could admit no collateral circumstances which might presumptively make it more probable that he, not they, should be wrong. Truth, they say, follows not the counting of noses, nor is it only another name for a majority vote. It is a relation that antedates experience, between our opinions and an independent something which the pragmatist account ignores, a relation which, tho the opinions of individuals should to all eternity deny it, would still remain to qualify them as false. To talk of opinions without referring to this independent something, the anti-pragmatist assures us, is to play Hamlet with Hamlet's part left out.

But when the pragmatist speaks of opinions, does he mean any such insulated and unmotivated abstractions as are here supposed? Of course not, he means men's opinions in the flesh, as they have really formed themselves, opinions surrounded by their grounds and the influences they obey and exert, and along with the whole environment of social communication of which they are a part and out of which they take their rise. Moreover the 'experience' which the pragmatic definition postulates *is* the independent something which the anti-pragmatist accuses him of ignoring. Already have men grown unanimous in the opinion that such experience is 'of' an independent reality, the existence of which all opinions must acknowledge, in order to be true. Already do they agree that in the long run it is useless to resist experience's pressure; that the more of it a man has, the better position he stands in, in respect of truth; that some men, having had more experience, are therefore better authorities than others; that some are also wiser by nature and better able to interpret the experience they have had; that it is one part of such wisdom to compare notes, discuss, and follow the opinion of our betters; and that the more systematically and thoroughly such comparison and weighing of opinions is pursued, the truer the opinions that survive are likely to be. *When the pragmatist talks of opinions, it is opinions as they thus concretely and livingly and interactingly and correlatively exist that he has in mind;* and when the anti-pragmatist tries to floor him because the word 'opinion' can also be taken abstractly and as if it had no environment, he simply ignores the soil out of which the whole discussion grows. His weapons cut the air and strike no blow. No one gets wounded in the war against caricatures of belief and skeletons of opinion of which the German onslaughts upon 'relativismus' consists. Refuse to use the word 'opinion' abstractly, keep it in its real environment, and the withers of pragmatism remain unwrung.

That men do exist who are 'opinionated,' in the sense that their opinions are self-willed, is unfortunately a fact that must be admitted, no matter what one's notion of truth in general may be. But that this fact should make it impossible for truth to form itself authentically out of the life of opinion is what no critic has yet proved. Truth may well consist of certain opinions, and does indeed consist of nothing but opinions, tho not every opinion need be true. No pragmatist needs to *dogmatize* about the consensus of opinion in the future being right—he need only *postulate* that it will probably contain more of truth than any one's opinion now.

XIV

M R. BERTRAND RUSSELL'S article entitled 'Transatlantic Truth,'[1] has all the clearness, dialectic subtlety, and wit which one expects from his pen, but it entirely fails to hit the right point of view for apprehending our position. When, for instance, we say that a true proposition is one the consequences of believing which are good, he assumes us to mean that any one who believes a proposition to be true must first have made out clearly that its consequences *are* good, and that his belief must primarily be in that fact,—an obvious absurdity, for that fact is the deliverance of a new proposition, quite different from the first one and is, more-over, a fact usually very hard to verify, it being 'far easier,' as Mr. Russell justly says, 'to settle the plain question of fact: "Have popes always been infallible?" than to settle the question whether the effects of thinking them infallible are on the whole good.'

We affirm nothing as silly as Mr. Russell supposes. Good consequences are not proposed by us merely as a sure sign, mark, or criterion, by which truth's presence is habitually as-certained, tho they may indeed serve on occasion as such a sign; they are proposed rather as the lurking *motive* inside of every truth-claim, whether the 'trower' be conscious of such motive, or whether he obey it blindly. They are proposed as the *causa existendi* of our beliefs, not as their logical cue or premise, and still less as their objective deliverance or content. They assign the only intelligible practical *meaning* to that dif-ference in our beliefs which our habit of calling them true or false comports.

No truth-claimer except the pragmatist himself need ever be aware of the part played in his own mind by consequences, and he himself is aware of it only abstractly and in general, and may at any moment be quite oblivious of it with respect to his own beliefs.

Mr. Russell next joins the army of those who inform their

[1] In the *Albany Review* for January, 1908.

readers that according to the pragmatist definition of the word 'truth' the belief that A exists may be 'true,' even when A does *not* exist. This is the usual slander, repeated to satiety by our critics. They forget that in any concrete account of what is denoted by 'truth' in human life, the word can only be used relatively to some particular trower. Thus, I may hold it true that Shakespere wrote the plays that bear his name, and may express my opinion to a critic. If the critic be both a pragmatist and a baconian, he will in his capacity of pragmatist see plainly that the workings of my opinion, I being what I am, make it perfectly true for me, while in his capacity of baconian he still believes that Shakespere never wrote the plays in question. But most anti-pragmatist critics take the word 'truth' as something absolute, and easily play on their reader's readiness to treat his own truths as the absolute ones. If the reader whom they address believes that A does not exist, while we pragmatists show that those for whom the belief that it exists works satisfactorily will always call it true, he easily sneers at the naïveté of our contention, for is not then the belief in question 'true,' tho what it declares as fact has, as the reader so well knows, no existence? Mr. Russell speaks of our statement as an 'attempt to get rid of fact' and naturally enough considers it 'a failure' (p. 410). 'The old notion of truth reappears,' he adds—that notion being, of course, that when a belief is true, its object does exist.

It is, of course, *bound* to exist, on sound pragmatic principles. Concepts signify consequences. How is the world made different for me by my conceiving an opinion of mine under the concept 'true'? First, an object must be findable there (or sure signs of such an object must be found) which shall agree with the opinion. Second, such an opinion must not be contradicted by anything else of which I am aware. But in spite of the obvious pragmatist requirement that when I have said truly that something exists, it *shall* exist, the slander which Mr. Russell repeats has gained the widest currency.

Mr. Russell himself is far too witty and athletic a ratiocinator simply to repeat the slander dogmatically. Being nothing if not mathematical and logical, he must prove the accusation *secundum artem*, and convict us not so much of error as of absurdity. I have sincerely tried to follow the windings of his mind in this procedure, but for the life of me I can only see in it another example of what I have called (above, p. 951) vicious abstractionism. The abstract world of mathematics and pure logic is so native to Mr. Russell that he thinks that we describers of the functions of concrete fact must also mean fixed mathematical terms and functions. A mathematical term, as *a*, *b*, *c*, *x*, *y*, sin., log., is self-sufficient, and terms of this sort, once equated, can be substituted for one another in endless series without error. Mr. Russell, and also Mr. Hawtrey, of whom I shall speak presently, seem to think that in our mouth also such terms as 'meaning,' 'truth,' 'belief,' 'object,' 'definition,' are self-sufficients with no context of varying relation that might be further asked about. What a word means is expressed by its definition, is n't it? The definition claims to be exact and adequate, does n't it? Then it can be substituted for the word—since the two are identical—can't it? Then two words with the same definition can be substituted for one another, n'est-ce pas? Likewise two definitions of the same word, *nicht wahr*, etc., etc., till it will be indeed strange if you can't convict some one of self-contradiction and absurdity.

The particular application of this rigoristic treatment to my own little account of truth as working seems to be something like what follows. I say 'working' is what the 'truth' of our ideas means, and call it a definition. But since meanings and things meant, definitions and things defined, are equivalent and interchangeable, and nothing extraneous to its definition can be meant when a term is used, it follows that whoso calls an idea true, and means by that word that it works, cannot mean anything else, can believe nothing but that it does work, and in particular can neither imply nor allow anything about its object or deliverance. 'According to the pragmatists,' Mr. Russell writes, 'to say "it is true that other people exist" means "it is useful to believe that other people exist." But if so, then these two phrases are merely different words for the same proposition; therefore when I believe the one I believe the other' (p. 400). [Logic, I may say in passing, would seem to require Mr. Russell to believe them both at once, but he ignores this consequence, and considers that 'other people exist' and 'it is useful to believe that they do *even if they don't,*' must be identical and therefore substitutable propositions in the pragmatist mouth.]

But may not real terms, I now ask, have accidents not expressed in their definitions? and when a real value is finally substituted for the result of an algebraic series of substituted definitions, do not all these accidents creep back? Beliefs have their objective 'content' or 'deliverance' as well as their truth, and truth has its implications as well as its workings. If any one believe that other men exist, it is both a content of his belief and an implication of its truth, that they should exist in fact. Mr. Russell's logic would seem to exclude, 'by definition,' all such accidents as contents, implications, and associates, and would represent us as translating all belief into a sort of belief in pragmatism itself—of all things! If I say that a speech is eloquent, and explain 'eloquent' as meaning the power to work in certain ways upon the audience; or if I say a book is original, and define 'original' to mean differing from other books, Russell's logic, if I follow it at all, would seem to doom me to agreeing that the speech is about eloquence, and the book about other books. When I call a belief true, and define its truth to mean its workings, I certainly do not mean that the belief is a belief *about* the workings. It is a belief about the object, and I who talk about the workings am a different subject, with a different universe of discourse, from that of the believer of whose concrete thinking I profess to give an account.

The social proposition 'other men exist' and the pragmatist proposition 'it is expedient to believe that other men exist' come from different universes of discourse. One can believe the second without being logically compelled to believe the first; one can believe the first without having ever heard of the second; or one can believe them both. The first expresses the object of a belief, the second tells of one condition of the belief's power to maintain itself. There is no identity of any kind, save the term 'other men' which they contain in common, in the two propositions; and to treat them as mutually substitutable, or to insist that *we* shall do so, is to give up dealing with realities altogether.

Mr. Ralph Hawtrey, who seems also to serve under the banner of abstractionist logic, convicts us pragmatists of absurdity by arguments similar to Mr. Russell's.[1]

As a favor to us and for the sake of the argument, he abandons the word 'true' to our fury, allowing it to mean nothing but the fact that certain beliefs are expedient; and he uses the word 'correctness' (as Mr. Pratt uses the word 'trueness') to designate a fact, not about the belief, but about the belief's object, namely that it is as the belief declares it. 'When therefore,' he writes, 'I say it is correct to say that Cæsar is dead, I mean "Cæsar is dead." This must be regarded as the definition of correctness.' And Mr. Hawtrey then goes on to demolish me by the conflict of the definitions. What is 'true' for the pragmatist cannot be what is 'correct,' he says, 'for the definitions are not logically interchangeable; or if we interchange them, we reach the tautology: "Cæsar is dead" means "it is expedient to believe that Cæsar is dead." But what is it expedient to believe? Why, "that Cæsar is dead." ' A precious definition indeed of 'Cæsar is dead.'

Mr. Hawtrey's conclusion would seem to be that the pragmatic definition of the truth of a belief in no way implies—what?—that the believer shall believe in his own belief's deliverance?—or that the pragmatist who is talking about him shall believe in that deliverance? The two cases are quite different. For the believer, Cæsar must of course really exist; for the pragmatist critic he need not, for the pragmatic deliverance belongs, as I have just said, to another universe of discourse altogether. When one argues by substituting definition for definition, one needs to stay in the same universe.

The great shifting of universes in this discussion occurs when we carry the word 'truth' from the subjective into the objective realm, applying it sometimes to a property of opinions, sometimes to the facts which the opinions assert. A number of writers, as Mr. Russell himself, Mr. G. E. Moore, and others, favor the unlucky word 'proposition,' which seems expressly invented to foster this confusion, for they

[1] See *The New Quarterly*, for March, 1908.

speak of truth as a property of 'propositions.' But in naming propositions it is almost impossible not to use the word 'that.' *That* Cæsar is dead, *that* virtue is its own reward, are propositions.

I do not say that for certain logical purposes it may not be useful to treat propositions as absolute entities, with truth or falsehood inside of them respectively, or to make of a complex like 'that-Cæsar-is-dead' a single term and call it a 'truth.' But the 'that' here has the extremely convenient ambiguity for those who wish to make trouble for us pragmatists, that sometimes it means the *fact* that, and sometimes the *belief* that, Cæsar is no longer living. When I then call the belief true, I am told that the truth means the fact; when I claim the fact also, I am told that my definition has excluded the fact, being a definition only of a certain peculiarity in the belief—so that in the end I have no truth to talk about left in my possession.

The only remedy for this intolerable ambiguity is, it seems to me, to stick to terms consistently. 'Reality,' 'idea' or 'belief,' and the 'truth of the idea or belief,' which are the terms I have consistently held to, seem to be free from all objection.

Whoever takes terms abstracted from all their natural settings, identifies them with definitions, and treats the latter *more algebraico*, not only risks mixing universes, but risks fallacies which the man in the street easily detects. To prove 'by definition' that the statement 'Cæsar exists' is identical with a statement about 'expediency' because the one statement is 'true' and the other is about 'true statements,' is like proving that an omnibus is a boat because both are vehicles. A horse may be defined as a beast that walks on the nails of his middle digits. Whenever we see a horse we see such a beast, just as whenever we believe a 'truth' we believe something expedient. Messrs. Russell and Hawtrey, if they followed their anti-pragmatist logic, would have to say here that we see *that it is* such a beast, a fact which notoriously no one sees who is not a comparative anatomist.

It almost reconciles one to being no logician that one thereby escapes so much abstractionism. Abstractionism of the worst sort dogs Mr. Russell in his own trials to tell positively what the word 'truth' means. In the third of his articles

on Meinong, in *Mind*, vol. xiii, p. 509 (1904), he attempts
this feat by limiting the discussion to three terms only, a
proposition, its content, and an object, abstracting from the
whole context of associated realities in which such terms are
found in every case of actual knowing. He puts the terms,
thus taken in a vacuum, and made into bare logical entities,
through every possible permutation and combination, tortures them on the rack until nothing is left of them, and after
all this logical gymnastic, comes out with the following por-
tentous conclusion as what he believes to be 'the correct view:
that there is no problem at all in truth and falsehood, that
some propositions are true and some false, just as some roses
are red and some white, that belief is a certain attitude towards propositions, which is called knowledge when they are
true, error when they are false'—and he seems to think that
when once this insight is reached the question may be considered closed forever!

In spite of my admiration of Mr. Russell's analytic powers,
I wish, after reading such an article, that pragmatism, even
had it no other function, might result in making him and
other similarly gifted men ashamed of having used such powers in such abstraction from reality. Pragmatism saves us at
any rate from such diseased abstractionism as those pages
show.

P. S. Since the foregoing rejoinder was written an article on
Pragmatism which I believe to be by Mr. Russell has appeared in the *Edinburgh Review* for April, 1909. As far as his
discussion of the truth-problem goes, altho he has evidently
taken great pains to be fair, it seems to me that he has in no
essential respect improved upon his former arguments. I will
therefore add nothing further, but simply refer readers who
may be curious to pp. 272–280 of the said article.

XV

AFTER CORRECTING the proofs of all that precedes I imagine a residual state of mind on the part of my reader which may still keep him unconvinced, and which it may be my duty to try at least to dispel. I can perhaps be briefer if I put what I have to say in dialogue form. Let then the anti-pragmatist begin: —

Anti-Pragmatist: — You say that the truth of an idea is constituted by its workings. Now suppose a certain state of facts, facts for example of antediluvian planetary history, concerning which the question may be asked: 'Shall the truth about them ever be known?' And suppose (leaving the hypothesis of an omniscient absolute out of the account) that we assume that the truth is never to be known. I ask you now, brother pragmatist, whether according to you there can be said to be any truth at all about such a state of facts. Is there a truth, or is there not a truth, in cases where at any rate it never comes to be known?

Pragmatist: — Why do you ask me such a question?

Anti-Prag.: — Because I think it puts you in a bad dilemma.

Prag.: — How so?

Anti-Prag.: — Why, because if on the one hand you elect to say that there is a truth, you thereby surrender your whole pragmatist theory. According to that theory, truth requires ideas and workings to constitute it; but in the present instance there is supposed to be no knower, and consequently neither ideas nor workings can exist. What then remains for you to make your truth of?

Prag.: — Do you wish, like so many of my enemies, to force me to make the truth out of the reality itself? I cannot: the truth is something known, thought or said about the reality, and consequently numerically additional to it. But probably your intent is something different; so before I say which horn of your dilemma I choose, I ask you to let me hear what the other horn may be.

Anti-Prag.: — The other horn is this, that if you elect to say that there is *no* truth under the conditions assumed, because there are no ideas or workings, then you fly in the face of common sense. Does n't common sense believe that every state of facts must in the nature of things be truly statable in some kind of a proposition, even tho in point of fact the proposition should never be propounded by a living soul?

Prag.: — Unquestionably common sense believes this, and so do I. There have been innumerable events in the history of our planet of which nobody ever has been or ever will be able to give an account, yet of which it can already be said abstractly that only one sort of possible account can ever be true. The truth about any such event is thus already generically predetermined by the event's nature; and one may accordingly say with a perfectly good conscience that it virtually pre-exists. Common sense is thus right in its instinctive contention.

Anti-Prag.: — Is this then the horn of the dilemma which you stand for? Do you say that there is a truth even in cases where it shall never be known?

Prag.: — Indeed I do, provided you let me hold consistently to my own conception of truth, and do not ask me to abandon it for something which I find impossible to comprehend. — You also believe, do you not, that there is a truth, even in cases where it never shall be known?

Anti-Prag.: — I do indeed believe so.

Prag.: — Pray then inform me in what, according to you, this truth regarding the unknown consists.

Anti-Prag.: — Consists? — pray what do you mean by 'consists'? It consists in nothing but itself, or more properly speaking it has neither consistence nor existence, it obtains, it *holds.*

Prag.: — Well, what relation does it bear to the reality of which it holds?

Anti-Prag.: — How do you mean, 'what relation'? It holds *of* it, of course; it knows it, it represents it.

Prag.: — Who knows it? What represents it?

Anti-Prag.: — The truth does; the truth knows it; or rather not exactly that, but any one knows it who *possesses* the truth. Any true idea of the reality *represents* the truth concerning it.

Prag.: — But I thought that we had agreed that no knower of it, nor any idea representing it was to be supposed.

Anti-Prag.:—Sure enough!

Prag.:—Then I beg you again to tell me in what this truth consists, all by itself, this *tertium quid* intermediate between the facts *per se*, on the one hand, and all knowledge of them, actual or potential, on the other. What is the shape of it in this third estate? Of what stuff, mental, physical, or 'epistemological,' is it built? What metaphysical region of reality does it inhabit?

Anti-Prag.:—What absurd questions! Is n't it enough to say that it *is true* that the facts are so-and-so, and false that they are otherwise?

Prag.:—'It' is true that the facts are so-and-so—I won't yield to the temptation of asking you *what* is true; but I do ask you whether your phrase that 'it is true that' the facts are so-and-so really means anything really additional to the bare *being* so-and-so of the facts themselves.

Anti-Prag.:—It seems to mean more than the bare being of the facts. It is a sort of mental equivalent for them, their epistemological function, their value in noetic terms.

Prag.:—A sort of spiritual double or ghost of them, apparently! If so, may I ask you *where* this truth is found.

Anti-Prag.:—Where? where? There is no 'where'—it simply obtains, absolutely obtains.

Prag.:—Not in any one's mind?

Anti-Prag.:—No, for we agreed that no actual knower of the truth should be assumed.

Prag.:—No actual knower, I agree. But are you sure that no notion of a potential or ideal knower has anything to do with forming this strangely elusive idea of the truth of the facts in your mind?

Anti-Prag.:—Of course if there be a truth concerning the facts, that truth is what the ideal knower would know. To that extent you can't keep the notion of it and the notion of him separate. But it is not him first and then it; it is it first and then him, in my opinion.

Prag.:—But you still leave me terribly puzzled as to the status of this so-called truth, hanging as it does between earth and heaven, between reality and knowledge, grounded in the reality, yet numerically additional to it, and at the same time antecedent to any knower's opinion and entirely independent thereof. Is it as independent of the knower as you suppose? It looks to me terribly dubious, as if it might be only another name for a potential as distinguished from an actual knowledge of the reality. Is n't your truth, after all, simply what any successful knower *would* have to know *in case he existed*? And in a universe where no knowers were even conceivable would any truth about the facts there as something numerically distinguishable from the facts themselves, find a place to exist in? To me such truth would not only be non-existent, it would be unimaginable, inconceivable.

Anti-Prag.:—But I thought you said a while ago that there *is* a truth of past events, even tho no one shall ever know it.

Prag.:—Yes, but you must remember that I also stipulated for permission to define the word in my own fashion. The truth of an event, past, present, or future, is for me only another name for the fact that *if* the event ever *does* get known, the nature of the knowledge is already to some degree predetermined. The truth which precedes actual knowledge of a fact means only what any possible knower of the fact will eventually find himself necessitated to believe about it. He must believe something that will bring him into satisfactory relations with it, that will prove a decent mental substitute for it. What this something may be is of course partly fixed already by the nature of the fact and by the sphere of its associations.

This seems to me all that you can clearly mean when you say that truth pre-exists to knowledge. It is knowledge anticipated, knowledge in the form of possibility merely.

Anti-Prag.:—But what does the knowledge know when it comes? Does n't it know the *truth*? And, if so, must n't the truth be distinct from either the fact or the knowledge?

Prag.:—It seems to me that what the knowledge knows is the fact itself, the event, or whatever the reality may be. Where you see three distinct entities in the field, the reality, the knowing, and the truth, I see only two. Moreover, I can see what each of my two entities is *known-as*, but when I ask myself what your third entity, the truth, is known-as, I can find nothing distinct from the reality on the one hand, and the ways in which it may be known on the other. Are you not probably misled by common language, which has found it convenient to introduce a hybrid name, meaning sometimes a kind of knowing and sometimes a reality known, to apply to either of these things interchangeably? And has philosophy anything to gain by perpetuating and consecrating the ambiguity? If you call the object of knowledge 'reality,' and call the manner of its being cognized 'truth,' cognized moreover on particular occasions, and variously, by particular human beings who have their various businesses with it, and if you hold consistently to this nomenclature, it seems to me that you escape all sorts of trouble.

Anti-Prag.:—Do you mean that you think you escape from my dilemma?

Prag.:—Assuredly I escape; for if truth and knowledge are terms correlative and interdependent, as I maintain they are, then wherever knowledge is conceivable truth is conceivable, wherever knowledge is possible truth is possible, wherever knowledge is actual truth is actual. Therefore when you point your first horn at me, I think of truth *actual*, and say it does n't exist. It does n't; for by hypothesis there is no knower, no ideas, no workings. I agree, however, that truth *possible* or *virtual* might exist, for a knower might possibly be brought to birth; and truth *conceivable* certainly exists, for, abstractly taken, there is nothing in the nature of antediluvian events that should make the application of knowledge to them inconceivable. Therefore when you try to impale me on your second horn, I think of the truth in question as a mere abstract possibility, so I say it does exist, and side with common sense.

Do not these distinctions rightly relieve me from embarrassment? And don't you think it might help you to make them yourself?

Anti-Prag.:—Never!—so avaunt with your abominable hair-splitting and sophistry! Truth is truth; and never will I degrade it by identifying it with low pragmatic particulars in the way you propose.

Prag.:—Well, my dear antagonist, I hardly hoped to convert an eminent intellectualist and logician like you; so enjoy, as long as you live, your own ineffable conception. Perhaps the rising generation will grow up more accustomed than you are to that concrete and empirical interpretation of terms in which the pragmatic method consists. Perhaps they may then wonder how so harmless and natural an account of truth as mine could have found such difficulty in entering the minds of men far more intelligent than I can ever hope to become, but wedded by education and tradition to the abstractionist manner of thought.

Index

SOME PROBLEMS
OF PHILOSOPHY

A Beginning of an Introduction to Philosophy

'. . . he [*Charles Renouvier*] *was one of the greatest of philosophic characters, and but for the decisive impression made on me in the seventies by his masterly advocacy of pluralism, I might never have got free from the monistic superstition under which I had grown up. The present volume, in short, might never have been written. This is why, feeling endlessly thankful as I do, I dedicate this text-book to the great Renouvier's memory.'* [1066]

Contents

CHAPTER X

CHAPTER XI

CHAPTER XII

CHAPTER XIII

APPENDIX

CHAPTER I

PHILOSOPHY AND ITS CRITICS

THE PROGRESS of society is due to the fact that individuals vary from the human average in all sorts of directions, and that the originality is often so attractive or useful that they are recognized by their tribe as leaders, and become objects of envy or admiration, and setters of new ideals.

Among the variations, every generation of men produces some individuals exceptionally preoccupied with theory. Such *Philosophy and those who write it* men find matter for puzzle and astonishment where no one else does. Their imagination invents explanations and combines them. They store up the learning of their time, utter prophecies and warnings, and are regarded as sages. Philosophy, etymologically meaning the love of wisdom, is the work of this class of minds, regarded with an indulgent relish, if not with admiration, even by those who do not understand them or believe much in the truth which they proclaim.

Philosophy, thus become a race-heritage, forms in its totality a monstrously unwieldy mass of learning. So taken, there is no reason why any special science like chemistry, or astronomy, should be excluded from it. By common consent, however, special sciences are to-day excluded, for reasons *What philosophy is* presently to be explained; and what remains is manageable enough to be taught under the name of philosophy by one man if his interests be broad enough.

If this were a German textbook I should first give my abstract definition of the topic, thus limited by usage, then proceed to display its *'Begriff, und Eintheilung,'* and its *'Aufgabe und Methode.'* But as such displays are usually unintelligible to beginners, and unnecessary after reading the book, it will conduce to brevity to omit that chapter altogether, useful though it might possibly be to more advanced readers as a summary of what is to follow.

I will tarry a moment, however, over the matter of definition. Limited by the omission of the special sciences, the name of philosophy has come more and more to denote ideas of universal scope exclusively. The principles of explanation that underlie all things without exception, the elements common to gods and men and animals and stones, the first *whence* and the last *whither* of the whole cosmic procession, the conditions of all knowing, and the most general rules of human action—these furnish the problems commonly deemed philosophic *par excellence*; and the philosopher is the man who finds the most to say about them. Philosophy is defined in the usual scholastic textbooks as 'the knowledge of things in general by their ultimate causes, so far as natural reason can attain to such knowledge.' This means that explanation of the universe at large, not description of its details, is what philosophy must aim at; and so it happens that a view of anything is termed philosophic just in proportion as it is broad and connected with other views, and as it uses principles not proximate, or intermediate, but ultimate and all-embracing, to justify itself. Any very sweeping view of the world is a philosophy in this sense, even though it may be a vague one. It is a *Weltanschauung*, an intellectualized attitude towards life. Professor Dewey well describes the constitution of all the philosophies that actually exist, when he says that philosophy expresses a certain attitude, purpose and temper of conjoined intellect and will, rather than a discipline whose boundaries can be neatly marked off.[1]

To know the chief rival attitudes towards life, as the history of human thinking has developed them, and to have heard Its value some of the reasons they can give for themselves, ought to be considered an essential part of liberal education. Philosophy, indeed, in one sense of the term is only a compendious name for the spirit in education which the word 'college' stands for in America. Things can be taught in dry dogmatic ways or in a philosophic way. At a technical school a man may grow into a first-rate instrument for doing a certain job, but he may miss all the graciousness of mind suggested by the term liberal culture. He may remain a cad, and not a gentleman, intellectually pinned down to his one narrow subject, literal, unable to suppose anything different from

[1] Compare the article 'Philosophy' in Baldwin's *Dictionary of Philosophy and Psychology*.

what he has seen, without imagination, atmosphere, or mental perspective.

Philosophy, beginning in wonder, as Plato and Aristotle said, is able to fancy everything different from what it is. It sees the familiar as if it were strange, and the strange as if it were familiar. It can take things up and lay them down again. Its mind is full of air that plays round every subject. It rouses us from our native dogmatic slumber and breaks up our caked prejudices. Historically it has always been a sort of fecundation of four different human interests, science, poetry, religion, and logic, by one another. It has sought by hard reasoning for results emotionally valuable. To have some contact with it, to catch its influence, is thus good for both literary and scientific students. By its poetry it appeals to literary minds; but its logic stiffens them up and remedies their softness. By its logic it appeals to the scientific; but softens them by its other aspects, and saves them from too dry a technicality. Both types of student ought to get from philosophy a livelier spirit, more air, more mental background. 'Hast any philosophy in thee, Shepherd?'—this question of Touchstone's is the one with which men should always meet one another. A man with no philosophy in him is the most inauspicious and unprofitable of all possible social mates.

I say nothing in all this of what may be called the gymnastic use of philosophic study, the purely intellectual power gained by defining the high and abstract concepts of the philosopher, and discriminating between them.

In spite of the advantages thus enumerated, the study of philosophy has systematic enemies, and they were never as numerous as at the present day. The definite conquests of science and the apparent indefiniteness of philosophy's results partly account for this; to say nothing of man's native rudeness of mind, which maliciously enjoys deriding long words and abstractions. 'Scholastic jargon,' 'mediæval dialectics,' are for many people synonyms of the word philosophy. With his obscure and uncertain speculations as to the intimate nature and causes of things, the philosopher is likened to a 'blind man in a dark room looking for a black cat that is not there.' His occupation

Its enemies and their objections

is described as the art of 'endlessly disputing without coming to any conclusion,' or more contemptuously still as the *'systematische Missbrauch einer eben zu diesem Zwecke erfundenen Terminologie.'*

Only to a very limited degree is this sort of hostility reasonable. I will take up some of the current objections in successive order, since to reply to them will be a convenient way of entering into the interior of our subject.

Objection *Objection 1.* Whereas the sciences make steady
that it is progress and yield applications of matchless util-
unpractical
answered ity, philosophy makes no progress and has no practical applications.

Reply. The opposition is unjustly founded, for the sciences are themselves branches of the tree of philosophy. As fast as questions got accurately answered, the answers were called 'scientific,' and what men call 'philosophy' to-day is but the residuum of questions still unanswered. At this very moment we are seeing two sciences, psychology and general biology, drop off from the parent trunk and take independent root as specialties. The more general philosophy cannot as a rule follow the voluminous details of any special science.

A backward glance at the evolution of philosophy will reward us here. The earliest philosophers in every land were
This encylopædic sages, lovers of wisdom, sometimes
objection in
the light of with, and sometimes without a dominantly ethical
history or religious interest. They were just men curious beyond immediate practical needs, and no particular problems, but rather the problematic generally, was their specialty. China, Persia, Egypt, India, had such wise men, but those of Greece are the only sages who until very recently have influenced the course of western thinking. The earlier Greek philosophy lasted, roughly speaking, for about two hundred and fifty years, say from 600 B. C. onwards. Such men as Thales, Heracleitus, Pythagoras, Parmenides, Anaxagoras, Empedocles, Democritus, were mathematicians, theologians, politicians, astronomers, and physicists. All the learning of their time, such as it was, was at their disposal. Plato and Aristotle continued their tradition, and the great mediæval philosophers only enlarged its field of application. If we turn to Saint

Thomas Aquinas's great 'Summa,' written in the thirteenth century, we find opinions expressed about literally everything, from God down to matter, with angels, men, and demons taken in on the way. The relations of almost everything with everything else, of the creator with his creatures, of the knower with the known, of substances with forms, of mind with body, of sin with salvation, come successively up for treatment. A theology, a psychology, a system of duties and morals, are given in fullest detail, while physics and logic are established in their universal principles. The impression made on the reader is of almost superhuman intellectual resources. It is true that Saint Thomas's method of handling the mass of fact, or supposed fact, which he treated, was different from that to which we are accustomed. He deduced and proved everything, either from fixed principles of reason, or from holy Scripture. The properties and changes of bodies, for example, were explained by the two principles of matter and form, as Aristotle had taught. Matter was the quantitative, determinable, passive element; form, the qualitative, unifying, determining, and active principle. All activity was for an end. Things could act on each other only when in contact. The number of species of things was determinate, and their differences discrete, etc., etc.[1]

By the beginning of the seventeenth century, men were tired of the elaborate *a priori* methods of scholasticism. Suarez's treatises availed not to keep them in fashion. But the new philosophy of Descartes, which displaced the scholastic teaching, sweeping over Europe like wildfire, preserved the same encyclopædic character. We think of Descartes nowadays as the metaphysician who said 'Cogito, ergo sum,' separated mind from matter as two contrasted substances, and gave a renovated proof of God's existence. But his contemporaries thought of him much more as we think of Herbert Spencer in our day, as a great cosmic evolutionist, who explained, by 'the redistribution of matter and motion,' and the laws of impact, the rotations of the heavens, the circulation of the

---

[1] J. Rickaby's *General Metaphysics* (Longmans, Green and Co.) gives a popular account of the essentials of St. Thomas's philosophy of nature. Thomas J. Harper's *Metaphysics of the School* (Macmillan) goes into minute detail.

blood, the refraction of light, apparatus of vision and of nervous action, the passions of the soul, and the connection of the mind and body.

Descartes died in 1650. With Locke's 'Essay Concerning Human Understanding,' published in 1690, philosophy for the first time turned more exclusively to the problem of knowledge, and became 'critical.' This subjective tendency developed; and although the school of Leibnitz, who was the pattern of a universal sage, still kept up the more universal tradition—Leibnitz's follower Wolff published systematic treatises on everything, physical as well as moral—Hume, who succeeded Locke, woke Kant 'from his dogmatic slumber,' and since Kant's time the word 'philosophy' has come to stand for mental and moral speculations far more than for physical theories. Until a comparatively recent time, philosophy was taught in our colleges under the name of 'mental and moral philosophy,' or 'philosophy of the human mind,' exclusively, to distinguish it from 'natural philosophy.'

But the older tradition is the better as well as the completer one. To know the actual peculiarities of the world we are born into is surely as important as to know what makes worlds anyhow abstractly possible. Yet this latter knowledge has been treated by many since Kant's time as the only knowledge worthy of being called philosophical. Common men feel the question 'What is Nature like?' to be as meritorious as the Kantian question 'How is Nature possible?' So philosophy, in order not to lose human respect, must take some notice of the actual constitution of reality. There are signs to-day of a return to the more objective tradition.[1]

Philosophy in the full sense is only *man thinking*, thinking about generalities rather than about particulars. But whether

Philosophy is only 'man thinking' about generalities or particulars, man thinks always by the same methods. He observes, discriminates, generalizes, classifies, looks for causes, traces analogies, and makes hypotheses. Philosophy, taken as something distinct from science or from practical affairs, follows no method peculiar to itself. All our thinking to-day has evolved gradually out of primitive human thought, and the only really

[1] For an excellent defence of it I refer my readers to Paulsen's *Introduction to Philosophy*, translated by Thilly (1895), pp. 19–44.

important changes that have come over its manner (as distinguished from the matters in which it believes) are a greater hesitancy in asserting its convictions, and the habit of seeking verification[1] for them whenever it can.

It will be instructive to trace very briefly the origins of our present habits of thought.

Auguste Comte, the founder of a philosophy which he called 'positive,'[2] said that human theory on any subject always took three forms in succession. In the theological stage of theorizing, phenomena are explained by spirits producing them; in the metaphysical stage, their essential feature is made into an abstract idea, and this is placed behind them as if it were an explanation; in the positive stage, phenomena are simply described as to their coexistences and successions. Their 'laws' are formulated, but no explanation of their natures or existence is sought after. Thus a *'spiritus rector'* would be a theological, —a 'principal of attraction' a metaphysical, —and a 'law of the squares' would be a positive theory of the planetary movements.

Origin of man's present ways of thinking

Comte's account is too sharp and definite. Anthropology shows that the earliest attempts at human theorizing mixed the theological and metaphysical together. Common things needed no special explanation, remarkable things alone, odd things, especially deaths, calamities, diseases, called for it. What made things act was the mysterious energy in them, and the more awful they were, the more of this *mana* they possessed. The great thing was to acquire *mana* oneself. 'Sympathetic magic' is the collective name for what seems to have been the primitive philosophy here. You could act on anything by controlling anything else that either was associated with it or resembled it. If you wished to injure an enemy, you should either make an image of him, or get some of his hair or other belongings, or get his name written. Injuring the substitute, you thus made him suffer correspondingly. If you wished the rain to come, you sprinkled the ground, if the wind, you whistled, etc. If you would have yams grow well in your garden, put a stone there that looks like a yam. Would

[1] Compare G. H. Lewes: *Aristotle* (1864), chap. 4.
[2] *Cours de philosophie positive*, 6 volumes, Paris, 1830–1842.

you cure jaundice, give turmeric, that makes things look yellow; or give poppies for troubles of the head, because their seed vessels form a 'head.' This 'doctrine of signatures' played a great part in early medicine. The various '-mancies' and '-mantics' come in here, in which witchcraft and incipient science are indistinguishably mixed. 'Sympathetic' theorizing persists to the present day. 'Thoughts are things,' for a contemporary school—and on the whole a good school—of practical philosophy. Cultivate the thought of what you desire, affirm it, and it will bring all similar thoughts from elsewhere to reinforce it, so that finally your wish will be fulfilled.[1]

Little by little, more positive ways of considering things began to prevail. Common elements in phenomena began to be singled out and to form the basis of generalizations. But these elements at first had necessarily to be the more dramatic or humanly interesting ones. The hot, the cold, the wet, the dry in things explained their behavior. Some bodies were naturally warm, others cold. Motions were natural or violent. The heavens moved in circles because circular motion was the most perfect. The lever was explained by the greater quantity of perfection embodied in the movement of its longer arm.[2] The sun went south in winter to escape the cold. Precious or beautiful things had exceptional properties. Peacock's flesh resisted putrefaction. The lodestone would drop the iron which it held if the superiorly powerful diamond was brought near, etc.

Such ideas sound to us grotesque, but imagine no tracks made for us by scientific ancestors, and what aspects would we single out from nature to understand things by? Not till the beginning of the seventeenth century did the more insipid kinds of regularity in things abstract men's attention away from the properties originally picked out. Few of us realize

[1] Compare Prentice Mulford and others of the 'new thought' type. For primitive sympathetic magic consult J. Jastrow in *Fact and Fable in Psychology*, the chapter on Analogy; F. B. Jevons: *Introduction to the History of Religion*, chap. iv; J. G. Frazer: *The Golden Bough*, i, 2; R. R. Marett: *The Threshold of Religion, passim*; A. O. Lovejoy: *The Monist*, xvi, 357.

[2] On Greek science, see W. Whewell's *History of the Inductive Sciences*, vol. i, book i; G. H. Lewes, *Aristotle, passim*.

how short the career of what we know as 'science' has been. Three hundred and fifty years ago hardly any one believed in the Copernican planetary theory. Optical combinations were not discovered. The circulation of the blood, the weight of air, the conduction of heat, the laws of motion were unknown; the common pump was inexplicable; there were no clocks; no thermometers; no general gravitation; the world was five thousand years old; spirits moved the planets; alchemy, magic, astrology, imposed on every one's belief. Modern science began only after 1600, with Kepler, Galileo, Descartes, Torricelli, Pascal, Harvey, Newton, Huygens, and Boyle. Five men telling one another in succession the discoveries which their lives had witnessed, could deliver the whole of it into our hands: Harvey might have told Newton, who might have told Voltaire; Voltaire might have told Dalton, who might have told Huxley, who might have told the readers of this book.

The men who began this work of emancipation were philosophers in the original sense of the word, universal sages. Galileo said that he had spent more years on philosophy than Science is months on mathematics. Descartes was a universal specialized philosopher in the fullest sense of the term. But the philosophy fertility of the newer conceptions made special departments of truth grow at such a rate that they became too unwieldy with details for the more universal minds to carry them, so the special sciences of mechanics, astronomy, and physics began to drop off from the parent stem.

No one could have foreseen in advance the extraordinary fertility of the more insipid mathematical aspects which these geniuses ferreted out. No one could have dreamed of the control over nature which the search for their concomitant variations would give. 'Laws' describe these variations; and all our present laws of nature have as their model the proportionality of v to t, and of s to t^2 which Galileo first laid bare. Pascal's discovery of the proportionality of altitude to barometric height, Newton's of acceleration to distance, Boyle's of airvolume to pressure, Descartes' of sine to sine in the refracted ray, were the first fruits of Galileo's discovery. There was no question of agencies, nothing animistic or sympathetic in this new way of taking nature. It was description only, of concomitant variations, after the particular quantities that varied had been successfully abstracted out. The result soon showed itself in a differentiation of human knowledge into two spheres, one called 'Science,' within which the more definite laws apply, the other 'General Philosophy,' in which they do not. The state of mind called positivistic is the result. 'Down with philosophy!' is the cry of innumerable scientific minds. 'Give us measurable facts only, phenomena, without the mind's additions, without entities or principles that pretend to explain.' It is largely from this kind of mind that the objection that philosophy has made no progress, proceeds.

It is obvious enough that if every step forward which philosophy makes, every question to which an accurate answer is found, gets accredited to science the residuum of unanswered problems will alone remain to constitute the domain of philosophy, and will alone bear her name. In point of fact this is just what is happening. Philosophy has become a collective name for questions that have not yet been answered to the satisfaction of all by whom they have been asked. It does not follow, because some of these questions have waited two thousand years for an answer, that no answer will ever be forthcoming. Two thousand years probably measure but one paragraph in that great romance of adventure called the history of the intellect of man. The extraordinary progress of the last three hundred years is due to a rather sudden finding of the way in which a certain order of questions ought to be attacked, questions admitting of mathematical treatment. But to assume therefore, that the only possible philosophy must be mechanical and mathematical, and to disparage all enquiry into the other sorts of question, is to forget the extreme diversity of aspects under which reality undoubtedly exists. To the spiritual questions the proper avenues of philosophic approach will also undoubtedly be found. They have, to some extent, been found already. In some respects, indeed, 'science' has made less progress than 'philosophy'—its most general conceptions would astonish neither Aristotle nor Descartes, could they revisit our earth. The composition of things from elements, their evolution, the conservation of energy, the idea of a universal determinism, would seem to them common-

Philosophy is the residuum of problems unsolved by science

place enough—the little things, the microscopes, electric lights, telephones, and details of the sciences, would be to them the awe-inspiring things. But if they opened our books on metaphysics, or visited a philosophic lecture room, everything would sound strange. The whole idealistic or 'critical' attitude of our time would be novel, and it would be long before they took it in.[1]

Objection 2. Philosophy is dogmatic, and pretends to settle things by pure reason, whereas the only fruitful mode of getting at truth is to appeal to concrete experience. Science collects, classes, and analyzes facts, and thereby far outstrips philosophy.

Reply. This objection is historically valid. Too many philosophers have aimed at closed systems, established *a priori*, claiming infallibility, and to be accepted or rejected only as totals. The sciences on the other hand, using hypotheses only, but always seeking to verify them by experiment and observation, open a way for indefinite self-correction and increase. At the present day, it is getting more and more difficult for dogmatists claiming finality for their systems, to get a hearing in educated circles. Hypothesis and verification, the watchwords of science, have set the fashion too strongly in academic minds.

Philosophy need not be dogmatic

Since philosophers are only men thinking about things in the most comprehensive possible way, they can use any method whatsoever freely. Philosophy must, in any case, complete the sciences, and must incorporate their methods. One cannot see why, if such a policy should appear advisable, philosophy might not end by forswearing all dogmatism whatever, and become as hypothetical in her manners as the most empirical science of them all.

Objection 3. Philosophy is out of touch with real life, for which it substitutes abstractions. The real world is various, tangled, painful. Philosophers have, almost without exception, treated it as noble, simple, and perfect, ignoring the complexity of fact, and indulging in a sort of optimism that exposes their systems to the contempt of common men, and

---

[1]The reader will find all that I have said, and much more, set forth in an excellent article by James Ward in *Mind*, vol. 15, no. lviii: 'The Progress of Philosophy.'

to the satire of such writers as Voltaire and Schopenhauer. The great popular success of Schopenhauer is due to the fact that, first among philosophers, he spoke the concrete truth about the ills of life.

Reply. This objection also is historically valid, but no reason appears why philosophy should keep aloof from reality permanently. Her manners may change as she successfully develops. The thin and noble abstractions may give way to more solid and real constructions, when the materials and methods for making such constructions shall be more and more securely ascertained. In the end philosophers may get into as close contact as realistic novelists with the facts of life.

Nor is it divorced from reality

In conclusion. In its original acceptation, meaning the completest knowledge of the universe, philosophy must include the results of all the sciences, and cannot be contrasted with the latter. It simply aims at making of science what Herbert Spencer calls a 'system of completely unified knowledge.'[1] In the more modern sense, of something contrasted with the sciences, philosophy means 'metaphysics.' The older sense is the more worthy sense, and as the results of the sciences get more available for co-ordination, and the conditions for finding truth in different kinds of question get more methodically defined, we may hope that the term will revert to its original meaning. Science, metaphysics, and religion may then again form a single body of wisdom, and lend each other mutual support.

Philosophy as metaphysics

At present this hope is far from its fulfillment. I propose in this book to take philosophy in the narrow sense of metaphysics, and to let both religion and the results of the sciences alone.

[1] See the excellent chapter in Spencer's *First Principles*, entitled: 'Philosophy Defined.'

CHAPTER II

THE PROBLEMS OF METAPHYSICS

N O EXACT definition of the term 'metaphysics' is possible, and to name some of the problems it treats of is the best way of getting at the meaning of the word. **Examples of metaphysical problems** It means the discussion of various obscure, abstract, and universal questions which the sciences and life in general suggest but do not solve; questions left over, as it were; questions, all of them very broad and deep, and relating to the whole of things, or to the ultimate elements thereof. Instead of a definition let me cite a few examples, in a random order, of such questions:—

What are 'thoughts,' and what are 'things'? and how are they connected?

What do we mean when we say 'truth'?

Is there a common stuff out of which all facts are made?

How comes there to be a world at all? and, Might it as well not have been?

Which is the most real kind of reality?

What binds all things into one universe?

Is unity or diversity more fundamental?

Have all things one origin? or many?

Is everything predestined, or are some things (our wills for example) free?

Is the world infinite or finite in amount?

Are its parts continuous, or are there vacua?

What is God?—or the gods?

How are mind and body joined? Do they act on each other?

How does anything act on anything else?

How can one thing change or grow out of another thing?

Are space and time beings?—or what?

In knowledge, how does the object get into the mind?—or the mind get at the object?

We know by means of universal notions. Are these also real? Or are only particular things real?

What is meant by a 'thing'?

'Principles of reason,'—are they inborn or derived?

Are 'beauty' and 'good' matters of opinion only? Or have they objective validity? And, if so, what does the phrase mean?

Such are specimens of the kind of question termed metaphysical. Kant said that the three essential metaphysical questions were:—

What can I know?

What should I do?

What may I hope?

A glance at all such questions suffices to rule out such a definition of metaphysics as that of Christian Wolff, who **Metaphysics defined** called it 'the science of what is possible,' as distinguished from that of what is actual, for most of the questions relate to what is actual fact. One may say that metaphysics inquires into the cause, the substance, the meaning, and the outcome of all things. Or one may call it the science of the most universal principles of reality (whether experienced by us or not), in their connection with one another and with our powers of knowledge. 'Principles' here may mean either entities, like 'atoms,' 'souls,' or logical laws like: 'A thing must either exist or not exist'; or generalized facts, like 'things can act only after they exist.' But the principles are so numerous, and the 'science' of them is so far from completion, that such definitions have only a decorative value. The serious work of metaphysics is done over the separate single questions. If these should get cleared up, talk of metaphysics as a unified science might properly begin. This book proposes to handle only a few separate problems, leaving others untouched.

These problems are for the most part real; that is, but few of them result from a misuse of terms in stating them. **Nature of metaphysical problems** 'Things,' for example, are or are not composed of one stuff; they either have or have not a single origin; they either are or are not completely predetermined, etc. Such alternatives may indeed be impossible of decision; but until this is conclusively proved of them, they confront us legitimately, and some one must take charge of them and keep account of the solutions that are proposed, even if he does not himself add new ones. The opinions of the learned regarding them must, in short, be classified and responsibly discussed. For instance, how many opinions are possible as to the origin of the world? Spencer says that the world must have been either eternal, or self-created, or created by an outside power. So for him there are only three. Is this correct? If so, which of the three views seems the most reasonable? and why? In a moment we are in the thick of metaphysics. We have to be metaphysicians even to decide with Spencer that neither mode of origin is thinkable and that the whole problem is unreal.

Some hypotheses may be absurd on their face, because they are self-contradictory. If, for example, infinity means 'what can never be completed by successive syntheses,' the notion of anything made by the successive addition of infinitely numerous parts, and yet completed, is absurd. Other hypotheses, for example that everything in nature contributes to a single supreme purpose, may be insusceptible either of proof or of disproof. Other hypotheses again, for instance that vacua exist, may be susceptible of probable solution. The classing of the hypotheses is thus as necessary as the classing of the problems, and both must be recognized as constituting a serious branch of learning.[1] There must in short be metaphysicians. Let us for a while become metaphysicians ourselves.

As we survey the history of metaphysics we soon realize that two pretty distinct types of mind have filled it with their *Rationalism and empiricism in metaphysics* warfare. Let us call them the rationalist and the empiricist types of mind. A saying of Coleridge's is often quoted, to the effect that every one is born either a platonist or an aristotelian. By aristotelian, he means empiricist, and by platonist, he means rationalist; but although the contrast between the two Greek philosophers exists in the sense in which Coleridge meant it, both of them were rationalists as compared with the kind of empiricism which Democritus and Protagoras developed; and Coleridge had better have taken either of those names instead of Aristotle as his empiricist example.

Rationalists are the men of principles, empiricists the men

[1] Consult here Paul Janet: *Principes de Métaphysique*, etc., 1897, leçons 1, 2.

of facts; but, since principles are universals, and facts are particulars, perhaps the best way of characterizing the two tendencies is to say that rationalist thinking proceeds most
willingly by going from wholes to parts, while empiricist
thinking proceeds by going from parts to wholes. Plato, the
archrationalist, explained the details of nature by their participation in 'ideas,' which all depended on the supreme idea of
the 'good.' Protagoras and Democritus were empiricists. The
latter explained the whole cosmos, including gods as well as
men, and thoughts as well as things, by their composition out
of atomic elements; Protagoras explained truth, which for
Plato was the absolute system of the ideas, as a collective
name for men's opinions.

Rationalists prefer to deduce facts from principles. Empiricists prefer to explain principles as inductions from facts. Is
thought for the sake of life? or is life for the sake of thought?
Empiricism inclines to the former, rationalism to the latter
branch of the alternative. God's life, according to Aristotle
and Hegel, is pure theory. The mood of admiration is natural
to rationalism. Its theories are usually optimistic, supplement-
ing the experienced world by clean and pure ideal constructions. Aristotle and Plato, the Scholastics, Descartes, Spinoza,
Leibnitz, Kant, and Hegel are examples of this. They claimed
absolute finality for their systems, in the noble architecture
of which, as their authors believed, truth was eternally em-
balmed. This temper of finality is foreign to empiricist minds.
They may be dogmatic about their method of building on
'hard facts,' but they are willing to be sceptical about any conclusions reached by the method at a given time. They aim at
accuracy of detail rather than at completeness; are contented
to be fragmentary; are less inspiring than the rationalists, often treating the high as a case of 'nothing but' the low ('nothing but' self-interest well understood, etc.), but they usually
keep more in touch with actual life, are less subjective, and
their spirit is obviously more 'scientific' in the hackneyed
sense of that term. Socrates, Locke, Berkeley, Hume, the
Mills, F. A. Lange, J. Dewey, F. C. S. Schiller, Bergson, and
other contemporaries are specimens of this type. Of course
we find mixed minds in abundance, and few philosophers are
typical in either class. Kant may fairly be called mixed. Lotze

and Royce are mixed. The author of this volume is weakly endowed on the rationalist side, and his book will show a strong leaning towards empiricism. The clash of the two ways of looking at things will be emphasized throughout the volume.[1]

I will now enter the interior of the subject by discussing special problems as examples of metaphysical inquiry; and in order not to conceal any of the skeletons in the philosophic closet, I will start with the worst problem possible, the so-called 'ontological problem,' or question of how there comes to be anything at all.

[1] Compare W. James: 'The Sentiment of Rationality,' in *The Will to Believe* (Longmans, Green and Co., 1899), p. 63 f.; *Pragmatism* (ibid.), chap. i; *A Pluralistic Universe* (ibid.), chap. i.

CHAPTER III

THE PROBLEM OF BEING

Hˢᵒʷ ᶜᵒᵐᵉˢ the world to be here at all instead of the nonentity which might be imagined in its place? Schopenhauer's remarks on this question may be considered classical. 'Apart from man,' he says, 'no being wonders at its own existence. When man first becomes conscious, he takes himself for granted, as something needing no explanation. But not for long; for, with the rise of the first reflection, that wonder begins which is the mother of metaphysics, and which made Aristotle say that men now and always seek to philosophize because of wonder— The lower a man stands in intellectual respects the less of a riddle does existence seem to him . . . but, the clearer his consciousness becomes the more the problem grasps him in its greatness. In fact the unrest which keeps the never stopping clock of metaphysics going is the thought that the non-existence of this world is just as possible as its existence. Nay more, we soon conceive the world as something the non-existence of which not only is conceivable but would indeed be preferable to its existence; so that our wonder passes easily into a brooding over that fatality which nevertheless could call such a world into being, and mislead the immense force that could produce and preserve it into an activity so hostile to its own interests. The philosophic wonder thus becomes a sad astonishment, and like the overture to Don Giovanni, philosophy begins with a minor chord.'[1]

Schopen-
hauer on
the origin
of the
problem

One need only shut oneself in a closet and begin to think of the fact of one's being there, of one's queer bodily shape in the darkness (a thing to make children scream at, as Stevenson says), of one's fantastic character and all, to have the wonder steal over the detail as much as over the general fact of being, and to see that it is only familiarity that blunts it. Not only that *anything* should be, but that *this* very thing

[1] *The World as Will and Representation*: Appendix 17, 'On the metaphysical need of man,' abridged.

should be, is mysterious! Philosophy stares, but brings no reasoned solution, for from nothing to being there is no logical bridge.

Attempts are sometimes made to banish the question rather than to give it an answer. Those who ask it, we are told, extend illegitimately to the whole of being the contrast to a **Various** supposed alternative non-being which only particular beings possess. These, indeed, were not, and now are. But being in general, or in some shape, always was, and you cannot rightly bring the whole of it into relation with a primordial nonentity. Whether as God or as material atoms, it is itself primal and eternal. But if you call any being whatever eternal, some philosophers have always been ready to taunt you with the paradox inherent in the assumption. Is past eternity completed? they ask: If so, they go on, it must have had a beginning; for whether your imagination traverses it forwards or backwards, it offers an identical content or stuff to be measured; and if the amount comes to an end in one way, it ought to come to an end in the other. In other words, since we now witness its end, some past moment must have witnessed its beginning. If, however, it had a beginning, when was that, and why?

(margin: Various treatments of the problem)

You are up against the previous nothing, and do not see how it ever passed into being. This dilemma, of having to choose between a regress which, although called infinite, has nevertheless come to a termination, and an absolute first, has played a great part in philosophy's history.

Other attempts still are made at exorcising the question. Non-being is not, said Parmenides and Zeno; only being is. Hence what is, is necessarily being—being, in short, is necessary. Others, calling the idea of nonentity no real idea, have said that on the absence of an idea can no genuine problem be founded. More curtly still, the whole ontological wonder has been called diseased, a case of *Grübelsucht* like asking, 'Why am I myself?' or 'Why is a triangle a triangle?'

Rationalistic minds here and there have sought to reduce the mystery. Some forms of being have been deemed more natural, so to say, or more inevitable and necessary than

Rationalist and empiricist treatments

others. Empiricists of the evolutionary type—Herbert Spencer seems a good example—have assumed that whatever had the least of reality, was weakest, faintest, most imperceptible, most nascent, might come easiest first, and be the earliest successor to nonentity. Little by little the fuller grades of being might have added themselves in the same gradual way until the whole universe grew up.

To others not the minimum, but the maximum of being has seemed the earliest First for the intellect to accept. 'The perfection of a thing does not keep it from existing,' Spinoza said, 'on the contrary, it founds its existence.'[1] It is mere prejudice to assume that it is harder for the great than for the little to be, and that easiest of all it is to be nothing. What makes things difficult in any line is the alien obstructions that are met with, and the smaller and weaker the thing the more powerful over it these become. Some things are so great and inclusive that to be is implied in their very nature. The anselmian or ontological proof of God's existence, sometimes called the cartesian proof, criticised by Saint Thomas, rejected by Kant, re-defended by Hegel, follows this line of thought. What is conceived as imperfect may lack being among its other lacks, but if God, who is expressly defined as *Ens perfectissimum*, lacked anything whatever, he would contradict his own definition. He cannot lack being therefore: He is *Ens necessarium, Ens realissimum*, as well as *Ens perfectissimum*.[2]

Hegel in his lordly way says: 'It would be strange if God were not rich enough to embrace so poor a category as Being, the poorest and most abstract of all.' This is somewhat in line with Kant's saying that a real dollar does not contain one cent more than an imaginary dollar. At the beginning of his logic Hegel seeks in another way to mediate nonentity with being. Since 'being' in the abstract, mere being, means nothing in particular, it is indistinguishable from 'nothing'; and he seems dimly to think that this constitutes an identity between the two notions, of which some use may be made in getting from one to the other. Other still queerer attempts show well the

[1] *Ethics*, part i, prop. xi, scholium.
[2] St. Anselm: *Proslogium*, etc. Translated by Deane: Chicago, 1903; Descartes: *Meditations*, p. 5; Kant: *Critique of Pure Reason, Transcendental Dialectic*, 'On the impossibility of an ontological proof, etc.'

rationalist temper. Mathematically you can deduce 1 from 0 by the following process: $\frac{0}{0} = \frac{1-1}{1-1} = 1$. Or physically if all being has (as it seems to have) a 'polar' construction, so that every positive part of it has its negative, we get the simple equation: $+1-1=0$, *plus* and *minus* being the signs of polarity in physics.

It is not probable that the reader will be satisfied with any of these solutions, and contemporary philosophers, even rationalistically minded ones, have on the whole agreed that no one has intelligibly banished the mystery of *fact*. Whether the original nothing burst into God and vanished, as night vanishes in day, while God thereupon became the creative principle of all lesser beings; or whether all things have foisted or shaped themselves imperceptibly into existence, the same amount of existence has in the end to be assumed and begged

The same amount of existence must be begged by all

by the philosopher. To comminute the difficulty is not to quench it. If you are a rationalist you beg a kilogram of being at once, we will say; if you are an empiricist you beg a thousand successive grams; but you beg the same amount in each case, and you are the same beggar whatever you may pretend. You leave the logical riddle untouched, of how the coming of whatever is, came it all at once, or came it piecemeal, can be intellectually understood.[1]

If being gradually *grew*, its quantity was of course not always the same, and may not be the same hereafter. To most

Conservation vs. creation

philosophers this view has seemed absurd, neither God, nor primordial matter, nor energy being supposed to admit of increase or decrease. The orthodox opinion is that the quantity of reality must at all costs be conserved, and the waxing and waning of our phenomenal experiences must be treated as surface appearances which leave the deeps untouched.

Nevertheless, within experience, phenomena come and go. There are novelties; there are losses. The world seems, on the concrete and proximate level at least, really to grow. So the

---

[1] In more technical language, one may say that fact or being is 'contingent,' or matter of 'chance,' so far as our intellect is concerned. The conditions of its appearance are uncertain, unforeseeable, when future, and when past, elusive.

question recurs: How do our finite experiences come into being from moment to moment? By inertia? By perpetual creation? Do the new ones come at the call of the old ones? Why do not they all go out like a candle?

Who can tell off-hand? The question of being is the darkest in all philosophy. All of us are beggars here, and no school can speak disdainfully of another or give itself superior airs. For all of us alike, Fact forms a datum, gift, or *Vorgefundenes*, which we cannot burrow under, explain or get behind. It makes itself somehow, and our business is far more with its What than with its Whence or Why.

CHAPTER IV

PERCEPT AND CONCEPT—THE IMPORT OF CONCEPTS

THE PROBLEM convenient to take up next in order will be that of the difference between thoughts and things. 'Things' are known to us by our senses, and are called 'presentations' by some authors, to distinguish them from the ideas or 'representations' which we may have when our senses are closed. I myself have grown accustomed to the words 'percept' and 'concept' in treating of the contrast, but concepts flow out of percepts and into them again, they are so

Their difference
interlaced, and our life rests on them so interchangeably and undiscriminatingly, that it is often difficult to impart quickly to beginners a clear notion of the difference meant. Sensation and thought in man are mingled, but they vary independently. In our quadrupedal relatives thought proper is at a minimum, but we have no reason to suppose that their immediate life of feeling is either less or more copious than ours. Feeling must have been originally self-sufficing; and thought appears as a superadded function, adapting us to a wider environment than that of which brutes take account. Some parts of the stream of feeling must be more intense, emphatic, and exciting than others in animals as well as in ourselves; but whereas lower animals simply react upon these more salient sensations by appropriate movements, higher animals remember them, and men react on them intellectually, by using nouns, adjectives, and verbs to identify them when they meet them elsewhere.

The great difference between percepts and concepts[1] is that percepts are continuous and concepts are discrete. Not discrete in their *being*, for conception as an *act* is part of the flux of feeling, but discrete from each other in their several *meanings*. Each concept means just what it singly means, and

---

[1] In what follows I shall freely use synonyms for these two terms. 'Idea,' 'thought,' and 'intellection' are synonymous with 'concept.' Instead of 'percept' I shall often speak of 'sensation,' 'feeling,' 'intuition,' and sometimes of 'sensible experience' or of the 'immediate flow' of conscious life. Since Hegel's time what is simply perceived has been called the 'immediate,' while the 'mediated' is synonymous with what is conceived.

nothing else; and if the conceiver does not know whether he means this or means that, it shows that his concept is imperfectly formed. The perceptual flux as such, on the contrary, *means* nothing, and is but what it immediately is. No matter how small a tract of it be taken, it is always a much-at-once, and contains innumerable aspects and characters which conception can pick out, isolate, and thereafter always intend. It shows duration, intensity, complexity or simplicity, interestingness, excitingness, pleasantness or their opposites. Data from all our senses enter into it, merged in a general extensiveness of which each occupies a big or little share. Yet all these parts leave its unity unbroken. Its boundaries are no more distinct than are those of the field of vision. Boundaries are things that intervene; but here nothing intervenes save parts of the perceptual flux itself, and these are overflowed by what they separate, so that whatever we distinguish and isolate conceptually is found perceptually to telescope and compenetrate and diffuse into its neighbors. The cuts we make are purely ideal. If my reader can succeed in abstracting from all conceptual interpretation and lapse back into his immediate sensible life at this very moment, he will find it to be what someone has called a big blooming buzzing confusion, as free from contradiction in its 'much-at-onceness' as it is all alive and evidently there.[1]

Out of this aboriginal sensible muchness attention carves out objects, which conception then names and identifies forever—in the sky 'constellations,' on the earth 'beach,' 'sea,' 'cliff,' 'bushes,' 'grass.' Out of time we cut 'days' and 'nights,' 'summers' and 'winters.' We say *what* each part of the sensible continuum is, and all these abstracted *whats* are concepts.[2]

The conceptual order

The intellectual life of man consists almost wholly in his substitution of a conceptual order for the perceptual order in which his

---

[1] Compare W. James: *A Pluralistic Universe*, pp. 758–761. Also *Psychology, Briefer Course*, pp. 157–166.

[2] On the function of conception consult: Sir William Hamilton's *Lectures on Logic*, 9, 10; H. L. Mansel, *Prolegomena Logica*, chap. i; A. Schopenhauer, *The World as Will*, etc., Supplements 6, 7 to book ii; W. James, *Principles of Psychology*, chap. xii; *Briefer Course*, chap. xiv. Also G. J. Romanes: *Mental*

experience originally comes. But before tracing the consequences of the substitution, I must say something about the conceptual order itself.[1]

Trains of concepts unmixed with percepts grow frequent in the adult mind; and parts of these conceptual trains arrest our attention just as parts of the perceptual flow did, giving rise to concepts of a higher order of abstractness. So subtile is the discernment of man, and so great the power of some men to single out the most fugitive elements of what passes before them, that these new formations have no limit. Aspect within aspect, quality after quality, relation upon relation, absences and negations as well as present features, end by being noted and their names added to the store of nouns, verbs, adjectives, conjunctions, and prepositions by which the human mind interprets life. Every new book verbalizes some new concept, which becomes important in proportion to the use that can be made of it. Different universes of thought thus arise, with specific sorts of relation among their ingredients. The world of common-sense 'things'; the world of material tasks to be done; the mathematical world of pure forms; the world of ethical propositions; the worlds of logic, of music, etc., all abstracted and generalized from long forgotten perceptual in-

---

Evolution in Man, chaps. iii, iv; Th. Ribot: *l'Evolution des Idées Générales*, chap. vi; Th. Ruyssen, *Essai sur l'Evolution psychologique du Jugement*, chap. vii; Laromiguière, *Leçons de Philosophie*, part 2, lesson 12. The account I give directly contradicts that which Kant gave which has prevailed since Kant's time. Kant always speaks of the aboriginal sensible flux as a 'manifold' of which he considers the essential character to be its disconnectedness. To get any togetherness at all into it requires, he thinks, the agency of the 'transcendental ego of apperception,' and to get any definite connections requires the agency of the understanding, with its synthetizing concepts or 'categories.' 'Die Verbindung (conjunctio) eines Mannigfaltigen kann überhaupt niemals durch Sinne in uns kommen, und kann also auch nicht in der reinen Form der sinnlichen Anschauung zugleich mit enthalten sein; denn sie ist ein Actus der Spontaneität der Einbildungskraft, und, da man diese, zum Unterschiede von der Sinnlichkeit, Verstand nennen muss, so ist alle Verbindung . . . eine Verstandeshandlung.' K. d. r. V., 2te, Aufg., pp. 129–130. The reader must decide which account agrees best with his own actual experience.

[1] The substitution was first described in these terms by S. H. Hodgson in his *Philosophy of Reflection*, i, 288–310.

stances, from which they have as it were flowered out, return and merge themselves again in the particulars of our present and future perception. By those *whats* we apperceive all our *thises*. Percepts and concepts interpenetrate and melt together, impregnate and fertilize each other. Neither, taken alone, knows reality in its completeness. We need them both, as we need both our legs to walk with.

From Aristotle downwards philosophers have frankly admitted the indispensability, for complete knowledge of fact, of both the sensational and the intellectual contribution.[1] For complete knowledge of fact, I say; but facts are particulars and connect themselves with practical necessities and the arts; and Greek philosophers soon formed the notion that a knowledge of so-called 'universals,' consisting of concepts of abstract forms, qualities, numbers, and relations was the only knowledge worthy of the truly philosophic mind. Particular facts decay and our perceptions of them vary. A concept never varies; and between such unvarying terms the relations must be constant and express eternal verities. Hence there arose a tendency, which has lasted all through philosophy, to contrast the knowledge of universals and intelligibles, as godlike, dignified, and honorable to the knower, with that of particulars and sensibles as something relatively base which more allies us with the beasts.[2]

---

[1] See, for example, book i, chap. ii, of Aristotle's *Metaphysics*.

[2] Plato in numerous places, but chiefly in books 6 and 7 of the *Republic*, contrasts perceptual knowledge as 'opinion' with real knowledge, to the latter's glory. For an excellent historic sketch of this platonistic view see the first part of E. Laas's *Idealismus und Positivismus*, 1879. For expressions of the ultra-intellectualistic view, read the passage from *Plotinus on the Intellect* in C. M. Bakewell's *Source-book in Ancient Philosophy*, N. Y. 1907, pp. 353 f.; Bossuet, *Traité de la Connaissance de Dieu*, chap. iv, §§ v, vi; R. Cudworth, *A Treatise concerning eternal and immutable Morality*, books iii, iv.—'Plato,' writes Prof. Santayana, 'thought that all the truth and meaning of earthly things was the reference they contained to a heavenly original. This heavenly original we remember to recognize even among the distortions, disappearances, and multiplications of its ephemeral copies. . . . The impressions themselves have no permanence, no intelligible essence, but are always either arising or ceasing to be. There must be, he tells us, an eternal and clearly definable object of which the visible appearances to us are the multiform semblance; now by one trait, now by another, the phantom before us reminds us of that half-forgotten celestial reality and makes us utter its name.

For rationalistic writers conceptual knowledge was not only the more noble knowledge, but it originated independently

Conceptual knowledge — the rationalist view of all perceptual particulars. Such concepts as God, perfection, eternity, infinity, immutability, identity, absolute beauty, truth, justice, necessity, freedom, duty, worth, etc., and the part they play in our mind, are, it was supposed, impossible to explain as results of practical experience. The empiricist view, and probably the true view, is that they do result from practical experience.[1] But a more important question than that as to the origin of our concepts is that as to their functional use and value;—is *that* tied down to perceptual experience, or out of all relation to it? Is conceptual knowledge self-sufficing and a revelation all by itself, quite apart from its uses in helping to a better understanding of the world of sense?

Rationalists say, Yes. For, as we shall see in later places (page 1017), the various conceptual universes referred to on page 1009 can be considered in complete abstraction from perceptual reality, and when they are so considered, all sorts of fixed relations can be discovered among their parts. From

---

. . . We and the whole universe exist only in the attempt to return to our perfection, to lose ourselves again in God. That ineffable good is our natural possession; and all we honor in this life is but a partial recovery of our birthright; every delightful thing is like a rift in the clouds, through which we catch a glimpse of our native heaven. And if that heaven seems so far away, and the idea of it so dim and unreal, it is because we are so far from perfect, so unversed in what is alien and destructive to the soul.' ('Platonic Love in some Italian Poets,' in *Interpretations of Poetry and Religion*, 1896.)

This is the interpretation of Plato which has been current since Aristotle. It should be said that its profundity has been challenged by Prof. A. J. Stewart. (Plato's *Doctrine of Ideas*, Oxford, 1909.)

Aristotle found great fault with Plato's treatment of ideas as heavenly originals, but he agreed with him fully as to the superior excellence of the conceptual or theoretic life. In chapters vii and viii of book x of the *Nicomachean Ethics* he extols contemplation of universal relations as alone yielding pure happiness. 'The life of God, in all its exceeding blessedness, will consist in the exercise of philosophic thought; and of all human activities, that will be the happiest which is most akin to the divine.'

[1] John Locke, in his *Essay concerning Human Understanding*, books i, ii, was the great popularizer of this doctrine. Condillac's *Traité des Sensations*, Helvetius's work, *De l'Homme*, and James Mill's *Analysis of the Human Mind*, were more radical successors of Locke's great book.

these the *a priori* sciences of logic, mathematics, ethics, and æsthetics (so far as the last two can be called sciences at all) result. Conceptual knowledge must thus be called a self-sufficing revelation; and by rationalistic writers it has always been treated as admitting us to a diviner world, the world of universal rather than that of perishing facts, of essential qualities, immutable relations, eternal principles of truth and right. Emerson writes: 'Generalization is always a new influx of divinity into the mind: hence the thrill that attends it.' And a disciple of Hegel, after exalting the knowledge of 'the General, Unchangeable, and alone Valuable' above that of 'the Particular, Sensible and Transient,' adds that if you reproach philosophy with being unable to make a single grass-blade grow, or even to know how it does grow, the reply is that since such a particular 'how' stands not above but below knowledge, strictly so-called, such an ignorance argues no defect.[1]

To this ultra-rationalistic opinion the empiricist contention that *the significance of concepts consists always in their relation to perceptual particulars* has been opposed. Made of percepts, or distilled from parts of percepts, their essential office, it has been said, is to coalesce with percepts again, bringing the mind back into the perceptual world with a better command of the situation there. Certainly whenever we *can* do this with our concepts, we do *more* with them than when we leave them flocking with their abstract and motionless companions. It is possible therefore, to join the rationalists in allowing conceptual knowledge to be self-sufficing, while at the same time one joins the empiricists in maintaining that the full *value* of such knowledge is got only by combining it with perceptual reality again. This mediating attitude is that which this book must adopt. But to understand the nature of concepts better we must now go on to distinguish their *function* from their *content*.

The concept 'man,' to take an example, is three things: 1,

Conceptual knowledge — the empiricist view

---

[1] Michelet, Hegel's *Werke*, vii, 15, quoted by A. Gratry, *De la Connaissance de l'Âme*, i, 231. Compare the similar claim for philosophy in W. Wallace's *Prolegomena to Hegel*, 2d ed., 1894, pp. 28–29, and the long and radical statement of the same view in book iv of Ralph Cudworth's *Treatise on Eternal and Immutable Morality*.

the word itself; 2, a vague picture of the human form which
The content has its own value in the way of beauty or not; and
and 3, an instrument for symbolizing certain objects
function of
concepts from which we may expect human treatment when
occasion arrives. Similarly of 'triangle,' 'cosine,'—they have
their substantive value both as words and as images suggested, but they also have a functional value whenever they
lead us elsewhere in discourse.

There are concepts, however, the image-part of which is so
faint that their whole value seems to be functional. 'God,'
'cause,' 'number,' 'substance,' 'soul,' for example, suggest no
definite picture; and their significance seems to consist entirely in their *tendency*, in the further turn which they may
give to our action or our thought.[1] We cannot rest in the
contemplation of their form, as we can in that of a 'circle' or
a 'man'; we must pass beyond.

Now however beautiful or otherwise worthy of stationary
contemplation the substantive part of a concept may be, the
more important part of its significance may naturally be held
to be the consequences to which it leads. These may lie either
The in the way of making us think, or in the way of
pragmatic making us act. Whoever has a clear idea of these
rule knows effectively what the concept practically signifies, whether its substantive content be interesting in its
own right or not.

This consideration has led to a method of interpreting concepts to which I shall give the name of *the Pragmatic Rule*.[2]

The pragmatic rule is that the meaning of a concept may
always be found, if not in some sensible particular which it
directly designates, then in some particular difference in the
course of human experience which its being true will make.
Test every concept by the question 'What sensible difference
to anybody will its truth make?' and you are in the best possible position for understanding what it means and for discussing its importance. If, questioning whether a certain
concept be true or false, you can think of absolutely nothing

[1] On this functional tendency compare H. Taine, *On Intelligence*, book i,
chap. ii (1870).

[2] Compare W. James, *Pragmatism*, chap. ii and *passim*; also Baldwin's *Dictionary of Philosophy*, article 'Pragmatism,' by C. S. Peirce.

that would practically differ in the two cases, you may assume that the alternative is meaningless and that your concept is no distinct idea. If two concepts lead you to infer the same particular consequence, then you may assume that they embody the same meaning under different names.

This rule applies to concepts of every order of complexity, from simple terms to propositions uniting many terms.

So many disputes in philosophy hinge upon ill-defined words and ideas, each side claiming its own word or idea to be true, that any accepted method of making meanings clear must be of great utility. No method can be handier of application than our pragmatic rule. If you claim that any idea is true, assign at the same time some difference that its being true will make in some possible person's history, and we shall know not only just what you are really claiming but also how important an issue it is, and how to go to work to verify the claim. In obeying this rule we neglect the substantive content of the concept, and follow its function only. This neglect might seem at first sight to need excuse, for the content often has a value of its own which might conceivably add lustre to reality, if it existed, apart from any modification wrought by it in the other parts of reality. Thus it is often supposed that 'Idealism' is a theory precious in itself, even though no definite change in the details of our experience can be deduced from it. Later discussion will show that this is a superficial view, and that particular consequences are the only criterion of a concept's meaning, and the only test of its truth.

Instances are hardly called for, they are so obvious. That A and B are 'equal,' for example, means either that 'you will find Examples   no difference' when you pass from one to the other, or that in substituting one for the other in certain operations 'you will get the same result both times.' 'Substance' means that 'a definite group of sensations will recur.' 'Incommensurable' means that 'you are always confronted with a remainder.' 'Infinite' means either that, or that 'you can count as many units in a part as you can in the whole.' 'More' and 'less' mean certain sensations, varying according to the matter. 'Freedom' means 'no feeling of sensible restraint.' 'Necessity' means that 'your way is blocked in all directions save one.'

'God' means that 'you can dismiss certain kinds of fear,' 'cause' that 'you may expect certain sequences,' etc. etc. We shall find plenty of examples in the rest of this book; so I go back now to the more general question of whether the whole import of the world of concepts lies in its relation to perceptual experience, or whether it be also an independent revelation of reality. Great ambiguity is possible in answering this question, so we must mind our Ps and Qs.

The first thing to notice is that in the earliest stages of human intelligence, so far as we can guess at them, thought proper must have had an exclusively practical use. Men classed their sensations, substituting concepts for them, in order to 'work them for what they were worth,' and to prepare for what might lie ahead. Class-names suggest consequences that have attached themselves on other occasions to other members of the class—consequences which the present percept will also probably or certainly show.[1] The present percept in its immediacy may thus often sink to the status of a bare sign of the consequences which the substituted concept suggests.

Origin of concepts in their utility

The substitution of concepts and their connections, of a whole conceptual order, in short, for the immediate perceptual flow, thus widens enormously our mental panorama. Had we no concepts we should live simply 'getting' each successive moment of experience, as the sessile sea-anemone on its rock receives whatever nourishment the wash of the waves may bring. With concepts we go in quest of the absent, meet the remote, actively turn this way or that, bend our experience, and make it tell us whither it is bound. We change its order, run it backwards, bring far bits together and separate near bits, jump about over its surface instead of plowing through its continuity, string its items on as many ideal diagrams as our mind can frame. All these are ways of *handling* the perceptual flux and *meeting* distant parts of it; and as far as this primary function of conception goes, we can only conclude it to be what I began by calling it, a faculty superadded to our barely perceptual consciousness for its use in practically

[1] For practical uses of conception compare W. James, *Principles of Psychology*, chap. xxii; I. E. Miller, *The Psychology of Thinking*, 1909, *passim*, but especially chaps. xv, xvi, xvii.

adapting us to a larger environment than that of which brutes take account.[1] We *harness* perceptual reality in concepts in order to drive it better to our ends.

Does our conceptual translation of the perceptual flux enable us also to understand the latter better? What do we mean by making us 'understand'? Applying our pragmatic rule to the interpretation of the word, we see that the better we understand anything the more we are able to *tell about it*. Judged by this test, concepts do make us understand our percepts better: knowing *what* these are, we can tell all sorts of farther truths about them, based on the relation of those whats to other whats. The whole system of relations, spatial, temporal, and logical, of our fact, gets plotted out. An ancient philosophical opinion, inherited from Aristotle, is that we do not understand a thing until we know it by its causes. When the maid-servant says that 'the cat' broke the tea-cup, she would have us conceive the fracture in a causally explanatory way. No otherwise when Clerk-Maxwell asks us to conceive of gas-electricity as due to molecular bombardment. An imaginary agent out of sight becomes in each case a part of the cosmic context in which we now place the percept to be explained; and the explanation is valid in so far as the new causal *that* is itself conceived in a context that makes its existence probable, and with a nature agreeable to the effects it is imagined to produce. All our scientific explanations would seem to conform to this simple type of the 'necessary cat.' The conceived order of nature built round the perceived order and explaining it theoretically, as we say, is only a system of hypothetically imagined *thats*, the *whats* of which harmoniously connect themselves with the *what* of any *that* which we immediately perceive.

The system is essentially a topographic system, a system of the distribution of things. It tells us what's what, and where's where. In so far forth it merely prolongs that opening up of the perspective of practical consequences which we found to be the primordial utility of the conceiving faculty: it adapts us to an immense environment. Working by the causes of

---

[1] Herbert Spencer in his *Psychology*, parts iii and iv, has at great length tried to show that such adaptation is the sole meaning of our intellect.

things we gain advantages which we never should have compassed had we worked by the things alone.

But in order to reach such results the concepts in the explanatory system must, I said, 'harmoniously connect.' What does that mean? Is this also only a practical advantage, or is it something more? It seems something more, for it points to the fact that when concepts of various sorts are once abstracted or constructed, new relations are then found between them, connecting them in peculiarly intimate, 'rational,' and unchangeable ways. In another book[1] I have tried to show that these rational relations are all products of our faculty of comparison and of our sense of 'more.'

In the a priori sciences

The sciences which exhibit these relations are the so-called *a priori* sciences of mathematics and logic.[2] But these sciences express relations of comparison and identification exclusively. Geometry and algebra, for example, first define certain conceptual objects, and then establish equations between them, substituting equals for equals. Logic has been defined as the 'substitution of similars'; and in general one may say that the perception of likeness and unlikeness generates the whole of 'rational' or 'necessary' truth. Nothing *happens* in the worlds of logic, mathematics or moral and æsthetic preference. The static nature of the relations in these worlds is what gives to the propositions that express them their 'eternal' character: The binomial theorem, e. g., expresses the value of any power of any sum of two terms, to the end of time.

These vast unmoving systems of universal terms form the new worlds of thought of which I spoke on page 1011. The terms are elements (or are framed of elements) abstracted from the perceptual flux; but in their abstract shape we note relations between them (and again between these relations) which enable us to set up various schemes of fixed serial orders or of 'more and more.' The terms are indeed man-made, but the order, being established solely by comparison, is fixed by the nature of the terms on the one hand and by our power

---

[1] *Principles of Psychology*, 1890, chap. xxviii.

[2] The 'necessary' character of the abstract truths which these sciences exhibit is well explained by G. H. Lewes: *Problems of Life and Mind*, Problem 1, chapters iv, xiii, especially p. 405 f. of the English edition (1874).

of perceiving relations on the other. Thus two abstract twos are always the same as an abstract four; what contains the container contains the contained of whatever material either be made; equals added to equals always give equal results, in the world in which abstract equality is the only property the terms are supposed to possess; the more than the more is more than the less, no matter in what direction of moreness we advance; if you dot off a term in one series every time you dot one off in another, the two series will either never end, or will come to an end together, or one will be exhausted first, etc. etc.; the result being those skeletons of 'rational' or 'necessary' truth in which our logic- and mathematics-books (sometimes our philosophy-books) arrange their universal terms.

The 'rationalization' of any mass of perceptual fact consists in assimilating its concrete terms, one by one, to so many terms of the conceptual series, and then in assuming that the relations intuitively found among the latter are what connect the former too. Thus we rationalize gas-pressure by identifying it with the blows of hypothetic molecules; then we see that the more closely the molecules are crowded the more frequent the blows upon the containing walls will become; then we discern the exact proportionality of the crowding with the number of blows; so that finally Mariotte's empirical law gets rationally explained. All our transformations of the sense-order into a more rational equivalent are similar to this one. We interrogate the beautiful apparition, as Emerson calls it, which our senses ceaselessly raise upon our path, and the items there refer us to their interpretants in the shape of ideal constructions in some static arrangement which our mind has already made out of its concepts alone. The interpretants are then substituted for the sensations, which thus get rationally conceived. To 'explain' means to coördinate, one to one, the *thises* of the perceptual flow with the *whats* of the ideal manifold, whichever it be.[1]

We may well call this a theoretic conquest over the order in which nature originally comes. The conceptual order into which we translate our experience seems not only a means of

[1] Compare W. Ostwald: *Vorlesungen über Naturphilosophie, Sechste Vorlesung.*

practical adaptation, but the revelation of a deeper level of reality in things. Being more constant, it is *truer*, less illusory than the perceptual order, and ought to command our attention more.

There is still another reason why conception appears such an exalted function. Concepts not only guide us over the map

Concepts bring new values

of life, but we *revalue* life by their use. Their relation to percepts is like that of sight to touch. Sight indeed helps us by preparing us for contacts while they are yet far off, but it endows us in addition with a new world of optical splendor, interesting enough all by itself to occupy a busy life. Just so do concepts bring their proper splendor. The mere possession of such vast and simple pictures is an inspiring good: they arouse new feelings of sublimity, power, and admiration, new interests and motivations.

Ideality often clings to things only when they are taken thus abstractly. "Causes, as anti-slavery, democracy, etc., dwindle when realized in their sordid particulars. Abstractions will touch us when we are callous to the concrete instances in which they lie embodied. Loyal in our measure to particular ideals, we soon set up abstract loyalty as something of a superior order, to be infinitely loyal to; and truth at large becomes a 'momentous issue' compared with which truths in detail are 'poor scraps, mere crumbling successes.' "[1] So strongly do objects that come as universal and eternal arouse our sensibilities, so greatly do life's values deepen when we translate percepts into ideas! The translation appears as far more than the original's equivalent.

---

[1] J. Royce: *The Philosophy of Loyalty*, 1908, particularly Lecture vii, § 5.

Emerson writes: 'Each man sees over his own experience a certain stain of error, whilst that of other men looks fair and ideal. Let any man go back to those delicious relations which make the beauty of his life, which have given him sincerest instruction and nourishment, he will shrink and moan. Alas! I know not why, but infinite compunctions embitter in mature life the remembrances of budding joy, and cover every beloved name. Everything is beautiful seen from the point of view of the intellect, or as truth, but all is sour, if seen as experience. Details are melancholy; the plan is seemly and noble. In the actual world—the painful kingdom of time and place—dwell care, and canker, and fear. With thought, with the ideal, is immortal hilarity, the rose of Joy. Round it all the muses sing. But grief clings to names and persons, and the partial interests of to-day and yesterday.' (*Essay on Love*.)

Summary   *Concepts thus play three distinct parts* in human life.

1. They steer us practically every day, and provide an immense map of relations among the elements of things, which, though not now, yet on some possible future occasion, may help to steer us practically;

2. They bring new values into our perceptual life, they reanimate our wills, and make our action turn upon new points of emphasis;

3. The map which the mind frames out of them is an object which possesses, when once it has been framed, an independent existence. It suffices all by itself for purposes of study. The 'eternal' truths it contains would have to be acknowledged even were the world of sense annihilated.

We thus see clearly what is gained and what is lost when percepts are translated into concepts. Perception is solely of the here and now; conception is of the like and unlike, of the future, of the past, and of the far away. But this map of what surrounds the present, like all maps, is only a surface; its features are but abstract signs and symbols of things that in themselves are concrete bits of sensible experience. We have but to weigh extent against content, thickness against spread, and we see that for some purposes the one, for other purposes the other, has the higher value. Who can decide offhand which is absolutely better, to live or to understand life? We must do both alternately, and a man can no more limit himself to either than a pair of scissors can cut with a single one of its blades.

CHAPTER V

PERCEPT AND CONCEPT—THE ABUSE OF CONCEPTS

IN SPITE of this obvious need of holding our percepts fast if our conceptual powers are to mean anything distinct, there has always been a tendency among philosophers to treat conception as the more essential thing in knowledge.[1] The Platonizing persuasion has ever been that the intelligible order ought to supersede the senses rather than interpret them. The senses, according to this opinion, are organs of wavering illusion that stand in the way of 'knowledge,' in the unalterable sense of that term. They are an unfortunate complication on which philosophers may safely turn their backs.

The intellectualist creed

'Your sensational modalities,' writes one of these, 'are but darkness, remember that. Mount higher, up to reason, and you will see light. Impose silence on your senses, your imagination, and your passions, and you will then hear the pure voice of interior truth, the clear and evident replies of our common mistress [reason]. Never confound that evidence which results from the comparison of ideas with the vivacity of those feelings which move and touch you. . . . We must follow reason despite the caresses, the threats and the insults of the body to which we are conjoined, despite the action of the objects that surround us. . . . I exhort you to recognize the difference there is between knowing and feeling, between our clear ideas, and our sensations always obscure and confused.'[2]

This is the traditional intellectualist creed. When Plato, its originator, first thought of concepts as forming an entirely separate world and treated this as the only object fit for the study of immortal minds, he lit up an entirely new sort of enthusiasm in the human breast. These objects were precious objects, concrete things were dross. Introduced by Dion,

---

[1]The traditional rationalist view would have it that to understand life, without entering its turmoil, is the absolutely better part. Philosophy's 'special work,' writes William Wallace, 'is to comprehend the world, not try to make it better' (*Prolegomena to the Study of Hegel's Philosophy*, 2d edition, Oxford, 1894, p. 29).

[2]Malebranche: *Entretiens sur la Métaphysique*, 3me. Entretien, viii, 9.

who had studied at Athens, to the corrupt and worldly court of the tyrant of Syracuse, Plato, as Plutarch tells us, 'was received with wonderful kindness and respect. . . . The citizens began to entertain marvellous hopes of a speedy reformation when they observed the modesty which now ruled the banquets, and the general decorum which reigned in all the court, their tyrant also behaving himself with gentleness and humanity. . . . There was a general passion for reasoning and philosophy, so much so that the very palace, it is reported, was filled with dust by the concourse of the students in mathematics who were working their problems there' in the sand. Some 'professed to be indignant that the Athenians, who formerly had come to Syracuse with a great fleet and numerous army, and perished miserably without being able to take the city, should now, by means of one sophister, overturn the sovereignty of Dionysius; inveigling him to cashier his guard of 10,000 lances, dismiss a navy of 400 galleys, disband an army of 10,000 horse and many times over that number of foot, and go seek in the schools an unknown and imaginary bliss, and learn by the mathematics how to be happy.'

Having now set forth the merits of the conceptual translation, I must proceed to show its shortcomings. We extend our

Defects of the conceptual translation view when we insert our percepts into our conceptual map. We learn *about* them, and of some of them we transfigure the value; but the map remains superficial through the abstractness, and false through the discreteness of its elements; and the whole operation, so far from making things appear more rational, becomes the source of quite gratuitous unintelligibilities. Conceptual knowledge is forever inadequate to the fulness of the reality to be known. Reality consists of existential particulars as well as of essences and universals and class-names, and of existential particulars we become aware only in the perceptual flux. The flux can never be superseded. We must carry it with us to the bitter

The insuperability of sensation end of our cognitive business, keeping it in the midst of the translation even when the latter proves illuminating, and falling back on it alone when the translation gives out. 'The insuperability of sensation' would be a short expression of my thesis.

To prove it, I must show: 1. That concepts are secondary formations, inadequate, and only ministerial; and 2. That they falsify as well as omit, and make the flux impossible to understand.

1. Conception is a secondary process, not indispensable to life. It presupposes perception, which is self-sufficing, as all lower creatures, in whom conscious life goes on by reflex adaptations, show.

To understand a concept you must know what it *means*. It means always some *this*, or some abstract portion of a *this*, with which we first made acquaintance in the perceptual world, or else some grouping of such abstract portions. All conceptual content is borrowed: to know what the concept 'color' means you must have *seen* red or blue, or green. To know what 'resistance' means, you must have made some effort; to know what 'motion' means, you must have had some experience, active or passive, thereof. This applies as much to concepts of the most rarified order as to qualities like 'bright' and 'loud.' To know what the word 'illation' means one must once have sweated through some particular argument. To know what a 'proportion' means one must have compared ratios in some sensible case. You can create new concepts out of old elements, but the elements must have been perceptually given; and the famous world of universals would disappear like a soap-bubble if the definite contents of feeling, the *thises* and *thats*, which its terms severally denote, could be at once withdrawn. Whether our concepts live by returning to the perceptual world or not, they live by having come from it. It is the nourishing ground from which their sap is drawn.

2. Conceptual treatment of perceptual reality makes it seem paradoxical and incomprehensible; and when radically and consistently carried out, it leads to the opinion that perceptual experience is not reality at all, but an appearance or illusion.

Briefly, this is a consequence of two facts: First, that when we substitute concepts for percepts, we substitute their rela-

Why concepts are inadequate — tions also. But since the relations of concepts are of static comparison only, it is impossible to substitute them for the dynamic relations with which the perceptual flux is filled. Secondly, the conceptual scheme, consisting as it does of discontinuous terms, can only cover the perceptual flux in spots and incompletely. The one is no full measure of the other, essential features of the flux escaping whenever we put concepts in its place.

This needs considerable explanation, for we have concepts not only of qualities and relations, but of happenings and actions; and it might seem as if these could make the conceptual order active.[1] But this would be a false interpretation. The concepts themselves are fixed, even though they designate parts that move in the flux; they do not act, even though they designate activities; and when we substitute them and their order, we substitute a scheme the intrinsically stationary nature of which is not altered by the fact that some of its terms symbolize changing originals. The concept of 'change,' for example, is always that fixed concept. If it changed, its original self would have to stay to mark what it had changed from; and even then the change would be a perceived continuous process, of which the translation into concepts could only consist in the judgment that later and earlier parts of it

---

[1]Prof. Hibben, in an article in the *Philosophic Review*, vol. xix, pp. 125 ff. (1910), seeks to defend the conceptual order against attacks similar to those in the text, which, he thinks, come from misapprehensions of the true function of logic. 'The peculiar function of thought is to represent the continuous,' he says, and he proves it by the example of the calculus. I reply that the calculus, in substituting for certain perceptual continuities its peculiar symbols, lets us follow changes point by point, and is thus their *practical*, but not their *sensible* equivalent. It cannot *reveal* any change to one who never felt it, but it can lead him to where the change would lead him. It may practically replace the change, but it cannot *reproduce* it. What I am contending for is that the non-reproducible part of reality is an essential part of the content of philosophy, whilst Hibben and the logicists seem to believe that conception, if only adequately attained to, might be all-sufficient. 'It is the peculiar duty and privilege of philosophy,' Mr. Hibben writes, 'to exalt the prerogatives of intellect.' He claims that universals are able to deal adequately with particulars, and that concepts do not so exclude each other, as my text has accused them of doing. Of course 'synthetic' concepts abound, with subconcepts included in them, and the *a priori* world is full of them. But they are all designative; and I think that no careful reader of my text will accuse me of identifying 'knowledge' with either perception or conception absolutely or exclusively. Perception gives 'intension,' conception gives 'extension' to our knowledge.

differed—such 'differences' being conceived as absolutely static relations.

Whenever we conceive a thing we *define* it; and if we still don't understand, we define our definition. Thus I define a certain percept by saying 'this is motion,' or 'I am moving'; and then I define motion by calling it the 'being in new positions at new moments of time.' This habit of telling what everything is becomes inveterate. The farther we push it, the more we learn *about* our subject of discourse, and we end by thinking that knowing the latter always consists in getting farther and farther away from the perceptual type of experience. This uncriticized habit, added to the intrinsic charm of the conceptual form, is the source of 'intellectualism' in philosophy.

Origin of intellectualism

But intellectualism quickly breaks down. When we try to exhaust motion by conceiving it as a summation of parts, *ad infinitum*, we find only insufficiency. Although, when you have a continuum given, you can make cuts and dots in it, *ad libitum*, enumerating the dots and cuts will not give you your continuum back. The rationalist mind admits this; but instead of seeing that the fault is with the concepts, it blames the perceptual flux. This, Kant contends, has no reality in itself, being a mere apparitional birth-place for concepts, to be substituted indefinitely. When these themselves are seen never to attain to a completed sum, reality is sought by such thinkers outside both of the perceptual flow and of the conceptual scheme. Kant lodges it before the flow, in the shape of so-called 'things in themselves';[1] others place it beyond perception, as an Absolute (Bradley), or represent it as a Mind whose ways of thinking transcend ours (Green, the Cairds, Royce). In either case, both our percepts and our concepts are held by such philosophers to falsify reality; but the concepts less than the percepts, for they are static, and by all rationalist authors the ultimate reality is supposed to be static also, while perceptual life fairly boils over with activity and change.

Inadequacy of intellectualism

[1] 'We must suppose Noumena,' says Kant, 'in order to set bounds to the objective validity of sense-knowledge' (*Krit. d. Reinen Vernunft*, 2d ed., p. 310). The old moral need of somehow rebuking 'Sinnlichkeit'!

If we take a few examples, we can see how many of the troubles of philosophy come from assuming that to be understood (or 'known' in the only worthy sense of the word) our flowing life must be cut into discrete bits and pinned upon a fixed relational scheme.

Example 1. *Activity and causation are incomprehensible*, for the conceptual scheme yields nothing like them. Nothing happens therein: concepts are 'timeless,' and can only be juxtaposed and compared. The concept 'dog' does not bite; the concept 'cock' does not crow. So Hume and Kant translate the fact of causation into the crude juxtaposition of two phenomena. Later authors, wishing to mitigate the crudeness, resolve the adjacency, whenever they can, into identity: cause and effect must be the same reality in disguise, and our perception of difference in these successions thus becomes an illusion. Lotze elaborately establishes that the 'influencing' of one thing by another is inconceivable. 'Influence' is a concept, and, as such, a distinct third thing, to be identified neither with the agent nor the patient. What becomes of it on its way from the former to the latter? And when it finds the latter, how does it act upon it? By a second influence which it puts forth in turn?—But then again how? and so forth, and so forth till our whole intuition of activity gets branded as illusory because you cannot possibly reproduce its flowing substance by juxtaposing the discrete. Intellectualism draws the dynamic continuity out of nature as you draw the thread out of a string of beads.

Example 2. *Knowledge is impossible*; for knower is one concept, and known is another. Discrete, separated by a chasm, they are mutually 'transcendent' things, so that how an object can ever get into a subject, or a subject ever get at an object, has become the most unanswerable of philosophic riddles. An insincere riddle, too, for the most hardened 'epistemologist' never really doubts that knowledge somehow does come off.

Example 3. *Personal identity is conceptually impossible*. 'Ideas' and 'states of mind' are discrete concepts, and a series of them in time means a plurality of disconnected terms. To such an atomistic plurality the associationists reduce our mental life. Shocked at the discontinuous character of their scheme, the spiritualists assume a 'soul' or 'ego' to melt the separate ideas into one collective consciousness. But this ego itself is but another discrete concept; and the only way not to pile up more puzzles is to endow it with an incomprehensible power of producing that very character of manyness-in-oneness of which rationalists refuse the gift when offered in its immediate perceptual form.

Example 4. *Motion and change are impossible.* Perception changes pulsewise, but the pulses continue each other and melt their bounds. In conceptual translation, however, a continuum can only stand for elements with other elements between them *ad infinitum*, all separately conceived; and such an infinite series can never be exhausted by successive addition. From the time of Zeno the Eleatic, this intrinsic contradictoriness of continuous change has been one of the worst skulls at intellectualism's banquet.

Example 5. *Resemblance, in the way in which we naïvely perceive it, is an illusion.* Resemblance must be *defined*; and when defined it reduces to a mixture of identity with otherness. To know a likeness understandingly we must be able to abstract the identical point distinctly. If we fail of this, we remain in our perceptual limbo of 'confusion.'

Example 6. *Our immediate life is full of the sense of direction, but no concept of the direction of a process is possible until the process is completed.* Defined as it is by a beginning and an ending, a direction can never be prospectively but only retrospectively known. Our perceptual discernment beforehand of the way we are going, and all our dim foretastes of the future, have therefore to be treated as inexplicable or illusory features of experience.

Example 7. *No real thing can be in two relations at once*; the same moon, for example, cannot be seen both by you and by me. For the concept 'seen by you' is not the concept 'seen by me'; and if, taking the moon as a grammatical subject and, predicating one of these concepts of it, you then predicate the other also, you become guilty of the logical sin of saying that a thing can both be A and not-A at once. Learned trifling again; for clear though the conceptual contradictions be, nobody sincerely disbelieves that two men see the same thing.

Example 8. *No relation can be comprehended or held to be real in the form in which we innocently assume it.* A relation is a distinct concept; and when you try to make two other concepts continuous by putting a relation between them, you only increase the discontinuity. You have now conceived three things instead of two, and have two gaps instead of one to bridge over. Continuity is impossible in the conceptual world.

Example 9. *The very relation of subject to predicate in our judgments, the backbone of conceptual thinking itself, is unintelligible and self-contradictory.* Predicates are ready-made universal ideas by which we qualify perceptual singulars or other ideas. Sugar, for example, we say 'is' sweet. But if the sugar was *already* sweet, you have made no step in knowledge; whilst if not so already, you are identifying it with a concept, with which, in its universality, the particular sugar cannot be identical. Thus neither the sugar as described, nor your description, is comprehensible.[1]

These profundities of inconceivability, and many others like them, arise from the vain attempt to reconvert the manifold into which our conception has resolved things, back into the continuum out of which it came. The concept 'many' is not the concept 'one'; therefore the manyness-in-oneness which perception offers is impossible to construe intellectually. Youthful readers will find such difficulties too whimsical to be taken seriously; but since the days of the Greek sophists these dialectic puzzles have lain beneath the surface of all our thinking like the shoals and snags in the Mississippi river; and the more intellectually conscientious the thinkers have been, the less they have allowed themselves to disregard them. But most philosophers have

Attitude of philosophers to the 'dialectic' difficulties

---

[1] I have cited in the text only such conceptual puzzles as have become classic in philosophy, but the concepts current in physical science have also developed mutual oppugnancies which (although not yet classic commonplaces in philosophy) are beginning to make physicists doubt whether such notions develop unconditional 'truth.' Many physicists now think that the concepts of 'matter,' 'mass,' 'atom,' 'ether,' 'inertia,' 'force,' etc. are not so much duplicates of hidden realities in nature as mental instruments to handle nature by after-substitution of their scheme. They are considered, like the kilogram or the imperial yard, 'artefacts,' not revelations. The literature here is copious: J. B. Stallo's *Concepts and Theories of Modern Physics* (1882); pp. 136–140 especially, are fundamental. Mach, Ostwald, Pearson, Duhem, Milhaud, LeRoy, Wilbois, H. Poincaré, are other critics of a similar sort.

noticed this or that puzzle only, and ignored the others. The pyrrhonian Sceptics first, then Hegel,[1] then in our day Bradley and Bergson, are the only writers I know who have faced them collectively, and proposed a solution applicable to them all.

The sceptics gave up the whole notion of truth light-heartedly, and advised their pupils not to care about it.[2] Hegel
The sceptics and Hegel wrote so abominably that I cannot understand him, and will say nothing about him here.[3] Bradley and Bergson write with beautiful clearness and their arguments continue all that I have said.

Mr. Bradley agrees that immediate feeling possesses a native wholeness which conceptual treatment analyzes into a
Bradley on percept and concept many, but cannot unite again. In every 'this' as merely felt, Bradley says, we 'encounter' reality, but we encounter it only as a fragment, see it, as it were, only 'through a hole.'[4] Our sole practicable way of extending and completing this fragment is by using our intellect with its universal ideas. But with ideas, that harmonious compenetration of manyness-in-oneness which feeling originally gave is no longer possible. Concepts indeed extend our *this*, but lose the inner secret of its wholeness; when ideal 'truth' is substituted for 'reality' the very nature of 'reality' disappears.

The fault being due entirely to the conceptual form in which we have to think things, one might naturally expect that one who recognizes its inferiority to the perceptual form as clearly as Mr. Bradley does, would try to save both forms for philosophy, delimiting their scopes, and showing how, as

[1] I omit Herbart, perhaps wrongly.

[2] See any history of philosophy, *sub voce* 'Pyrrho.'

[3] Hegel connects immediate perception with ideal truth by a ladder of intermediary concepts—at least, I suppose they are concepts. The best opinion among his interpreters seems to be that ideal truth does not abolish immediate perception, but preserves it as an indispensable 'moment.' Compare, e. g., H. W. Dresser: *The Philosophy of the Spirit*, 1908; Supplementary Essay: 'On the Element of Irrationality in the Hegelian Dialectic.' In other words Hegel does not pull up the ladder after him when he gets to the top, and may therefore be counted as a non-intellectualist, in spite of his desperately intellectualist *tone*.

[4] F. H. Bradley: *The Principles of Logic*, book i, chap. ii, pp. 29–32.

our experience works, they supplement each other. This is M. Bergson's procedure; but Bradley, though a traitor to orthodox intellectualism in holding fast to feeling as a revealer of the inner oneness of reality, has yet remained orthodox enough to refuse to admit immediate feeling into 'philosophy' at all. 'For worse or for better,' he writes, 'the man who stays on particular feeling must remain outside philosophy.' The philosopher's business, according to Mr. Bradley, is to qualify the real 'ideally' (i. e. by concepts), and never to look back. The 'ideas' meanwhile yield nothing but a patchwork, and show no unity like that which the living perception gave. What shall one do in these perplexing circumstances? Unwilling to go back, Bradley only goes more desperately forward. He makes a flying leap ahead, and assumes, beyond the vanishing point of the whole conceptual perspective, an 'absolute' reality, in which the coherency of feeling and the completeness of the intellectual ideal shall unite in some indescribable way. Such an absolute totality-in-unity *can* be, it *must* be, it *shall* be, it *is* he says. Upon this incomprehensible metaphysical object the Bradleyan metaphysic establishes its domain.[1]

The sincerity of Bradley's criticisms has cleared the air of metaphysics and made havoc with old party lines. But, critical as he is, Mr. Bradley preserves one prejudice uncriticized. Perception 'untransmuted,' he believes, must not, cannot, shall not, enter into final 'truth.'

Criticism of Bradley

Such loyalty to a blank direction in thought, no matter where it leads you, is pathetic: concepts disintegrate—no matter, their way must be pursued; percepts are integral—no matter, they must be left behind. When anti-sensationalism has become an obstinacy like this, one feels that it draws near its end.

Since it is only the conceptual form which forces the dialectic contradictions upon the innocent sensible reality, the remedy would seem to be simple. Use concepts when they help, and drop them when they hinder understanding; and take reality bodily and integrally up into philosophy in exactly the perceptual shape in which it comes. The aboriginal flow of

---

[1] Mr. Bradley has expressed himself most pregnantly in an article in volume xviii, N. S. of *Mind*, p. 489. See also his *Appearance and Reality*, *passim*, especially the Appendix to the second edition.

feeling sins only by a quantitative defect. There is always much-at-once of it, but there is never enough, and we desiderate the rest. The only way to get the rest without wading through all future time in the person of numberless perceivers, is to substitute our various conceptual systems which, monstrous abridgments though they be, are nevertheless each an equivalent, for some partial aspect of the full perceptual reality which we can never grasp.

This, essentially, is Bergson's view of the matter, and with it I think that we should rest content.[1]

I will now sum up compendiously the result of what precedes. If the aim of philosophy were the taking full possession Summary of all reality by the mind, then nothing short of the whole of immediate perceptual experience could be the subject-matter of philosophy, for only in such experience is reality intimately and concretely found. But the philosopher, although he is unable as a finite being to compass more than a few passing moments of such experience, is yet able to extend his knowledge beyond such moments by the ideal symbol of the other moments.[2] He thus commands vicariously innumerable perceptions that are out of range. But the concepts by which he does this, being thin extracts from perception, are always insufficient representatives thereof; and, although they yield wider information, must never be treated after the rationalistic fashion, as if they gave a deeper quality of truth. The deeper features of reality are found only in perceptual experience. Here alone do we acquaint ourselves with continuity, or the immersion of one thing in another, here alone with self, with substance, with qualities, with activity in its various modes, with time, with cause, with change, with novelty, with tendency, and with freedom. Against all such

[1] Bergson's most compendious statement of his doctrine is in the 'Introduction à la Métaphysique,' in the *Revue de Métaphysique et de Morale*, 1903, p. i. For a brief comparison between him and Bradley, see an essay by W. James, in the *Journal of Philosophy*, vol. vii, no. 2.

[2] It would seem that in 'mystical' ways, he may extend his vision to an even wider perceptual panorama than that usually open to the scientific mind. I understand Bergson to favor some such idea as this. See W. James: 'A Suggestion about Mysticism,' *Journal of Philosophy*, vii, 4. The subject of mystical knowledge, as yet very imperfectly understood, has been neglected both by philosophers and scientific men.

features of reality the method of conceptual translation, when candidly and critically followed out, can only raise its *non possumus*, and brand them as unreal or absurd.

CHAPTER VI

PERCEPT AND CONCEPT—SOME COROLLARIES

THE FIRST COROLLARY of the conclusions of the fore-going chapter is that *the tendency known in philosophy as empiricism, becomes confirmed*. Empiricism proceeds from parts to wholes, treating the parts as fundamental both in the order of being and in the order of our knowledge.[1] In human experience the parts are percepts, built out into wholes by our conceptual additions. The percepts are singulars that change incessantly and never return exactly as they were before. This brings an element of concrete novelty into our experience. This novelty finds no representation in the conceptual method, for concepts are abstracted from experiences already seen or given, and he who uses them to divine the new can never do so but in ready-made and ancient terms. Whatever actual novelty the future may contain (and the singularity and individuality of each moment makes it novel) escapes conceptual treatment altogether. Properly speaking, concepts are post-mortem preparations, sufficient only for retrospective understanding; and when we use them to define the universe prospectively we ought to realize that they can give only a bare abstract outline or approximate sketch, in the filling out of which perception must be invoked.

I. Novelty becomes possible

Rationalistic philosophy has always aspired to a rounded-in view of the whole of things, a closed system of kinds, from which the notion of essential novelty being possible is ruled out in advance. For empiricism, on the other hand, reality cannot be thus confined by a conceptual ring-fence. It over-flows, exceeds, and alters. It may turn into novelties, and can be known adequately only by following its singularities from moment to moment as our experience grows. Empiricist philosophy thus renounces the pretension to an all-inclusive

[1] Naturally this applies in the present place only to the greater whole which philosophy considers; the universe namely, and its parts, for there are plenty of minor wholes (animal and social organisms, for example) in which both the being of the parts and our understanding of the parts are founded.

vision. It ekes out the narrowness of personal experience by concepts which it finds useful but not sovereign; but it stays inside the flux of life expectantly, recording facts, not formulating laws, and never pretending that man's relation to the totality of things as a philosopher is essentially different from his relation to the parts of things as a daily patient or agent in the practical current of events. Philosophy, like life, must keep the doors and windows open.

In the remainder of this book we shall hold fast to this empiricist view. We shall insist that, as reality is created temporally day by day, concepts, although a magnificent sketch-map for showing us our bearings, can never fitly supersede perception, and that the 'eternal' systems which they form should least of all be regarded as realms of being to know which is a kind of knowing that casts the knowledge of particulars altogether into the shade. That rationalist assumption is quite beside the mark. Thus does philosophy prove again that essential identity with science which we argued for in our first chapter.[1]

The last paragraph does not mean that concepts and the relations between them are not just as 'real' in their 'eternal' way as percepts are in their temporal way. What is
2. Conceptual systems are distinct realms of reality
it to be 'real'? The best definition I know is that which the pragmatist rule gives: 'anything is real of which we find ourselves obliged to take account in any way.'[2] Concepts are thus as real as percepts, for we cannot live a moment without taking account of them. But the 'eternal' kind of being which they enjoy is inferior to the temporal kind, because it is so static and schematic and lacks so many characters which temporal reality possesses. Philosophy must thus recognize many realms of reality which mutually interpenetrate. The conceptual systems of mathematics, logic, æsthetics, ethics, are such realms, each strung

[1] One way of stating the empiricist contention is to say that the 'alogical' enters into philosophy on an equal footing with the 'logical.' Mr. Belfort Bax, in his book, *The Roots of Reality* (1907), formulates his empiricism (such as it is) in this way. (See particularly chap. iii.) Compare also E. D. Fawcett: *The Individual and Reality*, *passim*, but especially part ii, chaps. iv and v.

[2] Prof. A. E. Taylor gives this pragmatist definition in his *Elements of Metaphysics* (1903), p. 51. On the nature of logical reality, cf. B. Russell: *Principles of Mathematics*.

upon some peculiar form of relation, and each differing from perceptual reality in that in no one of them is history or happening displayed. Perceptual reality involves and contains all these ideal systems, and vastly more besides.

A concept, it was said above, means always the same thing: Change means always change, white always white, a circle always a circle. On this self-sameness of conceptual objects the static and 'eternal' character of our systems of ideal truth is based; for a relation, once perceived to obtain, must obtain always, between terms that do not alter. But many persons find difficulty in admitting that a concept used in different contexts can be intrinsically the same. When we call both snow and paper 'white' it is supposed by these thinkers that there must be two predicates in the field. As James Mill says:[1] 'Every colour is an individual colour, every size is an individual size, every shape is an individual shape. But things have no individual colour in common, no individual shape in common; no individual size in common; that is to say, they have neither shape, colour, nor size in common. What, then, is it which they have in common which the mind can take into view? Those who affirmed that it was something, could by no means tell. They substituted words for things; using vague and mystical phrases, which, when examined, meant nothing.' The truth, according to this nominalist author, is that the only thing that can be possessed in common by two objects is the same *name*. Black in the coat and black in the shoe are the same in so far forth as both shoe and coat are called black—the fact that on this view the name can never twice be the 'same' being quite overlooked. What now does the concept 'same' signify? Applying, as usual, the pragmatic rule, we find that when we call two objects the same we mean either (a) that no difference can be found between them when compared, or (b) that we can substitute the one for the other in certain operations without changing the result. If we are to discuss sameness profitably we must bear these pragmatic meanings in mind.

Do then the snow and the paper show no difference in color? And can we use them indifferently in operations?

3. The self-sameness of ideal objects

_____
[1] *Analysis of the Human Mind* (1869), i, 249.

They may certainly replace each other for reflecting light, or be used indifferently as backgrounds to set off anything dark, or serve as equally good samples of what the word 'white' signifies. But the snow may be dirty, and the paper pinkish or yellowish without ceasing to be called 'white'; or both snow and paper in one light may differ from their own selves in another and still be 'white,'—so the no-difference criterion seems to be at fault. This physical difficulty (which all house painters know) of matching two tints so exactly as to show no difference seems to be the sort of fact that nominalists have in mind when they say that our ideal meanings are never twice the same. Must we therefore admit that such a concept as 'white' can never keep exactly the same meaning?

It would be absurd to say so, for we know that under all the modifications wrought by changing light, dirt, impurity in pigment, etc., there is an element of color-quality, different from other color-qualities, which we mean that our word *shall* inalterably signify. The impossibility of isolating and fixing this quality physically is irrelevant, so long as we can isolate and fix it mentally, and decide that whenever we say 'white,' that identical quality, whether applied rightly or wrongly, is what we shall be held to mean. Our meanings can be the same as often as we intend to have them so, quite irrespective of whether what is meant be a physical possibility or not. Half the ideas we make use of are of impossible or problematic things,—zeros, infinites, fourth dimensions, limits of ideal perfection, forces, relations sundered from their terms, or terms defined only conceptually, by their relations to other terms which may be equally fictitious. 'White' means a color quality of which the mind appoints the standard, and which it can decree to be there under all physical disguises. *That* white is always the same white. What sense can there be in insisting that although we ourselves have fixed it as the same, it cannot be the same twice over? It works perfectly for us on the supposition that it is there self-identically; so the nominalist doctrine is false of things of that conceptual sort, and true only of things in the perceptual flux.

What I am affirming here is the platonic doctrine that concepts are singulars, that concept-stuff is inalterable, and that physical realities are constituted by the various concept-stuffs of which they 'partake.' It is known as 'logical realism' in the history of philosophy; and has usually been more favored by rationalistic than by empiricist minds. For rationalism, concept-stuff is primordial and perceptual things are secondary in nature. The present book, which treats concrete percepts as primordial and concepts as of secondary origin, may be regarded as somewhat eccentric in its attempt to combine logical realism with an otherwise empiricist mode of thought.[1]

I mean by this that they are made of the same kind of stuff, and melt into each other when we handle them together. How could it be otherwise when the concepts are like evaporations out of the bosom of perception, into which they condense again whenever practical service summons them? No one can tell, of the things he now holds in his hand and reads, how much comes in through his eyes and fingers, and how much, from his apperceiving intellect, unites with that and makes of it this particular 'book'? The universal and the particular parts of the experience are literally immersed in each other, and both are indispensable. Conception is not like a painted hook, on which no real chain can be hung; for we hang concepts upon percepts, and percepts upon concepts interchangeably and indefinitely; and the relation of the two is much more like what we find in those cylindrical 'panoramas' in which a painted background continues a real foreground so cunningly that one fails to detect the joint. The world we practically live in is one in which it is impossible, except by theoretic retrospection, to disentangle the contributions of intellect from those of sense. They are wrapt and rolled together as a gunshot in the mountains is wrapt and rolled in fold on fold of echo and reverberative clamor. Even so do intellectual reverberations enlarge and prolong the perceptual experience which they envelop, associating it with remoter parts of existence. And the ideas of these in turn work like those resonators that pick out

4. Concepts and percepts are consubstantial

---

[1] For additional remarks in favor of the sameness of conceptual objects, see W. James in *Mind*, vol. iv, 1879, pp. 331–335; F. H. Bradley: *Ethical Studies* (1876), pp. 151–154, and *Principles of Logic* (1883), pp. 260 ff., 282 ff. The nominalist view is presented by James Mill, as above, and by John Stuart Mill in his *System of Logic*, 8th ed. i, 77.

partial tones in complex sounds. They help us to decompose our percept into parts and to abstract and isolate its elements.

The two mental functions thus play into each other's hands. Perception prompts our thought, and thought in turn enriches our perception. The more we see, the more we think; while the more we think, the more we see in our immediate experiences, and the greater grows the detail and the more significant the articulateness of our perception.[1] Later, when we come to treat of causal activity, we shall see how practically momentous is this enlargement of the span of our knowledge through the wrapping of our percepts in ideas. It is the whole coil and compound of both by which effects are determined, and they may then be different effects from those to which the perceptual nucleus would by itself give rise. But the point is a difficult one and at the present stage of our argument this brief mention of it must suffice.

Readers who by this time agree that our conceptual systems are secondary and on the whole imperfect and ministerial forms of being, will now feel able to return and embrace the flux of their hourly experience with a hearty feeling that, however little of it at a time be given, what is given is absolutely real. Rationalistic thought, with its exclusive interest in the unchanging and the general, has always de-realized the passing pulses of our life. It is no small service on empiricism's part to have exorcised rationalism's veto, and reflectively justified our instinctive feeling about immediate experience. 'Other world?' says Emerson, 'there is no other world,'—than this one, namely, in which our several biographies are founded.

5. An objection replied to

> 'Natur hat weder Kern noch Schale;
> Alles ist sie mit einem male.
> Dich prüfe du nur allermeist,
> Ob du Kern oder Schale seist.'

---

[1] Cf. F. C. S. Schiller: 'Thought and Immediacy,' in the *Journal of Philosophy*, etc., iii, 234. The interpretation goes so deep that we may even act as if experience consisted of nothing but the different kinds of concept-stuff into which we analyze it. Such concept-stuff may often be treated, for purposes of action and even discussion, as if it were a full equivalent for reality. But it is needless to repeat, after what precedes, that no amount of it can ever be a *full* equivalent, and that in point of genesis it remains a secondary formation.

The belief in the genuineness of each particular moment in which we feel the squeeze of this world's life, as we actually do work here, or work is done upon us, is an Eden from which rationalists seek in vain to expel us, now that we have criticized their state of mind.

But they still make one last attempt, and charge us with self-stultification.

'Your belief in the particular moments,' they insist, 'so far as it is based on reflective argument (and is not a mere omission to doubt, like that of cows and horses) is grounded in abstraction and conception. Only by using concepts have you established percepts in reality. The concepts are the vital things, then, and the percepts are dependent on them for the character of "reality" with which your reasoning endows them. You stand self-contradicted: concepts appear as the sole triumphant instruments of truth, for you have to employ their proper authority, even when seeking to install perception in authority above them.'

The objection is specious; but it disappears the moment one recollects that in the last resort a concept can only be *designative*; and that the concept 'reality,' which we restore to immediate perception, is no new conceptual creation, but only a kind of practical relation to our Will, *perceptively experienced*,[1] which reasoning had temporarily interfered with, but which, when the reasoning was neutralized by still further reasoning, reverted to its original seat as if nothing had happened. That concepts can neutralize other concepts is one of their great practical functions. This answers also the charge that it is self-contradictory to use concepts to undermine the credit of conception in general. The best way to show that a knife will not cut is to try to cut with it. Rationalism itself it is that has so fatally undermined conception, by finding that, when worked beyond a certain point, it only piles up dialectic contradictions.[2]

[1] Compare W. James: *Principles of Psychology*, chap. xxi, 'The Perception of Reality.'

[2] Compare further, as to this objection, a note in W. James: *A Pluralistic Universe*, pp. 742–744.

CHAPTER VII

THE ONE AND THE MANY

THE FULL NATURE, as distinguished from the full amount, of reality, we now believe to be given only in the perceptual flux. But, though the flux is continuous from next to next, non-adjacent portions of it are separated by parts that intervene, and such separation seems in a variety of cases to work a positive disconnection. The latter part, e. g., may contain no element surviving from the earlier part, may be unlike it, may forget it, may be shut off from it by physical barriers, or what not. Thus when we use our intellect for cutting up the flux and individualizing its members, we have (provisionally and practically at any rate) to treat an enormous number of these as if they were unrelated or related only remotely, to one another. We handle them piecemeal or distributively, and look at the entire flux as if it were their sum or collection. This encourages the empiricist notion, that the parts are distinct and that the whole is a resultant.

Pluralism vs. monism

This doctrine rationalism opposes, contending that the whole is fundamental, that the parts derive from it and all belong with one another, that the separations we uncritically accept are illusory, and that the entire universe, instead of being a sum, is the only genuine unit in existence, constituting (in the words often quoted from d'Alembert) *'un seul fait et une grande vérité.'*

The alternative here is known as that between pluralism and monism. It is the most pregnant of all the dilemmas of philosophy, although it is only in our time that it has been articulated distinctly. Does reality exist distributively? or collectively?—in the shape of *eaches, everys, anys, eithers*? or only in the shape of an *all* or *whole*? An identical content is compatible with either form obtaining, the Latin *omnes*, or *cuncti*, or the German *alle* or *sämmtliche* expressing the alternatives familiarly. Pluralism stands for the distributive, monism for the collective form of being.

Please note that pluralism need not be supposed at the outset to stand for any particular kind or amount of disconnection between the many things which it assumes. It only has the negative significance of contradicting monism's thesis that there is absolutely *no* disconnection. The irreducible outness of *any*thing, however infinitesimal, from *any*thing else, in *any* respect, would be enough, if it were solidly established, to ruin the monistic doctrine.

I hope that the reader begins to be pained here by the extreme vagueness of the terms I am using. To say that there is 'no disconnection,' is on the face of it simply silly, for we find practical disconnections without number. My pocket is disconnected with Mr. Morgan's bank-account, and King Edward VII's mind is disconnected with this book. Monism must mean that all such apparent disconnections are bridged over by some deeper absolute union in which it believes, and this union must in some way be more real than the practical separations that appear upon the surface.

In point of historical fact monism has generally kept itself vague and mystical as regards the ultimate principle of unity. To be One is more wonderful than to be many, so the principle of things must be One, but of that One no exact account is given. Plotinus simply calls it the One. 'The One is all things and yet no one of them. . . . For the very reason that none of them was in the One, are all derived from it. Furthermore, in order that they may be real existences, the One is not an existence, but the father of existences. And the generation of existence is as it were the first act of generation. Being perfect by reason of neither seeking nor possessing nor needing anything, the One overflows, as it were, and what overflows forms another hypostasis. . . . How should the most perfect and primal good stay shut up in itself as if it were envious or impotent? . . . Necessarily then something comes from it.'[1]

Kinds of monism

Mystical monism

This is like the Hindoo doctrine of the Brahman, or of the Âtman. In the Bhagavat-gita the holy Krishna speaking for the One, says: 'I am the immolation. I am the sacrificial rite. I am the libation offered to ancestors. I am the drug. I am the incantation. I am the sacrificial butter also. I am the fire.

[1] Compare the passages in C. M. Bakewell's *Source-Book in Ancient Philosophy*, pp. 363–370, or the first four books of the Vth Ennead generally, in M. N. Bouillet's translation.

I am the incense. I am the father, the mother, the sustainer, the grandfather of the universe—the mystic doctrine, the purification, the syllable "Om" . . . the path, the supporter, the master, the witness, the habitation, the refuge, the friend, the origin, the dissolution, the place, the receptacle, the inexhaustible seed. I heat (the world). I withhold and pour out the rain. I am ambrosia and death, the existing and the non-existing. . . . I am the same to all beings. I have neither foe nor friend. . . . Place thy heart on me, worshipping me, sacrificing to me, saluting me."[1]

I call this sort of monism mystical, for it not only revels in formulas that defy understanding,[2] but it accredits itself by appealing to states of illumination not vouchsafed to common men. Thus Porphyry, in his life of Plotinus, after saying that he himself once had such an insight, when 68 years old, adds that whilst he lived with Plotinus, the latter four times had the happiness of approaching the supreme God and consciously uniting with him in a real and ineffable act.

The regular mystical way of attaining the vision of the One is by ascetic training, fundamentally the same in all religious systems. But this ineffable kind of Oneness is not strictly philosophical, for philosophy is essentially talkative and explicit, so I must pass it by.

The usual philosophic way of reaching deeper oneness has been by the conception of substance. First used by the Greeks, this notion was elaborated with great care during the Middle Ages. Defined as any being that exists per se, so that Monism of it needs no further subject in which to inhere (*Ens substance ita per se existens, ut non indigeat alio tamquam*

[1] J. C. Thomson's translation, chap. iv.

[2] Al-Ghazzali, the Mohammedan philosopher and mystic, gives a more theistic version of essentially the same idea: 'Allah is the guider aright and the leader astray; he does what he wills and decides what he wishes; there is no opposer of his decision and no repeller of his decree. He created the Garden, and created for it a people, then used them in obedience. And he created the Fire, and created for it a people, then used them in rebellion. . . . Then he said, as has been handed down from the Prophet: "These are in the Garden, and I care not; and these are in the Fire, and I care not." So he is Allah, the Most High, the King, the Reality. He is not asked concerning what he does; but they are asked.' (D. B. MacDonald's translation, in *Hartford Seminary Record*, January, 1910.) Compare for other quotations, W. James: *The Varieties of Religious Experience*, pp. 375–381.

subjecto, cui inhaereat, ad existendum) a 'substance' was first distinguished from all 'accidents' (which do require such a subject of inhesion —*cujus esse est inesse*). It was then identified with the 'principle of individuality' in things, and with their 'essence,' and divided into various types, for example into first and second, simple and compound, complete and incomplete, specific and individual, material and spiritual substances. God, on this view, is a substance, for he exists *per se*, as well as *a se*; but of secondary beings, he is the creator, not the substance, for once created, they also exist *per se* though not *a se*. Thus, for scholasticism, the notion of substance is only a partial unifier, and in its totality, the universe forms a pluralism from the substance-point-of-view.[1]

Spinoza broke away from the scholastic doctrine. He began his 'Ethics' by demonstrating that only one substance is possible, and that that substance can only be the infinite and necessary God.[2] This heresy brought reprobation on Spinoza, but it has been favored by philosophers and poets ever since.

[1] Consult the word 'substance' in the index of any scholastic manual, such as J. Rickaby: *General Metaphysics*; A. Stöckl: *Lehrbuch d. Phil.*; or P. M. Liberatore: *Compendium Logicæ et Metaphysicæ*.

[2] Spinoza has expressed his doctrine briefly in part i of the Appendix to his *Ethics*: 'I have now explained,' he says, 'the nature of God, and his properties; such as that he exists necessarily; that he is unique; that what he is and does flows from the sole necessity of his nature; that he is the free cause of all things whatever; that all things are in God and depend on him in such wise that they can neither be nor be conceived without him; and finally, that all things have been predetermined by God, not indeed by the freedom of his will, or according to his good pleasure, but in virtue of his absolute nature or his infinite potentiality.'—Spinoza goes on to refute the vulgar notion of *final causes*. God pursues no ends—if he did he would lack something. He acts out of the logical necessity of the fulness of his nature.—I find another good monistic statement in a book of the spinozistic type:—'. . . The existence of every compound object in manifestation does not lie in the object itself, but lies in the universal existence which is an absolute unit, containing in itself all that is manifested. All the particularized beings, therefore, . . . are incessantly changing one into the other, coming and going, forming and dissolving through the one universal cause of the *potential universe*, which is the absolute unit of universal existence, depending on the one general law, the one mathematical bond, which is the absolute being, and it changes not in all eternity. Thus, . . . it is the universe as a whole, *in its potential being*, from which the physical universe is individualized; and its being is a mathematical inference from a mathematical or an intellectual universe which was and ever is previously formed by an intellect standing and existing by itself.

The pantheistic spinozistic unity was too sublime a prospect not to captivate the mind. It was not till Locke, Berkeley, and Hume began to put in their 'critical' work that the suspicion began to gain currency that the notion of substance might be only a word masquerading in the shape of an idea.[1]

Locke believed in substances, yet confessed that 'we have no such clear idea at all, but only an uncertain supposition of we know not what, which we take to be the substratum, or support of those ideas we do not know.'[2] He criticized the notion of personal substance as the principles of self-sameness in our different minds. *Experientially*, our personal identity consists, he said, in nothing more than the functional and perceptible fact that our later states of mind continue and remember our earlier ones.[3]

Critique of substance

Berkeley applied the same sort of criticism to the notion of bodily substance. 'When I consider,' he says, 'the two parts ("being" in general, and "supporting accidents") which make the signification of the words "material substance," I am convinced there is no distinct meaning annexed to them. . . . Suppose an intelligence without the help of external bodies to be affected with the same train of sensations that you are, imprinted in the same order, and with like vividness in his mind. I ask whether that intelligence hath not all the reason to believe the existence of corporeal substances, represented by his ideas, and exciting them in his mind, that you can

---

This mathematical or intellectual universe I call Absolute Intellectuality, the God of the Universe.'

(Solomon J. Silberstein: *The Disclosures of the Universal Mysteries*, New York, 1906, pp. 12–13.)

[1] No one believes that such words as 'winter,' 'army,' 'house,' denote substances. They designate collective facts, of which the parts are held together by means that can be experimentally traced. Even when we can't define what groups the effects together, as in 'poison,' 'sickness,' 'strength,' we don't assume a substance, but are willing that the word should designate some phenomenal agency yet to be found out. Nominalists treat all substances after this analogy, and consider 'matter,' 'gold,' 'soul,' as but the names of so many grouped properties, of which the bond of union must be, not some unknowable substance corresponding to the name, but rather some hidden portion of the whole phenomenal fact.

[2] *Essay concerning Human Understanding*, book i, chap. iv, § 18.

[3] Ibid., book ii, chap. xxvii, §§ 9–27.

possibly have for believing the same thing.'[1] Certain *grouped sensations*, in short, are all that corporeal substances are *known-as*, therefore the only meaning which the word 'matter' can claim is that it denotes such sensations and their groupings. They are the only verifiable aspect of the word.

The reader will recognize that in these criticisms our own pragmatic rule is used. What difference in practical experience is it supposed to make that we have each a personal substantial principle? This difference, that we can remember and appropriate our past, calling it 'mine.' What difference that in this book there is a substantial principle? This, that certain optical and tactile sensations cling permanently together in a cluster. The fact that certain perceptual experiences do seem to *belong together* is thus all that the word substance means. Hume carries the criticism to the last degree of clearness. 'We have no idea of substance,' he says, 'distinct from that of a collection of particular qualities, nor have we any other meaning when we either talk or reason concerning it. The idea of a substance . . . is nothing but a collection of simple ideas that are united by the imagination and have a particular name assigned them by which we are able to recall that collection.'[2] Kant's treatment of substance agrees with Hume's in denying all positive content to the notion. It differs in insisting that, by attaching shifting percepts to the permanent name, the category of substance unites them *necessarily* together, and thus makes nature intelligible.[3] It is impossible to assent to this. The grouping of qualities becomes no more intelligible when you call substance a 'category' than when you call it a bare word.

Let us now turn our backs upon ineffable or unintelligible ways of accounting for the world's oneness, and inquire

Pragmatic analysis of oneness

whether, instead of being a principle, the 'oneness' affirmed may not merely be a name like 'substance,' descriptive of the fact that certain *specific and verifiable connections* are found among the parts of the experiential

---

[1] *Principles of Human Knowledge*, part i, §§17, 20.

[2] *Treatise on Human Nature*, part 1, § 6.

[3] *Critique of Pure Reason*: First Analogy of Experience. For further criticism of the substance-concept see J. S. Mill: *A System of Logic*, book i, chap. iii, §§ 6–9; B. P. Bowne: *Metaphysics*, part 1, chap. i. Bowne uses the words being and substance as synonymous.

flux. This brings us back to our pragmatic rule: Suppose there is a oneness in things, what may it be known-as? What differences to you and me will it make?

Our question thus turns upside down, and sets us on a much more promising inquiry. We can easily conceive of things that shall have no connection whatever with each other. We may assume them to inhabit different times and spaces, as the dreams of different persons do even now. They may be so unlike and incommensurable, and so inert towards one another, as never to jostle or interfere. Even now there may actually be whole universes so disparate from ours that we who know ours have no means of perceiving that they exist. We conceive their diversity, however; and by that fact the whole lot of them form what is known in logic as one 'universe of discourse.' To form a universe of discourse argues, as this example shows, no further kind of connection. The importance attached by certain monistic writers to the fact that any chaos may become a universe by being merely named, is to me incomprehensible. We must seek something better in the way of oneness than this susceptibility of being mentally considered together, and named by a collective noun.

What connections may be perceived concretely or in point of fact, among the parts of the collection abstractly designated as our 'world'?

There are innumerable modes of union among its parts, some obtaining on a larger, some on a smaller scale. Not all the parts of our world are united *mechanically*, for some can move without the others moving. They all seem united by *gravitation*, however, so far as they are material things. Some again of these are united *chemically*, while others are not; and the like is true of thermic, optical, electrical, and other *physical* connections. These connections are specifications of what we mean by the word oneness when we apply it to our world. We should not call it one unless its parts were connected in these and other ways. But then it is clear that by the same logic we ought to call it 'many,' so far as its parts are disconnected in these same ways, chemically inert towards one another or non-conductors to electricity, light and heat. In all these modes of union, some parts of the world prove to be conjoined with other parts, so that if you

Kinds of oneness

choose your line of influence and your items rightly, you may travel from pole to pole without an interruption. If, however, you choose them wrongly, you meet with obstacles and non-conductors from the outset, and cannot travel at all. There is thus neither absolute oneness nor absolute manyness from the physical point of view, but a mixture of well-definable modes of both. Moreover, neither the oneness nor the manyness seems the more essential attribute, they are co-ordinate features of the natural world.

There are plenty of other practical differences meant by calling a thing One. Our world, being strung along in time and space, has *temporal and spatial unity.* But time and space relate things by determinately sundering them, so it is hard to say whether the world ought more to be called 'one' or 'many' in this spatial or temporal regard.

The like is true of the *generic oneness* which comes from so many of the worlds being similar. When two things are similar you can make inferences from the one which will hold good of the other, so that this kind of union among things, so far as it obtains, is inexpressibly precious from the logical point of view. But an infinite heterogeneity among things exists alongside of whatever likeness of kind we discover; and our world appears no more distinctly or essentially as a One than as a Many, from this generic point of view.

We have touched on the noetic unity predicable of the world in consequence of our being able to mean the whole of it at once. Widely different from unification by an abstract designation, would be the concrete noetic union wrought by an all-knower of perceptual type who should be acquainted at one stroke with every part of what exists. In such an absolute all-knower idealists believe. Kant, they say, virtually replaced the notion of Substance, by the more intelligible notion of Subject. The 'I am conscious of it,' which on some witness's part must accompany every possible experience, means in the last resort, we are told, one individual witness of the total frame of things, world without end, amen. You may call his undivided act of omniscience instantaneous or eternal, whichever you like, for time is its object just as everything else is, and itself is not in time.

We shall find reasons later for treating noetic monism as an

unverified hypothesis. Over against it there stands the noetic
pluralism which we verify every moment when we
seek information from our friends. According to
this, everything in the world might be known by
somebody, yet not everything by the same knower, or in one
single cognitive act,—much as all mankind is knit in one network of acquaintance, A knowing B, B knowing C,—Y
knowing Z, and Z possibly knowing A again, without the
possibility of anyone knowing everybody at once. This 'concatenated' knowing, going from next to next, is altogether
different from the 'consolidated' knowing supposed to be exercised by the absolute mind. It makes a coherent type of
universe in which the widest knower that exists may yet remain ignorant of much that is known to others.

Unity by concate- nation

There are other systems of concatenation besides the noetic
concatenation. We ourselves are constantly adding to the
connections of things, organizing labor-unions, establishing
postal, consular, mercantile, railroad, telegraph, colonial, and
other systems that bind us and things together in ever wider
reticulations. Some of these systems involve others, some do
not. You cannot have a telephone system without air and copper connections, but you can have air and copper connections
without telephones. You cannot have love without acquaintance, but you can have acquaintance without love, etc. The
same thing, moreover, can belong to many systems, as when
a man is connected with other objects by heat, by gravitation,
by love, and by knowledge.

From the point of view of these partial systems, the world
hangs together from next to next in a variety of ways, so that
when you are off of one thing you can always be on to something else, without ever dropping out of your world. Gravitation is the only positively known sort of connection among
things that reminds us of the consolidated or monistic form
of union. If a 'mass' should change anywhere, the mutual
gravitation of all things would instantaneously alter.

Teleological and æsthetic unions are other forms of systematic union. The world is full of partial purposes, of partial
stories. That they all form chapters of one supreme
purpose and inclusive story is the monistic conjecture. They *seem*, meanwhile, simply to run along-

Unity of purpose, meaning

side of each other—either irrelevantly, or, where they interfere, leading to mutual frustrations,—so the appearance of
things is invincibly pluralistic from this purposive point of
view.

It is a common belief that all particular beings have one
origin and source, either in God, or in atoms all equally old.
There is no real novelty, it is believed, in the universe, the
Unity of   new things that appear having either been eternally
origin   prefigured in the absolute, or being results of the
same *primordia rerum*, atoms, or monads, getting into new
mixtures. But the question of being is so obscure anyhow,
that whether realities have burst into existence all at once, by
a single 'bang,' as it were; or whether they came piecemeal,
and have different ages (so that real novelties may be leaking
into our universe all the time), may here be left an open question, though it is undoubtedly intellectually economical to
suppose that all things are equally old, and that no novelties
leak in.

These results are what the Oneness of the Universe is
known-as. They *are* the oneness, pragmatically considered. A
Summary   world coherent in any of these ways would be no
chaos, but a universe of such or such a grade. (The grades
might differ, however. The parts, e. g., might have space-
relations, but nothing more; or they might also gravitate; or
exchange heat; or know, or love one another, etc.)

Such is the cash-value of the world's unity, empirically realized. Its total unity is the sum of all the partial unities. It
consists of them and follows upon them. Such an idea, however, outrages rationalistic minds, which habitually despise all
this practical small-change. Such minds insist on a deeper,
more through-and-through union of all things in the absolute, 'each in all and all in each,' as the prior condition of
these empirically ascertained connections. But this may be
only a case of the usual worship of abstractions, like calling
'bad weather' the cause of to-day's rain, etc., or accounting
for a man's features by his 'face,' when really the rain *is* the
bad weather, is what you *mean* by 'bad weather,' just as the
features are what you mean by the face.

To sum up, the world is 'one' in some respects, and 'many'
in others. But the respects must be distinctly specified, if

either statement is to be more than the emptiest abstraction. Once we are committed to this soberer view, the question of the One or the Many may well cease to appear important. The amount either of unity or of plurality is in short only a matter for observation to ascertain and write down, in statements which will have to be complicated, in spite of every effort to be concise.

CHAPTER VIII

THE ONE AND THE MANY *(continued)* —
VALUES AND DEFECTS

W^{E MIGHT} dismiss the subject with the preceding chapter[1] were it not for the fact that further consequences follow from the rival hypotheses, and make of the alternative of monism or pluralism what I called it on page 1040, the most 'pregnant' of all the dilemmas of metaphysics.

To begin with, the attribute 'one' seems for many persons

The monistic theory to confer a value, an ineffable illustriousness and dignity upon the world, with which the conception of it as an irreducible 'many' is believed to clash.

Secondly, a through-and-through noetic connection of everything with absolutely everything else is in some quarters held to be indispensable to the world's rationality. Only then might we believe that all things really do *belong* together, instead of being connected by the bare conjunctions 'with' or 'and.' The notion that this latter pluralistic arrangement may obtain is deemed 'irrational'; and of course it does make the world partly alogical or non-rational from a purely intellectual point of view.

Monism thus holds the oneness to be the more vital and essential element. The entire cosmos must be a consolidated

The value of absolute oneness unit, within which each member is determined by the whole to be just that, and from which the slightest incipiency of independence anywhere is ruled out. With Spinoza, monism likes to believe that all things follow from the essence of God as necessarily as from the nature of a triangle it follows that the angles are equal to two right angles. The whole is what yields the parts, not the parts the whole. The universe is *tight*, monism claims, not loose; and you must take the irreducible whole of it just as it is offered, or have no part or lot in it at all. The only alternative allowed by monistic writers is to confess the world's non-rationality—and no philosopher can permit himself to

---

[1] For an amplification of what precedes, the lecture on 'The One and the Many' in W. James: *Pragmatism* (1907), may be referred to.

do that. The form of monism regnant at the present day in philosophic circles is *absolute idealism*. For this way of thinking, the world exists no otherwise than as the object of one infinitely knowing mind. The analogy that suggests the hypothesis here is that of our own finite fields of consciousness, which at every moment envisage a much-at-once composed of parts related variously, and in which both the conjunctions and the disjunctions that appear are there only in so far as we are there as their witnesses, so that they are both 'noetically' and monistically based.

We may well admit the sublimity of this noetic monism and of its vague vision of an underlying connection among all phenomena without exception.[1] It shows itself also able to confer religious stability and peace, and it invokes the authority of mysticism in its favor. Yet, on the other hand, like many another concept unconditionally carried out, Its defects it introduces into philosophy puzzles peculiar to itself, as follows: —

1. It does not account for our finite consciousness. If nothing exists but as the Absolute Mind knows it, how can anything exist otherwise than as that Mind knows it? That Mind knows each thing in one act of knowledge, along with every other thing. Finite minds know things without other things, and this ignorance is the source of most of their woes. We are thus not simply objects to an all-knowing subject: we are subjects on our own account and know differently from its knowing.

2. It creates a problem of evil. Evil, for pluralism, presents only the practical problem of how to get rid of it. For monism the puzzle is theoretical: How—if Perfection be the source, should there be Imperfection? If the world as known to the Absolute be perfect, why should it be known otherwise, in myriads of inferior finite editions also? The perfect edition surely was enough. How do the breakage and dispersion and ignorance get in?

3. It contradicts the character of reality as perceptually experienced. Of our world, change seems an essential in-

---

[1] In its essential features, Spinoza was its first prophet, Fichte and Hegel were its middle exponents, and Josiah Royce is its best contemporary representative.

gredient. There is history. There are novelties, struggles, losses, gains. But the world of the Absolute is represented as unchanging, eternal, or 'out of time,' and is foreign to our powers either of apprehension or of appreciation. Monism usually treats the sense-world as a mirage or illusion.

4. It is fatalistic. Possibility, as distinguished from necessity on the one hand and from impossibility on the other, is an essential category of human thinking. For monism, it is a pure illusion; for whatever is is necessary, and aught else is impossible, if the world be such a unit of fact as monists pretend.

Our sense of 'freedom' supposes that some things at least are decided here and now, that the passing moment may contain some novelty, be an original starting-point of events, and not merely transmit a push from elsewhere. We imagine that in some respects at least the future may not be co-implicated with the past, but may be really addable to it, and indeed addable in one shape *or* another, so that the next turn in events can at any given moment genuinely be ambiguous, i. e., possibly this, but also possibly that.

Monism rules out this whole conception of possibles, so native to our common-sense. The future and the past are linked, she is obliged to say; there can be no genuine novelty anywhere, for to suppose that the universe has a constitution simply additive, with nothing to link things together save what the words 'plus,' 'with,' or 'and' stand for, is repugnant to our reason.

Pluralism, on the other hand, taking perceptual experience at its face-value, is free from all these difficulties. It protests against working our ideas in a vacuum made of conceptual abstractions. Some parts of our world, it admits, cannot exist out of their wholes; but others, it says, can. To some extent The pluralistic theory the world *seems* genuinely additive: it may really be so. We cannot explain conceptually *how* genuine novelties can come; but if one did come we could experience *that* it came. We do, in fact, experience perceptual novelties all the while. Our perceptual experience overlaps our conceptual reason: the *that* transcends the *why*. So the common-sense view of life, as something really dramatic, with work done, and things decided here and now, is acceptable to pluralism. 'Free will' means nothing but real novelty; so pluralism accepts the notion of free will.

But pluralism, accepting a universe unfinished, with doors and windows open to possibilities uncontrollable in advance, gives us less religious certainty than monism, with its absolutely closed-in world. It is true that monism's religious certainty is not rationally based, but is only a faith that 'sees the All-Good in the All-Real.' In point of fact, however, monism is usually willing to exert this optimistic faith: its world is certain to be saved, yes, is saved already, unconditionally and from eternity, in spite of all the phenomenal appearances of risk.[1]

Its defects A world working out an uncertain destiny, as the phenomenal world appears to be doing, is an intolerable idea to the rationalistic mind.

Pluralism, on the other hand, is neither optimistic nor pessimistic, but melioristic, rather. The world, it thinks, may be saved, on condition that its parts shall do their best. But shipwreck in detail, or even on the whole, is among the open possibilities.

There is thus a practical lack of balance about pluralism, which contrasts with monism's peace of mind. The one is a more moral, the other a more religious view; and different men usually let this sort of consideration determine their belief.[2]

Its advantages So far I have sought only to show the respective implications of the rival doctrines without dogmatically deciding which is the more true. It is obvious that pluralism has three great advantages:—

1. It is more 'scientific,' in that it insists that when oneness is predicated, it shall mean definitely ascertainable conjunctive forms. With these the disjunctions ascertainable among things are exactly on a par. The two are co-ordinate aspects of reality. To make the conjunctions more vital and primordial than the separations, monism has to abandon verifiable experience and proclaim a unity that is indescribable.

[1] For an eloquent expression of the monistic position, from the religious point of view, read J. Royce: *The World and the Individual*, vol. ii, lectures 8, 9, 10.

[2] See, as to this religious difference, the closing lecture in W. James's *Pragmatism*.

2. It agrees more with the moral and dramatic expressiveness of life.

3. It is not obliged to stand for any particular amount of plurality, for it triumphs over monism if the smallest morsel of disconnectedness is once found undeniably to exist. 'Ever not quite' is all it says to monism; while monism is obliged to prove that what pluralism asserts can in no amount whatever possibly be true—an infinitely harder task.

The advantages of monism, in turn, are its natural affinity with a certain kind of religious faith, and the peculiar emotional value of the conception that the world is a unitary fact.

So far has our use of the pragmatic rule brought us towards understanding this dilemma. The reader will by this time feel for himself the essential practical difference which it involves. The word 'absence' seems to indicate it. The monistic principle implies that nothing that is can in any way whatever be absent from anything else that is. The pluralistic principle, on the other hand, is quite compatible with some things being absent from operations in which other things find themselves singly or collectively engaged. *Which* things are absent from which other things, and *when*,—these of course are questions which a pluralistic philosophy can settle only by an exact study of details. The past, the present, and the future in perception, for example, are absent from one another, while in imagination they are present or absent as the case may be. If the time-content of the world be not one monistic block of being, if some part, at least, of the future, is added to the past without being virtually one therewith, or implicitly contained therein, then it is absent really as well as phenomenally and may be called an absolute novelty in the world's history in so far forth.

Towards this issue, of the reality or unreality of the novelty that appears, the pragmatic difference between monism and pluralism seems to converge. That we ourselves may be authors of genuine novelty is the thesis of the doctrine of free-will. That genuine novelties can occur means that from the point of view of what is already given, what comes may have to be treated as a matter of *chance*. We are led thus to ask the question: In what manner

Monism, pluralism, and novelty

does new being come? Is it through and through the consequence of older being or is it matter of chance so far as older
being goes?—which is the same thing as asking: Is it original,
in the strict sense of the word?

We connect again here with what was said at the end of
Chapter III. We there agreed that being is a datum or gift
and has to be begged by the philosopher; but we left the
question open as to whether he must beg it all at once or beg
it bit by bit or in instalments. The latter is the more consistently empiricist view, and I shall begin to defend it in the
chapter that follows.

CHAPTER IX

THE PROBLEM OF NOVELTY

THE IMPOTENCE to explain being which we have attributed to all philosophers is, it will be recollected, a conceptual impotence. It is when thinking abstractly of the whole of being at once, as it confronts us ready-made, that we feel our powerlessness so acutely. Possibly, if we followed the empiricist method, considering the parts rather than the whole, and imagining ourselves inside of them perceptually, the subject might defy us less provokingly. We are thus brought back to the problem with which Chapter VII left off. When perceptible amounts of new phenomenal being come to birth, must we hold them to be in all points predetermined and necessary outgrowths of the being already there, or shall we rather admit the possibility that originality may thus instil itself into reality?

If we take concrete perceptual experience, the question can be answered in only one way. 'The same returns not, save to bring the different.' Time keeps budding into new moments, every one of which presents a content which in its individu-
Perceptual ality never was before and will never be again. Of
novelty no concrete bit of experience was an exact duplicate ever framed. 'My youth,' writes Delbœuf, 'has it not taken flight, carrying away with it love, illusion, poetry, and freedom from care, and leaving with me instead science, austere always, often sad and morose, which sometimes I would willingly forget, which repeats to me hour by hour its grave lessons, or chills me by its threats? Will time, which untiringly piles deaths on births, and births on deaths, ever remake an Aristotle or an Archimedes, a Newton or a Descartes? Can our earth ever cover itself again with those gigantic ferns, those immense equisetaceans, in the midst of which the same antediluvian monsters will crawl and wallow as they did of yore? . . . No, what has been will not, cannot, be again. Time moves on with an unfaltering tread, and never strikes twice an identical hour. The instants of which the existence of the world is composed are all dissimilar,—and what-

ever may be done, something remains that can never be reversed.'[1]

The everlasting coming of concrete novelty into being is so obvious that the rationalizing intellect, bent ever on explaining what is by what was, and having no logical principle but identity to explain by, treats the perceptual flux as a phenomenal illusion, resulting from the unceasing re-combination in new forms of mixture, of unalterable elements, coeval with Science and the world. These elements are supposed to be the novelty only real beings; and, for the intellect once grasped by the vision of them, there can be nothing genuinely new under the sun. The world's history, according to molecular science, signifies only the 'redistribution' of the unchanged atoms of the primal firemist, parting and meeting so as to appear to us spectators in the infinitely diversified configurations which we name as processes and things.[2]

So far as physical nature goes few of us experience any temptation to postulate real novelty. The notion of eternal elements and their mixture serves us in so many ways, that

[1] J. Delbœuf: *Revue Philosophique*, vol. ix, p. 138 (1880). On the infinite variety of reality, compare also W. T. Marvin: *An Introduction to Systematic Philosophy*, New York, 1903, pp. 22–30.

[2] The Atomistic philosophy, which has proved so potent a scientific instrument of explanation, was first formulated by Democritus, who died 370 B. C. His life overlapped that of Aristotle, who took what on the whole may be called a biological view of the world, and for whom 'forms' were as real as elements. The conflict of the two modes of explanation has lasted to our day, for some chemists still defend the Aristotelian tradition which the authority of Descartes had interrupted for so long, and deny our right to say that 'water' is not a simple entity, or that oxygen and hydrogen atoms persist in it unchanged. Compare W. Ostwald: *Die Ueberwindung des wissenschaftlichen Materialismus* (1895), p. 12: 'The atomistic view assumes that when in iron-oxide, for example, all the sensible properties both of iron and oxygen have vanished, iron and oxygen are nevertheless there but now manifest other properties. We are so used to this assumption that it is hard for us to feel its oddity, nay, even its absurdity. When, however, we reflect that all we know of a given kind of matter is its properties, we realize that the assertion that the matter is still there, but without any of those properties, is not far removed from nonsense.' Compare the same author's *Principles of Inorganic Chemistry*, English translation, 2d ed. (1904), p. 149 ff. Also P. Duhem: 'La Notion de Mixte,' in the *Revue de Philosophie*, vol. i, p. 452 ff. (1901).—The whole notion of the eternal fixity of elements is melting away before the new discoveries about radiant matter. See for radical statements G. Le Bon: *L'Évolution de la Matière*.

we adopt unhesitatingly the theory that primordial being is inalterable in its attributes as well as in its quantity, and that the laws by which we describe its habits are uniform in the strictest mathematical sense. These are the absolute conceptual foundations, we think, spread beneath the surface of perceptual variety. It is when we come to human lives, that our

Personal experience and novelty

point of view changes. It is hard to imagine that 'really' our own subjective experiences are only molecular arrangements, even though the molecules be conceived as beings of a psychic kind. A material fact may indeed be different from what we feel it to be, but what sense is there in saying that a feeling, which has no other nature than to be felt, is not as it *is* felt? Psychologically considered, our experiences resist conceptual reduction, and our fields of consciousness, taken simply as such, remain just what they appear, even though facts of a molecular order should prove to be the signals of the appearance. Biography is the concrete form in which all that is is immediately given; the perceptual flux is the authentic stuff of each of our biographies, and yields a perfect effervescence of novelty all the time. New men and women, books, accidents, events, inventions, enterprises, burst unceasingly upon the world. It is vain to resolve these into ancient elements, or to say that they belong to ancient kinds, so long as no one of them in its full individuality ever was here before or will ever come again. Men of science and philosophy, the moment they forget their theoretic abstractions, live in their biographies as much as any one else, and believe as naïvely that fact even now is making, and that they themselves, by doing 'original work,' help to determine what the future shall become.

I have already compared the live or perceptual order with the conceptual order from this point of view. Conception knows no way of explaining save by deducing the identical from the identical, so if the world is to be conceptually rationalized no novelty can really come. This is one of the traits in that general bankruptcy of conceptualism, which I enumerated in Chapter V—conceptualism can *name* change and growth, but can translate them into no terms of its own, and is forced to contradict the indestructible sense of life within us by denying that reality grows.

It may seem to the youthful student a rather 'far cry' from the question of the possibility of novelty to the 'problem of the infinite,' but in the history of speculation, the two problems have been connected. Novelty seems to violate continuity; continuity seems to involve 'infinitely' shaded gradation; infinity connects with number; and number with fact in general—for facts have to be numbered. It has thus come to pass that the nonexistence of an infinite number has been held to necessitate the finite character of the constitution of fact; and along with this its discontinuous genesis, or, in other words, its coming into being by discrete increments of novelty however small.

Novelty and the infinite

Thus we find the problem of the infinite already lying across our path. It will be better at this point to interrupt our discussion of the more enveloping question of novelty at large, and to get the minor problem out of our way first. I turn then to the problem of the infinite.

CHAPTER X

NOVELTY AND THE INFINITE—THE CONCEPTUAL VIEW

THE PROBLEM is as to which is the more rational supposition, that of continuous or that of discontinuous additions to whatever amount or kind of reality already exists.

On the discontinuity-theory, time, change, etc., would grow by finite buds or drops, either nothing coming at all, or **The discontinuity-theory** certain units of amount bursting into being 'at a stroke.' Every feature of the universe would on this view have a finite numerical constitution. Just as atoms, not half- or quarter-atoms are the minimum of matter that can be, and every finite amount of matter contains a finite number of atoms, so any amounts of time, space, change, etc., which we might assume would be composed of a finite number of minimal amounts of time, space, and change.

Such a discrete composition is what actually obtains in our perceptual experience. We either perceive nothing, or something already there in sensible amount. This fact is what in psychology is known as the law of the 'threshold.' Either your experience is of no content, of no change, or it is of a perceptible amount of content or change. Your acquaintance with reality grows literally by buds or drops of perception. Intellectually and on reflection you can divide these into components, but as immediately given, they come totally or not at all.

If, however, we take time and space as concepts, not as perceptual data, we don't well see how they can have this atomistic constitution. For if the drops or atoms are themselves without duration or extension it is inconceivable that by adding any number of them together times or spaces **The continuity-theory** should accrue. If, on the other hand, they are minute durations or extensions, it is impossible to treat them as real minima. Each temporal drop must have a later and an earlier half, each spatial unit a right and a left half, and these halves must themselves have halves, and so on *ad infinitum*, so that with the notion that the constitution of things is continuous and not discrete, that of a divisibility *ad* *infinitum* is inseparably bound up. This infinite divisibility of some facts, coupled with the infinite expansibility of others (space, time, and number) has given rise to one of the most obstinate of philosophy's dialectic problems. Let me take up, in as simple a way as I am able to, the *problem of the infinite*.

There is a pseudo-problem, 'How can the finite know the infinite?' which has troubled some English heads.[1] But one might as well make a problem of 'How can the fat know the lean?' When we come to treat of knowledge, such problems will vanish. The real problem of the infinite began with the famous arguments against motion, of Zeno the Eleatic. The school of Pythagoras was pluralistic. 'Things are numbers,' the master had said, meaning apparently that reality was made of points which one might number.[2] Zeno's arguments were meant to show, not that motion could not really take place, but that it could not truly be conceived as taking place by the successive occupancy of points. If a flying arrow occupies at Zeno's each point of time a determinate point of space, its paradoxes motion becomes nothing but a sum of rests, for it exists not, out of any point; and *in* the point it does n't move. Motion cannot truly occur as thus discretely constituted.

Still better known than the 'arrow' is the 'Achilles' paradox. Suppose Achilles to race with a tortoise, and to move twice as fast as his rival, to whom he gives an inch of head-start. By the time he has completed that inch, or in other words advanced to the tortoise's starting point, the tortoise is half an inch ahead of him. While Achilles is traversing that half inch, the tortoise is traversing a quarter of an inch, etc. So that the successive points occupied by the runners simultaneously form a convergent series of distances from the starting point of Achilles. Measured in inches, these distances would run as follows:

$$1 + \frac{1}{2} + \frac{1}{4} + \frac{1}{8} + \frac{1}{16} \cdots + \frac{1}{n} \cdots \frac{1}{\infty}$$

Zeno now assumes that space must be infinitely divisible. But

---

[1] In H. Calderwood's *Philosophy of the Infinite* one will find the subordinate difficulties discussed, with almost no consciousness shown of the important ones.

[2] I follow here J. Burnet: *Early Greek Philosophers* (the chapter on the Pythagoreans), and Paul Tannery: 'Le concept scientifique du continu' in the *Revue Philosophique*, xx, 385.

if so, then the number of points to be occupied cannot all be enumerated in succession, for the series begun above is interminable. Each time that Achilles gets to the tortoise's last point it is but to find that the tortoise has already moved to a further point; and although the interval between the points quickly grows infinitesimal, it is mathematically impossible that the two racers should reach any one point at the same moment. If Achilles could overtake the tortoise, it would be at the end of two inches; and if his speed were two inches a second, it would be at the end of the first second;[1] but the argument shows that he simply cannot overtake the animal. To do so would oblige him to exhaust, by traversing one by one, the whole of them, a series of points which the law of their formation obliges to come never to an end.

Zeno's various arguments were meant to establish the 'Eleatic' doctrine of real being, which was monistic. The 'minima sensibilia' of which space, time, motion, and change consist for our perception are not real 'beings,' for they subdivide themselves *ad infinitum*. The nature of real being is to be entire or continuous. Our perception, being of a hopeless 'many,' thus is false.

Our own mathematicians have meanwhile constructed what they regard as an adequate continuum, composed of points or numbers. When I speak again of that I shall have occasion to return to the Achilles-fallacy, so called. At present I will pass without transition to the next great historic attack upon the problem of the infinite, which is the section on the 'Antinomies' in Kant's 'Critique of Pure Reason.'

Kant's views need a few points of preparation, as follows:—

1. That real or objective existence must be determinate existence may be regarded as an axiom in ontology. We may **Kant's** be dim as to just how many stars we see in the **antinomies** Pleiades, or doubtful whose count to believe regarding them; but seeing and belief are subjective affections, and the stars by themselves, we are sure, exist in definite numbers. 'Even the hairs of our head are numbered,' we feel

---

[1] This shows how shallow is that common 'exposure' of Zeno's 'sophism,' which charges it with trying to prove that to overtake the tortoise, Achilles would require an infinitely long time.

certain, though no man shall ever count them.[1] Any existent reality, taken in itself, must therefore be countable, and to any group of such realities some definite number must be applicable.

2. Kant defines infinity as 'that which can never be completely measured by the successive addition of units'—in other words, as that which defies complete enumeration.

3. Kant lays it down as axiomatic that if anything is 'given,' as an existent reality, the whole sum of the 'conditions' required to account for it must similarly be given, or have been given. Thus if a cubic yard of space be 'given,' all its parts must equally be given. If a certain date in past time be real, then the previous dates must also have been real. If an effect be given, the whole series of its causes must have been given, etc., etc.

But the 'conditions' in these cases defy enumeration: the parts of space are less and less *ad infinitum*, times and causes form series that are infinitely regressive for our counting, and of no such infinite series can a 'whole' be formed. Any such series has a variable value, for the number of its terms is indefinite; whereas the conditions under consideration ought, if the 'whole sum of them' be really given, to exist (by the principle, 1, above) in fixed numerical amount.[2]

[1] Of the origin in our experience of this singularly solid postulate, I will say nothing here.

[2] The contradiction between the infinity in the *form* of the conditions, and the numerical determinateness implied in the *fact* of them, was ascribed by Kant to the 'antinomic' form of our experience. His solution of the puzzle was by the way of 'idealism,' and is one of the prettiest strokes in his philosophy. Since the conditions cannot exist in the shape of a totalized amount, it must be, he says, that they do not exist independently or *an sich*, but only as phenomena, or *for us*. Indefiniteness of amount is not incompatible with merely phenomenal existence. *Actual* phenomena, whether conditioned or conditioning, are there for us only in finite amount, as given to perception at any given moment; and the infinite form of them means only that we can go on perceiving, conceiving or imagining more and more about them, world without end. It does not mean that what we go on thus to represent shall have been there already by itself, apart from our acts of representation. Experience, for idealism, thus falls into two parts, a phenomenal given part which is finite, and a conditioning infinite part which is not given, but only possible to experience hereafter. Kant distinguishes this second part, as only *aufgegeben* (or set to us as a task), from the first part as *gegeben* (or already extant).

Such was the form of the puzzle of the infinite, as Kant propounded it. The reader will observe a bad ambiguity in the statement. When he speaks of the 'absolute totality of the synthesis' of the conditions, the words suggest that a completed collection of them must exist or have existed. When we hear that 'the whole sum of them must be given,' we interpret it to mean that they must be given in the form of a whole sum, whereas all that the logical situation requires is that *no one of them should be lacking*, an entirely different demand, and one that can be gratified as well in an infinitely growing as in a terminated series. The same things can always be taken ei-

Ambiguity of Kant's statement of the problem ther collectively or distributively, can be talked of either as 'all,' or as 'each,' or as 'any.' Either statement can be applied equally well to what exists in finite number; and 'all that is there' will be covered both times. But things which appear under the form of endless series can be talked of only distributively, if we wish to leave none of them out. When we say that 'any,' 'each,' or 'every' one of Kant's conditions must be fulfilled, we are therefore on impeccable ground, even though the conditions should form a series as endless as that of the whole numbers, to which we are forever able to add one. But if we say that 'all' must be fulfilled, and imagine 'all' to signify a sum harvested and gathered-in, and represented by a number, we not only make a requirement utterly uncalled for by the logic of the situation, but we create puzzles and incomprehensibilities that otherwise would not exist, and that may require, to get rid of them again, hypotheses as violent as Kant's idealism.

In the works of Charles Renouvier, the strongest philosopher of France during the second half of the nineteenth century, the problem of the infinite again played a pivotal part. Starting from the principle of the numerical determinateness of reality (supra, page 1063)—the *'principe du nombre,'* as he called it—and recognizing that the series of numbers 1, 2, 3, 4, . . . etc., leads to no final 'infinite' number, he concluded that such realities as present beings, past events and causes,

Renouvier's solution steps of change and parts of matter, must needs exist in limited amount. This made of him a radical pluralist. Better, he said, admit that being gives itself to us abruptly, that there are first beginnings, absolute numbers, and definite cessations, however intellectually opaque to us they may seem to be, than try to rationalize all this arbitrariness of fact by working-in explanatory conditions which would involve in every case the self-contradiction of things being paid-in and completed, although they are infinite in formal composition.

With these principles, Renouvier could believe in absolute novelties, unmeditated beginnings, gifts, chance, freedom, **His solution favors novelty** and acts of faith. Fact, for him, overlapped; conceptual explanation fell short; reality must in the end be begged piecemeal, not everlastingly deduced from other reality. This, the empiricist, as distinguished from the rationalist view, is the hypothesis set forth at the end of our last chapter.[1]

[1] I think that Renouvier made mistakes, and I find his whole philosophic manner and apparatus too scholastic. But he was one of the greatest of philosophic characters, and but for the decisive impression made on me in the seventies by his masterly advocacy of pluralism, I might never have got free from the monistic superstition under which I had grown up. The present volume, in short, might never have been written. This is why, feeling endlessly thankful as I do, I dedicate this text-book to the great Renouvier's memory. Renouvier's works make a very long list. The fundamental one is the *Essais de Critique Générale* (first edition, 1854–1864, is in four, second edition, 1875, in six volumes). Of his latest opinions *Le Personnalisme* (1903) gives perhaps the most manageable account; while the last chapter of his *Esquisse d'une Classification des Systèmes* (entitled 'Comment je suis arrivé à ces conclusions') is an autobiographic sketch of his dealings with the problem of the infinite. *Derniers entretiens*, dictated while dying, at the age of eighty-eight, is a most impressive document, coming as if from a man out of Plutarch.

CHAPTER XI

K ANT'S AND Renouvier's dealings with the infinite are fine
examples of the way in which philosophers have always
been wont to infer matters of fact from conceptual considerations. Real novelty would be a matter of fact; and so would
be the idealistic constitution of experience; but Kant and
Renouvier deduce these facts from the purely logical impossibility of an infinite number of conditions getting completed.
It seems a very short cut to truth; but if the logic holds firm,
it may be a fair cut,[1] and the possibility obliges us to scrutinize the situation with increasing care. Proceeding so to do,
we immediately find that in the class of infinitely conditioned
things, we must distinguish two sub-classes, as follows:—

1. Things conceived as *standing*, like space, past time, existing beings.

2. Things conceived as *growing*, like motion, change,
activity.

In the standing class there seems to be no valid objection
to admitting both real existence, and a numerical copiousness
demanding infinity for its description. If, for instance, we consider the stars, and assume the number of them to be infinite, we need only suppose
that to each several term of the endless series 1, 2, 3, 4, . . .
n . . . , there corresponds one star. The numbers, growing
endlessly, would then never exceed the stars standing there
to receive them. Each number would find its own star waiting from eternity to be numbered; and this *in infinitum*,
some star that ever was, matching each number that shall be
used. As there is no 'all' to the numbers so there need be
none to the stars. One cannot well see how the existence of
each star should oblige the whole class 'star' to be of one

The standing infinite

---

[1]Let me now say that we shall ourselves conclude that change completed
by steps infinite in number is inadmissible. This is hardly inferring fact from
conceptual considerations, it is only concluding that a certain conceptual hypothesis regarding the fact of change will not work satisfactorily. The field is
thus open for any other hypothesis; and the one which we shall adopt is
simply that which the face of perceptual experience suggests.

number rather than of another, or require it to be of any terminated number. What I say here of stars applies to the component parts of space and matter, and to those of past time.[1]

So long as we keep taking such facts piecemeal, and talk of them distributively as 'any' or 'each,' the existence of them in infinite form offers no logical difficulty. But there is a psychological tendency to slip from the distributive to the collective way of talking, and this produces a sort of mental flicker and dazzle out of which the dialectic difficulties emerge. 'If each condition be there,'—we say, 'then all are there, for there cannot be eaches that do not make an all.' Rightly taken, the phrase 'all are there,' means only that 'not one is absent.' But in the mouths of most people, it surreptitiously foists in the wholly irrelevant notion of a bounded total.

Its pragmatic definition

There are other similar confusions. 'How,' it may be asked, in Locke's words, can a 'growing measure' fail to overtake a 'standing bulk'? And standing existence must some time be overtaken by a growing number-series, must be finished or finite in its numerical determination. But this again foists in the notion of a bound. What is given as 'standing' in the cases under review is not a 'bulk,' but *each* star, atom, past date or what not; and to call these eaches a 'bulk,' is to beg the very point at issue. But probably the real reason why we object to a standing infinity is the reason that made Hegel speak of it as the 'false' infinite. It is that the vertiginous chase after ever more space, ever more past time, ever more subdivision, seems endlessly stupid. What need is there, what use is there,

---

[1] Past time may offer difficulty to the student as it has to better men! It has terminated in the present moment, paid itself out and made an 'amount.' But this amount can be counted in both directions; and in both, one may think it ought to give the same result. If, when counted forward, it came to an end in the present, then when counted backward, it must, we are told, come to a like end in the past. It must have had a beginning, therefore, and its amount must be finite. The sophism here is gross, and amounts to saying that what has one bound must have two. The 'end' of the forward counting *is* the 'beginning' of the backward counting, and is the *only* beginning logically implied. The ending of a series in no way prejudices the question whether it were beginningless or not; and this applies as well to tracts of time as to the abstract regression which 'negative' numbers form.

for so much? Not that any amount of anything is absolutely too big to be; but that some amounts are too big for our imagination to wish to caress them. So we fall back with a feeling of relief on some form or other of the finitest hypothesis.[1]

If now we turn from static to growing forms of being, we find ourselves confronted by much more serious difficulties. Zeno's and Kant's dialectic holds good wherever, before an end can be reached, a succession of terms, endless by definition, must needs have been *successively* counted out. This is the case with every process of change, however small; with every event which we conceive as unrolling itself continuously. What is continuous must be divisible *ad infinitum*; and from division to division here you cannot proceed by addition (or by what Kant calls the successive synthesis of units) and touch a farther limit. You can indeed define what the limit ought to be, but you cannot reach it *by this process*. That Achilles should occupy *in succession* 'all' the points in a single continuous inch of space, is as inadmissible a conception as that he should count the series of whole numbers 1, 2, 3, 4, etc., to infinity and reach an end. The terms are not 'enumerable' in that order; and the order it is that makes the whole difficulty. An infinite 'regression' like the rearward perspective of time offers no such contradiction, for it comes not in that order. Its 'end' is what we start with; and each successive note 'more' which our imagination has to add, *ad infinitum*, is thought of as already having been paid in and not as having yet to be paid before the end can be attained. Starting with our end, we have to wait for nothing. The infinity here is of the 'standing' variety. It is, in the word of Kant's pun, *gegeben*, not *aufgegeben*: in the other case, of a continuous process to be

The growing infinite

---

[1] The reader will note how emphatically in all this discussion, I am insisting on the distributive or piecemeal point of view. The distributive is identical with the pluralistic, as the collective is with the monistic conception. We shall, I think, perceive more and more clearly as this book proceeds, that *piecemeal existence is independent of complete collectibility*, and that some facts, at any rate, exist only distributively, or in form of a set of eaches which (even if in infinite number) need not in any intelligible sense either experience themselves, or get experienced by anything else, as members of an All.

traversed, it is on the contrary *aufgegeben*: it is a task—not only for our philosophic imagination, but for any real agent who might try physically to compass the entire performance. Such an agent is bound by logic to find always a remainder, something ever yet to be paid, like the balance due on a debt with even the interest of which we do not catch up.

'*Infinitum in actu pertransiri nequit,*' said scholasticism; and every continuous quantum to be gradually traversed is conceived as such an infinite. The quickest way to avoid the contradiction would seem to be to give up that conception, and to treat real processes of change no longer as being continuous, but as taking place by finite not infinitesimal steps, like the successive drops by which a cask of water is filled, when whole drops fall into it at once or nothing. This is the radically pluralist, empiricist, or perceptualist position, which I characterized in speaking of Renouvier (above, pages 1065–1066). We shall have to end by adopting it in principle ourselves, qualifying it so as to fit it closely to perceptual experience.

The growing infinite must be treated as discontinuous

Meanwhile we are challenged by a certain school of critics who think that what in mathematics is called 'the new infinite' has quashed the old antinomies, and who treat anyone whom the notion of a completed infinite in any form still bothers, as a very *naïf* person. *Naïf* though I am in mathematics, I must, notwithstanding the dryness of the subject, add a word in rebuttal of these criticisms, some of which, as repeated by novices, tend decidedly towards mystification.

Objections

The 'new infinite' and the 'number-continuum' are outgrowths of a general attempt to accomplish what has been called the 'arithmetization' (ἀριθμὸς meaning number) of all quantity. Certain *quanta* (grades of intensity or other difference, amounts of space) have until recently been supposed to be immediate data of perceptive sensibility or 'intuition'; but philosophical mathematicians have now succeeded in getting a conceptual equivalent for them in the shape of collections of numbers created by interpolation between one another indefinitely. We can halve any line in space, and halve its halves and so on. But between the cuts thus made and numbered, room is left for

(1) The number-continuum

infinite others created by using 3 as a divisor, for infinite
others still by using 5, 7, etc., until all possible 'rational' divisions of the line shall have been made. Between these it is
now shown that interpolation of cuts numbered 'irrationally'
is still possible *ad infinitum*, and that with these the line at
last gets filled *full*, its continuity now being wholly translated into these numbered cuts, and their number being infinite. 'Of the celebrated formula that continuity means
"unity in multiplicity," the multiplicity alone subsists, the
unity disappears,'[1]—as indeed it does in all conceptual translations—and the original intuition of the line's extent gets
treated, from the mathematical point of view, as a 'mass of
uncriticized prejudice' by Russell, or sneered at by Cantor as
a 'kind of religious dogma.'[2]

So much for the number-continuum. As for 'the new infinite': that means only a new definition of infinity. If we compare the indefinitely-growing number-series, 1, 2, 3, 4, − − − n,
− − − in its entirety, with any component part of it, like 'even'
numbers, 'prime' numbers, or 'square' numbers, we
are confronted with a paradox. No one of the parts,
thus named, of the number-series, is equal to the
whole collectively taken; yet any one of them is 'similar' to
the whole, in the sense that you can set up a one-to-one relation between *each* of its elements and *each* element of the
whole, so that part and whole prove to be of what logicians
call the same 'class,' numerically. Thus, in spite of the fact that
even numbers, prime numbers, and square numbers are much
fewer and rarer than numbers in general, and only form a part
of numbers *überhaupt* they appear to be equally copious for
purposes of counting. The terms of each such partial series
can be numbered by using the natural integers in succession.
There is, for instance, a first prime, a second prime, etc., *ad
infinitum*; and queerer-sounding still, since *every* integer, odd
or even, can be doubled, it would seem that the even numbers
thus produced cannot in the nature of things be less multitudinous than that series of both odd and even numbers of
which the whole natural series consists.

These paradoxical consequences result, as one sees imme-

(2) The 'new infinite'

[1] H. Poincaré: *La Science et l'hypothèse*, p. 30.
[2] B. Russell: *The Philosophy of Mathematics*, i, 260, 287.

diately, from the fact that the infinity of the number-series is
of the 'growing' variety (above, page 1069). They
were long treated as a *reductio ad absurdum* of the
notion that such a variable series spells infinity in
act, or can ever be translated into standing or collective
form.[1] But contemporary mathematicians have taken the bull
by the horns. Instead of treating such paradoxical properties
of indefinitely growing series as *reductiones ad absurdum*,
they have turned them into the proper definition of infinite
classes of things. Any class is now called infinite if its parts
are numerically similar to itself. If its parts are numerically
dissimilar, it is finite. This definition now separates the conception of the class of finite from that of infinite objects.

The new
infinite
paradoxical

Next, certain concepts, called 'transfinite numbers,' are now
created by definition. They are decreed to belong to the infinite
class, and yet not to be formed by adding one to
one *ad infinitum*, but rather to be postulated outright as coming *after each and all of the numbers formed by such
addition*.[2] Cantor gives the name of 'Omega' to the lowest of
these possible transfinite numbers. It would, for instance, be
the number of the point at which Achilles overtakes the tortoise—if he does overtake him—by exhausting all the intervening points successively. Or it would be the number of the
stars, in case their counting could not terminate. Or again it
would be the number of miles away at which parallel lines
meet—if they do meet. It is, in short, a 'limit' to the whole
class of numbers that grow one by one, and like other limits,

'Transfinite
numbers'

[1] The fact that, taken distributively, or paired each to each, the terms in
one endlessly growing series should be made a match for those in another
(or 'similar' to them) is quite compatible with the two series being collectively of vastly unequal amounts. You need only make the steps of difference,
or distances, between the terms much longer in one series than in the other,
to get numerically similar multitudes, with greatly unequal magnitudes of
content. Moreover the moment either series should stop growing, the 'similarity' would cease to exist.

[2] The class of all numbers that 'come before the first transfinite' is a definitely limited conception, provided we take the numbers as *eaches* or *anys*,
for then any one and every of them will have by definition to come *before* the
transfinite number comes—even though they form no whole and there be
no last one of them, and though the transfinite have no immediate predecessor. The transfinite is, in a word, not an ordinal conception, at least it does
not continue the order of entire numbers.

it proves a useful conceptual bridge for passing us from one range of facts to another.

The first sort of fact we pass to with its help is the number of the number-continuum or point-continuum described Their uses and defects above (page 1070) as generated by infinitely re-peated subdivision. The making of the subdivisions is an infinitely growing process; but the number of subdivisions that can be made has for its limit the transfinite number Omega just imagined and defined; thus is a growing assimilated to a standing multitude; thus is a number that is variable practically equated (by the process of passing to the limit) with one that is fixed; thus do we circumvent the law of indefinite addition, or division which previously was the only way in which infinity was constructable, and reach a constant infinite at a bound. This infinite number may now be substituted for any continuous finite quantum, however small the latter may perceptually appear to be.

When I spoke of my 'mystification,' just now, I had partly in mind the contemptuous way in which some enthusiasts for the 'new infinite' treat those who still cling to the superstition that 'the whole is greater than the part.' Because any point whatever in an imaginary inch is now conceivable as being matched by some point in a quarter-inch or half-inch, this numerical 'similarity' of the different *quanta*, taken point-wise, is treated as if it signified that half-inches, quarter-inches, and inches are mathematically identical things anyhow, and that their differences are facts which we may scientifically neglect. I may misunderstand the newest expounders of Zeno's famous 'sophism,' but what they say seems to me virtually to be equivalent to this.

Mr. Bertrand Russell (whom I do not accuse of mystification, for Heaven knows he tries to make things clear!) treats the Achilles-puzzle as if the difficulty lay only in seeing how the paths traversed by the two runners (measured after the race is run, and assumed then to consist of nothing but points Russell's solution of Zeno's paradox by their means of position coincident with points upon a common scale of time) should have the same time-measure if they be not themselves of the same length. But the two paths are of different lengths; for owing to the tortoise's head-start, the tortoise's path is only a part of the path of Achilles. How, then, if time-points are to be the medium of measurement, can the longer path *not* take the longer time?

The remedy, for Mr. Russell, if I rightly understand him, lies in noting that the sets of points in question are conceived as being infinitely numerous in both paths, and that where infinite multitudes are in question, to say that the whole is greater than the part is false. For each and every point traversed by the tortoise there is one point traversed by Achilles, at the corresponding point of time; and the exact correspondence, point by point, of either one of the three sets of points with both the others, makes of them similar and equally copious sets from the numerical point of view. There is thus no recurrent 'remainder' of the tortoise's head-start with which Achilles cannot catch up, which he can reduce indefinitely, but cannot annul. The books balance to the end. The last point in Achilles's path, the last point in the tortoise's, and the last time-instant in the race are terms which mathematically coincide. With this, which seems to be Mr. Russell's way of analyzing the situation, the puzzle is supposed to disappear.[1]

It seems to me however that Mr. Russell's statements dodge the real difficulty, which concerns the 'growing' variety of infinity exclusively, and not the 'standing' variety, which is all that he envisages when he assumes the race already to have been run and thinks that the only problem that remains is that of numerically equating the paths. The real difficulty may almost be called physical, for it attends the process of *formation* of the paths. Moreover, two paths are not needed—that of either runner alone, or even the lapse of empty time, involves the difficulty, which is that of touching a goal when an interval needing to be traversed first keeps permanently reproducing itself and getting in your way. Of course the same quantum can be produced in various manners. This page which I am now painfully writing, letter after letter, will be printed at a single stroke. God, as the

The solution criticized

[1] Mr. Russell's own statements of the puzzle as well as of the remedy are too technical to be followed verbatim in a book like this. As he finds it necessary to paraphrase the puzzle, so I find it convenient to paraphrase him, sincerely hoping that no injustice has been done.

orthodox believe, created the space-continuum, with its infinite parts already standing in it, by an instantaneous *fiat*. Past time now stands in infinite perspective, and may conceivably have been created so, as Kant imagined, for our retrospection only, and all at once. 'Omega' was created by a single decree, a single act of definition in Prof. Cantor's mind. But whoso actually *traverses* a continuum, can do so by no process continuous in the mathematical sense. Be it short or long, each point must be occupied in its due order of succession; and if the points are necessarily infinite, their end cannot be reached, for the 'remainder,' in this kind of process, is just what one cannot 'neglect.' 'Enumeration' is, in short, the sole possible method of occupation of the series of positions implied in the famous race; and when Mr. Russell solves the puzzle by saying as he does, that 'the definition of whole and part without enumeration is the key to the whole mystery,'[1] he seems to me deliberately to throw away his case.[2]

[1] *The Philosophy of Mathematics*, i, 361.—Mr. Russell gives a *Tristram Shandy* paradox as a counterpart to the Achilles. Since it took T. S. (according to Sterne) two years to write the history of the first two days of his life, common sense would conclude that at that rate the life never could be written. But Mr. Russell proves the contrary; for, as days and years have no last term, and the *n*th day is written in the *n*th year, any assigned day will be written about, and no part of the life remain unwritten. But Mr. Russell's proof cannot be applied to the real world without the physical hypothesis which he expresses by saying: 'If Tristram Shandy lives forever, and does not weary of his task.' In all real cases of continuous change a similarly absurd hypothesis must be made: the agent of the change must live forever, in the sense of outliving an endless set of points of time, and 'not wearying' of his impossible task.

[2] Being almost blind mathematically and logically, I feel considerable shyness in differing from such superior minds, yet what can one do but follow one's own dim light? The literature of the new infinite is so technical that it is impossible to cite details of it in a non-mathematical work like this. Students who are interested should consult the tables of contents of B. Russell's *Philosophy of Mathematics*, of L. Couturat's *Infini Mathématique*, or his *Principes des Mathématiques*. A still more rigorous exposition may be found in E. V. Huntington, *The Continuum as a Type of Order*, in the *Annals of Mathematics*, vols. vi and vii (reprint for sale at publication-office, Harvard University). Compare also C. S. Peirce's paper in the *Monist*, ii, 537–546, as well as the presidential address of E. W. Hobson in the *Proceedings of the London Mathematical Society*, vol. xxxv. For more popular discussions see J. Royce, *The World and the Individual*, vol. i, Supplementary Essay; Keyser: *Journal of Philosophy*, etc., i, 29, and *Hibbert Journal*, vii, 380–390; S. Waterlow in

After this disagreeable polemic, I conclude that the new infinite need no longer block the way to the empiricist opin-

Conclu-
sions

ion which we reached provisionally on page 1070. Irrelevant though they be to facts the 'conditions' of which are of the 'standing' sort, the criticisms of Leibnitz, Kant, Cauchy, Renouvier, Evellin and others, apply legitimately to all cases of supposedly continuous growth or change. The 'conditions' here have to be fulfilled seriatim; and if the series which they form were endless, its limit, if 'successive synthesis' were the only way of reaching it, could simply not be reached. Either we must stomach logical contradiction, therefore, in these cases; or we must admit that the limit is reached in these successive cases by finite and perceptible units of approach—drops, buds, steps, or whatever we please to term them, of change, coming wholly when they do come, or coming not at all. Such seems to be the nature of concrete experience, which changes always by sensible amounts, or stays unchanged. The infinite character we find in it is woven into it by our later conception indefinitely repeating the act of subdividing any given amount supposed. The facts do not resist the subsequent conceptual treatment; but we need not believe that the treatment necessarily reproduces the operation by which they were originally brought into existence.

The antinomy of mathematically continuous growth is thus

1. Con-
ceptual
transfor-
mation of
perceptual
experience
turns the
infinite into
a problem

but one more of those many ways in which our conceptual transformation of perceptual experience makes it less comprehensible than ever. That being should immediately and by finite quantities add itself to being, may indeed be something which an onlooking intellect fails to understand; but that being should be identified with the consummation of an endless chain of units (such as 'points'), no one of which contains any amount whatever of the being (such as

Aristotelian Soc. Proceedings, 1910; Leighton: *Philosophical Review*, xiii, 497; and finally the tables of contents of H. Poincaré's three recent little books, *La Science et l'hypothèse*, Paris; *The Value of Science* (authorized translation by G. B. Halsted), New York, 1907; *Science et Méthode*, Paris, 1908. The liveliest short attack which I know upon infinites completed by successive synthesis, is that in G. S. Fullerton's *System of Metaphysics*, chapter xi.

'space') expected to result, this is something which our intellect not only fails to understand, but which it finds absurd. The substitution of 'arithmetization' for intuition thus seems, if taken as a description of reality, to be only a partial success. Better accept, as Renouvier says, the opaquely given data of perception, than concepts inwardly absurd.[1]

So much for the 'problem of the infinite,' and for the interpretation of continuous change by the new definition of infinity. We find that the picture of a reality changing by steps finite in number and discrete, remains quite as acceptable to our understanding and as congenial to our imagination as before; so, after these dry and barren chapters, we take up our main topic of inquiry just where we had laid it down. Does reality grow by abrupt increments of novelty, or not? The

2. It leaves the problem of novelty where it was

contrast between discontinuity and continuity now confronts us in another form. The mathematical definition of continuous quantity as 'that between any two elements or terms of which there is another term' is directly opposed to the more empirical or perceptual notion that anything is continuous when its parts appear as immediate next neighbors, with absolutely nothing between. Our business lies hereafter with the perceptual

---

[1] The point-continuum illustrates beautifully my complaint that the intellectualist method turns the flowing into the static and discrete. The buds or steps of process which perception accepts as primal gifts of being, correspond logically to the 'infinitesimals' (minutest *quanta* of motion, change or what not) of which the latest mathematics is supposed to have got rid. Mr. Russell accordingly finds himself obliged, just like Zeno, to treat motion as an unreality: 'Weierstrass,' he says, 'by strictly banishing all infinitesimals has at last shown that we live in an unchanging world, and that the arrow, at every moment of its flight, is truly at rest' (*op. cit.*, p. 347). 'We must entirely reject the notion of a state of motion,' he says elsewhere; 'motion consists merely in the occupation of different places at different times. . . . There is no transition from place to place, no consecutive moment, or consecutive position, no such thing as velocity except in the sense of a real number which is the limit of a certain set of quotients' (p. 473). The mathematical 'continuum,' so called, becomes thus an absolute discontinuum in any physical or experiential sense. Extremes meet; and although Russell and Zeno agree in denying perceptual motion, for the one a pure unity, for the other a pure multiplicity takes its place. It is probable that Russell's denial of change, etc. is meant to apply only to the mathematical world. It would be unfair to charge him with writing metaphysics in these passages, although he gives no warning that this may not be the case.

account, but before we settle definitively to its discussion, another classic problem of philosophy had better be got out of the way. This is the 'problem of causation.'

CHAPTER XII

NOVELTY AND CAUSATION—THE CONCEPTUAL VIEW

IF REALITY changes by finite sensible steps, the question
whether the bits of it that come are radically new, remains
unsettled still. Remember our situation at the end of Chapter
III. Being *überhaupt* or at large, we there found to be unde-
duceable. For our *intellect* it remains a casual and contingent
quantum that is simply found or begged. May it be begged
bit by bit, as it adds itself? Or must we beg it only once, by
assuming it either to be eternal or to have come in an instant
that co-implicated all the rest of time? Did or did not 'the
first morning of creation write what the last dawn

The
'principle of
causality'

of reckoning shall read'? With these questions monism and pluralism stand face to face again. The classic obstacle to pluralism has always been what is known as the
'principle of causality.' This principle has been taken to mean
that the effect in some way already exists in the cause. If this
be so, the effect cannot be absolutely novel, and in no radical
sense can pluralism be true.

We must therefore review the facts of causation. I take
them in conceptual translation before considering them in
perceptual form. The first definite inquiry into causes was
made by Aristotle.[1]

The 'why' of anything, he said, is furnished by four principles: the material cause of it (as when bronze makes a

Aristotle on
causation

statue); the formal cause (as when the ratio of two
to one makes an octave); the efficient cause (as
when a father makes a child) and the final cause (as when one
exercises for the sake of health). Christian philosophy adopted
the four causes; but what one generally means by the cause
of anything is its 'efficient' cause, and in what immediately
follows I shall speak of that alone.

An efficient cause is scholastically defined as 'that which
produces something else by a real activity proceeding from
itself.' This is unquestionably the view of common sense; and

[1] Book 2, or book 5, chap. ii of his *Metaphysics*, or chap. iii of his *Physics*,
give what is essential in his views.

Scholasti-
cism on the
efficient
cause scholasticism is only common sense grown quite articulate. Passing over the many classes of efficient
cause which scholastic philosophy specifies, I will
enumerate three important sub-principles it is supposed to
follow from the above definition. Thus: 1. No effect can come
into being without a cause. This may be verbally taken; but
if, avoiding the word effect, it be taken in the sense that nothing can happen without a cause, it is the famous 'principle of
causality' which, when combined with the next two principles, is supposed to establish the block-universe, and to render the pluralistic hypothesis absurd.

2. The effect is always proportionate to the cause, and the
cause to the effect.

3. Whatever is in the effect must in some way, whether formally, virtually, or eminently, have been also in the cause.
('Formally' here means that the cause resembles the effect, as
when one motion causes another motion; virtually means that
the cause somehow involves that effect, without resembling
it, as when an artist causes a statue but possesses not himself
its beauty; 'eminently' means that the cause, though unlike
the effect, is superior to it in perfection, as when a man overcomes a lion's strength by greater cunning.)

Nemo dat quod non habet is the real principle from which
the causal philosophy flows; and the proposition *causa æquat
effectum* practically sums up the whole of it.[1]

It is plain that each moment of the universe must contain
all the causes of which the next moment contains effects, or
to put it with extreme concision, it is plain that each moment
in its totality causes the next moment.[2] But if the maxim

---

[1] Read for a concise statement of the school-doctrine of causation the account in J. Rickaby: *General Metaphysics*, book 2, chap. iii. I omit from my
text various subordinate maxims which have played a great part in causal
philosophy, as 'The cause of a cause is the cause of its effects'; 'The same
causes produce the same effects'; 'Causes act only when present'; 'A cause
must exist before it can act,' etc.

[2] This notion follows also from the consideration of conditioning circumstances being at bottom as indispensable as causes for producing effects. 'The
cause, philosophically speaking, is the sum total of the conditions positive
and negative,' says J. S. Mill (*Logic*, 8th edition, i, 383). This is equivalent to
the entire state of the universe at the moment that precedes the effect. But
neither is the 'effect' in that case the one fragmentary event which our atten-

holds firm that *quidquid est in effectu debet esse prius aliquo modo in causa*, it follows that the next moment can contain nothing genuinely original, and that the novelty that appears to leak into our lives so unremittingly, must be an illusion, ascribable to the shallowness of the perceptual point of view.

Scholasticism always respected common sense, and in this case escaped the frank denial of all genuine novelty by the vague qualification 'aliquo modo.' This allowed the effect also to differ, *aliquo modo*, from its cause. But conceptual necessities have ruled the situation and have ended, as usual, by driving nature and perception to the wall. A cause and its effect are two numerically discrete concepts, and yet in some inscrutable way the former must 'produce' the latter. How can it intelligibly do so, save by already hiding the latter in itself? Numerically two, cause and effect must be generically one, in spite of the perceptual appearances; and causation changes thus from a concretely experienced relation between differents into one between similars abstractly thought of as more real.[1]

The overthrow of perception by conception took a long time to complete itself in this field. The first step was the theory of 'occasionalism,' to which Descartes led the way by his doctrine that mental and physical substance, the one consisting purely of thought, the other purely of extension, were absolutely dissimilar. If this were so, any such causal intercourse as we instinctively perceive between mind and body ceased to be rational. For thinkers of that age,

Occasionalism

tion first abstracted under that name. It is that fragment, along with all its concomitants—or in other words it is the entire state of the universe at the second moment desired.

[1] Sir William Hamilton expresses this very compactly: 'What is the law of Causality? Simply this,—that when an object is presented phenomenally as commencing, we cannot but suppose that the complement (i. e. the amount) of existence, which it now contains, has previously been;—in other words, that all that we at present know as an effect must previously have existed in its causes; though what these causes are we may perhaps be altogether unable to surmise.' (End of Lecture 39 of the *Metaphysics*.) The cause becomes a reason, the effect a consequence; and since logical consequence follows only from the same to the same, the older vaguer causation-philosophy develops into the sharp rationalistic dogma that cause and effect are two names for one persistent being, and that if the successive moments of the universe be causally connected, no genuine novelty leaks in.

'God' was the great solvent of absurdities. He could get over every contradiction. Consequently Descartes' disciples Régis and Cordemoy, and especially Geulincx, denied the fact of psychological interaction altogether. God, according to them, immediately caused the changes in our mind of which events in our body, and those in our body of which events in our mind, appear to be the causes, but of which they are in reality only the signals or occasions.

Leibnitz took the next step forward in quenching the claim to truth of our perceptions. He freed God from the duty of lending all this hourly assistance, by supposing Him to have decreed on the day of creation that the changes in our several minds should coincide with those in our several bodies, after the manner in which clocks, wound up on the same day, thereafter keep time with one another. With this 'pre-established harmony' so-called, the conceptual translation of the immediate given, with its never failing result of negating both activity and continuity, is complete. Instead of the dramatic flux of personal life, a bare 'one to one correspondence' between the terms of two causally unconnected series is set up. God is the sole cause of anything, and the cause of everything at once. The theory is as monistic as the rationalist heart can desire, and of course novelty would be impossible if it were true.

David Hume made the next step in discrediting common-sense causation. In the chapters on 'the idea of necessary connection' both in his 'Treatise on Human Nature,' and in his 'Essays,' he sought for a positive picture of the 'efficacy of the power' which causes are assumed to exert, and failed to find it. He shows that neither in the physical nor in the mental world can we abstract or isolate the 'energy' transmitted from causes to effects. This is as true of perception as it is of imagination. 'All ideas are derived from and represent impressions. We never have any impression that contains any power or efficacy. We never therefore have any idea of power.' 'We never can by our utmost scrutiny discover anything but one event following another; without being able to comprehend any force or power, by which the cause operates, or any connection between it and its supposed effect. . . . The necessary conclusion seems to be that we have no idea of connection or power at all, and that these words are absolutely without any meaning, when employed either in philosophical reasonings or in common life.' 'Nothing is more evident than that the mind cannot form such an idea of two objects as to conceive any connection between them, or comprehend distinctly that power or efficacy by which they are united.'

The pseudo-idea of a connection which we have, Hume then goes on to show, is nothing but the misinterpretation of a mental custom. When we have often experienced the same sequence of events, 'we are carried by habit, upon the appearance of the first one, to expect its usual attendant, and to believe that it will exist. . . . This customary transition of the imagination is the sentiment or impression from which we form the idea of power or necessary connection. Nothing farther is in the case.' 'A cause is an object precedent and contiguous to another, and so united with it that the idea of the one determines the idea of the other.'

Nothing could be more essentially pluralistic than the elements of Hume's philosophy. He makes events rattle against their neighbors as drily as if they were dice in a box. He might with perfect consistency have believed in real novelties, and upheld freewill. But I said awhile ago that most empiricists had been half-hearted; and Hume was perhaps the most half-hearted of the lot. In his essay 'on liberty and necessity,' he insists that the sequences which we experience, though between events absolutely disconnected, are yet absolutely uniform, and that nothing genuinely new can flower out of our lives.

The reader will recognize in Hume's famous pages a fresh example of the way in which conceptual translations always
Criticism of   maltreat fact. Perceptually or concretely (as we shall
Hume   notice in more detail later) causation names the manner in which some fields of consciousness introduce other fields. It is but one of the forms in which experience appears as a continuous flow. Our names show how successfully we can discriminate within the flow. But the conceptualist rule is to suppose that where there is a separate name there ought to be a fact as separate; and Hume, following this rule, and finding no such fact corresponding to the word 'power,' concludes that the word is meaningless. By this rule every

conjunction and preposition in human speech is meaning-less —*in*, *on*, *of*, *with*, *but*, *and*, *if*, are as meaningless as *for*, and *because*. The truth is that neither the elements of fact nor the meanings of our words are separable as the words are. The original form in which fact comes is the perceptual *durch-einander*, holding terms as well as relations in solution, or interfused and cemented. Our reflective mind abstracts divers aspects in the muchness, as a man by looking through a tube may limit his attention to one part after another of a land-scape. But abstraction is not insulation; and it no more breaks reality than the tube breaks the landscape. Concepts are notes, views taken on reality,[1] not pieces of it, as bricks are of a house. Causal activity, in short, may play its part in growing fact, even though no substantive 'impression' of it should stand out by itself. Hume's assumption that any factor of real-ity must be separable, leads to his preposterous view, that no relation can be real. 'All events,' he writes, 'seem entirely loose and separate. One event follows another, but we never can observe any tie between them. They seem conjoined, but never connected.' Nothing, in short, belongs with anything else. Thus does the intellectualist method pulverize perception and triumph over life. Kant and his successors all espoused Hume's opinion that the immediately given is a disconnected 'manifold.' But unwilling simply to accept the manifold, as Hume did, they invoked a superior agent in the shape of what Kant called the 'transcendental ego of apperception' to patch its bits together by synthetic 'categories.' Among these cate-gories Kant inscribes that of 'causality,' and in many quarters he passes for a repairer of the havoc that Hume made.

His chapter on Cause[2] is the most confusedly written part of his famous Critique, and its meaning is often hard to catch. As I understand his text, he leaves things just where Hume did, save that where Hume says 'habit' he says 'rule.' They Kant both cancel the notion that phenomena called causal ever exert 'power,' or that a single case would ever have sug-gested cause and effect. In other words Kant contradicts com-mon sense as much as Hume does and, like Hume, translates

---

[1] These expressions are Bergson's.

[2] Entitled 'The Second Analogy of Experience,' it begins on page 232 of the second edition of his *Critique of Pure Reason*.

causation into mere time-succession; only, whereas the order in time was essentially 'loose' for Hume and only subjectively uniform, Kant calls its uniformity 'objective as obtaining in conformity to a law, which our *Sinnlichkeit* receives from our *Verstand*.' Non-causal sequences can be reversed; causal ones follow in conformity to rule.[1]

The word *Verstand* in Kant's account must not be taken as if the rule it is supposed to set to sensation made us understand things any better. It is a brute rule of sequence which reveals no 'tie.' The non-rationality of such a 'category' leaves it worthless for purposes of insight. It removes dynamic causation and substitutes no other explanation for the sequences found. It yields external descriptions only, and assimilates all cases to those where we discover no reason for the law ascertained.

Our 'laws of nature' do indeed in large part enumerate bare coexistences and successions. Yellowness and malleability coexist in gold; redness succeeds on boiling in lobsters; coagulation in eggs; and to him who asks for the Why of these uniformities, science only replies: 'Not yet'! Meanwhile the Positivism laws are potent for prediction, and many writers on science tell us that this is all we can demand. To explain, according to the way of thinking called positivistic, is only to substitute wider or more familiar, for narrower or less familiar laws, and the laws at their widest only express uniformities empirically found. Why does the pump suck up water? Because the air keeps pressing it into the tube. Why does the air press in? Because the earth attracts it. Why does the earth

[1] Kant's whole notion of a 'rule' is inconstruable by me. What or whom does the rule bind? If it binds the phenomenon that follows (the 'effect') we fall back into the popular dynamic view, and any single case would exhibit causal action, even were there no other cases in the world.—Or does it bind the observer of the single case? But his own sensations of sequence are what bind him. Be a sequence causal or non-causal, if it is sensible, he cannot turn it backwards as he can his ideas. Or does the rule bind future sequences and determine them to follow in the same order which the first sequence observed? Since it obviously does not do this when the observer judges wrongly that the first sequence is causal, all we can say is that it is a rule whereby his expectations of uniformity follow his causal judgments, be these latter true or false. But wherein would this differ from the humian position? Kant, in short, flounders, and in no truthful sense can one keep repeating that he has 'refuted Hume.'

attract it? Because it attracts everything—such attraction being in the end only a more universal sort of fact. Laws, according to their view, only generalize facts, they do not connect them in any intimate sense.[1]

Against this purely inductive way of treating causal sequences, a more deductive interpretation has recently been urged. If the later member of a succession could be deduced by logic from the earlier member, in the particular sequence the 'tie' would be unmistakable. But logical ties carry us only from sames to sames; so this last phase of scientific method is at bottom only the scholastic principle of *Causa æquat effectum*, brought into sharper focus and illustrated more concretely. It is thoroughly monistic in its aims, and if it could be worked out in detail it would turn the real world into the procession of an eternal identity, with the appearances, of which we are perceptually conscious, occurring as a sort of by-product to which no 'scientific' importance should be attached.[2] In any case no real growth and no real novelty could effect an entrance into life.[3]

Deductive theories of causation

---

[1] For expressions of this view the student may consult J. S. Mill's *Logic*, book 3, chap. xii; W. S. Jevons's *Principles of Science*, book 6; J. Venn's *Empirical Logic*, chap. xxi, and K. Pearson's *Grammar of Science*, chap. iii.

[2] 'Consciousness,' writes M. Couturat, to cite a handy expression of this mode of thought, 'is properly speaking, the realm of the unreal. . . . What remains in our subjective consciousness, after all objective facts have been projected and located in space and time, is the rubbish and residuum of the construction of the universe, the formless mass of images that were unable to enter into the system of nature and put on the garment of reality' (*Revue de Métaphysique*, etc., v, 244).

[3] I avoid amplifying this conception of cause and effect. An immense number of causal facts can indeed be explained satisfactorily by assuming that the effect is only a later position of the cause; and for the remainder we can fall back on the *aliquo modo* which gave such comfort in the past. Such an interpretation of nature would, of course, relegate variety, activity, and novelty to the limbo of illusions, as fast as it succeeded in making its static concepts cancel living facts. It is hard to be sincere, however, in following the conceptual method ruthlessly; and of the writers who think that in science causality must mean identity, some willingly allow that all such scientific explanation is more or less artificial, that identical 'molecules' and 'atoms' are like identical 'pounds' and 'yards,' only pegs in a conceptual arrangement for hanging percepts on in 'one to one relations,' so as to predict facts in 'elegant' or expeditious ways. This is the view of the conceptual universe which our own discussion has insisted on; and, taking scientific logic in this way, no harm is

This negation of real novelty seems to be the upshot of the conceptualist philosophy of causation. This is why I called it on page 1079 the classic obstacle to the acceptance of plural-ism's additive world. The principle of causality be-gins as a hybrid between common sense and intel-lectualism:—what actively produces an effect, it says, must 'in some way' contain the 'power' of it already. But as nothing corresponding to the concept of power can be insulated, the activity-feature of the sequence erelong gets suppressed, and the vague latency, supposed to exist *aliquo modo* in the causal phenomenon, of the effect about to be produced, is developed into a static relation of identity be-tween two concepts which the mind substitutes for the per-cepts between which the causal tie originally was found.[1]

Summary
and
conclusion

The resultant state of 'enlightened opinion' about cause, is, as I have called it before, confused and unsatisfactory. Few philosophers hold radically to the identity view. The view of the logicians of science is easier to believe but not easier to believe metaphysically, for it violates instinct almost as strongly. Mathematicians make use, to connect the various in-terdependencies of quantities, of the general concept of func-tion. That A is a function of B (A equals B) means that with

---

done. Almost no one is radical in using scientific logic metaphysically. Read-ers wishing for more discussion of the monistic view of cause, may consult G. H. Lewes: *Problems of Life and Mind*, problem 5, chap. iii; A. Riehl: *Der philosophische Kriticismus* (1879), 2ter Absn., Kap. 2; G. Heymans: *Die Gesetze u. Elemente d. wissenschaftlichen Denkens*, par. 83–85. Compare also B. P. Bowne: *Metaphysics*, revised edition, part i, chap. iv. Perhaps the most in-structive general discussion of causation is that in C. Sigwart: *Logic*, 2d edi-tion, par. 73. Chap. v of book 3 in J. S. Mill's *Logic* may be called classical.

[1] I omit saying anything in my text about 'energetics.' Popular writers often appear to think that 'science' has demonstrated a monistic principle called 'energy,' which they connect with activity on the one hand and with quantity on the other. So far as I understand this difficult subject, 'energy' is not a principle at all, still less an active one. It is only a collective name for certain amounts of immediate perceptual reality, when such reality is measured in definite ways that allow its changes to be written so as to get constant sums. It is not an ontological theory at all, but a magnificent economic schematic device for keeping account of the functional variations of the surface phe-nomena. It is evidently a case of '*non fingo* hypotheses,' and since it tolerates perceptual reality, it ought to be regarded as neutral in our causal debate.

every alteration in the value of A, an alteration in that of B is always connected. If we generalize so as also to include qualitative dependencies, we can conceive the universe as consisting of nothing but elements with functional relations between them; and science has then for its sole task the listing of the elements and the describing in the simplest possible terms the functional 'relations.'[1] Changes, in short, occur, and ring throughout phenomena, but neither reasons, nor activities in the sense of agencies, have any place in this world of scientific logic, which compared with the world of common sense, is so abstract as to be quite spectral, and merits the appellation (so often quoted from Mr. Bradley) of 'an unearthly ballet of bloodless categories.'

[1] W. Jerusalem: *Einleitung in die Philosophie*, 4te Aufl., 145.

CHAPTER XIII

NOVELTY AND CAUSATION — THE PERCEPTUAL VIEW

MOST PERSONS remain quite incredulous when they are told that the rational principle of causality has exploded our native belief in naïf activity as something real, and our assumption that genuinely new fact can be created by work done. 'Le sens de la vie qui s'indigne de tant de discours,' awakens in them and snaps its fingers at the 'critical' view. The present writer has also just called the critical view an incomplete abstraction. But its 'functional laws' and schematisms are splendidly useful, and its negations are true oftener than is commonly supposed. We feel as if our 'will' immediately moved our members, and we ignore the brain-cells whose activity that will must first arouse; we think we cause the bell-ring, but we only close a contact and the battery in the cellar rings the bell; we think a certain star's light is the cause of our now seeing it, but ether-waves are the causes, and the star may have been extinguished long ago. We call the 'draft,' the cause of our 'cold'; but without co-operant microbes the draft could do no harm. Mill says that causes must be unconditional antecedents, and Venn that they must be 'close' ones. In nature's numerous successions so many links are hidden, that we seldom know exactly which antecedent is unconditional or which is close. Often the cause which we name only fits some other cause for producing the phenomenon; and things, as Mill says, are frequently then most active when we assume them to be acted upon.

Defects of the perceptual view do not warrant scepticism

This vast amount of error in our instinctive perceptions of causal activity encourages the conceptualist view. A step farther, and we suspect that to suppose causal activity anywhere may be a blunder, and that only consecutions and juxtapositions can be real. Such sweeping scepticism is, however, quite uncalled for. Other parts of experience expose us to error, yet we do not say that in them is no truth. We see trains moving at stations, when they are really standing still, or falsely we feel ourselves to be moving, when we are giddy, without such

1089

errors leading us to deny that motion anywhere exists. It exists elsewhere; and the problem is to place it rightly. It is the same with all other illusions of sense.

There is doubtless somewhere an original perceptual experience of the kind of thing we mean by causation, and that kind of thing we locate in various other places, rightly or wrongly as the case may be. Where now is the typical experience originally got?

Evidently it is got in our own personal activity-situations. In all of these what we feel is that a previous field of 'consciousness' containing (in the midst of its complexity) the idea
The perceptual experience of causation of a result, develops gradually into another field in which that result either appears as accomplished, or else is prevented by obstacles against which we still feel ourselves to press. As I now write, I am in one of these activity situations. I 'strive' after words, which I only half prefigure, but which, when they shall have come, must satisfactorily complete the nascent sense I have of what they ought to be. The words are to run out of my pen, which I find that my hand actuates so obediently to desire that I am hardly conscious either of resistance or of effort. Some of the words come wrong, and then I do feel a resistance, not muscular but mental, which instigates a new instalment of my activity, accompanied by more or less feeling of exertion. If the resistance were to my muscles, the exertion would contain an element of strain or squeeze which is less present where the resistance is only mental. If it proves considerable in either kind I may leave off trying to overcome it; or, on the other hand, I may sustain my effort till I have succeeded in my aim.

It seems to me that in such a continuously developing experiential series our concrete perception of causality is found in operation. If the word have any meaning at all it must mean what there we live through. What 'efficacy' and 'activity' are *known-as* is what these appear.

The experiencer of such a situation feels the push, the obstacle, the will, the strain, the triumph, or the passive giving up, just as he feels the time, the space, the swiftness or intensity, the movement, the weight and color, the pain and pleasure, the complexity, or whatever remaining characters the situation may involve. He goes through all that can ever be imagined where activity is supposed. The word 'activity' has no content save these experiences of process, obstruction, striving, strain, or release, ultimate *qualia* as they are of the life given us to be known. No matter what 'efficacies' there may really be in this extraordinary universe it is impossible to conceive of any one of them being either lived through or authentically known otherwise than in this dramatic shape of something sustaining a felt purpose against felt obstacles, and overcoming or being overcome. What 'sustaining' means here is clear to anyone who has lived through the experience, but to no one else; just as 'loud,' 'red,' 'sweet,' mean something only to beings with ears, eyes, and tongues. The *percipi* in these originals of experience is the *esse*; the curtain is the picture. If there is anything hiding in the background, it ought not to be called causal agency, but should get itself another name.

In it 'final' and 'efficient' causation coincide

The way in which we feel that our successive fields continue each other in these cases is evidently what the orthodox doctrine means when it vaguely says that 'in some way' the cause 'contains' the effect. It contains it by proposing it as the end pursued. Since the desire of that end is the efficient cause, we see that in the total fact of personal activity final and efficient causes coalesce. Yet the effect is oftenest contained *aliquo modo* only, and seldom explicitly foreseen. The activity sets up more effects than it proposes literally. The end is defined beforehand in most cases only as a general direction, along which all sorts of novelties and surprises lie in wait. These words I write even now surprise me; yet I adopt them as effects of my scriptorial causality. Their being 'contained' means only their harmony and continuity with my general aim. They 'fill the bill' and I accept them, but the exact shape of them seems determined by something outside of my explicit will.

And novelties arise

If we look at the general mass of things in the midst of which the life of men is passed, and ask 'How came they here?' the only broad answer is that man's desires preceded and produced them. If not all-sufficient causes, desire and will were at any rate what John Mill calls unconditional causes, indispensable causes namely, without which the effects could not have come at all. Human causal activity is the only known unconditional antecedent of the works of civilization; so we find, as Edward Carpenter says,[1] something like a law of nature, the law that a movement from feeling to thought and thence to action, from the world of dreams to the world of things, is everywhere going on. Since at each phase of this movement novelties turn up, we may fairly ask, with Carpenter, whether we are not here witnessing in our own personal experience what is really the essential process of creation. Is not the world really growing in these activities of ours? And where we predicate activities elsewhere, have we a right to suppose aught different in kind from this?

To some such vague vision are we brought by taking our perceptual experience of action at its face-value, and following the analogies which it suggests.

I say vague vision, for even if our desires be an unconditional causal factor in the only part of the universe where we *Perceptual causation sets a problem* are intimately acquainted with the way creative work is done, desire is anything but a close factor, even there. The part of the world to which our desires lie closest is, by the consent of physiologists, the cortex of the brain. If they act causally, their first effect is there, and only through innumerable neural, muscular, and instrumental intermediaries is that last effect which they consciously aimed at brought to birth. Our trust in the face-value of perception was apparently misleading. There is no such continuity between cause-and-effect as in our activity-experiences was made to appear. There is disruption rather; and what we naïvely assume to be continuous is separated by causal successions of which perception is wholly unaware.

The logical conclusion would seem to be that even if the kind of thing that causation is, were revealed to us in our own activity, we should be mistaken on the very threshold if we supposed that the fact of it is there. In other words we seem in this line of experience to start with an illusion of place. It is as if a baby were born at a kinetoscope-show and his first experiences were of the illusions of movement that reigned in the place. The nature of movement would indeed be revealed to him, but the real facts of movement he would have to seek

[1] *The Art of Creation*, 1894, chap. i.

outside. Even so our will-acts may reveal the nature of causation, but just where the facts of causation are located may be a further problem.[1] With this further problem, philosophy leaves off comparing conceptual with perceptual experience, and begins enquiring into physical and psychological facts.

Perception has given us a positive idea of causal agency but it remains to be ascertained whether what first appears as such, is really such; whether aught else is really such; or finally, whether nothing really such exists. Since with this we are led immediately into the mind-brain relation, and since that is such a complicated topic, we had better interrupt our study of causation provisionally at the present point, meaning to complete it when the problem of the mind's relation to the body comes up for review.

This is the problem of the relation of mind to brain

Our outcome so far seems therefore to be only this, that the attempt to treat 'cause,' for conceptual purposes, as a separable link, has failed historically, and has led to the denial of efficient causation, and to the substitution for it of the bare descriptive notion of uniform sequence among events. Thus intellectualist philosophy once more has had to butcher our perceptual life in order to make it 'comprehensible.' Meanwhile the concrete perceptual flux, taken just as it comes, offers in our own activity-situations perfectly comprehensible instances of causal agency. The transitive causation in them does not, it is true, stick out as a separate piece of fact for conception to fix upon. Rather does a whole subsequent field grow continuously out of a whole antecedent field because it seems to yield new being of the nature called for, while the feeling of causality-at-work flavors the entire concrete sequence as salt flavors the water in which it is dissolved.

Conclusion

If we took these experiences as the type of what actual causation is, we should have to ascribe to cases of causation

---

[1]With this cause-and-effect are in what is called a transitive relation: as 'more than more is more than less,' so 'cause of cause is cause of effect.' In a chain of causes, intermediaries can drop out and (logically at least) the relation still hold between the extreme terms, the wider causal span enveloping, without altering the 'closer' one. This consideration may provisionally mitigate the impression of falsehood which psychophysical criticism finds in our consciousness of activity. The subject will come up later in more detail.

outside of our own life, to physical cases also, an inwardly experiential nature. In other words we should have to espouse a so-called 'pan-psychic' philosophy. This complication, and the fact that hidden brain-events appear to be 'closer' effects than those which consciousness directly aims at, lead us to interrupt the subject here provisionally. Our main result, up to this point, has been the contrast between the perceptual and the intellectualist treatment of it.[1]

[1] Almost no philosopher has admitted that perception can give us relations immediately. Relations have invariably been called the work of 'thought,' so cause must be a 'category.' The result is well shown in such a treatment of the subject as Mr. Shadworth Hodgson's, in his elaborate work the *Metaphysic of Experience*. 'What we call conscious activity is not a consciousness of activity in the sense of an immediate perception of it. Try to perceive activity or effort immediately, and you will fail; you will find nothing there to perceive' (i, 180). As there is nothing there to conceive either, in the discrete manner which Mr. Hodgson desiderates, he has to conclude that 'Causality *per se* (why need it be *per se*?) has no scientific or philosophic justification. . . . All cases of common-sense causality resolve themselves, on analysis, into cases of *post hoc, cum illo, evenit istud*. Hence we say that the search for causes is given up in science and philosophy, and replaced by the search for real conditions (i. e., phenomenal antecedents merely) and the laws of real conditioning. It must also be recognized that realities answering to the terms cause and causality *per se* are impossible and non-existent' (ii, 374–378).

The author whose discussion most resembles my own (apart from Bergson's, of which more later) is Prof. James Ward in his *Naturalism and Agnosticism* (see the words 'activity' and 'causality' in the index). Consult also the chapter on 'Mental Activity' in G. F. Stout's *Analytic Psychology*, vol. i. W. James's *Pluralistic Universe*, Appendix B, may also be consulted. Some authors seem to think that we do have an ideal conception of genuine activity which none of our experiences, least of all personal ones, match. Hence, and not because activity is a spurious idea altogether, are all the activities we imagine false. Mr. F. H. Bradley seems to occupy some such position, but I am not sure.

APPENDIX

FAITH AND THE RIGHT TO BELIEVE

'INTELLECTUALISM' is the belief that our mind comes upon a world complete in itself, and has the duty of ascertaining its contents; but has no power of re-determining its character, for that is already given.

Among intellectualists two parties may be distinguished. Rationalizing intellectualists lay stress on deductive and 'dialectic' arguments, making large use of abstract concepts and pure logic (Hegel, Bradley, Taylor, Royce). Empiricist intellectualists are more 'scientific,' and think that the character of the world must be sought in our sensible experiences, and found in hypotheses based exclusively thereon (Clifford, Pearson).

Both sides insist that in our conclusions personal preferences should play no part, and that no argument from what *ought to be* to what *is*, is valid. 'Faith,' being the greeting of our whole nature to a kind of world conceived as well adapted to that nature, is forbidden, until purely intellectual *evidence* that such *is* the actual world has come in. Even if evidence should eventually prove a faith true, the truth, says Clifford, would have been 'stolen,' if assumed and acted on too soon.

Refusal to believe anything concerning which 'evidence' has not yet come in, would thus be the rule of intellectualism. Obviously it postulates certain conditions, which for aught we can see need not necessarily apply to all the dealings of our minds with the Universe to which they belong.

1. It postulates that *to escape error* is our paramount duty. Faith *may* grasp truth; but also it *may* not. By resisting it always, we are sure of escaping error; and if by the same act we renounce our chance at truth, that loss is the lesser evil, and should be incurred.

2. It postulates that in every respect the universe is finished in advance of our dealings with it;

That the knowledge of what it thus is, is best gained by a

passively receptive mind, with no native sense of probability, or good-will towards any special result;

That 'evidence' not only needs no good-will for its reception; but is able, if patiently waited for, to neutralize ill-will;

Finally, that our beliefs and our acts based thereupon, although they are parts of the world, and although the world without them is unfinished, are yet such mere externalities as not to alter in any way the significance of the rest of the world when they are added to it.

In our dealings with many details of fact these postulates work well. Such details exist in advance of our opinion; truth concerning them is often of no pressing importance; and by believing nothing, we escape error while we wait. But even here we often *cannot* wait but must act, somehow; so we act on most *probable* hypothesis, trusting that the event may prove us wise. Moreover, not to act on one belief, is often equivalent to acting as if the opposite belief were true, so inaction would not always be as 'passive' as the intellectualists assume. It is one attitude of will.

Again, Philosophy and Religion have to interpret the total character of the world, and it is by no means clear that here the intellectualist postulates obtain. It may be true all the while (even though the evidence be still imperfect) that, as Paulsen says, 'the natural order is at bottom a moral order.' It may be true that work is still doing in the world-process, and that in that work we are called to bear our share. The character of the world's results may in part depend upon our acts. Our acts may depend on our religion,—on our not-resisting our faith-tendencies, or on our sustaining them in spite of 'evidence' being incomplete. These faith-tendencies in turn are but expressions of our good-will towards certain forms of result.

Such faith-tendencies are extremely active psychological forces, constantly outstripping evidence. The following steps may be called the 'faith-ladder':

1. There is nothing absurd in a certain view of the world being true, nothing self-contradictory;

2. It *might* have been true under certain conditions;

3. It *may* be true, even now;

4. It is *fit* to be true;
5. It *ought* to be true;
6. It *must* be true;
7. It *shall* be true, at any rate true for *me*.

Obviously this is no intellectual chain of inferences, like the *sorites* of the logic-books. Yet it is a slope of good-will on which in the larger questions of life men habitually live.

Intellectualism's proclamation that our good-will, our 'will to believe,' is a pure disturber of truth, is itself an act of faith of the most arbitrary kind. It implies the will to insist on a universe of intellectualist constitution, and the willingness to stand in the way of a pluralistic universe's success, such success requiring the good-will and active faith, theoretical as well as practical, of all concerned, to make it 'come true.'

Intellectualism thus contradicts itself. It is a sufficient objection to it, that if a 'pluralistically' organized, or 'co-operative' universe or the 'melioristic' universe above, were really here, the veto of intellectualism on letting our good-will ever have any vote would debar us from ever admitting that universe to be true.

Faith thus remains as one of the inalienable birthrights of our mind. Of course it must remain a practical, and not a dogmatic attitude. It must go with toleration of other faiths, with the search for the most probable, and with the full consciousness of responsibilities and risks.

It may be regarded as a formative factor in the universe, if we be integral parts thereof, and co-determinants, by our behavior, of what its total character may be.

HOW WE ACT ON PROBABILITIES

In most emergencies we have to act on probability, and incur the risk of error.

'Probability' and 'possibility' are terms applied to things of the conditions of whose coming we are (to some degree at least) ignorant.

If we are entirely ignorant of the conditions that make a thing come, we call it a 'bare' possibility. If we know that some of the conditions already exist, it is for us in so far forth a 'grounded' possibility. It is in that case *probable* just in proportion as the said conditions are numerous, and few hindering conditions are in sight.

When the conditions are so numerous and confused that we can hardly follow them, we treat a thing as probable in proportion to the *frequency* with which things of that *kind* occur. Such frequency being a fraction, the probability is expressed by a fraction. Thus, if one death in 10,000 is by suicide, the antecedent probability of my death being a suicide is 1–10,000th. If one house in 5000 burns down annually, the probability that my house will burn is 1–5000th, etc.

Statistics show that in most kinds of thing the frequency is pretty regular. Insurance companies bank on this regularity, undertaking to pay (say) 5000 dollars to each man whose house burns, provided he and the other house-owners each pay enough to give the company that sum, plus something more for profits and expenses.

The company, hedging on the large number of cases it deals with, and working by the long run, need run no risk of loss by the single fires.

The individual householder deals with his own single case exclusively. The probability of his house burning is only 1–5000, but if that lot befall he will lose everything. He has no 'long run' to go by, if his house takes fire, and he can't hedge as the company does, by taxing his more fortunate neighbors. But in this particular kind of risk, the company helps him out. It translates his one chance in 5000 of a big loss, into a certain loss 5000 times smaller, and the bargain is a fair one on both sides. It is clearly better for the man to lose *certainly*, but *fractionally*, than to trust to his 4999 chances of no loss, and then have the improbable chance befall.

But for most of our emergencies there is no insurance company at hand, and fractional solutions are impossible. Seldom can we *act* fractionally. If the probability that a friend is waiting for you in Boston is 1–2, how should you act on that probability? By going as far as the bridge? Better stay at home! Or if the probability is 1–2 that your partner is a villain, how should you act on that probability? By treating him as a villain one day, and confiding your money and your secrets to him the next? That would be the worst of all solutions. In all such cases we must act wholly for one *or* the other horn of the dilemma. We must go in for the more probable alternative as if the other one did not exist, and suffer the full penalty if the event belie our faith.

Now the metaphysical and religious alternatives are largely of this kind. We have but this one life in which to take up our attitude towards them, no insurance company is there to cover us, and if we are wrong, our error, even though it be not as great as the old hell-fire theology pretended, may yet be momentous. In such questions as that of the *character* of the world, of life being moral in its essential meaning, of our playing a vital part therein, etc., it would seem as if a certain *wholeness* in our faith were necessary. To calculate the probabilities and act fractionally, and treat life one day as a farce, and another day as a very serious business, would be to make the worst possible mess of it. Inaction also often counts as action. In many issues the inertia of one member will impede the success of the whole as much as his opposition will. To refuse, *e. g.*, to testify against villainy, is practically to help it to prevail.[1]

THE PLURALISTIC OR MELIORISTIC UNIVERSE

Finally, if the 'melioristic' universe were *really* here, it would require the active good-will of all of us, in the way of belief as well as of our other activities, to bring it to a prosperous issue.

The melioristic universe is conceived after a *social* analogy, as a pluralism of independent powers. It will succeed just in proportion as more of these work for its success. If none work, it will fail. If each does his best, it will not fail. Its destiny thus hangs on an *if*, or on a lot of *ifs*—which amounts to saying (in the technical language of logic) that, the world being as yet unfinished, its total character can be expressed only by *hypothetical* and not by *categorical* propositions.

(Empiricism, believing in possibilities, is willing to formulate its universe in hypothetical propositions. Rationalism, believing only in impossibilities and necessities, insists on the contrary on their being categorical.)

[1] Cf. Wm. James: *The Will to Believe*, etc., pp. 1–31, and 90–110.

As individual members of a pluralistic universe, we must recognize that, even though we do *our* best, the other factors also will have a voice in the result. If they refuse to conspire, our good-will and labor may be thrown away. No insurance company can here cover us or save us from the risks we run in being part of such a world.

We *must* take one of four attitudes in regard to the other powers: either

1. Follow intellectualist advice: wait for evidence; and while waiting, do nothing; or

2. *Mistrust* the other powers and, sure that the universe will fail, *let* it fail; or

3. *Trust* them; and at any rate do *our* best, in spite of the *if*; or, finally,

4. *Flounder*, spending one day in one attitude, another day in another.

This 4th way is no systematic solution. The 2d way spells faith in failure. The 1st way may in practice be indistinguishable from the 2d way. The 3d way seems the only wise way.

'*If* we do *our* best, *and* the other powers do *their* best, the world will be perfected'—this proposition expresses no actual fact, but only the complexion of a fact thought of as eventually possible. As it stands, *no* conclusion can be positively deduced from it. *A conclusion would require another premise of fact, which only we can supply. The original proposition per se has no pragmatic value whatsoever, apart from its power to challenge our will to produce the premise of fact required.* Then indeed the perfected world emerges as a logical conclusion.

We can *create* the conclusion, then. We can and we may, as it were, jump with both feet off the ground into or towards a world of which we trust the other parts to meet our jump—and *only so* can the *making* of a perfected world of the pluralistic pattern ever take place. Only through our precursive trust in it can it come into being.

There is no inconsistency anywhere in this, and no 'vicious circle' unless a circle of poles holding themselves upright by leaning on one another, or a circle of dancers revolving by holding each other's hands, be 'vicious.'

The faith circle is so congruous with human nature that the only explanation of the veto that intellectualists pass upon it must be sought in the offensive character *to them* of the faiths of certain concrete persons.

Such possibilities of offense have, however, to be put up with on empiricist principles. The long run of experience may weed out the more foolish faiths. Those who held them will then have failed: but without the wiser faiths of the others the world could never be perfected.

(Compare G. Lowes Dickinson: "Religion, a Criticism and a Forecast," N. Y. 1905, Introduction; and chaps. iii, iv.)

Index

ESSAYS

Contents

The Ph.D. Octopus

S OME YEARS AGO we had at our Harvard Graduate School a very brilliant student of Philosophy, who, after leaving us and supporting himself by literary labor for three years, received an appointment to teach English Literature at a sister-institution of learning. The governors of this institution, however, had no sooner communicated the appointment than they made the awful discovery that they had enrolled upon their staff a person who was unprovided with the Ph.D. degree. The man in question had been satisfied to work at Philosophy for her own sweet (or bitter) sake, and had disdained to consider that an academic bauble should be his reward.

His appointment had thus been made under a misunderstanding. He was not the proper man; and there was nothing to do but to inform him of the fact. It was notified to him by his new President that his appointment must be revoked, or that a Harvard doctor's degree must forthwith be procured.

Although it was already the Spring of the year, our Subject, being a man of spirit, took up the challenge, turned his back upon literature (which in view of his approaching duties might have seemed his more urgent concern) and spent the weeks that were left him, in writing a metaphysical thesis and grinding his psychology, logic and history of philosophy up again, so as to pass our formidable ordeals.

When the thesis came to be read by our committee, we could not pass it. Brilliancy and originality by themselves won't save a thesis for the doctorate; it must also exhibit a heavy technical apparatus of learning; and this our candidate had neglected to bring to bear. So, telling him that he was temporarily rejected, we advised him to pad out the thesis properly, and return with it next year, at the same time informing his new President that this signified nothing as to his merits, that he was of ultra Ph.D. quality, and one of the strongest men with whom we had ever had to deal.

To our surprise we were given to understand in reply that the quality *per se* of the man signified nothing in this connection, and that three magical letters were the thing seriously required. The College had always gloried in a list of faculty members who bore the doctor's title, and to make a gap in the galaxy, and admit a common fox without a tail, would be a degradation impossible to be thought of. We wrote again, pointing out that a Ph.D. in philosophy would prove little anyhow as to one's ability to teach literature; we sent separate letters in which we outdid each other in eulogy of our candidate's powers, for indeed they were great; and at last, *mirabile dictu*, our eloquence prevailed. He was allowed to retain his appointment provisionally, on condition that one year later at the farthest his miserably naked name should be prolonged by the sacred appendage the lack of which had given so much trouble to all concerned.

Accordingly he came up here the following spring with an adequate thesis (known since in print as a most brilliant contribution to metaphysics), passed a first-rate examination, wiped out the stain, and brought his college into proper relations with the world again. Whether his teaching, during that first year, of English Literature was made any the better by the impending examination in a different subject, is a question which I will not try to solve.

I have related this incident at such length because it is so characteristic of American academic conditions at the present day. Graduate schools still are something of a novelty, and higher diplomas something of a rarity. The latter, therefore, carry a vague sense of preciousness and honor, and have a particularly "up-to-date" appearance, and it is no wonder if smaller institutions, unable to attract professors already eminent, and forced usually to recruit their faculties from the relatively young, should hope to compensate for the obscurity of the names of their officers of instruction by the abundance of decorative titles by which those names are followed on the pages of the catalogues where they appear. The dazzled reader of the list, the parent or student, says to himself, "this must be a terribly distinguished crowd—their titles shine like the stars in the firmament, Ph.D.'s, S.D.'s, and Litt.D.'s, bespangle the page as if they were sprinkled over it from a pepper caster."

Human nature is once for all so childish that every reality becomes a sham somewhere, and in the minds of Presidents and Trustees the Ph.D. degree is in point of fact already looked upon as a mere advertising resource, a manner of throwing dust in the Public's eyes. "No instructor who is not a Doctor" has become a maxim in the smaller institutions which represent demand; and in each of the larger ones which represent supply, the same belief in decorated scholarship expresses itself in two antagonistic passions, one for multiplying as much as possible the annual output of doctors, the other for raising the standard of difficulty in passing, so that the Ph.D. of the special institution shall carry a higher blaze of distinction than it does elsewhere. Thus we at Harvard are proud of the number of candidates whom we reject, and of the inability of men who are not *distingués* in intellect to pass our tests.

America is thus as a nation rapidly drifting towards a state of things in which no man of science or letters will be accounted respectable unless some kind of badge or diploma is stamped upon him, and in which bare personality will be a mark of outcast estate. It seems to me high time to rouse ourselves to consciousness, and to cast a critical eye upon this decidedly grotesque tendency. Other nations suffer terribly from the Mandarin disease. Are we doomed to suffer like the rest?

Our higher degrees were instituted for the laudable purpose of stimulating scholarship, especially in the form of "original research." Experience has proved that great as the love of truth may be among men, it can be made still greater by adventitious rewards. The winning of a diploma certifying mastery and marking a barrier successfully passed, acts as a challenge to the ambitious; and if the diploma will help to gain bread-winning positions also, its power as a stimulus to work is tremendously increased. So far, we are on innocent ground; it is well for a country to have research in abundance, and our graduate schools do but apply a normal psychological spur. But the institutionizing on a large scale of any natural combination of need and motive always tends to run into technicality and to develop a tyrannical Machine with unforeseen powers of exclusion and corruption. Observation of the workings of our Harvard system for 20 years past has brought some of these drawbacks home to my consciousness, and I should like to call the attention of the readers of the

MONTHLY to this disadvantageous aspect of the picture, and to make a couple of remedial suggestions, if I may.

In the first place, it would seem that to stimulate study, and to increase the *gelehrtes Publikum*, the class of highly educated men in our country, is the only positive good, and consequently the sole direct end at which our graduate schools, with their diploma-giving powers, should aim. If other results have developed they should be deemed secondary incidents, and if not desirable in themselves, they should be carefully guarded against.

To interfere with the free development of talent, to obstruct the natural play of supply and demand in the teaching profession, to foster academic snobbery by the *prestige* of certain privileged institutions, to transfer accredited value from essential manhood to an outward badge, to blight hopes and promote invidious sentiments, to divert the attention of aspiring youth from direct dealings with truth to the passing of examinations,—such consequences, if they exist, ought surely to be regarded as drawbacks to the system, and an enlightened public consciousness ought to be keenly alive to the importance of reducing their amount. Candidates themselves do seem to be keenly conscious of some of these evils, but outside of their ranks or in the general public no such consciousness, so far as I can see, exists; or if it does exist, it fails to express itself aloud. Schools, Colleges, and Universities, appear enthusiastic over the entire system, just as it stands, and unanimously applaud all its developments.

I beg the reader to consider some of the secondary evils which I have enumerated. First of all, is not our growing tendency to appoint no instructors who are not also doctors an instance of pure sham? Will any one pretend for a moment that the doctor's degree is a guarantee that its possessor will be successful as a teacher? Notoriously his moral, social and personal characteristics may utterly disqualify him for success in the class-room; and of these characteristics his doctor's examination is unable to take any account whatever. Certain bare human beings will always be better candidates for a given place than all the doctor-applicants on hand; and to exclude the former by a rigid rule, and in the end to have to sift the latter by private inquiry into their personal peculiarities among those who know them, just as if they were not doctors at all, is to stultify one's own procedure. You may say that at least you guard against ignorance of the subject by considering only the candidates who are doctors; but how then about making doctors in one subject teach a different subject? This happened in the instance by which I introduced this article, and it happens daily and hourly in all our colleges. The truth is that the Doctor-Monopoly in teaching, which is becoming so rooted an American custom, can show no serious grounds whatsoever for itself in reason. As it actually prevails and grows in vogue among us, it is due to childish motives exclusively. In reality it is but a sham, a bauble, a dodge whereby to decorate the catalogues of schools and colleges.

Next, let us turn from the general promotion of a spirit of academic snobbery to the particular damage done to individuals by the system.

There are plenty of individuals so well endowed by nature that they pass with ease all the ordeals with which life confronts them. Such persons are born for professional success. Examinations have no terrors for them, and interfere in no way with their spiritual or worldly interests. There are others, not so gifted, who nevertheless rise to the challenge, get a stimulus from the difficulty, and become doctors, not without some baleful nervous wear and tear and retardation of their purely inner life, but on the whole successfully, and with advantage. These two classes form the natural Ph.D.'s, for whom the degree is legitimately instituted. To be sure, the degree is of no consequence one way or the other for the first sort of man, for in him the personal worth obviously outshines the title. To the second set of persons, however, the doctor-ordeal may contribute a touch of energy and solidity of scholarship which otherwise they might have lacked, and were our candidates all drawn from these classes, no oppression would result from the institution.

But there is a third class of persons who are genuinely, and in the most pathetic sense, the institution's victims. For this type of character the academic life may become, after a certain point, a virulent poison. Men without marked originality or native force, but fond of truth and especially of books and study, ambitious of reward and recognition, poor often, and needing a degree to get a teaching position, weak in the eyes of their examiners,—among these we find the veritable *chair à canon* of the wars of learning, the unfit in the academic struggle for existence. There are individuals of this sort for whom to pass one degree after another seems the limit of earthly aspiration. Your private advice does not discourage them. They will fail, and go away to recuperate, and then present themselves for another ordeal, and sometimes prolong the process into middle life. Or else, if they are less heroic morally they will accept the failure as a sentence of doom that they are not fit, and are broken-spirited men thereafter.

We of the University faculties are responsible for deliberately creating this new class of American social failures, and heavy is the responsibility. We advertise our "schools" and send out our degree-requirements, knowing well that aspirants of all sorts will be attracted, and at the same time we set a standard which intends to pass no man who has not native intellectual distinction. We know that there is no test, however absurd, by which, if a title or decoration, a public badge or mark, were to be won by it, some weakly suggestible or hauntable persons would not feel challenged, and remain unhappy if they went without it. We dangle our three magic letters before the eyes of these predestined victims, and they swarm to us like moths to an electric light. They come at a time of life when failure can no longer be repaired easily and when the wounds it leaves are permanent; and we say deliberately that mere work faithfully performed, as they perform it, will not by itself save them, they must in addition put in evidence the one thing they have not got, namely this quality of intellectual distinction. Occasionally, out of sheer human pity, we ignore our high and mighty standard and pass them. Usually, however, the standard, and not the candidate, commands our fidelity. The result is caprice, majorities of one on the jury, and on the whole a confession that our pretensions about the degree cannot be lived up to consistently. Thus, partiality in the favored cases; in the unfavored, blood on our hands; and in both a bad conscience,—are the results of our administration.

The more widespread becomes the popular belief that our diplomas are indispensable hall-marks to show the sterling metal of their holders, the more widespread these corruptions will become. We ought to look to the future carefully, for it takes generations for a national custom, once rooted, to be grown away from. All the European countries are seeking to diminish the check upon individual spontaneity which state examinations with their tyrannous growth have brought in their train. We have had to institute state examinations too; and it will perhaps be fortunate if some day hereafter our descendants, comparing machine with machine, do not sigh with regret for old times and American freedom, and wish that the régime of the dear old bosses might be reinstalled, with plain human nature, the glad hand and the marble heart, liking and disliking, and man-to-man relations grown possible again. Meanwhile, whatever evolution our state-examinations are destined to undergo, our universities at least should never cease to regard themselves as the jealous custodians of personal and spiritual spontaneity. They are indeed its only organized and recognized custodians in America today. They ought to guard against contributing to the increase of officialism and snobbery and insincerity as against a pestilence; they ought to keep truth and disinterested labor always in the foreground, treat degrees as secondary incidents, and in season and out of season make it plain that what they live for is to help men's souls, and not to decorate their persons with diplomas.

There seem to be three obvious ways in which the increasing hold of the Ph.D. Octopus upon American life can be kept in check.

The first way lies with the Universities. They can lower their fantastic standards (which here at Harvard we are so proud of) and give the doctorate as a matter of course, just as they give the bachelor's degree, for a due amount of time spent in patient labor in a special department of learning, whether the man be a brilliantly gifted individual or not. Surely native distinction needs no official stamp, and should disdain to ask for one. On the other hand, faithful labor, however commonplace, and years devoted to a subject, always deserve to be acknowledged and requited.

The second way lies with both the Universities and Colleges. Let them give up their unspeakably silly ambition to bespangle their lists of officers with these doctorial titles. Let them look more to substance and less to vanity and sham.

The third way lies with the individual student, and with his personal advisers in the Faculties. Every man of native power, who might take a higher degree, and refuses to do so, because examinations interfere with the free following out of his more immediate intellectual aims, deserves well of his country, and in a rightly organized community, would not be made to suffer for his independence. With many men the passing of these extraneous tests is a very grievous interference indeed. Private letters of recommendation from their instructors, which in any event are ultimately needful, ought, in these cases, completely to offset the lack of the bread-winning degree; and instructors ought to be ready to advise students against it upon occasion, and to pledge themselves to back them later personally, in the market-struggle which they have to face.

It is indeed odd to see this love of titles—and such titles—growing up in a country of which the recognition of individuality and bare manhood have so long been supposed to be the very soul. The independence of the State, in which most of our colleges stand, relieves us of those more odious forms of academic politics which continental European countries present. Anything like the elaborate University machine of France, with its throttling influences upon individuals is unknown here. The spectacle of the "Rath" distinction in its innumerable spheres and grades, with which all Germany is crawling today, is displeasing to American eyes; and displeasing also in some respects is the institution of knighthood in England, which, aping as it does an aristocratic title, enables one's wife as well as one's self so easily to dazzle the servants at the house of one's friends. But are we Americans ourselves destined after all to hunger after similar vanities on an infinitely more contemptible scale? And is individuality with us also going to count for nothing unless stamped and licensed and authenticated by some title-giving machine? Let us pray that our ancient national genius may long preserve vitality enough to guard us from a future so unmanly and so unbeautiful!

The Harvard Monthly, March 1903

Address at the Centenary of Ralph Waldo Emerson, May 25, 1903

THE PATHOS of death is this, that when the days of one's life are ended, those days that were so crowded with business and felt so heavy in their passing, what remains of one in memory should usually be so slight a thing. The phantom of an attitude, the echo of a certain mode of thought, a few pages of print, some invention, or some victory we gained in a brief critical hour, are all that can survive the best of us. It is as if the whole of a man's significance had now shrunk into the phantom of an attitude, into a mere musical note or phrase, suggestive of his singularity—happy are those whose singularity gives a note so clear as to be victorious over the inevitable pity of such a diminution and abridgment.

An ideal wraith like this, of Emerson's singularity, hovers over all Concord to-day, taking in the minds of those of you who were his neighbors and intimates a somewhat fuller shape, remaining more abstract in the younger generation, but bringing home to all of us the notion of a spirit indescribably precious. The form that so lately moved upon these streets and country roads, or awaited in these fields and woods the beloved Muse's visits, is now dust; but the soul's note, the spiritual voice, rises strong and clear above the uproar of the times, and seems securely destined to exert an ennobling influence over future generations.

What gave a flavor so matchless to Emerson's individuality was, even more than his rich mental gifts, their combination. Rarely has a man so known the limits of his genius or so unfailingly kept within them. "Stand by your order," he used to say to youthful students; and perhaps the paramount impression one gets of his life is of his loyalty to his own type and mission. The type was that of what he liked to call the scholar, the perceiver of pure truth, and the mission was that of the reporter in worthy form of each perception. The day is good, he said, in which we have the most perceptions. There are times when the cawing of a crow, a weed, a snowflake, or a farmer planting in his field, become symbols to the intellect of truths equal to those which the most majestic phenomena can open. Let me mind my own charge, then, walk alone, consult the sky, the field and forest, sedulously waiting every morning for the news concerning the structure of the universe which the good Spirit will give me.

This was the first half of Emerson, but only half, for his genius was insatiate for expression, and his truth had to be clad in the right verbal garment. The form of the garment was so vital with Emerson that it is impossible to separate it from the matter. They form a chemical combination,— thoughts which would be trivial expressed otherwise are important through the nouns and verbs to which he married them. The style is the man, it has been said: the man Emerson's mission culminated in his style, and if we must define him in one word, we have to call him Artist. He was an artist whose medium was verbal and who wrought in spiritual material.

This duty of spiritual seeing and reporting determined the whole tenor of his life. It was to shield it from invasion and distraction that he dwelt in the country, and that he consistently declined to entangle himself with associations or to encumber himself with functions which, however he might believe in them, he felt were duties for other men and not for him. Even the care of his garden, "with its stoopings and fingerings in a few yards of space," he found "narrowing and poisoning," and took to long free walks and saunterings instead, without apology. "Causes" innumerable sought to enlist him as their "worker"—all got his smile and word of sympathy, but none entrapped him into service. The struggle against slavery itself, deeply as it appealed to him, found him firm: "God must govern his own world, and knows his way out of this pit without my desertion of my post, which has none to guard it but me. I have quite other slaves to face than those Negroes, to wit, imprisoned thoughts far back in the brain of man, and which have no watchman or lover or defender but me." This in reply to the possible questions of his conscience. To hot-blooded moralists with more objective ideas of duty, such a fidelity to the limits of his genius must often have made him seem provokingly remote and unavailable; but we who can see things in more liberal perspective must unqualifiedly approve the results. The faultless tact with which he kept his safe limits while he so dauntlessly asserted himself within them is an example fitted to give heart to other theorists and artists the world over.

The insight and creed from which Emerson's life followed can be best summed up in his own verse: —

> "So nigh is grandeur to our dust,
> So near is God to man!"

Through the individual fact there ever shone for him the effulgence of the Universal Reason. The great Cosmic Intellect terminates and houses itself in mortal men and passing hours. Each of us is an angle of its eternal vision, and the only way to be true to our Maker is to be loyal to ourselves. "O rich and various Man!" he cries, "thou palace of sight and sound, carrying in thy senses the morning and the night and the unfathomable galaxy; in thy brain the geometry of the city of God; in thy heart the bower of love and the realms of right and wrong."

If the individual open thus directly into the Absolute, it follows that there is something in each and all of us, even the lowliest, that ought not to consent to borrowing traditions and living at second hand. "If John was perfect, why are you and I alive?" writes Emerson. "As long as any man exists there is some need of him; let him fight for his own." This faith that in a life at first hand there is something sacred is perhaps the most characteristic note in Emerson's writings. The hottest side of him is this non-conformist persuasion, and if his temper could ever verge on common irascibility, it would be by reason of the passionate character of his feelings on this point. The world is still new and untried. In seeing freshly, and not in hearing of what others saw, shall a man find what truth is. "Each one of us can bask in the great morning which rises out of the Eastern Sea, and be himself one of the children of the light." "Trust thyself, every heart vibrates to that iron string. There is a time in each man's education when he must arrive at the conviction that imitation is suicide; when he must take himself for better or worse as his portion; and know that though the wide universe is full of good, no kernel of nourishing corn can come to him but through his toil bestowed on that plot of ground which it was given him to till."

The matchless eloquence with which Emerson proclaimed the sovereignty of the living individual electrified and emancipated his generation, and this bugle-blast will doubtless be regarded by future critics as the soul of his message. The present man is the aboriginal reality, the Institution is derivative, and the past man is irrelevant and obliterate for present issues. "If any one would lay an axe to your tree with a text from I John, v. 7, or a sentence from Saint Paul, say to him," Emerson wrote, " 'My tree is Ygdrasil, the tree of life.' Let him know by your security that your conviction is clear and sufficient, and, if he were Paul himself, that you also are here and with your Creator." "Cleave ever to God," he insisted, "against the name of God;"—and so, in spite of the intensely religious character of his total thought, when he began his career it seemed to many of his brethren in the clerical profession that he was little more than an iconoclast and desecrator.

Emerson's belief that the individual must in reason be adequate to the vocation for which the Spirit of the world has called him into being is the source of those sublime pages, hearteners and sustainers of our youth, in which he urges his hearers to be incorruptibly true to their own private conscience. Nothing can harm the man who rests in his appointed place and character. Such a man is invulnerable; he balances the universe, balances it as much by keeping small when he is small as by being great and spreading when he is great. "I love and honor Epaminondas," said Emerson, "but I do not wish to be Epaminondas. I hold it more just to love the world of this hour than the world of his hour. Nor can you, if I am true, excite me to the least uneasiness by saying, 'He acted and thou sittest still.' I see action to be good when the need is, and sitting still to be also good. Epaminondas, if he was the man I take him for, would have sat still with joy and peace, if his lot had been mine. Heaven is large, and affords space for all modes of love and fortitude." "The fact that I am here certainly shows me that the Soul has need of an organ here, and shall I not assume the post?"

The vanity of all super-serviceableness and pretense was never more happily set forth than by Emerson in the many passages in which he develops this aspect of his philosophy. Character infallibly proclaims itself. "Hide your thoughts!— hide the sun and moon. They publish themselves to the universe. They will speak through you though you were dumb. They will flow out of your actions, your manners and your face. . . . Don't say things: What you are stands over you the while and thunders so that I cannot say what you say to the contrary. . . . What a man *is* engraves itself upon him in letters of light. Concealment avails him nothing, boasting nothing. There is confession in the glances of our eyes; in our smiles; in salutations; and the grasp of hands. His sin bedaubs him, mars all his good impression. Men know not why they do not trust him, but they do not trust him. His vice glasses the eye, casts lines of mean expression in the cheek, pinches the nose, sets the mark of the beast upon the back of the head, and writes, O fool! fool! on the forehead of a king. If you would not be known to do a thing, never do it; a man may play the fool in the drifts of a desert, but every grain of sand shall seem to see.—How can a man be concealed? How can he be concealed?"

On the other hand, never was a sincere word or a sincere thought utterly lost. "Never a magnanimity fell to the ground but there is some heart to greet and accept it unexpectedly. . . . The hero fears not that if he withstood the avowal of a just and brave act, it will go unwitnessed and unloved. One knows it,—himself,—and is pledged by it to sweetness of peace and to nobleness of aim, which will prove in the end a better proclamation than the relating of the incident."

The same indefeasible right to be exactly what one is, provided one only be authentic, spreads itself, in Emerson's way of thinking, from persons to things and to times and places. No date, no position is insignificant, if the life that fills it out be only genuine:—

"In solitude, in a remote village, the ardent youth loiters and mourns. With inflamed eye, in this sleeping wilderness, he has read the story of the Emperor Charles the Fifth, until his fancy has brought home to the surrounding woods the faint roar of cannonades in the Milanese, and marches in Germany. He is curious concerning that man's day. What filled it? The crowded orders, the stern decisions, the foreign despatches, the Castilian etiquette? The soul answers—Behold his day here! In the sighing of these woods, in the quiet of these gray fields, in the cool breeze that sings out of these northern mountains; in the workmen, the boys, the maidens you meet,—in the hopes of the morning, the ennui of noon, and sauntering of the afternoon; in the disquieting comparisons; in the regrets at want of vigor; in the great idea and the puny execution:—behold Charles the Fifth's day; another, yet the same; behold Chatham's, Hampden's, Bayard's, Alfred's, Scipio's, Pericles's day,—day of all that are born of women. The difference of circumstance is merely costume. I am tasting the self-same life,—its sweetness, its greatness, its pain,—which I so admire in other men. Do not foolishly ask the inscrutable, obliterated past what it cannot tell,—the details of that nature, of that day, called Byron or Burke;—but ask it of the enveloping Now. . . . Be lord of a day and you can put up your history books."

Thus does "the deep to-day which all men scorn" receive from Emerson superb revindication. "Other world! there is no other world." All God's life opens into the individual particular, and here and now, or nowhere, is reality. "The present hour is the decisive hour, and every day is doomsday."

Such a conviction that Divinity is everywhere may easily make of one an optimist of the sentimental type that refuses to speak ill of anything. Emerson's drastic perception of differences kept him at the opposite pole from this weakness. After you have seen men a few times, he could say, you find most of them as alike as their barns and pantries, and soon as musty and as dreary. Never was such a fastidious lover of significance and distinction, and never an eye so keen for their discovery. His optimism had nothing in common with that indiscriminate hurrahing for the Universe with which Walt Whitman has made us familiar. For Emerson, the individual fact and moment were indeed suffused with absolute radiance, but it was upon a condition that saved the situation—they must be worthy specimens,—sincere, authentic, archetypal; they must have made connection with what he calls the Moral Sentiment, they must in some way act as symbolic mouthpieces of the Universe's meaning. To know just which thing does act in this way, and which thing fails to make the true connection, is the secret (somewhat incommunicable, it must be confessed) of seership, and doubtless we must not expect of the seer too rigorous a consistency. Emerson himself was a real seer. He could perceive the full squalor of the individual fact, but he could also see the transfiguration. He might easily have found himself saying of some present-day agitator against our Philippine conquest what he said of this or that reformer of his own time. He might have called him, as a private person, a tedious bore and canter. But he would infallibly have added what he then added: "It is strange and horrible to say this, for I feel that under him and his partiality and exclusiveness is the earth and the sea, and all that in them is, and the axis round which the Universe revolves passes through his body where he stands."

Be it how it may, then, this is Emerson's revelation:—The point of any pen can be an epitome of reality; the commonest person's act, if genuinely actuated, can lay hold on eternity. This vision is the head-spring of all his outpourings; and it is for this truth, given to no previous literary artist to express in such penetratingly persuasive tones, that posterity will reckon him a prophet, and, perhaps neglecting other pages, piously turn to those that convey this message. His life was one long conversation with the invisible divine, expressing itself through individuals and particulars:—"So nigh is grandeur to our dust, so near is God to man!"

I spoke of how shrunken the wraith, how thin the echo, of men is after they are departed. Emerson's wraith comes to me now as if it were but the very voice of this victorious argument. His words to this effect are certain to be quoted and extracted more and more as time goes on, and to take their place among the Scriptures of humanity. " 'Gainst death and all oblivious enmity shall you pace forth," beloved Master. As long as our English language lasts, men's hearts will be cheered and their souls strengthened and liberated by the noble and musical pages with which you have enriched it.

Riverside Press for the Social Circle in Concord, June 1903

The True Harvard[1]

WHEN A MAN gets a decoration from a foreign institution, he may take it as an honor. Coming as mine has come to-day, I prefer to take it for that far more valuable thing, a token of personal good will from friends. Recognizing the good will and the friendliness, I am going to respond to the chairman's call by speaking exactly as I feel.

I am not an alumnus of the College. I have not even a degree from the Scientific School, in which I did some study forty years ago. I have no right to vote for Overseers, and I have never felt until to-day as if I were a child of the house of Harvard in the fullest sense. Harvard is many things in one—a school, a forcing house for thought, and also a social club; and the club aspect is so strong, the family tie so close and subtle among our Bachelors of Arts that all of us here who are in my plight, no matter how long we may have lived here, always feel a little like outsiders on Commencement day. We have no class to walk with, and we often stay away from the procession. It may be foolish, but it is a fact. I don't believe that my dear friends Shaler, Hollis, Lanman, or Royce ever have felt quite as happy or as much at home as my friend Barrett Wendell feels upon a day like this.

I wish to use my present privilege to say a word for these outsiders with whom I belong. Many years ago there was one of them from Canada here—a man with a high-pitched voice, who could n't fully agree with all the points of my philosophy. At a lecture one day, when I was in the full flood of my eloquence, his voice rose above mine, exclaiming: "But, doctor, doctor! to be serious for a moment . . .", in so sincere a tone that the whole room burst out laughing. I want you now to be serious for a moment while I say my little say. We are glorifying ourselves to-day, and whenever the name of Harvard is emphatically uttered on such days, frantic cheers go up. There are days for affection, when pure sentiment and loyalty come rightly to the fore. But behind our mere animal feeling for old schoolmates and the Yard and the bell, and Memorial and the clubs and the river and the Soldier's Field,

[1]Speech at the Harvard Commencement Dinner, June 24, 1903.

there must be something deeper and more rational. There ought at any rate to be some possible ground in reason for one's boiling over with joy that one is a son of Harvard, and was not, by some unspeakably horrible accident of birth, predestined to graduate at Yale or at Cornell.

Any college can foster club loyalty of that sort. The only rational ground for preëminent admiration of any single college would be its preëminent spiritual tone. But to be a college man in the mere clubhouse sense—I care not of what college—affords no guarantee of real superiority in spiritual tone.

The old notion that book learning can be a panacea for the vices of society lies pretty well shattered to-day. I say this in spite of certain utterances of the President of this University to the teachers last year. That sanguine-hearted man seemed then to think that if the schools would only do their duty better, social vice might cease. But vice will never cease. Every level of culture breeds its own peculiar brand of it as surely as one soil breeds sugar-cane, and another soil breeds cranberries. If we were asked that disagreeable question, "What are the bosom-vices of the level of culture which our land and day have reached?" we should be forced, I think, to give the still more disagreeable answer that they are swindling and adroitness, and the indulgence of swindling and adroitness, and cant, and sympathy with cant—natural fruits of that extraordinary idealization of "success" in the mere outward sense of "getting there," and getting there on as big a scale as we can, which characterizes our present generation. What was Reason given to man for, some satirist has said, except to enable him to invent reasons for what he wants to do. We might say the same of education. We see college graduates on every side of every public question. Some of Tammany's stanchest supporters are Harvard men. Harvard men defend our treatment of our Filipino allies as a masterpiece of policy and morals. Harvard men, as journalists, pride themselves on producing copy for any side that may enlist them. There is not a public abuse for which some Harvard advocate may not be found.

In the successful sense, then, in the worldly sense, in the club sense, to be a college man, even a Harvard man, affords

no sure guarantee for anything but a more educated clever-
ness in the service of popular idols and vulgar ends. Is there
no inner Harvard within the outer Harvard which means definitely more than this—for which the outside men who come
here in such numbers, come? They come from the remotest
outskirts of our country, without introductions, without
school affiliations; special students, scientific students, graduate students, poor students of the College, who make their
living as they go. They seldom or never darken the doors of
the Pudding or the Porcellian; they hover in the background
on days when the crimson color is most in evidence, but they
nevertheless are intoxicated and exultant with the nourishment they find here; and their loyalty is deeper and subtler
and more a matter of the inmost soul than the gregarious
loyalty of the clubhouse pattern often is.

Indeed, there is such an inner spiritual Harvard; and the
men I speak of, and for whom I speak to-day, are its true
missionaries and carry its gospel into infidel parts. When they
come to Harvard, it is not primarily because she is a club. It
is because they have heard of her persistently atomistic constitution, of her tolerance of exceptionality and eccentricity,
of her devotion to the principles of individual vocation and
choice. It is because you cannot make single one-ideaed regiments of her classes. It is because she cherishes so many vital
ideals, yet makes a scale of value among them; so that even
her apparently incurable second-rateness (or only occasional
first-rateness) in intercollegiate athletics comes from her
seeing so well that sport is but sport, that victory over Yale is
not the whole of the law and the prophets, and that a popgun
is not the crack of doom.

The true Church was always the invisible Church. The true
Harvard is the invisible Harvard in the souls of her more
truth-seeking and independent and often very solitary sons.
Thoughts are the precious seeds of which our universities
should be the botanical gardens. Beware when God lets loose
a thinker on the world—either Carlyle or Emerson said
that—for all things then have to rearrange themselves. But
the thinkers in their youth are almost always very lonely creatures. "Alone the great sun rises and alone spring the great
streams." The university most worthy of rational admiration

is that one in which your lonely thinker can feel himself least lonely, most positively furthered, and most richly fed. On an occasion like this it would be poor taste to draw comparisons between the colleges, and in their mere clubhouse quality they cannot differ widely:—all must be worthy of the loyalties and affections they arouse. But as a nursery for independent and lonely thinkers I do believe that Harvard still is in the van. Here they find the climate so propitious that they can be happy in their very solitude. The day when Harvard shall stamp a single hard and fast type of character upon her children, will be that of her downfall. Our undisciplinables are our proudest product. Let us agree together in hoping that the output of them will never cease.

Harvard Graduate Magazine, September 1903

Address on the Philippine Question

M R. CHAIRMAN: I think we have candidly to admit that in the matter of our Philippine conquest we here and our friends outside have failed to produce much immediate effect. 'Duty and Destiny' have rolled over us like a Juggernaut car whose unwieldy bulk the majority of our countrymen were pushing and pulling forward, and our outcries and attempts to scotch the wheels with our persons haven't acted in the least degree as a brake. Nevertheless, if we look round us today we see a great change from the conditions that prevailed when the outbreak of hostilities first called us into being. Religious emotion and martial hysterics are both over with the public, and the sober fit is on.

In the physiologies which I studied when I was young, the function of incorporating foreign bodies into one's organism was divided into four stages—prehension, deglutition, digestion and assimilation. We prehended our prey, or took it into our mouth, when President McKinley posted his annexation edict, and insalivated with pious phrases the alternative he offered to our late allies of instant obedience or death. The morsel thus lubricated, deglutition went on slowly during those three years and more when our army was slaughtering and burning, and famine, fire, disease and depopulation were the new allies we invoked. But if the swallowing took three years, how long ought the process of digestion, that teaching of the Filipinos to be 'fit' for rule, that solution of recalcitrant lumps into a smooth 'chyle,' with which our civil commission is charged—how long ought that to take? It will take a decade, at least. As for assimilation, that is altogether an affair of the day after tomorrow. The most sanguine expect no real assimilation of our prey to us or of us to our prey for fifty years to come, and no one who knows history expects that it can genuinely come at all.

Meanwhile, in spite of the indifference of the newspapers and in spite of the administrative barring out of news, our public has actually grown a little educated and reflective since the war began. It is fair to say that the more idealistic of our expansionists have put this forward from the outset as one chief reason why the Islands should be annexed. We were remaining too provincial-minded, they said, here in the United States, and this new responsibility would cultivate our consciousness of international affairs. But the consciousness which the experience has cultivated is a consciousness that all the anti-imperialistic prophecies were right. One by one we have seen them punctually fulfilled:—The material ruin of the Islands; the transformation of native friendliness to execration; the demoralization of our army, from the war office down—forgery decorated, torture whitewashed, massacre condoned; the creation of a chronic anarchy in the Islands, with ladronism still smouldering, and the lives of American travelers and American sympathizers unsafe in the country out of sight of army posts; the deliberate reinflaming on our part of ancient tribal animosities, the arming of Igorrote savages and Macabebe semi-savages, too low to have a national consciousness, to help us hunt the highest portions of the population down; the inoculation of Manila with a floating Yankee scum; these things, I say, or things like them, were things which everyone with any breadth of understanding clearly foretold; while the incapacity of our public for taking the slightest interest in anything so far away was from the outset a foregone conclusion.

It is only fair to President McKinley and his coadjutors and successor to say that their better angels also had a finger in the pie, and that the institution of our civil commission has gone far toward redeeming our national reputation for good sense. The only trouble is that this agency has come too late for any solid success. We are trying to do with our right hand what with our left hand, the army, we had made impossible in advance. When we landed at Manila we found a passionate native cordiality, which would have met us half way in almost any scheme of protectorate and co-operation which we might have proposed. But, 'like the base Indian,' we threw that pearl of a psychological moment away, and embarked, callous and cold, and business-like, as we flattered ourselves, upon our sinister plan of a preliminary military deglutition of them, just to show them what 'Old Glory' meant. Let our civil commission do what it will now, the hands will not move backward on the dial, the day of genuine co-operation with the

Filipinos is forever past. We cannot even be certain that the well-meaning commission will be anything but what the army thinks it, a sop to sentimentalists at home, and in the Islands a safe cover for the treacherous natives to hatch a new rebellion out.

This, then, is where we are today. The first act is over, and what is done can't be undone. Difficult as it is to keep hot words of accusation from rising to our lips whenever we think of the men who threw away so splendid an American opportunity—threw it away with our own action in the Cuba case before us as the only precedent we had to follow,—nevertheless it is bad politics to dwell too long upon events of yesterday. We opponents of an imperialist policy must simply hand over our brief for the past to the historians' keeping,— the historians who are already at work upon the chronicle, and who will shape the verdict of posterity upon the whole affair. We have made their labors easier. Time will unwind yet many a secret, but our Secretary and his fellow-workers have let few facts now attainable escape their channels of publicity, and for that service to truth they deserve our heartiest thanks.

Let us drop yesterday and its sins, then, and forget them. The attitude of 'I told you so' is sterile, and wise men know when to change their tune. To the ordinary citizen the word anti-imperialist suggests a thin-haired being just waked up from the day before yesterday, brandishing the Declaration of Independence excitedly, and shrieking after a railroad train thundering toward its destination to turn upon its tracks and come back. Anti-imperialism, people think, is something petrified, a religion, a thing that results in martyrdom, for which to 'discuss' means only to prophesy and denounce. If, so far, some of us have struck a slightly monotonous attitude, we have our good excuse. The wounds which our love of country received in those days of February, 1899, are of a kind that do not quickly heal. They ache too persistently to allow us easily to forget. Forget we must, however, we must attend to the practical possibilities of today.

And what are they? Immediate scuttling is certainly not among them, and anyone who should now urge it would, speaking practically, be a fool. Nations are masses with too enormous a momentum to reverse their motion with a jerk.

They must be brought round in a curve. It seems even doubtful whether it would be for the Islands' interest to have our government immediately withdraw. What they need now is quiet for a few years, time to repair war's ravages, and to acquire some habits of administration which might outlast our stay. Not today, then, but tomorrow, is what we ought to work for—abandonment of the islands as soon as, in our delicious phraseology, we have made them 'fit,' and meanwhile as steady a pressure as we can bring to bear towards determining our people to face that prospect, and towards making Congress say the decisive word.

The Democrats have already espoused our principles, and many of us think, therefore, that the one thing left for us is to espouse the Democratic cause. Against this there is the objection that the Democrats are only half sincere in the matter—it is largely an opposition issue to gain the independent vote—and there is the still stronger objection that the Republicans themselves have not half made up their minds that the Islands ought to be retained. The better self of the Republicans, their subliminal consciousness, so to speak, is already on our side. The party was railroaded into its conquistadore career by the McKinley administration. The war short-circuited political reflection, and we had first of all to back up the Flag. But we may be sure that today the state of mind, even of our leaders, is full of misgivings, and that if we don't put them too much on the defensive, time will do our work.

The vital fact of the situation for us is that neither presidents nor Congress have as yet dared to face the responsibility of making any permanent colonial professions to which in pride or consistency we might find ourselves obliged to live up. Our adventure has literally been a wayward spree of power, wholly detached from any definite policy or plan. The instinct for self-preservation which in this has ruled us, is wiser far than a greater sense for national dignity would have been. The policy of drift has never been abandoned. If we should grant the Islands independence tomorrow, no man could show a scrap of paper to prove that we had broken a pledge to anybody, or had backed out of a single clause in our program.

Our tactics in this situation, Mr. Chairman, would therefore seem to be the simplest in the world. We must individually do all we can to circulate two phrases, so that the public ear becomes inured—"Independence for the Philippine Islands," and "Treat the Filipinos like the Cubans," and we must do all we can to force the hands of both parties to a positive declaration before its next presidential campaign. The Republicans will certainly not make a declaration for perpetual retention, and every open shying from that issue helps public opinion the other way. Constant dropping wears the marble. Phrases repeated have a way of turning into facts.

I hope you have not all forgotten the great speech on 'Public Opinion' which Wendell Phillips made in 1852. Read it again, anyhow, for it is full of inspiration for us here. "Hearts and sentiments are alive," said Phillips, "and we know that the gentlest of Nature's growths or motions will in time burst asunder or wear away the proudest dead-weight man can put upon them. You may build your capitol of granite, and pile it as high as the Rocky Mountains, but if it is founded on or mixed up with iniquity, the pulse of a girl will in time beat it down. . . . . . This heart of mine, which beats so uninterruptedly in the bosom, if its force could be directed against a granite pillar, would wear it to dust in the course of a man's life. Your capitol, Daniel Webster," continued Phillips—if he had been speaking here he would have used other names— "Your capitol is marble, but the pulse of every humane man is beating against it. God will give us time and the pulses of men shall beat it down. The day must be ours, thank God, for the hearts, the hearts, are on our side."

Phillips's era saw the heart of man in perhaps a little simpler light than we can. We used to believe then that we were of a different clay from other nations, that there was something deep in the American heart that answered to our happy birth, free from that hereditary burden which the nations of Europe bear, and which obliges them to grow by preying on their neighbors. Idle dream! pure Fourth of July fancy, scattered in five minutes by the first temptation. In every national soul there lie potentialities of the most barefaced piracy, and our own American soul is no exception to the rule. Angelic impulses and predatory lusts divide our heart exactly as they divide the hearts of other countries. It is good to rid ourselves of cant and humbug, and to know the truth about ourselves. Political virtue does not follow geographical divisions. It follows the eternal division inside of each country between the more animal and the more intellectual kind of men, between the tory and the liberal tendencies, the jingoism and animal instinct that would run things by main force and brute possession, and the critical conscience that believes in educational methods and in rational rules of right.

As a group of citizens calling to our country to return to the principles which it was suckled in, I believe that we Anti-Imperialists are already a back number. We had better not print that name upon our publications any longer. The country has once for all regurgitated the Declaration of Independence and the Farewell Address, and it won't swallow again immediately what it is so happy to have vomited up. It has come to a hiatus. It has deliberately pushed itself into the circle of international hatreds, and joined the common pack of wolves. It relishes the attitude. We have thrown off our swaddling clothes, it thinks, and attained our majority. We are objects of fear to other lands. This makes of the old liberalism and the new liberalism of our country two discontinuous things. The older liberalism was in office, the new is in the opposition. Inwardly it is the same spirit, but outwardly the tactics, the questions, the reasons, and the phrases have to change. American memories no longer serve as catchwords. The great international and cosmopolitan liberal party, the party of conscience and intelligence the world over, has, in short, absorbed us; and we are only its American section, carrying on the war against the powers of darkness here, playing our part in the long, long campaign for truth and fair dealing which must go on in all the countries of the world until the end of time. Let us cheerfully settle into our interminable task. Everywhere it is the same struggle under various names,—light against darkness, right against might, love against hate. The Lord of life is with us, and we cannot permanently fail.

Proceedings of the Fifth Annual Meeting of the New England Anti-Imperialist League, December 1903

The Chicago School[1]

THE REST of the world has made merry over the Chicago man's legendary saying that 'Chicago hasn't had time to get round to culture yet, but when she does strike her, she'll make her hum.' Already the prophecy is fulfilling itself in a dazzling manner. Chicago has a School of Thought!—a school of thought which, it is safe to predict, will figure in literature as the School of Chicago for twenty-five years to come. Some universities have plenty of thought to show, but no school; others plenty of school, but no thought. The University of Chicago, by its Decennial Publications, shows real thought and a real school. Professor John Dewey, and at least ten of his disciples, have collectively put into the world a statement, homogeneous in spite of so many coöperating minds, of a view of the world, both theoretical and practical, which is so simple, massive, and positive that, in spite of the fact that many parts of it yet need to be worked out, it deserves the title of a new system of philosophy. If it be as true as it is original, its publication must be reckoned an important event. The present reviewer, for one, strongly suspects it of being true.

The briefest characterization is all that will be attempted here. Criticism from various quarters will doubtless follow, for about the new system as a bone of contention discussion is bound to rage.

Like Spencer's philosophy, Dewey's is an evolutionism; but unlike Spencer, Dewey and his disciples have so far (with the exception of Dewey's admirable writings on ethics) confined themselves to establishing certain general principles without applying them to details. Unlike Spencer, again, Dewey is a pure empiricist. There is nothing real, whether

[1] 1. *Studies in Logical Theory*, John Dewey, with the coöperation of members and fellows of the Department of Philosophy. The Decennial Publications, second series, Volume XI., Chicago. The University of Chicago Press, 1903. 2. *The Definition of the Psychical*, George H. Mead. 3. *Existence, Meaning and Reality*, A. W. Moore. 4. *Logical Conditions of a Scientific Treatment of Morality*, John Dewey. 5. *The Relations of Psychology to Philosophy*, James Rowland Angell. Reprints from Volume III. of the first series of Decennial Publications, *ibid.*, 1903.

being or relation between beings, which is not direct matter of experience. There is no Unknowable or Absolute behind or around the finite world. No Absolute, either, in the sense of anything eternally constant; no term is static, but everything is process and change.

Like Spencer, again, Dewey makes biology and psychology continuous. 'Life,' or 'experience,' is the fundamental conception; and whether you take it physically or mentally, it involves an adjustment between terms. Dewey's favorite word is 'situation.' A situation implies at least two factors, each of which is both an independent variable and a function of the other variable. Call them E (environment) and O (organism) for simplicity's sake. They interact and develop each other without end; for each action of E upon O changes O, whose reaction in turn upon E changes E, so that E's new action upon O gets different, eliciting a new reaction, and so on indefinitely. The situation gets perpetually 'reconstructed,' to use another of Professor Dewey's favorite words, and this reconstruction is the process of which all reality consists.

I am in some doubt as to whether, in the last resort, Dewey thinks monistically or pluralistically of this reality. He often talks of 'experience' in the singular as if it were one universal process and not a collective name for many particular processes. But all his special statements refer to particular processes only, so I will report him in pluralistic terms.

No biological processes are treated of in this literature, except as incidental to ethical discussion, and the ethical discussions would carry us too far afield. I will confine myself therefore to the psychological or epistemological doctrines of the school.

Consciousness is functionally active in readjustment. In perfectly 'adapted' situations, where adjustments are fluent and stereotyped, it exists in minimal degree. Only where there is hesitation, only where past habit will not run, do we find that the situation awakens explicit thought. Thought is thus incidental to change in experience, to conflict between the old and new. The situation must be reconstructed if activity is to be resumed, and the rejudging of it mentally is the reconstruction's first stage. The nucleus of the *Studies in Logical Theory* becomes thus an account of the judging process.

"In psychological terms we may say, in explanation of the judging process, that some stimulus to action has failed to function properly as a stimulus, and that the activity which was going on has been interrupted. Response in the accustomed way has failed. In such a case there arises a division in experience into sensation content as subject and ideal content as predicate. In other words, . . . upon failure of the accustomed stimulus to be adequate . . . activity ceases, and is resumed in an integral form only when a new habit is set up to which the new or altered stimulus is adequate. It is in this process of reconstruction that subject and predicate appear." The old subject (the *that* of the situation) stands for the interrupted habit, the new subject (the *that* with the new *what* added) stands for the new habit begun. The predicate is thus essentially hypothetical—the situations to which the use of it leads may have quickly to be reconstructed in turn. In brief, S is a stimulus intellectually irritating; P is an hypothesis in reponse; SP is a mental action, which normally is destined to lead or pass into action in a wider sense. The sense of 'objectivity' in the S emerges emphatically only when the P is problematic and the action undefined. Then only does the S arrest attention, and its contrast with the self become acute. 'Knowing,' therefore, or the conscious relation of the object to the self, is thus only an incident in the wider process of 'adjustment,' which includes unconscious adjustments as well.

This leads Professor Dewey and his disciples to a peculiar view of 'fact.' What is a fact? A fact and a theory have not different natures, as is usually supposed, the one being objective, the other subjective. They are both made of the same material, experience-material namely, and their difference relates to their way of functioning solely. What is fact for one epoch, or for one inquirer, is theory for another epoch or another inquirer. It is 'fact' when it functions steadily; it is 'theory' when we hesitate. 'Truth' is thus in process of formation like all other things. It consists not in conformity or correspondence with an externally fixed archetype or model. Such a thing would be irrelevant even if we knew it to exist. Truth consists in a character inclosed within the 'situation.' Whenever a situation has the maximum of stability, and seems most satisfactory to its own subject-factor, it is true for him.

If accused here of opening the door to systematic protago-reanism, Professor Dewey would reply that the concrete facts themselves are what keep his scepticism from being systematic in any practically objectionable sense. Experience is contin-ually enlarging, and the object-factors of our situations are always getting problematic, making old truths unsatisfactory, and obliging new ones to be found. The object-factors more-over are common to ourselves and others; and our truths have to be mated with those of our fellow men. The real safeguard against caprice of statement and indetermination of belief is that there is a 'grain' in things against which we can't practi-cally go. But as the grain creates itself from situation to situ-ation, so the truth creates itself *pari passu*, and there is no eternally standing system of extra-subjective verity to which our judgments, ideally and in advance of the facts, are obliged to conform.

There are two great gaps in the system, which none of the Chicago writers have done anything to fill, and until they are filled, the system, as a system, will appear defective. There is no cosmology, no positive account of the order of physical fact, as contrasted with mental fact, and no account of the fact (which I assume the writers to believe in) that different subjects share a common object-world. These lacunæ can hardly be inadvertent—we shall doubtless soon see them filled in some way by one or another member of the school.

I might go into much greater technical detail, and I might in particular make many a striking quotation. But I prefer to be exceedingly summary, and merely to call the reader's atten-tion to the importance of this output of Chicago University. Taking it *en gros*, what strikes me most in it is the great sense of concrete reality with which it is filled. It seems a promising *via media* between the empiricist and transcendentalist ten-dencies of our time. Like empiricism, it is individualistic and phenomenalistic; it places truth *in rebus*, and not *ante rem*. It resembles transcendentalism, on the other hand, in making value and fact inseparable, and in standing for continuities and purposes in things. It employs the genetic method to which both schools are now accustomed. It coincides remark-ably with the simultaneous movement in favor of 'pragma-tism' or 'humanism' set up quite independently at Oxford by

Messrs. Schiller and Sturt. It probably has a great future, and is certainly something of which Americans may be proud. Professor Dewey ought to gather into another volume his scattered essays and addresses on psychological and ethical topics, for now that his philosophy is systematically formulated, these throw a needed light.

The Psychological Bulletin, January 15, 1904

Does 'Consciousness' Exist?

'THOUGHTS' AND 'THINGS' are names for two sorts of object, which common sense will always find contrasted and will always practically oppose to each other. Philosophy, reflecting on the contrast, has varied in the past in her explanations of it, and may be expected to vary in the future. At first, 'spirit and matter,' 'soul and body,' stood for a pair of equipollent substances quite on a par in weight and interest. But one day Kant undermined the soul and brought in the transcendental ego, and ever since then the bipolar relation has been very much off its balance. The transcendental ego seems nowadays in rationalist quarters to stand for everything, in empiricist quarters for almost nothing. In the hands of such writers as Schuppe, Rehmke, Natorp, Münsterberg—at any rate in his earlier writings, Schubert-Soldern and others, the spiritual principle attenuates itself to a thoroughly ghostly condition, being only a name for the fact that the 'content' of experience *is known*. It loses personal form and activity—these passing over to the content—and becomes a bare *Bewusstheit* or *Bewusstsein überhaupt*, of which in its own right absolutely nothing can be said.

I believe that 'consciousness,' when once it has evaporated to this estate of pure diaphaneity, is on the point of disappearing altogether. It is the name of a nonentity, and has no right to a place among first principles. Those who still cling to it are clinging to a mere echo, the faint rumor left behind by the disappearing 'soul' upon the air of philosophy. During the past year, I have read a number of articles whose authors seemed just on the point of abandoning the notion of consciousness,[1] and substituting for it that of an absolute experience not due to two factors. But they were not quite radical enough, not quite daring enough in their negations. For twenty years past I have mistrusted 'consciousness' as an entity; for seven or eight years past I have suggested its nonexistence to my students, and tried to give them its pragmatic

[1] Articles by Baldwin, Ward, Bawden, King, Alexander and others. Dr. Perry is frankly over the border.

equivalent in realities of experience. It seems to me that the
hour is ripe for it to be openly and universally discarded.

To deny plumply that 'consciousness' exists seems so absurd
on the face of it—for undeniably 'thoughts' do exist—that I
fear some readers will follow me no farther. Let me then immediately explain that I mean only to deny that the word
stands for an entity, but to insist most emphatically that it
does stand for a function. There is, I mean, no aboriginal
stuff or quality of being, contrasted with that of which material objects are made, out of which our thoughts of them are
made; but there is a function in experience which thoughts
perform, and for the performance of which this quality of
being is invoked. That function is *knowing*. 'Consciousness' is
supposed necessary to explain the fact that things not only
are, but get reported, are known. Whoever blots out the notion of consciousness from his list of first principles must still
provide in some way for that function's being carried on.

I

My thesis is that if we start with the supposition that there
is only one primal stuff or material in the world, a stuff of
which everything is composed, and if we call that stuff 'pure
experience,' then knowing can easily be explained as a particular sort of relation towards one another into which portions
of pure experience may enter. The relation itself is a part of
pure experience; one of its 'terms' becomes the subject or
bearer of the knowledge, the knower,[1] the other becomes the
object known. This will need much explanation before it can
be understood. The best way to get it understood is to contrast it with the alternative view; and for that we may take
the recentest alternative, that in which the evaporation of the
definite soul-substance has proceeded as far as it can go without being yet complete. If neo-Kantism has expelled earlier
forms of dualism, we shall have expelled all forms if we are
able to expel neo-Kantism in its turn.

For the thinkers I call neo-Kantian, the word consciousness
to-day does no more than signalize the fact that experience is
indefeasibly dualistic in structure. It means that not subject,

[1] In my 'Psychology' I have tried to show that we need no knower other
than the 'passing thought.'

not object, but object-plus-subject is the minimum that can actually be. The subject-object distinction meanwhile is entirely different from that between mind and matter, from that between body and soul. Souls were detachable, had separate destinies; things could happen to them. To consciousness as such nothing can happen, for, timeless itself, it is only a witness of happenings in time, in which it plays no part. It is, in a word, but the logical correlative of 'content' in an Experience of which the peculiarity is that *fact comes to light* in it, that *awareness of content* takes place. Consciousness as such is entirely impersonal—'self' and its activities belong to the content. To say that I am self-conscious, or conscious of putting forth volition, means only that certain contents, for which 'self' and 'effort of will' are the names, are not without witness as they occur.

Thus, for these belated drinkers at the Kantian spring, we should have to admit consciousness as an 'epistemological' necessity, even if we had no direct evidence of its being there.

But in addition to this, we are supposed by almost every one to have an immediate consciousness of consciousness itself. When the world of outer fact ceases to be materially present, and we merely recall it in memory, or fancy it, the consciousness is believed to stand out and to be felt as a kind of impalpable inner flowing, which, once known in this sort of experience, may equally be detected in presentations of the outer world. "The moment we try to fix our attention upon consciousness and to see *what*, distinctly, it is," says a recent writer, "it seems to vanish. It seems as if we had before us a mere emptiness. When we try to introspect the sensation of blue, all we can see is the blue; the other element is as if it were diaphanous. Yet it can be distinguished, if we look attentively enough, and know that there is something to look for."[1] "Consciousness" (Bewusstheit), says another philosopher, "is inexplicable and hardly describable, yet all conscious experiences have this in common that what we call their content has this peculiar reference to a center for which 'self' is the name, in virtue of which reference alone the content is subjectively given, or appears. . . . While in this way con-

[1] G. E. Moore: *Mind*, Vol. XII., N. S., p. 450.

sciousness, or reference to a self, is the only thing which distinguishes a conscious content from any sort of being that might be there with no one conscious of it, yet this only ground of the distinction defies all closer explanations. The existence of consciousness, although it is the fundamental fact of psychology, can indeed be laid down as certain, can be brought out by analysis, but can neither be defined nor deduced from anything but itself."[1]

'Can be brought out by analysis,' this author says. This supposes that the consciousness is one element, moment, factor—call it what you like—of an experience of essentially dualistic inner constitution, from which, if you abstract the content, the consciousness will remain revealed to its own eye. Experience, at this rate, would be much like a paint of which the world pictures were made. Paint has a dual constitution, involving, as it does, a menstruum[2] (oil, size or what not) and a mass of content in the form of pigment suspended therein. We can get the pure menstruum by letting the pigment settle, and the pure pigment by pouring off the size or oil. We operate here by physical subtraction; and the usual view is, that by mental subtraction we can separate the two factors of experience in an analogous way—not isolating them entirely, but distinguishing them enough to know that they are two.

II

Now my contention is exactly the reverse of this. *Experience, I believe, has no such inner duplicity; and the separation of it into consciousness and content comes, not by way of subtraction, but by way of addition*—the addition, to a given concrete piece of it, of other sets of experiences, in connection with which severally its use or function may be of two different kinds. The paint will also serve here as an illustration. In a pot in a paint-shop, along with other paints, it serves in its entirety as so much saleable matter. Spread on a canvas, with other

[1] Paul Natorp: 'Einleitung in die Psychologie,' 1888, pp. 14, 112.

[2] "Figuratively speaking, consciousness may be said to be the one universal solvent or menstruum, in which the different kinds of psychic acts and facts are contained, whether in concealed or in obvious form." G. T. Ladd: 'Psychology, Descriptive and Explanatory,' 1894, p. 30.

paints around it, it represents, on the contrary, a feature in a picture and performs a spiritual function. Just so, I maintain, does a given undivided portion of experience, taken in one context of associates, play the part of a knower, of a state of mind, of 'consciousness'; while in a different context the same undivided bit of experience plays the part of a thing known, of an objective 'content.' In a word, in one group it figures as a thought, in another group as a thing. And, since it can figure in both groups simultaneously we have every right to speak of it as subjective and objective both at once. The dualism connoted by such double-barrelled terms as 'experience,' 'phenomenon,' 'datum,' '*Vorfindung*'—terms which, in philosophy at any rate, tend more and more to replace the single-barrelled terms of 'thought' and 'thing'—that dualism, I say, is still preserved in this account, but reinterpreted, so that, instead of being mysterious and elusive, it becomes verifiable and concrete. It is an affair of relations, it falls outside, not inside, the single experience considered, and can always be particularized and defined.

The entering wedge for this more concrete way of understanding the dualism was fashioned by Locke when he made the word 'idea' stand indifferently for thing and thought, and by Berkeley when he said that what common sense means by realities is exactly what the philosopher means by ideas. Neither Locke nor Berkeley thought his truth out into perfect clearness, but it seems to me that the conception I am defending does little more than consistently carry out the 'pragmatic' method which they were the first to use.

If the reader will take his own experiences, he will see what I mean. Let him begin with a perceptual experience, the 'presentation,' so called, of a physical object, his actual field of vision, the room he sits in, with the book he is reading as its center; and let him for the present treat this complex object in the common-sense way as being 'really' what it seems to be, namely, a collection of physical things cut out from an environing world of other physical things with which these physical things have actual or potential relations. Now at the same time it is just *those self-same things* which his mind, as we say, perceives; and the whole philosophy of perception from Democritus's time downwards has been just one long wrangle over the paradox that what is evidently one reality should be in two places at once, both in outer space and in a person's mind. 'Representative' theories of perception avoid the logical paradox, but on the other hand they violate the reader's sense of life, which knows no intervening mental image but seems to see the room and the book immediately just as they physically exist.

The puzzle of how the one identical room can be in two places is at bottom just the puzzle of how one identical point can be on two lines. It can, if it be situated at their intersection; and similarly, if the 'pure experience' of the room were a place of intersection of two processes, which connected it with different groups of associates respectively, it could be counted twice over, as belonging to either group, and spoken of loosely as existing in two places, although it would remain all the time a numerically single thing.

Well, the experience is a member of diverse processes that can be followed away from it along entirely different lines. The one self-identical thing has so many relations to the rest of experience that you can take it in disparate systems of association, and treat it as belonging with opposite contexts. In one of these contexts it is your 'field of consciousness'; in another it is 'the room in which you sit,' and it enters both contexts in its wholeness, giving no pretext for being said to attach itself to consciousness by one of its parts or aspects, and to outer reality by another. What are the two processes, now, into which the room-experience simultaneously enters in this way?

One of them is the reader's personal biography, the other is the history of the house of which the room is part. The presentation, the experience, the *that* in short (for until we have decided *what* it is it must be a mere *that*) is the last term of a train of sensations, emotions, decisions, movements, classifications, expectations, etc., ending in the present, and the first term of a series of similar 'inner' operations extending into the future, on the reader's part. On the other hand, the very same *that* is the *terminus ad quem* of a lot of previous physical operations, carpentering, papering, furnishing, warming, etc., and the *terminus a quo* of a lot of future ones, in which it will be concerned when undergoing the destiny of a physical room. The physical and the mental operations form curiously incompatible groups. As a room, the experience has occupied that spot and had that environment for thirty years. As your field of consciousness it may never have existed until now. As a room, attention will go on to discover endless new details in it. As your mental state merely, few new ones will emerge under attention's eye. As a room, it will take an earthquake, or a gang of men, and in any case a certain amount of time, to destroy it. As your subjective state, the closing of your eyes, or any instantaneous play of your fancy will suffice. In the real world, fire will consume it. In your mind, you can let fire play over it without effect. As an outer object, you must pay so much a month to inhabit it. As an inner content, you may occupy it for any length of time rent-free. If, in short, you follow it in the mental direction, taking it along with events of personal biography solely, all sorts of things are true of it which are false, and false of it which are true if you treat it as a real thing experienced, follow it in the physical direction, and relate it to associates in the outer world.

III

So far, all seems plain sailing, but my thesis will probably grow less plausible to the reader when I pass from percepts to concepts, or from the case of things presented to that of things remote. I believe, nevertheless, that here also the same law holds good. If we take conceptual manifolds, or memories, or fancies, they also are in their first intention mere bits of pure experience, and, as such, are single *thats* which act in one context as objects, and in another context figure as mental states. By taking them in their first intention, I mean ignoring their relation to possible perceptual experiences with which they may be connected, which they may lead to and terminate in, and which then they may be supposed to 'represent.' Taking them in this way first, we confine the problem to a world merely 'thought-of' and not directly felt or seen. This world, just like the world of percepts, comes to us at first as a chaos of experiences, but lines of order soon get traced. We find that any bit of it which we may cut out as an example is connected with distinct groups of associates, just as our perceptual experiences are, that these associates link themselves with it by different relations,[1] and that one forms the inner history of a person, while the other acts as an impersonal 'objective' world, either spatial and temporal, or else merely logical or mathematical, or otherwise 'ideal.'

The first obstacle on the part of the reader to seeing that these non-perceptual experiences have objectivity as well as subjectivity will probably be due to the intrusion into his mind of *percepts*, that third group of associates with which the non-perceptual experiences have relations, and which, as a whole, they 'represent,' standing to them as thoughts to things. This important function of the non-perceptual experiences complicates the question and confuses it; for, so used are we to treat percepts as the sole genuine realities that, unless we keep them out of the discussion, we tend altogether to overlook the objectivity that lies in non-perceptual experiences by themselves. We treat them, 'knowing' percepts as they do, as through and through subjective, and say that they are wholly constituted of the stuff called consciousness, using this term now for a kind of entity, after the fashion which I am seeking to refute.[2]

Abstracting, then, from percepts altogether, what I maintain is, that any single non-perceptual experience tends to get counted twice over, just as a perceptual experience does, figuring in one context as an object or field of objects, in another as a state of mind: and all this without the least internal self-diremption on its own part into consciousness and content. It is all consciousness in one taking; and, in the other, all content.

I find this objectivity of non-perceptual experiences, this complete parallelism in point of reality between the presently felt and the remotely thought, so well set forth in a page of Münsterberg's 'Grundzüge,' that I will quote it as it stands.

"I may only think of my objects," says Professor Münsterberg; "yet, in my living thought they stand before me exactly

---

[1] Here as elsewhere the relations are of course *experienced* relations, members of the same originally chaotic manifold of non-perceptual experience of which the related terms themselves are parts.

[2] Of the representative function of non-perceptual experience as a whole, I will say a word in a subsequent article: it leads too far into the general theory of knowledge for much to be said about it in a short paper like this.

as perceived objects would do, no matter how different the two ways of apprehending them may be in their genesis. The book here lying on the table before me, and the book in the next room of which I think and which I mean to get, are both in the same sense given realities for me, realities which I acknowledge and of which I take account. If you agree that the perceptual object is not an idea within me, but that percept and thing, as indistinguishably one, are really experienced *there*, *outside*, you ought not to believe that the merely thought-of object is hid away inside of the thinking subject. The object of which I think, and of whose existence I take cognizance without letting it now work upon my senses, occupies its definite place in the outer world as much as does the object which I directly see.

"What is true of the here and the there, is also true of the now and the then. I know of the thing which is present and perceived, but I know also of the thing which yesterday was but is no more, and which I only remember. Both can determine my present conduct, both are parts of the reality of which I keep account. It is true that of much of the past I am uncertain, just as I am uncertain of much of what is present if it be but dimly perceived. But the interval of time does not in principle alter my relation to the object, does not transform it from an object known into a mental state. . . . The things in the room here which I survey, and those in my distant home of which I think, the things of this minute and those of my long-vanished boyhood, influence and decide me alike, with a reality which my experience of them directly feels. They both make up my real world, they make it directly, they do not have first to be introduced to me and mediated by ideas which now and here arise within me. . . . This not-me character of my recollections and expectations does not imply that the external objects of which I am aware in those experiences should necessarily be there also for others. The objects of dreamers and hallucinated persons are wholly without general validity. But even were they centaurs and golden mountains, they still would be 'off there,' in fairy land, and not 'inside' of ourselves."[1]

[1] 'Grundzüge der Psychologie,' Vol. I., p. 48.

This certainly is the immediate, primary, naïf, or practical way of taking our thought-of world. Were there no perceptual world to serve as its 'reductive,' in Taine's sense, by being 'stronger' and more genuinely 'outer' (so that the whole merely thought-of world seems weak and inner in comparison), our world of thought would be the only world, and would enjoy complete reality in our belief. This actually happens in our dreams, and in our day-dreams so long as percepts do not interrupt them.

And yet, just as the seen room (to go back to our late example) is *also* a field of consciousness, so the conceived or recollected room is *also* a state of mind; and the doubling-up of the experience has in both cases similar grounds.

The room thought-of, namely, has many thought-of couplings with many thought-of things. Some of these couplings are inconstant, others are stable. In the reader's personal history the room occupies a single date—he saw it only once perhaps, a year ago. Of the house's history, on the other hand, it forms a permanent ingredient. Some couplings have the curious stubbornness, to borrow Royce's term, of fact; others show the fluidity of fancy—we let them come and go as we please. Grouped with the rest of its house, with the name of its town, of its owner, builder, value, decorative plan, the room maintains a definite foothold, to which, if we try to loosen it, it tends to return, and to reassert itself with force.[1] With these associates, in a word, it coheres, while to other houses, other towns, other owners, etc., it shows no tendency to cohere at all. The two collections, first of its cohesive, and, second, of its loose associates, inevitably come to be contrasted. We call the first collection the system of external realities, in the midst of which the room, as 'real,' exists; the other we call the stream of our internal thinking, in which, as a 'mental image,' it for a moment floats.[2] The room thus

[1]Cf. A. L. Hodder: 'The Adversaries of the Skeptic,' N. Y., 1899, pp. 94–99.

[2]For simplicity's sake I confine my exposition to 'external' reality. But there is also the system of ideal reality in which the room plays its part. Relations of comparison, of classification, serial order, value, also are stubborn, assign a definite place to the room, unlike the incoherence of its places in the mere rhapsody of our successive thoughts.

again gets counted twice over. It plays two different rôles, being *Gedanke* and *Gedachtes*, the thought-of-an-object, and the object-thought-of, both in one; and all this without paradox or mystery, just as the same material thing may be both low and high, or small and great, or bad and good, because of its relations to opposite parts of an environing world.

As 'subjective' we say that the experience represents; as 'objective' it is represented. What represents and what is represented is here numerically the same; but we must remember that no dualism of being represented and representing resides in the experience *per se*. In its pure state, or when isolated, there is no self-splitting of it into consciousness and what the consciousness is 'of.' Its subjectivity and objectivity are functional attributes solely, realized only when the experience is 'taken,' *i. e.*, talked-of, twice, considered along with its two differing contexts respectively, by a new retrospective experience, of which that whole past complication now forms the fresh content.

The instant field of the present is at all times what I call the 'pure' experience. It is only virtually or potentially either object or subject as yet. For the time being, it is plain, unqualified actuality or existence, a simple *that*. In this *naïf* immediacy it is of course *valid*; it is *there*, we *act* upon it; and the doubling of it in retrospection into a state of mind and a reality intended thereby, is just one of the acts. The 'state of mind,' first treated explicitly as such in retrospection, will stand corrected or confirmed, and the retrospective experience in its turn will get a similar treatment; but the immediate experience in its passing is always 'truth,'[1] practical truth, *something to act on*, at its own movement. If the world were then and there to go out like a candle, it would remain truth absolute and objective, for it would be 'the last word,' would have no critic, and no one would ever oppose the thought in it to the reality intended.[2]

[1] Note the ambiguity of this term, which is taken sometimes objectively and sometimes subjectively.

[2] In the *Psychological Review* for July of this year, Dr. R. B. Perry has published a view of Consciousness which comes nearer to mine than any other with which I am acquainted. As present, Dr. Perry thinks, every field of experience is so much 'fact.' It becomes 'opinion' or 'thought' only in retro-

I think I may now claim to have made my thesis clear. Consciousness connotes a kind of external relation, and does not denote a special stuff or way of being. *The peculiarity of our experiences, that they not only are, but are known, which their 'conscious' quality is invoked to explain, is better explained by their relations—these relations themselves being experiences—to one another.*

IV

Were I now to go on to treat of the knowing of perceptual by conceptual experiences, it would again prove to be an affair of external relations. One experience would be the knower, the other the reality known; and I could perfectly well define, without the notion of 'consciousness,' what the knowing actually and practically amounts to—leading-towards, namely, and terminating-in percepts, through a series of transitional experiences which the world supplies. But I will not treat of this, space being insufficient.[1] I will rather consider a few objections that are sure to be urged against the entire theory as it stands.

V

First of all, this will be asked: "If experience has not 'conscious' existence, if it be not partly made of 'consciousness,' of what then is it made? Matter we know, and thought we know, and conscious content we know, but neutral and simple 'pure experience' is something we know not at all. Say *what* it consists of—for it must consist of something—or be willing to give it up!"

To this challenge the reply is easy. Although for fluency's

---

spection, when a fresh experience, thinking the same object, alters and corrects it. But the corrective experience becomes itself in turn corrected, and thus experience as a whole is a process in which what is objective originally forever turns subjective, turns into our apprehension of the object. I strongly recommend Dr. Perry's admirable article to my readers.

[1] I have given a partial account of the matter in *Mind*, Vol. X., p. 27, 1885, and in the *Psychological Review*, Vol. II., p. 105, 1895. See also C. A. Strong's article in the JOURNAL OF PHILOSOPHY, PSYCHOLOGY AND SCIENTIFIC METHODS, Vol. I., p. 253, May 12, 1904. I hope myself very soon to recur to the matter in this JOURNAL.

sake I myself spoke early in this article of a stuff of pure experience, I have now to say that there is no *general* stuff of
which experience at large is made. There are as many stuffs as
there are 'natures' in the things experienced. If you ask what
any one bit of pure experience is made of, the answer is always the same: "It is made of *that*, of just what appears, of
space, of intensity, of flatness, brownness, heaviness, or what
not." Shadworth Hodgson's analysis here leaves nothing to
be desired. Experience is only a collective name for all these
sensible natures, and save for time and space (and, if you like,
for 'being') there appears no universal element of which all
things are made.

VI

The next objection is more formidable, in fact it sounds
quite crushing when one hears it first.

"If it be the self-same piece of pure experience, taken twice
over, that serves now as thought and now as thing"—so the
objection runs—"how comes it that its attributes should differ so fundamentally in the two takings. As thing, the experience is extended; as thought, it occupies no space or place.
As thing, it is red, hard, heavy; but who ever heard of a red,
hard or heavy thought? Yet even now you said that an experience is made of just what appears, and what appears is just
such adjectives. How can the one experience in its thing-func-
tion be made of them, consist of them, carry them as its own
attributes, while in its thought-function it disowns them and
attributes them elsewhere. There is a self-contradiction here
from which the radical dualism of thought and thing is the
only truth that can save us. Only if the thought is one kind
of being can the adjectives exist in it 'intentionally' (to use
the scholastic term); only if the thing is another kind, can
they exist in it constitutively and energetically. No simple subject can take the same adjectives and at one time be qualified
by it, and at another time be merely 'of' it, as of something
only meant or known."

The solution insisted on by this objector, like many other
common-sense solutions, grows the less satisfactory the more
one turns it in one's mind. To begin with, *are* thought and
thing as heterogenous as is commonly said?

No one denies that they have some categories in common. Their relations to time are identical. Both, moreover, may have parts (for psychologists in general treat thoughts as having them); and both may be complex or simple. Both are of kinds, can be compared, added and subtracted and arranged in serial orders. All sorts of adjectives qualify our thoughts which appear incompatible with consciousness being, as such, a bare diaphaneity. For instance, they are natural and easy, or laborious. They are beautiful, happy, intense, interesting, wise, idiotic, focal, marginal, insipid, confused, vague, precise, rational, casual, general, particular, and many things besides. Moreover, the chapters on 'Perception' in the Psychology-books are full of facts that make for the essential homogeneity of thought with thing. How, if 'subject' and 'object' were separated 'by the whole diameter of being,' and had no attributes in common, could it be so hard to tell, in a presented and recognized material object, what part comes in through the sense-organs and what part comes 'out of one's own head'? Sensations and apperceptive ideas fuse here so intimately that you can no more tell where one begins and the other ends, than you can tell, in those cunning circular panoramas that have lately been exhibited, where the real foreground and the painted canvas join together.[1]

Descartes for the first time defined thought as the absolutely unextended, and later philosophers have accepted the description as correct. But what possible meaning has it to say that, when we think of a foot-rule or a square yard, extension is not attributable to our thought? Of every extended object the *adequate* mental picture must have all the extension of the object itself. The difference between objective and subjective extension is one of relation to a context solely. In the mind the various extents maintain no necessarily stubborn order relatively to each other, while in the physical world they bound each other stably, and, added together, make the great enveloping Unit which we believe in and call real Space. As

---

[1] Spencer's proof of his 'Transfigured Realism' (his doctrine that there is an absolutely non-mental reality) comes to mind as a splendid instance of the impossibility of establishing radical heterogeneity between thought and thing. All his painfully accumulated points of difference run gradually into their opposites, and are full of exceptions.

'outer,' they carry themselves adversely, so to speak, to one another, exclude one another and maintain their distances; while, as 'inner,' their order is loose, and they form a *durcheinander* in which unity is lost.[1] But to argue from this that inner experience is absolutely inextensive seems to me little short of absurd. The two worlds differ, not by the presence or absence of extension, but by the relations of the extensions which in both worlds exist.

Does not this case of extension now put us on the track of truth in the case of other qualities? It does; and I am surprised that the facts should not have been noticed long ago. Why, for example, do we call a fire hot, and water wet, and yet refuse to say that our mental state, when it is 'of' these objects, is either wet or hot? 'Intentionally,' at any rate, and when the mental state is a vivid image, hotness and wetness are in it just as much as they are in the physical experience. The reason is this, that, as the general chaos of all our experiences gets sifted, we find that there are some fires that will always burn sticks and always warm our bodies, and that there are some waters that will always put out fires; while there are other fires and waters that will not act at all. The general group of experiences that *act*, that do not only possess their natures intrinsically, but wear them adjectively and energetically, turning them against one another, comes inevitably to be contrasted with the group whose members, having identically the same natures, fail to manifest them in the 'energetic' way. I make for myself now an experience of blazing fire; I place it near my body; but it does not warm me in the least. I lay a stick upon it, and the stick either burns or remains green, as I please. I call up water, and pour it on the fire, and absolutely no difference ensues. I account for all such facts by calling this whole train of experiences unreal, a mental train. Mental fire is what won't burn real sticks; mental water is what won't necessarily (though of course it may) put out even a mental fire. Mental knives may be sharp, but they won't cut real wood. Mental triangles are pointed, but their points won't wound. With 'real' objects, on the contrary, con-

[1] I speak here of the complete inner life in which the mind plays freely with its materials. Of course the mind's free play is restricted when it seeks to copy real things in real space.

sequences always accrue; and thus the real experiences get sifted from the mental ones, the things from our thoughts of them, fanciful or true, and precipitated together as the stable part of the whole experience-chaos, under the name of the physical world. Of this our perceptual experiences are the nucleus, they being the originally *strong* experiences. We add a lot of conceptual experiences to them, making these strong also in imagination, and building out the remoter parts of the physical world by their means; and around this core of reality the world of laxly connected fancies and mere rhapsodical objects floats like a bank of clouds. In the clouds, all sorts of rules are violated which in the core are kept. Extensions there can be indefinitely located; motion there obeys no Newton's laws.

VII

There is a peculiar class of experiences to which, whether we take them as subjective or as objective, we *assign* their several natures as attributes, because in both contexts they affect their associates actively, though in neither quite as 'strongly' or as sharply as things affect one another by their physical energies. I refer here to *appreciations*, which form an ambiguous sphere of being, belonging with emotion on the one hand, and having objective 'value' on the other, yet seeming not quite inner nor quite outer, as if a diremption had begun but had not made itself complete.

Experiences of painful objects, for example, are usually also painful experiences; perceptions of loveliness, of ugliness, tend to pass muster as lovely or as ugly perceptions; intuitions of the morally lofty are lofty intuitions. Sometimes the adjective wanders as if uncertain where to fix itself. Shall we speak of seductive visions or of visions of seductive things? Of wicked desires or of desires for wickedness? Of healthy thoughts or of thoughts of healthy objects? Of good impulses, or of impulses towards the good? Of feelings of anger, or of angry feelings? Both in the mind and in the thing, these natures modify their context, exclude certain associates and determine others, have their mates and incompatibles. Yet not as stubbornly as in the case of physical qualities, for beauty and ugliness, love and hatred, pleasant and painful can, in certain complex experiences, coexist.

If one were to make an evolutionary construction of how a lot of originally chaotic pure experiences became gradually differentiated into an orderly inner and outer world, the whole theory would turn upon one's success in explaining how or why the quality of an experience, once active, could become less so, and, from being an energetic attribute in some cases, elsewhere lapse into the status of an inert or merely internal 'nature.' This would be the 'evolution' of the psychical from the bosom of the physical, in which the esthetic, moral and otherwise emotional experiences would represent a halfway stage.

VIII

But a last cry of *non possumus* will probably go up from many readers. "All very pretty as a piece of ingenuity," they will say, "but our consciousness itself intuitively contradicts you. We, for our part, *know* that we are conscious. We *feel* our thought, flowing as a life within us, in absolute contrast with the objects which it so unremittingly escorts. We can not be faithless to this immediate intuition. The dualism is a fundamental *datum*: Let no man join what God has put asunder."

My reply to this is my last word, and I greatly grieve that to many it will sound materialistic. I can not help that, however, for I, too, have my intuitions and I must obey them. Let the case be what it may in others, I am as confident as I am of anything that, in myself, the stream of thinking (which I recognize emphatically as a phenomenon) is only a careless name for what, when scrutinized, reveals itself to consist chiefly of the stream of my breathing. The 'I think' which Kant said must be able to accompany all my objects, is the 'I breathe' which actually does accompany them. There are other internal facts besides breathing (intracephalic muscular adjustments, etc., of which I have said a word in my larger Psychology), and these increase the assets of 'consciousness,' so far as the latter is subject to immediate perception; but breath, which was ever the original of 'spirit,' breath moving outwards, between the glottis and the nostrils, is, I am persuaded, the essence out of which philosophers have constructed the entity known to them as consciousness. *That entity is fictitious, while thoughts in the concrete are fully real. But thoughts in the concrete are made of the same stuff as things are.*

I wish I might believe myself to have made that plausible in this article. In another article I shall try to make the general notion of a world composed of pure experiences still more clear.

The Journal of Philosophy, Psychology and Scientific Methods,
September 1, 1904

A World of Pure Experience

I T IS DIFFICULT not to notice a curious unrest in the philosophic atmosphere of the time, a loosening of old landmarks, a softening of oppositions, a mutual borrowing from one another on the part of systems anciently closed, and an interest in new suggestions, however vague, as if the one thing sure were the inadequacy of the extant school-solutions. The dissatisfaction with these seems due for the most part to a feeling that they are too abstract and academic. Life is confused and superabundant, and what the younger generation appears to crave is more of the temperament of life in its philosophy, even though it were at some cost of logical vigor and of formal purity. Transcendental idealism is inclining to let the world wag incomprehensibly, in spite of its Absolute Subject and his unity of purpose. Berkeleyan idealism is abandoning the principle of parsimony and dabbling in panpsychic speculations. Empiricism flirts with teleology; and, strangest of all, natural realism, so long decently buried, raises its head above the turf, and finds glad hands outstretched from the most unlikely quarters to help it to its feet again. We are all biased by our personal feelings, I know, and I am personally discontented with extant solutions, so I seem to read the signs of a great unsettlement, as if the upheaval of more real conceptions and more fruitful methods were imminent, as if a true landscape might result, less clipped, straight edged and artificial.

If philosophy be really on the eve of any considerable rearrangement, the time should be propitious for any one who has suggestions of his own to bring forward. For many years past my mind has been growing into a certain type of *Weltanschauung*. Rightly or wrongly, I have got to the point where I can hardly see things in any other pattern. I propose, therefore, to describe the pattern as clearly as I can consistently with great brevity, and to throw my description into the bubbling vat of publicity where, jostled by rivals and torn by critics, it will eventually either disappear from notice, or else, if better luck befall it, quietly subside to the profundities, and serve as a possible ferment of new growths or a nucleus of new crystallization.

I. RADICAL EMPIRICISM

I give the name of 'radical empiricism' to my *Weltan-schauung*. Empiricism is known as the opposite of rationalism. Rationalism tends to emphasize universals and to make wholes prior to parts in the order of logic as well as in that of being. Empiricism, on the contrary, lays the explanatory stress upon the part, the element, the individual, and treats the whole as a collection and the universal as an abstraction. My description of things, accordingly, starts with the parts and makes of the whole a being of the second order. It is essentially a mosaic philosophy, a philosophy of plural facts, like that of Hume and his descendants, who refer these facts neither to Substances in which they inhere nor to an Absolute Mind that creates them as its objects. But it differs from the Humian type of empiricism in one particular which makes me add the epithet radical.

To be radical, an empiricism must neither admit into its constructions any element that is not directly experienced, nor exclude from them any element that is directly experienced. For such a philosophy, *the relations that connect experiences must themselves be experienced relations, and any kind of relation experienced must be accounted as 'real' as anything else in the system*. Elements may indeed be redistributed, the original placing of things getting corrected, but a real place must be found for every kind of thing experienced, whether term or relation, in the final philosophic arrangement.

Now, ordinary empiricism, in spite of the fact that conjunctive and disjunctive relations present themselves as being fully coordinate parts of experience, has always shown a tendency to do away with the connections of things, and to insist most on the disjunctions. Berkeley's nominalism, Hume's statement that whatever things we distinguish are as 'loose and separate' as if they had 'no manner of connection,' James Mill's denial that similars have anything 'really' in common, the resolution of the causal tie into habitual sequence, John Mill's account of both physical things and selves as composed of discontinuous possibilities, and the general pulverization of all Experience by association and the mind-dust theory, are examples of what I mean.

The natural result of such a world-picture has been the efforts of naturalism to correct its incoherencies by the addition of trans-experiential agents of unification, substances, intellectual categories and powers, or Selves; whereas, if empiricism had only been radical and taken every thing that comes without disfavor, conjunction as well as separation, each at its face value, the results would have called for no such artificial correction. *Radical empiricism*, as I understand it, *does full justice to conjunctive relations*, without, however, treating them as rationalism always tends to treat them, as being true in some supernal way, as if the unity of things and their variety belonged to different orders of truth and vitality altogether.

II. CONJUNCTIVE RELATIONS

Relations are of different degrees of intimacy. Merely to be 'with' one another in a universe of discourse is the most external relation that terms can have, and seems to involve nothing whatever as to farther consequences. Simultaneity and time-interval come next, and then space-adjacency and distance. After them, similarity and difference, carrying the possibility of many inferences. Then relations of activity, tying terms into series involving change, tendency, resistance, and the causal order generally. Finally, the relation experienced between terms that form states of mind, and are immediately conscious of continuing each other. The organization of the Self as a system of memories, purposes, strivings, fulfilments or disappointments, is incidental to this most intimate of all relations, the terms of which seem in many cases actually to compenetrate and suffuse each other's being.

Philosophy has always turned on grammatical particles. With, near, next, like, from, towards, against, because, for, through, my—these words designate types of conjunctive relation arranged in a roughly ascending order of intimacy and inclusiveness. *A priori*, we can imagine a universe of withness but no nextness; or one of nextness but no likeness, or of likeness with no activity, or of activity with no purpose, or of purpose with no ego. These would be universes, each with its own grade of unity. The universe of human experience is, by one or another of its parts, of each and all these grades. Whether or not it possibly enjoys some still more absolute grade of union does not appear upon the surface.

Taken as it does appear, our universe is to a large extent chaotic. No one single type of connection runs through all the experiences that compose it. If we take space-relations, they fail to connect minds into any regular system. Causes and purposes obtain only among special series of facts. The self relation seems extremely limited and does not link two different selves together. *Prima facie*, if you should liken the universe of absolute idealism to an aquarium, a crystal globe in which goldfish are swimming, you would have to compare the empiricist universe to something more like one of those dried human heads with which the Dyaks of Borneo deck their lodges. The skull forms a solid nucleus; but innumerable feathers, leaves, strings, beads, and loose appendices of every description float and dangle from it, and save that they terminate in it, seem to have nothing to do with one another. Even so my experiences and yours float and dangle, terminating, it is true, in a nucleus of common perception, but for the most part out of sight and irrelevant and unimaginable to one another. This imperfect intimacy, this bare relation of *withness* between some parts of the sum total of experience and other parts, is the fact that ordinary empiricism overemphasizes against rationalism, the latter always tending to ignore it unduly. Radical empiricism, on the contrary, is fair to both the unity and the disconnection. It finds no reason for treating either as illusory. It allots to each its definite sphere of description, and agrees that there appear to be actual forces at work which tend, as time goes on, to make the unity greater.

The conjunctive relation that has given most trouble to philosophy is *the co-conscious transition*, so to call it, by which one experience passes into another when both belong to the same self. About the facts there is no question. My experiences and your experiences are 'with' each other in various external ways, but mine pass into mine, and yours pass into yours in a way in which yours and mine never pass into one another. Within each of our personal histories, subject, object, interest and purpose *are continuous or may be continuous*.[1] Personal histories are processes of change in time, and *the change itself is one of the things immediately experienced*. 'Change' in this case means continuous as opposed to discontinuous transition. But continuous transition is one sort of a conjunctive relation; and to be a radical empiricist means to hold fast to this conjunctive relation of all others, for this is the strategic point, the position through which, if a hole be made, all the corruptions of dialectics and all the metaphysical fictions pour into our philosophy. The holding fast to this relation means taking it at its face value, neither less nor more; and to take it at its face value means first of all to take it just as we feel it, and not to confuse ourselves with abstract talk *about* it, involving words that drive us to invent secondary conceptions in order to neutralize their suggestions and to make our actual experience again seem rationally possible.

What I do feel simply when a later moment of my experience succeeds an earlier one is that though they are two moments, the transition from the one to the other is *continuous*. Continuity here is a definite sort of experience; just as definite as is the *discontinuity-experience* which I find it impossible to avoid when I seek to make the transition from an experience of my own to one of yours. In this latter case I have to get on and off again, to pass from a thing lived to another thing only conceived, and the break is positively experienced and noted. Though the functions exerted by my experience and by yours may be the same (*e. g.*, the same objects known and the same purposes followed), yet the sameness has in this case to be ascertained expressly (and often with difficulty and uncertainty) after the break has been felt; whereas in passing from one of my own moments to another the sameness of object and interest is unbroken, and both the earlier and the later experience are of things directly lived.

There is no other *nature*, no other whatness than this absence of break and this sense of continuity in that most intimate of all conjunctive relations, the passing of one

---

[1] The psychology books have of late described the facts here with approximate adequacy. I may refer to the chapters on 'The Stream of Thought' and on the Self in my own 'Principles of Psychology,' as well as to S. H. Hodgson's 'Metaphysic of Experience,' Vol. I., Chap. VII. and VIII.

experience into another when they belong to the same self. And this whatness is real empirical 'content' just as the whatness of separation and discontinuity is real content in the contrasted case. Practically to experience one's personal continuum in this living way is to know the originals of the ideas of continuity and of sameness, to know what the words stand for concretely, to own all that they can ever mean. But all experiences have their conditions; and over-subtle intellects, thinking about the facts here, and asking how they are possible, have ended by substituting a lot of static objects of conception for the direct perceptual experiences. "Sameness," they have said, "must be a stark numerical identity; it can't run on from next to next. Continuity can't mean mere absence of gap; for if you say two things are in immediate contact, *at* the contact how can they be two? If, on the other hand, you put a relation of transition between them, that itself is a third thing, and needs to be related or hitched to its terms. An infinite series is involved," and so on. The result is that from difficulty to difficulty, the plain conjunctive experience has been discredited by both schools, the empiricists leaving things permanently disjoined, and the rationalist remedying the looseness by their Absolutes or Substances, or whatever other fictitious agencies of union they may have employed. From all which artificiality we can be saved by a couple of simple reflections: first, that conjunctions and separations are, at all events, coordinate phenomena which, if we take experiences at their face value, must be accounted equally real; and second, that if we insist on treating things as really separate when they are given as continuously joined, invoking, when union is required, transcendental principles to overcome the separateness we have assumed, then we ought to stand ready to perform the converse act. We ought to invoke higher principles of *dis*union also, to make our merely experienced *dis*junctions more truly real. Failing thus, we ought to let the originally given continuities stand on their own bottom. We have no right to be lopsided or to blow capriciously hot and cold.

III. THE COGNITIVE RELATION
The first great pitfall from which such a radical standing by

experience will save us is an artificial conception of the *relations between knower and known*. Throughout the history of philosophy the subject and its object have been treated as absolutely discontinuous entities; and thereupon the presence of the latter to the former, or the 'apprehension' by the former of the latter, has assumed a paradoxical character which all sorts of theories had to be invented to overcome. Representative theories simply shoved the subject-object gap a step farther, getting it now between the object and the representation. Common-sense theories left the gap untouched, declaring our mind able to clear it by a self-transcending leap. Transcendentalist theories left it impassible in the finite realm, and brought an Absolute in to perform the bridging act. All the while, in the very bosom of the finite experience, every conjunction required to make the relation intelligible is given in full. Either the knower and the known are:

(1) the self-same piece of experience taken twice over in different contexts; or they are

(2) two pieces of *actual* experience belonging to the same subject, with definite tracts of conjunctive transitional experience between them; or

(3) the known is a *possible* experience either of that subject or another, to which the said conjunctive transitions *would* lead, if sufficiently prolonged.

To discuss all the types, the ways in which one experience may function as the knower of another, would be incompatible with the limits of this essay.[1] I have just treated of type 1, the kind of knowledge called perception, in an article in this JOURNAL for September 1, 1904. This is the type of case in which the mind enjoys direct 'acquaintance' with a present object. In the other types the mind has 'knowledge-about' an object not immediately there. Of type 2, the simplest sort of

---

[1] For brevity's sake I altogether omit mention of the type constituted by knowledge of the truth of general propositions. This type has been thoroughly and, so far as I can see, satisfactorily, elucidated in Dewey's 'Studies in Logical Theory' (Chicago, 1904). Such propositions are reducible to the S-is-P form; and the 'terminus' that verifies and fulfills is the $S = P$ as they feel in combination. Of course percepts may be involved in the mediating experiences, or in the 'satisfactoriness' of the P in its new position.

conceptual knowledge, I have given some account in two articles, published respectively in *Mind*, Vol. X., p. 27, 1885, and in the *Psychological Review*, Vol. II., p. 105, 1895.[1] Type 3 can always formally and hypothetically be reduced to type 2, so that a brief description of that type will put the present reader sufficiently at my point of view, and make him see what the actual experience-value and meaning of the mysterious cognitive relation may be.

Suppose me to be sitting here in my library at Cambridge, at ten minutes' walk from 'Memorial Hall,' and to be thinking truly of the latter object. My mind may have before it only the name, or it may have a clear image, or it may have a very dim image of the hall, but such intrinsic differences in the image make no difference in its cognitive function. Certain extrinsic phenomena, special experiences of conjunction, are what impart to the image, be it what it may, its knowing office.

For instance, if you ask me what hall I mean by my image, and I can tell you nothing, or if I fail to point or lead you towards the Harvard Delta, or if, being led by you, I am uncertain whether the Hall I see be what I had in mind or not, you would rightly deny that I had 'meant' that particular hall at all, even though my mental image might to some degree have resembled it. The resemblance would count in that case as coincidental merely, for all sorts of things of a kind resemble one another in this world without being held for that reason to take cognizance of one another.

On the other hand, if I can lead you to the hall, and tell you of its history and present uses; if in its presence I now feel my idea, however bad it may have been, to be *continued*; if the associates of the image and of the felt hall run parallel, so that each term of the one context corresponds serially, as I walk, with an answering term of the others; why then my soul was prophetic, and my idea must be, and by common consent would be, called cognizant of reality. That percept

---

[1] These articles and their doctrine, unnoticed apparently by any one else, have lately gained favorable comment from Professor Strong in this JOURNAL, for May 12, 1904. Dr. Dickinson S. Miller has independently thought out the same results, which Strong accordingly dubs the James-Miller theory of cognition.

was what *meant*, for into it my idea has passed by conjunctive experiences of sameness and fulfilled intention. Nowhere is there jar, but every later moment matches and corroborates an earlier.

In this matching and corroborating, taken in no transcendental sense, but denoting definitely felt transitions, lies all that the knowing of a percept by an idea can possibly contain or signify. Wherever such transitions are felt, the first experience *knows* the last one. Where they do not, or where even as possibles, they can not intervene, there can be no pretense of knowing. In this latter case the extremes will be connected, if connected at all, by inferior relations—bare likeness or succession, or by 'withness' alone. Knowledge thus lives inside the tissue of experience. It is *made*; and made by relations that unroll themselves in time. Whenever certain intermediaries are given, such that, as they develop towards their terminus, there is experience from point to point of one direction followed, and finally of one process fulfilled, the result is that their starting point thereby becomes a knower and their terminus an object meant or known. That is all that knowing (in the simple case considered) can be known-as, that is the whole of its nature, put into experiential terms. Whenever such is the sequence of our experiences we may freely say that we had the terminal object 'in mind' from the outset, even although *at* the outset nothing was there in us but a flat piece of substantive experience like any other, with no self-transcendency about it, and no mystery save the mystery of coming into existence and of being followed by other pieces of substantive experience, with conjunctively transitional experiences between. That is what we *mean* here by being 'in mind.' Of any deeper more real way of being in mind we have no positive conception, and we have no right to discredit our actual experience by talking of such a thing at all.

I know that many a reader will rebel at this. "Mere intermediaries," he will say, "even though they be feelings of continuously growing fulfilment, only *separate* the knower from the known, whereas what we have in knowledge is a kind of immediate touch of the one by the other, an 'apprehension' in the etymological sense of the word, a leaping of the chasm as by lightning, an act by which union is smitten into living being, over the head of the distinctness of its terms. All these dead intermediaries of yours are out of each other, and outside of their termini still."

But do not such dialectic difficulties remind us of the dog dropping his bone and snapping at its image in the water? If we knew any more real kind of union *aliunde*, we might be entitled to brand all our empirical unions as a sham. But unions by continuous transition are the only ones we know of, whether in this matter of a knowledge-about that terminates in an acquaintance, whether in personal identity, in logical predication through the copula 'is,' or elsewhere. If anywhere there were more absolute unions realized, they could only reveal themselves to us by just such conjunctive results. These are what the unions are *worth*, these are all that *we can ever practically mean* by union, by continuity. Is it not time to repeat what Lotze said of substances, that to *act like one* is to *be* one? Should we not say here that to be experienced as continuous is to be really continuous, in a world where experience and reality come to the same thing? In a picture gallery a painted hook will serve to hang a painted chain by, a painted cable will hold a painted ship. In a world where both the terms and their distinctions are affairs of experience, the conjunctions which we experience must be at least as real as anything else. They will be 'absolutely' real conjunctions, if we have no transphenomenal Absolute ready, to derealize the whole experienced world by, at a stroke. If, on the other hand, we had such an Absolute, not one of our opponents' theories of knowledge could remain standing any better than ours could; for the distinctions as well as the conjunctions of experience would impartially fall its prey. The whole question of how 'one' thing can know 'another' would cease to be a real one at all in a world where otherness itself was an illusion.[1]

So much for the essentials of the cognitive relation, where the knowledge is conceptual in type, or forms knowledge

[1] Mr. Bradley, not professing to know his absolute *aliunde*, nevertheless derealizes Experience by alleging it to be everywhere infected with self-contradiction. His arguments seem almost purely verbal, but this is no place for arguing that point out.

'about' an object. It consists in intermediary experiences (possible, if not actual) of continuously developing progress, and, finally, of fulfilment, when the sensible percept, which is the object, is reached. The object here not only *verifies* the idea, proves its function of knowing that object to be true, but the object's existence as the terminus of the chain of intermediaries *creates* the function. Whatever terminates that chain was, because it now is, what the idea 'had in mind.'

The towering importance of this kind of knowing for human life lies in the fact that an experience that knows another can figure as its *representative*, not in any quasi-miraculous 'epistemological' sense, but in the definite practical sense of being its *substitute* in various operations, yet leading to the same result. By experimenting on our conceptual experiences, or ideas of reality, we may save ourselves the trouble of experimenting on the real experience which they severally mean. The ideas form related systems, corresponding point for point to the systems which the realities form; and by letting an ideal term call up its associates systematically, we may be led to a terminus which the corresponding real term would have led to in case we had operated on the real world. This brings us to the general question of substitution, and some remarks on that subject seem to be the next thing in order.

IV. Substitution

In Taine's brilliant book on 'Intelligence,' substitution was for the first time named as a cardinal logical function, though of course the facts had always been familiar enough. What now, exactly, in an absolute system of experiences, does the 'substitution' of one of them for another mean?

According to radical empiricism, experience as a whole wears the form of a process in time, whereby innumerable particular terms lapse and are superseded by others that follow upon them by transitions which, whether disjunctive or conjunctive in content, are themselves experiences, and must in general be accounted at least as real as the terms which they relate. What the nature of the event called 'superseding' signifies, depends altogether on the kind of transition that obtains. Some experiences simply abolish their predecessors without continuing them in any way. Others follow them more livingly, are felt to increase or to enlarge their meaning, to carry out their purpose, or to bring us nearer to their goal. They 'represent' them, and may fulfil their function better than they fulfilled it themselves. But to 'fulfil a function' in a world of pure experience can be conceived and defined in only one possible way. In such a world transitions and arrivals (or terminations) are the only events that happen, though they happen by so many sorts of path. The only function that one experience can perform is to lead into another experience; and the only fulfilment we can speak of is the reaching of a certain kind of end. When one experience leads to (or can lead to) the same end as another, they agree in function. But the whole system of experiences as they are immediately given presents itself as a quasi-chaos through which one can pass out of an initial term in many directions and yet end in the same terminus, moving from next to next by a great many alternative paths.

Either one of these paths might be a functional substitute for another, and to follow one rather than another might on occasion be an advantageous thing to do. As a matter of fact, and in a general way, the paths that run through conceptual experiences, that is, through 'thoughts' or 'ideas' that 'know' the things in which they terminate, are highly advantageous paths to follow. Not only do they yield inconceivably rapid transitions; but, owing to the 'universal' Character[1] which they frequently possess, and to their capacity for association with one another in great systems, they outstrip the tardy consecutions of the things themselves, and sweep us on towards our ultimate termini in a far more labor-saving way than the following of trains of sensible perception ever could. Wonderful are the new cuts and the short-circuits which the thought-paths make. Most thought-paths, it is true, are substitutes for nothing actual; they end outside of the real world altogether, in wayward fancies, utopias, fictions or mistakes. But where they do reenter reality and terminate therein, we substitute them always; and with these substitutes we pass the greater number of our hours.

This is why I called our experiences, taken all together, a

[1]Of which all that need be said in this essay is that it also can be conceived as functional, and defined in terms of transitions, or of the possibility of such.

quasi-chaos. There is vastly more discontinuity in the sum total of experiences than we commonly suppose. The nucleus of every man's experience, the sense of his own body, is, it is true, an absolutely continuous perception; and equally continuous is his perception (though it may be very inattentive) of a material environment of that body, changing by gradual transition when the body moves. But the rest of the physical world is at all times absent from each of us, a conceptual object merely, into the perceptual realities of which our life inserts itself at points discrete and relatively rare. Round the nucleus, partly continuous and partly discrete, of what we call the physical world of actual perception, innumerable hosts of thinkers, pursuing their several lines of physically true cogitation trace paths that intersect one another only at discontinuous perceptual points, and the rest of the time are quite incongruent; and around the whole of the nucleus of relative 'reality,' as around the Dyak's head of my late metaphor, there floats the vast *nimbus* of experiences that are wholly subjective, that are non-substitutional, that find not even an eventual ending for themselves in the perceptual world—the mere day-dreams and joys and sufferings and wishes of the individual minds. These exist *with* one another, indeed, and with the objective nucleus, but out of them it is probable that to all eternity no inter-related system of any kind will ever be made.

This notion of the purely substitutional or conceptual physical world brings us to the most critical of all the steps in the development of a philosophy of pure experience. The paradox of self-transcendency in knowledge comes back upon us here, but I think that our notions of pure experience and of substitution, and our radically empirical view of conjunctive transitions, are *Denkmittel* that will carry us safely through the pass.

V. WHAT OBJECTIVE REFERENCE IS

Whosoever feels his experience as something substitutional, even while he has it, may be said to have an experience that reaches beyond itself. From inside of its own entity it postulates reality existing elsewhere. For the transcendentalist, who holds knowing to consist in a *salto mortale* across an 'epistemological chasm,' such an idea presents no difficulty, but it seems at first sight as if it might be inconsistent with an

empiricism like our own. Have we not explained conceptual
knowledge to be wholly constituted by things that fall outside
of the knowing experience itself—by intermediary experiences and by a terminus that fulfills? Can the knowledge be
there before these elements that constitute its being have
come? And, if knowledge be not there, how can objective
reference occur?

The key to this difficulty lies in the distinction between
knowing as verified and completed, and the same knowing as
in transit and on its way. To recur to the Memorial Hall example of my former article, it is only when our idea of the
Hall has actually terminated in the percept that we know 'for
certain' that from the beginning it was truly cognitive of *that*.
Until established by the end of the process, its quality of
knowing that, or indeed of knowing anything, could still be
doubted; and yet the knowing really *was* there, as the result
now shows. We were virtual knowers of the Hall long before
we were nailed down and certified to have been its actual
knowers by the percept's retroactive validating power.

Now the immensely greater part of all our knowing never
gets beyond this virtual stage. It never is completed or nailed
down. I speak not merely of our ideas of imperceptibles like
ether-waves or dissociated 'ions,' or of 'ejects' like the contents of our neighbors' minds; I speak also of ideas which we
might verify if we would take the trouble, but which we hold
for true although unterminated perceptually, because nothing
says 'no' to us, and there is no contradicting truth in sight.
To continue thinking unchallenged is, ninety-nine times out
of a hundred, our practical substitute for knowing in the
completed sense. As each experience runs by cognitive transition into the next one, and we nowhere feel a collision with
what we elsewhere count as fact, we commit ourselves to the
current as if the port were sure. We live, as it were, upon the
front edge of an advancing wave-crest, and our sense of a
determinate direction in falling forward is all we cover of the
future of our path. It is as if a differential quotient should be
conscious and treat itself as an adequate substitute for a
traced-out curve. Our experience, *inter alia*, is of variations of
rate and of direction, and lives in these transitions more than
in the journey's end. The truncated experiences are sufficient

to act upon—what more could we have *done* at those moments even if later verification were complete?

This is what, as a radical empiricist, I say to the charge that the objective reference which is so flagrant a character of our experiences involves a chasm and a mortal leap. A positively conjunctive transition involves neither chasm nor leap. Being the very original of what we mean by continuity, it makes a continuum wherever it appears. I know full well that such brief words as these will leave the hardened transcendentalist unshaken. Conjunctive experiences *separate* their terms, he will still say: they are third things interposed, that have themselves to be conjoined by new links, and to invoke them makes our trouble infinitely worse. To 'feel' our motion forward is impossible. Motion implies terminus; and how can terminus be felt before we have arrived? The barest start and sally forwards, the barest tendency to leave the instant, involves the chasm and the leap. Conjunctive transitions are the most superficial of appearances, illusions of our sensibility which philosophical reflection pulverizes at a touch. Conception is our only trustworthy instrument, conception and the Absolute working hand in hand. Conception disintegrates experience utterly, but its disjunctions are easily overcome again when the Absolute takes up the task.

Such transcendentalists I must leave, provisionally at least, in full possession of their creed. I have no space for polemics in this article, so I shall simply formulate the empiricist doctrine as my hypothesis, leaving it to work or not work as it may.

Objective reference, I say then, is a mere incident of the fact that so much of our experience comes as an insufficient and is of process and transition. Our fields of experience have no more definite boundaries than have our fields of view. Both are fringed forever by a *more* that continuously develops, and that continuously supersedes them as life proceeds. The relations, generally speaking, are as real here as the terms are, and the only complaint of the transcendentalist's with which I could at all sympathize would be his charge that, by first making knowledge to consist in external relations as I have done, and by then confessing that nine-tenths of the time these are not actually there, so that our knowledge for the most part keeps only virtual, I have knocked the solid bottom out of the whole business, and palmed off a mere substitute of knowledge for the genuine thing. Only the admission that our ideas are self-transcendent already, such a critic might say, in advance of the experiences that are to terminate them, can bring solidity back to knowledge in a world like this, in which transitions and terminations are only by exception carried out.

This seems to me an excellent place for applying the pragmatic method. When a dispute arises, that method consists in auguring what practical consequences would be different if one side rather than the other were true. If no difference can be thought of, the dispute is a quarrel over words.

What then would the *salto mortale*, the immediate self-transcendency affirmed as something existing independently of experiential mediation or termination, be known as, what would it practically result in, were it true?

It could only result in our orientation, in the turning of our expectations and practical tendencies into the right path; and the right path here, so long as we and the object are not yet face to face (or can never get face to face, as in the case of ejects), would be the path that led us into the object's nearest neighborhood. Where direct acquaintance is lacking, 'knowledge about' is the next best thing, and such knowledge an acquaintance with what actually lies about the object, and is most closely related to it, puts within our grasp. Ether-waves and your anger, for example, are things in which my thoughts will never perceptually terminate, but my concepts of them lead me to their very brink, to the chromatic fringes and to the hurtful words and deeds which are their really next effects.

Even if our ideas did in themselves carry the postulated self-transcendency, it would still remain true that their putting us into possession of such really next effects *would be the sole cash-value of the self-transcendency for us*. And this cash-value, it is needless to say, is *verbatim et literatim* what our empiricist account pays in. On pragmatist principles therefore, a dispute over self-transcendency here would be a pure logomachy. Call our concepts of ejective things self-transcendent or the reverse, it makes no difference, so long as we don't differ about the nature of that exalted virtue's fruits.

Fruits for us, humanistic fruits, of course. If an Absolute were proved to exist for other reasons, it might well appear that *his* knowledge is terminated in innumerable cases where ours is still incomplete. That, however, would be a fact indifferent to our knowledge. The latter would grow neither worse nor better, whether we acknowledged such an Absolute or left him out.

So the notion of a knowledge still *in transitu* and on its way joins hands here with that notion of a 'pure experience' which I tried to explain in my recent article entitled 'Does Consciousness Exist?' The instant field of the present is always experience in its 'pure' state, plain unqualified actuality, a simple *that*, as yet undifferentiated into thing and thought, and only virtually classifiable as objective fact or as some one's opinion about fact. This is as true when the field is conceptual as when it is perceptual. 'Memorial Hall' is 'there' in my idea as much as when I stand before it. I proceed to act on its account in either case. Only in the later experience that supersedes the present one is this *naif* immediacy retrospectively split into two parts, a 'consciousness' and its 'content,' and the content corrected or confirmed. While still pure, or present, any experience—mine, for example, of what I write about in these very lines—passes for 'truth.' The morrow may reduce it to 'opinion.' The transcendentalist in all his particular knowledges is as liable to this reduction as I am: his Absolute does not save him. Why, then, need he quarrel with an account of knowing that merely leaves it liable to this inevitable condition? Why insist on its being a static relation out of time when it practically seems so much a function of our active life? For a thing to be valid, says Lotze, is the same as to make itself valid. When the whole universe seems only to be making itself valid and to be still incomplete (else why its ceaseless changing?) why, of all things, should knowing be exempt? Why should it not be making itself valid like everything else? That some parts of it may be already valid or verified beyond dispute, the empirical philosopher, of course, like any one else, may always hope.

VI.   THE CONTERMINOUSNESS OF DIFFERENT MINDS
With transition and prospect thus enthroned in pure ex-

perience, it is impossible to subscribe to the idealism of the English school. Radical empiricism has, in fact, more affinities with natural realism than with the views of Berkeley or of Mill, and this can be easily shown.

For the Berkeleyan school, ideas (the verbal equivalent of what I term experiences) are discontinuous. The content of each is wholly immanent, and there are no transitions with which they are consubstantial and through which their beings may unite. Your Memorial Hall and mine, even when both are percepts, are wholly out of connection with each other. Our lives are a congeries of solipsisms, out of which in strict logic only a God could compose a universe even of discourse. No dynamic currents run between my objects and your objects. Never can our minds meet in the *same*.

The incredibility of such a philosophy is flagrant. It is 'cold, strained, and unnatural' in a supreme degree; and it may be doubted whether even Berkeley himself, who took it so religiously, really believed, when walking through the streets of London, that his spirit and the spirits of his fellow wayfarers had absolutely different towns in view.

To me the decisive reason in favor of our minds meeting in *some* common objects at least is that, unless I make that supposition, I have no motive for assuming that your mind exists at all. Why do I postulate your mind? Because I see your body acting in a certain way. Its gestures, facial movements, words and conduct generally, are 'expressive,' so I deem it actuated as my own is, by an inner life like mine. This argument from analogy is my *reason*, whether an instinctive belief runs before it or not. But what is 'your body' here but a percept in *my* field? It is only as animating *that* object, *my* object, that I have any occasion to think of you at all. If the body that you actuate be not the very body that I see there, but some duplicate body of your own with which that has nothing to do, we belong to different universes, you and I, and for me to speak of you is folly. Myriads of such universes even now may coexist, irrelevant to one another; my concern is solely with the universe with which my own life is connected.

In that perceptual part of my universe which I call your body, your mind and my mind meet and may be called conterminous. Your mind actuates that body and mine sees it; my thoughts pass into it as into their harmonious cognitive fulfillment; your emotions and volitions pass into it as causes into their effects.

But that percept hangs together with all our other physical percepts. They are of one stuff with it; and if it be our common possession, they must be so likewise. For instance, your hand lays hold of one end of a rope and my hand lays hold of the other end. We pull against each other. Can our two hands be mutual objects in this experience, and the rope not be mutual also? What is true of the rope is true of any other percept. Your objects are over and over again the same as mine. If I ask you *where* some object of yours is, our old Memorial Hall, for example, you point to *my* Memorial Hall with *your* hand which *I* see. If you alter an object in your world, put out a candle, for example, when I am present, *my* candle *ipso facto* goes out. It is only as altering my objects that I guess you to exist. If your objects do not coalesce with my objects, if they be not identically where mine are, they must be proved to be positively somewhere else. But no other location can be assigned for them, so their place must be what it seems to be, the same.[1]

Practically, then, our minds meet in a world of objects which they share in common, which would still be there, if one or several of the minds were destroyed. I can see no formal objection to this supposition's being literally true. On the principles which I am defending, a 'mind' or 'personal consciousness' is the name for a series of experiences run together by certain definite transitions, and an objective reality is a series of similar experiences knit by different transitions. If one and the same experience can figure twice, once in a mental and once in a physical context (as I have tried, in my article on 'Consciousness,' to show that it can), one does not see why it might not figure thrice, or four times, or any number of times, by running into as many different mental contexts, just as the same point, lying at their intersection, can be continued into many different lines. Abolishing any number of contexts would not destroy the experience itself or its other

[1] The notion that our objects are inside of our respective heads is not seriously defensible, so I pass it by.

contexts, any more than abolishing some of the point's linear continuations would destroy the others, or destroy the point itself.

I well know the subtle dialectic which insists that a term taken in another relation must needs be an intrinsically different term. The crux is always the old Greek one, that the same man can't be tall in relation to one neighbor, and short in relation to another, for that would make him tall and short at once. In this essay I can not stop to refute this dialectic, so I pass on, leaving my flank for the time exposed. But if my reader will only allow that the same '*now*' both ends his past and begins his future; or that, when he buys an acre of land from his neighbor, it is the same acre that successively figures in the two estates; or that when I pay him a dollar, the same dollar goes into his pocket that came out of mine; he will also in consistency have to allow that the same object may conceivably play a part in, as being related to the rest of, any number of otherwise entirely different minds. This is enough for my present point: the common-sense notion of minds sharing the same object offers no special logical or epistemological difficulties of its own; it stands or falls with the general possibility of things being in conjunctive relation with other things at all.

In principle, then, let natural realism pass for possible. Your mind and mine *may* terminate in the same percept, not merely against it, as if it were a third external thing, but by inserting themselves into it and coalescing with it, for such is the sort of conjunctive union that appears to be experienced when a perceptual terminus 'fulfills.' Even so, two hawsers may embrace the same pile, and yet neither one of them touch any other part, except that pile, of what the other hawser is attached to.

It is therefore not a formal question, but a question of empirical fact solely, whether, when you and I are said to know the 'same' Memorial Hall, our minds do terminate at or in a numerically identical percept. Obviously, as a plain matter of fact, they do *not*. Apart from color-blindness and such possibilities, we see the Hall in different perspectives. You may be on one side of it and I on another. The percept of each of us, as he sees the surface of the Hall, is moreover only his provisional terminus. The next thing beyond my percept is not your mind, but more percepts of my own into which my first percept develops, the interior of the Hall, for instance, or the inner structure of its bricks and mortar. If our minds were in a literal sense *con*terminous, neither could get beyond the percept which they had in common, it would be an ultimate barrier between them—unless indeed they became 'co-conscious' over a still larger part of their content, which (thought-transference apart) is not supposed to be the actual case. In point of fact the ultimate common barrier can always be pushed, by both minds, farther than any actual percept, until at last it resolves itself into the mere notion of imperceptibles like molecules or ether, so that, where we do terminate in percepts, our knowledge is only speciously completed, being, in theoretic strictness, only a virtual knowledge of those remoter objects which conception carries out.

Is natural realism, permissible in logic, refuted then by empirical fact? Do our minds have no object in common after all?

Yes, they certainly have *Space* in common. On pragmatic principles we are obliged to predicate sameness wherever we can predicate no assignable point of difference. If two named things have every equality and function indiscernible, and are at the same time in the same place, they must be written down as numerically one thing under two different names. But there is no test discoverable, so far as I know, by which it can be shown that the place occupied by your percept of Memorial Hall differs from the place occupied by mine. The percepts themselves may be shown to differ; but if each of us be asked to point out where his percept is, we point to an identical spot. All the relations, whether geometrical or causal, of the Hall originate or terminate in that spot wherein our hands meet, and where each of us begins to work if he wishes to make the Hall change before the other's eyes. Just so it is with our bodies. That body of yours which you actuate and feel from within must be in the same spot as the body of yours which I see or touch from without. 'There' for me means where I place my finger. If you do not feel my finger's contact to be 'there' in *my* sense, when I place it on your body, where then do you feel it? Your inner actuations of your body also meet my finger *there*: it is *there* that you resist its push, or shrink back, or sweep the finger aside with your hand. Whatever farther knowledge either of us may acquire of the real constitution of the body which we thus feel, you from within and I from without, it is in that same place that the newly conceived or perceived constituents have to be located, and it is *through* that space that your and my mental intercourse with each other has always to be carried on, by the mediation of impressions which I convey thither, and of the reactions thence which those impressions may provoke from you.

In general terms, then, whatever differing contents our minds may eventually fill a place with, the place itself is a numerically identical content of the two minds, a piece of common property in which, through which, and over which they join. The receptacle of certain of our experiences being thus common, the experiences themselves might some day become common also. If that day ever did come, our thoughts would terminate in a complete empirical identity, there would be an end, so far as *those* experiences went, to our discussions about truth. No points of difference appearing, they would have to count as the same.

VII. CONCLUSION.

With this we have the outlines of a philosophy of pure experience before us. At the outset of my essay, I called it a mosaic philosophy. In actual mosaics the pieces are held together by their bedding, for which bedding the Substances, transcendental Egos, or Absolutes of other philosophies may be taken to stand. In radical empiricism there is no bedding; it is as if the pieces clung together by their edges, the transitions experienced between them forming their cement. Of course such a metaphor is misleading, for in actual experience the more substantive and the more transitive parts run into each other continuously, there is in general no separateness needing to be overcome by an external cement; and whatever separateness is actually experienced is not overcome, it stays and counts as separateness to the end. But the metaphor serves to symbolize the fact that Experience itself, taken at large, can grow by its edges. That one moment of it proliferates into the next by transitions which, whether conjunctive or disjunctive, continue the experiential tissue, can not, I contend, be denied. Life is in the transitions as much as in the terms connected; often, indeed, it seems to be there more emphatically, as if our spurts and sallies forward were the real firing-line of the battle, were like the thin line of flame advancing across the dry autumnal field which the farmer proceeds to burn. In this line we live prospectively as well as retrospectively. It is 'of' the past, inasmuch as it comes expressly as the past's continuation; it is 'of' the future in so far as the future, when it comes, will have continued *it*.

These relations of continuous transition experienced are what make our experiences cognitive. In the simplest and completest cases the experiences are cognitive of one another. When one of them terminates a previous series of them with a sense of fulfillment, it, we say, is what those other experiences 'had in view.' The knowledge, in such a case, is verified, the truth is 'salted down.' Mainly, however, we live on speculative investments, or on our prospects only. But living on things *in posse* is as good as living in the actual, so long as our credit remains good. It is evident that for the most part it is good, and that the universe seldom protests our drafts.

In this sense we at every moment can continue to believe in an existing *beyond*. It is only in special cases that our confident rush forward gets rebuked. The beyond must of course always in our philosophy be itself of an experiential nature. If not a future experience of our own or a present one of our neighbor, it must be a thing in itself in Dr. Prince's and Professor Strong's sense of the term—that is, it must be an experience *for* itself whose relation to other things we translate into the action of molecules, ether-waves, or whatever else the physical symbols may be.[1] This opens the chapter of the relations of radical empiricism to panpsychism, into which I can not enter now.

The beyond can in any case exist simultaneously—for it

[1] Our minds and these ejective realities would still have space (or pseudo-space, as I believe Professor Strong calls the medium of interaction between 'things-in-themselves') in common. These would exist *where*, and begin to act *where*, we locate the molecules, etc., and *where* we perceive the sensible phenomena explained thereby.

can be experienced *to have existed* simultaneously—with the experience that practically postulates it by looking in its direction, or by turning or changing in the direction of which it is the goal. Pending that actuality of union, in the virtuality of which the 'truth,' even now, of the postulation consists, the beyond and its knower are entities split off from each other. The world is in so far forth a pluralism of which the unity is not fully experienced as yet. But, as fast as verification comes, trains of experience, once separate, run into one another; and that is why I said, earlier in my article, that the unity of the world is on the whole undergoing increase. The universe continually grows in quantity by new experiences that graft themselves upon the older mass; but these very new experiences often help the mass to a more consolidated form.

These are the main features of a philosophy of pure experience. It has innumerable other aspects and arouses innumerable questions, but the points I have touched on seem enough to make an entering wedge. In my own mind such a philosophy harmonizes best with a radical pluralism, with novelty and indeterminism, moralism and theism, and with the 'humanism' lately sprung upon us by the Oxford and the Chicago schools.[1] I can not, however, be sure that all these doctrines are its necessary and indispensable allies. It presents so many points of difference, both from the common sense and from the idealism that have made our philosophic language, that it is almost as difficult to state it as it is to think it out clearly, and if it is ever to grow into a respectable system, it will have to be built up by the contributions of many cooperating minds. It seems to me, as I said at the outset of this essay, that many minds are, in point of fact, now turning in a direction that points towards radical empiricism. If they are carried farther by my words, and if then they add their stronger voices to my feebler one, the publication of this essay will have been worth while.

[1] I have said something of this latter alliance in an article entitled 'Humanism and Truth,' in *Mind*, October, 1904.

Answers to a Questionnaire

IT IS BEING realized as never before that religion, as one of the most important things in the life both of the community and of the individual, deserves close and extended study. Such study can be of value only if based upon the personal experiences of many individuals. If you are in sympathy with such study and are willing to assist in it, will you kindly write out the answers to the following questions and return them with this questionnaire, as soon as you conveniently can, to JAMES B. PRATT, 20 Shepard Street, Cambridge, Mass.

Please answer the questions at length and in detail. Do not give philosophical generalizations, but your own personal experience.

1. What does religion mean to you personally? Is it
   (1) A belief that something exists? *Yes.*
   (2) An emotional experience? *Not powerfully so, yet a* social *reality.*
   (3) A general attitude of the will toward God or toward righteousness? *It involves these.*
   (4) Or something else?
If it has several elements, which is for you the most important? *The social appeal for corroboration, consolation, etc., when things are going wrong with my causes (my truth denied), etc.*

2. What do you mean by God? *A combination of Ideality and (final) efficacity.*
   (1) Is He a person—if so, what do you mean by His being a person? *He must be cognizant and responsive in some way.*
   (2) Or is He only a Force? *He must do.*
   (3) Or is God an attitude of the Universe toward you? *Yes, but more conscious. "God," to me, is not the only spiritual reality to believe in. Religion means primarily a universe of spiritual relations surrounding the earthly practical ones, not merely relations of "value," but agencies and their activities. I suppose that the chief premise for my hospitality towards the religious testimony of others is my*

*conviction that "normal" or "sane" consciousness is so small
a part of actual experience. What e'er be true, it is not
true exclusively, as philistine scientific opinion assumes. The
other kinds of consciousness bear witness to a much wider
universe of experiences, from which our belief selects and
emphasizes such parts as best satisfy our needs.*

How do you apprehend his relation to mankind
   and to you personally?

If your position on any of these matters is uncertain, please state the fact.

                                Uncertain.

3. Why do you believe in God? Is it
   (1) From some argument? *Emphatically, no.*
  Or (2) Because you have experienced His presence? *No,
      but rather because I need it so that it "must" be true.*
  Or (3) From authority, such as that of the Bible or of
      some prophetic person? *Only the whole tradition of re-
      ligious people, to which something in me makes admiring
      response.*
  Or (4) From any other reason? *Only for the social reasons.*
    If from several of these reasons, please indicate carefully the
order of their importance.

    4. Or do you not so much *believe* in God as want to *use*
Him? *I can't use him very definitely, yet I believe.* Do you
accept Him not so much as a real existent Being, but rather
as an ideal to live by? *More as a more powerful ally of my own
ideals.* If you should become thoroughly convinced that
there was no God, would it make any great difference in
your life—either in happiness, morality, or in other respects? *Hard to say. It would surely make some difference.*

    5. Is God very real to you, as real as an earthly friend,
though different? *Dimly real; not as an earthly friend.*

    Do you feel that you have experienced His presence? If so,
please describe what you mean by such an experience.
Never.

    How vague or how distinct is it? How does it affect you
mentally and physically?

    If you have had no such experience, do you accept the tes-
timony of others who claim to have felt God's presence directly? Please answer this question with special care and in as
great detail as possible. *Yes! The whole line of testimony on this*

point is so strong that I am unable to pooh-pooh it away. No doubt there is a germ in me of something similar that makes response.

6. Do you pray, and if so, why? That is, is it purely from habit, and social custom, or do you really believe that God hears your prayers? *I can't possibly pray—I feel foolish and artificial.*

Is prayer with you one-sided or two-sided—*i.e.*, do you sometimes feel that in prayer you receive something—such as strength or the divine spirit—from God? Is it a real communion?

7. What do you mean by "spirituality"? *Susceptibility to ideals, but with a certain freedom to indulge in imagination about them. A certain amount of "other worldly" fancy. Otherwise you have mere morality, or "taste."*

Describe a typical spiritual person. *Phillips Brooks.*

8. Do you believe in personal immortality? *Never keenly; but more strongly as I grow older.* If so, why? *Because I am just getting fit to live.*

9. Do you accept the Bible as *authority* in religious matters? Are your religious faith and your religious life based on it? If so, how would your belief in God and your life toward Him and your fellow men be affected by loss of faith in the *authority* of the Bible? *No. No. No. It is so human a book that I don't see how belief in its divine authorship can survive the reading of it.*

10. What do you mean by a "religious experience"? *Any moment of life that brings the reality of spiritual things more "home" to one.*

1904; Printed in *The Letters of William James*, 1920

How Two Minds Can Know One Thing

IN AN ARTICLE in this JOURNAL entitled 'Does Consciousness Exist?'[1] I have tried to show that when we call an
experience 'conscious,' that does not mean that it is suffused
throughout with a peculiar modality of being ('psychic'
being) as stained glass may be suffused with light, but rather
that it stands in certain determinate relations to other portions of experience extraneous to itself. These form one peculiar 'context' for it; while, taken in another context of
experiences, we class it as a fact in the physical world. This
'pen,' for example, is, in the first instance, a bald *that*, a datum, fact, phenomenon, content, or whatever other neutral or
ambiguous name you may prefer to apply. I called it in that
article a 'pure experience.' To get classed either as a physical
pen or as some one's percept of a pen, it must assume a *function*, and that can only happen in a more complicated world.
So far as in that world it is a stable feature, holds ink, marks
paper and obeys the guidance of a hand, it is a physical pen.
That is what we mean by being 'physical,' in a pen. So far as
it is instable, on the contrary, coming and going with the
movements of my eyes, altering with what I call my fancy,
continuous with subsequent experiences of its 'having been'
(in the past tense), it is the percept of a pen in my mind.
Those peculiarities are what we mean by being 'conscious,' in
a pen.

In Section VI. of another article[2] I tried to show that the
same *that*, the same numerically identical pen of pure experience, can enter simultaneously into many conscious contexts,
or, in other words, be an object for many different minds. I
admitted that I had not space to treat of certain possible objections in that article; but in a subsequent article[3] I took
some of the objections up. At the end of that article I said
that still more formidable-sounding objections remained; so,

[1] Vol. I., p. 477, September 1, 1904.

[2] 'A World of Pure Experience,' *ibid.*, Vol. I., p. 564, October 13, 1904.

[3] 'The Thing and its Relations,' in the present volume of this JOURNAL,
p. 29.

to leave my pure-experience theory in as strong a state as possible, I propose to consider those objections now.

I

The objections I previously tried to dispose of were purely logical or dialectical. No one identical term, whether physical or psychical, it had been said, could be the subject of two relations at once. This thesis I sought to prove unfounded. The objections that now confront us arise from the nature supposed to inhere in psychic facts specifically. Whatever may be the case with physical objects, a fact of consciousness, it is alleged (and indeed very plausibly), can not, without self-contradiction, be treated as a portion of two different minds, and for the following reasons.

In the physical world we make with impunity the assumption that one and the same material object can figure in an indefinitely large number of different processes at once. When, for instance, a sheet of rubber is pulled at its four corners, a unit of rubber in the middle of the sheet is affected by all four of the pulls. It *transmits* them each, as if it pulled in four different ways at once itself. So, an air-particle or an ether-particle 'compounds' the different directions of movement imprinted on it without obliterating their several individualities. It delivers them distinct, on the contrary, at as many several 'receivers' (ear, eye or what not) as may be 'tuned' to that effect. The apparent paradox of a distinctness like this surviving in the midst of compounding is a thing which, I fancy, the analyses made by physicists have by this time sufficiently cleared up.

But if, on the strength of these analogies, one should ask: "Why, if two or more lines can run through one and the same geometrical point, or if two or more distinct processes of activity can run through one and the same physical thing so that it simultaneously plays a rôle in each and every process, might not two or more streams of personal consciousness include one and the same unit of experience so that it would simultaneously be a part of the experience of all the different minds?" one would be checked by thinking of a certain peculiarity by which phenomena of consciousness differ from physical things.

While physical things, namely, are supposed to be permanent and to have their 'states,' a fact of consciousness exists but once and *is* a state. Its *esse* is *sentiri*; it is only so far as it is felt; and it is unambiguously and unequivocally exactly *what* is felt. The hypothesis under consideration would, however, oblige it to be felt equivocally, felt now as part of my mind and again at the same time *not* as a part of my mind, but of yours (for my mind is *not* yours), and this would seem impossible without doubling it into two distinct things, or, in other words, without reverting to the ordinary dualistic philosophy of insulated minds each knowing its object representatively as a third thing,—and that would be to give up the pure-experience scheme altogether.

Can we see, then, any way in which a unit of pure experience might enter into and figure in two diverse streams of consciousness without turning itself into the two units which, on our hypothesis, it must not be?

II

There is a way; and the first step towards it is to see more precisely how the unit enters into either one of the streams of consciousness alone. Just what, from being 'pure,' does its becoming 'conscious' *once* mean?

It means, first, that new experiences have supervened; and, second, that they have borne a certain assignable relation to the unit supposed. Continue, if you please, to speak of the pure unit as 'the pen.' So far as the pen's successors do but repeat the pen or, being different from it, are 'energetically'[1] related to it, it and they will form a group of stably existing physical things. So far, however, as its successors differ from it in another well-determined way, the pen will figure in their context, not as a physical, but as a mental fact. It will become a passing 'percept,' *my* percept of that pen. What now is that decisive well-determined way?

In the chapter on 'The Self,' in my 'Principles of Psychology,' I explained the continuous identity of each personal consciousness as a name for the practical fact that new

---

[1] For an explanation of this expression see above, Vol. I., p. 489.

experiences[1] come which look back on the old ones, find them 'warm,' and greet and appropriate them as 'mine.' These operations mean, when analyzed empirically, several tolerably definite things, viz.:

1. That the new experience has past time for its 'content,' and in that time a pen that 'was';

2. That 'warmth' was also about the pen, in the sense of a group of feelings ('interest' aroused, 'attention' turned, 'eyes' employed, etc.) that were closely connected with it and that now recur and evermore recur with unbroken vividness, though from the pen of now which may be only an image all such vividness may have gone;

3. That these feelings are the nucleus of 'me';

4. That whatever once was associated with them was, at least for that one moment, 'mine'—my implement if associated with hand-feelings, my 'percept' only, if only eye-feelings and attention-feelings were involved.

The pen, realized in this retrospective way as my percept, thus figures as a fact of 'conscious' life. But it does so only so far as 'appropriation' has occurred; and appropriation is *part of the content of a later experience* wholly additional to the originally 'pure' pen. *That* pen, virtually both objective and subjective, is at its own moment actually and intrinsically neither. It has to be looked back upon and *used*, in order to be classed in either distinctive way. But its use, so called, is in the hands of the other experience, while *it* stands, throughout the operation, passive and unchanged.

If this pass muster as an intelligible account of how an experience originally pure can enter into one consciousness, the next question is as to how it might conceivably enter into two.

III

Obviously no new kind of condition would have to be supplied. All that we should have to postulate would be a second subsequent experience, collateral and contemporary with the first subsequent one, in which a similar act of appropriation should occur. The two acts would interfere neither with one

[1] I call them 'passing thoughts' in the book—the passage in point goes from pages 330 to 342 of Vol. I.

another nor with the originally pure pen. It would sleep undisturbed in its own past, no matter how many such successors went through their several appropriative acts. Each would know it as 'my' percept, each would class it as a 'conscious' fact.

Nor need their so classing it interfere in the least with their classing it at the same time as a physical pen. Since the classing in both cases depends upon the taking of it in one group or another of associates, if the superseding experience were of wide enough 'span' it could think the pen in both groups simultaneously, and yet distinguish the two groups. It would then see the whole situation conformably to what we call 'the representative theory of cognition,' and that is what we all spontaneously do. As a man philosophizing 'popularly,' I believe that what I see myself writing with is double—I think it in its relations to physical nature, and also in its relations to my personal life; I see that it is in my mind, but that it also is a physical pen.

The paradox of the same experience figuring in two consciousnesses seems thus no paradox at all. To be 'conscious' means not simply to be, but to be reported, known, to have awareness of one's being added to that being; and this is just what happens when the appropriative experience supervenes. The pen-experience in its original immediacy is not aware of itself, it simply *is*, and the second experience is required for what we call awareness of it to occur.[1] The difficulty of understanding what happens here is, therefore, not a logical difficulty: there is no contradiction involved. It is an ontological difficulty rather. Experiences come on an enormous scale, and if we take them all together, they come in a chaos of incommensurable relations that we can not straighten out. We have to abstract different groups of them, and handle these separately if we are to talk of them at all. But how the experiences ever *get themselves made*, or *why* their characters and relations

[1] Shadworth Hodgson has laid great stress on the fact that the minimum of consciousness demands two subfeelings, of which the second retrospects the first. (Cf. the section 'Analysis of Minima' in his 'Philosophy of Reflection,' I., 248; also the chapter entitled 'The Moment of Experience' in his 'Metaphysic of Experience,' Vol. I.) 'We live forward, we understand backward' is a phrase of Kierkegaard's which Höffding quotes.

are just such as appear, we can not begin to understand. Granting, however, that, by hook or crook, they *can* get themselves made, and can appear in the successions that I have so schematically described, then we have to confess that even although (as I began by quoting from the adversary) 'a feeling only is as it is felt,' there is still nothing absurd in the notion of its being felt in two different ways at once, as yours, namely, and as mine. It is, indeed, 'mine' only as it is felt as mine, and 'yours' only as it is felt as yours. But it is felt as neither *by itself*, but only when 'owned' by our two several remembering experiences, just as one undivided estate is owned by several heirs.

IV

One word, now, before I close, about the corollaries of the views set forth. Since the acquisition of conscious quality on the part of an experience depends upon a context coming to it, it follows that the sum total of all experiences, having no context, can not strictly be called conscious at all. It is a *that*, an Absolute, a 'pure' experience on an enormous scale, undifferentiated and undifferentiable into thought and thing. This the post-Kantian idealists have always practically acknowledged by calling their doctrine an *Identitätsphilosophie*. The question of the *Beseelung* of the All of things ought not, then, even to be asked. No more ought the question of its *truth* to be asked, for truth is a relation inside of the sum total, obtaining between thoughts and something else, and thoughts, as we have seen, can only be contextual things. In these respects the pure experiences of our philosophy are, in themselves considered, so many little absolutes, the philosophy of pure experience being only a more comminuted *Identitätsphilosophie*.

Meanwhile, a pure experience can be postulated with any amount whatever of span or field. If it exert the retrospective and appropriative function on any other piece of experience, the latter thereby enters into its own conscious stream. And in this operation time intervals make no essential difference. After sleeping, my retrospection is as perfect as it is between two successive waking moments of my time. Accordingly if, millions of years later, a similarly retrospective experience should anyhow come to birth, my present thought would form a genuine portion of its long-span conscious life. 'Form a portion,' I say, but not in the sense that the two things could be entitatively or substantively one—they can not, for they are numerically discrete facts—but only in the sense that the *functions* of my present thought, its knowledge, its purpose, its content and 'consciousness,' in short, being inherited, would be continued practically unchanged. Speculations like Fechner's, of an Earth-soul, of wider spans of consciousness enveloping narrower ones throughout the cosmos, are, therefore, philosophically quite in order, provided they distinguish the functional from the entitative point of view, and do not treat the minor consciousness under discussion as a kind of standing material of which the wider ones *consist*.

The Journal of Philosophy, Psychology and Scientific Methods,
March 30, 1905

Humanism and Truth Once More

MR. JOSEPH'S CRITICISM, in the last number of MIND, of my article 'Humanism and Truth' is a useful contribution to the general clearing up. He has seriously tried to comprehend what the pragmatic movement may intelligibly mean; and if he has failed, it is the fault neither of his patience nor of his sincerity, but rather of stubborn tricks of thought which he could not easily get rid of. Minute polemics, in which the parties try to rebut every detail of each of the other's charges, are a useful exercise only to the disputants. They can but breed confusion in a reader. I will therefore ignore as much as possible the text of both our articles (mine was inadequate enough) and treat once more the general objective situation.

As I apprehend the movement towards humanism, it is based on no particular discovery or principle that can be driven into one precise formula which thereupon can be impaled upon a logical skewer. It is much more like one of those secular changes that come upon public opinion overnight, as it were, borne upon tides 'too full for sound or foam,' that survive all the crudities and extravagances of their advocates, that you can pin to no one absolutely essential statement, nor kill by any one decisive stab.

Such have been the changes from aristocracy to democracy, from classic to romantic taste, from theistic to pantheistic feeling, from static to evolutionary ways of understanding life—changes of which we all have been spectators. Scholasticism still opposes to such changes the method of confutation by single decisive reasons, showing that the new view involves self-contradiction, or traverses some fundamental principle. This is like stopping a river by planting a stick in the middle of its bed. Round your obstacle flows the water and 'gets there all the same'. In reading Mr. Joseph, I am not a little reminded of those Catholic writers who refute Darwinism by telling us that higher species cannot come from lower because *minus nequit gignere plus,* or that the notion of transformation is absurd, for it implies that species tend to their own destruction, and that would violate the principle that every reality tends to persevere in its own shape. The point of view is too myopic, too tight and close to take in the inductive argument. You cannot settle questions of fact by formal logic. I feel as if Mr. Joseph almost pounced on my words singly, without giving the sentences time to get out of my mouth.

The one condition of understanding humanism is to become inductive-minded oneself, to drop rigorous definitions, and follow lines of least resistance 'on the whole'. "In other words," Mr. Joseph may probably say, "resolve your intellect into a kind of slush." "Even so," I make reply,—"if you will consent to use no politer word." For humanism, conceiving the more 'true' as the more 'satisfactory' (Dewey's term), has to renounce sincerely rectilinear arguments and ancient ideals of rigour and finality. It is in just this temper of renunciation, so different from that of pyrrhonistic scepticism, that the spirit of humanism essentially consists. Satisfactoriness has to be measured by a multitude of standards, of which some, for aught we know, may fail in any given case; and what is 'more' satisfactory than any alternative in sight, may to the end be a sum of *pluses* and *minuses*, concerning which we can only trust that by ulterior corrections and improvements a maximum of the one and a minimum of the other may some day be approached. It means a real change of heart, a break with absolutistic hopes, when one takes up this view of the conditions of belief.

That humanism's critics have never imagined this attitude inwardly, is shown by their invariable tactics. They do not get into it far enough to see objectively and from without what their own opposite notion of truth is. Mr. Joseph is possessed by some such notion; he thinks his readers to be full of it, he obeys it, works from it, but never even essays to tell us what it is. The nearest he comes to doing so is where (on p. 37) he says it is the way "we ought to think," whether we be psychologically compelled to or not.

Of course humanism agrees to this: it is only a manner of calling truth an ideal. But humanism explicates the summarising word 'ought' into a mass of pragmatic motives from the midst of which our critics think that truth itself takes flight. Truth is a name of double meaning. It stands now for an abstract something defined only as that to which our thought

ought to conform; and again it stands for the concrete propositions within which we believe that conformity already
reigns—they being so many 'truths'. Humanism sees that the
only conformity we ever have to deal with concretely is that
between our subjects and our predicates, using these words
in a very broad sense. It sees moreover that this conformity is
'validated' (to use Mr. Schiller's term) by an indefinite number of pragmatic tests that vary as the predicates and subjects
vary. If an S gets superseded by an SP that gives our mind a
completer sum of satisfactions, we always say, humanism
points out, that we have advanced to a better position in regard to truth.

Now many of our judgments thus attained are retrospective. The S'es, so the judgment runs, were SP's already ere the
fact was humanly recorded. Common sense, struck by this
state of things, now rearranges the whole field; and traditional philosophy follows her example. The general requirement that predicates must conform to their subject, they
translate into an ontological theory. A most previous Subject
of all is substituted for the lesser subjects and conceived of as
an archetypal Reality; and the conformity required of predicates in detail is reinterpreted as a relation which our whole
mind, with all its subjects and predicates together, must get
into with respect to this Reality. It, meanwhile, is conceived
as eternal, static, and unaffected by our thinking. Conformity
to a non-human Archetype like this is probably the notion of
truth which my opponent shares with common sense and
philosophic rationalism.

When now Humanism, fully admitting both the naturalness and the grandeur of this hypothesis, nevertheless points
to its sterility, and declines to chime in with the substitution,
keeping to the concrete and still lodging truth between the
subjects and the predicates in detail, it provokes the outcry
which we hear and which my critic echoes.

One of the commonest parts of the outcry is that humanism is subjectivistic altogether—it is supposed to labour under a necessity of 'denying trans-perceptual reality'. It is not
hard to see how this misconception of humanism may have
arisen; and humanistic writers, partly from not having sufficiently guarded their expressions, and partly from not having

yet "got round" (in the poverty of their literature) to a full discussion of the subject, are doubtless in some degree to blame. But I fail to understand how any one with a working grasp of their principles can charge them wholesale with subjectivism. I myself have never thought of humanism as being subjectivistic farther than to this extent, that, inasmuch as it treats the thinker as being himself one portion of reality, it must also allow that *some* of the realities that he declares for true are created by his being there. Such realities of course are either acts of his, or relations between other things and him, or relations between things, which, but for him, would never have been traced. Humanists are subjectivistic, also in this, that, unlike rationalists (who think they carry a warrant for the absolute truth of what they now believe in in their present pocket), they hold all present beliefs as subject to revision in the light of future experience. The future experience, however, may be of things outside the thinker; and that this is so the humanist may believe as freely as any other kind of empiricist philosopher.

The critics of humanism (though here I follow them but darkly) appear to object to any infusion whatever of subjectivism into truth. All must be archetypal; every truth must pre-exist to its perception. Humanism sees that an enormous quantity of truth must be written down as having pre-existed to its perception by us humans. In countless instances we find it most satisfactory to believe that, though we were always ignorant of the fact, it always *was* a fact that S was SP. But humanism separates this class of cases from those in which it is more satisfactory to believe the opposite, *e.g.* that S is ephemeral, or P a passing event, or SP created by the perceiving act. Our critics seem on the other hand, to wish to universalise the retrospective type of instance. Reality for them must pre-exist to every assertion for which truth is claimed. And, not content with this overuse of one particular type of judgment, our critics claim its monopoly. They appear to wish to cut off Humanism from its rights to any retrospection at all.

Humanism says that satisfactoriness is what distinguishes the true from the false. But satisfactoriness is both a subjective quality, and a present one. *Ergo* (the critics appear to reason) an object, *quâ* true, must always for humanism be both present and subjective, and a humanist's belief can never be in anything that lives outside of the belief itself or antedates it. Why so preposterous a charge should be so current, I find it hard to say. Nothing is more obvious than the fact that both the objective and the past existence of the object may be the very things about it that most seem satisfactory, and that most invite us to believe them. The past tense can figure in the humanist's world, as well of belief as of representation, quite as harmoniously as in the world of any one else.

Mr. Joseph gives a special turn to this accusation. He charges me (on p. 32) with being self-contradictory when I say that the main categories of thought were evolved in the course of experience itself. For I use these very categories to define the course of experience by. Experience, as I talk about it, is a product of their use; and yet I take it as true anteriorly to them. This seems to Mr. Joseph to be an absurdity. I hope it does not seem such to his readers; for if experiences can suggest hypotheses at all (and they notoriously do so) I can see no absurdity whatever in the notion of a retrospective hypothesis having for its object the very train of experiences by which its own being, along with that of other things, has been brought about. If the hypothesis is 'satisfactory' we must, of course, believe it to have been true anteriorly to its formulation by ourselves. Every explanation of a present by a past seems to involve this kind of circle, which is not a vicious circle. The past is *causa existendi* of the present, which in turn is *causa cognoscendi* of the past. If the present were treated as *causa existendi* of the past, the circle might indeed be vicious.

Closely connected with this pseudo-difficulty is another one of wider scope and greater complication—more excusable therefore—which Mr. Joseph deals with (though in much too pettifogging and logic-chopping a way) on pages 33 and 34 of his article. Humanism, namely, asking how truth in point of fact is reached, and seeing that it is by ever substituting more satisfactory for less satisfactory opinions, is thereby led into a vague historic sketch of truth's development. The earliest 'opinions,' it thinks, must have been dim, unconnected 'feelings,' and only little by little did more and more orderly views of things replace them. Our own retrospective view of this whole evolution is now, let us say, the latest candidate for 'truth' as yet reached in the process. To be a satisfactory candidate, it must give some definite sort of a picture of what forces keep the process going. On the subjective side we have a fairly definite picture—sensation, association, interest, hypothesis, these account in a general way for the growth into a cosmos of the relative chaos with which the mind began.

But on the side of the object, so to call it roughly, our view is much less satisfactory. Of which of our many objects are we to believe that it truly *was* there and at work before the human mind began? Time, space, kind, number, serial order, cause, consciousness, are hard things not to objectify—even transcendental idealism leaves them standing as 'empirically real'. Substance, matter, force, fall down more easily before criticism, and secondary qualities make almost no resistance at all. Nevertheless, when we survey the field of speculation, from Scholasticism through Kantism to Spencerism, we find an ever-recurring tendency to convert the pre-human into a merely logical object, an unknowable *ding-an-sich*, that but starts the process, or a vague *materia prima* that but receives our forms.[1]

The reasons for this are not so much logical as they are material. We can postulate an extra-mental *that* freely enough (though some idealists have denied us the privilege), but when we have done so, the *what* of it is hard to determine satisfactorily, because of the oppositions and entanglements of the variously proposed *whats* with one another and with the history of the human mind. The literature of speculative cosmology bears witness to this difficulty. Humanism suffers from it no more than any other philosophy suffers, but it makes all our cosmogonic theories so unsatisfactory that some thinkers seek relief in the denial of any primal dualism. Absolute Thought or 'pure experience' is postulated, and endowed with attributes calculated to justify the belief that it may 'run itself'. Both these truth-claiming hypotheses are non-dualistic in the old mind-and-matter sense; but the one is monistic and the other pluralistic as to the world process

[1] Compare some elaborate articles by M. Le Roy and M. Wilbois in the *Revue de Métaphysique*, vols. viii., ix. and x.

itself. Some humanists are non-dualists of this sort—I myself am one *und zwar* of the pluralistic brand. But doubtless dualistic humanists also exist, as well as non-dualistic ones of the monistic wing.

Mr. Joseph pins these general philosophic difficulties on humanism alone, or possibly on me alone. My article spoke vaguely of a 'most chaotic pure experience' coming first, and building up the mind. But how can two structureless things interact so as to produce a structure? my critic triumphantly asks. Of course they can't, as purely so-named entities. We must make additional hypotheses. We must beg a minimum of structure for them. The *kind* of minimum that *might* have tended to increase towards what we now find actually developed is the philosophical desideratum here. The question is that of the most materially satisfactory hypothesis. Mr. Joseph handles it by formal logic purely, as if he had no acquaintance with the logic of hypothesis at all.

Mr. Joseph again is much bewildered as to what a humanist can mean when he uses the word knowledge. He tries to convict me (on p. 36) of vaguely identifying it with any kind of good. Knowledge is a difficult thing to define briefly, and Mr. Joseph shows his own constructive hand here even less than in the rest of his article. I have myself put forth on several occasions a radically pragmatist account of knowledge,[1] the existence of which account my critic probably does not know of—so perhaps I had better not say anything about knowledge until he reads and attacks that. I will say, however, that whatever the relation called knowing may itself prove to consist in, I can think of no conceivable kind of *object* which may not become an object of knowledge on humanistic principles as well as on the principles of any other philosophy.[2]

I confess that I am pretty steadily hampered by the habit, on the part of humanism's critics, of assuming that they have

[1] Most recently in two articles, "Does 'Consciousness' Exist?" and "A World of Pure Experience," in the *Journal of Philosophy*, New York, 1st Sept., 29th Sept. and 13th Oct., 1904.
[2] For a recent attempt, effective on the whole, at squaring humanism with knowing, I may refer to Prof. Woodbridge's very able address at the Saint Louis Congress, "The Field of Logic," printed in *Science*, N.Y., 4th November, 1904.

truer ideas than mine of truth and knowledge, the nature of which I must know of and cannot need to have re-defined. I have consequently to reconstruct these ideas in order to carry on the discussion (I have *e.g.* had to do so in some parts of this article) and I thereby expose myself to charges of caricature. In one part of Mr. Joseph's attack, however, I rejoice that we are free from this embarrassment. It is an important point and covers probably a genuine difficulty, so I take it up last.

When, following Schiller and Dewey, I define the true as that which gives the maximal combination of satisfactions, and say that satisfaction is a many-dimensional term that can be realised in various ways, Mr. Joseph replies, rightly enough, that the chief satisfaction of a rational creature must always be his thought that what he believes is *true*, whether the truth brings him the satisfaction of collateral profits or not. This would seem, however, to make of truth the prior concept, and to relegate satisfaction to a secondary place.

Again, if to be satisfactory is what is meant by being true, *whose* satisfactions, and *which* of his satisfactions, are to count? Discriminations notoriously have to be made; and the upshot is that only rational candidates and intellectual satisfactions stand the test. We are thus driven to a purely theoretic notion of truth, and get out of the pragmatic atmosphere altogether. And with this Mr. Joseph leaves us— truth is truth, and there is an end of the matter. But he makes a very pretty show of convicting me of self-stultification in according to our purely theoretic satisfactions any place in the humanistic scheme. They crowd the collateral satisfactions out of house and home, he thinks, and pragmatism has to go into bankruptcy if she recognises them at all.

There is no room for disagreement about the facts here; but the destructive force of the reasoning disappears as soon as we talk concretely instead of abstractly, and ask, in our quality of good pragmatists, just what the famous theoretic needs are known as and in what the intellectual satisfactions consist. Mr. Joseph, faithful to the habits of his party, makes no attempt at characterising them, but assumes that their nature is self-evident to all.

Are they not all mere matters of *consistency*—and emphatically *not* of consistency between an Absolute Reality and the mind's copies of it, but of actually felt consistency among judgments, objects, and manners of reacting, in the mind? And are not both our need of such consistency and our pleasure in it conceivable as outcomes of the natural fact that we are beings that develop mental *habits*—habit itself proving adaptively beneficial in an environment where the same objects, or the same kinds of objects, recur and follow 'law'? If this were so, what would have come first would have been the collateral profits of habit, and the theoretic life would have grown up in aid of these. In point of fact, this seems to have been the probable case. At life's origin, any present perception may have been 'true'—if such a word could then be applicable. Later, when reactions became organised, the reactions became 'true' whenever expectation was fulfilled by them. Otherwise they were 'false' or 'mistaken' reactions. But the same class of objects needs the same kind of reaction, so the impulse to react consistently must gradually have been established, with a disappointment felt whenever the results frustrated expectation. Here is a perfectly plausible germ for all our higher consistencies. Nowadays, if an object claims from us a reaction of the kind habitually accorded only to the opposite class of objects, our mental machinery refuses to run smoothly. The situation is intellectually unsatisfactory. To gain relief we seek either to preserve the reaction by re-interpreting the object, or, leaving the object as it is, we react in a way contrary to the way claimed of us. Neither solution is easy. Such a situation might be that of Mr. Joseph, with me claiming assent to humanism from him. He cannot apperceive it so as to permit him to gratify my claim; but there is enough appeal in the claim to induce him to write a whole article in justification of his refusal. If he should assent to humanism, on the other hand, that would drag after it an unwelcome, yea incredible, alteration of his previous mental beliefs. Whichever alternative he might adopt, however, a new equilibrium of intellectual consistency would in the end be reached. He would feel, whichever way he decided, that he was now thinking truly. But if, with his old habits unaltered, he should simply add to them the new one of advocating humanism quietly or noisily, his mind would be rent into two systems, each of which would accuse the other of false-hood. The resultant situation, being profoundly unsatisfactory, would also be instable.

Theoretic truth is thus no relation between our mind and archetypal reality. It falls *within* the mind, being the accord of some of its processes and objects with other processes and objects—'accord' consisting here in well-definable relations. So long as the satisfaction of feeling such an accord is denied us, whatever collateral profits may seem to inure from what we believe in are but as dust in the balance—provided always that we are highly organised intellectually, which the majority of us are not. The amount of accord which satisfies most men and women is merely the absence of violent clash between their usual thoughts and statements and the limited sphere of sense-perceptions in which their lives are cast. The theoretic truth that most of us think we 'ought' to attain to is thus the possession of a set of predicates that do not contradict their subjects. We preserve it as often as not by leaving other predicates and subjects out.

In some men theory is a passion, just as music is in others. The form of inner consistency is pursued far beyond the line at which collateral profits stop. Such men systematise and classify and schematise and make synoptical tables and invent ideal objects for the pure love of unifying. Too often the results, glowing with 'truth' for the inventors, seem pathetically personal and artificial to bystanders. Which is as much as to say that the purely theoretic criterion of truth can leave us in the lurch as easily as any other criterion.

I think that if Mr. Joseph will but consider all these things a little more concretely, he may find that the humanistic scheme and the notion of theoretic truth fall into line consistently enough to yield him also intellectual satisfaction.

Mind, April 1905

Is Radical Empiricism Solipsistic?

I F ALL the criticisms which the humanistic *Weltanschauung* is receiving were as *sachgemäss* as Mr. Bode's in this JOURNAL for March 2, the truth of the matter would more rapidly clear up. Not only is it excellently well written, but it brings its own point of view out clearly, and admits of a perfectly straight reply.

The argument (unless I fail to catch it) can be expressed as follows:

If a series of experiences be supposed, no one of which is endowed immediately with the self-transcendent function of reference to a reality beyond itself, no motive will occur within the series for supposing anything beyond it to exist. It will remain subjective, and contentedly subjective, both as a whole and in its several parts.

Radical empiricism, trying, as it does, to account for objective knowledge by means of such a series, egregiously fails. It can not explain how the notion of a physical order, as distinguished from a subjectively biographical order, of experiences, ever arose.

It pretends to explain the notion of a physical order, but does so by playing fast and loose with the concept of objective reference. On the one hand, it denies that such reference implies self-transcendency on the part of any one experience; on the other hand, it claims that experiences *point*. But, critically considered, there can be no pointing unless self-transcendency be also allowed. The conjunctive function of pointing, as I have assumed it, is, according to my critic, vitiated by the fallacy of attaching a bilateral relation to a term *a quo*, as if it could stick out substantively and maintain itself in existence in advance of the term *ad quem* which is equally required for it to be a concretely experienced fact. If the relation be made concrete, the term *ad quem* is involved, which would mean (if I succeed in apprehending Mr. Bode rightly) that this latter term, although not empirically there, is yet *noetically* there, in advance—in other words it would mean that any experience that 'points' must already have transcended itself, in the ordinary 'epistemological' sense of the word transcend.

Something like this, if I understand Mr. Bode's text, is the upshot of his state of mind. It is a reasonable sounding state of mind, but it is exactly the state of mind which radical empiricism, by its doctrine of the reality of conjunctive relations, seeks to dispel. I very much fear—so difficult does mutual understanding seem in these exalted regions—that my able critic has failed to understand that doctrine as it is meant to be understood. I suspect that he performs on all these conjunctive relations (of which the aforesaid 'pointing' is only one) the usual rationalistic act of substitution—he takes them not as they are given in their first intention, as parts constitutive of experience's living flow, but only as they appear in retrospect, each fixed as a determinate object of conception, static, therefore, and contained within itself.

Against this rationalistic tendency to treat experience as chopped up into discontinuous static objects, radical empiricism protests. It insists on taking conjunctions at their 'face-value,' just as they come. Consider, for example, such conjunctions as 'and,' 'with,' 'near,' '*plus*,' 'towards.' While we live in such conjunctions our state is one of *transition* in the most literal sense. We are expectant of a 'more' to come, and before the more *has* come, the transition, nevertheless, is directed *towards* it. I fail otherwise to see how, if one kind of more comes, there should be satisfaction and feeling of fulfillment; but disappointment if the more comes in another shape. One more will continue, another more will arrest or deflect the direction, in which our experience is moving even now. We can not, it is true, *name* our different living 'ands' or 'withs' except by naming the different terms towards which they are moving us, but we *live* their specifications and differences before those terms explicitly arrive. Thus, though the various 'ands' are all bilateral relations, each requiring a term *ad quem* to define it when viewed in retrospect and articulately conceived, yet in its living moment any one of them may be treated as if it 'stuck out' from its term *a quo* and pointed in a special direction, much as a compass-needle (to use Mr. Bode's excellent simile) points at the pole, even though it stirs not from its box.

In Professor Höffding's massive little article in a recent

number of this JOURNAL,[1] he quotes a saying of Kierke-gaard's to the effect that we live forwards, but we understand backwards. Understanding backwards is, it must be confessed, a very frequent weakness of philosophers, both of the ratio-nalistic and of the ordinary empiricist type. Radical empiri-cism alone insists on understanding forwards also, and refuses to substitute static concepts of the understanding for transi-tions in our moving life. A logic similar to that which my critic seems to employ here should, it seems to me, forbid him to say that our present is, while present, directed towards our future, or that any physical movement can have direction until its goal is actually reached.

At this point does it not seem as if the quarrel about self-transcendency in knowledge might drop? Is it not a purely verbal dispute? Call it self-transcendency or call it pointing, whichever you like—it makes no difference so long as real transitions towards real goals are admitted as things given *in* experience, and among experience's most indefeasible parts. Radical empiricism, unable to close its eyes to the transitions caught *in actu*, accounts for the self-transcendency or the pointing (whichever you may call it) as a process that occurs within experience, as an empirically mediated thing of which a perfectly definite description can be given. 'Epistemology,' on the other hand, denies this; and pretends that the self-transcendency is unmediated or, if mediated, then mediated in a super-empirical world. To justify this pretension, episte-mology has first to transform all our conjunctions into static objects, and this, I submit, is an absolutely arbitrary act. But in spite of Mr. Bode's maltreatment of conjunctions, as I un-derstand them—and as I understand him—I believe that at bottom we are fighting for nothing different, but are both defending the same continuities of experience in different forms of words.

There are other criticisms in the article in question, but, as this seems the most vital one, I will for the present, at any rate, leave them untouched.

[1] Vol. II., No. 4, pp. 85–92.

The Place of Affectional Facts in a World of Pure Experience

C OMMON SENSE and popular philosophy are as dualistic as it is possible to be. Thoughts, we all naturally think, are made of one kind of substance, and things of another. Consciousness, flowing inside of us in the forms of conception or judgment, or concentrating itself in the shape of passion or emotion, can be directly felt as the spiritual activity which it is, and known in contrast with the space-filling objective 'content' which it envelopes and accompanies. In opposition to this dualistic philosophy, I tried, in a recent article in this JOURNAL,[1] to show that thoughts and things are absolutely homogeneous as to their material, and that their opposition is only one of relation and of function. There is no thought-stuff different from thing-stuff, I said; but the same identical piece of 'pure experience' (which was the name I gave to the *materia prima* of everything) can stand alternately for a 'fact of consciousness' or for a physical reality, according as it is taken in one context or in another. For the right understanding of what follows, I shall have to presuppose that the reader will have read that earlier article.[2]

The commonest objection which the doctrine there laid down runs up against is drawn from the existence of our 'affections.' In our pleasures and pains, our loves and fears and angers, in the beauty, comicality, importance or preciousness of certain objects and situations, we have, I am told by many critics, a great realm of experience intuitively recognized as spiritual, made, and felt to be made, of consciousness exclusively, and different in nature from the space-filling kind of being which is enjoyed by physical objects. In Section VII. of that earlier article, I treated of this class of experiences very inadequately, because I had to be so brief. I now return to the subject, because I believe that, so far from invalidating my

[1] 'Does Consciousness Exist?' Vol. I., p. 477.
[2] It will be still better if he shall have also read the article entitled 'A World of Pure Experience,' which follows that one and develops its ideas still farther. See this JOURNAL, Vol. I., pp. 533, 561.

general thesis, these phenomena, when properly analyzed, afford it powerful support.

The central point of the pure-experience theory is that 'outer' and 'inner' are names for two groups into which we sort experiences according to the way in which they act upon their neighbors. Any one 'content,' such as *hard*, let us say, can be assigned to either group. In the outer group it is 'strong,' it acts 'energetically' and aggressively. Here whatever is hard interferes with the space its neighbors occupy. It dents them; is impenetrable by them; and we call the hardness then a physical hardness. In the mind, on the contrary, the hard thing is nowhere in particular, it dents nothing, it suffuses through its mental neighbors, as it were, and interpenetrates them. Taken in this group we call both it and them 'ideas' or 'sensations'; and the basis of the two groups respectively is the different type of interrelation, the mutual impenetrability, on the one hand, and the lack of physical interference and interaction, on the other.

That what in itself is one and the same entity should be able to function thus differently in different contexts is a natural consequence of the extremely complex reticulations in which our experiences come. To her offspring a tigress is tender, but cruel to every other living thing—both cruel and tender, therefore, at once. A mass in movement resists every force that operates contrariwise to its own direction, but to forces that pursue the same direction, or come in at right angles, it is absolutely inert. It is thus both energetic and inert; and the same is true (if you vary the associates properly) of every other piece of experience. It is only towards certain specific groups of associates that the physical energies, as we call them, of a content are put forth. In another group it may be quite inert.

It is possible to imagine a universe of experiences in which the only alternative between neighbors would be either physical interaction or complete inertness. In such a world the mental or the physical *status* of any piece of experience would be unequivocal. When active, it would figure in the physical, and when inactive, in the mental group.

But the universe we live in is more chaotic than this, and there is room in it for the hybrid or ambiguous group of our affectional experiences, of our emotions and appreciative perceptions. In the paragraphs that follow I shall try to show:

(1) That the popular notion that these experiences are intuitively given as purely inner facts is hasty and erroneous; and

(2) That their ambiguity illustrates beautifully my central thesis that subjectivity and objectivity are affairs not of what an experience is aboriginally made of, but of its classification. Classifications depend on our temporary purposes. For certain purposes it is convenient to take things in one set of relations, for other purposes in another set. In the two cases their contexts are apt to be different. In the case of our affectional experiences we have no permanent and steadfast purpose that obliges us to be consistent, so we find it easy to let them float ambiguously, sometimes classing them with our feelings, sometimes with more physical realities, according to caprice or to the convenience of the moment. Thus would these experiences, so far from being an obstacle to the pure-experience philosophy, serve as an excellent corroboration of its truth.

First of all, then, it is a mistake to say, with the objectors whom I began by citing, that anger, love and fear are affections purely of the mind. That, to a great extent at any rate, they are simultaneously affections of the body is proved by the whole literature of the James-Lange theory of emotion. All our pains, moreover, are local, and we are always free to speak of them in objective as well as in subjective terms. We can say that we are aware of a painful place, filling a certain bigness in our organism, or we can say that we are inwardly in a 'state' of pain. All our adjectives of worth are similarly ambiguous—I instanced some of the ambiguities on page 490 of the former article. Is the preciousness of a diamond a quality of the gem? or is it a feeling in our mind? Practically we treat it as both or as either, according to the temporary direction of our thought. 'Beauty,' says Professor Santayana, 'is pleasure objectified'; and in Sections 10 and 11 of his work, 'The Sense of Beauty,' he treats in a masterly way of this equivocal realm. The various pleasures we receive from an object may count as 'feelings' when we take them singly, but when they combine in a total richness, we call the result the 'beauty' of the object, and treat it as an outer attribute which our mind perceives. We discover beauty just as we discover the physical properties of things. Training is needed to make us expert in either line. Single sensations also may be ambiguous. Shall we say an 'agreeable degree of heat,' or an 'agreeable feeling' occasioned by the degree of heat? Either will do; and language would lose most of its esthetic and rhetorical value were we forbidden to project words primarily connoting our affections upon the objects by which the affections are aroused. The man is really hateful; the action really mean; the situation really tragic—all in themselves and quite apart from our opinion. We even go so far as to talk of a weary road, a giddy height, a jocund morning or a sullen sky; and the term 'indefinite' while usually applied only to our apprehensions, functions as a fundamental physical qualification of things in Spencer's 'law of evolution,' and doubtless passes with most readers for all right.

Psychologists, studying our perceptions of movement, have unearthed experiences in which movement is felt in general but not ascribed correctly to the body that really moves. Thus in optical vertigo, caused by unconscious movements of our eyes, both we and the external universe appear to be in a whirl. When clouds float by the moon, it is as if both clouds and moon and we ourselves shared in the motion. In the extraordinary case of amnesia of the Rev. Mr. Hanna, published by Sidis and Goodhart in their important work on 'Multiple Personality' (New York: Appleton, 1905) we read that when the patient first recovered consciousness and "noticed an attendant walk across the room, he identified the movement with his own. He did not yet discriminate between his own movements and those outside himself" (p. 102). Such experiences point to a primitive stage of perception in which discriminations afterwards needful have not yet been made. A piece of experience of a determinate sort is there, but there at first as a 'pure' fact. Motion originally simply *is*; only later is it confined to this thing or to that. Something like this is true of every experience, however complex, at the moment of its actual presence. Let the reader arrest himself in the act of reading this article now. *Now* this is a pure experience, a phenomenon, or datum, a mere *that* or content of fact. *'Reading'*

simply is, is there; and whether there for some one's consciousness, or there for physical nature, is a question not yet put.
At the moment, it is there for neither; later we shall probably
judge it to have been there for both.

With the affectional experiences which we are considering,
the relatively 'pure' condition lasts. In practical life no urgent
need has yet arisen for deciding whether to treat them as rigorously mental or as rigorously physical facts. So they remain
equivocal; and, as the world goes, their equivocality is one of
their great conveniences.

The shifting place of 'secondary qualities' in the history of
philosophy is another excellent proof of the fact that 'inner'
and 'outer' are not coefficients with which experiences come
to us aboriginally stamped, but are rather results of a later
classification performed by us for particular needs. The common-sense stage of thought is a perfectly definite practical
halting-place, the place where we ourselves can proceed to act
unhesitatingly. On this stage of thought things act on each
other as well as on us by means of their secondary qualities.
Sound, as such, goes through the air and can be intercepted.
The heat of the fire passes over, as such, into the water which
it sets a-boiling. It is the very light of the arc-lamp which
displaces the darkness of the midnight street, etc. By engendering and translocating just these qualities, actively efficacious as they seem to be, we ourselves succeed in altering
nature so as to suit us; and until more purely intellectual, as
distinguished from practical, needs had arisen, no one ever
thought of calling these qualities subjective. When, however,
Galileo, Descartes, and others found it best for philosophic
purposes to class sound, heat and light along with pain and
pleasure as purely mental phenomena, they could do so with
impunity.

Even the primary qualities are undergoing the same fate.
Hardness and softness are effects on us of atomic interactions,
and the atoms themselves are neither hard nor soft, nor solid
nor liquid. Size and shape are deemed subjective by Kantians;
time itself is subjective according to many philosophers; and
even the activity and causal efficacy which lingered in physics
long after secondary qualities were banished are now treated
as illusory projections outwards of phenomena of our own

consciousness. There are no activities or effects in nature, for the most intellectual contemporary school of physical speculation. Nature exhibits only *changes*, which habitually coincide with one another so that their habits are describable in simple 'laws.'

There is no original spirituality or materiality of being, intuitively discerned, then; but only a translocation of experiences from one world to another; a grouping of them with one set or another of associates for definitely practical or intellectual ends.

I will say nothing here of the persistent ambiguity of *relations*. They are undeniable parts of pure experience; yet, while common sense and what I call radical empiricism stand for their being objective, both rationalism and the usual empiricism claim that they are exclusively the 'work of the mind'—the finite mind or the absolute mind, as the case may be.

Turn now to those affective phenomena which more directly concern us.

We soon learn to separate the ways in which things appeal to our interests and emotions from the ways in which they act upon one another. It does not *work* to assume that physical objects are going to act on one another by their sympathetic or antipathetic qualities. The beauty of a thing or its value is no force that can be plotted in a polygon of compositions, nor does its 'use' or 'significance' affect in the minutest degree its vicissitudes or destiny at the hands of physical nature. Chemical 'affinities' are a purely verbal metaphor; and, as I just said, even such things as forces, tensions and activities can at a pinch be regarded as anthropomorphic projections. So far, then, as the physical world means the collection of contents that determine in each other certain regular changes, the whole collection of our appreciative attributes has to be treated as falling outside of it. If we mean by physical nature whatever lies beyond the surface of our bodies, these attributes are inert throughout the whole extent of physical nature.

Why then do men leave them as ambiguous as they do, and not class them decisively as purely spiritual?

The reason would seem to be that, although they are inert as regards the rest of physical nature, they are not inert as regards that part of physical nature which our own skin covers. It is those very appreciative attributes of things, their dangerousness, beauty, rarity, utility, etc., that primarily appeal to our attention. In our commerce with nature these attributes are what give *emphasis* to objects; and for an object to be emphatic, whatever spiritual fact it may mean, means also that it produces immediate bodily effects upon us, alterations of tone and tension, of heart-beat and breathing, of vascular and visceral action. The 'interesting' aspects of things are thus not wholly inert physically, though they be active only in these small corners of physical nature which our bodies occupy. That, however, is enough to save them from being classed as absolutely non-objective.

The attempt, if any one should make it, to sort experiences into two absolutely discrete groups, with nothing but inertness in one of them and nothing but activities in the other, would thus receive one check. It would receive another as soon as we examined the more distinctively mental group; for though in that group it be true that things do not act on one another by their physical properties, do not dent each other or set fire to each other, they yet act on each other in the most energetic way by those very characters which are so inert extracorporeally. It is by the interest and importance that experiences have for us, by the emotions they excite, and the purposes they subserve, by their affective values, in short, that their consecution in our several conscious streams, as 'thoughts' of ours, is mainly ruled. Desire introduces them; interest holds them; fitness fixes their order and connection. I need only refer for this aspect of our mental life, to Wundt's article 'Ueber psychische Causalität,' which begins Volume X. of his *Philosophische Studien*.[1]

It thus appears that the ambiguous or amphibious *status* which we find our epithets of value occupying is the most natural thing in the world. It would, however, be an unnat-

---

[1] It is enough for my present purpose if the appreciative characters but *seem* to act thus. Believers in an activity *an sich*, other than our mental experiences of activity, will find some farther reflections on the subject in my address on 'The Experience of Activity' in the *Psychological Review* for January, 1905.

ural status if the popular opinion which I cited at the outset were correct. If 'physical' and 'mental' meant two different kinds of intrinsic nature, immediately, intuitively, and infallibly discernible, and each fixed forever in whatever bit of experience it qualified, one does not see how there could ever have arisen any room for doubt or ambiguity. But if, on the contrary, these words are words of sorting, ambiguity is natural. For then, as soon as the relations of a thing are sufficiently various it can be sorted variously. Take a mass of carrion, for example, and the 'disgustingness' which for us is part of the experience. The sun caresses it, and the zephyr wooes it as if it were a bed of roses. So the disgustingness fails to *operate* within the realm of suns and breezes,—it does not function as a physical quality. But the carrion 'turns our stomach' by what seems a direct operation—it *does* function physically, therefore, in that limited part of physics. We can treat it as physical or as non-physical, as a mass or as a perception, according as we take it in the narrower or in the wider context, and conversely, of course, we must treat it as non-mental or as mental.

Our body itself is the palmary instance of the ambiguous. Sometimes I treat my body purely as a part of outer nature. Sometimes, again, I think of it as 'mine,' I sort it with the 'me,' and then certain local changes and determinations in it pass for spiritual happenings. Its breathing is my 'thinking,' its sensorial adjustments are my 'attention,' its kinesthetic alterations are my 'efforts,' its visceral perturbations are my 'emotions.' The obstinate controversies that have arisen over such statements as these (which sound so paradoxical, and which can yet be made so seriously) prove how hard it is to decide by bare introspection what it is in experiences that shall make them either spiritual or material. It surely can be nothing intrinsic in the individual experiences. It is their way of behaving towards each other, their system of relations, their function; and all these things vary with the context in which we find it opportune to consider them.

I think I may conclude, then (and I hope that my readers are now ready to conclude with me), that the pretended spirituality of our emotions and of our attributes of value, so far from proving an objection to the philosophy of pure experience, does, when rightly discussed and accounted for, serve as one of its best corroborations.

The Journal of Philosophy, Psychology and Scientific Methods,
May 25, 1905

On Some Mental Effects of the Earthquake

WHEN I DEPARTED from Harvard for Stanford University last December, almost the last good-by I got was that of my old Californian friend B.: "I hope they'll give you a touch of earthquake while you're there, so that you may also become acquainted with *that* Californian institution."

Accordingly, when, lying awake at about half past five on the morning of April 18th in my little "flat" on the campus of Stanford, I felt the bed begin to waggle, my first consciousness was one of gleeful recognition of the nature of the movement. "By Jove," I said to myself, "here's B.'s old earthquake, after all!" And then, as it went *crescendo*, "And a jolly good one it is, too!" I said.

Sitting up involuntarily, and taking a kneeling position, I was thrown down on my face as it went *fortior* shaking the room exactly as a terrier shakes a rat. Then everything that was on anything else slid off to the floor, over went bureau and chiffonier with a crash, as the *fortissimo* was reached, plaster cracked, an awful roaring noise seemed to fill the outer air, and in an instant all was still again, save the soft babble of human voices from far and near that soon began to make itself heard, as the inhabitants in costumes *negligés* in various degrees sought the greater safety of the street and yielded to the passionate desire for sympathetic communication.

The thing was over, as I understand the Lick Observatory to have declared, in forty-eight seconds. To me it felt as if about that length of time, although I have heard others say that it seemed to them longer. In my case, sensation and emotion were so strong that little thought, and no reflection or volition, were possible in the short time consumed by the phenomenon.

The emotion consisted wholly of glee and admiration; glee at the vividness which such an abstract idea or verbal term as "earthquake" could put on when translated into sensible reality and verified concretely; and admiration at the way in which the frail little wooden house could hold itself together in spite of such a shaking. I felt no trace whatever of fear; it was pure delight and welcome.

"*Go* it," I almost cried aloud, "and go it *stronger!*"

I ran into my wife's room, and found that she, although awakened from sound sleep, had felt no fear, either. Of all the persons whom I later interrogated, very few had felt any fear while the shaking lasted, although many had had a "turn," as they realized their narrow escapes from bookcases or bricks from chimney-breasts falling on their beds and pillows an instant after they had left them.

As soon as I could think, I discerned retrospectively certain peculiar ways in which my consciousness had taken in the phenomenon. These ways were quite spontaneous, and, so to speak, inevitable and irresistible.

First, I personified the earthquake as a permanent individual entity. It was *the* earthquake of my friend B.'s augury, which had been lying low and holding itself back during all the intervening months, in order, on that lustrous April morning, to invade my room, and energize the more intensely and triumphantly. It came, moreover, directly to *me*. It stole in behind my back, and once inside the room, had me all to itself, and could manifest itself convincingly. Animus and intent were never more present in any human action, nor did any human activity ever more definitely point back to a living agent as its source and origin.

All whom I consulted on the point agreed as to this feature in their experience. "It expressed intention," "It was vicious," "It was bent on destruction," "It wanted to show its power," or what not. To me, it wanted simply to manifest the full meaning of its *name*. But what was this "It"? To some, apparently, a vague demonic power; to me an individualized being, B.'s earthquake, namely.

One informant interpreted it as the end of the world and the beginning of the final judgment. This was a lady in a San Francisco hotel, who did not think of its being an earthquake till after she had got into the street and some one had explained it to her. She told me that the theological interpretation had kept fear from her mind, and made her take the shaking calmly. For "science," when the tensions in the earth's crust reach the breaking-point, and strata fall into an altered equilibrium, earthquake is simply the collective *name* of all the cracks and shakings and disturbances that happen. They *are* the earthquake. But for me *the* earthquake was the *cause* of the disturbances, and the perception of it as a living agent was irresistible. It had an overpowering dramatic convincingness.

I realize now better than ever how inevitable were men's earlier mythologic versions of such catastrophes, and how artificial and against the grain of our spontaneous perceiving are the later habits into which science educates us. It was simply impossible for untutored men to take earthquakes into their minds as anything but supernatural warnings or retributions.

A good instance of the way in which the tremendousness of a catastrophe may banish fear was given me by a Stanford student. He was in the fourth story of Encina Hall, an immense stone dormitory building. Awakened from sleep, he recognized what the disturbance was, and sprang from the bed, but was thrown off his feet in a moment, while his books and furniture fell round him. Then, with an awful, sinister, grinding roar, everything gave way, and with chimneys, floor-beams, walls and all, he descended through the three lower stories of the building into the basement. "This is my end, this is my death," he felt; but all the while no trace of fear. The experience was too overwhelming for anything but passive surrender to it. (Certain heavy chimneys had fallen in, carrying the whole center of the building with them.)

Arrived at the bottom, he found himself with rafters and débris round him, but not pinned in or crushed. He saw daylight, and crept toward it through the obstacles. Then, realizing that he was in his nightgown, and feeling no pain anywhere, his first thought was to get back to his room and find some more presentable clothing. The stairways at Encina Hall are at the ends of the building. He made his way to one of them, and went up the four flights, only to find his room no longer extant. Then he noticed pain in his feet, which had been injured, and came down the stairs with difficulty. When he talked with me ten days later he had been in hospital a week, was very thin and pale, and went on crutches, and was dressed in borrowed clothing.

So much for Stanford, where all our experiences seem to have been very similar. Nearly all our chimneys went down, some of them disintegrating from top to bottom; parlor floors were covered with bricks; plaster strewed the floors; furniture was everywhere upset and dislocated; but the wooden dwellings sprang back to their original position, and in house after house not a window stuck or a door scraped at top or bottom. Wood architecture was triumphant! Everybody was excited, but the excitement at first, at any rate, seemed to be almost joyous. Here at last was a *real* earthquake after so many years of harmless waggle! Above all, there was an irresistible desire to talk about it, and exchange experiences.

Most people slept outdoors for several subsequent nights, partly to be safer in case of a recurrence, but also to work off their emotion, and get the full unusualness out of the experience. The vocal babble of early-waking girls and boys from the gardens of the campus, mingling with the birds' songs and the exquisite weather, was for three or four days a delightful sunrise phenomenon.

Now turn to San Francisco, thirty-five miles distant, from which an automobile ere long brought us the dire news of a city in ruins, with fires beginning at various points, and the water-supply interrupted. I was fortunate enough to board the only train of cars—a very small one—that got up to the city; fortunate enough also to escape in the evening by the only train that left it. This gave me and my valiant feminine escort some four hours of observation. My business is with "subjective" phenomena exclusively; so I will say nothing of the material ruin that greeted us on every hand—the daily papers and the weekly journals have done full justice to that topic. By midday, when we reached the city, the pall of smoke was vast and the dynamite detonations had begun, but the troops, the police and the firemen seemed to have established order, dangerous neighborhoods were roped off everywhere and picketed, saloons closed, vehicles impressed, and every one at work who *could* work.

It was indeed a strange sight to see an entire population in the streets, busy as ants in an uncovered ant-hill scurrying to save their eggs and larvæ. Every horse, and everything on wheels in the city, from hucksters' wagons to automobiles, was being loaded with what effects could be scraped together from houses which the advancing flames were threatening.

The sidewalks were covered with well-dressed men and women, carrying baskets, bundles, valises, or dragging trunks to spots of greater temporary safety, soon to be dragged farther, as the fire kept spreading!

In the safer quarters, every door-step was covered with the dwelling's tenants, sitting surrounded with their more indispensable chattels, and ready to flee at a minute's notice. I think every one must have fasted on that day, for I saw no one eating. There was no appearance of general dismay, and little of chatter or of incoördinated excitement.

Every one seemed doggedly bent on achieving the job which he had set himself to perform; and the faces, although somewhat tense and set and grave, were inexpressive of emotion. I noticed only three persons overcome, two Italian women, very poor, embracing an aged fellow countrywoman, and all weeping. Physical fatigue and *seriousness* were the only inner states that one could read on countenances.

With lights forbidden in the houses, and the streets lighted only by the conflagration, it was apprehended that the criminals of San Francisco would hold high carnival on the ensuing night. But whether they feared the disciplinary methods of the United States troops, who were visible everywhere, or whether they were themselves solemnized by the immensity of the disaster, they lay low and did not "manifest," either then or subsequently.

The only very discreditable thing to human nature that occurred was later, when hundreds of lazy "bummers" found that they could keep camping in the parks, and make alimentary storage-batteries of their stomachs, even in some cases getting enough of the free rations in their huts or tents to last them well into the summer. This charm of pauperized vagabondage seems all along to have been Satan's most serious bait to human nature. There was theft from the outset, but confined, I believe, to petty pilfering.

Cash in hand was the only money, and millionaires and their families were no better off in this respect than any one. Whoever got a vehicle could have the use of it; but the richest often went without, and spent the first two nights on rugs on the bare ground, with nothing but what their own arms had rescued. Fortunately, those nights were dry and comparatively

warm, and Californians are accustomed to camping conditions in the summer, so suffering from exposure was less great
than it would have been elsewhere. By the fourth night,
which was rainy, tents and huts had brought most campers
under cover.

I went through the city again eight days later. The fire was
out, and about a quarter of the area stood unconsumed. Intact sky-scrapers dominated the smoking level majestically and
superbly—they and a few walls that had survived the overthrow. Thus has the courage of our architects and builders
received triumphant vindication!

The inert elements of the population had mostly got away,
and those that remained seemed what Mr. H. G. Wells calls
"efficients." Sheds were already going up as temporary start-
ing-points of business. Every one looked cheerful, in spite of
the awful discontinuity of past and future, with every familiar
association with material things dissevered; and the discipline
and order were practically perfect.

As these notes of mine must be short, I had better turn to
my more generalized reflections.

Two things in retrospect strike me especially, and are the
most emphatic of all my impressions. Both are reassuring as
to human nature.

The first of these was the rapidity of the improvisation of
order out of chaos. It is clear that just as in every thousand
human beings there will be statistically so many artists, so
many athletes, so many thinkers, and so many potentially
good soldiers, so there will be so many potential organizers
in times of emergency. In point of fact, not only in the great
city, but in the outlying towns, these natural order-makers,
whether amateurs or officials, came to the front immediately.
There seemed to be no possibility which there was not some
one there to think of, or which within twenty-four hours was
not in some way provided for.

A good illustration is this: Mr. Keith is the great landscape-
painter of the Pacific slope, and his pictures, which are many,
are artistically and pecuniarily precious. Two citizens, lovers
of his work, early in the day diverted their attention from all
other interests, their own private ones included, and made it
their duty to visit every place which they knew to contain a

Keith painting. They cut them from their frames, rolled them up, and in this way got all the more important ones into a place of safety.

When they then sought Mr. Keith, to convey the joyous news to him, they found him still in his studio, which was remote from the fire, beginning a new painting. Having given up his previous work for lost, he had resolved to lose no time in making what amends he could for the disaster.

The completeness of organization at Palo Alto, a town of ten thousand inhabitants close to Stanford University, was almost comical. People feared exodus on a large scale of the rowdy elements of San Francisco. In point of fact, very few refugees came to Palo Alto. But within twenty-four hours, rations, clothing, hospital, quarantine, disinfection, washing, police, military, quarters in camp and in houses, printed information, employment, all were provided for under the care of so many volunteer committees.

Much of this readiness was American, much of it Californian; but I believe that every country in a similar crisis would have displayed it in a way to astonish the spectators. Like soldiering, it lies always latent in human nature.

The second thing that struck me was the universal equanimity. We soon got letters from the East, ringing with anxiety and pathos; but I now know fully what I have always believed, that the pathetic way of feeling great disasters belongs rather to the point of view of people at a distance than to the immediate victims. I heard not a single really pathetic or sentimental word in California expressed by any one.

The terms "awful," "dreadful" fell often enough from people's lips, but always with a sort of abstract meaning, and with a face that seemed to admire the vastness of the catastrophe as much as it bewailed its cuttingness. When talk was not directly practical, I might almost say that it expressed (at any rate in the nine days I was there) a tendency more toward nervous excitement than toward grief. The hearts concealed private bitterness enough, no doubt, but the tongues disdained to dwell on the misfortunes of self, when almost everybody one spoke to had suffered equally.

Surely the cutting edge of all our usual misfortunes comes from their character of loneliness. We lose our health, our wife or children die, our house burns down, or our money is made way with, and the world goes on rejoicing, leaving us on one side and counting us out from all its business. In California every one, to some degree, was suffering, and one's private miseries were merged in the vast general sum of privation and in the all-absorbing practical problem of general recuperation. The cheerfulness, or, at any rate, the steadfastness of tone, was universal. Not a single whine or plaintive word did I hear from the hundred losers whom I spoke to. Instead of that there was a temper of helpfulness beyond the counting.

It is easy to glorify this as something characteristically American, or especially Californian. Californian education has, of course, made the thought of all possible recuperations easy. In an exhausted country, with no marginal resources, the outlook on the future would be much darker. But I like to think that what I write of is a normal and universal trait of human nature. In our drawing-rooms and offices we wonder how people ever *do* go through battles, sieges and shipwrecks. We quiver and sicken in imagination, and think those heroes superhuman. Physical pain, whether suffered alone or in company, is always more or less unnerving and intolerable. But mental pathos and anguish, I fancy, are usually effects of distance. At the place of action, where all are concerned together, healthy animal insensibility and heartiness take their place. At San Francisco the need will continue to be awful, and there will doubtless be a crop of nervous wrecks before the weeks and months are over, but meanwhile the commonest men, simply because they *are* men, will go on, singly and collectively, showing this admirable fortitude of temper.

The Youth's Companion, June 7, 1906

The Energies of Men[1]

W E HABITUALLY hear much nowadays of the difference between structural and functional psychology. I am not sure that I understand the difference, but it probably has something to do with what I have privately been accustomed to distinguish as the analytical and the clinical points of view in psychological observation. Professor Sanford, in a recently published "Sketch of a Beginner's Course in Psychology," recommended "the physician's attitude" in that subject as the thing the teacher should first of all try to impart to the pupil. I fancy that few of you can have read Professor Pierre Janet's masterly works in mental pathology without being struck by the little use he makes of the machinery usually relied on by psychologists, and by his own reliance on conceptions which in the laboratories and in scientific publications we never hear of at all.

Discriminations and associations, the rise and fall of thresholds, impulses and inhibitions, fatigue,—these are the terms into which our inner life is analyzed by psychologists who are not doctors, and in which, by hook or crook, its aberrations from normality have to be expressed. They can indeed be described, after the fact, in such terms, but always lamely; and everyone must feel how much is unaccounted for, how much left out.

When we turn to Janet's pages, we find entirely other forms of thought employed. Oscillations of the level of mental energy, differences of tension, splittings of consciousness, sentiments of insufficiency and of unreality, substitutions, agitations and anxieties, depersonalizations—such are the elementary conceptions which the total view of his patient's life imposes on this clinical observer. They have little or nothing to do with the usual laboratory categories. Ask a scientific psychologist to predict what symptoms a patient must have when his 'supply of mental energy' diminishes, and he can utter only the word 'fatigue.' He could never predict such consequences as Janet subsumes under his one term 'psych-

[1]Delivered as the Presidential Address before the American Philosophical Association at Columbia University, December 28, 1906.

asthenia'—the most bizarre obsessions and agitations, the most complete distortions of the relation between the self and the world.

I do not vouch for Janet's conceptions being valid, and I do not say that the two ways of looking at the mind contradict each other or are mutually incongruous; I simply say that they are incongru*ent*. Each covers so little of our total mental life that they do not even interfere or jostle. Meanwhile the clinical conceptions, though they may be vaguer than the analytic ones, are certainly more adequate, give the concreter picture of the way the whole mind works, and are of far more urgent practical importance. So the 'physician's attitude,' the 'functional psychology,' is assuredly the thing most worthy of general study to-day.

I wish to spend this hour on one conception of functional psychology, a conception never once mentioned or heard of in laboratory circles, but used perhaps more than any other by common, practical men—I mean the conception of the *amount of energy available* for running one's mental and moral operations by. Practically every one knows in his own person the difference between the days when the tide of this energy is high in him and those when it is low, though no one knows exactly what reality the term energy covers when used here, or what its tides, tensions, and levels are in themselves. This vagueness is probably the reason why our scientific psychologists ignore the conception altogether. It undoubtedly connects itself with the energies of the nervous system, but it presents fluctuations that cannot easily be translated into neural terms. It offers itself as the notion of a quantity, but its ebbs and floods produce extraordinary qualitative results. To have its level raised is the most important thing that can happen to a man, yet in all my reading I know of no single page or paragraph of a scientific psychology book in which it receives mention—the psychologists have left it to be treated by the moralists and mind-curers and doctors exclusively.

Every one is familiar with the phenomenon of feeling more or less alive on different days. Every one knows on any given day that there are energies slumbering in him which the incitements of that day do not call forth, but which he might display if these were greater. Most of us feel as if we lived habitually with a sort of cloud weighing on us, below our highest notch of clearness in discernment, sureness in reasoning, or firmness in deciding. Compared with what we ought to be, we are only half-awake. Our fires are damped, our drafts are checked. We are making use of only a small part of our possible mental and physical resources. In some persons this sense of being cut off from their rightful resources is extreme, and we then get the formidable neurasthenic and psychasthenic conditions, with life grown into one tissue of impossibilities, that the medical books describe.

Part of the imperfect vitality under which we labor can be explained by scientific psychology. It is the result of the inhibition exerted by one part of our ideas on other parts. Conscience makes cowards of us all. Social conventions prevent us from telling the truth after the fashion of the heroes and heroines of Bernard Shaw. Our scientific respectability keeps us from exercising the mystical portions of our nature freely. If we are doctors, our mind-cure sympathies, if we are mind-curists, our medical sympathies are tied up. We all know persons who are models of excellence, but who belong to the extreme philistine type of mind. So deadly is their intellectual respectability that we can't converse about certain subjects at all, can't let our minds play over them, can't even mention them in their presence. I have numbered among my dearest friends persons thus inhibited intellectually, with whom I would gladly have been able to talk freely about certain interests of mine, certain authors, say, as Bernard Shaw, Chesterton, Edward Carpenter, H. G. Wells, but it wouldn't do, it made them too uncomfortable, they wouldn't play, I had to be silent. An intellect thus tied down by literality and decorum makes on one the same sort of impression that an able-bodied man would who should habituate himself to do his work with only one of his fingers, locking up the rest of his organism and leaving it unused.

In few of us are functions not tied-up by the exercise of other functions. G. T. Fechner is an extraordinary exception that proves the rule. He could use his mystical faculties while being scientific. He could be both critically keen and devout. Few scientific men can pray, I imagine. Few can carry on any living commerce with 'God.' Yet many of us are well aware how much freer in many directions and abler our lives would be, were such important forms of energizing not sealed up. There are in everyone potential forms of activity that actually are shunted out from use.

The existence of reservoirs of energy that habitually are not tapped is most familiar to us in the phenomenon of 'second wind.' Ordinarily we stop when we meet the first effective layer, so to call it, of fatigue. We have then walked, played, or worked 'enough,' and desist. That amount of fatigue is an efficacious obstruction, on this side of which our usual life is cast. But if an unusual necessity forces us to press onward, a surprising thing occurs. The fatigue gets worse up to a certain critical point, when gradually or suddenly it passes away, and we are fresher than before. We have evidently tapped a level of new energy, masked until then by the fatigue-obstacle usually obeyed. There may be layer after layer of this experience. A third and a fourth 'wind' may supervene. Mental activity shows the phenomenon as well as physical, and in exceptional cases we may find, beyond the very extremity of fatigue distress, amounts of ease and power that we never dreamed ourselves to own, sources of strength habitually not taxed at all, because habitually we never push through the obstruction, never pass those early critical points.

When we do pass, what makes us do so?

Either some unusual stimulus fills us with emotional excitement, or some unusual idea of necessity induces us to make an extra effort of will. *Excitements, ideas, and efforts*, in a word, are what carry us over the dam.

In those hyperesthetic conditions which chronic invalidism so often brings in its train, the dam has changed its normal place. The pain-threshold is abnormally near. The slightest functional exercise gives a distress which the patient yields to and stops. In such cases of 'habit-neurosis' a new range of power often comes in consequence of the bullying-treatment, of efforts which the doctor obliges the patient, against his will, to make. First comes the very extremity of distress, then follows unexpected relief. There seems no doubt that we are each and all of us to some extent victims of habit-neurosis.

We have to admit the wider potential range and the habitually narrow actual use. We live subject to inhibition by degrees of fatigue which we have come only from habit to obey. Most of us may learn to push the barrier farther off, and to live in perfect comfort on much higher levels of power.

Country people and city people, as a class, illustrate this difference. The rapid rate of life, the number of decisions in an hour, the many things to keep account of, in a busy city-man's or woman's life, seem monstrous to a country-brother. He doesn't see how we live at all. But settle him in town; and in a year or two, if not too old, he will have trained himself to keep the pace as well as any of us, getting more out of himself in any week than he ever did in ten weeks at home. The physiologists show how one can be in nutritive equilib-rium, neither losing nor gaining weight, on astonishingly dif-ferent quantities of food. So one can be in what I might call 'efficiency-equilibrium' (neither gaining nor losing power when once the equilibrium is reached), on astonishingly dif-ferent quantities of work, no matter in what dimension the work may be measured. It may be physical work, intellectual work, moral work, or spiritual work.

Of course there are limits: the trees don't grow into the sky. But the plain fact remains that men the world over pos-sess amounts of resource, which only very exceptional individ-uals push to their extremes of use.

The excitements that carry us over the usually effective dam are most often the classic emotional ones, love, anger, crowd-contagion, or despair. Life's vicissitudes bring them in abun-dance. A new position of responsibility, if it do not crush a man, will often, nay, one may say, will usually, show him to be a far stronger creature than was supposed. Even here we are witnessing (some of us admiring, some deploring—I must class myself as admiring) the dynamogenic effects of a very exalted political office upon the energies of an individual who had already manifested a healthy amount of energy be-fore the office came.

Mr. Sydney Olivier has given us a fine fable of the dyna-mogenic effects of love in a fine story called "The Empire Builder," in the *Contemporary Review* for May, 1905. A young naval officer falls in love at sight with a missionary's daughter on a lost island, which his ship accidentally touches. From that day onward he must see her again; and he so moves Heaven and earth and the Colonial Office and the Admiralty to get sent there once more, that the island finally is annexed to the empire in consequence of the various fusses he is led to make. People must have been appalled lately in San Francisco to find the stores of bottled up energy and endurance they possessed.

Wars, of course, and shipwrecks, are the great revealers of what men and women are able to do and bear. Cromwell's and Grant's careers are the stock examples of how war will wake a man up. I owe to Professor Norton's kindness the permission to read to you part of a letter from Colonel Baird-Smith, written shortly after the six weeks' siege of Delhi in 1857, for the victorious issue of which that excellent officer was chiefly to be thanked. He writes as follows:—

. . . "My poor wife had some reason to think that war and disease between them had left very little of a husband to take under nursing when she got him again. An attack of camp-scurvy had filled my mouth with sores, shaken every joint in my body, and covered me all over with sores and livid spots so that I was marvellously unlovely to look upon. A smart knock on the ankle-joint from the splinter of a shell that burst in my face, in itself a mere bagatelle of a wound, had been of necessity neglected under the pressing and incessant calls upon me, and had grown worse and worse till the whole foot below the ankle became a black mass and seemed to threaten mortification. I insisted however on being allowed to use it till the place was taken, mortification or no; and though the pain was sometimes horrible, I carried my point and kept up to the last. On the day after the assault I had an unlucky fall on some bad ground, and it was an open question for a day or two whether I hadn't broken my arm at the elbow. Fortunately it turned out to be only a very severe sprain, but I am still conscious of the wrench it gave me. To crown the whole pleasant catalogue, I was worn to a shadow by a constant diarrhea, and consumed as much opium as would have done credit to my father-in-law.[1] However, thank God I have

[1] Thomas De Quincey.

a good share of Tapleyism in me and come out strong under difficulties. I think I may confidently say that no man ever saw me out of heart, or ever heard one croaking word from me even when our prospects were gloomiest. We were sadly scourged by the cholera and it was almost appalling to me to find that out of twenty-seven officers present, I could only muster fifteen for the operations of the attack. However, it was done, and after it was done came the collapse. Don't be horrified when I tell you that for the whole of the actual siege, and in truth for some little time before, I almost lived on brandy. Appetite for food I had none, but I forced myself to eat just sufficient to sustain life, and I had an incessant craving for brandy as the strongest stimulant I could get. Strange to say, I was quite unconscious of its affecting me in the slightest degree. *The excitement of the work was so great that no lesser one seemed to have any chance against it, and I certainly never found my intellect clearer or my nerves stronger in my life.* It was only my wretched body that was weak, and the moment the real work was done by our becoming complete masters of Delhi, I broke down without delay and discovered that if I wished to live I must continue no longer the system that had kept me up until the crisis was past. With it passed away as if in a moment all desire to stimulate, and a perfect loathing of my late staff of life took possession of me."

Such experiences show how profound is the alteration in the manner in which, under excitement, our organism will sometimes perform its physiological work. The metabolisms become different when the reserves have to be used, and for weeks and months the deeper use may go on.

Morbid cases, here as elsewhere, lay the normal machinery bare. In the first number of Dr. Morton Prince's *Journal of Abnormal Psychology*, Dr. Janet has discussed five cases of morbid impulse, with an explanation that is precious for my present point of view. One is a girl who eats, eats, eats all day. Another walks, walks, walks, and gets her food from an automobile that escorts her. Another is a dipsomaniac. A fourth pulls out her hair. A fifth wounds her flesh and burns her skin. Hitherto such freaks of impulse have received Greek names (as bulimia, dromomania, etc.) and been scientifically disposed of as "episodic syndromata of hereditary degeneration." But it turns out that Janet's cases are all what he calls psychasthenics, or victims of a chronic sense of weakness, torpor, lethargy, fatigue, insufficiency, impossibility, unreality, and powerlessness of will; and that in each and all of them the particular activity pursued, deleterious though it be, has the temporary result of raising the sense of vitality and making the patient feel alive again. These things reanimate; they would reanimate *us*; but it happens that in each patient the particular freak-activity chosen is the only thing that does reanimate; and therein lies the morbid state. The way to treat such persons is to discover to them more usual and useful ways of throwing their stores of vital energy into gear.

Colonel Baird-Smith, needing to draw on altogether extraordinary stores of energy, found that brandy and opium were ways of throwing them into gear.

Such cases are humanly typical. We are all to some degree oppressed, unfree. We don't come to our own. It is there, but we don't get at it. The threshold must be made to shift. Then many of us find that an excentric activity—a 'spree,' say— relieves. There is no doubt that to some men sprees and excesses of almost any kind are medicinal, temporarily at any rate, in spite of what the moralists and doctors say.

But when the normal tasks and stimulations of life don't put a man's deeper levels of energy on tap, and he requires distinctly deleterious excitements, his constitution verges on the abnormal. The normal opener of deeper and deeper levels of energy is the will. The difficulty is to use it; to make the effort which the word volition implies. But if we *do* make it (or if a god, though he were only the god Chance, makes it through us), it will act dynamogenically on us for a month. It is notorious that a single successful effort of moral volition, such as saying 'no' to some habitual temptation, or performing some courageous act, will launch a man on a higher level of energy for days and weeks, will give him a new range of power.

The emotions and excitements due to usual situations are the usual inciters of the will. But these act discontinuously; and in the intervals the shallower levels of life tend to close in and shut us off. Accordingly the best practical knowers of the human soul have invented the thing known as methodical ascetic discipline to keep the deeper levels constantly in reach. Beginning with easy tasks, passing to harder ones, and exercising day by day, it is, I believe, admitted that disciples of asceticism can reach very high levels of freedom and power of will.

Ignatius Loyola's spiritual exercises must have produced this result in innumerable devotees. But the most venerable ascetic system, and the one whose results have the most voluminous experimental corroboration, is undoubtedly the Yoga system in Hindostan. From time immemorial, by Hatha Yoga, Raja Yoga, Karma Yoga, or whatever code of practice it might be, Hindu aspirants to perfection have trained themselves, month in and out, for years. The result claimed, and certainly in many cases accorded by impartial judges, is strength of character, personal power, unshakability of soul. But it is not easy to disentangle fact from tradition in Hindu affairs. So I am glad to have a European friend who has submitted to Hatha Yoga training, and whose account of the results I am privileged to quote. I think you will appreciate the light it throws on the question of our unused reservoirs of power.

My friend is an extraordinarily gifted man, both morally and intellectually, but has an instable nervous system, and for many years has lived in a circular process of alternate lethargy and over-animation: something like three weeks of extreme activity, and then a week of prostration in bed. An unpromising condition, which the best specialists in Europe had failed to relieve; so he tried Hatha Yoga, partly out of curiosity, and partly with a sort of desperate hope. What follows is a short extract from a letter sixty pages long which he addressed me a year ago.

"Thus I decided to follow Vivekananda's advice: 'Practice hard: whether you live or die by it doesn't matter.' My improvised chela and I began with starvation. I do not know whether you did try it ever . . . but voluntary starvation is very different from involuntary, and implies more temptations. We reduced first our meals to twice a day and then to once a day. The best authorities agree that in order to control the body fasting is essential, and even in the Gospel the worst spirits are said to obey only those who fast and pray. We reduced very much the amount of food, disregarding chemical theories about the need of albumen, sometimes living on olive oil and bread; or on fruits alone; or on milk and rice; in very small quantities—much less than I formerly ate at one meal. I began to get lighter every day, and lost 20 pounds in a few weeks; but this could not stop such a desperate undertaking . . . rather starve than live as a slave! Then besides we practised *asana* or postures, breaking almost our limbs. Try to sit down on the floor and to kiss your knees without bending them, or to join your hands on the usually unapproachable upper part of your back, or to bring the toe of your right foot to your left ear without bending the knees . . . these are easy samples of posture for a Yogi.

"All the time also breathing exercises: keeping the breath in and out up to two minutes, breathing in different rhythms and positions. Also very much prayer and Roman Catholic practices combined with the Yoga, in order to leave nothing untried and to be protected against the tricks of Hindu devils! Then concentration of thought on different parts of the body, and on the processes going on within them. Exclusion of all emotions, dry logical reading, as intellectual diet, and working out logical problems . . . I wrote a Handbook of Logic as a *Nebenprodukt* of the whole experiment.[1]

"After a few weeks I broke down and had to interrupt everything, in a worse state of prostration than ever . . . My younger chela went on unshaken by my fate; and as soon as I arose from bed I tried again, decided to fight it out, even feeling a kind of determination such as I had never felt before, a certain absolute will of victory at any price and faith in it. Whether it is my own merit or a divine grace, I cannot judge for certain, but I prefer to admit the latter. I had been ill for seven years, and some people say this is a term for many punishments. However base and vile a sinner I had been, perhaps my sins were about to be forgiven, and Yoga was only an exterior opportunity, an object for concentration of will. I do not yet pretend to explain much of what I have gone through, but the fact is that since I arose from bed on August 20, no new crisis of prostration came again, and I have now the

---

[1] This handbook was published last March.

strongest conviction that no crisis will ever return. If you consider that for the past years there has been not a single month without this lethargy, you will grant that even to an outside observer four successive months of increasing health are an objective test. In this time I underwent very severe penances, reducing sleep and food and increasing the task of work and exercise. My intuition was developed by these practices: there came a sense of certainty, never known before, as to the things needed by the body and the mind, and the body came to obey like a wild horse tamed. Also the mind learned to obey, and the current of thought and feeling was shaped according to my will. I mastered sleep and hunger, and the flights of thought, and came to know a peace never known before, an inner rhythm of unison with a deeper rhythm above or beyond. Personal wishes ceased, and the consciousness of being the instrument of a superior power arose. A calm certainty of indubitable success in every undertaking imparts great and real power. I often guessed the thoughts of my companion . . . we observed generally the greatest isolation and silence. We both felt an unspeakable joy in the simplest natural impressions, light, air, landscape, any kind of simplest food; and above everything in rhythmical respiration, which produces a state of mind without thought or feeling, and still very intense, indescribable.

"These results began to be more evident in the fourth month of uninterrupted training. We felt quite happy, never tired, sleeping only from 8 P. M. to midnight, and rising with joy from our sleep to another day's work of study and exercise. . . .

"I am now in Palermo, and have had to neglect the exercises in the last few days, but I feel as fresh as if I were in full training and see the sunny side of all things. I am not in a hurry, rushing to complete ———."

And here my friend mentions a certain life-work of his own about which I had better be silent. He goes on to analyze the exercises and their effects in an extremely practical way, but at too great length for me to entertain you with. Repetition, alteration, periodicity, parallelism (or the association of the idea of some desirable vital or spiritual effect with each movement), etc., are laws which he deems highly important. "I am sure," he continues, "that everybody who is able to concentrate thought and will, and to eliminate superfluous emotions, sooner or later becomes a master of his body and can overcome every kind of illness. This is the truth at the bottom of all mind-cures. Our thoughts have a plastic power over the body."

You will be relieved, I doubt not, to hear my excentric correspondent here make connection at last with something you know by heart, namely, "suggestive therapeutics." Call his whole performance, if you like, an experiment in methodical self-suggestion. That only makes it more valuable as an illustration of what I wish to impress in as many ways as possible upon your minds, that we habitually live inside our limits of power. Suggestion, especially under hypnosis, is now universally recognized as a means, exceptionally successful in certain persons, of concentrating consciousness, and, in others, of influencing their body's states. It throws into gear energies of imagination, of will, and of mental influence over physiological processes, that usually lie dormant, and that can only be thrown into gear at all in chosen subjects. It is, in short, dynamogenic; and the cheapest terms in which to deal with our amateur Yogi's experience is to call it auto-suggestive.

I wrote to him that I couldn't possibly attribute any sacramental value to the particular Hatha Yoga processes, the postures, breathings, fastings, and the like, and that they seemed to me but so many manners, available in his case and his chela's, but not for everybody, of breaking through the barriers which life's routine had concreted round the deeper strata of the will, and gradually bringing its unused energies into action.

He replied as follows: "You are quite right that the Yoga exercises are nothing else than a methodical way of increasing our will. Because we are unable to will at once the most difficult things, we must imagine steps leading to them. Breathing being the easiest of the bodily activities, it is very natural that it offers a good scope for exercise of will. The control of thought could be gained without breathing-discipline, but it is simply easier to control thought simultaneously with the control of breath. Anyone who can think clearly and persistently of one thing needs not breathing exercises. You are quite right that we are not using all our power and that we often learn how much we *can* only when we *must*. . . . The power that we do not use up completely can be brought [more and more] into use by what we call *faith*. Faith is like the manometer of the will, registering its pressure. If I could believe that I can levitate, I could do it. But I cannot believe, and therefore I am clumsily sticking to earth . . . Now this faith, this power of credulity, can be educated by small efforts. I can breathe at the rate of say twelve times a minute. I can easily believe that I can breathe ten times a minute. When I have accustomed myself to breathe ten times a minute, I learn to believe it will be easy to breathe six times a minute. Thus I have actually learned to breathe at the rate of once a minute. How far I shall progress I do not know. . . . The Yogi goes on in his activity in an even way, without fits of too much or too little, and he is eliminating more and more every unrest, every worry—growing into the infinite by regular training, by small additions to a task which has grown familiar. . . . But you are quite right that religious crises, love-crises, indignation-crises, may awaken in a very short time powers similar to those reached by years of patient Yoga practice. . . . The Hindus themselves admit that Samadhi can be reached in many ways and with complete disregard of every physical training."

Allowance made for every enthusiasm and exaggeration, there can be no doubt of my friend's regeneration—relatively, at any rate. The second letter, written six months later than the first (ten months after beginning Yoga practice, therefore), says the improvement holds good. He has undergone material trials with indifference, travelled third class on Mediterranean steamers, and fourth class on African trains, living with the poorest Arabs and sharing their unaccustomed food, all with equanimity. His devotion to certain interests has been put to heavy strain, and nothing is more remarkable to me than the changed moral tone with which he reports the situation. Compared with certain earlier letters, these read as if written by a different man, patient and reasonable instead of vehement, self-subordinating instead of imperious. The new tone persists in a communication received only a fortnight ago (fourteen months after beginning training)—there is, in fact, no doubt that profound modification has occurred in the running of his mental machinery. The gearing has changed, and his will is available otherwise than it was. Available without any new ideas, beliefs, or emotions, so far as I can make out, having been implanted in him. He is simply more balanced where he was more unbalanced.

You will remember that he speaks of faith, calling it a 'manometer' of the will. It sounds more natural to call our will the manometer of our faiths. Ideas set free beliefs, and the beliefs set free our wills (I use these terms with no pretension to be 'psychological'), so the will-acts register the faith-pressure within. Therefore, having considered the liberation of our stored-up energy by emotional excitements and by efforts, whether methodical or unmethodical, I must now say a word about *ideas* as our third great dynamogenic agent. Ideas contradict other ideas and keep us from believing them. An idea that thus negates a first idea may itself in turn be negated by a third idea, and the first idea may thus regain its natural influence over our belief and determine our behavior. Our philosophic and religious development proceeds thus by credulities, negations, and the negating of negations.

But whether for arousing or for stopping belief, ideas may fail to be efficacious, just as a wire at one time alive with electricity, may at another time be dead. Here our insight into causes fails us, and we can only note results in general terms. In general, whether a given idea shall be a live idea, depends more on the person into whose mind it is injected than on the idea itself. The whole history of 'suggestion' opens out here. Which are the suggestive ideas for this person, and which for that? Beside the susceptibilities determined by one's education and by one's original peculiarities of character, there are lines along which men simply as men tend to be inflammable by ideas. As certain objects naturally awaken love, anger, or cupidity, so certain ideas naturally awaken the energies of loyalty, courage, endurance, or devotion. When these ideas are effective in an individual's life, their effect is often very great indeed. They may transfigure it, unlocking innumerable powers which, but for the idea, would never have come into play. 'Fatherland,' 'The Union,' 'Holy Church,' the 'Monroe Doctrine,' 'Truth,' 'Science,' 'Liberty,'

Garibaldi's phrase 'Rome or Death,' etc., are so many examples of energy-releasing abstract ideas. The *social* nature of all such phrases is an essential factor of their dynamic power. They are forces of detent in situations in which no other force produces equivalent effects, and each is a force of detent only in a specific group of men.

The memory that an oath or vow has been made will nerve one to abstinences and efforts otherwise impossible: witness the 'pledge' in the history of the temperance movement. A mere promise to his sweetheart will clean up a youth's life all over—at any rate for a time. For such effects an educated susceptibility is required. The idea of one's 'honour,' for example, unlocks energy only in those who have had the education of a gentleman, so called.

That delightful being, Prince Pueckler-Muskau, writes to his wife from England that he has invented "a sort of artificial resolution respecting things that are difficult of performance." "My device," he says, "is this: I give my word of honour most solemnly to myself to do or to leave undone this or that. I am of course extremely cautious in the use of this expedient, but when once the word is given, even though I afterwards think I have been precipitate or mistaken, I hold it to be perfectly irrevocable, whatever inconveniences I foresee likely to result. If I were capable of breaking my word after such mature consideration, I should lose all respect for myself—and what man of sense would not prefer death to such an alternative? . . . When the mysterious formula is pronounced, no alteration in my own views, nothing short of physical impossibility, must, for the welfare of my soul, alter my will. . . . I find something very satisfactory in the thought that man has the power of framing such props and weapons out of the most trivial materials, indeed out of nothing, merely by the force of his will, which thereby truly deserves the name of omnipotent."[1]

Conversions, whether they be political, scientific, philosophic, or religious, form another way in which bound energies are let loose. They unify, and put a stop to ancient mental

[1]*Tour in England, Ireland, and France*, Philadelphia, 1833, p. 435.

interferences. The result is freedom, and often a great enlargement of power. A belief that thus settles upon an individual always acts as a challenge to his will. But, for the particular challenge to operate, he must be the right challeng*ee*. In religious conversions we have so fine an adjustment that the idea may be in the mind of the challengee for years before it exerts effects; and why it should do so then is often so far from obvious that the event is taken for a miracle of grace, and not a natural occurrence. Whatever it is, it may be a highwater mark of energy, in which 'noes,' once impossible, are easy, and in which a new range of 'yeses' gain the right of way.

We are just now witnessing—but our scientific education has unfitted most of us for comprehending the phenomenon—a very copious unlocking of energies by ideas, in the persons of those converts to 'New Thought,' 'Christian Science,' 'Metaphysical Healing,' or other forms of spiritual philosophy, who are so numerous among us to-day. The ideas here are healthy-minded and optimistic; and it is quite obvious that a wave of religious activity, analogous in some respects to the spread of early Christianity, Buddhism, and Mohammedanism is passing over our American world. The common feature of these optimistic faiths is that they all tend to the suppression of what Mr. Horace Fletcher calls "fear thought." Fear thought he defines as "the self-suggestion of inferiority"; so that one may say that these systems all operate by the suggestion of power. And the power, small or great, comes in various shapes to the individual, power, as he will tell you, not to 'mind' things that used to vex him, power to concentrate his mind, good cheer, good temper, in short, to put it mildly, a firmer, more elastic moral tone. The most genuinely saintly person I have ever known is a friend of mine now suffering from cancer of the breast. I do not assume to judge of the wisdom or unwisdom of her disobedience to the doctors, and I cite her here solely as an example of what ideas can do. Her ideas have kept her a practically well woman for months after she should have given up and gone to bed. They have annulled all pain and weakness and given her a cheerful active life, unusually beneficent to others to whom she has afforded help.

How far the mind-cure movement is destined to extend its

influence, or what intellectual modifications it may yet
undergo, no one can foretell. Being a religious movement, it
will certainly outstrip the previsions of its rationalist critics,
such as we here may be supposed to be.

I have thus brought a pretty wide induction to bear upon
my thesis, and it appears to hold good. The human individual
lives usually far within his limits; he possesses powers of various sorts which he habitually fails to use. He energizes below
his maximum, and he behaves below his optimum. In elementary faculty, in coördination, in power of inhibition and control, in every conceivable way, his life is contracted like the
field of vision of an hysteric subject—but with less excuse,
for the poor hysteric is diseased, while in the rest of us it is
only an inveterate *habit*—the habit of inferiority to our full
self—that is bad.

Expressed in this vague manner, everyone must admit my
thesis to be true. The terms have to remain vague; for though
every man of woman born knows what is meant by such
phrases as having a good vital tone, a high tide of spirits, an
elastic temper, as living energetically, working easily, deciding
firmly, and the like, we should all be put to our trumps if
asked to explain in terms of scientific psychology just what
such expressions mean. We can draw some child-like psycho-
physical diagrams, and that is all. In physics the conception
of 'energy' is perfectly defined. It is correlated with the conception of 'work.' But mental work and moral work, although we cannot live without talking about them, are terms
as yet hardly analyzed, and doubtless mean several heterogeneous elementary things. Our muscular work is a voluminous
physical quantity, but our ideas and volitions are minute
forces of release, and by 'work' here we mean the substitution
of higher *kinds* for lower *kinds* of detent. Higher and lower
here are qualitative terms, not translatable immediately into
quantities, unless indeed they should prove to mean newer or
older forms of cerebral organization, and unless newer should
then prove to mean cortically more superficial, older, cortically more deep. Some anatomists, as you know, have pretended this; but it is obvious that the intuitive or popular idea

of mental work, fundamental and abolutely indispensable as it is in our lives, possesses no degree whatever of scientific clearness to-day.

Here, then, is the first problem that emerges from our study. Can any one of us refine upon the conceptions of mental work and mental energy, so as later to be able to throw some definitely analytic light on what we mean by 'having a more elastic moral tone,' or by 'using higher levels of power and will'? I imagine that we may have to wait long before progress in this direction is made. The problem is too homely; one doesn't see just how to get in the electric keys and revolving drums that alone make psychology scientific to-day.

My fellow-pragmatist in Florence, G. Papini, has adopted a new conception of philosophy. He calls it the *doctrine of action* in the widest sense, the study of all human powers and means (among which latter, *truths* of every kind whatsoever figure, of course, in the first rank). From this point of view philosophy is a *Pragmatic*, comprehending, as tributary departments of itself, the old disciplines of logic, metaphysic, physic, and ethic.

And here, after our first problem, two other problems burst upon our view. My belief that these two problems form a program of work well worthy of the attention of a body as learned and earnest as this audience, is, in fact, what has determined me to choose this subject, and to drag you through so many familiar facts during the hour that has sped.

The first of the two problems is *that of our powers*, the second *that of our means*. We ought somehow to get a topographic survey made of the limits of human power in every conceivable direction, something like an ophthalmologist's chart of the limits of the human field of vision; and we ought then to construct a methodical inventory of the paths of access, or keys, differing with the diverse types of individual, to the different kinds of power. This would be an absolutely concrete study, to be carried on by using historical and biographical material mainly. The limits of power must be limits that have been realized in actual persons, and the various ways of unlocking the reserves of power must have been exemplified in individual lives. Laboratory experimentation can play but a small part. Your psychologist's *Versuchsthier*, outside of hypnosis, can never be called on to tax his energies in ways as extreme as those which the emergencies of life will force on him.

So here is a program of concrete individual psychology, at which anyone in some measure may work. It is replete with interesting facts, and points to practical issues superior in importance to anything we know. I urge it therefore upon your consideration. In some shape we have all worked at it in a more or less blind and fragmentary way; yet before Papini mentioned it I had never thought of it, or heard it broached by anyone, in the generalized form of a program such as I now suggest, a program that might with proper care be made to cover the whole field of psychology, and might show us parts of it in a very fresh light.

It is just the generalizing of the problem that seems to me to make so strong an appeal. I hope that in some of you the conception may unlock unused reservoirs of investigating power.

The Philosophical Review, January 1907

The Social Value of the College-Bred

AN ADDRESS MADE AT A MEETING OF THE ASSOCIATION
OF AMERICAN ALUMNAE AT RADCLIFFE COLLEGE,
NOVEMBER 7, 1907

O F WHAT USE is a college training? We who have had it seldom hear the question raised—we might be a little nonplussed to answer it offhand. A certain amount of meditation has brought me to this as the pithiest reply which I myself can give: The best claim that a college education can possibly make on your respect, the best thing it can aspire to accomplish for you, is this: that it should *help you to know a good man when you see him*. This is as true of women's as of men's colleges; but that it is neither a joke nor a one-sided abstraction I shall now endeavor to show.

What talk do we commonly hear about the contrast between college education and the education which business or technical or professional schools confer? The college education is called higher because it is supposed to be so general and so disinterested. At the "schools" you get a relatively narrow practical skill, you are told, whereas the "colleges" give you the more liberal culture, the broader outlook, the historical perspective, the philosophic atmosphere, or something which phrases of that sort try to express. You are made into an efficient instrument for doing a definite thing, you hear, at the schools; but, apart from that, you may remain a crude and smoky kind of petroleum, incapable of spreading light. The universities and colleges, on the other hand, although they may leave you less efficient for this or that practical task, suffuse your whole mentality with something more important than skill. They redeem you, make you well-bred; they make "good company" of you mentally. If they find you with a naturally boorish or caddish mind, they cannot leave you so, as a technical school may leave you. This, at least, is pretended; this is what we hear among college-trained people when they compare their education with every other sort. Now, exactly how much does this signify?

It is certain, to begin with, that the narrowest trade or

professional training does something more for a man than to make a skilful practical tool of him—it makes him also a judge of other men's skill. Whether his trade be pleading at the bar or surgery or plastering or plumbing, it develops a critical sense in him for that sort of occupation. He understands the difference between second-rate and first-rate work in his whole branch of industry; he gets to know a good job in his own line as soon as he sees it; and getting to know this in his own line, he gets a faint sense of what good work may mean anyhow, that may, if circumstances favor, spread into his judgments elsewhere. Sound work, clean work, finished work: feeble work, slack work, sham work—these words express an identical contrast in many different departments of activity. In so far forth, then, even the humblest manual trade may beget in one a certain small degree of power to judge of good work generally.

Now, what is supposed to be the line of us who have the higher college training? Is there any broader line—since our education claims primarily not to be "narrow"—in which we also are made good judges between what is first-rate and what is second-rate only? What is especially taught in the colleges has long been known by the name of the "humanities," and these are often identified with Greek and Latin. But it is only as literatures, not as languages, that Greek and Latin have any general humanity-value; so that in a broad sense the humanities mean literature primarily, and in a still broader sense the study of masterpieces in almost any field of human endeavor. Literature keeps the primacy; for it not only *consists* of masterpieces, but is largely *about* masterpieces, being little more than an appreciative chronicle of human master-strokes, so far as it takes the form of criticism and history. You can give humanistic value to almost anything by teaching it historically. Geology, economics, mechanics, are humanities when taught with reference to the successive achievements of the geniuses to which these sciences owe their being. Not taught thus, literature remains grammar, art a catalogue, history a list of dates, and natural science a sheet of formulas and weights and measures.

The sifting of human creations!—nothing less than this is what we ought to mean by the humanities. Essentially this

means biography; what our colleges should teach is, therefore, biographical history, that not of politics merely, but of
anything and everything so far as human efforts and conquests are factors that have played their part. Studying in this
way, we learn what types of activity have stood the test of
time; we acquire standards of the excellent and durable. All
our arts and sciences and institutions are but so many quests
of perfection on the part of men; and when we see how diverse the types of excellence may be, how various the tests,
how flexible the adaptations, we gain a richer sense of what
the terms "better" and "worse" may signify in general. Our
critical sensibilities grow both more acute and less fanatical.
We sympathize with men's mistakes even in the act of penetrating them; we feel the pathos of lost causes and misguided
epochs even while we applaud what overcame them.

Such words are vague and such ideas are inadequate, but
their meaning is unmistakable. What the colleges—teaching
humanities by examples which may be special, but which
must be typical and pregnant—should at least try to give us,
is a general sense of what, under various disguises, *superiority*
has always signified and may still signify. The feeling for a
good human job anywhere, the admiration of the really admirable, the disesteem of what is cheap and trashy and imper-
manent—this is what we call the critical sense, the sense for
ideal values. It is the better part of what men know as wisdom. Some of us are wise in this way naturally and by genius;
some of us never become so. But to have spent one's youth
at college, in contact with the choice and rare and precious,
and yet still to be a blind prig or vulgarian, unable to scent
out human excellence or to divine it amid its accidents, to
know it only when ticketed and labeled and forced on us by
others, this indeed should be accounted the very calamity and
shipwreck of a higher education.

The sense for human superiority ought, then, to be considered our line, as boring subways is the engineer's line and the
surgeon's is appendicitis. Our colleges ought to have lit up in
us a lasting relish for the better kind of man, a loss of appetite
for mediocrities, and a disgust for cheapjacks. We ought to
smell, as it were, the difference of quality in men and their
proposals when we enter the world of affairs about us. Expert-

ness in this might well atone for some of our awkwardness at accounts, for some of our ignorance of dynamos. The best claim we can make for the higher education, the best single phrase in which we can tell what it ought to do for us, is, then, exactly what I said: it should enable us to *know a good man when we see him.*

That the phrase is anything but an empty epigram follows from the fact that if you ask in what line it is most important that a democracy like ours should have its sons and daughters skilful, you see that it is this line more than any other. "The people in their wisdom"—this is the kind of wisdom most needed by the people. Democracy is on its trial, and no one knows how it will stand the ordeal. Abounding about us are pessimistic prophets. Fickleness and violence used to be, but are no longer, the vices which they charge to democracy. What its critics now affirm is that its preferences are inveterately for the inferior. So it was in the beginning, they say, and so it will be world without end. Vulgarity enthroned and institutionalized, elbowing everything superior from the highway, this, they tell us, is our irremediable destiny; and the picture-papers of the European continent are already drawing Uncle Sam with the hog instead of the eagle for his heraldic emblem. The privileged aristocracies of the foretime, with all their iniquities, did at least preserve some taste for higher human quality and honor certain forms of refinement by their enduring traditions. But when democracy is sovereign, its doubters say, nobility will form a sort of invisible church, and sincerity and refinement, stripped of honor, precedence, and favor, will have to vegetate on sufferance in private corners. They will have no general influence. They will be harmless eccentricities.

Now, who can be absolutely certain that this may not be the career of democracy? Nothing future is quite secure; states enough have inwardly rotted; and democracy as a whole may undergo self-poisoning. But, on the other hand, democracy is a kind of religion, and we are bound not to admit its failure. Faiths and utopias are the noblest exercise of human reason, and no one with a spark of reason in him will sit down fatalistically before the croaker's picture. The best of us are filled with the contrary vision of a democracy stumbling through every error till its institutions glow with justice and its customs shine with beauty. Our better men *shall* show the way and we *shall* follow them; so we are brought round again to the mission of the higher education in helping us to know the better kind of man whenever we see him.

The notion that a people can run itself and its affairs anonymously is now well known to be the silliest of absurdities. Mankind does nothing save through initiatives on the part of inventors, great or small, and imitation by the rest of us— these are the sole factors active in human progress. Individuals of genius show the way, and set the patterns, which common people then adopt and follow. *The rivalry of the patterns is the history of the world.* Our democratic problem thus is statable in ultra-simple terms: Who are the kind of men from whom our majorities shall take their cue? Whom shall they treat as rightful leaders? We and our leaders are the x and the y of the equation here; all other historic circumstances, be they economical, political, or intellectual, are only the background of occasion on which the living drama works itself out between us.

In this very simple way does the value of our educated class define itself: we more than others should be able to divine the worthier and better leaders. The terms here are monstrously simplified, of course, but such a bird's-eye view lets us immediately take our bearings. In our democracy, where everything else is so shifting, we alumni and alumnae of the colleges are the only permanent presence that corresponds to the aristocracy in older countries. We have continuous traditions, as they have; our motto, too, is *noblesse oblige*; and, unlike them, we stand for ideal interests solely, for we have no corporate selfishness and wield no powers of corruption. We ought to have our own class-consciousness. "Les intellectuels"! What prouder club-name could there be than this one, used ironically by the party of "red blood," the party of every stupid prejudice and passion, during the anti-Dreyfus craze, to satirize the men in France who still retained some critical sense and judgment! Critical sense, it has to be confessed, is not an exciting term, hardly a banner to carry in processions. Affections for old habit, currents of self-interest, and gales of passion are the forces that keep the human ship moving; and the pressure of the judicious pilot's hand upon the tiller is a relatively insignificant energy. But the affections, passions, and interests are shifting, successive, and distraught; they blow in alternation while the pilot's hand is steadfast. He knows the compass, and, with all the leeways he is obliged to tack toward, he always makes some headway. A small force, if it never lets up, will accumulate effects more considerable than those of much greater forces if these work inconsistently. The ceaseless whisper of the more permanent ideals, the steady tug of truth and justice, give them but time, *must* warp the world in their direction.

This bird's-eye view of the general steering function of the college-bred amid the driftings of democracy ought to help us to a wider vision of what our colleges themselves should aim at. If we are to be the yeast-cake for democracy's dough, if we are to make it rise with culture's preferences, we must see to it that culture spreads broad sails. We must shake the old double reefs out of the canvas into the wind and sunshine, and let in every modern subject, sure that any subject will prove humanistic, if its setting be kept only wide enough.

Stevenson says somewhere to his reader: "You think you are just making this bargain, but you are really laying down a link in the policy of mankind." Well, your technical school should enable you to make your bargain splendidly; but your college should show you just the place of that kind of bargain—a pretty poor place, possibly—in the whole policy of mankind. That is the kind of liberal outlook, of perspective, of atmosphere, which should surround every subject as a college deals with it.

We of the colleges must eradicate a curious notion which numbers of good people have about such ancient seats of learning as Harvard. To many ignorant outsiders, that name suggests little more than a kind of sterilized conceit and incapacity for being pleased. In Edith Wyatt's exquisite book of Chicago sketches called "Every One his Own Way" there is a couple who stand for culture in the sense of exclusiveness, Richard Elliot and his feminine counterpart—feeble caricatures of mankind, unable to know any good thing when they see it, incapable of enjoyment unless a printed label gives them leave. Possibly this type of culture may exist near Cambridge and Boston, there may be specimens there, for priggishness is just like painter's colic or any other trade-disease. But every good college makes its students immune against this malady, of which the microbe haunts the neighborhood-printed pages. It does so by its general tone being too hearty for the microbe's life. Real culture lives by sympathies and admirations, not by dislikes and disdains—under all misleading wrappings it pounces unerringly upon the human core. If a college, through the inferior human influences that have grown regnant there, fails to catch the robuster tone, its failure is colossal, for its social function stops: democracy gives it a wide berth, turns toward it a deaf ear.

"Tone," to be sure, is a terribly vague word to use, but there is no other, and this whole meditation is over questions of tone. By their tone are all things human either lost or saved. If democracy is to be saved it must catch the higher, healthier tone. If we are to impress it with our preferences, we ourselves must use the proper tone, which we, in turn, must have caught from our own teachers. It all reverts in the end to the action of innumerable imitative individuals upon each other and to the question of whose tone has the highest spreading power. As a class, we college graduates should look to it that *ours* has spreading power. It ought to have the highest spreading power.

In our essential function of indicating the better men, we now have formidable competitors outside. McClure's Magazine, the American Magazine, Collier's Weekly, and, in its fashion, the World's Work, constitute together a real popular university along this very line. It would be a pity if any future historian were to have to write words like these: "By the middle of the twentieth century the higher institutions of learning had lost all influence over public opinion in the United States. But the mission of raising the tone of democracy, which they had proved themselves so lamentably unfitted to exert, was assumed with rare enthusiasm and prosecuted with extraordinary skill and success by a new educational power; and for the clarification of their human sympathies and elevation of their human preferences, the people at large acquired the habit of resorting exclusively to the guidance of certain private literary adventures, commonly designated in the market by the affectionate name of ten-cent magazines."

Must not we of the colleges see to it that no historian shall ever say anything like this? Vague as the phrase of knowing a good man when you see him may be, diffuse and indefinite as one must leave its application, is there any other formula that describes so well the result at which our institutions *ought* to aim? If they do that, they do the best thing conceivable. If they fail to do it, they fail in very deed. It surely is a fine synthetic formula. If our faculties and graduates could once collectively come to realize it as the great underlying purpose toward which they have always been more or less obscurely groping, a great clearness would be shed over many of their problems; and, as for their influence in the midst of our social system, it would embark upon a new career of strength.

McClure's Magazine, February 1908

The Confidences of a "Psychical Researcher"

THE LATE Professor Henry Sidgwick was celebrated for the rare mixture of ardor and critical judgment which his character exhibited. The liberal heart which he possessed had to work with an intellect which acted destructively on almost every particular object of belief that was offered to its acceptance. A quarter of a century ago, scandalized by the chaotic state of opinion regarding the phenomena now called by the rather ridiculous name of "psychic"—phenomena of which the supply reported seems inexhaustible, but which scientifically trained minds mostly refuse to look at—he established, along with Professor Barrett, Frederic Myers and Edmund Gurney, the Society for Psychical Research. These men hoped that if the material were treated rigorously and, as far as possible, experimentally, objective truth would be elicited, and the subject rescued from sentimentalism on the one side and dogmatizing ignorance on the other. Like all founders, Sidgwick hoped for a certain promptitude of result; and I heard him say, the year before his death, that if anyone had told him at the outset that after twenty years he would be in the same identical state of doubt and balance that he started with, he would have deemed the prophecy incredible. It appeared impossible that that amount of handling evidence should bring so little finality of decision.

My own experience has been similar to Sidgwick's. For twenty-five years I have been in touch with the literature of psychical research, and have had acquaintance with numerous "researchers." I have also spent a good many hours (though far fewer than I ought to have spent) in witnessing (or trying to witness) phenomena. Yet I am theoretically no "further" than I was at the beginning; and I confess that at times I have been tempted to believe that the Creator has eternally intended this department of nature to remain *baffling*, to prompt our curiosities and hopes and suspicions all in equal measure, so that, although ghosts and clairvoyances, and raps and messages from spirits, are always seeming to exist and can never be fully explained away, they also can never be susceptible of full corroboration.

The peculiarity of the case is just that there are so many sources of possible deception in most of the observations that the whole lot of them *may* be worthless, and yet that in comparatively few cases can aught more fatal than this vague general possibility of error be pleaded against the record. Science meanwhile needs something more than bare possibilities to build upon; so your genuinely scientific inquirer—I don't mean your ignoramus "scientist"—has to remain unsatisfied. It is hard to believe, however, that the Creator has really put any big array of phenomena into the world merely to defy and mock our scientific tendencies; so my deeper belief is that we psychical researchers have been too precipitate with our hopes, and that we must expect to mark progress not by quarter-centuries, but by half-centuries or whole centuries.

I am strengthened in this belief by my impression that just at this moment a faint but distinct step forward is being taken by competent opinion in these matters. "Physical phenomena" (movements of matter without contact, lights, hands and faces "materialized," etc.) have been one of the most baffling regions of the general field (or perhaps one of the least baffling *prima facie*, so certain and great has been the part played by fraud in their production); yet even here the balance of testimony seems slowly to be inclining towards admitting the supernaturalist view. Eusapia Paladino, the Neapolitan medium, has been under observation for twenty years or more. Schiaparelli, the astronomer, and Lombroso were the first scientific men to be converted by her performances. Since then innumerable men of scientific standing have seen her, including many "psychic" experts. Every one agrees that she cheats in the most barefaced manner whenever she gets an opportunity. The Cambridge experts, with the Sidgwicks and Richard Hodgson at their head, rejected her *in toto* on that account. Yet her credit has steadily risen, and now her last converts are the eminent psychiatrist, Morselli, the eminent physiologist, Botazzi, and our own psychical researcher, Carrington, whose book on "The Physical Phenomena of Spiritualism" (*against* them rather!) makes his conquest strategically important. If Mr. Podmore, hitherto the prosecuting attorney of the S. P. R. so far as physical phenomena are concerned, becomes converted also, we may indeed sit up and look around us.

Getting a good health bill from "Science," Eusapia will then throw retrospective credit on Home and Stainton Moses, Florence Cook (Prof. Crookes's medium), and all similar wonder-workers. The balance of *presumptions* will be changed in favor of genuineness being possible at least, in all reports of this particularly crass and low type of supernatural phenomenon.

Not long after Darwin's "Origin of Species" appeared I was studying with that excellent anatomist and man, Jeffries Wyman, at Harvard. He was a convert, yet so far a half-hesitating one, to Darwin's views; but I heard him make a remark that applies well to the subject I now write about. When, he said, a theory gets propounded over and over again, coming up afresh after each time orthodox criticism has buried it, and each time seeming solider and harder to abolish, you may be sure that there is truth in it. Oken and Lamarck and Chambers had been triumphantly despatched and buried, but here was Darwin making the very same heresy seem only more plausible. How often has "Science" killed off all spook philosophy, and laid ghosts and raps and "telepathy" away underground as so much popular delusion. Yet never before were these things offered us so voluminously, and never in such authentic-seeming shape or with such good credentials. The tide seems steadily to be rising, in spite of all the expedients of scientific orthodoxy. It is hard not to suspect that here may be something different from a mere chapter in human gullibility. It may be a genuine realm of natural phenomena.

Falsus in uno, falsus in omnibus, once a cheat, always a cheat, such has been the motto of the English psychical researchers in dealing with mediums. I am disposed to think that, as a matter of policy, it has been wise. Tactically it is far better to believe much too little than a little too much; and the exceptional credit attaching to the row of volumes of the S. P. R.'s Proceedings, is due to the fixed intention of the editors to proceed very slowly. Better a little belief tied fast, better a small investment *salted down*, than a mass of comparative insecurity.

But, however wise as a policy the S. P. R.'s maxim may have been, as a test of truth I believe it to be almost irrelevant. In most things human the accusation of deliberate fraud and falsehood is grossly superficial. Man's character is too sophistically mixed for the alternative of "honest or dishonest" to be a sharp one. Scientific men themselves will cheat —at public lectures—rather than let experiments obey their well-known tendency towards failure. I have heard of a lecturer on physics, who had taken over the apparatus of the previous incumbent, consulting him about a certain machine intended to show that, however the peripheral parts of it might be agitated, its center of gravity remained immovable. "It *will* wobble," he complained. "Well," said the predecessor, apologetically, "to tell the truth, whenever *I* used that machine I found it advisable to *drive a nail* through the center of gravity." I once saw a distinguished physiologist, now dead, cheat most shamelessly at a public lecture, at the expense of a poor rabbit, and all for the sake of being able to make a cheap joke about its being an "American rabbit"—for no other, he said, could survive such a wound as he pretended to have given it.

To compare small men with great, I have myself cheated shamelessly. In the early days of the Sanders Theater at Harvard, I once had charge of a heart on the physiology of which Prof. Newell Martin was giving a popular lecture. This heart, which belonged to a turtle, supported an index-straw which threw a moving shadow, greatly enlarged, upon the screen, while the heart pulsated. When certain nerves were stimulated, the lecturer said, the heart would act in certain ways which he described. But the poor heart was too far gone and, although it stopped duly when the nerve of arrest was excited, that was the final end of its life's tether. Presiding over the performance, I was terrified at the fiasco, and found myself suddenly acting like one of those military geniuses who on the field of battle convert disaster into victory. There was no time for deliberation; so, with my forefinger under a part of the straw that cast no shadow, I found myself impulsively and automatically imitating the rhythmical movements which my colleague had prophesied the heart would undergo. I kept the experiment from failing; and not only saved my colleague (and the turtle) from a humiliation that but for my presence of mind would have been their lot, but I established in the audience the true view of the subject. The lecturer was stating this; and the misconduct of one half-dead specimen of heart ought not to destroy the impression of his words. "There is no worse lie than a truth misunderstood," is a maxim which I have heard ascribed to a former venerated President of Harvard. The heart's failure would have been misunderstood by the audience and given the lie to the lecturer. It was hard enough to make them understand the subject anyhow; so that even now as I write in cool blood I am tempted to think that I acted quite correctly. I was acting for the *larger* truth, at any rate, however automatically; and my sense of this was probably what prevented the more pedantic and literal part of my conscience from checking the action of my sympathetic finger. To this day the memory of that critical emergency has made me feel charitable towards all mediums who make phenomena come in one way when they won't come easily in another. On the principles of the S. P. R., my conduct on that one occasion ought to discredit everything I ever do, everything for example, I may write in this article,—a manifestly unjust conclusion.

Fraud, conscious or unconscious, seems ubiquitous throughout the range of physical phenomena of spiritism, and false pretense, prevarication and fishing for clues are ubiquitous in the mental manifestations of mediums. If it be not everywhere fraud simulating reality, one is tempted to say, then the reality (if any reality there be) has the bad luck of being fated everywhere to simulate fraud. The suggestion of humbug seldom stops, and mixes itself with the best manifestations. Mrs. Piper's control, "Rector," is a most impressive personage, who discerns in an extraordinary degree his sitter's inner needs, and is capable of giving elevated counsel to fastidious and critical minds. Yet in many respects he is an arrant humbug—such he seems to me at least—pretending to a knowledge and power to which he has no title, nonplussed by contradiction, yielding to suggestion, and covering his tracks with plausible excuses. Now the non-"researching" mind looks upon such phenomena simply according to their face-pretension and never thinks of asking what they may signify below the surface. Since they profess for the most part to be revealers of spirit life, it is either as being absolutely that, or as being absolute frauds, that they are judged. The result is an inconceivably shallow state of public opinion on the subject. One set of persons, emotionally touched at hearing the names of their loved ones given, and consoled by assurances that they are "happy," accept the revelation, and consider spiritualism "beautiful." More hard-headed subjects, disgusted by the revelation's contemptible contents, outraged by the fraud, and prejudiced beforehand against all "spirits," high or low, avert their minds from what they call such "rot" or "bosh" entirely. Thus do two opposite sentimentalisms divide opinion between them! A good expression of the "scientific" state of mind occurs in Huxley's "Life and Letters":

"I regret," he writes, "that I am unable to accept the invitation of the Committee of the Dialectical Society. . . . I take no interest in the subject. The only case of 'Spiritualism' I have ever had the opportunity of examining into for myself was as gross an imposture as ever came under my notice. But supposing these phenomena to be genuine—they do not interest me. If anybody would endow me with the faculty of listening to the chatter of old women and curates in the nearest provincial town, I should decline the privilege, having better things to do. And if the folk in the spiritual world do not talk more wisely and sensibly than their friends report them to do, I put them in the same category. The only good that I can see in the demonstration of the 'Truth of Spiritualism' is to furnish an additional argument against suicide. Better live a crossing-sweeper, than die and be made to talk twaddle by a 'medium' hired at a guinea a *Seance*."[1]

Obviously the mind of the excellent Huxley has here but two whole-souled categories, namely revelation or imposture, to apperceive the case by. Sentimental reasons bar revelation out, for the messages, he thinks, are not romantic enough for that; fraud exists anyhow; therefore the whole thing is nothing but imposture. The odd point is that so few of those who talk in this way realize that they and the spiritists are using the same major premise and differing only in the minor. The major premise is: "Any spirit-revelation must be romantic." The minor of the spiritist is: "This *is* romantic"; that of the

[1] T. H. Huxley, "Life and Letters," I, 240.

Huxleyan is: "this is dingy twaddle"—whence their opposite conclusions!

Meanwhile the first thing that anyone learns who attends seriously to these phenomena is that their causation is far too complex for our feelings about what is or is not romantic enough to be spiritual to throw any light upon it. The causal factors must be carefully distinguished and traced through series, from their simplest to their strongest forms, before we can begin to understand the various resultants in which they issue. Myers and Gurney began this work, the one by his serial study of the various sorts of "automatism," sensory and motor, the other by his experimental proofs that a split-off consciousness may abide after a post-hypnotic suggestion has been given. Here we have subjective factors; but are not transsubjective or objective forces also at work? Veridical messages, apparitions, movements without contact, seem *prima facie* to be such. It was a good stroke on Gurney's part to construct a theory of apparitions which brought the subjective and the objective factors into harmonious co-operation. I doubt whether this telepathic theory of Gurney's will hold along the whole line of apparitions to which he applied it, but it is unquestionable that some theory of that mixed type is required for the explanation of all mediumistic phenomena; and that when all the psychological factors and elements involved have been told off—and they are many—the question still forces itself upon us: Are these all, or are there indications of any residual forces acting on the subject from beyond, or of any "metapsychic" faculty, (to use Richet's useful term) exerted by him? This is the problem that requires real expertness, and this is where the simple sentimentalisms of the spiritist and scientist leave us in the lurch completely.

"Psychics" form indeed a special branch of education, in which experts are only gradually becoming developed. The phenomena are as massive and wide-spread as is anything in Nature, and the study of them is as tedious, repellent and undignified. To reject it for its unromantic character is like rejecting bacteriology because *penicillium glaucum* grows on horse-dung and *bacterium termo* lives in putrefaction. Scientific men have long ago ceased to think of the dignity of the materials they work in. When imposture has been checked off as far as possible, when chance coincidence has been allowed for, when opportunities for normal knowledge on the part of the subject have been noted, and skill in "fishing" and following clues unwittingly furnished by the voice or face of bystanders have been counted in, those who have the fullest acquaintance with the phenomena admit that in good mediums *there is a residuum of knowledge displayed* that can only be called supernormal: the medium taps some source of information not open to ordinary people. Myers used the word "telepathy" to indicate that the sitter's own thoughts or feelings may be thus directly tapped. Mrs. Sidgwick has suggested that if living minds can be thus tapped telepathically, so possibly may the minds of spirits be similarly tapped—if spirits there be. On this view we should have one distinct theory of the performances of a typical test-medium. They would be all originally due to an odd *tendency to personate*, found in her dream life as it expresses itself in trance. [Most of us reveal such a tendency whenever we handle a "ouija-board" or a "planchet," or let ourselves write automatically with a pencil.] The result is a "control," who purports to be speaking; and all the resources of the automatist, including his or her trance-faculty of telepathy, are called into play in building this fictitious personage out plausibly. On such a view of the control, the medium's *will to personate* runs the whole show; and if spirits be involved in it at all, they are passive beings, stray bits of whose memory she is able to seize and use for her purposes, without the spirit being any more aware of it than the sitter is aware of it when his own mind is similarly tapped.

This is one possible way of interpreting a certain type of psychical phenomenon. It uses psychological as well as "spiritual" factors, and quite obviously it throws open for us far more questions than it answers, questions about our subconscious constitution and its curious tendency to humbug, about the telepathic faculty, and about the possibility of an existent spirit-world.

I do not instance this theory to defend it, but simply to show what complicated hypotheses one is inevitably led to consider, the moment one looks at the facts in their complexity and turns one's back on the *naïve* alternative of "revelation or imposture," which is as far as either spiritist thought or ordinary scientist thought goes. The phenomena are endlessly complex in their factors, and they are so little understood as yet that off-hand judgments, whether of "spirits" or of "bosh" are the one as silly as the other. When we complicate the subject still farther by considering what connection such things as rappings, apparitions, poltergeists, spirit-photographs, and materializations may have with it, the bosh end of the scale gets heavily loaded, it is true, but your geniune inquirer still is loath to give up. He lets the data collect, and bides his time. He believes that "bosh" is no more an ultimate element in Nature, or a really explanatory category in human life than "dirt" is in chemistry. Every kind of "bosh" has its own factors and laws; and patient study will bring them definitely to light.

The only way to rescue the "pure bosh" view of the matter is one which has sometimes appealed to my own fancy, but which I imagine few readers will seriously adopt. If, namely, one takes the theory of evolution radically, one ought to apply it not only to the rock-strata, the animals and the plants, but to the stars, to the chemical elements, and to the laws of nature. There must have been a far-off antiquity, one is then tempted to suppose, when things were really chaotic. Little by little, out of all the haphazard possibilities of that time, a few connected things and habits arose, and the rudiments of regular performance began. Every variation in the way of law and order added itself to this nucleus, which inevitably grew more considerable as history went on; while the aberrant and inconstant variations, not being similarly preserved, disappeared from being, wandered off as unrelated vagrants, or else remained so imperfectly connected with the part of the world that had grown regular as only to manifest their existence by occasional lawless intrusions, like those which "psychic" phenomena now make into our scientifically organized world. On such a view, these phenomena ought to remain "pure bosh" forever, that is, they ought to be forever intractable to intellectual methods, because they should not yet be organized enough in themselves to follow any laws. Wisps and shreds of the original chaos, they would be connected enough with the cosmos to affect its periphery every now and then, as by a momentary whiff or touch or gleam, but not enough ever to be followed up and hunted down and bagged. Their relation to the cosmos would be tangential solely.

Looked at dramatically, most occult phenomena make just this sort of impression. They are inwardly as incoherent as they are outwardly wayward and fitful. If they express anything, it is pure "bosh," pure discontinuity, accident, and disturbance, with no law apparent but to interrupt, and no purpose but to baffle. They seem like stray vestiges of that primordial irrationality, from which all our rationalities have been evolved.

To settle dogmatically into this bosh-view would save labor, but it would go against too many intellectual prepossessions to be adopted save as a last resort of despair. Your psychical researcher therefore bates no jot of hope, and has faith that when we get our data numerous enough, some sort of rational treatment of them will succeed.

When I hear good people say (as they often say, not without show of reason), that dabbling in such phenomena reduces us to a sort of jelly, disintegrates the critical faculties, liquefies the character, and makes of one a *gobe-mouche* generally, I console myself by thinking of my friends Frederic Myers and Richard Hodgson. These men lived exclusively for psychical research, and it converted both to spiritism. Hodgson would have been a man among men anywhere; but I doubt whether under any other baptism he would have been that happy, sober and righteous form of energy which his face proclaimed him in his later years, when heart and head alike were wholly satisfied by his occupation. Myers's character also grew stronger in every particular for his devotion to the same inquiries. Brought up on literature and sentiment, something of a courtier, passionate, disdainful, and impatient naturally, he was made over again from the day when he took up psychical research seriously. He became learned in science, circumspect, democratic in sympathy, endlessly patient, and above all, happy. The fortitude of his last hours touched the heroic, so completely were the atrocious sufferings of his body cast into insignificance by his interest in the cause he lived for. When a man's pursuit gradually makes his face shine and grow handsome, you may be sure it is a worthy one. Both Hodgson and Myers kept growing ever handsomer and stronger-looking.

Such personal examples will convert no one, and of course they ought not to. Nor do I seek at all in this article to convert any one to my belief that psychical research is an important branch of science. To do that, I should have to quote evidence; and those for whom the volumes of S. P. R. Proceedings already published count for nothing would remain in their dogmatic slumber, though one rose from the dead. No, not to convert readers, but simply to *put my own state of mind upon record publicly* is the purpose of my present writing. Some one said to me a short time ago that after my twenty-five years of dabbling in "Psychics," it would be rather shameful were I unable to state any definite conclusions whatever as a consequence. I had to agree; so I now proceed to take up the challenge and express such convictions as have been engendered in me by that length of experience, be the same true or false ones. I may be dooming myself to the pit in the eyes of better-judging posterity; I may be raising myself to honor; I am willing to take the risk, for what I shall write is *my* truth, as I now see it.

I began this article by confessing myself baffled. I *am* baffled, as to spirit-return, and as to many other special problems. I am also constantly baffled as to what to think of this or that particular story, for the sources of error in any one observation are seldom fully knowable. But weak sticks make strong faggots; and when the stories fall into consistent sorts that point each in a definite direction, one gets a sense of being in presence of genuinely natural types of phenomena. As to there being such real natural types of phenomena ignored by orthodox science, I am not baffled at all, for I am fully convinced of it. One cannot get demonstrative proof here. One has to follow one's personal sense, which, of course, is liable to err, of the dramatic probabilities of nature. Our critics here obey their sense of dramatic probability as much as we do. Take "raps" for example, and the whole business of objects moving without contact. "Nature," thinks the scientific man, is not so unutterably silly. The cabinet, the darkness, the tying, suggest a sort of human rat-hole life exclusively and "swindling" is for him the dramatically sufficient explanation. It probably is, in an indefinite majority of instances; yet it is to me dramatically improbable that the swindling should not have accreted round some originally genuine nucleus. If we look at human imposture as a historic phenomenon, we find it always imitative. One swindler imitates a previous swindler, but the first swindler of that kind imitated some one who was honest. You can no more create an absolutely new trick than you can create a new word without any previous basis.—You don't know how to go about it. Try, reader, yourself, to invent an unprecedented kind of "physical phenomenon of spiritualism." When *I* try, I find myself mentally turning over the regular medium-stock, and thinking how I might improve some item. This being the dramatically probable human way, I think differently of the whole type, taken collectively, from the way in which I may think of the single instance. I find myself believing that there is "something in" these never ending reports of physical phenomena, although I haven't yet the least positive notion of the something. It becomes to my mind simply a very worthy problem for investigation. Either I or the scientist is of course a fool, with our opposite views of probability here; and I only wish he might feel the liability, as cordially as I do, to pertain to both of us.

I fear I look on Nature generally with more charitable eyes than his, though perhaps he would pause if he realized as I do, how vast the fraudulency is which in consistency he must attribute to her. Nature is brutal enough, Heaven knows; but no one yet has held her non-human side to be *dishonest*, and even in the human sphere deliberate deceit is far rarer than the "classic" intellect, with its few and rigid categories, was ready to acknowledge. There is a hazy penumbra in us all where lying and delusion meet, where passion rules beliefs as well as conduct, and where the term "scoundrel" does not clear up everything to the depths as it did for our forefathers. The first automatic writing I ever saw was forty years ago. I unhesitatingly thought of it as deceit, although it contained vague elements of supernormal knowledge. Since then I have come to see in automatic writing one example of a department of human activity as vast as it is enigmatic. Every sort of person is liable to it, or to something equivalent to it; and whoever encourages it in himself finds himself personating someone else, either signing what he writes by fictitious name, or spelling out, by ouija-board or table-tips, messages from the departed. Our subconscious region seems, as a rule, to be dominated either by a crazy "will to make-believe," or by some curious external force impelling us to personation. The first difference between the psychical researcher and the inexpert person is that the former realizes the commonness and typicality of the phenomenon here, while the latter, less informed, thinks it so rare as to be unworthy of attention. *I wish to go on record for the commonness.*

The next thing I wish to go on record for is *the presence*, in the midst of all the humbug, *of really supernormal knowledge*. By this I mean knowledge that cannot be traced to the ordinary sources of information—the senses namely, of the automatist. In really strong mediums this knowledge seems to be abundant, though it is usually spotty, capricious and unconnected. Really strong mediums are rarities; but when one starts with them and works downwards into less brilliant regions of the automatic life, one tends to interpret many slight but odd coincidences with truth as possibly rudimentary forms of this kind of knowledge.

What is one to think of this queer chapter in human nature? It is odd enough on any view. If all it means is a preposterous and inferior monkey-like tendency to forge messages, systematically embedded in the soul of all of us, it is weird; and weirder still that it should then own all this supernormal information. If on the other hand the supernormal information be the key to the phenomenon, it ought to be superior; and then how ought we to account for the "wicked partner," and for the undeniable mendacity and inferiority of so much of the performance? We are thrown, for our conclusions, upon our instinctive sense of the dramatic probabilities of nature. My own dramatic sense tends instinctively to picture the situation as an interaction between slumbering faculties in the automatist's mind and a cosmic environment of *other consciousness* of some sort which is able to work upon them. If there were in the universe a lot of diffuse soul-stuff, unable of itself to get into consistent personal form, or to take permanent possession of an organism, yet always craving to do so, it might get its head into the air, parasitically, so to speak, by profiting by weak spots in the armor of human minds, and slipping in and stirring up there the sleeping tendency to personate. It would induce habits in the subconscious region of the mind it used thus, and would seek above all things to prolong its social opportunities by making itself agreeable and plausible. It would drag stray scraps of truth with it from the wider environment, but would betray its mental inferiority by knowing little how to weave them into any important or significant story.

This, I say, is the dramatic view which my mind spontaneously takes, and it has the advantage of falling into line with ancient human traditions. The views of others are just as dramatic, *for the phenomenon is actuated by will of some sort anyhow*, and wills give rise to dramas. The spiritist view, as held by Messrs. Hyslop and Hodgson, sees a "will to communicate," struggling through inconceivable layers of obstruction in the conditions. I have heard Hodgson liken the difficulties to those of two persons who on earth should have only dead-drunk servants to use as their messengers. The scientist, for his part, sees a "will to deceive," watching its chance in all of us, and able (possibly?) to use "telepathy" in its service.

Which kind of will, and how many kinds of will are most inherently probable? Who can say with certainty? The only certainty is that the phenomena are enormously complex, especially if one includes in them such intellectual flights of mediumship as Swedenborg's, and if one tries in any way to work the physical phenomena in. That is why I personally am as yet neither a convinced believer in parasitic demons, nor a spiritist, nor a scientist, but still remain a psychical researcher waiting for more facts before concluding.

Out of my experience, such as it is (and it is limited enough) one fixed conclusion dogmatically emerges, and that is this, that we with our lives are like islands in the sea, or like trees in the forest. The maple and the pine may whisper to each other with their leaves, and Conanicut and Newport hear each other's fog-horns. But the trees also commingle their roots in the darkness underground, and the islands also hang together through the ocean's bottom. Just so there is a continuum of cosmic consciousness, against which our individuality builds but accidental fences, and into which our several minds plunge as into a mother-sea or reservoir. Our "normal" consciousness is circumscribed for adaptation to our external earthly environment, but the fence is weak in spots, and fitful influences from beyond leak in, showing the otherwise unverifiable common connection. Not only psychic research, but metaphysical philosophy, and speculative biology are led in their own ways to look with favor on some such "panpsychic" view of the universe as this. Assuming this common reservoir of consciousness to exist, this bank upon which we all draw, and in which so many of earth's memories must in some way be stored, or mediums would not get at them as they do, the question is, What is its own structure? What is its inner topography? This question, first squarely formulated by Myers, deserves to be called "Myers's problem" by scientific men hereafter. What are the conditions of individuation or insulation in the mother-sea? To what tracts, to what active systems functioning separately in it, do personalities correspond? Are individual "spirits" constituted there? How numerous, and of how many hierarchic orders may these then be? How permanent? How transient? And how confluent with one another may they become?

What again, are the relations between the cosmic consciousness and matter? Are there subtler forms of matter which upon occasion may enter into functional connection with the individuations in the psychic sea, and then, and then only, show themselves?—So that our ordinary human experience, on its material as well as on its mental side, would appear to be only an extract from the larger psycho-physical world?

Vast, indeed, and difficult is the inquirer's prospect here, and the most significant data for his purpose will probably be just these dingy little mediumistic facts which the Huxleyan minds of our time find so unworthy of their attention. But when was not the science of the future stirred to its conquering activities by the little rebellious exceptions to the science of the present? Hardly, as yet, has the surface of the facts called "psychic" begun to be scratched for scientific purposes.

It is through following these facts, I am persuaded, that the greatest scientific conquests of the coming generation will be achieved. *Kühn ist das Mühen, herrlich der Lohn!*

The American Magazine, October 1909

Bradley or Bergson?

D R. BRADLEY has summed up his *Weltanschauung* in last October's *Mind*, in an article which for sincerity and brevity leaves nothing to be desired. His thought and Bergson's run parallel for such a distance, yet diverge so utterly at last that a comparison seems to me instructive. The watershed is such a knife-edge that no reader who leans to one side or the other can after this plead ignorance of the motives of his choice.

Bradley's first great act of candor in philosophy was his breaking loose from the Kantian tradition that immediate feeling is all disconnectedness. In his "Logic" as well as in his "Appearance" he insisted that in the flux of feeling we directly encounter reality, and that its form, as thus encountered, is the continuity and wholeness of a transparent much-at-once. This is identically Bergson's doctrine. In affirming the "end-osmosis" of adjacent parts of "living" experience, the French writer treats the minimum of feeling as an immediately intuited much-at-once.

The idealist tradition is that feelings, aboriginally discontinuous, are woven into continuity by the various synthetic concepts which the intellect applies. Both Bradley and Bergson contradict this flatly; and although their tactics are so different, their battle is the same. They destroy the notion that conception is essentially a unifying process. For Bergson all concepts are discrete; and though you can get the discrete out of the continuous, out of the discrete you can never construct the continuous again. Concepts, moreover, are static, and can never be adequate substitutes for a perceptual flux of which activity and change are inalienable features. Concepts, says Bergson, make things less, not more, intelligible, when we use them seriously and radically. They serve us practically more than theoretically. Throwing their map of abstract terms and relations round our present experience, they show its bearings and let us plan our way.

Bradley is just as independent of rationalist tradition, and is more thoroughgoing still in his criticism of the conceptual function. When we handle felt realities by our intellect they grow, according to him, less and less comprehensible; activity becomes inconstruable, relation contradictory, change inadmissible, personality unintelligible, time, space, and causation impossible—nothing survives the Bradleyan wreck.

The breach which the two authors make with previous rationalist opinion is complete, and they keep step with each other perfectly up to the point where they diverge. Sense-perception first develops into conception; and then conception, developing its subtler and more contradictory implications, comes to an end of its usefulness for both authors, and runs itself into the ground. Arrived at this conviction, Bergson *drops* conception—which apparently has done us all the good it can do; and, turning back towards perception with its transparent multiplicity-in-union, he takes its data integrally up into philosophy, as a kind of material which nothing else can replace. The fault of our perceptual data, he tells us, is not of nature, but only of extent; and the way to know reality intimately is, according to this philosopher, to sink into those data and get *our sympathetic imagination to enlarge their bounds. Deep* knowledge is not of the conceptually mediated, but of the immediate type. Bergson thus allies himself with old-fashioned empiricism, on the one hand, and with mysticism, on the other. His breach with rationalism could not possibly be more thorough than it is.

Bradley's breach is just as thorough in its first two steps. The form of oneness in the flow of feeling is an attribute of reality which even the absolute must preserve. Concepts are an organ of misunderstanding rather than of understanding; they turn the "reality" which we "encounter" into an "appearance" which we "think." But with all this anti-rationalist *matter*, Bradley is faithful to his anti-empiricist *manner* to the end. Crude unmediated feelings shall never form a part of "truth." "Judgment, on our view," he writes, "transcends and must transcend the immediate unity of feeling upon which it can not cease to depend. Judgment has to qualify the real ideally. . . . This is the fundamental inconsistency of judgment, . . . for ideas can not qualify reality as reality is qualified immediately in feeling. . . . The reality as conditioned in feeling has been in principle abandoned, while other conditions have not been found."[1]

Abandoned in "principle," Mr. Bradley says; and, in sooth, nothing but a sort of religious principle against admitting "untransformed" feeling into philosophy would seem to explain his procedure from here onwards. "At the entrance of philosophy," he says, "there appears to be a point at which the roads divide. By the one way you set out to seek truth in ideas. . . . On this road what is sought is ideas, and nothing else is current. . . . If you enter here you are committed to this principle. . . . [This] whole way doubtless may be delusion; but, if you choose to take this way . . . no possible appeal to designation [i. e., to feeling] in the end is permitted. . . . This I take to be the way of philosophy. . . . It is not the way of life or of common knowledge, and to commit oneself to such a principle may be said to depend upon choice. The way of life starts from and in the end it rests on dependence upon feeling. . . . Outside of philosophy there is no consistent course but to accept the unintelligible. For worse or for better the man who stands on particular feeling must remain outside of philosophy. . . . I recognize that in life and in ordinary knowledge one can never wholly cease to rest on this ground. But how to take over into ultimate theory and to use there this certainty of feeling, *while still leaving that untransformed*, I myself do not know. I admit that philosophy, as I conceive it, is one-sided. I understand the dislike of it and the despair of it while this its defect is not remedied. But to remedy the defect by imparting bodily into philosophy the 'this' and 'thine,' as they are felt, to my mind brings destruction on the spot."[2]

Mr. Bradley's "principle" seems to be only that of doggedly following a line once entered on to the bitterest of ends. We encounter reality in feeling, and find that when we develop it into ideas it becomes more intelligible in certain definite respects. We then have "truth" instead of reality; which truth, however, pursued beyond a certain practical point, develops into the whole bog of unintelligibilities

[1] *Mind*, October, 1909, p. 498.
[2] *Ibid.*, pp. 500–502.

through which the critical part of "Appearance and Reality" wades. The wise and natural course at this point would seem to be to drop the notion that truth is a *thoroughgoing* improvement on reality, to confess that its value is limited, and to hark back. But there is nothing that Mr. Bradley, religiously loyal to the direction of development once entered upon, will not do sooner than this. Forward, forward, let us range! He makes the desperate transconceptual leap, assumes *beyond* the whole ideal perspective an ultimate "suprarelational" and trans-conceptual reality in which somehow the wholeness and certainty and unity of feeling, which we turned our backs on forever when we committed ourselves to the leading of ideas, are supposed to be resurgent in transfigured form; and shows us as the only authentic object of philosophy, with its "way of ideas," an absolute which "can be" and "must be" and therefore "is." "It *shall* be" is the only candid way of stating its relation to belief; and Mr. Bradley's statement comes very near to that.

How could the elements of a situation be made more obvious? Or what could bring to a sharper focus the factor of personal choice involved?

The way of philosophy is not the way of life, Mr. Bradley admits, but for the philosopher, he continues, it seems to be *all there is*—which is like saying that the way of starvation is not the way of life, but to the starveling it is all there is. Be it so! Though what *obliges* one to become either such a philosopher or such a starveling does not clearly appear. The only motive I can possibly think of for choosing to be a philosopher on these painful terms is the old and obstinate intellectualist prejudice in favor of universals. They are loftier, nobler, more rational objects than the particulars of sense. In their direction, then, and away from feeling, should a mind conscious of its high vocation always turn its face. Not to enter life is a *higher vocation* than to enter it, on this view.

The motive is pathetically simple, and any one can take it in. On the thin watershed between life and philosophy, Mr. Bradley tumbles to philosophy's call. Down he slides, to the dry valley of "absolute" mare's nests and abstractions, the habitation of the fictitious suprarelational being which his will prefers. Never was there such a case of will-to-believe;

for Mr. Bradley, unlike other anti-empiricists, deludes himself neither as to feeling nor as to thought: the one reveals for him the inner *nature* of reality perfectly, the other falsifies it utterly as soon as you carry it beyond the first few steps. Yet once committed to the conceptual direction, Mr. Bradley thinks we can't reverse, we can save ourselves only by hoping that the absolute will re-realize unintelligibly and "somehow," the unity, wholeness, certainty, etc., which feeling so immediately and transparently made us acquainted with at first.

Bergson and the empiricists, on the other hand, tumble to life's call, and turn into the valley where the green pastures and the clear waters always were. If in sensible particulars reality reveals the manyness-in-oneness of its constitution in so convincing a way, why then withhold, if you will, the name of "philosophy" from perceptual knowledge, but recognize that perceptual knowledge is at any rate the *only complete kind of knowledge*, and let "philosophy" in Bradley's sense pass for the one-sided affair which he candidly confesses that it is. When the alternative lies between knowing life in its full thickness and activity, as one acquainted with its *me's* and *thee's* and *now's* and *here's*, on the one hand, and knowing a transconceptual evaporation like the absolute, on the other, it seems to me that to choose the latter knowledge merely because it has been named "philosophy" is to be superstitiously loyal to a name. But if names are to be used eulogistically, rather let us give that of philosophy to the fuller kind of knowledge, the kind in which perception and conception mix their lights.

As one who calls himself a radical empiricist, I can find no possible excuse for not inclining towards Bergson's side. He and Bradley together have confirmed my confidence in non-"transmuted" percepts, and have broken my confidence in concepts down. It seems to me that their parallel lines of work have converged to a sharp alternative which now confronts everybody, and in which the reasons for one's choice must plainly appear and be told. Be an empiricist or be a transconceptualist, whichever you please, but at least say why! I sincerely believe that nothing but inveterate anti-empiricist prejudice accounts for Mr. Bradley's choice; for at the point where he stands in the article I have quoted, I can discover no sensible reason why he should prefer the way he takes. If he should ever take it into his head to *revoke*, and drop into the other valley, it would be a great day for English thought. As Kant is supposed to have extinguished all previous forms of rationalism, so Bergson and Bradley, between them, might lay post-Kantian rationalism permanently underground.

The Journal of Philosophy, Psychology and Scientific Methods,
January 20, 1910

A Suggestion About Mysticism

Much INTEREST in the subject of religious mysticism has been shown in philosophic circles of late years. Most of the writings I have seen have treated the subject from the outside, for I know of no one who has spoken as having the direct authority of experience in favor of his views. I also am an outsider, and very likely what I say will prove the fact loudly enough to readers who possibly may stand within the pale. Nevertheless, since between outsiders one is as good as another, I will not leave my suggestion unexpressed.

The suggestion, stated very briefly, is that states of mystical intuition may be only very sudden and great extensions of the ordinary "field of consciousness." Concerning the causes of such extensions I have no suggestion to make; but the extension itself would, if my view be correct, consist in an immense spreading of the margin of the field, so that knowledge ordinarily transmarginal would become included, and the ordinary margin would grow more central. Fechner's "wave-scheme" will diagrammatize the alteration, as I conceive it, if we suppose that the wave of present awareness, steep above the horizontal line that represents the plane of the usual "threshold," slopes away below it very gradually in all directions. A fall of the threshold, however caused, would, under these circumstances, produce the state of things which we see on an unusually flat shore at the ebb of a spring-tide. Vast tracts usually covered are then revealed to view, but nothing rises more than a few inches above the water's bed, and great parts of the scene are submerged again, whenever a wave washes over them.

Some persons have naturally a very wide, others a very narrow, field of consciousness. The narrow field may be represented by an unusually steep form of the wave. When by any accident the threshold lowers, in persons of this type—I speak here from direct personal experience—so that the field widens and the relations of its center to matters usually subliminal come into view, the larger panorama perceived fills the mind with exhilaration and sense of mental power. It is a refreshing experience; and—such is now my hypothesis—we only have to suppose it to occur in an exceptionally extensive form, to give us a mystical paroxysm, if such a term be allowed.

A few remarks about the field of consciousness may be needed to give more definiteness to my hypothesis. The field is composed at all times of a mass of present sensation, in a cloud of memories, emotions, concepts, etc. Yet these ingredients, which have to be named separately, are not separate, as the conscious field contains them. Its form is that of a much-at-once, in the unity of which the sensations, memories, concepts, impulses, etc., coalesce and are dissolved. The present field as a whole came continuously out of its predecessor and will melt into its successor as continuously again, one sensation-mass passing into another sensation-mass and giving the character of a gradually changing *present* to the experience, while the memories and concepts carry time-coefficients which place whatever is present in a temporal perspective more or less vast.

When, now, the threshold falls, what comes into view is not the next mass of *sensation*; for sensation requires new physical stimulations to produce it, and no alteration of a purely mental threshold can create these. Only in case the physical stimuli were already at work subliminally, preparing the next sensation, would whatever sub-sensation was already prepared reveal itself when the threshold fell. But with the memories, concepts, and conational states, the case is different. Nobody knows exactly how far we are "marginally" conscious of these at ordinary times, or how far beyond the "margin" of our present thought trans-marginal consciousness of them may exist.[1] There is at any rate no definite bound set between what is central and what is marginal in consciousness, and the margin itself has no definite bound *a parte foris*. It is like the field of vision, which the slightest movement of

[1] Transmarginal or subliminal, the terms are synonymous. Some psychologists deny the existence of such consciousness altogether (A. H. Pierce, for example, and Münsterberg apparently). Others, *e. g.*, Bergson, make it exist and carry the whole freight of our past. Others again (as Myers) would have it extend (in the "telepathic" mode of communication) from one person's mind into another's. For the purposes of my hypothesis I have to postulate its existence; and once postulating it, I prefer not to set any definite bounds to its extent.

the eye will extend, revealing objects that always stood there to be known. My hypothesis is that a movement of the threshold downwards will similarly bring a mass of subconscious memories, conceptions, emotional feelings, and perceptions of relation, etc., into view all at once; and that if this enlargement of the nimbus that surrounds the sensational present is vast enough, while no one of the items it contains attracts our attention singly, we shall have the conditions fulfilled for a kind of consciousness in all essential respects like that termed mystical. It will be transient, if the change of threshold is transient. It will be of reality, enlargement, and illumination, possibly rapturously so. It will be of unification, for the present coalesces in it with ranges of the remote quite out of its reach under ordinary circumstances; and the sense of *relation* will be greatly enhanced. Its form will be intuitive or perceptual, not conceptual, for the remembered or conceived objects in the enlarged field are supposed not to attract the attention singly, but only to give the sense of a tremendous *muchness* suddenly revealed. If they attracted attention separately, we should have the ordinary steep-waved consciousness, and the mystical character would depart.

Such is my suggestion. Persons who *know* something of mystical experience will no doubt find in it much to criticize. If any such shall do so with definiteness, it will have amply served its purpose of helping our understanding of mystical states to become more precise.

The notion I have tried (at such expense of metaphor) to set forth was originally suggested to me by certain experiences of my own, which could only be described as very sudden and incomprehensible enlargements of the conscious field, bringing with them a curious sense of cognition of real fact. All have occurred within the past five years; three of them were similar in type; the fourth was unique.

In each of the three like cases, the experience broke in abruptly upon a perfectly commonplace situation and lasted perhaps less than two minutes. In one instance I was engaged in conversation, but I doubt whether the interlocutor noticed my abstraction. What happened each time was that I seemed all at once to be reminded of a past experience; and this reminiscence, ere I could conceive or name it distinctly, developed into something further that belonged with it, this in turn into something further still, and so on, until the process faded out, leaving me amazed at the sudden vision of increasing ranges of distant fact of which I could give no articulate account. The mode of consciousness was perceptual, not conceptual—the field expanding so fast that there seemed no time for conception or identification to get in its work. There was a strongly exciting sense that my knowledge of past (or present?) reality was enlarging pulse by pulse, but so rapidly that my intellectual processes could not keep up the pace. The *content* was thus entirely lost to retrospection—it sank into the limbo into which dreams vanish as we gradually awake. The feeling—I won't call it belief—that I had had a sudden *opening*, had seen through a window, as it were, distant realities that incomprehensibly belonged with my own life, was so acute that I can not shake it off to-day.

This conviction of fact-revealed, together with the perceptual form of the experience and the inability to make articulate report, are all characters of mystical states. The point of difference is that in my case certain special directions only, in the field of reality, seemed to get suddenly uncovered, whereas in classical mystical experiences it appears rather as if the whole of reality were uncovered at once. *Uncovering* of some sort is the essence of the phenomenon, at any rate, and is what, in the language of the Fechnerian wave-metaphor, I have used the expression "fall of the threshold" to denote.

My fourth experience of uncovering had to do with dreams. I was suddenly intromitted into the cognizance of a pair of dreams that I could not remember myself to have had, yet they seemed somehow to connect with me. I despair of giving the reader any just idea of the bewildering confusion of mind into which I was thrown by this, the most intensely peculiar experience of my whole life. I wrote a full memorandum of it a couple of days after it happened, and appended some reflections. Even though it should cast no light on the conditions of mysticism, it seems as if this record might be worthy of publication, simply as a contribution to the descriptive literature of pathological mental states. I let it follow, therefore, as originally written, with only a few words altered to make the account more clear.

"San Francisco, Feb. 14th 1906.—The night before last, in my bed at Stanford University, I woke at about 7:30 A.M., from a quiet dream of some sort, and whilst gathering my waking wits, seemed suddenly to get mixed up with reminiscences of a dream of an entirely different sort, which seemed to telescope, as it were, into the first one, a dream very elaborate, of lions, and tragic. I concluded this to have been a previous dream of the same sleep; but the apparent mingling of two dreams was something very queer, which I had never before experienced.

"On the following night (Feb. 12–13) I awoke suddenly from my first sleep, which appeared to have been very heavy, in the middle of a dream, in thinking of which I became suddenly confused by the contents of two other dreams that shuffled themselves abruptly in between the parts of the first dream, and of which I couldn't grasp the origin. Whence come *these dreams*? I asked. They were close to *me*, and fresh, as if I had just dreamed them; and yet they were far away *from the first dream*. The contents of the three had absolutely no connection. One had a cockney atmosphere, it had happened to some one in London. The other two were American. One involved the trying on of a coat (was this the dream I seemed to wake from?) the other was a sort of nightmare and had to do with soldiers. Each had a wholly distinct emotional atmosphere that made its individuality discontinuous with that of the others. And yet, in a moment, as these three dreams alternately telescoped into and out of each other, and I seemed to myself to have been their common dreamer, they seemed quite as distinctly *not* to have been dreamed in succession, in that one sleep. *When*, then? Not on a previous night, either. *When*, then? and *which* was the one out of which I had just awakened? *I could no longer tell:* one was as close to me as the others, and yet they entirely repelled each other, and I seemed thus to belong to three different dream-systems at once, no one of which would connect itself either with the others or with my waking life. I began to feel curiously confused and *scared*, and tried to wake myself up wider, but I seemed already wide-awake. Presently cold shivers of dread ran over me: *am I getting into other people's dreams?* Is this a 'telepathic' experience? Or an invasion of double (or treble) personality? Or is it a thrombus in a cortical artery? and the beginning of a general mental 'confusion' and disorientation which is going on to develop who knows how far?

"Decidedly I was losing hold of my 'self,' and making acquaintance with a quality of mental distress that I had never known before, its nearest analogue being the sinking, giddying anxiety that one may have when, in the woods, one discovers that one is really 'lost.' Most human troubles look towards a terminus. Most fears point in a direction, and concentrate towards a climax. Most assaults of the evil one may be met by bracing oneself against something, one's principles, one's courage, one's will, one's pride. But in this experience all was diffusion from a centre, and foothold swept away, the brace itself disintegrating all the faster as one needed its support more direly. Meanwhile vivid perception (or remembrance) of the various dreams kept coming over me in alternation. Whose? *whose?* WHOSE? Unless I can *attach* them, I am swept out to sea with no horizon and no bond, getting *lost*. The idea aroused the 'creeps' again, and with it the fear of again falling asleep and renewing the process. It had begun the previous night, but then the confusion had only gone one step, and had seemed simply curious. *This* was the second step—where might I be after a third step had been taken? My teeth chattered at the thought.

"At the same time I found myself filled with a new pity towards persons passing into dementia with *Verwirrtheit*, or into invasions of secondary personality. *We* regard them as simply *curious*; but what *they* want in the awful drift of their being out of its customary self, is any principle of steadiness to hold on to. We ought to assure them and reassure them that we will stand by them, and recognize the true self in them to the end. We ought to let them know that we are with *them* and not (as too often we must seem to them) a part of the world that but confirms and publishes their deliquescence.

"Evidently I was in full possession of my reflective wits; and whenever I thus objectively thought of the situation in which I was, my anxieties ceased. But there was a tendency to relapse into the dreams and reminiscences, and to relapse vividly; and then the confusion recommenced, along with the emotion of dread lest it should develop farther.

"Then I looked at my watch. Half past twelve! Midnight, therefore. And this gave me another reflective idea. Habitually, on going to bed, I fall into a very deep slumber from which I never naturally awaken until after two. I never awaken, therefore, from a midnight dream, as I did to-night, so of midnight dreams my ordinary consciousness retains no recollection. My sleep seemed terribly heavy as I woke to-night. Dream states carry dream memories—why may not the two succedaneous dreams (whichever two of the three *were* succedaneous) be memories of *twelve o'clock dreams of previous nights*, swept in, along with the just-fading dream, into the just-waking system of memory? Why, in short, may I not be tapping, in a way precluded by my ordinary habit of life, *the midnight stratum* of my past experiences?

"This idea gave great relief—I felt now as if I were in full possession of my *anima rationalis*. I turned on my light, resolving to read myself to sleep. But I didn't read, I felt drowsy instead, and, putting out the light, soon was in the arms of Morpheus.

"I woke again two or three times before daybreak with no dream-experiences, and finally, with a curious, but not alarming, confusion between two dreams, similar to that which I had had the previous morning, I awoke to the new day at seven.

"Nothing peculiar happened the following night, so the thing seems destined not to develop any further."[1]

The distressing confusion of mind in this experience was the exact opposite of mystical illumination, and equally unmystical was the definiteness of what was perceived. But the exaltation of the sense of relation was mystical (the perplexity

---

[1] I print the rest of my memorandum in the shape of a note:—

"Several ideas suggest themselves that make the observation instructive.

"First, the general notion, now gaining ground in mental medicine, that certain mental maladies may be foreshadowed in dream-life, and that therefore the study of the latter may be profitable.

"Then the specific suggestion, that states of 'confusion,' loss of personality, *apraxia*, etc., so often taken to indicate cortical lesion or degeneration of dementic type, may be very superficial functional affections. In my own case the confusion was *foudroyante*—a state of consciousness unique and unparalleled in my 64 years of the world's experience; yet it alternated quickly with perfectly rational states, as this record shows. It seems, therefore, merely as if

all revolved about the fact that the three dreams *both did and did not belong in the most intimate way together*); and the sense that *reality was being uncovered* was mystical in the highest degree. To this day I feel that those extra dreams were dreamed in reality, but when, where, and by whom, I can not guess.

In the *Open Court* for December, 1909, Mr. Frederick Hall narrates a fit of ether-mysticism which agrees with my formula very well. When one of his doctors made a remark to the other, he chuckled, for he realized that these friends "believed they saw real things and causes, but they *didn't*, and I did. . . . I was where the causes *were* and to see them required no more mental ability than to recognize a color as blue. . . . The knowledge of how little [the doctors] actually did see, coupled with their evident feeling that they saw all there was, was funny to the last degree. . . . [They] knew as little of the real causes as does the child who, viewing a passing train and noting its revolving wheels, supposes that they, turning of themselves, give to coaches and locomotive their momentum. Or imagine a man seated in a boat, surrounded by dense fog, and out of the fog seeing a flat stone leap from the crest of one wave to another. *If he had always sat thus*, his explanations must be very crude as compared with those of a man whose eyes could pierce fog, and who saw upon the shore the boy skipping stones. In some such way the remarks of the two physicians seemed to me like the last two 'skips' of a stone thrown from my side. . . . All that was essential in the remark I knew before it was made. Thus to discover

---

the threshold between the rational and the morbid state had, in my case, been temporarily lowered, and as if similar confusions might be very near the line of possibility in all of us.

"There are also the suggestions of a telepathic entrance into some one else's dreams, and of a doubling up of personality. In point of fact I don't know now 'who' had those three dreams, or which one 'I' first woke up from, so quickly did they substitute themselves back and forth for each other, discontinuously. Their discontinuity was the pivot of the situation. My sense of it was as 'vivid' and 'original' an experience as anything Hume could ask for. And yet they kept telescoping!

"Then there is the notion that by waking at certain hours we may tap distinct strata of ancient dream-memory."

convincingly and for myself, that the things which are unseen are those of real importance, this was sufficiently stimulating."

It is evident that Mr. Hall's marginal field got enormously enlarged by the ether, yet so little defined as to its particulars that what he perceived was mainly the thoroughgoing causal integration of its whole content. That this perception brought with it a tremendous feeling of importance and superiority is a matter of course.

I have treated the phenomenon under discussion as if it consisted in the uncovering of tracts of *consciousness*. Is the consciousness already there waiting to be uncovered? and is it a veridical revelation of reality? These are questions on which I do not touch. In the subjects of the experience the "emotion of conviction" is always strong, and sometimes absolute. The ordinary psychologist disposes of the phenomenon under the conveniently "scientific" head of *petit mal*, if not of "bosh" or "rubbish." But we know so little of the noetic value of abnormal mental states of any kind that in my own opinion we had better keep an open mind and collect facts sympathetically for a long time to come. We shall not *understand* these alterations of consciousness either in this generation or in the next.

The Journal of Philosophy, Psychology and Scientific Methods,
February 17, 1910

The Moral Equivalent of War

THE WAR against war is going to be no holiday excursion or camping party. The military feelings are too deeply grounded to abdicate their place among our ideals until better substitutes are offered than the glory and shame that come to nations as well as to individuals from the ups and downs of politics and the vicissitudes of trade. There is something highly paradoxical in the modern man's relation to war. Ask all our millions, north and south, whether they would vote now (were such a thing possible) to have our war for the Union expunged from history, and the record of a peaceful transition to the present time substituted for that of its marches and battles, and probably hardly a handful of eccentrics would say yes. Those ancestors, those efforts, those memories and legends, are the most ideal part of what we now own together, a sacred spiritual possession worth more than all the blood poured out. Yet ask those same people whether they would be willing in cold blood to start another civil war now to gain another similar possession, and not one man or woman would vote for the proposition. In modern eyes, precious though wars may be, they must not be waged solely for the sake of the ideal harvest. Only when forced upon one, only when an enemy's injustice leaves us no alternative, is a war now thought permissible.

It was not thus in ancient times. The earlier men were hunting men, and to hunt a neighboring tribe, kill the males, loot the village and possess the females, was the most profitable, as well as the most exciting, way of living. Thus were the more martial tribes selected, and in chiefs and peoples a pure pugnacity and love of glory came to mingle with the more fundamental appetite for plunder.

Modern war is so expensive that we feel trade to be a better avenue to plunder; but modern man inherits all the innate pugnacity and all the love of glory of his ancestors. Showing war's irrationality and horror is of no effect upon him. The horrors make the fascination. War is the *strong* life; it is life *in extremis*; war-taxes are the only ones men never hesitate to pay, as the budgets of all nations show us.

History is a bath of blood. The Iliad is one long recital of how Diomedes and Ajax, Sarpedon and Hector *killed*. No detail of the wounds they made is spared us, and the Greek mind fed upon the story. Greek history is a panorama of jingoism and imperialism—war for war's sake, all the citizens being warriors. It is horrible reading, because of the irrationality of it all—save for the purpose of making "history"—and the history is that of the utter ruin of a civilization in intellectual respects perhaps the highest the earth has ever seen.

Those wars were purely piratical. Pride, gold, women, slaves, excitement, were their only motives. In the Peloponnesian war, for example, the Athenians ask the inhabitants of Melos (the island where the "Venus of Milo" was found), hitherto neutral, to own their lordship. The envoys meet, and hold a debate which Thucydides gives in full, and which, for sweet reasonableness of form, would have satisfied Matthew Arnold. "The powerful exact what they can," said the Athenians, "and the weak grant what they must." When the Meleans say that sooner than be slaves they will appeal to the gods, the Athenians reply: "Of the gods we believe and of men we know that, by a law of their nature, wherever they can rule they will. This law was not made by us, and we are not the first to have acted upon it; we did but inherit it, and we know that you and all mankind, if you were as strong as we are, would do as we do. So much for the gods; we have told you why we expect to stand as high in their good opinion as you." Well, the Meleans still refused, and their town was taken. "The Athenians," Thucydides quietly says, "thereupon put to death all who were of military age and made slaves of the women and children. They then colonized the island, sending thither five hundred settlers of their own."

Alexander's career was piracy pure and simple, nothing but an orgy of power and plunder, made romantic by the character of the hero. There was no rational principle in it, and the moment he died his generals and governors attacked one another. The cruelty of those times is incredible. When Rome finally conquered Greece, Paulus Aemilius was told by the Roman Senate to reward his soldiers for their toil by "giving" them the old kingdom of Epirus. They sacked seventy cities and carried off a hundred and fifty thousand inhabitants as slaves. How many they killed I know not; but in Etolia they killed all the senators, five hundred and fifty in number. Brutus was "the noblest Roman of them all," but to reanimate his soldiers on the eve of Philippi he similarly promises to give them the cities of Sparta and Thessalonica to ravage, if they win the fight.

Such was the gory nurse that trained societies to cohesiveness. We inherit the warlike type; and for most of the capacities of heroism that the human race is full of we have to thank this cruel history. Dead men tell no tales, and if there were any tribes of other type than this they have left no survivors. Our ancestors have bred pugnacity into our bone and marrow, and thousands of years of peace won't breed it out of us. The popular imagination fairly fattens on the thought of wars. Let public opinion once reach a certain fighting pitch, and no ruler can withstand it. In the Boer war both governments began with bluff, but couldn't stay there, the military tension was too much for them. In 1898 our people had read the word WAR in letters three inches high for three months in every newspaper. The pliant politician McKinley was swept away by their eagerness, and our squalid war with Spain became a necessity.

At the present day, civilized opinion is a curious mental mixture. The military instincts and ideals are as strong as ever, but are confronted by reflective criticisms which sorely curb their ancient freedom. Innumerable writers are showing up the bestial side of military service. Pure loot and mastery seem no longer morally avowable motives, and pretexts must be found for attributing them solely to the enemy. England and we, our army and navy authorities repeat without ceasing, arm solely for "peace," Germany and Japan it is who are bent on loot and glory. "Peace" in military mouths to-day is a synonym for "war expected." The word has become a pure provocative, and no government wishing peace sincerely should allow it ever to be printed in a newspaper. Every up-to-date Dictionary should say that "peace" and "war" mean the same thing, now *in posse*, now *in actu*. It may even reasonably be said that the intensely sharp competitive *preparation* for war by the nations *is the real war*, permanent, unceasing; and that the battles are only a sort of public verification of the mastery gained during the "peace"-interval.

It is plain that on this subject civilized man has developed a sort of double personality. If we take European nations, no legitimate interest of any one of them would seem to justify the tremendous destructions which a war to compass it would necessarily entail. It would seem as though common sense and reason ought to find a way to reach agreement in every conflict of honest interests. I myself think it our bounden duty to believe in such international rationality as possible. But, as things stand, I see how desperately hard it is to bring the peace-party and the war-party together, and I believe that the difficulty is due to certain deficiencies in the program of pacificism which set the militarist imagination strongly, and to a certain extent justifiably, against it. In the whole discussion both sides are on imaginative and sentimental ground. It is but one utopia against another, and everything one says must be abstract and hypothetical. Subject to this criticism and caution, I will try to characterize in abstract strokes the opposite imaginative forces, and point out what to my own very fallible mind seems the best utopian hypothesis, the most promising line of conciliation.

In my remarks, pacificist tho' I am, I will refuse to speak of the bestial side of the war-régime (already done justice to by many writers) and consider only the higher aspects of militaristic sentiment. Patriotism no one thinks discreditable; nor does any one deny that war is the romance of history. But inordinate ambitions are the soul of every patriotism, and the possibility of violent death the soul of all romance. The militarily patriotic and romantic-minded everywhere, and especially the professional military class, refuse to admit for a moment that war may be a transitory phenomenon in social evolution. The notion of a sheep's paradise like that revolts, they say, our higher imagination. Where then would be the steeps of life? If war had ever stopped, we should have to reinvent it, on this view, to redeem life from flat degeneration.

Reflective apologists for war at the present day all take it religiously. It is a sort of sacrament. Its profits are to the vanquished as well as to the victor; and quite apart from any question of profit, it is an absolute good, we are told, for it is human nature at its highest dynamic. Its "horrors" are a cheap price to pay for rescue from the only alternative supposed, of a world of clerks and teachers, of co-education and zoophily, of "consumer's leagues" and "associated charities," of industrialism unlimited, and feminism unabashed. No scorn, no hardness, no valor any more! Fie upon such a cattleyard of a planet!

So far as the central essence of this feeling goes, no healthy minded person, it seems to me, can help to some degree partaking of it. Militarism is the great preserver of our ideals of hardihood, and human life with no use for hardihood would be contemptible. Without risks or prizes for the darer, history would be insipid indeed; and there is a type of military character which every one feels that the race should never cease to breed, for every one is sensitive to its superiority. The duty is incumbent on mankind, of keeping military characters in stock—of keeping them, if not for use, then as ends in themselves and as pure pieces of perfection,—so that Roosevelt's weaklings and mollycoddles may not end by making everything else disappear from the face of nature.

This natural sort of feeling forms, I think, the innermost soul of army-writings. Without any exception known to me, militarist authors take a highly mystical view of their subject, and regard war as a biological or sociological necessity, uncontrolled by ordinary psychological checks and motives. When the time of development is ripe the war must come, reason or no reason, for the justifications pleaded are invariably fictitious. War is, in short, a permanent human *obligation*. General Homer Lea, in his recent book "the Valor of Ignorance," plants himself squarely on this ground. Readiness for war is for him the essence of nationality, and ability in it the supreme measure of the health of nations.

Nations, General Lea says, are never stationary—they must necessarily expand or shrink, according to their vitality or decrepitude. Japan now is culminating; and by the fatal law in question it is impossible that her statesmen should not long since have entered, with extraordinary foresight, upon a vast policy of conquest—the game in which the first moves were her wars with China and Russia and her treaty with England, and of which the final objective is the capture of the Philip-

pines, the Hawaiian Islands, Alaska, and the whole of our
Coast west of the Sierra Passes. This will give Japan what her
ineluctable vocation as a state absolutely forces her to claim,
the possession of the entire Pacific Ocean; and to oppose
these deep designs we Americans have, according to our author, nothing but our conceit, our ignorance, our commercialism, our corruption, and our feminism. General Lea makes
a minute technical comparison of the military strength which
we at present could oppose to the strength of Japan, and concludes that the islands, Alaska, Oregon, and Southern California, would fall almost without resistance, that San Francisco
must surrender in a fortnight to a Japanese investment, that
in three or four months the war would be over, and our republic, unable to regain what it had heedlessly neglected to
protect sufficiently, would then "disintegrate," until perhaps
some Caesar should arise to weld us again into a nation.

A dismal forecast indeed! Yet not unplausible, if the mentality of Japan's statesmen be of the Caesarian type of which
history shows so many examples, and which is all that General
Lea seems able to imagine. But there is no reason to think
that women can no longer be the mothers of Napoleonic or
Alexandrian characters; and if these come in Japan and find
their opportunity, just such surprises as "the Valor of Ignorance" paints may lurk in ambush for us. Ignorant as we still
are of the innermost recesses of Japanese mentality, we may
be foolhardy to disregard such possibilities.

Other militarists are more complex and more moral in their
considerations. The "Philosophie des Krieges," by S. R.
Steinmetz is a good example. War, according to this author,
is an ordeal instituted by God, who weighs the nations in its
balance. It is the essential form of the State, and the only
function in which peoples can employ all their powers at once
and convergently. No victory is possible save as the resultant
of a totality of virtues, no defeat for which some vice or weakness is not responsible. Fidelity, cohesiveness, tenacity, heroism, conscience, education, inventiveness, economy, wealth,
physical health and vigor—there isn't a moral or intellectual
point of superiority that doesn't tell, when God holds his as-
sizes and hurls the peoples upon one another. *Die Weltge-
schichte ist das Weltgericht*; and Dr. Steinmetz does not believe

that in the long run chance and luck play any part in apportioning the issues.

The virtues that prevail, it must be noted, are virtues anyhow, superiorities that count in peaceful as well as in military competition; but the strain on them, being infinitely intenser in the latter case, makes war infinitely more searching as a trial. No ordeal is comparable to its winnowings. Its dread hammer is the welder of men into cohesive states, and nowhere but in such states can human nature adequately develop its capacity. The only alternative is "degeneration."

Dr. Steinmetz is a conscientious thinker, and his book, short as it is, takes much into account. Its upshot can, it seems to me, be summed up in Simon Patten's word, that mankind was nursed in pain and fear, and that the transition to a "pleasure-economy" may be fatal to a being wielding no powers of defense against its disintegrative influences. If we speak of the *fear of emancipation from the fear-regime*, we put the whole situation into a single phrase; fear regarding ourselves now taking the place of the ancient fear of the enemy.

Turn the fear over as I will in my mind, it all seems to lead back to two unwillingnesses of the imagination, one aesthetic, and the other moral: unwillingness, first to envisage a future in which army-life, with its many elements of charm, shall be forever impossible, and in which the destinies of peoples shall nevermore be decided quickly, thrillingly, and tragically, by force, but only gradually and insipidly by "evolution"; and, secondly, unwillingness to see the supreme theatre of human strenuousness closed, and the splendid military aptitudes of men doomed to keep always in a state of latency and never show themselves in action. These insistent unwillingnesses, no less than other esthetic and ethical insistencies have, it seems to me, to be listened to and respected. One cannot meet them effectively by mere counter-insistency on war's expensiveness and horror. The horror makes the thrill; and when the question is of getting the extremest and supremest out of human nature, talk of expense sounds ignominious. The weakness of so much merely negative criticism is evident—pacificism makes no converts from the military party. The military party denies neither the bestiality nor the horror, nor the expense; it only says that these things tell but half the story. It only says that war is *worth* them; that, taking human nature as a whole, its wars are its best protection against its weaker and more cowardly self, and that mankind cannot *afford* to adopt a peace-economy.

Pacificists ought to enter more deeply into the esthetical and ethical point of view of their opponents. Do that first in any controversy, says J. J. Chapman, *then move the point*, and your opponent will follow. So long as anti-militarists propose no substitute for war's disciplinary function, no *moral equivalent* of war, analogous, as one might say, to the mechanical equivalent of heat, so long they fail to realize the full inwardness of the situation. And as a rule they do fail. The duties, penalties, and sanctions pictured in the utopias they paint are all too weak and tame to touch the military-minded. Tolstoy's pacificism is the only exception to this rule, for it is profoundly pessimistic as regards all this world's values, and makes the fear of the Lord furnish the moral spur provided elsewhere by the fear of the enemy. But our socialistic peace-advocates all believe absolutely in this world's values; and instead of the fear of the Lord and the fear of the enemy, the only fear they reckon with is the fear of poverty if one be lazy. This weakness pervades all the socialistic literature with which I am acquainted. Even in Lowes Dickinson's exquisite dialogue,[1] high wages and short hours are the only forces invoked for overcoming man's distaste for repulsive kinds of labor. Meanwhile men at large still live as they always have lived, under a pain-and-fear economy—for those of us who live in an ease-economy are but an island in the stormy ocean—and the whole atmosphere of present-day utopian literature tastes mawkish and dishwatery to people who still keep a sense for life's more bitter flavors. It suggests, in truth, ubiquitous inferiority.

Inferiority is always with us, and merciless scorn of it is the keynote of the military temper. "Dogs, would you live forever?" shouted Frederick the Great. "Yes," say our utopians, "let us live forever, and raise our level gradually." The best thing about our "inferiors" to-day is that they are as tough as nails, and physically and morally almost as insensitive. Uto-

[1] Justice and Liberty, N. Y., 1909

pianism would see them soft and squeamish, while militarism would keep their callousness, but transfigure it into a meritorious characteristic, needed by "the service," and redeemed by that from the suspicion of inferiority. All the qualities of a man acquire dignity when he knows that the service of the collectivity that owns him needs them. If proud of the collectivity, his own pride rises in proportion. No collectivity is like an army for nourishing such pride; but it has to be confessed that the only sentiment which the image of pacific cosmopolitan industrialism is capable of arousing in countless worthy breasts is shame at the idea of belonging to *such* a collectivity. It is obvious that the United States of America as they exist to-day impress a mind like General Lea's as so much human blubber. Where is the sharpness and precipitousness, the contempt for life, whether one's own, or another's? Where is the savage "yes" and "no," the unconditional duty? Where is the conscription? Where is the blood-tax? Where is anything that one feels honored by belonging to?

Having said thus much in preparation, I will now confess my own utopia. I devoutly believe in the reign of peace and in the gradual advent of some sort of a socialistic equilibrium. The fatalistic view of the war-function is to me nonsense, for I know that war-making is due to definite motives and subject to prudential checks and reasonable criticisms, just like any other form of enterprise. And when whole nations are the armies, and the science of destruction vies in intellectual refinement with the sciences of production, I see that war becomes absurd and impossible from its own monstrosity. Extravagant ambitions will have to be replaced by reasonable claims, and nations must make common cause against them. I see no reason why all this should not apply to yellow as well as to white countries, and I look forward to a future when acts of war shall be formally outlawed as between civilized peoples.

All these beliefs of mine put me squarely into the anti-militarist party. But I do not believe that peace either ought to be or will be permanent on this globe, unless the states pacifically organized preserve some of the old elements of army-discipline. A permanently successful peace-economy cannot be a simple pleasure-economy. In the more or less socialistic future towards which mankind seems drifting we must still subject ourselves collectively to those severities which answer to our real position upon this only partly hospitable globe. We must make new energies and hardihoods continue the manliness to which the military mind so faithfully clings. Martial virtues must be the enduring cement; intrepidity, contempt of softness, surrender of private interest, obedience to command, must still remain the rock upon which states are built—unless, indeed, we wish for dangerous reactions against commonwealths fit only for contempt, and liable to invite attack whenever a centre of crystallization for military-minded enterprise gets formed anywhere in their neighborhood.

The war-party is assuredly right in affirming and reaffirming that the martial virtues, although originally gained by the race through war, are absolute and permanent human goods. Patriotic pride and ambition in their military form are, after all, only specifications of a more general competitive passion. They are its first form, but that is no reason for supposing them to be its last form. Men now are proud of belonging to a conquering nation, and without a murmur they lay down their persons and their wealth, if by so doing they may fend off subjection. But who can be sure that *other aspects of one's country* may not, with time and education and suggestion enough, come to be regarded with similarly effective feelings of pride and shame? Why should men not some day feel that it is worth a blood-tax to belong to a collectivity superior in *any* ideal respect? Why should they not blush with indignant shame if the community that owns them is vile in any way whatsoever? Individuals, daily more numerous, now feel this civic passion. It is only a question of blowing on the spark till the whole population gets incandescent, and on the ruins of the old morals of military honour, a stable system of morals of civic honour builds itself up. What the whole community comes to believe in grasps the individual as in a vise. The war-function has graspt us so far; but constructive interests may some day seem no less imperative, and impose on the individual a hardly lighter burden.

Let me illustrate my idea more concretely. There is nothing to make one indignant in the mere fact that life is hard, that men should toil and suffer pain. The planetary conditions once for all are such, and we can stand it. But that so many men, by mere accidents of birth and opportunity, should have a life of *nothing else* but toil and pain and hardness and inferiority imposed upon them, should have *no* vacation, while others natively no more deserving never get any taste of this campaigning life at all,—*this* is capable of arousing indignation in reflective minds. It may end by seeming shameful to all of us that some of us have nothing but campaigning, and others nothing but unmanly ease. If now—and this is my idea—there were, instead of military conscription a conscription of the whole youthful population to form for a certain number of years a part of the army enlisted against *Nature*, the injustice would tend to be evened out, and numerous other goods to the commonwealth would follow. The military ideals of hardihood and discipline would be wrought into the growing fibre of the people; no one would remain blind as the luxurious classes now are blind, to man's real relations to the globe he lives on, and to the permanently sour and hard foundations of his higher life. To coal and iron mines, to freight trains, to fishing fleets in December, to dishwashing, clothes-washing, and window-washing, to roadbuilding and tunnel-making, to foundries and stoke-holes, and to the frames of skyscrapers, would our gilded youths be drafted off, according to their choice, to get the childishness knocked out of them, and to come back into society with healthier sympathies and soberer ideas. They would have paid their blood-tax, done their own part in the immemorial human warfare against nature, they would tread the earth more proudly, the women would value them more highly, they would be better fathers and teachers of the following generation.

Such a conscription, with the state of public opinion that would have required it, and the many moral fruits it would bear, would preserve in the midst of a pacific civilization the manly virtues which the military party is so afraid of seeing disappear in peace. We should get toughness without callousness, authority with as little criminal cruelty as possible, and painful work done cheerily because the duty is temporary, and threatens not, as now, to degrade the whole remainder of one's life. I spoke of the "moral equivalent" of war. So far, war has been the only force that can discipline a whole community, and until an equivalent discipline is organized, I believe that war must have its way. But I have no serious doubt that the ordinary prides and shames of social man, once developed to a certain intensity, are capable of organizing such a moral equivalent as I have sketched, or some other just as effective for preserving manliness of type. It is but a question of time, of skillful propagandism, and of opinion-making men seizing historic opportunities.

The martial type of character can be bred without war. Strenuous honour and disinterestedness abound elsewhere. Priests and medical men are in a fashion educated to it, and we should all feel some degree of it imperative if we were conscious of our work as an obligatory service to the state. We should be *owned*, as soldiers are by the army, and our pride would rise accordingly. We could be poor, then, without humiliation, as army officers now are. The only thing needed henceforward is to inflame the civic temper as past history has inflamed the military temper. H. G. Wells, as usual, sees the centre of the situation. "In many ways," he says, "military organization is the most peaceful of activities. When the contemporary man steps from the street, of clamorous insincere advertisement, push, adulteration, underselling and intermittent employment, into the barrack-yard, he steps on to a higher social plane, into an atmosphere of service and co-operation and of infinitely more honourable emulations. Here at least men are not flung out of employment to degenerate because there is no immediate work for them to do. They are fed and drilled and trained for better services. Here at least a man is supposed to win promotion by self-forgetfulness and not by self-seeking. And beside the feeble and irregular endowment of research by commercialism, its little short-sighted snatches at profit by innovation and scientific economy, see how remarkable is the steady and rapid development of method and appliances in naval and military affairs! Nothing is more striking than to compare the progress of civil conveniences which has been left almost entirely to the trader, to the progress in military apparatus during the last few decades. The house-appliances of to-day for example, are little better than they were fifty years ago. A house of to-day is still almost as ill-ventilated, badly heated by wasteful fires, clumsily arranged and furnished as the house of 1858. Houses a couple of hundred years old are still satisfactory places of residence, so little have our standards risen. But the rifle or battleship of fifty years ago was beyond all comparison inferior to those we possess; in power, in speed, in convenience alike. No one has a use now for such superannuated things."[1]

Wells adds[2] that he thinks that the conceptions of order and discipline, the tradition of service and devotion, of physical fitness, unstinted exertion, and universal responsibility, which universal military duty is now teaching European nations, will remain a permanent acquisition, when the last ammunition has been used in the fireworks that celebrate the final peace. I believe as he does. It would be simply preposterous if the only force that could work ideals of honour and standards of efficiency into English or American natures should be the fear of being killed by the Germans or the Japanese. Great indeed is Fear; but it is not, as our military enthusiasts believe and try to make us believe, the only stimulus known for awakening the higher ranges of men's spiritual energy. The amount of alteration in public opinion which my utopia postulates is vastly less than the difference between the mentality of those black warriors who pursued Stanley's party on the Congo with their cannibal war-cry of "Meat! Meat" and that of the "general-staff" of any civilized nation. History has seen the latter interval bridged over: the former one can be bridged over much more easily.

[1] First and Last Things, 1908, p. 215.
[2] Ibid., p. 226.

Association for International Conciliation: Leaflet No. 27,
February 1910

A Pluralistic Mystic

NOT FOR the ignoble vulgar do I write this article, but only for those dialectic-mystic souls who have an irresistible taste, acquired or native, for higher flights of metaphysics. I have always held the opinion that one of the first duties of a good reader is to summon other readers to the enjoyment of any unknown author of rare quality whom he may discover in his explorations. Now for years my own taste, literary as well as philosophic, has been exquisitely titillated by a writer the name of whom I think must be unknown to the readers of this article; so I no longer continue silent about the merits of BENJAMIN PAUL BLOOD.

Mr Blood inhabits a city otherwise, I imagine, quite unvisited by the Muses, the town called Amsterdam, situated on the New York Central Railroad. What his regular or bread-winning occupation may be I know not, but it can't have made him super-wealthy. He is an author only when the fit strikes him, and for short spurts at a time; shy, moreover, to the point of publishing his compositions only as private tracts, or in letters to such far-from-reverberant organs of publicity as the *Gazette* or the *Recorder* of his native Amsterdam, or the *Utica Herald* or the *Albany Times*. Odd places for such subtile efforts to appear in, but creditable to American editors in these degenerate days! Once, indeed, the lamented W. T. Harris of the old *Journal of Speculative Philosophy* got wind of these epistles, and the result was a revision of some of them for that review ("Philosophic Reveries," 1889). Also a couple of poems were reprinted from their leaflets by the editor of *Scribner's Magazine* ("The Lion of the Nile," 1888, and "Nemesis," 1899). But apart from these three dashes before the footlights, Mr Blood has kept behind the curtain all his days.[1]

The author's maiden adventure was the *Anæsthetic Reve-*

---

[1] "Yes! Paul is quite a correspondent!" said a good citizen of Amsterdam, from whom I inquired the way to Mr Blood's dwelling many years ago, after alighting from the train. I had sought to identify him by calling him an "author," but his neighbour thought of him only as a writer of letters to the journals I have named.

lation, a pamphlet printed privately at Amsterdam in 1874. I forget how it fell into my hands, but it fascinated me so "weirdly" that I am conscious of its having been one of the stepping-stones of my thinking ever since. It gives the essence of Blood's philosophy, and shows most of the features of his talent—albeit one finds in it little humour and no verse. It is full of verbal felicity, felicity sometimes of precision, sometimes of metaphoric reach; it begins with dialectic reasoning, of an extremely Fichtean and Hegelian type, but it ends in a trumpet-blast of oracular mysticism, straight from the insight wrought by anæsthetics—of all things in the world—and unlike anything one ever heard before. The practically unanimous tradition of "regular" mysticism has been unquestionably *monistic*; and inasmuch as it is the characteristic of mystics to speak, not as the scribes, but as men who have "been there" and seen with their own eyes, I think that this sovereign manner must have made some other pluralistic-minded students hesitate, as I confess that it has often given pause to me. One cannot criticise the vision of a mystic—one can but pass it by, or else accept it as having some amount of evidential weight. I felt unable to do either with a good conscience until I met with Mr Blood. His mysticism, which may, if one likes, be understood as monistic in this earlier utterance, develops in the later ones a sort of "left-wing" voice of defiance, and breaks into what to my ear has a radically pluralistic sound. I confess that the existence of this novel brand of mysticism has made my cowering mood depart. I feel now as if my own pluralism were not without the kind of support which mystical corroboration may confer. Monism can no longer claim to be the only beneficiary of whatever right mysticism may possess to lend *prestige*.

This is my philosophic, as distinguished from my literary interest, in introducing Mr Blood to this more fashionable audience: his philosophy, however mystical, is in the last resort not dissimilar from my own. I must treat him by "extracting" him, and simplify—certainly all too violently—as I extract. He is not consecutive as a writer, aphoristic and oracular rather; and being moreover sometimes dialectic, sometimes poetic, and sometimes mystic in his manner, sometimes monistic and sometimes pluralistic in his matter, I have to run my own risk in making him orate *pro domo mea*, and I am not quite unprepared to hear him say, in case he ever reads these pages, that I have entirely missed his point. No matter; I will proceed.

I

I will separate his diverse phases and take him first as a pure dialectician. Dialectic thought of the Hegelian type is a whirlpool into which some persons are sucked out of the stream which the straightforward understanding follows. Once in the eddy, nothing but rotary motion can go on. All who have been in it know the feel of its swirl—they know thenceforward that thinking unreturning on itself is but one part of reason, and that rectilinear mentality, in philosophy at any rate, will never do. Though each one may report in different words of his rotational experience, the experience itself is almost childishly simple, and whosoever has been there instantly recognises other authentic reports. To have been in that eddy is a freemasonry of which the common password is a "fie" on all the operations of the simple popular understanding.

In Hegel's mind the vortex was at its liveliest, and any one who has dipped into Hegel will recognise Mr Blood to be of the same tribe. "That Hegel was pervaded by the great truth," Blood writes, "cannot be doubted. The eyes of philosophy, if not set directly on him, are set towards the region which he occupied. Though he may not be the final philosopher, yet pull him out, and all the rest will be drawn into his vacancy."

Drawn into the same whirlpool, Mr Blood means. Nondialectic thought takes facts as singly given, and accounts for one fact by another. But when we think of "*all* fact," we see that nothing of the nature of fact can explain it, "for that were but one more added to the list of things to be accounted for. . . . The beginning of curiosity, in the philosophic sense," Mr Blood again writes, "is the stare of being at itself, in the wonder why anything is at all, and what this being signifies. Naturally we first assume the void, and then wonder how, with no ground and no fertility, anything should come into it." We treat it as a positive nihility, "a barrier from which all our batted balls of being rebound."

Upon this idea Mr Blood passes the usual transcendentalist criticism. There *is* no such separate opposite to being; yet we never think of being as such—of pure being as distinguished from specific forms of being—save as what stands relieved against this imaginary background. Being has no *outline* but that which non-being makes, and the two ideas form an inseparable pair. "Each limits and defines the other. Either would be the other in the same position, for here (where there is as yet no question of content, but only of being itself) the position is all and the content is nothing. Hence arose that paradox: 'Being is by nothing more real than not-being.'"

"Popularly," Mr Blood goes on, "we think of all that is as having got the better of non-being. If all were not—*that*, we think, were easy: there were no wonder then, no tax on ingenuity, nothing to be accounted for. This conclusion is from the thinking which assumes all reality as immediately given, assumes knowledge as a simple physical light, rather than as a distinction involving light and darkness equally. We assume that if the light were to go out, the show would be ended (and so it would); but we forget that if the darkness were to go out, that would be equally calamitous. It were bad enough if the master had lost his crayon, but the loss of the blackboard would be just as fatal to the demonstration. Without darkness light would be useless—universal light as blind as universal darkness. Universal thing and universal no-thing were indistinguishable. Why, then, assume the positive, the immediately affirmative, as alone the ingenious? Is not the mould as shapely as the model? The original ingenuity does not show in bringing light out of darkness, nor in bringing things out of nothing, but in evolving, through the just opposition of light and darkness, this wondrous picture, in which the black and white lines have equal significance—in evolving from life and death at once, the conscious spirit. . . .

"It is our habit to think of life as dear, and of death as cheap (though Tithonus found them otherwise), or, continuing the simile of the picture, that paper is cheap while drawing is expensive; but the engraver had a different estimation in one sense, for all his labour was spent on the white ground, while he left untouched those parts of the block which make

the lines in the picture. If being and non-being are both necessary to the presence of either, neither shall claim priority or
preference. Indeed, we may fancy an intelligence which, instead of regarding things as simply owning entity, should regard chiefly their background as affected by the holes which
things are making in it. Even so, the paper-maker might see
your picture as intrusive!"

Thus "does the negation of being appear as indispensable
in the making of it." But to anyone who should appeal to
particular forms of being to refute this paradox, Mr Blood
admits that "to say that a picture, or any other sensuous
thing, is the same as the want of it, were to utter nonsense
indeed: there is a difference equivalent to the whole stuff and
merit of the picture; but in so far as the picture can be there
for thought, as something either asserted or negated, its presence or its absence are the same and indifferent. By *its* absence
we do not mean the absence of anything else, nor absence in
general; and how, forsooth, does its absence differ from these
other absences, save by containing a complete description of
the picture? The hole is as round as the plug; and from our
thought the 'picture' cannot get away. The negation is specific
and descriptive, and what it destroys it preserves for our
conception."

The result is that, whether it be taken generally or taken
specifically, all that which *either is or is not* is or is not *by
distinction or opposition*. "And observe the life, the process,
through which this slippery doubleness endures. Let us suppose the present tense, that gods and men and angels and
devils march all abreast in this present instant, and the only
real time and date in the universe is now. And what *is* this
instant now? Whatever else, it is *process*—becoming and departing; with what between? Simply division, difference; the
present has no breadth, for if it had, that which we seek
would be the middle of that breadth. There is no precipitate,
as on a stationary platform, of the process of becoming, no
residuum of the process of departing, but between the two is
a curtain, *the apparition of difference*, which is all the world."

I am using my scissors somewhat at random on my
author's paragraphs, since one place is as good as another for

entering a ring by, and the expert reader will discern at once the authentic dialectic circling. Other paragraphs show Mr Blood as more Hegelian still, and thoroughly idealistic:—

"Assume that knowing is distinguishing, and that distinction is of difference; if one knows a difference, one knows it as of entities which afford it, and which also he knows; and he must know the entities and the difference apart—one from the other. Knowing all this, he should be able to answer the twin question, 'What is the difference *between sameness and difference*?' It is a 'twin' question, because the two terms are equal in the proposition, and each is full of the other. . . .

"Sameness has 'all the difference in the world'—from difference; and difference is an entity as difference—it being identically that. They are alike and different at once, since either is the other when the observer would contrast it with the other—so that the sameness and the difference are 'subjective,' are the property of the observer: his is the 'limit' in their unlimited field. . . .

"We are thus apprised that distinction involves and carries its own identity; and that ultimate distinction—distinction in the last analysis—is self-distinction—'self-knowledge,' as we realise it consciously every day. Knowledge is self-referred: to know is to know that you know, and to be known as well.

" 'Ah! but *both in the same time*?' inquires the logician. A subject-object knowing itself as a seamless unit, while yet its two items show a real distinction: this passes all understanding."

But the whole of idealism goes to the proof that the two sides *cannot* succeed one another in a time-process. "To say you know, and you know that you know, is to add nothing in the last clause; it is as idle as to say that you lie, and you know that you lie," for if you know it not you lie not.

Philosophy seeks to grasp totality, "but the power of grasping or consenting to totality involves the power of thought to make itself its own object. Totality itself may indeed be taken by the naïve intellect as an immediate topic, in the sense of being just an *object*, but it cannot be just that; for the knower, as other or opposite, would still be within that totality. The 'universe' by definition must contain all opposition.

If distinction should vanish, what would remain? To what other could it change as a whole? How can the loss of distinction make a *difference*? Any loss, at its utmost, offers a new status with the old, but obviously it is too late now to efface distinction by a *change*. There is no possible conjecture, but such as carries with it the subjective that holds it; and when the conjecture is of distinction in general, the subjective fills the void with distinction of itself. The ultimate, ineffaceable distinction is self-distinction, self-consciousness. . . . 'Thou art the unanswered question, couldst see thy proper eye.' . . . . The thought that must be is the very thought of our experience; the ultimate opposition, the to be *and* not to be, is personality, spirit—somewhat that is in knowing that it is, and is nothing else but this knowing in its vast relations.[1]

"Here lies the bed-rock; here the brain-sweat of twenty-five centuries crystallises to a jewel five words long: 'THE UNIVERSE HAS NO OPPOSITE.' For there the wonder of that which is, rests safe in the perception that all things *are* only through the opposition which is their only fear."

"The inevitable generally," in short, is exactly and identically that which in point of fact is actually here.

This is the familiar nineteenth-century development of Kant's idealistic vision. To me it sounds monistic enough to

[1]"How shall a man know he is alive—since in thought the knowing constitutes the being alive, without knowing that thought (life) from its opposite, and so knowing both, and so far as being is knowing, being both? Each defines and relieves the other, each is impossible in thought without the other; therefore each has no distinction save as presently contrasting with the other, and each by itself is the same, and nothing. Clearly, then, consciousness is neither of one nor of the other nor of both, but a knowing subject perceiving them and itself together and as one. . . . So, in coming out of the anæsthetic exhilaration . . . . we want to tell something; but the effort instantly proves that something will stay back and do the telling—one must utter one's own throat, one must eat one's own teeth, to express the being that possesses one. The result is ludicrous and astounding at once—astounding in the clear perception that this is the ultimate mystery of life, and is given you as the old Adamic secret, which you then feel that all intelligence must sometime know or have known; yet ludicrous in its familiar simplicity, as somewhat that any man should always perceive at his best, if his head were only level, but which in our ordinary thinking has grown into a thousand creeds and theories dignified as religion and philosophy."

charm the monist in me unreservedly. I listen to the felici-
tously-worded concept-music circling round itself, as on some
drowsy summer noon one listens under the pines to the mur-
muring of leaves and insects, and with as little thought of
criticism.

But Mr Blood strikes a still more vibrant note: "No more
can be than rationally is; and this was always true. There is
no reason for what is not; but for what there is reason, that
is and ever was. Especially is there no becoming of reason,
and hence no reason for becoming, to a sufficient intelligence.
In the sufficient intelligence all things always are, and are rational. To say there is something yet to be which never was,
not even in the sufficient intelligence wherein the world is
rational and not a blind and orphan waif, is to ignore all reason. Aught that might be assumed as contingently coming to
be could only have 'freedom' for its origin; and 'freedom' has
not fertility or invention, and is not a reason for any special
thing, but the very vacuity of a ground for anything in preference to its room. Neither is there in bare time any principle
or originality whereby anything should come or go. . . .

"Such idealism enures greatly to the dignity and repose of
man. No blind fate, prior to what is, shall necessitate that all
first be and afterward be known, but knowledge is first, with
fate in her own hands. When we are depressed by the weight
and immensity of the immediate, we find in idealism a wondrous consolation. The alien positive, so vast and overwhelming by itself, reduces its pretensions when the whole negative
confronts it on our side.[1] It matters little for its greatness
when an equal greatness is opposed. When one remembers
that the balance and motion of the planets are so delicate that
the momentary scowl of an eclipse may fill the heavens with
tempest, and even affect the very bowels of the earth—when
we see a balloon, that carries perhaps a thousand pounds, leap
up a hundred feet at the discharge of a sheet of note paper—

---

[1]Elsewhere Mr Blood writes of the "force of the negative" thus:—"As
when a faded lock of woman's hair shall cause a man to cut his throat in a
bedroom at five o'clock in the morning; or when Albany resounds with legislation, but a little henpecked judge in a dusty office at Herkimer or Johns-
town sadly writes across the page the word 'unconstitutional'—and the glory
of the Capitol has faded."

or feel it stand deathly still in a hurricane, because it goes with the hurricane, sides with it, and ignores the rushing world below—we should realise that one tittle of pure originality would outweigh this crass objective, and turn these vast masses into mere breath and tissue-paper show."[1]

But whose is the originality? There is nothing in what I am treating as this phase of our author's thought to separate it from the old-fashioned rationalism. There must be a reason for every fact; and so much reason, so fact. The reason is always the whole foil and background and negation of the fact, the whole remainder of reality. "A man may feel good only by feeling better. . . . Pleasure is ever in the company and contrast of pain; for instance, in thirsting and drinking, the pleasure of the one is the exact measure of the pain of the other, and they cease precisely together—otherwise the patient would drink more. The black and yellow gonfalon of Lucifer is indispensable in any spiritual picture." Thus do truth's two components seem to balance, vibrating across the centre of indifference; "being and non-being have equal value and cost," and "mainly are convertible in their terms."[2]

This sounds radically monistic; and monistic also is the first

[1] Elsewhere Blood writes:—"But what then, in the name of common sense, *is* the external world? If a dead man could answer he would say Nothing, or as Macbeth said of the air-drawn dagger, 'there is no such thing.' But a live man's answer might be in this way: What is the multiplication table when it is not written down? It is a necessity of thought; it was not created, it cannot but be; every intelligence which goes to it, and thinks, must think in that form or think falsely. So the universe is the static necessity of reason; it is not an object for any intelligence to find, but it is half object and half subject; it never cost anything as a whole; it never *was* made, but always *is* made, in the Logos, or expression of reason—the Word; and slowly but surely it will be understood and uttered in every intelligence, until he is one with God or reason itself. As a man, for all he knows, or has known, stands at any given instant the realisation of only one thought, while all the rest of him is invisibly linked to that in the necessary form and concatenation of reason, so the man as a whole of exploited thoughts is a moment in the front of the concatenated reason of the universal whole; and this whole is personal only as it is personally achieved. This is the Kingdom that is 'within you,' and the *God* which 'no man hath seen at any time.'"

[2] There are passages in Blood that sound like a well-known essay by Emerson. For instance:—"Experience burns into us the fact and the necessity of universal compensation. The philosopher takes it from Heraclitus, in the insight that everything exists through its opposite; and the bummer comforts

account of the Ether-revelation, in which we read that "thenceforth each is all, in God. . . . The One remains, the many change and pass; and every one of us is the One that remains."

II

It seems to me that any transcendental idealist who reads this article ought to discern in the fragmentary utterances which I have quoted thus far, the note of what he considers the truer dialectic profundity. He ought to extend the glad hand of fellowship to Mr Blood; and if he finds him afterwards palavering with the enemy, he ought to count him, not as a simple ignoramus or Philistine, but as a renegade and relapse. He cannot possibly be treated as one who sins because he never has known better, or as one who walks in darkness because he is congenitally blind.

Well, Mr Blood, explain it as one may, does turn towards the darkness as if he had never seen the light. Just listen for a moment to such irrationalist deliverances on his part as these:—

"Reason is neither the first nor the last word in this world. Reason is an equation; it gives but a pound for a pound. Nature is excess; she is evermore, without cost or explanation.

> 'Is heaven so poor that *justice*
> Metes the bounty of the skies?
> So poor that every blessing

---

himself for his morning headache as only the rough side of a square deal. We accept readily the doctrine that pain and pleasure, evil and good, death and life, chance and reason, are necessary equations—that there must be just as much of each as of its other.

"It grieves us little that this great compensation cannot at every instant balance its beam on every individual centre, and dispense with an under dog in every fight; we know that the parts must subserve the whole; we have faith that our time will come; and if it comes not at all in this world, our lack is a bid for immortality, and the most promising argument for a world hereafter. 'Though He slay me, yet will I trust in Him.'

"This is the faith that baffles all calamity, and ensures genius and patience in the world. Let not the creditor hasten the settlement: let not the injured man hurry toward revenge; there is nothing that draws bigger interest than a wrong, and to 'get the best of it' is ever in some sense to get the worst."

Fills the debit of a cost?
That all process is returning?
And all gain is of the lost?'

Go back into reason, and you come at last to fact, nothing more—a given-ness, a something to wonder at and yet admit, like your own will. And all these tricks for logicising originality, self-relation, absolute process, subjective contradiction, will wither in the breath of the mystical fact—they will swirl down the corridors before the besom of the everlasting Yea."

Or again: "The monistic notion of a oneness, a centred wholeness, ultimate purpose, or climacteric result of the world, has wholly given way. Thought evolves no longer a centred whole, a One, but rather a numberless many, adjust it how we will."

Or still again: "The pluralists have talked philosophy to a standstill—Nature is contingent, excessive and mystical essentially."

Have we here contradiction simply, a man converted from one faith to its opposite? Or is it only dialectic circling, like the opposite points on the rim of a revolving disc, one moving up, one down, but replacing one another endlessly, while the whole disc never moves? If it be this latter—Mr Blood himself uses the image—the dialectic is too pure for me to catch: a deeper man must mediate the monistic with the pluralistic Blood. Let my incapacity be castigated, if my "Subject" ever reads this article, but let me treat him from now onwards as the simply pluralistic mystic which my reading of the rest of him suggests. I confess to some dread of my own fate at his hands. In making so far an ordinary transcendental idealist of him, I have taken liberties, running separate sentences together, inverting their order, and even altering single words—for all which I beg pardon; but in treating my author from now onwards as a pluralist, interpretation is easier, and my hands can be less stained (if they *are* stained) with exegetic blood.

I have spoken of his verbal felicity, and alluded to his poetry. Before passing to his mystic gospel, I will refresh the reader (doubtless now fatigued with so much dialectic) by a

sample of his verse. "The Lion of the Nile" is an allegory of
the "champion spirit of the world" in its various incarnations.
Thus it begins:—

"Whelped on the desert sands, and desert bred
 From dugs whose sustenance was blood alone—
 A life translated out of other lives,
 I grew the king of beasts; the hurricane
 Leaned like a feather on my royal fell;
 I took the Hyrcan tiger by the scruff
 And tore him piecemeal; my hot bowels laughed
 And my fangs yearned for prey. Earth was my lair:
 I slept on the red desert without fear:
 I roamed the jungle depths with less design
 Than e'en to lord their solitude; on crags
 That cringe from lightning—black and blasted fronts
 That crouch beneath the wind-bleared stars, I told
 My heart's fruition to the universe,
 And all night long, roaring my fierce defy,
 I thrilled the wilderness with aspen terrors,
 And challenged death and life. . . ."

Again:

"Naked I stood upon the raked arena
 Beneath the pennants of Vespasian,
 While seried thousands gazed—strangers from Caucasus,
 Men of the Grecian Isles, and Barbary princes,
 To see me grapple with the counterpart
 Of that I had been—the raptorial jaws,
 The arms that wont to crush with strength alone,
 The eyes that glared vindictive.—Fallen there,
 Vast wings upheaved me; from the Alpine peaks
 Whose avalanches swirl the valley mists
 And whelm the helpless cottage, to the crown
 Of Chimborazo, on whose changeless jewels
 The torrid rays recoil, with ne'er a cloud
 To swathe their blistered steps, I rested not,
 But preyed on all that ventured from the earth,
 An outlaw of the heavens.—But evermore
 Must death release me to the jungle shades;

And there like Samson's grew my locks again
In the old walks and ways, till scapeless fate
Won me as ever to the haunts of men,
Luring my lives with battle and with love.". . .

I quote less than a quarter of the poem, of which the rest is just as good, and I ask: Who of us all handles his English vocabulary better than Mr Blood?[1]

His proclamations of the mystic insight have a similar verbal power:—

"There is an invariable and reliable condition (or uncondition) ensuing about the instant of recall from anæsthetic stupor to 'coming to,' in which the genius of being is revealed. . . . No words may express the imposing certainty of the patient that he is realising the primordial Adamic surprise of Life.

"Repetition of the experience finds it ever the same, and as if it could not possibly be otherwise. The subject resumes his normal consciousness only to partially and fitfully remember its occurrence, and to try to formulate its baffling import,— with but this consolatory afterthought: that he has known the oldest truth, and that he has done with human theories as to the origin, meaning, or destiny of the race. He is beyond instruction in 'spiritual things.' . . . .

"It is the instant contrast of this 'tasteless water of souls' with formal thought as we 'come to,' that leaves in the patient an astonishment that the awful mystery of Life is at last but a homely and a common thing, and that aside from mere for-

---

[1]Or what thinks the reader of the verbiage of these verses?—addressed in a mood of human defiance to the cosmic Gods—

"Whose lightnings tawny leap from furtive lairs,
To helpless murder, while the ships go down
Swirled in the crazy stound, and mariners' prayers
Go up in noisome bubbles—such to *them*;—
Or when they tramp about the central fires,
Bending the strata with æonian tread
Till steeples totter, and all ways are lost,—
Deem they of wife or child, or home or friend,
Doing these things as the long years lead on
Only to other years that mean no more,
That cure no ill, nor make for use or proof—
Destroying ever, though to rear again."

mality the majestic and the absurd are of equal dignity. The astonishment is aggravated as at a thing of course, missed by sanity in overstepping, as in too foreign a search, or with too eager an attention: as in finding one's spectacles on one's nose, or in making in the dark a step higher than the stair. My first experiences of this revelation had many varieties of emotion; but as a man grows calm and determined by experience in general, so am I now not only firm and familiar in this once weird condition, but triumphant—divine. To minds of sanguine imagination there will be a sadness in the tenor of the mystery, as if the key-note of the universe were low, for no poetry, no emotion known to the normal sanity of man, can furnish a hint of its primeval prestige, and its all-but appalling solemnity; but for such as have felt sadly the instability of temporal things there is a comfort of serenity and ancient peace, while for the resolved and imperious spirit there are majesty and supremacy unspeakable. Nor can it be long until all who enter the anæsthetic condition (and there are hundreds every secular day) will be taught to expect this revelation, and will date from its experience their initiation into the Secret of Life. . . . .

"This has been my moral sustenance since I have known of it. In my first printed mention of it I declared: 'The world is no more the alien terror that was taught me. Spurning the cloud-grimed and still sultry battlements whence so lately Jehovan thunders boomed, my grey gull lifts her wing against the nightfall, and takes the dim leagues with a fearless eye.' And now, after twenty-seven years of this experience, the wing is greyer, but the eye is fearless still, while I renew and doubly emphasise that declaration. I know, as having known, the meaning of Existence; the sane centre of the universe—at once the wonder and the assurance of the soul."

After this rather literary interlude I return to Blood's philosophy again. I spoke a while ago of its being an "irrationalistic" philosophy in its latest phase. Behind every "fact" rationalism postulates its "reason." Blood parodizes this demand in true nominalistic fashion. "The goods are not enough, but they must have the invoice with them. There must be a *name*, something *to read*. I think of Dickens's horse that always fell down when they took him out of the shafts; or of the fellow who felt weak when naked, but strong in his overcoat."—No bad mockery, this, surely, of rationalism's habit of explaining things by putting verbal doubles of them beneath them as their ground!

"All that philosophy has sought as cause, or reason," he says, "pluralism subsumes in the status and the given fact, where it stands as plausible as it may ever hope to stand. There may be disease in the presence of a question as well as in the lack of an answer. We do not wonder so strangely at an ingenious and well-set-up effect, for we feel such in ourselves; but a cause, reaching out beyond the verge [of fact] and dangling its legs in nonentity, with the hope of a rational foothold, should realise a strenuous life. Pluralism believes in truth and reason, but only as mystically realised, as lived in experience. Up from the breast of a man, up to his tongue and brain, comes a free and strong determination, and he cries, originally, and in spite of his whole nature and environment, 'I will.' This is the Jovian fiat, the pure cause. This is reason; this or nothing shall explain the world for him. For how shall he entertain a reason bigger than himself? . . . Let a man stand fast, then, as an axis of the earth; the obsequious meridians will bow to him, and gracious latitudes will measure from his feet."

This seems to be Blood's mystical answer to his own monistic statement which I quoted above, that "freedom" has no fertility, and is no reason for any special thing.[1] "Philosophy,"

[1] I subjoin a poetic apostrophe of Mr Blood's to freedom:

"Let it ne'er be known.
If in some book of the Inevitable,
Dog-eared and stale, the future stands engrossed
E'en as the past. There shall be news in heaven,
And question in the courts thereof; and chance
Shall have its fling, e'en at the [ermined] bench.
. . . .
Ah, long ago, above the Indian ocean,
Where wan stars brood over the dreaming East,
I saw, white, liquid, palpitant, the Cross;
And faint and far came bells of Calvary
As planets passed, singing that they were saved,
Saved from themselves: but ever low Orion—
For hunter too was I, born of the wild,

Mr Blood writes to me in a letter, "is past. It was the long endeavour to logicise what we can only realise practically or in immediate experience. I am more and more impressed that Heraclitus insists on the equation of reason and unreason, or chance, as well as of being and not-being, etc. This throws the secret beyond logic, and makes mysticism outclass philosophy. The insight that mystery—the MYSTERY—as such is final, is the hymnic word. If you use reason pragmatically, and deny it absolutely, you can't be beaten—be assured of that. But the *Fact* remains, and of course the Mystery."[1]

> And the game flavour of the infinite
> Tainted me to the bone—he waved me on,
> On to the tangent field beyond all orbs,
> Where form nor order nor continuance
> Hath thought nor name; there unity exhales
> In want of confine, and the protoplasm
> May beat and beat, in aimless vehemence,
> Through vagrant spaces, homeless and unknown.
>   .   .   .   .   .
> There ends One's empire!—but so ends not all;
> One knows not all; my griefs at least are mine—
> By me their measure, and to me their lesson;
> E'en I am one—(poor deuce to call the Ace!)
> And to the open bears my gonfalon,
> Mine ægis, Freedom!—Let me ne'er look back
> Accusing, for the withered leaves and lives
> The sated past hath strewn, the shears of fate,
> But forth to braver days.
>   O, Liberty,
> Burthen of every sigh!—thou gold of gold,
> Beauty of the beautiful, strength of the strong!
> My soul for ever turns agaze for thee.
> There is no purpose of eternity
> For faith or patience; but thy buoyant torch
> Still lighted from the Islands of the Blest,
> O'erbears all present for potential heavens
> Which are not—ah, so more than all that are!
> Whose chance postpones the ennui of the skies!
> Be thou my genius—be my hope in thee!
> For this were heaven: to be, and to be free."

[1] In another letter Mr Blood writes:—"I think we are through with 'the Whole,' and with 'causa sui,' and with the 'negative unity' which assumes to identify each thing as being what it lacks of everything else. You can, of course, build out a chip by modelling the sphere it was chipped from;—but

The "Fact," as I understand the writer here to mean it, remains in its native disseminated shape. From every realised amount of fact some other fact is *absent*, as being uninvolved. "There is nowhere more of it consecutively, perhaps, than appears upon this present page." There is, indeed, to put it otherwise, no more one all-enveloping fact than there is one all-enveloping spire in an endlessly growing spiral, and no more one all-generating fact than there is one central point in which an endlessly converging spiral ends. Hegel's "bad infinite" belongs to the eddy as well as to the line. "Progress?" writes our author. "And to what? Time turns a weary and a wistful face; has he not traversed an eternity? and shall another give the secret up? We have dreamed of a climax and a consummation, a final triumph where a world shall burn *en barbecue*; but there is not, cannot be, a purpose of eternity; it shall pay mainly as it goes, or not at all. The show is on; and what a show, if we will but give our attention! Barbecues, bonfires, and banners? Not twenty worlds a minute would keep up our bonfire of the sun; and what banners of our fancy could eclipse the meteor pennants of the pole, or the opaline splendours of the everlasting ice? . . . . Doubtless we *are* ostensibly progressing, but there have been prosperity and high-jinks before. Nineveh and Tyre, Rome, Spain, and Venice also had their day. We are going, but it is a question of our standing the pace. It would seem that the news must become less interesting or tremendously more so—'a breath can make us, as a breath has made.' "

Elsewhere we read: "Variety, not uniformity, is more likely to be the key to progress. The genius of being is whimsical rather than consistent. Our strata show broken bones of histories all forgotten. How can it be otherwise? There can be no purpose of eternity. It is process all. The most sublime result, if it appeared as the ultimatum, would go stale in an hour—it could not be endured."

---

if it wasn't a sphere? What a weariness it is to look back over the twenty odd volumes of the *Journal of Speculative Philosophy*, and see Harris's mind wholly filled by that one conception of self-determination—everything to be thought as 'part of a system'—a 'whole' and 'causa sui.'—I should like to see such an idea get into the head of Edison or Geo. Westinghouse."

Of course from an intellectual point of view this way of thinking must be classed as scepticism. "Contingency forbids any inevitable history, and conclusions are absurd. Nothing in Hegel has kept the planet from being blown to pieces." Obviously the mystical "security," the "apodal sufficiency" yielded by the anæsthetic revelation, are very different moods of mind from aught that rationalism can claim to father— more active, prouder, more heroic. From his ether intoxica-tion Blood may feel towards ordinary rationalists "as Clive felt towards those millions of Orientals in whom honour had no part." On page 1303, above, I quoted from his "Nemesis" —"Is heaven so poor that justice," etc. The writer goes on, addressing the goddess of "compensation" or rational balance:—

> "How shalt thou poise the courage
>   That covets all things hard?
> How pay the love unmeasured
>   That could not brook reward?
> How prompt self-loyal honour
>   Supreme above desire,
> That bids the strong die for the weak,
>   The martyrs sing in fire?
> Why do I droop in bower
>   And sigh in sacred hall?
> Why stifle under shelter?
>   Yet where, through forest tall,
> The breath of hungry winter
>   In stinging spray resolves,
> I sing to the north wind's fury
>   And shout with the coarse-haired wolves?
>   .   .   .   .   .   .
> What of thy priests' confuting,
>   Of fate and form and law,
> Of being and essence and counterpoise,
>   Of poles that drive and draw?
> Ever some compensation,
>   Some pandering purchase still
> But the vehm of achieving reason
>   Is the all-patrician Will!"

Mr Blood must manage to re-write the last two lines; but the contrast of the two securities, his and the rationalist's, is plain enough. The rationalist sees safe conditions. But Mr Blood's revelation, whatever the conditions be, helps him to stand ready for a life among them. In this, his attitude seems to resemble that of Nietzsche's *amor fati*! "Simply," he writes to me, "*we do not know*. But when we say we do not know, we are not to say it weakly and meekly, but with confidence and content. . . . Knowledge is and must ever be *secondary*—a witness rather than a principal—or a 'principle'!—in the case. Therefore mysticism for me!"

"Reason," he prints elsewhere, "is but an item in the duplex potency of the mystery, and behind the proudest consciousness that ever reigned, Reason and Wonder blushed face to face. The legend sinks to burlesque if in that great argument which antedates man and his mutterings, Lucifer had not a fighting chance. . . .

"It is given to the writer and to others for whom he is permitted to speak—and we are grateful that it is the custom of gentlemen to believe one another—that the highest thought is not a milk-and-water equation of so much reason and so much result—'no school sum to be cast up.' We have realised the highest divine thought of itself, and there is in it as much of wonder as of certainty; inevitable, and solitary and safe in one sense, but queer and cactus-like no less in another sense, it appeals unutterably to experience alone.

"There are sadness and disenchantment for the novice in these inferences, as if the keynote of the universe were low, but experience will approve them. Certainty is the root of despair. The inevitable stales, while doubt and hope are sisters. Not unfortunately the universe is wild—game flavoured as a hawk's wing. Nature is miracle all. She knows no laws; the same returns not, save to bring the different. The slow round of the engraver's lathe gains but the breadth of a hair, but the difference is distributed back over the whole curve, never an instant true—ever not quite."

"Ever not quite!'—this seems to wring the very last panting word out of rationalistic philosophy's mouth. It is fit to be pluralism's heraldic device. There is no complete generalisation, no total point of view, no all-pervasive unity, but everywhere some residual resistance to verbalisation, formulation, and discursification, some genius of reality that escapes from the pressure of the logical finger, that says "hands off," and claims its privacy, and means to be left to its own life. In every moment of immediate experience is somewhat absolutely original and novel. "We are the first that ever burst into this silent sea." Philosophy must pass from words, that reproduce but ancient elements, to life itself, that gives the integrally new. The "inexplicable," the "mystery," as what the intellect, with its claim to reason out reality, thinks that it is in duty bound to resolve, and the resolution of which Blood's revelation would eliminate from the sphere of our duties, remains; but it remains as something to be met and dealt with by faculties more akin to our activities and heroisms and willingnesses, than to our logical powers. This is the anæsthetic insight, according to our author. Let *my* last word, then, speaking in the name of intellectual philosophy, be *his* word:—"There is no conclusion. What has concluded, that we might conclude in regard to it? There are no fortunes to be told, and there is no advice to be given.—Farewell!"

The Hibbert Journal, July 1910

Index

Chronology

1842   Born January 11 at Astor House, New York City hotel, first child of Henry James and Mary Walsh James, and named William after paternal grandfather. (Grandfather William James emigrated from northern Ireland in 1789 at age seventeen, settled in Albany, New York, and became a merchant, banker, and landowner, leaving an estate valued at three million dollars at his death in 1832. Father, Henry, born 1811, received $1,250 annuity under terms of grandfather's will, which placed all capital in trust for twenty-one years and forbade eventual distribution to any heir leading a "grossly immoral, idle or dishonorable life." Father joined several of the eleven heirs in contesting the will and received a major distribution of the estate's capital while studying at Princeton Theological Seminary in 1837. After visiting England and Ireland, he abandoned the seminary, began to devote himself to the independent study of theology, and in 1840 married Mary Robertson Walsh, thirty-year-old daughter of a prosperous New York family of Scots-Irish descent.) Family moves to house on Washington Place, New York City, shortly after James's birth. Father meets Ralph Waldo Emerson in March (beginning long friendship), and Emerson "blesses" James during visit to their home.

1843   Brother Henry born April 15. Father's litigation results in second major distribution of estate's capital, providing annual income of $10,000 and enabling family to go abroad. They sail from New York to Liverpool in October, accompanied by mother's sister Catherine Walsh (Aunt Kate), and settle in London. Father meets J. J. Garth Wilkinson, leading English exponent and translator of Emanuel Swedenborg.

1844   Family moves to Paris and then to cottage in Windsor, England. Father has breakdown ("a perfectly insane and abject terror . . . an ever growing tempest of doubt, anxiety, and despair, with absolutely no relief from any truth I had ever encountered save a most pale and distant glimmer of the divine existence") in May and finds consolation in writings of Swedenborg.

1845   Family returns to America and lives alternately in New
        York and at 50 North Pearl Street, Albany, a few doors
        from grandmother Catherine Barber James, uncle Augus-
        tus James, and numerous cousins. Brother Garth Wilkin-
        son (Wilky) born July 21 in New York City.

1846   Brother Robertson (Bob or Rob) born August 29 in Al-
        bany. James attends kindergarten on North Pearl Street.

1847   Family moves to apartment at 11 Fifth Avenue, New York
        City, two blocks from maternal grandmother, Elizabeth
        Robertson Walsh.

1848–54 Spring, father buys and family moves into brownstone at
        58 West 14th Street. Sister Alice born August 7, 1848. Fa-
        ther's *Moralism and Christianity* published in 1850, first of
        many books, influenced by Swedenborg, on religious,
        moral, and social questions (father also lectures). Relatives
        and father's friends and acquaintances, including Horace
        Greeley, George Ripley, Charles Anderson Dana, William
        Cullen Bryant, Bronson Alcott, and Emerson, are frequent
        guests. James explores neighborhood with friends and
        sometimes Henry (though James once rejects Henry's
        company saying, "*I* play with boys who curse and
        swear!"). Receives instruction from tutors and three pri-
        vate schools in Lower Broadway and Greenwich Village.
        Attends theatrical performances, Barnum's American Mu-
        seum, and numerous art shows, including Thorwaldsen's
        sculptures of Christ and disciples at 1853 Crystal Palace ex-
        hibition. Enjoys art lessons with Benjamin Coe and begins
        to draw in his spare time. (Henry later describes him sit-
        ting and "drawing and drawing, always drawing,
        . . . and not at all with a plodding patience . . . but
        easily, freely, and, as who should say, infallibly.")

1855   Family, with Aunt Kate, sails for England on June 27 be-
        cause father believes children will receive better education
        in Europe, and travels through London, Paris, and Lyons
        to Geneva. Attends multilingual (English, French, and
        German) boarding school near Geneva with Wilky, Bob,
        and orphaned cousins Robert and William Temple, while
        Henry recuperates from malarial fever and receives in-
        struction at home in Geneva. October, family leaves for
        London, where Robert Thomson (later Robert Louis Ste-
        venson's tutor) is engaged.

1856   Family returns to Paris in June, where another tutor is hired and children briefly attend an experimental, coeducational, international school influenced by theories of Fourier. Frequently visits the Louvre and Luxembourg Palace and is fascinated by work of Delacroix; reproduces his *Barque de Dante* with aid of lithograph.

1857   Family summers in Boulogne-sur-Mer on the English Channel. James attends Collège Impérial, local public school, and does well at science. Family returns to Paris in fall, where James is admitted to studio of painter Léon Cogniet, but financial effects of American depression of 1857 force them to return to Boulogne-sur-Mer, where they can live more cheaply. Receives microscope as Christmas gift from father.

1858   James continues science studies at the Collège Impérial while taking and developing photographs, collecting and studying marine animals, administering mild electrical shocks to family and friends, mixing and heating chemicals, and occasionally trying out effects of drugs on himself. June, family returns to America, stopping in New York and Albany before settling in Newport, Rhode Island. James becomes friends with future actor, playwright, and director James Steele MacKaye and future literary scholar and translator Thomas Sergeant Perry, grandson of naval hero Oliver Hazard Perry. Swims, rows, goes fishing, and is taught to box by MacKaye. Becomes close to orphaned Temple cousins, now living in Newport, especially Katharine (Kitty) and Mary (Minny). Begins sketching at painter William Hunt's studio in early fall. Studies at Berkeley Institute, school run by local curate, and reads Arthur Schopenhauer and Joseph Renan.

1859   Interest in art deepens. Meets painter John La Farge, who comes to Newport to study with Hunt. Father decides to return to Europe; writes to a friend that he dreads "those inevitable habits of extravagance and insubordination, which appear to be characteristic of American youth." October, family sails to France and settles in Geneva. James studies science at the Geneva Academy (now University of Geneva); takes anatomy course, attends dissections, and sketches cadavers (later writes that he "never had any" early education).

1860   July, takes walking tour of Mont Blanc region with
        Henry, then goes to Bonn, where he lives with local fam-
        ily and studies German. Tells father that he wants to re-
        turn to United States so that he can resume painting with
        Hunt; father reluctantly agrees. James writes to a friend,
        "I have fully decided to try the career of a painter. In a
        year or two I shall know definitely whether I am suited to
        it or not. If not, it will be easy to withdraw. There is
        nothing on earth more deplorable than a bad artist." Fam-
        ily returns to Newport in October and rents house at 13
        Kay Street. James and La Farge study under Hunt six days
        a week, occasionally joined in class by Henry. Wilky and
        Bob attend experimental school in Concord, run by mili-
        tant abolitionist Franklin Sanborn, with children of Emer-
        son, Nathaniel Hawthorne, and John Brown. Father
        suffers from mysterious fainting spells during winter.

1861   Decides in early summer to abandon painting and enters
        Lawrence Scientific School at Harvard in September.
        Studies chemistry under Charles William Eliot (who later
        recalls that while James was "not wholly devoted" to his
        work and suffered from "a delicacy of nervous constitu-
        tion," his "excursions into other sciences and realms of
        thought were not infrequent; his mind was excursive, and
        he liked experimenting, particularly novel experiment-
        ing"). Impressed by Lowell Lectures of naturalist Louis
        Agassiz. Meets law student Oliver Wendell Holmes, Jr.
        (who soon enlists in the Union Army), and becomes
        friends with Charles Sanders Peirce, fellow student at the
        Lawrence School, and Thomas Ward, distant cousin and
        student at Harvard College.

1862   Spends summer in Newport. Returns to Cambridge in
        the fall with Henry, who enters Harvard Law School.
        Brothers live in separate boarding houses but regularly
        dine together. September, Wilky enlists in the 44th Mas-
        sachusetts Regiment and is sent to North Carolina. James
        continues study of chemistry under Eliot, eating special
        breads to test effects of different yeasts on his urine.

1863   Withdraws from school and lives at home in Newport
        during spring and summer, reading widely in literature,
        science, history, and philosophy, including German mate-
        rialist philosopher Ludwig Büchner's *Kraft und Stoff*

(*Force and Matter*), philologist Max Müller's *History of Ancient Sanskrit Literature*, and Jonathan Edwards's *Original Sin*. Applies with Henry for position working with free blacks in the South, but plan is never carried out. Wilky becomes adjutant to Robert Gould Shaw, commander of the 54th Massachusetts, one of the first black regiments in the Union Army. Bob enlists and soon joins the 55th Massachusetts, another black regiment. Henry withdraws from law school. July 18, Wilky badly wounded during attack on Fort Wagner in which Shaw and many of his men are killed. Near death, he is brought to Newport, where James helps care for him and sketches him as he lies unconscious. James returns to Lawrence Scientific School in the fall and studies comparative anatomy and physiology under Jeffries Wyman. (Later praises Wyman as "the paragon . . . of goodness, disinterestedness, and single-minded love of the truth.")

1864   Enters Harvard School of Medicine at beginning of year. Writes to a friend, "I embraced the medical profession a couple of months ago. My first impressions are that there is much humbug therein, and that, with the exception of surgery . . . a doctor does more by the moral effect of his presence on the patient and family, than by anything else. He also extracts money from them." Continues study of anatomy under Wyman. Moves in May into new family residence at 13 Ashburton Place, Boston. Becomes friend of Oliver Wendell Holmes, Jr., who is at Harvard Law School after three years in the Union Army. Wilky, partially recovered, returns to his regiment in December.

1865   Joins expedition to Brazil organized by Agassiz to collect specimens for his zoological museum (now Harvard Museum of Comparative Zoology); expenses are paid by father and Aunt Kate. April 1, leaves New York with Agassiz and his wife, Elizabeth, four naturalists, and five other student assistants, including Thomas Ward. James is severely seasick during voyage. Contracts varioloid (mild form of smallpox) shortly after arrival in Rio de Janeiro. Suffers temporary blindness and is quarantined for four weeks (after recovery eyes remain sensitive to strain). Despondent from illness and tedium of collecting and packing specimens, resolves to return home, writing family in early June that he is "cut out for a speculative rather than an active life," but decides to remain with expedition after health improves. Goes up Amazon in August and makes three collecting trips along river and its Tapajós, Içá, and Jutaí tributaries. Expedition nears Peruvian frontier in September, but does not cross due to rumors of impending war. James is impressed by Agassiz's energy and determination, but disagrees with some of his scientific views. Returns to coast in December and sails for the United States soon after Christmas.

1866   Returns to Boston in February and resumes medical studies in March. Enjoys company of Oliver Wendell Holmes, Jr., and Holmes's future wife, Fanny Dixwell. Works as summer intern at Massachusetts General Hospital. Mid-July to early September, joins parents, Henry, and Alice at shore house in Swampscott, Massachusetts. Father begins to invest heavily in Florida cotton plantation run by Wilky and Bob, which uses paid black labor and has an integrated school on its grounds. James continues studies at Harvard Medical School in the fall, where his friends include future social reformer Charles Putnam, his brother James Putnam, later a leading neurologist, and future physiologist Henry Bowditch. Engages in philosophical discussions with Peirce (beginning of lifelong intellectual dialogue), Holmes, Ward, and Chauncey Wright (meetings evolve by early 1870s into informal "metaphysical club," with all but Ward as members). Becomes friends with William Dean Howells (will read and praise many of Howells's novels). Moves into new family residence at 20 Quincy Street, across from Harvard Yard, in November. Suffers from back pain, eyestrain, insomnia, digestive problems, and profound depression throughout winter; finds his home "loathsome" and contemplates suicide. Alice goes to New York for treatment of her persistent nervous symptoms.

1867   April, sails for Europe hoping to improve health and to study German and physiology. Visits Paris and spends summer in Dresden, reading German (including Goethe's *Faust*, essays by art historian Herman Grimm, and German translation of George Henry Lewes's *Aristotle*) and touring art galleries, and at nearby Bad Teplitz (now Teplice, Czechoslovakia), drinking mineral water and taking thermal baths. September, goes to Berlin to enter its university, and is joined in October by Thomas Sergeant Perry, who shares his rooms at 12 Mittelstrasse. James takes five courses and attends three lectures on physiology during the fall and is especially interested in teaching of pioneering electrophysiologist Emil Du Bois–Reymond. Reads German works on physiology and psychology and becomes interested in experimental neurology; writes Ward that "perhaps the time has come for psychology to begin to be a science. . . ." Unable to do laboratory work due to continuing eye and back problems. Writes review of Herman Grimm's novel *Unüberwindliche Mächte* (*Invincible Powers*) and sends it to Henry, asking him to revise it; review appears unsigned in *The Nation*, November 28. Sees historian George Bancroft, family acquaintance and American minister to Berlin, who introduces him to Grimm (son of folklorist Wilhelm Grimm) and his wife, Gisela von Arnim (daughter of Goethe's friend Bettina von Arnim). Meets philosopher Wilhelm Dilthey through Grimm.

1868   Breaks off studies in Berlin and returns to Bad Teplitz, January. Writes to Bob (who, depressed and in poor health, has left Florida plantation and taken job as railroad clerk in Iowa) that he feels "rather ashamed at my age to stand in the presence of you and Wilky without having earned a cent." Goes to Dresden in March, returning to Bad Teplitz for three weeks in late April and early May. Reads extensively (Shakespeare, Homer, Renan, Hippolyte Taine, Immanuel Kant, Paul Janet, Gotthold Lessing, Charles Darwin, and especially Goethe and Johann von Schiller), despite persistent depression. Writes sympathetically to Alice, who has suffered serious nervous collapse, including comic descriptions of his boarding house residents. Sends Henry criticism of his recently published stories "Poor Richard," "The Story of a Masterpiece," and "The Romance of Certain Old Clothes." Goes to Heidelberg in late June to study experimental psychology under Wilhelm Wundt and Hermann von Helmholtz but returns to Berlin six days later "under the influence of a blue despair." Visits Geneva and takes baths at Divonne in French Savoy without effect; writes to Thomas Ward of episodes of suicidal depression: "sometimes when I despair of ever doing anything, say: 'Why not step out into the green darkness?' " Reads French philosopher Charles

Renouvier and is impressed by his "vigor of style and compression . . . unequaled by anyone." Spends two weeks in Paris with Henry Bowditch. Returns to Cambridge in November. Writes five unsigned book reviews during year for *The Nation*, *Atlantic Monthly*, and *North American Review*, including two of Darwin's *The Variation of Animals and Plants under Domestication*.

1869   January, begins to review for medical school final examination. February, Henry leaves for year-long European tour. March, reviews E. Sargent's *Planchette*, book on spiritualism, for the *Boston Daily Advertiser*. Submits thesis on effects of cold on the human body, based on published sources, May 21, and passes ninety-minute oral examination given by nine professors, June 21, completing requirements for M.D. (Despite degree, never practices.) Vacations at farmhouse in Pomfret, Connecticut, with parents and Alice, where he enjoys "the life of an absolute caterpillar" and the company of twenty-two-year-old Elizabeth (Lizzie) Boott. Sketches and reads (or skims) widely in science, literature, and philosophy (including works by Johann Fichte, Ivan Turgenev, Herbert Spencer, George Henry Lewes, George Sand, Schopenhauer, Auguste Comte's *Cours de philosophie positive*, John Stuart Mill's *The Subjection of Women*, and Robert Browning's *The Ring and the Book*), recording quotations, reactions, and philosophical and psychological speculations in notebooks. Becomes severely depressed after return to Cambridge in the fall; writes Bob in November that he has resolved never to marry for fear of passing nervous disabilities on to his children.

1870   January, outlines plan of reading in neurophysiology and pathology for the coming year, and resolves to finish reading his father's works. Temporarily inflames eyelids with overdose of chloral hydrate, new hypnotic drug taken "for the fun of it as an experiment. . . ." Suffers from back pains, severe depression, and deep philosophic uncertainty. March 9, learns that beloved cousin Minny Temple has died of tuberculosis; writes in diary, March 22, "Minny, your death makes me feel the nothingness of all our egotistic fury." Encouraged by further reading of Renouvier, writes in diary on April 30, "My first act of free will shall be to believe in free will." Resolves to avoid "speculation" for the remainder of the year and to devote himself to "action" and belief in "my individual reality and creative power." Nervous symptoms and poor health persist. Henry returns to Quincy Street from Europe in May. James spends summer on Mount Desert Island, Maine, returning to Cambridge in the fall. Restricts his reading, limited to four hours a day due to eyestrain, to newspapers, novels, and biographies; writes to Bowditch in December of his "morbid shrinking" from intellectual conversation and that he is "long since dead and buried in that respect."

1871   April, enrolls in Harvard-sponsored lecture series on "Optical Phenomena and the Eye," given by B. Joy Jeffries. Wilky leaves Florida plantation, which has failed due to bad weather, falling prices, poor management, and racist harassment, and joins brother Bob, now in Milwaukee.

1872   Henry, Alice, and Aunt Kate leave for European tour in May. James vacations in Maine during summer. Accepts offer from Charles William Eliot, now president of Harvard, to teach undergraduate course in comparative physiology in spring of 1873. Writes Henry, "The appointment to teach physiology is a perfect God-send to me just now . . . a dealing with men instead of my own mind, and a diversion from those introspective studies which had bred a sort of philosophical hypochondria in me of late. . . ." Can read only three or four hours a day, and is afflicted by insomnia and general nervousness. Fall, review of Taine's *On Intelligence* published in *The Nation*. Begins to correspond with Renouvier on philosophical problems. Attends Bowditch's Harvard Medical School lectures and works in physiology laboratory. Undergoes "crisis" in late autumn (possibly the event James later disguised in *The Varieties of Religious Experience* as that of a French correspondent of his: "Whilst in this state of philosophical pessimism and general depression of spirits . . . suddenly there fell upon me without any warning, just as if it came out of the darkness, a horrible fear of my own existence. . . . I became a mass of quivering fear. After this the universe was changed for me altogether. . . ."). Bob marries Mary Holton in Milwaukee, November 18, and visits Cambridge with her later in month.

1873   Enjoys teaching and reads Wordsworth with pleasure dur-
        ing spring. After period of uncertainty, accepts appoint-
        ment from Harvard president Eliot to teach full year of
        comparative anatomy and physiology at salary of $600,
        despite reluctance to move into anatomy and away from
        "mental science." Travels along New England coast during
        summer. Decides to postpone teaching for a year due to
        continuing poor health (back pain, insomnia, and ner-
        vousness). Borrows $1,000 from Aunt Kate and sails to
        Liverpool in October, stopping in London and Paris be-
        fore joining Henry (who has stayed in Europe) in Flor-
        ence. Writes Wilky, "My old love of art returns, but not
        in full force. The years have weakened it, I am afraid."
        Goes to Rome with Henry in late November; visits Coli-
        seum by night and finds it "inhuman and horrible." Re-
        turns to Florence in late December, sick with fever.

1874   Recovers and leaves Florence in February, visiting Venice,
        Munich, and Dresden. Returns to Cambridge in March.
        June, visits brothers in Milwaukee and meets Wilky's new
        wife, Caroline Cary James. Teaches comparative vertebrate
        anatomy and physiology in fall (gives course through
        1878–79) and becomes director of the Museum of Com-
        parative Anatomy and the anatomy laboratory after death
        of Jeffries Wyman in September. Helps found new
        "metaphysical club," primarily devoted to the study of
        Hegel; members include George Howison, professor of
        logic at the Massachusetts Institute of Technology, W. T.
        Harris, editor of *The Journal of Speculative Philosophy* and
        a leading American exponent of Hegel, and George
        Herbert Palmer, assistant professor of philosophy at
        Harvard (soon joined by Scottish philosopher Thomas
        Davidson, who becomes friend of James). Writes seven
        unsigned reviews for general and professional journals of
        works on physiology, psychology, and philosophy (con-
        tinues to write reviews and notices regularly over the
        next twenty-five years).

1875   Writes article on vivisection, defending it in principle
        while attacking its abuses, for *The Nation*. Fall, gives grad-
        uate course on the relationship between physiology and
        psychology (teaches it through 1877–78), which includes
        first laboratory work in psychology in the United States.
        Writes tribute to Chauncey Wright for *The Nation* after

his death in September. Inhales amyl nitrate during visit to Harvard chemistry laboratory to satisfy curiosity about its effects.

1876   Introduced by Thomas Davidson to Alice Howe Gibbens (born 1849), teacher at Miss Sanger's School for Girls in Boston, after father mentions her to James, beginning long and sometimes troubled courtship. Appointed assistant professor of physiology at annual salary of $2,000, February. June, writes article on Scottish philosopher Alexander Bain and Renouvier for *The Nation*. September, submits anonymous letter to *The Nation* criticizing neglect of philosophy in American universities. Has G. Stanley Hall as graduate student (in 1878 Hall receives first Harvard Ph.D. in psychology). Teaches undergraduate course on physiological psychology, using Herbert Spencer's *Principles of Psychology* as text while criticizing it thoroughly during lectures.

1877   Summer, visited in Cambridge by Josiah Royce, graduate student at Johns Hopkins University, seeking advice on whether he should continue career in philosophy; James encourages him to persist. Again teaches undergraduate and graduate psychology courses, now under the auspices of the philosophy department. Considers offer of psychology professorship from Daniel Gilman, first president of Johns Hopkins.

1878   Delivers ten lectures on "The Brain and the Mind" at Johns Hopkins in February. April, Alice James has severe attack of hysteria. James and Alice Gibbens become engaged in May. June, signs contract with Henry Holt and Company for a text on psychology, proposing to finish by fall of 1880. Marries Alice Gibbens in Boston, July 10, and spends honeymoon at Keene Valley, New York, in the Adirondack Mountains, where he owns farmhouse with Bowditch and Charles and James Putnam. Works on book during honeymoon, to the amusement of his friends. Shortly after marriage, "Brute and Human Intellect" (first of nineteen articles that will be drawn from work on psychology text) and "Remarks on Spencer's Definition of Mind as Correspondence" appear in *Journal of Speculative Philosophy* and "Quelques Considérations sur la méthode subjective" in Renouvier's journal *Critique Philosophique*.

Fall, Jameses rent furnished rooms at 387 Harvard Street, Cambridge. Lectures on psychology at Lowell Institute in Boston. Continuing eye trouble prevents reading or writing at night. Writes, "I have found in marriage a calm and repose I never knew before."

1879   First son, Henry (Harry), born May 18. Family spends summer on Maine coast. Teaches psychology course and two philosophy courses (on Renouvier and on the philosophy of evolution) at Harvard, and gives one lecture a week on physiology and hygiene. Decides to stay at Harvard, but writes Henry complaining of scientific isolation and need for contact with German experimental psychologists. Publishes essays "Are We Automata?" and "The Sentiment of Rationality" in British journal *Mind*.

1880   Travels in Europe during summer while wife and son stay at mother-in-law's Cambridge home at 18 Garden Street. Visits Henry in London in June and meets British philosopher Shadworth Hodgson before leaving for Amsterdam in July. Sees G. Stanley Hall in Heidelberg (where Hall is studying psychology) and travels in Switzerland before going to France, where he visits Renouvier near Grenoble on August 15. Returns to Cambridge in the fall. Appointed assistant professor of philosophy. Replaces Renouvier course with psychology course using Bain's *Mental Science*. Family moves from Harvard Street to rooms on Louisburg Square in Boston. "The Association of Ideas" appears in *Popular Science Monthly*, containing first use of term "stream of consciousness." Writes Renouvier that his "principal amusement this winter has been resisting the inroads of Hegelism in our University."

1881   Goes to Milwaukee when Bob, deeply depressed and drinking heavily, decides to leave his family. Accompanies him back to Boston, where Bob stays alternately with parents and James before collapsing completely (returns to Milwaukee after short stay in asylum). Continues physiology lectures, teaches classes on "The Human Intellect" and contemporary philosophy, and gives graduate course in advanced psychology. November, Henry visits, meeting Alice and Harry for first time; Henry and Alice like each other immediately. James, father, mother, Henry, sister

Alice, and Wilky (now bankrupt and unable to work because of severe rheumatism) reunited for Christmas.

1882   Mother dies of bronchial asthma after brief illness, January
30. Funeral brings five siblings together for last time.
James buys small house at 15 Appian Way in Cambridge.
"On Some Hegelisms" appears in *Mind*, including observations made by James under influence of nitrous oxide.
Applies for and is granted year's leave of absence at half
pay in order to rest and meet with European philosophers
and psychologists. Arranges for Josiah Royce, then teaching English at Berkeley, to take his place (leads to permanent Harvard professorship for Royce). Second son,
William (Billy), born June 17. September, travels to Europe while wife and sons stay with her mother. Sees
Henry in London and then goes through Germany to Vi-
enna. Spends three weeks in Venice in October, viewing
art and suffering from constant insomnia. Visits Prague
and meets physiologist Ewald Hering, psychologist Carl
Stumpf (beginning long friendship), and physicist and
philosopher Ernst Mach. November, discusses brain vivisection during visit to Berlin veterinary school and attends
lectures of physiologist Wilhelm Ludwig and experimental
psychologist Wilhelm Wundt in Leipzig. Stays at home of
Belgian philosopher and psychologist Joseph Rémy Léo-
pold Delbœuf in Liège before going to Paris. Writes to
Henry of his German trip: "I certainly got a most distinct
impression of my own *information* in regard to *modern*
philosophic matters being broader than that of any one I
met, and our Harvard post of observation being more cosmopolitan." Attends lectures of Jean Charcot at his neurological clinic before receiving telegram from wife telling
of father's rapidly weakening condition. Joins Henry in
England, where they decide that Henry will sail for America while James waits in London for further news. Writes
farewell letter to father, December 14, while staying in
Henry's rooms on Bolton Street ("All my intellectual life
I derive from you; and though we have often seemed at
odds in the expression thereof, I'm sure there's a harmony
somewhere, and that our strivings will combine"). Attends dinner of the "Scratch Eight," philosophy discussion
group; members include Hodgson, George Croom Robertson, first editor of *Mind*, and Leslie Stephen. Father

dies in Boston, December 18, before Henry arrives; Henry reads letter aloud beside father's grave, December 31.

1883   James remains in England at family's urging, trying to work on long-delayed psychology text, and continues to see the "Scratch Eight." Father leaves estate of $95,000. Will names Henry as executor, limits Bob's share, and excludes Wilky on grounds that money already given him for plantation and other unsuccessful ventures constitute his inheritance. James objects when Henry and sister Alice agree to divide estate equally, proposing more complex arrangement based on needs of his wife and children and wealth of Wilky's wife's family, but then agrees to equal division among the five siblings. Goes to Paris in February and returns to Cambridge in March. Lectures at Concord School of Philosophy in early summer. Spends latter part of summer with family at Keene Valley. Takes over as executor of father's estate when Henry leaves for England in late August. Teaches three philosophy courses (on evolution, the human intellect, and English philosophy) and course in advanced psychology. Has George Santayana as undergraduate philosophy student. Hurries to Milwaukee to see Wilky, who is critically ill with kidney and heart disease. Arrives October 1 and finds him temporarily improved but highly nervous; leaves the following day so that Wilky can rest. Wilky dies November 15.

1884   Third son, Herman, born January 31. Lectures at Harvard Divinity School on "The Dilemma of Determinism." Family goes to Keene Valley for summer, where James works on one-volume selection from father's work and writes long introduction. "On Some Omissions of Introspective Psychology" appears in *Mind*. September, contracts fever that affects eyes for weeks. Gives dictation to Bob, who has again left his family. Sister Alice sails for England with close friend Katherine Loring in November. James becomes corresponding member of English Society for Psychical Research and organizes informal Boston branch. *The Literary Remains of the Late Henry James* published by Houghton, Mifflin at end of year.

1885   March, wife ill with scarlet fever and family is quarantined. June, wife and son Herman fall sick with whooping cough; other children are sent away to country. Herman develops pneumonia and dies July 9; buried next to James's father. James writes to a cousin, "He was a broad, generous, patient little nature, with a noble head who would doubtless have done credit to his name if he had lived. . . . The great part of the experience to me has been the sight of Alice's devotion. I thought I knew her, but I didn't, nor did I fully know the meaning of that old human word *motherhood*." Spends summer on farm at Jaffrey, New Hampshire, with family, and alone in Cambridge, writing. Becomes full professor of philosophy, at salary of $4,000. Teaches two psychology courses and conducts experiments in hypnotism, enlisting students as subjects. December, family moves to mother-in-law's house on Garden Street while Mrs. Gibbens is in Italy recuperating from severe illness (they will remain there after her return).

1886　　May, enjoys Henry's *The Bostonians* and praises it in letter to him. Summer, report on séances conducted by Helen Berry and by Mrs. William J. Piper appears in *Proceedings of the American Society for Psychical Research*. Family spends summer at Jaffrey, New Hampshire. Unable to make progress on psychology book, goes alone to Portsmouth, New Hampshire, Cambridge, and White Mountains. Purchases large farmhouse and ninety acres of land on Lake Chocorua, near Conway, New Hampshire, for $8,000. Teaches courses on logic and psychology, on English empirical philosophy, and on advanced psychological research. "The Perception of Time" appears in *Journal of Speculative Philosophy*.

1887　　Seeking relief from insomnia, makes repeated visits to "mind-cure doctress," but problem persists. March 24, daughter Margaret Mary (Peggy) born. Works with architect on remodeling house at Chocorua, at expense of $2,000. Goes to Chocorua in early summer to begin garden and is joined by family when house is finished in mid-July. Goes mountain climbing in the Adirondacks at end of summer. Repeats previous year's courses, with shift toward Berkeley, Hume, and Reid in English philosophy course. "The Perception of Space" appears in four issues of *Mind*, "The Laws of Habit" and "Some Human Instincts" in *Popular Science Monthly*, and "What Is an Instinct?" in *Scribner's Magazine*.

1888   Winter, remains in Cambridge while wife and children go to Aiken, South Carolina, hoping to alleviate Billy's asthma. May, family returns to Cambridge and summers in Chocorua. September, returns to Cambridge and is joined by family in October. Teaches new ethics course in place of English empirical philosophy; extensive preparatory reading slows work on psychology book.

1889   Has new house built for family in Cambridge at 95 Irving Street and directs its design. Catherine Walsh (Aunt Kate) dies, March 6. James and wife attend funeral in New York and James inherits $10,000. Late June, sails alone for Ireland. Visits Trinity College, Dublin, tours Scotland, and arrives in London in mid-July. Goes with Henry to visit sister Alice, now permanent invalid, at Royal Leamington Spa, Warwickshire. Attends International Congress of Physiological Psychology in Paris, early August. Meets Théodore Flournoy, Swiss experimental psychologist teaching at University of Geneva, and begins lasting friendship. Returns to England and sees Henry and Alice before sailing for America in late August. Family moves into new Irving Street house in fall. Teaches undergraduate course on logic and psychology and graduate course in experimental psychology. Becomes first Alford Professor of Psychology at Harvard in November. Helps International Congress of Experimental Psychology conduct census of hallucinations in the United States based on questionnaires sent to randomly chosen individuals.

1890   Works to complete psychology text, organizing and revising previously published material and writing new sections. After last of many late-night writing sessions, finally sends finished manuscript to Henry Holt, May 22. Writes brother Henry, "As 'Psychologies' go, it is a good one, but psychology is in such an ante-scientific condition that the whole present generation of them is predestined to become unreadable old medieval lumber, as soon as the first genuine tracks of insight are made." Corrects proofs in Cambridge during summer before joining family in Chocorua in August. *The Principles of Psychology*, published in two volumes by Henry Holt and Company in late September, receives wide acclaim and is quickly adopted as a text at many American and British universities, though a few reviewers criticize its lively style and occasional irreverence. Teaches undergraduate philosophy courses on metaphysics and on Descartes, Spinoza, and Leibniz, an undergraduate psychology course using *The Principles* as text, and graduate psychology seminar on pleasure and pain. Fourth son, Francis Tweedy (later renamed Alexander Robertson and called Aleck), born December 22.

1891   Begins correspondence with John Dewey. Spends summer abridging and rewriting *The Principles of Psychology* for one-volume version in Holt's "Briefer Course" series, designed for use as introductory text. July, learns that sister Alice has breast tumor. Writes to her, "When that which is *you* passes out of the body, I am sure that there will be an explosion of liberated force and life till then eclipsed and kept down. . . . Everyone will feel the shock, but you yourself will be more surprised than anybody else." September, goes to England for ten days to see Alice for the last time. Attends London opening of Henry's stage version of *The American* and advises Alice to try hypnotism as means of controlling her pain. Teaches introductory psychology, logic and psychology, and graduate psychology seminar.

1892   Accompanied by graduate student W.E.B. Du Bois (a student of James's in the late 1880s, soon to be the first black Harvard Ph.D.), visits twelve-year-old Helen Keller at her school in Boston and gives her an ostrich feather (later corresponds with her). *Psychology* (eventually known as *Psychology: Briefer Course*), shorter version of *The Principles*, published by Henry Holt in January. Gives series of lectures on psychology to Cambridge schoolteachers. Receives farewell telegram from sister Alice, March 5; she dies March 6. James is left $20,000 in her will. Arranges for Hugo Münsterberg, young German experimental psychologist, to take over Harvard's psychological laboratory for three-year trial period. Sails with family to Antwerp, May 25, beginning sabbatical leave. Meets Münsterberg in Freiburg to discuss Harvard appointment and then goes to Lucerne and Gryon, alpine village near Lake Geneva, in July. Enjoys Switzerland but finds travel with children exhausting. Arranges for Harry and Billy to live with local pastors, and goes to Vers-chez-les-Blanc, near Lausanne, where Théodore Flournoy and his family are staying. Henry visits in August and meets his youngest nephew and niece for first time, but sees little of James, who goes on previously arranged walking tour with F.W.H. Myers of the English Society for Psychical Research. Family moves to Florence in late September. James takes walks with former student Bernhard Berenson and meets Mark Twain. Sees Caroline James (Wilky's widow) and their children, Cary and Alice, who are traveling in Europe, but relations are strained. December, attends anniversary festival in honor of Galileo at the University of Padua, and receives honorary doctoral degree.

1893   Enrolls Harry in boarding school near Munich and sees Carl Stumpf. March, with Henry's approval, has lines from Dante's *Paradiso* ("And she from martyrdom and from exile found this peace") inscribed in Italian on urn for Alice's ashes in Cambridge family plot. Family returns to Switzerland in April. Declines editorship of *Psychological Review*, new publication of American Psychological Association, but becomes frequent contributor. Family returns to Cambridge in August. Teaches introductory psychology, philosophy course on cosmology (primarily devoted to theories of evolution and materialism), and graduate seminar on mental pathology. Writes Henry in September that "the coming back makes one feel strangely sad and hardens one in the resolution never to go away again unless one can go to end one's days. Such a divided soul is very bad." Makes eighteen visits to "mind-curer" for relief of melancholia and insomnia; condition improves, but James is unsure if treatment is responsible. December, accepts honorary appointment as president of English Society for Psychical Research and is elected president of the American Association of Psychologists.

1894   March, reads privately printed copy of sister Alice's diary. Writes Henry that it made "a unique and tragic impression of personal power venting itself on no opportunity. And such really *deep* humor." Opposes bill (eventually tabled) introduced in the Massachusetts legislature aimed at restricting practice of mental therapy to licensed medical doctors. Writes in *Boston Evening Transcript*, March 24: "I assuredly hold no brief for any of these healers . . . But their *facts* are patent and startling; and anything that interferes with the multiplication of such facts, and with our freest opportunity of observing and studying them, will, I believe, be a public calamity." Writes favorable notice for *Psychological Review* of Sigmund Freud and Josef Breuer's first paper on hysteria. Repeats courses from previous year, and gives cosmology course at newly founded Radcliffe College (will teach at Radcliffe until 1902). December, delivers presidential address, "The Knowing of Things Together," to American Association of Psychologists meeting in Princeton (published in *Psychological Review* in 1895).

1895   Resumes directorship of psychology laboratory for one year when Münsterberg returns to Germany. Delivers address "Is Life Worth Living?" to Harvard Young Men's Christian Association (published in October *International Journal of Ethics*). Lectures on psychology to schoolteachers in Boston, New York, and at summer school in Colorado Springs. Teaches introductory and advanced undergraduate psychology courses and graduate seminar in the psychology of feeling. December, deeply disturbed by widespread jingoism aroused by Anglo-American crisis over Venezuelan–British Guianese border dispute.

1896   January, in response to statement by Theodore Roosevelt (then police commissioner of New York City), defends right to dissent in foreign affairs in letter to the *Harvard Crimson*. Spring, delivers address "The Will to Believe" to philosophical clubs at Yale and Brown. Takes government-supplied peyote, obtained from Dr. S. Weir Mitchell, as experiment while preparing Chocorua house for tenant in June; becomes violently nauseated but does not experience expected hallucinatory effects. Worries about finances and supplements salary by repeating psychology lectures for schoolteachers in upstate New York, Vermont, and Chicago during summer before vacationing in Wisconsin. Reads *War and Peace* and *Anna Karenina*; writes Flournoy that "now I feel as if I knew *perfection* in the representation of human life." Fall, delivers eight lectures at Lowell Institute in Boston on exceptional mental states; subjects include hypnotism, hysteria, multiple personality, demoniacal possession, and genius. Teaches introductory and abnormal psychology, philosophy of nature (similar to earlier cosmology course), and gives graduate seminar on Kant. Persuades Gertrude Stein, his student at Radcliffe, to pursue study of psychology by going to medical school.

1897   *The Will to Believe, and Other Essays in Popular Philosophy* published by Longmans, Green & Co. in March. Declines Gifford Lectureship in Natural Theology at University of Aberdeen (hoping to be offered Gifford Lectureship at University of Edinburgh, which would allow more time for preparation and is better paying) and nominates Royce in his place. Is freed of responsibility for psychology laboratory by Münsterberg's return to Harvard and decides to concentrate increasingly on philosophy (appointment changed to professor of philosophy in August). Delivers oration at dedication of Augustus Saint-Gaudens's monument to Robert Gould Shaw, commander of the 54th Massachusetts, May 31. Family spends summer at Chocorua. Teaches philosophy of nature and advanced graduate psychology. November, gives Ingersoll Lecture on Human Immortality (published by Houghton, Mifflin in 1898 as *Human Immortality: Two Supposed Objections to the Doctrine*).

1898   January, warned by Henry that Bob is returning from England in highly unstable mental condition. James persuades him to enter Dansville Asylum, near Buffalo, and accompanies him there (Bob stays for several years). Accepts appointment as Gifford Lecturer at University of Edinburgh for 1899–1900 and 1900–01. March, argues before Massachusetts legislative committee against new medical licensing bill (measure is defeated). Becomes alarmed by growing annexationist sentiment in wake of American victories in Spanish-American War. July, goes to Keene Valley with friends and undergoes "a regular Walpurgis Nacht" while unable to sleep on hiking trip. (Writes to Alice that "it seemed as if the Gods of all the nature-mythologies were holding an indescribable meeting in my breast with the moral Gods of the inner life. The two kinds of Gods have nothing in common—the Edinburgh lectures made quite a hitch ahead. . . . It was one of the happiest lonesome nights of my existence, and I understand now what a poet is.") Overexerts himself the following day while hiking in mountains with younger companions. August, travels by train to British Columbia, goes through Washington and Oregon, and visits Yosemite. Delivers lecture "Philosophical Conceptions and Practical Results" at University of California at Berkeley, August 26; speaks for first time of "pragmatism" as a philosophic principle, attributing term to Charles Peirce. Teaches metaphysics and advanced seminar on abnormal psychology. November, severe chest pains lead to diagnosis of valvular lesion and permanent heart damage, attributed to hiking experiences of summer. Decides to rent Chocorua for following summer and take sabbatical in Europe while preparing Gifford Lectures.

1899   Becomes fervent public opponent of American policy in the Philippines and active member of Anti-Imperialist League. Accuses imperialists of treating Filipinos "as if they were a painted picture, an amount of mere matter in our way. They are too remote from us ever to be realized as they exist in their inwardness." *Talks to Teachers on Psychology: and to Students on Some of Life's Ideals*, based on oft-repeated 1892 Cambridge lectures, published by Henry Holt. June, gets lost while walking in Keene Valley until late at night, further damaging health. Sails with wife and daughter for Europe, July 15 (Aleck stays with Mrs. Gibbens; Harry and Billy, now Harvard undergraduates, are working as forest rangers in Washington). Goes to Bad Nauheim, spa near Frankfurt-am-Main, seeking treatment for heart condition and nervous exhaustion. Remains for seven weeks, takes baths, sits in park, and begins to read religious biographies in preparation for Gifford Lectures, but is unable to write. Closely follows Dreyfus Affair in *Le Figaro* and is outraged by Dreyfus's second conviction. September, goes to Switzerland and then to England. Visits Henry at Lamb House, his home in Rye, Sussex, for first time. Lives as invalid with Alice (daughter is at boarding school) in Henry's London flat at 34 De Vere Gardens from October until December. Dictates letters to Alice to save eyes from strain, makes slight progress on lectures and fears that he may die before they are completed, but is cheered when weather improves. December, goes on doctor's advice to take baths at West Malvern, Worcestershire, but condition worsens. Resigns lectureship and asks Harvard for second year of leave. Spends end of year in Rye and improves slightly.

1900   Leaves England with Alice, January 10, and goes to Costebelle, near Hyères, in Provence. After week in hotel, moves with British psychic researcher F.W.H. Myers and his family into nearby chateau, loaned to them by physiologist Charles Richet. Visited by Josiah Royce, who gives James first volume of his *The World and the Individual*. James quickly reads it and writes to Royce, praising its "ease, unfailing clearness, its sincerity and affability" while stating that he "finds the arguments you use as incoercive as ever, and the Absolute still remains for me a hypothesis to be tested by its uses, rather than a doctrine to be submitted to for its credentials." Receives one-year postponement of Gifford Lectureship and additional year of leave from Harvard at half pay. Writes in bed for a few hours in mornings; starts fourth lecture by end of April. While visiting Flournoy family in Geneva, writes letter to the *Springfield Republican* containing translation of French naval officer's critical account of the American occupation of the Philippines. Goes for six weeks to Bad Nauheim in May, but baths do not improve condition and he is unable to write. Spends summer in Geneva and Lucerne and resumes work on fourth lecture in July. Returns to Bad Nauheim in late August for further treatment. Saddened by death of philosopher Thomas Davidson in September. Goes to Rome in October after doctor advises against spending winter in England. Continues work on lectures, writing for two hours in the morning, and makes encouraging progress; sends manuscripts to Henry for his typist to copy. November, begins injecting new lymph compound (mixture of male goat lymph glands, spinal cords, and brains and bull sperm) to treat heart and nervous symptoms. (Pleased by results, later takes daily injections for six weeks twice a year.) Stays in same hotel as anthropologist James Frazer and discusses religious and psychological questions with him.

1901   Joined in Rome by gravely ill F.W.H. Myers, who dies in James's hotel, January 17; James is profoundly impressed by his courage in the face of death. Writes Henry that he has finished eighth lecture, January 25. Leaves Rome in March, visiting Perugia, Assisi, Lucerne, and Geneva; arrives in Rye in early April, where James, Alice, and Henry are joined by Harry in May. Buys new clothes in London before going to Edinburgh. Gives first lecture on May 16 to responsive audience of 250 and is encouraged as audiences grow to 300, but often has to rest in bed between lectures and take digitalis. Impressed by Scotland's beauty ("the air itself an *object*, holding watery vapor, tenuous smoke, and ancient sunshine in solution, so as to yield the most exquisite minglings and gradations . . ."). Delivers tenth and final lecture of first series, June 17. Returns to Bad Nauheim in late June, after visiting Henry in Rye; writes him in mid-July that the "baths stir up my aortic feeling and make me depressed." Goes to Vosges mountains in August to recover. Sees E. L. Godkin, former editor of *The Nation*, now crippled by stroke, in England before sailing for the United States on August 31. Teaches advanced course on the psychology of religious life one hour per week at salary of $2,000 per year. Despite fatigue and insomnia, writes two-thirds of second series of Gifford Lectures by end of year.

1902　　Finishes second lecture series while preparing both sets for publication. Sails for England with Alice, April 1. Receives honorary LL.D. from University of Edinburgh and visits Godkin in Devonshire and Henry at Rye. Gives ten lectures at Edinburgh, May 13–June 9, before enthusiastic audiences of up to 400. Sails for Boston, June 10, and goes with family to Chocorua for summer. Gifford Lectures published in June as *The Varieties of Religious Experience: A Study in Human Nature* by Longmans, Green & Co., and quickly earn international praise (11,500 copies are printed in first year of publication, and sales help James's finances considerably). Delivers two lectures at Harvard Summer School of Theology, July. Teaches course on the philosophy of nature. December, begins correspondence with French philosopher Henri Bergson by praising his *Matière et mémoire* (*Matter and Memory*) as a work that "makes a sort of Copernican revolution as much as Berkeley's *Principles* or Kant's *Critique* did" and sending him a copy of *The Varieties of Religious Experience*.

1903　　March, "The Ph.D. Octopus" appears in *Harvard Monthly*. Goes to Asheville, North Carolina, in April to recuperate from tonsillitis. Greatly enjoys rereading works of Emerson in preparation for address delivered at Emerson centenary celebration in Concord, May 25. June, sends Henry copy of W.E.B. Du Bois's *The Souls of Black Folk*;

describes it as "a decidedly moving book" and recommends that Henry read it for his planned American trip. Gives speech "The True Harvard" at commencement dinner, June 24, praising university's tolerance and respect for individualism (published in September *Harvard Graduates' Magazine*). Letter on lynching appears in the *Springfield Republican*, July 23, and is widely reprinted ("It is where the impulse is collective, and the murder is regarded as a punitive or protective duty, that the peril to civilization is greatest"). Goes to Chocorua in July and spends most of summer there, planning major work of philosophy. Writes friend in August: "I am convinced that the desire to formulate truths is a virulent disease. It has contracted an alliance lately in me with a feverish personal ambition, which I never had before, and which I recognize as an unholy thing in such a connexion. I actually dread to die until I have settled the Universe's hash in one more book . . . ! Childish idiot—as if formulas about the Universe could ruffle its majesty, and as if the common-sense world and its duties were not eternally the really real! . . ." Gives five talks on "Radical Empiricism as a Philosophy" at Glenmore, informal summer philosophy school in the Adirondacks founded by Thomas Davidson. Teaches graduate seminar in metaphysics. Resigns from Harvard at end of the year.

1904   Persuaded by Harvard president Eliot to continue teaching reduced course load. Writes Flournoy in June that two attacks of influenza and general fatigue have prevented him from writing more than thirty-two pages of new philosophy book. Visited by Henry at Chocorua for first time in September, at start of his extended American stay; James is pleased by his brother's appreciation of the landscape. Sees several foreign scholars and scientists, including Pierre Janet, on their way to and from St. Louis World Exposition. September, "Does 'Consciousness' Exist?" and "A World of Pure Experience" appear in *Journal of Philosophy, Psychology and Scientific Methods*, beginning series of articles elaborating doctrine of radical empiricism. Teaches first semester of course in metaphysics. November, visited by Henry in Cambridge.

1905   "How Two Minds Can Know One Thing" appears in March issue of *Journal of Philosophy, Psychology and Scien-*

tific Methods. Sails for Europe alone, March 11, and travels in southern Italy and Greece; cries at sight of Parthenon ("It sets a standard for other human things, showing that absolute rightness is not out of reach"). Attends Philosophical Congress in Rome at end of April, and is especially well-received by group of Italian pragmatic philosophers. Writes and delivers address "La Notion de Conscience" to Congress in French. Travels in Italy and France and visits Flournoy in Geneva. Meets Bergson for first time in Paris, May 28, and sees philosopher F.C.S. Schiller at Oxford before sailing for the United States at the beginning of June. "Is Radical Empiricism Solipsistic?" appears in *Journal of Philosophy, Psychology and Scientific Methods* in April and "The Place of Affectional Facts in a World of Pure Experience" in May. Visited by Henry in June before his return to England. Lectures at University of Chicago summer school in early July, vacations in Keene Valley, and gives talks at Glenmore. Ill with influenza during August and is unable to write. Teaches first four weeks of introductory philosophy course and fall semester of undergraduate metaphysics course. Writes Henry in October criticizing *The Golden Bowl* for its narration "by interminable elaboration of suggestive reference" and suggesting that he write a novel with "absolute straightness in the style. . . ." Henry replies by asking that James not read his works due to their greatly different sensibilities.

1906   Visits Grand Canyon on way to California, arriving in Palo Alto, January 8, to begin one-semester appointment at Stanford University. Teaches introductory course in philosophy with 300 enrolled students. Joined by Alice in early February. Delivers address "The Moral Equivalent of War" to university assembly, February 25. During great earthquake of April 18, experiences "glee at the vividness which such an abstract idea or verbal term as 'earthquake' could put on when translated into sensible reality and verified concretely. . . ." Goes with colleague, psychology professor Lillian Martin, into San Francisco in late morning to search for her sister (whom she finds). Sees city in flames and closely observes reactions to disaster, returning to Palo Alto in evening. Writes to Henry, "Everyone at San Francisco seemed in a good hearty frame of mind; there was work for every moment of the day and a kind of uplift in the sense of a 'common lot' that took away the sense of loneliness that (I imagine) gives the sharpest edge to the more usual kind of misfortune that may befall a man." University closes due to earthquake damage and James and Alice leave for Cambridge on April 26. "On Some Mental Effects of the Earthquake" appears in June issue of *Youth's Companion*. Considers writing textbook that will systematically express his philosophy. Spends summer in Cambridge, Keene Valley, Chocorua, and on the Maine coast. Praises former mental patient Clifford Beers's manuscript indicting mental health system (book is published as *A Mind That Found Itself* in 1908). Heart condition worsens. September, in response to magazine article by H. G. Wells, writes to Wells criticizing American "callousness to abstract justice" and "the moral flabbiness born of the exclusive worship of the bitch-goddess SUCCESS. That—with the squalid interpretation put on the word success—is our national disease." Teaches one-semester course on general problems in philosophy. Gives eight Lowell Lectures on "Pragmatism," November 14–December 8. Delivers presidential address "The Energies of Men" to the American Philosophical Association in New York, December 28 (published in January 1907 *Philosophical Review*).

1907   Resigns professorship January 11 and is presented with silver loving cup at last lecture on January 22. Repeats "Pragmatism" lectures at Columbia University, January 29–February 8, with over 1,000 attending. Begins to suffer from persistent angina. Becomes active supporter of Clifford Beers's efforts to organize National Committee for Mental Hygiene (founded in 1909, with James serving as trustee). Visits daughter Peggy, now student at Bryn Mawr. *Pragmatism: A New Name for Some Old Ways of Thinking*, based on Lowell and Columbia lectures, published in June by Longmans, Green & Co. Writes Bergson praising his *L'Évolution créatrice* (*Creative Evolution*) and compares its literary qualities to those of *Madame Bovary*. Spends summer in Chocorua, Cambridge, Lincoln, Massachusetts, and Keene Valley. Awarded $3,000 a year pension by Carnegie fund. Delivers address "The Social Value of the College-Bred" to Association of American Alumnae at Radcliffe (published in *McClure's Magazine*, February 1908). November, accepts invitation to give eight Hibbert

Lectures at Manchester College, Oxford, on "The Present Situation in Philosophy." Works on lectures in December and delivers address "The Meaning of the Word Truth" to the American Philosophical Association meeting at Cornell University at the end of the month.

1908   Ill with grippe in January. Finishes writing six Hibbert Lectures by mid-April, despite persistent vertigo and insomnia and uncertainty about continuing to write in a "picturesque and popular style." Sails for Liverpool with Alice on April 21. Delivers Hibbert Lectures to large audiences, May 4–28 and receives honorary D.Sc. degree on May 12. Travels throughout England in late spring and summer; meets Bertrand Russell and Lady Ottoline Morrell, receives honorary Litt.D. from University of Durham, and tours Lake District, though health prevents him from hiking. Spends late July and August with Henry in Rye, where they are joined by Harry, Peggy, and Aleck. Sends Beers $1,000 to help with costs of mental hygiene movement. Meets G. K. Chesterton and H. G. Wells. Visits Belgium, the Netherlands, and northern France before returning to England in September. Sees Henry again and goes to Devon coast before sailing for Boston, October 6. Has sample of lymph compound sent to Flournoy, and writes that he attributes most of his ability to work since 1901 to its effects (Flournoy tries it without significant results). Has portrait done in oils by son Billy (who is starting career as a painter). Repeats Hibbert Lectures at Harvard, November 6–30, to audiences of 600. December, works on lengthy report evaluating seventy-five alleged communications by the deceased psychical researcher Richard Hodgson through medium Mrs. Piper.

1909   Suffers from recurring "violent" heart pain triggered by exertion or "any mental hesitation, trepidation, or flurry." "Report on Mrs. Piper's Hodgson-Control" published in *Proceedings* of the English and American Societies for Psychical Research. Begins writing philosophy text in late March. April, Hibbert Lectures published as *A Pluralistic Universe* by Longmans, Green & Co. Spends summer in Chocorua reading proofs for collection of thirteen previously published and two new essays, published as *The Meaning of Truth: A Sequel to "Pragmatism"* by Longmans, Green & Co. in October. Cardiac pain interferes with work on new philosophy book. September, meets Sigmund Freud, Carl Gustav Jung, and Ernest Jones at conference organized by G. Stanley Hall at Clark University in Worcester, Massachusetts, and tells them that "the future of psychology belongs to your work." (Later writes Flournoy that although Freud impressed him as a man "obsessed by fixed ideas," he hopes that Freud and his pupils will "push their ideas to their utmost limits.") October, "The Confidences of a 'Psychical Researcher,'" expressing fundamental uncertainty on subject, published in *American Magazine*. Works on articles despite increasing pain, nervous tension, and angina-related breathing difficulties.

1910   Portrait, painted by cousin Ellen Emmet Rand, unveiled at testimonial dinner held at 95 Irving Street, January 18. "Bradley or Bergson?" appears in *The Journal of Philosophy, Psychology and Scientific Methods* in January and "A Suggestion about Mysticism" in February. "The Moral Equivalent of War," revised version of 1906 Stanford address, issued as pamphlet by the Association for International Conciliation. Continues to work on philosophy book. Learns in February that Henry is seriously ill. Asks Harry (now an attorney involved in family affairs) to go to England; his letters convince James that Henry has had a nervous breakdown. Decides in March to advance planned trip to Europe for heart treatment so that he and Alice can be with Henry. Before leaving, writes at top of faculty list in his copy of the Harvard catalogue: "Infinite compunctions cover every beloved name. Forgive me!" Sails on March 29 and reaches Rye on April 7. Stays with Henry before going to Paris alone on May 5 to receive electrical therapy for his arteries. Sees Bergson, Edith Wharton, Henry Adams, and others; treatments are ineffectual. Exhausted, leaves for Bad Nauheim May 17. Takes baths and is joined by Henry and Alice in early June, but condition does not improve (Alice writes that "William cannot walk and Henry cannot smile"). Goes to Switzerland with Alice and Henry in late June, visiting Zurich, Lucerne, and Geneva, but James finds high altitudes painful and breathing difficulties worsen. Learns in Geneva of brother Bob's death from heart attack in Concord on July 3. Returns to London on July 17 and Rye on July 23. "A Pluralistic Mystic," tribute to philosopher Benjamin Paul

Blood, published in July *Hibbert Journal*. Gives up hopes of completing philosophy book and writes instructions on July 26 for its publication: "Say that I hoped by it to round out my system, which now is too much like an arch built only on one side." (Published as *Some Problems in Philosophy* by Longmans, Green in May 1911, edited by his son Henry James, Jr., Horace Kallen, and Ralph Barton Perry.) James, Alice, and Henry sail from England, August 12, land in Quebec August 18, and reach Chocorua the following day. James, in intense pain, has Alice promise that she will "go to Henry when his time comes." Dies of heart failure, 2:30 P.M., August 26. Funeral service held at Appleton Chapel in Harvard Yard, August 30. Body is cremated and ashes are interred in Cambridge family plot.

Note on the Texts

This volume includes the following works by William James published between 1902 and 1911: *The Varieties of Religious Experience: A Study in Human Nature. Being the Gifford Lectures on Natural Religion Delivered at Edinburgh in 1901–1902*; *Pragmatism: A New Name for Some Old Ways of Thinking. Popular Lectures on Philosophy*; *A Pluralistic Universe. Hibbert Lectures at Manchester College on the Present Situation in Philosophy*; *The Meaning of Truth: A Sequel to 'Pragmatism'*; *Some Problems of Philosophy: A Beginning of an Introduction to Philosophy*; and a selection of twenty short pieces written during that period.

When James first accepted the offer of the Gifford Lectureship early in 1898, the lectures that make up *The Varieties of Religious Experience: A Study in Human Nature* were scheduled to be delivered in two courses of ten each at the University of Edinburgh during the winters of 1899–1900 and 1900–01. By the time James sailed for Europe in July 1899, the date of delivery for the first course had been changed to the late spring of 1900. Pressure of work and then his developing heart problems had prevented him from working on the lectures earlier, but he hoped that treatment at the spa at Bad Nauheim would give him the strength to write again. His health continued to fail, and in December 1899 he resigned the lectureship. The Gifford Committee refused his resignation, however, and on May 16, 1901, after repeated postponements and continued severe illness, James delivered his first lecture. The course was very successful, and by the time he gave the last lecture on June 17 his health had improved. He returned home to Cambridge in September and soon began work on the second course of ten lectures. The writing this time proceeded smoothly, and that fall he also began to have the lectures set in type at H. O. Houghton's Riverside Press in Cambridge for publication in New York and London by Longmans, Green, and Co. in June 1902. By late March he had finished the index and corrected the proofs. The second course of lectures was delivered in Edinburgh from May 13 to

June 9, 1902, and before the lectures were finished he received the first copy of the completed book. It was immediately successful, and new printings were made from the plates in August, October, November, and December 1902; January, March, and November 1903; April and September 1904; February 1905; February and November 1906; May 1907; February and September 1908; August 1909; and June and October 1910. The thirty-eighth printing in 1935 was the last to be made from these plates.

James's annotated copy of the first printing, in the Houghton Library at Harvard University, records corrections and revisions he wanted to make in the text. Only about half were made in later printings, and a few of these had to be slightly altered to fit existing lines. Omitting or adding words, unless at the end of a paragraph, could be complicated and expensive. For example, at 74.7–9, James wanted to revise "and our *articulately verbalized* philosophy is but its showy translation *into formulas*. The *unreasoned and* immediate assurance is the deep thing in us, the *reasoned* argument is but a surface exhibition" by omitting the italicized words and inserting "verbalized" after "showy." Since dropping six words would have involved considerable cutting of the plates and would have affected more than one page, the change was not made. Though not marked in his copy, James also corrected the footnote on page 115 and added quotation marks to the case studies on pages 117–20; apparently some early readers assumed that the case studies were from James's own experience, and a correction slip was inserted into some copies of the first printing and the corrections made in the second. The present volume prints the text of William James's annotated copy of the first printing of the first edition, Harvard *AC85.J2376.902v(c), incorporating all the corrections and revisions he marked in it, as well as the alterations noted on pages 115 and 117–20.

Pragmatism: A New Name for Some Old Ways of Thinking evolved from a series of lectures James began in 1905. The first three courses of lectures were delivered from notes: five lectures at Wellesley College, February 28 to March 10, 1905; five lectures at the University of Chicago, June 30 to July 7, 1905;

and a series of lectures at Glenmore in Keene, New York, July 28 to August 3, 1905. In preparation for eight lectures to be given at the Lowell Institute in Boston from November 14 to December 8, 1906, James began the actual writing that would become the book, and he was still writing the later lectures after he began delivering the first ones. The lectures were repeated to large audiences at Columbia University from January 29 to February 8, 1907, and James continued to make revisions in them. Three of the lectures, I, II, and VI, were prepared for periodical publication during this time, but with the stipulation that they not be published until after his appearance at Columbia. Lecture I, "The Present Dilemma in Philosophy," appeared under the title "A Defence of Pragmatism: I. Its Mediating Office" in *Popular Science Monthly* for March 1907; Lecture II, "What Pragmatism Means," under the title "A Defence of Pragmatism: II. What Pragmatism Means" in *Popular Science Monthly* for April 1907; and Lecture VI, "Pragmatism's Conception of Truth," in *The Journal of Philosophy, Psychology and Scientific Methods* for March 14, 1907. James revised these three lectures directly on the journal offprints and eventually submitted them in that form for book publication. A fourth article, used as the basis for Lecture III, "Some Metaphysical Problems Pragmatically Considered," had been published earlier under the title "The Pragmatic Method" in *The Journal of Philosophy, Psychology and Scientific Methods* for December 9, 1904; this revision in turn had been a revision of "Philosophical Conceptions and Practical Results," in *The University of California Chronicle* for September 1898, reprinted for the Philosophical Union of the University of California (Berkeley: The University Press, 1898). This article was also prepared for book publication by revising journal pages that were supplemented by newly prepared manuscript. The remaining four lectures were submitted in heavily revised manuscript. James took the manuscript to the printer, H. O. Houghton's Riverside Press in Cambridge, in March 1907. The book was published in New York and London by Longmans, Green, and Co. from sheets printed at the Riverside Press in June 1907. *Pragmatism* went through eight further printings during James's lifetime: July (twice),

October and November 1907; February and September 1908; March 1909; and April 1910.

In his own copy of the first printing, now at the Houghton Library at Harvard, James marked seventy-eight changes to be made by the printer, but only six of these were made in the plates during the successive reprintings, and one of the changes, the correcting of the spelling of "Vivekanda" to "Vivekananda" at 552.22, also necessitated a change of the word "shores" to "land" to make room in the line. The spelling of "Vivekananda" was also corrected in two other places and in the index, though James did not mark them in his own copy; slight alterations in James's wording were again necessary to make room for the additional syllable. No other corrections were made. The present volume prints the text of James's own corrected copy of the first printing of the first edition of *Pragmatism*, Harvard *AC85.J2376.907p(c), and includes all the revisions and corrections he marked in it.

On November 29, 1907, James accepted an offer to give a course of eight Hibbert Lectures at Manchester College in Oxford in the spring of 1908 and immediately set to work. By the time he sailed for England in April 1908 he had written almost all of the lectures that were to become *A Pluralistic Universe*. He left the bulk of the manuscript to be set at H. O. Houghton's Riverside Press. Proof was sent to him for correction while he was still at Oxford. The first lecture was delivered May 4 and the last May 28, 1908, attracting audiences larger than those of any previous lecturer on philosophy at Oxford. During the rest of the summer he continued to correct proof sent to him by the Riverside Press. He also prepared four of the lectures for successive publication in *The Hibbert Journal*, condensing and omitting some material, as well as cutting introductory remarks and other forms of direct address to the audience in order to shorten the pieces to fit the *Journal* format. Lecture VIII, "Conclusions," appeared as "Pluralism and Religion" (July 1908); Lecture III as "Hegel and His Method" (October 1908); Lecture IV, "Concerning Fechner," as "The Doctrine of the Earth-Soul and of Beings Intermediate Between Man and God. An Account of the Philosophy of G. T. Fechner"

(January 1909); and Lecture VI, "Bergson and His Critique of Intellectualism," as "The Philosophy of Bergson" (April 1909). On his return to Cambridge, he repeated the lectures at Harvard, beginning November 6 and ending November 30, 1908. Three appendices were added to the lectures for book publication. Two were slightly revised versions of earlier articles: Appendix A, "The Thing and Its Relations," had appeared in *The Journal of Philosophy, Psychology and Scientific Methods* for January 19, 1905; and Appendix B, "The Experience of Activity," in *The Psychological Review* for January 1905. The third, "On the Notion of Reality as Changing," appeared for the first time as Appendix C in *A Pluralistic Universe*.

James continued to make revisions even after the book was already in type. Apparently when he first gave the manuscript to Houghton for setting, it did not include the notes, because—in contrast to the form of his other books—the notes in the first edition of *A Pluralistic Universe* are in a section by themselves following the lectures and before the appendices. The book was published April 1909 in New York and London by Longmans, Green, and Co. Sheets printed by the Riverside Press in Cambridge were used for both American and English publication. A second printing (with unaltered text) was made in August 1909, but a third printing was not called for until March 1912, and there were far fewer printings of *A Pluralistic Universe* than there had been of *The Varieties of Religious Experience* or *Pragmatism*. The text of James's own corrected copy of the first printing of the first edition at the Houghton Library, Harvard University (WJ 200.25.3), including the twelve corrections and revisions he marked in it, is printed in the present volume. Each note has been placed at the foot of the page containing the passage referred to, following the form of the other books.

Soon after finishing work on *A Pluralistic Universe* James began assembling and revising a group of previously published journal essays for inclusion in *The Meaning of Truth: A Sequel to 'Pragmatism.'* His own notes to the first eight chapters and Chapter XII identify the original appearances of these nine essays. Chapter XI, "The Absolute and the Strenuous

Life," appeared in *The Journal of Philosophy, Psychology and Scientific Methods*, September 26, 1907 (not 1906 as in James's footnote). Chapter IX, "The Meaning of the Word Truth," was revised either from the privately printed pamphlet or from the version printed in *Mind*, July 1908. Chapter X, "The Existence of Julius Cæsar," was printed in *The Journal of Philosophy, Psychology and Scientific Methods*, March 26, 1908. Chapter XIII, "Abstractionism and 'Relativismus,'" originally appeared in *Popular Science Monthly*, May 1909. James added transitional sentences and paragraphs to the original articles, extracted parts of others, and reworked phrases and punctuation. The Preface, Chapter XIV, "Two English Critics," and Chapter XV, "A Dialogue," were written for the volume. No index was prepared for this work. The manuscript was delivered by James to the Riverside Press in Cambridge April 7, 1909. *The Meaning of Truth* was published in New York and London by Longmans, Green, and Co. in October 1909. Sheets from the Riverside Press were again used for both American and English publication. Second and third printings followed in November, and a fourth printing appeared in January 1911. James's own copy of the first printing contains a list of six corrections and revisions he wanted to make: one of them was made in the second printing and four others in the third. The printer also made one unauthorized change: James wanted to emend "anything else I am aware of" to "anything else of which I am aware" (963.33), but the printer, to make this revision fit, shortened it to "anything of which I am aware." The present volume prints the text of James's private copy of the first printing of the first edition, Harvard *AC85.J2376.909m(b), and incorporates the six changes that James wanted made.

James did not live to see *Some Problems of Philosophy* into print. His written instructions for publishing the book noted that "it is fragmentary and unrevised. . . . Say that I hoped by it to round out my system, which now is too much like an arch built only on one side." Before his death he appointed Horace M. Kallen to see it through the press. Kallen was aided by William James's son Henry and Ralph Barton Perry. The book was set and printed at the Riverside Press in Cambridge and was published in New York and London by Longmans, Green, and Co. in May 1911. This volume presents the text of the first printing of the first edition.

The twenty short pieces included in the present volume are a selection from the years 1903–10. The texts printed here are those of the original periodical appearances (except "Answers to a Questionnaire," which was published in *The Letters of William James*), and they incorporate the few corrections made by James in his private file copies (identified in parentheses below) now in the James collection at the Houghton Library at Harvard University:

"The Ph.D. Octopus," *The Harvard Monthly*, March 1903, pp. 1–9. (*80–55)

"Address at the Centenary of Ralph Waldo Emerson, May 25, 1903," *The Centenary of the Birth of Ralph Waldo Emerson as Observed in Concord . . . Printed at The Riverside Press for the Social Circle in Concord, June 1903*, pp. 67–77.

"The True Harvard," *Harvard Graduate's Magazine*, September 1903, pp. 5–8.

"Address on the Philippine Question," *Proceedings of the Fifth Annual Meeting of the New England Anti-Imperialist League*, December 1903, pp. 21–26.

"The Chicago School," *The Psychological Bulletin*, January 15, 1904, pp. 1–5.

"Does 'Consciousness' Exist?" *The Journal of Philosophy, Psychology and Scientific Methods*, September 1, 1904, pp. 477–91. (WJ 110.42)

"A World of Pure Experience," *The Journal of Philosophy, Psychology and Scientific Methods*, September 29, 1904, pp. 533–43, and October 13, 1904, pp. 561–70.

"Answers to a Questionnaire" (1904), *The Letters of William James*, edited by Henry James III, Boston: The Atlantic Monthly Press, 1920, volume II, pp. 212–15.

"How Two Minds Can Know One Thing," *The Journal of Philosophy, Psychology and Scientific Methods*, March 30, 1905, pp. 176–81. (WJ 110.42)

"Humanism and Truth Once More," *Mind*, April 1905, pp. 190–98. (Phil.22.4.6*)

"Is Radical Empiricism Solipsistic?" *The Journal of Philoso-*

phy, Psychology and Scientific Methods, April 27, 1905, pp. 235–38.

"The Place of Affectional Facts in a World of Pure Experience," *The Journal of Philosophy, Psychology and Scientific Methods*, May 25, 1905, pp. 281–87. (WJ 110.42)

"On Some Mental Effects of the Earthquake," *Youth's Companion*, June 7, 1906, pp. 283–84.

"The Energies of Men," *The Philosophical Review*, January 1907, pp. 1–20.

"The Social Value of the College-Bred," *McClure's Magazine*, February 1908, pp. 419–22.

"The Confidences of a 'Psychical Researcher,'" *American Magazine*, October 1909, pp. 580–89.

"Bradley or Bergson?" *The Journal of Philosophy, Psychology and Scientific Methods*, January 20, 1910, pp. 29–33.

"A Suggestion About Mysticism," *The Journal of Philosophy, Psychology and Scientific Methods*, February 17, 1910, pp. 85–92.

"The Moral Equivalent of War," *Association for International Conciliation: Leaflet No. 27*, February 1910, pp. 3–20.

"A Pluralistic Mystic," *The Hibbert Journal*, July 1910, pp. 739–59.

This volume is concerned with presenting the texts described here; it does not attempt to reproduce features of the typographic design of the original printings, such as the display capitalization of chapter openings. The original indexes for *The Varieties of Religious Experience*, *Pragmatism*, *A Pluralistic Universe*, and *Some Problems of Philosophy* are reproduced here, corrected only to correspond to corrections or emendations made in the texts of those editions. Two indexes are newly supplied: one for *The Meaning of Truth* (which appeared without one), and the other for the Essays section. Whenever James refers to book-length works included in the present volume, his page citations are changed to the corresponding pages here. His page citations referring to periodical publications, however, have not been replaced, even when the particular article is included here, since to do so would involve more extensive changes. In such instances, page references to the present volume are provided in the notes.

The texts selected for printing in this volume are reproduced without other changes except for the correction of typographical errors. Spelling, punctuation, and capitalization
often are expressive features, and they are not altered even
when apparently inconsistent or irregular. James, for example,
will sometimes use a shortened form of a word (such as
"tho") and yet occasionally will also use the full form
("though"). The following is a list of the typographical errors
corrected, cited by page and line number: 12:12–13, Pyschol-
ogy; 37.11, your; 37.25, warns; 42.4, Nietszche; 146.38, ZONIA;
175.10, church,; 198.39–40, astonishing; 199.30, EDWARD'S;
204.14, vi; 221.25, change; 230.38, Whitfield's; 233.12, Peek;
252.38, C. H. HILTY; 277.37, MOUNIN; 281.37, *pedocchi*; 282.35,
and blunted; 313.4, jusqù'à; 341.5, XIII; 379.28, teeming;
379.37, BOUILLIER'S; 412.22, asscending; 432.4, Itgân; 472.17b,
ELWOOD; 475.18a, PEEK; 476.24a, SANDAYS; 481.31, J. MIL-
HAUD; 485.22, [Index omitted]; 526.3, Nestor . . . ; 553.6,
There . . . ; 578.35, thing; 579.2, current,; 593.25, of; 601.24,
collar; 602.1, Vivekanda's; 606.18, Vivekanda's; 606.28, men
and women; 607.37, rest; 619.12, ken; 624.6b, VIVEKANDA;
715.36, however; 745.4, *regel*; 782.24, *näif*; 792.2, it!]; 793.18,
reality; 815.21, 'agapasticism; 815.39, casual; 884.2, prediction;
886.34, common; 887.3, fulfils?[]; 916.27, transcended"; 922.2–
3, epitemologizing; 988.3, *Misbrauch*; 990.2, passings; 990.5,
1609; 991.18, metaphysical; 991.18, theological; 992.1, tumeric;
992.37, Marrett; 998.6, Kan[]; 999.32–33, philosphers; 1001.13,
Pragmatism,; 1004.38, *Prosologium*; 1004.38, Doane; 1008.39,
J. G. Romanes; 1009.32, Uberhaupt; 1009.33, form; 1009.35,
mann; 1010.25, *Interpretations of Poetry and Religion*; 1010.34,
amd; 1015.39, J. E. Miller; 1020.24, better; 1028.40, Pearson;
1030.18, totality-in unity; 1031.38, this; 1039.35, "The; 1040.11,
whatnot; 1040.21, one-another; 1041.40, F. Bouillier's; 1042.6,
world); 1058.32, *Materialisms*; 1071.13, criticized; 1971.19, numbers; 1075.36, Conturat's; 1075.44, Waterton; 1076.39, G. M.
Fullerton's; 1077.26, notion; 1081.1, *effecta*; 1082.3, Guelinex;
1085.3, it; 1085.40, human; 1086.23, Conturat; 1086.28, *Révue*;
1087.27, *d*,; 1087.40, hypothesis; 1090.37, of; 1094.23, conditioning.'; 1098.35, Bostion; 1115.7, colleges?; 1136.37, *Philosophy*;
1141.11, of; 1149.14, see."; 1153.8, not.; 1166.36, aparently;
1166.39, according; 1169.24, SUSTITUTION; 1183.19, righteous-

ness!; 1194.12, term); 1198.20, *ding-and-sich*; 1203.2, *Weltau-schauung*; 1227.13, then; 1240.31, ophthamologist's; 1245.11, wisdom'; 1255.12, Letters:"; 1272.30, other; 1281.20, women; 1282.14, found,; 1282.38, Aemilius,; 1283.40, permament; 1295.29, Morrison. Errors corrected second printing: 223.7, previous (*LOA*); 474.26, its (*LOA*); 888.23, already;; 1071.39, *La science et l'hypothese.*

Notes

In the notes below, the reference numbers denote page and line of the present volume (the line count includes chapter headings). No note is made for material included in a standard desk-reference book. Notes at the foot of the page in the text are James's own. For more detailed notes, references to other studies, and further biographical background, see *The Letters of William James*, 2 volumes (Boston: The Atlantic Monthly Press, 1920), edited by Henry James III; Ralph Barton Perry, *The Thought and Character of William James*, 2 volumes (Boston: Little, Brown and Company, 1935); Gay Wilson Allen, *William James* (New York: The Viking Press, 1967); Howard M. Feinstein, *Becoming William James* (Ithaca: Cornell University Press, 1984); Gerald E. Myers, *William James: His Life and Thought* (New Haven: Yale University Press, 1986); and the individual volumes in *The Works of William James* published by Harvard University Press, Cambridge, Mass., edited by Frederick H. Burkhardt, Fredson Bowers, and Ignas K. Skrupskelis: *The Varieties of Religious Experience* (1985), *Pragmatism* (1975), *A Pluralistic Universe* (1977), *The Meaning of Truth* (1975), *Some Problems of Philosophy* (1979), and selected essays in *Essays in Radical Empiricism* (1976), *Essays in Philosophy* (1978), *Essays in Religion and Morality* (1982), *Essays in Psychology* (1983), *Essays in Psychical Research* (1986), and *Essays, Comments, and Reviews* (1987).

THE VARIETIES OF RELIGIOUS EXPERIENCE

2.2   E. P. G.]   Elizabeth Putnam Gibbens, James's mother-in-law.

3.32–4.1   Starbuck . . . Ward]   Starbuck (1866–1947), an American psychologist; Rankin, the librarian at the Mount Hermon Boys' School in Northfield, Massachusetts; Rand (1856–1934), an American bibliographer of philosophy, editor, and instructor at Harvard University; Ward (b. 1844), an American banker and old school friend of James.

17.35–37   "I . . . solids."]   From Spinoza's *Ethics* Pt. III, Intro.; Pt. IV, prop. 57, scholium.

21.39   Dr. Binet-Sanglé]   Charles Binet-Sanglé (1868–1941).

23.36   Dr. Moreau]   Jacques Joseph Moreau (1804–84).

40.9   a friend]   To Cardinal François Joachim de Pierre de Bernes on December 22, 1766.

47.24 Imitation of Christ] Fifteenth-century mystical work, probably by Thomas à Kempis.

53.13–17 "Entbehren . . . singt."] Johann Wolfgang Goethe, *Faust*, I, 1549–53: "You must do without! Do without! / That is the eternal refrain / That rings in everyone's ears, / That, for our whole life long / Every hour hoarsely sings to us."

63.14 In . . . book] *The Principles of Psychology* (1890).

64.15 dreaming.' "¹] After this word James wrote in the bottom margin of his own first-edition copy: "cf Janet's Obsessens et Psychasthenie, p. 431 et. passim."

72.20–23 idol . . . through.] In the margin of his first-edition copy James notes: "Janet's pts."

103.15 *Diätetik der Seele*] Literally "Dietetics of the Soul." Taken from the title of a popular mental hygiene book by Austrian physician, poet, and philosopher Ernst von Feuchtersleben (1806–49).

103.18–20 'Thoughts . . . pages;] Slogan used by journalist and essayist Prentice Mulford (1834–91) in his tracts.

104.4–6 *Things* . . . sound,] Here, in the margin of his copy of the book, James wrote: "Mc T. p. 238," referring to John McTaggart Ellis McTaggart's *Studies in Hegelian Cosmology* (1901). See, for example, on page 238: "It is our destiny to become perfect, *sub specie temporis*, because it is our nature to be eternally perfect, *sub specie aeternitatis*. We become perfect in our own right. . . . In Hegel's own words—'the consummation of the infinite End . . . consists merely in removing the illusion which makes it seem yet unaccomplished.' " See also *A Pluralistic Universe*, 693.15–23 in the present volume.

105.20–21 makes . . . before.] Here James wrote in his own copy of the book: "Cf Luther on Galatians p. 396."

108.16 Mgr. Gay] Paul Lejeune is quoting Charles Gay (1815–92).

123.6 Staupitz] Johann von Staupitz (d. 1524), vicar-general of the German Augustinians and teacher and patron of Martin Luther.

128.25 God's . . . world."] From Robert Browning's "Pippa Passes."

129.31–36 "I . . . forever."] James is quoting a conversation with Johann Peter Eckermann on January 27, 1824, from Eckermann's *Gespräche mit Goethe* (*Conversations with Goethe*) (1836–48).

130.1–12 "I . . . Paradise."] From Jules Michelet, *The Life of Luther Written by Himself*, trans. William Hazlitt (1862).

130.24–27 "There . . . allotted."] Robert Louis Stevenson, "A Christmas Sermon," *Across the Plains with Other Memories and Essays* (1892).

131.11−24   "What . . . many."]   Ecclesiastes 1:3; 2:11; 3:19−20; 9:5−6;
11:7−8.

149.25−150.30   "Whilst . . . bearing."]   James later wrote to Swiss philosopher Frank Abauzit, who was translating *The Varieties* into French, that
this account "is my own case—acute neurasthenic attack with phobia. I naturally disguised the *provenance*! So you may translate freely. . . ." The epi-
sode is believed to have occurred in the early 1870s.

159.10−13   "Fils . . . citerne."]   "L'An neuf de l'Hégire" (1858), lines 75−
78: "Son, I am the low field of sublime struggles: / Sometimes man is noble,
sometimes man is base; / Evil and good alternate in my mouth, / As in some
desert the sand and the cistern."

159.14−15   "What . . . I,"]   Romans 7:19.

159.31   "not . . . wantonness,"]   Romans 13:13−14.

192.34−35   Laycock . . . Carpenter]   Thomas Laycock (1812−76), British
physician, first to formulate theory of the reflex action of the brain, further
developed by William Carpenter (1813−85), British physiologist, and others.

194.18   John Nelson]   Nelson (1707−74), a British Methodist converted
by John Wesley, wrote a journal describing his experiences as an evangelist.

199.26   Nettleton's]   Asahel Nettleton (1783−1844), an American revivalist in Connecticut, Massachusetts, and New York.

204.16−17   Colonel Gardiner]   James Gardiner (1688−1784), Scottish military officer. See further discussion of Gardiner on p. 247 in this volume.

212.7   Edwards says]   In *The Treatise on Religious Affections* (1746).

217.5   Mason]   Rufus Osgood Mason (1830−1903), author of *Telepathy
and the Subliminal Self* (1897).

219.37   Edwards says elsewhere]   In *Some Thoughts on the Revival of Religion in New England* (1742).

221.31   Emerson writes:]   In "Spiritual Laws," *Essays: First Series*.

225.37   la Vie]   The title of the book by Wilfred Monod is *Il Vit: Six
méditations sur le mystère Chrétien pour la fête de l'Ascension*.

227.34   Hudson Taylor]   Taylor (1832−1905) was an English missionary
and founder of the China Inland Mission.

233.12   Mr. Peck]   Jonas Oramel Peck (1836−94), an American clergyman.

236.24   DAN YOUNG]   American Methodist minister (b. 1773) who
preached in New England before moving to Ohio with a group of followers,
where he established a cotton mill and iron company.

242.20   "Lass . . . sind!"]   "Let them go begging if they are hungry."
From Heinrich Heine, "Die Grenadiere."

242.29   Sighele]   Scipio Sighele (1868–1913), Italian anthropologist.

245.6–8   "Wo . . . Morgenroth."]   From "Morgengebet" by Joseph von Eichendorff (1788–1857): "Where is the wretchedness and the distress / That yesterday still threatened to sap my strength? / The red dawn makes me ashamed of this."

255.38   Bougaud]   Émile Bougaud (1824–88), Roman Catholic bishop.

291.25–26   "Wer . . . nichts!"]   From Gotthold Ephraim Lessing's play *Nathan der Weise*, I, v. When approached by a friar, the Knight Templar thinks he will be asked to give alms and replies, "Wer nur selbst was hätte, bei Gott, bei Gott, ich habe nichts!" ("If only oneself had anything, by God, by God, I have nothing!")

302.24–27   Luther . . . Unitarianism.]   From Emerson's "The Sovereignty of Ethics," in *Lectures and Biographical Sketches*.

304.28–29   "Heartily . . . arrive."]   Emerson, "Give All To Love."

311.12   *abgeschmackt*]   "Inept."

340.13–14   Agnes . . . Pattisons]   Agnes Elizabeth Jones (1832–68), British nurse who died of a fever caught while caring for the poor in a workhouse. Margaret Mary Hallahan (1803–68), founder of the first English house of the Third Dominican Order, helped establish five convents with schools for the poor, orphanages, and a hospital for incurables. Dorothy Wyndlow Pattison (1832–78), known as "Sister Dora," British member of the sisterhood of the Good Samaritan, surgical nurse and philanthropist.

345.32   *Sehnsucht*]   "Longing."

345.38   B. P. Blood]   Benjamin Paul Blood (1832–1919), philosopher, mystic, and poet, was born and lived in Amsterdam, New York. See "A Pluralistic Mystic," pp. 1294–1313 in this volume.

350.22–23   'The One . . . pass;']   Percy Bysshe Shelley, *Adonais*, LII.

350.32   *Aufgabe*]   "Task."

354.16   'Domine non sum digna']   "God, I am not worthy."

354.45   dream."]   Here William James later added a note in his copy of the book: "Cf. a verse from V. Hugo's a Villequier: . . . Peut-être faites vous des choses inconnues / Où la douleur de l'homme entre comme élément." ("Perhaps you are doing unknown things / Where the sadness of man plays a part.")

356.21   Malwida von Meysenbug]   German socialist author and political refugee (1816–1903), whose circle of friends included Nietzsche, Wagner, Garibaldi, and Mazzini.

371.3–16   "I believe . . . love."]   From "Song of Myself," 5 in *Leaves of Grass* (1891–92).

366.38   Vallgornera]   Thomas de Vallgornera (1595–1665), Dominican theologian.

371.38   Andrew Jackson Davis's]   Davis (1826–1920), an American clairvoyant also known as the "Poughkeepsie Seer," gave a series of lectures while in hypnotic trance and later assembled his first major work, *The Principles of Nature, Her Divine Revelations*, from verbatim accounts of the lectures. He claimed his later works were written under the influence of various spirits, including that of Emanuel Swedenborg.

377.6–7   "Gott ist . . . dir."]   "God is a pure nothing, no here nor there moves him; / The more you clutch at him, the more he twists away from you."

379.24–26   "Ich . . . sein."]   "I am as large as God; he is as small as me; He can't be over me; I can't be under him."

381.5   'the . . . primeval.']   Whitman, "Song of Myself," 24, iv, *Leaves of Grass* (1891–92).

384.34   'seraph and snake']   Emerson, "The Daemonic Love" in *Poems*: "And with snake and seraph talked."

386.24–25   "Oh . . . away!"]   From Browning, "By the Fireside," stanza 39, in *Men and Women* (1855).

395.40–396.1   *effectus . . . causam*]   "The effect is never greater than the cause."

396.11   freedom.]   After this word James wrote in the bottom margin of his copy of the book: "cf McTaggart's Hegelian Cosmology p. 237." On page 237 of *Studies in Hegelian Cosmology* (1901) McTaggart quotes Hegel: " 'The harmony of this contradiction must accordingly be represented as something which is a presupposition for the subject. The Notion, in getting to know the divine unity, knows that God essentially exists in-and-for-Himself, and consequently what the subject thinks, and its activity, have no meaning in themselves, but are and exist only in virtue of that presupposition.' "

397.9–10   *bonum . . . partis*]   "The good of the whole is greater than the good of the part."

412.27–413.1   "man . . . meet."]   The last line in Emerson's "Good-bye": "For what are they all, in their high conceit, / When man in the bush with God may meet?"

414.31–32   'meek . . . good,']   From the last stanza of Emerson's "Brahma," in *May-Day and Other Pieces*.

422.42   Bishop of Ripon]   William Boyd Carpenter (1841–1918).

438.16   *Tout . . . pardonner*]   "To know all is to forgive all."

452.32–37   Walt . . . defeated."]   The first line is from "Me Imperturbe" and the next two are the last lines of "As I Lay with My Head in Your Lap Camerado." The poems were next to each other in James's edition.

457.32–34   which . . . volume.]   For the second printing, James revised and expanded the note here to: "which is already announced by Messrs. Longmans, Green & Co. as being in press. Mr. Myers for the first time proposed as a general psychological problem the exploration of the subliminal region of consciousness throughout its whole extent, and made the first methodical steps in its topography by treating as a natural series a mass of subliminal facts hitherto considered only as curious isolated facts, and subjecting them to a systematized nomenclature. How important this exploration will prove, future work upon the path which Myers has opened can alone show." To make room for the note, everything after the numbers in the following note was deleted.

PRAGMATISM

481.33   BLONDEL . . . DE SAILLY]   Bernard De Sailly was a pen name of French neo-Catholic modernist philosopher Maurice Blondel (1861–1949).

488.2–3   founder of pragmatism]   Charles Sanders Peirce (1839–1914).

488.20   per . . . nefas]   "Through right or wrong."

495.9   quaesitum]   "That which is searched for."

502.9–10   'who . . . man.']   From "So Long," Leaves of Grass: "Camerado! This is no book; / Who touches this, touches a man."

502.27–28   'Statt . . . hinein']   Goethe, Faust, I, v, 414–15: "Instead of living nature / in which God placed human beings . . ."

511.38   Ruyssen]   James substituted Theodore Ruyssen (1868–1967), a French philosopher, in his own copy, for Dutch philosopher Gerardus Heymans (1857–1930), whose name had appeared in the first edition.

518.9   nulla . . . retrorsum]   "No tracks lead back out."

529.14–15   'the same . . . blame,']   Robert Browning, in stanza 17, "A Lovers' Quarrel," in Men and Women (1855): "Foul be the world or fair / More or less, how can I care? / 'T is the world the same / For my praise or blame, / And endurance is easy there."

538.8   Messrs. . . . McTaggart]   George Fullerton (1859–1925); John McTaggart Ellis McTaggart (1865–1925). See The Meaning of Truth, pp. 952–57 in this volume.

539.28–29   'Watchman . . . bear,']   From a hymn by Sir John Bowring (1792–1872), "Watchman, Tell Us of the Night."

539.36–38   "Deus . . . intelligens,"]   This is James's compilation of scholastic definitions of God: "God is being, from itself, above and beyond all kinds, necessary, one, infinitely perfect, simple, unchanging, great, eternal, the principle of thought."

549.23   *denkmittel*]   "Conceptual device, instrument of thought."

552.27–553.11   "Where . . . deserves."]   James is quoting from "God in Everything."

553.21–36   "When . . . else.' "]   This quote is from *On "The Atman"* (1896).

561.12–13   *gewühl . . . wahrnehmungen*,]   "A swarm of appearances, a rhapsody of perceptions." The second phrase is from Immanuel Kant, *The Critique of Pure Reason*, B 195 = A 156.

564.15   *durcheinander*]   "At random, in a muddle."

566.28   *aequabiliter fluit*]   "Flows evenly."

567.14–15   *sibi permissi*]   "Devoted to themselves."

567.29–30   *regel der verbindung*]   "Law of association."

581.24   *in rebus*]   "In things."

582.20   *ante rem*]   "Before the thing."

582.29–32   Sagt . . . besitzen?"]   In *Die Geschichte und die Wurzel des Satzes von der Erhaltung der Arbeit* (*History and Root of the Principle of the Conversion of Work*) (1872): "Says little Hans to Cousin Fritz, / Why is it, Cousin Fritz / That the richest people in the world, / Possess the most gold?"

584.13   Danish thinker]   Sören Kierkegaard, as quoted by Harald Höff-ding in "A Philosophic Confession" in *The Journal of Philosophy, Psychology and Scientific Methods* (1905).

588.40–589.1   If . . . day,]   From "Self-Reliance," in *Essays: First Series.*

592.36   ΰλη]   "Material."

599.11–12   '*Die . . . daseins*']   "The increased value of what is thrust upon us." Rudolf Eucken uses this phrase in *Geistige Strömungen der Gegenwart* (3rd edition, 1904).

601.40–602.1   'eternal . . . agitation.']   From *The Excursion*, Bk. IV, 1146–47: "And central peace, subsisting at the heart / Of endless agitation."

615.9   "Top . . . schlag!"]   "Okay! Onwards and onwards!"

617.33–36   "A . . . gale."]   This epigram of Theodorides of Syracuse appears in *Selections from the Greek Anthology* (1889), ed. Graham R. Tomson (pseud.).

618.24   *primus inter pares*]   "First among equals."

A PLURALISTIC UNIVERSE

638.9–10   *oberflächliches . . . unwissenschaftlich.*]   "Superficial nonsense and completely unscientific."

642.3   *toto genere*]   "As a whole species."

644.22   *socius*]   "Companion."

647.1   gedanke and gedachtes]   "Thoughts and that which is thought."

647.7–8   *identitätsphilosophie*]   "Philosophy of identity." Royce used this phrase in an address, "The Conception of God" (1895), published in 1897 along with discussions by G. H. Howison, Joseph LeConte, and S. E. Mezes.

651.1   *Quatenus . . . est*]   "Insofar as he is infinite."

651.1–2   *quatenus . . . constituit.*]   "Insofar as he has formed man's understanding."

651.11   *sub . . . eternitatis*]   "Under the aspect of eternity."

651.19–21   to . . . sky]   "Revere the Maker; fetch thine eye / Up to his style, and manners of the sky." From Emerson's "Threnody."

651.23–25   'Aus . . . leiden.']   Goethe, *Faust*, I, 1663–64: "From this earth spring my joys, / and its sun shines upon my sorrows."

652.29–30   'I . . . whole,']   From "Each and All": "Over me soared the eternal sky, / Full of light and of deity; / Again I saw, again I heard, / The rolling river, the morning bird; — / Beauty through my senses stole; / I yielded myself to the perfect whole."

657.4   *secundum quid*]   "According to something; relatively; in a qualified sense."

657.14   Sigwart]   German philosopher Christoph Sigwart (1830–1904), author of *Logik* (1873–78).

657.22   *le . . . boire,*]   "The wine is poured, it must be drunk."

662.27   *quand même*]   "Nevertheless; all the same."

662.38–40   'All . . . universe.']   David Ritchie (1843–97) is quoted from "The One and the Many," *Mind* (1898).

669.11   *ens perfectissimum*]   "Perfect being."

669.12–16   'It . . . Being.']   From *The Logic of Hegel*, trans. William Wallace (1874).

669.27–28   'to . . . crimes.']   From Byron's "The Corsair": "He left a Corsair's name to other times, / Linked with one virtue and a thousand crimes."

673.8–9   *Summum . . . injuria*]   "Greatest right, greatest wrong."

675.32   *inconcussum*]   "Unshaken."

676.18   *methode . . . negativität*]   "Method of absolute negativity."

676.21   death . . . then]   Shakespeare, Sonnet CXLVI: "So shalt thou feed on death, that feeds on men, / And Death once dead, there's no more dying then."

681.25–26   central . . . agitation.]   Wordsworth, *The Excursion*. Compare with 601.40–602.1.

693.12–14   'can . . . endeavor.']   From Alfred Edward Taylor's *Elements of Metaphysics* (1903).

694.6–7   'all . . . conclusions,']   In *Studies in the Hegelian Dialectic* (1896).

694.27   *machtspruch*]   "Power speech."

696.35–36   *so . . . ausgehalten*]   "Then I could not have endured that time."

707.37   'Büchlein . . . tode,']   "Booklet on life after death."

710.11   as . . . wine]   From Alfred, Lord Tennyson, *Locksley Hall*, 152.

713.10   Barratt]   Alfred Barratt (1844–81).

724.24–25   Wo . . . ein.]   Goethe, *Faust*, I, 1995–96: "Where concepts fail / a word conveniently puts itself in their place at just the right time."

727.16   *an sich*]   "In itself."

728.32–33   *unerbittlich consequent*]   "Relentlessly consequential."

732.1   *l'art . . . dire*]   "The art of saying it well."

732.8   an american reviewer]   American philosopher Boyd Henry Bode (1873–1953) reviewed *L'Évolution créatrice* in *Philosophical Review* (1908).

738.5–6   *dinge . . . sich*]   "Things in themselves."

738.34–35   *ens rationis*]   "Rational being."

739.32   danish writer]   Sören Kierkegaard. See note 584.13.

741.16   barbed-wire . . . Arthur]   Barbed-wire entanglements were part of the Russian fortifications at the 1904 siege of Port Arthur during the Russo-Japanese War.

745.4–5   *regeln . . . verknüpfung*]   "Rules of combination."

748.1   *durcheinander*]   "At random, in a muddle."

751.16   *devenir réel*]   "Becoming real."

751.30   *Am . . . tat*]   *Faust*, I, 1237: "In the beginning was the fact," translating "tat" (which also means "deed" or "act") as "fact."

764.17   *abschluss*]   "Closure, conclusion."

766.13   lights . . . morn]   Shakespeare, *Measure for Measure*, I, iv, 4.

774.35–36   'Nous . . . réel.']   "We are of the real in the real." Maurice Blondel, "Le Point de départ de la recherche philosophique," part II, *Annales de Philosophie Chrétienne* (1906).

777.4   *multum in parvo*]   "Much in little."

778.15   *all-einheit*]   "All-unity."

781.12–13   'Ring . . . in.']   Alfred, Lord Tennyson, "In Memoriam," CVI, 19: "Ring out the want, the care, the sin, / The faithless coldness of the times; / Ring out, ring out my mournful rhymes, / But ring the fuller minstrel in."

782.19–20   'A world . . . experience,']   See pp. 1159–82 in this volume.

788.32   H. Spir]   Afrikan Spir (1837–90), Ukrainian-born philosopher who wrote in German.

790.37   Hodder's]   Alfred Hodder (1866–1907), an American lawyer and author who took his doctorate at Harvard in the early 1890s.

790.39   MacLennan's]   Simon Fraser MacLennan (1870–1938), American philosopher and colleague of John Dewey at the University of Chicago.

795.3   *proprius motus*]   "Of one's own motion or initiative."

797.3   . . . Mr. Bradley]   The first three introductory paragraphs were dropped by James when he prepared this essay for inclusion here. They were:

Brethren of the Psychological Association:

In casting about me for a subject for your President this year to talk about it has seemed to me that our experiences of activity would form a good one; not only because the topic is so naturally interesting, and because it has lately led to a good deal of rather inconclusive discussion, but because I myself am growing more and more interested in a certain systematic way of handling questions, and want to get others interested also, and this question strikes me as one in which, although I am painfully aware of my inability to communicate new discoveries or to reach definitive conclusions, I yet can show, in a rather definite manner, how the method works.

The way of handling things I speak of, is, as you already will have suspected, that known sometimes as the pragmatic method, sometimes as humanism, sometimes as Deweyism, and in France, by some of the disciples of Bergson, as the Philosophie nouvelle. Professor Woodbridge's *Journal of Philosophy* seems unintentionally to have become a sort of meeting place for those who follow these tendencies in America. There is only a dim identity among them; and the most that can be said at present is that some sort of gestation seems to be in the atmosphere, and that almost any day a man with a genius for finding the right word for things may hit upon some unifying and conciliating formula that will make so much vaguely similar aspiration crystallize into more definite form.

I myself have given the name of 'radical empiricism' to that version of the tendency in question which I prefer; and I propose, if you will now let me, to illustrate what I mean by radical empiricism, by applying it to activity as an example, hoping at the same time incidentally to leave the general problem of activity in a slightly—I fear very slightly—more manageable shape than before.

797.14–18   'I . . . it.'] James Ward (1843–1925) is quoted from "Mr. F. H. Bradley's Analysis of Mind," *Mind* (1887).

797.20–21   *verständigung . . . 'grundsätzlich ausgeschlossen'*] "An understanding with him is fundamentally impossible."

799.28   *ideenflucht*] "Flight of ideas."

799.28–29   *rhapsodie der wahrnehmungen*] "Rhapsody of perceptions."

800.4   *gestaltqualität*] "Quality of the form."

800.5   *fundirte inhalt*] "The given content."

802.20   *Verborum gratiâ*] "For example."

802.21   Loveday] British philosopher Thomas Loveday (1875–1966).

802.28–30   'In . . . tätigkeit'] "In the sense of activity lies the least valid proof of a psychic activity." Citation from Münsterberg's "Über Aufgaben und methoden der Psychologie," *Schriften der Gesellschaft für psychologische Forschung* (1891).

804.16   *überhaupt*] "In general."

805.3–4   you . . . mankind] Robert Louis Stevenson, "Lay Morals."

805.20   *Cessante . . . effectus*] "The cause ceasing, the effect also ceases."

809.32–33   article . . . exist?'] See pp. 1141–58 in this volume.

813.6   *dictum . . . nullo*] "Principle of all or nothing."

816.3   A friend of mine] Henry Adams. See, for example, the last chapters in *The Education of Henry Adams.*

THE MEANING OF TRUTH

825.3–4   oh . . . sun!] From Thomas Hood, "The Bridge of Sighs," with slight variation.

829.27−29   Gardiner . . . Schinz]   Harry Norman Gardiner (1855−1927); Charles Montague Bakewell (1867−1957), professor at Yale who had studied under James, Josiah Royce, George Santayana, and George Herbert Palmer, and later wrote the introduction to James's *Selected Papers in Philosophy* (1916); Dominique Parodi (1870−1955); William Mackintire Salter (1853−1931), American ethical culture lecturer, philosopher, and author; André Lalande (1867−1963); François Mentré (1877−1950); Albert Schinz (1870−1943), Swiss-born professor of French literature who taught in the United States and published works on pragmatism and Rousseau.

834.20−21   *semper . . . sentire*]   "Always the same, to feel and not to feel."

835.9   dirempted]   "To separate, divide; break off."

836.5   *Erkenntnisstheoretiker*]   "Epistemologists."

839.17   *ab extra*]   "From without."

840.18   *ins . . . hinein*]   "Into the blue."

843.38   Professor D. S. Miller]   Dickinson Sergeant Miller (1868−1963), American philosopher and psychic researcher, was a student of James and George Fullerton at Harvard.

844.28   *grübelsucht*]   "Excessive deliberation."

852.1   *Nirgends . . . Sohlen*]   "Nowhere is there a place to which the uncertain soles of the feet can cling."

858.15   *ignoratio elenchi*]   "Ignorance of the point in dispute; the fallacy of appearing to refute an opponent by arguing an unraised point."

858.33   'too . . . foam,']   Alfred, Lord Tennyson, "Crossing the Bar": "Too full for sound and foam."

859.9   *minus . . . plus*]   "The lesser cannot engender the greater."

860.6   *Barbara* and *Celarent*]   Mnemonic names of traditional valid syllogisms in logic.

862.14   *denkmittel*]   "Conceptual device, instrument of thought."

864.8−9   *adæquatio . . . rei*]   "Adequate to the intellect and to things."

866.23   *brutum fulmen*]   "Empty threat."

866.27−28   *ante rem*]   "Before the thing."

866.28   *in rebus*]   "In things."

868.15   *inbegriff*]   "Substance."

869.10−11   cognitio . . . cognoscentis]   "Knowing comes through the assimilation of the known and the knower."

869.27–41 'Autant . . . *importe.*'] "As much as the Revolution, 'the Affair' is from henceforth one of our 'origins.' If it has not opened the abyss, it has at least rendered patent and visible the long underground labor that silently prepared the separation between our two camps today, and which at last, with a sudden blow, split the France of the traditionalists (principle-asserters, unity-seekers, builders of a priori systems) and the France in love with the positive fact and free inquiry;—the revolutionary and romantic France, if you will, which exalts the individual, which would not see one just man perish, even to save the nation, and which seeks truth in each subordinate part as well as in the whole. . . . Duclaux could not conceive that anyone would prefer something to the truth. But he saw about him profoundly sincere people who, weighing political necessity and the life of a man, acknowledged to him how lightly they evaluated a simple individual existence, innocent as it was. These were the classicists, people to whom totality alone matters."

869.42 Mme. Em D.] Madame Emile Duclaux (Agnes Mary Frances Robinson) (1857–1944), an English writer.

870.14 *'Die . . . daseins,'*] "The elevation of existence as we know it."

877.20 *schlechthin*] "Simply."

881.36 'A World . . . Experience,'] See pp. 1159–82 in this volume.

883.37 *aliunde*] "From some other direction."

886.18–19 *salto mortale*] "Mortal leap."

893.18 *identitätsphilosophie*] "Philosophy of identity."

893.39–40 'Does . . . Experience'] See pp. 1141–58 and 1159–82 in this volume.

900.24 *erkenntnisstheorie*] "Epistemology."

907.19 *pari passu*] "By an equal progress."

908.11–12 *und zwar*] "That is."

911.32 *in se*] "In itself."

928.33 *in posse*] "In possible existence."

928.36–37 Aennchen von Tharau] An opera by German composer Heinrich Hoffmann (1842–1902), first produced in 1878.

934.38–39 "Es . . . sein."] By Josef Victor von Scheffel (1826–86), *Der Trompeter von Säkkingen*: "It would have been so beautiful / It was not meant to be."

937.11 *actio in distans*] "Action at a distance."

939.4 Professor Pratt . . . book] *What Is Pragmatism?* (1909).

942.23–24   *valeur . . . dite*]   "Cognitive value properly speaking."

943.3–4   *connaissance objective*]   "Objective knowledge."

946.15   *grenzbegriff*]   "Limiting concept."

946.17   *endgültig*]   "Final; ultimate."

947.30–31   *connaissance . . . dite.*]   "Knowledge properly speaking."

948.11   *ebenbürtig*]   "Of equally high birth."

955.2   *zerrissenheit*]   "Inner strife, lack of inner unity."

959.35   'Es . . . Welt,']   "There must be a world."

SOME PROBLEMS OF PHILOSOPHY

985.29–30   '*Begriff* . . . *Methode.*']   "Concept and classification"; "task and method."

987.20   'Hast . . . Shepherd?']   Shakespeare, *As You Like It*, III, ii, 21–22.

987.39–40   a 'blind . . . there.']   Attributed to British jurist Charles, Baron Bowen (1835–94), with "black hat" instead of "black cat." For the second printing James's son Henry authorized the change of "cat" to "hat," but since James may have intended "cat" this revision is not made here.

988.2–4   '*systematische* . . . *Terminologie.*']   "The systematic misuse of a terminology invented for these very purposes."

991.17   '*spiritus rector*']   "Guiding spirit."

999.28–30   A saying . . . aristotelian.]   From July 2, 1830, in *Specimens of the Table Talk* (1836).

1003.34   *Grübelsucht*]   "Excessive deliberation."

1006.8   *Vorgefundenes*]   "Given."

1009.32–37   'Die . . . Verstandeshandlung.']   From *Critique of Pure Reason*, B 129–130: "The combination (conjunction) of a manifold in general can never come to us through the senses, and cannot, therefore, be already contained in the pure form of sensible intuition. For it is an act of spontaneity of the faculty of representation; and since this faculty, to distinguish it from sensibility, must be entitled understanding, all combination . . . is an act of the understanding." (Translation from Norman Kemp Smith's edition of *Critique of Pure Reason* [1929].)

1012.8–9   'Generalization . . . it.']   In "Circles," *Essays: First Series*.

1019.30–41   Emerson . . . *Love.*)]   In *Essays: First Series*.

1021.1   CHAPTER V]   The editor of the 1911 posthumous edition added a footnote stating: "[This chapter and the following chapter do not appear as separate chapters in the manuscript. Ed.]"

1025.39   'Sinnlichkeit']   "Sensuousness."

1038.27–28   'Other . . . world,']   In the "Sovereignty of Ethics," *Lectures and Biographical Sketches*.

1038.30–33   'Natur . . . seist.']   Goethe, "Allerdings" ("Certainly"): "Nature has neither kernel nor shell / It is both at the same time / Just make sure you examine yourself / To see if you're either kernel or shell."

1040.24–25   *'un . . . vérité.'*]   "One sole fact and one great truth." Jean le Rond d'Alembert, *Discourse preliminaire de l'Encyclopedie* (1751).

1051.1   CHAPTER VIII]   A footnote by the editor in the 1911 edition states: "[This chapter was not indicated as a separate chapter in the manuscript. Ed.]"

1061.1   CHAPTER X]   A footnote to the 1911 edition states: "[In the author's manuscript this chapter and the succeeding chapters were labelled 'sub-problems,' and this chapter was entitled 'The Continuum and the Infinite.' Ed.]"

1063.37   'Even . . . numbered,']   Cf. Matthew 10:30.

1067.1   CHAPTER XI]   A footnote by the editor in the 1911 edition states: "[This chapter was not indicated as a separate chapter in the manuscript. Ed.]"

1067.7   experience;]   James intended to write a chapter on idealism and added a footnote here: "For an account of idealism the reader is referred to chapter below." In the 1911 edition this appears with the additional note by the editor: "[Never written. Ed.]"

1070.7   *'Infinitum . . . nequit,'*]   "The infinite cannot be traversed in actuality."

1075.44   S. Waterlow]   British diplomat Sydney Waterlow (1878–1944).

1076.6   Evellin]   French philosopher François Evellin (1836–1910).

1076.34   Leighton]   Joseph Alexander Leighton (1870–1954).

1079.1   CHAPTER XII]   A footnote by the editor of the 1911 edition states: "[In the author's manuscript this chapter bore the heading—'Second Sub-problem—Cause and Effect.' Ed.]"

1079.11–13   'the first . . . read']   *Rubáiyát of Omar Khayyam*, trans. Edward Fitzgerald, 3rd. ed., LXXIII.

1080.23   *Nemo . . . habet*]   "No one gives what he does not have."

1080.24–25   *causa . . . effectum*]   "The cause equals the effect."

1081.1–2   *quidquid . . . causa*]   "Whatever is in the effect must be first in some way in the cause."

1082.2–3   Régis . . . Cordemoy]   Pierre Régis (1632–1707) and Gerard de Cordemoy (1620–84).

1089.7–8   'Le . . . discours,']   "The sense of life is indignant at such speech."

1094.20   *post . . . istud*]   "After this, with that, resulting from that."

1095.1   APPENDIX]   A footnote in the 1911 edition reads: "[The following pages, part of a syllabus printed for the use of students in an introductory course in philosophy, were found with the MS. of this book, with the words, 'To be printed as part of the Introduction to Philosophy,' noted thereon in the author's handwriting. Ed.]"

ESSAYS

1116.2–3   *chair à canon*]   "Cannon fodder."

1119.29   "Stand . . . order,"]   In "The Man of Letters," in *Lectures and Biographical Sketches*.

1119.34–35   The day . . . perceptions.]   In "Inspiration," in *Letters and Social Aims*.

1119.35–1120.2   There . . . open.]   Cf. "Powers and Laws of Thought," pt. III, in *Natural History of Intellect*.

1120.6–7   his . . . expression,]   "Genius is not a lazy angel contemplating itself and things. It is insatiable for expression." "Powers and Laws of Thought," pt. III, in *Natural History of Intellect*.

1020.24–27   "with . . . apology.]   Cf. "Wealth," in *The Conduct of Life*.

1120.31–36   "God . . . me."]   From Emerson's Journal, August 1852, quoted by Edward Waldo Emerson, in *Emerson in Concord* (1889).

1121.7–8   "So . . . man!"]   "Voluntaries," III, *Poems*.

1121.13–18   "O rich . . . wrong."]   "The Method of Nature," in *Nature; Addresses, and Lectures*.

1121.22–24   "If John . . . own."]   "Nominalist and Realist," in *Essays: Second Series*.

1121.32–34   "Each . . . light."]   "The Method of Nature," in *Nature; Addresses, and Lectures*: ". . . but we also can bask in the great morning which rises forever out of the eastern sea."

1121.34–1122.2   "Trust . . . till."]   These sentences appear separately and in different order in "Self-Reliance," *Essays: First Series*.

1122.9–14   "If . . . Creator."]   "The Sovereignty of Ethics," *Lectures and Biographical Sketches*.

1122.14–15   "Cleave . . . God;"]   "Powers and Laws of Thought," *Natural History of Intellect*.

1122.28–36   "I love . . . fortitude."]   "Spiritual Laws," *Essays: First Series*.

1122.36–38   "The fact . . . post?"]   "Spiritual Laws," *Essays: First Series*.

1123.2–6   "Hide . . . face.]   "Literary Ethics," *Nature; Addresses, and Lectures*.

1123.6–8   Don't . . . contrary.]   "Social Aims," in *Letters and Social Aims*, where the passage reads "cannot hear what you say to the contrary."

1123.8–20   What . . . concealed?"]   "Spiritual Laws," *Essays: First Series*.

1123.22–24   "Never . . . unexpectedly.]   "Spiritual Laws," *Essays: First Series*.

1123.24–28   The hero . . . incident."]   "Spiritual Laws," *Essays: First Series*.

1123.34–1124.17   "In solitude . . . books."]   "Literary Ethics," *Nature; Addresses, and Lectures*.

1124.18   "the deep . . . scorn"]   "Work and Days," *Society and Solitude*.

1124.19–20   "Other . . . world."]   "Sovereignty of Ethics," *Lectures and Biographical Sketches*.

1124.21–22   "The present . . . doomsday."]   See "Work and Days," *Society and Solitude*.

1124.38   Moral Sentiment]   Found throughout Emerson's essays. See, for example, "The Divinity School Address," in *Nature; Addresses, and Lectures*.

1125.10–14   "It is . . . stands."]   Taken and abridged from James Elliot Cabot, *A Memoir of Ralph Waldo Emerson* (1887), vol. II, 427. Cabot does not give the source for his quote, but Emerson's Journal V for May 1844–March 1845 has an entry that contains part of the material: ". . . the whole class of professed Philanthropists—it is strange and horrible to say—are an altogether odious set of people, whom one would be sure to shun as the worst bores & canters."

1125.31–32   " 'Gainst . . . forth,"]   Shakespeare, Sonnet LV.

1126.3–4   Coming . . . to-day]   James received an honorary LL.D. degree from Harvard University on June 24, 1903.

1128.35–36   Beware . . . world]   Emerson in "Circles," *Essays: First Series*: "Beware when the great God lets loose a thinker on this planet."

1128.39–40   "Alone . . . streams."]   Matthew Arnold, in "In Utrumque Paratus" ("Prepared for Either Event").

1131.34   'like . . . Indian,'] Shakespeare, *Othello*, V, ii, 346: "Like the base Indian, threw a pearl away."

1139.34   *in rebus*] "In things."

1139.34   *ante rem*] "Before the thing."

1165.28–30   I have . . . 1904.] See "Does 'Consciousness' Exist?," pp. 1141–58 in this volume.

1166.1–3   I have . . . 1895.] See "The Function of Cognition," in *The Meaning of Truth*, pp. 833–52 in this volume, and "The Knowing of Things Together," reproduced in part in *The Meaning of Truth* as "The Tigers in India," pp. 853–56 in this volume.

1168.7   *aliunde*] "From another source."

1171.31   *Denkmittel*] "Conceptual device, instrument of thought."

1183.1   *Answers to a Questionnaire*] James's answers are given in italic.

1186.35   Vol. . . . 1904.] See pp. 1141–58 in this volume.

1186.37–38   'The Thing . . . 29.] See Appendix A in *A Pluralistic Universe*, pp. 782–96 in this volume.

1188.37   For . . . 489.] See p. 1155 in this volume.

1191.23   *Beseelung*] "Inspiration."

1193.2   MR. JOSEPH . . . MIND] Horace W. B. Joseph (1867–1943) in an article titled "Prof. James on 'Humanism and Truth.' "

1193.3   'Humanism and Truth'] See *The Meaning of Truth*, pp. 857–80.

1193.36   *minus . . . plus*] "Less can't generate more."

1197.27   *causa existendi*] "Cause of existence."

1197.28   *causa cognoscendi*] "Cause of knowledge."

1198.20   *ding-an-sich*] "Thing-in-itself."

1198.21   *materia prima*] "Primal matter."

1199.2   *und zwar*] "In fact."

1199.34–35   "Does . . . Experience,"] See pp. 1141–58 and 1159–82 in this volume.

1203.3   *sachgemäss*] "Pertinent."

1203.3   Mr. Bode's] Boyd Henry Bode (1873–1953) in an article titled " 'Pure Experience' and the External World."

1203.29   *a quo*] "From which."

1203.31   *ad quem*] "To which."

1204.40–1205.1   Professor . . . JOURNAL]   Harald Höffding in an article titled "A Philosophic Confession."

1206.34   'Does . . . Exist?']   See pp. 1141–58 in this volume.

1206.35–36   'A World . . . Experience']   See pp. 1159–82 in this volume.

1208.31–32   page 490]   See p. 1156 in this volume.

1212.38   *an sich,*]   "In itself."

1212.40   'The Experience . . . 1905']   See *A Pluralistic Universe*, Appendix B, pp. 797–812 in this volume.

1215.4   California friend B.]   Charles M. Bakewell. See note 829.27–29.

1215.15   *fortior*]   "Stronger."

1220.35   Mr. Keith]   William Keith (1839–1911), a friend of John Muir and John Burroughs.

1227.31–36   Even . . . came.]   Theodore Roosevelt, then president of the United States.

1229.39   dromomania]   Mania for roaming or running. (James's use of the word here is cited in the Supplement to the *Oxford English Dictionary*.)

1231.22   My friend]   Wincenty Lutoslawski (1863–1954), Polish platonic philosopher, who later taught at Wilno. James met him in 1893 when Lutoslawski visited him at Cambridge.

1231.34   chela]   "Disciple."

1232.23   *Nebenprodukt*]   "By-product."

1241.2   *Versuchstier*]   "Laboratory animal."

1247.22–24   Stevenson . . . mankind."]   Robert Louis Stevenson, "Lay Morals."

1259.22   *gobe-mouche*]   "A fly-catcher," i.e. a credulous simpleton, who swallows anything.

1265.3   *Kühn . . . Lohn!*]   "Daring is the effort; magnificent the reward."

1273.32   *a parte foris*]   "From the part outside."

1277.26   *Verwirrtheit*]   "Confusion."

1278.16   *anima rationalis*]   "Rational spirit."

1278.39   *foudroyante*]   "Calamitous."

1286.39–40   *Die . . . Weltgericht*]   "The unfolding of history is the unfolding of right."

1296.1   *pro domo mea*]   Literally "for my house," that is, from James's perspective.

1309.41   'causa sui']   "Cause of itself."

1312.6   Nietzsche's *amor fati*]   "Love of fate." Cf. the Epilogue to *Nietzsche Contra Wagner* (1895): "As my inmost nature teaches me, whatever is necessary—as seen from the heights and in the sense of a great economy—is also the useful par excellence: one should *love* it. *Amor fati*: that is my inmost nature." (Walter Kaufmann's translation.)

Cataloging Information

James, William, 1842–1910.
    Writings 1902–1910.
    Edited by Bruce Kuklick.

    (The Library of America ; 38)
    Contents: The varieties of religious experience — Pragmatism
— A pluralistic universe — The meaning of truth — Some
problems of philosophy — Essays.
    Includes indexes.
    1. Philosophy. 2. Pragmatism. 3. Experience (Religion).
4. Psychology, Religious. 5. Religion.
I. Kuklick, Bruce, 1941–   . II. Title: The varieties of religious
experience. III. Title: Pragmatism. IV. Title: A pluralistic
universe. V. Title: The meaning of truth. VI. Title: Some
problems of philosophy. VII. Series.
B945.J21   1988   191   87–3301
ISBN 0–940450–38–0

THE LIBRARY OF AMERICA SERIES

This book is set in 10 point Linotron Galliard,
a face designed for photocomposition by Matthew Carter
and based on the sixteenth-century face Granjon. The paper
is acid-free Ecusta Nyalite and meets the requirements for perma-
nence of the American National Standards Institute. The binding
material is Brillianta, a 100% woven rayon cloth made by
Van Heek-Scholco Textielfabrieken, Holland. The com-
position is by Haddon Craftsmen, Inc., and The
Clarinda Company. Printing and binding
by R. R. Donnelley & Sons Company.
Designed by Bruce Campbell.